PEARSON   ALWAYS LEARNING

Baker College Composition

A Custom Approach
Revised Edition

Taken from:
Reading and Writing in the Academic Community, Fourth Edition
by Mary Lynch Kennedy and Hadley M. Smith

The Allyn & Bacon Guide to Writing, Sixth Edition
by John D. Ramage, John C. Bean, and June Johnson

Writing and Reading Across the Curriculum, Eleventh Edition
by Laurence Behrens and Leonard J. Rosen

Good Reasons with Contemporary Arguments, Fifth Edition
by Lester Faigley and Jack Selzer

Writing Arguments: A Rhetoric with Readings, Brief Eighth Edition
by John D. Ramage, John C. Bean, and June Johnson

Writing: A Guide for College and Beyond, Brief Second Edition
by Lester Faigley

Perspectives on Argument, Sixth Edition
by Nancy V. Wood

The Allyn & Bacon Guide to Writing, Fifth Edition
by John D. Ramage, John C. Bean, and June Johnson

The Prentice Hall Essential Guide for College Writers, Ninth Edition
by Stephen Reid

Taken from:

Reading and Writing in the Academic Community,
Fourth Edition
by Mary Lynch Kennedy and Hadley M. Smith
Copyright © 2010, 2006, 2001 by Mary Lynch
Kennedy and Hadley M. Smith
Published by Prentice Hall, a Pearson Education
Company
Upper Saddle River, New Jersey 07458

The Allyn & Bacon Guide to Writing, Sixth Edition
by John D. Ramage, John C. Bean, and June Johnson
Copyright © 2012, 2009, 2006 by Pearson
Education, Inc.
Published by Longman
New York, New York 10036

Writing and Reading Across the Curriculum,
Eleventh Edition
by Laurence Behrens and Leonard J. Rosen
Copyright © 2011, 2008, 2005 by Laurence
Behrens and Leonard J. Rosen
Published by Longman, a Pearson Education
Company

Good Reasons with Contemporary Arguments,
Fifth Edition
by Lester Faigley and Jack Selzer
Copyright © 2012, 2009, 2007, 2004
by Pearson Education, Inc.
Published by Longman

Writing Arguments: A Rhetoric with Readings,
Brief Eighth Edition
by John D. Ramage, John C. Bean, and June Johnson
Copyright © 2010 by Pearson Education, Inc.
Published by Longman

Writing: A Guide for College and Beyond,
Brief Second Edition
by Lester Faigley
Copyright © 2010 by Pearson Education, Inc.
Published by Longman

Perspectives on Argument, Sixth Edition
by Nancy V. Wood
Copyright © 2009 by Pearson Education, Inc.
Published by Prentice Hall

The Allyn & Bacon Guide to Writing, Fifth Edition
by John D. Ramage, John C. Bean, and June Johnson
Copyright © 2009 by Pearson Education, Inc.
Published by Longman

*The Prentice Hall Essential Guide for College
Writers*, Ninth Edition
by Stephen Reid
Copyright © 2011 by Pearson Education, Inc.
Published by Prentice Hall

Pearson Learning Solutions, 501 Boylston Street, Suite 900, Boston, MA 02116
A Pearson Education Company
www.pearsoned.com

Printed in the United States of America

5 6 7 8 9 10 V354 17 16 15 14 13

000200010270802793

CB/JW

ISBN 10: 1-256-40339-3
ISBN 13: 978-1-256-40339-5

Acknowledgments

This custom text is dedicated to all Baker College Composition Students.

This text is part of a vision of composition that resulted from a Communication and Collaboration AQIP Project.

We are most grateful for the Directors of College Writing, at each of the campuses, who were instrumental in customizing our composition sequence and text:

Allen Park—Jill Morris
Auburn Hills--Lisa Friedrich-Harris
Cadillac--Jenifer Witt
Clinton Township- Jenna Caruso
Flint—Kim Rosebohm
Jackson—Cheryl Cox
Muskegon—Gerald Browning
Online—Kirk Astle
Owosso—Jacqueline Dalley
Port Huron— Teri Horton

We also wish to acknowledge the subcommittee whose dedication and collaboration made possible the creation of this custom text:

Brian Hudson, full time faculty at Auburn Hills
Lisa Friedrich-Harris
Jenifer Witt
Jenna Caruso
Jacqueline Dalley
Teri Horton

Brief Contents

Contents

18 HOW DO I PRESENT MY POSITION?   763

Baker College Composition

A Custom Approach

Revised Edition

Baker College
Allen Park

What Is the Writing Process?

WHICH SCENARIO BEST DESCRIBES YOUR PAST EXPERIENCES WITH WRITING?

A. You receive a writing assignment that is due in two weeks. Not long before the essay is due (sometimes the night before), you read the assigned material, take a few notes, and sit down at the computer to pound out a finished product. If you have time, you read over the essay for typos before handing it in. A week later, maybe longer, the teacher returns your paper. You check out the grade, glance at the teacher's comments, and stash the essay in your notebook.

B. You receive an assignment that directs you to write an essay in stages. The first draft is due in one week, a second draft a week later, and perhaps a final draft a week after that. Before you compose the preliminary draft, you do some prewriting activities, reading the assigned material and responding to it in your course journal. You use these prewriting notes to write your essay. When you bring your essay to class, you give it to a group of peers or to the teacher. These reviewers make suggestions for revision. You rethink the paper, make revisions, and resubmit it. The teacher returns the paper with comments and a grade. You check out the grade; read over the comments, especially those referring to the improvements you made; and store the essay in your notebook.

These scenarios represent two different approaches to writing. Scenario A focuses on the finished product, whereas scenario B values the *process* as much as the product. The product-oriented writer tries to create a perfect, polished essay in one try. The process-oriented writer works at assignments in phases: *prewriting, drafting, revising,* and *editing.* The product-oriented writer considers composing a solitary activity. The process-oriented writer engages in collaborative activities, sometimes in prewriting discussions and often in peer review groups.

Whenever you generate ideas, read texts, and organize your materials for writing, you engage in prewriting. When you begin to compose the paper, you enter the *drafting* phase. After you complete a draft and receive some feedback from your teacher or peers, you rework your paper in the *revising* phase. You expand on important points, delete irrelevant material, and clarify anything that confused your readers. Finally, you move to *editing*. At this phase, you focus on the surface features of your writing, checking for problems with usage, spelling, punctuation, and mechanics.

Writers do not necessarily proceed from one stage to the next in a systematic fashion. The process is recursive. The various activities can occur at any point in the process. Revising can take place while you are drafting your essay or after you have completed a full-blown draft. As we wrote this textbook, we revised some of it at the drafting stage, most of it at the revision stage as we completed each chapter, and a few parts at a later date after we had completed the entire manuscript.

You need not work through the reading and writing process in lockstep fashion, marching methodically from one stage to the next. But you should be aware that some types of pacing are more productive than others. When you are drafting your essay, if you stop every few minutes to fret about spelling, punctuation, or correct usage, you may end up with disjointed, disconnected prose. The beauty of the process approach to writing is it allows you to concentrate on generating ideas while you are drafting. Editing comes later.

You should also be aware that writers may use different composing styles, depending on their purposes. A writer completing a complex history assignment may spend much more time on prewriting activities—reading, underlining and annotating the materials, and taking notes—than would a writer who is composing an essay drawing on prior knowledge or personal experience.

Resistance to Process Writing

The following excerpt comes from an e-mail received from a student the morning an essay was due:

> . . . It's [name deleted] from your academic writing course. I had grand ambitions tonight of pulling the classic college-esque 'all-nighter' to finish a biology project, chemistry lab report, and your writing paper. Unfortunately, things aren't going as smoothly as I planned—it's 5 AM and the chem report is almost done, while the bio project and paper are as blank as I'd imagine your facial expression will be when reading this. With class in 4 hours and 15 minutes (its actually 5:09 right now according to my computer clock), I am doubting how much I will get done on your assignment. I have 387 words, but it's mostly fragmented paragraphs with incomplete ideas. If i manage to crawl into your class this morning the shell of a shell of the man i usually am (that's not a

typo, but you may have to read it a few times to understand it. Actually, I really have no idea how much of my language in this makes sense at all. The amount of caffeine that i've consumed is enough to kill a small horse, and my eyes are having trouble focusing), I will most likely have a shitty essay at best, with some pretty cool ideas that never get expanded upon. My essay is about the relationship and integration of television and the internet, and I'm having a lot of trouble finding articles to support my claim. I've used ProQuest, Lexis-Nexis, EbscoHost, and Google. I've never used databases before, and I'm having a lot of trouble finding review articles on the relation between the internet and society, tv and society, and just statistics about either (i.e., how many people own/watch tv, the amount of time the average user spends on the internet, etc.). I know how terrible it is that I'm sending this so late in the game. I hate to put professors in positions like this. The only time I can meet this week is on Friday after 11 AM.

The worst part about this is the entire e-mail is 533 words, which is longer than my essay.

Many students believe that they write best "under pressure." Some intentionally begin work on essays the night before a due date because they think that approach works well for them. Even those who admit that they are not able to write well under pressure often believe that they might develop that ability with practice. Virtually all students claim to know someone who is able to start working on an essay the night before it is due and by morning produce A-quality work.

While students may want to believe that last minute drafting is effective, the evidence indicates that successful writers rely on a process that involves multiple drafts and extends over time. Virtually all teachers of writing are committed to the process approach because the research in our discipline demonstrates the importance of process. The following excerpt, taken from a recent research study, indicates the consensus of those who study writing:

> Writing in marathon sessions is a kind of blocked practice that students and perhaps even some of their professors use to meet deadlines. Such writing binges can cause anxiety, exhaustion, and writer's block (Boice, 1985, 1997). Professional writers typically compose on a consistent schedule of a few hours per day at most (Kellogg, 2006).

In addition to the conclusions of scholarly inquiry into writing, anecdotal evidence from hundreds of famous writers indicates that even the most proficient wordsmiths, those with years of successful publishing experience, must go through a process of drafting and revision that cannot be compressed into a short time frame. For example, consider Joyce Carol Oates, known for her excellence as a writer of novels, short stories, poems, essays, and reviews. Since Oates is one of the most prolific writers of our times, we might assume that she has mastered the art of writing under pressure. However, at a reading she gave in

2003 at Ithaca College, Oates explained that she depends upon a writing process that extends over time. She compared writing a first draft to pushing a peanut over a filthy floor using only her nose. Only after she crosses the floor can she get up, see where she has been to get "the big picture," and then begin revising. Oates also stated that a writer can only write a good first sentence after he or she has written the last sentence; in other words, revision produces good sentences. She described her process for writing a novel as writing the first half and then rewriting that half while simultaneously writing the second half. She also reported that the short story she read to us earlier in the evening had been written and published years before, but she still made revisions for the reading up until twenty minutes before she took the stage. Other accomplished writers' descriptions of the writing process echo that of Oates. Writing takes time. Good writing results from getting down a draft and then returning to it repeatedly and tinkering with it until it works. There are no shortcuts.

As Anne Lamott (1994) points out in her best selling book *Bird by Bird*, developing writers should take heart in the fact that first drafts are always rough:

> Almost all good writing begins with terrible first efforts. You need to start somewhere. Start by getting something—anything—down on paper. A friend of mine says that the first draft is the down draft—you just get it down. The second draft is the up draft—you fix it up. You try to say what you have to say more accurately. And the third draft is the dental draft, where you check every tooth, to see if it's loose or cramped or decayed, or even, God help us, healthy. (pp. 25–26)

We are encouraged by Oates' and Lamott's testimonies as they indicate to us that everyone, even the best writers, struggle with first drafts but that anyone who commits to the writing process will improve. Don't expect too much from your first drafts, but, on the other hand, don't be discouraged by them.

Prewriting

Prewriting is also called *invention*. A root of *invention* is the Latin word *invenire*, meaning to discover or find. It is the period in which writers discover what they want to say. They explore what they already know about a topic, searching for ideas, using problem-solving methods, making connections, and conducting inquiries.

As a college writer, you will spend a substantial amount of time prewriting: analyzing your assignments, specifying your purposes for writing, establishing your audience, and reading your sources. As you read each source, decide what you want to obtain from it. Remember to look beyond content. Also consider form, organization, stylistic features, and rhetorical context. As you underline, annotate, and take notes, plan how you will use the reading source in your essay.

Then reread part or all of the text, reread your notes, record additional notes, and do more planning. When you have done all this rereading, noting, and planning, you are ready to write your first draft.

For assignments that require you to use sources in your writing, the key to success lies at the prewriting stage. This is the period just before you sit down at the computer to type out a complete draft of your paper. It is the time for reading and rereading the text, annotating, taking notes, and planning your essay. You will find that it is far more efficient to select relevant parts of the reading source, bring your prior topic knowledge into play, and organize your ideas at this stage than to rack your brain and refer continually to the reading source *while* you are drafting your essay.

ANALYZE THE ASSIGNMENT

When you receive your assignment, put on your rhetorical glasses and think about audience and purpose. Work within the context of the rhetorical situation: just as the author of the source you are about to read has written to his or her readers for a reason, you are writing your essay for a reason. You are trying to affect or influence your readers in a certain way.

Consider student Nora Gold, who received the following assignment in her first-year writing course:

> How should our society balance the rights and responsibilities of developing teens? Write a 1000-word essay in which you take a position on an issue concerning the legal rights of minors in American society. You might consider the laws and governmental policies specific to minors that pertain to one of the following issues: alcohol use, abortion, consent to sexual activity, voting, municipal curfews, or sentencing youthful offenders. Conduct research on your topic and use at least three sources in your essay. Write for an general audience unfamiliar with the sources you cite.

This assignment asks the writer to take a position and write an argument essay. Whenever you analyze an assignment, determine the essay type or "genre" that is called for. Other genres that we cover in this textbook include summary essays, response essays, analysis essays, and research papers.

You may need to ask your instructor for more detail about aspects of the assignment. For instance, we have noticed that our colleagues in various disciplines use the term "critique" in distinct ways: some assume that a critique includes both a summary of a source as well as a response to it, while others think that a critique should include only analysis of the source and no summary. Some instructors believe that papers should be written for a general readership while others want papers directed to those knowledgeable about the field. You need to pose questions about the assignment up front rather than wait until the essay is well under way, as some students are inclined to do.

Some genres are particular to academic disciplines. For example, in the world of business, cost–benefits analysis is a common form for written expression. Proposed corporate ventures are often presented in this balance sheet approach, where potential gains are weighed against risks and potential losses. All academic disciplines are characterized by certain thinking strategies or methodologies. An important part of learning to write in a particular discipline is identifying and becoming skilled at using the methods of analysis specific to that field of study.

Another way to better understand writing assignments is to think about how the instructor expects you to use the course content in your writing. Bloom's Taxonomy of Educational Objectives provides a means of achieving this understanding. Educational psychologist Benjamin Bloom analyzed the intellectual demands of academic tasks and came up with the following classifications: knowledge, comprehension, application, analysis, synthesis, judgment. In the following list, we use Bloom's scheme as the basis for questions you might ask about the goals of your writing assignments:

ANALYZING WRITING ASSIGNMENTS USING BLOOM'S TAXONOMY

- knowledge: Am I aware of the information presented in the course?
- comprehension: Do I understand fully the information presented in the course?
- application: Can I apply the information presented in the course outside the context in which I learned it?
- analysis: Can I break down concepts taught in the course into their components and understand the relationships among those components?
- synthesis: Can I make connections among various parts of the course content to arrive at a conclusion of my own?
- judgment: Can I arrive at and defend my own viewpoints about the course content?

Keep in mind that any given assignment may touch on more than one of the categories in Bloom's Taxonomy. For example, a judgment might be supported by analysis and synthesis of course content elements.

Don't hesitate to ask for explanations of your assignments, but make sure your questions have meaningful content. Avoid the "Just tell me what you want" demand. Try asking your instructor the following questions:

QUESTIONS TO ASK INSTRUCTORS ABOUT WRITING ASSIGNMENTS

- For whom am I writing? The professor? My classmates? Someone else?
- Do you have a sample of a strong student essay that you can show me?
- Which documentation style shall I use?
- Which organizational plans will work best for this assignment?
- What percentage of the essay should be taken from sources and what percentage should be my own ideas?

ESTABLISH A FOCUS

From among the options mentioned in the assignment, Nora is drawn to the topic of youth curfews, since she grew up in a community that enforces a midnight curfew on teens under seventeen years of age, and she has been involved in many discussions of that law, particularly with her parents.

As do most teens in her community, Nora opposes the curfew law. Several of her friends were caught violating the curfew on weekends and were detained at the police station until their parents picked them up, an experience that the teens felt was embarrassing and unfair. On the other hand, Nora knows the curfew was instituted following a series of late night accidents which claimed teens' lives. The parents of one of those who died mounted the campaign for the curfew. As Nora thinks about the goal of her essay, she realizes it will not be enough to merely reiterate her opinion and relate the experiences of her friends. In order to appeal to a broad audience, one that includes both young and older readers, she will need to do more than explain her own viewpoint; she will need to draw on outside sources that will substantiate her point of view.

In this particular example, the student starts out the writing process with an opinion she has developed in the past and identifies an audience that is not inclined to agree with her and needs to be convinced. We should note, however, that many times students begin the writing process with an assigned topic about which they have no opinion. In those cases, opinions emerge through reading and responding to sources. Even in cases where writers begin with a viewpoint they want to defend, it is advantageous to consider a range of opinions at the prewriting stage. Strong arguments are grounded in a clear understanding of and response to viewpoints contrary to the writer's.

Two weeks before her essay is due, Nora begins to collect information on her topic. She reasons that her topic will be covered in newspaper and magazine articles since it is an issue of public concern; consequently, she decides to check databases at her college library that cover periodicals written for a broad readership. She travels on the Internet to the Web site of her college library and accesses Proquest Research Library, a database that she has used in the past to access journal and magazine articles. She tries "Curfews" as a subject search term, and Proquest responds with a list of related subject headings including "Curfews and teens." She selects "Curfews and teens," and Proquest provides a long list of related articles, starting with the most recently published. Nora reads through the titles of the articles that were published over the last ten years and selects those that seem most relevant to her topic. She then conducts similar searches on General OneFile, another general purpose database, and on Lexis-Nexus, a database that emphasizes legal content. On all three databases, Nora locates numerous articles related to her topic.

While youth curfews is relatively easy to research, other topics may require a more sophisticated approach. In this case, Nora is able to locate material easily; her work is to sift through the sources and select those that best serve her purposes as a writer. She narrows down the list of articles to those that seem most promising and then prints them out.

READ AND RESPOND TO SOURCES

As Nora reads the articles she has printed out, she writes marginal comments that record her responses to the text. Here is an excerpt of her response to the article "Nunez and Beyond: An Examination of Nunez v. City of San Diego and the Future of Nocturnal Juvenile Curfew Ordinances " by Jeff Beaumont:

This is exactly what I want to prove.

The Supreme Court needs to take leadership on this issue. But then, the current Court is conservative and might not place as much value on youth rights as I do.

Apparently, Bellotti v. Baird has to do with abortions. How does this case relate to curfews?

Juvenile curfews implicate serious constitutional issues involving minors' and parents' fundamental rights. They infringe on minors' First Amendment freedoms of speech and association, as well as the fundamental right of free movement. Minors—like adults—possess these fundamental rights, and any infringement therein requires strict scrutiny. However, because the United States Supreme Court has not yet ruled on the constitutionality of nocturnal juvenile curfews, lower federal courts addressing these fundamental rights issues have been unable to meet a consensus. Federal courts' inconsistent and divergent treatment of minors' rights in relation to those of adults is a result of the erroneous application of Bellotti v. Baird in the context of juvenile curfews. Federal courts, such as the Ninth Circuit, continue to apply Bellotti despite the absence of the Supreme Court's willingness to extend Bellotti beyond the context of abortions. Even assuming that the Supreme Court would extend Bellotti, juvenile curfews do not implicate "the peculiar vulnerability of children; their inability to make critical decisions in an informed, mature manner; and the importance of the parental role in childrearing." Moreover, the imposition of juvenile curfews on minors burdens—not strengthens—parents' fundamental right to rear their children. Thus, as one court stated, juvenile curfews are like "a bull in a china shop of constitutional values."

I could use this quotation!

When she is finished reading Beaumont's article, Nora jots down her thoughts on how she might use the material in her essay. Here is an excerpt from Nora's journal:

> Beaumont supports the idea that curfews violate the constitutional rights of young people. One point he raises that I hadn't read elsewhere is that curfews interfere with minors' First Amendment rights. He says that curfews "significantly restrict minors' access to public forums, thereby preventing minors from exercising their First Amendment freedoms." This makes sense. If you can't go out in public, then it limits your ability to express yourself or get information from others.
>
> Beaumont and other writers on this topic refer to the Bellotti v. Baird case. According to Beaumont, the case involved a Massachusetts law that required minors to obtain their parents' consent before they could have abortions. I understand that the abortion and curfew issues both involve the constitutional rights of minors and thus might have some common ground, but I don't think it will help my argument to bring up the abortion issue. People react so strongly to the debate over abortion rights that it might be a distraction from what I want to say about curfews.

Nora's marginal notes and journal entries are examples of active reading strategies. Her goal at this stage is to record her thoughts about the readings, material that she will be able to draw on as she begins her preliminary writing.

PREWRITING STRATEGIES

BRAINSTORM

Another way to determine what you are looking for is to brainstorm a list. For example, below is a list of observations and questions on Lyme disease:

- A friend had Lyme disease for a year and went to many doctors before it was diagnosed.
- Why is Lyme disease hard to diagnose?
- Overpopulation of deer spreads Lyme disease.
- Are deer the only animals that spread the ticks that transmit Lyme disease?
- What methods can control the deer population in suburbs?
- How can you control ticks in yards?

WRITE NONSTOP

Another way to find out how much you know about a topic is to write nonstop.

1. Put a tentative topic at the top of the page. Then write as fast as you can for five to ten minutes.

2. Don't stop to correct mistakes. Let your ideas flow wherever they take you, even if they take you well outside the boundaries of your topic. The idea is that the constant flow of words will generate ideas—some useful and some not.

3. If you get stuck, write the same sentence over again, or write about how hungry you are or how hard it is to write. Thoughts will eventually start reappearing.

4. After you've finished, read what you have written and underline any key ideas.

5. Select one of the ideas and put it at the top of the page. Then write nonstop again for five to ten minutes.

MAKE AN IDEA MAP

Start with the general subject you plan to write about. State it in a few words. Draw a box around it.

Obesity in children

Next think about what can be said about this topic. At this point you don't want specifics but general categories.

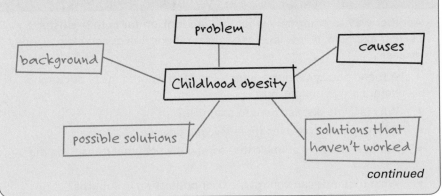

continued

The third stage is to generate topics about each category.

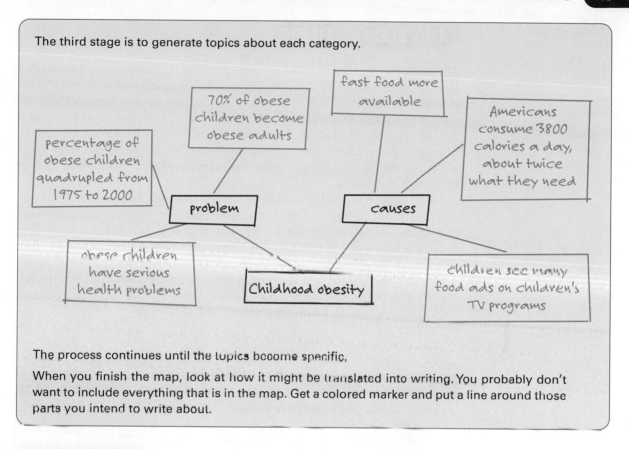

The process continues until the topics become specific.

When you finish the map, look at how it might be translated into writing. You probably don't want to include everything that is in the map. Get a colored marker and put a line around those parts you intend to write about.

Drafting

You can see that throughout the prewriting phase, you continually shift back and forth between your role as reader and your role as writer. As you begin drafting, the writer role takes on more importance, but you don't give up the reader role. Throughout the drafting stage, you may find it necessary to refer to the reading sources to retrieve a quotation, verify a piece of information, or flesh out a note.

Before you begin to write a first draft, reflect on the prior knowledge you have already brought into play. You have tapped your prior knowledge of the topic to produce a pool of responses to the reading source, and you have invoked your prior knowledge of organization and structure to discover an organizational plan. At this point, you will summon up two other types of prior knowledge: (1) knowledge of the basic features of writing—elements like titles, introductions, sentences, paragraphs, transitions and connecting ideas, and conclusions—and (2) knowledge of strategies for summarizing, paraphrasing, and quoting sources.

DEVELOP A THESIS

The preliminary or *working thesis* is the central idea that you intend to develop in your paper. You might think of it as a capsule summary of your entire essay. It reflects your rhetorical purpose and the effect you want to have on the audience. It may also indicate your organizational plan. In an argumentative essay, it may express your level of agreement (or disagreement) with the source or indicate ways you will extend or build on the source. We call the thesis *preliminary* at the prewriting stage because writers often revise their thesis statements later in the writing process.

One of the principal characteristics of the academic essay is that it is *thesis-driven*. This means that the thesis is revealed early in the essay and everything that follows serves to support it. You may find this convention unappealing because it forces you to reveal the end before you have told the story and thus may sound like a formula for boredom. All the same, the convention of beginning with a thesis statement is strong in the academic tradition, and your readers will expect you to observe this practice. The thesis for an academic essay should accomplish the following goals.

GOALS OF A THESIS STATEMENT

- Provide a comprehensive statement of the writer's intentions and the central idea
- Indicate the complexity of the writer's thinking
- Suggest how the essay will be organized
- Be consistent with the discussion in the body of the essay and with the conclusion

---

You may be asking, "How can I come up with a thesis statement at the outset of the drafting process if I'm not yet sure about the point I wish to make in my essay?" If this is the case, review marginal notes and journal entries as follows.

- **See if one type of response predominates.**
- **See if a good number of responses were triggered by a particular source idea.**
- **Classify your responses.** Select workable categories and discard the rest. You might highlight the responses in which you agree or disagree with the author of the source and then work only with these as you draft your essay.

Another way to work toward a thesis statement is by *freewriting*, which involves writing nonstop for ten minutes or more without worrying about spelling, grammar, or punctuation. The goal is to force yourself to get words down and thus get past the psychological barrier of the blank page or screen. Allow ideas to flow freely and follow your stream of consciousness. For this technique to work, you have to keep writing without a pause for at least ten minutes. Once you have completed your ten-minute writing blitz, you read through what you have written, searching for main ideas that might form part of your thesis statement.

In his book *Writing With Power*, Peter Elbow (1998), a renowned expert on writing instruction, describes the value of freewriting:

> Freewriting makes writing easier by helping you with the root psychological or existential difficulty in writing: finding words in your head and putting them down on a blank sheet of paper. So much writing time and energy is spent *not* writing: wondering, worrying, crossing out, having second, third, and fourth thoughts. (p.14)

Nora decides to use freewriting as she works on her thesis statement. She first reviews her assignment and looks through her written responses to the articles she read. Then she puts her readings and notes aside and writes nonstop for ten minutes, attempting to capture the main idea that she wants to develop in her essay. Later, she looks through her freewriting and notices that the following excerpt seems to capture what she wants to say in her essay:

> I didn't find a single source that included any information that really proves that teen curfews help reduce crime or make young people any safer. What good are they? Why have them at all? Politicians, of course, love curfews. If they pass curfews, they seem like they are tough on crime, which gets them votes. So it seems they are willing to stomp on the civil liberties of teenagers just for a few votes! This is totally unfair!

Using this freewriting excerpt as a starting point, Nora develops the following preliminary thesis statement:

> Even though curfews are supposed to reduce youth crime, there is no real evidence that they work. What is clear is that curfews infringe on the civil liberties of young people. Apparently, politicians are willing to sacrifice those civil liberties in order to appear tough on crime.

This preliminary thesis statement serves as a starting point for Nora as she writes the first draft of her essay. Subsequent revisions result in the thesis statement as it appears in her final draft:

> Teen curfew laws, such as the one enforced in San Diego, are being established in cities across the United States for the alleged purpose of reducing youth crime. These laws will do little to deter those teens who are criminally inclined and are unfair to the millions of young people

who have done nothing to deserve being held under house arrest. Enforcing teen curfews amounts to penalizing young people so that adults can enjoy a false sense of security and politicians can give the impression that they are tough on crime.

You may be surprised that this preliminary thesis statement is three sentences long since you may have been told that a thesis statement should be a single sentence. The length and the complexity of a thesis statement depend on the writer's rhetorical purpose. Thesis statements in academic essays are often two, three, or more sentences. If you have a complex reaction to the topic, the thesis of your essay may be lengthy. Consider a thesis statement that took up the entire second paragraph of student Steven Siegele's essay:

> The courts have ruled that people under the age of eighteen have constitutional rights that may be affected by curfew laws. Curfews potentially impinge on First Amendment rights to freedom of expression and assembly, the Fourth Amendment principle of probable cause, and the 14th Amendment right to equal protect under the law. In addition, it has been argued that curfews violate parents' right to determine what is best for their children, a right which, according to the Supreme Court, is protected by the Constitution. On the other hand, the Supreme Court has ruled in many cases that individual rights must sometimes take a back seat to what is good for society in general. As was once stated by the Court, freedom of speech does not give one the right to yell "Fire" in a crowded theater. Curfews are justified only when the authorities can demonstrate clearly that they do more good than harm.

As his thesis indicates, Steven wants his audience to understand how the courts need to balance individual rights with the greater good of society. His point is to urge caution in establishing that balance. He has a complicated objective, and it takes an entire paragraph to express it. Some thesis statements are much more compact, like the one written by student Colin Smith:

> I oppose curfews because they single out people for harassment based on their age alone. We should be judged by our actions, not by the number of years we've lived.

Lisa Rodriguez's thesis is longer than Colin's but shorter than Steven's paragraph:

> As long as the rate of crime in our society remains unacceptably high, we must continue to provide the police with the means to maintain law and order. Curfews are one of the tools that the police need to control urban crime. I do feel, however, that the penalties for curfew violation should be relatively mild. Curfews should serve primarily as a justification for police to stop and check up on teens who are out on the streets.

As our examples indicate, the length and the complexity of a thesis statement depend on the writer's rhetorical purpose.

You may be surprised that several of these thesis statements contain the first-person pronouns—*our, we, I.* Personal pronouns are appropriate in certain types of academic writing, particularly in response essays. It is difficult to write from personal experience without using *we, I, my,* or *me.* These pronouns also help writers label their own views so that they are not confused with those of the source authors. Personal pronouns appear in respected professional journals, but they are discouraged in some academic writing contexts. In the sciences, lab reports are generally written to sound objective and impersonal ("The sample was analyzed for trace elements" rather than "I analyzed the sample for trace elements"). Ask your professor if you are unsure about using personal pronouns in your assignment.

We should stress that your preliminary thesis statement is subject to change throughout the writing process. Too often students think that they have to make sense of the topic and come up with a full-blown thesis before they begin to write the essay. Writing is a creative process that advances your thinking. Often your ideas about a topic will develop as you draft the essay. If you hold tenaciously to your initial thesis, you won't be able to take advantage of the new thinking that the writing process inspires.

We discuss revising entire essay drafts later in the chapter, but we briefly touch on thesis revision here because writers typically revisit their thesis statements repeatedly as they work on their initial drafts. One result of in-process revisions is to enrich the thesis and make it more comprehensive. In the following example, notice how the successive revisions of a preliminary thesis statement reflect increasing complexity of thought. The thesis is written in response to Jerry Farber's essay "A Young Person's Guide to the Grading System," which appears on pages 184–188.

Preliminary Thesis	I am against the grading system.
First Revision	I believe the grading system runs counter to the goals of education.
Second Revision	I believe grades are counterproductive because they focus students' attention on scores rather than knowledge.
Third Revision	Even though many students believe that they need grades for motivation, grades are counterproductive because they distract students from the most important goal of education: gaining knowledge.

In the third revision, the writer takes a stand, "grades are counterproductive...." She also acknowledges an opposing position, "many students...." This thesis indicates the writer's path of development. She will support her own position against grades, but she will also respond to students who favor grades. The wording of the thesis tells readers that they can expect the writer to organize the essay as an argument. In general, you will help readers if you can write a thesis that indicates your organizational plan.

The following table lists the most common organizational plans. Notice how the intended organizational plan for the essay is signaled in each of the following thesis statements. The topic for this example is affirmative action in college admissions. Notice also that the thesis statements do not express the writers' viewpoints on affirmative action. Although the term *thesis* is often used to refer to an argumentative position, it has a much broader meaning in the academic community. The thesis statement specifies your *intention* in writing—what you hope to accomplish but not always your opinion. In many cases, your intention in writing will not be to win an argument but rather to present an issue objectively for the benefit of your readers, and that intention would still be labeled your thesis statement.

Organizational Plan	Thesis Statement
Time order	During the 1960s and early 1970s, it was widely accepted that affirmative action policies were beneficial, particularly in the college admission process. After the *Bakke* decision in 1978, however, arguments against affirmative action grew louder and reached a crescendo in the 1990s.
Comparison and contrast	The supporters and critics of using affirmative action in college admission decisions disagree on a range of social issues. Among them are what constitutes merit, how America should address class-based education deprivation, and which rights are protected by the Fourteenth Amendment.
Case in point	Opponents of affirmative action would argue that my adopted brother from Guatemala and I should receive the same treatment in the college admission process. On the other hand, proponents of affirmative action would maintain that my brother should be given special advantages.

Each of these thesis statements provides the reader with a roadmap for how the essay will proceed and will help the reader follow the writer's train of thought as the essay develops. A strong thesis statement establishes the basis for a unified and coherent essay.

As you approach the end of the revision process, make sure that your thesis is consistent and comprehensive. It must be consistent with the discussion in the body of your essay and with the perspective that comes through in your conclusion. If the drafting process has altered your perspective on the issue, modify the thesis so that it is consistent with this shift. Read the introduction and then immediately read the conclusion to check for consistency. The thesis should be comprehensive enough to capture the major viewpoints the essay presents.

A final piece of advice is to avoid a banal thesis statement that includes an opinion but makes only a superficial attempt to come to grips with the topic. Imagine that you are writing an essay in response to an article that defends human cloning. After reading the article, you decide you are opposed to human cloning and write the following thesis statement:

> I am opposed to human cloning because it involves asexual reproduction of a human being.

This statement indicates opposition to human cloning and then provides a brief definition of cloning as if it were a reason to reject the technology. It leaves readers with a question: Why does the writer find "asexual reproduction" troubling? Since there are a number of possible answers to this question, readers can only guess how the writer would answer it.

The next sample thesis includes a reason for the writer's belief but still does not indicate that the writer weighed the evidence or thought about the issue in any depth.

> I oppose human cloning because it is an unnatural process that no normal person would be willing to undergo.

The offhand dismissal of proponents of cloning makes the writer seem immature. You risk losing the respect of your reader at the outset if your thesis indicates a superficial approach to the topic. Take advantage of the thesis statement to indicate the full complexity of your viewpoint, as in the following example:

> I oppose human cloning for the same reason that I oppose selective breeding and other eugenic technologies because it is based on the assumption that some individuals' genes are better than those of others. If this assumption becomes widely accepted, it will jeopardize the basic human rights of those who are judged genetically inferior.

SELECT AN ORGANIZATIONAL PLAN

After you come up with a preliminary thesis, your next step is to decide which organizational format to use. Table 1.1 identifies the most common patterns and gives a brief description of the purpose of each.

Table 1.1   Patterns for Developing and Organizing Ideas

Pattern	Writer's Purpose
Time order, narration, process	To present ideas or events in a chronological sequence; to tell what happened (narration) or to describe a sequence of actions (process)
Antecedent and consequence, cause and effect	To present causes (antecedents) or examine effects or outcomes (consequences); to reveal the causes of a particular outcome or phenomenon or to explain its consequences, usually by explaining the relationship between the causes and the effects
Description	To present the physical attributes, parts, or setting of the topic, often out of a desire to give a personal impression of the person, place, or thing being described
Statement and response	To present a statement and give a reaction, often in a question-and-answer, problem-and-solution, or remark-and-reply format
Comparison and contrast	To present the similarities or differences between objects, approaches, or viewpoints
Example	To present illustrations or instances that support an idea
Analysis or classification	To divide the topic into parts (analyze) or to group parts or facets of the topic according to some principle or characteristic (classify)
Definition	To explain a word, concept, or principle
Analogy	To show the similarity between things that otherwise bear little or no resemblance; to explain something by comparing it point by point with something similar

An organizational plan you may have learned in middle school or high school is the five-paragraph theme.

Introduction   Introduce your topic. At the end of the paragraph, state your thesis.

Three body paragraphs   In each paragraph, present a reason why you hold your position.

Conclusion   Sum up your main points, speculate about the implications of what you have just said, or call your readers to action.

The five-paragraph format is appropriate in some cases, but don't rely on it in college-level papers. One of the principal reasons this format is taught so widely is that it provides a general-purpose organizational plan students can rely on when writing under time pressure, especially during standardized tests, when they do not have the leisure to think carefully about the organizational structure that best fits the situation. The five-paragraph plan may serve as a security blanket when you are under pressure to produce a coherent essay in a very limited time, but it also shackles your writing. Your ideas about the topic should determine how you organize your essay, but your ideas will be distorted if you force them into an inappropriate pattern. Our recommendation is that you approach exams with a handful of writing plans in mind rather than a single all-purpose format.

As Nora considers how she will develop her thesis, she realizes that there are four principal assertions she intends to defend:

1. Curfews don't actually reduce youth crime.
2. After-school programs can help reduce youth crime.
3. Politicians propose curfews to give the appearance of being tough on crime.
4. Curfews lead to reductions in the civil liberties of young people.

As she thinks about these four assertions, she realizes that they all involve cause-and-effect relationships. For each of the four, she will have to demonstrate a causal relationship between two factors. She also considers how the four assertions connect together and reorders them as follows:

1. Curfews lead to reductions in the civil liberties of young people.

    Nora reasons that her entire argument rests on this point: if adults do not perceive that curfews have serious negative consequences, then they would be inclined to give them a try.

2. Curfews don't actually reduce youth crime.

    Once she has demonstrated the negative consequences of curfews, then Nora reasons she can weigh those consequences against the dubious claims that curfews reduce crime.

3. Politicians propose curfews to give the appearance of being tough on crime.

> Nora figures that some readers may question her point 2, since they assume that curfews would not be established if they weren't effective. Her point 3 responds to that concern by identifying the political motives behind curfews.

4. After-school programs can help reduce youth crime.

> Nora thinks that presenting an alternative method of reducing youth crime and demonstrating that it works is a logical way to end her discussion. She reasons that in response to points 1 to 3, some skeptical readers might say to themselves, "But we can't just do nothing at all about youth crime." Point 4 provides a possible solution that might be applied in the future.

Nora now has a rough plan for how she will organize the first draft of her essay. Of course, she may modify this initial plan as the essay develops. As she writes her first draft, she may discover new ways of connecting ideas that did not occur to her before she began to write.

WRITE A FIRST DRAFT

Next, we will describe drafting an essay sequentially, starting with the title and ending with the conclusion. We do not mean to suggest that you will follow this order. The title may be a later addition to the essay. You may find it easier to write the introduction after you compose the body. Whatever you do, don't stare at the blank page waiting for the title or first sentence to come to you. Start wherever you feel ready to write, and return later to the parts that caused initial hesitation. As Nora begins to draft her essay, she decides to begin with point 2 from her organizational plan: demonstrating that curfews do not reduce crime. She begins with point 2 because she is confident that she has collected enough information to prove this point and has a good notion of what she wants to say in this section of her essay. She starts with the section of the essay that she feels she is best prepared to write.

● **TITLE YOUR ESSAY**   Wait to title your essay until after you have revised your first draft. That way, if you've changed direction, you will not have to retitle it. Your title should express the position you take in the essay or relate to your thesis in some other way. Create titles that indicate your perspective and, if possible, capture the essence of the issue you are addressing. For example, assume that you are writing an essay in response to "Time to Do Everything But Think," an article written by *New York Times* columnist David Brooks (2007) on the topic of technology. A straightforward title like "A Response to David Brooks's 'Time to Do Everything But Think'" fails to indicate that the topic un-

TITLING YOUR ESSAY

- Let the title reflect your organizational plan. An essay that develops according to the comparison-and-contrast pattern might be titled "The Wireless Human: Master or Slave?"

- Borrow an apt phrase from the reading source or from your essay. In paragraph 5 of his article, Brooks states, "He's a speed freak, an info junkie." An essay written in response to Brooks might be titled "Info Junkies."

- State the general topic and then, after a colon, your perspective or stance—for example, "Wireless Communication: A New Technology That Is Dominating Our Lives."

- Phrase the title as a question—for example, "Will Wireless Technology Change Society?"

- Use another well-known quotation or saying, such as "Faster Than a Speeding Bullet: The Wireless Culture."

der discussion is the social impact of wireless communication. Compare this matter-of-fact title to the examples in the box above.

Nora uses the third of these options and titles her essay "Curfew Laws: Demonizing Teens." She wants her title to announce the topic and to suggest her perspective on the issue. She also hopes the provocative phrase "Demonizing Teens" will capture her audience's attention.

● **ESTABLISH A STYLE**   Before you write your first draft, you should make a conscious decision about the writing style that will be appropriate for your assignment and audience. Academic writing always involves making decisions about style based on content and audience. At this early stage of the writing process, you will set general stylistic goals. Don't get bogged down in wording, turns of phrase, and sentence structure. When you are revising and editing your essay, you will revisit the issue of style and use specific strategies for improving the style of your paper.

To illustrate how writers tailor style to content, we'd like you to read excerpts from two articles in the same issue of *College English*, a journal written for English professors. Each of the writers, Eleanor Berry (2007) and Lee Ann Carroll (2009), addresses the same group of readers, but because of the nature of her subject matter, each conceives of her audience in a distinct way.

While the method of grammatical analysis and the notion of counterpoint as constituting a prosody, as developed and deployed by Wesling and Hartman, serve to illuminate ways that poets eschewing meter can induce an experience of rhythm and affect readers' attention and construction of meaning, they do not fully address the need for a means of classifying the many modes of versification encompassed by the term "free verse." (p. 110)

It is not that students know too few stories, but that they know too many. Students experience every day how the lines between genres are blurred—in news presented as entertainment, docu-dramas, shock-jockey talk shows as the most public forums for political debate. Contrasting different forms over the course of a semester makes clearer how conventions both permit and constrain us to speak in different ways. (p. 201)

Professor Berry discusses poetic forms, a discipline that has a history and a related vocabulary. She sees her audience as scholars with knowledge of poetic forms and the field's specialized vocabulary. Professor Carroll writes about a broader topic, the teaching of first-year composition. She views her readers as classroom teachers, and she uses everyday language and an informal voice to speak to them. Both examples fit underneath a broad umbrella of academic writing styles that range from conversational to highly formal, from terse to expansive. Some students view the academic writing style as a starchy, uncomfortable uniform that they must don to write course papers. It should be seen as a vast wardrobe that allows the writer to make choices about content and audience.

As the examples from *College English* show, academic writers may employ different styles for readers of the same publication. But the readership has to be comfortable with diversification. Some readerships are not, and the journals that appeal to them expect uniformity in writing style and even give prospective authors style sheets that they must follow. Just as scholars have to adjust their writing style to the publication, students have to tailor their style to particular assignments. Prior to writing her essay, Nora Gold revisits her assignment:

How should our society balance the rights and responsibilities of developing teens? Write a 1000-word essay in which you take a position on an issue concerning the legal rights of minors in American society. You might consider the laws and governmental policies specific to minors that pertain to one of the following issues: alcohol use, abortion, consent to sexual activity, voting, municipal curfews, or sentencing youthful offenders. Conduct research on your topic and use at least three sources in your essay. Write for a general audience unfamiliar with the sources you cite.

Nora notes that the last sentence of the assignment specifies "a general audience," so she knows she is not writing exclusively for the professor, for other students in her writing or sociology classes, or for other members of the college community. She figures that she should use words that will be accessible to a relatively wide range of readers and should avoid academic jargon that might put off nonacademics. She looks through the sources she intends to draw on and decides to model her style on articles from *The Economist* and *National Catholic Reporter*, respected publications intended for wide readerships. She notes that some of her source articles are taken from academic publications, *New York University Law Review* and *Harvard Law Review*, and she concludes that she should present ideas from those sources in language that will make them accessible to a broader audience.

Some people speak of a writer's style as his or her trademark. They talk about Hemingway's clipped sentences and repeated adjectives and Faulkner's long, convoluted sentences. The truth is that writers make stylistic choices based on the publication and audience. Asked to write for *People* magazine, Eleanor Berry would not adopt the scholarly style she uses for her article in *College English*.

To show you how an academic writer alters her style to accommodate the publication and its intended audience, we reprinted the opening paragraphs from articles written by Sherry Turkle, a professor of sociology at M.I.T. and an expert on machine–human interaction. The first article appeared in *UNESCO Courier*, a publication meant for a general adult readership. The second article was published in *Social Research*, a venue for academic research studies in the social sciences. The readers of this journal are college professors and social scientists. Note the differences in Turkle's writing styles.

From *UNESCO Courier*

Children have always used their toys and playthings to create models for understanding their world. Fifty years ago, the genius of Swiss psychologist Jean Piaget showed it is the business of childhood to take objects and use how they "work" to construct theories of space, time, number, causality, life and mind. At that time, a child's world was full of things that could be understood in simple, mechanical ways. A bicycle could be understood in terms of its pedals and gears, a windup car in terms of its clockwork springs. Children were able to take electronic devices such as basic radios and (with some difficulty) bring them into this "mechanical" system of understanding. (Turkle, 2007, p. 24)

From *Social Research*

Computers offer themselves as models of mind and as "objects to think with" for thinking about the self. They do this in several ways. There is, first of all, the world of artificial intelligence research—Marvin Minsky once called it the enterprise of "trying to get computers to do things that would be considered intelligent if done by people." In the course of this effort, some artificial intelligence researchers explicitly endeavor to build machines that model the human mind. Second, there is the world of computational objects in the culture—the toys, the games, the simulation packages, the computational environments accessed through

Internet connections. These objects are evocative; interacting with them provokes reflection on the nature of the self.

For many decades computers had a clear cultural identity as linear, logical, mechanistic machines. Here I tell a story of a change in the cultural identity of the computer and consequently in the kind of mirror that computers offer for thinking about the self. Computational theories of intelligence now support decentered and emergent views of mind; experience with today's computational objects encourages rethinking identity in terms of multiplicity and flexibility. (Turkle, 2009, p. 146)

These two passages are not dramatically different, but the stylistic distinctions make sense given each publication's audience. In the first excerpt, Turkle uses straightforward language and provides examples—a bicycle, a windup car, a radio—that will appeal to a broad readership. She makes a point of identifying Jean Piaget for a population who may be unfamiliar with this developmental psychologist. In the passage from *Social Research*, Turkle quotes a fellow scholar, uses enumeration, and adopts a serious tone. Reread the closing sentence of the passage from *Social Research:* "Computational theories of intelligence now support decentered and emergent views of mind; experience with today's computational objects encourages rethinking identity in terms of multiplicity and flexibility." Language of this complexity does not appear anywhere in the *UNESCO Courier* excerpt. Readers unfamiliar with the field of artificial intelligence will not understand "decentered and emergent views of the mind." But the passage from *Social Research* remains an example of good academic writing. Those who read in the field of artificial intelligence will recognize its efficient use of language and the validity of Turkle's stylistic choices.

STRATEGIES FOR IMPROVING STYLE

- Avoid inflated language.
- Vary the structure and length of your sentences.
- Strengthen your verbs.
- Make your writing concise by cutting ineffective words and expressions and eliminating needless repetition.
- Liven up your writing with detail.
- Avoid sexist language.

Play it safe and discuss issues of style with your professors before you write your papers. Many professors assign only one or two papers per course, so you don't have the luxury of writing the first paper without assistance just to see how the instructor will respond, a strategy that many students use in high school. When you receive your first writing assignment, ask the professor to describe his or her expectations for style. Ask about the level of formality the professor expects, and find out about any special stylistic requirements, such as use of discipline-specific vocabulary or avoidance of passive voice. See if your professor can give you examples of successful student papers from past semesters. These models will tell you a lot about stylistic expectations.

While you should write in a style that meets the demands of particular courses, don't lose sight of your personal development as a stylist. See yourself as expanding your stylistic options rather than just complying with a temporary set of style guidelines that you will abandon at the semester's end. When adjusting to a professor's stylistic preferences, you are still growing as a writer and learning approaches that will prove useful down the road.

● **WRITE AN INTRODUCTION**   Introductions prepare readers for what comes next. In your introduction, you will accomplish several objectives. We have listed them in the following box.

HOW TO WRITE EFFECTIVE INTRODUCTIONS

- Use an opener that will interest the reader.
- Announce the topic.
- Disclose a thesis or attitude toward the topic.
- Establish your style and voice.

Let's see how Nora Gold develops the introduction to her essay on page 49.

Notice how Nora leads the reader smoothly and logically from one idea to the next. She begins by engaging the reader with an example that illustrates dramatically how curfews are unreasonable and unfair. The opening example also introduces the topic of her essay and suggests her viewpoint. Then she mentions that curfews are established to reduce youth crime, a goal that clearly was not served in her opening example; thus, she has begun to contrast her position with those of her opponents. She next begins to develop her thesis, stating that curfews do not deter criminals; they punish those who mean no harm. Finally, she suggests why ineffective and unfair curfews are established: they give the appearance of addressing a politically sensitive issue. Nora's writing style is consistent throughout the paragraph: she establishes a serious tone that seems appropriate for an issue of social concern. Her style is certainly appropriate for an academic essay, yet she avoids sounding stilted.

The opening sentences of an essay should engage the readers and encourage them to read on. The opening also establishes the writer's voice as formal or informal, academic or conversational. Some forms of academic writing require you to open your paper in a designated way and write in a very professional voice. Formal research studies often open with a one-paragraph abstract that summarizes the study's principal findings in straightforward, objective language. Response essays allow for much more freedom, for example, an informal opening that speaks directly to the reader. If you have difficulty deciding how to begin, use one of the techniques from the following list. The examples of essay openers were written in response to an assignment on the topic of cloning human beings.

Essay Openers

Technique	Example
Quotation (from the reading source or elsewhere)	"Human embryos are life-forms, and there is nothing to stop anyone from marketing them now, on the same shelves with Cabbage Patch dolls" (Ehrenreich, 1995, p. 86). Perhaps we are headed to a future where, as Ehrenreich suggests in her article "The Economics of Cloning," we will purchase rather than bear our children.
Question	Many parents want their children to have certain family characteristics—their grandfather's hair, their aunt's height, their father's eyes—but would you want a child who was an exact replica, a clone, of you or your spouse?
Anecdote, brief story, or scenario	Imagine you were born a clone, an exact copy of your mother or father, rather than a combination of genetic material from them both.
Fact or statistic	When human embryos were first cloned, President Clinton issued an executive order banning any further human cloning in government-sponsored research.
Generalization	Despite our fascination with genetic technologies, many of us recoil from the idea of cloning human beings.
Contradiction	Although cloning may multiply the odds that infertile couples will conceive, it may also multiply the chances of a genetic disaster.

Technique	Example
Thesis statement	Cloning human beings threatens our very future as a species.
Background	Cloning, a biological process that makes it possible to produce an exact replica of a living organism, has been applied to simple life forms for years. Now it is possible to clone complex animals, even humans.

Avoid using paper openers that will bore or turn off your readers. If your opening sentences alienate readers, it is difficult to win them back in the paragraphs that follow. The following paper openers are used too often and sound trite.

Overused Openings You Should Avoid	
Opening	**Example**
Clichés or platitudes	As we consider the rapid growth of wireless communication, we should keep in mind that fools rush in where angels fear to tread.
Dictionary definitions of well-known words	According to *Webster's International Dictionary*, *thinking* means. . . .
Restatement of the assignment	In "Time to Do Everything But Think," David Brooks attempts to demonstrate that wireless. . . .
An obvious statement of your purpose	In this essay, I give my reactions to David Brooks's article "Time to Do Everything But Think."

Reread the preliminary thesis you wrote at the prewriting stage and decide if you want to revise it before incorporating it into your introduction. Make sure that it still captures the principal perspective that you want to develop. The thesis statement is often located at the end of the introduction—after the opening, explanation of the general topic, and identification of the source—but it can occur anywhere within the introduction, even in the very first line. Wherever you place it, be sure to provide your reader with enough context to understand it fully. As we explained, a thesis statement may be several sentences long.

The introduction can include more than one paragraph. Long academic essays often have an introduction that contains many paragraphs. Shorter essays can also have multi-paragraph introductions. For lengthy, complex thesis statements, a two-paragraph introduction may work best. Another consideration is to use a dramatized scenario or vignette to open a paper that runs to several paragraphs. Follow the opening paragraphs with a paragraph that zeroes in on the topic and presents the thesis.

● **WRITE THE BODY OF THE ESSAY** The essay you compose at this stage should be a preliminary draft, not a polished, final copy. Think of this first draft as a discovery draft, an opportunity to find out more about what you want to say.

As you draft the body, follow the organizational plan you chose at the prewriting stage—time order, statement and response, point-by-point, or another pattern. Develop sections and paragraphs that fit into your plan. If your prewriting plan proves unworkable or you discover a new direction for the paper, rethink your organizational strategy.

Recall that before she began to draft her essay, Nora determined that she would develop four central points in the following order:

1. Curfews lead to reductions in the civil liberties of young people.
2. Curfews don't actually reduce youth crime.
3. Politicians propose curfews to give the appearance of being tough on crime.
4. After-school programs can help reduce youth crime.

Also recall that Nora concluded that each of these four points involved establishing cause-and-effect relationships. Nora's approach is to work on these points separately and then, when all four are completed, write the transitions that connect them.

Paragraphs. Develop paragraphs that are unified and coherent. Make sure that each paragraph develops a central idea and that all the sentences contribute to this idea in some way. As you read the following paragraph, notice how each sentence develops the point that curfew laws violate teens' constitutional rights.

> From several different perspectives, youth curfews represent an attack on Americans' civil liberties. The Supreme Court has ruled that "neither the 14th Amendment nor the Bill of Rights is for adults alone" (as cited in Herman, 2007, p. 546). The most obvious constitutional problem is that curfews grant police the power to detain citizens for nothing more than appearing young (Budd, 1999). This blatant age discrimination is arguably a violation of the constitutional principle of equal protection under the law, a Fourteenth Amendment right (Diviaio, 2007). Some curfew laws include provisions that fly in the face of Fourth Amendment protections against unreasonable search and seizure. For instance, a law passed in Cicero, Illinois, gives police the right to seize the vehicles of teenagers who violate the local curfew ("Lights Out," 1999). Court challenges to curfew laws have defended teens' "fundamental right to free movement" (Herman, 2007, p. 546) as well as their rights to travel to and from evening jobs and even to stand or sit on

their own sidewalks ("Juvenile Curfews," 2005). Finally, some curfew laws may violate teens' First Amendment rights if they restrict opportunities for young people to attend religious services or school meetings held in the evening ("Juvenile Curfews," 2005).

At the outset of the paragraph, Nora asserts that curfew laws curtail civil liberties, and subsequent sentences identify the specific rights (Fourteenth, Fourth, and First Amendment rights) that are affected. The overall structure of the paragraph is a claim backed up by several supporting examples. That structure stands out for the reader and results in a paragraph that is unified.

Also strive to make your paragraphs coherent. In a coherent paragraph, repeated words and ideas, rewording of ideas, and transitional expressions (*also, for example, thus, similarly, consequently,* and so on) show the reader the logical links among the sentences. We give you additional pointers on coherence later in this chapter.

● **INTEGRATE SOURCE MATERIAL**   As you draft the body of your essay, include relevant material from sources in the form of summaries, paraphrases, and quotations. Later in this book, we discuss in detail how to summarize sources and how to paraphrase and quote from sources. We also discuss how to document summaries, paraphrases, and quotations so that your audience will be able to identify the sources from which they are taken. At this point, we will merely list several principles of using sources that are crucial at the drafting stage:

USING SOURCES AS YOU DRAFT YOUR ESSAY

- Each quotation must be enclosed within quotation marks. Do not alter the wording of the quotation except when you interpolate or cut material, adding ellipses.

- Every summary and paraphrase must be converted from the language of the original into your own words. Change both vocabulary and sentence structure.

- Every summary, paraphrase, and quotation must be cited to the source from which it was derived. The citation must appear within the text of the essay and must indicate precisely the extent of the material taken from the source. Typically, an in-text citation gives the source author's last name or, for a source without an identified author, the source title, as well as the year of publication. If a direct quotation is used, the page number from which the quotation was taken follows the publication year. A full bibliographic reference to the source must appear in the References page at the end of the essay.

Note in the following paragraph how Nora Gold integrates documentation into her paragraph:

Paraphrase from Diviaio

Paraphrase from the article "Juvenile Curfews"

Paraphrase from the article "Mall Madness"

Paraphrase from the article "Mall Madness"

More and more frequently, American communities are relying on curfews in their efforts to battle youth- and gang-related crime. Over seventh percent of the largest two hundred cities in the United States had youth curfews by the late 1990s (Diviaio, 2007). Typical curfew hours are 11:00 p.m. on weeknights and 12:00 p.m. on Fridays and Saturdays, and these restrictions usually apply to individuals under eighteen ("Juvenile Curfews," 2005). In addition to curfews passed by city and town governments, certain privately owned shopping malls have established teen curfews. According to the International Council of Shopping Centers, shopping malls in no fewer than ten states have established youth curfews ("Mall Madness," 2008). In many cases, mall curfews deny entry on Friday and Saturday after 6:00 p.m. to anyone under eighteen unless they are under the supervision of someone over twenty-one ("Mall Madness," 2008). The combination of strict public and private sector curfews could essentially confine teens to home and school unless they are accompanied by an adult.

Make sure that as you draft, you put summaries and paraphrases into your own language and that you document all material that comes from sources. If you partially reword source material as you draft, assuming that you will change the wording more when you revise, you run the risk of forgetting which sections need further work. Similarly, if you leave out documentation as you draft, you may, at the revising stage, find it hard to determine what material came from which source. These oversights can lead to charges of plagiarism, a serious academic offense that can lead to expulsion.

Notice that Nora identifies her sources in *parenthetical citations*. Immediately after she draws on information from a source, Nora inserts within parentheses either the author's name or, in the case of articles published anonymously, an abbreviated version of the article's title.

● **WRITE THE CONCLUSION**   Human beings seem hard-wired to want beginnings and endings. Just as readers need an introduction to orient them to your essay, they need an ending that leaves them with a sense of closure. Your closing paragraph should do more than summarize your argument or restate your thesis. Use one of the following techniques.

TECHNIQUES FOR WRITING CONCLUDING PARAGRAPHS

- Stress the significance of your thesis rather than simply repeating it. Encourage your readers to look beyond the thesis to an important future goal.
- Predict consequences.
- Call your readers to action.
- Come full circle to an idea mentioned in the introduction.
- Use any of the devices for paper openers (see pages 28–29).

Read Nora Gold's closing paragraph on page 51. Notice how she uses three distinct techniques to achieve closure: (1) stressing the significance of her essay topic, (2) predicting consequences, and (3) coming full circle back to her opening example. Writers often construct conclusions using more than one closing technique.

● **CONSTRUCT A LIST OF SOURCES** As you complete your initial draft, make sure you construct a list of the sources that you referred to in your essay. Nora's list of sources appears on page 52. Don't leave the References page for the night before the essay is due, as you may not have enough time to locate lost citations or to check style manuals for complex citation formats.

Revising

The essence of editing is easy come easy go. Unless you really say to yourself, "What the hell. There's plenty more where that came from, let's throw it away," you can't really edit. You have to be a big spender. Not tightass. (Elbow, 1998, p. 39)

Every word omitted keeps another reader with you. Every word retained saps strength from the others. Think of throwing away not as negative—not as crumpling up sheets of paper in helplessness and rage—but as a positive, creative, generative act. Learn to play the role of the sculptor pulling off layers of stone with his chisel to reveal a figure beneath. Leaving things out makes the backbone or structure show better. (Elbow, 1998, p. 41)

In the preceding passages taken from the book *Writing Without Teachers*, Peter Elbow describes the essence of revision: you must be willing to let go of much or even all of what appears in your first draft. It is, of course, hard work to hammer out a draft, and it is difficult to part with the words that you struggled to produce. All the same, you need to approach revision with the idea that everything is subject to change or even deletion.

After you have composed a draft of your essay, set it aside and come back to it in a day or two. You will acquire fresh insights in the interim. It is also beneficial to have someone else read your draft and give you feedback. Your teacher may arrange to have peer review groups in class. If not, if it is all right with your instructor, ask your roommate, a family member, or a friend to review your draft.

The reviewer of your essay will find the following questions helpful. The same questions can guide your own rereading of your draft.

✓ *Checklist for Revising a First Draft*

_____ 1. Does the essay have an appropriate title?

2. As you consider style and voice,

_____ do you hear the writer's voice throughout the entire essay? (Can you describe it?)

_____ is the style of the essay appropriate for its content and audience?

3. Does the introduction accomplish the following:

_____ use an opener that will interest the reader?

_____ announce the topic?

_____ disclose a thesis or attitude toward the topic?

_____ establish a style and voice?

4. As you consider the overall organization of the essay,

_____ is the writer's rhetorical purpose clear? (How does the writer attempt to influence or affect readers?)

_____ does everything in the draft lead to or follow from one central thesis? (If not, which ideas appear to be out of place?)

_____ is the organizational plan or form appropriate for this kind of paper? (If not, can you suggest another format?)

_____ does the writer provide transitions or connecting ideas? (If not, where are they needed?)

5. As you consider the writer's use of sources,

_____ throughout the essay, when referring to the source, does the writer supply necessary documentation?

_____ are there clear transitions or connectives that differentiate the writer's own ideas from those of the source author?

_____ does the paper end with a list of sources used?

_____ 6. Does the conclusion do more than simply restate the main idea? Does it leave the reader with a sense of closure?

The process of getting advice on your writing may be difficult both for you and for your reviewer. Many of us tighten up in response to criticism; some even feel compelled to defend themselves. Reviewers are typically aware that their comments may not be well received and thus may hesitate to point out difficulties in drafts. We recommend that you ask for an honest response to your writing, listen carefully to the feedback you get, take notes, and then return to those notes in a day or two. At that point, you will be in a position to benefit from the feedback you received without feeling too defensive.

Once you have feedback from one or more readers and have reread the draft yourself, devise a revision plan and begin a second draft of your essay. You may want to start with the introduction and work through sequentially to the conclusion, or you may decide to start with the sections of the essay that, based on the feedback you received and your own rereading of draft, seem to need the most work.

There is no generic formula for revision, since each initial draft has its unique strengths and weaknesses. We can, however, provide a case in point and describe the revision process of student Jane Wolf. We will show the first draft and revision of Jane's essay and then discuss the changes that she made. Jane wrote this essay for her introductory computer science course. The assignment was to read a book on the social consequences of computers and then submit a short essay of response to the book. Jane selected *The Intimate Machine,* in which Neil Frude argues that humans may one day have fulfilling emotional relationships with intelligent machines.

FIRST DRAFT

INTIMATE MACHINE PAPER   2

Intimate Machine Paper: First Draft

1   A book titled *The Intimate Machine* describes a machine that could be

programmed to act like a friend. The machine would "be programmed to behave

in a congenial manner" and "to be charming, stimulating, and easygoing," to

"sometimes take the initiative," and "to have a personality of its own" (Frude,

1983, p. 169). The machine would provide people with many of the benefits of

friendship. It would carry on a conversation and take an active interest in

humans. It could even become intimate with them. Such an idea is not so far-

fetched. People already use machines for therapeutic purposes, and they play

chess with computers. People may be shocked by the idea of having a machine

as a friend, but they should not condemn something that could benefit so many

lonely people. I disagree with Frude, and I worry that machines have already

replaced too many people today. I think it is far better for people to befriend

people than to become intimate with machines.

INTIMATE MACHINE PAPER   3

2   Machines already function as therapists and teammates. They also teach classes. When my economics professor cannot make the class, he sends us a video lecture to watch in his place. Machines have also replaced bank tellers, telephone operators, and checkout cashiers. If this trend continues, we will soon have robot waiters, nurses, and mechanics, and, finally, machine friends. We will have less and less human contact in our daily lives.

3   I would argue that it is important to bring more and more people together than to separate them by introducing machines as friends. A lonely person may get some enjoyment from conversing with a "charming, stimulating, and easygoing" machine, but the satisfaction would be much greater if the person had genuine human contact. It is true that the machine would always be available, but the person would know that it had not come of its own free will.

4   Some people will find the prospect of having a friendly, intimate machine tempting. But I would urge them to reconsider their position. Instead of putting so much research time and money into developing friendly machines, why not study ways to bring people together and enhance human relations? People need spontaneous, human love, not a programmed simulation.

REVISED DRAFT

How do you regard your personal computer, as a "tool," a "colleague" or a "friend"? You might be surprised that anyone would consider a machine a friend, but in ?

INTIMATE MACHINE PAPER   2

Do We Want Programmed Friends?
Intimate Machine Paper: First Draft

1   A book entitled *The Intimate Machine* ~~describes a~~ machine ~~that~~ could be

Neil Frude (1983) explains that s

programmed to act like ~~a~~ friend. The machine would "~~be programmed to~~ behave

s

in a congenial manner" and "~~to~~ be charming, stimulating, and easygoing," ~~to~~

It would   it would

"sometimes take the initiative," and "~~to have~~ a personality of its own"

Frude claims that

(p. 169). The machine would provide ~~people~~ with many of the benefits of

us

friendship. It would carry on a conversation and take an active interest in

with us

our affairs. We

~~humans~~ It could even become intimate ~~with them~~. Such an idea is not so far-

says Frude.

fetched. People already use machines for therapeutic purposes, and they play

Frude points out that we

chess with computers. ~~People~~ may be shocked by the idea of having a machine

we

as a friend, but ~~they~~ should not condemn something that could benefit

so many lonely people. I disagree with Frude ~~and~~ I worry that machines

have already replaced too many people ~~today~~. ~~I think~~ it is far better for people to

befriend people than to become intimate with machines.

As Frude (1983) points out

2   Machines already function as therapists and ~~teammates~~. They also teach

partners for games

is unable to attend

classes. When my economics professor ~~cannot make the~~ class, he sends ~~us~~ a

video lecture to watch in his place. Machines have also replaced bank tellers,

telephone operators, and checkout cashiers. If this trend continues, we

INTIMATE MACHINE PAPER 3

will soon have robot waiters, nurses, and mechanics, and,' finally, machine
and less understanding of each other's wants and needs
friends. We will have less and less human contact in our daily lives. ^

3   *I*
~~I would argue that~~ ȷt is important to bring ~~more and more~~ people together *rather*
^

than ~~to~~ separate them by introducing machines as friends. A lonely person may
talking to a machine about politics or sharing a secret or juicy
get some enjoyment ~~from conversing with a "charming, stimulating, and~~
piece of gossip *there were*
~~easygoing" machine~~, but the satisfaction would be much greater if ~~the person~~
A human friend would respond less predictably and would
~~had~~ genuine human contact. It is true that the machine would *probably have more*
^ *authentic stories to tell.*
always be available, but the person would know that it had
Nor would it be able to turn itself on. It would be
not come on its own free will. *totally dependent on the human user.*

4   Some people will find the prospect of having a friendly, intimate machine

tempting. But I would urge them to reconsider their position. Instead of putting

so much research time and money into developing friendly machines, why not

study ways to bring people together and enhance human relations? People need

spontaneous, human love, not a programmed simulation.

INTIMATE MACHINE PAPER 4

References

Frude, N. (1983). *The intimate machine.* New York: New American Library.

REVISE THE TITLE AND OPENING

Starting with the title, let us discuss some of the additions, deletions, and other
changes Jane made. As we mentioned earlier, you will probably title your essay
after you have revised your preliminary draft. Jane decided to phrase her title as
a question: "Do We Want Programmed Friends?" Notice that she did not underline or italicize the essay title or place it in quotation marks.

Next, compare the opening sentences of the two drafts.

First Draft

A book titled *The Intimate Machine* describes a machine that could be programmed to act like a friend.

Revised Draft

How do you regard your personal computer--as a "tool," a "colleague," or a "friend?"

The first draft begins with a statement of fact. Although this is an acceptable way to open an essay, Jane thought it was too formal, so she decided to address the reader with a question instead. Notice that the new opening also does a better job of establishing the writer's voice.

REVISE THE BODY PARAGRAPHS

If you refer to Jane's preliminary draft, you will see that the main way she altered the body paragraphs was by adding details. Paragraph 2 was already adequately developed with examples, but Jane needed to add details in order to flesh out paragraph 3. Both of these body paragraphs follow directly from the introduction. In paragraph 2, Jane develops the statement, "I worry that machines have already replaced too many people," and in paragraph 3, she explains why it is "better for people to befriend people than to become intimate with machines."

In this response essay, Jane could have developed the body paragraphs by quoting, paraphrasing, or summarizing pertinent ideas from the source and forging a connection between those ideas and her own thoughts. Also, she could have used any of the patterns of development (cause and effect, comparison and contrast, example, and so forth; see Table 1.1 on page 20) to develop her body paragraphs.

REVISE THE CONCLUSION

Jane left her closing paragraph untouched because she was satisfied with its form and content. She brings her essay to a close by acknowledging that some people may not share her view and calling on her readers to change their outlook and set new priorities for the future.

ADD ATTRIBUTION

Comparing Jane's two drafts, you can see that in the revised version, she signals her reader each time she presents one of Frude's points. In the first draft, the reader is not always sure where Frude's ideas end and Jane's begin. The addition of attribution—"Frude claims that . . . ," " . . . says Frude," "Frude points out . . ."— helps the reader make this differentiation.

IMPROVE FOCUS AND DEVELOPMENT

Well-written papers have a clear, sharply defined focus. When you reread your first draft, check to see if you present a consistent perspective throughout the entire piece. Make sure that you have not started off with a thesis that expresses your intention but then drifted away from it in the subsequent paragraphs. Also make sure that you have not started off with one intention as expressed in your thesis but ended up with another position.

If you drifted away from your original goal, examine each sentence to determine how the shift took place. You may need to eliminate whole chunks of irrelevant material, add more content, or rearrange some of the parts. If this is the case, ask yourself these questions:

- What should I add so that my audience can follow my train of thought more easily?
- What should I eliminate that does not contribute to my central focus?
- What should I move that is out of place or needs to be grouped with material elsewhere in the paper?

After you make these changes, read over your work to make sure that the new version makes sense, conforms to your organizational plan, and shows improvement.

IMPROVE COHERENCE

When you are satisfied with your focus and development, check that the ideas in the essay connect with each other. Your readers should be able to follow your train of thought by referring to preceding sentences, looking ahead to subsequent sentences, and being mindful of transitions and other connective devices. The following are some common connective devices.

- Repeating words or parts of words
- Substituting synonyms or related words

- Using personal pronouns and demonstrative pronouns *(this, that)* with easily recognizable referents
- Using explicit or implied transitions that signal relationships such as addition, exemplification, opposition, similarity, cause, effect, or time order
- Substituting a general term for a more specific term or terms

To illustrate, here is a paragraph from an essay student Maura Kennedy wrote in response to John Knowles's novel *A Separate Peace.* We have highlighted and labeled some of the connective devices. See if you can find others.

A Separate Peace shows that sarcasm helps us to escape from stating the truth straightforwardly. Gene, the [Repeats word] weaker character, uses sarcasm to express disapproval, [Synonym] whereas Finny, the symbol of strength, blatantly states his [Repeats word] disapproval. Gene uses sarcasm because he feels resentment toward Finny. His indignation stems from [Synonym] jealousy. This becomes evident after Finny charms his way out of trouble for wearing the Devon tie as a belt. Gene explains, "He had gotten away with everything. I felt a sudden stab of disappointment." Later, he adds, "That was because I just wanted to see some more excitement; that [Pronoun] must have been it" (Knowles, 2008, p. 21). Although Gene's [Repeats word] jealousy almost causes him to dislike Finny, he cannot admit [Pronoun] this painful fact, and he covers it up.

Labels on the left: Transition: contrast / Transition: cause / Pronoun / Demonstrative pronoun / Transition: Time / Transition: contrast / General term

MOVE FROM WRITER-BASED TO READER-BASED PROSE

We have stressed the importance of considering your audience as you make stylistic decisions. One way to do this, as composition theorist Linda Flower points out, is to learn to distinguish between writer-based prose and reader-based prose. When you are getting your ideas down on paper, you put words down in the order in which they come to you. You record what makes sense to you, but you exert minimal effort to communicate these ideas to someone else. This type of egocentric writing is called *writer-based prose*. It is meaningful personally, but it may not make sense to a larger audience. In contrast, *reader-based prose* clearly conveys the writer's ideas to other people. The writer does not assume that the reader will understand automatically, so she provides information that will facilitate the reader's comprehension. It is easy to forget about audience amid all the complications of producing the first draft of an academic essay. That's why first drafts are quite often writer-based. An important function of revising is to convert this writer-based prose to something the reader can readily understand.

For an illustration of writer-based prose, read the following excerpt from a student's early draft. The topic is technological advancements, and Emily is responding to an article written by Bill Joy, cofounder and chief scientist of Sun Microsystems. The assignment asked students to select an article from their anthology and write a response that would appeal to their classmates. As you read, make note of features that are writer-based.

HUMANS AND TECHNOLOGY   2

Humans and Technology

The article deals with the author's ideas about the interaction between

humans and technology in the next century. Joy (2007) backs up his views with

numerous examples and with references to conversations he has had with

experts in the field. After reading his article, I feel that I agree with many of the

points Joy raises.

From the outset, the student assumes the audience is familiar with both the assignment and the article on which it is based. The introduction begins, "The article deals with . . ." as if the reader knows in advance the article that will be discussed. The first sentence indicates that "the author" has "ideas" about "the interaction between humans and technology," but the student doesn't tell us about the nature of those ideas. What is Bill Joy's position? Does he fear or embrace technology? The introduction doesn't answer these questions. The student is writing for someone who already knows the author's viewpoint, not for classmates who may not have read the article. Similar failures to consider the audience occur throughout the paragraph.

Note how Emily transforms her introductory paragraph from writer-based prose to reader-based prose.

HUMANS AND TECHNOLOGY   2

Human Obsolescence

In "Why the Future Doesn't Need Us," Bill Joy (2007), the cofounder and chief scientist of Sun Microsystems, expresses his fear that twentieth-century technology might exterminate the human species.

His particular concern is that the world might be overrun by genetically engineered life forms capable of reproduction or self-replicating computerized robots. Joy (2007) backs up his views with strong evidence by providing numerous examples and references to respected scientists and computer experts, such as Ray Kurzweil and Hans Moravec. I agree with Joy that researchers must consider carefully how the technologies they produce will affect the larger society.

What does the revision tell you that the first draft does not? You learn the title of the article, the author's name and affiliation, Joy's position on technology, and Emily's reaction to that position. If you lay the two drafts side by side, you will see that Emily has cracked open the vague words in the first version. "Article" has been expanded to "Why the Future Doesn't Need Us"; "author" has become "Bill Joy, cofounder and Chief Scientist of Sun Microsystems"; "ideas" has become "his fear that twentieth-century technology might exterminate the human species" and "that the world might be overrun by genetically engineered life forms capable of reproduction or self-replicating computerized robots"; "experts" has become "Ray Kurzweil and Hans Moravec"; and "points" has become "researchers must consider carefully how the technologies they produce will affect the larger society." Emily has learned to write with detail.

As you revise your first drafts, make sure you have provided your readers with context or background for the material you have taken from sources. Add lots of detail and specific information. Unless the assignment indicates that the audience has read the sources, do not assume that your readers share your prior knowledge and experience.

REVISE SENTENCES FOR CLARITY AND STYLE

Earlier in this chapter in our discussion of stylistic choices, we stressed the importance of clear expression. Revise any sentences in your draft that might not communicate your ideas clearly to a reader. A classmate or friend can help you locate the sentences that need work by reading through your draft and putting a checkmark in the margin next to each sentence that seems unclear. Some of the sentences your reader checks may sound fine to you since you know your intended meaning, but you need to rework those sentences all the same. When someone can't follow a sentence you have written, the problem is with the sentence, not the reader.

As you revise sentences, it will help to keep in mind the following advice that Joseph Williams (2006) provides in his book *Style: Lessons in Clarity and Grace*, ninth edition:

> Express actions [in sentences] in verbs. . . . Make the subjects of those verbs the characters associated with those actions. (p. 51)

This basic principle of revision will help you restructure confusing sentences so that the central meaning stands out for your reader.

Proofreading

We use the term "proofreading" to refer to the process of checking for details: spelling, punctuation, word usage, and grammar. Of course, you often catch your own mistakes as you write and revise, so proofreading typically begins early in the writing process, as soon as you begin to get words on the page. That said, focusing too intently on proofreading in early drafts may interrupt your train of thought and sap your creativity. Much of the published advice on writing recommends getting your thoughts down, expanding on them fully, and organizing them coherently before you worry about matters of correctness. Even for those who prefer to edit as they write, it is important to proofread carefully as the final step in the writing process.

All students have the experience of handing in papers they have proofread carefully, only to receive them back with instructors' comments pointing out errors that seem obvious to the students in retrospect. Professors miss errors in their own writing. As we worked on our textbook, we detected several errors that had been repeated in previous editions, errors that we and our editors did not see while proofreading the manuscripts and page proofs of the earlier editions.

Why do we overlook, at least on occasion, obvious errors in our written work? Part of the answer, undoubtedly, has to do with the way our brains process information when we read. We think of our eyes as smoothly scanning the printed page, but our eyes actually move across the page in small jumps, called saccades. We take in information from the page only when the eye is still, not when it is making a jump. When the eye takes in information from the page, the brain processes the meaning and structure of the text and makes predictions on what will come next. Based on these predictions, the brain instructs the eye to make successive saccades across the page, pulling in new information from the page and filling in any gaps to make meaning. This process of filling in the gaps makes it possible for us to read quickly rather than having to stop to perceive each word and figure out how it fits into the context of the surrounding text. But another result is that we sometimes make unconscious predictions about what will come up next in the text that are off the mark. These faulty predictions may make us stumble over words when we are reading out loud. Once we catch the problem, we backtrack to get the right words. If, however, the inaccurate prediction fits into the structure and meaning of the rest of the sentence, we may never notice that the word or phrase that the brain expected was different from what appeared on the page. The brain's efforts to fill the gaps as we read accounts for our unconscious ability to mentally "correct" errors as we proofread but still fail to correct the written text. In other words, we read what we meant, not what we actually wrote.

So how do we proofread if our brains work against us by hiding our own errors? The key to accurate proofreading is to establish a list of the errors you typically make and then develop a method for locating each of those errors in your drafts. For many common errors, the "Find" or "Search" functions on word processing programs can help you locate and correct problems. For example, if you tend to confuse "there" and "their," use the Find function to locate each occurrence of those words in your draft and check to make sure you use the correct spelling in each instance. This method counteracts your natural tendency to mentally "correct" errors since you are not processing the sentences in a meaningful sequence but rather just focusing on sentence parts.

Keep a list of your own problem areas. The night before you submit an essay, proofread it by using the Find function to locate each of these potential problem areas in your draft.

Another way to circumvent your brain's auto correction mechanism is to proofread your sentences in reverse order, beginning with the last sentence in the essay and working backward to the first. This technique breaks up the logical sequence of your sentences, which reduces the likelihood that your brain will attempt to make those subconscious predictions of what is coming next; consequently, it is easier to notice errors.

SPELLING

Use the spelling checker, but be aware that it will not detect all errors. For example, consider the following sentence:

The orchestra preformed works by Bach and Hayden.

The third word in the sentence should be "performed" rather than "preformed." "Preformed" is actually a word which refers to something that is formed in advance of use, so the spelling checker will not mark it as an error. For the most part, spelling software is not sophisticated enough to analyze the context of words.

A WORD ABOUT AUTO CORRECT

If you use the "Auto Correct" function of your spelling checker, the software will change spellings automatically as you type. While this feature helps you get ideas down without having to interrupt your flow of thought to look up spellings, it may introduce errors by guessing incorrectly. A comparative study of error patterns in first-year college writing found that "wrong word" errors have increased dramatically over the last two decades, and the study authors suggest that spelling checkers may be responsible (Lunsford & Lunsford). For example, if you are working rapidly and mistakenly type "defintly" rather than "definitely," the spelling checker may insert the correction as "defiantly." A common problem with the Auto correct function is that the spelling checker will interpret a person's name as a misspelling and then attempt to correct it, for example, changing the last name "Littel" to "Little." As we have stressed earlier, it is important in academic writing to cite the source of borrowed ideas or language. Be careful that the authors' names you cite are spelled correctly.

As with other proofreading concerns, you can reduce your spelling errors by keeping a list of frequent misspellings and then searching for those misspelling using the Find function of your word processor.

Good editing skills depend on your knowledge of sentence structure, punctuation, usage, and spelling, but even more important is your commitment to getting it right and your willingness to invest time attending to detail. As we explained earlier, even if you know grammatical conventions thoroughly, you'll make mistakes in initial drafts because your primary focus is on getting thoughts down on paper, not on comma placement and spelling. As you edit your papers, you have to train your eyes and brain to detect commonplace errors. Otherwise, you will be using your time inefficiently.

Submitting the Final Draft

When you have finished proofreading your paper, print out your final draft on the best quality printer you have access to. Use black ink only. If you are relying on your own printer, don't wait until the night before the essay is due to make sure you have black ink in your printer cartridge. Check each page for ink smears, paper tears, and other printing errors. Make sure that each page is there, including the References page.

The advice in the preceding paragraph may seem self-evident, but students who have worked hard on essays sometimes undermine their efforts by failing to check the final draft for obvious problems. If you submit an essay that is missing pages, you may lose credit since, from the instructor's perspective, the essay is not finished until it can be evaluated.

A Summary of the Writing Process

Prewriting
- Analyze the assignment
- Establish a focus
- Read and respond to sources

Drafting
- Develop a thesis
- Select an organizational plan
- Write a first draft
  - Title your essay
  - Establish a style
  - Write an introduction
  - Write the body of the essay
  - Integrate source material
  - Write the conclusion
  - Construct a list of sources

Revising
- Revise the title and opening
- Revise the body paragraphs
- Revise the conclusion
- Add attribution
- Improve focus and development
- Improve cohesion
- Move from writer-based to reader-based prose
- Revise sentences for clarity and style

Proofreading

Submitting the final draft

Here is a copy of Nora Gold's final draft. As you read through it, notice how she combines material from a number of reading sources in order to make a statement about teen curfews.

CURFEW LAWS: DEMONIZING TEENS   2

Curfew Laws: Demonizing Teens

1   In the summer of 1996, sixteen-year-old Asha Sidhu was arrested by the San Diego police, taken to the station, interrogated by officers, accused of various offenses, and held for hours, all without her parents being informed (Allen, 1997). What crime did she commit? She was out after the 10:00 p.m. curfew. Even though she was only two blocks from her home and was out with her parents' permission, the San Diego curfew law gave the police the right to treat this honor student as if she were a common criminal. Teen curfew laws, such as the one enforced in San Diego, are being established in cities across the United States for the alleged purpose of reducing youth crime. These laws will do little to deter those teens who are criminally inclined and are unfair to the millions of young people who have done nothing to deserve being held under house arrest. Enforcing teen curfews amounts to penalizing young people so that adults can enjoy a false sense of security and politicians can give the impression that they are tough on crime.

CURFEW LAWS: DEMONIZING TEENS   3

2   More and more frequently, American communities are relying on curfews

in their efforts to battle youth- and gang-related crime. Over seventy percent of

the largest two hundred cities in the United States had youth curfews by the

late 1990s (Diviaio, 2007). Typical curfew hours are 11:00 p.m. on weeknights

and 12:00 p.m. on Fridays and Saturdays, and these restrictions usually apply to

individuals under eighteen ("Juvenile Curfews," 2005). In addition to curfews

passed by city and town governments, certain privately owned shopping malls

have established teen curfews. According to the International Council of

Shopping Centers, shopping malls in no fewer than ten states have established

youth curfews ("Mall Madness," 2008). In many cases, mall curfews deny entry

on Friday and Saturday after 6:00 p.m. to anyone under eighteen unless they are

under the supervision of someone over twenty-one ("Mall Madness," 2008). The

combination of strict public- and private-sector curfews could essentially confine

teens to home and school unless they are accompanied by an adult.

3   From several different perspectives, youth curfews represent an attack on

Americans' civil liberties. The Supreme Court has ruled that "neither the 14th

Amendment nor the Bill of Rights is for adults alone" (as cited in Herman, 2007,

p. 1882). The most obvious constitutional problem is that curfews grant police

the power to detain citizens for nothing more than appearing young (Budd,

1999). This blatant age discrimination is arguably a violation of the

constitutional principle of equal protection under the law, a Fourteenth

Amendment right (Diviaio). Some curfew laws include provisions that fly in the

face of Fourth Amendment protections against unreasonable search and seizure.

For instance, a law passed in Cicero, Illinois, gives police the right to seize the

vehicles of teenagers who violate the local curfew ("Lights Out," 1999). Court

challenges to curfew laws have defended teens' "fundamental right to free

movement" (Herman) as well as their rights to travel to and from evening jobs

and even to stand or sit on their own sidewalks ("Juvenile Curfews," 2005).

Finally, some curfew laws may violate teens' First Amendment rights if they restrict opportunities for young people to attend religious services or school meetings held in the evening ("Juvenile Curfews").

4   Some people might argue that it is worth sacrificing the constitutional rights of teenagers in order to protect all Americans, young and old, from crime. There is, however, little evidence that curfews make our country any safer. On the surface, it seems unlikely that curfews would deter anyone with serious criminal intentions. Budd (1999) points out that teens who are willing to risk spending years in jail for committing serious crimes, such as burglary or assault, are unlikely to fear the relatively minor penalties for violating curfew laws. Crime statistics support this notion. According to Budd, no studies have provided empirical evidence that curfews actually work. For example, San Diego officials claim their curfew law helped reduce juvenile crime; Budd points out, however, that the crime rate decline occurred only during hours of the day not covered by the curfew. According to legal scholar Danielle Diviaio (2007), research studies indicate that curfews are not a significant factor in deterring crime. These studies show, among other things, that "curfews do not work because (1) most crime happens during non-curfew hours, (2) juveniles who do not fear getting caught for a crime will not fear violating juvenile curfew laws" (p. 813). In the case of *Ramos v. Town of Vernon,* the court ruled that the government could not prove that the curfew law under consideration had any impact on gang activity or youth safety.

5   If curfews appear to violate teens' rights and do not even accomplish their intended purpose of reducing crime, why are more and more cities establishing curfews? One reason that curfews appeal to politicians and adult citizens is that they give the appearance of attacking crime without asking the taxpayers to provide much additional funding. According to Rice University sociologist Steven Kleinberg, "People feel insecure economically, and so there's resistance to dealing with delinquency through measures that require an investment..In this climate of thought, it's a helpful belief to say, 'It's their [teens'] fault'" (Allen, 1997, p. 5). Curfews remain in place because Americans under age eighteen

cannot vote and thus lack the political power to resist unfair laws. As Budd

(1999) points out, "Such a blunt and overreaching crime-fighting technique

would clearly be unenforceable against adults" (p. 25). Legal scholar David

Herman (2007) points out that children cannot make effective use of the

democratic process to overturn laws that were passed for political motives:

> Even if it turns out that a curfew does nothing to prevent juvenile crime
>
> and victimization, children are unlikely to be able to bring about the
>
> repeal of the ineffective ordinance. The law will remain in place,
>
> therefore, although it imposes great restrictions on children's freedom
>
> with little appreciable benefit. . . . There is a danger . . . that the
>
> curfews are actually enacted to benefit adults' interest in aesthetics,
>
> peace and quiet, or even their distaste for the lifestyles of certain young
>
> people. . . . While reducing juvenile crime and victimization may be
>
> compelling interests, removing unpleasant-looking youths from the
>
> nighttime streets is not. (pp. 1888–1889)

Sociologists have argued that youth crime can be addressed effectively

only through programs that help teens develop into productive adults, such as

after-school tutoring and sports, rather than laws that attempt to keep them off

the streets (Allen, 1997). Rather than addressing social problems that affect

teens, the focus of curfew laws is seemingly "to make adults feel better"

("Lights Out," 1999, p. 30). Surely, our efforts and money should go into

programs for troubled youth that appear to work rather than senseless curfew

enforcement, which, although inexpensive, does nothing.

"The image of dissolute youth roaming the streets in search of victims is

now a fixture of our political rhetoric, and curfews offer a satisfying and

uncomplicated solution" (Budd, 1999, p. 23). A curfew is a simplistic and

ineffective response to teen crime. Until we develop and support effective

programs to address poverty, domestic violence, drug abuse, and a host of other

social problems, teen crime will continue. Harassing thousands of innocent

teenagers, such as Asha Sidhu, will do nothing to make our streets safer.

CURFEW LAWS: DEMONIZING TEENS   6

References

Allen, J. (1997, January 10). U.S. teens face rash of get-tough actions as nation's

    fear grows. *National Catholic Reporter,* 4–5. Retrieved from General

    OneFile.

Budd, J. C. (1999, Fall). Juvenile curfews: The rights of minors vs. the rhetoric of

    public safety. *Human Rights*. Retrieved from www.americanbar.org/

Diviaio, D. (2007, Spring–Summer). The government is establishing your child's

    curfew. *St. John's Journal of Legal Commentary, 21*(3), 797–835. Retrieved

    from http://www.lexisnexis.com/hottopics/Inacademic/?

Herman, D. A. (2007, December). Juvenile curfews and the breakdown of the

    tiered approach to equal protection. *New York University Law Review, 82,*

    1857–1893. Retrieved from http://www.lexisnexis.com/hottopics/

    Inacademic/?

Juvenile curfews and the major confusion over minor rights. (2005, May).

    Harvard Law Review, 118, 2400–2421. Retrieved from

    http://www.lexisnexis.com/hottopics/Inacademic/?

Lights out. (1999, September). *The Economist,* 30.

Mall madness. (2008, January). *Know Your World Extra*, 8–9. Retrieved from

    http://www.proquest.com/en-US/products/default.shtml

PRACTICE

1. Write a one-paragraph description of how you wrote essays in high school. Consider the following questions: How did you come up with ideas for your writing? What organizational plans did you use? Did you create outlines? Did you write first drafts without notes? Did you ask friends, family members, or teachers to read your rough drafts? If so, what types of feedback did you receive, and how did you respond? When you proofread, what specific issues of usage, spelling, punctuation, and mechanics did you focus on?

   Now consider the overall writing process you have used. Over how many days did the process extend? What were the strengths of your approach to writing assignments? What were the weaknesses? Which parts of the process were the easiest for you, and which parts were the hardest? Write another paragraph in response to these questions.

   In class, compile a joint list of students' strengths and weaknesses. Discuss why students' responses vary.

2. Describe a particular situation in which you did not understand what a professor wanted in a writing assignment (don't use our class) and as a result produced a paper that was off target. What was the nature of your confusion? To what extent was the confusion your fault and to what extent did the professor make unwarranted assumptions about what would be obvious to students?

3. Study Nora's essay, and then answer the following questions.

   a. What is Nora's overall purpose? What point is she making? How does she get that message across to her readers?

   b. What aspects of the essay remind you of things you have been taught in the past about writing?

   c. What aspects of the essay are at odds with what you have been told about writing? Can you account for any discrepancy?

   d. How does Nora's essay differ from essays you have written in high school?

e. What is the relationship between Nora's ideas and those of the authors of the sources she cites?

f. Which approach is Nora using: simply telling her readers the contents of the reading sources, giving her readers a new understanding of information in the reading sources, or using that information as support for her own thesis or point of view?

4 Choose three of the exercises below and write for 10 minutes on each. Date and number each entry.

a. Make an "authority" list of activities, subjects, ideas, places, people, or events that you already know something about. List as many topics as you can. If your reaction is "I'm not really an *authority* on anything," then imagine you've met someone from another school, state, country, or historical period. With that person as your audience, what are you an "authority" on?

b. In two or three sentences, complete the following thought: "I have trouble writing because . . ."

c. In a few sentences, complete the following thought: "In my previous classes and from my own writing experience, I've learned that the three most important rules about writing are . . ."

d. Describe your own writing rituals. *When, where,* and *how* do you write best?

5 The following exercises will help you review and practice the topics covered in this chapter. In addition, you may discover a subject for your own writing. Write for ten minutes on each entry.

a. Reread your "authority" list. Choose one of those topics and then explain your purpose, identify a possible audience, and select a genre you would use.

b. **Writing Across the Curriculum.** If you have already been given a writing assignment in another course, explain the purpose, the intended audience, and the genre for that assignment. Be prepared to explain in class (or in a discussion forum) how you plan to complete that assignment.

6 **Individual task:** Bring to class a draft-in-progress essay. Pick out several paragraphs in the body of your essay and analyze them. For each paragraph, ask the following questions:

- Does my paragraph have a topic sentence near the beginning?
- If so, does my topic sentence accurately forecast what the paragraph says?
- Does my topic sentence link to my thesis statement or to a higher-order point that my paragraph develops?
- Does my paragraph have enough particulars to develop and support my topic sentence?

Group task: Then exchange your draft with a partner and do a similar analysis of your partner's selected paragraphs. Discuss your analyses of each other's paragraphs and then help each other plan appropriate revision strategies. If time permits, revise your paragraphs and show your results to your partner. [Note: Sometimes you can revise simply by adding a topic sentence to a paragraph, rewording a topic sentence, or making other kinds of local revisions. At other times, you may need to cross out whole paragraphs and start over, rewriting from scratch after you rethink your ideas.]

7 This exercise is designed to show you how transition words govern relationships between ideas. Working in groups or on your own, finish each of the following statements using ideas of your own invention. Make sure what you add fits the logic of the transition word.

a. Writing is difficult; therefore _____.

b. Writing is difficult; however, _____.

c. Writing is difficult because _____.

d. Writing is difficult. For example, _____.

e. Writing is difficult. To put it another way, _____.

f. Writing is difficult. Likewise, _____.

g. Although writing is difficult, _____.

8 In the following paragraph, various kinds of linking devices have been omitted. Fill in the blanks with words or phrases that would make the paragraph coherent. Clues are provided in brackets.

Writing an essay is a difficult process for most people. _____ [contrast] the process can be made easier if you learn to practice three simple techniques. _____ [sequence] learn the technique of nonstop writing. When you are first trying to think of ideas for an essay, put your pen to your paper and write nonstop for ten or fifteen minutes without letting your pen leave the paper. Stay loose and free. Let your pen follow the waves of thought. Don't worry about grammar or spelling. _____ [concession] this technique won't work for everyone, it helps many people get a good cache of ideas to draw on. A _____ [sequence] technique is to write your rough draft rapidly without worrying about being perfect. Too many writers try to get their drafts right the first time. _____ [contrast] by learning to live with imperfection, you will save yourself headaches and a wastepaper basket full of crumpled paper. Think of your first rough draft as a path hacked out of the jungle—as part of an exploration, not as a completed highway. As a _____ [sequence] technique, try printing out a triple-spaced copy to allow space for revision. Many beginning writers don't leave enough space to revise. _____ [consequence] these writers never get in the habit of crossing out chunks of their rough draft and writing revisions in the blank spaces. After you have revised your rough draft until it is too messy to work from anymore, you can _____ [sequence] enter your changes into your word processor and print out a fresh draft, again setting your text on triple-space. The resulting blank space invites you to revise.

9 While drafting and revising, writers frequently make crucial changes in their ideas and language. The first scribbled sentences, written primarily for ourselves, are often totally different from what we later present to other people in final, polished versions. Take, for example, the final version of Abraham Lincoln's Gettysburg Address. It begins with the famous lines "Four score and seven years ago our fathers brought forth on this continent a new nation. . . ." But his first draft might well have begun, "Eighty-seven years ago, several politicians and other powerful men in the American Colonies got together and decided to start a new country. . . ." It is difficult to imagine that language ingrained in our consciousness was once drafted, revised, drafted again, and edited, as the author or authors added, deleted, reordered, and otherwise altered words, sentences, and ideas. In fact, it usually was.

Carl Becker's study of the American Declaration of Independence assembles the early drafts of that famous document and compares them with the final version. Shown on the next page is Thomas Jefferson's first draft, with revisions made by Benjamin Franklin, John Adams, and other members of the Committee of Five that was charged with developing the new document.

Rough Draft of the Opening Sentences
of the Declaration of Independence
Thomas Jefferson

When in the course of human events it becomes necessary for ~~a~~ ^one^ people to

dissolve the political bands which have connected them with another, and to

~~advance from that subordination in which they have hitherto remained, & to~~

assume among the powers of the earth the ~~equal & independent~~ ^separate and equal^ station to which

the laws of nature & of nature's god entitle them, a decent respect to the opinions

of mankind requires that they should declare the causes which impel them to

^the separation.^
~~the change.~~

We hold these truths *to be* ~~*sacred & undeniable;*~~ ^self-evident^ that all men are created

equal ~~& independent;~~ that ~~from that equal creation they derive in rights~~ ^they are endowed by their creator with^ inherent

^rights; that^
& inalienable among ~~which~~ are ~~the preservation of~~ ^these^ life, ~~&~~ liberty, & the pursuit

of happiness. . . .

The Final Draft of the Opening Sentences of the Declaration
of Independence, as Approved on July 4, 1776

When in the Course of human events, it becomes necessary for one people

to dissolve the political bands which have connected them with another, and to

assume among the powers of the earth, the separate and equal station to which

the Laws of Nature and of Nature's God entitle them, a decent respect to the

opinions of mankind requires that they should declare the causes which impel

them to the separation.

We hold these truths to be self-evident, that all men are created equal, that

they are endowed by their Creator with certain inalienable Rights, that among

these are Life, Liberty and the pursuit of Happiness.

a. Select one change in a sentence that most improved the final version of the Declaration of Independence. Explain how the revised wording is more effective.

b. Find one change in a word or phrase that constitutes an alteration in meaning rather than just a choice of "smoother" or more appropriate language. How does this change affect the meaning?

c. Upon rereading this passage from the Declaration of Independence, one reader wrote, "I was really irritated by that 'all men are created equal' remark. The writers were white, free, well-to-do, Anglo-Saxon, mostly Protestant males discussing their own 'inalienable rights.' They sure weren't discussing the 'inalienable rights' of female Americans or of a million slaves or of nonwhite free Americans!" Revise the passage from the Declaration of Independence using this person as your audience.

d. On the Internet, visit the National Archives at http://www.nara.gov to see a photograph of the original Declaration of Independence and learn how the Dunlap Broadside of the Declaration was read aloud to troops. What does this historical context add to what you know about the Declaration of Independence? Do the revisions help make the document more revolutionary or propagandistic? In addition, this site has other treasures from the National Archives including the police blotter listing Abraham Lincoln's assassination, the first report of the *Titanic*'s collision with an iceberg, and Rosa Parks's arrest records. Do you think these documents are as important to our history and culture as the Declaration itself? Explain.

10 Before you hand in your essay, reflect on your writing and learning process. In your journal, spend a few minutes answering the following questions.

a. Describe the purpose and intended audience for your essay.

b. What was the best peer review advice that you received? What did you revise in your draft because of that advice? What piece of advice did you ignore? Why?

c. What caused you the most difficulty with this essay? How did you solve the problem—or attempt to solve it? With what parts are you still least satisfied?

d. What are the best parts of your paper? Refer to specific paragraphs—what do you like most about them?

e. If you added visual images or special document-design features to your essay, explain how they supported your purpose or rhetorical goals.

f. What was the most important thing you learned about writing or your writing process as you wrote this paper?

Courtesy of David R. Frazier Photolibrary, Inc./Alamy.

Mackinac Bridge
Mackinaw City, MI
St. Ignace, MI

How Do I Organize Academic Writing?

2

Writing Introductions

All writers must face the task of writing their paper's introduction and conclusion. How to start? What's the best way to approach your topic? With a serious tone, a light touch, an anecdote? How to end? How best to make the connection from your work back to the reader's world?

Many writers avoid such decisions by putting them off—and productively so. Bypassing careful planning for the introduction and conclusion, they begin writing the body of the piece; only after they've finished the body do they go back to write the opening and closing paragraphs. There's a lot to be said for this approach: Because you have presumably spent more time thinking and writing about the topic itself than about how you're going to introduce or conclude it, you are in a better position to set out your ideas. And often it's not until you've actually seen the piece on paper and read it over once or twice that a natural way of introducing or concluding it becomes apparent. You are generally in better psychological shape to write both the introduction and the conclusion after the major task of writing is behind you and you know exactly what your major points are.

The purpose of an introduction is to prepare the reader to enter the world of your paper. The introduction makes the connection between the more familiar world inhabited by the reader and the less familiar world of the writer's topic; it places a discussion in a context that the reader can understand. If you find yourself getting stuck on an introduction at the beginning of a first draft, skip over it for the moment. State your working thesis directly and move on to the body of the paper.

There are many strategies for opening a paper; we'll consider the most common ones.

QUOTATION

Here are the two introductory paragraphs to an article titled "The Radical Idea of Marrying for Love," from Stephanie Coontz's (2005) *Marriage: A History*.

> George Bernard Shaw described marriage as an institution that brings together two people "under the influence of the most violent, most insane, most delusive, and most transient of passions. They are required to swear that they will remain in that excited, abnormal, and exhausting condition continuously until death do them part."
>
> Shaw's comment was amusing when he wrote it at the beginning of the twentieth century, and it still makes us smile today, because it pokes fun at the unrealistic expectations that spring from a dearly held cultural ideal—that marriage should be based on intense, profound love and a couple should maintain their ardor until death do them part. But for thousands of years the joke would have fallen flat.* (p. 47)

The provocative quotation by Shaw is intended by Coontz to puncture our romantic assumptions about the role of love and passion in marriage. She follows the quotation with an explanation of why Shaw's statement "makes us smile" before setting out on her main undertaking in this article—as indicated in the final sentence of the second paragraph—a historical survey demonstrating that for most of the last few thousand years, love and marriage have had little to do with one another. Quoting the words of others offers you many points of departure for your paper: You can agree with the quotation. You can agree and expand. You can sharply disagree. You can use the quotation to set a context or tone.

HISTORICAL REVIEW

In many cases, the reader will be unprepared to follow the issue you discuss unless you provide some historical background. Consider this introduction to a paper on the film-rating system:

> Sex and violence on the screen are not new issues. In the Roaring Twenties there was increasing pressure from civic and religious groups to ban depictions of "immorality" from the screen. Faced with the threat of federal censorship, the film producers decided to clean their own house. In 1930, the Motion Picture Producers and Distributors of America

---

*"The Radical Idea of Marrying for Love," from *Marriage: A History*, by Stephanie Coontz, copyright 2005 by the S.J. Coontz Company. Viking Penguin, a division of Penguin Group (USA), Inc.

established the Production Code. At first, adherence to the Code was voluntary; but in 1934 Joseph Breen, newly appointed head of the MPPDA, gave the Code teeth. Henceforth all newly produced films had to be submitted for approval to the Production Code Administration, which had the power to award or withhold the Code seal. Without a Code seal, it was virtually impossible for a film to be shown anywhere in the United States, since exhibitors would not accept it. At about the same time, the Catholic Legion of Decency was formed to advise the faithful which films were and were not objectionable. For several decades the Production Code Administration exercised powerful control over what was portrayed in American theatrical films. By the 1960s, however, changing standards of morality had considerably weakened the Code's grip. In 1968, the Production Code was replaced with a rating system designed to keep younger audiences away from films with high levels of sex or violence. Despite its imperfections, this rating system has proved more beneficial to American films than did the old censorship system.

The paper examines the relative benefits of the rating system. By beginning with some historical background on the rating system, the writer helps readers understand his arguments. (Notice the chronological development of details.)

REVIEW OF A CONTROVERSY

A particular type of historical review provides the background on a controversy or debate. Consider this introduction:

> The *American Heritage Dictionary's* definition of civil disobedience is rather simple: "the refusal to obey civil laws that are regarded as unjust, usually by employing methods of passive resistance." However, despite such famous (and beloved) examples of civil disobedience as the movements of Mahatma Gandhi in India and the Reverend Martin Luther King, Jr., in the United States, the question of whether or not civil disobedience should be considered an asset to society is hardly clear cut. For instance, Hannah Arendt, in her article "Civil Disobedience," holds that "to think of disobedient minorities as rebels and truants is against the letter and spirit of a constitution whose framers were especially sensitive to the dangers of unbridled majority rule." On the other hand, a noted lawyer, Lewis Van Dusen, Jr., in his article "Civil Disobedience: Destroyer of Democracy," states that "civil disobedience, whatever the ethical rationalization, is still an assault on our democratic society, an affront to our legal order and an attack on our constitutional government." These two views are clearly incompatible. I believe, though, that

Van Dusen's is the more convincing. On balance, civil disobedience is dangerous to society.* (Jacques, 1993, p. 49)

The negative aspects of civil disobedience, rather than Van Dusen's essay, are the topic of this paper. But to introduce this topic, the writer has provided quotations that represent opposing sides of the controversy over civil disobedience, as well as brief references to two controversial practitioners. By focusing at the outset on the particular rather than on the abstract qualities of the topic, the writer hopes to secure the attention of her readers and involve them in the controversy that forms the subject of her paper.

FROM THE GENERAL TO THE SPECIFIC

Another way of providing a transition from the reader's world to the less familiar world of the paper is to work from a general subject to a specific one. The following introduction begins a paper on improving our air quality by urging people to trade the use of their cars for public transportation.

While generalizations are risky, it seems pretty safe to say that most human beings are selfish. Self-interest may be part of our nature, and probably aids the survival of our species, since self-interested pursuits increase the likelihood of individual survival and genetic reproduction. Ironically, however, our selfishness has caused us to abuse the natural environment upon which we depend. We have polluted, deforested, depleted, deformed, and endangered our earth, water, and air to such an extent that now our species' survival is gravely threatened. In America, air pollution is one of our most pressing environmental problems, and it is our selfish use of the automobile that poses the greatest threat to clean air, as well as the greatest challenge to efforts to stop air pollution. Very few of us seem willing to give up our cars, let alone use them less. We are spoiled by the individual freedom afforded us when we can hop into our gas-guzzling vehicles and go where we want, when we want. Somehow, we as a nation will have to wean ourselves from this addiction to the automobile, and we can do this by designing alternative forms of transportation that serve our selfish interests.† (Knight, 1998, p. 1)

*Michele Jacques, "Civil Disobedience: Van Dusen vs. Arendt," unpublished paper, 1993, 1. Used by permission.
†Travis Knight, "Reducing Air Pollution with Alternative Transportation," unpublished paper, 1998, 1. Used by permission.

ANECDOTE AND ILLUSTRATION: FROM THE SPECIFIC TO THE GENERAL

The following two paragraphs offer an anecdote in order to move from the specific to a general subject:

> The night of March 24, 1989, was cold and calm, the air crystalline, as the giant *Exxon Valdez* oil tanker pulled out of Valdez, Alaska, into the tranquil waters of Prince William Sound. In these clearest of possible conditions the ship made a planned turn out of the shipping channel and didn't turn back in time. The huge tanker ran aground, spilling millions of gallons of crude oil into the sound. The cost of the cleanup effort was over $2 billion. The ultimate cost of continuing environmental damage is incalculable. Furthermore, when the civil trial was finally over in the summer of 1995, the Exxon Corporation was assessed an additional $5 billion in punitive damages. Everyone I query in my travels vividly recalls the accident, and most have the impression that it had something to do with the master's alcohol consumption. No one is aware of the true cause of the tragedy. In its final report, the National Transportation Safety Board (NTSB) found that sleep deprivation and sleep debt were direct causes of the accident. This stunning result got a brief mention in the back pages of the newspapers.
>
> Out of the vast ocean of knowledge about sleep, there are a few facts that are so important that I will try to burn them into your brain forever. None is more important than the topic of sleep debt. If we can learn to understand sleep indebtedness and manage it, we can improve everyday life as well as avoid many injuries, *horribly diminished lives, and premature deaths.** (Dement, 1999, p. 78)

The previous introduction went from the general (the statement that human beings are selfish) to the specific (how to decrease air pollution). This one goes from the specific (a calamitous oil spill by a giant oil tanker in Alaskan waters) to the general (the enormous financial and human costs of "sleep debt," or not getting enough sleep). The anecdote is one of the most effective means at your disposal for capturing and holding your reader's attention. It is also one of the most commonly used types of introduction in popular articles. For decades, speakers have begun their remarks with a funny, touching, or otherwise appropriate story. (In fact, plenty of books are nothing but collections of such stories, arranged by subject.)

*From "The Promise of Sleep," copyright 1999 by William C. Dement. Used by permission of Dell Publishing, a division of Random House, Inc.

QUESTION

Frequently you can provoke the reader's attention by posing a question or a series of questions:

> **Which of the following people** would you say is the most admirable: Mother Teresa, Bill Gates, or Norman Borlaug? And which do you think is the least admirable? For most people, it's an easy question. Mother Teresa, famous for ministering to the poor in Calcutta, has been beatified by the Vatican, awarded the Nobel Peace Prize and ranked in an American poll as the most admired person of the 20th century. Bill Gates, infamous for giving us the Microsoft dancing paper clip and the blue screen of death, has been decapitated in effigy in "I Hate Gates" Web sites and hit with a pie in the face. As for Norman Borlaug . . . who the heck is Norman Borlaug?
>
> Yet a deeper look might lead you to rethink your answers. Borlaug, father of the "Green Revolution" that used agricultural science to reduce world hunger, has been credited with saving a billion lives, more than anyone else in history. Gates, in deciding what to do with his fortune, crunched the numbers and determined that he could alleviate the most misery by fighting everyday scourges in the developing world like malaria, diarrhea and parasites. Mother Teresa, for her part, extolled the virtue of suffering and ran her well-financed missions accordingly: their sick patrons were offered plenty of prayer but harsh conditions, few analgesics and dangerously primitive medical care.
>
> It's not hard to see why the moral reputations of this trio should be so out of line with the good they have done. . . . * (Pinker, 2008, p. 96)

In this introduction to "The Moral Instinct," Steven Pinker asks a question that appears to be easy; but the answer turns out to be more complex than the average reader would have suspected. Pinker uses the rest of the first paragraph to explain why the question appears to be so easy. (After all, no one was more widely admired than Mother Teresa; and for many people—especially Apple partisans!—former Microsoft CEO Bill Gates was an emblem of capitalist greed.) In the second paragraph, Pinker overturns these assumptions as he begins his exploration of the moral sense. Opening your paper with a question can be provocative because it places the reader in an active role. Put on the spot by the author, he or she must consider answers—in this case, Who is the most admirable? What kind of qualities or activities *should* we admire? An opening question, chosen well, will engage readers and launch them into your paper.

---

*Steven J. Pinker, "The Moral Instinct," *New York Times Magazine* 12 Jan. 2008.

STATEMENT OF THESIS

Perhaps the most direct method of introduction is to begin immediately with the thesis:

> The contemporary American shopping mall is the formal garden of late twentieth-century culture, a commodified version of the great garden styles of Western history with which it shares fundamental characteristics. Set apart from the rest of the world as a place of earthly delight like the medieval walled garden; filled with fountains, statuary, and ingeniously devised machinery like the Italian Renaissance garden; designed on grandiose and symmetrical principles like the seventeenth-century French garden; made up of the fragments of cultural and architectural history like the eighteenth-century irregular English garden; and set aside for the public like the nineteenth-century American park, the mall is the next phase of this garden history, a synthesis of all these styles that have come before. But it is now joined with the shopping street, or at least a sanitized and standardized version of one, something that never before has been allowed within the garden.* (Simon, 1992, p. 67)

This selection begins with a general assertion—that the American shopping mall is analogous to the great formal gardens of Western history. This idea is Richard Keller Simon's thesis, for an article titled "The Formal Garden in the Age of Consumer Culture," which he begins to develop in his second sentence with comparisons between the modern shopping mall and various types of gardens throughout history. In the paragraphs following this introduction, Simon draws correspondences between contemporary shopping malls in Houston, Philadelphia, and Palo Alto and such classic formal gardens as Henry VIII's Hampton Court. The "promenades, walls, vistas, mounts, labyrinths, statues, archways" of classic gardens, he writes, all have their analogs in the modern mall. Beginning with a thesis statement (as opposed to a quotation, question, or anecdote) works well when you want to develop an unexpected, or controversial, argument. The mall as a formal garden? Who would think so? We read on.

Or perhaps you open with the provocative assertion that "Reading is dead" in a paper examining the problem of declining literacy in the digital age. The reader sits up and takes notice, perhaps even protesting ("No, it's not—I read all the time!"). This strategy "hooks" a reader, who is likely to want to find out how you will support such an emphatic thesis.

One final note about our model introductions: They may be longer than introductions you have been accustomed to writing. Many writers (and readers)

---

*Excerpted from "The Formal Garden in the Age of Consumer Culture: A Reading of the Twentieth-Century Shopping Mall," copyright 1992 by Richard Keller Simon. Reprinted from *Mapping the American Culture,* ed. Wayne Franklin and Michael Steiner, by permission of the University of Iowa Press.

prefer a shorter, snappier introduction. The length of an introduction can depend on the length of the paper it introduces, and it is also largely a matter of personal or corporate style. There is no rule concerning the correct length of an introduction. If you feel that a short introduction is appropriate, use one. Or you may wish to break up what seems like a long introduction into two paragraphs.

Writing a Thesis

Whether it is explanatory, mildly argumentative, or strongly argumentative, the thesis is an assertion about that content—for instance, about what the content is, how it works, what it means, if it is valuable, if action should be taken, and so on. A thesis is similar, actually, to a paper's conclusion, but it lacks the conclusion's concern for broad implications and significance. The thesis is the product of your thinking; it therefore represents *your* conclusion about the topic on which you're writing, and therefore you have to have spent some time thinking (that is, in the invention stage) in order to arrive at the thesis that governs your paper.

For a writer in the drafting stages, the thesis establishes a focus, a basis on which to include or exclude information. For the reader of a finished product, the thesis anticipates the author's discussion. *A thesis, therefore, is an essential tool for both writers and readers of academic papers.*

THE COMPONENTS OF A THESIS

Like any other sentence, a thesis includes a subject and a predicate that makes an assertion about the subject. In the sentence "Lee and Grant were different kinds of generals," "Lee and Grant" is the subject and "were different kinds of generals" is the predicate. What distinguishes a thesis from any other sentence with a subject and a predicate is that *the thesis presents the controlling idea of the paper*. The subject of a thesis, and the assertion about it, must present the right balance between the general and the specific to allow for a thorough discussion within the allotted length of the paper. The discussion might include definitions, details, comparisons, contrasts—whatever is needed to illuminate a subject and support the assertion. (If the sentence about Lee and Grant were a thesis, the reader would assume that the rest of the paper contained comparisons and contrasts between the two generals.)

Bear in mind when writing theses that the more general your subject and the more complex your assertion, the longer your paper will be. The broadest theses require book-length treatments, as in this case:

Meaningful energy conservation requires a shrewd application of political, financial, and scientific will.

One could not write an effective ten-page paper based on this thesis. The
topic alone would require pages merely to define carefully what is meant by
"energy conservation" and then by "meaningful." Energy can be conserved in
homes, vehicles, industries, appliances, and power plants, and each of these
areas would need consideration. Having accomplished this task, the writer would then
turn his or her attention to the claim, which entails a discussion of how politics,
finance, and science individually and collectively influence energy conservation.
Moreover, the thesis requires the writer to argue that "shrewd application" of politics, finance, and science is required. The thesis may very well be accurate and
compelling. Yet it promises entirely too much for a ten-page paper.

To write an effective thesis and thus a controlled, effective paper, you need to
limit your subject and your claims about it, in that way arriving at a manageable
topic. You will convert that topic to a thesis when you make an assertion about
it—a *claim* that you will explain and support in the paper.

● **MAKING AN ASSERTION**   Thesis statements constitute an assertion or claim
that you wish to make *about* your paper's topic. If you have spent enough time
reading and gathering information, and brainstorming ideas about the assignment, you will be knowledgeable enough to have something to say based on a combination of your own thinking and the thinking of your sources.

If you have trouble making an assertion, devote more time to invention
strategies: Try writing your subject at the top of a page and then listing everything you now know and feel about it. Often from such a list you will discover an
assertion that you can then use to fashion a working thesis. A good way to gauge
the reasonableness of your claim is to see what other authors have asserted about
the same topic. Your keeping good notes on the views of others will provide you
with a useful counterpoint to your own views as you write and think about your
claim, and you may want to use those notes in your paper. Next, make several
assertions about your topic, in order of increasing complexity, as in the
following:

1. Fuel-cell technology has emerged as a promising approach to developing
   energy-efficient vehicles.
2. To reduce our dependence on nonrenewable fossil fuel, the federal
   government should encourage the development of fuel-cell vehicles.
3. The federal government should subsidize the development of fuel-cell
   vehicles as well as the hydrogen infrastructure needed to support them;
   otherwise, the United States will be increasingly vulnerable to recession
   and other economic dislocations resulting from our dependence on the
   continued flow of foreign oil.

Keep in mind that these are *working theses*. Because you haven't begun a paper
based on any of them, they remain *hypotheses* to be tested. You might choose one

and use it to focus your initial draft. After completing a first draft, you would revise it by comparing the contents of the paper to the thesis and making adjustments as necessary for unity. The working thesis is an excellent tool for planning broad sections of the paper, but—again—don't let it prevent you from pursuing related discussions as they occur to you.

● **STARTING WITH A WORKING THESIS** As a student, you are not yet an expert on the subject of your paper and, therefore, won't generally have the luxury of beginning your writing tasks with a definite thesis in mind. But let's assume that you *do* have an area of expertise, that you are in your own right a professional (albeit not in academic matters). We'll assume that you understand some nonacademic subject—say, backpacking—and have been given a clear purpose for writing: to discuss the relative merits of backpack designs. Your job is to write a recommendation for the owner of a sporting-goods chain, suggesting which line of backpacks the chain should carry. Because you already know a good deal about backpacks, you may have some well-developed ideas on the subject before you start doing additional research.

Yet even as an expert in your field, you will find that crafting a thesis is challenging. After all, a thesis is a summary, and it is difficult to summarize a presentation yet to be written—especially if you plan to discover what you want to say during the process of writing. Even if you know your material well, the best you can do at first is to formulate a working thesis—a hypothesis of sorts, a well-informed hunch about your topic and the claim to be made about it. After you have completed a draft, you can evaluate the degree to which your working thesis accurately summarizes the content of your paper. If the match is a good one, the working thesis becomes the thesis. If, however, sections of the paper drift from the focus of the working thesis, you'll need to revise the thesis and the paper itself to ensure that the presentation is unified. (You'll know that the match between content and thesis is a good one when every paragraph directly refers to and develops some element of the thesis.)

This model works whether you are writing about a subject in your area of expertise—backpacking, for example—or one that is more in your professor's territory, such as government or medieval poetry. The difference is that when approaching subjects that are less familiar to you, you will have to spend more time gathering data and brainstorming in order to make assertions about your subject.

● **USING THE THESIS TO PLAN A STRUCTURE** A working thesis will help you sketch the structure of your paper, for the structure flows directly from the thesis. Consider, for example, the third thesis on fuel-cell technology:

> The federal government should subsidize the development of fuel-cell vehicles as well as the hydrogen infrastructure needed to support them; otherwise, the United States will be increasingly vulnerable to recession and other economic dislocations resulting from our dependence on the continued flow of foreign oil.

This thesis is *strongly argumentative* or *persuasive*. The economic catastrophes mentioned by the writer indicate a strong degree of urgency in the need for the solution recommended: the federal subsidy of a national hydrogen infrastructure to support fuel-cell vehicles. If a paper based on this thesis is to be well developed, the writer must commit him- or herself to explaining (1) why fuel-cell vehicles are a preferred alternative to gasoline-powered vehicles; (2) why fuel-cell vehicles require a hydrogen infrastructure (i.e., the writer must explain that fuel cells produce power by mixing hydrogen and oxygen, generating both electricity and water in the process); (3) why the government needs to subsidize industry in developing fuel-cell vehicles; and (4) how continued reliance on fossil fuel technology could make the country vulnerable to economic dislocations. This thesis, therefore, helps the writer plan the paper, which should include a section on each of the four topics. Assuming that the paper follows the organizational plan we've proposed, the working thesis would become the final thesis, on the basis of which a reader could anticipate sections of the paper to come. In a finished product, the thesis becomes an essential tool for guiding readers.

Note, however, that this thesis is still provisional. It may turn out, as you do research or begin drafting, that the paper to which this thesis commits you will be too long and complex. You may therefore decide to drop the second clause of the thesis dealing with the country's vulnerability to economic dislocations and

HOW AMBITIOUS SHOULD YOUR THESIS BE?

Writing tasks vary according to the nature of the thesis.

- The *explanatory thesis* is often developed in response to short-answer exam questions that call for information, not analysis (e.g., "How does James Barber categorize the main types of presidential personality?").

- The *mildly argumentative thesis* is appropriate for organizing reports (even lengthy ones), as well as essay questions that call for some analysis (e.g., "Discuss the qualities of a good speech").

- The *strongly argumentative thesis* is used to organize papers and exam questions that call for information, analysis, *and* the writer's forcefully stated point of view (e.g., "Evaluate the proposed reforms of health maintenance organizations").

The strongly argumentative thesis, of course, is the riskiest of the three because you must state your position unequivocally and make it appear reasonable—which requires that you offer evidence and defend against logical objections. But such intellectual risks pay dividends, and if you become involved enough in your work to make challenging assertions, you will provoke challenging responses that enliven classroom discussions and your own learning.

focus on the need for the government to subsidize the development of fuel-cell vehicles and a hydrogen infrastructure, relegating the economic concerns to your conclusion (if at all). If you make this change, your final thesis could read: "The federal government should subsidize the development of fuel-cell vehicles as well as the hydrogen infrastructure needed to support them."

This revised thesis makes an assertive commitment to the subject even though the assertion is not as complex as the original. Still, it is more assertive than the second proposed thesis:

> To reduce our dependence on nonrenewable fossil fuel energy sources, the federal government should encourage the development of fuel-cell vehicles.

Here we have a *mildly argumentative* thesis that enables the writer to express an opinion. We infer from the use of the words "should encourage" that the writer endorses the idea of the government's promoting fuel-cell development. But a government that "encourages" development is making a lesser commitment than one that "subsidizes," which means that it allocates funds for a specific policy. So the writer who argues for mere encouragement takes a milder position than the one who argues for subsidies. Note also the contrast between the second thesis and the first one, in which the writer is committed to no involvement in the debate and suggests no government involvement whatsoever.

> Fuel-cell technology has emerged as a promising approach to developing energy-efficient vehicles.

This, the first of the three thesis statements, is *explanatory* or *informative*. In developing a paper based on this thesis, the writer is committed only to explaining how fuel-cell technology works and why it is a promising approach to energy-efficient vehicles. Given this thesis, a reader would *not* expect to find the author strongly recommending, for instance, that fuel-cell engines replace internal combustion engines in the near future. Neither does the thesis require the writer to defend a personal opinion; he or she need only justify the use of the relatively mild term "promising."

As you can see, for any topic you might explore in a paper, you can make any number of assertions—some relatively simple, some complex. It is on the basis of these assertions that you set yourself an agenda for your writing—and readers set for themselves expectations for reading. The more ambitious the thesis, the more complex will be the paper and the greater will be the readers' expectations.

To review: A thesis helps you organize your discussion, and it helps your reader anticipate it. Theses are distinguished by their carefully worded subjects and predicates, which should be just broad enough and complex enough to be developed within the length limitations of the assignment. Both novices and experts typically begin the initial draft of a paper with a working thesis—a statement that provides writers with structure enough to get started but with latitude enough to discover what they want to say as they write. Once you have completed a first draft, however, you test the "fit" of your thesis with what you have written. When you have a good fit, every element of the thesis is developed in the paper that follows. Discussions that drift from your thesis should be deleted, or the thesis revised to accommodate the new discussions.

WRITE A WORKING THESIS

Your thesis should follow the direction your assignment calls for. These examples show how the broad subject of databases and privacy can be approached from different directions, depending on your purpose.

● **DESCRIBE**   THESIS: My Amazon.com account has a list of every book I have purchased from them dating back ten years, plus Amazon records every item I browse but don't buy. No wonder Amazon's recommendations of what I might like are so uncannily accurate!

● **ANALYZE**   THESIS: Understanding how the concept of privacy is legally defined is critical for strengthening privacy laws.

● **INFORM**   THESIS: Imagine a government that compels its citizens to reveal vast amounts of personal data, including your physical description, your phone number, your political party, your parents' and spouse's names, where you work, where you live, what property you own, what it is worth, and every legal transaction in your life, and then making that data available to anyone on the Web—which is exactly what federal, state, and local governments are doing today in the United States.

● **ARGUE**   THESIS: Unlike the government, companies have almost no restrictions on what information they collect or what they do with that information. Laws should be passed that make companies responsible for the misuse of personal information and allow people to have greater participation in how that information is used.

● **EVALUATE**   THESIS: Using personal consumer data to refuse service or offer inferior service to customers who likely will not spend much money is an example of the misuse of personal information.

● **REFLECT**   THESIS: I had never thought about the consequences of data profiling until I read about Netflix's policy of "throttling" frequent users, which explained why deliveries of movies I had requested from Netflix grew slower and slower.

● **ANALYZE CAUSES**   THESIS: Many laws to protect privacy are on the books, but these laws are ineffective for the digital era because they were written to protect people from government spying and intrusion rather than from the collection and selling of personal information by companies.

EVALUATE YOUR WORKING THESIS

Ask yourself these questions about your working thesis.

1. Is it specific?
2. Is it manageable in terms of the assigned length and the amount of time you have?
3. Is it interesting to your intended readers?

● **EXAMPLE 1**   THESIS: Steroids are a problem in Major League Baseball.

- **Specific?** The thesis is too broad. What exactly is the problem? Is the problem the same now as it was a few years ago?
- **Manageable?** Because the thesis is not limited, it cannot be discussed adequately.
- **Interesting?** The topic is potentially interesting, but many people are aware that baseball players used steroids. How can you lead readers to think about the topic in a new way?

● **EXAMPLE 1 REVISED**   THESIS: Home run records from 1993 through 2004 should be placed in a special category because of the high use of steroids in Major League Baseball before testing began in 2004.

● **EXAMPLE 2**   THESIS: "Nanotechnology" refers to any technology that deals with particles measured in units of a nanometer, which is one billionth (10^{-9}) of a meter.

- **Specific?** The thesis is specific, but it is too narrow. It offers only a definition of nanotechnology.
- **Manageable?** The thesis states a fact.
- **Interesting?** Nanotechnology could be interesting if some of its potential effects are included.

● **EXAMPLE 2 REVISED**   THESIS: Nanotechnology may soon change concepts of social identity by making it possible for individuals to alter their physical appearances either through cosmetic surgery performed by nanorobots or changes in genetic sequences on chromosomes.

Conclusions

One way to view the conclusion of your paper is to see it as an introduction in reverse, a bridge from the world of your paper back to the world of your reader. A conclusion is the part of your paper in which you restate and (if necessary) expand on your thesis. Essential to many conclusions is the summary, which is not merely a repetition of the thesis but a restatement that takes advantage of the material you've presented. *The simplest conclusion is a summary of the paper, but you should want more than this.* Depending on your needs, you might offer a summary and then build onto it a discussion of the paper's significance or its implications for future study, for choices that individuals might make, for policy, and so on. You might also want to urge readers to change an attitude or modify behavior. Certainly, you are under no obligation to discuss the broader significance of your work (and a summary, alone, will satisfy the formal requirement that your paper have an ending); but the conclusions of better papers often reveal that authors are "thinking large" and want to connect their concerns with the broader concerns of society.

Two words of advice: First, no matter how clever or beautifully executed, a conclusion cannot salvage a poorly written paper. Second, by virtue of its placement, the conclusion carries rhetorical weight; it is the last statement a reader will encounter before turning from your work. Realizing this, writers who expand on the basic summary conclusion often wish to give their final words a dramatic flourish, a heightened level of diction. Soaring rhetoric and drama in a conclusion are fine as long as they do not unbalance the paper and call attention to themselves. Having labored long hours over your paper, you may be inclined at this point to wax eloquent. But keep a sense of proportion and timing; make your points quickly and end crisply.

STATEMENT OF THE SUBJECT'S SIGNIFICANCE

One of the more effective ways to conclude a paper is to discuss the larger significance of what you have written, providing readers with one more reason to regard your work as a serious effort. When using this strategy, you move from the specific concern of your paper to the broader concerns of the reader's world. Often, you will need to choose among a range of significances: A paper on the Wright brothers might end with a discussion of air travel as it affects economies, politics, or families; a paper on contraception might end with a discussion of its effect on sexual mores, population, or the church. But don't overwhelm your reader with the importance of your remarks. Keep your discussion well focused.

The following paragraph by June J. Pilcher and Amy S. Walters (1997) concludes a paper on how "sleep debt" hurts college students.

> In sum, our findings suggest that college students are not aware of the extent to which sleep deprivation impairs their ability to complete cognitive tasks successfully because they consistently overrate their concentration and effort, as well as their estimated performance. In addition, the current data suggest that 24 hours of sleep deprivation significantly affects only fatigue and confusion and does not have a more

general effect on positive or negative mood states. The practical implication of these findings is that many college students are unknowingly sabotaging their own performance by choosing to deprive themselves of sleep [while] they complete complex cognitive tasks.* (p. 123)

The first sentence (as the initial phrase indicates) summarizes the chief finding of the study on which the authors have written. They expand on this conclusion before ending with a statement of the subject's significance ("The practical implication of these findings is that . . . "). Ending the paper in this fashion is another way of saying, "The conclusions of this paper matter." If you have taken the trouble to write a good paper, the conclusions *do* matter. Don't be bashful: State the larger significance of the point(s) you have made. Just don't claim too great a significance for your work, lest by overreaching you pop the balloon and your reader thinks, "No, the paper's not *that* important."

CALL FOR FURTHER RESEARCH

In the scientific and social scientific communities, papers often end with a review of what has been presented (as, for instance, in an experiment) and the ways in which the subject under consideration needs to be further explored. *A word of caution:* If you raise questions that you call on others to answer, make sure you know that the research you are calling for hasn't already been conducted.

The following conclusion comes from a sociological report on the placement of elderly men and women in nursing homes.

Thus, our study shows a correlation between the placement of elderly citizens in nursing facilities and the significant decline of their motor and intellectual skills over the ten months following placement. What the research has not made clear is the extent to which this marked decline is due to physical as opposed to emotional causes. The elderly are referred to homes at that point in their lives when they grow less able to care for themselves—which suggests that the drop-off in skills may be due to physical causes. But the emotional stress of being placed in a home, away from family and in an environment that confirms the patient's view of himself as decrepit, may exacerbate—if not itself be a primary cause of—the patient's rapid loss of abilities. Further research is needed to clarify the relationship between depression and particular

*"How Sleep Deprivation Affects Psychological Variables Related to College Students' Cognitive Performance" by June J. Pilcher and Amy S. Walters, from *Journal of American College Health,* Vol. 46, issue 3, November 1997, pp. 121–126. Reprinted with permission of the Helen Dwight Reid Educational Foundation. Published by Heldref Publications, 1319 Eighteenth St., N.W., Washington, DC 20036-1802. Copyright 1997.

physical ailments as these affect the skills of the elderly in nursing facilities. There is little doubt that information yielded by such studies can enable health care professionals to deliver more effective services.*

Notice how this call for further study locates the author in a larger community of researchers on whom he depends for assistance in answering the questions that have come out of his own work. The author summarizes his findings (in the first sentence of the paragraph), states what his work has not shown, and then extends his invitation.

SOLUTION/RECOMMENDATION

The purpose of your paper might be to review a problem or controversy and to discuss contributing factors. In such a case, it would be appropriate, after summarizing your discussion, to offer a solution based on the knowledge you've gained while conducting research, as the writer of the following conclusion does. If your solution is to be taken seriously, however, your knowledge must be amply demonstrated in the body of the paper.

> The major problem in college sports today is not commercialism—it is the exploitation of athletes and the proliferation of illicit practices which dilute educational standards.
>
> Many universities are currently deriving substantial benefits from sports programs that depend on the labor of athletes drawn from the poorest sections of America's population. It is the responsibility of educators, civil rights leaders, and concerned citizens to see that these young people get a fair return for their labor both in terms of direct remuneration and in terms of career preparation for a life outside sports.
>
> Minimally, scholarships in revenue-producing sports should be designed to extend until graduation, rather than covering only four years of athletic eligibility, and should include guarantees of tutoring, counseling, and proper medical care. At institutions where the profits are particularly large (such as Texas A & M, which can afford to pay its football coach $280,000 a year), scholarships should also provide salaries that extend beyond room, board, and tuition. The important thing is that the athlete be remunerated fairly and have the opportunity to gain skills from a university environment without undue competition from a physically and psychologically demanding full-time job. This may well require that scholarships be extended over five or six years, including summers.

*Adam Price, "The Crisis in Nursing Home Care," unpublished paper, 2001. Used by permission.

> Such a proposal, I suspect, will not be easy to implement. The current amateur system, despite its moral and educational flaws, enables universities to hire their athletic labor at minimal cost. But solving the fiscal crisis of the universities on the backs of America's poor and minorities is not, in the long run, a tenable solution. With the support of concerned educators, parents, and civil rights leaders, and with the help from organized labor, the college athlete, truly a sleeping giant, will someday speak out and demand what is rightly his—and hers—a fair share of the revenue created by their hard work.*

In this conclusion, the author summarizes his article in one sentence: "The major problem in college sports today is not commercialism—it is the exploitation of athletes and the proliferation of illicit practices which dilute educational standards." In paragraph two, he continues with an analysis of the problem just stated and follows with a general recommendation that "educators, civil rights leaders, and concerned citizens" be responsible for the welfare of college athletes. In paragraph three, he makes a specific proposal, and in the final paragraph, he anticipates resistance to the proposal. He concludes by discounting this resistance and returning to the general point, that college athletes should receive a fair deal.

ANECDOTE

As you learned in the context of introductions, an anecdote is a briefly told story or joke, the point of which is to shed light on your subject. The anecdote is more direct than an allusion. With an allusion, you merely refer to a story ("Too many people today live in Plato's cave . . . "); with the anecdote, you retell the story. The anecdote allows readers to discover for themselves the significance of a reference to another source—an effort most readers enjoy because they get to exercise their creativity.

The following anecdote concludes a political-philosophical essay. First, the author sums up her argument in a paragraph, then she follows that with a brief story.

> Ironically, our economy is fueled by the very thing that degrades our value system. But when politicians call for a return to "traditional family values," they seldom criticize the business interests that promote and benefit from our coarsened values. Consumer capitalism values things over people; it thrives on discontent and unhappiness since discontented people make excellent consumers, buying vast numbers of things that may somehow "fix" their inadequacies. We buy more than we need, the economy chugs along, but such materialism is the real culprit behind our warped value systems. Anthony de Mello tells the following story:

---

*Mark Naison, "Scenario for Scandal," *Commonweal* 109.16 (1982).

Socrates believed that the wise person would instinctively lead a frugal life, and he even went so far as to refuse to wear shoes. Yet he constantly fell under the spell of the marketplace and would go there often to look at the great variety and magnificence of the wares on display.

A friend once asked him why he was so intrigued with the allures of the market. "I love to go there," Socrates replied, "to discover how many things I am perfectly happy without."*

The writer chose to conclude her article with this anecdote. She could have developed an interpretation, but this would have spoiled the dramatic value for the reader. The purpose of using an anecdote is to make your point with subtlety, to resist the temptation to interpret. When selecting an anecdote, keep in mind four guidelines: The anecdote should fit your content, it should be prepared for (readers should have all the information they need to understand it), it should provoke the readers' interest, and it should not be so obscure as to be unintelligible.

QUOTATION

A favorite concluding device is the quotation—the words of a famous person or an authority in the field on which you are writing. The purpose of quoting another is to link your work to theirs, thereby gaining for your work authority and credibility. The first criterion for selecting a quotation is its suitability to your thesis. But consider carefully what your choice of sources says about you. Suppose you are writing a paper on the American work ethic. If you could use a line by the comedian Jon Stewart or one by the current Secretary of Labor to make the final point of your conclusion, which would you choose and why? One source may not be inherently more effective than the other, but the choice certainly sets a tone for the paper. The following paragraph concludes an article on single-sex education:

But schools, inevitably, present many curriculums, some overt and some subtle; and critics argue that with Sax's*model comes a lesson that our gender differences are primary, and this message is at odds with one of the most foundational principles of America's public schools. Given the myriad ways in which our schools are failing, it may be hard to remember that public schools were intended not only to instruct children in reading and math but also to teach them commonality, tolerance and

*Frances Wageneck, "Family Values in the Marketplace," unpublished paper, 2000. Used by permission.
*Leonard Sax is a psychologist and physician who gave up medicine to devote himself to promoting single-sex public education.

what it means to be American. "When you segregate, by any means, you lose some of that," says Richard Kahlenberg, a senior fellow at the Century Foundation. "Even if one could prove that sending a kid off to his or her own school based on religion or race or ethnicity or gender did a little bit better job of raising the academic skills for workers in the economy, there's also the issue of trying to create tolerant citizens in a democracy"[†] (Weil, 2008, p. 88).

In the article leading up to this conclusion, Elizabeth Weil takes a somewhat skeptical view of the virtues of "teaching boys and girls separately." She concludes with an apt quotation by Richard Kahlenberg who, while conceding some value for single-sex education, supports Weil's own skepticism by suggesting that single-sex education may not create citizens as tolerant as those who have been through classes that include both genders.

Using quotations poses one potential problem: If you end with the words of another, you may leave the impression that someone else can make your case more eloquently than you. The language of the quotation will put your own prose into relief. If your prose suffers by comparison—if the quotations are the best part of your paper—you need to spend time revising. Avoid this kind of problem by making your own presentation a strong one.

QUESTION

Questions are useful for opening papers, and they are just as useful for closing them. Opening and closing questions function in different ways, however. The introductory question promises to be addressed in the article that follows. But the concluding question leaves issues unresolved, calling on the readers to assume an active role by offering their own answers. Consider the following two paragraphs, written to conclude an article on genetically modified (GM) food:

Are GM foods any more of a risk than other agricultural innovations that have taken place over the years, like selective breeding? Do the existing and potential future benefits of GM foods outweigh any risks that do exist? And what standard should governments use when assessing the safety of transgenic crops? The "frankenfood" frenzy has given life to a policy-making standard known as the "precautionary principle," which has been long advocated by environmental groups. That principle essentially calls for governments to prohibit any activity that raises concerns about human health or the environment, even if some

[†]Elizabeth Weil, "Teaching Boys and Girls Separately," *New York Times Magazine* 2 Mar. 2008.

cause-and-effect relationships are not fully established scientifically. As Liberal Democrat MP [Member of Parliament] Norman Baker told the BBC: "We must always apply the precautionary principle. That says that unless you're sure of adequate control, unless you're sure the risk is minimal, unless you're sure nothing horrible can go wrong, you don't do it."

But can any innovation ever meet such a standard of certainty—especially given the proliferation of "experts" that are motivated as much by politics as they are by science? And what about those millions of malnourished people whose lives could be saved by transgenic foods ("Frankenfoods Frenzy," 2000, p. 8)?*

Rather than end with a question, you may choose to *raise* a question in your conclusion and then answer it, based on the material you've provided in the paper. The answered question challenges a reader to agree or disagree with you and thus places the reader in an active role. The following brief conclusion ends a student paper titled "Is Feminism Dead?"

So the answer to the question "Is the feminist movement dead?" is no, it's not. Even if most young women today don't consciously identify themselves as "feminists"—due to the ways in which the term has become loaded with negative associations—the principles of gender equality that lie at feminism's core are enthusiastically embraced by the vast number of young women, and even a large percentage of young men.

SPECULATION

When you speculate, you ask about and explore what has happened or what might happen. Speculation involves a spinning out of possibilities. It stimulates readers by immersing them in your discussion of the unknown, implicitly challenging them to agree or disagree. The following paragraph concludes a brief article, "The Incandescent Charisma of the Lonely Light Bulb" by Dan Neil. The author laments the passing of the familiar electric light bulb (in favor of lower wattage compact fluorescent lights) as one more indication of the end of the analog age and the triumph of the digital: "The demise of the light bulb marks the final transition from electrics to electronics":

The passing of any technology provokes nostalgia. I'm sure someone bemoaned the rise of the push-button phone and eulogized the rotary dialer. (*What a beautiful sound, the "shickity-shick" of a well-spun*

---

*"Frankenfoods Frenzy," *Reason* 13 Jan. 2000.

*number. . . . *) But the Edisonian light bulb is a more fundamental thing—so much the proverbial better idea that it came to symbolize the eureka moment, the flash of insight, when it appeared over a cartoon character's head. The fact is, how we light the world inevitably affects how we see the world. I predict we're going to miss the soft, forgiving light of the incandescent bulb with its celestial geometry. *I predict a more harshly lighted future.** (Neil, 2008, p. 70)

The author's concluding speculation may not be entirely serious (though a few people do lament the passing of the manual typewriter and the phonograph record), but it does highlight what is often lost, and subsequently missed, in the relentless journey of technological progress. If you have provided the necessary information prior to a concluding speculation, you will send readers back into their lives (and away from your paper) with an implicit challenge: Do they regard the future as you do? Whether they do or do not, you have set an agenda. You have got them thinking.

*Dan Neil, "The Incandescent Charisma of the Lonely Light Bulb," *Los Angeles Times Magazine* 3 Feb. 2008: 70.

STUDENT MODELS

Got Roddick?   ←————————————————————

The heading is in the correct APA format. The paper is free of major errors.

Angela Yamashita

Dr. Sanchez

English 15—October 13, 2008

GOT RODDICK?   2

The title plays off the theme of the ad and suggests the content.

Got Roddick?

The writer gets off to a fast start, introducing her subject in the first sentence.

Andy Roddick is one of the hottest professional athletes today. In 2003 he became the youngest American to finish ranked number one in the ATP rankings, and he's known not only for his excellent playing skills but also for his good looks and easygoing attitude. Ex-boyfriend to popular singer Mandy Moore, Roddick has been thrown into the spotlight and is now a teenage crush.

The writer engages her subject.

It was his picture that stopped me while leafing through *Seventeen* and made me take a longer look. Roddick stands staring at the viewer, racquet over his

Angela describes the ad with specifics.

shoulder, leaning against the net on the court. More prominent than his white pants, white tennis shirt, and white towel draped around his neck is the white milk mustache above his upper lip. The ad reads: "Now serving. I'm into power. So I drink milk. It packs 9 essential nutrients into every glass. Which comes in handy whether you're an athlete or an energetic fan." At the bottom of the page is the ad slogan (also in white) "Got Milk?"

The "Got Milk?" campaign has published numerous ads that try to convince adults to drink more milk. Everyone from rock groups to actors to athletes have participated in this campaign. In today's caffeine-obsessed society of coffee and soda drinkers, America's Dairy Farmers and Milk Processors (2003)

Angela provides background information.

(the association that sponsors the "Got Milk?" campaign) felt the need to reverse the decline in milk consumption by advertising milk in a new way. The catchy "Got Milk?" proved to be highly successful, and the campaign has been

Angela cites the source of her information.

mimicked by many others including "Got cookies?" "Got fish?" "Got sports?" and even "Got Jesus?" (Philpot, 2002, D3). The Andy Roddick (2003) ad is typical of the "Got Milk?" series, urging people young and old to drink milk to remain healthy and strong. The Roddick ad primarily uses the appeals of ethos and

Thesis of paper

pathos to persuade its audience. (The one gesture toward logos in the ad is the mention that milk has nine nutrients.)

GOT RODDICK? 3

"Got Milk?" ad featuring Andy Roddick

Angela includes the ad along with the caption.

To establish the ethos of their ads, America's Dairy Farmers and Milk Processors use celebrity endorsements. The "Got Milk?" campaign has enlisted a range of celebrities popular with young audiences from Amy Grant to Austin Powers, Britney Spears to Brett Favre, T-Mac (Tracy McGrady) to Bernie Mac. Choosing Andy Roddick, the dominant young male player in American tennis, fits squarely in this lineup. Admired by a strong following of young adults (girls for his looks, boys for his athletic ability), Roddick is an ideal spokesman for establishing that milk is a healthy drink. Implicit in the ad is that milk will help you become a better athlete and better looking too.

Repeating "ethos" makes a smooth transition.

Angela explains why Andy Roddick was chosen as a spokesperson.

The ad conveys pathos not simply through Roddick's good looks. His pose is casual, almost slouching, yet his face is serious, one that suggests that he not only means business about playing tennis but also about his drink of choice. The words "I'm into power" don't mess around. They imply that you too can be more powerful by drinking milk. "Now serving" is also in your face, making a play on the word "serving" both as a tennis and a drink term.

Angela analyzes the appeals to pathos.

Angela looks closely at the language the ad uses.

GOT RODDICK?   4

The effectiveness of the "Got Milk?" campaign is demonstrated in gallons of milk sold. The campaign began in California in 1993 at a time when milk sales were rapidly eroding. A San Francisco ad agency developed the milk mustache idea, which is credited for stopping the downward trend in milk consumption in California. In 1995 the campaign went national. By 2000 national sales of milk remained consistent in contrast to annual declines in the early 1990s (Stamler, 2001). "Got Milk?" gave milk a brand identity that it had previously lacked, allowing it to compete with the well-established identities of Pepsi and Coca-Cola. Milk now has new challengers with more and more people going out to Starbuck's and other breakfast bars. Nonetheless, the original formula of using celebrities like Andy Roddick who appeal to younger audiences continues to work. Milk isn't likely to go away soon as a popular beverage.

The history of the "Got Milk?" campaign is given briefly and the source is documented.

Angela's style is efficient and appropriate for college readers.

The ending provides new ideas for readers to think about rather than simply summarizing what has been said.

GOT RODDICK?   5

References

Angela includes a list of references in the correct APA format. If readers want to look at her sources, they should be able to find them easily.

Got Milk? (2003). Andy Roddick. (Advertisement) Milk Processor Education
    Program.

Philpot, R. (2002, May). Copycats mimic "got milk" ads. *Milwaukee Journal Sentinel,*
    D3. Retrieved from http://www.lexisnexis.com/hottopics/Inacademic/?

Stamler, B. (2001, July). Got sticking power? *New York Times,* C11. Retrieved from
    http://www.lexisnexis.com/hottopics/Inacademic/?

PRACTICE

1 **Write a bold thesis**

Too much of what we read says what we've all heard before. Instead of serving up what readers likely know, try challenging readers. For example, in *Everything Bad Is Good for You*, Steven Johnson argues that video games are not a total waste of time but teach children valuable problem-solving skills.

Think of something that many people accept as common sense or general wisdom—that junk food is bad for you, reality television is garbage, or graffiti is vandalism—and argue the opposite. Or that something thought of as boring might be really interesting: bird watching, classical Indian music, or ancient Greek drama. Write a thesis that stands that common wisdom on its head.

Then write a paragraph about how you might argue for your controversial thesis. What evidence might you supply?

2 **Individual task:** Choose an essay you are currently working on or have recently completed and examine your title and introduction. Ask yourself these questions:

- What audience am I imagining? What do I assume are my readers' initial interests that will lead them to read my essay (the old information I must hook into)? What is new in my essay?
- Do I have an attention-grabber? Why or why not?
- Where do I state or imply the question or problem that my essay addresses?
- Do I explain why the question is problematic and significant? Why or why not?
- For my audience to understand the problem, do I provide too much background information, not enough, or just the right amount?
- What strategies do I use to forecast the whole?

Based on your analysis of your present title and introduction, revise as appropriate.

Group task: Working with a partner or in small groups, share the changes you made in your title or introduction and explain why you made the changes.

3 Choose a paper you have just written and write an alternative conclusion using one of the strategies discussed in this lesson. Then share your original and revised conclusions in groups. Have group members discuss which one they consider most effective and why.

Baker College
Auburn Hills

How Do I Work with Outside Sources?

3

Summarizing, Paraphrasing, and Quoting

Since many writing assignments require you to draw on books, articles, lecture notes, and other written texts, it's important to learn how to use sources to their best advantage. The ability to take information from sources and use it in a piece of writing addressed to one's own audience is useful not only in academic writing, but in business and professional settings. When writers prepare annual reports for stockholders in large corporations, they summarize hundreds of individual reports, studies, and analyses. They repackage information that was originally produced for accountants, managers, engineers, and other professionals so that the general public can easily understand it. For in-house business documents, writers often take information that was originally intended for one audience, for instance, technical experts, and make it intelligible for another audience, say, the sales staff. Much of the writing that goes on in business, government, and other professions involves reducing, processing, and translating information for a designated audience or purpose.

Writers use three basic techniques to represent information they acquire from sources. First, they *summarize* the information by focusing on key elements and compacting or omitting details. Whether summaries are brief or comprehensive, they are attempts to capture the overall message. Second, they *paraphrase* selected parts of sources by translating the text into their own words. Finally, they *quote* directly from original sources. In this chapter, we focus on paraphrasing and quoting.

Setting Rhetorical Goals

When you summarize, paraphrase, and quote, even though you are working with another person's ideas, you are still guided by your own *rhetorical purpose*. Recall that *your rhetorical purpose is your reason for writing and the desired effect that you hope to have on your audience.* When you incorporate sources into your writing, you do not passively transfer them from one document to another. You make many decisions about how to tailor them to your own purpose.

Your rhetorical purpose dictates the amount of source material to include in your paper and the form the material will take. Your purpose provides you with answers to a number of questions:

- Will you summarize the author's thesis and entire supporting argument or simply summarize the main points?
- Will you paraphrase the author's thesis or other important points?
- Will you quote selectively from the text you are borrowing?

Students sometimes think that when they summarize, paraphrase, and quote a text, they must convey it exactly as it is written. Accuracy is important whenever you draw on a source. You cannot distort the message to make it appear that the text states something its author did not intend. However, the way you use the source depends on your own intentions. Two writers can draw on the same text in very different ways.

Consider two assignments. For the first assignment, your psychology professor asks you to write a three-page paper summarizing major theories for the causes of schizophrenia. You scan relevant sections of your assigned readings and class notes and write brief summaries of each theory. Given the page requirement, you make each summary concise, providing only enough information for the reader to understand the broad outlines of the theory. For the second assignment, your professor asks you to write a four-page argument defending what you believe is the most plausible explanation for schizophrenia. For this assignment, you summarize the passages describing the theory you favor and paraphrase and quote evidence that supports the theory. You also consider evidence that argues against competing theories. Your essay will contain details that you do not include in the paper that summarizes the principal theories. To illustrate, we use excerpts from student papers written in response to these two assignments. Student A summarizes a passage from R. D. Laing's book *The Politics of Experience* as part of her three-page summary of chief theories for the causes of schizophrenia. Student B writes a four-page defense of Laing's theory.

Student A

R. D. Laing (2005) maintains that schizophrenia is not a disease but rather a means to escape or even resolve an impossible situation. According to this view, people become schizophrenic when they are caught in a double bind, usually in a family setting, so that any course of action (or inaction) they take leads to psychic stress. They extract themselves from these unlivable situations by "going crazy." Laing supports his theory by analyzing the families of schizophrenics and attempting to identify the double binds that he believes produced the patients' conditions.

Student B

In the 1960s, R. D. Laing (2007) began to question the traditional assumption that schizophrenia is a physiological illness. Traditional psychiatric practices relied heavily on using drugs that reduce schizophrenic symptoms while largely ignoring the underlying causes. Laing, however, identified the actual root of the problem: the family. By analyzing the dynamics of schizophrenics' families, he demonstrated that schizophrenia results when a family creates an environment that places one family member in a double bind. In this untenable situation, all of the unfortunate victim's options for acting or thinking lead to emotionally unacceptable consequences, and schizophrenia becomes a refuge from an impossible life. Laing's theory goes to the heart of the schizophrenic's problem and thus suggests to the therapist a course of action, whereas treating the symptoms of schizophrenia with drugs leaves the basic cause intact.

Both students provide essentially the same information about Laing's theory. But Student A writes an objective summary while Student B reveals that he advocates Laing's views and rejects the medical model for schizophrenia. As this example demonstrates, the task at hand and the writer's rhetorical purpose determine how the source material is used.

Even though we urge you to let your rhetorical purpose determine how you use sources in your writing, we caution you not to distort sources deliberately. As an academic writer, you have the right to defend your opinion, but you should never use sources in a way that changes or hides their intended meaning. This is sometimes done in advertising. Ad writers twist the meaning of a source to suit their rhetorical purpose of convincing readers to purchase a product. When they cite experiments that demonstrate a product's usefulness or superiority, sometimes they refer only to the parts of the studies that portray the product in the most favorable light. Staff writers for *Consumer Reports,* a magazine published by a nonprofit organization, might summarize the same studies in their entirety and thereby reveal the limitations of the product. Or they might compare the studies with other experiments that prove that other products work as well or better. Academic writers are expected to conform to a standard of objectivity that is more like the one for *Consumer Reports* than the one for advertising. Certainly, scholars often write about controversial matters and present source material in ways that best support their personal views, but they are always expected to represent the source material accurately. Make sure that you do not twist the words of authors you use as sources or put your own words into their mouths.

Considering Your Audience

When you summarize, paraphrase, and quote portions of sources, you tailor the material for your own audience. Your readers may have needs that differ from the needs of the readers of the original text. It is important to envision your own audience as you work with the sources.

Before you incorporate sources into your writing, ask the following questions.

QUESTIONS ABOUT AUDIENCE

- Are you writing for your professor or for a broader audience?
- Is your audience in the academic community?
- Are you writing for a general audience or for specialists?
- What will your audience already know about the topic?
- Will you need to explain basic concepts or provide background for the source material to make sense?
- Will your audience be biased either for or against what the source says?
- Can you predict how your audience will react to the source?
- What is the overall impact that you want to have on your audience?
- How will your writing inform, influence, or change your audience?

Answers to these questions help you clarify your readers' needs so that you can present the source information in ways they can comprehend.

To see how considerations of audience affect summary writing, read two passages excerpted from summaries of Stephen Goode and Timothy W. Maier's article "Inflating the Grades." In the margin of your book, speculate on the audience for whom each passage is intended.

Passage 1

According to Goode and Maier (1998), the use of student evaluations as a measure of teaching success may provide a motive for grade inflation. Students often give good teaching evaluations to teachers who give them good grades on their work. The pressure to inflate grades is particularly strong, Goode and Maier point out, on part-time faculty members, who typically have short-term contracts and no job security. If their student evaluations are not strong, these part-timers may very well lose their jobs, so they may be reluctant to risk the anger of students who are displeased with their grades. Full-time faculty members in permanent, tenure-track positions may, from their position of greater security, resist the pressure for higher grades. They are more willing to take the stance of Professor Mark Edmundson of the University of Virginia: "I do feel a certain amount of pressure. Fending it off is part of the job" (as cited in Goode and Maier, 1998, p. 10).

Passage 2

On the surface, grade inflation might seem like a benefit to students who will get a higher GPA for less effort. But Goode and Maier (1998) point out that grade inflation may actually diminish the value of college students' academic achievements. According to Kiki Petrosino, a student at the University of Virginia, "I've got the good grades. But part of me would like so much to have my A stand out. I wish my A would mean more" (as cited in Goode and Maier, p. 11). Goode and Maier list a number of campuses where the percentage of A's and B's is very high, in some cases over 80%. Under these circumstances, good grades cease to mean very much. But it will be difficult to revive the value of the A unless students are "willing to accept the possibility of a C grade" (Goode and Maier, p. 11).

The first passage is excerpted from a report to college presidents on the causes of grade inflation. The second comes from an article in a campus newspaper on the consequences of grade inflation for students. You may have noticed that even though both passages summarize the same text, their emphasis, tone, form, and content are tailored for the designated audiences.

Notice that in both passages "as cited in" appears within parentheses. This phrase indicates that the Goode and Maier text contains quotations that are used in the summary passages. For example, the second passage quotes Kiki Petrosino, a University of Virginia student whom Goode and Maier apparently interviewed and quoted in their article. The student who wrote Passage 2 must make sure her readers know that the Petrosino quotation appears in Goode and Maier's text. It is not a quotation the writer came up with on her own. She informs her readers of the origin of the quotation by putting "as cited in Goode and Maier" and the page number in parentheses.

Sometimes readers have difficulty understanding ideas attributed to sources. If you anticipate this happening, use additional texts or your own knowledge to provide background, definitions, or context that will help your readers understand what the source is saying. For example, assume that you are writing a paper on racial profiling, the police practice of targeting nonwhites as potential criminals, which has been the subject of recent public discussion. Your primary source is a lengthy article on racial profiling. A section of the article compares racial profiling perpetrated by police officers to the actions of Bernhard Goetz, New York City's notorious "subway vigilante," but the article does not explain the Goetz incident. If you don't know the details of the Goetz incident yourself, you have to look for another source that provides this background information. Then you must explain to your readers that Goetz was a white civilian who in 1984 shot four African American teenagers who he thought intended to mug him in a New York City subway car.

If you're sure that your readers will not need background information, you can reduce summarizing or paraphrasing to the simple process of transforming material meant for one audience to material comprehensible to other readers. Later in this chapter, we describe this process in more detail. The important thing to remember is to identify the specified audience whenever you receive a writing assignment. If the audience is not stipulated, ask the professor for guidance or define an appropriate audience on your own. Avoid writing only to yourself. Egocentric writing does not communicate effectively to anyone else. Egocentric summary writing can serve as a prompt to help you recall the source, but it is of little help to someone who has not read the original text. When you draw on textual sources, always have your audience clearly in mind.

Identifying Your Sources

As we mentioned in the opening paragraph of this chapter, all types of writers draw from sources when they compose texts. The difference between academic writers, news writers, and writers for popular magazines is that academic writers *always* attribute the source material to its author and provide their readers with information about the original publication. Writers for newspapers, magazines, and other popular materials rarely use footnotes, parenthetical citations, or reference lists. No matter what type of source academic writers use— newspaper, popular magazine, scholarly journal, book, reference material, sound recording, image, interview, Web site, blog, e-mail, or other online material— their standard operating procedure is to identify each piece of information that is borrowed from sources. You should strictly observe the convention of citing and documenting sources in all your college courses. Failure to adhere to it, even in short pieces of writing, is unacceptable and considered to be plagiarism.

Often students have trouble adjusting to the academic convention of acknowledging sources because they are accustomed to nonprint media and popular forms of writing in which sources are not cited and documented. Television ads claim, "Tests show that . . ." without specifying where and by whom these tests were conducted. Newspapers quote sources without revealing their identity. *Time* and *Newsweek* often quote authorities without citing pages and providing documentation. The general public overlooks the importance of identifying sources, but academic readers are demanding. They want to know which ideas are original, which ideas are from elsewhere, and where each borrowed idea originated.

To illustrate how academic writing differs from popular writing in its handling of sources, we excerpted two passages, one from Michael Budds's "From Fine Romance to Good Rockin'—and Beyond: Look What They've Done to My Song," a chapter from a scholarly book, and the other from Philip O'Donnell's "Ours and Theirs: Redefining Japanese Pop Music," an article from *World and I,* a popular magazine.

Budds

Serious loss of income and loss of control forced industry executives to adopt a defensive posture. Leaders of the recording industry went so far as to condemn the music of their competitors as socially irresponsible and morally corrupting. The editors of *Billboard* and *Variety,* trade magazines of the profession, called for self-policing and raised the specter of government censorship as the ultimate solution to the dilemma.[6]

[6]See the editorials "Control the Dim-Wits," *Billboard* LXVI (25 Sept. 1954); and Abel [Green], "A Warning to the Music Business," *Variety* CXCVII:12 (23 Feb. 1955), 2.

O'Donnell

According to the Recording Industry Association of Japan (RIAJ), foreign artists in 1992 had a market share of less than 24 percent. That figure has remained relatively constant for over a decade, and domestic music has been consistently outselling imports for thirty years.

Budds acknowledges his sources, "the editors of *Billboard* and *Variety.*" The [6] at the end of Budds's final sentence is called a superscript. It refers the reader to endnote 6, where Budds cites the specific sources, editorials from *Billboard* and *Variety.* If readers wish, they can locate and consult the two sources. O'Donnell offers statistics from the Recording Industry Association of Japan, but he does not provide complete bibliographic information for this source. We are not criticizing O'Donnell or the magazine that printed his article. We're simply pointing out that standards for identifying, citing, and documenting sources are less strict in the popular press than in academic publications. As a student writer, you must adhere to academic standards for citing sources, not to the less rigorous standards in the magazines and newspapers that you read regularly.

The precise way in which source material is cited varies depending on the academic discipline, but there are general guidelines that cover most subject areas.

CONVENTIONS FOR CITING SOURCES IN ACADEMIC WRITING

- Cite each source you use and each piece or block of information you draw from the source.
- Identify where each fact or idea came from.
- Make documentation clear enough that readers can differentiate your ideas or assertions from those you have borrowed from the sources.
- Provide complete citations to sources in References page at the end of the piece.

These citations enable readers to locate the exact page on which the borrowed fact or idea appears in the original document. The citation should be thorough enough that readers can locate the original source in the library or online. Compare two students' summaries of David Rothenberg's "Learning in Finland: No Grades, No Criticism," an article from the *Chronicle of Higher Education.* In the first, the writer fails to attribute the source material to Rothenberg. In the second, the writer refers to Rothenberg by name and includes a date in parentheses.

Matt's Summary

In Finland, it is difficult to get admitted to the most prestigious universities, but once students are in, the competition stops. College students' work is never graded, and students can't fail a course, even if they do not submit the "required" work. When students submit work that falls short of expectations, they are rarely criticized or asked to revise. Finnish professors discourage competition among students, and critique is just not part of the Finnish educational culture. Students ultimately graduate by completing a final exam or project and may take as many years as they like to reach this goal.

Rob's Summary

According to David Rothenberg (1998), who spent a semester as a visiting professor in Finland, it is difficult to get admitted to the most prestigious Finnish universities, but once students are in, the competition stops. College students' work is never graded, and students can't fail a course, even if they do not submit the "required" work. Rothenberg notes that when students submit work that falls short of expectations, they are typically not criticized or asked to revise. Finnish professors discourage competition among students, and "critique is just not part of the Finnish educational culture" (Rothenberg, 1998, p. 101). Students ultimately graduate by completing a final exam or project, and Rothenberg explains that they may take as many years as they like to reach this goal.

Matt gives us no indication of the source of the ideas. Because Matt is appropriating Rothenberg's ideas and words as his own, he is guilty of plagiarism even if he lists Rothenberg's article on his reference page at the end of his essay. Rob does a good job of crediting his source. He begins by citing Rothenberg, and he cites him throughout the summary. Once the author's name, the year of publication, quotation marks, and the page number are added, we know immediately that Rob is summarizing and quoting from Rothenberg. Notice also how Rob attributes the material to Rothenberg, using tag words like "According to David Rothenberg," "Rothenberg notes," and "Rothenberg explains." In academic essays, citations may become quite numerous. If a writer alternates, sentence by sentence, among various sources, every sentence may need a reference. Consider the following excerpt from Josh White's essay on gun control and the Second Amendment. Josh draws on four sources.

As Doherty (2008) points out, a key issue in the debate over the constitutional right to bear arms is whether the Second Amendment protects an individual right to self-protection or rather establishes only a collective right to maintain state militias. A 2008 Harris poll indicated that two of every three American adults believe that under the Constitution, gun ownership is an individual right ("Does the Second Amendment," 2008). Opponents of gun control, notably the National Rifle Association, point out the other nine amendments in the Bill of Rights are clearly interpreted as protecting individual rather than collective rights, so the Second Amendment should be interpreted in the same way (Greenhouse, 2008). The justification for gun ownership is often self defense. One gay rights group has asserted in a brief to the U.S. Supreme Court that for gay Americans who are subject to bias-related attacks, "recognition of an individual right to keep and bear arms is literally a matter of life or death" (as cited in Rauch, 2008, p. 15). In general, the logic for seeing the Second Amendment as an individual right is its connection to the concept of self defense.

In three consecutive sentences, Josh paraphrases Doherty, summarizes an article identified by its title, and paraphrases Greenhouse. Later in the paragraph, Josh excerpts a quotation from an article by Rauch. Authors' and articles' names by themselves do not give readers all the information they need to locate and consult sources. At the end of the paper, a references page, organized alphabetically by authors' last names, provides the complete identification.

6

References

Does the second amendment provide the right to bear arms? U.S. adults think

so. (2008, June). *Business Wire*. Retrieved from http://www.lexisnexis

.com/hottopics/Inacademic/?

Doherty, B. (2008, March). Guns for D.C. *Reason*. Retrieved from

http://www.proquest.com/en-US/products/default.shtml

Greenhouse, L. (2008, January). Do you have a right to "bear arms"? *New York

Times Upfront*. Retrieved from http://www.proquest.com/

en-US/products/default.shtml

Rauch, J. (2008, March). The right kind of gun rights. *National Journal,* 15–16.

Retrieved from http://www.proquest.com/en-US/products/

default.shtml

Avoiding Plagiarism

Failure to identify the source is a form of *plagiarism.* Over the past decade, accusations of plagiarism for not citing sources damaged the careers of several prominent scholars and politicians. One of the most publicized cases was that of the Pulitzer Prize–winning Harvard historian Doris Kearns Goodwin. In 1987, Goodwin published a 900-page biography, *The Fitzgeralds and the Kennedys.* Although Goodwin included 3,500 footnotes in the book, she admitted that she failed to acknowledge a number of passages that she took from sources. Because of this oversight, Goodwin's reputation suffered. Students who plagiarize are assigned penalties ranging from a reduced grade for the assignment to automatic suspension or expulsion. Be sure to consult your writing instructor, college writing center, student handbook, or college catalog for details about how plagiarism cases are handled on your campus.

To avoid plagiarism, you must do more than cite and document your sources. You must set off direct quotations with quotation marks and entirely reword and document material you paraphrase or summarize. Be sure the vocabulary and the sentence structure are significantly different from the original. It is not enough to change the words but keep the same sentence structure and order of ideas. The following examples show adequate and inadequate paraphrases.

Original

The current constitutional debate over heavy metal rock and gangsta rap music is not just about the explicit language but also advocacy, an act of incitement to violence.

Inadequate Paraphrase

Today's constitutional debate about gangsta rap and heavy metal rock is not just about obscene language but also advocacy and incitement of acts of violence.

Adequate Paraphrase

Rap and heavy metal lyrics that contain obscenities and appear to promote violence have generated a constitutional debate over popular music.

The inadequate paraphrase reshuffles the words from the original but retains the vocabulary, sentence structure, and order of ideas. There is no acceptable middle ground between an adequate paraphrase and a direct quotation. You must either reword or quote word for word. An inadequate paraphrase is considered a form of plagiarism, since it is interpreted as an attempt to pass off another writer's sentence structure and word choice as your own.

While it is hard to define precisely how much rewording is necessary to avoid plagiarism, the following guidelines can help.

GUIDELINES FOR REWORDING SOURCE MATERIAL

- As a rule of thumb, do not repeat more than three consecutive words from the original without putting them in quotation marks. You may occasionally need to repeat a three word phrase, but whenever possible, substitute synonyms for the original words.
- Change, as best you can, the original order in which concepts are presented. For example, if the author you are paraphrasing presents a generalization and then backs it up with an example, try using the example as a lead-in to the generalization. For a sentence, relocate a phrase from the beginning of the sentence to a position near the end, or vice versa.

In our discussion of paraphrasing later in this chapter, we provide more specific techniques for rewording source material.

Remember that entirely rewording the material you obtain from a source does not make it yours. You must still cite the source so that the reader knows exactly where the information came from. Failing to document a paraphrase or summary is considered plagiarism.

The Paraphrasing Process

Paraphrasing is a powerful operation for academic writing, but students do not use it enough. Too often, beginning academic writers rely on direct quoting when they use sources. Quotations are necessary only when you have a clear reason for including the precise wording of the original. We discuss some of the reasons for quoting in the next section of this chapter. A drawback of quoting is that it is a passive process of mechanically copying portions of the text. Paraphrasing is an active process that forces you to grapple with the author's ideas. In this way, paraphrasing promotes comprehension. It is no wonder that many professors ask students to paraphrase rather than quote textual sources. They know that students who can paraphrase ideas are students who understand ideas.

Whereas a summary contains only the *most important* information from the source, a paraphrase includes *all* the information. Writers paraphrase to record the total meaning of a passage. Notice the difference between the paraphrase and the summary in the following example, which draws on a sentence from Steven Vogel's (1997) "Grades and Money."

Vogel's Sentence

Students expect that their grade will indicate the amount of time they have put into the course, as if they were hourly workers, and many faculty agree that it's important to consider "effort" when they "award" grades (Vogel, 1997, p. 89).

Paraphrase

Professors often reward students' efforts with higher grades, and indeed, most students assume that they should receive grades that reflect how much time they invest in schoolwork, just as if they were being paid by the hour (Vogel, 1997).

Summary

Students and many professors think grades should reflect effort to some degree (Vogel, 1997).

If you want to include only the gist or main idea of a source, summarize it. If you want to capture the meaning of the text in its entirety, paraphrase it. In general, writers paraphrase relatively small sections of text, often a sentence or two. When dealing with larger chunks of information, they summarize.

Begin the paraphrasing process by articulating your rhetorical purpose and defining your audience, as when summarizing. The act of clarifying how you intend to use the paraphrase and the effect you hope it will have on your audience will prepare you to paraphrase effectively.

Earlier in this chapter, we discussed how extensively you must alter the wording of the original when you paraphrase. Change both vocabulary and sentence structure, and don't repeat more than three consecutive words from the original.

STRATEGIES FOR PARAPHRASING

As with summarizing, you can sometimes paraphrase simply by rewriting the original passage for a new audience. Envision your readers and then change the original text to make it more suitable for them. Suppose that your objective is to paraphrase for an audience of middle-school students the following sentence from an article by visual anthropologist Joanna Cohan Scherer.

> Neither the photograph itself as an artifact, nor the viewer's interpretations of the subject of the photograph, nor an understanding of the photographer's intention alone can give holistic meaning to images.

Because you do not want to talk over the students' heads, you put the sentence into simpler language.

> As Scherer (2008) points out, if we want to fully understand the meaning of a photograph, we need to consider what actually appears in the image, but we must also take into account the photographer's goal and the various interpretations that viewers might give to the photograph.

You could simply rewrite the original, as here, keeping in mind that the audience might not understand terms like *artifact*. As the example demonstrates, paraphrasing often requires you to express abstract ideas in a more concrete form. But for many assignments, you need a more systematic approach to paraphrasing. When a passage includes difficult concepts or complex language, it may be hard to reword it and still preserve the original meaning. In these cases, try the following paraphrasing procedures.

IMPORTANT PARAPHRASING STRATEGIES

- Locate the individual statements or major idea units in the original.
- Change the order of major ideas, maintaining the logical connections among them.
- Substitute synonyms for words in the original, making sure the language in your paraphrase is appropriate for your audience.
- Combine or divide sentences as necessary.
- Compare the paraphrase to the original to ensure that the rewording is sufficient and the meaning has been preserved.

- Weave the paraphrase into your essay in accordance with your rhetorical purpose.
- Document the paraphrase.

Sometimes you may use only some of these seven strategies, and you may apply them in any order. For illustrative purposes, we paraphrase a sentence from John Leo's article, "When Life Imitates Video," using all the strategies in the order listed. Let's assume that we are writing for an audience of first-year college students. The excerpt refers to the possible role that violent video games played in motivating the Columbine High School massacre in Littleton, Colorado.

> If we want to avoid more Littleton-style massacres, we will begin taking the social effects of the killing games more seriously.

● **LOCATE INDIVIDUAL STATEMENTS OR MAJOR IDEA UNITS**   First, we determine how many major ideas are presented in the passage. We find two central units of information: (1) avoiding more school massacres and (2) taking seriously the impact of violent video games.

1. If we want to avoid more Littleton-style massacres, . . .
2. we will begin taking the social effects of the killing games more seriously.

● **CHANGE THE ORDER OF MAJOR IDEAS, MAINTAINING THE LOGICAL CONNECTIONS AMONG THEM**   Now we change the order of the two units of information, placing the second before the first. To accommodate this switch, we substitute "If we begin" for "we will" and "we may" for "If we want to" so that the recommendation to take seriously the social impact of killing games fits at the beginning of the sentence.

1. If we begin taking the social effects of the killing games more seriously, . . .
2. we may avoid more Littleton-style massacres.

● **SUBSTITUTE SYNONYMS FOR WORDS IN THE ORIGINAL**   At this stage, it is important to think about audience. Leo's original language is relatively easy to understand. If the language of the original source is too formal or sophisticated, you may want to make it more accessible to your readers. In addition, you may need to provide a context for certain types of material that you excerpt from sources.

Whenever you replace original text with synonyms, try to come up with synonyms without consulting a dictionary or thesaurus. Many students who have trouble substituting words rush to reference books and copy synonyms without considering how they fit into the general sense of the sentence. This is a mistake. Paraphrases filled with synonyms taken indiscriminately from a dictionary or thesaurus are awkward and confusing. Here is a procedure for finding synonyms on your own.

COMING UP WITH YOUR OWN SYNONYMS

1. Think of a word or phrase in your vocabulary that comes as close as possible to the meaning of the original word.

2. Read the original sentence, substituting your synonym for the original word. Reread the sentence to see if it makes sense. If the new word changes the meaning, come up with another synonym and try the substitution again.

3. Compare the dictionary definitions of the original word and your synonym. If the definitions do not correspond, come up with another synonym and try the substitution again.

When you are paraphrasing a passage that contains a word you don't understand, you have to supplement these strategies. Before you consult a dictionary or thesaurus, try to figure out the approximate meaning of the unfamiliar word based on its relationship to the other words in the sentence. We call this procedure using *contextual clues* to discover meaning. Use contextual clues to figure out a synonym for the italicized word in the following sentence.

> After meeting someone for the first time, we often retain a *gestalt* of what the person is like but cannot remember specific details such as eye color.

From the sentence, you learn that a *gestalt* is something other than a memory of specific details, so you can infer that it means an overall impression. Check a dictionary to see if the definition we derived from context is appropriate.

Contextual clues will not give you a complete definition of an unknown word, but they will help you unlock enough of the meaning to know what synonym to substitute for it. Always test a synonym that you figure out from contextual clues by substituting it for the word it replaces in the original sentence. If you are not sure the synonym fits, consult a dictionary to check your understanding of the original word. Also, check your synonym against the synonyms listed in the dictionary or thesaurus.

As we mentioned, if you copy a synonym without examining its fit in the original sentence, your paraphrase may not sound right, and it may distort the meaning of the original. As a last resort, consult the dictionary, using the following procedure.

LOCATING SYNONYMS IN A DICTIONARY

1. Read *all* the definitions for the word. (Do not read the synonyms.)

2. When the dictionary lists more than one definition, reread the original sentence to see which definition works best in the context.

3. Try to come up with your own synonym based on the definition.

4. Replace the original word with your synonym. Does the sentence still have its original meaning?

5. If the dictionary gives synonyms for the original word, compare them to your synonym. Do they mean the same thing?

If you use a thesaurus, make sure that you follow steps 4 and 5 so that you do not pick inappropriate synonyms. Remember that no two words mean exactly the same thing, and a synonym listed in a thesaurus is not necessarily an appropriate substitute for the original word in all contexts. Returning to our example, by substituting synonyms, doing a little more rearranging, and providing context where necessary, we arrive at the following paraphrase:

> If we consider seriously how violent video games affect society, we may be able to prevent future Littleton-style tragedies (Leo, 2005).

You do not have to find a substitute for every word in the sentence you are paraphrasing. You can repeat words that are essential to the meaning or have no appropriate synonyms, such as the term *Littleton-style* in our example.

● **COMBINE OR DIVIDE SENTENCES AS NECESSARY**   Since our paraphrase is well-coordinated, there is no pressing need to divide it. But for illustration, we split it into two smaller units.

> We should consider seriously how violent video games affect society. Then we may be able to prevent future Littleton-style tragedies (Leo, 2005).

● **COMPARE THE PARAPHRASE TO THE ORIGINAL**   At this juncture, before we incorporate the paraphrase into our essay, we compare it to Leo's original sentence and make any necessary revisions.

Original

> If we want to avoid more Littleton-style massacres, we will begin taking the social effects of the killing games more seriously.

Paraphrase

> If we consider seriously how violent video games affect society, we may be able to prevent future Littleton-style tragedies (Leo, 2005).

As you compare your paraphrase to the original, ask yourself the following questions.

QUESTIONS FOR REVISING PARAPHRASES

- Did you leave out important ideas in the original source?
- Did you change the meaning of the original text by adding your own interpretation or superfluous ideas?
- Did you follow the original text too closely by neglecting to rearrange main idea units?
- Did you include too many words from the original text or repeat more than three words in a row?
- Did you substitute inappropriate synonyms that change the original meaning of the text?
- Did you choose words that are inappropriate for your audience?

● **WEAVE THE PARAPHRASE INTO YOUR ESSAY**   We are now ready to weave the paraphrase into our essay in a way that helps further our rhetorical purpose. Consider the following example.

Essay Excerpt

So what is causing the current outburst of deadly violence in American public schools? One explanation is that the current school-age generation has been entranced by violent entertainment, including television, films, and video games. In the wake of the massacre at Columbine High School in Littleton, Colorado, John Leo (2005) wrote that if we considered seriously how violent video games affect society, we might be able to prevent future Littleton-style tragedies. It is hard to imagine that children who spend hours each day "killing" in cyberspace will not be affected by the experience.

We cannot be sure that a paraphrase is successful without seeing it in context. The paraphrase must accurately reword the author's message and also fit smoothly in the passage of the essay for which it was intended. To achieve this fit in our example, we had to identify the overall subject of Leo's piece. We did this by adding "In the wake of the massacre at Columbine High School in Littleton, Colorado, John Leo wrote that. . . ." This phrase also attributes the material to Leo (2005).

● **DOCUMENT THE PARAPHRASE**   Remember that failing to document a paraphrase is considered plagiarism. Always indicate the author of the source, the date of the information you paraphrased, and a complete entry on the References page.

In addition to the seven paraphrasing strategies we have discussed, you can use graphic overviews as paraphrasing tools. If you are paraphrasing complex sentences or groups of sentences, construct a graphic overview of the text and then derive your paraphrase from the overview. But keep in mind that a paraphrase includes all the points from the original rather than just the key ideas.

Direct Quoting

When you draw on sources, make an effort to summarize or paraphrase rather than quote directly. As a general rule, repeat sources word for word only when there is an obvious rhetorical advantage to quoting, for example, when rewording the original will weaken your argument or prevent you from including particularly elegant language.

Sometimes students quote for convenience because they think it's too much trouble to paraphrase the source. But it is to your advantage to negotiate a difficult text and render its meaning in your own words. When you quote excessively, you relinquish rhetorical control and give it to the source author. You can also end up with a series of strung-together quotations in an essay that seems purposeless and disjointed.

REASONS FOR DIRECT QUOTING

Given these admonitions, when is it advisable to quote? We discuss five common purposes for quoting and give an example of each.

WHEN TO USE DIRECT QUOTATIONS
- To retain the meaning and authenticity of the original source
- To lend support to an analysis or evaluation
- To capture exactly language that supports your point
- To employ a stylistic device
- To capture language that is unusual, well crafted, striking, or memorable

A typical reason for quoting is to retain the meaning or authenticity of the original source. Assume that you are writing about whether youth curfews violate teens' constitutional rights. In your essay, you decide to quote directly from relevant parts of the United States Constitution. In this case, it would not be effective to paraphrase the Constitution, since the exact wording is crucial to its interpretation. When precise wording affects your argument, you may need to quote.

Another purpose for quoting involves analysis and evaluation. When you analyze and evaluate texts, you need to identify specific passages that support your position. For now, we illustrate with an excerpt from an essay in which Helen Chang analyzes journalist Linda Grant's book, *Sexing the Millennium: Women and the Sexual Revolution*.

> Although Grant (1995) makes some good points about the significance of the sexual revolution for many women's lives, one flaw in her argument lies in her overly general and sweeping definition of "women." The women Grant refers to are for the most part white and middle-class. A case in point is her statement that prior to the 1960s, women who had jobs were "sexless, repressed—spinsters whom, by implication, no man wanted or loved" (p. 2). Perhaps this was true for the privileged classes, but many poor women did work and also had children and husbands who valued them.

If Helen had paraphrased Grant's words instead of quoting them directly, Grant's description would have lost its punch and Helen would have weakened her argument.

A third purpose for quoting is to capture exactly language that supports your point. In his essay "From Fine Romance to Good Rockin'—and Beyond: Look What They've Done to My Song," musicologist Michael Budds explains that with the advent of rock and roll, popular music lyrics became more sexually explicit. He illustrates this shift by quoting directly from a Tin Pan Alley song and then contrasting the song with early rock-and-roll lyrics. Excerpts from the lyrics Budds quotes make his point quite vividly.

Tin Pan Alley (from "All the Things You Are," lyrics by Jerome Kern)

Some day my happy arms will hold you,
And some day I'll know that moment divine
When all the things you are, are mine.

Rock and Roll (from "Sixty-Minute Man," lyrics by William Ward and Rose Marks)

If your man ain't treatin' you right, come up here and see old Dan.
I rock 'em, roll 'em all night long: I'm a sixty-minute man.

By quoting directly from the lyrics, Budds lends a sense of reality to his discussion. The exact language of the lyrics tells the reader much more about the treatment of sexuality in each song than paraphrased language would reveal.

Another reason to use a direct quotation is as a stylistic device. A common technique for opening or closing a paper is to supply a direct quotation.

Consider how Charles Krauthammer, a staff writer for *Time* magazine, ends his article, "First and Last, Do No Harm," with a quotation from the Hippocratic Oath that for centuries has been the pledge doctors take when they enter the medical profession:

"I will give no deadly medicine to anyone if asked."
—The Hippocratic Oath

A final reason for quoting is to capture language that you find especially effective or memorable. Notice how our student Karla Allen employs Charles Dickens's memorable lines.

In Charles Dickens's (1859) words, "It was the best of times, it was the worst of times" (p. 3). While big corporations were reaping larger profits than ever before, many smaller companies and individuals found themselves out of work.

ALTERING QUOTATIONS

There will be times when you wish to alter a direct quotation by omitting or inserting words. These changes are permissible as long as you follow conventions that alert your audience to what you are doing. In the following example, we give a sentence from Michael Moffatt's "College Life: Undergraduate Culture and Higher Education," an article published in the *Journal of Higher Education,* and an excerpt from a student paper that quotes part of the sentence. The student uses *points of ellipsis,* a set of three spaced periods, to show where words have been omitted.

Original

As it is elsewhere in American middle-class culture, friendliness is the central code of etiquette in student culture, the expected code of conduct in student collectivities such as dorm-floor groups and fraternities, the one taken-for-granted politesse whose systematic breach almost always generates anger and even outrage in students. (Moffatt, 1999, pp. 52–53)

Student Essay

While students may tolerate outrageous and idiosyncratic behavior in the residence halls, they will not put up with unfriendliness. According to Moffatt (1999), "As it is elsewhere in American middle-class culture, friendliness is the central code of etiquette in student culture...whose systematic breach almost always generates anger and even outrage in students" (pp. 52–53).

In cases where you need to show omission at the end of quoted material, use a period followed by the three spaced points of ellipsis.

Sometimes, you will find it necessary to insert your own words into a quotation. When you *interpolate* in this way, signal this to your audience by placing your words between brackets. Notice how our student Spencer Levy uses this convention when he quotes the final sentence from Toni Cade Bambara's short story, "The Lesson."

Original

But ain't nobody gonna beat me at nuthin.

Student Essay

At the end of the story, when we hear Sylvia boasting that "nobody [is] gonna beat me at nuthin," we know that she does not need our sympathy; she simply deserves our praise.

By inserting the verb *is,* Spencer works the quotation into the structure of his sentence. Brackets also enable you to explain or identify quoted material. In the following example, a student uses brackets to provide context for a quotation from Jerry Farber's essay "A Young Person's Guide to the Grading System."

Farber (1969) points out that "many of us understand all this [that grades are just a game we play to please teachers] and yet remain convinced that we need to be graded in order to learn" (p. 385).

The student inserts "that grades are just a game we play to please teachers" in order to explain "all this." Remember that the only time it is permissible to change a quotation or interject your own words is when you use ellipsis points or brackets.

DOCUMENTING QUOTATIONS

Enclose short quotations (less than 40 words) in double quotation marks. Set longer quotations (40 words or more) apart from your text by indenting them one half inch, as has been done for the following quotation from Rand Cooper's article "The Dignity of Helplessness: What Sort of Society Would Euthanasia Create?," which appeared in *Commonweal* magazine.

THE DIGNITY OF HELPLESSNESS   4

At the end of his article, Cooper (2003) reminds us that physician-assisted suicide may affect not only the individuals who choose this option but the rest of society as well:

> A sense of this deep privacy drives the right-to-die movement in America today. And yet to step outside the rights framework is to ask how institutionalizing assisted suicide will affect not only those who die, but those who live on; not only individuals, but society. The fact is, our deaths are both solo journeys toward an ultimate mystery and strands in the tapestries of each other's lives. Which side of this reality will we emphasize? Whose death is it, anyway? The debate about assisted suicide should begin at the place where that question ceases to be a rhetorical one. (p. 14)

Cooper is right that most deaths have a strong impact on those who are left behind. In this sense, we have a responsibility to consider others when we make choices about our own deaths. While we tend to think of death as a private matter, it most certainly does have a public dimension.

Notice that for a long quotation, the parenthetical citation goes outside the final punctuation. For short quotations, place the parenthetical citation between the final quotation marks and the closing punctuation:

> Farber (1969) points out that "many of us understand all this [that grades are just a game we play to please teachers] and yet remain convinced that we need to be graded in order to learn" (p. 385).

In our example, the phrase "Farber points out" leads in to the quotation and acknowledges the author. Many other verbs can be used to introduce quotations:

acknowledges	analyzes	assesses
addresses	answers	believes
adds	argues	categorizes
admits	ascertains	cites
agrees (disagrees)	asks	compares (contrasts)

concludes	furnishes	remarks
concurs	identifies	replies
considers	inquires	reports
critiques	investigates	reviews
defines	lists	says
delineates	makes the case	shows
demonstrates	measures	states
describes	notes	stipulates
determines	observes	stresses
discovers	points out	suggests
emphasizes	postulates	summarizes
envisions	presents	surveys
evaluates	proposes	synthesizes
examines	proves	traces
explores	questions	views
expounds on	rationalizes	warns
finds	refers to	writes

These verbs can be used as lead-ins to summaries and paraphrases as well as quotations.

As we mentioned, when you use a direct quotation that appears in a source, you must acknowledge both the person who originally said or wrote the words and the author of the source in which you found the quotation. For example, assume that you want to use a quotation that appears in John Leo's *U.S. News & World Report* article, "When Life Imitates Video." Leo quotes David Grossman, a retired army officer and psychologist, who claims that violent video games increase incidents of violence:

Sentence from Leo's Article

"We have to start worrying about what we are putting into the minds of our young," says Grossman.

Documentation in Student Essay

According to David Grossman, a retired army officer and psychologist, "We have to start worrying about what we are putting into the minds of our young" (as cited in Leo, 1999, p. 14).

The student must link both Grossman's and Leo's names to the quotation in order for the documentation to be complete.

If the sentence contains quotation marks, substitute single quotation marks for the double quotation marks that appear in the original. Then enclose the entire block you are quoting within double quotation marks, as shown below:

Sentence from Leo's Article

One ad for a Sony game says: "Get in touch with your gun-toting, testosterone-pumping, cold-blooded murdering side."

Documentation in Student Essay

According to Leo (2001), "One ad for a Sony game says: 'Get in touch with your gun-toting, testosterone-pumping, cold-blooded murdering side'" (p. 14).

If you paraphrase the speaker tag and quote only the embedded quotation, all you need is the set of double quotation marks:

Documentation in Student Essay

According to Leo (2001), a Sony computer game advertisement urges kids to "get in touch with your gun-toting, testosterone-pumping, cold-blooded murdering side" (p. 14).

WEAVING QUOTATIONS INTO YOUR ESSAY

There are a number of ways to weave a quotation into your writing. You can acknowledge the author right in your text, or you can place the name in parentheses. When you acknowledge the author in the text, you can cite the name before the quotation, within the quotation, or after it. For example, let's say you are quoting the following sentence from Vogel's article:

We let grades count as money—we let education count as money—because money, nowadays, is the only value we know.

Here are five options for incorporating quotations into your essay. Option A allows you to insert the quotation without acknowledging the author in the body of the text. Instead, you place the name in parentheses.

A. "We let grades count as money—we let education count as money—because money, nowadays, is the only value we know" (Vogel, 1997, p. 392).

When you use option A, remember to connect your own ideas to the quotation. Don't just plop the quotation into your essay. Lead in to it by providing transitions or connecting ideas. Inexperienced writers sprinkle their papers with direct quotations that appear to have little connection with the rest of the text. If you have difficulty coming up with connecting ideas, use option B, C, D, or E. In these options, you acknowledge the author within the text.

B. Vogel (1996) argues, "We let grades count as money—we let education count as money—because money, nowadays, is the only value we know" (p. 392).

C. "We let grades count as money—we let education count as money—because," Vogel argues, "money, nowadays, is the only value we know" (1996, p. 392).

D. "We let grades count as money—we let education count as money—because money, nowadays, is the only value we know," Vogel claims (1996, p. 392).

A final option is to introduce a quotation with a complete sentence followed by a colon.

E. Vogel (1996) reminds us that the problem with grades in higher education reflects the values of the larger society: "We let grades count as money—we let education count as money—because money, nowadays, is the only value we know" (p. 392).

You will find the following rules about capitalization and punctuation useful when you quote

CAPITALIZATION

1. If the quotation is a complete sentence, begin it with a capital letter.

   > According to Leo (2001), "Video games are much more powerful versions of the military's primitive discovery about overcoming the reluctance to shoot" (p. 14).

2. If the quotation is not a complete sentence, begin it with a lowercase letter.

   > Video games that include cops as targets are, according to Leo (2001), "exploiting resentments toward law enforcement and making real-life shooting of cops more likely" (p. 14).

3. If the quotation is preceded by the word *that* and the quoted words become part of the structure of your own sentence, omit the comma and begin the quotation with a lowercase letter.

   > Leo (2001) points out that "adolescent feelings of resentment, powerlessness, and revenge pour into the killing games" (p. 14).

4. If you break up a quotation and insert a speaker tag, do not capitalize the opening word of the latter part of the quotation unless it begins a complete sentence or is a proper noun.

   > "Did the sensibilities created by the modern video kill games," asks Leo (2001), "play a role in the Littleton massacre?" (p. 14).

PUNCTUATION

1. Set off the quoted material with double quotation marks: "..."
2. Set off quoted material within a quotation with single quotation marks.

> Leo (2001) notes that "psychologist David Grossman of Arkansas State
> University, a retired Army officer, thinks 'point and shoot' video games
> have the same effect as military strategies used to break down a soldier's
> aversion to killing" (p. 14).

3. Separate the verb of acknowledgment from a short quotation with a
comma and from a long quotation with a colon.

> Leo (2001) asks, "Can it be that all this constant training in make-believe
> killing has no social effects?" (p. 14).

> Many parents assert that their children are aware of the difference
> between video games and real life; however, these games may have
> more impact on children's values than most parents realize. Leo (2001)
> points out:
>> We are now a society in which the chief form of play for millions of
>> youngsters is making large numbers of people die. Hurting and
>> maiming others is the central fun activity in video games played so
>> addictively by the young. A widely cited survey of 900 fourth-
>> through-eighth-grade students found that almost half of the
>> children said their favorite electronic games involve violence. Can
>> it be that all this constant training in make-believe killing has no
>> social effects? (p. 14)

4. Close a quotation by placing the period or comma after the parenthetical
documentation of the page number.

> According to Leo (2001), many Americans believe that video games are
> just a "harmless activity among children who know the difference between
> fantasy and reality" (p. 14).

5. When you acknowledge a source, set off the title with italics or quotation
marks. Italics tells your audience that you are quoting from a long source:
a book, full-length play, journal, magazine, or long poem. Quotation
marks signal a shorter work: a chapter or section in a book, an article in a
journal or magazine, a poem, or a short story.

> In his novel, *The Stranger,* Albert Camus (1997) describes. . . .

> James Joyce's (2003) short story, "The Dead," concerns. . . .

> In Chapter 2, "Sources," Kennedy and Smith (1998) discuss. . . .

> *Romeo and Juliet,* a play by Shakespeare (1597) turned into a film by
> Zeffirelli (1968), shows how. . . .

Incorporating Quotations and Paraphrases into Essays

Usually, when you quote or paraphrase, your rhetorical purpose is to do much more than reproduce the content of a text. Most likely, you intend to incorporate the material in your essay. For example, you might include paraphrase or quotations from Vogel's "Grades and Money" in an essay in which you react to, analyze, or evaluate Vogel's article. For the reaction essay, you might take the stance of a college student, professor, or administrator. The source material has to fit your point of view and purpose.

Integrating quotations and paraphrases into your essay becomes more complex when you use more than one source. When you draw from a variety of sources that address the same topic, it is challenging to keep the information from each source distinct when you incorporate it in your paper. The bedrock principle of documentation is to make sure your reader is able to identify the source of every piece of information that you include in your paper. Students sometimes attempt to avoid confusion in documentation by presenting sources one at a time, each in its own paragraph. While this approach helps to avoid ambiguity, it works against synthesis, the practice of combining various ideas to derive a fresh viewpoint. This practice is valued highly in academia because it is an important component in independent and creative thinking. By isolating each source in its own paragraph, you make synthesis awkward at best. It is essential to develop the skill to work with several sources simultaneously while still providing accurate documentation for all the borrowed ideas.

In order to synthesize source material within a single paragraph while still documenting responsibly, it may help to think of the paragraph as a quilt in which information and ideas from various sources are combined into an interesting pattern. While you are concerned with the overall design, you still want the individual pieces to stand out. Read the following excerpt from an essay on random drug testing in public schools to see how our student, Kate Kobre, combines various sources but still highlights the boundaries between them.

Summary of two sources

> Juvenile courts were first established in America in the late nineteenth century based on the beliefs that children were less responsible than adults for their actions and were more open to rehabilitation (Drizin, 2004; Talbot, 2007). In recent years, however, these beliefs have been called into question. Over the past decade, thousands of American teenagers have been tried and sentenced as adults, including sentences of death and life in prison without parole, for crimes they committed before they turned eighteen. Across the

Kate's generalization

nation, examples abound of youngsters being tried as adults. In Michigan, a fourteen-year-old boy who was mentally retarded was charged for hitting another youth and stealing two dollars from him (Young, 2008). In Kentucky, a fourteen-year-old involved in a robbery received a ten-year prison sentence that he may have to serve in adult prison (Stansky, 2004). In Arizona, a fourteen-year-old boy who used an unloaded antique shotgun to scare off his property three boys who had come to beat him up was placed in an adult prison, where he may stay for as long as thirty years (Talbot, 2007). The number of cases where children are sentenced as adults will most likely grow as more states pass and enforce laws designed to get tough on young criminals. Three states allow prosecutors to request that children ten or older be tried as adults and ten states have no lower age limits at all ("Should Children," 2004).

Sentencing children to adult prisons is a misguided practice because it keeps them from receiving the opportunities for rehabilitation that juvenile detention centers typically provide. Talbot (2007) reports on a case in Florida where a thirteen-year-old girl named Jessica was involved in a robbery and then sentenced to an adult prison where she will remain until she is at least twenty-two. In the adult facility, Jessica will have no opportunity to receive therapy and is not required to continue her schooling. Her guidance comes primarily from her surrogate prison mother, a twenty-nine-year-old who is serving a life sentence for cutting the throats of two elderly people during a robbery. Her prison meals lack the dietary elements, such as milk, that are essential for a teenager's development. Jessica's case illustrates that our society has become increasingly willing to write off young criminals rather than trying to improve their lives. I share the belief of Janet Reno (2002), former United States Attorney General, that "we can save each child if we only put enough effort into it, enough know-how, enough continuity in the child's life" (p. 207). Our focus should be on providing more effective rehabilitation rather than maximizing the level of punishment.

Documentation marks source boundaries

Beginning of information from Talbot

References to a person featured in Talbot's article

End of information from Talbot

Kate's opinion

Evidence from sources to support Kate's generalization

Kate's opinion

Example that supports Kate's opinion

Kate's opinion

Quotation that supports Kate's opinion

In the first paragraph, Kate links sources in a relatively straightforward manner. The first sentence contains background information on the development of juvenile courts. The parenthetical citation at the end of the sentence contains two sources separated by a semicolon. This indicates that the background information Kate is summarizing is contained in both of the sources. In the second sentence, Kate generalizes about trends in youth sentencing. In subsequent sentences, she provides evidence that supports this generalization. She follows each piece of evidence with parenthetical documentation, including the author's name or an abbreviated article title, which indicates the source of the evidence. These parenthetical citations serve as boundaries that show clearly what information came from which source.

The second paragraph begins with a sentence containing Kate's opinion about youth sentencing. In the next four sentences, she describes a supporting example that is taken from an article written by Talbot. It is not necessary to include documentation within every sentence that pertains to the example. The phrase "Talbot (2007) reports" signals the beginning of the material taken from Talbot, and the sentence goes on to identify "Jessica," the young woman who, Talbot explains, was sentenced to adult prison. The next sentence, which combines information from various sentences in Talbot's article, is not cited to a source, but the sentence's content, particularly the name "Jessica," links it quite obviously to Talbot. The word "Her" that begins the next two sentences refers to Jessica, and the subject matter of both sentences clearly comes from Talbot's article. Beginning the next sentence with "I" and including a new source "Janet Reno (2002)," establishes a boundary between the sentences describing Jessica and the new sentence in which Kate states her opinion.

We noted that in the second paragraph, Kate cites Talbot at the beginning of the block of information she takes from Talbot's article. Cite the source as soon as you begin to draw on it. A common mistake that students make is paraphrasing or summarizing a source over several sentences and failing to cite it until the end of the last sentence. This is what the student does in the following paragraph.

As states toughen punishments for juvenile offenders, an increasing number of children end up in prisons designed for adults. These children in the general prison population are targets for physical and sexual abuse and, as a result, are more likely to commit suicide than adult prisoners. Children receive fewer educational opportunities in adult prisons than they do in juvenile facilities and have less access to counseling and rehabilitation programs. Their role models are the adult prisoners. A case in point is Jessica, who committed a robbery at thirteen for which she will remain in adult prison until she is twenty-two. Jessica receives no schooling and has been "adopted" by a twenty-nine-year-old woman who committed multiple murders (Talbot, 2007).

The documentation at the end of the paragraph links the case in point to Talbot's article, but the reader has no way of knowing whether or not Talbot is the source for the rest of the information in the paragraph. The paragraph refers to specific facts, such as the incidence of suicides in prison, that the writer must have derived from a source. But the reader doesn't know whether the source is Talbot or some other author the student fails to document. Make sure that all documentation is unambiguous.

READINGS

Is There a There in Cyberspace?

John Perry Barlow

John Perry Barlow, a lyricist for the Grateful Dead, operated his family's cattle ranch in Wyoming from 1971 to 1988. He is one of the founders of the Electronic Frontier Foundation, an advocacy group for preserving free speech in digital media. Barlow has been called the Thomas Jefferson of the online community for his famous essay, "A Declaration of the Independence of Cyberspace." An essayist and lecturer, Barlow is a Fellow at Harvard Law School's Berkman Center for Internet and Society.

"Is There a There in Cyberspace?" was originally published in a special issue of Utne Reader *entitled "Cyberhood vs. Neighborhood" in spring 1995.*

Prereading

Write nonstop for fifteen minutes about what you already know about the differences between online communities and real life communities.

> *"There is no there there."*
> Gertrude Stein (speaking of Oakland)

> *"It ain't no Amish barn-raising in therep"*
> Bruce Sterling (speaking of cyberspace)

1 I am often asked how I went from pushing cows around a remote Wyoming ranch to my present occupation (which *Wall Street Journal* recently described as "cyberspace cadet"). I haven't got a short answer, but I suppose I came to the virtual world looking for community.

2 Unlike most modern Americans, I grew up in an actual place, an entire nonintentional community called Pinedale, Wyoming. As I struggled for nearly a generation to keep my ranch in the family, I was motivated by the belief that such places were the spiritual home of humanity. But I knew their future was not promising.

3 At the dawn of the 20th century, over 40 percent of the American workforce lived off the land. The majority of us lived in towns like Pinedale. Now fewer than 1 percent of us extract a living from the soil. We just became too productive for our own good.

4 Of course, the population followed the jobs. Farming and ranching communities are now home to a demographically insignificant percentage

...continued Is There a There in Cyberspace?, **John Perry Barlow**

of Americans, the vast majority of whom live not in ranch houses but in more or less identical split level "ranch homes" in more or less identical suburban "communities." Generica.

5   In my view, these are neither communities nor homes. I believe the combination of television and suburban population patterns is simply toxic to the soul. I see much evidence in contemporary America to support this view.

6   Meanwhile, back at the ranch, doom impended. And, as I watched the community in Pinedale growing ill from the same economic forces that were killing my family's ranch, the Bar Cross, satellite dishes brought the cultural infection of television. I started looking around for evidence that community in America would not perish altogether.

7   I took some heart in the mysterious nomadic City of the Deadheads, the virtually physical town that follows the Grateful Dead around the country. The Deadheads lacked place, touching down briefly wherever the band happened to be playing, and they lacked continuity in time, since they had to suffer a new diaspora every time the band moved on or went home. But they had many of the other necessary elements of community, including a culture, a religion of sorts (which, though it lacked dogma, had most of the other, more nurturing aspects of spiritual practice), a sense of necessity, and most importantly, shared adversity.

8   I wanted to know more about the flavor of their interaction, what they thought and felt, but since I wrote Dead songs (including "Estimated Prophet" and "Cassidy"), I was a minor icon to the Deadheads, and was thus inhibited, in some socially Heisenbergian way, from getting a clear view of what really went on among them.

9   Then, in 1987, I heard about a "place" where Deadheads gathered where I could move among them without distorting too much the field of observation. Better, this was a place I could visit without leaving Wyoming. It was a shared computer in Sausalito, California, called the Whole Earth 'Lectronic Link, or WELL. After a lot of struggling with modems, serial cables, init strings, and other Computer arcana that seemed utterly out of phase with such notions as Deadheads and small towns, I found myself looking at the glowing yellow word "Login:" beyond which lay my future.

10   "Inside" the WELL were Deadheads in community. There were thousands of them there, gossiping, complaining (mostly about the Grateful Dead), comforting and harassing each other, bartering, engaging in religion (or at least exchanging their totemic set lists), beginning and ending love affairs, praying for one another's sick kids. There was, it seemed, everything one might find going on in a small town, save dragging Main Street and making out on the back roads.

11   I was delighted. I felt I had found the new locale of human community—never mind that the whole thing was being conducted in mere words by minds from whom the bodies had been amputated. Never mind that all these people were deaf, dumb, and blind as paramecia or that their town had neither seasons nor sunsets nor smells.

12   Surely all these deficiencies would be remedied by richer, faster communications media. The featureless log-in handles would gradually acquire video faces (and thus expressions), shaded 3-D body puppets (and thus body language). This "space" which I recognized at once to be a primitive form of the cyberspace William Gibson predicted in his sci-fi novel *Neuromancer,* was still without apparent dimensions of vistas. But virtual reality would change all that in time.

13   Meanwhile, the commons, or something like it, had been rediscovered. Once again, people from the 'burbs had a place where they could encounter their friends as my fellow Pinedalians did at the post office and the Wrangler Café. They had a place where their hearts could remain as the companies they worked for shuffled their bodies around America. They could put down roots that could not be ripped out by forces of economic history. They had a collective stake. They had a community.

14   It is seven years now since I discovered the WELL. In that time, I co-founded an organization, the Electronic Frontier Foundation, dedicated to protecting its interests and those of other virtual communities like it from raids by physical governments. I've spent countless hours typing away at its residents, and I've watched the larger context that contains it, the Internet, grow at such an explosive rate that, by 2004, every human on the planet will have an e-mail address unless the growth curve flattens (which it will).

15   My enthusiasm for virtuality has cooled. In fact, unless one counts interaction with the rather too large society of those with whom I exchange electronic mail, I don't spend much time engaging in virtual community, at all. Many of the near-term benefits I anticipated from it seem to remain as far in the future as they did when I first logged in. Perhaps they always will.

16   Pinedale works, more or less, as it is, but a lot is still missing from the communities of cyberspace, whether they be places like the WELL, the fractious newsgroups of USENET, the silent "auditoriums" of America Online, or even enclaves on the promising World Wide Web.

17   What is missing? Well, to quote Ranjit Makkuni of Xerox Corporation's Palo Alto Research Center, "the *prana* is missing," *prana* being the Hindu term for both breath and spirit. I think he is right about this and that perhaps the central question of the virtual age is whether or not *prana* can somehow be made to fit through any disembodied medium.

18   *Prana* is, to my mind, the literally vital element in the holy and unseen ecology of relationship, the dense mesh of invisible life, on whose surface carbon-based life floats like a thin film. It is at the heart of the

fundamental and profound difference between information and experience. Jaron Lanier has said that "information is alienated experience," and, that being true, *prana* is part of what is removed when you create such easily transmissible replicas of experience as, say, the evening news.

19   Obviously a great many other, less spiritual, things are also missing entirely, like body language, sex, death, tone of voice, clothing, beauty (or homeliness), weather, violence, vegetation, wildlife, pets, architecture, music, smells, sunlight, and that ol' harvest moon. In short, most of the things that make my life real to me.

20   Present, but in far less abundance than in the physical world, which I call "meat space," are women, children, old people, poor people, and the genuinely blind. Also mostly missing are the illiterate and the continent of Africa. There is not much human diversity in cyberspace, which is populated, as near as I can tell, by white males under 50 with plenty of computer terminal time, great typing skills, high math SATs, strongly held opinions on just about everything, and an excruciating face-to-face shyness, especially with the opposite sex.

21   But diversity is as essential to healthy community as it is to healthy ecosystems (which are, in my view, different from communities only in unimportant aspects). I believe that the principal reason for the almost universal failure of the intentional communities of the '60s and '70s was a lack of diversity in their members. It was a rare commune with any old people in it, or people who were fundamentally out of philosophical agreement with the majority.

22   Indeed, it is the usual problem when we try to build something that can only be grown. Natural systems, such as human communities, are simply too complex to design by the engineering principles we insist on applying to them. Like Dr. Frankenstein, western civilization is now finding its rational skills inadequate to the task of creating and caring for life. We would do better to return to a kind of agricultural mind-set in which we humbly try to re-create the conditions from which life has sprung before. And leave the rest to God.

23   Given that it has been built so far almost entirely by people with engineering degrees, it is not so surprising that cyberspace has the kind of overdesigned quality that leaves out all kinds of elements nature would have provided invisibly.

24   Also missing from both the communes of the '60s and from cyberspace are a couple of elements that I believe are very important, if not essential, to the formation and preservation of a real community: an absence of alternatives and a sense of genuine adversity, generally shared. What about these?

25   It is hard to argue that anyone would find losing a modem literally hard to survive, while many have remained in small towns, have tolerated their intolerances and created entertainment to enliven their culturally

arid lives simply because it seemed there was no choice but to stay. There are many investments—spiritual, material, and temporal—one is willing to put into a home one cannot leave. Communities are often the beneficiaries of these involuntary investments.

26   But when the going gets rough in cyberspace, it is even easier to move than it is in the 'burbs, where, given the fact that the average American moves some 12 times in his or her life, moving appears to be pretty easy. You cannot only find another bulletin board service (BBS) or newsgroup to hang out in; you can, with very little effort, start your own.

27   And then there is the bond of joint suffering. Most community is a cultural stockade erected against a common enemy that can take many forms. In Pinedale, we bore together, with an understanding needing little expression, the fact that Upper Green River Valley is the coldest spot, as measured by annual mean temperature, in the lower 48 states. We knew that if somebody was stopped on the road most winter nights, he would probably die there, so the fact that we might loathe him was not sufficient reason to drive on past his broken pickup.

28   By the same token, the Deadheads have the Drug Enforcement Administration, which strives to give them 20-year prison terms without parole for distributing the fairly harmless sacrament of their faith. They have an additional bond in the fact that when their Microbuses die, as they often do, no one but another Deadhead is likely to stop to help them.

29   But what are the shared adversities of cyberspace? Lousy user interfaces? The flames of harsh invective? Dumb jokes? Surely these can all be survived without the sanctuary provided by fellow sufferers.

30   One is always free to yank the jack, as I have mostly done. For me, the physical world offers far more opportunity for *prana* rich connections with my fellow creatures. Even for someone whose body is in a state of perpetual motion, I feel I can generally find more community among the still-embodied.

31   Finally, there is that shyness factor. Not only are we trying to build community here among people who have never experienced any in my sense of the term, we are trying to build community among people who, in their lives, have rarely used the word *we* in a heartfelt way. It is a vast club, and many of the members—following Groucho Marx—wouldn't want to join a club that would have them.

32   And yet...

33   How quickly physical community continues to deteriorate. Even Pinedale, which seems to have survived the plague of ranch failures, feels increasingly cut off from itself. Many of the ranches are now owned by corporate types who fly their Gulfstreams in to fish and are rarely around during the many months when the creeks are frozen over and neighbors are needed. They have kept the ranches alive financially, but they actively discourage their managers from the interdependence my former colleagues and I require. They keep agriculture on life support, still alive but lacking a functional heart.

---

34 And the town has been inundated with suburbanites who flee here, bringing all their terrors and suspicions with them. They spend their evenings as they did in Orange County, watching television or socializing in hermetic little enclaves of fundamentalist Christianity that seem to separate them from us and even, given their sectarian animosities, from one another. The town remains. The community is largely a wraith of nostalgia.

35 So where else can we look for the connection we need to prevent our plunging further into the condition of separateness Nietzsche called sin? What is there to do but to dive further into the bramble bush of information that, in its broadest forms, has done so much to tear us apart?

36 Cyberspace, for all its current deficiencies and failed promises, is not without some very real solace already.

37 Some months ago, the great love of my life, a vivid young woman with whom I intended to spend the rest of it, dropped dead of undiagnosed viral cardiomyopathy two days short of her 30th birthday. I felt as if my own heart had been as shredded as hers.

38 We had lived together in New York City. Except for my daughters, no one from Pinedale had met her. I needed a community to wrap around myself against colder winds than fortune had ever blown at me before. And without looking, I found I had one in the virtual world.

39 On the WELL, there was a topic announcing her death in one of the conferences to which I posted the eulogy I had read over her before burying her in her own small town of Nanaimo, British Columbia. It seemed to strike a chord among the disembodied living on the Net. People copied it and sent it to one another. Over the next several months I received almost a megabyte of electronic mail from all over the planet, mostly from folks whose faces I have never seen and probably never will.

40 They told me of their own tragedies and what they had done to survive them. As humans have since words were first uttered, we shared the second most common human experience, death, with an openheartedness that would have caused grave uneasiness in physical America, where the whole topic is so cloaked in denial as to be considered obscene. Those strangers, who had no arms to put around my shoulders, no eyes to weep with mine, nevertheless saw me through. As neighbors do.

41 I have no idea how far we will plunge into this strange place. Unlike previous frontiers, this one has no end. It is so dissatisfying in so many ways that I suspect we will be more restless in our search for home here than in all our previous explorations. And that is one reason why I think we may find it after all. If home is where the heart is, then there is already some part of home to be found in cyberspace.

42   So…does virtual community work or not? Should we all go off to cyberspace or should we resist it as a demonic form of symbolic abstraction? Does it supplant the real or is there, in it, reality itself?

43   Like so many true things, this one doesn't resolve itself to a black or a white. Nor is it gray. It is, along with the rest of life, black/white. Both/neither. I'm not being equivocal or whishy-washy here. We have to get over our Manichean sense that everything is either good or bad, and the border of cyberspace seems to me a good place to leave that old set of filters.

44   But really it doesn't matter. We are going there whether we want to or not. In five years, everyone who is reading these words will have an e-mail address, other than the determined Luddites who also eschew the telephone and electricity.

45   When we are all together in cyberspace we will see what the human spirit, and the basic desire to connect, can create there. I am convinced that the result will be more benign if we go there open-minded, open-hearted, and excited with the adventure than if we are dragged into exile.

46   And we must remember that going to cyberspace, unlike previous great emigrations to the frontier, hardly requires us to leave where we have been. Many will find, as I have, a much richer appreciation of physical reality for having spent so much time in virtuality.

47   Despite its current (and perhaps in some areas permanent) insufficiencies, we should go to cyberspace with hope. Groundless hope, like unconditional love, may be the only kind that counts.

In Memoriam, Dr. Cynthia Homer (1964–1994).

Suddenly Teen Pregnancy Is Cool?

Cathy Gulli

Cathy Gulli is an associate editor and regular contributor to Maclean's *magazine.*

The article was originally published in Maclean's *magazine.* Maclean's *is a leading Canadian magazine. Published weekly, it focuses on Canadian current affairs. "Suddenly Teen Pregnancy Is Cool?" was the cover story for a January 2008 issue of the magazine.*

Prereading

Read the introductory paragraph of the article and respond to Cathy Gulli's question: "How could a wealthy preteen idol . . . be just several months away from adolescent, out-of-wedlock motherhood?"

...continued Suddenly Teen Pregnancy Is Cool?, **Cathy Gulli**

1 When Jamie Lynn Spears, the 16-year-old sister of Britney, announced that she was pregnant last month in *OK!*, the magazine sold a record two million copies and had to run a second printing of the issue to keep up with demand. How could a wealthy preteen idol with her own hit Nickelodeon show, and the good sister to her chaotic older kin, be just several months away from adolescent, out-of-wedlock motherhood? "I didn't believe it because Jamie Lynn's always been so conscientious. She's never late for her curfew," lamented mother Lynne Spears. She got over the shock in a week, and then Jamie Lynn, ever conscientious, notified the press that she would be having, keeping and raising the baby with her mama in Louisiana. "I'm just trying to do the right thing," said the star of Zoey 101.

2 Only a few days earlier, the film *Juno* had been released to instant and unanimous applause from such diverse sources as *The New Yorker, Christianity Today* and *Film Freak Central*. Suddenly the heroine of a hit movie—a comedy no less—could be a smart, motivated, white, middle-class girl, just 16, who matter-of-factly chooses to have a baby and an open adoption rather than an abortion. No big deal.

3 Unplanned pregnancy is now a pop-culture staple. Movies like *Knocked Up* and *Waitress,* and celebrity moms including Nicole Richie and Jessica Alba, are part of a trend that's sweeping teen culture along with it: *American Idol* star Fantasia Barrino became a mom at 17, and the last season of *Degrassi: The Next Generation* ended with Emma realizing she might be pregnant. "The media is awash in it," says David Landry, senior research associate at the Guttmacher Institute in New York, a nonprofit organization focused on sexual and reproductive health. Even *Grey's Anatomy* had a teen pregnancy storyline last year, and just last week so did *Gossip Girl.*

4 "As an idea, teen pregnancy is more socially accepted," says Andrea O'Reilly, a women's studies professor at York University in Toronto, and director of the Association for Research on Mothering. Evidence of a less outraged reaction was best summarized by Hollywood's most sought-after paparazzi muse, Lindsay Lohan: "Why does everyone think it's such a big deal?" she replied when asked what she thought of Jamie Lynn's situation.

5 Then came the statistical data confirming that something—something real—was happening: in 2006, for the first time in 15 years, the teen birth rate in America actually increased, said a report by the National Center for Health Statistics (NCHS), a branch of the U.S. Centers for Disease Control. Meanwhile, in England, the number of pregnancies among females under age 18 also rose in 2005—to the highest point since 1998, according to the U.K.'s Department for Children, Schools and Families.

6   So far, the numbers aren't rising in Canada, but our statistics are a couple of years old—from 2005. Some experts say that when data does become available, we'll see the same rise as our neighbours. "Overall trends for these three countries tend to mirror each other," says Alex McKay, research coordinator of the Sex Information and Education Council of Canada. "If we're seeing an increase in the teen birth rate in the U.S. and the U.K.," he continues, "it is quite likely we may see the same thing occur in Canada."

7   In an era when not getting pregnant should be easy, explanations for the jump in births among teens are speculative, if not elusive. Data on abortion rates or contraception use are outdated, so there's little way of knowing for sure how much of the increase is due to a rise in unprotected sex or a possible decline in abortion rates. Some experts say it's just a blip, a statistical aberration we'll see corrected next year. Others believe the problem is institutional, that ineffective abstinence-only programs are to blame in the U.S. Or that we may have simply maxed out how much teen pregnancy can be prevented. "Whenever you try to improve things it's easiest in the beginning," says Bill Albert, deputy director of the National Campaign to Prevent Teen and Unplanned Pregnancy, based in Washington.

8   Those who see the signs of something more profound offer a range of explanations: a celebrity culture that downplays the hard work of motherhood; ever-changing family structures that normalize non-traditional arrangements; children who live at home longer than ever with parental support and aren't expected, if they have kids of their own, to marry the father.

9   Invariably though, it seems teen pregnancy has become more accepted. A Denver high school is considering implementing a four-week maternity leave for students so they can recover and get used to the baby without penalties for missing class. In Canada, there is a recognition that teen moms should receive more help too: "Schools try to offer flexibility to young mothers," says Marcia Powers-Dunlop, chief of social work with the Toronto District School Board's northwest region. Consequently, many girls don't drop out, she's observed, "because there isn't the stigma that there once was." Jamie Lynn, for her part, was photographed recently toting a GED study book to get her high-school equivalency degree.

10   "There's a redefining of motherhood," says O'Reilly. "Teen moms are saying, why can't I be a mother now?" She believes that as older women are gaining acceptance as new mothers, adolescent girls are claiming their maternal rights too. "Before, the time of motherhood was so restricted. Now it's okay at 48. So why not at 18?" The feminist motherhood movement, as O'Reilly refers to the growing show of support for moms of all ages, has people questioning societal expectations about when is the right time to have children. "It's part of a larger revisioning of motherhood: queer mothers, old mothers, young mothers. That wasn't possible 20 years ago."

11   Suffice to say, the rising American teen birth rate in 2006 is some-thing of an eye-opener. Between 1991 and 2005, the United States saw a 34 per cent decrease in the birth rate among those aged 15 to 19. But in 2006, that relatively steady decline was reversed. Suddenly, among 15- to 17-year-olds, the rate was up three per cent to 22 babies per 1,000 females, and 18- and 19-year-olds jumped four per cent to 73 births for every 1,000. "That took us by surprise," admits Stephanie J. Ventura, head of the reproductive statistics branch at NCHS. And the rise was spread over almost every ethnic group except for Asians; births among black, native, Hispanic and white teenagers rose. While no specific data was col-lected on the income of teen mothers, Albert says that with three in 10 girls getting pregnant by age 20, "you realize this is not [just] 'poor folk.' The problem is spread wide."

12   In England and Wales, the birth rate per 1,000 females under age 20 rose to 45.5 in 2006 compared to 44.8 the year before. Not a huge leap, but it's already one of the highest rates in the developed world. The United Nations' last comprehensive tally of G8 countries, from 2004, showed the U.K. has the third-highest teen birth rate, with 26.8 births per 1,000, slightly lower than Russia (28.2) and well above Japan (5.6), France (7.8), Italy (6.7) and Germany (11). The U.S. soars above them all, at 41.8 per 1,000 females.

13   Canada ranks exactly in the middle, with a teen birth rate of 13.4 per 1,000 as of 2005 (or 14.5 in 2003, as stated in the UN report), but that's still down 45 per cent over the last decade. Domestically, we've come a long way. In 1995, teens aged 15 to 19 had 24.3 births per 1,000. And among the under-15 age group, the number of births per 1,000 plummeted nearly 60 per cent between 1995 and 2004. (Teen births, of course, are not the same thing as teen pregnancies, which include births and abortions and there-fore capture the broader picture of how many adolescents are actually deal-ing with pregnancy, one way or another. Like birth rates, pregnancy rates also showed declines through the late 1990s and early to mid-2000s in the U.S., the U.K. and Canada, but the latest numbers are between two and five years old.)

14   What no one knows in Canada, for now, is what's been happening in the last couple of years. McKay suggests Canada should consider rises in other countries as foreshadowing of what could be happening here. "Although there are profound differences between Canada and the United States," he says, "both countries have seen a persistent long-term decline in teen pregnancy rates over the last quarter-century." That both our southern neighbour and England have seen reversals means "there's a fairly big probability we will see the same," he continues. Adds David Quist, executive director of the Ottawa-based Institute of Marriage and Family Canada, an arm of Focus on the Family: "Often Canada follows the U.S. in trends like this."

15   And the U.S., before seeing the jump in its teen birth rate in 2006, first witnessed a flattening out. "The rate of decline had slowed in the last few years," explains Ventura, "so maybe that was an early indication that it was about to reverse." Similarly, England's birth rate has barely budged since 2000.

16   In Canada, the declining teen birth rate has also levelled off—from 14.9 births per 1,000 in 2002 to 13.6 in 2004 to 13.4 births one year later.

17   So what if this isn't a blip? It could be that teens are just following what is really a nationwide trend in the U.S. Across all ages (from 15 to 44) the birth rate is up, according to the NCHS. Between 2005 and 2006, more women had babies than had since 1961—in excess of 4.2 million. And the 2006 fertility rate was the highest it had been since 1971. Explanations for the overall increase are as elusive as for the rising teen birth rate.

18   "The short answer is none of us really know why the rates went up," says Albert. For teens, many blame the rise on abstinence only programs, which have bloomed in the U.S. since 1996, with more than $1 billion in federal funding. Critics say they deny teens information that could help them make safer decisions when they do have sex. "There is precious little evidence to suggest that abstinence-only interventions work," says Albert. But he's reluctant to put much stock in arguments for or against abstinence-only, since these programs existed during the major declines between 1996 and 2005.

19   In Canada, the federal government has assembled guidelines for sex education, but programs differ by school board, school and classroom, says McKay. He believes programs are not uniform enough across the country to make a consistent contribution to the health of Canadian youth. "The extent and quality of sex education varies from excellent to non-existent. And unfortunately, the non-existent is more common," he says.

20   Poor access to emergency contraception and abortion also may explain the increase in teen births. "There are more limits now on abortions—[longer] waiting periods, fewer abortion providers," says Landry. As well, they often require travel, parental permission, and large fees. Plus, he adds, teens may be more reluctant to terminate because it has become "such a politicized, divisive issue." Meanwhile, pharmacies can sell the morning after pill only to females 18 or older; younger girls need a doctor's note, a problem since the medication must be administered within 72 hours of having sex.

21   The situation isn't much better in Canada. The morning-after pill, while readily available, requires a consultation with a pharmacist, which costs up to $45 plus the drug fee. And according to a 2007 report by the Canadian Federation for Sexual Health, less than one in six hospitals provided abortions in 2006, and many provinces do not have full health insurance coverage for terminations done in clinics. Without the option to terminate a pregnancy, we'll see a rise in births, says O'Reilly.

22 | Or it could be that teen birth rates have simply gone as low as they can. After all, says Landry, the vast majority of adolescents have sex: "In some ways, it's amazing that we have had this long a run in the decline in birth rates." After several years of getting the message about teen pregnancy out to the most receptive adolescents, "it may be that we're down to very difficult cases," says Albert.

23 | It doesn't seem to be the case that teens generally are less sexually prudent than earlier generations. The age of first sexual experience hasn't gotten any younger—17 in the U.S., and 16.5 in Canada. The use of condoms and hormonal birth controls had increased as of 2002 in the States, and in Canada, contraception use has risen—nearly 87 per cent of teens have safe sex. (This further suggests that abstinence-only programs may not work.) And adolescents here aren't having any more sex than earlier generations either. "In some ways, [teens] tend to be more conservative now than they were in the past," says McKay.

24 | During the 1960s and '70s, sex was a rite of passage equated with youthful rebellion and liberation, he surmises. Today, many "teens have sex for reasons associated with pleasure, relationships and exploration. It's done in a different context."

25 | The fact that "babies!" tops the list of news categories at www .people.com suggests that pregnancy—celebrity, teen, unplanned, out-of-wedlock, whatever—has moved into a new realm of acceptance. "It's no longer a scary word," says Ottawa-based sex therapist Sue McGarvie. "It's been normalized." Entertainment tabloids, which have long featured style-watch lists, have turned their attention to the latest accessory in Hollywood—protruding bellies. And teens, heavy consumers of such media, are getting the message that "having a baby is the new handbag," says Nicole Fischer, 17, who lives in Calgary and just gave birth to her son Cristian five months ago.

26 | "Popular culture is showing a more positive representation of young mothers," says O'Reilly. Today, having an unexpected baby can be more of an image-enhancer than a shameful faux pas. It's part of a larger trend to make motherhood chic and happening, she says: "If you're 18, you want a baby on your hip, a miniskirt, and a guitar on your back." In many ways, celebrities have helped prove that motherhood isn't "the end of coolness or sexiness for women, or the end of the line," says Ariel Gore, a Portland, Ore.–based blogger and author of *Breeder: Real-Life Stories from the New Generation of Mothers,* among other books.

27 | Trite as it may sound, Albert says social norms are shaped by star culture. "The Britneys of this world and the Angelina Jolies may have an effect. To ignore it would be Polly-annaish." Of course, to say it's all positive would also be wrong, says O'Reilly. "The glamour and romance

quickly goes—when you're having morning sickness [or] in childbirth for two days. That whole [Hollywood mom] culture worries me," she continues, "because that's not how motherhood is."

28   However misguided, Powers-Dunlop says that some teens "no longer think there's a big deal" about having sex—and so, presumably, getting pregnant. As someone in daily contact with adolescents, she says that premarital sex now is a way of life. It is not unusual for her to get calls about 12- and 13-year-olds who are expecting babies. "That would have been unheard of a while ago," she says. "And yet it's no longer cause for panic."

29   Celebs aside, rising teen birth rates may also have to do with home life, Powers-Dunlop adds, where casual sex may be observed among single parents. "There's a lot of families separating and divorcing, and parents having new partners but not getting married. There's a message that this is a natural," she explains. "It's no longer love then sex." In fact, the ever-more diverse family structures happening today— gay parents, multi-faith and race marriages, open relationships, step and half-siblings, and single-parent adoption or in vitro fertilization—may relieve some of the old shock of teen parenthood.

30   And now that more adult children live at home with their folks for longer—60 per cent of Canadians aged 20 to 24 did last year—teens may feel they'll have more support in raising their child, just like Jamie Lynn Spears is counting on her mother's help. (Fischer, meanwhile, is living with the family of her boyfriend, who fathered the baby.)

31   One trend observed by Pauline Paterson, director of the YWCA's girls and family programs in Scarborough, Ont., is a phenomenon called "multi-daddying." Teen moms are actually having more than one baby with various fathers as a way of forming bonds with new men in their lives—and it's yet another way that adolescents are putting their stamp on parenthood and establishing new family models.

32   Of course, few people would say they encourage adolescent motherhood. Actress Eva Mendes, during the launch of her antifur PETA ads, said of unplanned births, "It's an epidemic and I don't want to catch it!" Lily Allen, the 22-year-old singer, admonished teen pregnancy in *Marie Claire*. Soon after, she announced that she was surprised but "thrilled" to be expecting a child too.

33   The main difference these days is that the severe shame and stigmatization teens used to face when they got pregnant has lessened—if only slightly, says Kayla Clark, 18, who got pregnant despite using two forms of birth control. She gave birth to son William almost two years ago. That change is partly because parents, teachers and health care workers are realizing that much worse things can befall an adolescent. "Now parents worry about serious drugs, HIV or AIDS," says O'Reilly, not to mention gang violence. In *Juno*, for example, the parents heaved a huge sigh of relief when the big news their daughter had come to confess turned out

to be pregnancy—they were terrified she had been expelled or was addicted to drugs.

34   There's also recognition that offering support to pregnant teens doesn't necessarily have to mean it's being encouraged. "Taking away the stigma isn't going to cause a bunch of young women to get pregnant," says Gore. She suggests the rising birth rate may be a backlash to the intense campaigns against teen pregnancy throughout the last decade. Adolescents may be rebelling against the idea that they can't be parents. Gore also believes that teens may be more open to motherhood after witnessing their own moms suffer health problems or constant fatigue because they put off having kids until later in life. "I don't think there's anything intrinsically wrong with teen parenting," Gore says. Her beef is with the need for more social services to help adolescent mothers cope.

35   There are some indications support is taking priority. Louise Dean Centre in Calgary is one of only a few schools in Canada that cater exclusively to pregnant teens and young mothers aged 14 to 20. "They feel more comfortable that [motherhood] hasn't ended their life," says teacher Alison Orpe. "It's just taken it in a different direction." And groups for adolescent moms, like the one run by Scarborough's YWCA, provide a dinner and community support twice a week for teens and their babies. The group is constantly at maximum capacity, with 150 attending.

36   Fischer, who says she was "the perfect child" of her family, and got pregnant after having sex for the first time, is among the students at Louise Dean. She has big plans to become a legal assistant. "My grades are up and I know I'm going to college," she says. "I know there is a way out. But you have to be responsible enough to make the choices."

37   Increasingly, teens are proving that they can pull off adolescence and motherhood at once. "There are some huge pregnancy success stories," McGarvie says. "It's not necessarily all bad." Many young mothers are finding "motivation, tenacity and purpose" in their new role, continues O'Reilly, and this propels them to stay in school so they can later find work and establish a good life for their growing family. As much as we may not like to admit it, adds McKay, "there are many young women who are perfectly capable of bearing a child in their late teens and leading healthy and productive lives for themselves and providing a good upbringing for their children."

38   Part of this empowerment is tied up in the fact that unplanned pregnancy no longer automatically means that girls must have a secret abortion or put their baby up for closed adoption—as *Juno* shows. Nor do they automatically have to marry the father of their baby. McKay says we are undergoing a profound transformation in the control women are exhibiting over their reproductive fate. Clark lives on her own with the

baby in subsidized housing and will begin studying exercise science at the University of Lethbridge in September. She says that while she debated both termination and open adoption, she couldn't bear giving up her claim to motherhood. "I couldn't be part of life knowing that I [wouldn't be] a mom anymore," she says.

39   "It's a rescripting of what we know as a teen mom," says O'Reilly. Historically, they were demonized, or worse: they were known as "the disappeared," she says. "You were shipped off to Aunt Martha's" for an abortion or to put the baby up for adoption. Now, "there's more cultural permission to be a young mother than 10 or 20 years ago," believes O'Reilly. "It's not a death sentence."

PRACTICE

1 Read John Perry Barlow's "Is There a There in Cyberspace?" on pages 119–125. As you read, look for indications of the audience Barlow has in mind. Is he writing for a college-educated audience? For computer addicts? For everyday Americans? For technophobes? Write a paragraph that describes Barlow's intended audience. Be sure to defend your answer with references to Barlow's text.

    a. Explain the significance of the two quotations that preface Barlow's essay.

    b. If you were to insert subtitles into this article, where would you place them and what would they be?

2 Read Cathy Gulli's article "Suddenly Teen Pregnancy Is Cool" on pages 125–133. As you read, pause at each place where Gulli uses a fact or idea that you believe comes from another source. Each time you pause, write "yes" in the margin if you think Gulli provides enough information for you to locate the original source and "no" if she does not. Can you make any generalizations about when Gulli chooses to identify sources as opposed to when she does not cite a source? If you were to convert Gulli's popular magazine article into an academic paper, how many sources would appear in the list of references?

    a. How would you describe Gulli's point of view, voice, and tone? Does Gulli use the first person (I, we), the second person (you), or the third person (he, she, it, they)?

3 Change the order of the ideas in each of the following sentences. An example is shown.

> When Boris Pasternak was awarded the Nobel Prize for his novel *Doctor Zhivago,* Soviet authorities pressured him to reject the prize.

> Soviet authorities pressured Boris Pasternak to reject the Nobel Prize when he was awarded it for his novel *Doctor Zhivago.*

    a. As the Industrial Revolution progressed, exploitation of child labor became a serious social problem.

    b. Although there are currently several theories concerning the origin of the universe, the Big Bang theory is the one most widely held.

    c. Despite the common belief that the brush is the primary tool of the painter, many well-known paintings were created entirely with pallet knives.

    d. Even though the secretary of defense disagreed sharply with the president's foreign policy, she did not resign from office.

4 Rewrite the following paragraph from James Monaco's book *How to Read a Film* by substituting synonyms for the underlined words and phrases. Come up with your own synonyms for familiar words. If contextual clues do not unlock the meaning of unfamiliar words, use the procedure for finding synonyms in a dictionary or thesaurus.

The theoretical <u>interrelationship</u> between painting and film <u>continues to this day.</u> The Italian Futurist movement produced obvious parodies of the motion picture; <u>contemporary</u> photographic hyperrealism continues to comment on the <u>ramifications</u> of the camera esthetic. But the connection between the two arts has never been as <u>sharp</u> and <u>clear</u> as it was during the Cubist Period. The primary <u>response</u> of painting to the <u>challenge</u> of film has been the <u>conceptualism</u> that Cubism first <u>liberated</u> and that is not <u>common</u> to all the arts. The work of <u>mimesis</u> has been left, in the main, to the <u>recording</u> arts. The arts of representation and <u>artifact</u> have moved on to a new, more abstract <u>sphere.</u> The <u>strong challenge</u> film presented to the pictorial arts was certainly a function of its <u>mimetic capabilities,</u> but it was <u>also due to</u> the one factor that made film <u>radically different</u> from painting: film moved. (Monaco, 2006, p. 25)

5 Here we present a sentence from a textbook and sample student paraphrases. Compare each paraphrase to the original to see if the writer needs to make revisions. Ask yourself the questions for revising paraphrases.

Somatic cells, while tiny compact worlds within themselves, nevertheless do not exist in isolation; instead, cells bond together, according to their special function, and thereby form definite units or structures called tissues (Luckman & Sorensen, 1974, p. 138).

PARAPHRASES

a. A tissue is formed by the bonding of different somatic cells according to their common functions (Luckman & Sorensen, 1974).

b. Tissues that are definite units or structures are formed by cells that bond together. They bond according to the special functions they have. Somatic cells are an example of small cells that bond together to form a tissue instead of remaining separate (Luckman & Sorensen, 1974).

c. Somatic cells, like any other cells, do not live alone. They join together with other cells depending on their specific functions and form a substance called tissue (Luckman & Sorensen, 1974).

d. Tissues are formed when somatic cells collide outside their small worlds. In order for these cells to be bonded, they must match in a certain way (Luckman & Sorensen, 1974).

e. Tissues are formed by the bonding together of somatic cells according to their special functions (Luckman & Sorensen, 1974).

6 For this exercise, we reproduced two excerpts from student essays that draw on Steven Vogel's "Grades and Money." For each excerpt, convert the quotation to a paraphrase by using the strategies described in the text. Remember that in addition to accurately rewording the author's ideas, you have to make sure the paraphrase fits smoothly into the existing paragraph. If you have not read Vogel's article, it will help to know that Vogel is a college professor of philosophy who claims that students have come to see grades as "money," the currency of higher education. According to Vogel, professors "pay" students for their academic work with grades, and thus grades are valued more than learning.

a. The tragic aspect of the A–F grading system is that it devalues education. Under this system, students attend college not to learn but rather to accumulate an impressive portfolio of grades. Students see grades, not knowledge, as the payoff for hard academic work. "If grades are money, then learning is a cost—a painful effort one undergoes only for the reward it produces" (Vogel, 1996, p. 391). Thus it is not that students need grades to motivate them to learn but rather that achieving the grades has itself become the ultimate goal of higher education.

b. Most students expect relatively high grades in courses where they work hard. Perhaps the exception is mathematics, where some students readily admit a lack of aptitude, but even students who recognize that they are struggling in a particular subject expect decent grades if they are trying. At the same time, students who are doing well in a subject are often not content with any grades below an A. "These honor students are in some ways the worst in terms of their fixation on grades and their constant and creative search to find ways to manipulate the system: their skill at doing so, after all, has gotten them where they are today" (Vogel, 1996, p. 392). Since virtually all students, from the academically talented to the academically challenged, think they deserve higher grades, professors are under constant pressure to compromise their standards.

7 Explain why students used direct quotations in each of the following examples.

a. Computer expert Alan Kay once stated that "although the personal computer can be guided in any direction we choose, the real sin would be to make it act like a machine" (Frude, 2006, p. 24). As Kay indicates, we should take advantage of recent advances in artificial intelligence to produce a computer that simulates human thinking.

b. The Supreme Court's recent decisions on search warrants seem to support the logic that "if you have nothing to hide, you have nothing to fear" (Stephens, 2007, p. 22).

c. "I'm going [to the party] because I've been invited. . . . And I've been invited because Luciana is my friend. So there." [Her mother replied], "That one's not your friend. You know what you are to them? The maid's daughter, that's what!" (Heker, 1999, p. 432). This brief yet dramatic confrontation draws the reader immediately into the theme of Liliana Heker's story, "The Stolen Party."

d. One of the physician's most fundamental rights is the right to choose patients. In Section VI of the Code of Ethics, the American Medical Association guarantees that "a physician is free, except in emergencies, to choose whom to serve" (Zuger & Miles, 1926, p. 44).

8 What follow are four different ways that a writer can use the same passage from a source to support a point about the greenhouse effect. Working in groups or as a whole class, rank the four methods from "most effective" to "least effective." Assume that you are writing a researched argument addressed to your college classmates.

a. *Quotation with parenthetical citation*

The greenhouse effect will have a devastating effect on the earth's environment: "Potential impacts include increased mortality and illness due to heat stress and worsened air pollution, as in the 1995 Chicago heat wave that killed hundreds of people. . . . Infants, children and other vulnerable populations—especially in already-stressed regions of the world—would likely suffer disproportionately from these impacts" (Hall, 2008, p. 19).

b. *Quotation with attributive tag*

The greenhouse effect will have a devastating effect on the earth's environment. David C. Hall (2008), president of Physicians for Social Responsibility, claims the following: "Potential impacts include increased mortality and illness due to heat stress and worsened air pollution, as in the 1995 Chicago heat wave that killed hundreds of people. . . . Infants, children and other vulnerable populations— especially in already-stressed regions of the world—would likely suffer disproportionately from these impacts" (p. 19).

c. *Paraphrase with parenthetical citation*

The greenhouse effect will have a devastating effect on the earth's environment. One of the most frightening effects is the threat of diseases stemming from increased air pollution and heat stress. Infants and children would be most at risk (Hall, 2008).

d. *Paraphrase with attributive tag*

The greenhouse effect will have a devastating effect on the earth's environment. One of the most frightening effects, according to David C. Hall (2008), president of Physicians for Social Responsibility, is the threat of diseases stemming from increased air pollution and heat stress. Infants and children would be most at risk.

9 Read the passage below. Unlike the ethical summary of McGrath's article produced by Writer 1 on page 139, the writer of the following passage would likely be accused of plagiarism.

Summary of McGrath's Article (An Example of Plagiarism)

It is commonly assumed that violence is part of our Wild West heritage. But Roger McGrath (2007), in his article "The Myth of Violence in the Old West," shows that frontier violence was very different from violence today. He explains that in a typical frontier town, violence involved gunslingers who were "willing combatants," whereas today's typical victims—the old, the young, the weak, and the female—were unaffected by crime. The greatest deterrent to crime in Bodie was the fact that so many people were armed. Armed guards prevented bank robberies and stagecoach holdups, and armed citizens stopped burglary. On the other hand, McGrath explains, Bodie had a high homicide rate. Most of the town's residents were young single males who adhered to a code of conduct that frequently required them to fight. Alcohol also played a major role. Therefore murders were much more frequent than in any U.S. city today. Thus, according to McGrath, there is little resemblance between violence on the frontier and violence in today's cities, so we cannot blame current violence on our tumultuous frontier past.

Working in small groups or as a whole class, respond to the following questions.

a. How does this passage cross the line into plagiarism? (You'll need to compare the passage to Writer 1's ethical summary on p. 139.)

b. The writer of this passage might say, "How can this be plagiarism? I cited my source and gave page numbers." How would you explain the problem to this writer?

c. Psychologically or cognitively, what may have caused this writer to misuse the source? How might this writer's note-taking process or composing process have differed from that of Writer 1 on page 139? In other words, what happened that got this writer into trouble?

Writer 1: An Analytical Paper on Cause of Violence on Contemporary Society

Many people believe that our Wild West heritage is one of the causes of contemporary violence. But Roger McGrath (2011), in his article "The Myth of Violence in the Old West," shows that today's violence is much different from frontier violence. He explains that in a typical frontier town, violence involved gunslingers who were "willing combatants," whereas today's typical victims—"the old, the young, the weak, and the female"—were unaffected by crime (p. 554). Because the presence of an armed populace deterred robbery and burglary, theft was much less common in the Old West than today. On the other hand, McGrath explains, killings were fueled by guns, alcohol, and a code of conduct that invited fighting, so murders were much more frequent than in any U.S. city today. Thus, according to McGrath, there is little resemblance between violence on the frontier and violence in today's cities, so we cannot blame current violence on a tumultuous frontier past.

Identification of source

Summary of McGrath's argument

Page number of original material

Writer 1's own argument

Pictured Rocks
Munising, MI

How Do I Read Critically?

4

Reading Academic Texts

College students sometimes have difficulty comprehending assigned reading. Even when they understand the text, they find it hard to communicate that understanding in writing. Why do students who were accomplished readers in high school experience problems with reading comprehension? Read each of the following passages and then summarize the main ideas.

Passage 1

Man is spirit. But what is spirit? Spirit is the self. But what is the self? The self is a relation which relates itself to its own self, or it is that in the relation [which accounts for it] that the relation relates itself to its own self; the self is not the relation but [consists in the fact] that the relation relates itself to its own self. Man is a synthesis of the infinite and the finite, of the temporal and the eternal, of freedom and necessity, in short it is a synthesis. A synthesis is a relation between two factors. So regarded, man is not yet a self. (Kierkegaard, 2008, p. 146)

Passage 2

One of childhood's saddest figures is the one who hangs around the fringes of every group, walks home alone after school, and sobs in despair, "Nobody wants to play with me." Children can be unpopular for many reasons, sometimes because they are withdrawn or rebellious. They may walk around with a "chip on the shoulder," showing unprovoked aggression and hostility. Or they may act silly and babyish, showing off in immature ways. Or they may be anxious and uncertain, exuding such a pathetic lack of confidence that they repel other children, who don't find them fun to be with. (Papalia & Olds, 2001, p. 233)

Most students have difficulty with the passage by the Danish philosopher Kierkegaard but no problem with the passage by Papalia and Olds.

Kierkegaard's vocabulary is no more complex than that of Papalia and Olds, so what accounts for the disparity in comprehensibility? A fundamental difference between the two passages is that Kierkegaard's definition of "self" is theoretical and abstract, whereas Papalia and Olds's description of unpopular children is grounded in everyday experience. Readers comprehend not just by recognizing vocabulary but also by relating the content to prior knowledge and experience. As you read Passage 2, you may picture an unpopular child whom you know. Because you already have the background knowledge to make this image concrete, the text is easy to understand. As you read Passage 1, you are stumped. Since you haven't thought much about the philosophical definition of self, the text is enigmatic.

Another factor that contributes to comprehension is text organization. The Papalia and Olds passage is easy to understand because it follows a logical, conventional pattern. It starts with the effect of unpopularity—the lonely child—and goes on to list the causes of the problem. The Kierkegaard passage is difficult to grasp because it doesn't follow a familiar pattern.

You can make sense of the child passage because you have a working knowledge of the concept of *unpopularity* and the organizational pattern of cause and effect. Your stored mental images of these phenomena are called *schemata*. You have schemata for any number of things, for example, how a college course is conducted. When you entered the classroom on the first day of your writing course, you probably took a seat, faced the front of the room, and waited for your professor to begin since you have experienced that routine innumerable times in your career as a student. If your professor had not come to the front of the room but rather had taken a seat in the back, opened his book, and began reading quietly, you would undoubtedly have felt confused, because the circumstances would not fit with your mental schema for how a class functions. We acquire schemata from our experiences in the world and we rely on our schemata to make sense of new situations we encounter. If new circumstances are at odds with our existing schemata, we try as best we can to make tentative links to what we already know.

Strategies designed to improve reading comprehension typically begin with activities that involve surveying the reading source to get an idea of its content and generating preliminary links between that content and the reader's prior knowledge. These prereading activities activate the reader's preexisting schemata for the source topic and thus prepare the ground for understanding the text. In the past, you have probably learned one or more prereading strategies. When you have difficulty understanding a text, it is because you lack the appropriate background and cannot make connections between its content and your mental schemata.

A Comprehensive Strategy for the Reading Process

Despite the gaps that exist between texts and prior knowledge, it is possible to improve your reading comprehension. The key is to approach texts from several perspectives. In this chapter, we describe a powerful reading strategy that will enable you to do so.

Comprehensive Reading Strategy
- Grasp the *content:* the main idea, and details.
- Determine how the text functions: its *genre, organization,* and *stylistic features.*
- Identify the *rhetorical context:* the context in which the author is writing and the effect he or she means to achieve.

As you use each strategy, ask yourself the following questions.

Strategy	Questions
Reading for content	What is the main idea?
	How is the main idea supported and developed?
	What other content is important?
Reading for genre, organization, and stylistic features	Is the text in an identifiable genre?
	How do the different parts function?
	How is the text organized?
	What are the text's distinctive stylistic features?
Reading for rhetorical context	What is the author's purpose?
	How is the author trying to affect the audience?
	What are the circumstances surrounding the production of the text?

When you use these strategies, you read in three different but not necessarily separate ways. All three approaches can be used simultaneously and harmoniously. For the purposes of this discussion, however, we present the strategies one by one.

READING FOR CONTENT

When we read for content, we read for concepts, main ideas, and supporting information. This reading requires versatility and various degrees of exertion. We scan the front page of the newspaper to find out the latest developments in a current political crisis; we thumb through *Consumer Reports* to locate facts on a car we're interested in buying; we study a textbook to learn details about an important historical event; and we debate with the premise of a journal article we wish to incorporate in our own writing.

When you read for content, you must be *active*. This means reading with a purpose instead of passively processing print. An example of active reading is reading a scholarly article to discern the author's position on a topic you are researching for a term paper. Your purpose is clear: to find expert opinions you can quote in support of your argument. The following strategies will help you to be an active reader.

Strategies That Promote Active Reading
- Call up your prior knowledge, experience, and feelings about the topic.
- Preview the text and derive questions that will guide your reading.
- Annotate the text and take notes.

● CALLING UP PRIOR KNOWLEDGE, EXPERIENCE, AND FEELINGS
Prior knowledge and experience enable you to construct meaning for new information. You will comprehend difficult texts with ease if you can relate them to existing conceptual frameworks. This is why people who have read extensively in a subject find it easy to understand complex texts written in that area. Prior knowledge prepares them to receive new information. Prior experience may bias you in certain ways, but it makes comprehension possible. As a process-oriented reader, you will benefit from your prior knowledge and experience *before* you read, *while* you are reading, and *after* you have completed the text.

Using Prior Knowledge in the Reading Process
- Tap your prior knowledge *before* you read.
- Probe for links between the content and your prior knowledge *while* you are reading.
- Look for additional links *after* you have read through the text.

These strategies enable you to take full advantage of what you already know as you unpack the meaning of the text. At the same time, they make you aware of how prior knowledge and experience influence your reading. Two ways to tap prior knowledge and experience are freewriting and brainstorming.

Freewriting involves writing anything that comes to mind about a topic. Write nonstop for ten minutes and don't worry about usage, spelling, or mechanics. Jot down whatever is in your head. Here is an excerpt from the freewriting a student completed prior to reading Moses's "Race, Higher Education, and American Society" on p. 170 of this book. She is writing in response to the title of the Moses article.

> When I was looking at colleges, all the material we received from their admissions offices stressed diversity. All the brochures showed students of various races and ethnic backgrounds, which appealed to me. One of the main reasons I wanted to attend college away from home was to meet people who are not just the same as those I grew up with. It's not that I was tired of my friends from back home, but I felt that I needed to move out of my comfort zone and give myself room for personal growth. My parents also wanted me to attend a college with a diverse student body. They thought the experience would prepare me better for the American workforce of the future that will be increasingly diverse. That's why they had me study Spanish in high school rather than French as they did. When I actually visited campuses, I found that they were actually less diverse than my high school, which came as a big surprise. It seems that the colleges I was considering wanted diversity but that it was still a goal that they were working toward. Perhaps the article by Moses will explain why campuses are still less diverse than American society as a whole.

Brainstorming uses a process of free association. To begin the process, skim the text for key words or phrases that are pivotal to the assignment. Then list the associations that come to mind when you think about these target concepts. Don't bother to write complete sentences; just list words and phrases. Give your imagination free rein. Here's a short list of words and phrases a student generated after skimming Moses's article:

What I learned in the past about the role of race in American education

- Brown v. Topeka Board of Education Supreme Court decision
- separate but equal
- affirmative action
- reverse discrimination
- test scores and college admissions
- recruiting for diversity: fair to everyone?
- school desegregation: Little Rock, South Boston
- the documentary film Eyes on the Prize shown on PBS
- comparison of urban and suburban high schools
- busing
- athletic recruitment and race
- elimination of affirmative action in California and Texas
- student organizations based on race and ethnic background: racist?
- campus housing units that are based on race and ethic background: racist?
- ethnic studies majors and minors at colleges
- diversity awareness programs in the dorms
- college speakers that focus on issues of diversity

Freewriting and brainstorming help you to access prior knowledge of key concepts and make fuller sense of your background. These procedures also make you more conscious of your opinions and biases so you won't inadvertently confuse your views with those of the author. All the same, because you comprehend texts by relating known concepts to new ideas, you can never be completely objective. Your understanding is always a function of what you already know.

● **PREVIEWING AND DERIVING QUESTIONS**   After you have tapped your prior knowledge, set some goals for what you expect to get from the text. Then preview the text by reading the introduction, headings, and any print in special type. If you are reading a textbook, use the reader aids that accompany each chapter: preview outlines, introductory and concluding sections, and review questions. Then generate questions about the content. For example, what do you expect to find out? What more do you want to know about the topic? Answer these questions as you read. This tactic works best if you write out the questions beforehand and record the answers as you come to them. If you enter the questions and answers in a reading journal or log, you can reread them at a later date. Too often, students spend hours reading information-rich texts only to find several days later that they remember nothing and must reread the material. The extra time it takes to preview a text and formulate reading questions represents a real savings compared to the extra time needed for rereading the text.

● **ANNOTATING THE TEXT AND TAKING NOTES**   Another strategy that promotes active reading is to enter into a dialogue with the author by *annotating* the text as you read. *Annotating* means making marginal notes, underlining or highlighting important concepts, and recording brief responses to what the author says. The following example shows a student's annotations of paragraph 6 from Yolanda Moses's article. The student uses the right margin to highlight important concepts and record personal reactions.

Modern anthropology's roots lie in nineteenth-century European natural history traditions, with their focus on the classification and comparison of human populations and their search for indicators of "mental capacity." Cultural anthropologists such as L.H. Morgan and E.B. Tylor worked with physical anthropologists of the time to "scientifically" reconstruct human prehistory and to rank human groups along a unilinear evolutionary path from "savagery" to "civilization." Morgan considered mental development crucial to a group's evolutionary progress. Physical indicators of evolutionary rank were developed, including such attributes as the degree of facial projection and the position of

View of 19th century anthropologists on race.

Morgan and Tylor

Does this imply that we are still evolving? That we are smarter, in general, than ancient Egyptians and ancient Greeks?

the foramen magnum. Measurements of cranial dimensions and proportions ("the cephalic index") were initially proposed as indicators of advancement. Cranial size and the weight and morphological complexity of the brain were other measures used to infer the "mental capacity" of various groups (e.g., "races," sexes, immigrant groups) according to their "natural" "intellectual endowments," which presumably identified their overall evolutionary rank (Mukhopadhyay & Moses, 1997, p. 518).

Is this called phrenology?

Totally unfair!!!

An effective annotation technique is to use prior knowledge to *elaborate* the text. *Elaborations* are associations, extensions, illustrations, or evaluations. Elaborate by suggesting situations the author has not envisioned and by providing analogies, examples, or counterexamples. Here is how a student elaborates on ideas in paragraph 27 of Moses's article.

As I stated earlier, in this section I am going to discuss how salient words such as "merit" and "quality" are used in the admissions process and how a single standardized test such as the SAT figures more prominently, not less, in the arguments used by conservatives to describe why minorities are not qualified (read "worthy") to attend elite institutions. The SAT exam and the vocabulary of "worthiness" that tends to be used in connection with it create an artificial environment that reinforces the myth that individual merit and intelligence can only be measured by scores on such tests. The fact that minorities and women consistently do worse on these tests is assumed to mean that there must be some underlying immutable, natural reason for this.

Why use SAT scores at all for college admissions? Why not rely primarily on high school grades? Don't the grades, accumulated over many years of education, say more about how a person will perform in college than a single test taken on one particular day? Some people just don't test well when under time pressure. The two people from my high school class who got the highest scores on the SAT are really not the classmates I would feel confident going to in the future as my doctor or lawyer. Test taking skill is only a small part of what makes someone a good student who will go on to be a competent professional.

As you annotate, don't overuse highlighting markers. When you read through a text the first time, you may have difficulty deciding what's important.

Every concept seems worthy of special attention. But if you highlight a large percentage of the text, you'll have a lot to reread when you study for an exam or search for ideas for papers. Another problem is that highlighting is a passive, mechanical activity. It only gives the illusion that you are engaged with the text. Instead of highlighting, write out summary statements and reactions. Writing forces you to process information, restate it in your own words, and react to it. The ultimate goals of annotating are to involve you intellectually with the text and give you access to it without rereading. Writing marginal notes is the best way to accomplish this.

The most successful strategy for reading difficult texts is to use the preview-and-question method or some other type of note-taking method along with marginal annotations. Keep in mind, however, that sometimes one system is more practical than the other. Since you can't annotate library materials, you have to take separate notes.

If texts are easy to read and have straightforward content, you can streamline note-taking and annotating procedures to capture only the most basic ideas. But remember that it's natural to forget much of what you've read; even relatively simple ideas slip from memory unless you write them down.

Whether you take separate notes or annotate, it's helpful to write out your reactions to the text. Designate a notebook as your reading journal or log. Reactions can include agreements and disagreements, questions for the author, and judgments on the text's relevance or acceptability. The written responses are another way of relating your prior knowledge to the author's ideas. Reacting as you read is especially important if you intend to write a paper that gives your views on the text. To get the juices flowing, ask the following questions.

QUESTIONS FOR REACTION

- What do you already know about this topic from books, magazines, television, school or college courses, personal experience, or conversation?
- What is the relationship between your prior knowledge and the content being presented in the text?
- Do you have personal opinions or biases on this topic? With what parts of the author's discussion do you agree or disagree?

Answering these questions will help you link content to relevant information that you already know.

Notice how the goals of summarizing and reacting are represented both in marginal notes and in a journal entry for paragraph 12 of Moses's article:

Over the past five to seven years, practitioners have been revisiting and reexamining the nature of race in both biological and cultural anthropology (e.g., Harrison 1995; Goodman 1996; Lieberman and Jackson 1995; Blakey 1987; Marks 1995; Sacks 1994; Shanklin 1994). The conclusion of most of us is that "race" does not exist as a biological phenomenon, but rather that it is socially and culturally constructed. Having said that, we also have said how important it is to understand that this statement does not explain why people *look* different. Most lay people, and some cultural anthropologists, do not know how to explain human variability in ways that are easily understood. So, in the absence of reasonable anthropological explanation, many people tend to fall back on what they know, or what they think they know. The media and peers tend to reinforce uninformed stereotypes, and eventually these stereotypes become belief. For example, why were the sociobiological themes of Shockley's and Jensen's writings so popular with conservatives in the 1970s, and why was *The Bell Curve* such a best-seller only recently? Just a few years ago I proposed that it was because both books reinforce easy stereotypes that have long been held in this society, namely, that people of color and women are inferior to White males, and that our cultural institutions subliminally reinforce these notions in many ways, from advertising to loan policies, to work laws, to wages.

Current views on basis of race: cultural or biological?

Current anthropologist: race is culturally constructed.

Hard to explain human variability.

Racial stereotypes are definitely reinforced in the media. Music videos (including, ironically, those on BET) often reinforce the stereotype of the Black male as a "gangsta." Black woman are often presented as sexual objects in these videos. "Uninformed stereotypes" to be sure!

I've never heard of The Bell Curve. I'll Google it.

Journal Notes

Modern anthropologists agree that the concept of race is created by our culture, not our biological makeup. This reminds me of the movie Black and White, which focused on a group of affluent White teenagers who were making a conscious decision to become "Black," by adopting speech patterns and stereotypical behavior associated with African Americans. The film portrayed the teens as more or less "posers" with a shallow understanding of Black culture. One of the points the film seems to make is that you can't just choose to be Black, that racial identity is formed by how society treats you as you grow up, which is based, in part, on your skin color.

Also useful is a *double-entry journal.* For this type of journal, you create two columns. In the left-hand column, you copy key passages from the text. In the right-hand column, you write your reactions, questions, interpretation, or evaluation.

Reading actively by taking notes, annotating, and reacting is important when your ultimate goal is to write about the text. Notes and annotations are the raw material for summaries and paraphrases, two forms of writing. Responses recorded in marginal notes and freewriting are the basis for response essays. We discuss how you can move from these initial responses to essays of personal reaction and analysis. Active reading not only helps you understand the ideas in reading sources, it sets you well on the way to writing source-based essays.

READING FOR GENRE, ORGANIZATION, AND STYLISTIC FEATURES

To become a proficient college reader and writer, you have to pay attention to what authors are *doing* as well as saying. In addition to reading for content, you need to consider the genre, the organizational pattern, and the stylistic features of the text.

Just as you have prior knowledge related to content, you have expectations about the ways authors set up their texts. Since you've had at least twelve years of reading practice by the time you enter college, you know a great deal about genres, structures, and features of texts. You already know that stories have elements like setting, plot, and theme; business letters contain an inside address and salutation; poems sometimes rhyme and have uneven lines; and newspaper articles are constructed with the most important facts in the first paragraph and the less essential information later in the piece. In other words, you have developed conceptual frameworks for each genre. This type of knowledge is crucial to reading comprehension.

● **GENRE** Your knowledge of the word *genre* may be restricted to your English teachers' discussions of textual forms: the genre of the novel, the short story, or the poem. Today, genre is understood as a broader concept. It refers to a wide range of standardized activities. In the classroom setting, you could speak of pedagogical genres—for example, the genre of show-and-tell in primary school and the genre of the in-place final examination in the university. Each of these activities has recognizable features and conventions. Each is a regularized or structured response to a recurring event. Everything we write can be described in terms of genre. These written genres are the focus of our discussion.

Most likely, you have no difficulty recognizing the literary genres we mentioned above or nonliterary genres like the news article, editorial, or biography. As you become more familiar with academic writing, you will be able to identify specialized genres like the psychological research article, the scientific lab report, and the philosophical essay of reflection.

Table 4.1   Classroom Genres in Academic Writing

Essay Type	Characteristics
Summary Essay	Includes title, author, thesis, and key elements of the text. The essay reflects the organizational pattern of the source and closes by placing the source in a larger context.
Response Essay	Includes identification of the text to which the writer is responding, indication of the focus of the essay, commentary, and reactions.
Comparison-and-Contrast Essay	Presents a thesis based on the elements being compared or contrasted. The essay usually follows one of two patterns of organization. In the *point-by-point* pattern, the writer shifts back and forth between the elements being compared; in the *block* pattern, the writer explains one item completely before turning to the other.
Synthesis Essay	Includes a thesis or unifying theme around which the writer organizes material selected from two or more texts. The writer sets the context for the reader by giving appropriate background information on the reading sources. Clear connectives differentiate the writer's ideas from those of the authors of the other texts.
Argumentative Essay	Includes an argumentative thesis, background information on the issue, support for the position being argued, mention of positions in opposition to the writer's, and response to opposition.
Analysis Essay	Includes identification of the text being analyzed, background information, statement of the writer's purpose for writing, summary of main points of the source, and examination of the author's presentation. Shows how the author's technique and various parts of the text contribute to the theme and the author's purpose.
Evaluation Essay	Includes identification of the text being evaluated, background information, statement of the writer's purpose for writing, summary of the main points of the source, and consideration of the author's presentation. The essay includes comments on the author's success in achieving his or her purpose, usually by reviewing stylistic features and techniques. Discusses overall strengths and weaknesses.
Research Paper	Starts with a question or problem that requires collecting facts, opinions, and perspectives from books, magazines, newspapers, or other sources. The author makes sense of information derived from a variety of sources. May include literature review, analysis, or evaluation.

Readers familiar with the genres of academic writing have expectations about organization, textual features, and authors' intentions. When reading an argument essay, they assume the writer will lay out both sides of the controversial issue, make concessions to people holding opposing views and refute their claims, and marshal convincing evidence to support the thesis. Knowledge of genre is indispensable if you want to read with full comprehension. Make a conscious effort to learn new genres whenever possible.

● **PATTERNS OF ORGANIZATION AND DEVELOPMENT**   Just as you come to college already knowing something about genre, you also bring knowledge of the basic organization of texts. You can identify introductions, conclusions, theses or main idea statements, and topic sentences of paragraphs. In your own essays, you've used organizational plans, such as cause and effect or comparison and contrast. Writers use a variety of these patterns, depending on their purpose for writing. Review the organizational plans for academic writing that we presented in Table 1.1 (page 20).

Occasionally, writers tell their readers how they are going to organize material. In the introductory paragraph of her article, Moses informs us that she will explore three premises.

> "Race, higher education, and American society" are three topics that I care deeply about and have written and talked about separately on many other occasions. In this article I want to bring them together in a way that helps me to lay out three major observations that I have been thinking about as I go about my work as an anthropologist, as a spokesperson for higher education—especially public education—and as someone who still believes in the potential of American society to deliver its promise of an equitable, culturally pluralistic society. (p. 459)

When writers explain what they are doing or direct you to read in a certain way, you know what to expect. When they don't supply this information, you have to determine the pattern of development yourself.

A key to unlocking the meaning of a text is to identify the pattern of organization. A writer may use a single organizational pattern, but more likely he or she will use overlapping patterns. An initial, quick reading often gives you a sense of the text's overall organizational pattern. Keep this pattern in mind, and then, when you do a close reading, annotate the places where the author has used other patterns of development. Consider how one of our students annotated a paragraph from an article by musicologist Michael J. Budds:

Time order — In retrospect, it seems possible to identify a number of factors that help explain this radical change in musical taste. First of all, the popular song tradition of Tin Pan Alley, which had been centered in New York City and had flourished for more than three generations, began to show signs of wear. The — *Cause and effect*

Example —
search for fresh and compelling expression within the rather well-defined style became increasingly difficult. The traumatic events of World War II, moreover, made the sanitized worldview delivered in the snappy dance songs and dreamy love ballads that were hallmarks of the genre seem inappropriate or irrelevant to the new generation of youngsters. At the same time that Tin Pan Alley was reaching its peak in the songs of Gershwin, Kern, Rodgers, and Porter, two minority song traditions that had evolved from longstanding folk practice—the urban blues of black America and the country and western songs of rural white Southerners—entered the popular arena and reached a larger audience thanks to a process of commercialization that included recordings, radio stations, and more venues for live performance. The inexpensive portable transistor radio, a by-product of wartime technology, enabled young people to acquaint themselves with rhythm and blues as well as country and western music without parental knowledge or supervision.

The general plan for the paragraph is cause and effect; Budds identifies the various causes of a "radical change in musical taste." But within this overall pattern, Budds describes a time-ordered sequence of events and gives examples.

● **STYLISTIC FEATURES**   In addition to identifying the genre and organizational pattern of texts, proficient readers pay attention to stylistic features. They look at the writer's sentences and word choice, tone, and reliance on other textual sources. For a clearer understanding of stylistic features, first read the following passages and then read our comparison of Moses's and Farber's styles of writing.

Moses (paragraph 7)

Efforts to refine devices for measuring linked physical and mental traits existed well into the twentieth century. Such endeavors stimulated the development of psychometrics and the intelligence tests first used in World War I on nearly two million American military recruits. Consistent with Euro-American racial ideology, these tests were eventually put to civilian use. Psychologists interpreted results of these tests as indicators of heredity-based, innate intelligence and compared group scores to support ideologies of natural racial superiority and inferiority

(Mukhopadhyay & Moses 1997:518). Anthropology helped establish an elaborate set of ideological principles, based on racial and biological determinism, which to this day deeply influence how the world understands human variation and its relations to human behavior. This racial worldview has provided a rationale for slavery, colonial and neocolonial domination, racial segregation, and discrimination and miscegenation laws, and it has fueled the eugenics and anti-immigration movements in the United States.

Farber (paragraph 4)

Learning happens when you *want* to know. Ask yourself: did you need grades to learn how to drive? To learn how to talk? To learn how to play chess—or play the guitar—or dance—or find your way around a new city? Yet these are things we do very well—much better than we handle that French or Spanish that we were graded on for years in high school. Some of us, though, are certain that, while we might learn to drive or play chess without grades, we still need them to force us to learn the things we don't really want to learn—math, for instance. But is that really true? If for any reason you really want or need some math—say, algebra—you can learn it without being graded. And if you don't want it and don't need it, you'll probably never get it straight, grades or not. Just because you pass a subject doesn't mean you've learned it. How much time did you spend on algebra and geometry in high school? Two years? How much do you remember? Or what about grammar? How much did all those years of force-fed grammar do for you? You learn to talk (without being graded) from the people around you, not from gerunds and modifiers. And as for writing—if you ever do learn to write well, you can bet your sweet ass it won't be predicate nominatives that teach you. Perhaps those subjects that we would never study without being graded are the very subjects that we lose hold of as soon as the last test is over.

Comparison of the Stylistic Features of the Texts

Moses	*Farber*
All relatively long sentences. Sentences contain lengthy phrases or clauses.	Varied sentence length. Sentences are medium length or short, some only two to four words. He uses intentional fragments.
Some words, such as "psychometrics," are challenging. Language is formal.	Accessible, everyday words. Language is very informal.
Formal tone.	Informal tone.

Third-person point of view.	Second-person point of view, addressing the reader directly with the pronoun *you*.
Cites other sources and relies on readers' knowledge of history and scholarly concepts such as "neocolonialism."	Includes no references to outside sources. Makes a number of appeals to the reader's experience

Our analysis is based on five features of the text: *choice of sentences, words, tone, point of view,* and *reliance on other textual sources.* We looked first at sentence type, length, and complexity. All of Moses's sentences are straightforward statements, whereas almost half of Farber's sentences are questions addressed to the reader. Moses's sentences are relatively long, and some contain lengthy phrases: "Consistent with Euro-American racial ideology." Farber varies the length of his sentences between medium-sized and very short sentences. Some of Farber's sentences contain dependent clauses, but these longer sentences are balanced by intentional sentence fragments like "Or what about grammar?" that add to the informal tone.

Our next consideration was the authors' word choice. Moses uses words such as *miscegenation* and *eugenics.* Farber uses common, everyday language and an informal vocabulary bordering on vulgarity in *you can bet your sweet ass.* In general, Farber's language is down to earth while Moses includes words that are not commonly used outside the academic community.

The above features—sentence type, length, and complexity as well as word choice—contribute to the author's voice and tone. Moses's tone is formal and scholarly; Farber's is informal and chatty. Another feature contributing to tone is point of view. Moses writes in the third person; Farber addresses the reader in the second person, *you.*

The last stylistic feature we examined is called *intertextuality.* Intertextuality is the relationship between texts. It refers to the way writers relate other texts to their own text, often by incorporating the other texts in the form of direct quotations, paraphrases, summaries, or other types of references. Moses bolsters her position by referring to a previous publication. She also relies on the readers' knowledge of academic concepts, such as *biological determinism.* Farber doesn't refer to prior publications or academic concepts. Instead, he asks questions that evoke his readers' personal experiences.

Our textual analysis leads us to conclude that Moses writes in a formal style characteristic of many genres of academic writing. She uses long sentences, sophisticated language, a scholarly tone, and references to prior publications. In contrast, Farber has a relaxed, conversational style that we associate with informal writing.

We have provided a detailed analysis of the Moses and Farber passages in order to show you the roles stylistic features play in writing. We don't expect you to perform an exhaustive textual analysis each time you read a text. However, knowledge of the five stylistic features we have discussed—sentence type, length, and complexity; word choice; tone; point of view; and intertextuality—will better enable you to read critically and appreciate how the writer's style contributes to the text. On the occasions when you wish to delve deeper, ask yourself the following questions.

QUESTIONS FOR ANALYZING THE STYLISIC FEATURES OF TEXTS

- Does the writer vary the type of sentences? Do all the sentences function as statements, or do some ask questions, give commands, or express exclamations?
- What does the length of the sentences convey?
- What can you say about sentence complexity? Are the sentences simple and unpretentious or complex, remote, and scholarly?
- Does the writer put verbs into active or passive voice?
- Does the writer use difficult or specialized words?
- How would you describe the point of view, voice, and tone? Does the writer use the first person (I, we), the second person (you), or the third person (he, she, it, they)?
- How often does the writer draw on other sources? How do the references to other texts further the writer's agenda?
- What do your answers to the preceding questions indicate about the author's writing style? Write a paragraph summarizing the style.

Your professors will undoubtedly assign texts that are more like Moses's than Farber's. As Moses does, scholarly writers frequently draw on evidence from prior publications or original research, taking care to cite and document their sources. They adopt formal tones and use lengthy, rather complex sentences. They often use specialized vocabulary or technical terms as well. But you will also be assigned texts by academic writers who use conversational, less formal writing styles like Farber's. One style is not necessarily more appropriate than the other.

It is difficult to make generalizations about academic writing style or describe it as a distinct entity. In academia, there are many different writing styles ranging from the prescribed style of the scientific research article in an upper level chemistry course to the relaxed style of free verse in an introduction to creative writing. Disciplines such as economics, finance, and accounting require textual features like headings and subheadings, enumeration, and figures and charts. Other disciplines, like engineering, stress the importance of visual and numeral texts.

In your own work, you will learn to write in styles that are appropriate to the rhetorical situation. The lab reports you write in biology will be formal, with concise sentences describing procedural matters. The personal essays you compose in English will be less formal with free-flowing sentences rich in descriptive detail.

● **INTERTEXTUALITY**   Of all the stylistic features we have discussed, the one that best characterizes academic discourse is the practice of drawing on other texts. Academic texts depend on other texts for their meaning. Sometimes writers simply refer to other sources, but more often they paraphrase, quote, or summarize them, always citing the author and providing bibliographic information for their readers. Let us illustrate with another example from Moses's article:

> Greater access to higher education for minorities has translated into better performance on standard school tests for their children. Grissmer, Kirby, Berends, and Williamson (1994) showed tremendous increases in the verbal and math proficiency scores of Black thirteen-to-seventeen-year-olds between 1970 and 1990 as measured by the National Assessment of Educational Progress (NAEP) Test. (p. 463)

Moses refers to ideas in Grissmer, Kirby, Berends, and Williamson's book, *Student Achievement and the Changing Family*, published in 1994. She names the scholars and puts in parentheses the date of the publication. If readers want to know the book's title or if they wish to learn more about the research, they can consult the alphabetical list of references on the last pages of the Moses selection and then locate the book in the library.

Another distinctive feature of academic writing is content endnotes or footnotes. When writers want to give their readers additional information but don't want to interrupt the flow of the text, they provide a reference numeral in the text and include the extra information in a footnote or in a list titled "Notes" at the end of the selection. Here is an example from Michael J. Budds's scholarly article on popular music.

> Song texts of mainstream America had long been influenced by the high culture of Europe, however watered down for middle-class consumption. Romantic love, the subject of the vast majority of all songs, was treated in a highly idealistic, typically sentimental manner. Although rarely profound, the language tended toward the poetic, preferring a high-priced vocabulary filled with euphemism and fully respectful of an unwritten, but widely sanctioned code of public propriety. Songs with texts overstepping this sensibility were banned by radio stations or deleted from the musical scores of Broadway and Hollywood.[7] Early in the nineteenth century, for example, Stephen Foster's Jeanie was "borne like a vapor on the summer air."

7. The grand exception appears to be songwriter/composer Cole Porter (1891–1964), whose witty but suggestive lyrics earned for him the nickname "the genteel pornographer" from Cecil Smith in *Musical Comedy in America* (New York: Theatre Arts Books, 1950).

The convention of drawing on other texts is not confined to academic writing. Writers whose work originally appeared in newspapers or popular magazines tend to cite, paraphrase, quote, and summarize sources without supplying bibliographic information for the reader. The convention of meticulously citing sources is not always observed outside the academic community. Sometimes magazine writers even cite facts without explaining where they came from, and depending on their editorial policies, some newspapers publish stories based on the statements of unnamed sources.

READING FOR RHETORICAL CONTEXT

For proficient readers, the rhetorical context of a text is as important as its content and stylistic features. The word *rhetorical* relates to *rhetoric*. Many people who hear the word *rhetoric* think of pretentious language. "Politicians' speeches are all rhetoric" means that politicians use empty or inflated language. Either they do not say very much or they divert attention from where it should be. When we speak of rhetoric in this book, we do not mean pompous language. We mean *an author's attempt to use language to achieve an intended effect on an audience.* An important word here is *intended*. Both writing and reading are intentional. They are deliberate actions, guided by a purpose or goal.

We wrote this textbook with a clear purpose: to show you how to become competent readers and writers in the academic community. As you read this book, you should have a clear purpose: to learn how to write for your college courses. Without purpose, the acts of reading and writing are meaningless.

When you are reading for content, genre, organization, and stylistic features, you are focusing on the text itself. This type of analysis is called *textual analysis*. But another type of analysis is also important: *contextual analysis*. Contextual analysis examines *the author's purpose and motivation for writing the text, the intended audience, the circumstances surrounding the text's production, the author's position toward other writers and other texts, and the larger conversation of which the text is part.* As rhetoric scholar Jack Selzer (2008) argues,

> Textual analysis, strictly speaking, need not attend to such matters; it can proceed as if the item under consideration "speaks for all time" somehow, as if it is a sort of museum piece unaffected by time and space just as surely as, say, an ancient altarpiece once housed in a church might be placed on a pedestal in a museum. Museums have their functions, and they certainly permit people to observe and appreciate objects in an important way. But just as certainly as museums often fail to retain a vital sense of an art work's original context and cultural meaning; in that sense museums can diminish understanding as much as they contribute to it. Contextual rhetorical analysis, however, as an attempt to understand communications through the lens of their environments, does attend to the setting or scene out of which any com-

munication emerges. It does strive to understand an object of analysis as an integral part of culture. (p. 292)

Equally as important as the environment in which the text was written is the environment in which the text is read. You also need to consider the rhetorical context of the act of reading—the reader's purpose and the circumstances surrounding the reading. In this section, we present sets of questions for analyzing both contexts as a means of improving comprehension. You can answer some of these questions by drawing inferences from the text itself. Other questions require you to undertake research. We first discuss the context of the text itself and then move on to the context of your own act of reading.

● **CONTEXT OF THE TEXT**   To illustrate the process of analyzing the rhetorical context of a text, we walk you through an analysis of Jerry Farber's "A Young Person's Guide to the Grading System" on pages 184–188. Take time to read the essay carefully before you continue.

> ## QUESTIONS FOR ANALYZING THE RHETORICAL CONTEXT OF A TEXT
>
> - For whom is the author writing, and what do you perceive as the effect the author intends to have on this audience?
> - What do you know about the author's background and credibility?
> - What prompted the author to write the text? Can you identify a circumstance, event, or social practice?
> - How is the author drawing on other writers and other texts? How does he or she view what others have said about the topic?

To answer these questions, you have to take two courses of action. You have to step inside the author's head to discover his or her intentions, and you have to conduct research into the circumstances surrounding the text's production. In some cases, the writer's motives are obvious. When you receive an advertisement in the mail, you know that the ad writers want to convince you to buy something. They are also attempting to please their employers and earn a paycheck. True, they may have other motives that you can't discern—for instance, striving to win a promotion or an advertising industry award—but their primary goals are clear. The goals of academic writers are not as obvious as those of advertisers. The text itself gives you insights into the imperative—the feeling, view, incident, or phenomenon—that inspired the author to write, but you also need to do some research.

For whom is the author writing, and what do you perceive as the effect the author intends to have on this audience? This is a crucial question for determining the rhetorical context. A proficient writer tailors the text to the needs of a particular group of readers. If you can identify the audience, you're well on your way to determining what the author is trying to accomplish. An important factor is where the text was published. Was it published in book form or as an article in an academic journal or a popular magazine? Academic writers write for the university community, whereas staff writers for news magazines like *Newsweek* or *Time* direct their articles to a general audience. Certain writers address readers of a particular political persuasion. Writers for *The National Review* anticipate a readership that is conservative, whereas writers for *The Nation* expect their readers to be liberal.

Farber's essay originally appeared in book form as part of a collection of essays he published in 1970. In the essay, he mentions educational reform at all levels, but most of his comments relate to the undergraduate college. He speaks directly to students, referring to their experiences with the grading system, but he also addresses an audience other than students. In his last paragraph, he asks, "But what about the students themselves? Can they live without grades? Can they learn without them?" Here he addresses an audience concerned about students—perhaps professors, college administrators, or parents.

Next, we ask about Farber's impact on these two audiences. What does he expect them to do or think after reading the essay? This question gets to the heart of writers' goals. Some writers want to prompt overt changes in the behavior of readers. For example, the writer of an article on ozone depletion warns readers to reduce their use of air conditioners and aerosol cans. Other authors intend to change opinions. The author of a biography of Mozart encourages readers to accept a new interpretation of the composer's significance. Many writers work to make more subtle changes in readers' perspectives. A journalist provides conflicting information on a Supreme Court decision. She does not want her readers to favor or oppose the court decision. In the tradition of news reporting, she wants to provide them with accurate and detailed information that will help them arrive at sound decisions of their own. The writer's intended impact is to prompt independent and informed thought in the reader.

Farber's intentions are clear. He wants to persuade his readers to adopt his position on grades and his broader plan for an educational system that depends less on what he terms "Mickey-Mouse requirements." In contrast, Moses's essay is not overtly argumentative in tone. Yet Moses intends to influence her audience. Presumably, she wants her readers to derive from her article a new way of understanding certain aspects of American culture. Specifically, she wants to provide her readers with a theoretical framework for understanding the role race plays in American higher education.

What do you know about the author's background and credibility? The introductory material preceding the Farber selection gives a brief biographical sketch.

Jerry Farber, a civil rights activist and professor of English and comparative literature at San Diego State University, is author of many books and articles of social and literary criticism. His work had an impact on the student movement of the late 1960s and early 1970s. The following essay was published in 1970 in a collection of essays and stories entitled *The Student as Nigger.* Farber is using the analogy in the title to describe students as slaves of teachers and administrators.

Further research tells us that Farber (born 1935) wrote for the *Los Angeles Free Press* from 1965 to 1968 and taught at California State University at Los Angeles from 1962 to 1968 and later at the University of Paris. He is the author of two other books, *The University of Tomorrowland* (1972) and *A Field Guide to the Aesthetic Experience* (1982). This information makes clear that Farber is a credible author and scholar. We found this biographical material by going to www.google.com and searching for *Jerry Farber* and *The Student as Nigger,* the author's name and the title of the book in which the essay was published.

What prompted the author to write the text? Can you identify a circumstance, event, or social practice? As was the case for question one, we can answer this question in part by analyzing the text itself, but we also have to do some research. Farber focuses the essay on a common educational practice: grading. He argues passionately that he is vehemently opposed to the A through F grading system. We can infer that he wrote the essay to express his outrage, to convince his readers that grades hinder learning, and to provoke them to support educational reform. Farber wrote the essay over forty years ago. To discover more about the circumstances, events, and social practices of the time, we set out to do some research.

We found that the Lone Star College Kingwood Library maintains a comprehensive Web site devoted to American cultural history in the nineteenth and twentieth centuries, including a series of Web guides for each decade. A visit to *http://lonestar.edu/decades.html* and a click on *1960–1969* tells us that college campuses were highly volatile centers of debate in the 1960s. It was a time of social unrest: civil rights demonstrations, antiwar rallies, and unprecedented student protest directed toward many facets of American society, including education. Knowing the historical period when Farber wrote enables us to put his essay in a rich, multilayered context. Even though the essay still has relevance today, it is part of a larger cultural conversation that took place five decades ago. Another useful Web site for historical research is Best of History Web Sites: *http://www.besthistorysites.net.*

How is the author drawing on other writers and other texts? How does he or she view what others have said about the topic? Many academic texts are multivocal because they represent the voices of many different writers. As we noted earlier, academic writers often draw on the words and utterances of other writers. Sometimes the author simply mentions another writer or text. Other times the text is quoted, paraphrased, or summarized. Writers draw on other texts to acknowledge what other individuals have written about the topic, to provide the reader with background, to support their position, and to develop their argument.

We can categorize the ways authors use sources to build arguments according to the following scheme. A writer constructs a *one-dimensional argument* by presenting a thesis and supporting it with texts that argue a similar viewpoint. A writer creates a *two-dimensional argument* by drawing on sources for direct support and also for counterarguments. A two-dimensional argument anticipates and deals with views that are contrary to those of the writer. Farber makes a two-dimensional argument: he anticipates what supporters of grades might say about his proposal to eliminate grades and responds to their concerns. Farber does not refer to other writers or make explicit use of other texts. As we explained earlier, we cannot make generalizations about academic writing.

● **RHETORICAL CONTEXT OF YOUR READING**   As a critical reader, you should be just as aware of the circumstances surrounding the process of your own reading as you are of the circumstances surrounding the production of the assigned text. Keep in mind that there are degrees of separation between you and the author. Liz Mandrell addresses English teachers in "Zen and the Art of Grade Motivation," an article originally published in *English Journal*. It is important to acknowledge that the audience the writer had in mind is not the only audience that ends up reading the text.

When you read a text, either one that is assigned or one chosen independently, be sure to enunciate clear-cut goals. For novels and popular magazines, your goal is pure enjoyment. For academic texts, your goal is more functional. In college writing courses, you will be asked to read sources and then write about them. If your assignment is to summarize the source, you will read with the goal of extracting and rewording the author's main ideas. If your assignment is to respond to the text, you will read for the purpose of generating reactions to the author's argument. Effective readers tailor their reading goals and strategies to the task at hand.

Reading to write, reading a text in preparation for a writing assignment, also requires a clear rhetorical purpose. This purpose should guide your reading as well as your writing. It should speak to the two roles you are assuming: reader and writer.

The first step in reading to write is making sure that you fully understand the writing assignment. Examine the assignment carefully. Underline key words that are crucial to your aim and purpose in writing. Ask yourself the following questions.

QUESTIONS TO ASK ABOUT ASSIGNMENTS

- What is the topic or issue you will be writing about?
- As you read, can you find key words or phrases that signal material that is relevant to your topic?
- Who is the audience for your paper, and what are this audience's needs?
- Does the assignment require you to adopt a particular perspective on the issue, a recognizable genre, or a particular plan of development?
- Do you already hold a position on the issue that you intend to develop or defend?

Answering these questions helps you develop a mind-set for the assignment. Then you can fit relevant parts of the text into this mental image as you read.

For example, assume that you are asked to write an essay in which you summarize and respond to Moses's article on race and higher education. In this case, you will read with two distinct purposes: to identify Moses's main points and to relate your own opinion and knowledge about race and education to Moses's discussion. Your notes and annotations will reflect these two reading goals. However, if your assignment is to write an essay explaining the evolution of affirmative action in higher education, your reading will focus on turning points in the history of that issue. Your reading goals will also change depending on whether your essay is intended for an audience of professors or an audience of students.

When you receive a writing assignment, articulate a rhetorical purpose that will drive your reading of the text. The purpose will suggest a method of structuring the textual information. Consider the following rhetorical purposes and the corresponding plans for organizing the material in Moses's article.

Purpose	Plan
Explain anthropologists' assertion that race is culturally rather than biologically determined	Group by the arguments for and against both biological and cultural determinism
Argue for or against affirmative action	Group by reasons affirmative action is either helpful or harmful to society
Explain the history of the anthropological scholarship on race	Group anthropological concepts in time order
Describe the impact that the concept of biological determinism has had on American society	Group by various aspects of American culture that have been influenced by the concept of biological determinism

When you read with the goal of fitting the source information into a specific rhetorical plan, you read more efficiently and you're better able to extract relevant ideas from complex texts. A major advantage of rhetorical reading is that it is active and goal-driven. If you read just to get through the required number of pages, you will recall little, especially if the text is challenging. Rhetorical reading is purposeful reading. It increases the likelihood that you will comprehend the material, and it lays the groundwork for writing.

Reading and Interpretation

In this chapter, we recommended a variety of reading strategies. As we mentioned earlier, there is more than one way to understand a text. Scholars argue long and hard about the meaning of a single passage in a text important to their discipline. Or they discover a new interpretation of a text that was long assumed to be adequately understood. It should come as no surprise that when students with varying degrees of prior knowledge read the same text, they may interpret it differently. Similarly, students who read for a particular purpose interpret a text differently from readers with other goals. A text may have several interpretations, some of which conflict. Often class discussions center on comparing and contrasting various interpretations of texts.

Sometimes our students argue that the author's intended meaning is sacrosanct and more important than the reader's interpretation. Even if this were true, we can't be sure that we have arrived at the definitive interpretation of the text. We cannot contact an author each time we are in doubt about what his or her text means. Viewing the author as the ultimate judge of debates about meaning does not help us solve the everyday problems of interpretation. Once ideas appear in print, readers have to interpret them as best they can.

Are we implying that you are a prisoner of your prior knowledge and experience, doomed to a subjective interpretation of every text you read? Not necessarily. Many texts have unambiguous meanings upon which most readers agree. In this chapter, our objective is to make you aware of the factors that influence your interpretation of texts so that you can see beyond the bounds of your own experiences. Once you recognize you are reading Farber's article from the perspective of a student in the twenty-first century, you are free to speculate about how students in the 1960s and 1970s reacted to the essay. As you become more aware of how the rhetorical situation affects your understanding, you become a better reader.

Table 4.2 Summary of the Guidelines for the Reading Process

1. Call up your prior knowledge and feelings about the topic.
2. Preview the text and derive questions that will guide your close reading.

As You Read

1. Annotate the text and take notes.
2. Identify the genre. Given the genre, what expectations do you have about the way the article will be organized?
3. Identify how the author has organized his or her ideas. What is the principal pattern of development? Does it overlap with other patterns?
4. Identify the stylistic features of the text by answering the following questions:
   - Does the writer vary the type of sentences? Do all the sentences function as statements, or do some ask questions, give commands, or express exclamations?
   - What does the length of the sentences convey?
   - What can you say about sentence complexity? Are the sentences simple and unpretentious or complex, remote, and scholarly?

- Does the writer put verbs in active or passive voice?
- Does the writer use difficult or specialized words?
- How would you describe the point of view, voice, and tone? Does the writer use the first person (I, we), the second person (you), or the third person (he, she, it, they)?
- How often does the writer draw on other sources? How do the references to other texts further the writer's agenda?

After You Read

Identify the rhetorical context of the text by answering following questions:

- For whom is the author writing, and what do you perceive as the effect the author intends to have on this audience?
- What do you know about the author's background and credibility?
- What prompted the author to write the text? Can you identify a circumstance, event, or social practice?
- How is the author drawing on other writers and other texts? How does he or she view what others have said about the topic?

Identify the rhetorical context of your own reading by answering the following questions:

- What is the topic or issue you will be writing about?
- As you read, can you find key words or phrases that signal material that is relevant to your topic?
- Who is the audience for your paper, and what are this audience's needs?
- Does the assignment require you to adopt a particular perspective on the issue, a recognizable genre, or a particular plan of development?
- Do you already hold a position on the issue that you intend to develop or defend?

Tackling Difficult Course Readings

The Yolanda Moses article that we analyzed in this chapter is a first-rate example of academic writing: Moses writes for an educated audience interested in the role of race in American higher education. She maintains a scholarly tone, and she includes numerous references to publications in the field. Even though the article is scholarly, it is readable because the subject matter is familiar and the language is accessible. But not all the reading you are assigned in college courses will be as easy to understand. Consider the opening paragraph of Paulo Freire's (1967) *The Pedagogy of the Oppressed*, a classic academic text frequently assigned in education courses:

> While the problem of humanization has always, from an axiological point of view, been man's central problem, it now takes on the character of an inescapable concern. Concern for humanization leads at once to the recognition of dehumanization, not only as an ontological possibility but as a historical reality. And as man perceives the extent of dehumanization, he asks himself if humanization is a viable possibility. Within history, in concrete, objective contexts, both humanization and dehumanization are possibilities for man as an uncompleted being conscious of his incompletion. (p. 1)

This passage poses comprehension problems comparable to the ones we confronted when we read the Kierkegaard passage. Kierkegaard assumes his readers are already familiar with ongoing academic discussions of the definition of self. Freire assumes his readers are familiar with "the problem of humanization." The Freire passage presents the additional challenge of difficult vocabulary, with words like *axiological* and *ontological*. In fairness to Freire, we should mention that his book is translated into English from his native language of Portuguese. We don't know if the text is more readable in the original, but we do know that the English translation is difficult reading for students in our teacher education programs.

The strategies we covered earlier in the chapter will help you unpack the meaning of demanding academic texts, but you need additional techniques as well.

Strategies for Comprehending Complex Texts

1. Allow adequate time to read.
2. Work with classmates.
3. Use a dictionary.
4. Read sentence by sentence.
5. Ask questions in class.

1. Allow adequate time to read. A significant barrier to understanding complex texts is attempting to complete the reading the night before it is due. If you open your books only when tests are looming and you don't make academic reading part of your daily schedule, you will find yourself skimming complex readings with minimal comprehension.

Complex academic texts take longer to read than magazine articles, newspapers, or novels. Paulo Freire's short book, *The Pedagogy of the Oppressed,* would take a period of days, possibly weeks, to comprehend, whereas a thriller novel of the same length could be read in a single sitting.

No shortcut will significantly reduce reading time for complex texts. Study-skill strategies like skimming and reading headings and subheadings do not work well for dense academic prose. Academic readings vary in difficulty, so preview your reading assignments well in advance of the deadlines. That way you can gauge how much time you will need to complete them. As a rule of thumb, start difficult readings several days before they are due.

2. Work with classmates. Gather several classmates together for study sessions devoted to the collaborative reading of complex texts. Your professors may encourage or even require you to participate in collaborative learning groups that meet outside of regular class hours. If not, go ahead and form groups of your own. Group members pool their intellectual resources to unlock the meaning of difficult texts, and they encourage and motivate each other to succeed. Reading complex texts is hard work; it helps to share the load.

The group activity can be as simple as taking turns reading aloud, stopping at points where anyone loses the train of thought. Or group members could read silently, stopping periodically, perhaps at the end of a page, to discuss the content. If you wish to structure the activity, you could engage in an exercise called **reciprocal reading** with a group of three. Group members read the text independently, marking the spots where comprehension breakdown occurs. When the group convenes, the members take turns reading the designated passages aloud. After reading a passage, the student does what we call a **think aloud.** She rereads the passage out loud, sentence by sentence, and tells the others the thoughts that are going through her head. In other words, she makes audible to her listeners the mental process she engages in while reading. In so doing, she demonstrates where and how her comprehension broke down. Then the other two members of the group take turns assuming the role of reader, reading the passage and then thinking aloud. After all three think alouds, the group members reach a consensus on their comprehension and interpretation of the difficult text. If questions and doubts persist, they consult with the professor.

Although collaborative reading is a slow process, it is more efficient than working alone. Within a group, you are less likely to become frustrated and lay the complex text aside. The encouragement and fellowship of the group keeps you on task. In our culture, we view reading as a solitary activity that is best done in complete silence. It doesn't have to be that way. In the Middle Ages, literate Europeans read aloud, even when no one else was around. Hearing the words provides another avenue for understanding the content.

3. Use a dictionary. Since spell checkers are widely available, many students think they don't need a dictionary. But a college-level dictionary is invaluable, especially for looking up the definitions of complex words like *humanization, axiological,* and *ontological,* from the Freire passage we examined earlier. Using

Webster's New World Dictionary of the American Language, third college edition, we obtained the following definitions for Freire's terms:

> humanize: to make humane; make kind, merciful, considerate, etc.; civilize; refine

> axiology: the branch of philosophy dealing with the nature of values and the types of value, as in morals, aesthetics, religion, and metaphysics

> ontology: the branch of metaphysics dealing with the nature of being, reality or ultimate substance

The definition of *ontology* includes the word *metaphysics,* defined as "the branch of philosophy that deals with first principles and seeks to explain the nature of being or reality." Dictionary definitions take us a long way toward understanding Freire's paragraph. We conclude that it means

> The problem of getting people to treat each other humanely has always been philosophers' most important concern, but now it has become a central problem for everyone.

4. Read sentence by sentence. You may need to tackle dense texts sentence by sentence in order to avoid becoming overwhelmed by the language. Part of the difficulty in reading the Freire paragraph is that one difficult sentence follows another. Because of this cascade effect, readers become increasingly confused as they proceed through the paragraph. Try to unpack each sentence rather than read a paragraph or more and then pause to consider what was said. Armed with our dictionary definitions, we were able to decipher Freire's passage one sentence at a time. Try to figure out each sentence by yourself before reading our paraphrases. Freire's text is followed by the paraphrase.

> While the problem of humanization has always, from an axiological point of view, been man's central problem, it now takes on the character of an inescapable concern.

> > The problem of getting people to treat each other humanely has always been philosophers' most important concern, but now it has become a central problem for everyone.

> Concern for humanization leads at once to the recognition of dehumanization, not only as an ontological possibility but as a historical reality.

> > Once we begin to focus on getting people to treat others humanely, we become more aware of inhuman behavior, both as a theoretical possibility and as an occurrence in everyday life.

> And as man perceives the extent of dehumanization, he asks himself if humanization is a viable possibility.

> There is so much inhumane behavior in the world that one begins to wonder if it is possible to get people to treat each other humanely.

Within history, in concrete, objective contexts, both humanization and dehumanization are possibilities for man as an uncompleted being conscious of his incompletion.

> In actuality, people are capable of behaving both humanely and inhumanely, but we realize that we have the potential to develop further.

When the language is simplified, Freire's assertions are not so daunting. By looking up a few key terms and zeroing in on the text sentence by sentence, we get to the core of Freire's ideas.

5. Ask questions in class. Students who have difficulty understanding assigned readings lay low in class discussions because they want to avoid embarrassment. To succeed in college, you need to become an active learner who admits to having problems with comprehension. On the days you are confused about the reading assignment, you should be active in class. Here are questions to ask your professor.

1. How was the author educated?
2. What is his or her principal field?
3. Who is the intended audience? For whom did the author write the text?
4. What basic background knowledge do we need to understand the text?
5. How is the author using p (insert a word)?
6. In this sentence, does the author mean (give your paraphrase of the text)?

These questions show the professor that you are making an effort to understand the reading. Avoid questions that pass responsibility off to the professor, such as "Freire's too hard to read. What is his point?" Make sure you actually do the reading instead of relying on your professor to explain the concepts contained in the texts. Some students can do well in high-school courses without reading their textbooks, since all the content is covered in class. College professors may not go over reading assignments that they expect students to have already read and fully understood. Instead, they supplement the reading with additional material and offer commentary. The responsibility for keeping up with and comprehending course readings is on your shoulders, not your professor's.

READINGS

Race, Higher Education, and American Society

Yolanda T. Moses

Yolanda T. Moses is Professor of Anthropology at the University of California–Riverside. Her research interests include cultural change and the relationship between cultural diversity and public policy. She has served as president of the City University of New York, the American Association for Higher Education, and the American Anthropological Association. In addition, she has been a member of the board of trustees of the Ford Foundation and Dean and Professor of Anthropology at California State Polytechnic University–Pomona. She is the coauthor of How Real Is Race?: A Sourcebook on Race, Culture, and Biology *(2007) and* Strategies in Teaching Anthropology *(1999).*

The article was originally published in The Journal of Anthropological Research, *a scholarly journal that publishes original research from across the globe in all areas of anthropology. It is based on a JAR Distinguished Lecture that was originally delivered by Professor Moses and later edited into publishable form by Lawrence Straus.*

Prereading

How much does race matter on your college campus? Is diversity promoted or merely tolerated? Are there any racial tensions or animosities? Are any of the deeper racial problems in our society reflected in your school? Freewrite for ten minutes in response to these questions.

This article explores three connected premises: first, that folk beliefs about the immutable nature of race are prevalent in society today; second, that there is a social and cultural reluctance to discuss the American racialized worldview; and, third, that there is the potential for American policy makers and society at large to reembrace biological determinism and social Darwinism at the millennium. The author suggests that anthropologists have a major role to play in educating a wider public about race, cultural pluralism, and diversity in education. Anthropologists should do this by (1) articulating for a general audience what race is and what it is not; (2) providing an anthropological analysis of higher education as a public right or a public good; (3) providing an anthropological analysis of the contemporary American culture of education and educational success; and (4) explaining American paradoxical behavior concerning affirmative action.

1   "Race, higher education, and American society" are three topics that I care deeply about and have written and talked about separately on many other occasions. In this article I want to bring them together in a way that helps me to lay out three major observations that I have been thinking about as I go about my work as an anthropologist, as a spokesperson for higher education—especially public higher education—and as someone who still believes in the potential of American society to deliver on its promise of an equitable, culturally pluralistic society.

2   The first observation is that the folk beliefs about the fixed, immutable nature of biological "race" are alive and well in American culture today. Anthropologists have made pronouncements that there is no such thing as biological race, that "it's not race, it's clines," and that race is socially and culturally constructed (Brace, 1982; Goodman, 1996; Mukhopadhyay and Moses, 1997). But I contend that recent academic policies and/or state initiatives (for example, in California and Washington State) that in effect restrict access by people of color, women, and poor Whites to higher education are not *logical* from an educational, quality-of-life, or economic perspective. They neither correlate with national polls on diversity nor do they correlate necessarily with the values of the presidents, faculties, and staffs on campuses across the country that must enforce these policies. Something else is going on. I am concerned that well-meaning educators may unwittingly buy into social Darwinist theories which will then be used by those who want to keep "the other" (minorities and women) in their place.

3   The second and even more disturbing observation is how this racial worldview is not even talked about directly—but it is hidden in buzzwords within a vocabulary of respectability. This vocabulary is made up of words like "excellence," "quality," or "qualified"—as in "we want to hire the most qualified person." The word "merit" is used as if it is itself a unilinear measure, and the Scholastic Aptitude Test (SAT) has taken on almost holy dimensions in its applications, *contrary* to what research shows about its lack of predictability for measuring the success of women or people of color. Why is this happening now, at this point of time in American cultural history?

4   Third, and perhaps the most disturbing of all, is the potential for reasonable people at the end of the twentieth century and of the millennium to get back into a nineteenth-century biologically determinist mode of

accepting the notions of fixed racial, gender, and class hierarchies all over again. We have seen that in the nineteenth century, these stereotypes and "scientific truths" helped to justify the social, economic, and political status quo in European colonies in Africa and Asia, as well as in the Americas (Smedley 1993). What is the motivation today, precisely at a time when American demographics are more complex than ever?

5   Finally, I will discuss ways in which anthropologists *can* and do make a difference in educating ourselves, our students, and a wider public about how to get clarity and understanding concerning the issues of race, racism, human diversity, and American cultural values. We must give voice to that which remains unspoken and is *deafening* in its silence.

RACE: IS IT BIOLOGICAL OR CULTURAL?

Race—A New Paradigm

6   Modern anthropology's roots lie in nineteenth-century European natural history traditions, with their focus on the classification and comparison of human populations and their search for indicators of "mental capacity." Cultural anthropologists such as L.H. Morgan and E.B. Tylor worked with physical anthropologists of the time to "scientifically" reconstruct human prehistory and to rank human groups along a unilinear evolutionary path from "savagery" to "civilization." Morgan considered mental development crucial to a group's evolutionary progress. Physical indicators of evolutionary rank were developed, including such attributes as the degree of facial projection and the position of the foramen magnum. Measurements of cranial dimensions and proportions ("the cephalic index") were initially proposed as indicators of advancement. Cranial size and the weight and morphological complexity of the brain were other measures used to infer the "mental capacity" of various groups (e.g., "races," sexes, immigrant groups) according to their "natural" "intellectual endowments," which presumably identified their overall evolutionary rank (Mukhopadhyay and Moses 1997:518).

7   Efforts to refine devices for measuring linked physical and mental traits existed well into the twentieth century. Such endeavors stimulated the development of psychometrics and the intelligence tests first used in World War I on nearly two million American military recruits. Consistent with Euro-American racial ideology, these tests were eventually put to civilian use. Psychologists interpreted results of these tests as indicators of heredity-based, innate intelligence and compared group scores to support ideologies of natural racial superiority and inferiority (Mukhopadhyay and Moses 1997:518). Anthropology helped establish an elaborate set of ideological principles, based on racial and biological determinism, which to this day deeply influence how the world under-

stands human variation and its relations to human behavior. This racial worldview has provided a rationale for slavery, colonial and neocolonial domination, racial segregation, and discrimination and miscegenation laws, and it has fueled the eugenics and anti-immigration movements in the United States.

8   On the other hand, anthropology—both cultural and biological—played a major role in twentieth-century attempts to transform and dismantle the American racial worldview. From Franz Boas, who as early as 1897 questioned the key assumption in American racial ideology, to the rise of population genetics in the 1930s to 1950s, American anthropologists have sought to dismantle the Euro-American racial worldview. A paradigm shift was in the making, from old typological and morphological definitions of static races to the consideration of dynamic populations with overlapping physical distributions of traits. Yet even the rise of population genetics was not sufficient to eradicate the old racial worldview. To those who wanted to maintain "racial" purity, population genetics actually offered a way to potentially identify and eradicate "bad" genes, such as the genes for homosexuality, criminal behavior, etc.

9   During the 1940s, anthropologists reexamined the racial worldview themes in view of Nazism and genocide. In the 1950s and the 1960s, anthropologists focused on the problems with the old racial classifications and argued for the socially and culturally constructed meaning of "race." Ashley Montagu was instrumental in disseminating new anthropological insights to the wider, nonanthropological community. Research by anthropologists in the 1960s and 1970s helped to refine the "deficit" models, which argued that African American schoolchildren lacked the verbal capacities of their Euro-American counterparts. By the 1980s, anthropology appeared to have successfully challenged—at least within the profession—central elements in the racial worldview, particularly the existence of "biological races" within the species *Homo sapiens*, as well as the common belief that American racial categories are universal, longstanding, and rooted in nature.

10   Unfortunately this shift within the anthropological community appears to have had little external impact. The American racial worldview seems to be alive and well in the popular imagination, among some of our most prominent political leaders, in the halls of academia, and even among some of our anthropological colleagues. This is strikingly apparent in the widespread attention paid to the book *The Bell Curve* (Herrnstein and Murray 1994), a 1990s version of racial determinism. It is also telling in the more popular pronouncements of radio talk-show hosts and newspaper articles that treat race as if it were still an operative biological phenomenon. "Racism"—the attitudinal, behavioral, and institutional manifestation of the American racial ideology—continues to be pervasive in American society. We anthropologists clearly must do a better job at disseminating our findings about race to a wider audience.

...*continued* Race, Higher Education, and American Society, **Yolanda T. Moses**

11   As we shift to make "race" once again the center of anthropological inquiry and praxis, we will engage both cultural and biological anthropologists in the common enterprise of reintroducing a more unified anthropological voice into contemporary conversations on race and human diversity. Here I would like to discuss the concept of "race" as it relates to the controversies in higher education that swirl around notions of intelligence and the question of who is still lacking access to higher education in this country.

12   Over the past five to seven years, practitioners have been revisiting and reexamining the nature of race in both biological and cultural anthropology (e.g., Harrison 1995; Goodman 1996; Lieberman and Jackson 1995; Blakey 1987; Marks 1995; Sacks 1994; Shanklin 1994). The conclusion of most of us is that "race" does not exist as a biological phenomenon, but rather that it is socially and culturally constructed. Having said that, we also have said how important it is to understand that this statement does not explain why people *look* different. Most lay people, and some cultural anthropologists, do not know how to explain human variability in ways that are easily understood. So, in the absence of reasonable anthropological explanation, many people tend to fall back on what they know, or what they think they know. The media and peers tend to reinforce uninformed stereotypes, and eventually these stereotypes become belief. For example, why were the sociobiological themes of Shockley's and Jensen's writings so popular with conservatives in the 1970s, and why was *The Bell Curve* such a best-seller only recently? Just a few years ago I proposed that it was because both books reinforce easy stereotypes that have long been held in this society, namely, that people of color and women are inferior to White males, and that our cultural institutions subliminally reinforce these notions in many ways, from advertising to loan policies, to work laws, to wages.

13   No one, of course, would admit to doing this, and some of it may even be subliminal, but the result is that stereotypes about particular people having certain innate characteristics get reinforced. You fill in the blanks: "Asians are smart," "Blacks are good athletes," "Latins are good lovers," etc. We live in a society preconditioned to the suggestion of fixed racial and biological categories. In times of scarcity, these stereotypes often serve as justifications to restrict access to the benefits of society.

14   How does this play out in higher education? There is the tendency for elected officials in conservative governments not to put funds where they think they are not going to do any good. This part is fiscal conservatism, but it also reflects a nineteenth-century racialized view of minorities that underlies recent challenges to affirmative action and access to universities—a belief that certain people cannot learn. This viewpoint manifests itself in popular initiatives such as Proposition 209

in California, which incidentally was coordinated by an anthropologist, Glen Custred. It has also been evident in recent cases in Texas and Michigan. I argue that these activities really mask the truth and perpetuate myths about the realities of racism in this country in general and in higher education in particular. Four of these myths are: (1) we don't need help for people of color and women because racism and sexism have ended, (2) university curricula already have been sufficiently broadened, (3) the potential for underrepresented minorities to succeed is limited since they are inherently inferior, and (4) grades and test scores constitute "merit."

THE ROLE OF HIGHER EDUCATION IN AMERICAN SOCIETY

15 The United States was originally founded as a nation that provided educational opportunities for wealthy, elite, White males. Women, people of color, and poor White males were not originally written into the Constitution as full citizens. It took the Thirteenth, Fourteenth, and Fifteenth Amendments for slaves and the Nineteenth Amendment for women to become voters in this country. Race, class, and gender issues have always been parts of the landscape of American cultures; it is still so today. Race, class, and gender have also always played roles in higher education in this country. Over the years the development of the U.S. populist notions of higher education took hold in the following ways:

16 1. The creation of municipal colleges began to address the fact that there were vast numbers of poor, immigrant people who could not afford a college education. (The City College of New York was founded in 1847, although women were not included until 1870, when Hunter College was founded.)

17 2. The Morrill Act of 1868 created land-grant colleges and universities. It established state universities that began as resources for farmers, stressing agricultural field stations. Early entrants were farmers, who were not selected against for putative reasons of academic "merit."

18 3. With World War II and the G.I. Bill, the federal government once again provided an opportunity for an even wider group of Americans to take advantage of higher education than ever before. These were generally working-class White males and people of color who had served their country in the military and who were rewarded with the opportunity to obtain postsecondary education. My father, for example, was a beneficiary of the G.I. Bill, both to attend refrigeration school and to buy a new house. He got his certificate, but he was unable to get a job in his newly acquired trade. This move of millions of Americans into colleges and universities was unprecedented and led to the further democratization of higher education in the U.S.

...*continued* Race, Higher Education, and American Society, **Yolanda T. Moses**

19   4. The 1954 *Brown v. Topeka* Supreme Court decision and the Civil
        Rights Movement of the 1960s for the first time brought Blacks,
        women, and other underrepresented minorities into universities
        that had discriminatory admissions policies, especially in the South
        and in the Southwest.

20   There are over 3,700 institutions of higher education in the United
        States. From the inception of our populist notions of democracy and
        education, there has been differential access to them. Sociologists Gun-
        nar Myrdal and W.E.B. Dubois both said that "race" would be the major
        problem for us to solve in the twentieth century. How does the most suc-
        cessful country in the world step up to the plate to talk about race and to
        tackle racism at the individual, institutional, and societal levels? If we do
        not do so, I would suggest, as others do, that our status as a great nation
        will be diminished. As a nation, we must embrace the diversity that is our
        destiny. Our universities and colleges are the place to engage the central
        issues of our cultural variety.

21   The demographics of colleges and universities have changed during
        the last three decades. For example, the percentage of women attending
        college in the United States has increased from 44 percent in 1961 to
        53 percent in 1991. In 1961 Whites comprised 97 percent of the total col-
        lege population; in 1994 they comprised only 78 percent. Blacks com-
        prised 2 percent in 1961; in 1994, 12 percent. The number of Latinos
        attending college has also increased over the past ten years. While women
        and men had previously been graduating at the same rates, over the past
        two years, data show that women have now surpassed men in college
        graduation rates—29 percent versus 26 percent (Day and Curry 1998).
        Greater access to higher education for minorities has translated into bet-
        ter performance on standard school tests for their children. Grissmer,
        Kirby, Berends, and Williamson (1994) showed tremendous increases in
        the verbal and math proficiency scores of Black thirteen-to-seventeen-
        year-olds between 1970 and 1990 as measured by the National Assess-
        ment of Educational Progress (NAEP) Test. While the scores of Whites
        increased approximately 0.1 standard deviation over that time period,
        those of Blacks increased by more than 0.6 standard deviations, and
        those of Hispanic seventeen-year-old students increased 0.2 standard
        deviations in math and more than 0.5 standard units in verbal skills
        (Grissmer et al. 1994).

22   Despite these gains, the majority of students of color, when they do
        go to college, go to community colleges and less-selective four-year col-
        leges and universities. So, if the majority of students of color go on to
        less-selective colleges and universities, then why is there a need for affir-
        mative action in higher education? Affirmative action came into exis-

tence as an Executive Order of the President of the United States to make equal opportunity a reality for those who were not able to immediately step up to the "starting line." President Lyndon Johnson justified the need for affirmative action at a speech at Howard University:

23

> You do not wipe away the scourge of centuries by saying: You are now free to go where you want, and do as you desire. . . . You do not take a person who for years has been hobbled by chains and liberate him, bring him to the starting line of a race and then say you are free to compete with all of the others, and still justly believe that you have been completely fair. (Citizens' Commission on Civil Rights 1984; quoted in Wightman n.d.:27)

24

Opponents of affirmative action argue that the Civil Rights Movement encouraged us to advocate a color-blind society in exchange for equality. Jones (1997:524) points out that, to the contrary, the Civil Rights Movement actually encouraged the removal of race as a barrier to opportunity and sought to minimize its negative impact. Affirmative action has been highly criticized because of the aggressive racial- and gender-based admissions policies that elite universities have put in place to recruit more students of color and women. If you will recall, back in 1978, in the highly celebrated Bakke decision, the issue revolved around whether a White male, Alan Bakke, had been deprived of a slot in medical school in favor of a less-qualified minority person. In ruling on this case, the Supreme Court said that a college or university could use race as one of many factors in admissions. I remember being at the Stanford University Center for Advanced Studies in the Behavioral Sciences in the summer of 1978, where I participated in a summer program called "Biological Difference and Social Inequality." The Bakke case was very much the topic of conversation. There was a split among the interdisciplinary team of researchers in the program as to whether they supported the idea. Some said that individual merit should count and that, despite past discrimination, "race" (or gender) should not be given preferential consideration in the university admissions process.

25

Today, twenty-one years later, the concept of affirmative action is just as highly contested with the lawsuits that have been filed in Texas (Hopwood) and in Michigan (Center for Individual Rights). Americans tend to favor the idea of equal opportunity but shy away from and dislike the idea of quotas and preferential treatment. Race and gender should not be given special consideration in admissions according to the Regents of the University of California, as well as other trustees of universities across the country.

26

I propose that both race and class beliefs are operating to help to maintain the status quo of exclusivity as to who goes to elite universities and colleges. In addition to a potential for increased income, graduation from an elite institution bestows upon the graduate the "right" friends, the best networks, the "right" contacts, the "right" job opportunities, and the general ability to develop relationships with people and a lifestyle that spell out "he is upper or upper-middle class" and "he/she fits in." The old cliché, "it's not what you know, it's who you know," takes on added meaning. How you walk and talk, whom you date, what parties you go to, what fraternities you pledge, etc., are often a part of the package you get when you are lucky enough to get into an elite university. I argue that affirmative action measures put White males and to a certain extent White females at a disadvantage when race is taken into account, and White males are likewise somewhat disadvantaged when gender is taken into account. Affirmative action programs create criteria which their networks, alumni, connections, legacy, social milieu, contacts, and parents' donations can't help them under affirmative action, while privilege is disadvantaged. So arguments of "fairness," "color blindness," and "race neutrality" become the buzzwords. Thus White males and females become disadvantaged, discriminated against by the system that has been set up to correct historical systemic discrimination. The sacrosanct ideal of individual rights is being pitted against what is best for the society.

RACE, CLASS, AND TEST SCORES

27   As I stated earlier, in this section I am going to discuss how salient words such as "merit" and "quality" are used in the admissions process and how a single standardized test such as the SAT figures more prominently, not less, in the arguments used by conservatives to describe why minorities are not qualified (read "worthy") to attend elite institutions. The SAT exam and the vocabulary of "worthiness" that tends to be used in connection with it create an artificial environment that reinforces the myth that individual merit and intelligence can only be measured by scores on such tests. The fact that minorities and women consistently do worse on these tests is assumed to mean that there must be some underlying immutable, natural reason for this.

28   The conservative arguments conveniently tend to ignore that "race" and "racism" are class issues and cut across class barriers as well. Education and money often cannot overcome the discrimination that even wealthy people of color (Blacks, Latinos, and Native Americans) experience in this country (Jones 1997). All group characteristics play a defining role in determining the experience and access to opportunities for an individual. Though this disparity exists across all class levels, the literature shows that the disadvantages of the poor are really exacerbated by race. While it is true that many Euro-American people are poor, it is almost exclusively Latinos and African Americans who live in concentrated poverty (Taylor 1998).

29   The isolated urban ghettos in which poor Blacks and Latinos live present fewer opportunities for educational or economic opportunity than the more economically integrated neighborhoods where low-income Whites tend to live. These neighborhoods where Blacks and Latinos tend to live were created over a long period of time through discriminatory policies and practices (Taylor 1998). The research literature also shows how positive the impact is on low-income minority students who attend school in economically and racially integrated settings. But since Blacks and Latinos tend to live in areas with a high concentration of poverty, the schools they attend tend to afford little or no opportunity for them to receive a superior education. This type of evidence counters the assumption that all low-income children, regardless of "race" or ethnicity, are disadvantaged equally. This is one of the premises underlying replacing the use of "race" with "class" as a plus factor in admissions criteria at the University of California and elsewhere.

Merit and Test Scores

30   Wightman (n.d.) looks at the history of standardized test use and the evolution of tests as the principal screening device in determining admission to higher education. She argues that those who are against affirmative action and other race-conscious policies base their arguments on the common notion that there are concrete ways of measuring merit that are fairly precise and scientific. And they argue that any departures from these supposedly valid tests result in unfair discrimination against individuals who are more deserving. Wightman shows that although a test may be statistically sound, policies based on such narrow definitions of merit tend to exclude students whose qualifications do not give them the experiences they need. These policies reinforce the status quo and continue to create a homogenous student body. Wightman's (n.d.) findings can be summarized as follows:

31   1. Factors that determine *merit* and *capacity for success*—a mixture of ability, talent, and motivation—are *not* measured by standardized tests.

32   2. Misuse of test scores for purposes beyond which they were validated have had a systematic, adverse impact on minority applicants to higher education institutions. There is a consistent difference of one standard deviation between Blacks and Whites, but this difference has not been presented as attributable to environmental factors and says nothing about capacity to achieve if given the opportunity. We are left with the perception that there is something "natural" about the differences.

33   3. A predictable differential validity exists among the different "racial" and ethnic groups that take these tests. Its origins are unknown. If

the source of this differential predictive validity is unknown, then its well-documented existence calls into question the utility of considering the test scores of *all* applicants in a uniform way (especially if the goal is to be inclusive and not exclusive).

34   4. Evidence shows that minorities are excluded when only test scores and grade-point averages are given in *substantial numbers*. However, when admitted, despite lower numerical indicators, most students succeeded.

35   I argue the point that "merit" is a cultural construct that has historically benefited certain elite people. Merit has always been multidimensional, but it has become more and more unidimensional as it is used to keep the club elite. Bowen and Bok (1998) show that letting minorities in through aggressive affirmative action has worked and worked well in the elite colleges and universities. Though we are only talking about a small group of people who get into these programs, Bowen and Bok's book, *The Shape of the River* (1998), shows that affirmative action policies have worked for the past twenty-five years to bring a small elite group of minorities into the most prestigious colleges and universities in the country. In the final part of the article, I would like to revisit this issue of access to elite universities and colleges.

IS IT RACE OR RACISM?

36   I have painted a picture in this article that Americans and American popular culture are reinforcing some of the premises that we used in the nineteenth century to justify the social hierarchy and the power base of Europeans in a colonialized world of White landowners, to justify slavery, and later to establish Jim Crow laws in the United States, in order to maintain the status quo of Whites in a social hierarchy that had put them in a privileged position. Those systems of social inequality were maintained through a pervasive and widely held belief that some groups were more wanting than others and that Whites should benefit from their superior *racial* status by having superior social status.

37   Today, while it is not quite so blatant, still there is the denial of the continuing impact of institutional racism: policies and practices in every segment of American society that work to keep poor people poor and poor people of color doubly disenfranchised.

38   One prime example that I use from my own institution is that since 1847, when the taxpayers of New York City had to support "The Free Academy," which later became City College, there has been a distrust of "those people" and their ability to learn. In the nineteenth century, the immigrants were from Southern and Eastern Europe. Today they are

from the world diaspora (especially Latin America, Africa, and Southeast Asia), as well as from the poor neighborhoods of New York City.

39   The current anti-affirmative action arguments place the blame on the shoulders of the minority groups, rather than society, to make the claim as to why disparities exist in grades and test scores between people of color (except Asians) and Whites. By ignoring centuries of institutional racism, as well as evidence that discrimination in housing, employment, health, and education continue to exist, the only supposed causes that are left are biological or natural.

40   Anthropologists must guard against this tendency in American culture to *not* talk about race and racism. The silence is deafening. How can we as anthropologists participate in the discussions about the importance of diversity and access in higher education? How can we provide opportunities for our students and the public at large to understand difference and differential performance in a nonbiological racialized way? I will discuss these issues in the last section.

CONCLUSION

41   What is it that anthropology brings to the discussion of access, "race," cultural pluralism, and diversity in higher education?

42   The first thing we bring to the discussion is a clear articulation for public use of what "race" is and what it is not. Based on the path I have taken with this article, it is clear that we must point out to the general public that the concept of biological "race" no longer exists, that "race" is culturally constructed, and that "racism" is alive and well both in American society in general and in higher education in particular.

43   Second, anthropology can provide the lenses through which the country can examine its often paradoxical behavior toward higher education in a democratic society. Is it a public right or a public good? Who should have access to it and under what conditions? From elite universities to open-access institutions, where are the contradictions and paradoxes, what are the policy issues that need to be addressed?

44   Third, anthropologists should be able to describe the contemporary culture of education and educational success. In our postcapitalist, consumer-oriented society, what students need to do to be successful is often at odds with what popular culture reinforces. Young people in contemporary American culture are reinforced to be consumers of goods and services, to have a short attention span, and not to want to work hard on homework. Hence, science and mathematics are not pursued in high schools because they are harder and take more time to do the required work. American students, by and large, are not less intelligent than high school students in the countries where more math and science work is required; they are just more lazy and less challenged.

45   So, how does this scenario play out along class, race, and ethnic lines?

46   Upper- and upper-middle-class students tend to get tutored, mentored, and advised by family members who have gone to college on how to prepare for the SAT and for the college admission process, as well as on how to negotiate the environment once the student gets there.

47   First-generation immigrant students present a different picture. They are often successful in secondary and postsecondary school because their families have not been in the United States long enough to have absorbed negative educational value habits. In addition, the families of first-generation immigrant students, while seeking better economic and political conditions, are often slow to give up their own cultural values. So the students often get reinforcement for success from their families' values, rather than negative reinforcement from their peer groups or from society at large. This may also help to explain why certain immigrant groups (such as Asian, Eastern European, South American, and Caribbean students) often do better than students who have spent their lives going through domestic inner-city school systems.

48   Working-class students of all ethnicities are at a disadvantage under this system. They are not always challenged or motivated to study because the payoffs (a good college education and employment) seem far away and there is no clear path for them to see how to achieve them. Working-class students who do make it to university are at risk, because they do not understand the educational culture nor do they have the familial support systems to help them. As a matter of fact, some African American and Latino students have been shown to actually shy away from being seen as successful in high school (Fordham 1996). Colleges and universities that have been successful with this cohort of students have used a variety of measures, including the involvement of peers, faculty, and parents as mentors and role models.

49   Fourth, we can explain why people are so upset with affirmative action policies that support the ideology of equal opportunity. After all, affirmative action is really only operative in elite institutions, where access to this kind of education is a limited good and where the people who have historically had access are now at a disadvantage under a system of racial/gender preferences. The executive branch of the government has mandated that societal needs override individual "merit" to achieve a level playing field for all citizens. This kind of anthropological analysis challenges biologically deterministic arguments about merit and shows how systems of inequality can construct biological categories to maintain favored position status. Anthropology has a critical role to play in the study of and advocacy for the establishment of a more just American society and culture, one in which diversity is not only accepted but genuinely regarded as a common good.[1]

Note

1. The text of the *JAR* Distinguished Lecture was edited into publishable form by Lawrence Straus

References Cited

Blakey, M.L., 1987, Skull Doctors: Intrinsic Social and Political Bias in the History of American Physical Anthropology, with Special Reference to the Work of Aleš Hrdlička. Critique of Anthropology 7(2):7–35.

Bowen, W., and D. Bok, 1998, The Shape of the River: Long-Term Consequences of Considering Race in College and University Admissions. Princeton, N.J.: Princeton University Press.

Brace, C.L., 1982, Comment on Redefining Race: The Potential Demise of a Concept in Physical Anthropology. Current Anthropology 23:648–49.

Day, J., and A. Curry, 1998, Educational Attainment in the United States: March 1997. Pp. 20–505 in Current Population Reports: Population Characteristics, Census Bureau. Washington, D.C.. U.S. Department of Commerce, Economic and Statistics Administration.

Fordham, S., 1996, Blacked Out: Dilemmas of Race, Identity and Success at Capital High. Chicago: University of Chicago Press.

Goodman, A., 1996, The Resurrection of Race: The Concept of Race in Physical Anthropology in the 1990s. Pp. 174–86 in Race and Other Misadventures: Essays in Honor of Ashley Montague in His Ninetieth Year (ed. by L.T. Reynolds and L. Lieberman). Dix Hills, N.Y.: General Hall Publishers.

Grissmer, D., S.N. Kirby, M. Berends, and S. Williamson, 1994, Student Achievement and the Changing Family. Santa Monica, Calif.: Rand.

Harrison, F., 1995, The Persistent Power of "Race" in the Cultural and Political Economics of "Racism." Annual Review of Anthropology 24:47–74.

Herrnstein, R.J., and C. Murray, 1994, The Bell Curve: Intelligence and Class Structure in American Life. New York: Free Press.

Jensen, A.R., 1974, How Biased Are Culture Loaded Tests? Genetic Psychology Monographs 90:185–244.

Jones, J.A., 1997, Prejudice and Racism. 2nd ed. New York: McGraw Hill.

Lieberman, L., and F. Jackson, 1995, Race and Three Models of Human Origin. American Anthropologist 97:237–42.

Marks, J., 1995, Human Biodiversity: Genes, Race and History. New York: Aldine de Gruyter.

Mukhopadhyay, C., and Y.T. Moses, 1997, Reestablishing Race in Anthropological Discourse. American Anthropologist 99(3):527–33.

Sacks, K., 1994, How Did Jews Become White Folks? Pp. 78–102 in Race (ed. by S. Gregory and R. Sanjek). New Brunswick, N.J.: Rutgers University Press.

Shanklin, E., 1994, Anthropology and Race. Belmont, Calif.: Wadsworth Publishing.

Shockley, W., 1987, Jensen's Data on Spearman's Hypotheses: No Artifact. Behavioral and Brain Sciences 10:512.

...continued Race, Higher Education, and American Society, **Yolanda T. Moses**

Smedley, A., 1993, Race in North America: Origin and Evolution of a Worldview. Boulder, Colo.: Westview Press.

Taylor, W.L., 1998, Racism and the Poor: Integration and Affirmative Action as Mobility Strategies. In Locked in the Poorhouse: Cities, Race, and Poverty in the United States (ed. by F.R. Harris and L.A. Curtis). Lanham, Md.: Rowman and Littlefield Publishers.

Wightman, L., n.d., Standardized Testing and Equal Access: A Tutorial. In A Compelling Interest: Weighing the Evidence on Racial Dynamics in Higher Education (ed. by M. Chang, D. Witt, J. Jones, and K. Hakuta). Unpublished work in author's possession.

A Young Person's Guide to the Grading System

Jerry Farber

Jerry Farber, a professor of English and comparative literature at San Diego State University, is the author of many books and articles of social and literary criticism. His work had an impact on the student movement of the late 1960s and early 1970s.

Farber's essay was first published in 1969 in a collection of essays and stories entitled The Student as Nigger. *Farber uses the analogy in the title to describe students as slaves of teachers and administrators.*

Prereading

In the first paragraph of his essay, Farber asks the reader to consider what grades do for learning. Freewrite for ten minutes in response to this prompt.

1   There's no question that the grading system is effective in training people to do what they're told. The question is: What does it do for learning?

2   Grades focus our attention. But on what? On the test. Academic success, as everyone knows, is something that we measure not in knowledge but in grade points. What we get on the final is all-important; what we retain after the final is irrelevant. Grades don't make us want to enrich our minds; they make us want to please our teachers (or at least put them on). Grades are a game. When the term is over, you shuffle the deck and

begin a new round. Who reads his textbooks after the grades are in? What's the point? It doesn't go on your score.

3   Oddly enough, many of us understand all of this and yet remain convinced that we need to be graded in order to learn. When we get to college, twelve years of slave work have very likely convinced us that learning is dull, plodding and unpalatable. We may think we need to be graded: we assume that without the grades we'd never go through all that misery voluntarily. But, in fact, we've been had. We've been prodded with phony motivations so long that we've become insensitive to the true ones. We're like those sleeping pill addicts who have reached the point where they need strong artificial inducement to do what comes naturally. We're grade junkies—convinced that we'd never learn without the A's and F's to keep us going. Grades have prevented us from growing up. No matter how old a person is—when he attends school, he's still a child, tempted with lollipops and threatened with spankings.

4   Learning happens when you *want* to know. Ask yourself: did you need grades to learn how to drive? To learn how to talk? To learn how to play chess—or play the guitar—or dance—or find your way around a new city? Yet these are things we do very well—much better than we handle that French or Spanish that we were graded on for years in high school. Some of us, though, are certain that, while we might learn to drive or play chess without grades, we still need them to force us to learn the things we don't really want to learn—math, for instance. But is that really true? If for any reason you really want or need some math—say, algebra—you can learn it without being graded. And if you don't want it and don't need it, you'll probably never get it straight, grades or not. Just because you pass a subject doesn't mean you've learned it. How much time did you spend on algebra and geometry in high school? Two years? How much do you remember? Or what about grammar? How much did all those years of force-fed grammar do for you? You learn to talk (without being graded) from the people around you, not from gerunds and modifiers. And as for writing—if you ever do learn to write well, you can bet your sweet ass it won't be predicate nominatives that teach you. Perhaps those subjects that we would never study without being graded are the very subjects that we lose hold of as soon as the last test is over.

5   Still, some of us maintain that we need grades to give us self-discipline. But do you want to see real self-discipline? Look at some kid working on his car all weekend long. His parents even have to drag him in for dinner. And yet, if that kid had been compelled to work on cars all his life and had been continually graded on it, then he'd swear up and down that he needed those grades to give him self-discipline.

6   It is only recently—and out of school—that I have begun to understand self-discipline in writing. It grows out of freedom, not out of coercion. Self-discipline isn't staying up all night to finish a term paper; that's slave work.

Self-discipline is revising one paragraph fanatically for weeks—for no other reason than that you yourself aren't happy with it. Self-discipline is following a problem through tedious, repetitive laboratory experiments, because there's no other way of finding out what you want to know. Or it can be surfing all day long every single day for an entire summer until you are good at it. Self-discipline is nothing more than a certain way of pleasing yourself, and it is the last thing anyone is likely to learn for a grade.

7   Coercion inside school probably leads many of us to develop our self-discipline in areas untouched by the classroom. Who knows? If movie-going, dancing and surfing were the only required subjects, there might well be a poetic renaissance. I suspect that most kids fool around with writing on their own at some point—diaries, poetry, whatever—but this interest rarely survives school. When you learn that writing is intellectual slave work, it's all over.

8   Do you think you're a lazy student? No wonder! Slaves are almost always lazy.

9   Suppose I go to college; I want to be a chemist or a high school teacher or an accountant. Are grades really my only reason for learning the field? Is getting graded going to turn me on to my subject? Or is it more likely to turn me off? How sad this is. History is so engrossing. Literature is so beautiful. And school is likely to turn them dull or even ugly. Can you imagine what would happen if they graded you on sex? The race would die out.

10   Wouldn't it be great to be free to learn? Without penalties and threats, without having to play childish competitive games for gold and silver stars? Can you even imagine what the freedom to learn might be like?

11   Perhaps this kind of freedom sounds attractive to you but you're convinced that it isn't suited to our society. Even if the grading system can be shown to work against learning, you may assume that grades are still necessary to *evaluate* people—to screen people for various kinds of work.

12   But think about it. Do you really believe that the best way to determine someone's qualifications is to grade him—A, B, C, D, F—week by week, day by day, in everything he studies for sixteen years of school? Is this monstrous rigmarole honestly necessary in order to determine who gets which jobs?

13   There are far better ways to determine a person's qualifications. Many fields already do their own screening by examination; the bar exam is one instance. In some areas—journalism, for example—supervised on-the-job experience would probably be the most effective screening and qualifying technique. Other fields might call for a combination of methods. Engineers, for example, could be qualified through

apprenticeship plus a demonstration of reasonable competency on exams at various levels—exams on which they would, of course, get an unlimited number of tries.

14   In a great many fields, no screening technique is necessary at all. Countless employers, public and private, require a college degree for no really good reason, simply because it enables their personnel departments to avoid making any meaningful individual evaluation and because it indicates some degree of standardization. There is no reason why a person should be forced to spend four years of his life in college just to get a decent job and then discover that he would have been much better off working in the field itself for four years and pursuing his own learning interests on a less rigid and formal basis.

15   Still it might be argued that eliminating grades entirely would require too sudden a shift in our society. I would maintain that the sudden shift is desirable. In any case, though, society is not likely to face the simultaneous abandonment of grading by every school in the country. Furthermore, on a campus where there is enormous resistance to abolishing grades, one could put forth a fairly good half-way compromise—the Credit system—which is, from my point of view, worth trying even though it falls short of what should be the real goal: no grades at all.

16   Under this system, some courses could be made totally free of grading: basic algebra, say, or drawing or poetry writing. The rest would be run on a Credit basis. If you meet the minimum requirements of a course, you get credit for it. No A's or C's or silver stars. Just credit. And if you don't meet the requirements, nothing happens. You don't lose anything or get penalized; you just don't get credit for that course. This is NOT the Pass-Fail System. Pass-Fail is a drag; if you don't pass a course, you get hurt. Under the Credit system you simply either get credit or you don't. All that your record shows is the courses you've earned credit for (not the ones you've attempted). And when you get credit for enough courses, you can get some kind of certification or credential, if you want one, according to the number and type of courses you've taken. And there should be not just a few assembly-line four-year degrees: AB, BS, and so on; there should be scores of more meaningful and varied certifications and degrees. Or maybe there should be none at all, just a list of the courses for which you have credit.

17   What's wrong with that? College becomes something more like a place for learning and growth, not fear and anxiety. It becomes a learning community, not a gladiatorial arena where you're pitted in daily battle against your fellow students. In elementary and secondary schools, of course, there is an even weaker pretext for grading and even more to be gained by its abolishment.

18   And we mustn't be too quick to assume that abolishing A's and F's would make our colleges still more overcrowded. If we eliminate the pointless Mickey-Mouse requirements that are foisted on everyone, if we eliminate the gold-star games and all the administrative paperwork and

class busywork that go along with them, if we reduce the overwhelming pressure for a meaningless, standardized degree, then perhaps we'll end up with learning facilities that can accommodate even more students than the number that get processed in the factories that we currently operate.

19   And if an employer wants not just degrees but grade-point averages too, the colleges will explain that that's not what they are there for. Graduate schools, for their part, will probably not present a serious problem. They already put heavy emphasis on criteria other than GPA's. They stress interviews, personal recommendations: most of them already give their own entrance exams anyway. Besides, the best graduate schools will probably be delighted to get some *live* students for a change.

PRACTICE

❶ Read "Race, Higher Education, and American Society" by Yolanda T. Moses. As you read, write "yes" in the margin next to passages that match up with your prior knowledge and "no" next to passages that are unrelated to your experience. Are the passages marked "yes" easier to understand than those marked "no"? Estimate the percentage of the selection that is recognizable and the percentage that is unfamiliar.

Next, read Jerry Farber's essay "A Young Person's Guide to the Grading System" and annotate the margin as you did for the Moses reading. Again, estimate the percentage of the selection that is recognizable and the percentage that is unfamiliar. Based on the percentages for Farber and Moses, which selection should be easier to understand? Which do you think you actually did understand better?

a. Since the article is complex, Moses lays out a plan for her readers and uses sequencers and certain words and phrases to focus the readers' attention. Point out the places where Moses provides this assistance to her audience.

b. Would you describe Farber's tone as formal and reverent or informal and irreverent? Cite examples from the text to support your view.

c. In paragraph 18, Farber uses the device of repetition. What other stylistic devices does he use in his essay? Give examples.

d. Instead of giving his readers a ready-made "guide" to grading, Farber engages them in a conversation about grades. Explain how he engages his readers and draws them into the conversation.

2 Select one of the readings in this chapter. Identify the genre and list the characteristics on which you based your decision.

3 Break into groups of four. Each group selects one of the readings from this chapter or another chapter. Each member of the group is responsible for preparing a response to one of the four questions for analyzing the rhetorical context of a text on page 159. After each member contributes his or her response, the group leader synthesizes the four responses and reports to the class.

4 The purpose of this exercise is to give you practice using the three reading strategies we presented in this chapter: (1) reading for content; (2) reading for genre, organization, and stylistic features; and (3) reading for rhetorical context. Read one of the selections in this chapter or another chapter. Record answers *before* you read, *as* you read, and *after* you have read the article.

5 Working with four or five other students, use the Strategies for Comprehending Complex Texts on page 166 to write a summary of the following passage from Walter J. Ong's classic work *The Presence of the Word: Some Prolegomena for Cultural and Religious History:*

The alphabet, useful and indispensable as it has certainly proved to be, itself entails to some extent delusional systematization if not necessarily schizophrenia properly so called. The alphabet, after all, is a careful pretense. Letters are simply not sounds, do not have the properties of sounds. As we have seen, their whole existence and economy of operation is in a temporally neuter space rather than within the living stream of time. With alphabetic writing, a kind of pretense, a remoteness from actuality, becomes institutionalized.

Baker College
Cadillac

How Do I Think Critically About Writing?

5

WHEN NEW STUDENTS ASK US ABOUT THE RULES FOR GOOD COLLEGE WRITING, THEY ARE OFTEN SURPRISED BY HISTORY PROFESSOR RODNEY KILKUP'S UNEXPECTED ADVICE IN THE MARGIN TO THE RIGHT. TO BECOME A BETTER WRITER, SAYS Kilcup, the most crucial thing is to have "a good, interesting question." We love Professor Kilcup's advice because we'd like you to think of good writers as critical thinkers who pose questions and problems.

As we show throughout this text, writing is closely allied to critical thinking and to the innate satisfaction you take in exercising your curiosity, creativity, and problem-solving ability. Writing helps you discover and express ideas that you would otherwise never think or say. Unlike speaking, writing gives you time to think deeply and long about an idea. Because you can revise writing, it lets you pursue a problem in stages, with each draft reflecting a deeper, clearer, or more complex level of thought. Moreover, the skills you learn in a writing course are transferable to all majors and to your professional careers. Research has shown that managers, accountants, lawyers, engineers, and other professionals spend, on average, forty-four percent of their professional time writing. In sum, writing has lifelong importance: It stimulates, challenges, and stretches your mental powers while giving you a voice in important academic, civic, and professional conversations.

> " It seems to me, then, that the way to help people become better writers is not to tell them that they must first learn the rules of grammar, that they must develop a four-part outline, that they must consult the experts and collect all the useful information. These things may have their place. But none of them is as crucial as having a good, interesting question. "
>
> —RODNEY KILCUP
> HISTORIAN

In this chapter, you will learn three important concepts about writing:

Good writing can vary from closed to open forms.

Good writers address problems rather than topics.

Good writers think rhetorically about purpose, audience, and genre.

Good Writing Can Vary from Closed to Open Forms

In our experience, beginning college writers are often discomforted by the ambiguity of the rules governing writing. They often wish for some consistent rules: "Never use 'I' in a formal paper" or "Start every paragraph with a topic sentence." The problem is that different kinds of writing have different criteria for effectiveness, leaving the writer with rhetorical choices rather than with hard-and-fast formulas for success. You'll be able to appreciate this insight for yourself through the following exercise.

Read the following short pieces of nonfiction prose. The first is a letter to the editor written by a professional civil engineer in response to a newspaper editorial arguing for the development of wind-generated electricity. The second short piece is entitled "A Festival of Rain." It was written by the American poet and religious writer Thomas Merton, a Trappist monk. After reading the two samples carefully, proceed to the questions at the end of the chapter.

A Letter to the Editor

David Rockwood

1   Your editorial on November 16, "Get Bullish on Wind Power," is based on fantasy rather than fact. There are several basic reasons why wind-generated power can in no way serve as a reasonable major alternative to other electrical energy supply alternatives for the Pacific Northwest power system.

2   First and foremost, wind power is unreliable. Electric power generation is evaluated not only on the amount of energy provided, but also on its ability to meet system peak load requirements on an hourly, daily, and weekly basis. In other words, an effective power system would have to provide enough electricity to meet peak demands in a situation when the

wind energy would be unavailable—either in no wind situations or in severe blizzard conditions, which would shut down the wind generators. Because wind power cannot be relied on at times of peak needs, it would have to be backed up by other power generation resources at great expense and duplication of facilities.

3   Secondly, there are major unsolved problems involved in the design of wind generation facilities, particularly for those located in rugged mountain areas. Ice storms, in particular, can cause sudden dynamic problems for the rotating blades and mechanisms which could well result in breakdown or failure of the generators. Furthermore, the design of the facilities to meet the stresses imposed by high winds in these remote mountain regions, in the order of 125 miles per hour, would indeed escalate the costs.

4   Thirdly, the environmental impact of constructing wind generation facilities amounting to 28 percent of the region's electrical supply system (as proposed in your editorial) would be tremendous. The Northwest Electrical Power system presently has a capacity of about 37,000 megawatts of hydro power and 10,300 megawatts of thermal, for a total of about 48,000 megawatts. Meeting 28 percent of this capacity by wind power generators would, most optimistically, require about 13,400 wind towers, each with about 1,000 kilowatt (one megawatt) generating capacity. These towers, some 100 to 200 feet high, would have to be located in the mountains of Oregon and Washington. These would encompass hundreds of square miles of pristine mountain area, which, together with interconnecting transmission facilities, control works, and roads, would indeed have major adverse environmental impacts on the region.

5   There are many other lesser problems of control and maintenance of such a system. Let it be said that, from my experience and knowledge as a professional engineer, the use of wind power as a major resource in the Pacific Northwest power system is strictly a pipe dream.

A Festival of Rain

Thomas Merton

1   Let me say this before rain becomes a utility that they can plan and distribute for money. By "they" I mean the people who cannot understand that rain is a festival, who do not appreciate its gratuity, who think that what has no price has no value, that what cannot be sold is not real, so that the only way to make something *actual* is to place it on the market. The time will come when they will sell you even your rain. At the moment it is still free, and I am in it. I celebrate its gratuity and its meaninglessness.

...continued A Festival of Rain, **Thomas Merton**

2   The rain I am in is not like the rain of cities. It fills the woods with an immense and confused sound. It covers the flat roof of the cabin and its porch with insistent and controlled rhythms. And I listen, because it reminds me again and again that the whole world runs by rhythms I have not yet learned to recognize, rhythms that are not those of the engineer.

3   I came up here from the monastery last night, sloshing through the corn fields, said Vespers, and put some oatmeal on the Coleman stove for supper. . . . The night became very dark. The rain surrounded the whole cabin with its enormous virginal myth, a whole world of meaning, of secrecy, of silence, of rumor. Think of it: all that speech pouring down, selling nothing, judging nobody, drenching the thick mulch of dead leaves, soaking the trees, filling the gullies and crannies of the wood with water, washing out the places where men have stripped the hillside! What a thing it is to sit absolutely alone, in a forest, at night, cherished by this wonderful, unintelligible, perfectly innocent speech, the most comforting speech in the world, the talk that rain makes by itself all over the ridges, and the talk of the watercourses everywhere in the hollows!

4   Nobody started it, nobody is going to stop it. It will talk as long as it wants, this rain. As long as it talks I am going to listen.

5   But I am also going to sleep, because here in this wilderness I have learned how to sleep again. Here I am not alien. The trees I know, the night I know, the rain I know. I close my eyes and instantly sink into the whole rainy world of which I am a part, and the world goes on with me in it, for I am not alien to it.

Figure 5.1
A Continuum
of Essay Types:
Closed to
Open Forms

Closed Forms

Top-down thesis-based prose
- thesis explicitly stated in introduction
- all parts of essay linked clearly to thesis
- body paragraphs develop thesis
- body paragraphs have topic sentences
- structure forecasted

Delayed-thesis prose
- thesis appears near end
- text reads as a mystery
- reader held in suspense

DISTINCTIONS BETWEEN CLOSED AND OPEN FORMS OF WRITING

David Rockwood's letter and Thomas Merton's mini-essay are both examples of nonfiction prose. But as these examples illustrate, nonfiction prose can vary enormously in form and style. From the perspective of structure, we can place nonfiction prose along a continuum that goes from closed to open forms of writing (see Figure 5.1).

● **CLOSED-FORM PROSE** Of our two pieces of prose, Rockwood's letter illustrates tightly closed writing and falls at the far left end of the continuum because it has these elements:

- An explicit thesis in the introduction that informs readers of the point of the whole essay (i.e., wind-generated power isn't a reasonable alternative energy source in the Pacific Northwest)
- Unified and coherent paragraphs (i.e., "First and foremost, wind power is unreliable. . . . Secondly, there are major unsolved problems. . . . Thirdly, . . .")
- Sustained development of that thesis without digressions

Once the thesis is stated, readers know the point of the essay and can predict its structure. (You might note that the five-paragraph essay sometimes taught in high school is a by-the-numbers way to teach closed-form prose.) Because its structure is transparent and predictable, the success of closed-form prose rests entirely on its ideas, which must "surprise" readers by asserting something new, challenging, doubtful, or controversial. It aims to change readers' view of the subject through the power of reason, logic, and evidence. Closed-form prose

Open Forms

Thesis-seeking prose
- essay organized around a question rather than a thesis
- essay explores the problem or question, looking at it in many ways
- writer may or may not arrive at thesis

Theme-based narrative
- often organized chronologically or has storylike elements
- often used to heighten or deepen a problem, or show its human significance
- often has an implicit theme rather than a thesis
- often violates rules of closed-form prose by using literary techniques

is what most college professors write in their scholarly research, what they most often expect from their students, and what is most common in professional and business contexts.

● **OPEN-FORM PROSE**   In contrast, Merton's "A Festival of Rain" falls toward the right end of the closed-to-open continuum because it exhibits these features:

- No reduction to a single, summarizable thesis (Merton clearly opposes the consumer culture that will try to "sell" you the rain, but what exactly does Merton mean by "festival" or by rain's "gratuity and its meaninglessness"?)
- The use of story or narrative as an organizing principle (i.e., the story of Merton's leaving the monastery to sleep in the rain-drenched cabin) through which a point emerges suggestively

Although open-form prose does not announce its thesis and support it with reasons and evidence, it does have a focus. As Merton's piece illustrates, the focus is more like a theme in fiction that readers might discuss and even dispute than like a thesis in argument.

Consider also the extent to which Merton violates the rules for closed-form prose. Instead of using transitions between paragraphs, Merton juxtaposes passages that tell the story of his camping trip ("I came up here from the monastery last night . . .") with passages that make cryptic, interpretive comments about his experience ("The rain I am in is not like the rain of cities"). Unlike paragraphs in closed-form prose, which typically begin with topic sentences and are developed with supporting details, the paragraphs in Merton's piece have no clear hierarchical structure; paragraph four, in fact, is only two lines long. These open-form elements often appear in personal essays, in blogs, in newspaper or magazine feature stories or character profiles, or in professional nonfiction.

● **FLEXIBILITY OF "RULES" ALONG THE CONTINUUM**   As you can see from the continuum in Figure 5.1, essays can fall anywhere along the scale. Not all thesis-with-support writing has to be top down, stating its thesis explicitly in the introduction. In some cases writers choose to delay the thesis, creating a more exploratory, open-ended, "let's think through this together" feeling before finally stating the main point late in the essay. In some cases writers explore a problem without *ever* finding a satisfactory thesis, creating an essay that is thesis seeking rather than thesis supporting, an essay aimed at deepening the question, refusing to accept an easy answer. Such essays may replicate their authors' process of exploring a problem and include digressions, speculations, conjectures, multiple perspectives, and occasional invitations to the reader to help solve the problem. When writers reach the far right-hand position on the continuum, they no longer state an explicit thesis. Instead, like novelists or short story writers, they embed their points in plot, imagery, dialogue, and so forth, leaving their readers to *infer* a theme from the text. This kind of writing is often called "literary nonfiction."

WHERE TO PLACE YOUR WRITING ALONG THE CONTINUUM

Clearly, essays at opposite ends of this continuum operate in different ways and obey different rules. Because each position on the continuum has its appropriate uses, the writer's challenge is to determine which sort of writing is most appropriate in a given situation. Most college papers (but not all) and much professional writing are written in closed form. Thus if you were writing a business proposal, a legal brief, or an academic paper for a scholarly audience, you would typically choose a closed-form structure, and your finished product would include elements such as the following:

- An explicit thesis in the introduction
- Forecasting of structure
- Cohesive and unified paragraphs with topic sentences
- Clear transitions between sentences and between parts
- No digressions

But if you were writing to express your conflicted relationship with, say, a parent or friend or to reflect on your first discovery of racism or homophobia, you would probably move toward the open end of the continuum and violate one or more of these conventions. Instead of a thesis-support structure, you might use the power of compelling stories, vivid characterization, dialogue, and evocative language to convey your ideas.

If we return now to the question about good writing posed at the beginning of this chapter, we can see that having a thesis statement, topic sentences, good transitions, and unified and coherent paragraphs are not qualities of "good prose" but simply of "closed-form prose." What makes a piece of closed-form prose "good," as we will see in the next section, is the extent to which it addresses a problem or question that matters to the reader and brings to the reader something new, surprising, or provocative. In contrast, we have seen that open-form prose can be "good" without having a thesis-driven, hierarchical structure. Open-form prose conveys its pleasures and insights through narrative strategies rather than through thesis-with-support strategies.

Good Writers Address Problems Rather Than Topics

In the previous section, we explained how the rules for good writing vary along a continuum from closed to open forms. In this section, we return to the close connection between writing and critical thinking. From chapter one, you are probably familiar with the term **thesis statement**, which is the main point a writer wants to make in an essay. However, you may not have thought much about the *question* that lies behind the thesis, which is the problem or issue that the writer is wrestling with. Behind every thesis statement is an explicit or implied **thesis question**, which is the problem or issue to which the thesis responds. An essay's thesis statement is actually the writer's proposed answer to this question, and it is this question that has propelled the writer's thinking.

Thus, the problem that matters to engineer David Rockwood is whether wind power can be a viable alternative energy source. Rockwood writes to make his answer ("No!") persuasive to readers. Thomas Merton's question is more complex and subtle, one that leads him to use open-form narrative strategies. His question seems to be: What is the effect of a consumer economy on our understanding of meaning and value? He wants to raise readers' awareness of a problem with corporate capitalism (where corporations want to sell you even the rain), which alienates us from nature and from our deepest selves.

This focus on a writer's motivating problem or question differs somewhat from the common view that writers first choose a topic and then narrow it down. Of course, writers have broad areas of interest (which we might call topics), but what they are seeking isn't the topic itself but a cluster of problems or questions within the topic. Instead of "narrowing a topic," they seek a problem that grips their curiosity and gets them thinking.

SHARED PROBLEMS UNITE WRITERS AND READERS

For college professors, "a good, interesting question" is at the heart of good writing. Professors want students to become gripped by problems because they themselves are gripped by problems. For example, at a workshop for new faculty members, we asked participants to write a brief description of the question or problem that motivated their Ph.D. dissertation or a recent conference paper or article. Here is how a biochemistry professor responded:

During periods of starvation, the human body makes physiological adaptations to preserve essential protein mass. Unfortunately, these adaptations don't work well during long-term starvation. After the body depletes its carbohydrate storage, it must shift to depleting protein in order to produce glucose. Eventually, this loss of functional protein leads to metabolic dysfunction and death. Interestingly, several animal species are capable of surviving for extensive periods without food and water while conserving protein and maintaining glucose levels. How do the bodies of these animals accomplish this feat? I wanted to investigate the metabolic functioning of these animals, which might lead to insights into the human situation.

As you progress through your college career, you will find yourself increasingly engaged with the kinds of questions that motivate your professors. All around college campuses you'll find clusters of professors and students asking questions about all manner of problems ranging from puzzles in the reproductive cycles of worms and bugs to the use of nanotechnology to fight global warming, from the changing portrayal of race and gender in American films to the impact of digital technology on the dissemination of news. At the heart of all these communities of writers and readers is an interest in common questions and the hope for better or different answers. Writers write because they have something new or surprising or challenging to say in response to a question. Readers read because they share the writer's interest in the problem and want to deepen their understanding.

WHERE DO PROBLEMS COME FROM?

So where do these problems come from? How does a writer get hooked on a problem? Although this question is complex at a philosophical level, we can offer two relatively simple and helpful answers: Sometimes you encounter a problem that is already "out there" in a conversation already in progress in some human community. Some enduring problems have been sparking conversations that have lasted for thousands of years: Do humans have free will? What constitutes ethical action? What is the origin of the universe? Why do good people have to suffer? Thousands of less sweeping problems are being discussed by human communities all the time. In many of your college courses, you'll be introduced to long-standing problems that you hadn't encountered before and that may hook you and draw you into their spell. In these cases, a problem that is already "out there" initiates your search for a possible answer and invites you to join the conversation.

But sometimes you actually find, pose, or articulate a problem yourself, fresh from your own brain. In this case you start a conversation, rather than join an existing one. (It may turn out later that other people have asked the same question, but you didn't know that at the time.) For example, you find your own problem whenever you see something puzzling in the natural world, note curious or unexplained features in a cultural phenomenon or artifact, or discover conflicts or contradictions within your own way of looking at the world.

In Table 5.1 we describe some of the ways that writers can become gripped by a problem that may lead to engaged writing.

Table 5.1 How Writers Become Gripped by a Problem		
Occasion That Leads to Problem	Your Interior Mental State	Example
The problem is already "out there." *(You enter a conversation already in progress)*		
You encounter others arguing about a problem, and you don't know where you stand.	• You are equally persuaded by different views or dissatisfied with all the views • Part of you thinks X but another part thinks Y (you feel divided)	I don't know where I stand on the question of whether health care should be rationed. In *To Kill a Mockingbird*, I can't decide whether Atticus Finch is a good father.
You aren't satisfied with a common view of something or you disagree with someone on an issue.	• Your skepticism or intuition pushes against some popular view • You are committed to a view different from someone else's • Note: *You must go beyond simply having an opinion. You aren't gripped by a problem until you have seen the possible strengths of other views and the possible weaknesses of your own.*	My teacher's explanation of the causes for anorexia doesn't seem quite right to me. Shanita says that we should build more nuclear power plants to combat global warming, but I say nuclear power is too dangerous.
Someone gives you a question that you can't yet answer.	• You feel overwhelmed with unknowns • You feel that you can't begin to answer until you do more exploration and research • If you know enough to start proposing hypotheses, you aren't satisfied with any of your approaches	Your boss asks you whether the company should enact the proposed marketing plan. Your history professor asks you, "To what extent does Frederick Jackson Turner's frontier hypothesis reflect a Euro-centric world view?"

Occasion That Leads to Problem	Your Interior Mental State	Example
You pose the problem yourself. *(You initiate the conversation)*		
You see something puzzling in a natural or cultural phenomenon.	• Something deviates from what you would expect or is otherwise unexplainable • You begin testing possible solutions or answers. (Often you want to talk to someone—to start a conversation about the problem)	Why is this fungus appearing on some of these tomatoes but not on the others? Why is Twitter more popular among middle-aged adults than teenagers?
You see something unexpected, puzzling, or unexplained in a poem, painting, or other human artifact.	• You can't see why the artist/maker did something in such a way • You wonder why this particular artifact is different from other artifacts that you thought would be similar	Why does Merton call rain "meaningless"? If Hamlet really loves Ophelia, then why does he treat her like a whore in the nunnery scene?
You articulate something inconsistent or contradictory in your own view of the world.	• You feel unsettled by your own inconsistent views or values • You probe more deeply into your own identity and place in the world	I agree with Merton's argument against consumerism, but I really want a large plasma TV. Is consumerism really bad? Am I a materialist?

Good Writers Think Rhetorically About Purpose, Audience, and Genre

So far, we have used the term "rhetoric" or "thinking rhetorically"—without defining it. Now is the time for us to explain what we mean by *rhetoric*.

WHAT IS RHETORIC?

At the broadest level, **rhetoric** is the study of how human beings use language and other symbols to influence the attitudes, beliefs, and actions of others. One prominent twentieth-century rhetorician, Kenneth Burke, calls rhetoric "a symbolic means of inducing cooperation in beings that by nature respond to symbols." To understand what Burke means by "symbols," consider the difference in flirting behavior between peacocks and humans. When male peacocks flirt, they spread their fantastic tail feathers, do mating dances, and screech weirdly to attract females, but the whole process is governed by instinct. Peacocks don't have to choose among different symbolic actions such as buying an Armani tail versus buying a knockoff from Wal-Mart or driving to the mating grounds in the right car. Unlike a peacock, however, a flirting human must make symbolic choices, all of which have meaning. Consider the different flirting messages humans send to each other by their choice of clothes, their method of transportation, their choice of major, their favorite music. Even word choices (for example, academic jargon words versus street slang) or texting behavior give further hints of a person's identity, values, and social groups. Rhetoricians study, among other things, how these symbols arise within a given culture and how they influence others.

In a narrower sense, rhetoric is the art of making messages persuasive. Perhaps the most famous definition of rhetoric comes from the Greek philosopher Aristotle, who defined rhetoric as "the ability to see, in any particular case, all the available means of persuasion." An effective speaker's task, in Aristotle's view, is to persuade listeners to accept the speaker's views on a question of action or belief. But to do so, the speaker must first understand all the arguments on all sides of the question ("all the available means of persuasion"). If we imagine the interaction of several speakers, each proposing different answers to a question, and if we imagine all the speakers listening to each other respectfully and open-mindedly, we can see how productive human conversation could emerge. The study of rhetoric can therefore help people write, speak, read, and listen more effectively.

At an operational level, writers can be said to "think rhetorically" whenever they are consciously aware of writing to an audience for a purpose within a genre. (A *genre*, to be explained in more detail shortly, is a recurring type of writing with distinguishing features and conventions such as a letter to the editor, a scholarly article, a business memo, or a blog.) To think rhetorically, writers consider questions like these:

- *Purpose:* What am I trying to accomplish in this paper? What do I want my readers to know, believe, see, or do?
- *Audience:* Who are my intended readers, and what are their values and assumptions? What do they already know or believe about my subject? How much do they care about it?
- *Genre:* What kind of document am I writing? What are its requirements for structure, style, and document design?

Let's look more closely at each of these components of a writer's rhetorical context.

HOW WRITERS THINK ABOUT PURPOSE

In this section, we want to help you think more productively about your purpose for writing, which can be examined from several different perspectives: your rhetorical aim, the motivating occasion that gets you going, and your desire to change your reader's view. All three perspectives will help you make your awareness of purpose work for you and increase your savvy as a writer. Let's look at each in turn.

● **PURPOSE AS RHETORICAL AIM** One powerful way to think about purpose is through the general concept of "rhetorical aim." In this text, we identify six different rhetorical aims of writing: to express, to explore, to inform, to analyze and synthesize, to persuade, and to reflect. Thinking of each piece of writing in terms of one or more of these rhetorical aims can help you understand typical ways that your essay can be structured and developed and can help you clarify your relationship with your audience. Table 5.2 gives you an overview of each of the six rhetorical aims and sketches out how the subject matter differs

Table 5.2   Purpose as Rhetorical Aim

Rhetorical Aim	Focus of Writing	Relationship to Audience	Forms and Genres
Express or share May also include an artistic aim	Your own life, personal experiences, reflections	You share aspects of your life; you invite readers to walk in your shoes, to experience your insights	**Form:** Has many open-form features **Sample genres:** journal, blog, personal Web site, or online profile; personal essays or literacy narratives, often with artistic features
Explore or inquire	A significant subject-matter problem that puzzles you	You take readers on your own intellectual journey by showing your inquiry process (raising questions, seeking evidence, considering alternative views)	**Form:** Follows open form in being narrative based; is thesis seeking rather than thesis supporting **Sample genres:** freewriting; research logs; articles and books focused on process of discovery

(continued)

Table 5.2 *Continued*

Rhetorical Aim	Focus of Writing	Relationship to Audience	Forms and Genres
Inform or explain	Factual knowledge addressing a reader's need or curiosity	You provide knowledge that your readers need or want, or you arouse curiosity and provide new, surprising information. You expect readers to trust your authority	**Form:** Usually has a closed-form structure **Sample genres:** encyclopedia articles; instruction booklets; sales reports; technical reports; informative magazine articles; informative Web sites
Analyze, synthesize, or interpret	Complex subject matter that you can break down into parts and put together in new ways for greater understanding	Using critical thinking and possibly research, you challenge readers with a new way of understanding your subject. Skeptical readers expect you to support your thesis with good particulars.	**Form:** Typically has a closed-form structure **Sample genres:** scholarly articles; experimental reports; many kinds of college research papers; public affairs magazine articles; many kinds of blogs
Persuade	Subject-matter questions that have multiple controversial answers	You try to convince readers, who may not share your values and beliefs, to accept your stance on an issue by providing good reasons and evidence and attending to alternative views.	**Form:** Usually closed form, but may employ many open-form features for persuasive effect **Sample genres:** letters to the editor; op-ed pieces; advocacy pieces in public affairs magazines; advocacy Web sites; researched academic arguments
Reflect	Subject matter closely connected to your interests and experience; often involves self-evaluation of an experience	Writing for yourself as well as for a reader, you seek to find personal meaning and value in an experience or course of study. You assume a sympathetic and interested reader.	**Form:** Anywhere on the closed-to-open-form continuum **Sample genres:** memoirs, workplace self-evaluations; introductory letter for a portfolio; personal essays looking back on an experience

from aim to aim, how the writer's task and relationship to readers differ according to aim, and how a chosen aim affects the writing's genre and its position on the spectrum from open to closed forms.

● **PURPOSE AS A RESPONSE TO A MOTIVATING OCCASION** Another important way to think about purpose is to think about each piece of writing as a response to a particular motivating occasion. Almost all writing is compelled by some sort of motivating occasion or exigency.* This exigency can be external (someone giving you a task and setting a deadline) or internal (your awareness of a problem stimulating your desire to bring about some change in people's views). Thus, when engineer David Rockwood read a newspaper editorial supporting wind-power projects, his own belief in the impracticality of wind power motivated him to write a letter to the editor in rebuttal. But he also knew that he had to write the letter within one or two days or else it stood no chance of being published. His exigency thus included both internal and external factors.

College students' motivations for writing can be equally mixed: In part, you write to meet an assignment deadline; in part, you write to please the teacher and get a good grade. But ideally you also write because you have become engaged with an intellectual problem and want to say something significant about it. Our point here is that your purposes for writing are always more complex than the simple desire to meet an assignment deadline.

● **PURPOSE AS A DESIRE TO CHANGE YOUR READER'S VIEW** Perhaps the most useful way to think about purpose is to focus on the change you want to bring about in your audience's view of the subject. When you are given a college writing assignment, this view of purpose engages you directly with the intellectual problem specified in the assignment. For most essays, you can write a one-sentence, nutshell statement about your purpose.

> My purpose is to give my readers a vivid picture of my difficult struggle with Graves' disease.
>
> My purpose is to explain how Thoreau's view of nature differs in important ways from that of contemporary environmentalists.
>
> My purpose is to persuade the general public that wind-generated electricity is not a practical energy alternative in the Pacific Northwest.

In closed-form academic articles, technical reports, and other business and professional pieces, writers often place explicit purpose statements in their introductions along with the thesis. In most other forms of writing, the writer uses a behind-the-scenes purpose statement to achieve focus and direction but seldom states the purpose explicitly. Writing an explicit purpose statement for a paper is a powerful way to nutshell the kind of change you want to bring about in your reader's view of the subject.

---

*An *exigency* is an urgent or pressing situation requiring immediate attention. Rhetoricians use the term to describe the event or occasion that causes a writer to begin writing.

HOW WRITERS THINK ABOUT AUDIENCE

In our discussion of purpose, we have already had a lot to say about audience. What you know about your readers—their familiarity with your subject matter, their reasons for reading, their closeness to you, their values and beliefs—affects most of the choices you make as a writer.

In assessing your audience, you must first determine who that audience is—a single reader (for example, your boss), a select group (a scholarship committee; attendees at an undergraduate research conference), or a general audience. If you imagine a general audience, you will need to make some initial assumptions about their views and values. Doing so creates an "implied audience," giving you a stable rather than a moving target so that you can make decisions about your own essay. Once you have identified your audience, you can use the following strategies for analysis.

Strategies for Analyzing Audience

Questions to Ask about Your Audience	Reasons for Asking the Question
How busy are my readers?	• Helps you decide on length, document design, and open versus closed features • In workplace writing, busy readers often require closed-form prose with headings that allow for skimming
What are my readers' motives for reading?	• If the reader has requested the document, you need only a short introduction • In most cases, your opening must hook your reader's interest
What is my relationship with my readers?	• Helps you decide on a formal or informal style • Helps you select tone—polite and serious or loose and slangy
What do my readers already know about my topic? Do my readers have more or less expertise than I have, or about the same expertise?	• Helps you determine what will be old/familiar information for your audience versus new/unfamiliar information • Helps you decide how much background and context to include • Helps you decide to use or avoid in-group jargon and specialized knowledge
How interested are my readers in my topic? Do my readers already care about it?	• Helps you decide how to write the introduction • Helps you determine how to make the problem you address interesting and significant to your reader
What are my readers' attitudes toward my thesis? Do my readers share my beliefs and values?	• Helps you make numerous decisions about tone, structure, reference to alternative views, and use of evidence • Helps you decide on the voice and persona you want to project

To appreciate the importance of audience, consider how a change in audience can affect the content of a piece. Suppose you want voters to approve a bond issue to build a new baseball stadium. If most voters are baseball fans, you can appeal to their love of the game, the pleasure of a new facility, and so forth. But non-baseball fans won't be moved by these arguments. To reach them, you must tie the new stadium to their values. You can argue that it will bring new tax revenues, clean up a run-down area, revitalize local businesses, or stimulate tourism. Your purpose remains the same—to persuade taxpayers to fund the stadium—but the content of your argument changes if your audience changes.

In college, you often seem to be writing for an audience of one—your instructor. However, most instructors try to read as a representative of a broader audience. To help college writers imagine these readers, many instructors try to design writing assignments that provide a fuller sense of audience. They may ask you to write for the readers of a particular magazine or journal, or they may create case assignments with built-in audiences (for example, "You are an accountant in the firm of Numbers and Fudge; one day you receive a letter from   ") If your instructor does not specify an audience, you can generally assume the audience to be what we like to call "the generic academic audience"—student peers who have approximately the same level of knowledge and expertise in the field as you do, who are engaged by the question you address, and who want to read your writing and be surprised in some way.

HOW WRITERS THINK ABOUT GENRE

The term *genre* refers to categories of writing that follow certain conventions of style, structure, approach to subject matter, and document design. Table 5.3 shows different kinds of genres.

The concept of genre creates strong reader expectations and places specific demands on writers. How you write any given letter, report, or article is influenced by the structure and style of hundreds of previous letters, reports, or articles written in the same genre. If you wanted to write for *Reader's Digest*, for example, you would have to use the conventions that appeal to its older, conservative readers: simple language, subjects with strong human interest, heavy reliance on anecdotal evidence in arguments, an upbeat and optimistic perspective, and an approach that reinforces the conservative *ethos* of individualism, self-discipline, and family. If you wanted to write for *Seventeen* or *Rolling Stone*, however, you would need to use quite different conventions.

To illustrate the relationship of a writer to a genre, we sometimes draw an analogy with clothing. Although most people have a variety of different types of clothing in their wardrobes, the genre of activity for which they are dressing (Saturday night movie date, job interview, wedding) severely constrains their choice and expression of individuality. A man dressing for a job interview might express his personality through choice of tie or quality and style of business suit; he probably wouldn't express it by wearing a Hawaiian shirt and sandals. Even

Table 5.3   Examples of Genres

Personal Writing	Academic Writing	Popular Culture	Public Affairs, Civic Writing	Professional Writing	Literature
Letter Diary/journal Memoir Blog Text message E-mail Facebook profile Personal essay Literacy narrative	Scholarly article Research paper Scientific report Abstract or summary Book review Essay exam Annotated bibliography Textual analysis	Articles for magazines such as *Seventeen*, *Ebony*, or *Vibe* Advertisements Hip-hop lyrics Fan Web sites Bumper stickers Reviews of books, films, plays, music	Letter to the editor Newspaper editorial Op-ed piece Advocacy Web site Political blog Magazine article on civic issue	Cover letter for a job application Résumé Business memo Legal brief Brochure Technical manual Instruction booklet Proposal Report Press release	Short story Novel Graphic novel Play Sonnet Epic poem Literary podcast

when people deviate from a convention, they tend to do so in a conventional way. For example, teenagers who do not want to follow the genre of "teenager admired by adults" form their own genre of purple hair and pierced body parts. The concept of genre raises intriguing and sometimes unsettling questions about the relationship of the unique self to a social convention or tradition.

These same kinds of questions and constraints perplex writers. For example, academic writers usually follow the genre of the closed-form scholarly article. This highly functional form achieves maximum clarity for readers by orienting them quickly to the article's purpose, content, and structure. Readers expect this format, and writers have the greatest chance of being published if they meet these expectations. In some disciplines, however, scholars are beginning to publish more experimental, open-form articles. They may slowly alter the conventions of the scholarly article, just as fashion designers alter styles of dress.

This chapter has introduced you to three transferable rhetorical concepts aimed at deepening your thinking about "good writing" in college.

- *Good writing can vary from closed to open forms.* Closed-form prose has an explicit thesis statement, topic sentences, unified and coherent paragraphs, and good transitions. At the other end of the continuum is open-form prose, which often uses narrative techniques such as storytelling, evocative language, surprising juxtapositions, and other features that violate the conventions of closed-form prose. Closed-form prose is "good" only if its ideas bring something new, provocative, or challenging to the reader.

- *Good writers address problems rather than topics.* Writers write because they have something surprising or challenging to say in response to a question that matters to the reader. Writers can pose their own problematic questions about a subject or become engaged in controversies or issues that are already "out there."

- *Good writers think rhetorically about purpose, audience, and genre.* In thinking about purpose, writers consider their rhetorical aim, their motivating occasion, or their desire to bring about change in their readers' view. They also think about their audience, analyzing how much their readers already know about (and care about) their subject and assessing their readers' values, beliefs, and assumptions. Writers attend to genre by thinking about the conventions of content, structure, and style associated with the kind of document they are writing.

PRACTICE

1 Working in small groups or as a whole class, try to reach consensus on the following specific tasks:

a. What are the main differences between the two types of writing, closed form and open form? If you are working in groups, help your recorder prepare a presentation describing the differences between Rockwood's writing (p. 194) and Merton's writing (p. 195).

b. Create a metaphor, simile, or analogy that best sums up your feelings about the most important differences between Rockwood's and Merton's writing: "Rockwood's writing is like . . ., but Merton's writing is like. . . ."

c. Explain why your metaphors are apt. How do your metaphors help clarify or illuminate the differences between the two pieces of writing?

2 The purpose of this brief write-to-learn assignment is to let you experience firsthand how rhetorical context influences a writer's choices. The whole assignment, which has three parts, should not be more than two double-spaced pages long.

a. *A Text Message to a Friend.* Write a text message to a friend using the abbreviations, capitalization, and punctuation style typically used for text messages. Explain that you are going to miss an upcoming social event (movie, football game, dance, trip to the local diner or coffee house) because you are feeling sick. Then ask your friend to text you during the event to schedule another get-together. (Make up details as you need them.)

b. *An E-Mail Message to a Professor.* Compose an e-mail message to your professor explaining that you cannot meet an assignment deadline because you are sick and asking for an extension. Create a subject line appropriate for this new context.

c. *Reflection on the Two Messages.* Using items 1 and 2 as illustrative examples, explain to someone who has not read this text why a difference in your rhetorical context caused you to make different choices in these two messages. In your explanation, use the terms "purpose," "audience," and "genre." Your goal is to teach your audience the meanings of these terms.

3 Write a letter to your instructor in which you reflect on the extent to which the ideas in this chapter are new to you or have caused you to think about writing in new or different ways. Structure your letter in the following way:

- Describe for your instructor a piece of writing you did in high school or elsewhere that represents your most engaged work or about which you are most proud. Explain the context of this piece of writing (class or professional setting, nature of the assignment, length, and so forth) and provide a brief summary of your intentions and argument. Explain why this piece of writing particularly engaged you.

- Then analyze this piece of writing and your own thinking processes in producing it in light of the following three questions from this chapter:
  - Where would you place this piece of writing on the continuum from closed to open forms? Why?
  - To what extent was this piece of writing rooted in a "good, interesting question"? Explain.
  - To what extent did you think about purpose, audience, and genre as you wrote this piece?

- Finally, explain to your instructor the extent to which this chapter caused you to think about writing in any new or different ways.

Eagle Harbor Lighthouse
Eagle Harbor, MI

How Do I Conduct Quality Research?

6

Although the "research paper" is a common writing assignment in college, students are often baffled by their professor's expectations. The problem is that students often think of research writing as presenting information rather than as creating an argument.

One of our business school colleagues calls these sorts of research papers "data dumps": The student backs a truckload full of fresh data up to the professor's desk, dumps it, and says: "Here's your load of info on 'world poverty,' Prof. You make sense of it."

But a research paper shouldn't be a data dump. Like any other argument, it should use its information to support a contestable claim. Formal researched arguments have much in common with arguments in a popular magazine. However, there is one major difference between a formal research paper and an informal magazine article—the presence of citations and a bibliography. In academic research, the purpose of in-text citations and a complete bibliography is to enable readers to follow the trail of the author's research. The proper formats for citations and bibliographic entries are simply conventions within an academic discipline to facilitate the reader's retrieval of the original sources.

Fortunately, you will find that writing an argument as a formal research paper draws on the same argumentation skills you have been using all along—the ability to pose a good question at issue within a community, to formulate a contestable claim, and to support your claim with audience-based reasons and evidence. What special skills are required? The main ones are these:

- The ability to use your research effectively to frame your issue and to support your claim, revealing your reputable *ethos* and knowledge of the issue. Sources should be woven seamlessly into your argument, which is written in your own voice throughout.
- The ability to tap the resources of libraries and the Internet.
- The ability to evaluate sources for credibility, bias, and accuracy. Special care is needed to evaluate anything retrieved from the "free-access" portion of the World Wide Web.

- The ability to summarize, quote, or paraphrase sources and to avoid plagiarism through citations and attributive tags such as "according to Jones" or "Peterson says."
- The ability to cite and document sources according to appropriate conventions.

This chapter should help you develop these skills.

Formulating a Research Question

The best way to avoid writing a data dump is to begin with a good research question—the formulation of a problem or issue that your essay will address. The research question, usually in the form of an issue question, will give you a guiding purpose in doing your library research. Let's say you are interested in how toys affect the development of gender identity in children. You can see that this topic is big and unfocused. Your research will be much easier if you give yourself a clear direction through a focused research question. For example, you might formulate a specific question like one of these:

- Why have Barbie dolls been so continuously popular?
- Does the Barbie doll reinforce traditional ideas of womanhood or challenge them?
- Is culture or biology the stronger force in making little boys interested in trucks and guns?
- Do boys' toys such as video games, complex models, electronic gadgets, and science sets develop intellectual and physical skills more than girls' toys do?

The sooner you can settle on a research question, the easier it will be to find the source materials you need in a time-saving, efficient manner.

A good way to begin formulating a research question is to freewrite for ten minutes or so, reflecting on recent readings that have stimulated your interest, on recent events that have sparked arguments, or on personal experiences that may open up onto public issues. If you have no idea for a topic, try starting with the trigger question: "What possible topics am I interested in?" If you already have an idea for a topic area, explore why you are interested in it. Search for the personal connections or the particular angles that most intrigue you.

When student writer Megan Matthews began brainstorming possible issues for a research project, she was initially interested in the problem of storing nuclear waste, but in the middle of a freewrite she switched her focus to a newspaper article she had seen on how the hearing of whales may be threatened by the Navy's sonar technology for detecting enemy submarines. After a few hours of research, both in the library and on the Web, Megan produced the following freewrite in her research notebook:

A Freewrite from Megan's Research Notebook

I'm really becoming interested in the whale issue. The Navy has its own site with a Q&A that contradicts some of its earlier findings, and NOAA [National Oceanic and Atmospheric Administration] issued approval for the military to "harass and disturb" marine mammals despite expressing earlier reservations. Hmmm. Very interesting. Is this new sonar really necessary for security? No one seems to answer that! How many whales could suffer? How dangerous to whales is this sonar? Have they really done enough testing?

Note how Megan has moved from a topic orientation (I am researching whales and Navy sonar) to a question orientation (I am doing research to find the answers to questions that I have posed). Once you get engaged with questions, then your research has a purpose guided by your own critical thinking.

Understanding Differences in the Kinds of Sources

To be an effective researcher, you need to understand the differences among the many kinds of books, articles, and Web sites you are apt to encounter. In this section, we explain these different kinds of resources. By the term *rhetorical overview*, we indicate a way of looking at sources that makes you fully conscious of the writer's context, bias, and intentions:

- For any given piece, what is the writer's purpose and who is the intended audience?
- What is the writer's bias, perspective, or angle of vision?
- What is being *left out* of this source as well as included?

Once you are aware of the many kinds of sources available—and of the kinds of library or Web search strategies needed to find them—you will be a savvy and responsible researcher.

Table 6.1   A Rhetorical Overview of Print Sources

Genre and Publisher	Author and Angle of Vision	How to Recognize Them
Books		
Scholarly Books • University/academic presses • Nonprofit • Selected through peer review	**Author:** Professors, researchers **Angle of vision:** Scholarly advancement of knowledge	• University press on title page • Specialized academic style • Documentation and bibliography
Trade Books (Nonfiction) • Commercial publishers (for example, Penguin Putnam) • Selected for profit potential	**Author:** Journalists, freelancers, scholars aiming at popular audience **Angle of vision:** Varies from informative to persuasive; often well researched, sometimes shoddy	• Covers designed for marketing appeal • Popular style • Usually documented in an informal rather than an academic style
Reference Books—Many in Electronic Format • Publishers specializing in reference material • For-profit through library sales	**Author:** Commissioned scholars **Angle of vision:** Balanced, factual overview	• Titles containing words such as encyclopedia, dictionary, or guide • Found in reference section of library or online
Periodicals		
Scholarly Journals • University/academic presses • Nonprofit • Articles chosen through peer review • Examples: *Journal of Abnormal Psychology, Review of Metaphysics*	**Author:** Professors, researchers, independent scholars **Angle of vision:** Scholarly advancement of knowledge; presentation of research findings; development of new theories and applications	• Not sold on magazine racks • No commercial advertising • Specialized academic style • Documentation and bibliography • Cover often has table of contents • Often can be found in online databases or on the Web

Genre and Publisher	Author and Angle of Vision	How to Recognize Them
Public Affairs Magazines • Commercial, "for-profit" presses • Manuscripts reviewed by editors • Examples: *Harper's, Commonweal, National Review*	**Author:** Staff writers, freelancers, scholars for general audiences **Angle of vision:** Aims to deepen public understanding of issues; magazines often have political bias of left, center, or right	• Long, well-researched articles • Ads aimed at upscale professionals • Often has reviews of books, theater, film, and the arts • Often can be found in online databases or on the Web
Trade Magazines • Commercial, "for-profit" presses • Focused on a profession or trade • Examples: *Advertising Age, Automotive Rebuilder, Farm Journal*	**Author:** Staff writers, industry specialists **Angle of vision:** Informative articles for practitioners; advocacy for the profession or trade	• Title indicating trade or profession • Articles on practical job concerns • Ads geared toward a particular trade or profession
Newsmagazines and Newspapers • Newspaper chains and publishers • Examples: *Time, Newsweek, Washington Post, Los Angeles Times*	**Author:** Staff writers and journalists; occasional freelancers **Angle of vision:** News reports aimed at balance and objectivity; editorial pages reflect perspective of editors; op-ed pieces reflect different perspectives	• Readily familiar by name, distinctive cover style • Widely available on newsstands, by subscription, and on the Web • Ads aimed at broad, general audience
Popular Niche Magazines • Large conglomerates or small presses with clear target audience • Focused on special interests of target audience • Examples: *Seventeen, People, TV Guide, Car and Driver, Golf Digest*	**Author:** Staff or freelance writers **Angle of vision:** Varies—in some cases content and point of view are dictated by advertisers or the politics of the publisher	• Glossy paper, extensive ads, lots of visuals • Popular; often distinctive style • Short, undocumented articles • Credentials of writer often not mentioned

Table 6.2   A Rhetorical Overview of Web Sites

Type of Site	Author/Sponsor and Angle of Vision	Characteristics
Com or .Biz (A Commercial Site Created by a Business or Corporation)		
• Either of these suffixes signals a for-profit operation; this group includes major periodicals and publishers of reference materials • Purpose is to enhance image, attract customers, market products and services, provide customer service • Creators are paid by salary or fees and often motivated by desire to design innovative sites	**Author:** Difficult to identify individual writers; sponsoring company often considered the author **Angle of vision:** Purpose is to promote the point of view of the corporation or business; links are to sites that promote same values	• Links are often to other products and services provided by company • Photographs and other visuals used to enhance corporate image
.Org (A Nonprofit Organization or Advocacy Group)		
• May function as a major information portal, such as NPR.org, a think tank, or a museum (for example, the Heritage Foundation or the Museum of Modern Art) • Sometimes purpose is to provide accurate, balanced information (for example, the American Red Cross site) • Frequently, purpose is to advocate for or explain the organization (for example, the Ford Foundation or local charity sites); thus, advocacy for fund-raising or political views is likely (for example, People for the Ethical Treatment of Animals [PETA] site or blog portals [Cursor.org])	**Author:** Often hard to identify individual writers; sponsoring organization often considered the author; some sites produced by amateurs with passionate views; others produced by well-paid professionals **Angle of vision:** Purpose is to promote views of sponsoring organization and influence public opinion and policy; many encourage donations through the site	• Advocacy sites sometimes don't announce purpose on home page • You may enter a node of an advocacy site through a link from another site and not realize the political slant • Facts/data selected and filtered by site's angle of vision • Often uses visuals for emotional appeal

Type of Site	Author/Sponsor and Angle of Vision	Characteristics
.Edu (An Educational Site Associated with a College or University)		
• Wide range of purposes • Home page aimed at attracting prospective students and donors • Inside the site are numerous subsites devoted to research, pedagogy, libraries, student employment, and so forth	**Author:** Professors, staff, students **Angle of vision:** Varies from personal sites of professors and students to sites of research centers and libraries; can vary from scholarly and objective to strong advocacy on issues	• Often an .edu site has numerous "subsites" sponsored by the university library, art programs, research units • Links to .pdf documents may make it difficult to determine where you are in the site—e.g., professor's course site, student site, administrative site
.Gov or .Mil (Sponsored by a Government Agency or Military Unit)		
• Provides enormous range of basic data about government policy, bills in Congress, economic forecasts, and so forth • Aims to create good public relations for agency or military unit	**Author:** Development teams employed by the agency; sponsoring agency is usually considered the author	• Typical sites (for example, http://www.energy.gov, the site of the U.S. Dept. of Energy) are extremely layered and complex and provide hundreds of links to other sites
	Angle of vision: Varies— informational sites publish data and government documents with an objective point of view; agency sites also promote agency's agenda— e.g., Dept. of Energy, Dept. of Labor	• Valuable for research • Sites often promote values/assumptions of sponsoring agency
Personal Web Sites (.Name or .Net)		
• An individual contracts with server to publish the site; many personal Web sites have .edu affiliation • Promotes hobbies, politics; provides links according to personal preferences	**Author:** Anyone can create a personal Web site **Angle of vision:** Varies from person to person	• Credentials/bias of author often hard to determine • Irresponsible sites may have links to excellent sites; tracing links is complicated

BOOKS VERSUS PERIODICALS VERSUS WEB SITES

When you conduct library research, you often leave the library with an arm-load of books and a stack of articles that you have either photocopied from journals or magazines or downloaded from a computer and printed out. At home, you will have no trouble determining who wrote the books and for what purpose, but your photocopied or downloaded articles can pose problems. What is the original source of the article in your hands? If you photocopied the articles from actual journals or magazines in your library, then you can be sure that they are "periodical print sources" (*periodical* means a publication, such as a scholarly journal or magazine, issued at regular intervals—that is, periodically). If you downloaded them from a computer—which may have been connected either to a licensed database leased by the library or to the World Wide Web—they may be electronic copies of periodical print sources or they may be material posted on the Web but never published in a print periodical.

When you download a print article from a computer, you should be aware that you lose many contextual clues about the author's purpose and bias—clues that you can pick up from the original magazine or journal itself by its appearance, title, advertisements (if any), table of contents, and state-ment of editorial policy. When you download something from the Web that has never appeared in print, you have to be wary about its source. Because print publications are costly to produce, print articles generally go through some level of editorial review. In contrast, anyone can post almost anything on the Web. You need to become savvy at recognizing these distinctions in order to read sources rhetorically and to document them accurately in your references page.

SCHOLARLY BOOKS VERSUS TRADE BOOKS

Note in Table 6.1 the distinction between scholarly books, which are peer reviewed and published by nonprofit academic presses, and trade books, which are published by for-profit presses with the intention of making money. By "peer reviewed," which is a highly prized concept in academia, we mean the selection process by which scholarly manuscripts get chosen for publication. When manuscripts are submitted to an academic publisher, the editor sends them for independent review to experienced scholars who judge the rigor and accuracy of the research and the significance and value of the argument. The process is highly competitive and weeds out much shoddy or trivial work.

In contrast, trade books are not peer reviewed by independent scholars. Instead, they are selected for publication by editors whose business is to make a profit. Fortunately, it can be profitable for popular presses to publish superbly researched and argued intellectual material because college-educated people, as lifelong learners, create a demand for intellectually satisfying trade books written for the general reader rather than for the highly specialized reader. These can be excellent sources for undergraduate research, but you need to separate the trash from the treasure. Trade books are aimed at many different audiences and market segments and can include sloppy, unreliable, and heavily biased material.

SCHOLARLY JOURNALS VERSUS MAGAZINES

Like scholarly books, scholarly journals are academic, peer-reviewed publications. Although they may look like magazines, they almost never appear on newsstands; they are nonprofit publications subsidized by universities for disseminating high-level research and scholarship.

In contrast, magazines are intended to make a profit through sales and advertising revenues. Fortunately for researchers, a demand exists for intellectually satisfying magazines, just as for sophisticated trade books. Many for-profit magazines publish highly respectable, useful material for undergraduate or professional researchers, but many magazines publish shoddy material. As Table 6.1 shows, magazines fall in various categories aimed at different audiences.

PRINT SOURCES VERSUS CYBERSPACE SOURCES

Another crucial distinction exists between print sources and cyberspace sources. Much of what you can retrieve from a computer was originally published in print. What you download is simply an electronic copy of a print source, either from a library-leased database or from someone's Web site. (The next section shows you how to tell the difference.) In such cases, you often need to consider the article's original print origins for appropriate cues about its rhetorical context and purpose. But much cyberspace material, having never appeared in print, may never have undergone either peer review or editorial review. To distinguish between these two kinds of cyberspace sources, we call one kind a "print/cyberspace source" (something that has appeared in print and is made available on the Web or through library-leased databases) and the other a "cyberspace-only source." When you use a cyberspace-only source, you've got to take special care in figuring out who wrote it, why, and for what audience.

Finding Books: Searching Your Library's Online Catalog

Your library's holdings are listed in its online catalog. Most of the entries are for books, but an academic library also has a wealth of other resources such as periodical collections, government records and reports, newspapers, videos and cassettes, maps, encyclopedias, and hundreds of specialized reference works that your reference librarian can help you use.

Indexed by subject, title, and author, the online catalog gives you titles of books and other library-owned resources relevant to your research area. Note that the catalog lists the titles of journals and magazines in the library's periodical collection (for example, *Journal of Abnormal Psychology, Atlantic Monthly*), but does *not* list the titles of individual articles within these periodicals. As we explain next, you can search the contents of periodicals by using a licensed database. Methods of accessing and using online catalogs vary from institution to institution, so you'll need to learn the specifics of your library's catalog through direct experience.

Finding Articles: Searching a Licensed Database

For many research projects, useful sources are print articles from your library's periodical collection, including scholarly journals, public affairs magazines, newspapers or newsmagazines, and niche magazines related to your research area. Some of these articles are available free on the World Wide Web, but most of them are not. Rather, they may be located physically in your library's periodical collection (or through interlibrary loan) or located electronically in databases leased by your library.

WHAT IS A LICENSED DATABASE?

Electronic databases index articles in thousands of periodicals. You can search the database by author, title, subject, keyword, date, genre, and other characteristics. In most cases the database contains an abstract of each article, and in many cases it contains the full text of the article, which you can download and print. Because access to these databases is restricted to fee-paying customers,

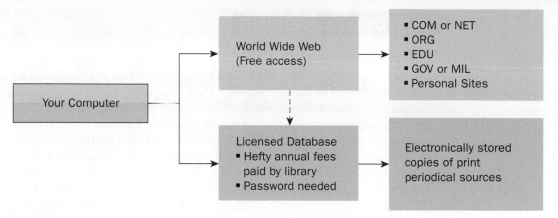

Figure 6.1   Licensed Database versus Free-Access Portions of Internet

they can't be searched through Web engines like Yahoo! or Google. Most university libraries allow students to access these databases by using a password. You can therefore use the Internet to connect your computer to licensed databases as well as to the World Wide Web (see Figure 6.1).

Although the methods of accessing licensed databases vary from institution to institution, we can offer some widely applicable guidelines. Most likely your library has online one or more of the following databases:

- *EBSCOhost:* Includes citations and abstracts from journals in most disciplines as well as many full-text articles from more than 3,000 journals; its *Academic Search Elite* function covers material published as long ago as the early 1980s.
- *UMI ProQuest Direct:* Gives access to the full text of articles from journals in a variety of subject areas; includes full-text articles from newspapers.
- *InfoTrac:* Is often called "Expanded Academic Index," and is similar to EBSCOhost and UMI ProQuest in its coverage of interdisciplinary subjects.
- *FirstSearch Databases:* Incorporate multiple specialized databases in many subject areas, including WorldCat, which contains records of books, periodicals, and multimedia formats from libraries worldwide.
- *LexisNexis Academic Universe:* Is primarily a full-text database covering current events, business, and financial news; includes company profiles and legal, medical, and reference information.

Generally, one of these databases is the "default database" chosen by your library for most article searches. Your reference librarian will be able to direct you to the most useful licensed database for your purpose.

KEYWORD SEARCHING

To use an online database, you need to be adept at keyword searching. When you type a word or phrase into a search box, the computer will find sources that contain the same words or phrases. If you want the computer to search for a phrase, put it in quotation marks. Thus if you type *street people* using quotation marks, the computer will search for those two words occurring together. If you type in *street people* without quotation marks, the computer will look for the word *street* and the word *people* occurring in the same document but not necessarily together. Use your imagination to try a number of related terms. If you are researching gendered toys and you get too many hits using the keyword *toys,* try *gender toys, Barbie, G.I. Joe, girl toys, boy toys, toys psychology,* and so forth. You can increase the flexibility of your searches by using Boolean terms to expand, narrow, or limit your search (see Table 6.3 for an explanation of Boolean searches).

ILLUSTRATION OF A DATABASE SEARCH

As an illustration of a database search, we'll draw again on Megan's process as she researched the effect of Navy sonar on whales. Using the database EBSCOhost, Megan entered the keywords *Navy sonar* AND *whales,* which revealed the five articles shown in Figure 6.2. As the Results list shows, this EBSCO database carries the full text of articles 1 and 3; for articles 2 and 4, Megan will have to check the

Table 6.3 Boolean Search Commands

Command and Function	Research Example	What to Type	Search Result
X OR Y (Expands your search)	You are researching Barbie dolls and decide to include G.I. Joe figures.	"Barbie doll" OR "GI Joe"	Articles that contain either phrase
X AND Y (Narrows your search)	You are researching the psychological effects of Barbie dolls and are getting too many hits under *Barbie dolls.*	"Barbie dolls" AND psychology	Articles that include both the phrase "Barbie dolls" and the word *psychology*
X NOT Y (Limits your search)	You are researching girls' toys and are tired of reading about Barbie dolls. You want to look at other popular girls' toys.	"girl toys" NOT Barbie	Articles that include the phrase "girl toys" but exclude *Barbie*

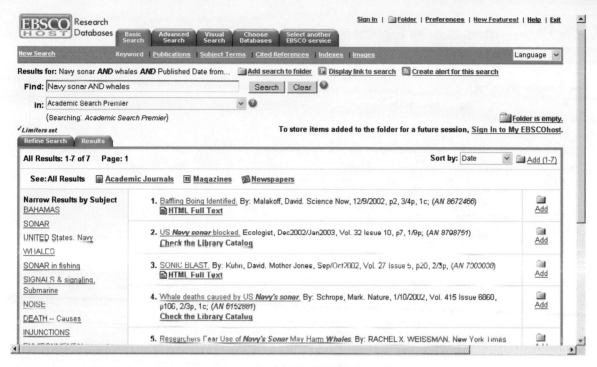

Figure 6.2   Results List from a Search Using EBSCOhost

library's catalog to locate the print periodical in the stacks. To get more information about article 3, "Sonic Blast," Megan clicked on its title, which revealed the screen shown in Figure 6.3 on page 228. This screen gives citation information and provides a brief abstract of the article. If she were interested in reading it, Megan could click on the Full Text link for the whole article.

the screen shown in Figure 6.3 on page 228.

After you've identified useful articles, locate those available in your library's print periodical collection. (This way you won't lose important contextual cues for reading them rhetorically.) For those unavailable in your library, print, download, or e-mail them from the database or order them from interlibrary loan.

Finding Cyberspace Sources: Searching the World Wide Web

Another valuable resource is the World Wide Web. In this section we begin by explaining in more detail the logic of the Internet—the difference between restricted portions of the Internet, such as licensed databases, and the

Figure 6.3   Sample Display for an Article on EBSCOhost

amorphous, ever-changing, "free-access" portion, commonly called the "World Wide Web" (see again Figure 6.1). We then offer suggestions for searching the Web.

THE LOGIC OF THE INTERNET

To understand the logic of Web search engines, you need to know that the Internet is divided into restricted sections open only to those with special access rights and a "free-access" section. Web engines such as Yahoo! or Google search only the free-access portion of the Internet. When you type keywords into a Web search engine, it searches for matches in material made available on the Web by all the users of the world's network of computers—government agencies, corporations, advocacy groups, information services, individuals with their own Web sites, and many others.

The following example will quickly show you the difference between a licensed database search and a Web search. When Megan entered the keywords *Navy sonar* AND *whales* into EBSCOhost, she received five "hits"—the titles of five articles on this subject appearing in print periodicals. In contrast, when she entered the same keywords into the Web search engine Yahoo!, she received 709,000 hits; when she tried the search engine Google, she got even more. The Web search engines are picking up, in addition to articles that someone may have posted on the Web, all references to Navy sonar and whales that appear in advocacy Web sites, government publications, newspapers, blogs, chat rooms, student papers posted on the Web, and so forth.

USING WEB SEARCH ENGINES

Although the hits from a Web search frequently include useless, shoddy, trivial, or irrelevant material, the Web's resources are breathtaking. At your fingertips you have access to government documents, legislative and corporate white papers, court cases, persuasive appeals of advocacy groups, consumer information—the list is almost endless.

The World Wide Web can be searched by a variety of engines that collect and categorize individual Web files and search them for keywords. Most of these engines will find not only text files but also graphic, audio, and video files. Different engines search the Web in different ways, so it is important that you try a variety of search engines when you look for information. Again, if you are in doubt, your reference librarian can help you choose the most productive search engine for your needs.

DETERMINING WHERE YOU ARE ON THE WEB

As you browse the Web looking for resources, clicking from link to link, try to figure out what site you are actually in at any given moment. This information is crucial, both for properly documenting a Web source and for reading the source rhetorically.

To know where you are on the Web, begin by recognizing the codes contained in a site's URL (uniform resource locator). The generic structure of a typical URL looks like this:

Here is a specific example:

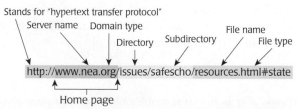

The file name "resources" is linked through a series of directories and subdirectories to the home page of the National Education Association (www.nea.org).

Often, when you click on a link in one site, you will be sent to a totally different site. To determine the home page of this new site, simply note the root URL immediately following the "www."* To view the home page directly, delete the codes to the right of the initial home page URL in your computer's location window and hit Enter. You will then be linked directly to the site's home page. Being able to examine a site's home page helps you read the site rhetorically and document it properly.

Reading Your Sources Rhetorically

Even when you have a research question that interests you, it's easy to feel overwhelmed when you return from a library with a stack of books and magazine or journal articles. How do you begin reading all this material? There is no one right answer to this question. At times you need to read slowly with analytical closeness. At other times you can skim a source, looking only for its gist or for a needed piece of information.

READING WITH YOUR OWN GOALS IN MIND

How you read a source depends to a certain extent on where you are in the research process. Early in the process, when you are in the thesis-seeking, exploratory stage, your goal is to achieve a basic understanding about your research problem. You need to become aware of different points of view, learn what is unknown or controversial about your research question, see what values or assumptions are in conflict, and build up your store of background knowledge.

Given these goals, at the early stages of research you should select, where possible, easy-to-read, overview kinds of sources to get you into the conversation. In some cases, even an encyclopedia or specialized reference work can be a good start for getting general background.

As you get deeper into your research, your questions become more focused, and the sources you read become more specialized. Once you formulate a thesis and plan a structure for your paper, you can determine more clearly the sources you need and read them with purpose and direction.

---

*Not all URLs begin with "www" after the first set of double slashes. Our description doesn't include variations from the most typical URL types. You can generally find the home page of any site by eliminating all codes to the right of the first slash mark following the initial set of double slashes.

READING WITH RHETORICAL AWARENESS

To read your sources rhetorically, you should keep two basic questions in mind:

(1) What was the source author's purpose in writing this piece?
(2) What might be my purpose in using this piece?

Table 6.4 sums up the kinds of questions a rhetorical reader typically considers.

Table 6.4 reinforces a point we've made throughout this text: all writing is produced from an angle of vision that privileges some ways of seeing and filters out other ways. You should guard against reading your sources as if they present hard, undisputed facts or universal truths. For example, if one of your sources says that

Table 6.4 Questions Asked by Rhetorical Readers	
What Was the Source Author's Purpose in Writing This Piece?	**What Might Be My Purpose in Using This Piece In My Own Argument?**
• Who is this author? What are his or her credentials and affiliations? • What audience was this person addressing? • What is the genre of this piece? (If you downloaded the piece from the World Wide Web, did it originally appear in print?) • If this piece appeared in print, what is the reputation and bias of the journal, magazine, or press? Was the piece peer reviewed? • If this piece appeared only on the Web, who or what organization sponsors the Web site (check the home page)? What is the reputation and bias of the sponsor? • What is the author's thesis or purpose? • How does this author try to change his or her audience's view? • What is this writer's angle of vision or bias? • What is omitted or censored from this text? • How reliable and credible is this author? • What facts, data, and other evidence does this author use and what are the sources of these data? • What are this author's underlying values, assumptions, and beliefs?	• How has this piece influenced or complicated my own thinking? • How does this piece relate to my research question? • How will my own intended audience react to this author? • How might I use this piece in my own argument? • Is it an opposing view that I might summarize? • Is it an alternative point of view that I might compare to other points of view? • Does it have facts and data that I might use? • Would a summary of all or part of this argument support or oppose one or more of my own points? • Could I use this author for testimony? (If so, how should I indicate this author's credentials?) • If I use this source, will I need to acknowledge the author's bias and angle of vision?

"Saint John's wort [an herb] has been shown to be an effective treatment for depression," some of your readers might accept that statement as fact—but many wouldn't. Skeptical readers would want to know who the author is, where his views have been published, and what he uses for evidence. Let's say the author is someone named Samuel Jones. Skeptical readers would ask whether Jones is relying on published research, and if so, whether the studies have been peer reviewed in reputable, scholarly journals and whether the research has been replicated by other scientists. They would also want to know whether Jones has financial connections to companies that produce herbal remedies and supplements. Rather than settling the question about Saint John's wort as a treatment for depression, a quotation from Jones may open up a heated controversy about medical research.

Reading rhetorically is thus a way of thinking critically about your sources. It influences the way you take notes, evaluate sources, and shape your argument.

Taking Effective Notes

Taking good research notes serves two functions:

1. Taking notes encourages you to read actively because you must summarize your sources' arguments, record usable information, and extract short quotations.
2. Taking notes encourages you to do exploratory thinking—to write down ideas as they occur to you, to analyze sources as you read them, and to join your sources in conversation.

There are many ways to take notes, but we can offer several techniques that have worked especially well for other writers.

1. You can use a double-entry journal. Divide a page in half, entering your informational notes on one side and your exploratory writing on the other.
2. You can record notes on index cards or in a computer file and then write out your exploratory thinking in a separate research journal.
3. You can record informational notes on your computer in a regular font and then use a boldfaced font for exploratory writing.

No matter the method, your objective is to create a visual way to distinguish your informational notes from your exploratory thinking.

A common practice of beginning researchers—one that experienced researchers almost never use—is *not* taking notes as they read and *not* doing any exploratory writing. We've seen students photocopy a dozen or more articles, but then write nothing as they read (sometimes they highlight passages with a marker), planning to rely later on memory to navigate through the sources. This practice reduces your ability to synthesize your sources and create your argument. When you begin drafting your paper, you'll have no notes to refer to, no record of your thinking-in-progress. Your only recourse is to revisit all your sources, thumbing through them one at a time—a practice that leads to passive cutting and pasting.

To make your notes purposeful, you need to imagine how a given source might be used in your research paper. Table 6.5 shows how notes are a function of your purpose.

When you use a source's exact words, be meticulous in copying them exactly and marking the quoted passage with prominent quotation marks. If you record information without directly quoting it, be sure that you restate it completely in your own words to avoid later problems with plagiarism. Next, check that you have all the bibliographic information you may need for a citation including the page numbers for each entry in your notes and the sponsor of each Web site.

Table 6.5   Note Taking According to Purpose

How Source Might Be Used in Your Paper	Notes to Take
Background information about research problem or issue	Summarize the information; record specific data.
Part of a section reviewing different points of view on your question	Summarize the source's argument; note its bias and perspective. In exploratory notes, jot down ideas on how and why different sources disagree.
As an opposing view that you must summarize and respond to	Summarize the argument fully and fairly. In and exploratory notes, speculate about why you disagree with the source and whether you can refute the argument, concede to it, or compromise with it.
As data, information, or testimony to be used as evidence to support your thesis	Record the data or information; summarize or paraphrase the supporting argument with occasional quotations of key phrases; directly quote short passages for supporting testimony; note the credentials of the writer or person quoted. In exploratory notes, record new ideas as they occur to you.
As data, information, or testimony that counters your position or raises doubts about your thesis	Take notes on counterevidence. In exploratory notes, speculate on how you might respond to the counterevidence.

Evaluating Sources

When you read sources for your research project, you need to evaluate them as you go along. As you read each potential source, ask yourself questions about the author's angle of vision, degree of advocacy, reliability, and credibility.

ANGLE OF VISION

By "angle of vision," we mean the way that a piece of writing gets shaped by the underlying values, assumptions, and beliefs of the author so that the text reflects a certain perspective, worldview, or belief system. The angle of vision is revealed by internal factors such as the author's word choice (especially notice the connotations of words), selection and omission of details, overt statements, figurative language, and grammatical emphasis, and by external factors such as the politics of the author, the genre of the source, the politics of the publisher, and so forth.

When reading a source, see whether you can detect underlying assumptions or beliefs that suggest a writer's values or political views: Is this writer conservative or liberal? Predisposed toward traditional "family values" or new family structures? Toward technology or toward the simple life? Toward free markets or regulatory controls on the economy? Toward business interests or labor? Toward the environment or jobs? Toward order or freedom?

You can also get useful clues about a writer's angle of vision by looking at external data. What are the writer's credentials? Is the writer affiliated with an advocacy group or known for a certain ideology? (If you know nothing about an author who seems important to your research, try typing the author's name into a Web search engine. You may discover useful information about the author's other publications or about the writer's reputation in various fields.) Also pay attention to publishing data. Where was this source originally published? What is the reputation and editorial slant of the publication in which the source appears? For example, editorial slants of magazines can range from very liberal to very conservative. Likewise, publications affiliated with advocacy organizations (the Sierra Club, the National Rifle Association) will have a clear editorial bias.* Table 6.6 shows our own assessment of the political biases of various popular magazines and media commentators.

---

*If you are uncertain about the editorial bias of a particular magazine or newspaper, consult the *Gale Directory of Publications and Broadcast Media* or *Magazines for Libraries,* which, among other things, identify the intended audience and political biases of a wide range of magazines and newspapers.

Table 6.6   Angles of Vision in U.S. Media and Think Tanks: A Sampling Across the Political Spectrum[1]

Commentators

Left	Left Center	Center	Right Center	Right
Barbara Ehrenreich	E.J. Dionne	Amitai Etzioni	David Brooks	Pat Buchanan
Al Franken	Ellen Goodman	Thomas Friedman	Midge Decter	Tucker Carlson
Bob Herbert	Nicholas Kristof	Kathleen Hall Jamieson	William Kristol	Linda Chavez
Michael Moore	William Raspberry	Kevin Phillips	William Safire	Ann Coulter
Bill Moyers	Mark Shields	Leonard Pitts	Andrew Sullivan	Rush Limbaugh
Salim Muwakkil	Fareed Zakaria	William Saletan	George Will	Bill O'Reilly
Daniel Schorr		Bob Woodward		Kathleen Parker

Newspapers and Magazines[2]

Left/Liberal	Center	Right/Conservative
The American Prospect	*Atlantic Monthly*	*American Spectator*
Harper's	*Business Week*	*Fortune*
Los Angeles Times	*Christian Science Monitor*	*National Review*
Mother Jones	*Commentary*	*Reader's Digest*
The Nation	*Commonweal*	*Reason*
New York Times	*Foreign Affairs*	*Wall Street Journal*
Salon	*New Republic*	*Washington Times*
Sojourners	*Slate*	*Weekly Standard*
	Washington Post	

Blogs

Liberal/Left	Moderate/Independent	Right/Conservative
americablog.com	newmoderate.blogspot.com	andrewsullivan.theatlantic.com
atrios.blogspot.com	politics-central.blogspot.com	conservativeblogger.com
crooksandliars.com	rantingbaldhippie.com	instapundit.com
dailykos.com	stevesilver.net	littlegreenfootballs.com
digbysblog.blogspot.com	themoderatevoice.com	michellemalkin.com
firedoglake.com	watchingwashington.blogspot.com	polipundit.com
huffingtonpost.com		powerlineblog.com
mediamatters.com		redstate.com
salon.com/opinion/greenwald/		
talkingpointsmemo.com		

[1]For further information about the political leanings of publications or think tanks, ask your librarian about *Gale Directory of Publications and Broadcast Media* or *NIRA World Directory of Think Tanks.*
[2]Newspapers are categorized according to positions they take on their editorial page.

(continued)

Table 6.6   Continued

Think Tanks		
Left/Liberal	Center	Right/Conservative
Center for Defense Information	The Brookings Institution	American Enterprise Institute
Center for Media and Democracy (sponsors Disinfopedia.org)	Carnegie Endowment for International Peace	Cato Institute (Libertarian)
Institute for Policy Studies	Council on Foreign Relations	Center for Strategic and International Studies
Open Society Institute (Soros Foundation)	Jamestown Foundation	Heritage Foundation (sponsors Townhall.com)
Urban Institute	National Bureau of Economic Research	Project for the New American Century
	Progressive Policy Institute	

DEGREE OF ADVOCACY

By "degree of advocacy" we mean the extent to which an author unabashedly takes a persuasive stance on a contested position as opposed to adopting a more neutral, objective, or exploratory stance. When a writer strongly advocates a position, you need to weigh carefully the writer's selection of evidence, interpretation of data, and fairness to opposing views. Although objectivity is itself an "angle of vision" and no one can be completely neutral, it is always useful to seek out authors who offer a balanced assessment of the evidence. Evidence from a more detached and neutral writer may be more trusted by your readers than the arguments of a committed advocate. For example, if you want to persuade corporate executives of the dangers of global warming, evidence from scholarly journals may be more persuasive than evidence from an environmentalist Web site or from a freelance writer in a leftist popular magazine like *Mother Jones*.

RELIABILITY

"Reliability" refers to the accuracy of factual data in a source as determined by external validation. If you check a writer's "facts" against other sources, do you find that the facts are correct? Does the writer distort facts, take them out of context, or otherwise use them unreasonably? In some controversies, key data are highly disputed—for example, the number of homeless people in the United States, the frequency of date rape, or the risk factors for many diseases. A reliable writer acknowledges these controversies and doesn't treat disputed data as fact. Furthermore, if you check out the sources used by a reliable writer, they'll reveal accurate and careful research—respected primary sources rather than hearsay or secondhand reports.

CREDIBILITY

"Credibility" is similar to "reliability" but is based on internal rather than external factors. It refers to the reader's trust in the writer's honesty, goodwill, and trustworthiness and is apparent in the writer's tone, reasonableness, fairness in summarizing opposing views, and respect for different perspectives (what we have called *ethos*). Audiences differ in how much credibility they will grant to certain authors. Nevertheless a writer can achieve a reputation for credibility, even among bitter political opponents, by applying to issues a sense of moral courage, integrity, and consistency of principle.

Understanding the Rhetoric of Web Sites

In the previous section we focused on reading sources rhetorically by asking questions about a source's angle of vision, degree of advocacy, reliability, and credibility. In this section we turn to the skills of effectively evaluating and using Web sources by understanding the special rhetoric of Web sites.

THE WEB AS A UNIQUE RHETORICAL ENVIRONMENT

Although many Web sites are highly professional and expensive to produce, the Web is also a great vehicle for democracy, giving voice to the otherwise voiceless. Anyone with a cause and a rudimentary knowledge of Web page design can create a Web site. Before the invention of the Web, people with a message had to stand on street corners passing out fliers or put money into newsletters or advocacy advertisements. The Web, in contrast, is cheap. The result is a rhetorical medium that differs in significant ways from print.

ANALYZING THE PURPOSE OF A SITE AND YOUR OWN RESEARCH PURPOSE

When you conduct research on the Web, your first question should be, "Who placed this piece on the Web and why?" You can begin answering this question by analyzing the site's home page, where you will often find navigational buttons linking to "Mission," "About Us," or other identifying information about the site's sponsors. You can also get hints about the site's purpose by asking, What kind of Web site is it? As we explained earlier, different kinds of Web sites have different purposes, often revealed by the domain identifier following the server name (.com, .net, .org, .gov, .mil). As you evaluate the Web site, also consider your own purpose for using it. For instance, are you trying to get an initial understanding of various points of view on an issue, or are you looking for reliable information? An advocacy site may be an excellent place for researching a point of view but a doubtful source of data and evidence for your own argument.

SORTING SITES BY DOMAIN TYPE

One powerful research strategy for reading Web sites rhetorically is to use the "advanced search" feature of a search engine to sort sites by domain type. As an example, consider again Megan's research dilemma when she plugged *Navy sonar* AND *whales* into Yahoo! and received 709,000 "hits." How could she begin to navigate through such a huge number? Using Yahoo!'s "advanced search" feature, Megan sorted through her hits by domain, selecting one type of domain at a time:

- The **.com sites** were primarily the sites of newspapers, news services, and whale-watching tourist sites. These sites tended to repeat the same news stories and offer superficial coverage.
- The **.org sites** were primarily the sites of environmental advocacy groups, such as the National Resources Defense Council, the Sierra Club, the League for Coastal Protection, and the Cetacean Society International—all dedicated to protecting marine life. These advocacy sites were strongly pro-whale; in their arguments against Navy sonar they either discounted or ignored issues of national security.
- The **.edu sites** of colleges and universities were primarily references to course descriptions and syllabi that included this controversy as a source of study. Megan didn't find these helpful.
- The **.gov sites** revealed documents on whales and sonar submitted to congressional hearings; they also revealed key government agencies

involved in the sonar dispute: the National Marine Fisheries Service and the National Oceanic and Atmospheric Administration.

- The **.mil sites** gave access to white papers and other documents provided by the Navy to justify its use of low-frequency sonar.

This overview of the territory helped Megan understand the angle of vision or bias of different sources. The .org sites focused on protecting marine life. In contrast, the .mil and the .gov sites helped her understand the national security issue. In the middle, trying to balance the competing demands of the environment, national security, and preservation of commerce, were the sites of government agencies not directly connected to the military. All of these sites provided valuable information, and most of them included links to scientific and research studies.

CRITERIA FOR EVALUATING A WEB SITE

Given this overview of the territory, Megan still had to decide which specific sites to use for her research. One of the most challenging parts of using the Web is determining whether a site offers gold or glitter. Sometimes the case may not be clear-cut. How do you sort out reliable, worthwhile sites from unreliable ones? We offer the following criteria developed by scholars and librarians as points to consider when you are using Web sites.

1. AUTHORITY

- Is the author or sponsor of the Web site clearly identified?
- Does the site identify the occupation, position, education, experience, and credentials of the site's authors?
- Does the introductory material reveal the author's or sponsor's motivation for publishing this information on the Web?
- Does the site provide contact information for the author or sponsor such as an e-mail or organization address?

2. OBJECTIVITY OR CLEAR DISCLOSURE OF ADVOCACY

- Is the site's purpose (to inform, explain, or persuade) clear?
- Is the site explicit about declaring its author's or sponsor's point of view?
- Does the site indicate whether authors are affiliated with a specific organization, institution, or association?
- Does the site indicate whether it is directed toward a specific audience?

3. COVERAGE

- Are the topics covered by the site clear?
- Does the site exhibit suitable depth and comprehensiveness for its purpose?
- Is sufficient evidence provided to support the ideas and opinions presented?

4. ACCURACY

- Are the sources of information stated? Can you tell whether this information is original or taken from someplace else?
- Does the information appear to be accurate? Can you verify this information by comparing this source with other sources in the field?

5. CURRENCY

- Are dates included in the Web site?
- Do the dates apply to the material itself or to its placement on the Web? Is the site regularly revised and updated?
- Is the information current, or at least still relevant, for the site's purpose?

To illustrate how these criteria can help you evaluate a Web site, consider how they could be applied to "Environmental Groups Sue to Stop Global Deployment of Navy Low Frequency Sonar System," a press release Megan found on the site of the National Resources Defense Council (see Figure 6.4). Is the article trustworthy and reliable, or is it from a fringe environmental group likely to suppress or distort evidence? Using the criteria for evaluating Web sites, Megan was able to identify the strengths and weaknesses of this site in light of her research purpose.

1. *Authority.* The sponsor of the site is clearly the NRDC. Because the NRDC presents the material as a press release, Megan assumed that their motivation is to provide information for the news media that favors their position on the sonar issue. The site does provide contact information so that journalists and others can get in touch with NRDC staff.

2. *Objectivity or clear disclosure of advocacy.* What type of organization is NRDC? The site is clearly that of an advocacy group, as indicated by the logo and motto in the left-hand panel: "The Earth's Best Defense." Megan located the home page, clicked on "About Us," and discovered that the National Resources Defense Council has been around for almost forty years. The "About Us" section states:

NRDC is the nation's most effective environmental action group, combining the grassroots power of 1.2 million members and online

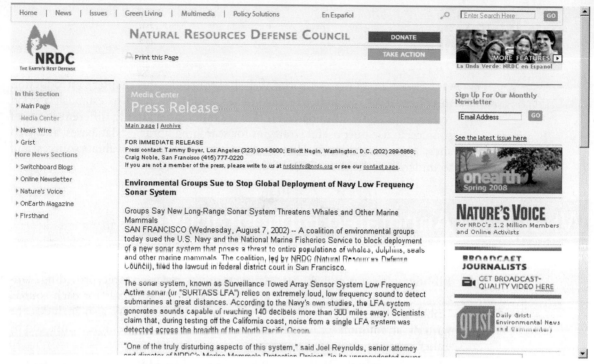

Figure 6.4   First Screen from Article on NRDC Web Site

activists with the courtroom clout and expertise of more than 350 lawyers, scientists and other professionals.

The site does very well on the criterion "clear disclosure of advocacy."

3. *Coverage.* The site is unusually broad and deep. It covers hundreds of different environmental issues and has multimedia features, blogs, games for children, and in-depth technical articles written for specialists.

4. *Accuracy.* Megan also determined that the site was accurate. Technical articles had bibliographies, and references to factual data had notes about sources. She discovered that information on this site corroborated well with references to the same data from other sites.

5. *Currency.* The site was current. News items within the site had clear indications of dates. This is an active, ongoing site.

Megan concluded that the site was an excellent source for both arguments and data from a pro-environmental perspective. She could use it to understand potential dangers of Navy sonar to whales and other marine life. However, the site was not helpful for understanding the national security and Navy reasons for needing low-frequency sonar.

Conclusion

Our discussion of the rhetoric of Web sites concludes this chapter's introduction to college-level research. We have talked about the need to establish a good research question; to understand the key differences among different kinds of sources; to use purposeful strategies for searching libraries, databases, and Web sites; to use your rhetorical knowledge when you read and evaluate sources; and to understand the rhetoric of Web sites.

What Is an Annotated Bibliography?

Bibliographies are alphabetized lists of sources on a given topic, providing readers with the names of authors, titles, and publication details for each source. Unlike a plain list of sources, an **annotated bibliography** also includes the writer's "annotation" or commentary on each source. These annotations can be either *summary-only* or *evaluative*.

- A **summary-only annotation** provides a capsule of the source's contents without any additional comments from the bibliography's author.
- An **evaluative annotation** adds the author's critique or assessment of the work, including comments about the source's rhetorical context, its particular strengths or weaknesses, and its usefulness or value.

Whichever type is used, the length of the annotation is a function of its audience and purpose. Brief annotations comprise only a few sentences (one standard approach—to be described later—uses three sentences) while longer annotations can be up to 150 words. Brief annotations are most common when the annotated bibliography has numerous entries; longer annotations, which allow for fuller summaries and more detailed analyses, are often more helpful for readers but can make an annotated bibliography too long if there are many sources.

Annotated bibliographies serve several important functions. First, writing an annotated bibliography engages researchers in exploratory thinking by requiring that they read sources rhetorically like experts, entering critically into scholarly conversations. Annotated bibliographies can also be valuable time-saving tools for new researchers in a field. By providing overview information about potential sources, they help new researchers determine whether a particular source might be useful for their own purposes. Think of source annotations as analogous to short movie reviews that help you select your next film. (What's this movie about? How good is it?) Additionally, annotated bibliographies can establish the writer's *ethos* by showing the depth, breadth, and competence of the writer's research. (A good annotated bibliography proves that you have read and thought about your sources.)

Features of Annotated Bibliography Entries

Each entry has two main parts, the bibliographic citation and the annotation. The **bibliographic citation** should follow the conventions of your assigned documentation style such as the Modern Language Association (MLA) or the American Psychological Association (APA).

An **evaluative annotation** (the most common kind) typically includes three elements. In a three-sentence evaluative annotation, each element is covered in one sentence.

- *Rhetorical information,* including the source's rhetorical context, particularly its genre and (if not implied by the genre) its purpose and audience. Is this source a scholarly article? An op-ed piece? A blog? What is the author's purpose and who is the intended audience? Are there any political biases that need to be noted?
- *A summary of the source's content.* In some cases, a writer simply lists what is covered in the source. Whenever possible, however, summarize the source's actual argument. (Note: In a *summary-only* annotation, this summary is the only element included.)
- *The writer's evaluation of the source.* What are the source's particular strengths or weaknesses? How useful is the source for specific purposes? How might the writer use the source for his or her research project? (Or, if the annotated bibliography comes at the end of the project, how did the writer use the source?)

Examples of Annotation Entries

Here are examples of different kinds of annotations:

Summary-Only Annotation

Bowley, G. (2006, October). The high priestess of Internet friendship. *Financial Times Weekend Magazine.* Retrieved from LexisNexis Academic.

In this feature story, Bowley explains the development of OSNs from their origins in *Friendster* to their current popularity in *MySpace* and *Facebook*. He also traces further developments of OSNs and explains their difficulties in making profits through commercial advertising. Finally, Bowley uses interviews with researchers to show how young people use OSNs to maintain social relationships and to play with different identities through self-expression.

Evaluative Annotation

Bowley, G. (2006, October). The high priestess of Internet friendship. *Financial Times Weekend Magazine.* Retrieved from LexisNexis Academic.

This article is a feature story in the "Arts and Weekend" section of the *Financial Times Weekend Magazine.* Bowley's information comes from interviews with researchers who study online social networks (OSNs). Bowley explains the development of OSNs from their origins in *Friendster* to their current popularity in *MySpace* and *Facebook*, traces further developments of OSNs, and explains their difficulties in making profits through commercial advertising. Bowley also shows how young people use OSNs to maintain social relationships and to play with different identities through self-expression. A particularly valuable section mentions the dangers of OSNs, such as sexual predators. However, Danah Boyd, a researcher whom Bowley quotes extensively, defends OSNs as a place where young people can explore their identities and "negotiate this new world." This article gives a mostly positive view of OSNs and goes beyond other articles by showing how OSNs provide a new space for "identity production."

Three-Sentence Evaluative Annotation

Bowley, G. (2006, October). The high priestess of Internet friendship. *Financial Times Weekend Magazine.* Retrieved from LexisNexis Academic.

This article is a journalistic feature story written for readers of a major business and finance newspaper. It gives the history of online social networks (OSN) including *Friendster*, *MySpace*, and *Facebook*, explains their difficulties in making money through commercial advertising, and shows how young people use OSNs to maintain social relationships and to play with different identities through self-expression. This is a valuable article that gives a mostly positive view of OSNs by showing how they provide a new space for "identity production" and self-expression.

Writing a Critical Preface for Your Annotated Bibliography

Scholars who publish annotated bibliographies typically introduce them with a critical preface that explains the scope and purpose of the bibliography. When you write a critical preface for your own annotated bibliography, you have a chance to highlight your critical thinking and show the purposeful way that you conducted your research. Typically the critical preface includes the following information:

- A contextual overview that shows the purpose of the annotated bibliography and suggests its value and significance for the reader
- The research question posed by the author
- The dates during which the bibliography was compiled
- An overview of the number of items in the bibliography and the kinds of material included

Shaping, Drafting, and Revising

The key to producing a good annotated bibliography is to take good research notes as you read. Before composing your annotated bibliography, make sure that you understand your instructor's preferences for the number of entries required and for the length and kinds of annotations. Arrange the bibliography in alphabetical order as you would in a "References" (APA format) list.

Questions for Peer Review

The following questions are based on the assumption that your instructor requires evaluative annotations and a critical preface. Adjust the questions to fit a different assignment.

CRITICAL PREFACE

1. Where does the writer explain the following: The purpose and significance of the bibliography? The research question that motivated the research? The dates of the research? The kinds of sources included?

2. How could the critical preface be improved?

BIBLIOGRAPHIC CITATIONS

3. Does each citation follow APA conventions? Pay particular attention to the formatting of sources downloaded from a licensed database or from the Web.

4. Are the sources arranged alphabetically?

ANNOTATIONS

5. Where does each annotation include the following: Information about genre or rhetorical context? A capsule summary of the source's contents? An evaluative comment?

6. Identify any places where the annotations are confusing or unclear or where the writer could include more information.

7. How could one or more of the annotations be improved?

STUDENT MODELS

What Is the Effect of Online Social Networks

on Communication Skills?

An Annotated Bibliography

STUDENT MODEL #1

What Is the Effect of Online Social Networks on Communication Skills?

An Annotated Bibliography

Critical Preface

1   Today, online social networks (OSNs) such as *MySpace* and *Facebook* have become staples in the lives of most American young people. Although I was conscious that OSNs were impacting the way young people communicate with each other, I was largely unaware of the specific ways that the people used these OSNs or how their communication skills were being affected by this new technology. For this research project, I set out to discover how online social networks influence the way young people communicate with each other. I posed several specific questions that I hoped my research could help me answer: (1) Why are OSNs so popular? (2) How do young people use OSNs? (3) How do OSNs affect communication skills? And (4) To what extent might OSNs be harmful or detrimental? These questions deserve to be examined because as more people move toward these new modes of communication, these networks will increasingly influence society as a whole.

2   I conducted this research during a one-week period in late February 2007. The bibliography contains different kinds of sources: two articles from popular magazines or newspapers; three articles from scholarly journals; and one survey report from a major Internet site devoted to research on people's use of the Internet. These sources gave me preliminary answers to all my initial research questions. They show why young people are attracted to OSNs and why and how they use them. Particularly valuable for my research are the articles by

Taken from: *The Allyn & Bacon Guide to Writing,* Sixth Edition by John D. Ramage, John C. Bean, and June Johnson.

Lampe, Ellison, and Steinfield (2006) showing the positive potential of OSNs and the article by Chou, Condron, and Belland (2005) showing the possible negative potential if persons become addicted to OSNs.

References

Chou, C., Condron, L., & Belland, J. C. (2005). A review of the research on Internet addiction. *Educational Psychology Review, 17*(4), 363–389. Retrieved from http://www.ebscohost.com/academic/academic-search-complete

This lengthy academic article written for scholars reviews research on Internet addiction. It has four sections: (1) explanations of how Internet addiction is defined and assessed; (2) problems created by Internet addiction and variables such as gender or psychosocial traits associated with addiction; (3) explanations for why the Internet creates addictions; and (4) ways to treat Internet addiction. For my project, section 2 on problems was most valuable. In one study 13% of respondents reported that Internet use interfered with their personal lives or academic performance. Although Internet addiction didn't seem as harmful as other addictions, the authors observed that too much dependence on online relationships can interfere with real relationships. The tables in this article show the key findings from dozens of research studies.

Lampe, D., Ellison, N., & Steinfield, C. (2006). A Face(book) in the crowd: Social searching versus social browsing. *Proceedings of the 2006 20th Anniversary Conference on Computer Supported Cooperative Work,* 167–170. Retrieved from portal.acm.org/

This scholarly research report is based on questionnaires about *Facebook* usage received from 1,440 first-year students at Michigan State University in fall 2006. The researchers investigated whether students used *Facebook* primarily to meet new people ("social browsers") or to maintain or develop friendships with persons whom they had already met ("social searchers.") The findings

contradicted the popular view that *Facebook* users are social browsers. Rather,

the majority of respondents used the network to keep in touch with existing

friends or to find out additional information about classmates or other recent

acquaintances. This article has useful data about perceived audiences for

profiles (peers rather than professors or administrators) and about primary

reasons for using *Facebook*. The article provided insights into why *Facebook*

is popular.

Lenhart, A., & Madden, M. (2007, January). Social networking websites and teens:

An overview. *Pew Internet & American Life Project.* Retrieved from Pew

Research Center.

This source is an online memo from researchers working for the Pew Internet

and American Life Project, a non-profit research organization. It reports the

results of a telephone survey of a random national sample of 935 youths aged

12 to 17 in fall 2006. The document has numerous tables showing

demographic data about teens' use of OSNs, the most popular sites, the

frequency of use, and the reasons teens give for using the sites. Because of

the scientific method of polling, this article provides reliable data for

understanding how teens currently use OSNs.

PRACTICE

1 Explain how James includes the three common elements of an evaluative annotation (genre/rhetorical context, summary of content, evaluation) in each of his annotations. How might James use information and points in this annotated bibliography in his researched argument?

2 Choose a topic that you are considering for your research project, and find one credible scholarly article that was published very recently—this year if possible. Check the works cited or reference page to see what sources were cited by that author. Starting with the most recent, locate sources that seem closest to your own topic and check their reference pages as well. Record trends in the research on this topic: names of authors who seem to be most often cited, key terms that are important (look especially at titles and abstracts), and any other information you can glean from a quick skimming. Then use this information to help set up your own research plan and search terms. Be prepared to explain in class what other relevant books, articles, or Web sites you found using this research method and how you located them.

3 Pairs of Students: Becoming Familiar with the Library

Visit the library with a classmate or with your entire class and learn how to access the online catalog, the subscription databases of periodical articles, and the World Wide Web. Find out how to print full-text articles in the library or send them to your e-mail address at home. Arrange for passwords, if those are required. Then learn to locate the following: books and bound periodicals in the stacks; current periodicals; microfilm or microfiche, including how to use the viewers; and the government documents. Finally, locate the reference desk and the reference librarians, who are always willing to help you with a research project.

4 The Researched Position Paper: Writing an Annotated Bibliography

a. *Collect ten quality sources about your issue.* Make certain that your sources express several different perspectives or ways of thinking about your issue. Copy all the publisher's information needed to cite your sources in APA format, and assemble your bibliography in alphabetical order. Unless your instructor indicates otherwise, an annotated bibliography should include both print and online sources and should represent more than two perspectives on the issue in these bibliographical items.

b. *Survey, skim, and read selected parts of each source.*

c. *Write a summary, a response, and an indication of how you might use each source in your paper after each item.* The example on pages 248–250 provides selected items from a student's annotated bibliography and demonstrates how to record information from different types of sources, how to summarize, how to respond to the sources, and how to indicate where you might use them in your paper.

d. The Researched Position Paper: Evaluating Your Research

Look back over your bibliography and the other research and ideas you have gathered and complete the questions that follow below. Make certain all of the information you want to use is complete and that you have the information you need to cite all sources. Add, correct, or eliminate any material that might weaken your argument.

- Do I have enough information to be convincing? What can I add?
- Is my information reliable and convincing? How can I make it more so?
- Is anything exaggerated or oversimplified? How can I be more accurate?
- Do I rely too much on my own authority ("This is true because I say it is") instead of giving support? Can I add opinions of other authorities to be more convincing?
- Am I weakening this argument with too much emotional material? Should any of it be eliminated?

Composition !

Baker College
Clinton Township

How Do I Write a Summary?

7

What Is a Summary?

The best way to demonstrate that you understand the information and the ideas in any piece of writing is to compose an accurate and clearly written summary of that piece. By a *summary* we mean a *brief restatement, in your own words, of the content of a passage* (a group of paragraphs, a chapter, an article, a book). This restatement should focus on the *central idea* of the passage. The briefest of summaries (one or two sentences) will do no more than this. A longer, more complete summary will indicate, in condensed form, the main points in the passage that support or explain the central idea. It will reflect the order in which these points are presented and the emphasis given to them. It may even include some important examples from the passage. But it will not include minor details. It will not repeat points simply for the purpose of emphasis. And it will not contain any of your own opinions or conclusions. A good summary, therefore, has three central qualities: *brevity, completeness,* and *objectivity.*

Can a Summary Be Objective?

Objectivity could be difficult to achieve in a summary. By definition, writing a summary requires you to select some aspects of the original and leave out others. Since deciding what to select and what to leave out calls for your personal judgment, your summary really is a work of interpretation. And, certainly, your interpretation of a passage may differ from another person's.

One factor affecting the nature and quality of your interpretation is your *prior knowledge* of the subject. For example, if you're attempting to summarize an anthropological article and you're a novice in that field, then your summary of the article will likely differ from that of your professor, who has spent twenty years studying this particular area and whose judgment about what is more or less significant is undoubtedly more reliable than your own. By the same token, your personal or professional *frame of reference* may also affect your interpretation. A union representative and a management representative attempting to summarize the latest management offer would probably come up with two very different accounts. Still, we believe that in most cases it's possible to produce a reasonably objective summary of a passage if you make a conscious, good-faith effort to be unbiased and to prevent your own feelings on the subject from coloring your account of the author's text.

Using the Summary

In some quarters, the summary has a bad reputation—and with reason. Summaries are often provided by writers as substitutes for analyses. As students, many of us have summarized books that we were supposed to *review critically*. All the same, the summary does have a place in respectable college work. First, writing a summary is an excellent way to understand what you read. This in itself is an important goal of academic study. If you don't understand your source material, chances are you won't be able to refer to it usefully in a paper. Summaries help you understand what you read because they force you to put the text into your own words. Practice with writing summaries also develops your general writing habits, because a good summary, like any other piece of good writing, is clear, coherent, and accurate.

Second, summaries are useful to your readers. Let's say you're writing a paper about the McCarthy era in the United States, and in part of that paper you want to discuss Arthur Miller's *The Crucible* as a dramatic treatment of the subject. A summary of the plot would be helpful to a reader who hasn't seen or read—or who doesn't remember—the play. Or perhaps you're writing a paper about the politics of recent American military interventions. If your reader isn't likely to be familiar with American actions in Kosovo and Afghanistan, it would be a good idea to summarize these events at some early point in the paper. In many cases (an exam, for instance), you can use a summary to demonstrate your knowledge of what your professor already knows; when writing a paper, you can use a summary to inform your professor about some relatively unfamiliar source.

Third, summaries are required frequently in college-level writing. For example, on a psychology midterm, you may be asked to explain Carl Jung's theory of the collective unconscious and to show how it differs from Sigmund Freud's theory of the personal unconscious. You may have read about Jung's theory in your textbook or in a supplementary article, or your instructor may have outlined it in her lecture. You can best demonstrate your understanding of it by summarizing it. Then you'll proceed to contrast it with Freud's theory—which, of course, you must also summarize.

WHERE DO WE FIND WRITTEN SUMMARIES?

Here are just a few of the types of writing that involve summary:

Academic Writing

- **Critique papers** summarize material in order to critique it.
- **Synthesis papers** summarize to show relationships between sources.
- **Analysis papers** summarize theoretical perspectives before applying them.
- **Research papers**: note-taking and reporting research require summary.
- **Literature reviews**: overviews of work are presented in brief summaries.
- **Argument papers** summarize evidence and opposing arguments.
- **Essay exams** demonstrate understanding of course materials through summary.

Workplace Writing

- **Policy briefs** condense complex public policy.
- **Business plans** summarize costs, relevant environmental impacts, and other important matters.
- **Memos, letters, and reports** summarize procedures, meetings, product assessments, expenditures, and more.
- **Medical charts** record patient data in summarized form.
- **Legal briefs** summarize relevant facts and arguments of cases.

The Reading Process

It may seem to you that being able to tell (or retell) in summary form exactly what a passage says is a skill that ought to be taken for granted in anyone who can read at high school level. Unfortunately, this is not so. For all kinds of reasons, people don't always read carefully. In fact, it's probably safe to say that usually they don't. Either they read so inattentively that they skip over words, phrases, or even whole sentences, or, if they do see the words in front of them, they see them without registering their significance.

When a reader fails to pick up the meaning and implications of a sentence or two, usually there's no real harm done. (An exception: You could lose credit on an exam or paper because you failed to read or to realize the significance of a crucial direction by your instructor.) But over longer stretches—the paragraph, the section, the article, or the chapter—inattentive or haphazard reading interferes with your goals as a reader: to perceive the shape of the argument, to grasp the central idea, to determine the main points that compose it, to relate the parts of the whole, and to note key examples. This kind of reading takes a lot more energy and determination than casual reading. But in the long run it's an energy-saving method because it enables you to retain the content of the material and to draw upon that content in your own responses. In other words, it allows you to develop an accurate and coherent written discussion that goes beyond summary.

CRITICAL READING FOR SUMMARY

- *Examine the context.* Note the credentials, occupation, and publications of the author. Identify the source in which the piece originally appeared. This information helps illuminate the author's perspective on the topic he or she is addressing.

- *Note the title and subtitle.* Some titles are straightforward; the meanings of others become clearer as you read. In either case, titles typically identify the topic being addressed and often reveal the author's attitude toward that topic.

- *Identify the main point.* Whether a piece of writing contains a thesis statement in the first few paragraphs or builds its main point without stating it up front, look at the entire piece to arrive at an understanding of the overall point being made.

- *Identify the subordinate points.* Notice the smaller subpoints that make up the main point, and make sure you understand how they relate to the main point. If a particular subpoint doesn't clearly relate to the main point you've identified, you may need to modify your understanding of the main point.

- *Break the reading into sections.* Notice which paragraphs make up a piece's introduction, body, and conclusion. Break up the body paragraphs into sections that address the writer's various subpoints.

- *Distinguish between points, examples, and counterarguments.* Critical reading requires careful attention to what a writer is *doing* as well as what he or she is *saying.* When a writer quotes someone else, or relays an example of something, ask yourself why this is being done. What point is the example supporting? Is another source being quoted as support for a point or as a counterargument that the writer sets out to address?

- *Watch for transitions within and between paragraphs.* In order to follow the logic of a piece of writing, as well as to distinguish between points, examples, and counterarguments, pay attention to the transitional words and phrases writers use. Transitions function like road signs, preparing the reader for what's next.

- *Read actively and recursively.* Don't treat reading as a passive, linear progression through a text. Instead, read as though you are engaged in a dialogue with the writer: Ask questions of the text as you read, make notes in the margin, underline key ideas in pencil, put question or exclamation marks next to passages that confuse or excite you. Go back to earlier points once you finish a reading, stop during your reading to recap what's come so far, and move back and forth through a text.

How to Write Summaries

Every article you read will present its own challenge as you work to summarize it. As you'll discover, saying in a few words what has taken someone else a great many can be difficult. But like any other skill, the ability to summarize improves with practice. Here are a few pointers to get you started. They represent possible stages, or steps, in the process of writing a summary. These pointers are not meant to be ironclad rules; rather, they are designed to encourage habits of thinking that will allow you to vary your technique as the situation demands.

GUIDELINES FOR WRITING SUMMARIES

- *Read the passage carefully.* Determine its structure. Identify the author's purpose in writing. (This will help you distinguish between more important and less important information.) Make a note in the margin when you get confused or when you think something is important; highlight or underline points sparingly, if at all.

- *Reread.* This time divide the passage into sections or stages of thought. The author's use of paragraphing will often be a useful guide. *Label,* on the passage itself, each section or stage of thought. *Underline* key ideas and terms. Write notes in the margin.

- *Write one-sentence summaries,* on a separate sheet of paper, of each stage of thought.

- *Write a thesis—a one- or two-sentence summary of the entire passage.* The thesis should express the central idea of the passage, as you have determined it from the preceding steps. You may find it useful to follow the approach of most newspaper stories—naming the *what, who, why, where, when,* and *how* of the matter. For persuasive passages, summarize in a sentence the author's conclusion. For descriptive passages, indicate the subject of the description and its key feature(s). Note: In some cases, *a suitable thesis statement may already be in the original passage.* If so, you may want to quote it directly in your summary.

(continued)

> ### GUIDELINES FOR WRITING SUMMARIES *CONT.*
>
> - ***Write the first draft of your summary*** by (1) combining the thesis with your list of one-sentence summaries or (2) combining the thesis with one-sentence summaries *plus* significant details from the passage. In either case, eliminate repetition and less important information. Disregard minor details or generalize them (e.g., Bill Clinton and George W. Bush might be generalized as "recent presidents"). Use as few words as possible to convey the main ideas.
> - ***Check your summary against the original passage*** and make whatever adjustments are necessary for accuracy and completeness.
> - ***Revise your summary,*** inserting transitional words and phrases where necessary to ensure coherence. Check for style. *Avoid a series of short, choppy sentences.* Combine sentences for a smooth, logical flow of ideas. Check for grammatical correctness, punctuation, and spelling.

Demonstration: Summary

To demonstrate these points at work, let's go through the process of summarizing a passage of expository material—that is, writing that is meant to inform and/or persuade. Read the following selection carefully. Try to identify its parts and understand how they work together to create an overall statement.

Will Your Job Be Exported?

Alan S. Blinder

Alan S. Blinder is the Gordon S. Rentschler Memorial Professor of Economics at Princeton University. He has served as vice chairman of the Federal Reserve Board and was a member of President Clinton's original Council of Economic Advisers.

The great conservative political philosopher Edmund Burke, who probably would not have been a reader of *The American Prospect*, once observed, "You can never plan the future by the past."* But when it comes to preparing the American workforce for the jobs of the future, we may be doing just that.

*Edmund Burke (1729–1797) was a conservative British statesman, philosopher, and author. *The American Prospect,* in which "Will Your Job Be Exported?" first appeared in the November 2006 issue, describes itself as "an authoritative magazine of liberal ideas."

For about a quarter-century, demand for labor appears to have shifted toward the college-educated and away from high school graduates and dropouts. This shift, most economists believe, is the primary (though not the sole) reason for rising income inequality, and there is no end in sight. Economists refer to this phenomenon by an antiseptic name: skill-biased technical progress. In plain English, it means that the labor market has turned ferociously against the low skilled and the uneducated.

In a progressive society, such a worrisome social phenomenon might elicit some strong policy responses, such as more compensatory education, stepped-up efforts at retraining, reinforcement (rather than shredding) of the social safety net, and so on. You don't fight the market's valuation of skills; you try to mitigate its more deleterious effects. We did a bit of this in the United States in the 1990s, by raising the minimum wage and expanding the Earned Income Tax Credit.* Combined with tight labor markets, these measures improved things for the average worker. But in this decade, little or no mitigation has been attempted. Social Darwinism has come roaring back.†

With one big exception: We have expended considerable efforts to keep more young people in school longer (e.g., reducing high-school dropouts and sending more kids to college) and to improve the quality of schooling (e.g., via charter schools and No Child Left Behind‡). Success in these domains may have been modest, but not for lack of trying. You don't have to remind Americans that education is important; the need for educational reform is etched into the public consciousness. Indeed, many people view education as the silver bullet. On hearing the question "How do we best prepare the American workforce of the future?" many Americans react reflexively with: "Get more kids to study science and math, and send more of them to college."

Which brings me to the future. As I argued in a recent article in *Foreign Affairs* magazine, the greatest problem for the next generation of American workers may not be lack of education, but rather "offshoring"—the movement of jobs overseas, especially to countries

---

*The Earned Income Tax Credit, an anti-poverty measure enacted by Congress in 1975 and revised in the 1980s and 1990s, provides a credit against federal income taxes for any filer who claims a dependent child.

†Social Darwinism, a largely discredited philosophy dating from the Victorian era and espoused by Herbert Spenser, asserts that Charles Darwin's observations on natural selection apply to human societies. Social Darwinists argue that the poor are less fit to survive than the wealthy and should, through a natural process of adaptation, be allowed to die out.

‡Charter schools are public schools with specialized missions to operate outside of regulations that some feel restrict creativity and performance in traditional school settings. The No Child Left Behind Act of 2001 (NCLB) mandates standards-based education for all schools receiving federal funding. Both the charter schools movement and NCLB can be understood as efforts to improve public education.

with much lower wages, such as India and China. Manufacturing jobs have been migrating overseas for decades. But the new wave of off-shoring, of *service* jobs, is something different.

Traditionally, we think of service jobs as being largely immune to foreign competition. After all, you can't get your hair cut by a barber or your broken arm set by a doctor in a distant land. But stunning advances in communication technology, plus the emergence of a vast new labor pool in Asia and Eastern Europe, are changing that picture radically, sub-jecting millions of presumed-safe domestic service jobs to foreign com-petition. And it is not necessary actually to move jobs to low-wage countries in order to restrain wage increases; the mere threat of off-shoring can put a damper on wages.

Service-sector offshoring is a minor phenomenon so far, Lou Dobbs notwithstanding; probably well under 1 percent of U.S. service jobs have been outsourced.* But I believe that service-sector offshoring will even-tually exceed manufacturing-sector offshoring by a hefty margin—for three main reasons. The first is simple arithmetic: There are vastly more service jobs than manufacturing jobs in the United States (and in other rich countries). Second, the technological advances that have made service-sector offshoring possible will continue and accelerate, so the range of services that can be moved offshore will increase ineluctably. Third, the number of (e.g., Indian and Chinese) workers capable of performing ser-vice jobs offshore seems certain to grow, perhaps exponentially.

I do not mean to paint a bleak picture here. Ever since Adam Smith and David Ricardo, economists have explained and extolled the gains in living standards that derive from international trade.[†] Those arguments are just as valid for trade in services as for trade in goods. There really *are* net gains to the United States from expanding service-sector trade with India, China, and the rest. The offshoring problem is not about the adverse nature of what economists call the economy's eventual equilib-rium. Rather, it is about the so-called transition—the ride from here to there. That ride, which could take a generation or more, may be bumpy. And during the long adjustment period, many U.S. wages could face downward pressure.

Thus far, only American manufacturing workers and a few low-end service workers (e.g., call-center operators) have been competing, at least potentially, with millions of people in faraway lands eager to work for

---

*Lou Dobbs, a conservative columnist and political commentator for CNN, is well known for his anti-immigration views.

[†]Adam Smith (1723–1790), Scottish author of *An Inquiry into the Nature and Causes of the Wealth of Nations* (1776), established the foundations of modern economics. David Ricardo (1772–1823) was a British businessman, statesman, and economist who founded the classical school of economics and is best known for his studies of monetary policy.

what seems a pittance by U.S. standards. But offshoring is no longer limited to low-end service jobs. Computer code can be written overseas and e-mailed back to the United States. So can your tax return and lots of legal work, provided you do not insist on face-to-face contact with the accountant or lawyer. In writing and editing this article, I communicated with the editors and staff of *The American Prospect* only by telephone and e-mail. Why couldn't they (or I, for that matter) have been in India? The possibilities are, if not endless, at least vast.

10   What distinguishes the jobs that cannot be offshored from the ones that can? The crucial distinction is not—and this is the central point of this essay—the required levels of skill and education. These attributes have been critical to labor-market success in the past, but may be less so in the future. Instead, the new critical distinction may be that some services either require personal delivery (e.g., driving a taxi and brain surgery) or are seriously degraded when delivered electronically (e.g., college teaching—at least, I hope!), while other jobs (e.g., call centers and keyboard data entry) are not. Call the first category personal services and the second category impersonal services. With this terminology, I have three main points to make about preparing our workforce for the brave, new world of the future.

First, we need to think about, plan, and redesign our educational system with the crucial distinction between personal service jobs and impersonal service jobs in mind. Many of the impersonal service jobs will migrate offshore, but the personal service jobs will stay here.

Second, the line that divides personal services from impersonal services will move in only one direction over time, as technological progress makes it possible to deliver an ever increasing array of services electronically.

Third, the novel distinction between personal and impersonal jobs is quite different from, and appears essentially unrelated to, the traditional distinction between jobs that do and do not require high levels of education.

For example, it is easy to offshore working in a call center, typing transcripts, writing computer code, and reading X-rays. The first two require little education; the last two require quite a lot. On the other hand, it is either impossible or very difficult to offshore janitorial services, fast-food restaurant service, college teaching, and open-heart surgery. Again, the first two occupations require little or no education, while the last two require a great deal. There seems to be little or no correlation between educational requirements (the old concern) and how "offshorable" jobs are (the new one).

15   If so, the implications could be startling. A generation from now, civil engineers (who must be physically present) may be in greater demand in the United States than computer engineers (who don't). Similarly, there might be more divorce lawyers (not offshorable) than tax lawyers (partly offshorable). More imaginatively, electricians might earn more than computer programmers. I am not predicting any of this; lots

...*continued* Will Your Job Be Exported?, **Alan S. Blinder**

of things influence relative demands and supplies for different types of labor. But it all seems within the realm of the possible as technology continues to enhance the offshorability of even highly skilled occupations. What does seem highly likely is that the relative demand for labor in the United States will shift away from impersonal services and toward personal services, and this shift will look quite different from the familiar story of skill-biased technical progress. So Burke's warning is worth heeding.

I am *not* suggesting that education will become a handicap in the job market of the future. On the contrary, to the extent that education raises productivity and that better-educated workers are more adaptable and/or more creative, a wage premium for higher education should remain. Thus, it still makes sense to send more of America's youth to college. But, over the next generation, the kind of education our young people receive may prove to be more important than how much education they receive. In that sense, a college degree may lose its exalted "silver bullet" status.

Looking back over the past 25 years, "stay in school longer" was excellent advice for success in the labor market. But looking forward over the next 25 years, more subtle occupational advice may be needed. "Prepare yourself for a high-end personal service occupation that is not offshorable" is a more nuanced message than "stay in school." But it may prove to be more useful. And many non-offshorable jobs—such as carpenters, electricians, and plumbers—do not require college education.

The hard question is how to make this more subtle advice concrete and actionable. The children entering America's educational system today, at age 5, will emerge into a very different labor market when they leave it. Given gestation periods of 13 to 17 years and more, educators and policy-makers need to be thinking now about the kinds of training and skills that will best prepare these children for their future working lives. Specifically, it is essential to educate America's youth for the jobs that will actually be available in America 20 to 30 years from now, not for the jobs that will have moved offshore.

Some of the personal service jobs that will remain in the United States will be very high-end (doctors), others will be less glamorous though well paid (plumbers), and some will be "dead end" (janitor). We need to think long and hard about the types of skills that best prepare people to deliver high-end personal services, and how to teach those skills in our elementary and high schools. I am not an education specialist, but it strikes me that, for example, the central thrust of No Child Left Behind is pushing the nation in exactly the wrong direction. I am all for accountability. But the nation's school system will not build the creative, flexible, people-oriented workforce we will need in the future by drilling kids incessantly with rote preparation for standardized tests in the vain hope that they will perform as well as memory chips.

20   Starting in the elementary schools, we need to develop our young-sters' imaginations and people skills as well as their "reading, writing, and 'rithmetic." Remember that kindergarten grade for "works and plays well with others"? It may become increasingly important in a world of per-sonally delivered services. Such training probably needs to be continued and made more sophisticated in the secondary schools, where, for exam-ple, good communications skills need to be developed.

More vocational education is probably also in order. After all, nurses, carpenters, and plumbers are already scarce, and we'll likely need more of them in the future. Much vocational training now takes place in com-munity colleges; and they, too, need to adapt their curricula to the job market of the future.

While it is probably still true that we should send more kids to col-lege and increase the number who study science, math, and engineering, we need to focus on training more college students for the high-end jobs that are unlikely to move offshore, and on developing a creative work-force that will keep America incubating and developing new processes, new products, and entirely new industries. Offshoring is, after all, mostly about following and copying. America needs to lead and innovate instead, just as we have in the past.

Educational reform is not the whole story, of course. I suggested at the outset, for example, that we needed to repair our tattered social safety net and turn it into a retraining trampoline that bounces displaced work-ers back into productive employment. But many low-end personal ser-vice jobs cannot be turned into more attractive jobs simply by more training—think about janitors, fast-food workers, and nurse's aides, for example. Running a tight labor market would help such workers, as would a higher minimum wage, an expanded Earned Income Tax Credit, universal health insurance, and the like.

Moving up the skill ladder, employment is concentrated in the pub-lic or quasi-public sector in a number of service occupations. Teachers and health-care workers are two prominent examples. In such cases, gov-ernment policy can influence wages and working conditions directly by upgrading the structure and pay of such jobs—developing more profes-sional early-childhood teachers and fewer casual daycare workers for example—as long as the taxpayer is willing to foot the bill. Similarly, some service jobs such as registered nurses are in short supply mainly because we are not training enough qualified personnel. Here, too, pub-lic policy can help by widening the pipeline to allow more workers through. So there are a variety of policy levers that might do some good—if we are willing to pull them.

25   But all that said, education is still the right place to start. Indeed, it is much more than that because the educational system affects the entire population and because no other institution is nearly as important when it comes to preparing our youth for the world of work. As the first

---

...continued Will Your Job Be Exported?, **Alan S. Blinder**

industrial revolution took hold, America radically transformed (and democratized) its educational system to meet the new demands of an industrial society. We may need to do something like that again. There is a great deal at stake here. If we get this one wrong, the next generation will pay dearly. But if we get it (close to) right, the gains from trade promise coming generations a prosperous future.

The somewhat inchoate challenge posed here—preparing more young Americans for personal service jobs—brings to mind one of my favorite Churchill quotations: "You can always count on Americans to do the right thing—after they've tried everything else." It is time to start trying.

READ, REREAD, HIGHLIGHT

Let's consider our recommended pointers for writing a summary.

As you reread the passage, note in the margins of the essay important points, shifts in thought, and questions you may have. Consider the essay's significance as a whole and its stages of thought. What does it say? How is it organized? How does each part of the passage fit into the whole? What do all these points add up to?

Here is how several paragraphs from the middle of Blinder's article might look after you have marked the main ideas by highlighting and by marginal notations.

Service-sector offshoring is a minor phenomenon so far, Lou Dobbs notwithstanding; probably well under 1 percent of U.S. service jobs have been outsourced. But I believe that service-sector offshoring will eventually exceed manufacturing-sector offshoring by a hefty margin—for three main reasons. The first is simple arithmetic: There are vastly more service jobs than manufacturing jobs in the United States (and in other rich countries). Second, the technological advances that have made service-sector offshoring possible will continue and accelerate, so the range of services that can be moved offshore will increase ineluctably. Third, the number of (e.g., Indian

Offshored service jobs will eclipse lost manufacturing jobs—3 reasons

and Chinese) workers capable of performing service jobs offshore seems <u>certain to grow</u>, perhaps exponentially.

I do not mean to paint a bleak picture here. Ever since Adam Smith and David Ricardo, economists have explained and extolled the gains in living standards that derive from international trade. Those arguments are just as valid for trade in services as for trade in goods. There really *are* net gains to the United States from expanding service-sector trade with India, China, and the rest. The offshoring problem is not about the adverse nature of what economists call the economy's eventual equilibrium. Rather, it is about the so-called transition—the ride from here to there. That ride, which could take a generation or more, may be bumpy. And during the long adjustment period, many U.S. wages could face downward pressure.

Long-term economy will be ok. Short-to-middle term will be "bumpy"

Thus far, only American manufacturing workers and a few low-end service workers (e.g., call-center operators) have been competing, at least potentially, with millions of people in faraway lands eager to work for what seems a pittance by U.S. standards. But offshoring is no longer limited to low-end service jobs. <u>Computer code</u> can be written overseas and e-mailed back to the United States. So can your <u>tax return</u> and lots of <u>legal work</u>, provided you do not insist on face-to-face contact with the <u>accountant</u> or lawyer. In writing and editing this article, I communicated with the editors and staff of *The American Prospect* only by telephone and e-mail. Why couldn't they (or I, for that matter) have been in India? The possibilities are, if not endless, at least vast.

High-end jobs to be lost

What distinguishes the jobs that cannot be offshored from the ones that can? The crucial distinction is not—and this is the central point of this essay—the required levels of skill and education. These attributes have been critical to labor-market success in the past, but may be less so in the future. Instead, the new critical distinction may be that some services either require personal delivery (e.g., driving a taxi and brain surgery) or are seriously degraded when delivered electronically (e.g., college teaching—at least, I hope!), while other jobs (e.g., call centers and keyboard data entry) are not. Call the first category personal services and the second category impersonal services. With this terminology, I have three main points to make about preparing our workforce for the brave, new world of the future.

First, we need to think about, plan, and redesign our educational system with the crucial distinction between personal service jobs and impersonal service jobs in mind. Many of the impersonal service jobs will migrate offshore, but the personal service jobs will stay here.

Second, the line that divides personal services from impersonal services will move in only one direction over time, as technological progress makes it possible to deliver an ever-increasing array of services electronically.

Third, the novel distinction between personal and impersonal jobs is quite different from, and appears essentially unrelated to, the traditional distinction between jobs that do and do not require high levels of education.

B's main point: Key distinction: Personal service jobs stay; impersonal jobs go

3 points re: prep of future workforce

Movement: impersonal → personal

Level of ed. not related to future job security

DIVIDE INTO STAGES OF THOUGHT

When a selection doesn't contain sections with topic headings, as is the case with "Will Your Job Be Exported?" how do you determine where one stage of thought ends and the next one begins? Assuming that what you have read is coherent and unified, this should not be difficult. (When a selection is unified, all of its parts pertain to the main subject; when a selection is coherent, the parts follow one another in logical order.) Look particularly for transitional sentences at the beginning of paragraphs. Such sentences generally work in one or both of two ways: (1) they summarize what has come before; (2) they set the stage for what is to follow.

Look at the sentences that open paragraphs 5 and 10: "Which brings me to the future" and "What distinguishes the jobs that cannot be offshored from the ones that can?" In both cases Blinder makes a clear announcement. Grammatically speaking, "Which brings me to the future" is a fragment, not a sentence. Experienced writers will use fragments on occasion to good effect, as in this case. The fragment clearly has the sense of a complete thought: the pronoun "which" refers readers to the content of the preceding paragraphs, asking readers to summarize that content and then, with the predicate "brings me to the future," to move forward into the next part of the article. Similarly, the question "What distinguishes the jobs that cannot be offshored from the ones that can?" implicitly asks readers to recall an important distinction just made (the definitions of off-shorable and non-offshorable jobs) and then clearly moves readers forward to new, related content. As you can see, the openings of paragraphs 5 and 10 announce new sections in the article.

Each section of an article generally takes several paragraphs to develop. Between paragraphs, and almost certainly between sections of an article, you will usually find transitions that help you understand what you have just read and what you are about to read. For articles that have no subheadings, try writing your own section headings in the margins as you take notes. Blinder's article can be divided into five sections.

Section 1: *Recent past: education of workers important*—For twenty-five years, the labor market has rewarded workers with higher levels of education (paragraphs 1–4).

Section 2: *Future: ed level won't always matter—workers in service sector will lose jobs offshore*—Once thought immune to outsourcing, even highly trained service workers will lose jobs to overseas competition (paragraphs 5–9).

Section 3: *Which service jobs at highest risk?*—<u>Personal</u> service workers are safe; <u>impersonal</u> service workers, both highly educated and not, will see jobs offshored (paragraphs 10–15).

Section 4: *Educating the future workforce*—Emphasizing the <u>kind</u>, not amount, of education will help to prepare workers for jobs of the future (paragraphs 16–22).

Section 5: *Needed policy reforms*—Government can improve conditions for low-end service workers and expand opportunities for higher-end service workers; start with education (paragraphs 23–26).

WRITE A BRIEF SUMMARY OF EACH STAGE OF THOUGHT

The purpose of this step is to wean you from the language of the original passage, so that you are not tied to it when writing the summary. Here are brief summaries, one for each stage of thought in "Will Your Job Be Exported?"

Section 1: Recent past: education of workers important (paragraphs 1–4).

For the past twenty-five years, the greater a worker's skill or level of education, the better and more stable the job.

Section 2: Future: ed level won't always matter—workers in service sector will lose jobs offshore (paragraphs 5–9).

Advances in technology have brought to the service sector the same pressures that forced so many manufacturing jobs offshore to China and India. The rate of offshoring in the service sector will accelerate and "eventually exceed" job losses in manufacturing, says Blinder, and jobs requiring both relatively little education (like call-center staffing) and extensive education (like software development) will be lost to workers overseas.

Section 3: Which service jobs at highest risk? (paragraphs 10–15).

While "personal services" workers (like barbers and surgeons) will be relatively safe from offshoring because their work requires close physical proximity to customers, "impersonal services" workers (like call-center operators and radiologists), regardless of their skill or education, will be at risk because their work can be completed remotely without loss of quality and then delivered via phone or computer. Blinder believes that "the relative demand for labor in the United States will [probably] shift away from impersonal services and toward personal services."

Section 4: Educating the future workforce (paragraphs 16–22).

Blinder advises young people to plan for "a high-end personal service occupation that is not offshorable." He also urges educators to prepare the future workforce by anticipating the needs of a personal services economy and redesigning classroom instruction and vocational training accordingly.

Section 5: Needed policy reforms (paragraphs 23–26).

Blinder urges the government to develop policies that will improve wages and conditions for low-wage personal service workers (like janitors); to encourage more low-wage workers (like daycare providers) to retrain and take on better jobs; and to increase opportunities for professional and vocational training in high-demand areas (like nursing and carpentry).

WRITE A THESIS: A BRIEF SUMMARY OF THE ENTIRE PASSAGE

The thesis is the most general statement of a summary (or any other type of academic writing). It is the statement that announces the paper's subject and the claim that you or—in the case of a summary—another author will be making about that subject. Every paragraph of a paper illuminates the thesis by providing supporting detail or explanation. The relationship of these paragraphs to the thesis is analogous to the relationship of the sentences within a paragraph to the topic sentence. Both the thesis and the topic sentences are general statements (the thesis being the more general) that are followed by systematically arranged details.

To ensure clarity for the reader, *the first sentence of your summary should begin with the author's thesis, regardless of where it appears in the article itself.* An author may locate her thesis at the beginning of her work, in which case the thesis operates as a general principle from which details of the presentation follow. This is called a *deductive* organization: thesis first, supporting details second. Alternatively, an author may locate his thesis at the end of the work, in which case the author begins with specific details and builds toward a more general conclusion, or thesis. This is called an *inductive* organization. And, as you might expect, an author might locate the thesis anywhere between beginning and end, at whatever point it seems best positioned.*

A thesis consists of a subject and an assertion about that subject. How can we go about fashioning an adequate thesis for a summary of Blinder's article? Probably no two versions of Blinder's thesis statement would be worded identically, but it is fair to say that any reasonable thesis will indicate that Blinder's

---

*Blinder positions his thesis midway through his five-section article. He opens the selection by discussing the role of education in the labor market during the past twenty-five years (Section 1, pars. 1–4). He continues by summarizing an earlier article on the ways in which service jobs are following manufacturing jobs offshore (Section 2, pars. 5–9). He then presents a two-sentence thesis in answer to the question that opens paragraph 10: "What distinguishes the jobs that cannot be offshored from the ones that can?" The remainder of the article either develops this thesis (Section 3, pars. 10–15) or follows its implications for education (Section 4, pars. 16–22) and public policy (Section 5, pars. 23–26).

subject is the future loss to offshoring of American jobs in the service sector—that part of the economy that delivers services to consumers, from low end (e.g., janitorial services) to high end (e.g., neurosurgery). How does Blinder view the situation? How secure will service jobs be if Blinder's distinction between personal and impersonal services is valid? Looking back over our section summaries, we find that Blinder insists on three points: (1) that education and skill matter less than they once did in determining job quality and security; (2) that the distinction between personal and impersonal services will increasingly determine which jobs remain and which are offshored; and (3) that the distinction between personal and impersonal has implications for both the future of education and public policy.

Does Blinder make a statement anywhere in this passage that pulls all this together? Examine paragraph 10 and you will find his thesis—two sentences that answer his question about which jobs will and will not be sent offshore: "The crucial distinction is not—and this is the central point of this essay—the required levels of skill and education . . . . Instead, the new critical distinction may be that some services either require personal delivery (e.g., driving a taxi and brain surgery) or are seriously degraded when delivered electronically (e.g., college teaching—at least, I hope!), while other jobs (e.g., call centers and keyboard data entry) are not."

You may have learned that a thesis statement must be expressed in a single sentence. We would offer a slight rewording of this generally sound advice and say that a thesis statement must be *expressible* in a single sentence. For reasons of emphasis or style, a writer might choose to distribute a thesis across two or more sentences. Certainly, the sense of Blinder's thesis can take the form of a single statement: "The critical distinction is X, not Y." For reasons largely of emphasis, he divides his thesis into two sentences—in fact, separating these sentences with another sentence that explains the first part of the thesis: "These attributes [that is, skill and education] have been critical to labor-market success in the past, but may be less so in the future."

Here is a one-sentence version of Blinder's two-sentence thesis:

> The quality and security of future jobs in America's service sector will be determined by how "offshorable" those jobs are.

Notice that the statement anticipates a summary of the *entire* article: both the discussion leading up to Blinder's thesis and his discussion after. To clarify for our readers the fact that this idea is Blinder's and not ours, we might qualify the thesis as follows:

> In "Will Your Job Be Exported?" economist Alan S. Blinder argues that the quality and security of future jobs in America's service sector will be determined by how "offshorable" those jobs are.

The first sentence of a summary is crucially important, for it orients readers by letting them know what to expect in the coming paragraphs. In the example above, the first sentence refers directly to an article, its author, and the thesis for the upcoming summary. The author and title reference could also be indicated in the summary's title (if this were a free-standing summary), in which case their mention could be dropped from the thesis statement. And lest you become frustrated too quickly with how much effort it takes to come up with this crucial sentence, keep in mind that writing an acceptable thesis for a summary takes time. In this case, it took three drafts, roughly ten minutes, to compose a thesis and another few minutes of fine-tuning after a draft of the entire summary was completed. The thesis needed revision because the first draft was vague; the second draft was improved but too specific on a secondary point; the third draft was more complete but too general on a key point:

Draft 1: We must begin now to train young people for high-quality personal service jobs.

(Vague. The question of why we should begin training isn't clear, nor is the phrase "high-quality personal service jobs." Define this term or make it more general.)

Draft 2: Alan S. Blinder (2006) argues that unlike in the past, the quality and security of future American jobs will not be determined by skill level or education but rather by how "offshorable" those jobs are.

(Better, but the reference to "skill level or education" is secondary to Blinder's main point about offshorable jobs.)

Draft 3: In "Will Your Job Be Exported?" economist Alan S. Blinder (2006) argues that the quality and security of future jobs will be determined by how "offshorable" those jobs are.

(Close—but not "all" jobs. Blinder specifies which types of jobs are "offshorable.")

Final Draft: In "Will Your Job Be Exported?" economist Alan S. Blinder (2006) argues that the quality and security of future jobs in America's service sector will be determined by how "offshorable" those jobs are.

WRITE THE FIRST DRAFT OF THE SUMMARY

Let's consider two possible summaries of Blinder's article: (1) a short summary, combining a thesis with brief section summaries, and (2) a longer summary, combining thesis, brief section summaries, and some carefully chosen details. Again, keep in mind that you are reading final versions; each of the following summaries is the result of at least two full drafts. Highlighting indicates transitions added to smooth the flow of the summary.

● SUMMARY 1: COMBINE THESIS SENTENCE WITH BRIEF SECTION SUMMARIES

In "Will Your Job Be Exported?" economist Alan S. Blinder (2006) argues that the quality and security of future jobs in America's service sector will be determined by how "offshorable" those jobs are. For the past twenty-five years, the greater a worker's skill or level of education, the better and more stable the job. No longer. Advances in technology have brought to the service sector the same pressures that forced so many manufacturing jobs offshore to China and India. The rate of off-shoring in the service sector will accelerate, and jobs requiring both relatively little education (like call-center staffing) and extensive education (like software development) will increasingly be lost to workers overseas.

These losses will "eventually exceed" losses in manufacturing, but not all services jobs are equally at risk. While "personal services" workers (like barbers and surgeons) will be relatively safe from offshoring because their work requires close physical proximity to customers, "impersonal services" workers (like call-center operators and radiologists), regardless of their skill or education, will be at risk because their work can be completed remotely without loss of quality and then delivered via phone or computer. "[T]he relative demand for labor in the United States will [probably] shift away from impersonal services and toward personal services" (Blinder, 2006, p. 63).

Blinder (2006) recommends three courses of action: He advises young people to plan for "a high-end personal service occupation that is not offshorable" (p. 63). He urges educators to prepare the future workforce by anticipating the needs of a personal services economy and redesigning classroom instruction and vocational training accordingly. Finally, he urges the government to adopt policies that will improve existing personal services jobs by increasing wages for low-wage workers; retraining workers to take on better jobs; and increasing opportunities in high-demand, well-paid areas like nursing and carpentry. Ultimately, Blinder wants America to prepare a new generation to "lead and innovate" in an economy that will continue exporting jobs that require "following and copying."

THE STRATEGY OF THE SHORTER SUMMARY

This short summary consists essentially of a restatement of Blinder's thesis plus the section summaries, modified or expanded a little for stylistic purposes. You'll recall that Blinder locates his thesis midway through the article, in paragraph 10. But note that this model summary *begins* with a restatement of his thesis. Notice also the relative weight given to the section summaries within the model. Blinder's main point, his "critical distinction" between personal and impersonal services jobs, is summarized in paragraph 2 of the model. The other paragraphs combine summaries of relatively less important (that is, supporting or explanatory) material. Paragraph 1 combines summaries of the article's Sections 1 and 2; paragraph 3 combines summaries of Sections 4 and 5.

Between the thesis and the section summaries, notice the insertion of three (highlighted) transitions. The first—a fragment (*No longer*)—bridges the first paragraph's summaries of Sections 1 and 2 of Blinder's article. The second transition links a point Blinder makes in his Section 2 (*Losses in the service sector will "eventually exceed" losses in manufacturing*) with an introduction to the key point he will make in Section 3 (*Not all service jobs are equally at risk*). The third transition (*Blinder recommends three courses of action*) bridges the summary of Blinder's Section 3 to summaries of Sections 4 and 5. Each transition, then, links sections of the whole: each casts the reader back to recall points just made; each casts the reader forward by announcing related points about to be made. Our model ends with a summary of Blinder's motivation for writing, the sense of which is implied by the section summaries but nowhere made explicit.

● **SUMMARY 2: COMBINE THESIS SENTENCE, SECTION SUMMARIES, AND CAREFULLY CHOSEN DETAILS**   The thesis and brief section summaries could also be used as the outline for a more detailed summary. However, most of the details in the passage won't be necessary in a summary. It isn't necessary even in a longer summary of this passage to discuss all of Blinder's examples of jobs that are more or less likely to be sent offshore. It would be appropriate, though, to mention one example of such a job; to review his reasons for thinking "that service-sector offshoring will eventually exceed manufacturing-sector offshoring by a hefty margin"; and to expand on his point that a college education in itself will no longer ensure job security.

None of these details appeared in the first summary; but in a longer summary, a few carefully selected details might be desirable for clarity. How do you decide which details to include? First, working with Blinder's point that one's job type (personal services vs. impersonal services) will matter more for future job quality and security than did the once highly regarded "silver bullet" of education, you may want to cite some of the most persuasive evidence supporting this idea. For example, you could explore why some highly paid physicians, like radiologists, might find themselves competing for jobs with lower-paid physicians overseas. Further, your expanded summary might reflect the relative weight Blinder gives to education (seven paragraphs, the longest of the article's five sections).

You won't always know which details to include and which to exclude. Developing good judgment in comprehending and summarizing texts is largely a matter of reading skill and prior knowledge. Consider the analogy of the seasoned mechanic who can pinpoint an engine problem by simply listening to a characteristic sound that to a less-experienced person is just noise. Or consider the chess player who can plot three separate winning strategies from a board position that to a novice looks like a hopeless jumble. In the same way, the more practiced a reader you are, the more knowledgeable you become about the subject and the better able you will be to make critical distinctions between elements of greater and lesser importance. In the meantime, read as carefully as you can and use your own best judgment as to how to present your material.

Here's one version of a completed summary with carefully chosen details. Note that we have highlighted phrases and sentences added to the original, briefer summary.

In "Will Your Job Be Exported?" economist Alan S. Blinder (2006) argues that the quality and security of future jobs in America's service sector will be determined by how "offshorable" those jobs are. For the past twenty-five years, the greater a worker's skill or level of education, the better and more stable the job. Americans have long regarded education as the "silver bullet" that could propel motivated people to better jobs and a better life. No longer. Advances in technology have brought to the service sector the same pressures that forced so many manufacturing jobs offshore to China and India. The rate of offshoring in the service sector will accelerate, says Blinder, and jobs requiring both relatively little education (like call-center staffing) and extensive education (like software development) will increasingly be lost to workers overseas.

Blinder (2006) expects that job losses in the service sector will "eventually exceed" losses in manufacturing, for three reasons. Developed countries have more service jobs than manufacturing jobs; as technology speeds communications, more service jobs will be offshorable; and the numbers of qualified offshore workers is increasing. Service jobs lost to foreign competition may cause a "bumpy" period as the global economy sorts out what work gets done where, by whom. In time, as the global economy finds its "eventual equilibrium," offshoring will benefit the United States; but the consequences in the meantime may be painful for many.

That pain will not be shared equally by all service workers, however. While "personal service" workers (like barbers and surgeons) will be relatively safe from offshoring because their work requires close physical proximity to customers, "impersonal service" workers (like audio transcribers and radiologists), regardless of their skill or education, will be at risk because their work can be completed remotely without loss of quality and then delivered via phone or computer. In the coming decades, says Blinder (2006), "the relative demand for labor in the United States will [probably] shift away from impersonal services and toward personal services" (p. 63). This shift will be influenced by the desire to keep good jobs in the United States while exporting jobs that require "following and copying." Highly trained computer coders will face the same pressures of outsourcing as relatively untrained call-center attendants. A tax attorney whose work requires no face-to-face interaction with clients may see her work migrate overseas while a divorce attorney, who must interact with clients on a case-by-case basis, may face no such competition. Same educations, different outcomes: what determines their fates in a global economy is the nature of their work (that is, personal vs. impersonal), not their level of education.

Based on this analysis, Blinder (2006) recommends three courses of action: First, he advises young people to plan for "a high-end personal service occupation that is not offshorable" (p. 64). Many good jobs, like carpentry and plumbing, will not require a college degree. Next, Blinder urges educators to prepare the future workforce by anticipating the needs of a personal services economy and redesigning classroom instruction and vocational training accordingly. These efforts should begin in elementary school and develop imagination and interpersonal skills rather than capacities for rote memorization. Finally, Blinder urges the government to develop policies that will improve wages and conditions for low-wage personal services workers (like janitors); to encourage more low-wage workers (like daycare providers) to retrain and take on better service jobs; and to increase opportunities for professional and vocational training for workers in high-demand services areas (like nurses and electricians). Ultimately, Blinder wants America to prepare a new generation of workers who will "lead and innovate . . . just as we have in the past" (p. 60).

THE STRATEGY OF THE LONGER SUMMARY

Compared to the first, briefer summary, this effort (seventy percent longer than the first) includes Blinder's reasons for suggesting that job losses in the services sector will exceed losses in manufacturing. It emphasizes Blinder's point that job type (personal vs. impersonal services), not a worker's education level, will ensure job security. It includes Blinder's point that offshoring in the service sector is part of a larger global economy seeking "equilibrium." And it offers more on Blinder's thoughts concerning the education of future workers.

The final two of our suggested steps for writing summaries are (1) to check your summary against the original passage, making sure that you have included all the important ideas, and (2) to revise so that the summary reads smoothly and coherently. The structure of this summary generally reflects the structure of the original article—with one significant departure, as noted earlier. Blinder uses a modified inductive approach, stating his thesis midway through the article. The summary, however, states the thesis immediately, then proceeds deductively to develop that thesis.

How Long Should a Summary Be?

The length of a summary depends both on the length of the original passage and on the use to which the summary will be put. If you are summarizing an entire article, a good rule of thumb is that your summary should be no longer than one-fourth the length of the original passage. Of course, if you were summarizing an entire chapter or even an entire book, it would have to be much shorter than that. The longer summary above is one-quarter the length of Alan Blinder's original. Although it shouldn't be very much longer, you have seen that it could be quite a bit shorter.

The length as well as the content of the summary also depends on the *purpose* to which it will be put. Let's suppose you decided to use Blinder's piece in a paper that dealt with the loss of manufacturing jobs in the United States and the rise of the service economy. In this case, in an effort to explain the complexities of the service economy to your readers, you might summarize *only* Blinder's core distinction between jobs in personal services and impersonal services, likely mentioning that jobs in the latter category are at risk of offshoring. If, instead, you were writing a paper in which you argued that the forces of globalization will eventually collapse the world's economies into a single, global economy, you would likely give less attention to Blinder's distinction between personal and impersonal services. More to the point might be his observation that highly skilled, highly educated workers in the United States are now finding themselves competing with qualified, lower-wage workers in China and India. Thus, depending on your purpose, you would summarize either selected portions of a source or an entire source.

Respond to the following opinion survey, using a 1 to 5 scale, with 1 meaning "strongly agree" and 5 meaning "strongly disagree."

Item	Strongly Agree	Agree	Neutral	Disagree	Strongly Disagree
1. Global warming is a very serious problem.	1	2	3	4	5
2. Going green in my own lifestyle will have no effect on climate change—the magnitude of the problem is too great.	1	2	3	4	5
3. The only way to make a real difference in climate change is through hugely expensive actions taken by governments and businesses.	1	2	3	4	5
4. The best way to combat global warming is for individual Americans to go green in their own consumer choices.	1	2	3	4	5
5. Environmentally conscious people should change the way they eat.	1	2	3	4	5

READINGS

Why Bother?

Michael Pollan

1 **Why bother?** That really is the big question facing us as individuals hoping to do something about climate change, and it's not an easy one to answer. I don't know about you, but for me the most upsetting moment in *An Inconvenient Truth* came long after Al Gore scared the hell out of me, constructing an utterly convincing case that the very survival of life on earth as we know it is threatened by climate change. No, the really dark moment came during the closing credits, when we are asked to . . . change our light bulbs. That's when it got really depressing. The immense disproportion between the magnitude of the problem Gore had described and the puniness of what he was asking us to do about it was enough to sink your heart.

2 But the drop-in-the-bucket issue is not the only problem lurking behind the "why bother" question. Let's say I do bother, big time. I turn my life upside-down, start biking to work, plant a big garden, turn down the thermostat so low I need the Jimmy Carter* signature cardigan, forsake the clothes dryer for a laundry line across the yard, trade in the station wagon for a hybrid, get off the beef, go completely local. I could theoretically do all that, but what would be the point when I know full well that halfway around the world there lives my evil twin, some carbon-footprint *doppelgänger* in Shanghai or Chongqing who has just bought his first car (Chinese car ownership is where ours was back in 1918), is eager to swallow every bite of meat I forswear and who's positively itching to replace every last pound of CO_2 I'm struggling no longer to emit. So what exactly would I have to show for all my trouble?

3 A sense of personal virtue, you might suggest, somewhat sheepishly. But what good is that when virtue itself is quickly becoming a term of derision? And not just on the editorial pages of the *Wall Street Journal* or on the lips of the vice president,[†] who famously dismissed energy conservation as a "sign of personal virtue." No, even in the pages of the *New York Times* and the *New Yorker*, it seems the epithet "virtuous," when applied to an act of personal environmental responsibility, may be used only ironically. Tell me: How did it come to pass that virtue—a quality that for most of history has generally been deemed, well, a virtue—became a mark of liberal softheadedness? How peculiar, that doing the right thing

* Jimmy Carter was the Democratic president (1977–1981) who supported environmental policies, world peace, and human rights.
† Pollan is referring to Dick Cheney who served as George W. Bush's vice president from 2001–2009.

...continued Why Bother?, **Michael Pollan**

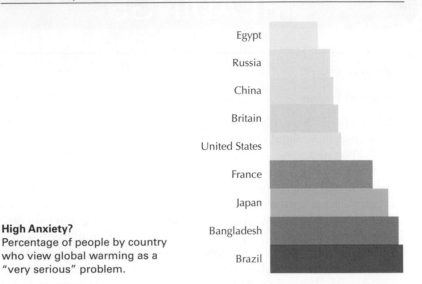

High Anxiety?
Percentage of people by country who view global warming as a "very serious" problem.

by the environment—buying the hybrid, eating like a locavore—should now set you up for the Ed Begley Jr.* treatment.

4   And even if in the face of this derision I decide I am going to bother, there arises the whole vexed question of getting it right. Is eating local or walking to work really going to reduce my carbon footprint? According to one analysis, if walking to work increases your appetite and you consume more meat or milk as a result, walking might actually emit more carbon than driving. A handful of studies have recently suggested that in certain cases under certain conditions, produce from places as far away as New Zealand might account for less carbon than comparable domestic products. True, at least one of these studies was co-written by a representative of agribusiness interests in (surprise!) New Zealand, but even so, they make you wonder. If determining the carbon footprint of food is really this complicated, and I've got to consider not only "food miles" but also whether the food came by ship or truck and how lushly the grass grows in New Zealand, then maybe on second thought I'll just buy the imported chops at Costco, at least until the experts get their footprints sorted out.

5   There are so many stories we can tell ourselves to justify doing nothing, but perhaps the most insidious is that, whatever we do manage to do, it will be too little too late. Climate change is upon us, and it has arrived well ahead of schedule. Scientists' projections that seemed dire a decade ago turn out to have been unduly optimistic: the warming and the melting is occurring much faster than the models predicted. Now truly terri-

* Ed Begley, Jr., is a prominent television star who has his own green living reality TV show, *Living with Ed Begley* has explored such topics as tapping the energy produced by people using exercise equipment.

fying feedback loops threaten to boost the rate of change exponentially, as the shift from white ice to blue water in the Arctic absorbs more sunlight and warming soils everywhere become more biologically active, causing them to release their vast stores of carbon into the air. Have you looked into the eyes of a climate scientist recently? They look really scared.

6   So do you still want to talk about planting gardens?

7   I do.

8   Whatever we can do as individuals to change the way we live at this suddenly very late date does seem utterly inadequate to the challenge. It's hard to argue with Michael Specter*, in a recent *New Yorker* piece on carbon footprints, when he says: "Personal choices, no matter how virtuous [N.B.!], cannot do enough. It will also take laws and money." So it will. Yet it is no less accurate or hardheaded to say that laws and money cannot do enough, either; that it will also take profound changes in the way we live. Why? Because the climate change crisis is at its very bottom a crisis of lifestyle— of character, even. The Big Problem is nothing more or less than the sum total of countless little everyday choices, most of them made by us (consumer spending represents 70 percent of our economy), and most of the rest of them made in the name of our needs and desires and preferences.

9   For us to wait for legislation or technology to solve the problem of how we're living our lives suggests we're not really serious about changing—something our politicians cannot fail to notice. They will not move until we do. Indeed, to look to leaders and experts, to laws and money and grand schemes, to save us from our predicament represents precisely the sort of thinking—passive, delegated, dependent for solutions on specialists—that helped get us into this mess in the first place. It's hard to believe that the same sort of thinking could now get us out of it.

10   Thirty years ago, Wendell Berry, the Kentucky farmer and writer, put forward a blunt analysis of precisely this mentality. He argued that the environmental crisis of the 1970s—an era innocent of climate change; what we would give to have back *that* environmental crisis!—was at its heart a crisis of character and would have to be addressed first at that level: at home, as it were. He was impatient with people who wrote checks to environmental organizations while thoughtlessly squandering fossil fuel in their everyday lives—the 1970s equivalent of people buying carbon offsets to atone for their Tahoes and Durangos. Nothing was likely to change until we healed the "split between what we think and what we do." For Berry, the "why bother" question came down to a moral imperative: "Once our personal connection to what is wrong becomes clear, then we have to choose: we can go on as before, recognizing our dishonesty and living with it the best we can, or we can begin the effort to change the way we think and live."

11   For Berry, the deep problem standing behind all the other problems of industrial civilization is "specialization," which he regards as the

*Michael Specter is a staff writer for the *New Yorker* and a national science reporter, who has most recently written a book, *Denialism,* about people's refusal to accept scientific evidence.

...continued Why Bother?, **Michael Pollan**

"disease of the modern character." Our society assigns us a tiny number of roles: we're producers (of one thing) at work, consumers of a great many other things the rest of the time, and then once a year or so we vote as citizens. Virtually all of our needs and desires we delegate to specialists of one kind or another—our meals to agribusiness, health to the doctor, education to the teacher, entertainment to the media, care for the environment to the environmentalist, political action to the politician.

12   As Adam Smith and many others have pointed out, this division of labor has given us many of the blessings of civilization. Specialization is what allows me to sit at a computer thinking about climate change. Yet this same division of labor obscures the lines of connection—and responsibility—linking our everyday acts to their real-world consequences, making it easy for me to overlook the coal-fired power plant that is lighting my screen, or the mountaintop in Kentucky that had to be destroyed to provide the coal to that plant, or the streams running crimson with heavy metals as a result.

13   Of course, what made this sort of specialization possible in the first place was cheap energy. Cheap fossil fuel allows us to pay distant others to process our food for us, to entertain us and to (try to) solve our problems, with the result that there is very little we know how to accomplish for ourselves. Think for a moment of all the things you suddenly need to do for yourself when the power goes out—up to and including entertaining yourself. Think, too, about how a power failure causes your neighbors—your community—to suddenly loom so much larger in your life. Cheap energy allowed us to leapfrog community by making it possible to sell our specialty over great distances as well as summon into our lives the specialties of countless distant others.

14   Here's the point: Cheap energy, which gives us climate change, fosters precisely the mentality that makes dealing with climate change in our own lives seem impossibly difficult. Specialists ourselves, we can no longer imagine anyone but an expert, or anything but a new technology or law, solving our problems. Al Gore asks us to change the light bulbs because he probably can't imagine us doing anything much more challenging, like, say, growing some portion of our own food. We can't imagine it, either, which is probably why we prefer to cross our fingers and talk about the promise of ethanol and nuclear power—new liquids and electrons to power the same old cars and houses and lives.

15   The "cheap-energy mind," as Wendell Berry called it, is the mind that asks, "Why bother?" because it is helpless to imagine—much less attempt—a different sort of life, one less divided, less reliant. Since the cheap-energy mind translates everything into money, its proxy, it prefers to put its faith in market-based solutions—carbon taxes and pollution-trading schemes. If we could just get the incentives right, it believes, the economy will properly value everything that matters and nudge our self-

interest down the proper channels. The best we can hope for is a greener version of the old invisible hand. Visible hands it has no use for.

16   But while some such grand scheme may well be necessary, it's doubtful that it will be sufficient or that it will be politically sustainable before we've demonstrated to ourselves that change is possible. Merely to give, to spend, even to vote, is not to do, and there is so much that needs to be done—without further delay. In the judgment of James Hansen, the NASA climate scientist who began sounding the alarm on global warming 20 years ago, we have only 10 years left to start cutting—not just slowing—the amount of carbon we're emitting or face a "different planet." Hansen said this more than two years ago, however; two years have gone by, and nothing of consequence has been done. So: eight years left to go and a great deal left to do.

17   Which brings us back to the "why bother" question and how we might better answer it. The reasons not to bother are many and compelling, at least to the cheap-energy mind. But let me offer a few admittedly tentative reasons that we might put on the other side of the scale:

18   If you do bother, you will set an example for other people. If enough other people bother, each one influencing yet another in a chain reaction of behavioral change, markets for all manner of green products and alternative technologies will prosper and expand. (Just look at the market for hybrid cars.) Consciousness will be raised, perhaps even changed: new moral imperatives and new taboos might take root in the culture. Driving an S.U.V. or eating a 24-ounce steak or illuminating your McMansion like an airport runway at night might come to be regarded as outrages to human conscience. Not having things might become cooler than having them. And those who did change the way they live would acquire the moral standing to demand changes in behavior from others—from other people, other corporations, even other countries.

19   All of this could, theoretically, happen. What I'm describing (imagining would probably be more accurate) is a process of viral social change, and change of this kind, which is nonlinear, is never something anyone can plan or predict or count on. Who knows, maybe the virus will reach all the way to Chongqing and infect my Chinese evil twin. Or not. Maybe going green will prove a passing fad and will lose steam after a few years, just as it did in the 1980s, when Ronald Reagan took down Jimmy Carter's solar panels from the roof of the White House.

20   Going personally green is a bet, nothing more or less, though it's one we probably all should make, even if the odds of it paying off aren't great. Sometimes you have to act as if acting will make a difference, even when you can't prove that it will. That, after all, was precisely what happened in Communist Czechoslovakia and Poland, when a handful of individuals like Václav Havel and Adam Michnik resolved that they would simply conduct their lives "as if" they lived in a free society. That improbable bet created a tiny space of liberty that, in time, expanded to take in, and then help take down, the whole of the Eastern bloc.

21   So what would be a comparable bet that the individual might make in the case of the environmental crisis? Havel himself has suggested that people begin to "conduct themselves as if they were to live on this earth forever and be answerable for its condition one day." Fair enough, but let me propose a slightly less abstract and daunting wager. The idea is to find one thing to do in your life that doesn't involve spending or voting, that may or may not virally rock the world but is real and particular (as well as symbolic) and that, come what may, will offer its own rewards. Maybe you decide to give up meat, an act that would reduce your carbon footprint by as much as a quarter. Or you could try this: determine to observe the Sabbath. For one day a week, abstain completely from economic activity: no shopping, no driving, no electronics.

22   But the act I want to talk about is growing some—even just a little—of your own food. Rip out your lawn, if you have one, and if you don't—if you live in a high-rise, or have a yard shrouded in shade—look into getting a plot in a community garden. Measured against the Problem We Face, planting a garden sounds pretty benign, I know, but in fact it's one of the most powerful things an individual can do—to reduce your carbon footprint, sure, but more important, to reduce your sense of dependence and dividedness: to change the cheap-energy mind.

23   A great many things happen when you plant a vegetable garden, some of them directly related to climate change, others indirect but related nevertheless. Growing food, we forget, comprises the original solar technology: calories produced by means of photosynthesis. Years ago the cheap-energy mind discovered that more food could be produced with less effort by replacing sunlight with fossil-fuel fertilizers and pesticides, with a result that the typical calorie of food energy in your diet now requires about 10 calories of fossil-fuel energy to produce. It's estimated that the way we feed ourselves (or rather, allow ourselves to be fed) accounts for about a fifth of the greenhouse gas for which each of us is responsible.

24   Yet the sun still shines down on your yard, and photosynthesis still works so abundantly that in a thoughtfully organized vegetable garden (one planted from seed, nourished by compost from the kitchen and involving not too many drives to the garden center), you can grow the proverbial free lunch—CO_2-free and dollar-free. This is the most-local food you can possibly eat (not to mention the freshest, tastiest and most nutritious), with a carbon footprint so faint that even the New Zealand lamb council dares not challenge it. And while we're counting carbon, consider too your compost pile, which shrinks the heap of garbage your household needs trucked away even as it feeds your vegetables and sequesters carbon in your soil. What else? Well, you will probably notice that you're getting a pretty good workout there in your garden, burning calories without having to get into the car to drive to the gym. (It is one of the absurdities of the modern division of labor that, having replaced

physical labor with fossil fuel, we now have to burn even more fossil fuel to keep our unemployed bodies in shape.) Also, by engaging both body and mind, time spent in the garden is time (and energy) subtracted from electronic forms of entertainment.

25   You begin to see that growing even a little of your own food is, as Wendell Berry pointed out 30 years ago, one of those solutions that, instead of begetting a new set of problems—the way "solutions" like ethanol or nuclear power inevitably do—actually beget other solutions, and not only of the kind that save carbon. Still more valuable are the habits of mind that growing a little of your own food can yield. You quickly learn that you need not be dependent on specialists to provide for yourself—that your body is still good for something and may actually be enlisted in its own support. If the experts are right, if both oil and time are running out, these are skills and habits of mind we're all very soon going to need. We may also need the food. Could gardens provide it? Well, during World War II, victory gardens supplied as much as 40 percent of the produce Americans ate.

26   **But there are sweeter** reasons to plant that garden, to bother. At least in this one corner of your yard and life, you will have begun to heal the split between what you think and what you do, to commingle your identities as consumer and producer and citizen. Chances are, your garden will re-engage you with your neighbors, for you will have produce to give away and the need to borrow their tools. You will have reduced the power of the cheap-energy mind by personally overcoming its most debilitating weakness: its helplessness and the fact that it can't do much of anything that doesn't involve division or subtraction. The garden's season-long transit from seed to ripe fruit—will you get a load of that zucchini?!—suggests that the operations of addition and multiplication still obtain, that the abundance of nature is not exhausted. The single greatest lesson the garden teaches is that our relationship to the planet need not be zero-sum, and that as long as the sun still shines and people still can plan and plant, think and do, we can, if we bother to try, find ways to provide for ourselves without diminishing the world.

STUDENT MODELS

STUDENT WRITING

Identification of the article, journal, and author

Gives overview summary of whole article

Attributive tag

Short quotations from article, APA documentation style; number in parentheses indicates page number of original article where quotation is found

Summary of "Why Bother?"

In "Why Bother?" published in the *New York Times Magazine,* environmental journalist Michael Pollan (2008) asks why, given the magnitude of the climate change problem, any individual should bother to go green, and argues that an individual's actions can bring multiple rewards for individuals, society, and the environment. Explaining that "the warming and the melting" (p. 90) are occurring much faster than earlier models had predicted, Pollan acknowledges the apparent powerlessness of individuals to make a difference. Not only are we uncertain what actions to take to preserve the planet, but we realize that whatever we do will be offset by growing carbon emissions from emerging nations. Our actions will be "too little too late" (p. 89). He asserts that our environmental problem is a "crisis of lifestyle"—"the sum total of countless little everyday choices" (p. 90) made possible by cheap fossil fuel, which has led to our increasingly specialized jobs. Nevertheless, to counteract our practical and moral distance from the environment caused by this specialization, Pollan urges individuals to go green. Although he concedes that "'laws and money'" (p. 90) are necessary, he still believes that individual actions may be influential by setting off a "process of viral social change" (p. 92). A particularly powerful act, he claims, is to convert yards into vegetable gardens. Growing your own vegetables, he argues, will help us overcome "specialization," eat locally, reduce carbon emissions, get healthy exercise, reconnect with neighbors, and restore our relationship with the earth. (227 words)

Bibliographic citation for Pollan's article using APA style. In a formal paper, the "References" list begins on a new page at the end of the paper.

References

Pollan, M. (2008, April). Why bother? In J. D. Ramage, J. C. Bean, & J. Johnson (Eds.). *The Allyn and Bacon Guide to Writing,* 6th ed. (pp. 88–94). New York: Pearson.

Summary of "Jennifer

and Rachel" by

Lee M. Silver

James Henderson

Professor Smith

Academic Writing I—September 28, 2006

STUDENT WRITING

"JENNIFER AND RACHEL"   2

Summary of "Jennifer and Rachel" by Lee M. Silver

1   How might our society change if individuals began to clone themselves to produce children rather than conceive through sexual relations? This question conjures up images of Aldous Huxley's *Brave New World,* where hordes of identical children were "hatched" and raised in uniform batches to fulfill specific social needs. According to Lee M. Silver (1997), author of "Jennifer and Rachel," human cloning will happen, but it will not pose the danger to our humanity or our social structure that Huxley predicted. Silver presents his own fictional account of cloning, but in his tale, a single woman named Jennifer clones herself to create a child that is entirely her own. He tells Jennifer's story to illustrate why someone might choose to be cloned, and then, through commentary on the scenario, he explains why we should not fear these products of our own brave new world.

2   Silver's (1997) scenario is set in the year 2049, when human cloning is technically possible but illegal in the United States. Jennifer, a financially secure woman, decides that she wants to give birth to a child and raise it alone. Several options for becoming pregnant are possible for Jennifer, but she chooses cloning because no one else's genetic material will be involved. This technology enables Jennifer to know automatically what her child's traits will be, an idea that appeals to her. After she makes her decision, she travels to the Cayman Islands, where the procedure takes place. Nine months later, Jennifer gives birth to her daughter. Rachel grows up very much like other children. Jennifer intends to tell Rachel the full story of her creation and birth as soon as she is old enough to understand the concept. Silver's (1997) scenario is certainly plausible; my cousin Louise, a single woman in her thirties, just adopted a child from Honduras, and no one questioned her desire to be a single parent. If cloning were available now, Louise might have used it.

3   After Silver (1997) presents the Jennifer and Rachel scenario, he anticipates

and responds to the objections that some people might have to Jennifer's choice to

clone herself. One objection is that as a clone of her mother, Rachel is denied the

right to grow up and develop her own identity. Since Jennifer and Rachel have the

same genes, will Rachel grow up to be just like her mother? Will she have the

freedom to develop a personality of her own? According to Silver, the fact that

Rachel and Jennifer have the same genetic makeup doesn't mean that their lives

will be the same. Rachel's childhood is bound to differ from that of her mother

because the environmental influences will not be the same. Mother and daughter

will be members of distinct generations and grow up under different social

circumstances, as is the case with other children and their parents. And after all,

what teenage girl tries to grow up to be just like her mom? While most parents

have certain expectations for their children, Silver sees no reason that Jennifer will

burden her clone daughter with unreasonable goals. Silver is probably thinking of

the many parents like my own who have their children's lives all plotted out for

them. And I'm most certainly not a clone!

4   Silver (1997) also notes that cloning may be perceived as a violation of religious

doctrines, and I know that the Vatican has, in fact, condemned human cloning. In

response to this objection, Silver points out that cloning does not involve tampering

with embryos, as abortion does, but rather involves only unfertilized eggs and regular

body cells that, without the cloning process, would never develop into embryos.

Though some people feel that the scientists who clone humans are "playing God,"

Silver points out that this claim applies equally to all reproductive technologies, not

just to cloning.

5   But the critics of cloning are not finished by any means; they next point

out that cloning has the potential to interfere with evolution and thus affect the

future progress of our species. In response, Silver (1997) argues that relatively

few people will find cloning attractive and hence that such a limited use of the

"JENNIFER AND RACHEL"   4

technology is unlikely to affect human evolution. As for the critics' claim that

evolution must be allowed to take its course, Silver maintains that "unfettered

evolution" won't necessarily guarantee improvement for the species.

6   The last objection to cloning that Silver (1997) addresses is that it might create

an underground market in designer clones. The genetic material of famous and

talented individuals might be stolen and cloned, and the resulting embryos could

then be sold to parents who want a child with outstanding characteristics. Silver

agrees that this practice is possible but maintains that it would most likely be

prohibited by law. He also questions whether many parents would want to raise other

people's clones rather than their own biological children. I imagine that it would be

very difficult to raise a child whose talents and skills far surpassed my own. Say my

son was Michael Jordan's clone. As a nine-year-old, what would little Mike think of my

lead feet and pitiful jump shot? In any case, Silver states that those parents who do

purchase designer clones may be disappointed since environmental influences will

ensure that the clones are significantly different from their biological parents.

7   Silver (1997) envisions a future where cloning will be one of the available

reproductive choices, and he suggests that some of us may have good reason to

give birth to a cloned child. Though many fear the idea of human cloning, Silver

believes that this process poses no significant risks to the clone children or to our

society at large. By the time I am ready to have a family, the Jennifer and Rachel

scenario may be more than just fiction, and the debate Silver outlines will be more

than a hypothetical exercise.

"JENNIFER AND RACHEL"   5

Reference

Silver, L. (1997). *Remaking Eden: Cloning and beyond in a brave new world.*

New York: Avon.

PRACTICE

1 This exercise asks you to work with the "Criteria for an Effective Summary Incorporated into Your Own Prose" (below) as you analyze the strengths and weaknesses of three summaries of the same article: "Protect Workers' Rights" by Bruce Raynor, published in the Washington Post on September 1, 2003. Imagine three student writers assigned to summarize this editorial in approximately 200 words. The first of the summaries below we have rated as excellent. Read the excellent summary first and then determine how successful the other summaries are.

Criteria for an effective summary incorporated into your own prose:

- Represents the original article accurately and fairly
- Is direct and concise, using words economically
- Remains objective and neutral, not revealing the writer's own ideas on the subject, but, rather, only the original author's points
- Gives the original article balanced and proportional coverage
- Uses the writer's own words to express the original author's ideas
- Distinguishes the summary writer's ideas from the original author's ideas by using attributive tags (such as "according to Pollan" or "Pollan argues that")
- Uses quotations sparingly, if at all, to present the original author's key terms or to convey the flavor of the original
- Is a unified, coherent piece of writing in its own right
- Cites and documents the text the writer is summarizing and any quotations used according to an appropriate documentation system

Summary 1 (an excellent summary of the Raynor article)

In Bruce Raynor's op-ed article "Protect Workers' Rights," originally published in the *Washington Post* on September 1, 2003, union official Raynor argues that workers everywhere are threatened by the current rules of globalization that allow corporations and governments to seek out the cheapest and least regulated labor around the world. Using the example of the Pillowtex Corporation that recently shut down its plant in Kannapolis, North Carolina, he shows how ending manufacturing that has played a long and major role in the economies of towns leaves workers without severance pay, medical insurance, money to pay taxes and mortgages, and other options for employment. According to Raynor, in the last three years, millions of jobs have been lost in all branches of American manufacturing. While policymakers advise these workers to seek education to retool for white-collar jobs, Raynor points out that fields such as telemarketing and the computer industry are also losing millions of jobs. Furthermore, outsourcing has caused a drop in wages in the United States. The same dynamic of jobs moving to countries with cheaper and less stringent safety and health regulation has recently caused Mexican and Bangladeshi workers to lose their jobs to Chinese workers. Raynor concludes with a call to protect the rights of workers everywhere by rewriting the "rules for the global economy" (p. A25). (214 words)

Reference

Raynor, B. (2003, September). Protect worker's rights. *Washington Post,* A25.

Summary 2

The closing of the Pillowtex Corporation's factories in the United States represents a loss of sixteen textile plants and about 6,500 jobs, according to Bruce Raynor (2003), president of UNITE, a union of textile workers.

The workers left in Kannapolis, North Carolina, former home of one of the largest Pillowtex plants, are experiencing financial problems as they are unable to buy medical insurance, pay their taxes or mortgages or find other jobs.

Raynor (2003) argues that the case of the Pillowtex workers is representative of workers in other industries such as metals, papers, and electronics and that "this is the longest decline since the Great Depression" with about three million jobs gone in the last three years.

He then explains that white-collar jobs are not safe either because millions of jobs in telemarketing, claims adjusting, and even government are predicted to go overseas in the next five years. Furthermore, Raynor (2003) states that the possibility of outsourcing jobs leads to lowering of wages within the United States, as "outsourcing has forced down hourly wage rates by 10 percent to 40 percent for many U.S. computer consultants" (p. A25).

However, according to Raynor (2003), the developing countries like Mexico and Bangladesh that have acquired manufacturing jobs are also threatened by countries like China who can offer employees who are willing to work for even lower wages and under worse conditions.

Raynor (2003) concludes that "a prosperous economy requires that workers be able to buy the products that they produce" (p. A25) and that workers everywhere need to be protected. (251 words)

Reference

Raynor, B. (2003, September). Protect worker's rights. *Washington Post,*
    A25.

Summary 3

    In his article "Protect Workers' Rights," Bruce Raynor (2003), president of UNITE, a textile workers' union, criticizes free trade and globalization for taking away workers' jobs. Using the Pillowtex Corporation's closing of its plant in Kannapolis, North Carolina, as his prime example, Raynor claims that outsourcing has destroyed the economy of this town and harmed workers across the United States. Raynor threatens that millions of white-collar jobs are also being lost and going to be lost in the next five years. Raynor complains that the whole national and global economy is falling apart and is going to get worse. He implies that the only solution is to keep jobs here in the United States. He maintains that workers around the world are also suffering when factories are moved from one developing country to another that has even more favorable conditions for the corporations. Raynor naively fails to factor in the role of consumers and the pressures on corporations into his defense of workers' rights. Clearly, Raynor loves unions and hates corporations; he probably fears that he is going to lose his own job soon. (183 words)

a. In what way do the opening sentences provide needed contextual information and then express the overall thesis of the text? What information could be added or more clearly stated?

b. How would you evaluate the writer's representation and coverage of the text's main ideas in terms of accuracy, balance, and proportion? What ideas have been omitted or overemphasized?

c. Has the writer treated the article fairly and neutrally? If judgments have crept in, where could the writer revise?

d. How could the summary use attributive tags more effectively to keep the focus on the original author's ideas?

e. Has the writer used quotations sparingly and cited them accurately? Has the writer translated points into his or her own words? Has the writer included a Reference entry?

f. Where might the writer's choice of words and phrasing of sentences be revised to improve the clarity, conciseness, and coherence of the summary?

2. In three to four sentences, summarize Pollan's main points.

a. Freewrite a response to this question: In what way has Pollan's article caused me to reconsider one or more of my answers to the opinion survey on page 278?

Thornton Lake
Thornton Lake, MI

How Do I Write a Response?

I N THE PAST, YOU UNDOUBTEDLY WROTE PERSONAL ESSAYS DRAWING ON LIFE EXPERIENCES. YOU MAY HAVE WRITTEN ON ASSIGNED TOPICS SUCH AS "AN INFLUENTIAL PERSON IN MY LIFE" OR "AN IMPORTANT LESSON I LEARNED." OR YOU MIGHT HAVE RESPONDED TO OPEN-ENDED ASSIGNMENTS THAT allowed you to write about relevant personal experiences; for example, "Compare your experiences to the those of the main character in the novel." In order to compose these personal essays, you had to search your memory to recall previous experiences and knowledge of the topic.

The writing assignments you receive in college will seldom ask you to write exclusively about memories and personal experiences. College professors expect students to write papers that draw on authoritative sources such as books and journal articles. That is not to say academic writers never make references to personal experiences. Occasionally, you will be asked to give personal reactions to readings. Such assignments will extend your understanding of the readings by allowing you to demonstrate the texts' relevance to your life. Consider the following assignment from a psychology class:

> As we have read in our textbook, research suggests that firstborn children experience greater anxiety throughout their lives than later-born children do. In a two-page essay, describe these research findings and test them against your own experience as a member and observer of families.

This assignment requires students to summarize material from the textbook and link it to their lives. Essays that cling to the textbook and make minimal use of personal experience will not work here; nor will essays that focus entirely on experiences. The assignment asks students to draw on two sources: the text and their own lived experience.

The writing tasks that we focus on in this chapter call for a balance between textual content and the writer's own expression. You are not being asked to offer opinions substantiated only by your own knowledge and experience. Your professors expect you to give an *informed* outlook. They want to hear your point of view about a text. You could approach these assignments in an elementary fashion by summarizing the text and tagging on a few sentences of commentary or reaction. But there are much more interesting ways to go about it.

To illustrate, let us look at a student essay. Diane Abramowitz was a student in a composition class that was studying the effect that technology has on our privacy. One of the sources she was required to read was "Invasion of Privacy," a *Time Magazine* article written by Joshua Quittner in 1997. Diane received the following assignment:

> In "Invasion of Privacy," Joshua Quittner (1997) explains that he is willing to risk his personal privacy in order to take advantage of technology. Use your experiences with technology to write an essay in response to the article.

The student paper reprinted here demonstrates how personal response to a source can form the basis for an essay. Notice that Diane Abramowitz does more than simply summarize the source and add personal reaction. As you read the essay, see if you can identify Diane's purpose.

STUDENT WRITING

HACKERS   2

Hackers

Opens with a scenario followed by a question

1   You turn on your computer and open your email expecting to read a few messages from your family and friends. Instead you find that your inbox is overflowing. It contains hundreds of messages. Some of them are returned messages with notifications about failure of delivery. Others are complaints accusing you of spamming. Does this scenario sound implausible? It's not. Until recently I was naïve enough to think that my email account was secure because I've never shared my password with anyone. Now I know that keeping my account password confidential is no guarantee that I will be exempt from email identity theft.

Describes personal experience

2   Three months ago someone stole my email address and sent a message to everyone in my address book. The message was advertising a company that sells discounted electronic products. When I contacted my email provider, I was told to change my password immediately. I was also told that I should select a new password that is difficult to decipher, for example, one that combines letters,

HACKERS   3

numbers, and symbols, because email thieves use programs that can easily figure

out many people's passwords. I was also told never to use my email password on a

website that requires a password, and I was advised to get a firewall to protect my

computer.

Joshua Quittner (1997) went through an experience similar to mine, but

instead of his e-mail it was his phone that was attacked. He recalls this event

in "Invasion of Privacy," an article published in *Time Magazine* in 1997. Quittner   *Introduces Quittner's*
                                                                                              article
(1997) explains that soon after he and his wife published a book on computer

hackers, someone redirected his incoming phone calls to an answering machine

containing an insulting message. The phone company was able to restore the

phone service initially, but the hacker struck again. Over the next six months,

the hacker interfered with Quittner's phone repeatedly, despite the best efforts

of the phone company. Even though Quittner found this incident annoying, he

concludes in his article that the usefulness of electronic technologies meant   *Quittner's main idea*

more to him than the privacy he lost by using them. While I agree with Quittner

that technology improves our everyday lives significantly, I am not resigned to   *Writer's thesis*

giving up my privacy in order to enjoy those advantages.

Quittner (1997) describes a wide range of technologies that have the

potential to compromise our privacy. He explains that we leave an electronic

record of our whereabouts and activities as we use ATM machines, E-Z Pass

lanes, and Internet shopping sites and even as we walk down the street past a

store that uses video surveillance. Our interests, preferences, and purchasing

habits are recorded as we browse the Web or make credit card purchases. A   *Summary of Quittner's*
                                                                                          article
skilled Internet researcher can, starting with only a name and address, uncover

much of the personal information that has been stored online. Quittner points

out that we can protect ourselves, to some extent, against invasions of privacy

by being more careful about the personal information we divulge and the

technologies we use. He also suggests that the online business community or

the government do more to protect individual privacy in cyberspace. In the final analysis, however, Quittner concludes that he is willing to risk losing some of his privacy in order to benefit from the power and convenience of technology. He has "nothing to hide" and just wants some control over who has access to his personal information.

5   In the years since Quittner (1997) wrote "Invasion of Privacy," the use of technology has increased at an astounding rate. He saw this coming when he wrote, "If things seem crazy now, think how much crazier they will be when everybody is wired as I am" (p. 30). Today everyone is wired. I grew up online, and every day I use a range of technologies that Quittner does not even mention in his article. I frequently use my cell phone to text message my friends. I send email messages on my cell as well as on my computer. I download music from iTunes onto my iPod. I share a good deal of personal information on Facebook and MySpace, and in one of my classes, I was required to record my reactions to the course readings on a blog. Without a doubt, technology has made communicating more convenient and, overall, it has improved my life.

Draws on personal experience to illustrate one of Quittner's points

6   Increased convenience has led to less personal privacy. While Quittner (1997) seems resigned to giving up some of his privacy, I don't think I should have to surrender my privacy when I go online. Despite the fact that I have a description of myself, photos, video clips, and lists of dozens of friends on Facebook, I value my privacy. I restrict my profiles to friends and family. Some of my friends do not even know that they have the option to edit their privacy settings and set limits on the amount of information they divulge to people. This option is very important to me. You can't be an individual without having secrets that you share only with those you trust. When someone trespasses into my online time, I feel that my rights have been violated. I don't want strangers to know what I am writing to my friends or relatives, and I don't want anyone looking over my shoulder while I'm surfing the Internet. Even though I am just browsing a Web page, I don't want to be followed around wherever I go to chat or browse. In legal terms, following people around is known as stalking. But what can the authorities do? At this point in time, there is legislation that

Challenges one of Quittner's claims and gives reasons for disagreeing

HACKERS   5

protects children's privacy on the Internet, but none that protects adults! Certainly,

local, state, and federal authorities must take immediate steps to ensure that

our right to privacy is protected. We don't have to accept, as Quittner does, that

our privacy rights and modern technology are simply incompatible.

7   Last year I rented a film called *The Net 2.0* (2006), a thriller about a

computer systems analyst whose identity is stolen. Her credit cards are

inoperable and all the money in her bank account disappears. The plot is about

how she struggles to reclaim her identity after she is accused of crimes she did

not commit. The movie is a sequel to *The Net* (1995), an earlier movie about

identity theft and hacking. These films are not science fiction. Online identity

theft is widespread and it occurs every day, but we are not powerless against it.

We all need to take precautions against it such as never divulging our

passwords, using passwords that are difficult to decipher, being careful when

we shop on sites like EBay, and never giving our personal information to people

we don't know.

8   "The only guys who insist on perfect privacy are hermits like the

Unabomber. I don't want to be cut off from the world. I have nothing to hide. I

just want some measure of control over what people know about me" (Quittner,

1997, p. 35). Although there is no such thing as perfect privacy, that doesn't

mean that we don't need and deserve as much privacy as possible. The

government and citizens themselves must take a much more active role in

ensuring that hackers do not threaten either our national or our personal

security. In the future, our individual freedom may depend as much on access to

cyberspace as it now does on access to the ballot box and the podium.

Reference to a film plot that illustrates a problem associated with Quittner's point of view

Speculates about the future

HACKERS   6

References

Quittner, J. (1997, August). Invasion of privacy. *Time.* 28–35.

Winkler, C. (Director). (2006). *The net 2.0* [Film]. United States: Columbia.

Winkler, I. (Director). (1995). *The net* [Film]. United States: Columbia.

Diane has a more complex goal than merely summarizing the source and giving a brief personal reaction. Let's zero in on her rhetorical purpose. From her comments, we know that she spends a great deal of time online, and she agrees with Joshua Quittner that this technology improves one's quality of life. But Diane takes issue with Quittner's willingness to surrender a degree of personal privacy in return for the advantages that technology has to offer. Her goal as a writer is to assert that one should be able to benefit from technology without giving up privacy rights. Notice that Diane supports her position by bringing her own knowledge into play. In the first paragraph, she describes how someone used her e-mail account to send out bogus messages to hundreds of e-mail addresses. Diane uses this personal experience to introduce Quittner's article, which begins with a description of his own experience with a malicious phone hacker. In the fourth paragraph, Diane explains that she has grown up online and she gives examples to show how much she relies on the Internet for day-to-day communication. Paragraph 5 includes Diane's personal feeling about having someone read her e-mail or monitor her Web-browsing habits. Her goal is to convey the sense of violation one experiences when victimized by electronic eavesdropping.

In the first, fourth, and fifth paragraphs, Diane describes experiences from her own life and her feelings about those experiences to demonstrate that online privacy violations should be taken seriously. In the sixth paragraph, she uses the film *The Net 2.0* as an example of how our lives can be affected if we fail to institute electronic privacy safeguards. As Diane's essay shows, personal knowledge includes not only direct experiences but also second-hand experiences and knowledge gleaned from books, magazines, film, television, radio, and audio recording. You may draw on a full range of personal knowledge when you write response essays.

Writing Response Essays

PREWRITING

Prewriting is the period when writers discover what they want to say. It includes everything you do before sitting down to pound out a first draft of your paper. When you are assigned a Response Essay, you will devote most of this time to reading the text and carefully considering your reactions to it. You will also organize these reactions, devise a preliminary thesis, and contemplate how you will support it. And you will select an organizational plan for your essay.

● **DO A FIRST READING TO GET A GENERAL IMPRESSION OF THE SOURCE**   After you have analyzed the assignment and determined that you are being asked to write an essay in response to a reading source, turn your attention to your purpose for reading. You will read the text for the purpose of generating reactions to the author's ideas. Your first reading may elicit little more than a general, impressionistic reaction. In the case of Joshua Quittner's article "Invasion of Privacy," our students' initial reactions ranged from "I care about my privacy and I don't want it to be invaded" to "Why worry about technology that makes our lives more convenient and safer?" After this initial reading, freewrite your reactions. Write nonstop for ten minutes or so, jotting down whatever comes to mind about the topic.

● **REREAD AND ELABORATE**   The second reading allows you to probe your memory and make associations between prior knowledge and experience and the propositions in the text. To elaborate, annotate in the margins of the text or take separate notes. Here a reader elaborates on two passages from Quittner's "Invasion of Privacy."

Quittner Text

Losing control of your telephone, of course, is the least of it. After all, most of us voluntarily give out our phone number and address when we allow ourselves to be listed in the White Pages. Most of us go a lot further than that. We register our whereabouts whenever we put a bank card in an ATM machine or drive through an E-Z Pass lane on the highway. We submit to being photographed every day—20 times a day on average if you live or work in New York City—by surveillance cameras. We make public our interests and our purchasing habits every time we shop by mail order or visit a commercial Website.

I don't know about you, but I do all this willingly because I appreciate what I get in return: the security of a safe parking lot, the convenience of cash when I need it, the improved service of mail-order houses that know me well enough to send me catalogs of stuff that interests me. And while I know we're supposed to feel just awful about giving up our vaunted privacy, I suspect (based on what the pollsters say) that you're as ambivalent about it as I am.

I don't do it willingly! I have no choice!

I think most students value their privacy. One of the most controversial issues on campus is that the college has the authority to enter at will any of our private dorm rooms.

Elaboration Notes

Since 9/11, the government has been accused of spying on U.S. citizens. I don't know if that's true or not, but surveillance cameras and closed circuit tvs are everywhere, even in schools.

We could have an unlisted phone number, but we don't have a choice about how information collected by an ATM, E-Z Pass, or surveillance camera is used. We should have the same choice of being unlisted with those services as we do with phones.

At home we get dozens of catalogs we don't want at all. I read that one catalog order can generate over 100 solicitations from other companies.

As you reread the source, elaborate as fully as you can. Even if some of these elaborations don't prove valuable to you, it is easier to write when you can select work from a rich pool of resources from which you can easily make selections.

You may be asking, "How can I forge connections between information in my memory and information in the reading source when I am dealing with a topic that is new to me?" When you don't have a pool of topic-related prior knowledge that you can draw forth readily, it helps to focus on your purpose for elaborating. Remind yourself of all the different forms your elaborations can take.

● **ESTABLISH PURPOSES AND FORMS OF ELABORATIONS**   Researchers who study composition have found that elaborations serve three purposes:

- To produce new ideas
- To develop critical viewpoints
- To develop ideas already stated by the author

Let us illustrate these three functions with another passage from Quittner's article. Here Quittner discusses the views of Sherry Turkle.

Text	Elaboration	Function
"It's a very schizophrenic time," says Sherry Turkle, professor of sociology at the Massachusetts Institute of Technology, who writes books about how computers and online communication are transforming society. She believes our culture is undergoing a kind of mass identity crisis, trying to hang on to a sense of privacy and intimacy in a global village of tens of millions. "We have very unstable notions about the boundaries of the individual," she says.	I see the "mass identity crisis" in youth fashion advertising. We're encouraged to develop a particular "look" that the fashion industry wants to sell. Part of the sales pitch is that this standardized "look" which will be worn by thousands of others is supposed to highlight the purchaser's individuality. Is it technology or is it our market economy that has created our society's identity crisis? My guess is that marketplace forces are at the root of the problem but that technology makes these forces even more powerful. "Be all that you can be."	Develops an idea already stated by the author Develops a critical view Produces a new idea

Notice the functions the elaboration serves. It extends Turkle's point about the impact of technology by linking it to the market economy; it poses a critical question about Turkle's conclusion; and it develops a new idea using Turkle's idea as a springboard. There are countless ways you can bring your own ideas to bear on the reading source. Some of them are as follows.

STRATEGIES FOR ELABORATING ON READING SOURCES

- Agree or disagree with a statement in the text and give reasons for your agreement or disagreement.
- Compare or contrast your reactions to the topic (for example, "At first I thought . . . , but now I think . . . ").

- Extend one of the author's points.
- Draw attention to what the author has neglected to say about the topic.
- Discover an idea implied by the text but not stated by the author.
- Provide additional details by fleshing out a point made by the author.
- Illustrate the text with an example, incident, scenario, or anecdote.
- Embellish the author's point with a vivid image, metaphor, or example.
- Test one of the author's claims.
- Compare one of the author's points with your own prior knowledge of the topic or with your own or others' experiences.
- Interpret the text in the light of your prior knowledge or applicable experiences.
- Personalize one of the author's statements.
- Question one of the author's points.
- Speculate about one of the author's points by

    Asking questions about the direct consequences of an idea
    Predicting consequences
    Drawing implications from an idea
    Applying the idea to a hypothetical situation
    Giving a concrete instance of a point made in the text
- Draw comparisons between the text and applicable books, articles, films, or other media.
- Classify items in the text under a superordinate category.
- Discover relationships between ideas in the text that are unstated by the author.
- Validate one of the author's points with an example or prior knowledge.
- Criticize a point in the text.
- Create hierarchies of importance among ideas in the text.
- Make a judgment about the relevance of a statement that the author has made.
- Impose a condition on a statement in the text (for example, "If . . . , then . . .").
- Qualify an idea in the text.
- Extend an idea with a personal recollection or reflection.
- Assess the usefulness and applicability of an idea.

● RESPONDING INDEPENDENTLY AND RESPONDING WITH OTHERS

During and after your reading, write brief marginal comments in the margins of the text and record longer reactions in your journal. We suggest that you use a double-entry journal in which you copy key passages from the text in the left-hand column and write your thoughts and opinions in the right-hand column. You may prefer a full-page format in which you write out your responses without copying down the text. If you use this format, be sure to make a note of the passages and pages to which you are responding. A useful prewriting activity is to share your responses with a partner or a small group. Exchange your journal with a classmate and comment on his or her reactions to the text. In the small group setting, ask each member of the group to select a sample of marginal annotations and journal entries and read them aloud. Group members will discuss responses that are similar in nature, and then they will come to consensus on a group response. You may choose to record your elaborations and extended journal entries in electronic form rather than pen and paper. You can share them with your classmates via email. Or your professor may ask you to post your comments on an electronic discussion board or class blog.

● **DEVELOP A THESIS** Even more important than generating your own ideas is deciding how to use them in your essay. If you already know the point you want to make, your rhetorical purpose will allow you to derive a *preliminary thesis* from your elaborations. Taking the Quittner assignment as an example, if you decide to argue that technological advances that make life more convenient should not come at the expense of individual privacy, you can prove your point by selecting elaborations that disagree with Quittner, draw attention to important factors he leaves out, challenge and question his ideas, make relevance judgments, or qualify his ideas and assess their applicability.

If you are not sure of the point you wish to make in your essay, review your elaborations as follows:

1. **See if one type of elaboration predominates.** Again, using the Quittner article as an example, let's assume that a good portion of your elaborations were drawn from your personal experiences. You could plan an essay in which you show how your experiences either validate or contradict Quittner's claims.

2. **See if a good number of elaborations were triggered by a particular source idea.** Let's say you elaborated at length on one of Quittner's assertions: "Popular culture shines its klieg light on the most intimate corners of our lives, and most of us play right along. If all we really wanted was to be left alone, explain the lasting popularity of Oprah and Sally and Ricki tell-all TV." If you wish, you may focus your paper on this single aspect of the topic.

3. **Classify your elaborations.** Select workable categories and discard the rest. You might highlight the elaborations in which you agree or disagree with the author of the source and then work only with these as you draft your essay.

To illustrate these procedures, we examine our student Kayla Robinson's elaborations on a set of paragraphs from Quittner's "Invasion of Privacy." As you study these elaborations, decide if one type of elaboration predominates. Are a number of elaborations triggered by a certain idea in the reading source? Do the elaborations fit into a classification scheme?

Text	Elaborations

Paragraph 4

I should also point out that as news director for Pathfinder, Time Inc.'s mega info mall, and a guy who makes his living on the Web, I know better than most people that we're hurtling toward an even more intrusive world. We're all being watched by computers whenever we visit Websites; by the mere act of "browsing" (it sounds so passive!) we're going public in a way that was unimaginable a decade ago. I know this because I'm a watcher too. When people come to my Website, without ever knowing their names, I can peer over their shoulders, recording what they look at, timing how long they stay on a particular page, following them around Pathfinder's sprawling offerings.

When I first read this paragraph, I didn't like the idea that someone is looking over my shoulder as I browse through Web sites. Since I'm alone when I browse, it feels like it should be private. But when I think about it, Web browsing is one of the least private activities because I am linked up to a network of literally millions of people and organizations. I know that commercial Web providers keep track of the people visiting their sites and they use small files called "cookies" to store information about my interests. That's why ads for sports products often pop up on my screen.

Paragraph 10

I don't know about you, but I do all this willingly because I appreciate what I get in return: the security of a safe parking lot, the convenience of cash when I need it, the improved service of mail-order houses that know me well enough to send me catalogs of stuff that interests me. And while I know we're supposed to feel just awful about giving up our vaunted privacy, I suspect (based on what the pollsters say) that you're as ambivalent about it as I am.

These conveniences appeal to me as well. I'd miss my ATM card and my e-mail more than the privacy I lose by using these technologies.

Paragraph 11

Popular culture shines its klieg lights on the most intimate corners of our lives, and most of us play right along. If all we really wanted was to be left alone, explain the lasting popularity of Oprah and Sally and Ricki tell-all TV. Memoirs top the best-seller lists, with books about incest and insanity and illness leading the way. Perfect strangers at cocktail parties tell me the most disturbing details of their abusive upbringings. Why?

What's a kleig light? I think it's sad that our society doesn't value privacy. TV reality shows have become popular, and there is a channel where you can watch live video of every moment of people's lives 24/7.

Paragraph 17

It all started in the 1950s, when, in order to administer Social Security funds, the U.S. government began entering records on big mainframe computers, using nine-digit identification numbers as data points. Then, even more than today, the citizenry instinctively loathed the computer and its injunctions against folding, spindling and mutilating. We were not numbers! We were human beings! These fears came to a head in the late 1960s, recalls Alan Westin, a retired Columbia University professor who publishes a quarterly report *Privacy and American Business.* "The techniques of intrusion and data surveillance had overcome the weak law and social mores that we had built up in the pre–World War II era," says Westin.

I didn't know this. How did they keep track of people before that? I heard that soon we'll be required to have national ID cards. What if this database of personal information is hacked?

Paragraph 23

"Most people would be astounded to know what's out there," says Carole Lane, author of *Naked in Cyberspace: How to Find Personal Information Online.* "In a few hours, sitting at my computer, beginning with no more than your name and address, I can find out what you do for a living, the names and ages of your spouse and children, what kind of car you drive, the value of your house and how much taxes you pay on it."

I don't like the idea that people can find out so much about me. Now all you have to do is google someone and you can find tons of information.

Paragraph 28

The real problem, says Kevin Kelly, executive editor of *Wired* magazine, is that although we say we value our privacy, what we really want is something very different: "We think that privacy is about information, but it's not—it's about relationships." The way Kelly sees it, there was no privacy in the traditional village or small town; everyone knew everyone else's secrets. And that was comfortable. I knew about you, and you knew about me. "There was a symmetry to the knowledge," he says. "What's gone out of whack is we don't know who knows about us anymore. Privacy has become asymmetrical."

I'm creeped out about this. Companies collect information about our shopping habits. Once it's on the Internet, personal information becomes the property of strangers.

Paragraph 35

"Technology has outpaced law," says Marc Rotenberg, director of the Washington-based Electronic Privacy Information Center. Rotenberg advocates protecting the privacy of E-mail by encrypting it with secret codes so powerful that even the National Security Agency's supercomputers would have a hard time cracking it. Such codes are legal within the U.S. but cannot be used abroad—where terrorists might use them to protect their secrets—without violating U.S. export laws. The battle between the Clinton Administration and the computer industry over encryption export policy has been raging for six years without resolution, a situation that is making it hard to do business on the Net and is clearly starting to fray some nerves. "The future is in electronic commerce," says Ira Magaziner, Clinton's point man on Net issues. All that's holding it up is "this privacy thing."

I'm afraid that the law will never catch up with the technology. Laws change so slowly and technology advances so rapidly. New methods of electronic snooping are invented every day. As soon as a law is created to control one method, two more will be invented.

Paragraph 38

I'm with Kelly. The only guys who insist on perfect privacy are hermits like the Unabomber. I don't want to be cut off from the world. I have nothing to hide. I just want some measure of control over what people know about me. I want to have my magic cookie and eat it too.

I had to look up Unabomber. The Unabomber was a guy named Ted Kaczynski who had once been a math professor. From late 1970 to the mid 1990s he mailed bombs to people working at universities and airports (that's why he's called "Unabomber") and subsequently killed three of the recipients. He wrote a manifesto about how technology was curtailing freedom. It was published in the New York Times.

Notice that the elaborations on these paragraphs express Kayla's reluctant acceptance of Quittner's ideas. A viewpoint emerges: although any loss of personal privacy is regrettable, the advantages of the new technology make it worth sacrificing a degree of privacy. Kayla also indicates that technology advances with such speed that it will leave in its wake any efforts to protect privacy. From these elaborations she derives the following preliminary thesis:

> Quittner's claim that technological advances are having a negative impact on personal privacy is, unfortunately, true. He is also correct that the benefits of the technology are worth the loss of privacy. Even if we wanted to stop the loss of privacy, it would not be possible, given the rapid progress of technology.

● **SELECT AN ORGANIZATIONAL PLAN**   After you come up with a preliminary thesis, your next step is to decide which organizational plan to use. A number of plans are appropriate for response essays, depending on the sources and your rhetorical purpose. Two patterns that are commonly used for response essays are summary and response and point-by-point response. Diane Abramowitz uses the summary and response pattern:

Paragraphs 2–3   Summary of Quittner's points

Paragraphs 4–6   Diane's commentary and reaction

Diane could have used the point-by-point response pattern by taking up each of Quittner's main points and responding to them one by one. To do this, Diane would alternate between her own ideas and those expressed by Quittner, perhaps in the following manner:

Paragraph 2   Brief Summary and commentary

Paragraphs 3–6   In each paragraph, summary of one of Quittner's points and response to it

Note how we use the summary and response and point-by-point alternating patterns to organize the elaborations.

Part of Essay	Summary and Response Pattern	Point-by-Point Pattern
Introductory paragraphs	Summarize Quittner's claim that we are sacrificing personal privacy in our pursuit of new technologies that make our lives more convenient and his belief that this trade-off is worthwhile. Explain your reluctant acceptance of Quittner's position.	Briefly summarize Quittner's claim that we are sacrificing personal privacy in our pursuit of new technologies that make our lives more convenient and his belief that this trade-off is worthwhile. Present your thesis.

Part of Essay	Summary and Response Pattern	Point-by-Point Pattern
Body paragraphs	Give reasons why the technological advances are worthwhile and why the losses in personal privacy are not that significant.	Alternate between Quittner's statements and your reactions. For example, first summarize the points Quittner makes in paragraphs 10 and 11 and give your reactions; then summarize the points Quittner makes in paragraph 17 and give your reactions; and so on.

Concluding
paragraph

The summary and response and point-by-point patterns are not the only ways to organize response essays. Your rhetorical purpose may provide the blueprint for your essay. Suppose that you disagree with Quittner's willingness to trade personal privacy for high-tech conveniences. You might develop your essay in a comparison-and-contrast format if you know of cases of devastating privacy violations that can be contrasted with the milder examples in Quittner's article. Or you might show the negative consequences of allowing convenience to take precedence over personal rights and thereby follow one of standard format for a cause-and-effect essay.

DRAFTING

To understand drafting better, reflect on the prior knowledge you have already brought into play. You have tapped your prior knowledge of the topic to produce a pool of elaborations on the reading source, and you have invoked your prior knowledge of organization and structure to discover an organizational plan. At this point, you will summon up two other types of prior knowledge: (1) knowledge of the basic features of writing—elements like titles, introductions, sentences, paragraphs, transitions and connecting ideas, and conclusions—and (2) knowledge of strategies for summarizing, paraphrasing, and quoting sources.

● **WRITE THE BODY OF THE RESPONSE ESSAY** The essay you compose at this stage should be a preliminary draft, not a polished, final copy. Think of this first draft as a discovery draft, an opportunity to find out more about what you want to say.

As you draft the body, follow the organizational plan you chose at the prewriting stage—summary and response, point-by-point, or another pattern. Develop sections and paragraphs that fit into your plan. If your prewriting plan proves unworkable or you discover a new direction for the paper, rethink your organizational strategy.

Summary.   The summary is an integral part of the response essay. Keep in mind that the type of summary you write depends on your rhetorical purpose. Ask yourself if your purpose is to provide your readers with a comprehensive summary that covers all the major aspects of the reading source. Or do you want simply to reduce the reading source to a series of gists?

Remember that your objective is to tailor the summary to the reaction. After you organize and classify your ideas and establish your direction, adapt the summary to your purpose. You need not summarize the entire article, only the sections that relate to your purpose. The summary should highlight the passages that prompted your reaction and refer only incidentally to other portions of the text.

Paragraphs.   Develop paragraphs that are unified and coherent. Make sure that each paragraph develops a central idea and that all the sentences contribute to this idea in some way. As you read the following paragraph, notice how each sentence develops the point that our everyday activities are becoming a matter of public record.

> As Quittner points out, we leave electronic trails behind us as we move through our everyday lives. When my computer alarm wakes me up at the preprogrammed time, I register my presence in cyberspace by logging on to my e-mail account to check for any messages and then moving on to a local weather Web site to help me decide what to wear. I'm still barely awake when the cashier swipes my ID at the campus coffee shop. On my way across campus, I stop by an ATM in the student center and get cash to repay a friend from whom I borrowed over the weekend. My first-period course meets in a networked classroom, and the professor asks us to log on to the course Web page to download the next assignment. It's only 9:00 a.m., and I've already created a trail, dropping electronic breadcrumbs at four different locations.

Also strive to make your paragraphs coherent. In a coherent paragraph, repeated words and ideas, rewording of ideas, and transitional expressions (*also, for example, thus, similarly, consequently,* and so on) show the reader the logical links among the sentences.

Expanding Your Rhetorical Goal

When you write the type of response essay discussed in this chapter, you are meeting the author of the reading source halfway. You are bringing your prior knowledge and experiences to bear on the ideas you read, and then as you compose the essay, you are forging connections between your own ideas and those of the author. The reader of your essay is well aware that the reading source has triggered your particular response.

If you have a good deal of knowledge about the topic or have generated a rich pool of elaborations, you may be able to compose a different type of response essay. The reading source will still trigger your reaction, but it will serve as a springboard or taking-off point rather than a mine from which you have unearthed a good portion of your material. In other words, the essay will be driven primarily by your own ideas and conception of the topic, and you will take your own angle or approach. Your readers will still be aware that the reading source has provided you with ideas, evidence, or support for your thesis, but they will see that you have taken the initiative and are not simply reacting to another person's ideas. Rather than summarizing and responding to a text (knowledge telling), you are transforming it for your own design and purpose (knowledge transforming). The following chart contrasts response essays of both types.

TOPIC: PRIVACY AND THE INTERNET

Stock Summary and Response Essay	Response Essay with a Self-Directed Purpose
Source author's conception of the topic is the driving force behind the writer's essay.	The writer's conception of the topic drives the essay.
Writer's points are prompted by or derived from passages in the reading source.	The writer uses some of the source author's ideas, but the emphasis is on developing the writer's own points.
The writer is engaged in knowledge-telling, referring to passages in the text and reacting to them.	The writer is engaged in knowledge-transforming, using the text as a springboard for his or her take on the topic.

Now let us look at a response essay that is written with a self-directed rhetorical purpose and then discuss its characteristics. Our student, Lili Wong, received the following assignment:

> Write a thoughtful essay in response to "When Poop Goes Primetime," the first chapter of Daniel J. Solove's *The Future of Reputation: Gossip, Rumor, and Privacy on the Internet.* Address your essay to classmates who have also done the reading. Solove's book is available online. You can download a PDF of Chapter 1 at http://docs.law.gwu.edu/facweb/dsolove/Future-of-Reputation/text.htm.

Solove's book examines the tension between free speech and individual rights. We are free to disclose personal information online and free to post information about other people, but this freedom has a profound impact on privacy. Solove opens *The Future of Reputation: Gossip, Rumor, and Privacy on the Internet* with a description of an incident that occurred on a subway train in South Korea. A young woman's dog pooped in the subway car, and despite complaints from the other passengers she refused to clean up the dog's mess. Someone on the train photographed the incident and posted the photos on a blog where many readers made accusatory and sometimes scathing comments. The story spread from the Korean blog to blogs in the United States and other countries, and as Solove remarks, soon everyone on the planet was reading about "the dog poop girl." Eventually the young woman's identity became known and she and her family were harassed. Distraught and shamed, she dropped out of the university she was attending. The remainder of Solove's chapter discusses how online freedom of expression is curtailing our privacy and in some cases having destructive effects on our lives. You might want to go to the Web site and read Chapter 1 of Solove's book before you examine Lili's response essay.

STUDENT WRITING

FACING THE INEVITABLE TRUTH   2

Facing the Inevitable Truth

1   The Internet profoundly intrudes upon your privacy, and there is very little you can do about it. Even if it were possible to survive without a computer, to never surf the Net, never write an email message, and never place an order online, you would still have an online presence. I could easily use free search tools to locate a great deal of personal information about you. Public records have been computerized, and well over a billion of them are available at Government Registry Online Records Retrieval (http://www.governmentregistry.org). Using this site, I can find birth and marriage certificates, property records,

FACING THE INEVITABLE TRUTH   3

court records, arrest records, military status, as well as tons of other information

about people. Your phone number and address are easily located online, and

Google Maps will even provide me with a photo of your apartment building. In

return, you can obtain a detailed profile of me, and since I have grown up online

as you have, when you google Lili Wong, you will have access to an amazing

amount of my personal information.

2   Every time you boot up your computer and open your browser, you

sacrifice your privacy and even risk the possibility of endangering your

reputation. If you are like me, you do not have the technological know-how to

safeguard your privacy. But even if you did, you still could not prevent people

from posting information about you. The truth is that you have little control

over the Internet. Daniel J. Solove (2007), an associate professor of law at

George Washington University Law School, explains that the Internet is a fairly

recent phenomenon. Solove (2007) compares it to an adolescent who is young,

wild, and ungovernable. In *The Future of Reputation, Gossip, Rumor, and Privacy*

on the Internet, he writes

> The future of the Internet involves not only the clash between freedom
>
> and control but also a struggle within the heart of freedom itself. The
>
> more freedom people have to spread information online, the more likely
>
> that people's private secrets will be revealed in ways that can hinder
>
> their opportunities in the future. In many respects, the teenage Internet
>
> is taking on all the qualities of an adolescent—brash, uninhibited, unruly,
>
> fearless, experimental, and often not mindful of the consequences of its
>
> behavior. And as with a teenager, the Net's greater freedom can be both
>
> a blessing and a curse. (pp. 5–6)

I have friends who act like teenagers when they're on the "teenage Internet."

They will do anything to get attention. They do not think about personal risk

when they have online interactions with strangers, and they have no regard for

anonymity when they post intimate secrets on blogs and social networking sites.

FACING THE INEVITABLE TRUTH   4

3   In some instances, you are guilty for voluntarily giving up your privacy. Phone conversations used to be private. If you wished to make a phone call in a public place, you entered a phone booth and closed the door behind you before you dialed the number. Years ago people wouldn't think of talking on the phone in front of strangers. Now you can easily eavesdrop on countless cell phone conversations every day. Growing up I kept a diary under lock and key, and I complained loudly the day my younger brother broke into it and read my cherished entries. Today I read blogs where people post risque photos and divulge shocking details about their private lives. They have no secrets. Until I got to college, the only people I knew intimately were my close circle of friends. I remember my middle school distributed a paper facebook to help us get to know each other, but all it contained was a headshot and short paragraph on each student. Today when I sign onto Facebook, I can access the personal profiles, blogs, photos, and videos of mere acquaintances. All of this openness comes at a price. I know that when I willingly divulge personal information on public blogs and social networking sites, I have to accept the consequences. I have heard that recruiters and employers check these sites and also do Google searches on prospective employees. A friend of mine was denied a job because of Facebook photos showing his alcohol and drug use. In cyberspace, privacy is an unreasonable expectation.

4   In other instances, you do not voluntarily give up your privacy. It is stolen from you. Solove (2007) gives an example of this with the story of the "dog poop girl." The girl was traveling on the subway with her dog. The dog pooped on the floor, and she refused to clean up after it. A passenger on the train photographed the incident and posted the pictures on the Internet. Someone found out the girl's identity. Bloggers criticized and ridiculed her and eventually severely damaged her reputation. What is interesting about this case is that it

FACING THE INEVITABLE TRUTH   5

could not have happened without technology. Personal data, even photos, are no

longer private. As Solove (2007) explains:

> Many of us today—especially children and teenagers—are spending
>
> more of our lives on the Internet. And the more we're online, the more
>
> likely details about our lives will slip out into cyberspace. This risk is
>
> increased because it is not just we ourselves who might leak
>
> information—data about us can be revealed by our friends or enemies,
>
> spouses or lovers, employers or employees, teachers or students ...
>
> and even by strangers on the subway. We live in an age when many
>
> fragments of information about our lives are being gathered by new
>
> technologies, horded by companies in databases, and scattered across
>
> the Internet. Even people who have never gone online are likely to
>
> have some personal information on the Internet. (pp. 9–10)

It is next to impossible to privatize your name to prevent it from popping up on

search engines. You can take precautions to limit access to your profiles on

Facebook and MySpace, but there is not much you can do to prevent other

people from posting photos or information about you without your consent. It is

foolish to have expectations of privacy.

5   The bottom line is that there is no semblance of privacy on the Internet.

When you send email, use search engines, and shop online, you no longer

own your personal information. Disregard for privacy on the part of web-

based corporations is rampant. They cavalierly collect information about your

web browsing and online shopping habits and use it for online profiling. The

Internet has been called transparent, but this is not an accurate description

because you don't know who is collecting information about you or what they

are doing with it. Unfortunately, you cannot reclaim your privacy. The

information that has been gathered about you is forever archived.

FACING THE INEVITABLE TRUTH 6

6   Perhaps trustworthy privacy protections will appear in the future, but at this point in time they don't exist. Solove (2007) is optimistic because he believes that the law has the potential to stop people from posting personal information without obtaining the person's consent. However, the law will not prevent you and me from divulging personal information ourselves. Solove admits that "any solution will be far from perfect, as we are dealing with a social tapestry of immense complexity, and the questions of how to modulate reputation, gossip, shame, privacy, norms, and free speech have confounded us for centuries" (p. 13). Privacy in cyberspace is an illusion. Accept this as the inevitable truth.

FACING THE INEVITABLE TRUTH 7

Reference

Solove, D. J. (2007). *The future of reputation: Gossip, rumor, and privacy on the Internet.* New Haven: Yale UP. Retrieved from http://docs.law.gwu.edu/facweb/dsolove/Future-of-Reputation/text.htm

In this essay, Lili moves beyond a simple response to the reading source. One of Solove's claims—that the lack of privacy on the Internet has profound consequences for us—triggers her essay. But in developing the essay, Lili uses more of her own knowledge and experiences than information from the reading source. Her purpose is to add to what the author has said about the topic. She includes three quotations from the text but uses them to develop her own points. She does not limit her response to the ideas that already appear in the chapter.

To develop an essay of this type, you can follow the same preparatory procedures as for a stock summary and response essay. The difference lies in the way you use your elaborations. As we saw earlier, elaborations can become the blueprint for the standard response essay. You can often find an essay lurking in your notes. When this does not occur, either of two straightforward patterns (summary and response or point by point; see page 308) can serve as a prefabricated plan for the essay. If you have a more personal rhetorical purpose, however, try either of these two approaches:

- Pull back from your elaborations and try to reconceptualize or transform them.
- Write a preliminary draft that takes you in a new direction and triggers new ideas.

Either procedure involves a substantial amount of ruminating, reflecting on the material you have already developed, and deciding how to use and expand it in a more interesting way. The following questions will prove helpful.

QUESTIONS FOR DEVELOPING A RESPONSE ESSAY WITH A SELF-DIRECTED PURPOSE

- How can you make this material more interesting, relevant, eventful, or meaningful?
- What new angle or point of view can you take with regard to this material?
- Can you create a rhetorical situation in which you are writing to move or influence a certain group of readers for a specific reason?
- Can you address a more definite audience?
- How can you better engage the reader?
- Can you fashion a richer rhetorical situation?

After you have come up with a thesis and a fresh approach, be sure to review the source to determine how it will figure in your essay. You won't be able to proceed as you would for a stock summary and response essay because you won't be following a prefabricated plan. You will use your elaboration notes, the source, and perhaps a preliminary draft as the raw materials for your essay.

Table 8.1   Summary of the Guidelines for Responding to Sources

Prewriting: Planning and Preparatory Activities

1. Read the assignment, and formulate your rhetorical purpose.
   - Why are you writing the response essay, and what desired effect do you hope to have on your audience?
   - How much of the source should you summarize, and what form will the summary take?
2. Consider your audience.
   - Are you writing for your professor or for a broader audience?
   - Is your audience in the academic community?
   - Are you writing for a general audience or for specialists?
   - What will your audience already know about the topic?
   - Will you need to explain basic concepts or provide background for the source material to make sense?
   - Will your audience be biased either for or against what the source says?
   - Can you predict how your audience will react to the source?
   - What is the overall impact that you want to have on your audience?
   - How will your writing inform, influence, or change your audience?
3. Read the source to get a general impression of the content; genre, organization, features; and rhetorical concerns.
   - Reading for information: What is the author's thesis or main point? What are other important points?
   - Reading for genre, organization, and stylistic features: How does the author get his or her points across? What is the method of presentation? What is the pattern of organization?
   - Reading for rhetorical concerns: What is the author's purpose? How does the author intend to influence the audience? Who is the author, and what is his or her background? What is the rhetorical context? To whom is the piece addressed? In what type of publication is it published? What is the author's relationship to the audience?
4. Reread and elaborate.
   - Tap your memory, and make associations between your prior knowledge and the ideas in the reading source.
   - Review your elaborations, and develop your thesis.
     See if one type of elaboration predominates.
     See if a number of elaborations were triggered by a particular idea in the reading source.
     Classify them.

- Decide on a suitable organizational format.
  Summarize the relevant parts of the source, and state your position.
  Develop your commentary, or briefly summarize the source and
  give your view.
  As you develop your position, alternate between the ideas in the
  reading source and your response, or use an organizational pattern
  that is appropriate for your rhetorical purpose.

Drafting

1. Write an opening paragraph in which you accomplish the following goals:
   - Use an opening that will interest the reader.
   - Announce the topic and disclose a thesis or attitude toward it (the
     thesis may come later).
   - Indicate the source title, author, and author's credentials and provide
     some summary information about the source.
   - Establish your own voice.
2. Arrange your elaboration notes in paragraphs, and develop each paragraph
   to its fullest.
3. Compose a concluding paragraph in which you use one of the following
   techniques:
   - Stress the significance of your thesis rather than simply repeating it.
     Encourage your readers to look beyond the thesis to an important
     future goal.
   - Predict consequences.
   - Call your readers to action.
   - Use any of the devices for paper openers.

Revising

1. If possible, have a classmate or friend read over your first draft.
2. If no one is available, leave your work for a day or two and then answer the
   questions yourself.

Editing

1. When you are satisfied with your revision, read your paper aloud. Then
   reread it line by line and sentence by sentence. Check for correct usage,
   punctuation, spelling, mechanics, manuscript form, and typos.
2. Run the spell checker. Then print out the paper and review the spelling
   yourself. Even the best spell checkers will not catch every error.
3. If your editing skills are not strong, have a friend read over your work.

READINGS

On Teenagers and Tattoos

Andrés Martin, M.D.

The skeleton dimensions I shall now proceed to set down are copied verbatim from my right arm, where I had them tattooed: as in my wild wanderings at that period, there was no other secure way of preserving such valuable statistics.

Melville/Moby-Dick CII

1   Tattoos and piercings have become a part of our everyday landscape. They are ubiquitous, having entered the circles of glamour and the mainstream of fashion, and they have even become an increasingly common feature of our urban youth. Legislation in most states restricts professional tattooing to adults older than 18 years of age, so "high end" tattooing is rare in children and adolescents, but such tattoos are occasionally seen in older teenagers. Piercings, by comparison, as well as self-made or "jailhouse" type tattoos, are not at all rare among adolescents or even among schoolage children. Like hairdo, makeup, or baggy jeans, tattoos and piercings can be subject to fad influence or peer pressure in an effort toward group affiliation. As with any other fashion statement, they can be construed as bodily aids in the inner struggle toward identity consolidation, serving as adjuncts to the defining and sculpting of the self by means of external manipulations. But unlike most other body decorations, tattoos and piercings are set apart by their irreversible and permanent nature, a quality at the core of their magnetic appeal to adolescents.

2   Adolescents and their parents are often at odds over the acquisition of bodily decorations. For the adolescent, piercings or tattoos may be seen as personal and beautifying statements, while parents may construe them as oppositional and enraging affronts to their authority. Distinguishing bodily adornment from self-mutilation may indeed prove challenging, particularly when a family is in disagreement over a teenager's motivations and a clinician is summoned as the final arbiter. At such times it may be most important to realize jointly that the skin can all too readily become but another battleground for the tensions of the age, arguments having less to do with tattoos and piercings than with core issues such as separation from the family matrix. Exploring the motivations and significance underlying tattoos (Grumet, 1983) and piercings can go a long way toward resolving such differences and can become a novel and additional way of getting to know teenagers. An interested and nonjudgmental appreciation of teenagers' sur-

face presentations may become a way of making contact not only in their terms but on their turfs: quite literally on the territory of their skins.

The following three sections exemplify some of the complex psychological underpinnings of youth tattooing.

IDENTITY AND THE ADOLESCENT'S BODY

Tattoos and piercing can offer a concrete and readily available solution for many of the identity crises and conflicts normative to adolescent development. In using such decorations, and by marking out their bodily territories, adolescents can support their efforts at autonomy, privacy, and insulation. Seeking individuation, tattooed adolescents can become unambiguously demarcated from others and singled out as unique. The intense and often disturbing reactions that are mobilized in viewers can help to effectively keep them at bay, becoming tantamount to the proverbial "Keep Out" sign hanging from a teenager's door.

Alternatively, [when teenagers feel] prey to a rapidly evolving body over which they have no say, self-made and openly visible decorations may restore adolescents' sense of normalcy and control, a way of turning a passive experience into an active identity. By indelibly marking their bodies, adolescents can strive to reclaim their bearings within an environment experienced as alien, estranged, or suffocating or to lay claim over their evolving and increasingly unrecognizable bodies. In either case, the net outcome can be a resolution to unwelcome impositions: external, familial, or societal in one case; internal and hormonal in the other. In the words of a 16-year-old girl with several facial piercings, and who could have been referring to her body just as well as to the position within her family, "If I don't fit in, it is because *I* say so."

INCORPORATION AND OWNERSHIP

Imagery of a religious, deathly, or skeletal nature, the likenesses of fierce animals or imagined creatures, and the simple inscription of names are some of the time-tested favorite contents for tattoos. In all instances, marks become not only memorials or recipients for clearly held persons or concepts; they strive for incorporation, with images and abstract symbols gaining substance on becoming a permanent part of the individual's skin. Thickly embedded in personally meaningful representations and object relations, tattoos can become not only the ongoing memento of a relationship, but at times even the only evidence that there ever was such a bond. They can quite literally become the relationship itself. The turbulence and impulsivity of early attachments and infatuations may become grounded, effectively bridging oblivion through the visible reality of tattoos.

Case Vignette. A, a 13-year-old boy, proudly showed me his tattooed deltoid. The coarsely depicted roll of the dice marked the day and month of his birth. Rather disappointed, he then uncovered an immaculate back, going on to draw for me the great "piece" he envisioned for it. A menacing figure held a hand of cards: two aces, two eights, and a card with two sets of dates. A's father had belonged to "Dead Man's Hand," a motorcycle gang named after the set of cards (aces and eights) that the legendary Wild Bill Hickock had held in the 1890s when shot dead over a poker table in Deadwood, South Dakota. A had only the vaguest memory of and sketchiest information about his father, but he knew he had died in a motorcycle accident: the fifth card marked the dates of his birth and death.

8

The case vignette also serves to illustrate how tattoos are often the culmination of a long process of imagination, fantasy, and planning that can start at an early age. Limited markings, or relatively reversible ones such as piercings, can at a later time scaffold toward the more radical commitment of a permanent tattoo.

THE QUEST FOR PERMANENCE

9

The popularity of the anchor as a tattoo motif may historically have had to do less with guild identification among sailors than with an intense longing for rootedness and stability. In a similar vein, the recent increase in the popularity and acceptance of tattoos may be understood as an antidote or counterpoint to our urban and nomadic lifestyles. Within an increasingly mobile society, in which relationships are so often transient—as attested by the frequencies of divorce, abandonment, foster placement, and repeated moves, for example—tattoos can be a readily available source of grounding. Tattoos, unlike many relationships, can promise permanence and stability. A sense of constancy can be derived from unchanging marks that can be carried along no matter what the physical, temporal, or geographical vicissitudes at hand. Tattoos stay, while all else may change.

10

Case Vignette. A proud father at 17, B had had the smiling face of his 3-month-old baby girl tattooed on his chest. As we talked at a tattoo convention, he proudly introduced her to me, explaining how he would "always know how beautiful she is today" when years from then he saw her semblance etched on himself.

11

The quest for permanence may at other times prove misleading and offer premature closure to unresolved conflicts. At a time of normative uncertainties, adolescents may maladaptively and all too readily commit to a tattoo and its indefinite presence. A wish to hold on to a current certainty may lead the adolescent to lay down in ink what is valued and cherished one day but may not necessarily be in the future. The frequency of self-made tattoos among hospitalized, incarcerated, or gang-affiliated youths suggests such motivations: a sense of stability may be a particularly dire need under temporary, turbulent, or volatile conditions. In addition, through their designs teenagers may assert a sense of bonding and allegiance to a group larger than themselves. Tattoos may attest to powerful experiences, such as adolescence itself, lived and even survived together. As with *Moby Dick's* protagonist Ishmael, they may bear witness to the "valuable statistics" of one's "wild wandering(s)": those of adolescent exhilaration and excitement on the one hand; of growing pains, shared misfortune, or even incarceration on the other.

12   Adolescents' bodily decorations, at times radical and dramatic in their presentation, can be seen in terms of figuration rather than disfigurement, of the natural body being through them transformed into a personalized body (Brain, 1979). They can often be understood as self-constructive and adorning efforts, rather than prematurely subsumed as mutilatory and destructive acts. If we bear all of this in mind, we may not only arrive at a position to pass more reasoned clinical judgment, but become sensitized through our patients' skins to another level of their internal reality.

References

Brain, R. (1979). *The Decorated Body.* New York: Harper & Row.

Grumet, G. W. (1983). Psychodynamic implications of tattoos. *Am J Orthopsychiatry,* 53:482–492.

30 Little Turtles

Thomas L. Friedman

1   Indians are so hospitable. I got an ovation the other day from a roomful of Indian 20-year-olds just for reading perfectly the following paragraph: "A bottle of bottled water held 30 little turtles. It didn't matter that each turtle had to rattle a metal ladle in order to get a little bit of noodles, a total turtle delicacy. The problem was that there were many turtle battles for less than oodles of noodles."

2   I was sitting in on an "accent neutralization" class at the Indian call center 24/7 Customer. The instructor was teaching the would-be Indian call center operators to suppress their native Indian accents and speak with a Canadian one—she teaches British and U.S. accents as well, but these youths will be serving the Canadian market. Since I'm originally from Minnesota, near Canada, and still speak like someone out of the movie "Fargo," I gave these young Indians an authentic rendition of "30 Little Turtles," which is designed to teach them the proper Canadian pronunciations. Hence the rousing applause.

3   Watching these incredibly enthusiastic young Indians preparing for their call center jobs—earnestly trying to soften their t's and roll their r's—is an uplifting experience, especially when you hear from their friends already working these jobs how they have transformed their lives. Most of them still live at home and turn over part of their salaries to their parents, so the whole family benefits. Many have credit cards and have become real consumers, including of U.S. goods, for the first time. All of them seem to have gained self-confidence and self-worth.

...*continued* 30 Little Turtles, **Thomas L. Friedman**

4   A lot of these Indian young men and women have college degrees, but would never get a local job that starts at $200 to $300 a month were it not for the call centers. Some do "outbound" calls, selling things from credit cards to phone services to Americans and Europeans. Others deal with "inbound" calls—everything from tracing lost luggage for U.S. airline passengers to solving computer problems for U.S. customers. The calls are transferred here by satellite or fiber optic cable.

5   I was most taken by a young Indian engineer doing tech support for a U.S. software giant, who spoke with pride about how cool it is to tell his friends that he just spent the day helping Americans navigate their software. A majority of these call center workers are young women, who not only have been liberated by earning a decent local wage (and therefore have more choice in whom they marry), but are using the job to get M.B.A.'s and other degrees on the side.

6   I gathered a group together, and here's what they sound like: M. Dinesh, who does tech support, says his day is made when some American calls in with a problem and is actually happy to hear an Indian voice: "They say you people are really good at what you do. I am glad I reached an Indian." Kiran Menon, when asked who his role model was, shot back: "Bill Gates— [I dream of] starting my own company and making it that big." I asked C. M. Meghna what she got most out of the work: "Self-confidence," she said, "a lot of self-confidence, when people come to you with a problem and you can solve it—and having a lot of independence." Because the call center teams work through India's night—which corresponds to America's day— "your biological clock goes haywire," she added. "Besides that, it's great."

7   There is nothing more positive than the self-confidence, dignity and optimism that comes from a society knowing it is producing wealth by tapping its own brains—men's and women's—as opposed to one just tapping its own oil, let alone one that is so lost it can find dignity only through suicide and "martyrdom."

8   Indeed, listening to these Indian young people, I had a déjà vu. Five months ago, I was in Ramallah, on the West Bank, talking to three young Palestinian men, also in their 20's, one of whom was studying engineering. Their hero was Yasir Arafat. They talked about having no hope, no jobs and no dignity, and they each nodded when one of them said they were all "suicide bombers in waiting."

9   What am I saying here? That it's more important for young Indians to have jobs than Americans? Never. But I am saying that there is more to outsourcing than just economics. There's also geopolitics. It is inevitable in a networked world that our economy is going to shed certain low-wage, low-prestige jobs. To the extent that they go to places like India or Pakistan— where they are viewed as high-wage, high-prestige jobs—we make not only a more prosperous world, but a safer world for our own 20-year-olds.

STUDENT MODELS

Can a Green Thumb Save the Planet?

A Response to Michael Pollan

Kyle Madsen (student)

When I was a child, our household had one garbage can, in which my family and I would deposit all of our cardboard, plastic, glass, and paper waste. No one on my block had ever heard of recycling or using energy saving bulbs, and we never considered turning down our thermostats during the frozen winters and ice storms that swept our region from November to March. It wasn't that we didn't care about what we were doing to our environment. We just didn't know any better. However, once I got to college all that changed. My university's policies requested that students separate glass bottles and pizza boxes from plastic candy wrappers and old food containers. Thanks in large part to the chilling success of Al Gore's (2006) documentary *An Inconvenient Truth*, many of my old neighbors were starting to catch on as well, and now my home town is as devoted to its recycling as any major metropolitan area. Still, even though we as a country have come a long way in just a few years, there is a long way to go. Environmental journalist Michael Pollan (2008) in his article "Why Bother?" for the *New York Times Magazine* examines why working to slow the threat of climate change is such a daunting task.

In "Why Bother?" Michael Pollan (2008) explores how we have arrived at our current climate change crisis and argues why and how we should try to change our individual actions. Pollan sums up the recent scientific evidence for rapid climate change and then focuses on people's feeling overwhelmed in the face of this vast environmental problem. He presents his interpretation of how we have contributed to the problem and why we feel powerless. Pollan asserts that the climate-change crisis is "the sum total of countless everyday choices" made by consumers globally and that it is "at its very bottom a crisis of lifestyle—of character, even" (p. 90). Our reliance on "cheap fossil fuel" has contributed to both the problem and to our sense of helplessness. In the final part of his article, Pollan concedes that "laws and money" (p. 90) are necessary to create change, but he still advocates acting on our values and setting an example, which might launch a green social revolution. According to Pollan, "The idea is to find one thing to do in your life that does not involve spending or voting . . . that will offer its own rewards" (p. 93). He concludes by encouraging readers to plant gardens in order to reduce carbon emissions, to lessen

Introduces topic/ problem and shows writer's investment in caring for the environment

Identifies Pollan's article and Pollan's purpose

Summary of Pollan's article

our "sense of dependence and dividedness" (p. 93)—to empower our-selves to contribute positively to our environment.

Thesis statement focused on rhetorical points

Although Pollan (2008) has created an argument with strong logical, ethical, and emotional appeals, his very dominant angle of vision—seen in his assumptions, alarmist language, and exclusive focus on garden-growing—may fail to win neutral readers. I also think Pollan's argument loses impact by not discussing more realistic alternatives such as pursuing smart consumerism and better environmental education for children.

Second part of thesis focused on ideas critique

With-the-grain rhetorical point focused on the logos and ethos of Pollan's argument

Pollan builds a forceful case in his well-argued and knowledgeable interpretation of our climate-change problem as a "crisis of lifestyle—of character, even" (p. 90). His frank confrontation of the problem of how to motivate people is compelling, especially when he admits the contrast between "the magnitude of the problem" and the "puniness" of individual action (p. 91). Pollan both deepens his argument and constructs a positive ethos by drawing on the ideas of environmental ethicist Wendell Berry and classical economist Adam Smith to explain how modern civilization has developed through the division of labor (specialization), which has brought us many advantages but also cut us off from community and envi-ronmental responsibility. In this part of his argument, Pollan helps readers understand how our dependence on cheap oil and our lifestyle choices have enhanced our roles as limited, specialized producers and major con-sumers. Pollan's development of his theory of the "cheap-energy mind" (p. 92) and his reasonable support of this idea are the strongest part of his argument and the most relevant to readers like me. I have thought that we have become small cogs in an overbearing machine of consumption and only larger cogs such as the government can have enough influence on the overall system to make change happen. From time to time, I have won-dered what I as one person could really do. This sense of insignificance, which Pollan theorizes, has made me wait until my regular light bulbs burned out before considering replacing them with energy-efficient ones.

Brief reflective comment

With-the-grain rhetorical point focused on the pathos of Pollan's argument

Another strength of Pollan's (2008) argument is the way he builds bridges to his audience through his appeals to *pathos*. He understands how overwhelmed the average person can feel when confronted with the climate-change problem. Pollan never criticizes his readers for not being as concerned as he is. Instead he engages them in learning with him. He explores with readers the suggestion of walking to work, a task on par with light bulb changing, when he writes, even if "I decide that I am going to bother, there arises the whole vexed question of getting it right. Is eating local or walking to work really going to reduce my carbon footprint?" (p. 89). By asking questions like these, he speaks as a concerned citizen who tries to create a dialogue with his audience about the problem of cli-mate change and what individuals can do.

However, despite his outreach to readers, Pollan's (2008) angle of vision may be too dominant and intense for some readers. He assumes that his

New York Times Magazine readers already share his agreement with the most serious views of climate change held by many scientists and environmentalists, people who are focusing on the "truly terrifying feedback loops" (p. 90) in weather and climate. He also assumes that his readers hold similar values about local food and gardening. This intense angle of vision may leave out some readers. For example, I am left wondering why gardening is more effective than, say, converting to solar power. He also tries to shock his readers into action with his occasional alarmist or overly dramatic use of language. For example, he tries to invoke fear: "Have you looked into the eyes of a climate scientist recently? They look really scared" (p. 90). However, how many regular people have run-ins with climate scientists?

 In addition, after appearing very in tune with readers in the first part of his argument, in the final part he does not address his readers' practical concerns. He describes in great detail the joys of gardening—specifically how it will connect readers not only to the earth, but to friends and neighbors as well—yet he glosses over the amount of work necessary to grow a garden. He writes, "Photosynthesis still works so abundantly that in a thoughtfully organized vegetable garden (one planted from seed, nourished by compost from the kitchen and involving not too many drives to the gardening center), you can grow the proverbial free lunch" (Pollan, 2008, pp. 93–94). However, not everyone has a space for a garden or access to a public one to grow tomatoes themselves, and it takes hours of backbreaking labor to grow a productive vegetable garden—hardly a free lunch. Average Americans work upwards of sixty hours per week, so it is unrealistic to expect them to spend their free time working in a garden. In not addressing readers' objections to gardening or suggesting other ways to mend our cheap oil values, I think Pollan proposes simply another situation for semi-concerned individuals to again say, "Why bother?"

 Also, besides gardens, I think Pollan (2008) could emphasize other avenues of change such as sustainable consumerism. In different places in the article, he mentions that individuals can use their consumer lifestyles to achieve a more sustainable way of life, but he chooses to insist that gardening be the main means. I would have liked him to discuss how we as consumers could buy more fuel-efficient cars, avoid plastic packaging, drink tap water, and buy products from green industries. This "going green" trend has already taken root in many of America's top industries—at least in their advertising and public relations campaigns. We can't leave a Starbucks without inadvertently learning about what they are doing to offset global warming. But we consumers need to know which industries really are going green in a significant way so that we can spend our shopping dollars there. If Pollan is correct, environmentally conscientious consumers can demand a change from the corporations they rely on, so why not use the same consumerism that got us into this mess to get us out?

Against-the-grain rhetorical point focused on angle of vision

Transition to ideas critique, an against-the-grain point critiquing Pollan's ideas—Pollan doesn't acknowledge the impracticality of expecting people to grow their own vegetables.

Another point critiquing Pollan's ideas. Madsen proposes sustainable consumerism as an alternative to gardening.

Another point addressing Pollan's ideas—environmental education in the schools as an alternative to gardening.

Besides sustainable consumerism, I think we should emphasize the promotion of better environmental education for our children. Curriculum in K–12 classrooms presented by teachers rather than information from television or newspapers will shape children's commitment to the environment. A good example is the impact of Recycle Now, an organization aimed at implementing recycling and global awareness in schools. According to Dave Lawrie (2009), a curriculum expert featured on their Web site, "Recycling at school is a hands-on way to show pupils that every single person can help to improve the environment. Everyone in our school has played a part in making a difference" (p. 5). With serious education, kids will learn the habits of respecting the earth, working in gardens, and using energy-saving halogen bulbs, making sustainability and environmental stewardship a way of life.

Short conclusion bringing closure to the essay.

While Pollan (2007) is correct in pushing us into action now, asking Americans to grow a garden, when changing a light bulb seems daunting, is an unrealistic and limited approach. However, Pollan persuasively addresses the underlying issues in our attitudes toward the climate crisis and works to empower readers to become responsible and involved. Whether it be through gardening, supporting green businesses, or education, I agree with Pollan that the important thing is that you learn to bother for yourself.

References

Citation of References in the essay using APA format

Lawrie, D. (2009, November). Bringing the curriculum to life. *RecycleNow.*

Pollan, M. (2008, April). Why bother? In J. D. Ramage, J. C. Bean, & J. Johnson (Eds.), *The Allyn and Bacon guide to writing,* 6th ed. (pp. 88–94). New York: Pearson.

Questioning Thomas L. Friedman's Optimism
in "30 Little Turtles"

Stephanie Malinowski

1   You are struggling to fix a problem that arises when you are downloading new computer software on to your computer. You're about to give up on the whole thing when an idea hits you: call the software com-

pany itself to ask for assistance. Should you be surprised when the person who answers the phone to help you is based in India? Should Americans support or question outsourcing?

In "30 Little Turtles," an op-ed piece that appeared in the *New York Times* on February 29, 2004, journalist and foreign affairs columnist Thomas L. Friedman (2004) argues that outsourcing call center jobs from the Western world to India is transforming the lives of Indian workers and benefiting geopolitics. Friedman supports his argument by detailing his experience visiting a call center in India. He claims that the Indians working to serve Canadian and American markets are happy with how their work has improved their lives. Friedman points out that the working Indian women feel liberated now that they are making a decent wage and can afford such things as a college education. He describes Indian workers' view of their jobs, using words such as "self-confidence" and "independence." At the end of his article, Friedman states that he doesn't favor Indian employment over American employment but that outsourced jobs in countries like India or Pakistan create both prosperity and global security. Although Friedman's article clearly conveys to its audience how some Indian workers are benefiting from outsourcing, his argument relies heavily on personal experience and generalizations. I also think his condescending attitude hurts his argument, and he concludes his article too abruptly, leaving readers with questions.

Friedman (2004) succeeds in portraying the positive side of outsourcing to his *New York Times* readers who may be questioning the rationale for outsourcing. Friedman interviews the recipients of American jobs to see outsourcing from their perspective and enlightens Americans trying to understand how outsourcing is benefiting workers in other countries. Friedman's opening is vivid and captures the readers' interest by detailing his experience inside an Indian call center. He quotes the Indian workers expressing the joys of working for American and Canadian people. These workers testify to the financial and personal gains these jobs have brought. One woman says that she feels good about her job and herself "when people come to you with a problem and you can solve it" (p. 125). The article is so full of optimism that the reader can't help but empathize with the Indians and feel happy that outsourcing has transformed their lives. Through these emotional appeals, Friedman succeeds in making readers who may have big reservations about outsourcing think about the human dimension of outsourcing.

However, Friedman (2004) also makes large generalizations based on his few personal experiences, lessening the credibility of his article. The first sentence of the article reads, "Indians are so hospitable" (p. 124). So are *all* Indians "so hospitable"? Friedman seems to make this generalization about national character based on the fact that he was applauded by a room full of Indians after reading a tongue twister paragraph in a perfect

Canadian accent. I can see why Friedman appreciates his warm reception, but "feel good" moments can hardly provide evidence for the soundness of global economic policies. Friedman generalizes further about what he sees and hears in the call center room. He talks about the Indian employees in these terms: "All of them seem to have gained self-confidence and self-worth" (p. 124). From this single observation, Friedman makes the assumption that almost every Indian working an outsourcing job must be gaining, and that the overall experience has done wonders for their lives. However, other articles that I have read have mentioned that call center work is basically a deadend job and that $200 a month is not a big salary. Later in his conclusion, Friedman states that "we make not only a more prosperous world, but a safer world for our own 20-year-olds" (p. 125). Can this conclusion be drawn from one visit to a call center where Indians expressed gratitude for their outsourcing work?

5   An even bigger problem with Friedman's (2004) article is the condescending way in which he describes the Indian workers. I think he portrays the culture as being incompetent before the American and Canadian outsourcing jobs came to improve their accents and their lives. One statement that conveys condescension is this remark: "Watching these incredibly enthusiastic young Indians preparing for their call center jobs—earnestly trying to soften their t's and roll their r's—is an uplifting experience . . ." (p. 124). This passage reminds me of the delight and pride of parents witnessing their children's growth milestones. Friedman is casting the accent neutralization of the Indian workers as overcoming a barrier in order to reach success. Friedman's condescending tone is apparent again when he restates the words of one American caller to an Indian worker, "They say you people are really good at what you do. I am glad I reached an Indian" (p. 125). I see Friedman's reason for including this quote; he wants the reader to know that Indian workers are being valued for their work. However, the words that the American uses, which Friedman deliberately chooses to include in his article, "you people," suggest that Indians are a whole other kind of people different from American workers in their skills. Friedman's condescension also appears when he says that these are "low-wage, low-prestige jobs" (p. 125). This remark is full of problems because it puts down the Indians taking the jobs and the Americans who have lost them, and it misrepresents the outsourcing scene that now includes many highly skilled prestigious jobs.

6   I also think that Friedman (2004) weakens his article by concluding abruptly and introducing new ideas to readers that leave them with unanswered questions. Friedman asks the reader, "What am I saying here? That it's more important for young Indians to have jobs than Americans?" (p. 125). This point seems like a relevant question to investigate, but its weakness is that Friedman never even mentions any

place in his article the loss that American workers are experiencing. At the end of the article, readers are left with questions. For example, the last sentence reads, "we make not only a more prosperous world, but a safer world for our own 20-year-olds" (p. 125). Although Friedman is implying that outsourcing improves our relationships with other countries and enhances our national safety, nowhere in the article does he substantiate this claim. He seems to have thrown this statement into the conclusion just to end the article on a happy note.

7   Giving a human face to outsourcing is a good idea; however, Friedman (2004) does not support his main argument well, and this article comes across as a simplistic, unexplored view of outsourcing. I and other readers are left needing to look for answers to serious questions about outsourcing elsewhere.

Reference

Friedman, T. L. (2004, February). 30 little turtles. In J. D. Ramage, J. C. Bean, & J. Johnson (Eds.), *The Allyn & Bacon guide to writing*, 6th ed. (pp. 124–125). New York: Pearson.

PRACTICE

❶ What follows is a short passage by writer Annie Dillard in response to a question about how she chooses to spend her time. This passage often evokes heated responses from our students.

> I don't do housework. Life is too short. . . . I let almost all my indoor plants die from neglect while I was writing the book. There are all kinds of ways to live. You can take your choice. You can keep a tidy house, and when St. Peter asks you what you did with your life, you can say, "I kept a tidy house, I made my own cheese balls."

Individual task: Read the passage and then briefly freewrite your reaction to it.

Group task: Working in groups or as a whole class, develop answers to the following questions:

a. What values does Dillard assume her audience holds?

b. What kinds of readers are apt to feel excluded from that audience?

c. If you are not part of the intended audience for this passage, what in the text evokes resistance?

❷ Summarize in one or two sentences Martin's main points in "On Teenagers and Tattoos" (p. 320).

a. Working in small groups or as a whole class, compare the note-taking strategies you used while reading this piece. (a) How many people wrote marginal notes? How many underlined or highlighted? (b) Compare the contents of these notes. Did people highlight the same passage or different passages? (c) Individually, look at your annotations and highlights and try to decide why you wrote or marked what you did. Share your reasons for making these annotations. The goal of this exercise is to make you more aware of your thinking processes as you read.

b. To what extent did this article change people's thinking about the reasons teenagers choose to tattoo their bodies? What were the most insightful points in this article?

c. Assume that you are looking for substantial, detailed information about changes in American attitudes toward tattooing. What parts of this article are useful? How might a psychiatrist writing about tattoos today differ from Martin in 1997?

Baker College
Flint

How Do I Write an Analysis?

I N AN *ANALYSIS* YOU STUDY THE PARTS OF SOMETHING TO UNDERSTAND HOW IT WORKS, WHAT IT MEANS, OR WHY IT MIGHT BE SIGNIFICANT. THE WRITER OF AN ANALYSIS USES AN ANALYTICAL TOOL: A *PRINCIPLE* OR *DEFINITION* ON THE BASIS OF WHICH AN OBJECT, AN EVENT, OR A BEHAVIOR CAN BE DIVIDED into parts and examined. Here are excerpts from two analyses of the movie version of L. Frank Baum's *The Wizard of Oz*:

> At the dawn of adolescence, the very time she should start to distance herself from Aunt Em and Uncle Henry, the surrogate parents who raised her on their Kansas farm, Dorothy Gale experiences a hurtful reawakening of her fear that these loved ones will be rudely ripped from her, especially her Aunt (Em—M for Mother!).*

> [*The Wizard of Oz*] was originally written as a political allegory about grass-roots protest. It may seem harder to believe than Emerald City, but the Tin Woodsman is the industrial worker, the Scarecrow [is] the struggling farmer, and the Wizard is the president, who is powerful only as long as he succeeds in deceiving the people.†

As these paragraphs suggest, what you discover through an analysis depends entirely on the principle or definition you use to make your insights. Is *The Wizard of Oz* the story of a girl's psychological development, or is it a story about politics? The answer is *both*. In the first example, the psychiatrist Harvey Greenberg applies the principles of his profession and, not surprisingly, sees *The Wizard of Oz* in psychological terms. In the second example, a newspaper reporter applies the political theories of Karl Marx and, again not surprisingly, discovers a story about politics.

Different as they are, these analyses share an important quality: Each is the result of a specific principle or definition used as a tool to divide an object

*Harvey Greenberg, *The Movies on Your Mind* (New York: Dutton, 1975).
†Peter Dreier, "The Politics of Oz," *San Francisco Chronicle*, 24 Sept. 1989.

into parts in order to see what it means and how it works. The writer's choice of analytical tool simultaneously creates and limits the possibilities for analysis. Thus, working with the principles of Freud, Harvey Greenberg sees *The Wizard of Oz* in psychological, not political, terms; working with the theories of Karl Marx, Peter Dreier understands the movie in terms of the economic relationships among characters. It's as if the writer of an analysis who adopts one analytical tool puts on a pair of glasses and sees an object in a specific way. Another writer, using a different tool (and a different pair of glasses), sees the object differently.

You might protest: Are there as many analyses of *The Wizard of Oz* as there are people to read the book or to see the movie? Yes, or at least as many analyses as there are analytical tools. This does not mean that all analyses are equally valid or useful. Each writer must convince the reader. In creating an essay of analysis,

---

WHERE DO WE FIND WRITTEN ANALYSES?

Here are just a few of the types of writing that involve analysis:

Academic Writing

- **Experimental and lab reports** analyze the meaning or implications of the study results in the discussion section.
- **Research papers** analyze information in sources or apply theories to material being reported.
- **Process analyses** break down the steps or stages involved in completing a process.
- **Literary analyses** examine characterization, plot, imagery, or other elements in works of literature.
- **Essay exams** demonstrate understanding of course material by analyzing data using course concepts.

Workplace Writing

- **Grant proposals** analyze the issues you seek funding for in order to address them.
- **Reviews of the arts** employ dramatic or literary analysis to assess artistic works.
- **Business plans** break down and analyze capital outlays, expenditures, profits, materials, and the like.
- **Medical charts** record analytical thinking and writing in relation to patient symptoms and possible options.
- **Legal briefs** break down and analyze facts of cases and elements of legal precedents and apply legal rulings and precedents to new situations.
- **Case studies** describe and analyze the particulars of a specific medical, social service, advertising, or business case.

the writer must organize a series of related insights, using the analytical tool to examine first one part and then another of the object being studied. To read Harvey Greenberg's essay on *The Wizard of Oz* is to find paragraph after paragraph of related insights—first about Aunt Em, then the Wicked Witch, then Toto, and then the Wizard. All these insights point to Greenberg's single conclusion: that "Dorothy's 'trip' is a marvelous metaphor for the psychological journey every adolescent must make." Without Greenberg's analysis, we would probably not have thought about the movie as a psychological journey. This is precisely the power of an analysis: its ability to reveal objects or events in ways we would not otherwise have considered.

The writer's challenge is to convince readers that (1) the analytical tool being applied is legitimate and well matched to the object being studied; and (2) the analytical tool is being used systematically to divide the object into parts and to make a coherent, meaningful statement about these parts and the object as a whole.

WHEN *YOUR* PERSPECTIVE GUIDES THE ANALYSIS

In some cases a writer's analysis of a phenomenon or a work of art may not result from anything as structured as a principle or a definition. It may follow from the writer's cultural or personal outlook, perspective, or interests. Imagine reading a story or observing the lines of a new building and being asked to analyze it— not based on someone else's definition or principle, but on your own. Analyses in this case continue to probe the parts of things to understand how they work and what they mean. And they continue to be carefully structured, examining one part of a phenomenon at a time. The essential purpose of the analysis, to *reveal*, remains unchanged. This goal distinguishes the analysis from the critique, whose main purpose is to *evaluate* and *assess validity*.

Consider this passage from an op-ed article by Terri Martin Hekker, "The Satisfactions of Housewifery and Motherhood in an Age of 'Do Your Own Thing,'" which appeared in the *New York Times* in 1977:

> I come from a long line of women . . . who never knew they were unfulfilled. I can't testify that they were happy, but they *were* cheerful. And if they lacked "meaningful relationships," they cherished relations who meant something. They took pride in a clean, comfortable home and satisfaction in serving a good meal because no one had explained to them that the only work worth doing is that for which you get paid.
>
> They enjoyed rearing their children because no one ever told them that little children belonged in church basements and their mothers belonged somewhere else. They lived, very frugally, on their husbands' paychecks because they didn't realize that it's more important to have a

bigger house and a second car than it is to rear your own children. And they were so incredibly ignorant that they died never suspecting they'd been failures.

That won't hold true for me. I don't yet perceive myself as a failure, but it's not for want of being told I am.

The other day, years of condescension prompted me to fib in order to test a theory. At a party where most of the guests were business associates of my husband, a Ms. Putdown asked me who I was. I told her I was Jack Hekker's wife. That had a galvanizing effect on her. She took my hand and asked if that was all I thought of myself—just someone's wife? I wasn't going to let her in on the five children but when she persisted I mentioned them but told her that they weren't mine, that they belonged to my dead sister. And then I basked in the glow of her warm approval.

It's an absolute truth that whereas you are considered ignorant to stay home to rear *your* children, it is quite heroic to do so for someone else's children. Being a housekeeper is acceptable (even to the Social Security office) as long as it's not *your* house you're keeping. And treating a husband with attentive devotion is altogether correct as long as he's not *your* husband.

Sometimes I feel like Alice in Wonderland. But lately, mostly, I feel like an endangered species.

Hekker's view of the importance of what she calls "housewifery"—the role of the traditional American wife and mother—derives from her own personal standards and ideals, which themselves derive from a cultural perspective that she admits is no longer in fashion in the late 1970s. This cultural and personal perspective places great value on such aspects of marriage and motherhood as having "a clean, comfortable home," the satisfaction of "serving a good meal," and the enjoyment of rearing "your own children," and it places less value on "having a big house and a second car." She refuses to consider herself a failure (as she believes others do) because she takes pride in identifying herself as her husband's wife. Hekker's analysis of her own situation, in contrast to the situation of the more "liberated" working wife, throws a revealing light on the cultural conflicts of that period regarding marriage.

Almost thirty years after she wrote this op-ed article, Hekker's perspective had dramatically shifted. Her shattering experiences in the wake of her unexpected divorce had changed her view—and as a result, her analysis—of the status, value, and prospects of the traditional wife:

Like most loyal wives of our generation, we'd contemplated eventual widowhood but never thought we'd end up divorced. And "divorced" doesn't begin to describe the pain of this process. "Canceled" is more like it. . . . If I had it to do over again, I'd still marry the man I married and have my children: they are my treasure and a powerful support system for me and for one another. But I would have used the years after my youngest started school to further my education. I could have amassed two doctorates using the time and energy I gave myself to charitable and community causes and been better able to support myself.

Hekker's new analysis of the role of the traditional wife (published in the *New York Times* in 2006) derives from her changed perspective, based on her own experience and the similar experiences of a number of her divorced friends. Notice, again, that the analysis is meant to *reveal*.

If you find yourself writing an analysis guided by your own insights, not by someone else's, then you owe your reader a clear explanation of your guiding principles and the definitions by which you will probe the subject under study. Continue using the Guidelines for Writing Analyses (see p. 350), modifying this advice as you think fit to accommodate your own personal outlook, perspective, or interests. Above all, remember to structure your analysis with care. Proceed systematically and emerge with a clear statement about what the subject means, how it works, or why it might be significant.

Demonstration: Analysis

Two examples of analyses follow. The first was written by a professional writer; the second was written by a student in response to an assignment in his sociology class. Each analysis illustrates the two defining features of analysis just discussed: a statement of an analytical principle or definition, and the use of that principle or definition in closely examining an object, behavior, or event. As you read, try to identify these features. An exercise with questions for discussion follows at the end of the chapter in the Practice section.

The Plug-In Drug

Marie Winn

This analysis of television viewing as an addictive behavior appeared originally in Marie Winn's book The Plug-In Drug: Television, Computers, and Family Life *(2002). A writer and media critic, Winn has been interested in the effects of television on both individuals and the larger culture. In this passage, she carefully defines the term addiction and then applies it systematically to the behavior under study.*

The word *addiction* is often used loosely and wryly in conversation. People will refer to themselves as "mystery-book addicts" or "cookie addicts." E. B. White wrote of his annual surge of interest in gardening: "We are hooked and are making an attempt to kick the habit." Yet nobody really believes that reading mysteries or ordering seeds by catalogue is serious enough to be compared with addictions to heroin or alcohol. In these cases the word "addiction" is used jokingly to denote a tendency to overindulge in some pleasurable activity.

People often refer to being "hooked on TV." Does this, too, fall into the lighthearted category of cookie eating and other pleasures that people pursue with unusual intensity? Or is there a kind of television viewing that falls into the more serious category of destructive addiction?

Not unlike drugs or alcohol, the television experience allows the participant to blot out the real world and enter into a pleasurable and passive mental state. To be sure, other experiences, notably reading, also provide a temporary respite from reality. But it's much easier to stop reading and return to reality than to stop watching television. The entry into another world offered by reading includes an easily accessible return ticket. The entry via television does not. In this way television viewing, for those vulnerable to addiction, is more like drinking or taking drugs— once you start it's hard to stop.

Just as alcoholics are only vaguely aware of their addiction, feeling that they control their drinking more than they really do ("I can cut it out any time I want—I just like to have three or four drinks before dinner"), many people overestimate their control over television watching. Even as they put off other activities to spend hour after hour watching television, they feel they could easily resume living in a different, less passive style. But somehow or other while the television set is present in their homes, it just stays on. With television's easy gratifications available, those other activities seem to take too much effort.

5   A heavy viewer (a college English instructor) observes:

> I find television almost irresistible. When the set is on, I cannot
> ignore it. I can't turn it off. I feel sapped, will-less, enervated. As
> I reach out to turn off the set, the strength goes out of my arms.
> So I sit there for hours and hours.

Self-confessed television addicts often feel they "ought" to do other things—but the fact that they don't read and don't plant their garden or sew or crochet or play games or have conversations means that those activities are no longer as desirable as television viewing. In a way, the lives of heavy viewers are as unbalanced by their television "habit" as drug addicts' or alcoholics' lives. They are living in a holding pattern, as it were, passing up the activities that lead to growth or development or a sense of accomplishment. This is one reason people talk about their television viewing so ruefully, so apologetically. They are aware that it is an unproductive experience, that by any human measure almost any other endeavor is more worthwhile.

It is the adverse effect of television viewing on the lives of so many people that makes it feel like a serious addiction. The television habit distorts the sense of time. It renders other experiences vague and curiously unreal while taking on a greater reality for itself. It weakens relationships by reducing and sometimes eliminating normal opportunities for talking, for communicating.

And yet television does not satisfy, else why would the viewer continue to watch hour after hour, day after day? "The measure of health," wrote the psychiatrist Lawrence Kubie, "is flexibility . . . and especially the freedom to cease when sated." But heavy television viewers can never be sated with their television experiences. These do not provide the true nourishment that satiation requires, and thus they find that they cannot stop watching.

Edward Peselman wrote the following paper as a first-semester sophomore, in response to this assignment from his English professor:

Read Chapter 3, "The Paradoxes of Power," in Randall Collins's *Sociological Insight: An Introduction to Non-Obvious Sociology* (2nd ed., 1992). Use any of Collins's observations to examine the sociology of power in a group with which you are familiar. Write for readers much like yourself: freshmen or sophomores who have taken one course in sociology. Your object in this paper is to use Collins as a way of learning something "nonobvious" about a group to which you belong or have belonged.

MODEL ANALYSIS

THE COMING APART OF A DORM SOCIETY   2

The Coming Apart of a Dorm Society

1   During my first year of college, I lived in a dormitory, like most freshmen

on campus. We inhabitants of the dorm came from different cultural and

economic backgrounds. Not surprisingly, we brought with us many of the traits

found in people outside of college. Like many on the outside, we in the dorm

sought personal power at the expense of others. The gaining and maintaining of

power can be an ugly business, and I saw people hurt and in turn hurt others all

Taken from: *Writing and Reading Across the Curriculum,* Eleventh Edition by Laurence Behrens and Leonard J. Rosen.

for the sake of securing a place in the dorm's prized social order. Not until one of us challenged that order did I realize how fragile it was.

2   Randall Collins (1992), a sociologist at the University of California, Riverside, defines the exercise of power as the attempt "to make something happen in society" (p. 61). A society can be understood as something as large and complex as "American society"; something more sharply defined, such as a corporate or organizational society; or something smaller still—a dorm society like my own, consisting of six 18-year-old men who lived at one end of a dormitory floor in an all-male dorm.

3   In my freshman year, my society was a tiny but distinctive social group in which people exercised power. I lived with two roommates, Dozer and Reggie. Dozer was an emotionally unstable, excitable individual who vented his energy through anger. His insecurity and moodiness contributed to his difficulty in making friends. Reggie was a friendly, happy-go-lucky sort who seldom displayed emotions other than contentedness. He was shy when encountering new people, but when placed in a socially comfortable situation he would talk for hours.

4   Eric and Marc lived across the hall from us and therefore spent a considerable amount of time in our room. Eric could be cynical and was often blunt: He seldom hesitated when sharing his frank and sometimes unflattering opinions. He commanded a grudging respect in the dorm. Marc could be very moody and, sometimes, was violent. His temper and stubborn streak made him particularly susceptible to conflict. The final member of our miniature society was Benjamin, cheerful yet insecure. Benjamin had certain characteristics which many considered effeminate, and he was often teased about his sexuality— which in turn made him insecure. He was naturally friendly but, because of the abuse he took, he largely kept to himself. He would join us occasionally for a pizza or late-night television.

5   Together, we formed an independent social structure. Going out to parties together, playing cards, watching television, playing ball: These were the activities through which we got to know each other and through which we established the basic pecking order of our community. Much like a colony of baboons, we established a hierarchy based on power relationships. According to Collins (1992), what a powerful person wishes to happen must be achieved by controlling others. Collins's observation can help to define who had how much power in our social group. In the dorm, Marc and Eric clearly had the most power. Everyone feared them and agreed to do pretty much what they wanted. Through violent words or threats of violence, they got their way. I was next in line: I wouldn't dare to manipulate Marc or Eric, but the others I could manage through occasional quips. Reggie, then Dozer, and finally Benjamin.

6   Up and down the pecking order, we exercised control through macho taunts and challenges. Collins (1992) writes that "individuals who manage to be powerful and get their own way must do so by going along with the laws of social organization, not by contradicting them" (p. 61). Until mid-year, our dorm motto could have read: "You win through rudeness and intimidation." Eric gained power with his frequent and brutal assessments of everyone's behavior. Marc gained power with his temper—which, when lost, made everyone run for cover. Those who were not rude and intimidating drifted to the bottom of our social world. Reggie was quiet and unemotional, which allowed us to take advantage of him because we knew he would back down if pressed in an argument. Yet Reggie understood that on a "power scale" he stood above Dozer and often shared in the group's tactics to get Dozer's food (his parents were forever sending him care packages). Dozer, in turn, seldom missed opportunities to take swipes at Benjamin, with references to his sexuality. From the very first week of school, Benjamin could never—and never wanted to—compete against Eric's bluntness or Marc's temper. Still, Benjamin hung out with us. He lived in

our corner of the dorm, and he wanted to be friendly. But everyone, including Benjamin, understood that he occupied the lowest spot in the order.

7   That is, until he left mid-year. According to Collins (1992), "any social arrangement works because people avoid questioning it most of the time" (p. 74). The inverse of this principle is as follows: When a social arrangement is questioned, that arrangement can fall apart. The more fragile the arrangement (the flimsier the values on which it is based), the more quickly it will crumble. For the entire first semester, no one questioned our rude, macho rules, and because of them we pigeon-holed Benjamin as a wimp. In our dorm society, gentle men had no power. To say the least, ours was not a compassionate community. From a distance of one year, I am shocked to have been a member of it. Nonetheless, we had created a mini-society that somehow served our needs.

8   At the beginning of the second semester, we found Benjamin packing up his room. Marc, who was walking down the hall, stopped by and said something like: "Hey buddy, the kitchen get too hot for you?" I was there, and I saw Benjamin turn around and say: "Do you practice at being such a _____, or does it come naturally? I've never met anybody who felt so good about making other people feel lousy. You'd better get yourself a job in the army or in the prison system, because no one else is going to put up with your _____." Marc said something in a raised voice. I stepped between them, and Benjamin said: "Get out." I was cheering.

9   Benjamin moved into an off-campus apartment with his girlfriend. This astonished us, first because of his effeminate manner (we didn't know he had a girlfriend) and second because none of the rest of us had been seeing girls much (though we talked about it constantly). Here was Benjamin, the gentlest among us, and he blew a hole in our macho society. Our social order never really recovered, which suggests its flimsy values. People in the dorm mostly went their own ways during the second semester. I'm not surprised, and I was more than a little grateful. Like most people in the dorm, save for Eric and Marc, I both

got my lumps and I gave them, and I never felt good about either. Like Benjamin, I wanted to fit in with my new social surroundings. Unlike him, I didn't have the courage to challenge the unfairness of what I saw.

10   By chance, six of us were thrown together into a dorm and were expected, on the basis of proximity alone, to develop a friendship. What we did was sink to the lowest possible denominator. Lacking any real basis for friendship, we allowed the forceful, macho personalities of Marc and Eric to set the rules, which for one semester we all subscribed to—even those who suffered.

11   The macho rudeness couldn't last, and I'm glad it was Benjamin who brought us down. By leaving, he showed a different and a superior kind of power. I doubt he was reading Randall Collins (1992) at the time, but he somehow had come to Collins's same insight: As long as he played by the rules of our group, he suffered because those rules placed him far down in the dorm's pecking order. Even by participating in pleasant activities, like going out for pizza, Benjamin supported a social system that ridiculed him. Some systems are so oppressive and small-minded that they can't be changed from the inside. They've got to be torn down. Benjamin had to move, and in moving he made me (at least) question the basis of my dorm friendships.

THE COMING APART OF A DORM SOCIETY   7

Reference

Collins, R. (1992). *Sociological insight: An introduction to non-obvious sociology* (2nd ed.). New York: Oxford UP.

How to Write Analyses

CONSIDER YOUR PURPOSE

Whether you are assigned a topic to write on or are left to your own devices, you inevitably face this question: What is my idea? Like every paper, an analysis has at its heart an idea you want to convey. For Edward Peselman, it was the idea that a social order based on flimsy values is not strong enough to sustain a direct challenge to its power and thus will fall apart eventually. From beginning to end, Peselman advances this one idea: first, by introducing readers to the dorm society he will analyze; next, by introducing principles of analysis (from Randall Collins); and finally, by examining his dorm relationships in light of those principles. The entire set of analytical insights coheres as a paper because the insights are *related* and point to Peselman's single idea.

Peselman's paper offers a good example of the personal uses to which analysis can be put. Notice that he gravitates toward events in his life that confuse him and about which he wants some clarity. Such topics can be especially fruitful for analysis because you know the particulars well and can provide readers with details; you view the topic with some puzzlement; and, through the application of your analytical tool, you may come to understand it. When you select topics to analyze from your own experience, you provide yourself with a motivation to write and learn. When you are motivated in this way, you spark the interest of readers.

Using Randall Collins as a guide, Edward Peselman returns again and again to the events of his freshman year in the dormitory. We sense that Peselman himself wants to understand what happened in that dorm. He writes, "I saw people hurt and in turn hurt others all for the sake of securing a place in the dorm's prized social order." Peselman does not approve of what happened, and the analysis he launches is meant to help him understand.

LOCATE AN ANALYTICAL PRINCIPLE

When you are given an assignment that asks for analysis, use two specific reading strategies to identify principles and definitions in source materials.

- **Look for a sentence that makes a general statement about the way something works.** The statement may strike you as a rule or a law. The line that Edward Peselman quotes from Randall Collins has this quality: "[A]ny social arrangement works because people avoid questioning it most of the time." Such statements are generalizations—conclusions to sometimes complicated and extensive arguments. You can use these conclusions to guide your own analyses as long as you are aware that for some audiences you will need to re-create and defend the arguments that resulted in these conclusions.

- **Look for statements that take this form: X can be defined as (or X consists of) A, B, and C.** The specific elements of the definition—A, B, and C—are what you use to identify and analyze parts of the object being studied. You've seen an example of this approach in Marie Winn's multipart definition of addiction, which she uses to analyze television viewing. As a reader looking for definitions suitable for conducting an analysis, you might come across Winn's definition of addiction and then use it for your own purposes, perhaps to analyze the playing of video games as an addiction.

Essential to any analysis is the validity of the principle or definition being applied, the analytical tool. Make yourself aware, as both writer and reader, of a tool's strengths and limitations. Pose these questions of the analytical principles and definitions you use: Are they accurate? Are they well accepted? Do *you* accept them? What are the arguments against them? What are their limitations? Since every principle or definition used in an analysis is the end product of an argument, you are entitled—even obligated—to challenge it. If the analytical tool is flawed, the analysis that follows from it will be flawed.

A page from Randall Collins's *Sociological Insight* follows; Edward Peselman uses a key sentence from this extract as an analytical tool in his essay on power relations in his dorm. Notice that Peselman underlines the sentence he will use in his analysis.

1. Try this experiment some time. When you are talking to someone, make them explain everything they say that isn't completely clear. The result, you will discover, is a series of uninterrupted interruptions:

   A: Hi, how are you doing?
   B: What do you mean when you say "how"?
   A: You know. What's happening with you?
   B: What do you mean, "happening"?
   A: Happening, you know, what's going on.
   B: I'm sorry. Could you explain what you mean by "what"?
   A: What do you mean, what do I mean? Do you want to talk to me or not?

2. It is obvious that this sort of questioning could go on endlessly, at any rate if the listener doesn't get very angry and punch you in the mouth. But it illustrates two important points. First, virtually everything can be called into question. We are able to get along with other people not because

everything is clearly spelled out, but because we are willing to take most things people say without explanation. Harold Garfinkel, who actually performed this sort of experiment, points out that there is an infinite regress of assumptions that go into any act of social communication. Moreover, some expressions are simply not explainable in words at all. A word like "you," or "here," or "now" is what Garfinkel calls "indexical." You have to know what it means already; it can't be explained.

3.   "What do you mean by 'you'?"

4.   "I mean *you, you!*" About all that can be done here is point your finger.

5.   The second point is that people get mad when they are pressed to explain things that they ordinarily take for granted. This is because they very quickly see that explanations could go on forever and the questions will never be answered. If you really demanded a full explanation of everything you hear, you could stop the conversation from ever getting past its first sentence. The real significance of this for a sociological understanding of the way the world is put together is not the anger, however. It is the fact that people try to avoid these sorts of situations. They tacitly recognize that we have to avoid these endless lines of questioning. Sometimes small children will start asking an endless series of "whys," but adults discourage this.

6.   In sum, <u>any social arrangement works because people avoid questioning it most of the time.</u> That does not mean that people do not get into arguments or disputes about just what ought to be done from time to time. But to have a dispute already implies there is a considerable area of agreement. An office manager may dispute with a clerk over just how to take care of some business letter, but they at any rate know more or less what they are disputing about. They do not get off into a . . . series of questions over just what is meant by everything that is said. You could very quickly dissolve the organization into nothingness if you followed that route: there would be no communication at all, even about what the disagreement is over.

7.   Social organization is possible because people maintain a certain level of focus. If they focus on one thing, even if only to disagree about it, they are taking many other things for granted, thereby reinforcing their social reality.*

*Randall Collins, *Sociological Insight: An Introduction to Non–obvious Sociology,* 2nd ed. (New York: Oxford UP, 1992) 73–74.

The statement that Peselman has underlined—"any social arrangement works because people avoid questioning it most of the time"—is the end result of an argument that takes Collins several paragraphs to develop. Peselman agrees with the conclusion and uses it in paragraph 7 of his analysis. Observe that for his own purposes Peselman does *not* reconstruct Collins's argument. He selects *only* Collins's conclusion and then imports that into his analysis, which concerns an entirely different subject. Once he identifies in Collins a principle he can use in his analysis, he converts the principle into questions that he then directs to his topic, life in his freshman dorm. Two questions follow directly from Collins's insight:

1. What was the social arrangement in the dorm?
2. How was this social arrangement questioned?

Peselman clearly defines his dormitory's social arrangement in paragraphs 3–6 (with the help of another principle borrowed from Collins). Beginning with paragraph 7, he explores how one member of his dorm questioned that arrangement:

> That is, until he left mid-year. According to Collins, "any social arrangement works because people avoid questioning it most of the time". The inverse of this principle is as follows: When a social arrangement is questioned, that arrangement can fall apart. The more fragile the arrangement (the flimsier the values on which it is based), the more quickly it will crumble. For the entire first semester, no one questioned our rude, macho rules, and because of them we pigeon-holed Benjamin as a wimp. In our dorm society, gentle men had no power. To say the least, ours was not a compassionate community. From a distance of one year, I am shocked to have been a member of it. Nonetheless, we had created a mini-society that somehow served our needs.

FORMULATE A THESIS

An analysis is two-part. The first part states and establishes the writer's agreement with a certain principle or definition.

● **PART ONE**   This first part essentially takes this form:

Claim #1: Principle X (or definition X) is valuable.

Principle X can be a theory as encompassing and abstract as the statement that *myths are the enemy of truth*. Principle X can be as modest as the definition of a term such as *addiction* or *comfort*. As you move from one subject area to another, the principles and definitions you use for analysis will change, as these assignments illustrate:

Sociology: Write a paper in which you place yourself in American society by locating both your absolute position and relative rank on each single criterion of social *stratification used by Lenski & Lenski. For each criterion, state whether you have attained your social position by yourself or if you have "inherited" that status from your parents.*

Literature: *Apply principles of Jungian psychology to Hawthorne's "Young Goodman Brown." In your reading of the story, apply Jung's principles of the* shadow, persona, *and* anima.

Physics: *Use Newton's second law* (F = ma) *to analyze the acceleration of a fixed pulley, from which two weights hang:* m_1 *(.45 kg) and* m2 *(.90 kg). Explain in a paragraph the principle of Newton's law and your method of applying it to solve the problem. Assume your reader is not comfortable with mathematical explanations: do not use equations in your paragraph.*

GUIDELINES FOR WRITING ANALYSES

Unless you are asked to follow a specialized format, especially in the sciences or the social sciences, you can present your analysis as a paper by following the guidelines below. As you move from one class to another, from discipline to discipline, the principles and definitions you use as the basis for your analyses will change, but the following basic components of analysis will remain the same.

- *Create a context for your analysis.* Introduce and summarize for readers the object, event, or behavior to be analyzed. Present a strong case about why an analysis is needed: Give yourself a motivation to write, and give readers a motivation to read. Consider setting out a problem, puzzle, or question to be investigated.

- *Introduce and summarize the key definition or principle that will form the basis of your analysis.* Plan to devote an early part of your analysis to arguing for the validity of this principle or definition if your audience is not likely to understand it or if they are likely to think that the principle or definition is not valuable.

- *Analyze your topic.* Systematically apply elements of this definition or principle to parts of the activity or object under study. You can do this by posing specific questions, based on your analytic principle or definition, about the object. Discuss what you find part by part (organized perhaps by question), in clearly defined sections of the essay.

- *Conclude by stating clearly what is significant about your analysis.* When considering your analytical paper as a whole, what new or interesting insights have you made concerning the object under study? To what extent has your application of the definition or principle helped you to explain how the object works, what it might mean, or why it is significant?

Finance: *Using Guidford C. Babcock's "Concept of Sustainable Growth" [Financial Analysis 26 (May–June 1970): 108–14], analyze the stock price appreciation of the XYZ Corporation, figures for which are attached.*

The analytical tools to be applied in these assignments must be appropriate to the discipline. Writing in response to the sociology assignment, you would use sociological principles developed by Lenski and Lenski. In your literature class, you would use principles of Jungian psychology; in physics, Newton's second law; and in finance, a particular writer's concept of "sustainable growth." But whatever discipline you are working in, the first part of your analysis will clearly state which (and whose) principles and definitions you are applying. For audiences unfamiliar with these principles, you will need to explain them; if you anticipate objections, you will need to argue that they are legitimate principles capable of helping you conduct the analysis.

● **PART TWO**   In the second part of an analysis, you *apply* specific parts of your principle or definition to the topic at hand. Regardless of how it is worded, this second argument in an analysis can be rephrased to take this form:

> **Claim #2:** By applying principle (or definition) X, we can understand *(topic)* as *(conclusion based on analysis)*.

This is your thesis, the main idea of your analytical paper. Fill in the first blank with the specific object, event, or behavior you are examining. Fill in the second blank with your conclusion about the meaning or significance of this object, based on the insights you made during your analysis. Mary Winn completes the second claim of her analysis this way:

> By applying my multipart definition, we can understand *television viewing* as *an addiction.*

DEVELOP AN ORGANIZATIONAL PLAN

You will benefit enormously in the writing of a first draft if you plan out the logic of your analysis. Turn key elements of your analytical principle or definition into questions and then develop the paragraph-by-paragraph logic of the paper.

● **TURNING KEY ELEMENTS OF A PRINCIPLE OR A DEFINITION INTO QUESTIONS**   Prepare for an analysis by phrasing questions based on the definition or principle you are going to apply, and then directing those questions to the activity or object to be studied. The method is straightforward: State as clearly as possible the principle or definition to be applied. Divide the principle or definition into its parts and, using each part, form a question. For example, Marie Winn develops a multipart definition of addiction, each part of which is readily turned into a question that she directs at a specific behavior: television viewing. Her analysis of television viewing can be understood as *responses* to each of her analytical questions. Note that in her brief analysis, Winn does not first define addiction and then analyze television viewing. Rather, *as* she defines aspects of addiction, she analyzes television viewing.

● **DEVELOPING THE PARAGRAPH-BY-PARAGRAPH LOGIC OF YOUR PAPER**   The following paragraph from Edward Peselman's essay illustrates the typical logic of a paragraph in an analytical essay:

> Up and down the pecking order, we exercised control through macho taunts and challenges. Collins writes that "individuals who manage to be powerful and get their own way must do so by going along with the laws of social organization, not by contradicting them" (p. 61). Until mid-year, our dorm motto could have read: "You win through rudeness and intimidation." Eric gained power with his frequent and brutal assessments of everyone's behavior. Marc gained power with his temper—which, when lost, made everyone run for cover. Those who were not rude and intimidating drifted to the bottom of our social world. Reggie was quiet and unemotional, which allowed us to take advantage of him because we knew he would back down if pressed in an argument. Yet Reggie understood that on a "power scale" he stood above Dozer and often shared in the group's tactics to get Dozer's food (his parents were forever sending him care packages). Dozer, in turn, seldom missed opportunities to take swipes at Benjamin, with references to his sexuality. From the very first week of school, Benjamin could never—and never wanted to—compete against Eric's bluntness or Marc's temper. Still, Benjamin hung out with us. He lived in our corner of the dorm, and he wanted to be friendly. But everyone, including Benjamin, understood that he occupied the lowest spot in the order.

We see in this paragraph the typical logic of analysis:

- *The writer introduces a specific analytical tool.* Peselman quotes a line from Randall Collins:

  > "[I]ndividuals who manage to be powerful and get their own way must do so by going along with the laws of social organization, not by contradicting them."

- *The writer applies this analytical tool to the object being examined.* Peselman states his dorm's law of social organization:

  > Until mid-year, our dorm motto could have read: "You win through rudeness and intimidation."

- *The writer uses the tool to identify and then examine the meaning of parts of the object.* Peselman shows how each member (the "parts") of his dorm society conforms to the laws of "social organization":

  > Eric gained power with his frequent and brutal assessments of everyone's behavior. Marc gained power with his temper— which, when lost, made everyone run for cover. Those who

were not rude and intimidating drifted to the bottom
of our social world.

An analytical paper takes shape when a writer creates a series of such paragraphs and then links them with an overall logic. Here is the logical organization of Edward Peselman's paper:

- Paragraph 1: Introduction states a problem—provides a motivation to
  write and to read.
- Paragraph 2: Randall Collins is introduced—the author whose work will
  provide principles for analysis.
- Paragraphs 3–4: Background information is provided—the cast of
  characters in the dorm.
- Paragraphs 5–9: The analysis proceeds—specific parts of dorm life are
  identified and found significant, using principles from Collins.
- Paragraphs 10–11: Summary and conclusion are provided—the
  freshman dorm society disintegrates for reasons set out in the analysis.
  A larger point is made: Some oppressive systems must be torn down.

DRAFT AND REVISE YOUR ANALYSIS

You will usually need at least two drafts to produce a paper that presents your idea
clearly. The biggest changes in your paper will typically come between your first
and second drafts. No paper that you write, including an analysis, will be complete until you revise and refine your single compelling idea: your analytical conclusion about what the object, event, or behavior being examined means or how
it is significant. You revise and refine by evaluating your first draft, bringing to it
many of the same questions you pose when evaluating any piece of writing:

- Are the facts accurate?
- Are my opinions supported by evidence?
- Are the opinions of others authoritative?
- Are my assumptions clearly stated?
- Are key terms clearly defined?
- Is the presentation logical?
- Are all parts of the presentation well developed?
- Are significant opposing points of view presented?

Address these same questions to the first draft of your analysis, and you will have
solid information to guide your revision.

● **WRITE AN ANALYSIS, NOT A SUMMARY** The most common error
made in writing analyses—an error that is *fatal* to the form—is to present readers with a summary only. For analyses to succeed, you must *apply* a principle or

definition and reach a conclusion about the object, event, or behavior you are examining. By definition, a summary includes none of your own conclusions. Summary is naturally a part of analysis; you will need to summarize the object or activity being examined and, depending on the audience's needs, summarize the principle or definition being applied. But in an analysis you must take the next step and share insights that suggest the meaning or significance of some object, event, or behavior.

● **MAKE YOUR ANALYSIS SYSTEMATIC**   Analyses should give the reader the sense of a systematic, purposeful examination. Marie Winn's analysis illustrates the point: She sets out specific elements of addictive behavior in separate paragraphs and then uses each, within its paragraph, to analyze television viewing. Winn is systematic in her method, and we are never in doubt about her purpose.

Imagine another analysis in which a writer lays out four elements of a definition and then applies only two, without explaining the logic for omitting the others. Or imagine an analysis in which the writer offers a principle for analysis but directs it to only a half or a third of the object being discussed, without providing a rationale for doing so. In both cases the writer would be failing to deliver on a promise basic to analyses: Once a principle or definition is presented, it should be thoroughly and systematically applied.

● **ANSWER THE "SO WHAT?" QUESTION**   An analysis should make readers *want* to read. It should give readers a sense of getting to the heart of the matter, that what is important in the object or activity under analysis is being laid bare and discussed in revealing ways. If when rereading the first draft of your analysis, you cannot imagine readers saying, "I never thought of _____ this way," then something may be seriously wrong. Reread closely to determine why the paper might leave readers flat and exhausted, as opposed to feeling that they have gained new and important insights. Closely reexamine your own motivations for writing. Have *you* learned anything significant through the analysis? If not, neither will readers, and they will turn away. If you have gained important insights through your analysis, communicate them clearly. At some point, pull together your related insights and say, in effect, "Here's how it all adds up."

● **ATTRIBUTE SOURCES APPROPRIATELY**   In an analysis you work with one or two sources and apply insights from them to some object or phenomenon you want to understand more thoroughly. Because you are not synthesizing a great many sources, and because the strength of an analysis derives mostly from *your* application of a principle or definition, the opportunities for not appropriately citing sources are diminished. Take special care to cite and quote, as necessary, the one or two sources you use throughout the analysis.

CRITICAL READING FOR ANALYSIS

- ***Read to get a sense of the whole in relation to its parts.*** Whether you are clarifying for yourself a principle or a definition to be used in an analysis, or you are reading a text that you will analyze, understand how parts function to create the whole. If a definition or principle consists of parts, use them to organize sections of your analysis. If your goal is to analyze a text, be aware of its structure: Note the title and subtitle; identify the main point and subordinate points and where they are located; break the material into sections.

- ***Read to discover relationships within the object being analyzed.*** Watch for patterns. When you find them, be alert—for they create an occasion to analyze, to use a principle or definition as a guide in discussing what the patterns may mean.

   In fiction, a pattern might involve responses of characters to events or to each other, the recurrence of certain words or phrasings, images, themes, or turns of plot (to name a few).

   In poetry, a pattern might involve rhyme schemes, rhythm, imagery, figurative or literal language, and more.

The challenge to you as a reader is first to see a pattern (perhaps using a guiding principle or definition to do so) and then to locate other instances of that pattern. Reading carefully in this way prepares you to conduct an analysis.

Analysis: A Tool for Understanding

As this chapter has demonstrated, analysis involves applying principles as a way to probe and understand. With incisive principles guiding your analysis, you will be able to pose questions, observe patterns and relationships, and derive meaning. Do not forget that this meaning will be one of several possible meanings. Someone else, or even you, using different analytical tools, could observe the same phenomena and arrive at very different conclusions regarding meaning or significance. We end the chapter, then, as we began it: with the two brief analyses of *The Wizard of Oz.* The conclusions expressed in one look nothing like the conclusions expressed in the other, save for the fact that both seek to interpret the same movie. And yet we can say that both are useful, that both reveal meaning.

> At the dawn of adolescence, the very time she should start to distance herself from Aunt Em and Uncle Henry, the surrogate parents who raised her on their Kansas farm, Dorothy Gale experiences a hurtful reawakening of her fear that these loved ones will be rudely ripped from her, especially her Aunt (Em—M for Mother!).*

> [*The Wizard of Oz*] was originally written as a political allegory about grass-roots protest. It may seem harder to believe than Emerald City, but the Tin Woodsman is the industrial worker, the Scarecrow [is] the struggling farmer, and the Wizard is the president, who is powerful only as long as he succeeds in deceiving the people.†

You have seen in this chapter how it is possible for two writers, analyzing the same object or phenomenon but applying different analytical principles, to reach vastly different conclusions about what the object or phenomenon may mean or why it is significant. *The Wizard of Oz* is both an inquiry into the psychology of adolescence and a political allegory. What else the classic film may be awaits revealing with the systematic application of other analytical tools. The insights you gain as a writer of analyses depend entirely on your choice of tools and the subtlety with which you apply them.

*Greenberg, Movies.
†Dreier, "Politics."

READINGS

The Satisfactions of Housewifery and Motherhood/Paradise Lost (Domestic Division)

Terry Martin Hekker

We begin with a matched set of op-ed columns written nearly 30 years apart for the New York Times *by the same author. At the time her December 20, 1977, column "The Satisfactions of Housewifery and Motherhood" was published, Terry Martin Hekker was a housewife living in South Nyack, New York, who had been married 22 years to her husband, John Hekker, a lawyer and South Nyack village judge. The column deals with Hekker's experiences as a "stay-at-home" mom at a time—the late 1970s—when many women were opting to enter the workforce rather than stay home to raise their children. As a result of the extraordinary response to Hekker's column—some of which she describes in her follow-up 2006 piece, "Paradise Lost"—she expanded the essay into a book,* Ever Since Adam and Eve, *published by William Morrow in 1979. "Paradise Lost" was published on January 1, 2006. Like her first column, it aroused much comment in op-ed pieces and blogs around the nation.*

(1977)

My son lied about it on his college application. My husband mutters it under his breath when asked. And I had grown reluctant to mention it myself.

The problem is my occupation. But the statistics on women that have come out since the Houston conference have given me a new outlook. I have ceased thinking of myself as obsolete and begun to see myself as I really am—an endangered species. Like the whooping crane and the snow leopard, I deserve attentive nurturing and perhaps a distinctive metal tag on my foot. Because I'm one of the last of the dying breed of human females designated, "Occupation: Housewife."

I know it's nothing to crow about. I realize that when people discuss their professions at parties I am more of a pariah than a hooker or a loan shark is. I have been castigated, humiliated and scorned. In an age of do-your-own-thing, it's clear no one meant me. I've been told (patiently and a little louder than necessary, as one does with a small child) that I am an anachronism (except that they avoid such a big word). I have been made to feel so outmoded that I wouldn't be surprised to discover that, like a carton of yogurt, I have an expiration date stamped on my bottom.

I once treasured a small hope that history might vindicate me. After all, nursing was once just such a shameful occupation, suitable for only the lowest women. But I abandoned any thought that my occupation would ever become fashionable again, just as I had to stop counting on full-figured women coming back into style. I'm a hundred years too late on both counts.

5   Now, however, thanks to all these new statistics, I see a brighter future for myself. Today, fewer than 16 percent of American families have a full-time housewife-mother. Comparing that with previous figures, at the rate it's going I calculate I am less than eight years away from being the last housewife in the country. And then I intend to be impossible.

I shall demand enormous fees to go on talk shows, and will charge for my autograph. Anthropologists will study my feeding and nesting habits through field glasses and keep notebooks detailing my every move. That is, if no one gets the bright idea that I'm so unique that I must be put behind sealed glass like the Book of Kells. In any event, I can expect to be a celebrity and to be pampered. I cannot, though, expect to get even.

There's no getting even for years of being regarded as stupid or lazy, or both. For years of being considered unproductive (unless you count five children, which no one does). For years of being viewed as a parasite, living off a man (except by my husband whose opinion doesn't seem to matter). For years of fetching other women's children after they'd thrown up in the lunchroom, because I have nothing better to do, or probably there is nothing I do better, while their mothers have "careers." (Is clerking in a drug store a bona fide career?) For years of caring for five children and a big house and constantly being asked when I'm going to work.

I come from a long line of women, most of them more Edith Bunker* than Betty Friedan,† who never knew they were unfulfilled. I can't testify that they were happy, but they *were* cheerful. And if they

---

*Edith Bunker (wife of Archie Bunker) was a character in the 1970s sitcom *All in the Family;* in the first few years of the series, she was a traditional stay-at-home housewife.
†Betty Friedan (1921–2006) was an author and activist; her 1963 book *The Feminine Mystique,* documenting the stifling and vaguely dissatisfied lot of the mid-20th century traditional housewife, launched the "second wave" feminist revolution.

lacked "meaningful relationships," they cherished relations who meant something. They took pride in a clean, comfortable home and satisfaction in serving a good meal because no one had explained to them that the only work worth doing is that for which you get paid.

They enjoyed rearing their children because no one ever told them that little children belonged in church basements and their mothers belonged somewhere else. They lived, very frugally, on their husbands' paychecks because they didn't realize that it's more important to have a bigger house and a second car than it is to rear your own children. And they were so incredibly ignorant that they died never suspecting they'd been failures.

That won't hold true for me. I don't yet perceive myself as a failure, but it's not for want of being told I am.

10   The other day, years of condescension prompted me to fib in order to test a theory. At a party where most of the guests were business associates of my husband, a Ms. Putdown asked me who I was. I told her I was Jack Hekker's wife. That had a galvanizing effect on her. She took my hand and asked if that was all I thought of myself—just someone's wife? I wasn't going to let her in on the five children but when she persisted I mentioned them but told her that they weren't mine, that they belonged to my dead sister. And then I basked in the glow of her warm approval.

It's an absolute truth that whereas you are considered ignorant to stay home to rear *your* children, it is quite heroic to do so for someone else's children. Being a housekeeper is acceptable (even to the Social Security office) as long as it's not *your* house you're keeping. And treating a husband with attentive devotion is altogether correct as long as he's not *your* husband.

Sometimes I feel like Alice in Wonderland. But lately, mostly, I feel like an endangered species.

Paradise Lost (Domestic Division)

(2006)
A while back, at a baby shower for a niece, I overheard the expectant mother being asked if she intended to return to work after the baby was born. The answer, which rocked me, was, "Yes, because I don't want to end up like Aunt Terry."

That would be me.

In the continuing case of Full-Time Homemaker vs. Working Mother, I offer myself as Exhibit A. Because more than a quarter-century ago I wrote an Op-Ed article for *The New York Times* on the satisfaction

...continued Paradise Lost (Domestic Division), **Terry Martin Hekker**

of being a full-time housewife in the new age of the liberated woman. I wrote it from my heart, thoroughly convinced that homemaking and raising my children was the most challenging and rewarding job I could ever want.

"I come from a long line of women," I wrote, "most of them more Edith Bunker than Betty Friedan, who never knew they were unfulfilled. I can't testify that they were happy, but they were cheerful. They took pride in a clean, comfortable home and satisfaction in serving a good meal because no one had explained that the only work worth doing is that for which you get paid."

5 I wasn't advocating that mothers forgo careers to stay home with their children; I was simply defending my choice as a valid one. The mantra of the age may have been "Do your own thing," but as a full-time homemaker, that didn't seem to mean me.

The column morphed into a book titled *Ever Since Adam and Eve,* followed by a national tour on which I, however briefly, became the authority on homemaking as a viable choice for women. I ultimately told my story on *Today* and to Dinah Shore, Charlie Rose and even to Oprah, when she was the host of a local TV show in Baltimore.

In subsequent years I lectured on the rewards of homemaking and housewifery. While others tried to make the case that women like me were parasites and little more than legalized prostitutes, I spoke to rapt audiences about the importance of being there for your children as they grew up, of the satisfactions of "making a home," preparing family meals and supporting your hard-working husband.

So I was predictably stunned and devastated when, on our 40th wedding anniversary, my husband presented me with a divorce. I knew our first anniversary would be paper, but never expected the 40th would be papers, 16 of them meticulously detailing my faults and flaws, the reason our marriage, according to him, was over.

We had been married by a bishop with a blessing from the pope in a country church filled with honeysuckle and hope. Five children and six grandchildren later we were divorced by a third-rate judge in a suburban courthouse reeking of dust and despair.

10 Our long marriage had its full share of love, complications, illnesses, joy and stress. Near the end we were in a dismal period, with my husband in treatment for alcoholism. And although I had made more than my share of mistakes, I never expected to be served with divorce papers. I was stunned to find myself, at this stage of life, marooned. And it was small comfort that I wasn't alone. There were many other confused women of my age and circumstance who'd been married just as long, sharing my situation.

I was in my teens when I first read Dickens's *Great Expectations,* with the tale of Miss Haversham, who, stood up by her groom-to-be, spent decades in her yellowing wedding gown, sitting at her cobweb-covered bridal banquet table, consumed with plotting revenge. I felt then that to be left waiting at the altar with a church full of people must be the most crushing thing that could happen to a woman.

I was wrong. No jilted bride could feel as embarrassed and humiliated as a woman in her 60's discarded by her husband. I was confused and scared, and the pain of being tossed aside by the love of my life made bitterness unavoidable. In those first few bewildering months, as I staggered and wailed through my life, I made Miss Haversham look like a good sport.

Sitting around my kitchen with two friends who had also been dumped by their husbands, I figured out that among the three of us we'd been married 110 years. We'd been faithful wives, good mothers, cooks and housekeepers who'd married in the 50's, when "dress for success" meant a wedding gown and "wife" was a tenured position.

Turns out we had a lot in common with our outdated kitchen appliances. Like them we were serviceable, low maintenance, front loading, self-cleaning and (relatively) frost free. Also like them we had warranties that had run out. Our husbands sought sleeker models with features we lacked who could execute tasks we'd either never learned or couldn't perform without laughing.

15   Like most loyal wives of our generation, we'd contemplated eventual widowhood but never thought we'd end up divorced. And "divorced" doesn't begin to describe the pain of this process. "Canceled" is more like it. It began with my credit cards, then my health insurance and checkbook, until, finally, like a used postage stamp, I felt canceled too.

I faced frightening losses and was overwhelmed by the injustice of it all. He got to take his girlfriend to Cancun, while I got to sell my engagement ring to pay the roofer. When I filed my first nonjoint tax return, it triggered the shocking notification that I had become eligible for food stamps.

The judge had awarded me alimony that was less than I was used to getting for household expenses, and now I had to use that money to pay bills I'd never seen before: mortgage, taxes, insurance and car payments. And that princely sum was awarded for only four years, the judge suggesting that I go for job training when I turned 67. Not only was I unprepared for divorce itself, I was utterly lacking in skills to deal with the brutal aftermath.

I read about the young mothers of today—educated, employed, self-sufficient—who drop out of the work force when they have children, and I worry and wonder. Perhaps it is the right choice for them. Maybe they'll be fine. But the fragility of modern marriage suggests that at least half of them may not be.

Regrettably, women whose husbands are devoted to their families and are good providers must nevertheless face the specter of future abandonment. Surely the seeds of this wariness must have been planted, even if they can't believe it could ever happen to them. Many have witnessed their own mothers jettisoned by their own fathers and seen divorced friends trying to rear children with marginal financial and emotional support.

...continued Paradise Lost (Domestic Division), **Terry Martin Hekker**

20 These young mothers are often torn between wanting to be home with their children and the statistical possibility of future calamity, aware that one of the most poverty-stricken groups in today's society are divorced older women. The feminine and sexual revolutions of the last few decades have had their shining victories, but have they, in the end, made things any easier for mothers?

I cringe when I think of that line from my Op-Ed article about the long line of women I'd come from and belonged to who were able to find fulfillment as homemakers "because no one had explained" to us "that the only work worth doing is that for which you get paid." For a divorced mother, the harsh reality is that the work for which you do get paid is the only work that will keep you afloat.

These days couples face complex negotiations over work, family, child care and housekeeping. I see my children dealing with these issues in their marriages, and I understand the stresses and frustrations. It becomes evident that where traditional marriage through the centuries had been a partnership based on mutual dependency, modern marriage demands greater self-sufficiency.

While today's young women know from the start they'll face thorny decisions regarding careers, marriage and children, those of us who married in the 50's anticipated lives similar to our mothers' and grandmothers'. Then we watched with bewilderment as all the rules changed, and the goal posts were moved.

If I had it to do over again, I'd still marry the man I married and have my children: they are my treasure and a powerful support system for me and for one another. But I would have used the years after my youngest started school to further my education. I could have amassed two doctorates using the time and energy I gave to charitable and community causes and been better able to support myself.

25 But in a lucky twist, my community involvement had resulted in my being appointed to fill a vacancy on our Village Board. I had been serving as titular deputy mayor of my hometown (Nyack, N.Y.) when my husband left me. Several weeks later the mayor chose not to run again because of failing health, and I was elected to succeed him, becoming the first female mayor.

I held office for six years, a challenging, full-time job that paid a whopping annual salary of $8,000. But it consumed me and gave me someplace to go every day and most nights, and as such it saved my sanity. Now, mostly retired except for some part-time work, I am kept on my toes by 12 amazing grandchildren.

My anachronistic book was written while I was in a successful marriage that I expected would go on forever. Sadly, it now has little relevance for modern women, except perhaps as a cautionary tale: never its intended purpose. So I couldn't imagine writing a sequel. But my friend Elaine did come up with a perfect title: "Disregard First Book."

The Collapse of Big Media: The Young and the Restless

David T. Z. Mindich

When news executives look at the decline over the past few decades in the number of people who read or watch the news, they're scared silly. But then they reassure themselves that the kids will come around. Conventional wisdom runs that as young men and women gain the trappings of adulthood—a job, a spouse, children, and a house—they tend to pick up the news habit, too. As CBS News president Andrew Heyward declared in 2002, "Time is on our side in that as you get older, you tend to get more interested in the world around you." Unfortunately for Heyward and other news executives, the evidence suggests that young people are not picking up the news habit—not in their teens, not in their twenties, not even in their thirties.

When they aren't reassuring themselves, editors and publishers are lying awake at night thinking about the dismaying trends of recent decades. In 1972, nearly half of 18-to-22-year-olds read a newspaper every day, according to research conducted by Wolfram Peiser, a scholar who studies newspaper readership. Today, less than a quarter do. That younger people are less likely to read than their elders is of grave concern, but perhaps not surprising. In fact, the baby boomers who came of age in the 1970s are less avid news consumers than their parents were. More ominous for the future of the news media, however, is Peiser's research showing that a particular age cohort's reading habits do not change much with time; in other words, as people age, they continue the news habits of their younger days. Thus, the real danger, Peiser says, is that cohort replacement builds in a general decline in newspaper reading. The deleterious effects of this phenomenon are clearly evident: In 1972, nearly three-quarters of the 34-to-37 age group read a paper daily. Those thirtysomethings have been replaced by successive crops of thirtysomethings, each reading less than its predecessor. Today, only about a third of this group reads a newspaper every day. This means that fewer parents are bringing home a newspaper or discussing current events over dinner. And fewer kids are growing up in households in which newspapers matter.

A similar decline is evident in television news viewership. In the past decade, the median age of network television news viewers has crept up from about 50 to about 60. Tune in to any network news show or CNN, and note the products hawked in the commercials: The pitches for Viagra, Metamucil, Depends, and Fixodent are not aimed at teenyboppers.

...continued The Collapse of Big Media, **David T. Z. Mindich**

Compounding the problem of a graying news audience is the proliferation of televisions within the typical household, which diminishes adult influence over what's watched. In 1970, six percent of all sixth graders had TVs in their bedrooms; today that number is an astonishing 77 percent. If you are in sixth grade and sitting alone in your room, you're probably not watching Peter Jennings.

One of the clearest signs of the sea change in news viewing habits was the uproar following the appearance last fall by Jon Stewart, host of *The Daily Show,* a parody of a news program, on CNN's *Crossfire,* a real one. With a median age of 34, *The Daily Show's* audience is the envy of CNN, so when Stewart told *Crossfire's* hosts that their show's predictable left/right approach to debates of current issues was "hurting America," one could have guessed that CNN bigwigs would pay attention. But who could have foreseen that CNN president Jonathan Klein would cancel *Crossfire?* "I agree wholeheartedly with Jon Stewart's overall premise," he told the *New York Times.* News executives are so desperate to get to consumers before the AARP does that they're willing to heed the advice of a comedian.

If the young (and not so young) are not reading newspapers or watching network television news, many assume that they are getting news online. Not so. Only 18 percent of Americans listed the Internet as a "primary news source" in a survey released earlier this year by the Pew Internet and American Life Project and the Pew Research Center for the People and the Press. And the theory that younger people are more reliant on the Internet for news than their elders doesn't hold up. Certainly an engaged minority of young people use the Net to get a lot of news, but studies show that most use it primarily for e-mailing, instant messaging, games, and other diversions. You only need to wander into a computer lab at your local college or high school and see what the students have on their screens for the dismal confirmation of these choices.

If the youth audience is tuned out of newspaper, television, and Internet news, what, exactly, is it tuning in to? To answer this question, I traveled the country in 2002 speaking with groups of young people about their news habits. My research confirmed what many people already suspect: that most young people tune in to situation comedies and "reality" TV to the exclusion of news. I was surprised, though, by the scope of the trend: Most of the young people I interviewed had almost no measurable interest in political news. At Brandeis University in Massachusetts, one student explained that watching the situation comedy *Friends* creates a "sense of emotional investment" and "instant gratification." This engagement contrasts with the "detachment" young people feel from public issues such as campaign finance reform and news sources such as CNN and Peter Jennings. And when the news and its purveyors are seen simply as alternative forms of entertainment, they can't compete with the likes of *CSI, Las Vegas, American Idol,* and *Fear Factor.*

The entertainment options competing with the news for the attention of the youth audience have multiplied exponentially. In the 1960s, there were only a handful of television stations in any given market. When Walter Cronkite shook the nation by declaring in a February 1968 report on the Vietnam War that the United States was "mired in stalemate," he spoke to a captive audience. New York City, for example, had only seven broadcast stations. At 10:30 p.m. on the night of Cronkite's remarks, channels 4 and 11 ran movies, channels 5 and 9 had discussion shows, and channel 7 was showing *N. Y. P. D.,* a cop show. In this media universe of limited competition, nearly 80 percent of all television viewers watched the nightly news, and from the late 1960s on, Cronkite won the lion's share of the total news audience. Today, young people can choose from hundreds of stations, less than a tenth of which are devoted to news. And that's not to mention the many competing diversions that weren't available in 1968, from video games to iPods. Amid this entertainment cornucopia, the combined network news viewership has shrunk significantly—from some 50 million nightly in the 1960s to about 25 million today. (In comparison, CNN's audience is minuscule, typically no more than a million or so viewers, while public television's *NewsHour with Jim Lehrer* generally reaches fewer than three million viewers.)

The effects of this diet are evident in how little Americans know about current events. True, Americans have been extremely uninformed for a long time. Most follow public affairs only in a vague way, and many don't bother to engage at all. In the 1950s and 1960s, at the height of the Cold War, a poll revealed that only 55 percent of Americans knew that East Germany was a communist country, and less than half knew that the Soviet Union was not part of NATO, report political scientists Michael X. Delli Carpini and Scott Keeter in *What Americans Know about Politics and Why It Matters* (1996). In short, there was never a golden age of informed citizenry. But in recent decades, Americans' ignorance has reached truly stupefying levels, particularly among young adults. A series of reports published over the past two decades by the Pew Research Center for the People and the Press (and its predecessor, the Times Mirror Center) suggest that young adults were once nearly as informed as their elders on a range of political issues. From 1944 to 1968, the interest of younger people in the news as reported in opinion surveys was less than five percent below that of the population at large. Political debates and elections in the 1940s, the Army-McCarthy hearings of the 1950s, and the Vietnam War in the 1960s generated as much interest among the young

...continued The Collapse of Big Media, **David T. Z. Mindich**

as among older people. But Watergate in the 1970s was the last in this series of defining events to draw general public attention. (Decades later, in 2001, the bombing of the World Trade Center towers revived general public engagement, at least for a few weeks.) Soon after Watergate, surveys began to show flagging interest in current affairs among younger people.

There is no single explanation for this sudden break. Many of the young people I spoke with in doing my research were disaffected with the political process and believed that it was completely insulated from public pressure. Why, in that case, keep up with public affairs? The blurring line between entertainment and journalism, along with corporate consolidation of big media companies, has also bred in some minds a deep skepticism about the news media's offerings. At bottom, however, the sense of community has declined as Americans are able to live increasingly isolated lives, spending long hours commuting to work and holing up in suburban homes cocooned from the rest of the world.

The extent of this withdrawal from civic involvement is evident in a poll conducted during the height of the 2004 Democratic presidential primaries. In response to the question, "Do you happen to know which of the presidential candidates served as an army general?" about 42 percent of the over-50 crowd could name Wesley Clark. Only 13 percent of those under 30 could. While these results reveal a general lack of political knowledge across ages, they also underscore the growing gap between ages.

The shrinking audience for news is undermining the health of many major news media outlets. The most recent symptom was the revelation last year that a number of major newspapers, notably the *Chicago Sun-Times* and New York's *Newsday,* had cooked their books, inflating circulation figures in order to mask declines and keep advertising revenues from falling. More insidious—and less widely decried—is the industry-wide practice of bolstering profits by reducing news content. In newspapers, this is done by cutting back on the number of reporters covering state government, Washington, and foreign affairs, and by shrinking the space in the paper devoted to news. The news media are, in a very real sense, making our world smaller. On the broadcast networks, this shrinkage is easily measurable: In 1981, a 30-minute nightly newscast on CBS, minus commercials, was 23 minutes and 20 seconds, according to Leonard Downie, Jr., and Robert G. Kaiser's *The News about the News: American Journalism in Peril* (2002). In 2000, the same newscast was down to 18 minutes and 20 seconds. That's a lot of missing news.

The failing health of the nation's news media is not only a symptom of Americans' low levels of engagement in political life. It is a threat to political life itself. "The role of the press," writes news media critic James W. Carey, "is simply to make sure that in the short run we don't get screwed." Independent, fair, and accurate reporting is what gives "We the People" our check on power. Reporters dig up corruption and confront power; they focus the public's attention on government policies and actions that are unwise, unjust, or simply ineffective. It was the news media that exposed the Watergate burglary and cover-up engineered by Richard Nixon, sparked the investigation of the Iran-contra affair during the watch of Ronald Reagan and George H. W. Bush, ferreted out Bill Clinton's Whitewater dealings, and turned a searchlight on George W. Bush's extrajudicial arrests of American citizens suspected of terrorism.

A shrinking audience impairs the news media's ability to carry out their watchdog role. It also permits the powers that be to undermine journalism's legitimate functions. Where was the public outrage when it was revealed that the current Bush administration had secretly paid journalists to carry its water, or when the White House denied a press pass to a real journalist, Maureen Dowd of the *New York Times*, and gave one to a political hack who wrote for purely partisan outlets using a false identity? The whole notion of the news media as the public's watchdog, once an unquestioned article of the American civic faith, is now in jeopardy. A recent study commissioned by the John S. and James L. Knight Foundation showed that more than a third of high school students feel that newspaper articles should be vetted by the federal government before publication.

If we are entering a post-journalism age—in which the majority of Americans, young and old, have little interaction with mainstream news media—the most valuable thing we are losing is the marketplace of ideas that newspapers and news broadcasts uniquely provide, that place where views clash and the full range of democratic choices is debated. You usually don't get that on a blog. You don't get that in the left-leaning *Nation* or on right-wing talk shows. But any newspaper worth its salt, and there are plenty, presents a variety of views, including ones antithetical to its editorial page positions. These papers are hardly immune from criticism—they sometimes err, get sloppy, or succumb to partisan or ideological bias—but they do strive to be accurate and independent sources of fact and opinion, and more often than not they fulfill that indispensable public function.

America's newspapers and television news divisions aren't going to save themselves by competing with reality shows and soap operas. The appetite for news, and for engagement with civic life itself, must be nurtured and promoted, and it's very much in the public interest to undertake the task. It's not the impossible assignment it may seem. During the course of my research, I met a group of boys in New Orleans who were very unlikely consumers of news: They were saturated with television programs and video games, they were poor, and they were in eighth grade. Yet they were all reading the *New York Times* online. Why? Because one of their teachers had assigned the newspaper to them to read when they were in sixth grade, and the habit stuck. There's no reason why print and broadcast news shouldn't be a bigger part of the school curriculum, or why there shouldn't be a short civics/current affairs section on the SAT for college-bound students, or why all high school seniors shouldn't have to take a nonbinding version of the civics test given to immigrants who want to become U.S. citizens. And why shouldn't broadcasters be required to produce a certain amount of children's news programming in return for their access to the public airwaves? These are only the most obvious possibilities.

Reporters, editors, producers, and media business executives will all need to make their own adjustments to meet the demands of new times and new audiences, but only by reaching a collective judgment about the value and necessity of vigorous news media in American democracy can we hope to keep our public watchdogs on guard and in good health.

Pesticides, Parasite May Cause Frog Deformities

Stentor Danielson

Over the past ten to fifteen years, more and more frogs have been discovered with deformed, missing, or extra hind legs. Concerned about these abnormalities, scientists worldwide have been searching for the cause. In this National Geographic *article from July 2002, science journalist Stentor Danielson looks at a careful study of the interplay between two potential causes: a waterborne parasite and common pesticides.*

Danielson begins by briefly laying out the problem and by explaining how his article will add to previous discussions: new research indicates that two potential causes need to be considered together in order to get a clear picture of what is happening.

Frogs with extra legs or missing legs have been showing up with greater frequency over the past decade, and scientists have been baffled by the cause.

Some researchers have concluded that pesticide runoff from farms is to blame; others say a common parasite is the culprit. Now, a new study suggests that both these factors in combination have disturbed normal development in many frogs, leading to the abnormalities.

The study, published today in the *Proceedings of the National Academy of Sciences*, was based on tests in both the laboratory and the field that were designed to examine the interaction of parasites and pesticides. The research team, led by Joseph Kiesecker, found that only frogs infected by the larvae of a parasite, the trematode worm, developed deformities, but infected frogs exposed to pesticide runoff experienced much higher levels of deformities.

"It is not uncommon now for 20 to 30 percent of the frogs at many locations to have limb deformities," said Kiesecker, an assistant professor of biology at Penn State University.

Abnormalities have been documented in 52 species of amphibians, mainly frogs, in 46 U.S. states and four Canadian provinces, according to the U.S. Geological Survey. Reports of deformed frogs have been particularly common in New England and the Upper Midwest and on the Pacific coast.

Statistics provide a sense of the scope of the phenomenon. Notice the use of a government source for this information—sources which are usually credible and respected by readers.

Although there is some disagreement about what levels of deformities occur naturally in frog populations, most researchers agree that current levels are above normal.

Kiesecker and other researchers have warned that the physiological problems seen in frogs may foreshadow similar effects on humans.

At the end of this introductory section, Danielson places an important point about the issue: it could directly affect humans.

INFECTED BY TREMATODES

During its life cycle, the parasitic trematode depends on several hosts, including pond snails. Tadpoles in ponds with snails pick up trematode larvae, called cercariae. In some cases the cercariae develop into hard cysts, which interfere with the tadpole's metamorphosis into a frog. When the cysts occur in tissue that later develops into legs, the cysts disrupt the animal's normal development and cause duplicate or missing legs.

Details about one of the causes are explained step-by-step.

The trematode also affects people—although not so dramatically as in developing frogs. It's the same parasite that causes "swimmer's itch," a common ailment in people who swim in ponds and lakes. Eventually, the human immune system defeats the cercariae, leaving the victim with just a rash.

PESTICIDES, PARASITE MAY CAUSE FROG DEFORMITIES

In tropical climates trematodes cause schistosomiasis, a disease that kills millions of people. The World Health Organization estimates that 120 million people worldwide suffer from schistosomiasis.

Kiesecker's team took tadpoles from Centre County, Pennsylvania, and placed them in six local ponds—three affected by pesticide runoff and three pesticide-free. In each pond, the tadpoles were separated into two groups. One group was placed inside a fine mesh that kept out cercariae.

Only the tadpoles that were exposed to cercariae developed deformities. "We learned from the first field experiment that tadpoles have to be exposed to trematode infection for limb deformities to develop," Kiesecker said.

Danielson explains how an experiment was designed to isolate possible causes of the limb mutations.

PESTICIDE PROBLEMS

Kiesecker's team then compared the rate of infection between trematode-exposed tadpoles in the different ponds. The team discovered that rates of infection were much higher in the ponds that received pesticide runoff.

...*continued* Pesticides, Parasite May Cause Frog Deformities, **Stentor Danielson**

This result parallels the finding of a study in 2000 in which frogs from the same pond—that is, those experiencing the same environmental conditions—were found to have similar deformities.

Scientists repeated the pond test under controlled laboratory conditions and got similar results, with more detailed findings. In scientific causal analysis, repeatability of results strengthens the case for causality.

To examine the effects of pesticides on cercariae development, the team conducted lab experiments on four groups of tadpoles—three groups exposed to three common pesticides and a control group. The pesticides were Atrazine, the most commonly used pesticide in North America; Malathion, a common household pesticide that also is used to control insect pests in agricultural fields; and Esfenvalerate, a synthetic pyrethroid pesticide. The tadpoles were all exposed to cercariae.

When they counted the number of cysts that formed in the tadpoles, the researchers found much higher levels in the tadpoles exposed to pesticides. The team also took blood samples before and after the experiments to determine whether the tadpoles' white blood cell count—a measure of immune system health—was affected.

"The tadpoles that we exposed to pesticides had fewer of this particular kind of white blood cell compared to the tadpoles that we did not expose to pesticides, suggesting that pesticides make these animals more susceptible to parasitic infections," Kiesecker said.

Pesticides have been found to have additional harmful effects on frogs. A study published in April in the *Proceedings of the National Academy of Sciences* found that Atrazine interfered with the sexual development of male frogs in the Midwest, reducing their levels of testosterone to below the levels found in female frogs.

"Atrazine-exposed frogs don't have normal reproductive systems," said Tyrone Hayes, the leader of a team from the University of California at Berkeley. "The males have ovaries in their testes and much smaller vocal organs."

HUMAN IMPACTS?

Kiesecker said society can learn a lot from the experiments because "amphibians are particularly sensitive to environmental changes that appear to be associated with the recent emergence of new diseases and resurgence of old diseases that infect humans."

Especially disturbing, he added, is that the concentrations of two of the pesticides that caused the deformities in frogs, Esfenvalerate and Atrazine, were low enough for the water to be considered safe for human consumption under Environmental Protection Agency standards.

Danielson closes by reminding readers of the possibility that the cause-and-effect relationship at work in frogs might have parallels for humans.

"Frogs may be a sentinel species that is warning us about the interplay between human-caused environmental change and disease susceptibility," he said, adding: "Hopefully, people will listen."

In other recent research on this problem, a study published in the July 1 issue of *Environmental Science & Technology* indicates that frog deformities may also occur as a result of exposure to ultraviolet (UV) radiation. At levels close to 60 percent of normal sunlight, frogs experienced deformities.

A survey of ponds in the Duluth, Minnesota, area showed that frogs in only three of 26 ponds were at risk of UV-induced deformities, because wetlands absorb a significant portion of the radiation. However, Steve Diamond of the Environmental Protection Agency's Duluth office and leader of the UV study said there may be cause for concern if human activities cause UV levels to rise.

Why Should I Be Nice to You? Coffee Shops and the Politics of Good Service
(Essay)

Emily Raine

Emily Raine recently received a Masters degree in Communication Studies at McGill University in Montreal. She also writes about graffiti and street art. This essay appeared in the online journal Bad Subjects *in 2005.*

> "There is no more precious commodity than the relationship of trust and confidence a company has with its employees."
>
> Starbucks Coffee Company Chairman Howard Schultz

I actually like to serve. I'm not sure if this comes from some innate inclination to mother and fuss over strangers, or if it's because the movement and sociability of service work provides a much-needed antidote to the solitude of academic research, but I've always found something about service industry work satisfying. I've done the gamut of service jobs, from fine dining to cocktail waitressing to hip euro-bistro counter work, and the only job where I've ever felt truly whipped was working as a barista at one of the now-ubiquitous specialty coffee chains, those bastions of jazz and public solitude that have spread through urban landscapes over the last ten years or so. The pay was poor, the shifts long and oddly dispersed, the work boring and monotonous, the managers demanding, and the customers regularly displayed that unique spleen that emerges in even the most pleasant people before they've had the morning's first coffee. I often felt like an aproned Coke machine, such was the effect my sparkling personality had on the clientele. And yet, some combination of service professionalism, fear of termination and an imperative to be "nice" allowed me to suck it up, smile and continue to provide that intangible trait that the industry holds above all else, good service.

Good service in coffee shops doesn't amount to much. Unlike table service, where interaction with customers spans a minimum of half an hour, the average contact with a café customer lasts less than ten seconds. Consider how specialty cafés are laid out: the customer service counter is arranged in a long line that clients move along to "use" the café. The linear coffee bar resembles an assembly line, and indeed, café labor is heavily grounded in the rationalism of Fordist manufacturing principles, which had already been tested for use in hospitality services by fast food chains. Each of the café workers is assigned a specific stage in the service process to perform exclusively, such as taking orders, using the cash registers, or handing clients cups of brewed coffee.

The specialization of tasks increases the speed of transactions and limits the duration of any one employee's interaction with the clientele. This means that in a given visit a customer might order from one worker, receive food from the next, then brewed coffee or tea from yet another, then pay a cashier before proceeding down the line of the counter, finishing the trip at the espresso machine which is always situated at its end. Ultimately, each of the café's products is processed and served by a different employee, who repeats the same preparation task for hours and attends to each customer only as they receive that one product.

Needless to say, the productive work in cafés is dreary and repetitive. Further, this style of service severely curtails interaction with the clientele, and the very brevity of each transaction precludes much chance for authentic friendliness or conversation—even asking about someone's day would slow the entire operation. The one aspect of service work that can be unpredictable—people—becomes redundant, and interaction with customers is reduced to a fatiguing eight-hour-long smile and the repetition of sentiments that allude to good service, such as injunctions to enjoy their purchases or to have a nice day. Rather than friendly exchanges with customers, barista workers' good service is reduced to a quick rictus in the customer's direction between a great deal of friendly interaction with the espresso machine.

As the hospitality industry really took off in the sixties, good service became one of the trademarks of its advertising claims, a way for brands to distinguish themselves from the rest of the pack. One needn't think too hard to come up with a litany of service slogans that holler the good graces of their personnel—at Starbucks where the baristas make the magic, at PSA where smiles aren't just painted on, or at McDonald's where smiles are free. Employee friendliness emerged as one of the chief distinguishing brand features of personal services, which means that the workers themselves become an aspect of the product for sale.

Our notions of good service revolve around a series of platitudes about professionalism—we're at your service, with a smile, where the customer's always right—each bragging the centrality of the customer to everything "we" do. Such claims imply an easy and equal exchange between two parties: the "we" that gladly serves and the "you" that happily receives. There is, however, always a third party involved in the service exchange, and that's whoever has hired the server, the body that ultimately decides just what the dimensions of good service will be.

Like most employees, a service worker sells labor to an employer at a set rate, often minimum wage, and the employer sells the product of that labor, the service itself, at market values. In many hospitality services, where gratuities make up the majority of employment revenue, the worker directly benefits from giving good service, which of course translates to good tips. But for the vast majority of service staff, and particularly those employed in venues yielding little or no gratuities—fast food outlets, café chains, cleaning and maintenance operations—this promises many workers little more than a unilateral imperative to be perpetually bright and amenable.

The vast majority of service personnel do not spontaneously produce an unaffected display of cheer and good will continuously for the duration of a shift. When a company markets its products on servers' friendliness, they must then monitor and control employees' friendliness, so good service is defined and enforced from above. Particularly in chains, which are premised upon their consistent reproduction of the same experience in numerous locations, organizations are obliged to impose systems to manage employees' interaction with their customers. In some chains, namely the fast food giants such as McDonald's and Burger King, employee banter is scripted into cash registers, so that as soon as a customer orders, workers are cued to offer, "would you like a dessert with that?" (an offer of dubious benefit to the customer) and to wish them a nice day. Ultimately, this has allowed corporations to be able to assimilate "good service"—or, friendly workers—into their overall brand image.

While cafés genuflect toward the notion of good service, their layouts and management styles preclude much possibility of creating the warmth that this would entail. Good service is, of course, important, but not if it interferes with throughput. What's more, these cafés have been at the forefront of a new wave of organizations that not only market themselves on service quality but also describe employees' job satisfaction as the seed from which this flowers.

Perhaps the most glaring example of this is Starbucks, where cheerful young workers are displayed behind elevated counters as they banter back and forth, calling out fancy Italian drink names and creating theatre out of their productive labor. Starbucks' corporate literature gushes not only about the good service its customers will receive, but about the great joy that its "partners" take in providing it, given the company's unique ability to "provide a great work environment and treat each other with respect and dignity," and where its partners are "emotionally and intellectually committed to Starbucks success." In the epigraph to this essay, Starbucks' chairman even describes the company's relationship with its workers as a commodity. Not only does Starbucks offer good service, but it attempts to guarantee something even better: good service provided by employees that are genuinely happy to give it.

Starbucks has branded a new kind of worker, the happy, wholesome, perfume-free barista. The company offers unusual benefits for service workers, including stock options, health insurance, dental plans and other perks such as product discounts and giveaways. Further, they do so very, very publicly, and the company's promotional materials are filled with moving accounts of workers who never dreamed that corporate America could care so much. With the other hand, though, the company has smashed unionization drives in New York, Vancouver and at its Seattle roaster; it schedules workers at oddly timed shifts that never quite add up to full-time hours; the company pays only nominally more than minimum wage, and their staffs are still unable to subsist schlepping lattes alone.

Starbucks is not alone in marketing itself as an enlightened employer. When General Motors introduced its Saturn line, the new brand was promoted almost entirely on the company's good relations with its staff. The company's advertising spots often featured pictures of and quotes from the union contract, describing their unique partnership between manufacturer, workers and union, which allowed blue-collar personnel to have a say in everything from automobile designs to what would be served for lunch. The company rightly guessed that this strategy would go over well with liberal consumers concerned about the ethics of their purchases. Better yet, Saturn could market its cars based on workers' happiness whether personnel were satisfied or not, because very few consumers would ever have the chance to interact with them.

At the specialty coffee chains, however, consumers have to talk to employees, yet nobody ever really asks. The café service counter runs like a smooth piece of machinery, and I found that most people preferred to pretend that they were interacting with an appliance. In such short transactions, it is exceedingly difficult for customers to remember the humanity of each of the four to seven people they might interact with to get their coffees. Even fast food counters have one server who processes each customer's order, yet in cafés the workers just become another gadget in the well-oiled café machine. This is a definite downside for the employees—clients are much ruder to café staff than in any other sector of the industry I ever worked in. I found that people were more likely to be annoyed than touched by any reference to my having a personality, and it took no small amount of thought on my part to realize why.

Barista workers are hired to represent an abstract category of worker, not to act as individuals. Because of the service system marked by short customer interaction periods and a homogenous staff, the services rendered are linked in the consumer imagination to the company and not to any one individual worker. Workers' assimilation into the company image makes employees in chain service as branded as the products they serve. The chain gang, the workers who hold these eminently collegiate after-school jobs, are proscribed sales scripts and drilled on customer service scenarios to standardize interactions with customers. The company issues protocols for hair length, color and maintenance, visible piercings and tattoos as well as personal hygiene and acceptable odorific products. Workers are made more interchangeable by the use of uniforms, which, of course, serve to make the staff just that. The organization is a constant intermediary in every transaction, interjecting its presence in every detail of the service experience, and this standardization amounts to an absorption of individuals' personalities into the corporate image.

Many of the measures that chains take to secure the homogeneity of their employees do not strike us as particularly alarming, likely because similar restrictions have been in place for several hundred years. Good service today has inherited many of the trappings of the good servant of yore, including prohibitions against eating, drinking, sitting or relaxing in front the served, entering and exiting through back doors and wearing uniforms to visually mark workers' status. These measures almost completely efface the social identities of staff during work hours, providing few clues to workers' status in their free time. Contact between service workers and their customers is thus limited to purely functional relations, so that the public only see them as workers, as makers of quality coffee, and never as possible peers.

Maintaining such divisions is integral to good service because this display of class distinctions ultimately underlies our notions of service quality. Good service means not only serving well, but also allowing customers to feel justified in issuing orders, to feel okay about being served—which, in turn, requires demonstrations of class difference and the smiles that suggest servers' comfort with having a subordinate role in the service exchange.

Unlike the penguin-suited household servant staffs whose class status was clearly defined, service industry workers today often have much more in common from a class perspective with those that they serve. This not only creates an imperative for them to wear their class otherness on their sleeves, as it were, but also to accept their subordinate role to those they serve by being unshakably tractable and polite.

Faith Popcorn has rather famously referred to the four-dollar latte as a "small indulgence," noting that while this is a lot to pay for a glass of hot milk, it is quite inexpensive for the feeling of luxury that can accompany it. In this service climate, the class status of the server and the served—anyone who can justify spending this much on a coffee—is blurry, indeed. Coffee shops that market themselves on employee satisfaction assert the same happy servant that allows politically conscientious consumers who are in many cases the workers' own age and class peers, to feel justified in receiving good service. Good service—as both an apparent affirmation of subordinate classes' desire to serve and as an enforced one-sided politeness—reproduces the class distinctions that have historically characterized servant-served relationships so that these are perpetuated within the contemporary service market.

The specialty coffee companies are large corporations, and for the twenty-somethings who stock their counters, barista work is too temporary to bother fighting the system. Mostly, people simply quit. Dissatisfied workers are stuck with engaging in tactics that will change nothing but allow them to make the best of their lot. These include minor infractions such as taking liberties with the uniforms or grabbing little bits of company time for their own pleasure, what Michel de Certeau calls *la perruque* and the companies themselves call "time theft." As my time in the chain gang wore on, I developed my own tactic, the only one I found that jostled the customers out of their complacency and allowed me to be a barista and a person.

There is no easy way to serve without being a servant, and I have always found that the best way to do so is to show my actual emotions rather than affecting a smooth display of interminable patience and good will. For café customers, bettering baristas' lots can be as simple as asking about their day, addressing them by name—any little gesture to show that you noticed the person behind the service that they can provide. My tactic as a worker is equally simple, but it is simultaneously an assertion of individual identity at work, a refusal of the class distinctions that characterize the service environment and a rebuttal to the companies that would promote my satisfaction with their system: be rude. Not arbitrarily rude, of course—customers are people, too, and nobody gains anything by spreading bad will. But on those occasions when customer or management behavior warranted a zinging comeback, I would give it.

Rudeness, when it is demanded, undermines companies' claims on workers' personal warmth and allows them to retain their individuality by expressing genuine rather than affected feelings in at-work interpersonal exchanges. It is a refusal of the class distinctions that underlie consumers' unilateral prerogative of rudeness and servers' unilateral imperative to be nice. It runs contrary to everything that we have been taught, not only about service but about interrelating with others. But this seems to be the only method of asserting one's person-hood in the service environment, where workers' personalities are all too easily reduced to a space-time, conflated with the drinks they serve. Baristas of the world, if you want to avoid becoming a green-aproned coffee dispensary, you're just going to have to tell people off about it.

STUDENT MODELS

Deinstitutionalization: The Past Idea

with the Present Misfortunes

Kimberley De Santis

Professor Kennedy

Composition 101—April 24, 2005

Deinstitutionalization: The Past Idea

with the Present Misfortunes

1   They embellish the streets night and day, harmless to society, their pain

self-evident. Confused by their environment, they walk without any destination.

They are the mentally ill homeless, and they reside on the streets of our cities.

Why are these sick people on the streets instead of in hospitals? Are there too

many occupants in psychiatric wards and not enough vacancies? Are there any

vacancies at all? There is much debate about why the homeless mentally ill are

in such large numbers on the streets. Many citizens blame the government for

the ingenious proposal of deinstitutionalization: the release of mentally ill

patients into the community. Beginning in the 1960s, mentally ill people were

dismissed from the institutional life and initiated into a lifestyle that they had

previously been denied. "Between 1955 and 1996, state mental hospital

populations fell from over 550,000 to 59,000" (Zaheer, 2001, p. 392). If

deinstitutionalization had been a complete success, the mentally ill would be

living in community apartments or houses and not sleeping on park benches.

2   In the past, hospitals housed both borderline and severely mentally ill

persons. The inhabitants had conditions such as schizophrenia, manic depressive

disorder, autism, panic disorder, and obsessive-compulsive disorder (Torrey,

1997). Out of those formally committed, 50% to 60% were schizophrenic, 10% to

15% were manic depressive, another 10% to 15% had organic brain diseases such

as epilepsy or Alzheimer's, and the remaining few had mental retardation. The

mentally ill led a life surrounded by other sick persons. Their diseases were not

uncommon, but they were placed in the psychiatric hospitals to avoid disruptions

that they might cause to mainstream society.

3   Although there was some concern about disengaging mentally ill patients

from institutions, the idea became intriguing. Throughout the 1960s, many people

felt that the institutionalization of mentally ill patients was morally wrong (Torrey,

1997). The government's idea of deinstitutionalization was welcomed. It allowed the mentally ill patients to be free of state hospitals and receive care in community-based living centers. President Jimmy Carter and his Commission of Mental Health defined deinstitutionalization as "the objective of maintaining the greatest degree of freedom, self-determination, autonomy, dignity and integrity of mind, and spirit for the individual while he or she participates in treatment or receives services" (Torrey, 1997, p. 11). Prior to 1964, mentally ill patients were placed in state hospitals on the assumption that they were in need of psychiatric treatment. Their mental well-being was determined by psychiatrists or psychologists, and sometimes the treatment was completely involuntary to individuals. Deinstitutionalization allowed those patients who were capable of an independent lifestyle to pursue residence within the community.

4   Nineteen sixty-four was a fruitful year for the mentally ill population. That year the federal Civil Rights Law was passed, stating that only patients who were a danger to themselves or others could be committed to institutions (Torrey, 1997). The placement of the individuals into the community ensured freedom that had been previously limited. Communal living allowed the mentally ill to have a sense of belonging and a feeling of acceptance in the public realm. For the first time, they could function as if they were part of the traditional society.

5   At the time, deinstitutionalization was considerably less expensive than institutional living. Community-based clinics averaged about $50 a day, as opposed to psychiatric hospital costs of at least $200 a day (Jaroszewski, 1996). As former residents were socialized into the community, they needed to learn to adjust to diverse lifestyles. Lifestyle stability was provided by several outpatient programs. Daily activities were monitored, and staff assisted the patients as much as needed (Jaroszewski). Everyday activities such as shopping, cooking, hygiene, the search for employment, paying rent, and cashing checks had to be taught so that the mentally ill would be successful living in the community (Long, 1990). These reforms benefited the mentally ill by giving them a sense of

security within the society. Society at large had always ignored the state hospitals and the "crazy" patients who occupied them. Deinstitutionalization allowed the patients to become part of the prevalent population. Mental illness was no longer taboo, nor were its victims.

6   Thorazine, the first antipsychotic medicine, allowed many mentally ill people to function as if they had no disease at all. Thorazine and other antipsychotic drugs introduced later did not cure the ailments, but they helped control the symptoms (Torrey, 1997). As a result, government and health officials felt it was safe to discharge patients into the community. It had been said that medicines and other treatments would be accessible to the needy persons who had been deinstitutionalized. However, what was not taken into consideration was how the released patients would actually receive the medication, rehabilitation, and counseling. Few services were available to the mentally ill, and hence many persons went untreated. According to psychiatrist E. Fuller Torrey, "Deinstitutionalization helped create the mental illness crisis: discharging people from psychiatric hospitals without ensuring they receive medication and rehabilitation for survival in the community" (p. 8). Thousands of mentally ill people were without treatment and unable to function appropriately in society.

7   Many of the patients who were discharged received inadequate care. A 1985 study of 132 patients with schizophrenia, mood disorders, and personality disorders proved that to be true. Thirty-three people were placed with irresponsible families or discharged to public shelters and addresses that turned out to be abandoned buildings or vacant lots. Thirty-four were homeless after one month, forty-four were homeless after three months, and thirty-two remained homeless after six months. Most were able to cash Social Security checks or veterans' benefits, but many had no income and lived on handouts. Many homeless individuals used illegal drugs and alcohol, and some were arrested for bizarre, threatening, or offensive behavior, as well as shoplifting,

prostitution, and trespassing (Long, 1990). Inadequate government care can be blamed for the misfortunes that the mentally ill individuals experienced.

8   It is often thought that deinstitutionalization was brought about so that the state no longer had to care directly for the mentally ill. As documented by the U.S. Department of Health and Human Services (1992), programs such as Medicaid, the federal Supplemental Security Income program (SSI), and the Supplemental Security Disability Insurance program (SSDI) provide direct entitlements to mentally ill disabled individuals who live in the community. Although these programs provide assistance, many mentally ill homeless live on the streets, and their numbers continue to rise. Therefore, one question to ask the government is, what can be done about this problem?

9   Changes have been made to make the governmental system more rational, systematic, and integrated, but "despite the efforts, the system remains a 'patchwork of settings,' providers, policies, administrative sponsors and founders" (U.S., 1992, p. 17). Services as such are dispersed through a variety of public and private agencies. These include mental hospitals, general hospitals, veterans' hospitals, community mental health centers, residential treatment centers, nursing homes, halfway houses, day treatment centers, board-and-care homes, outpatient clinics, office-based private practitioners (including psychologists, psychiatrists, and social workers), psychosocial rehabilitation programs, clubhouses, and self-help groups. Despite the number of care providers, there are still the problems of availability, accessibility, and appropriateness. Abolishing the needs of the mentally ill will be a difficult process. Aid, programs, and communal services provide some assistance, but a solution to remove the mentally ill from the streets is a long-term goal that has so far not been accomplished.

10   Deinstitutionalization marked a new beginning for the mentally ill. They were no longer involuntarily committed and hidden away in hospitals. People believed deinstitutionalization would benefit mentally ill patients by allowing them

to function as part of the mainstream. Unfortunately, deinstitutionalization has had

negative consequences. By 2001, "there [were] over 830,000 mentally ill people in

the criminal justice system either in jail, on probation, or on parole" (Zaheer, 2001,

p. 392). Another negative result is the homelessness. Thousands of mentally ill

persons struggle to live on their own on the streets of America. With the proposed

care overlooked, the homeless mentally ill now encounter problems that they are

incapable of solving. Lloyd M. Siegel stated in 1981, "Patients wander our streets,

lost in time, as if in a medieval city. We are protecting their civil liberties much

more adequately than we are protecting their minds and their lives" (Torrey,

1997, p. 142). The situation is even worse today. Shelters can accommodate only

a fortunate few, forcing many others to find shelter anywhere and by any

means. As Zaheer (2001) points out, "If the number of mentally ill people on the

streets and in jail is a measure of the success of deinstitutionalization, then no

one will disagree that it has been a complete failure" (p. 393).

11   We must learn from the experience of the last fifty years. We can no

longer push aside homeless mentally ill people just like the garbage and debris

they lie next to. More important, we have to rethink the problem and

acknowledge that it is bigger than homelessness. As Dr. John A. Talbott (2004)

explains:

> There must be a reconceptualization of the problem of the treatment and
>
> care of the severely and chronically mentally ill. Instead of considering the
>
> issue as one of where people should be housed, we must assess the needs
>
> of chronic patients and design or revise our services to meet those needs.
>
> And this means first and foremost that we must realize that we're not
>
> talking merely about psychotherapeutic needs but about medication,
>
> resistance to ongoing treatment, medical needs, housing, income,
>
> rehabilitation, social services, and what, for want of a better term, has
>
> become known as a community support system—that is, a system of supports

DEINSTITUTIONALIZATION　　　　　　　　　　　　　　　　　　　7

> that enables the chronically mentally ill person to receive the treatments and
>
> services he would receive if he were housed in a total institution. (p. 55)

If we do not take the measures Dr. Talbott (2004) recommends, the problems of

the mentally ill population will continue to worsen.

DEINSTITUTIONALIZATION　　　　　　　　　　　　　　　　　　　8

References

Jaroszewski, L. (1996). *Causes of homelessness: Mental health issues.* Spare

　　Change. Retrieved from http://www.way.net/wasnew96.html

Long, P. W. (1990, July/August). Mental illness and homelessness. *Harvard Mental Health Letter.* Retrieved from http://www.mentalhealth.com/

Talbott, J. A. (2004, October). Deinstitutionalization: Avoiding the disasters of

　　the past. Psychiatric Services, 55. Retrieved from http://www

　　.psychiatryonline.com

Torrey, E. F. (1997). *Out of the shadows: Confronting America's mental illness crisis.* New York: Wiley.

United States Dept. of Health and Human Services. National Institute of Mental

　　Health. (1992). Outcasts on main street: Report of the federal task force

　　on homelessness and severe mental illness. Washington: GPO.

Zaheer, D. A. (2001). Expanding California's coerced treatment for the mentally

　　ill: Is the promise of caring treatment in the community a lost hope?

　　Southern California Interdisciplinary Law Journal. Retrieved from

　　http://www.lexisnexis.com/hottopics/Inacademic/?

PRACTICE

1 In an analysis, an author first presents the analytical principle in full and then systematically applies parts of the principle to the object or phenomenon under study. In her brief analysis of television viewing, Marie Winn pursues an alternative, though equally effective, strategy by *distributing* parts of her analytical principle across the essay. Locate where Winn defines key elements of addiction. Locate where she uses each element as an analytical lens to examine television viewing as a form of addiction.

a. What function does paragraph 4 play in the analysis?

b. In the first two paragraphs, how does Winn create a funnel-like effect that draws readers into the heart of her analysis?

c. Recall a few television programs that genuinely moved you, educated you, humored you, or stirred you to worthwhile reflection or action. To what extent does Winn's analysis describe your positive experiences as a television viewer? (Consider how Winn might argue that from within an addicted state, a person may feel "humored, moved or educated" but is in fact—from a sober outsider's point of view—deluded.) If Winn's analysis of television viewing as an addiction does *not* account for your experience, does it follow that her analysis is flawed? Explain.

2 Make a log for one entire day on all the news you read, watch, or listen to: newspapers, radio, television news broadcasts, comedy reporting of news like *The Daily Show*, comic monologues commenting on events, news flashes at the bottom of other television programs, news on the Web, blogs, and personal news sources such as email. Make notes about what the news contained, and keep track of the time you spent reading, viewing, or listening. On the next day total the time for each category. Bring your analysis to class to compare with other students' totals. Do the results for the entire class surprise you in any way?

3 Mindich speaks of the decline in newspaper readership and television news viewing as a cultural crisis. Do you believe this trend is something to worry about? Why or why not?

Mindich's essay is an audience analysis in which he concludes that "Most of the young people I interviewed had almost no measurable interest in political news." First, from your experience do you agree with Mindich's claim? If you do agree, does having no measurable interest in political news mean that young people are not interested in news in general?

In the next-to-last paragraph, Mindich makes proposals that news should be a part of the school curriculum, high school seniors should take a civics test, and broadcasters should be required to produce a certain amount of children's news programming. Do you support these proposals? What suggestions do you have to raise the civic awareness of young people?

Tahquamenon Falls
Paradise, MI
Newberry, MI

How Do I Analyze Written Works?

THE REASON WE ANALYZE THINGS IS TO HELP US UNDERSTAND THEM BETTER. LET'S SAY YOU'RE WORKING HARD AT A PART-TIME JOB, BUT YOU DON'T SEEM TO BE SAVING MUCH MONEY. YOU INVESTIGATE THE CAUSES OF YOUR PROBLEM BY ITEMIZING YOUR weekly purchases. This systematic analysis of your spending habits reveals that a surprising portion of your paycheck is being spent on the take-out dinners you buy every night on your way home from work. Analysis serves many purposes. It enables you to identify and solve problems, examine how things work, and inquire into the complexities of various phenomena.

In college, you will be asked to write analyses of issues and texts. The procedure is the same. You break the subject up into elements, facets, or parts. For this process, you use the critical thinking and reading strategies presented throughout this book: examination of content; genre, organization, features; and rhetorical situation. In this chapter we explain how to analyze a text rhetorically, how to evaluate texts and images, and how to write an in-depth analysis and evaluation.

The focus of this chapter is:

- Rhetorical analysis
- Evaluation of written texts
- Analysis and evaluation of images
- In-depth analysis and evaluation

Analysis and Evaluation as Opposed to Response

Professors ask students to write analysis essays because they want to hear students' *own* interpretations of what they read. That's why it's important to come to your own conclusions rather than parrot the interpretations you hear in class lectures and discussions. Keep in mind that your professors expect you to base your interpretation on a systematic examination of the material, not on personal opinions or reactions. A reaction or response essay is different from an analysis essay. The response essay is based on your previous knowledge of and experiences with the topic. *Response essays focus on your reaction to content, whereas analysis essays focus on your estimation of how that content is conveyed.*

The *evaluation essay,* also called a *critique, critical essay,* or *review,* is similar to an analysis in that it requires you to do a systematic examination of the reading source. The primary difference is that the evaluation essay judges the strengths and weaknesses of the source according to established criteria. The analysis essay offers an interpretation; it does not assess the source's quality or worth.

Another difference between the two types of essays is that the evaluation essay has more of a persuasive edge than the analysis essay. For the evaluation, your aim is to get your reader to agree with you and in some cases, for instance, when you write a book review, to influence your reader to actually read the book.

The distinctions among essays of response, analysis, and evaluation are extremely important. Unless your assignment specifically calls for it, personal reaction is inappropriate in analyses and reviews.

Essay Type	Strategy	Goal
Response essay (subjective)	Obtain ideas from your personal knowledge and experience and apply them to the reading material.	Express informed opinions about the subject matter.
Analysis essay (objective)	Obtain ideas from your examination of the various elements of the reading source.	Interpret how the writer's techniques convey meaning.
Evaluation essay (objective)	Obtain ideas from your examination of the various elements of the reading source and judge them according to a set of established criteria.	Show the relative strengths and weaknesses of the work.

As illustrated, response essays are *subjective,* and essays of analysis and evaluation are *objective.* When you analyze and evaluate, you do not rely on personal reactions. You base your conclusions on a reasoned examination of standards that are acceptable to your readers. You already know many of these standards—you have been using them throughout this book. In this chapter, we discuss additional criteria that are commonly used in English and composition courses. You should keep in mind, however, that various academic fields have their own standards for analyzing and evaluating written work. When you take courses in the social sciences, you will see that the criteria in those fields differ somewhat from the criteria used in the humanities. Make a point to learn the criteria for quality writing in the various academic fields, and refer to them when you read and write in each area.

Rhetorical Analysis

Before we describe the process for composing a rhetorical analysis, we want you to take a look at an essay of this type. The essay was written in response to the following assignment:

> Write a systematic analysis of a reading selection of your choice. As you interpret the text, comment on the author's rhetorical strategies.

Steve Stout wrote his essay on "Skills and Pills," written by physician Kate Scannell when she was clinical director of AIDS services at a county hospital in San Francisco. Scannell explains that when she started working at the hospital, she treated her terminally ill patients the only way she knew how, with impersonal, aggressive medical service. She relates in detail her efforts to help Raphael, a young man who was near death. Each time Raphael asked Scannell for help, she responded with her "skills and pills." She was unaware that Raphael was not asking her to treat his disease but to put him out of his suffering. One night when Scannell was off duty, another physician granted Raphael his wish. After Raphael's death, Scannell was better able to communicate with her patients. She learned to practice medicine more compassionately, with her heart as well as her skills and pills.

THE ROLE OF IMAGERY IN "SKILLS AND PILLS"   2

The Role of Imagery in "Skills and Pills"   *Title (focus of essay)*

1   In her article "Skills and Pills," Kate Scannell (1988) describes the process   *Paper opener giving author, title, and topic*

she went through as a physician learning how to administer effectively to AIDS

patients. Throughout the article, she uses a series of images that serve to   *Initial identification of author by full name*

emphasize and illuminate the transformation she experienced, from a devotee of

medical technology to a compassionate caregiver who is aware of the limitations   *Thesis*

of medical science.

2   Scannell (1988), who was clinical director of services for AIDS patients at a   *Later identification of author by last name only*

county hospital in San Francisco, began working in the AIDS ward right after

THE ROLE OF IMAGERY IN "SKILLS AND PILLS"   3

Summary

Textual evidence supporting thesis

Use of present tense to explain how writer uses techniques

3

Summary paragraph

Summary paragraph

Block format for long quotation

medical school. Her initial response to AIDS was to give each patient full, aggressive treatment. Describing herself as an "ever-ready gunfighter," she says, "I stalked the hallways ready for surprise developments and acute medical problems to present themselves. [When they did,] I would shoot them down with my skills and pills" (p. 102). Scannell explains that she was listening to the voices of her old teachers in medical school, who had told her to use every intervention possible to keep her patients alive.

For months Scannell (1988) persisted in offering her brand of intensive, exhaustive medical service. Then one day she encountered Raphael. Raphael was a twenty-two-year-old AIDS patient, "a large, bloated, purple, knobby mass with eyes so swollen shut that he could not see" (p. 103). When Raphael asked Scannell to help him, she put her "diagnostic sharpshooting abilities" to work. Each time Raphael asked for more help, Scannell responded with more medical procedures. She said that when she left the hospital that evening, she knew that she had done everything conceivable to help her patient.

That night Raphael again asked for help. The attending physician responded very differently from Scannell (1988), however. Instead of giving Raphael skills and pills, he disconnected Raphael's intravenous and blood transfusions and gave him some morphine. "Raphael smiled and thanked the doctor for helping him, and then expired later that evening" (p. 104).

Raphael's death changed the way Scannell (1988) practiced medicine. She describes her transformation in terms of a clothing image:

> Like the vision of Raphael's spirit rising free from his disease-racked corpse in death, the clothing fashioned for me by years of traditional Western medical training fell off me like tattered rags. I began to hear my own voices and compassionate sensibilities once again, louder and clearer than the chorus of voices of my old mentors. (p. 104)

Scannell (1988) compares her self-discovery to an archaeological expedition. She says, "I got crushed under mounds of rubble that collected over the years of my

4

5

THE ROLE OF IMAGERY IN "SKILLS AND PILLS"   4

intense and all-consuming medical training" (p. 104). She describes this rubble

as consisting of increased medical technology, the dictum that physicians must

save lives at all costs, and the taboos against doctors using intuition or

compassion.

6   Transformed, Dr. Scannell (1988) no longer listened to the voices of her old

teachers, and she was no longer a sharpshooter. She listened instead to the

people behind the disease. She no longer offered these patients skills and pills;

instead, she gave them conversation and compassion.

*Paragraph with textual
evidence supporting
thesis*

Conclusion

THE ROLE OF IMAGERY IN "SKILLS AND PILLS"   6

Reference

Scannell, K. (1998). Skills and pills. In I. Rieder & P. Ruppett (Eds.), *AIDS: The

women* (pp. 103–105). San Francisco, CA: Clcis.

In this essay, Steve's aim is to show his readers how one of Scannell's rhetorical strategies, her use of imagery, operates in the article. His title indicates that he will focus on "the role of imagery," and his thesis reveals that he will explain how the imagery functions. The introductory paragraph reveals that he will show how Scannell's images serve to emphasize and illuminate the transformation she experienced. In paragraphs 2, 4, and 5, he describes how Scannell uses particular images, backing up his points with quotations from the article. The main purpose of paragraph 3 is to summarize relevant parts of the article. Note that Steve does not summarize the entire article. He gives only the background information readers need to comprehend the analysis.

Writing a Rhetorical Analysis Essay

Now that you have read a model analysis essay, you can practice writing one of your own. In the next section, we take you through the process Steve experienced as he wrote his analysis. The process we describe is applicable to any assignment that requires you to write a rhetorical analysis of nonfiction.

PREWRITING

Successful analysis requires careful planning. Assignments that direct you to analyze or evaluate a text are typically harder than assignments that ask you to react, compare and contrast, or argue because they require a more detailed examination of the reading source and a deeper knowledge of the author's writing techniques. Without sufficient planning, you may become lost or turn out an extended summary or reaction instead of an analysis. Without extensive preparation, it is almost impossible to write a satisfactory analytical piece.

● **CLARIFY THE ASSIGNMENT, SET YOUR RHETORICAL GOAL, AND CONSIDER YOUR AUDIENCE**   When you receive your assignment, pay attention to what it asks you to do. Some assignments, like the one our student Steve received, are open-ended and allow the writer to determine the aspects of the reading source that will be examined. Other assignments may stipulate the parts of the text on which you should focus. For example, a professor might ask you to discuss the role of language in a particular piece or to comment on the structure of a work and explain why it is organized as it is. If you have questions about the type of analysis the assignment calls for, be sure to ask your professor before you proceed.

After you have clarified the assignment, decide on your rhetorical purpose by asking yourself, Why am I writing this analysis essay? What desired effect do I hope to have on my audience? Your fundamental purpose is to give your readers your interpretation of the reading source and in so doing explain how one or more characteristics of the text contribute to its meaning. Looking back at Steve's essay, you can see that his objective is to demonstrate how various images in Scannell's "Skills and Pills" help the author convey that she has experienced a dramatic transformation.

The next decisions concern your audience. Ask yourself these questions:

- What will your readers already know about the source?
- How much of the source should you summarize, and what form will the summary take?
- Will you need to explain basic concepts and provide background for the material to make sense?
- What overall impact do you hope to have on your readers?

If your audience is familiar with the piece you are analyzing, supply only a minimal amount of background information. If your audience has not read the piece, as was the case with Steve, give some general background and summarize the parts of the source that are crucial to your analysis. It isn't necessary to summarize the entire text, only enough to persuade your readers that you have a valid, reasonable interpretation.

● **DO A FIRST READING TO GET A GENERAL IMPRESSION OF THE SOURCE** Your first reading may leave you with little more than a general impression of the reading source. You will get an overall sense of the subject, the author's approach, and the central point, but you probably won't pay much attention to other characteristics of the text unless they are very conspicuous. At this stage, you may want to freewrite your reactions, especially if the text evokes a strong response. A reader's first reaction to Scannell's "Skills and Pills" might have been, "Wow, that doctor certainly did an about-face!" The reader might also have been unsettled by Scannell's graphic description of Raphael's ravaged body.

● **REREAD AND ASK ANALYSIS QUESTIONS**   Analyzing a reading source is largely a matter of asking the right questions about it. The second reading allows you to ask questions, annotate the text, and take analysis notes. Essentially, you will work with the same questions concerning content; genre, organization, and features; and rhetorical concerns that you have been using throughout this book. But you will add to them and make them more probing and more detailed. Your objective is to delve deeper into the material. Don't trust your memory. Write the answers to the analysis questions in your journal or notebook. The answers to these questions will serve as the basis for your analysis essay.

● **EXAMINE CONTENT**   Start by examining the content. Locate the thesis or central point the author is making about the topic and identify other important points. Ask yourself which aspects of the topic are emphasized and which are downplayed or ignored. Next, examine the types of evidence the author uses, estimate whether they are sufficient, and determine whether they lead logically to the conclusions. Finally, ask whether the author acknowledges and refutes the views of individuals who might oppose his or her argument.

● **DETERMINE GENRE, ORGANIZATION, AND FEATURES**   Identify the genre of the text. In your everyday reading, you encounter other recognizable genres such as editorials, news stories, feature articles, biographies, memoirs, autobiographies, and letters to the editor. Ask yourself how the form contributes to the meaning of the text.

Then determine the organizational pattern. Is it chronological order or narrative; cause and effect; comparison and contrast, either point-by-point or block; argument, including position, reasons, opposition, and refutation; problem and solution; statement and response; question and answer; or classification? How does the organizational pattern contribute to the meaning of the piece? Would the meaning change if the parts were arranged differently, for example, if the narrative progressed from past to present instead of present to past; if the consequences were explained before the causes; or if reasons were ordered from least important to most important instead of vice versa?

Finally, zero in on the features of the text, asking yourself how they help convey the author's points. Search for memorable or significant devices that enable you to see the subject in a new perspective, and look closely at features like language, sentence elements, images and scenes, and references and allusions.

Determine whether the language serves to heighten and illuminate the topic. Does the author use precise wording, vivid details, words that appeal to the senses, and words with emotional intensity? Is figurative language (similes and metaphors) used? A *simile* occurs when the writer draws a comparison, using *like* or *as* to show the two elements that are being compared. Kate Scannell uses simile when she writes

> Like a very weary but ever-ready gunfighter, I stalked the hallways ready for surprise developments and acute medical problems to present themselves. (p. 102)

A *metaphor* is an implicit comparison because the *like* or *as* is not mentioned. Scannell uses metaphor when she writes

> The clothing fashioned for me by years of traditional Western medical training fell off me. (p. 104)

Here she likens the treatments, cures, and procedures that she learned in medical school to clothing. For another example, read Professor Steven Vogel's article, "Grades and Money." Throughout the article, Vogel uses the metaphor of money.

> In my college, like most others, grades *are* money. They're the currency around which everything revolves. (p. 89)

Next, examine sentence elements. Are you struck by rhythmic, balanced, symmetrical, and graceful sentences? Look for these characteristics in the following excerpt from an essay written by Gore Vidal about the "inventors" of the Constitution:

> But the Inventors were practical men and the federal constitution that they assembled in 1787 was an exquisite machine that, with a repair here and a twist there, has gone on protecting the property of the worthy for two hundred years while protecting in the Bill of Rights (that sublime afterthought) certain freedoms of speech and assembly which are still unknown even now to that irritable fount of America's political and actual being, old Europe. (p. 28)

How does this sentence help to convey the meaning of the text?

Also examine the author's use of images and scenes. *Images* are mental pictures. Recall the images Steve Stout examines in "Skills and Pills":

> Like the vision of Raphael's spirit rising free from his disease-racked corpse in death, the clothing fashioned for me by years of traditional Western medical training fell off me like tattered rags. I began to hear my own voices and compassionate sensibilities once again, louder and clearer than the chorus of voices of my old mentors. (p. 21)

> I got crushed under mounds of rubble that collected over the years of my intense and all-consuming medical training. (p. 22)

Scenes are also mental pictures, but they have enough detail in them that they could be acted out. As illustration, we'd like you to read three scenes from an essay written by Erica Mazor, one of our students. The focus of Erica's essay is the care of people who are mentally ill. To illustrate her point that physically ill individuals will be escorted to hospitals involuntarily whereas mentally ill people will not, Erica depicts three scenes:

- An elderly man rushes across the avenue and is hit by a bus and seriously injured. He pleads with the police to take him home instead of to the hospital. The police call an ambulance, and the man is quickly transported to a nearby emergency room.

- A young woman with chronic asthma has an attack on a crowded city street. A passerby offers to assist, but she refuses his help. Worried that she is seriously ill, the man hails a cab and escorts the woman to the nearest hospital.

- A middle aged woman, ravaged by paranoid schizophrenia, lies in the fetal position on a blanket on a subway platform. Commuters walk past her day after day. Finally, some people speak to her and offer to call the police. The woman yells at them to leave her alone. They walk away.

Each vignette enables the reader to visualize the characters and action, and in so doing, it drives home Erica's point. As you examine the text, ask yourself, Does the writer create memorable images and scenes that contribute to the meaning?

Finally, examine the author's references and allusions to determine if they illuminate or add significantly to the subject matter. Take account of the writer's formal references to other written sources as well as other types of references and allusions. An *allusion* is a reference to some other parallel concept. Describing the patients on her AIDS ward, Scannell writes:

Some patients were so emaciated by profound wasting that I could not shake disquieting memories of photographs I had seen as a little girl which depicted Auschwitz and Buchenwald prisoners.

Scannell's reference to prisoners of concentration camps intensifies her description of the patients' sad state. Notice Liz Mandrell's allusion in the following description:

Robin is a young Katie Couric, all smiles and perky nose, but racked with journalistic ambition and biting cynicism.

READINGS

Everyday Use (For Your Grandmama)

Alice Walker

1   I will wait for her in the yard that Maggie and I made so clean and wavy yesterday afternoon. A yard like this is more comfortable than most people know. It is not just a yard. It is like an extended living room. When the hard clay is swept clean as a floor and the fine sand around the edges lined with tiny, irregular grooves, anyone can come and sit and look up into the elm tree and wait for the breezes that never come inside the house.

2   Maggie will be nervous until after her sister goes: she will stand hopelessly in corners, homely and ashamed of the burn scars down her arms and legs, eying her sister with a mixture of envy and awe. She thinks her sister has held life always in the palm of one hand, that "no" is a word the world never learned to say to her.

3   You've no doubt seen those TV shows where the child who has "made it" is confronted, as a surprise, by her own mother and father, tottering in weakly from backstage. (A pleasant surprise, of course: What would they do if parent and child came on the show only to curse out and insult each other?) On TV mother and child embrace and smile into each other's faces. Sometimes the mother and father weep; the child wraps them in her arms and leans across the table to tell how she would not have made it without their help. I have seen these programs.

4   Sometimes I dream a dream in which Dee and I are suddenly brought together on a TV program of this sort. Out of a dark and soft-seated limousine I am ushered into a bright room filled with many people. There I meet a smiling, gray, sporty man like Johnny Carson who shakes my hand and tells me what a fine girl I have. Then we are on the stage and Dee is embracing me with tears in her eyes. She pins on my dress a large orchid, even though she has told me once that she thinks orchids are tacky flowers.

5   In real life I am a large, big-boned woman with rough, man-working hands. In the winter I wear flannel nightgowns to bed and overalls during the day. I can kill and clean a hog as mercilessly as a man. My fat keeps me hot in zero weather. I can work outside all day, breaking once to get water for washing; I can eat pork liver cooked over the open fire minutes after it comes steaming from the hog. One winter I knocked a bull calf straight in the brain between the eyes with a sledge hammer and had the meat hung up to chill before nightfall. But of course all this does not show on television. I am the way my daughter would want me to be: a

hundred pounds lighter, my skin like an uncooked barley pancake. My hair glistens in the hot bright lights. Johnny Carson has much to do to keep up with my quick and witty tongue.

6 But that is a mistake. I know even before I wake up. Who ever knew a Johnson with a quick tongue? Who can even imagine me looking a strange white man in the eye? It seems to me I have talked to them always with one foot raised in flight, with my head turned in whichever way is farthest from them. Dee, though. She would always look anyone in the eye. Hesitation was no part of her nature.

7 "How do I look, Mama?" Maggie says, showing just enough of her thin body enveloped in pink skirt and red blouse for me to know she's there, almost hidden by the door.

8 "Come out into the yard," I say.

9 Have you ever seen a lame animal, perhaps a dog run over by some careless person rich enough to own a car, sidle up to someone who is ignorant enough to be kind to him? That is the way my Maggie walks. She has been like this, chin on chest, eyes on ground, feet in shuffle, ever since the fire that burned the other house to the ground.

10 Dee is lighter than Maggie, with nicer hair and a fuller figure. She's a woman now, though sometimes I forget. How long ago was it that the other house burned? Ten, twelve years? Sometimes I can still hear the flames and feel Maggie's arms sticking to me, her hair smoking and her dress falling off her in little black papery flakes. Her eyes seemed stretched open, blazed open by the flames reflected in them. And Dee. I see her standing off under the sweet gum tree she used to dig gum out of; a look of concentration on her face as she watched the last dingy gray board of the house fall in toward the red-hot brick chimney. Why don't you do a dance around the ashes? I'd wanted to ask her. She had hated the house that much.

11 I used to think she hated Maggie, too. But that was before we raised the money, the church and me, to send her to Augusta to school. She used to read to us without pity; forcing words, lies, other folks' habits, whole lives upon us two, sitting trapped and ignorant underneath her voice. She washed us in a river of make-believe, burned us with a lot of knowledge we didn't necessarily need to know. Pressed us to her with the serious way she read, to shove us away at just the moment, like dimwits, we seemed about to understand.

12 Dee wanted nice things. A yellow organdy dress to wear to her graduation from high school; black pumps to match a green suit she'd made from an old suit somebody gave me. She was determined to stare down any disaster in her efforts. Her eyelids would not flicker for minutes at a time. Often I fought off the temptation to shake her. At sixteen she had a style of her own: and she knew what style was.

13 I never had an education myself. After second grade the school was closed down. Don't ask me why: in 1927 colored asked fewer questions

...continued Everyday Use (For Your Grandmama), **Alice Walker**

than they do now. Sometimes Maggie reads to me. She stumbles along good-naturedly but can't see well. She knows she is not bright. Like good looks and money, quickness passed her by. She will marry John Thomas (who has mossy teeth in an earnest face) and then I'll be free to sit here and I guess just sing church songs to myself. Although I never was a good singer. Never could carry a tune. I was always better at a man's job. I used to love to milk till I was hooked in the side in '49. Cows are soothing and slow and don't bother you, unless you try to milk them the wrong way.

14   I have deliberately turned my back on the house. It is three rooms, just like the one that burned, except the roof is tin; they don't make shingle roofs any more. There are no real windows, just some holes cut in the sides, like the portholes in a ship, but not round and not square, with rawhide holding the shutters up on the outside. This house is in a pasture, too, like the other one. No doubt when Dee sees it she will want to tear it down. She wrote me once that no matter where we "choose" to live, she will manage to come see us. But she will never bring her friends. Maggie and I thought about this and Maggie asked me, "Mama, when did Dee ever *have* any friends?"

15   She had a few. Furtive boys in pink shirts hanging about on washday after school. Nervous girls who never laughed. Impressed with her they worshipped the well-turned phrase, the cute shape, the scalding humor that erupted like bubbles in lye. She read to them.

16   When she was courting Jimmy T she didn't have much time to pay to us, but turned all her faultfinding power on him. He *flew* to marry a cheap city girl from a family of ignorant flashy people. She hardly had time to recompose herself.

17   When she comes I will meet—but there they are!

18   Maggie attempts to make a dash for the house, in her shuffling way, but I stay her with my hand. "Come back here," I say. And she stops and tries to dig a well in the sand with her toe.

19   It is hard to see them clearly through the strong sun. But even the first glimpse of leg out of the car tells me it is Dee. Her feet were always neat-looking, as if God himself had shaped them with a certain style. From the other side of the car comes a short, stocky man. Hair is all over his head a foot long and hanging from his chin like a kinky mule tail. I hear Maggie suck in her breath. "Uhnnnh," is what it sounds like. Like when you see the wriggling end of a snake just in front of your foot on the road. "Uhnnnh."

20   Dee next. A dress down to the ground, in this hot weather. A dress so loud it hurts my eyes. There are yellows and oranges enough to throw back the light of the sun. I feel my whole face warming from the heat waves it throws out. Earrings gold, too, and hanging down to her shoul-

ders. Bracelets dangling and making noises when she moves her arm up to shake the folds of the dress out of her armpits. The dress is loose and flows, and as she walks closer, I like it. I hear Maggie go "Uhnnnh" again. It is her sister's hair. It stands straight up like the wool on a sheep. It is black as night and around the edges are two long ponytails that rope about like small lizards disappearing behind her ears.

21   "Wa-su-zo-Tean-o!" she says, coming in on that gliding way the dress makes her move. The short stocky fellow with the hair to his navel is all grinning and he follows up with "Asalamalakim, my mother and sister!" He moves to hug Maggie but she falls back, right up against the back of my chair. I feel her trembling there and when I look up I see the perspiration falling off her chin.

22   "Don't get up," says Dee. Since I am stout it takes something of a push. You can see me trying to move a second or two before I make it. She turns, showing white heels through her sandals, and goes back to the car. Out she peeks next with a Polaroid. She stoops down quickly and lines up picture after picture of me sitting there in front of the house with Maggie cowering behind me. She never takes a shot without making sure the house is included. When a cow comes nibbling around the edge of the yard she snaps it and me and Maggie and the house. Then she puts the Polaroid in the back seat of the car, and comes up and kisses me on the forehead.

23   Meanwhile Asalamalakim is going through the motions with Maggie's hand. Maggie's hand is as limp as a fish, and probably cold, despite the sweat, and she keeps trying to pull it back. It looks like Asalamalakim wants to shake hands but wants to do it fancy. Or maybe he don't know how people shake hands. Anyhow, he soon gives up on Maggie.

24   "Well," I say. "Dee."

25   "No, Mama," she says. "Not 'Dee,' Wangero Leewanika Kemanjo!"

26   "What happened to 'Dee'?" I wanted to know.

27   "She's dead," Wangero said. "I couldn't bear it any longer, being named after the people who oppress me."

28   "You know as well as me you was named after your aunt Dicie," I said. Dicie is my sister. She named Dee. We called her "Big Dee" after Dee was born.

29   "But who was she named after?" asked Wangero.

30   "I guess after Grandma Dee," I said.

31   "And who was she named after?" asked Wangero.

32   "Her mother," I said, and saw Wangero was getting tired. "That's about as far back as I can trace it," I said. Though, in fact, I probably could have carried it back beyond the Civil War through the branches.

33   "Well," said Asalamalakim, "there you are."

34   "Uhnnnh," I heard Maggie say.

35   "There I was not," I said, "before 'Dicie' cropped up in our family, so why should I try to trace it that far back?"

36   He just stood there grinning, looking down on me like somebody inspecting a Model A car. Every once in a while he and Wangero sent eye signals over my head.

37   "How do you pronounce this name?" I asked.

38   "You don't have to call me by it if you don't want to," said Wangero.

39   "Why shouldn't I?" I asked. "If that's what you want us to call you, we'll call you."

40   "I know it might sound awkward at first," said Wangero.

41   "I'll get used to it," I said. "Ream it out again."

42   Well, soon we got the name out of the way. Asalamalakim had a name twice as long and three times as hard. After I tripped over it two or three times he told me to just call him Hakim-a-barber. I wanted to ask him was he a barber, but I didn't really think he was, so I didn't ask.

43   "You must belong to those beef-cattle peoples down the road," I said. They said "Asalamalakim" when they met you, too, but they didn't shake hands. Always too busy: feeding the cattle, fixing the fences, putting up salt-lick shelters, throwing down hay. When the white folks poisoned some of the herd the men stayed up all night with rifles in their hands. I walked a mile and a half just to see the sight.

44   Hakim-a-barber said, "I accept some of their doctrines, but farming and raising cattle is not my style." (They didn't tell me, and I didn't ask, whether Wangero (Dee) had really gone and married him.)

45   We sat down to eat and right away he said he didn't eat collards and pork was unclean. Wangero, though, went on through the chitlins and corn bread, the greens and everything else. She talked a blue streak over the sweet potatoes. Everything delighted her. Even the fact that we still used the benches her daddy made for the table when we couldn't afford to buy chairs.

46   "Oh, Mama!" she cried. Then turned to Hakim-a-barber. "I never knew how lovely these benches are. You can feel the rump prints," she said, running her hands underneath her and along the bench. Then she gave a sigh and her hand closed over Grandma Dee's butter dish. "That's it!" she said. "I knew there was something I wanted to ask you if I could have." She jumped up from the table and went over in the corner where the churn stood, the milk in it clabber by now. She looked at the churn and looked at it.

47   "This churn top is what I need," she said happily. "Didn't Uncle Buddy whittle it out of a tree you all used to have?"

48   "Yes," I said.

49   "Uh huh," she said happily. "And I want the dasher, too."

50   "Uncle Buddy whittle that, too?" asked the barber.

51   Dee (Wangero) looked up at me.

52   "Aunt Dee's first husband whittled the dash," said Maggie so low you almost couldn't hear her. "His name was Henry, but they called him Stash."

53   "Maggie's brain is like an elephant's," Wangero said, laughing. "I can use the churn top as a centerpiece for the alcove table," she said, sliding a plate over the churn, "and I'll think of something artistic to do with the dasher."

54   When she finished wrapping the dasher the handle stuck out. I took it for a moment in my hands. You didn't even have to look close to see where hands pushing the dasher up and down to make butter had left a kind of sink in the wood. In fact, there were a lot of small sinks; you could see where thumbs and fingers had sunk into the wood. It was beautiful light yellow wood, from a tree that grew in the yard where Big Dee and Stash had lived.

55   After dinner Dee (Wangero) went to the trunk at the foot of my bed and started rifling through it. Maggie hung back in the kitchen over the dishpan. Out came Wangero with two quilts. They had been pieced by Grandma Dee and then Big Dee and me had hung them on the quilt frames on the front porch and quilted them. One was in the Lone Star pattern. The other was Walk Around the Mountain. In both of them were scraps of dresses Grandma Dee had worn fifty and more years ago. Bits and pieces of Grandma Jarrell's Paisley shirts. And one teeny faded blue piece, about the size of a penny matchbox, that was from Great Grandpa Ezra's uniform that he wore in the Civil War.

56   "Mama," Wangero said sweet as a bird. "Can I have these old quilts?"

57   I heard something fall in the kitchen, and a minute later the kitchen door slammed.

58   "Why don't you take one or two of the others?" I asked. "These old things was just done by me and Big Dee from some tops your grandma pieced before she died."

59   "No," said Wangero. "I don't want those. They are stitched around the borders by machine."

60   "That'll make them last better," I said.

61   "That's not the point," said Wangero. "These are all pieces of dresses Grandma used to wear. She did all this stitching by hand. Imagine!" She held the quilts securely in her arms, stroking them.

62   "Some of the pieces, like those lavender ones, come from old clothes her mother handed down to her," I said, moving up to touch the quilts. Dee (Wangero) moved back just enough so that I couldn't reach the quilts. They already belonged to her.

63   "Imagine!" she breathed again, clutching them closely to her bosom.

64   "The truth is," I said, "I promised to give them quilts to Maggie, for when she marries John Thomas."

65   She gasped like a bee had stung her.

...continued Everyday Use (For Your Grandmama), **Alice Walker**

66   "Maggie can't appreciate these quilts!" she said. "She'd probably be backward enough to put them to everyday use."

67   "I reckon she would," I said. "God knows I been saving 'em for long enough with nobody using 'em. I hope she will!" I didn't want to bring up how I had offered Dee (Wangero) a quilt when she went away to college. Then she had told me they were old-fashioned, out of style.

68   "But they're *priceless!*" she was saying now, furiously; for she has a temper. "Maggie would put them on the bed and in five years they'd be in rags. Less than that!"

69   "She can always make some more," I said. "Maggie knows how to quilt."

70   Dee (Wangero) looked at me with hatred. "You just will not understand. The point is these quilts, *these* quilts!"

71   "Well," I said, stumped. "What would *you* do with them?"

72   "Hang them," she said. As if that was the only thing you *could* do with quilts.

73   Maggie by now was standing in the door. I could almost hear the sound her feet made as they scraped over each other.

74   "She can have them, Mama," she said, like somebody used to never winning anything, or having anything reserved for her. "I can 'member Grandma Dee without the quilts."

75   I looked at her hard. She had filled her bottom lip with checkerberry snuff and it gave her face a kind of dopey, hangdog look. It was Grandma Dee and Big Dee who taught her how to quilt herself. She stood there with her hands hidden in the folds of her skirt. She looked at her sister with something like fear but she wasn't mad at her. This was Maggie's portion. This was the way she knew God to work.

76   When I looked at her like that something hit me in the top of my head and ran down to the soles of my feet. Just like when I'm in church and the spirit of God touches me and I get happy and shout. I did something I never had done before: hugged Maggie to me, then dragged her on into the room, snatched the quilts out of Miss Wangero's hands and dumped them into Maggie's lap. Maggie just sat there on my bed with her mouth open.

77   "Take one or two of the others," I said to Dee.

78   But she turned without a word and went out to Hakim-a-barber.

79   "You just don't understand," she said, as Maggie and I came out to the car.

80   "What don't I understand?" I wanted to know.

81   "Your heritage," she said. And then she turned to Maggie, kissed her, and said, "You ought to try to make something of yourself, too, Maggie. It's really a new day for us. But from the way you and Mama still live you'd never know it."

82   She put on some sunglasses that hid everything above the tip of her nose and her chin.

83   Maggie smiled; maybe at the sunglasses. But a real smile, not scared. After we watched the car dust settle I asked Maggie to me bring me a dip of snuff. And then the two of us sat there just enjoying, until it was time to go in the house and go to bed.

Seven Variants of "Cinderella"

The existence of Chinese, French, German, African, and Native American versions of the popular Cinderella tale, along with 700 other versions worldwide, comes as a surprise to many. Which is the real "Cinderella"? The question is misleading in that each version is "real" for a particular group of people in a particular place and time. Certainly, you can judge among versions and select the most appealing. You can also draw comparisons and contrasts. Indeed, the grouping of the stories that we present here invites comparisons. You might wish to consider a few of the following categories as you read:

- Cinderella's innocence or guilt, concerning the treatment she receives at the hands of her stepsisters
- Cinderella's passive (or active) nature
- Sibling rivalry—the relationship of Cinderella with her sisters
- The father's role
- The rule that Cinderella must return from the ball by midnight
- The levels of violence
- The presence or absence of the fairy godmother
- Cinderella's relationship with the prince
- The characterization of the prince
- The presence of Cinderella's dead mother
- The function of magic
- The ending

Cinderella

Charles Perrault

Charles Perrault (1628–1703) was born in Paris of a prosperous family. He practiced law for a short time and then devoted his attentions to a job in government, in which capacity he was instrumental in promoting the advancement of the arts and sciences and in securing pensions for writers, both French and foreign. Perrault is best known as a writer for his Contes de ma mère l'oye (Mother Goose Tales), *a collection of fairy tales taken from popular folklore. He is widely suspected of having changed these stories in an effort to make them more acceptable to his audience—members of the French court.*

Once there was a nobleman who took as his second wife the proudest and haughtiest woman imaginable. She had two daughters of the same character, who took after their mother in everything. On his side, the husband had a daughter who was sweetness itself; she inherited this from her mother, who had been the most kindly of women.

No sooner was the wedding over than the stepmother showed her ill-nature. She could not bear the good qualities of the young girl, for they made her own daughters seem even less likable. She gave her the roughest work of the house to do. It was she who washed the dishes and the stairs, who cleaned out Madam's room and the rooms of the two Misses. She slept right at the top of the house, in an attic, on a lumpy mattress, while her sisters slept in panelled rooms where they had the most modern beds and mirrors in which they could see themselves from top to toe. The poor girl bore everything in patience and did not dare to complain to her father. He would only have scolded her, for he was entirely under his wife's thumb.

When she had finished her work, she used to go into the chimney-corner and sit down among the cinders, for which reason she was usually known in the house as Cinderbottom. Her younger stepsister, who was not so rude as the other, called her Cinderella. However, Cinderella, in spite of her ragged clothes, was still fifty times as beautiful as her sisters, superbly dressed though they were.

One day the King's son gave a ball, to which everyone of good family was invited. Our two young ladies received invitations, for they cut quite a figure in the country. So there they were, both feeling very pleased and very busy choosing the clothes and the hair-styles which would suit them best. More work for Cinderella, for it was she who ironed her sisters' underwear and goffered their linen cuffs. Their only talk was of what they would wear.

"I," said the elder, "shall wear my red velvet dress and my collar of English lace."

"I," said the younger, "shall wear just my ordinary skirt; but, to make up, I shall put on my gold-embroidered cape and my diamond clasp, which is quite out of the common."

The right hairdresser was sent for to supply double-frilled coifs, and patches were bought from the right patch-maker. They called Cinderella to ask her opinion, for she had excellent taste. She made useful suggestions and even offered to do their hair for them. They accepted willingly.

While she was doing it, they said to her:

"Cinderella, how would you like to go to the ball?"

"Oh dear, you are making fun of me. It wouldn't do for me."

"You are quite right. It would be a joke. People would laugh if they saw a Cinderbottom at the ball."

Anyone else would have done their hair in knots for them, but she had a sweet nature, and she finished it perfectly. For two days they were so excited that they ate almost nothing. They broke a good dozen laces trying to tighten their stays to make their waists slimmer, and they were never away from their mirrors.

At last the great day arrived. They set off, and Cinderella watched them until they were out of sight. When she could no longer see them, she began to cry. Her godmother, seeing her all in tears, asked what was the matter.

"If only I could . . . If only I could . . . " She was weeping so much that she could not go on.

Her godmother, who was a fairy, said to her: "If only you could go to the ball, is that it?"

"Alas, yes," said Cinderella with a sigh.

"Well," said the godmother, "be a good girl and I'll get you there."

She took her into her room and said: "Go into the garden and get me a pumpkin."

Cinderella hurried out and cut the best she could find and took it to her godmother, but she could not understand how this pumpkin would get her to the ball. Her godmother hollowed it out, leaving only the rind, and then tapped it with her wand and immediately it turned into a magnificent gilded coach.

Then she went to look in her mouse-trap and found six mice all alive in it. She told Cinderella to raise the door of the trap a little, and as each mouse came out she gave it a tap with her wand and immediately it turned into a fine horse. That made a team of six horses, each of fine mouse-coloured grey.

While she was wondering how she would make a coachman, Cinderella said to her:

"I will go and see whether there is a rat in the rat-trap, we could make a coachman of him."

...continued Cinderella, **Charles Perrault**

"You are right," said the godmother. "Run and see."

Cinderella brought her the rat-trap, in which there were three big rats. The fairy picked out one of them because of his splendid whiskers and, when she had touched him, he turned into a fat coachman, with the finest moustaches in the district.

25 Then she said: "Go into the garden and you will find six lizards behind the watering-can. Bring them to me."

As soon as Cinderella had brought them, her godmother changed them into six footmen, who got up behind the coach with their striped liveries, and stood in position there as though they had been doing it all their lives.

Then the fairy said to Cinderella:

"Well, that's to go to the ball in. Aren't you pleased?"

"Yes. But am I to go like this, with my ugly clothes?"

30 Her godmother simply touched her with her wand and her clothes were changed in an instant into a dress of gold and silver cloth, all sparkling with precious stones. Then she gave her a pair of glass slippers, most beautifully made.

So equipped, Cinderella got into the coach: but her godmother warned her above all not to be out after midnight, telling her that, if she stayed at the ball a moment later, her coach would turn back into a pumpkin, her horses into mice, her footmen into lizards, and her fine clothes would become rags again.

She promised her godmother that she would leave the ball before midnight without fail, and she set out, beside herself with joy.

The King's son, on being told that a great princess whom no one knew had arrived, ran out to welcome her. He handed her down from the coach and led her into the hall where his guests were. A sudden silence fell; the dancing stopped, the violins ceased to play, the whole company stood fascinated by the beauty of the unknown princess. Only a low murmur was heard: "Ah, how lovely she is!" The King himself, old as he was, could not take his eyes off her and kept whispering to the Queen that it was a long time since he had seen such a beautiful and charming person. All the ladies were absorbed in noting her clothes and the way her hair was dressed, so as to order the same things for themselves the next morning, provided that fine enough materials could be found, and skillful enough craftsmen.

The King's son placed her in the seat of honour, and later led her out to dance. She danced with such grace that she won still more admiration. An excellent supper was served, but the young Prince was too much occupied in gazing at her to eat anything. She went and sat next to her sisters and treated them with great courtesy, offering them oranges and lemons which the Prince had given her. They were astonished, for they did not recognize her.

While they were chatting together, Cinderella heard the clock strike a quarter to twelve. She curtsied low to the company and left as quickly as she could.

As soon as she reached home, she went to her godmother and, having thanked her, said that she would very much like to go again to the ball on the next night—for the Prince had begged her to come back. She was in the middle of telling her godmother about all the things that had happened, when the two sisters came knocking at the door. Cinderella went to open it.

"How late you are!" she said, rubbing her eyes and yawning and stretching as though she had just woken up (though since they had last seen each other she had felt very far from sleepy).

"If you had been at the ball," said one of the sisters, "you would not have felt like yawning. There was a beautiful princess there, really ravishingly beautiful. She was most attentive to us. She gave us oranges and lemons."

Cinderella could have hugged herself. She asked them the name of the princess, but they replied that no one knew her, that the King's son was much troubled about it, and that he would give anything in the world to know who she was. Cinderella smiled and said to them:

"So she was very beautiful? Well, well, how lucky you are! Couldn't I see her? Please, Miss Javotte, do lend me that yellow dress which you wear about the house."

"Really," said Miss Javotte, "what an idea! Lend one's dress like that to a filthy Cinderbottom! I should have to be out of my mind."

Cinderella was expecting this refusal and she was very glad when it came, for she would have been in an awkward position if her sister really had lent her her frock.

On the next day the two sisters went to the ball, and Cinderella too, but even more splendidly dressed than the first time. The King's son was constantly at her side and wooed her the whole evening. The young girl was enjoying herself so much that she forgot her godmother's warning. She heard the clock striking the first stroke of midnight when she thought that it was still hardly eleven. She rose and slipped away as lightly as a roe-deer. The Prince followed her, but he could not catch her up. One of her glass slippers fell off, and the Prince picked it up with great care.

Cinderella reached home quite out of breath, with no coach, no footmen, and wearing her old clothes. Nothing remained of all her finery, except one of her little slippers, the fellow to the one which she had dropped. The guards at the palace gate were asked if they had not seen a princess go out. They answered that they had seen no one go out except a very poorly dressed girl, who looked more like a peasant than a young lady.

When the two sisters returned from the ball, Cinderella asked them if they had enjoyed themselves again, and if the beautiful lady had been there.

...continued Cinderella, **Charles Perrault**

They said that she had, but that she had run away when it struck midnight, and so swiftly that she had lost one of her glass slippers, a lovely little thing. The Prince had picked it up and had done nothing but gaze at it for the rest of the ball, and undoubtedly he was very much in love with the beautiful person to whom it belonged.

They were right, for a few days later the King's son had it proclaimed to the sound of trumpets that he would marry the girl whose foot exactly fitted the slipper. They began by trying it on the various princesses, then on the duchesses and on all the ladies of the Court, but with no success. It was brought to the two sisters, who did everything possible to force their feet into the slipper, but they could not manage it. Cinderella, who was looking on, recognized her own slipper, and said laughing:

"Let me see if it would fit me!"

Her sisters began to laugh and mock at her. But the gentleman who was trying on the slipper looked closely at Cinderella and, seeing that she was very beautiful, said that her request was perfectly reasonable and that he had instructions to try it on every girl. He made Cinderella sit down and, raising the slipper to her foot, he found that it slid on without difficulty and fitted like a glove.

Great was the amazement of the two sisters, but it became greater still when Cinderella drew from her pocket the second little slipper and put it on her other foot. Thereupon the fairy godmother came in and, touching Cinderella's clothes with her wand, made them even more magnificent than on the previous days.

50

Then the two sisters recognized her as the lovely princess whom they had met at the ball. They flung themselves at her feet and begged her forgiveness for all the unkind things which they had done to her. Cinderella raised them up and kissed them, saying that she forgave them with all her heart and asking them to love her always. She was taken to the young Prince in the fine clothes which she was wearing. He thought her more beautiful than ever and a few days later he married her. Cinderella, who was as kind as she was beautiful, invited her two sisters to live in the palace and married them, on the same day, to two great noblemen of the Court.

Ashputtle

Jakob and Wilhelm Grimm

Jakob Grimm (1785–1863) and Wilhelm Grimm (1786–1859) are best known today for the 200 folktales they collected from oral sources and reworked in Kinder- und Hausmärchen *(popularly known as* Grimm's Fairy Tales*), which has been translated into 70 languages. The techniques Jakob and Wilhelm Grimm used to collect and comment on these tales became a model for other collectors, providing a basis for the science of folklore. Although the Grimm brothers argued for preserving the tales exactly as heard from oral sources, scholars have determined that they sought to "improve" the tales by making them more readable. The result, highly pleasing to lay audiences the world over, nonetheless represents a literary reworking of the original oral sources.*

A rich man's wife fell sick and, feeling that her end was near, she called her only daughter to her bedside and said: "Dear child, be good and say your prayers; God will help you, and I shall look down on you from heaven and always be with you." With that she closed her eyes and died. Every day the little girl went out to her mother's grave and wept, and she went on being good and saying her prayers. When winter came, the snow spread a white cloth over the grave, and when spring took it off, the man remarried.

His new wife brought two daughters into the house. Their faces were beautiful and lily-white, but their hearts were ugly and black. That was the beginning of a bad time for the poor stepchild. "Why should this silly goose sit in the parlor with us?" they said. "People who want to eat bread must earn it. Get into the kitchen where you belong!" They took away her fine clothes and gave her an old gray dress and wooden shoes to wear. "Look at the haughty princess in her finery!" they cried and, laughing, led her to the kitchen. From then on she had to do all the work, getting up before daybreak, carrying water, lighting fires, cooking and washing. In addition the sisters did everything they could to plague her. They jeered at her and poured peas and lentils into the ashes, so that she had to sit there picking them out. At night, when she was tired out with work, she had no bed to sleep in but had to lie in the ashes by the hearth. And they took to calling her Ashputtle because she always looked dusty and dirty.

One day when her father was going to the fair, he asked his two stepdaughters what he should bring them. "Beautiful dresses," said one. "Diamonds and pearls," said the other. "And you, Ashputtle. What would you like?" "Father," she said, "break off the first branch that brushes against your hat on your way home, and bring it to me." So he brought beautiful

...continued Ashputtle, **Jakob and Wilhelm Grimm**

dresses, diamonds, and pearls for his two stepdaughters, and on the way home, as he was riding through a copse, a hazel branch brushed against him and knocked off his hat. So he broke off the branch and took it home with him. When he got home, he gave the stepdaughters what they had asked for, and gave Ashputtle the branch. After thanking him, she went to her mother's grave and planted the hazel sprig over it and cried so hard that her tears fell on the sprig and watered it. It grew and became a beautiful tree. Three times a day Ashputtle went and sat under it and wept and prayed. Each time a little white bird came and perched on the tree, and when Ashputtle made a wish the little bird threw down what she had wished for.

Now it so happened that the king arranged for a celebration. It was to go on for three days and all the beautiful girls in the kingdom were invited, in order that his son might choose a bride. When the two step-sisters heard they had been asked, they were delighted. They called Ashputtle and said: "Comb our hair, brush our shoes, and fasten our buckles. We're going to the wedding at the king's palace." Ashputtle obeyed, but she wept, for she too would have liked to go dancing, and she begged her stepmother to let her go. "You little sloven!" said the stepmother. "How can you go to a wedding when you're all dusty and dirty? How can you go dancing when you have neither dress nor shoes?" But when Ashputtle begged and begged, the stepmother finally said: "Here, I've dumped a bowlful of lentils in the ashes. If you can pick them out in two hours, you may go." The girl went out the back door to the garden and cried out: "O tame little doves, O turtledoves, and all the birds under heaven, come and help me put

the good ones in the pot,
the bad ones in your crop."

Two little white doves came flying through the kitchen window, and then came the turtledoves, and finally all the birds under heaven came flapping and fluttering and settled down by the ashes. The doves nodded their little heads and started in, peck peck peck peck, and all the others started in, peck peck peck peck, and they sorted out all the good lentils and put them in the bowl. Hardly an hour had passed before they finished and flew away. Then the girl brought the bowl to her stepmother, and she was happy, for she thought she'd be allowed to go to the wedding. But the stepmother said: "No, Ashputtle. You have nothing to wear and you don't know how to dance; the people would only laugh at you." When Ashputtle began to cry, the stepmother said: "If you can pick two bowlfuls of lentils out of the ashes in an hour, you may come." And she thought: "She'll never be able to do it." When she had dumped the two bowlfuls of lentils in the ashes, Ashputtle went out the back door to the garden and cried out: "O tame little doves, O turtledoves, and all the birds under heaven, come and help me put

> *the good ones in the pot,*
> *the bad ones in your crop."*

Two little white doves came flying through the kitchen window, and then came the turtledoves, and finally all the birds under heaven came flapping and fluttering and settled down by the ashes. The doves nodded their little heads and started in, peck peck peck peck, and all the others started in, peck peck peck peck, and they sorted out all the good lentils and put them in the bowls. Before half an hour had passed, they had finished and they all flew away. Then the girl brought the bowls to her stepmother, and she was happy, for she thought she'd be allowed to go to the wedding. But her stepmother said: "It's no use. You can't come, because you have nothing to wear and you don't know how to dance. We'd only be ashamed of you." Then she turned her back and hurried away with her two proud daughters.

5   When they had all gone out, Ashputtle went to her mother's grave. She stood under the hazel tree and cried:

> *"Shake your branches, little tree,*
> *Throw gold and silver down on me."*

Whereupon the bird tossed down a gold and silver dress and slippers embroidered with silk and silver. Ashputtle slipped into the dress as fast as she could and went to the wedding. Her sisters and stepmother didn't recognize her. She was so beautiful in her golden dress that they thought she must be the daughter of some foreign king. They never dreamed it could be Ashputtle, for they thought she was sitting at home in her filthy rags, picking lentils out of the ashes. The king's son came up to her, took her by the hand and danced with her. He wouldn't dance with anyone else and he never let go her hand. When someone else asked for a dance, he said: "She is my partner."

She danced until evening, and then she wanted to go home. The king's son said: "I'll go with you, I'll see you home," for he wanted to find out whom the beautiful girl belonged to. But she got away from him and slipped into the dovecote. The king's son waited until her father arrived, and told him the strange girl had slipped into the dovecote. The old man thought: "Could it be Ashputtle?" and he sent for an ax and a pick and broke into the dovecote, but there was no one inside. When they went indoors, Ashputtle was lying in the ashes in her filthy clothes and a dim oil lamp was burning on the chimney piece, for Ashputtle had slipped out the back end of the dovecote and run to the hazel tree. There she had taken off her fine clothes and put them on the grave, and the bird had taken them away. Then she had put her gray dress on again, crept into the kitchen and lain down in the ashes.

...*continued* Ashputtle, **Jakob and Wilhelm Grimm**

Next day when the festivities started in again and her parents and stepsisters had gone, Ashputtle went to the hazel tree and said:

> "*Shake your branches, little tree,*
> *Throw gold and silver down on me.*"

Whereupon the bird threw down a dress that was even more dazzling than the first one. And when she appeared at the wedding, everyone marveled at her beauty. The king's son was waiting for her. He took her by the hand and danced with no one but her. When others came and asked her for a dance, he said: "She is my partner." When evening came, she said she was going home. The king's son followed her, wishing to see which house she went into, but she ran away and disappeared into the garden behind the house, where there was a big beautiful tree with the most wonderful pears growing on it. She climbed among the branches as nimbly as a squirrel and the king's son didn't know what had become of her. He waited until her father arrived and said to him: "The strange girl has got away from me and I think she has climbed up in the pear tree." Her father thought: "Could it be Ashputtle?" He sent for an ax and chopped the tree down, but there was no one in it. When they went into the kitchen, Ashputtle was lying there in the ashes as usual, for she had jumped down on the other side of the tree, brought her fine clothes back to the bird in the hazel tree, and put on her filthy gray dress.

On the third day, after her parents and sisters had gone, Ashputtle went back to her mother's grave and said to the tree:

> "*Shake your branches, little tree,*
> *Throw gold and silver down on me.*"

Whereupon the bird threw down a dress that was more radiant than either of the others, and the slippers were all gold. When she appeared at the wedding, the people were too amazed to speak. The king's son danced with no one but her, and when someone else asked her for a dance, he said: "She is my partner."

When the evening came, Ashputtle wanted to go home, and the king's son said he'd go with her, but she slipped away so quickly that he couldn't follow. But he had thought up a trick. He had arranged to have the whole staircase brushed with pitch, and as she was running down it the pitch pulled her left slipper off. The king's son picked it up, and it was tiny and delicate and all gold. Next morning he went to the father and said: "No girl shall be my wife but the one this golden shoe fits." The sisters were overjoyed, for they had beautiful feet. The eldest took the shoe to her room to try it on and her mother went with her. But the shoe was too small and she couldn't get her big toe in. So her mother handed her a knife and said: "Cut your toe off. Once you're queen you won't have to walk any more." The girl cut her toe off, forced her foot into the shoe, gritted her teeth against the pain, and went out to the king's son. He accepted her as his bride-to-be, lifted her up on his horse, and rode away with her. But they had to pass the grave. The two doves were sitting in the hazel tree and they cried out:

> *"Roocoo, roocoo,*
> *There's blood in the shoe.*
> *The foot's too long, the foot's too wide,*
> *That's not the proper bride."*

He looked down at her foot and saw the blood spurting. At that he turned his horse around and took the false bride home again. "No," he said, "this isn't the right girl; let her sister try the shoe on." The sister went to her room and managed to get her toes into the shoe, but her heel was too big. So her mother handed her a knife and said: "Cut off a chunk of your heel. Once you're queen you won't have to walk any more." The girl cut off a chunk of her heel, forced her foot into the shoe, gritted her teeth against the pain, and went out to the king's son. He accepted her as his bride-to-be, lifted her up on his horse, and rode away with her. As they passed the hazel tree, the two doves were sitting there, and they cried out:

> *"Roocoo, roocoo,*
> *There's blood in the shoe.*
> *The foot's too long, the foot's too wide,*
> *That's not the proper bride."*

He looked down at her foot and saw that blood was spurting from her shoe and staining her white stocking all red. He turned his horse around and took the false bride home again. "This isn't the right girl, either," he said. "Haven't you got another daughter?" "No," said the man, "there's only a puny little kitchen drudge that my dead wife left me. She couldn't possibly be the bride." "Send her up," said the king's son, but the mother said: "Oh, no, she's much too dirty to be seen." But he insisted and they had to call her. First she washed her face and hands, and when they were clean, she went upstairs and curtseyed to the king's son. He handed her the golden slipper and sat down on a footstool, took her foot out of her heavy wooden shoe, and put it into the slipper. It fitted perfectly. And when she stood up and the king's son looked into her face, he recognized the beautiful girl he had danced with and cried out: "This is my true bride!" The stepmother and the two sisters went pale with fear and rage. But he lifted Ashputtle up on his horse and rode away with her. As they passed the hazel tree, the two white doves called out:

> *"Roocoo, roocoo,*
> *No blood in the shoe.*
> *Her foot is neither long nor wide,*
> *This one is the proper bride."*

...*continued* Ashputtle, **Jakob and Wilhelm Grimm**

Then they flew down and alighted on Ashputtle's shoulders, one on the right and one on the left, and there they sat.

10

On the day of Ashputtle's wedding, the two stepsisters came and tried to ingratiate themselves and share in her happiness. On the way to church the elder was on the right side of the bridal couple and the younger on the left. The doves came along and pecked out one of the elder sister's eyes and one of the younger sister's eyes. Afterward, on the way out, the elder was on the left side and younger on the right, and the doves pecked out both the remaining eyes. So both sisters were punished with blindness to the end of their days for being so wicked and false.

A Chinese "Cinderella"

Tuan Ch'êng-shih

"The earliest datable version of the Cinderella story anywhere in the world occurs in a Chinese book written about 850–860 A.D." Thus begins Arthur Waley's essay on the Chinese "Cinderella" in the March 1947 edition of Folk-Lore. *The recorder of the tale is a man named Tuan Ch'êng-shih, whose father was an important official in Szechwan and who himself held a high post in the office arranging the ceremonies associated with imperial ancestor worship.*

Among the people of the south there is a tradition that before the Ch'in and Han dynasties there was a cave-master called Wu. The aborigines called the place the Wu cave. He married two wives. One wife died. She had a daughter called Yeh-hsien, who from childhood was intelligent and good at making pottery on the wheel. Her father loved her. After some years the father died, and she was ill-treated by her step-mother, who always made her collect firewood in dangerous places and draw water from deep pools. She once got a fish about two inches long, with red fins and golden eyes. She put it into a bowl of water. It grew bigger every day, and after she had changed the bowl several times she could find no bowl big enough for it, so she threw it into the back pond. Whatever food was left over from meals she put into the water to feed it. When she came to the pond, the fish always exposed its head and pillowed it on the bank; but when anyone else came, it did not come out. The step-mother knew about this, but when she watched for it, it did not once appear. So she tricked the girl, saying, "Haven't you worked hard! I am going to give you a new dress." She then made the girl change out of her tattered clothing. Afterwards she sent her to get water from another spring and reckoning that it was several hundred leagues, the step-mother at her leisure put on her daughter's clothes, hid a sharp blade up her sleeve, and went to the pond. She called to the fish. The fish at once put its head out, and she chopped it off and killed it. The fish was now more than ten feet long. She served it up and it tasted twice as good as an ordinary fish. She hid the bones under the dung-hill. Next day, when the girl came to the pond, no fish appeared. She howled with grief in the open countryside, and suddenly there appeared a man with his hair loose over his shoulders and coarse clothes. He came down from the sky. He consoled her, saying, "Don't howl! Your step-mother has killed the fish and its bones are under the dung. You go back, take the fish's bones and hide them in your room. Whatever you want, you have only to pray to them for it. It is bound to be granted." The girl followed his advice, and was able to provide herself with gold, pearls, dresses, and food whenever she wanted them.

When the time came for the cave-festival, the step-mother went, leaving the girl to keep watch over the fruit-trees in the garden. She waited till the step-mother was some way off, and then went herself, wearing a cloak of stuff spun from kingfisher feathers and shoes of gold. Her step-sister recognized her and said to the step-mother, "That's very like my sister." The step-mother suspected the same thing. The girl was aware of this and went away in such a hurry that she lost one shoe. It was picked up by one of the people of the cave. When the step-mother got home, she found the girl asleep, with her arms around one of the trees in the garden, and thought no more about it.

This cave was near to an island in the sea. On this island was a kingdom called T'o-han. Its soldiers had subdued twenty or thirty other islands and it had a coast-line of several thousand leagues. The cave-man sold the shoe in T'o-han, and the ruler of T'o-han got it. He told those about him to put it on; but it was an inch too small even for the one among them that had the smallest foot. He ordered all the women in his kingdom to try it on, but there was not one that it fitted. It was light as down and made no noise even when treading on stone. The king of T'o-han thought the cave-man had got it unlawfully. He put him in prison and tortured him, but did not end by finding out where it had come from. So he threw it down at the wayside. Then they went everywhere* through all the people's houses and arrested them. If there was a woman's shoe, they arrested them and told the king of T'o-han. He thought it strange, searched the inner-rooms and found Yeh-hsien. He made her put on the shoe, and it was true.

Yeh-hsien then came forward, wearing her cloak spun from halcyon feathers and her shoes. She was as beautiful as a heavenly being. She now

---

*Something here seems to have gone slightly wrong with the text. [Waley]

...continued A Chinese "Cinderella," **Tuan Ch'êng-shih**

___

began to render service to the king, and he took the fish-bones and Yeh-hsien, and brought them back to his country.

5   The step-mother and step-sister were shortly afterwards struck by flying stones, and died. The cave people were sorry for them and buried them in a stone-pit, which was called the Tomb of the Distressed Women. The men of the cave made mating-offerings there; any girl they prayed for there, they got. The king of T'o-han, when he got back to his kingdom, made Yeh-hsien his chief wife. The first year the king was very greedy and by his prayers to the fish-bones got treasures and jade without limit. Next year, there was no response, so the king buried the fish-bones on the seashore. He covered them with a hundred bushels of pearls and bordered them with gold. Later there was a mutiny of some soldiers who had been conscripted and their general opened (the hiding-place) in order to make better provision for his army. One night they (the bones) were washed away by the tide.

This story was told me by Li Shih-yuan, who has been in the service of my family a long while. He was himself originally a man from the caves of Yung-chou and remembers many strange things of the South.

The Maiden, the Frog, and the Chief's Son (An African "Cinderella")

The version of the "Cinderella" tale that follows was recorded in the Hausa (West African) language and published, originally, in 1911 by Frank Edgar. The tale remained unavailable to nonspeakers of Hausa until 1965, when Neil Skinner (of UCLA) completed an English translation.

There was once a man had two wives, and they each had a daughter. And the one wife, together with her daughter, he couldn't abide; but the other, with her daughter, he dearly loved.

Well, the day came when the wife that he disliked fell ill, and it so happened that her illness proved fatal, and she died. And her daughter was taken over by the other wife, the one he loved; and she moved into that wife's hut. And there she dwelt, having no mother of her own, just her father. And every day the woman would push her out, to go off to the bush to gather wood. When she returned, she had to pound up the *fura*. Then she had the *tuwo* to pound, and, after that, to stir. And then they wouldn't even let her eat the *tuwo*. All they gave her to eat were the burnt bits at the bottom of the pot. And day after day she continued thus.

Now she had an elder brother, and he invited her to come and eat regularly at his home—to which she agreed. But still when she had been to the bush, and returned home, and wanted a drink of water, they wouldn't let her have one. Nor would they give her proper food—only the coarsest of the grindings and the scrapings from the pot. These she would take, and going with them to a borrow-pit, throw them in. And the frogs would come out and start eating the scrapings. Then, having eaten them up, they would go back into the water; and she too would return home.

And so things went on day after day, until the day of the Festival arrived. And on this day, when she went along with the scrapings and coarse grindings, she found a frog squatting here; and realized that he was waiting for her! She got there and threw in the bits of food. Whereupon the frog said, "Maiden, you've always been very kind to us, and now we—but just you come along tomorrow morning. That's the morning of the Festival. Come along then, and we'll be kind to you, in our turn." "Fine," she said, and went off home.

5   Next morning was the Festival, and she was going off to the borrow-pit, just as the frog had told her. But as she was going, her half-sister's mother said to her, "Hey—come here, you good-for-nothing girl! You haven't stirred the *tuwo,* or pounded the *fura,* or fetched the wood or the water." So the girl returned. And the frog spent the whole day waiting for her. But she, having returned to the compound, set off to fetch wood. Then she fetched water, and set about pounding the *tuwo,* and stirred it till it was done and then took it off the fire. And presently she was told to take the scrapings. She did so and went off to the borrow-pit, where she found the frog. "Tut tut, girl!" said he, "I've been waiting for you here since morning, and you never came." "Old fellow," she said, "You see, I'm a slave." "How come?" he asked. "Simple," she said, "My mother died— died leaving me her only daughter. I have an elder brother, but he is married and has a compound of his own. And my father put me in the care of his other wife. And indeed he had never loved my mother. So I was moved into the hut of his other wife. And, as I told you, slavery is my lot. Every morning I have to go off to the bush to get wood. When I get back from that I have to pound the *fura,* and then I pound the *tuwo,* and then start stirring it. And even when I have finished stirring the *tuwo,* I'm not given it to eat—just the scrapings." Says the frog, "Girl, give us your hand." And she held it out to him, and they both leaped into the water.

Then he went and picked her up and swallowed her. (And he vomited her up.) "Good people," said he, "Look and tell me, is she straight or crooked?" And they looked and answered, "She is bent to the left." So he picked her up and swallowed her again and then brought her up, and

...continued The Maiden, the Frog, and the Chief's Son (An African "Cinderella")

again asked them the same question. "She's quite straight now," they said. "Good," said he.

Next he vomited up cloths for her, and bangles, and rings, and a pair of shoes, one of silver, one of gold. "And now," said he, "Off you go to the dancing." So all these things were given to her, and he said to her, "When you get there, and when the dancing is nearly over and the dancers dispersing, you're to leave your golden shoe, the right one, there." And the girl replied to the frog, "Very well, old fellow, I understand," and off she went.

Meanwhile the chief's son had caused the young men and girls to dance for his pleasure, and when she reached the space where they were dancing he saw her. "Well!" said the chief's son, "*There's* a maiden for you, if you like. Don't you let her go and join in the dancing—I don't care whose home she comes from. Bring her here!" So the servants of the chief's son went over and came back with her to where he was. He told her to sit down on the couch, and she took her seat there accordingly.

They chatted together for some time, till the dancers began to disperse. Then she said to the chief's son, "I must be going home." "Oh, are you off?" said he. "Yes," said she and rose to her feet. "I'll accompany you on your way for a little," said the chief's son, and he did so. But she had left her right shoe behind. Presently she said, "Chief's son, you must go back now," and he did so. And afterwards she too turned and made her way back.

10   And there she found the frog by the edge of the water waiting for her. He took her hand and the two of them jumped into the water. Then he picked her up and swallowed her, and again vomited her up; and there she was just as she had been before, a sorry sight. And taking her ragged things she went off home.

When she got there, she said, "Fellow-wife of my mother, I'm not feeling very well." And the other said, "Rascally slut! You have been up to no good—refusing to come home, refusing to fetch water or wood, refusing to pound the *fura* or make the *tuwo*. Very well then! No food for you today!" And so the girl set off to her elder brother's compound, and there ate her food, and so returned home again.

But meanwhile, the chief's son had picked up the shoe and said to his father, "Dad, I have seen a girl who wears a pair of shoes, one of gold, one of silver. Look, here's the golden one—she forgot it and left it behind. She's the girl I want to marry. So let all the girls of this town, young and old, be gathered together, and let this shoe be given to them to put on." "Very well," said the chief.

And so it was proclaimed, and all the girls, young and old, were collected and gathered together. And the chief's son went and sat there beside the shoe. Each girl came, and each tried on the shoe, but it fitted none of them, none of the girls of the town; until only the girl who had left it was left. Then someone said "Just a minute! There's that girl in so-and-so's compound, whose mother died." "Yes, that's right," said another, "Someone go and fetch her." And someone went and fetched her.

But the minute she arrived to try it on, the shoe itself of its own accord, ran across and made her foot get into it. Then said the chief's son, "Right, here's my wife."

At this, the other woman—the girl's father's other wife—said, "But the shoe belongs to my daughter; it was she who forgot it at the place of the dancing, not this good-for-nothing slut." But the chief's son insisted that, since he had seen the shoe fit the other girl, as far as he was concerned, she was the one to be taken to his compound in marriage. And so they took her there, and there she spent one night.

Next morning she went out of her hut and round behind it, and there saw the frog. She knelt respectfully and said, "Welcome, old fellow, welcome," and greeted him. Says he, "Tonight we shall be along to bring some things for you." "Thank you" said she, and he departed.

Well, that night, the frog rallied all the other frogs, and all his friends, both great and small came along. And he, their leader, said to them, "See here—my daughter is being married. So I want every one of you to make a contribution." And each of them went and fetched what he could afford, whereupon their leader thanked them all, and then vomited up a silver bed, a brass bed, a copper bed, and an iron bed, and went on vomiting up things for her—such as woollen blankets, and rugs, and satins, and velvets.

"Now," said he to the girl, "If your heart is ever troubled, just lie down on this brass bed," and he went on, "And when the chief's son's other wives come to greet you, give them two calabashes of cola-nuts and ten thousand cowrie shells; then, when his concubines come to greet you, give them one calabash of cola-nuts and five thousand cowries." "Very well," said she. Then he said, "And when the concubines come to receive corn for making *tuwo*, say to them, 'There's a hide-bag full, help yourselves.'" "Very well," she said. "And," he went on, "If your father's wife comes along with her daughter and asks you what it is like living in the chief's compound, say 'Living in the chief's compound is a wearisome business—for they measure out corn there with the shell of a Bambara groundnut.'"

So there she dwelt, until one day her father's favorite wife brought her daughter along at night, took her into the chief's compound, and brought the other girl out and took her to her own compound. There she said, "Oh! I forgot to get you to tell her all about married life in the chief's compound." "Oh, it's a wearisome business," answered our girl. "How so?" asked the older woman, surprised. "Well, they use the shell of a

...continued The Maiden, the Frog, and the Chief's Son (An African "Cinderella")

Bambara groundnut for measuring out corn. Then, if the chief's other wives come to greet you, you answer them with the 'Pf' of contempt. If the concubines come to greet you, you clear your throat, hawk, and spit. And if your husband comes into your hut, you yell at him." "I see," said the other—and her daughter stayed behind the chief's son's compound.

20   Next morning when it was light, the wives came to greet her—and she said "Pf" to them. The concubines came to greet her, and she spat at them. Then when night fell, the chief's son made his way to her hut, and she yelled at him. And he was amazed and went aside, and for two days pondered the matter.

Then he had his wives and concubines collected and said to them, "Look, now—I've called you to ask you. They haven't brought me the same girl. How did that one treat all of you?" "Hm—how indeed!" they all exclaimed. "Each morning, when we wives went to greet her, she would give us cola-nuts, two calabashes full, and cowries, ten thousand of them to buy tobacco flowers. And when the concubines went to greet her, she would give them a calabash of cola-nuts, and five thousand cowries to buy tobacco flowers with; and in the evening, for corn for *tuwo*, it would be a whole hide-bag full." "You see?" said he, "As for me, whenever I came to enter her hut, I found her respectfully kneeling. And she wouldn't get up from there, until I had entered and sat down on the bed."

"Hey," he called out, "Boys, come over here!" And when they came, he went into her hut and took a sword, and chopped her up into little pieces, and had them collect them and wrap them up in clothing; and then taken back to her home.

And when they got there, they found his true wife lying in the fire-place, and picking her up they took her back to her husband.

And next morning when it was light, she picked up a little gourd water-bottle and going around behind her hut, there saw the frog. "Welcome, welcome, old fellow," said she, and went on. "Old fellow, what I should like is to have a well built; and then you, all of you, can come and live in it and be close to me." "All right," said the frog, "You tell your husband." And she did so.

25   And he had a well dug for her, close to her hut. And the frogs came and entered the well and there they lived. That's all. *Kungurus kan kusu.*

Oochigeaskw—The Rough-Faced Girl
(A Native American "Cinderella")

The following version of the "Cinderella" tale was told, originally, in the Algonquin language. Native Americans who spoke Algonquian lived in the Eastern Woodlands of what is now the United States and in the northern, semiarctic areas of present-day Canada.

There was once a large village of the MicMac Indians of the Eastern Algonquins, built beside a lake. At the far end of the settlement stood a lodge, and in it lived a being who was always invisible. He had a sister who looked after him, and everyone knew that any girl who could see him might marry him. For that reason there were very few girls who did not try, but it was very long before anyone succeeded.

This is the way in which the test of sight was carried out: at evening-time, when the Invisible One was due to be returning home, his sister would walk with any girl who might come down to the lakeshore. She, of course, could see her brother, since he was always visible to her. As soon as she saw him, she would say to the girls:

"Do you see my brother?"

"Yes," they would generally reply—though some of them did say "No."

5   To those who said that they could indeed see him, the sister would say:

"Of what is his shoulder strap made?" Some people say that she would enquire:

"What is his moose-runner's haul?" or "With what does he draw his sled?"

And they would answer:

"A strip of rawhide" or "a green flexible branch," or something of that kind.

10   Then she, knowing that they had not told the truth, would say:

"Very well, let us return to the wigwam!"

When they had gone in, she would tell them not to sit in a certain place, because it belonged to the Invisible One. Then, after they had helped to cook the supper, they would wait with great curiosity, to see him eat. They could be sure he was a real person, for when he took off his moccasins they became visible, and his sister hung them up. But beyond this they saw nothing of him, not even when they stayed in the place all the night, as many of them did.

Now there lived in the village an old man who was a widower, and his three daughters. The youngest girl was very small, weak, and often ill: and yet her sisters, especially the elder, treated her cruelly. The second daughter was kinder, and sometimes took her side: but the wicked sister

...continued Oochigeaskw—The Rough-Faced Girl (A Native American "Cinderella")

would burn her hands and feet with hot cinders, and she was covered with scars from this treatment. She was so marked that people called her *Oochigeaskw,* the Rough-Faced Girl.

When her father came home and asked why she had such burns, the bad sister would at once say that it was her own fault, for she had dis-obeyed orders and gone near the fire and fallen into it.

15   These two elder sisters decided one day to try their luck at seeing the Invisible One. So they dressed themselves in their finest clothes, and tried to look their prettiest. They found the Invisible One's sister and took the usual walk by the water.

When he came, and when they were asked if they could see him, they answered: "Of course." And when asked about the shoulder strap or sled cord, they answered: "A piece of rawhide."

But of course they were lying like the others, and they got nothing for their pains.

The next afternoon, when the father returned home, he brought with him many of the pretty little shells from which wampum was made, and they set to work to string them.

That day, poor Little Oochigeaskw, who had always gone barefoot, got a pair of her father's moccasins, old ones, and put them into water to soften them so that she could wear them. Then she begged her sisters for a few wampum shells. The elder called her a "little pest," but the younger one gave her some. Now, with no other clothes than her usual rags, the poor little thing went into the woods and got herself some sheets of birch bark, from which she made a dress, and put marks on it for decoration, in the style of long ago. She made a petticoat and a loose gown, a cap, leg-gings, and a handkerchief. She put on her father's large old moccasins, which were far too big for her, and went forth to try her luck. She would try, she thought, to discover whether she could see the Invisible One.

20   She did not begin very well. As she set off, her sisters shouted and hooted, hissed and yelled, and tried to make her stay. And the loafers around the village, seeing the strange little creature, called out "Shame!"

The poor little girl in her strange clothes, with her face all scarred, was an awful sight, but she was kindly received by the sister of the Invis-ible One. And this was, of course, because this noble lady understood far more about things than simply the mere outside which all the rest of the world knows. As the brown of the evening sky turned to black, the lady took her down to the lake.

"Do you see him?" the Invisible One's sister asked.

"I do indeed—and he is wonderful!" said Oochigeaskw.

The sister asked:

25   "And what is his sled-string?"

The little girl said:

"It is the Rainbow."

"And, my sister, what is his bow-string?"

"It is The Spirit's Road—the Milky Way."

30 "So you *have* seen him," said his sister. She took the girl home with her and bathed her. As she did so, all the scars disappeared from her body. Her hair grew again, as it was combed, long, like a blackbird's wing. Her eyes were now like stars: in all the world there was no other such beauty. Then, from her treasures, the lady gave her a wedding garment, and adorned her.

Then she told Oochigeaskw to take the *wife's* seat in the wigwam: the one next to where the Invisible One sat, beside the entrance. And when he came in, terrible and beautiful, he smiled and said:

"So we are found out!"

"Yes," said his sister. And so Oochigeaskw became his wife.

Walt Disney's "Cinderella"

Adapted by Campbell Grant

Walter Elias Disney (1901–1966), winner of 32 Academy Awards, is famous throughout the world for his cartoon animations. After achieving recognition with cartoon shorts populated by such immortals as Mickey Mouse and Donald Duck, he produced the full-length animated film version of Snow White and the Seven Dwarfs *in 1937. He followed with other animations, including* Cinderella *(1950), which he adapted from Perrault's version of the tale. A* Little Golden Book, *the text of which appears here, was then adapted by Campbell Grant from the film.*

Once upon a time in a far-away land lived a sweet and pretty girl named Cinderella. She made her home with her mean old stepmother and her two stepsisters, and they made her do all the work in the house.

Cinderella cooked and baked. She cleaned and scrubbed. She had no time left for parties and fun.

But one day an invitation came from the palace of the king.

A great ball was to be given for the prince of the land. And every young girl in the kingdom was invited.

5 "How nice!" thought Cinderella. "I am invited, too."

But her mean stepsisters never thought of her. They thought only of themselves, of course. They had all sorts of jobs for Cinderella to do.

...*continued* Walt Disney's "Cinderella," **Adapted by Campbell Grant**

"Wash this slip. Press this dress. Curl my hair. Find my fan."

They both kept shouting, as fast as they could speak.

"But I must get ready myself. I'm going, too," said Cinderella.

"You!" they hooted. "The Prince's ball for you?"

And they kept her busy all day long. She worked in the morning, while her stepsisters slept. She worked all afternoon, while they bathed and dressed. And in the evening she had to help them put on the finishing touches for the ball. She had not one minute to think of herself.

Soon the coach was ready at the door. The ugly stepsisters were powdered, pressed, and curled. But there stood Cinderella in her workaday rags.

"Why, Cinderella!" said the stepsisters. "You're not dressed for the ball."

"No," said Cinderella. "I guess I cannot go."

Poor Cinderella sat weeping in the garden.

Suddenly a little old woman with a sweet, kind face stood before her. It was her fairy godmother.

"Hurry, child!" she said. "You are going to the ball!"

Cinderella could hardly believe her eyes! The fairy godmother turned a fat pumpkin into a splendid coach.

Next her pet mice became horses, and her dog a fine footman. The barn horse was turned into a coachman.

"There, my dear," said the fairy godmother. "Now into the coach with you, and off to the ball you go."

"But my dress—" said Cinderella.

"Lovely, my dear," the fairy godmother began. Then she really looked at Cinderella's rags.

"Oh, good heavens," she said. "You can never go in that." She waved her magic wand.

"*Salaga doola,*
Menchicka boola,
Bibbidi bobbidi boo!" she said.

There stood Cinderella in the loveliest ball dress that ever was. And on her feet were tiny glass slippers!

"Oh," cried Cinderella. "How can I ever thank you?"

"Just have a wonderful time at the ball, my dear," said her fairy godmother. "But remember, this magic lasts only until midnight. At the stroke of midnight, the spell will be broken. And everything will be as it was before."

"I will remember," said Cinderella. "It is more than I ever dreamed of."

Then into the magic coach she stepped, and was whirled away to the ball.

10

15

20

25

And such a ball! The king's palace was ablaze with lights. There was music and laughter. And every lady in the land was dressed in her beautiful best.

But Cinderella was the loveliest of them all. The prince never left her side, all evening long. They danced every dance. They had supper side by side. And they happily smiled into each other's eyes.

But all at once the clock began to strike midnight, Bong Bong Bong—

"Oh!" cried Cinderella. "I almost forgot!"

And without a word, away she ran, out of the ballroom and down the palace stairs. She lost one glass slipper. But she could not stop.

Into her magic coach she stepped, and away it rolled. But as the clock stopped striking, the coach disappeared. And no one knew where she had gone.

Next morning all the kingdom was filled with the news. The Grand Duke was going from house to house, with a small glass slipper in his hand. For the prince had said he would marry no one but the girl who could wear that tiny shoe.

Every girl in the land tried hard to put it on. The ugly stepsisters tried hardest of all. But not a one could wear the glass shoe.

And where was Cinderella? Locked in her room. For the mean old stepmother was taking no chances of letting her try on the slipper. Poor Cinderella! It looked as if the Grand Duke would surely pass her by.

But her little friends the mice got the stepmother's key. And they pushed it under Cinderella's door. So down the long stairs she came, as the Duke was just about to leave.

"Please!" cried Cinderella. "Please let me try."

And of course the slipper fitted, since it was her very own.

That was all the Duke needed. Now his long search was done. And so Cinderella became the prince's bride, and lived happily ever after—and the little pet mice lived in the palace and were happy ever after, too.

Cinderella

Anne Sexton

Anne Sexton (1928–1974) has been acclaimed as one of America's outstanding contemporary poets. In 1967, she won the Pulitzer Prize for poetry for Live or Die. *She published four other collections of her work, including* Transformations, *in which she recast, with a modern twist, popular European fairy tales such as "Cinderella." Sexton's poetry has appeared in the* New Yorker, Harper's, The Atlantic, *and* Saturday Review. *She received a Robert Frost*

...*continued* Cinderella, **Anne Sexton**

Fellowship (1959), a scholarship from Radcliffe College's New Institute for Independent Study (1961–1963), a grant from the Ford Foundation (1964), and a Guggenheim Award (1969). In her book All My Pretty Ones, Sexton quoted Franz Kafka: "The books we need are the kind that act upon us like a misfortune, that make us suffer like the death of someone we love more than ourselves. A book should serve as the axe for the frozen sea within us." Asked in an interview (by Patricia Marz) about this quotation, Sexton responded: "I think [poetry] should be a shock to the senses. It should almost hurt."

You always read about it;
the plumber with twelve children
who wins the Irish Sweepstakes.
From toilets to riches.
5 That story.

Or the nursemaid,
some luscious sweet from Denmark
who captures the oldest son's heart.
From diapers to Dior.
10 That story.

Or a milkman who serves the wealthy,
eggs, cream, butter, yogurt, milk,
the white truck like an ambulance
who goes into real estate
15 and makes a pile.
From homogenized to martinis at lunch.

Or the charwoman
who is on the bus when it cracks up
and collects enough from the insurance.
20 From mops to Bonwit Teller.
That story.

Once
the wife of a rich man was on her deathbed
and she said to her daughter Cinderella:
25 Be devout. Be good, Then I will smile
down from heaven in the seam of a cloud.
The man took another wife who had
two daughters, pretty enough
but with hearts like blackjacks.
30 Cinderella was their maid.

She slept on the sooty hearth each night
and walked around looking like Al Jolson.
Her father brought presents home from town,
jewels and gowns for the other women
35   but the twig of a tree for Cinderella.
She planted that twig on her mother's grave
and it grew to a tree where a white dove sat.
Whenever she wished for anything the dove
would drop it like an egg upon the ground.
40   The bird is important, my dears, so heed him.
Next came the ball, as you all know.
It was a marriage market.
The prince was looking for a wife.
All but Cinderella were preparing
45   and gussying up for the big event.
Cinderella begged to go too.
Her stepmother threw a dish of lentils
into the cinders and said: Pick them
up in an hour and you shall go.
50   The white dove brought all his friends;
all the warm wings of the fatherland came,
and picked up the lentils in a jiffy.
No, Cinderella, said the stepmother,
you have no clothes and cannot dance.
55   That's the way with stepmothers.

Cinderella went to the tree at the grave
and cried forth like a gospel singer:
Mama! Mama! My turtledove,
send me to the prince's ball!
60   The bird dropped down a golden dress
and delicate little gold slippers
Rather a large package for a simple bird.
So she went. Which is no surprise.

Her stepmother and sisters didn't
65   recognize her without her cinder face
and the prince took her hand on the spot
and danced with no other the whole day.
As nightfall came she thought she'd better
get home. The prince walked her home
70   and she disappeared into the pigeon house
and although the prince took an axe and broke
it open she was gone. Back to her cinders.
These events repeated themselves for three days.
However on the third day the prince
75   covered the palace steps with cobbler's wax
and Cinderella's gold shoe stuck upon it.

...continued Cinderella, **Anne Sexton**

Now he would find whom the shoe fit
and find his strange dancing girl for keeps.
He went to their house and the two sisters
80   were delighted because they had lovely feet.
The eldest went into a room to try the slipper on
but her big toe got in the way so she simply
sliced it off and put on the slipper.
The prince rode away with her until the white dove
85   told him to look at the blood pouring forth.
That is the way with amputations.
They don't just heal up like a wish.
The other sister cut off her heel
but the blood told as blood will.
90   The prince was getting tired.
He began to feel like a shoe salesman.
But he gave it one last try.
This time Cinderella fit into the shoe
like a love letter into its envelope.

95   At the wedding ceremony
the two sisters came to curry favor
and the white dove pecked their eyes out.
Two hollow spots were left
like soup spoons.

100   Cinderella and the prince
lived, they say, happily ever after,
like two dolls in a museum case
never bothered by diapers or dust,
never arguing over the timing of an egg,
105   never telling the same story twice,
never getting a middle-aged spread,
their darling smiles pasted on for eternity.

Regular Bobbsey Twins.
That story.

The Rise of Perrault's "Cinderella"

Bonnie Cullen

In this next selection, art historian Bonnie Cullen explains how, from among the hundreds of "Cinderellas" throughout the world, Charles Perrault's version came to be what many in the West think of as the canonical, or standard, one. Of the seven variants of "Cinderella" named in this article, six appear earlier in the chapter. A longer version of this article first appeared in The Lion and the Unicorn *(Volume 27, 2003).*

Why [did] Perrault's story, above all others, [become the dominant version of "Cinderella"]? Considering its origins, there were many contestants for the dominant tale. "Cinderella" is really a large family of tales first analyzed by folklorists in the nineteenth century. Studying more than 300 related narratives from Europe and Asia, Marian Roalfe Cox (1893) identified Cinderella stories according to the presence of certain themes: an abused child, rescue through some reincarnation of the dead mother, recognition, and marriage.

The earliest known Cinderella story is actually a literary version from ninth-century China. Already it has the familiar elements. Yeh-hsien (Cinderella) has lost both her father and mother and seeks consolation from a pet fish. Her cruel stepmother eats the fish and buries the bones. A man comes from the sky advising her to find and save the bones—she will get whatever she wishes for.

When her stepmother and stepsister leave for a festival, Yeh-hsien follows them in a cloak of kingfisher feathers and gold shoes. She loses a shoe, the shoe is found, and given to a king. A search for the foot small enough to fit the shoe ensues. Yeh-hsien is finally shown to be the rightful owner and marries the king (Ting, 1974).

In most early Cinderella tales, the dead mother hovers protectively, reincarnated as a cow, a fish, or a tree. Her relationship with the grieving daughter is as significant as the girl's triumph. Occasionally the protagonist is male. The shoe is not always the means of identification, although it is extremely common, as is the use of some magic garment (Philip, 1989).

5   By the sixteenth century, Cinderella appears in print in the West. One major debut is in Basile's (Canepa, 1999) seventeenth-century collection, *Il Pentamerone (Lo cunto de li cunti),* as the feisty "Gatta Cenerentola" or "Cat Cinderella." Zezolla (Cinderella) kills her wicked stepmother with the help of a governess, but when the governess marries Zezolla's father, the girl is mistreated again. A fairy in a tree supplies magic clothes and a coach for a feast where Zezolla captures a king's heart.

In Basile's (Canepa, 1999) tale, the dead mother is no longer a significant presence, although she might be vaguely identified with the fairy. While close to some oral versions, his bawdy narrative is full of intricate metaphors and clearly written for an adult audience. The book was published in Neapolitan dialect, which probably limited its dissemination in print (Canepa, 1999; Opie & Opie, 1992), although Basile's stories may have passed into the oral repertoire and traveled in other languages.

During the ancien régime of Louis the XIV, folktales were transformed into a new literary genre, the fairy tale. Narrated as a kind of conversational game in the salons of the *précieuses,* by the end of the century they were being written down (Zipes, *Beauties,* 1989; Warner, 1995). Two distinct versions of "Cinderella" issued from the pens of Charles Perrault and the Countess d'Aulnoy.

Marie-Catherine Le Jumel de Barneville, Baronne d'Aulnoy (1892), was a feminist and writer, the first to publish her stories as "fairy tales," or literary versions of popular folktales. Her Cinderella, "Finette Cendron," is both altruistic and spirited. When their parents abandon Finette and her sisters, she engineers daring escapes for all three. They plot against her, but Finette remains loyal. With a godmother's help she finds some magnificent clothing and triumphs at the ball. She loses a shoe and gallops back to claim it, but refuses to marry the prince until her parents' kingdom, which they lost, is restored.*

*An example of Finette's resourcefulness: Held captive in a castle, Finette devises a plan when a hungry ogre orders her and her two sisters to cook for him and his ogress (instead of eating them straightaway). It is the last request he makes:

"But," said [the ogre], turning to Finette, "when you have lit the fire, how can you tell if the oven be hot enough?" "My lord," she answered, "I throw butter in, and then I taste it with my tongue." "Very well," he said, "light the fire then." The oven was as big as a stable, for the ogre and ogress ate more bread than two armies. The princess made an enormous fire, which blazed like a furnace; and the ogre, who was standing by, ate a hundred lambs and a hundred sucking pigs while waiting for the new bread. [Finette's sisters] Fleur d'Amour and Belle-de-Nuit kneaded the dough. "Well," said the great ogre, "is the oven hot?" "My lord," replied Finette, "you will see presently." And so saying she threw a thousand pounds of butter into the oven. "I should try it with my tongue," she said, "but I am too little." "I am big enough," said the ogre, and bending down he went so far into the oven that he could not draw back again, so that he was burned to the bones. When the ogress came to the oven she was mightily astonished to find a mountain of cinders instead of her husband.

Fleur d'Amour and Belle-de-Nuit, who saw that she was in great distress, comforted her as they could, but they feared lest her grief should be consoled only too soon, and that regaining her appetite she would put them in a salad, as she had meant to do before. So they said to her: "Take courage, madam; you will find some king or some marquis who will be happy to marry you." At that she smiled a little, showing her teeth, which were longer than your finger. When they saw she was in a good humour, Finette said: "If you

Perrault's "Cendrillon" is quite a different lady. He dubs her chief virtue "la bonne grace," i.e., in the face of adversity she is generous, long-suffering, charming and good-humored; the ideal bride, from the gentleman's perspective.

10   A bland protagonist perhaps, but Perrault exhibits his wit. Cendrillon plays her own tricks on the sisters, asking one if she can borrow a dress to see the mysterious princess at the next ball. He also writes tongue-in-cheek. The slipper, evoking female virginity, is made of glass in his tale. Not only is it fragile and extremely pure, but Perrault hints that visual proof will be necessary.

Perrault's position as a member of the French Academy may have led him to adopt this tone for tales of the peasant class (Warner, 1995). He also shifts the spotlight to the fairy godmother, giving her a dominant role. In the ancien régime, fairies were equated with powerful women at court. D'Aulnoy's (1892) fairy is sympathetic and dignified, asking Finette to be her lady's maid and comb her hair. Her magic is in providing the necessary items, whether or not she is present. Perrault's elaborate description of rat-and-pumpkin tricks is a spoof: his fairy godmother is a witch.

• • •

When literary Cinderellas began to appear in English in the eighteenth century, it was Madame d'Aulnoy's (1892) story that took the lead. [An early version of her work appeared] in *A Collection of Novels and Tales, Written by that Celebrated Wit of France, the Countess d'Anois* (1721–22). Perrault's *Contes* did not appear in English until 1729.

By the nineteenth century, the tables had turned, apparently. Only seven English editions of d'Aulnoy's (1892) tales survive in the British Library; not all contain "Finette." There are over thirty editions of Perrault's "Cinderella" as a separate volume, besides its inclusion with the tales. Perrault's story was also adapted for pantomime and plays.

Perrault's version faced new competition, however. Searching for an antidote to bourgeois life—the stale "getting and spending," as Wordsworth put it—Romantics turned to nature. Might not the oral tales of

---

would but leave off wearing those horrible bear-skins, and dress a little more fashionably! We could arrange your hair beautifully, and you would be like a star." "Come then," she said, "let us see what you can do; but be sure that if I find any ladies more beautiful than myself I shall hack you into little bits." Thereupon the three princesses took off her cap, and began to comb and curl her hair, entertaining her all the while with their chatter. Then Finette took a hatchet, and with a great blow from behind, severed her head from her body.

For the complete version of d'Aulnoy's "Finette Cendron," go to http://www.surlalunefairytales .com/authors/aulnoy/1892/finettecendron.html.

country folk contain some primal wisdom? How closely they transcribed their originals is debated, but the Grimm brothers believed they were collecting rather than writing stories as they prepared their editions of *Die Kinder- und Hausmärchen* in 1812 (Warner, 1995). Their "Cinderella," "Aschenputtel," is indeed close to folk versions such as the Scottish tale, "Rashin Coatie" (Opie & Opie, 1992).

15   Mourning and revenge underlie "Aschenputtel": the heroine plants a tree on her mother's grave and tends it lovingly. A bird in the tree answers her calls for help. She begs for a dress, attends the feast and attracts the prince. The sisters cheat at the slipper test, cutting off parts of their feet, but birds reveal their deceit and at the wedding, peck out the sisters' eyes.

"Primal" tales had their opponents. With the first English translation, in volume two of *German Popular Stories* (1826), the brutal eye-pecking disappeared. During the previous century, the market for printed tales had expanded through chapbooks, devoured by a new audience of young readers as well as adults. By the end of the eighteenth century there was a movement in England to sanitize children's literature. Mrs. Trimmer (1802), reviewing children's books for middle-class families; argued that the often brutal tales "excite . . . groundless fears" and "serve no moral purpose" (pp. 185–86). This explains the intrusion of religious motifs, such as praying and church architecture, in chapbook illustration from the early nineteenth century, and the relative scarcity of expensive editions at the time.

Fairy tales would not go away, however. Those who wanted to imbue them with bourgeois morality faced equally vociferous champions of "pure" tales. "A child," Ruskin (1972) wrote, "should not need to chose between right and wrong. It should not be capable of wrong . . . " (p. 83). Innocent, children could be "fortif[ied] . . . against the glacial cold of selfish science" with the "inextinguishable life" of the folk tradition (p. 83). As Zipes (*Victorian,* 1987) points out, arguments about fairy tales became part of the greater "Condition of England" debate on the effects of the Industrial Revolution.

In the case of "Cinderella," it was a somewhat revised Perrault that prevailed in Victorian England.

• • •

One reason Perrault's tale [did so] was its suitability for a modern audience. During the nineteenth century, the market for literary fairy tales in England was increasingly urban and middleclass. Perrault focuses on the social sphere, rather than the forest. He delineates hairdos, costume, behavior at the ball and reactions to Cendrillon's appearance with the ironic tone of a society reporter.

20   D'Aulnoy's (1892) Finette is busy slaying ogres and galloping through the mud, while in "Aschenputtel" there is blood from the sisters' mutilated feet. Romantics like Ruskin (1972) favored the rugged terrain of folktales, but as Mrs. Trimmer's (1801–1805) remarks indicate, "polite" readers were concerned about "improving" young minds to function effectively in society.

More important, perhaps, Perrault's tale prevailed in English because it was the best vehicle for Victorian notions of femininity. D'Aulnoy's (1892) heroine liberates herself through female power, both magical and human. Folk Cinderellas like Aschenputtel also take action, advised by incarnations of their lost mothers. Perrault's Cendrillon is the least active, and he shifts the spotlight to her fairy godmother, whose magic is as amusing as it is powerful.

Whether or not the oral fairy tale had been a female genre, as Warner (1995) argues, by the nineteenth century the fairy tale in print was increasingly dominated by male writers and illustrators in an industry controlled by male publishers. That even some women writers followed the "party line" with canonical Cinderellas shows how powerful a formula it was for the middleclass market of nineteenth-century England.

It is interesting to note that Disney's revival of "Cinderella," which repeats the Victorian interpretation of Perrault's story, came out in 1950: a time when women, indispensable in the workforce during the war years, were being urged back home with imagery of ideal wives and mothers. There have been attempts to reclaim the tale in recent years in both print and film. Yet the canonical tale, with its Victorian ideology, persists.

References

Canepa, N. L. (1999). *From court to forest. Giambattista Basile's lo cunto de li cunti and the birth of the literary fairy tale.* Detroit: Wayne State UP.

Cox, M. R. (1893). *Cinderella; three hundred and forty-five variants.* London: Folk-lore Society (no. 31).

D'Aulnoy, M. C. B. (1892). *The fairy tales of Madame D'Aulnoy.* A. Macdonnell & Miss Lee (Trans.). London: Lawrence and Bullen.

Opie, I., & Opie, P. (1992). *The classic fairy tales.* Oxford: Book Club Associates.

Philip, N. (1989). *The Cinderella story.* Harmondsworth: Penquin.

Ruskin, J. (1972, May). *Fairy stories.* Lance Salway (Ed.). *Signal,* 81–86.

Ting, N-T. (1974). *The Cinderella cycle in China and Indo-China.* Helsinki: Suomalainen.

Trimmer, S. (1801–05). *The guardian of education.* 5 vols. London: J. Johnson.

Warner, M. (1995). *From the beast to the blond*. London: Vintage.

Zipes, J. D. (1989). *Beauties, beast and enchantment: Classic French fairy tales*. New York: New American Library.

———. (1987). *Victorian fairy tales: The revolt of the fairies and elves*. New York: Methuen.

The Princess Paradox

James Poniewozik

In this appraisal of Cinderella movies, beginning with The Princess Diaries (2001), *James Poniewozik explores some of the feminist themes that have found their way into updates of the classic tale. Moviemakers have reinvented Cinderella for the twenty-first century—almost: she's strong and resourceful, but she still loves her ball gowns. Poniewozik is media and television critic for* Time *magazine (and before that Salon.com). This article first appeared in* Time *on April 5, 2004.*

It's the recurring nightmare of high-minded modern parents of daughters. You ask your relatives to lay off the pink pinafores at the baby shower. You give your daughter Legos and soccer balls, not Barbies. You encourage her to play fire fighter and immerse her in Dora the Explorer videos. Then one Halloween rolls around, and your empowered, self-confident budding Marie Curie tells you that she wants to be . . . a princess.

Call it nature or nurture, harmless fantasy or insidious indoctrination, but Hollywood is discovering that it still pays not to fight the royal urge. Following 2001's $108 million—grossing *The Princess Diaries*, Hollywood has waved its wand and conjured a set of Cinderella stories for girls, including next month's *The Prince & Me* and *Ella Enchanted*, as well as *A Cinderella Story* in July and a sequel in August. That's not to mention other fairy-tale projects (*Shrek 2*) and transformational stories like *13 Going On 30*, in which a gawky teen is magically morphed into a fashion-plate magazine editor played by the perpetually miniskirted Jennifer Garner.

We've come a long way, it seems, from the girls-kick-ass culture of just a few years ago (*Charlie's Angels; Crouching Tiger, Hidden Dragon*) in which a 360 [degrees] flying-roundhouse kick was a girl's best friend.

(On the proto girl-power cartoon, *Powerpuff Girls*, one of the heroines' worst enemies was a spoiled brat named Princess Morbucks.) But brush off the fairy dust, and you find a new kind of Cinderella, one who would rather save Prince Charming, thank you, and who has learned the lessons of feminism—or at least learned to pay lip service to them. You can have the girly dream of glass slippers and true love, these films say, as well as the womanly ideal of self-determination and independence—and any contradictions between them are no match for the movies' magic.

Ella Enchanted, for instance, is a spoof of Cinderella in which the title character (*Diaries'* Anne Hathaway, Hollywood's queen of princesses) spends her free time protesting the discriminatory anti-elf and -giant policies of the family of Prince Charmont (Hugh Dancy). What she wants at first is not love but to free herself of a fairy's curse that forces her to be obedient. In *The Prince & Me* (what, *The Prince & I* would have been too egghead y?), Paige Morgan (Julia Stiles) is a workaholic soon-to-be medical student who rolls her eyes at friends rushing to get their M.R.S. degrees. When she falls for Eddie (Luke Mably), a rakish-but-sweet exchange student who turns out to be Danish Crown Prince Edvard, the prospect of becoming queen upsets her dreams of working for Doctors Without Borders. (Stiles, who played Ophelia in the 2000 film *Hamlet,* should know that dating the prince of Denmark can be a pain.) "The Cinderella story has always frustrated me," Stiles says. "What I like about *The Prince & Me* is that my character is a lot more active and is ready to live a life by herself and be independent."

5   SPOILER ALERT: Skip this paragraph if you don't want to know how these movies end. O.K., here's the shocker—they end happily. What is surprising, however, is that, in the original ending of *The Prince & Me*, Paige broke up with Edvard to go to med school (in the final version, she gets to have both the guy and the career). And what's downright shocking is that Paramount approved the first, decidedly non-fairy-tale ending. "But when I saw it," says director Martha Coolidge, "I knew it was wrong. What was wrong about it was not what we thought—whether she got together with him or not. The real issue was about him making a compromise and the monarchy making a compromise."

Reinventing fairy tales has been a favorite project of feminist authors from Angela Carter (*The Bloody Chamber*) to Marlo Thomas (*Free to Be . . . You and Me*), who understood that wish-fulfillment stories are about teaching people what they should wish for. Among an earlier generation of women, the wish was to be able to do everything men could. For the modern Cinderellas' audience, which takes that freedom as a given, the wish is to also be able—unashamedly—to fall in love and go to the ball. Indeed, in *Prince*, Paige realizes that she needs to be "rescued" from her disciplined but single-minded careerism as much as she needs to assert her independence. Girls asserting their right to choose the fairy-tale ending is not a bad thing, says Thomas, since now the movies are balanced by varied depictions of young women in films from *Whale Rider* to *Blue Crush*. "What women have tried to achieve for other women," she says, "is choice in every step of their lives."

But to succeed on both the feminist and the fantasy level, the new Cinderella has developed rules and conventions as strict as a Joseph Campbell template.* She should be pretty, but in a class-president way, not a head-cheerleader way. She should be able to stand up for herself (recall the *Crouching Tiger* moves of *Shrek's* Princess Fiona). She must be socially conscious—a result, says Meg Cabot, author of the *Princess Diaries* books, of Princess Diana's charitable work. And she should above all not want to be a princess—at least until she changes her mind. In *Diaries* . . . it's not the girl who must prove herself worthy of princesshood; princesshood must prove itself worthy of the girl.

There's something a little have-your-tiara-and-disdain-it-too about making your protagonists ambivalent about the very fantasy that people paid $9 to see them live out. But that may make the fantasy more palatable to parents and filmmakers: men and, especially, women who are educated professionals. "I don't want to sound like an archfeminist," says Sherry Lansing, chairman of Paramount, which produced *Prince*, "but it really is important that it imparts contemporary values. It's a good love that allows both people to remain whole in it." Still, the fantasy couple that this earnestness yields in *Prince* is more yuppie than romantic: she, committing to years of med school; he, giving up his love of car racing to strap on a necktie and negotiate labor disputes. Goodbye, Chuck and Di; hello, Abbey and Jed Bartlet.†

But it's easy for someone who has been through college to say a diploma and career are not cure-alls. The movies' audience of young girls makes the filmmakers much more message conscious—at least as far as

---

*Joseph Campbell (1904–1987) is best known for his work in comparative mythology. In *The Hero with a Thousand Faces* (1949), he traces how heroes in myths and folklore thousands of years old, from cultures around the world, progress through recognizable stages on their journeys away from the ordinary world, to a magical realm of adventure and severe challenge, then back to the ordinary. The classic versions of "Cinderella" that you have read in this chapter illustrate important features of what Campbell called a "monomyth"; here Poniewozik is suggesting, ironically, that the newer, filmed versions of "Cinderella" are similarly formulaic, though in ways calculated to sell tickets.

†Chuck and Di: As the older son of Queen Elizabeth II, Charles, Prince of Wales, is next in line to become King of England. "Di" is Diana, to whom Charles was married, then divorced. Jed (Josiah) and Abbey Bartlet: president and First Lady of the United States in the long-running television series *The West Wing*. Poniewozik is suggesting that Charles and Diana, a traditional royal couple, have given way in the popular imagination—or, at least, in the projected fantasies of the movie industry—to Abbey and Josiah Bartlet. Abbey is a Harvard Medical School graduate and practicing physician who will not hesitate to correct her husband.

the girls are concerned. The princes in these stories have fewer options than their Cinderellas. Edvard and Charmont are both reluctant to become king, but they learn, through the love of a good woman, to mature into the role and use it for good. The girls fight to control their destiny; the boys good-naturedly learn to accept theirs. Of course, they're not the target audience. "It's nice to have something that's not toxic or repellent to men," says Nina Jacobson, a top executive at Disney (*Diaries'* studio). "But we know we don't need guys to make a movie like that successful." You just need a feisty girl, a prophylactic dose of skepticism and a fabulous ball gown—about which no ambivalence is necessary.

STUDENT MODELS

WHO DO YOU WANT TO BE?

Finding Heritage in Walker's "Everyday Use"

"You just don't understand."
"What don't I understand?"
"Your heritage" (Walker, 2001, p. 297).

1   Whose heritage is Dee talking about? Is it her family's heritage or her ethnic heritage?

2   This exchange takes place near the end of Alice Walker's (2001) short story "Everyday Use" when Dee is saying goodbye to her mother and her sister Maggie after a brief visit and an argument about some quilts. That visit was almost like a treasure hunt for Dee. It seems that Dee, who now has the name Wangero Leewanika Kemanjo, came to visit because she wants to try to identify herself with the past. She wants to take parts of a butter churn and some family quilts back home with her, but Mama says "no" about the quilts because she promised them to Maggie. Dee thinks that Maggie can't "appreciate" the quilts and is "backward enough to put them to everyday use" (p. 297). This confrontation over the quilts suggests that Dee may have learned a lot in college about her ethnic background as an African American, but she does not understand or appreciate her own family's heritage.

3   At first, a reader might think that Dee/Wangero has come home to express her appreciation for her family's heritage. While Mama is waiting for her, she expects that Dee will want to tear down the family house because it is just like the one that burned down when she was a child there. Dee hated that house. But when Dee arrives, before she even tells her mother her new name, she begins taking "picture after picture" of her mother and Maggie, "making sure the house is included" (Walker, p. 294) in every one. It seems that Dee is proud to include the house in her heritage—but is it her ethnic heritage or her family heritage? What will she do with the pictures? Are they something to remember her family with or are they something "artistic" that she will use to display her ethnic heritage?

4   When Dee explains her new name to her mother, she seems to have forgotten part of her family heritage. Wangero says that "Dee" is "dead" because "I couldn't bear it any longer, being named after the people who oppress me" (Walker, p. 295). After her mother explains that she is actually named after Aunt Dee and Grandma Dee, Wangero Leewanika

Kemanjo may gain some appreciation of the family tradition because she says that Mama doesn't have to call her the new name "if you don't want to" (p. 295). But Mama shows her own respect for her own daughter by saying "I'll get used to it" (p. 296).

5   When the treasure hunt part of the visit begins after the dinner, Dee's concern for ethnic heritage becomes clear. Dee wants items from the past that she identifies with her ethnic heritage. She jumps up from the table and declares that she needs the churn top. She asks, "Didn't Uncle Buddy whittle it [the churn] out of a tree you all used to have?" (Walker, p. 296). She is talking about the churn top in terms of family heritage, but when she says that she intends to use it as a centerpiece on an alcove table, the reader understands that for Dee the churn is more significant for the ethnic heritage it represents. Many blacks could not afford to buy butter, so they had to make it themselves. (In fact, her mother is still using that churn to make butter.) She also wants the dasher from the churn. For Maggie and Mama, it is a tool in the present that represents family history. Maggie explains that Aunt Dee's first husband, Stash, whittled it; when Mama (the narrator) looks it over she notices the "small sinks" in the wood from the hands of people who had used it (including her own, no doubt). There is a strong contrast between their attitude toward the heirloom and Dee/Wangero's. She laughs at Maggie's story (family heritage), saying Maggie has a "brain . . . like an elephant's" and announces that she herself will "think of something artistic to do with the dasher" (p. 296). For all of them, the dasher represents the hard work blacks have had to struggle through, but for Mama and Maggie, it is a tool made by a family member to help with that work today. For Wangero it is an ethnic heritage object to display.

6   The final two items that Dee wants are the hand-stitched quilts that she digs out of Mama's trunk. They represent family heritage because they contain pieces of her ancestors' clothing, including a tiny piece from the blue uniform of a great-grandfather who fought in the Civil War. That family heritage is very strong for Mama, who was planning to give the quilts to Maggie as a wedding present. She remembers, but doesn't say anything, that Dee/Wangero had refused to take a quilt with her to college because they were old fashioned. Dee loses her temper over the idea of Maggie using the quilts on a bed because "in five years they'd be in rags" (Walker, p. 297). Mama says that then Maggie would make new ones. But Dee wants "*these* quilts," the ones with pieces of her own family's clothing. This may appear to be an appreciation of family heritage, but since Dee/Wangero wants to hang the quilts on the wall, not use them for a practical purpose, it seems that she wants to display a heritage that she doesn't want to live anymore.

7   Maggie is willing to give up the quilts, saying she can remember Grandma Dee without them, but Mama grabs the quilts back from Dee. The conflict here is not only about remembering but also about how to remember. Although Dee wants to preserve the original quilts with their antique pieces, she keeps separating herself from the family heritage that created them.

8   As Dee gets into the car to leave, she puts on a pair of sunglasses that hide "everything above the tip of her nose and her chin" (Walker, p. 297). If, as the saying goes, the eyes are the windows to the soul, then Dee is hiding her soul. By wearing the sunglasses, Dee is hiding who she truly is and just wants to be identified with the color of her skin, her ethnic heritage. She tells Maggie that "[i]t's really a new day for us" although "from the way you . . . live, you'd never know it" (p. 297).

9   Mama and Maggie may live in a very old-fashioned setting, using old-fashioned tools every day, but Dee/Wangero's attitude about her family and its heirlooms shows that actually she is the person who does not understand her heritage.

Reference

Walker, A. (2001). Everyday Use. In S. T. Range (Ed.), *Best short stories*, (pp. 294–297). New York: Whitfield.

Technology's Peril and Potential

Kate MacAulay (student)

Introduces focusing questions and context

Introduces the texts to be analyzed

Brief summary of Ritzer's text

Recently in English class, we have been focusing on the question, What effect is technology having on humanity and the quality of life in the twenty-first century? We have had heated discussions about the use of cell phones, palm pilots, beepers, e-mail, chat rooms, texting, and the Web. As part of my investigation of this question, I read two texts: a chapter from George Ritzer's (2000) book *The McDonaldization of Society*, entitled "The Irrationality of Rationality: Traffic Jams on Those 'Happy Trails,'" and an article published in the magazine *Wired* entitled "Who Am We?", by Sherry Turkle (1996). In his chapter, Ritzer, a sociology professor, explains how technology has rationalized businesses and many facets of

Taken from: *The Allyn & Bacon Guide to Writing*, Sixth Edition by John D. Ramage, John C. Bean, and June Johnson.

society following the McDonald's model. He argues that modern technology is causing loss of quality products, time, and relationships. In the McDonaldized system, where everything is designed logically for economy and convenience, things have become more artificial, and our relationships have become more superficial. In her article "Who Am We?", Sherry Turkle, a psychology professor at MIT, shows how computers and the Internet are transforming our views of ourselves and the way we interact socially. Focusing on computers' capacities for simulation and promoting interaction, Turkle has explored MUDs (multiuser domains), which allow people to create virtual identities. MUDs, Turkle believes, contribute to the formation of postmodern multiple selves and raise new questions about personal identity and morality. Although both Turkle and Ritzer identify problems in technology's influence and in society's responses to it, Turkle sees more potential and gain where Ritzer sees mostly peril and loss. Both articles made me question how we define our values and morality in this postmodern, technologically advanced world and persuaded me of the need for caution in embracing technology.

Brief summary of Turkle's text

Thesis statement with analytical points and synthesis points

Although Ritzer (2000) and Turkle (1996) both see technology as having some negative effects on human relations and the quality of life, they disagree about exactly where the most interesting and serious problems lie. Ritzer believes that the problems caused by technology are not problems within the individual, but problems imposed on the individual by McDonaldized systems. For example, Ritzer claims that fast-food restaurants encourage us to eat unhealthy food quickly and also contribute to "the disintegration of the family" (p. 141) by taking away family time. He also believes that rationalized systems create illusions of fun, reality, and friendliness. He talks about the "scripted interactions" (p. 138) that employees are supposed to have with customers, where they are told exactly what to say to every customer, making interactions less real. Further, rationalized systems are dehumanizing in the kinds of jobs they create that "don't offer much in the way of satisfaction or stability" (p. 137), benefiting only stockholders, owners, and employers.

Analytical point: compares and contrasts Ritzer's and Turkle's ideas

Analyzes and elaborates on Ritzer's ideas

In contrast, Turkle (1996) responds to technology's threat by focusing inward on technology's effect on the self and on relationships. While she is clearly intrigued by such Internet capabilities as multiuser domains, she acknowledges that this potential for multiple simultaneous identities threatens the wholeness of individuals, possibly damaging our emotional and psychological selves. Her concern is that people become addicted to these games because in the virtual world it is easy to create better "selves," to be what you wish you were. Turkle shows that people can lose themselves between the real world and the virtual world and be "imprisoned by the screens" (p. 199). Although the virtual world is exciting and fun, she notes that "[o]ur experiences there are serious play" (p. 199). She also examines cases of virtual characters who get into

Analyzes, contrasts, and elaborates on Turkle's ideas

Analytical point: compares and contrasts Ritzer's and Turkle's ideas

Analyzes and elaborates on Ritzer's ideas

Presents writer's independent thinking

Analyzes, contrasts, and elaborates on Turkle's ideas

Presents writer's independent thinking

Transition to writer's synthesis. Synthesis point discusses writer's own view

Elaborates on the connections the writer is making

relationships with other characters, including cyber-sex relationships. She ponders the issue of cyber-sex immorality and adultery.

Despite Turkle (2000) and Ritzer's (1996) agreement that technology can damage us as a society, they disagree on their overall outlook and on our power to respond positively to technology's influence. I find Ritzer's views almost entirely negative. He believes that we are irreversibly damaged by technological advances because we are completely caught up in the McDonaldized system, with few parts of society left unchanged. Almost all of the family-owned neighborhood restaurants or mom-and-pop grocery stores have been taken over by franchises like Red Robin or Safeway. The costs of these rationalized systems, he says, are "inefficiency, illusions of various types, disenchantment, dehumanization, and homogenization" (p. 124). In this chapter of his book, Ritzer doesn't mention any ways that our lives could be improved by these systems; he gives only examples of the way we are misled and damaged by them.

Turkle's (1996) approach strikes me as much more positive and balanced than Ritzer's (2000). Optimistically, she explains that MUDs can give people self-knowledge that they can apply to real life: "[t]he anonymity of MUDs gives people the chance to express multiple and often unexplored aspects of the self, to play with their identity and to try out new ones" (p. 152). Turkle sees an opportunity for us to grow as individuals and to learn to use technology in a positive way: "If we can cultivate awareness of what stands behind our screen personae, we are more likely to succeed in using virtual experience for personal transformation" (p. 199). I think Turkle's views are more complex than Ritzer's. She believes that we have to take responsibility for our own habits and psychological responses to technology. She encourages us to be aware of how we interact with technology and believes that we can grow as individuals using this technology.

After reading these articles, I have realized how the continuing advancement of technology raises new moral questions. In a McDonaldized system, where everything is designed for convenience, there seem to be many places for morals to be left out of the picture. For example, is it okay for us to exchange real human interaction for convenience and saving time? Is there something wrong with our ethics when interesting and fulfilling jobs are eliminated by machines or replaced by dead-end, low-paying Mcjobs? Turkle (1996) too shows us how virtual worlds pose new moral questions for us. In MUDs, people can form virtual relationships, even cyber-sex relationships. The people behind the characters are real people, even if they are acting as someone else. If a married person has a cyber-sex relationship on a MUD, is he or she cheating? If a person commits a virtual assault or other crime that has no real-world, physical effects, should he or she feel guilty or sinful for the intention? Ritzer (2000) and Turkle have made me see how important these questions are.

Reading the articles made me strongly believe that we must use this technology in moderation in order to preserve individual qualities and our relationships. From our class discussions, I remember what Scott said about the way that the Internet connects people. He said that people like his uncle, who was severely injured on the job, use the Internet as a way of "getting out" to meet people and socialize. He pointed out how the Microsoft Gaming Zone has brought his uncle into an ongoing backgammon tournament through which he has made friends. Meanwhile his aunt has gotten a lot of pleasure out of playing and problem solving in the world of MUDs.

Synthesis point discusses writer's own view

But my own experience has left me concerned about the danger we face as emotional, social beings in the face of technology. The other night at a family gathering, one of my cousins, after discussing car buying with some of the relatives, got the urge to research new car prices. He left the room, logged onto the Internet, and spent the rest of the evening looking at cars and prices. We saw him only once the whole evening when he came out to get a slice of pie. My cousin's withdrawal from the conversation made me think about Ritzer's and Turkle's concerns that technology decreases real interactions among people.

Synthesis point discusses writer's own view

Ritzer (2000) and Turkle (1996) offer us a warning that technology can be damaging if we don't recognize and overcome its dangers. I would encourage us not to let ourselves become dominated by technology, not to let it take our full attention just because it is there, and not to overlook the complex moral questions that technology poses. The convenience that technology offers—our e-mail, cell phones, and debit cards—should help us save time that can be spent in nurturing our relationships with other people. The real challenge is to find ways to become even better people because of technology.

Transition and final connections

Conclusion

References

Ritzer, G. (2000) *The McDonaldization of society*. Thousand Oaks, CA: Pine Forge.

Turkle, S. (1996, January). Who am we? *Wired*. 148–154.

Complete citation of articles in APA format

PRACTICE

Who Do You Want to Be?, p. 438

1 The assignment for this chapter asks for an essay built around a problematic and significant interpretive question. Do you think that Betsy Weiler adequately addresses the assignment? Has she been successful in articulating a problematic question and indicating its importance for our understanding of the story?

a. Does Weiler's thesis statement respond adequately to the question? Does she supply enough details to support her analysis? Would the paper be better with more analysis of literary elements? What should she add or cut?

b. What alternative answers to Weiler's interpretive question occur to you besides the ones she brings up? What evidence do you find in the text to support your analysis and interpretation?

c. What recommendations would you have for improving this essay?

The Princess Paradox, p. 434

2 What are the main differences between the prince and the princess in the new Cinderella movies, according to Poniewozik?

a. Poniewozik suggests that the makers of the new Cinderella movies want to "have-your-tiara-and-disdain-it-too." How so?

b. In what ways, according to Poniewozik, do more recent Cinderella movies suggest that we have come a "long way" from women as depicted in such action films as *Charlie's Angels* and *Crouching Tiger, Hidden Dragon*?

c. What is the "template" of the new Cinderella, according to Poniewozik?

d. Poniewozik quotes an industry executive responsible for one of the new "Cinderella" movies: "it really is important that it imparts contemporary values." Is this your view of folk tales—that they impart "contemporary values"? If not "contemporary," then what sort of values?

e. Poniewozik is not neutral regarding the new wave of Cinderella movies. Locate passages that suggest, if not state outright, his views. Explain your choices.

f. Recognizing it had a gold mine in Cinderella updates like *The Princess Diaries*, the movie industry quickly released other "contemporary" versions of the tale. To what extent do you think these updates have bent the traditional tale out of recognition?

g. Rent and watch one or more of the Cinderella remakes that Poniewozik mentions in this article. Then write a critique of the article or prepare talking points for a critique that you will share in discussion, in class. Do Poniewozik's observations hold up? In your critique, focus especially on the updates to Cinderella's character and the new "template" intended to make her a heroine for the twenty-first century.

h. You have read at least some variants of "Cinderella" in this chapter. Assuming that Poniewozik's characterization of the new movie versions is accurate, are you heartened by the changes to the main character? Disheartened? Explain.

Completion of these practice exercises requires location of additional outside sources.

3 Research the fairy tale literature of your ancestors, both the tales and any critical commentary that you can find on them. Once you have read the material, talk with older members of your family to hear any tales they have to tell. (Seek, especially, oral versions of stories you have already read.) In a paper, discuss the role that fairy tale literature has played, and continues to play, in your family.

a. Locate the book *Morphology of the Folktale* (1958) by Russian folklorist Vladimir Propp. Use the information you find there to analyze the elements of any three fairy tales of your choosing. In a paper, report on your analysis and evaluate the usefulness of Propp's system of classifying the key elements of fairy tale literature.

b. Bruno Bettelheim's *Uses of Enchantment* (1975) generated a great deal of reaction on its publication. Read Bettelheim and locate several reviews of his work. Based on your own reactions and on your reading of the reviews, write an evaluation in which you address Bettelheim's key assumption that fairy tale literature provides important insights into the psychological life of children.

c. Locate and study multiple versions of any fairy tale other than "Cinderella." Having read the versions, identify—and write your paper on—what you feel are the defining elements that make the tales variants of a single story. See if you can find the tale listed as a "type" in Aarne and Thompson's *The Types of Folk-Tales*. If you wish, argue that one version of the tale is preferable to others.

d. Jack Zipes, author of *Breaking the Magic Spell* (1979), takes the approach that fairy tales are far from innocuous children's stories; rather, they inculcate the unsuspecting with the value systems of the dominant culture. In a research paper, explicitly address the assumption that fairy tales are not morally or politically neutral but, rather, imply a distinct set of values.

c. Record, and then study, several hours of Saturday morning cartoons. Then locate and read a collection of Grimm's fairy tales. In a comparative analysis, examine the cartoons and the fairy tales along any four or five dimensions that you think are important. The point of your comparisons and contrasts will be to determine how well the two types of presentations stack up against each other. Which do you find more entertaining? Illuminating? Ambitious? Useful? (These criteria are suggestions only. You should generate your own criteria as part of your research.)

f. Arrange to read to your favorite young person a series of fairy tales. Based on your understanding of the selections in this chapter, develop a list of questions concerning the importance or usefulness of fairy tale literature to children. Read to your young friend on several occasions and, if possible, talk about the stories after you read them (or while you are reading). Then write a paper on your experience, answering as many of your initial questions as possible. (Be sure in your paper to provide a profile of the child with whom you worked; to review your selection of stories; and to list the questions you wanted to explore.)

Baker College
Jackson

How Do I Analyze Images?

THIS CHAPTER ASKS YOU TO THINK ABOUT THREE MAJOR KINDS OF COMMUNICATION THROUGH IMAGES—DOCUMENTARY OR NEWS PHOTOS, PAINTINGS, AND ADVERTISEMENTS—TO INCREASE YOUR VISUAL LITERACY SKILLS. BY VISUAL LITERACY, WE MEAN YOUR awareness of the importance of visual communication and your ability to interpret or make meaning out of images by examining their context and visual features. We focus on the ways that images influence our conceptual and emotional understanding of a phenomenon and the ways that they validate, reveal, and construct the world.

This chapter invites you to analyze images in order to understand their rhetorical and experiential effects. To **analyze** means to divide or dissolve the whole into its parts, examine these parts carefully, look at the relationships among them, and then use this understanding of the parts to better understand the whole—how it functions, what it means. When you analyze, your goal is to raise interesting questions about the image or object being analyzed—questions that perhaps your reader hasn't thought to ask—and then to provide tentative answers, supported by points and particulars derived from your own close examination.

The ability to analyze visual texts is particularly important because we are surrounded by images from photojournalism, the Internet, billboards, newspapers, television, and magazines. These images, as one critic has stated, "have designs on us." Although glamorous and disturbing images saturate our environment, we do not necessarily have a deep understanding of how they affect us.

By writing in a common academic genre—a comparative analysis of two visual texts—in this chapter you will learn to:

- analyze the persuasive effects of images and how these effects are created
- respond to visual images as a more informed citizen and perceptive cultural critic

Exploring Image Analysis

To introduce you to image analysis, we provide an exercise that asks you to interact with several news photographs on the issue of immigration reform.

Immigration reform is one of the most complex issues facing the United States today; the problem is particularly acute with respect to immigrants from Mexico and Central America. Immigrants are drawn to the United States by employment opportunities not found in their own countries. U.S. citizens benefit from immigrants' inexpensive labor, which helps keep the prices of services and goods low. In addition to a sizable Mexican-American citizenry, more than ten million illegal immigrants currently live in the United States. All these factors give rise to a number of controversial questions: Should the United States increase border security and focus on building impassable barriers? Should it deport illegal immigrants or explore easier routes to making them citizens? Should it crack down on employers of illegal immigrants or should it implement a guest worker program to legitimize immigrant labor?

Public debate about these issues is particularly susceptible to manipulation by the rhetorical appeal of images. The following exercise asks you to examine the news photos in Figures 11.1 through 11.4. Working individually or in groups, consider the rhetorical effect of these photos, first by recording your responses to them and then by speculating how you might use these images to increase the persuasiveness of different positions on immigration reform.

1. What objects, people, or places stand out in each photo? Does the photo look candid or staged, taken close-up or from a distance? How do the angle of the photo (taken from below or above the subject) and the use of color contribute to the effect?

2. What is the dominant impression conveyed by each photo?

3. Examine how the similarities and differences among the four photos convey different rhetorical impressions of immigrants, Latino culture, or the role of immigrants and ethnic diversity in U.S. culture.

4. Now imagine how you might use these photos to enhance the persuasiveness of particular claims. Choose one or two photos to support or attack each claim below and explain what the photo could contribute to the argument.

   • The United States should seal its border with Mexico by building a wall and increasing border patrols.

   • The United States should offer amnesty and citizenship to immigrants who are currently in the United States illegally.

Figure 11.1 Wall between Tijuana, Mexico and the United States

Figure 11.2 Immigrants Crossing the Border Illegally

Figure 11.3 Protestors Marching for Compassionate Treatment of Immigrants

Figure 11.4 Immigrants Saying Their Citizenship Pledge

Understanding Image Analysis: Documentary and News Photographs

Documentary and news photos are aimed at shaping the way we think and feel about an event or cultural/historical phenomenon. For example, consider the newspaper photos, TV news footage, or Internet videos of the billowing clouds of smoke and ash from the collapsing World Trade Center towers on September 11,

Figure 11.5 Terrorist Attack on the World Trade Center

Figure 11.6 World Trade Center Attack Seen from the Air

2001. Figures 11.5, 11.6, and 11.7 present three well-known documentary images of this event, taken from three different positions and at three slightly different moments as the event unfolded.

Although all three photos convey the severity of the terrorist attack, each has a different impact. Figure 11.5 records the event shortly before the north tower collapsed and just after the south tower was struck by the second plane, marked in the photo by the red flames. The sheer magnitude and horror of the moment-by-moment action unfolding before our eyes evoked shock, anger, and feelings of helplessness in Americans.

In contrast to the first image, which was taken from a distance below the towers, Figure 11.6 was taken by a police detective in a helicopter searching for survivors on the roof of the north tower before it collapsed. This photo suggests the apocalyptic explosion and implosion of a contemporary city. The destruction pictured here is too massive to be an ordinary event such as a fire in a major building, and yet the streams of ash and smoke don't reveal exactly what is happening.

Another well-publicized view of this event is that of the firefighters on the ground, seen in Figure 11.7. Here the firefighters, risking their lives while trying

Figure 11.7   Firefighters in the World Trade Center Wreckage

to rescue the people in the towers, have come to symbolize the self-sacrifice, courage, and also vulnerability of the human effort in the face of such colossal destruction. This image also suggests the terror and suspense of a science-fiction-like conflict. All three photos, while memorializing the same event, have different specific subjects, angles of vision, and emotional and mental effects.

The rest of this section introduces you to the ways that photographers think about their use of the camera and the effects they are trying to achieve.

ANGLE OF VISION AND CREDIBILITY OF PHOTOGRAPHS

Although the word "documentary" is associated with an objective, transparent, unmediated glimpse of reality, the relationship of documentary photography to its subject matter has always been complex. Historians are now reassessing early documentary photographs, exploring the class and race agendas of the photographers in the kinds of scenes chosen, the photographers' stance toward them, and the wording of the narratives accompanying the photographs. In other words, despite a photograph's appearance of capturing a moment of reality (whose reality?), its effect is always influenced by the photographer's rhetorical angle of vision conveyed through the framing and focusing power of the camera. Perhaps now more than ever, we are aware that the photographer's purpose and techniques actually shape the reality that viewers see. (Think of the multiple cameras tracking a football game and replaying a touchdown from different angles, often creating very different impressions of a particular play.)

The photographer's power to shape reality is enhanced by various strategies for making "unnatural" photographs seem "natural" or "real." For example, photographs can be manipulated or falsified in the following ways:

- staging images (scenes that appear spontaneous but are really posed)
- altering images (airbrushing, reshaping body parts)
- selecting images or parts of images (cropping photographs so that only certain parts are shown)
- mislabeling images (putting a caption on a photograph that misrepresents the image)
- constructing images (putting the head of one person on the body of another)

Research has revealed that many famous photographs were tampered with. As early as the Civil War, composite photos of generals were created by combining heads, bodies, and scenery and inserting figures into scenes. Today this manipulation is also conducted by amateur photographers using photo-editing software. The potential for altering images gives us additional reasons for considering the active role of the photographer and for investigating the credibility and purpose behind images.

HOW TO ANALYZE A DOCUMENTARY PHOTOGRAPH

Photographs are always created and interpreted within a social, political, and historical context—the original context in which the photograph was made and viewed and your own context as a current viewer and interpreter. At play are the assumptions, values, and cultural knowledge of the photographer, the original viewers, and the later viewers. Also at play are the sites in which the photograph is viewed—whether in an original news story, a museum, an upscale art exhibit, an expensive coffee-table book, a documentary film, an Internet site, or a textbook. These sites invite us to respond in different ways. For example, one site may call us to social action or deepen our understanding of an event, while another aims to elicit artistic appreciation or to underscore cultural differences.

● **EXAMINING THE RHETORICAL CONTEXTS OF A PHOTO**   A first step in analyzing a documentary photograph is to consider its various rhetorical contexts. The following chart will help you ask illuminating questions.

● **EXAMINING THE EFFECTS OF A PHOTO ON A VIEWER**   In addition to considering the contexts of photographs, we can explore how photographs achieve their effects—that is, how they move us emotionally or intellectually, how they imply arguments and cause us to see the subject in a certain way. An

Strategies for Analyzing the Rhetorical Contexts of Documentary Photographs

Context	Questions to Ask
Photographer's purpose and context in making the photograph	• What was the photographer's original intention/purpose in making the image (to report an event, convey information, persuade viewers to think about the event or people a certain way)? • What was the original historical, cultural, social, and political context in which the photograph was taken?
Original context for displaying the photograph	• Where was the photograph originally viewed (news story, photo essay, scientific report, public exhibit, advocacy Web site)? • How does the original title or caption, if any, reflect the context and shape impressions of the image?
Cultural contexts for interpreting the photograph	• How does the photograph's appearance in a particular place influence your impression of it? • How does your own cultural context differ from that of original viewers? • What assumptions and values do you bring to the context?

image might soothe us or repel us; it might evoke our sympathies, trigger our fears, or call forth a web of interconnected ideas, memories, and associations.

Before you begin a detailed analysis of a photograph, you will find it helpful to explore the photograph's immediate impact.

- What words come to mind when you view this photograph?
- What is the mood or overall feeling conveyed by the photo?
- Assuming that photographs "have designs on us," what is this photograph trying to get you to feel, think, do, or "see?"

The following chart will help you examine a photograph in detail in order to analyze how it achieves its persuasive effects.*

*We are indebted to Terry Barrett, Professor Emeritus of Art Education at Ohio State University, for his formulation of questions, "Looking at Photographs, Description and Interpretation," and to Claire Garoutte, Assistant Professor of Photography at Seattle University, for informing our discussion of context in analyzing documentary photographs.

Strategies for Analyzing the Persuasive Effects of Photographs and Other Images

What to Examine	Some Questions to Ask about Rhetorical Effect
Subject matter: People in portraits Portraits can be formal or informal and can emphasize character or social role. The gaze of the human subjects can imply power through direct eye contact and deference or shyness through lack of eye contact.	Is the emphasis on identity, character, and personality, or representative status (wife of wealthy merchant, king, soldier, etc.), or symbolic (an image of wisdom, daring, etc.)? What do details of clothing and setting (a room's furnishings, for example) reveal about historical period, economic status, national or ethnic identity?
Subject matter: People in scenes Scenes can make a statement about everyday life or capture some aspect of a news event or crisis.	What is the relationship of the people to each other and the scene? Can you re-create the story behind the scene? Does the scene look natural/realistic or staged/aesthetically attractive?
Subject matter: Landscape or nature Scenes can focus on nature or the environment as the dominant subject.	If the setting is outdoors, what are the features of the landscape: urban or rural, mountain or desert? What aspects of nature are shown? If people are in the image, what is the relationship between nature and the human figures? What vision of nature is the artist constructing—majestic, threatening, hospitable, tamed, orderly, wild?
Distance from subject: Close-ups tend to increase the intensity of the image and suggest the importance of the subject. Long shots tend to blend the subject into the environment.	Are viewers brought close to the subject or distanced from it? How does the distance from the subject contribute to the effect of the photo or painting?
Angle and orientation: The vantage point from which the photograph was taken and the positioning of the photographer to the subject determine the effect of images.	How does the angle influence what you see? Why do you think this angle was chosen? How would the photograph have changed if it had been taken from another angle?

What to Examine	Some Questions to Ask about Rhetorical Effect
Low angles make the subject look larger. High angles make the subject look smaller. A level angle implies equality. Front views tend to emphasize the persons in the image. Rear views often emphasize the scene or setting.	
Framing: Framing determines what is inside the image and what is closed off to viewers; it's a device to draw the attention of viewers.	How does the framing of the image direct your attention? What is included and what is excluded from the image? How does what the photo or painting allows you to see and know contribute to its effect? Why do you think this particular frame was chosen?
Light: The direction of the light determines the shadows and affects the contrasts, which can be subtle or strong. Lighting has different effects if it is natural or artificial, bright, soft, or harsh.	How does the light reveal details? What does the direction of the light contribute to the presence of shadows? How do these shadows affect the mood or feeling of the photo?
Focus: Focus refers to what is clearly in focus or in the foreground of the photo versus what is blurry. The range between the nearest and farthest thing in focus in the photo is referred to as the depth of field.	What parts of the image are clearly in focus? Are any parts out of focus? What effect do these choices have on viewers' impression of the image? How great is the depth of field and what effect does that have?
Scale, space, and shape: Size/scale and shape affect prominence and emphasis. Size and scale can be natural, minimized, or exaggerated. Use of space can be shallow, deep, or both. Both positive shapes and voids can draw viewers' attention.	How do the scale, space, and shape of objects direct viewers' attention and affect a feeling or mood? Are shapes geometric and angular or flowing and organic? Are shapes positive such as objects, or negative such as voids?

(*continued*)

Strategies for Analyzing the Persuasive Effects of Photographs and Other Images (continued)

What to Examine	Some Questions to Ask about Rhetorical Effect
Use of repetition, variety, and balance: Repetition of elements can create order, wholeness, and unity. Variety can create interest. Balance can create unity and harmony.	What elements are repeated in this image? What variety is present, say, in shapes? Does the visual weight of the photo seem to be distributed evenly on the sides, top, and bottom? What roles do repetition, variety, and balance play in the impression created by the photo?
Line: Lines can be curved and flowing, straight, or disjointed and angular. Lines can be balanced/symmetrical, stable, and harmonious, or disjointed and agitated.	Does the use of line create structure and convey movement/action or calm/stasis? How does the use of line control how viewers look at the photo or painting?
Color: Choice of black and white can reflect the site of publication, the date of the photo, or an artistic choice. Colors can contribute to the realism and appeal; harmonious colors can be pleasing; clashing or harsh colors can be disturbing.	How many colors are used? What is the relationship of the colors? Which colors dominate? Are the colors warm and vibrant or cool, bright, or dull? How are light and dark used? How does the use of color direct viewers' attention and affect the impression of the image? What emotional response do these colors evoke?

SAMPLE ANALYSIS OF A DOCUMENTARY PHOTOGRAPH

To illustrate how a documentary photograph can work on the viewer's mind and heart, we show you our own analysis of a photo titled *The Fall of the Berlin Wall* (Figure 11.8), taken by photojournalist Peter Turnley in 1989. At the time, the Berlin Wall, which separated communist East Berlin from democratic West Berlin, symbolized the oppression of communism. In 1987 President Ronald Reagan appealed to Mikhail Gorbachev, president of the Union of Soviet Socialist Republics, saying in a famous speech, "Mr. Gorbachev, tear down this wall." When the border opened in November 1989, marking the end of communist rule in Eastern Europe, East Berliners flooded into West Berlin, sparking weeks of celebration. Peter Turnley is a world-famous American photojournalist whose photos of major world events have appeared on the covers of *Newsweek* as well as

Figure 11.8   Fall of the Berlin Wall, 1989, by Peter Turnley

international magazines. This photograph appeared in a 1996 exhibit (and later a book) entitled *In Time of War and Peace* at the International Center of Photography in New York.

This documentary photograph of a celebratory scene following the opening of the Berlin Wall in 1989 uses elements of framing, orientation, focus, balance, and color to convey the dominant impression of a life-changing explosion of energy and emotion triggered by this significant event. This distance photo is divided into three horizontal bands—the sky, the wall, and the celebratory crowd—but the focal point is the yelling, triumphant German youth sitting astride the wall, wearing jeans, a studded belt, and a black jacket. The graffiti indicate that the photo was taken from the West Berlin side (East Berliners were not permitted to get close to the wall), and the light post between the two cranes was probably used to illuminate the no-man zone on the communist side.

Every aspect of the photograph suggests energy. In contrast with the mostly homogeneous sky, the wall and the crowd contain many diverse elements. The wall is heavily graffitied in many colors, and the crowd is composed of many people. The wall looks crowded, tattered, and dirty, something to be torn down rather than cleaned up. Most of the graffiti consist of tags, people's response to the ugly obstruction of the wall; West Berliners had no power to destroy the wall, but they could mark it up. The slightly blurred crowd of heads suggests that the people are in motion. At first it is hard to tell if they are angry protesters storming the wall or celebrators cheering on the German youth. The photograph captures this dual emotion—anger and joy—all at once.

At the center of the photograph is the German youth, whose dark jacket makes him stand out against the light blue sky. A few days earlier the wall had fenced him in (at that time, it would have been unthinkable even to approach the wall lest he be shot by border guards). Now he rides the wall like an American cowboy at a rodeo. He has conquered the wall. He has become transformed from prisoner to liberator. His cowboy gesture, reflecting European fascination with American cowboy movies, becomes the symbol of the ideological West, the land of freedom, now the wave of the future for these reunited countries. He holds in his hand a tool (a hammer or chisel?) used to chip away the wall symbolically, but the position of his arm and hand suggests a cowboy with a pistol.

What makes this photograph so powerful is the distance. Had Turnley used a telescopic lens to focus on the German youth up close, the photograph would have been about the youth himself, a personal story. But by placing the youth into a larger frame that includes the crowd, the long expanse of ugly wall, and the cranes and lamppost behind the wall, Turnley suggests both the enormous public and political nature of this event and the implications for individual lives. The youth appears to be the first of the energized crowd to demonstrate the conquering of the powerful barrier that had shaped so many German lives for almost three decades. Thus the composition of this photo packs many layers of meaning and symbolism into its depiction of this historical event.

Understanding Image Analysis: Paintings

When you analyze a painting, many of the strategies used for analyzing documentary photographs still apply. You still look carefully at the subject matter of the painting (the setting, the people or objects in the setting, the arrangement in space, the clothing, the gaze of persons, the implied narrative story, and so forth). Likewise, you consider the painter's distance from the subject, the angle of orientation, the framing, and other features that paintings share with photographs. Additionally, your analysis of paintings will be enriched if you consider, as you did with documentary photographs, the context in which the painting was originally created and originally viewed as well as your own cultural context and place of viewing.

But painters—by means of their choice of paints, their brushstrokes, their artistic vision, and their methods of representation—often do something quite different from photographers. For example, they can paint mythological or imaginary subjects and can achieve nonrepresentational effects not associated with a camera such as a medieval allegorical style or the striking distortions of Cubism. Also, the long history of painting and the ways that historical periods influence painters' choices of subject matter, medium, and style affect what viewers see and feel about paintings. Background on the artist, historical period, and style of paintings (for example, Baroque, Impressionism, Expressionism, and Cubism) can be found in sources such as the Oxford Art Online database. In analyzing paintings, art critics and historians often contrast paintings that have similar subject matter (for example, two portraits of a hero, two paintings of a biblical scene, two landscapes) but that create very different dominant impressions and effects on viewers.

HOW TO ANALYZE A PAINTING

Just as with photographs, you should ground your interpretation of a painting in close observation. Many of the elements introduced in the strategies chart for analyzing photographs can apply or be adapted to the analysis of paintings. In addition, you will want to examine the following elements of the paintings you are analyzing.

SAMPLE ANALYSIS OF A PAINTING

As an example of a visual analysis of a painting, we offer an interpretation of a famous painting by Pierre–Auguste Renoir (1841–1919), a French Impressionist painter of the late nineteenth century. The French Impressionists were recognized for their refusal to paint old themes; their embrace of scenes of modern

Strategies for Analyzing the Particular Elements of Paintings

Elements to Analyze	Questions to Ask about Rhetorical Effect
Design and shape of the painting: The width to height, division into parts, and proportional relationship of parts influence the impression of the painting.	What is viewer's impression of the shape of the painting and the relationship of its parts? How does line organize the painting? Is the painting organized along diagonal, horizontal, or vertical lines?
Medium, technique, and brushstrokes: The material with which the painting is made (for example, pen and ink, tempura/water colors, charcoal, oil paints on paper or canvas), and the thickness and style of brushstrokes determine the artistic effect.	In what medium is the artist working? How does the medium contribute to the impression of the painting? Are brushstrokes sharp and distinct or thick, layered, fused? Are they delicate and precise or vigorous? What effect does the awareness or lack of awareness of brushstrokes have on the appearance of the painting?

Figure 11.9 Renoir's *La Loge* (1874)

society, especially the city and suburbs; and their experimentation with light and brushstrokes as a way to capture fleeting impressions. Figure 11.9 shows Renoir's oil painting *La Loge* (The Theater Box), which he painted as his main contribution to the first exhibit of Impressionist paintings in 1874. Impressionist paintings were considered too *avant garde* to be displayed at the conservative state-controlled Salon, which was the official arbiter and channel of the work of established French artists.

Renoir's *La Loge* depicts social life in nineteenth-century urban society as an occasion to act out social roles. This painting of a man and a woman elegantly dressed in a theater box at the opera, a popular social spot of the period, suggests that attending the theater/opera entailed displaying one's wealth, being seen, and inspecting others as much as it did watching a performance. This painting focuses intensely on two members of the audience and specifically on the woman, who catches and holds our gaze. While the man in the background is looking at someone in the audience through his opera glasses, the woman looks directly at viewers and invites their attention.

Renoir has compelled viewers to dwell on this woman by a number of his choices in this painting. He has chosen to paint her in a tightly framed close-up image, which the slightly off-center woman dominates. Her face and eyes convey the impression that she and the viewer are staring at each other, while in the shadows the man's eyes are blocked by his opera glasses. Thus this painting combines the woman's portrait with a scene at the opera, even though most of the setting, the theater box, is excluded from the painting. (We know we are at the opera because of the painting's title and the man's and woman's accessories.) There seems to be a story behind the scene: what is the man looking at and why is he not noticing the woman as we, the viewers, are compelled to do? This depiction of a moment seems to be less a shared experience of relationship and more a site for performance: men engaged in looking, women inviting the gaze of others.

Another choice Renoir has made to focus viewers' attention on the woman is his striking use of color. In this painting, the color palette is not large—white, black, brown/gold/sepia, with her red lips and red flowers on her bodice. The white of her face and her upper body is the brightest, suggesting light shining on her. Renoir also highlights the woman with short, thick brushstrokes, which give her shimmering, elegant dress texture and the impression of silk, velvet, and lace. As additional signs of wealth, she wears earrings, a gold bracelet, a flower in her hair, and a flower at her bosom. The stark contrast of the black and white in her dress, the white of her face, and the red of her lips—and the agitated diagonal but converging lines of the stripes of her dress that, along with her arms angled out from her body, shape her into a diamond—all work to direct viewers' eyes to her bosom and most of all to her face. Although the expression of the woman is calm, smiling in mild amusement or subtle emotion, the painting captures intensity, perhaps excitement or anticipation, through the sharp contrast of the red, white, and black. The piece is fairly still and yet we are transfixed by this woman's eyes and lips. With the complex interaction of artistic elements in this painting, Renoir has invited viewers to experience an exciting scene of privileged nineteenth-century urban life.

Understanding Image Analysis: Advertisements

The images in advertisements are fascinating to analyze. Like other images, they employ the rhetorical strategies we described in the section on documentary photographs. Often, the ad's words (called the "copy") also contribute to its rhetorical effect. Moreover, ads make a more direct and constant demand on us than do documentary photographs and paintings. Advertising, a multibillion-dollar global industry whose business is communicating across a wide range of media to stimulate the purchase of products or services, comes to us in multiple forms: not just as slick, glamorous magazine ads, but also as direct mail, billboards, radio and television commercials, e-advertisements, banners, pop-ups,

Figure 11.10 A Billboard Ad

Figure 11.11 Ad on a City Bus

and spam. Figures 11.10 and 11.11, a billboard and a bus ad, illustrate the ordinary ubiquity of ads. Because of advertising's powerful role in shaping our culture and influencing our self-images, we have good reason to analyze the rhetorical strategies of advertisers.

HOW ADVERTISERS THINK ABOUT ADVERTISING

Although cultural critics frequently focus on ads as manipulative messages that need to be decoded to protect unwary consumers, we confess that we actually enjoy ads, appreciate how they hold down the consumer cost of media, and admire their often-ingenious creativity. (We suspect that others secretly enjoy ads also: Think of how the Super Bowl is popular both for its football and for its ads.) In this section, we take a look at advertising from a marketer's point of view in order to deepen your awareness of an ad's context and the many behind-the-scenes decisions and negotiations that produced it. Whether marketing professionals design an individual ad or a huge marketing campaign, they typically begin by asking questions.

● **WHO IS OUR TARGET AUDIENCE?**   At the outset, marketers identify one or more target audiences for their product or service. They often use sophisticated psychological research to identify segments of the population who share similar values, beliefs, and aspirations and then subdivide these categories according to age, gender, region, income level, ethnicity, and so forth. Think of the different way you'd pitch a product or service to, say, Wal-Mart shoppers versus Neiman Marcus shoppers, steak eaters versus vegans, or skateboarders versus geeks.

● **HOW MUCH MEDIA LANDSCAPE CAN WE AFFORD?**   While identifying their target audience, marketers also consider how much terrain they can afford to occupy on the enormous media landscape of billboards, newspapers, magazines, mailing lists, Internet pop-ups, TV and radio commercials, posters, naming rights for sports stadiums, T-shirts, coffee mugs, product placements in films, sandwich boards, or banners carried across the sky by propeller airplanes. Each of these sites has to be rented or purchased, with the price depending on the perceived quality of the location and the timing. For example, a thirty-second TV commercial during the 2010 Super Bowl cost $2.6 million, and a one-time full-page ad in a nationally circulated popular magazine can cost up to $500,000 or more. Overall, advertisers hope to attain the best possible positioning and timing within the media landscape at a price they can afford.

● **WHAT ARE THE BEST MEDIA FOR REACHING OUR TARGET AUDIENCE?**   A marketer's goal is to reach the target audience efficiently and with a minimum of overflow—that is, messages sent to people who are not likely buyers. Marketers are keenly aware of both media and timing: Note, for example, how daytime TV is dominated by ads for payday loans, exercise equipment, or technical colleges, while billboards around airports advertise rental cars. Women's fashion magazines advertise lingerie and perfume but not computers or life insurance, while dating services advertise primarily through Internet ads.

● **IS OUR GOAL TO STIMULATE DIRECT SALES OR TO DEVELOP LONG-TERM BRANDING AND IMAGE?**   Some ads are intended to stimulate retail sales directly: "Buy two, get one free." In some cases, advertisements use information and argument to show how their product or service is superior to that of their competitors. Most advertisements, however, involve parity products such as soft drinks, deodorants, breakfast cereals, or toothpaste. (*Parity products* are roughly equal in quality among competitors and so can't be promoted through any rational or scientific proof of superiority.) In such cases, advertisers' goal is to build brand loyalty based on a long-lasting relationship with consumers. Advertisers, best thought of as creative teams of writers and artists, try to convert a brand name appearing on a cereal box or a pair of jeans to a field of qualities, values, and imagery that lives inside the heads of its targeted consumers. Advertisers don't just want you to buy Nikes rather than Reeboks but also to see yourself as a Nike kind of person, who identifies with the lifestyle or values conveyed in Nike ads.

MIRRORS AND WINDOWS: THE STRATEGY OF AN EFFECTIVE ADVERTISEMENT

A final behind-the-scenes concept that will help you analyze ads is the marketers' principle of *"mirrors and windows,"* a psychological and motivational strategy to associate a product with a target audience's dreams, hopes, fears, desires, and wishes (often subconscious).

- ***The mirror effect*** refers to the way in which the ad mirrors the target audience's self-image, promoting identification with the ad's message. The target audience has to say, "I am part of the world that this ad speaks to. I have this problem (pimples, boring hair, dandelions, cell phone service without enough bars)."
- ***The window effect*** provides visions of the future, promises of who we will become or what will happen if we align ourselves with this brand. The ad implies a brief narrative, taking you from your ordinary self (mirror) to your new, aspirational self (window).

For example, the acne product Proactiv Solutions uses a very common mirrors/windows strategy. Proactiv infomercials create the mirror effect by featuring regular-looking teenagers with pimples and the window effect by using a gorgeous actress as endorsing spokesperson: If I use Proactiv Solutions, ordinary "me" will look beautiful like Jessica Simpson.

But the mirrors and windows principle can be used in much more subtle and creative ways. Consider the brilliance of the Geico insurance gecko ads promoting what advertisers call a "a resentful purchase"—that is, something you need to have but that doesn't give you material pleasure like a new pair of shoes or money in a savings account. Insurance, a hassle to buy, is also associated with fear—fear of needing it, fear of not having it, fear of not being able to get it again if you ever use it. In this light, think of the Geico campaign featuring the humorous, big-eyed gecko (friendly, cute) with the distinctive cockney voice (working-class swagger). When this chapter was being written, Geico billboards were sprouting up all over the country (see Figure 11.12), while large-print ads were appearing in popular magazines along with numerous TV and radio commercials. Here are some of the particular advantages of the gecko for Geico's layered advertising campaign across many media:

- ***"Gecko" sounds like "Geico."*** In fact, this sound-alike feature was the inspiration for the campaign.

Figure 11.12 Geico Gecko Billboard Ad

- ***The gecko is identifiable by both sight and sound.*** If you see a print ad or a billboard, you remember what the voice sounds like; if you hear a radio ad, you remember what the gecko looks like; on TV or YouTube, you get both sight and sound.
- ***The gecko is cheap.*** The cost of the computer simulations that produce the gecko is minimal in comparison to the royalties paid to celebrities for an advertising endorsement.
- ***The gecko is ethnically/racially neutral.*** Marketers didn't have to decide whether to choose a white versus black versus Asian spokesperson, yet a person of any race or nationality can identify with the little lizard. (think Kermit the Frog on *Sesame Street*). Feminist critics, however, might rightly ask why the gecko has to be male.
- ***The gecko is scandal-proof.*** When in 2010 the Tiger Woods imbroglio ruined the golfer's public image, the huge insurance company Accenture, along with TagHauer watches and other companies, had to drop his endorsement ads, forcing them at great expense to create new advertising campaigns and to lose media visibility in the interim.

Yet we must still ask why the gecko is a good advertising device for an insurance company. How does the gecko campaign incorporate mirrors and windows? Let's start with the mirror effect. It is easy to identify with the Geico ads because everyone has to buy insurance and because everyone wants to save money. (The gecko's main sales pitch is that Geico will save you 15 percent.) Moreover, our long cultural history of identifying with animated characters (*Sesame Street, ET*) makes it easy to project our own identities onto the gecko. Additionally, the cockney voice makes the gecko a bit of an outsider, someone breaking into corporate culture through sheer bravado. (Many people think of the gecko's accent as Australian more than cockney, giving the lizard a bit of sexy, macho Crocodile Dundee appeal.)

The ads also create a window effect, which comes from the way the gecko humanizes the insurance company, removing some of the fear and anxiety of buying insurance. You don't think of the gecko as *selling* you the insurance so much as *buying* it for you as your agent, hopping right up on the corporate desk and demanding your rights. Geico becomes a fun company, and you as consumer picture yourself going away with a pile of saved money. Recent ads have added another symbolic feature to the gecko—a pair of glasses—which makes him seem intellectual and responsible, more serious and grown-up. Meanwhile, another Geico campaign, the talking-money ad (see the billboard ad in Figure 11.12), extends the concept of a humorous, friendly creature, like the gecko, that turns Geico insurance into a savings, not an expense.

HOW TO ANALYZE AN ADVERTISEMENT

In addition to thinking about the decision making behind an ad, when you analyze a print ad you need to ask three overarching questions:

1. How does the ad draw in the target audience by helping them identify with the ad's problematic situation or story (mirror effect)?
2. How does the ad create a field of values, beliefs, and aspirations that serve as windows into a more fulfilled life?
3. How do the ad's images and words work together to create the desired persuasive effects?

For the images in an ad, all the strategies we have already described for documentary photographs and for paintings continue to apply—for example, angle of vision, framing, and so forth. (Review the strategies chart.) With many ads you also have to factor in the creative use of words—puns, connotations, and intertextual references to other ads or cultural artifacts. Note that in professionally created ads, every word, every punctuation mark, and every visual detail down to the props in the photograph or the placement of a model's hands are consciously chosen.

The following strategies chart focuses on questions particularly relevant to print ads.

Strategies for Analyzing the Compositional Features of Print Ads

What to Do	Some Questions to Ask
Examine the settings, furnishings, and all other details.	• Is the room formal or informal; neat, lived-in, or messy? • How is the room furnished and decorated? • If the setting is outdoors, what are the features of the landscape: urban or rural, mountain or meadow? • Why are particular animals or birds included? (Think of the differences between using a crow, a hummingbird, or a parrot.)
Consider the social meaning of objects.	• What is the emotional effect of the objects in a den: for example, duck decoys and fishing rods versus computers and high-tech printers? • What is the social significance (class, economic status, lifestyle, values) of the objects in the ad? (Think of the meaning of a groomed poodle versus a mutt or a single rose versus a fuchsia in a pot.)
Consider the characters, roles, and actions.	• Who are these people and what are they doing? What story line could you construct behind the image? • Are the models regular looking people, "beautiful people," or celebrities? • In product advertisements, are female models used instrumentally (depicted as mechanics working on cars or as a consumers buying cars) or are they used decoratively (bikini-clad and lounging on the hood of the latest truck)?
Observe how models are dressed, posed, and accessorized.	• What are the models' facial expressions? • What are their hairstyles and what cultural and social significance do they have? • How well are they dressed and posed?

(continued)

Strategies for Analyzing the Compositional Features of Print Ads (continued)

What to Do	Some Questions to Ask
Observe the relationships among actors and among actors and objects.	• How does the position of the models signal importance and dominance? • Who is looking at whom? • Who is above or below, in the foreground or background?
Consider what social roles are being played out and what values appealed to.	• Are the gender roles traditional or nontraditional? • Are the relationships romantic, erotic, friendly, formal, uncertain? • What are the power relationships among characters?
Consider how document design functions and how the words and images work together.	• What features of document design (variations of font style and size, placement on the page, formal or playful lettering) stand out? • How much of the copy is devoted to product information or argument about superiority of the product or service? • How much of the copy helps create a field of values, beliefs, aspirations? • How do the words contribute to the "story" implied in the visual images? • What is the style of the language (for example, connotations, double entendres, puns)?

SAMPLE ANALYSIS OF AN ADVERTISEMENT

With an understanding of possible photographic effects and the compositional features of ads, you now have all the background knowledge needed to begin doing your own analysis of ads. To illustrate how an analysis of an ad can reveal the ad's persuasive strategies, we show you our analysis of an ad for Coors Light (Figure 11.13) that ran in a variety of women's magazines in the mid-1990s. The marketers aimed to attract a new target audience—twenty-something or thirty-something middle-class women—and decided that print ads in magazines constituted the best medium.

Sam and Me.

Me and Sam? We're just friends. Best friends, actually, since Mrs. Ainsley's first grade class when I let the hamster loose and Sam took the rap for me. I mean Sam's seen me in braces and I've seen him eat pizza. There's just way too much history here. Sam's my friend. The one I go to when I really need someone to talk to. I bring the Coors Light and Sam brings his shoulder. And sometimes it's Sam bringing the Coors Light and I'm doing the listening. Me and Sam? Together? I've never even thought about it. Okay, so I've thought about it.

Coors Light.
Just between friends.

Coors LIGHT BEER

Figure 11.13   Beer Ad Aimed at Women

This Coors Light ad uses an unusual strategy to target young adult women. Unlike typical beer ads aimed at men, which feature beach girls in bikinis or men bonding together on fishing trips or in sports bars, this Coors Light ad with its "Sam and Me" theme associates beer drinking with the warm friendship of a man and a woman.

Part of the ad's emotional appeal is the totally relaxed "story" shown in the image. The ad reveals a man and a woman, probably in their early- to mid-twenties, in relaxed conversation; they are sitting casually on a tabletop, with their legs resting on chair seats. The woman is wearing casual pants, a summery cotton top, and informal shoes. Her shoulder-length hair has a healthy, mussed appearance, and a braid comes across the front of her shoulder. She is turned away from the man, leans on her knees, and holds a bottle of Coors Light. Her sparkling eyes are looking up, and she smiles happily, as if reliving a pleasant memory. The man is wearing slacks, a cotton shirt with the sleeves rolled up, and scuffed tennis shoes with white socks. He also has a reminiscing smile on his face, and he leans on the woman's shoulder. The words "Coors Light. Just between friends." appear immediately below the picture next to a Coors Light can.

This ad creates its mirror effect by making it easy for women to identify with its story, which includes a good-looking but nonglamorous model and which is told from a woman's point of view (the "me" is the woman in the photograph). The ad's window effect is its opening onto a happy future. It appeals to women's desire for close friendships and relationships. Everything about the picture signifies long-established closeness and intimacy—old friends rather than lovers. The way the man leans on the woman shows her strength and independence. Additionally, the way they pose, with the woman slightly forward and sitting up more than the man, results in their taking up equal space in the picture. In many ads featuring male-female couples, the man appears larger and taller than the woman; this picture signifies mutuality and equality.

The words of the ad help interpret the relationship. Sam and the woman have been friends since the first grade, and they are reminiscing about old times. The relationship is thoroughly mutual. Sometimes he brings the Coors Light and sometimes she brings it; sometimes she does the listening and sometimes he does; sometimes she leans on his shoulder and sometimes he leans on hers. Sometimes the ad says, "Sam and me"; sometimes it says, "me and Sam." Even the "bad grammar" of "Sam and me" (rather than "Sam and I") suggests the lazy, relaxed absence of pretense or formality. "Sam" is a "buddy" kind of name rather than a romantic-hero name. But the last three lines of the copy give just a hint of potential romance: "Me and Sam? Together? I've never even thought about it. Okay, so I've thought about it."

Whereas beer ads targeting men portray women as sex objects, this ad appeals to many women's desire for relationships and for romance based on friendship. Its window function is mutuality and love rather than sexual acquisition.

The Coors Light ad was designed to appeal to young adult women. But cultural critics might also point out that the ad reproduces a worldview in which heterosexuality is the norm and in which women find their identities in romance and marriage. From the perspective of cultural criticism, then, advertisements are powerful cultural forces that both reflect cultural values and help construct and reproduce those values, including our sense of what is normal and not normal and our ideas about gender, race, and class. Identifying these cultural values in ads is an important part of ad analysis.

Exploring and Generating Ideas for Your Analysis

For the subject of your analysis, your instructor may allow you to choose your own images or may provide them for you. If you choose your own, be sure to follow your instructor's guidelines. In choosing your visual texts, look for some important commonality that will enable you to concentrate on similarities and differences in your analysis:

- *Documentary or news photographs.* Analyze two photographs of an event from magazines with different political biases; two news photographs from articles addressing the same story from different angles of vision; or two images on Web sites presenting different perspectives on a recent controversial issue such as industrial farming or the war against terrorists.
- *Paintings.* Find two paintings with similar subject matter but different dominant impressions or emotional impacts.
- *Print ads.* Look for two ads for the same product (for example, cars, perfume, watches, shampoo) that are aimed at different target audiences or that make appeals to noticeably different value systems.

No matter what type of visual texts you are using, we suggest that you generate ideas and material for your analysis by using the question-asking strategies presented earlier in this chapter.

To help you generate more ideas, go detail by detail through your images, asking how the rhetorical effect would be different if some detail were changed:

- How would this documentary photo have a different effect if the homeless man were lying on the sidewalk instead of leaning against the doorway?
- Why did the artist blur images in the background rather than make them more distinct?
- What if the admakers had chosen a poodle rather than a black Lab? What if this model were a person of color rather than white?

Shaping and Drafting Your Analysis

Your closed-form essay should be fairly easy to organize at the big-picture level, but each part will require its own organic organization depending on the main points of your analysis. At the big-picture level, you can generally follow a structure like the one shown in Figure 11.14.

If you get stuck, we recommend that you write your rough draft rapidly, without worrying about gracefulness or correctness, merely trying to capture your initial ideas. Many people like to begin with the description of the two visual texts and then write the analysis before writing the introduction and conclusion. After you have written your draft, put it aside for a while before you begin revising.

Revising

Most experienced writers make global changes in their drafts when they revise, especially when they are doing analytical writing. The act of writing a rough draft generally leads to the discovery of more ideas. You may also realize that some of your original ideas aren't clearly developed or that the draft feels scattered or disorganized.

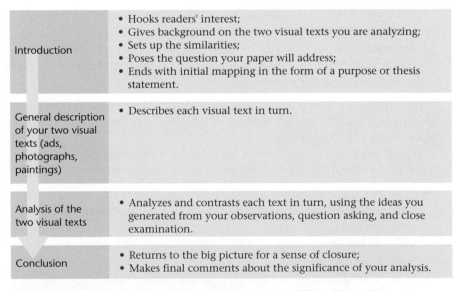

Introduction	• Hooks readers' interest; • Gives background on the two visual texts you are analyzing; • Sets up the similarities; • Poses the question your paper will address; • Ends with initial mapping in the form of a purpose or thesis statement.
General description of your two visual texts (ads, photographs, paintings)	• Describes each visual text in turn.
Analysis of the two visual texts	• Analyzes and contrasts each text in turn, using the ideas you generated from your observations, question asking, and close examination.
Conclusion	• Returns to the big picture for a sense of closure; • Makes final comments about the significance of your analysis.

Figure 11.14   Framework for an Analysis of Two Visuals

We recommend that you ask your classmates for a peer review of your draft early in the revising process to help you enhance the clarity and depth of your analysis.

Questions for Peer Review

Ask your peer reviewers to address these questions:

1. How well do the title, introduction, and thesis set up an academic analysis?

2. Where does the writer capture your interest and provide necessary background information? How might the writer more clearly pose the question to be addressed and map out the analysis?

3. Where could the writer describe the visual texts more clearly so that readers can "see" them?

4. How has the writer established the complexity of the texts and their commonalities and differences?

5. How well has the writer used the questions about angle of vision, artistic techniques, and compositional features presented in this chapter to achieve a detailed and insightful analysis of the texts? Where could the writer add more specific details about settings, props, furniture, posing of characters, facial expressions, manners of dress, and so forth?

6. In what ways could the writer improve this analysis by clarifying, deepening, expanding, or reorganizing the analysis? How has the writer helped you understand something new about these two texts?

READINGS

Mothers Against Drunk Driving

MADD—Mothers Against Drunk Driving—is one of the most respected nonprofit organizations in the United States. For the past 25 years MADD has championed the rights of victims of drunk driving and has promoted public awareness of the consequences of drunk driving. The ad on this page is one of many that were displayed on the MADD Web site (www.madd.org) in the summer of 2005.

Coming Home

Carolyn Kleiner Butler

To a war-weary nation, a U.S. POW's return from captivity in Vietnam in 1973 looked like the happiest of reunions.

Sitting in the back seat of a station wagon on the tarmac at Travis Air Force Base, in California, clad in her favorite fuchsia miniskirt, 15-year-old Lorrie Stirm felt that she was in a dream. It was March 17, 1973, and it had been six long years since she had last seen her father, Lt. Col. Robert L. Stirm, an Air Force fighter pilot who was shot down over Hanoi in 1967 and had been missing or imprisoned ever since. She simply couldn't believe they were about to be reunited. The teenager waited while her father stood in front of a jubilant crowd and made a brief speech on behalf of himself and other POW's who had arrived from Vietnam as part of "Operation Homecoming."

The minutes crept by like hours, she recalls, and then, all at once, the car door opened. "I just wanted to get to Dad as fast as I could," Lorrie says. She tore down the runway toward him with open arms, her spirits—and feet—flying. Her mother, Loretta, and three younger siblings—Robert Jr., Roger and Cindy—were only steps behind. "We didn't know if he would ever come home," Lorrie says. "That moment was all our prayers answered, all our wishes come true."

Associated Press photographer Slava "Sal" Veder, who'd been standing in a crowded bullpen with dozens of other journalists, noticed the sprinting family and started taking pictures. "You could feel the energy and the raw emotion in the air," says Veder, then 46, who had spent much of the Vietnam era covering antiwar demonstrations in San Francisco and Berkeley. The day was overcast, meaning no shadows and near-perfect light. He rushed to a makeshift darkroom in a ladies' bathroom on the base (United Press International had commandeered the men's). In less than half an hour, Veder and his AP colleague Walt Zeboski had developed six remarkable images of that singular moment. Veder's pick, which he instantly titled *Burst of Joy,* was sent out over the news-service wires, published in newspapers around the nation and went on to win a Pulitzer Prize in 1974.

It remains the quintessential homecoming photograph of the time. Stirm, 39, who had endured gunshot wounds, torture, illness, starvation and despair in North Vietnamese prison camps, including the infamous Hanoi Hilton, is pictured in a crisp new uniform. Because his back is to the camera, as Veder points out, the officer seems anonymous, an everyman who represented not only the hundreds of POW's released that

The story just before the photograph was taken

Lorrie's memories of her feelings when her dad returned

Shift to the photographer's story

The photographer's recollection of the emotions of that day

The story from the soldier's or father's point of view

...*continued* Coming Home, **Carolyn Kleiner Butler**

A hero's welcome: Lorrie, Robert Jr., Cindy, Loretta and Roger Stirm greet Lt. Col. Robert Stirm after his six years as a prisoner of war.

Events behind the moment of this photograph

spring but all the troops in Vietnam who would return home to the mothers, fathers, wives, daughters and sons they'd left behind. "It's a hero's welcome for guys who weren't always seen or treated as heroes," says Donald Goldstein, a retired Air Force lieutenant colonel and a coauthor of *The Vietnam War: The Stories and The Photographs,* of the Stirm family reunion picture. "After years of fighting a war we couldn't win, a war that tore us apart, it was finally over, and the country could start healing."

But there was more to the story than was captured on film. Three days before Stirm landed at Travis, a chaplain had handed him a Dear John letter from his wife. "I can't help but feel ambivalent about it," Stirm says today of the photograph. "I was very pleased to see my children—I loved them all and still do, and I know they had a difficult time—but there was a lot to deal with." Lorrie says, "So much had happened—there was so much that my dad missed out on—and it took a while to let him back into our lives and accept his authority." Her parents were divorced within a year of his return. Her mother remarried in 1974 and lives in Texas with her husband. Robert retired from the Air Force as a colonel in 1977 and worked as a corporate pilot and businessman. He married and was divorced again. Now 72 and retired, he lives in Foster City, California.

As for the rest of the family, Robert Jr. is a dentist in Walnut Creek, California; he and his wife have four children, the oldest of whom is a marine. Roger, a major in the Air Force, lives outside Seattle. Cindy Pierson, a waitress, resides in Walnut Creek with her husband and has a daughter in college. And Lorrie Stirm Kitching, now 47, is an executive administrator and mother of two sons. She lives in Mountain View, California, with her husband. All four of Robert Stirm Sr.'s children have a copy of *Burst of Joy* hanging in a place of honor on their walls. But he says he can't bring himself to display the picture.

How the lives of all the family members have changed

Three decades after the Stirm reunion, the scene, having appeared in countless books, anthologies and exhibitions, remains part of the nation's collective consciousness, often serving as an uplifting postscript to Vietnam. That the moment was considerably more fraught than we first assumed makes it all the more poignant and reminds us that not all war casualties occur on the battlefield.

Concluding comments leading up to Butler's thesis: Pictures do not always tell the complete story, and not all casualties occur on the battlefield.

"We have this very nice picture of a very happy moment," Lorrie says, "but every time I look at it, I remember the families that weren't reunited, and the ones that aren't being reunited today—many, many families—and I think, I'm one of the lucky ones."

Triple Self-Portrait

Charles Rosen and Henri Zerner

Triple Self-Portrait of 1960 is clever and witty. It is not simply a portrait of the artist by himself but represents the process of painting a self-portrait, and in the bargain Rockwell takes the opportunity to comment on his brand of "realism" and his relation to the history of art. A sheet of preparatory drawings in different poses is tacked onto the left of the canvas. The artist represents himself from the back; the canvas he works on already has a fully worked-out black-and-white drawing of his face with the pipe in his mouth, based on the central drawing of the sketch sheet. The artist gazes at his own reflection in a mirror propped up on a chair. The reflection we see in the mirror is similar to, but not identical with, the portrait sketched on the canvas. The artist wears glasses, and the glare of the lenses completely obliterates his gaze, while the portrait he works on is without glasses and a little younger-looking, certainly less tense than the reflection. Rockwell seems to confess that the reality of his depicted world, compelling as it may be, is in fact a make-believe.

Claim: The portrait is a clever and witty comment on his own art.

Layout and composition of portrait

Description of details

...continued Triple Self-Portrait, **Charles Rosen and Henri Zerner**

More description of details

Tacked on the upper right corner of the canvas is a series of reproductions of historical self-portraits: Dürer, Rembrandt, Van Gogh, and Picasso—grand company to measure oneself against, although the humorous tone of the image preserves it from megalomania. But there is a problem: "If Rockwell nodded humbly in Picasso's direction," as Robert Rosenblum suggests, how humbly was it? It is "most surprising," Rosenblum observes, that Rockwell chose "a particularly difficult Picasso that mixes in idealized self-portrait in profile with an id-like female monster attacking from within" rather than something easily recognizable. This was a cover for *The Saturday Evening Post*. The strength of Rockwell is

Interpreting the meaning and significance of the painting

that he knew his public, and knew that such subtleties would be entirely lost on its readers, that most of them would not recognize the Picasso as a self-portrait at all but would consider it as pretentious humbug compared to Rockwell's honest picture and those of the illustrious predecessors he claims. Nor does he seem to have been particularly anxious to change their minds, whatever he himself may have thought.

Face to Face with Tragedy

Clark Hoyt

1   It was hard to look at some of the pictures of suffering and death caused by the earthquake in Haiti—and impossible to turn away.

2   The top of one front page in the *Times* was dominated by a woman, her hand to her cheek, as if in shock, walking past partially covered corpses lined up along a dirty curb. The next day, an even larger photograph at the top of page 1 showed a man covered in gray dust, lying alone, dead, statue-like, on a stretcher made from a piece of tattered cardboard spread over a crude ladder. Inside that same paper, the Friday after the disaster, was a gruesome scene from the central morgue in Port-au-Prince: a man mourning the death of his 10-month-old daughter, lying in her diaper atop a pile of bodies.

3   Some readers were offended at these scenes and even more graphic pictures on the paper's Web site, calling them exploitive and sensationalistic. "The numerous photographs printed in the *Times* showing the dead strewn about the streets of Port-au-Prince are unnecessary, unethical, unkind and inhumane," wrote Randy Stebbins of Hammond, La. Christa Robbins of Chicago said, "I feel that the people who have suffered the most are being spectacularized by your blood-and-gore photographs, which do not at all inform me of the relief efforts, the political stability of the region or the extent of damage to families and infrastructure." She spoke for several readers when she added, "If this had happened in California, I cannot imagine a similar depiction of half-clothed bodies splayed out for the camera. What are you thinking?"

4   But other readers were grateful for the shocking pictures, even as they were deeply troubled by them. Mary Louise Thomas of Palatka, Fla., said a different photo of the baby, lying on her dead mother, caused her to cry out, "Oh, my God!" and to sob for an hour. "But run from it? Never," she said. People repelled by such images "should really try staring truth in the face occasionally and try to understand it," she wrote.

5   Mary Claire Carroll of Richmond, Vt., asked, "How else can you motivate or inspire someone like me to donate money" to help out in Haiti? Her son, she added, thinks Americans "are too sheltered and protected from the real world."

6   Every disaster that produces horrific scenes of carnage presents photographers and their editors with the challenge of telling the unsanitized truth without crossing into the offensive and truly exploitive. In 2004, when a giant undersea earthquake unleashed a tsunami that killed tens of thousands along Indian Ocean coastlines, the *Times* ran a dramatic

...continued Face to Face with Tragedy, **Clark Hoyt**

front-page photo of a woman overcome with grief amid rows of dead children, including her own. Some readers protested, but the newspaper's first public editor, Daniel Okrent, concluded that the paper was right to publish the picture. It told the story of the tsunami, he said.

7   I asked Kenneth Irby, leader of the visual journalism group at the Poynter Institute in Florida, for his assessment of the pictures from Haiti. Irby brings unusual perspectives to the task. He is a veteran photojournalist and an ordained minister, the pastor of an African Methodist Episcopal church in Palmetto, Fla. His wife's best friend is Haitian, and her family was still unaccounted for when we talked last week. "I think the *Times* coverage has been raw, truthful and tasteful," he told me, defending even the most graphic images.

8   Irby, who has been in touch with photographers in Haiti, said survivors want the world to see what has happened. "The actual loved ones, the bereaved, implore the journalists to tell their stories," he said.

9   That is exactly what Damon Winter told me. He is the *Times* photographer who took the pictures that elicited most of the protests to me and much praise on the paper's Web site. Winter, who won a Pulitzer Prize last year for his coverage of the Obama presidential campaign, was the first *Times* staff photographer on the scene, flying from New York to the Dominican Republic and then into Haiti aboard a chartered helicopter. He had never been to Haiti or covered a natural disaster.

10   "I have had so many people beg me to come to their home and photograph the bodies of their children, brothers, sisters, mothers, fathers," he said. "There are so many times that I have to apologize and say that I cannot, that I have photographed so many bodies already, and I think it breaks their hearts because they so desperately want people to know what has happened to them, what tremendous pain they are in, and that they desperately need help." Winter said it was important "that I do whatever I can to try and make our readers understand just how dire the situation is here."

11   Jessie De Witt, an international photo editor, said Winter sent the paper 26 pictures on his first day in Haiti, including the picture of the bodies along the curb that wound up on the front page. He sent 65 the next day, including the mourning father and the dead man on the stretcher. De Witt and her colleagues think carefully about photo selections. A picture of a dog eyeing a corpse is out, as are stacks of bodies without context. And they think about juxtaposition: an Armageddon-like scene of people scrambling for supplies from a ruined store was played against a quieter picture of people waiting patiently for medical treatment.

12   Michele McNally, the assistant managing editor in charge of photography, said she was going through all the photos from all sources, and Winter's photos of the single dead man and the grieving father "stopped me in my tracks." Bill Keller, the executive editor, said editors considered both for the front page, but chose the lone body, played big, because it was dramatic and there was "an intimacy that causes people to pause and dwell on the depth of the tragedy." Looking at one person, instead of many, "humanizes it," he said.

13   I asked McNally about Robbins's contention that such pictures would not appear in the paper if the victims were somewhere in the United States. If such pictures existed, she said, she would run them. When Hurricane Katrina hit New Orleans, the *Times* did publish a front-page picture of a body floating near a bridge where a woman was feeding her dog. But despite Katrina's toll, there were relatively few such images in the paper. Irby said that authorities in the United States are generally quick to cordon off disaster scenes.

14   Just as a picture of a grieving mother told the story of the tsunami in 2004, the disturbing images of the last two weeks have been telling the story of Haiti, and the *Times* is right to publish them. As Patricia Lay-Dorsey, a reader from Detroit, put it, Winter's "camera was my eye as much as it was his. And every one of his photos told the truth."

Disturbing Media Images of Haiti Earthquake Aftermath Tell Only Part of the Story

Manoucheka Celeste

1   As a Haitian, former journalist and media scholar, [I found] the earthquake in Haiti . . . both personally devastating and intellectually challenging.

2   The first earthquake to hit Haiti in more than 200 years was unbelievable, unexpected and unprecedented. The devastation is clear with more than 200,000 lives lost. The damage is real. As we saw, people around the world responded quickly and generously.

...continued Disturbing Media Images of Haiti Earthquake Aftermath, **Manoucheka Celeste**

3   This catastrophe presented an opportunity for media to respond in an unprecedented way. Some news outlets arrived before relief workers and doctors. We watched the horrors as they happened. I hoped that this was the moment when those of us trained in journalism would do something remarkable: Bring news of an unimaginable event in a way that disrupted the sensational and stereotypical ways that people in the "Third World" are represented.

4   What we got instead was much less humane. Videos of dead bodies, including children and the elderly, filled our television screens. For those of us who tuned in for information about friends and families, it was and is unbearable and despicable. Coverage went from sensational to ridiculous as CNN compared the literacy rates of Haiti and the United States. This was irrelevant as it continued to represent Haiti as a failed state.

5   The focus on poverty, with the repeated tagline "the poorest country in the Western Hemisphere" and references to crime and unrest, make it hard for viewers to imagine any other aspect of life in Haiti. People were called looters for taking food from collapsed buildings after not having eaten for days, framing their survival as a crime. The humanity needed in this moment is clearly missing.

6   Media scholars have long connected media coverage with public opinion, cultivating our attitudes and creating and reinforcing stereotypes. It is predominantly people of color who are shown negatively in news and entertainment. While the images mobilized some to help, they are damaging in the long term as they become ingrained in how we imagine Haitians. For many this is the first and last contact they will have with this population. The images matter as Haitians are shown as less than human. In mass media when images of Haiti and various countries in the African continent are shown, blackness becomes associated with helplessness, danger, poverty and hopelessness.

7   In the most disgusting moment in broadcast history, Pat Robertson proclaimed that Haiti had it coming because of its "deal with the devil," linking Haiti to "godlessness." What Robertson didn't consider was that "godlessness" was used as an excuse to kill and colonize peoples throughout history in the name of God, including Haiti, which, incidentally, is a heavily Christian country.

8   The question that plagues me and hopefully all audiences is: Who is able to die with dignity? In recent media history, there are few, but increasing instances where dead Americans are shown. From Columbine to Sept. 11, we rightfully protect the dead and rarely dare show them on television or in newspapers. Yet, the increasing presence of graphic and emotionally charged images, especially in broadcast media makes it seem normal or desirable.

9   This earthquake, despite the amazing pain that it has caused to so many, presents an unprecedented opportunity. Viewers and readers can demand that in people's darkest hour or once they lose their lives that they are treated with dignity.

10   We want the story without sensationalism and reinforcement of stereotypes. We want the media to value the lives of people who are "not us." As I waited for eight days to hear that my own mother and grandmother in Port-au-Prince are safe, I wanted to hold on to good memories of the person who brought me into the world and the one who taught me to be generous and tenacious. Let's seize the opportunity of this horrific tragedy to demand better from our news sources: dignity for everyone.

STUDENT MODELS

Two Photographs Capture Women's
Economic Misery

Lydia Wheeler (student)

1   During economic crises, the hardship of individuals is often presented to us as statistics and facts: number of bankruptcies, percentage of
the population living below the poverty line, and foreclosures or unemployment rates. Although this numerical data can be shocking, it usually
remains abstract and impersonal. In contrast, photographers such as
Stephen Crowley and Dorothea Lange help us visualize the human suffering involved in the economic conditions, skillfully evoking the emotional, as well as the physical, reality of their subjects. Crowley's (2010)
color photograph, first published January 2, 2010, in a *New York Times*
article titled "Living on Nothing but Food Stamps," is captioned "Isabel
Bermudez, who has two daughters and no cash income." Lange's (1936)
black and white photograph was commissioned by the Resettlement
Agency to document Americans living in the Great Depression; she originally captioned it *Destitute pea pickers in California; a 32 year old mother
of seven children. February 1936.* However, in March of the same year, the
San Francisco Times published Lange's photograph in an article demanding aid for workers like Florence Owens Thompson, the central subject
of the picture. Once published, the photograph became famous and was
nicknamed *Migrant Mother.* A close look at these two photos shows that
through their skillful use of photographic elements such as focus, framing, orientation, and shape, Stephen Crowley (2010) and Dorothea
Lange (1936) capture the unique emotional and physical realities of their
subjects, eliciting compassion and admiration, respectively.

2   Stephen Crowley's (2010) photograph of a mother sitting in a room,
perhaps the dining room of her house, and her young daughter standing
and reaching out to comfort her sets up contrasts and tensions that
underscore loss and convey grief. The accompanying article explains that
Isabel Bermudez, whose income from real estate once amply supported
her family, now has no income or prospect for employment and relies
entirely on food stamps. A careful examination of Crowley's photograph
implies this loss by hinting that Bermudez's wealth is insecure.

3   The framing, distance, and focus of Crowley's (2010) photograph
emphasize this vanished wealth and the emotional pain. The image is a
medium close up with its human subjects to the side, surrounding them
with empty space and hints of expensive furnishings. While part of the
foreground is sharply focused, the background is blurry and unfocused.

Isabel Bermudez, who has two daughters and no cash income, by Stephen Crowley

There is a suggestion that the room is spacious. Further, the high, decorative backs of the room's chairs, the repetitive design decorating the bookshelf on the frame's left, and the houseplant next to the bookshelf show that the room is well furnished, even luxurious. Bermudez and her daughter match their surroundings in being elegantly dressed. Bermudez looks across the room as if absorbed in her troubles; her daughter looks intently at her. Viewers' eyes are drawn to Bermudez's dark dress and her pearl necklace and earrings. However, the ostensible comfort of Bermudez and her surroundings starkly contrasts with her grief.

4   Crowley (2010) heightens this contrast and tension through the subjects' orientation and the space between them. The space between Bermudez and her daughter is one of the photograph's dominant features, but it contains only out-of-focus objects in the background. Neither figure is centered in the photo; neither looks at the camera. Consequently, the viewers' attention moves back and forth between them, creating a sense of uneasiness. The meaning of this photo is focused not on what Bermudez has but on what she has lost.

5   Crowley (2010) also evokes sympathy and compassion for his subjects with his choice of angle, scale, and detail. The photograph's slightly high angle makes viewers look down—literally—on Bermudez, making her appear vulnerable and powerless and reinforcing the pathos. The most striking bid for compassion is the tears streaming down Bermudez's well made-up face. The contrast between her tidy appearance and the tear tracks on her face suggest overwhelming sadness. The poignancy of her apparent breakdown is heightened by her somber daughter's attempt to

Destitute pea pickers in California; a 32 year old mother of seven children
[Migrant Mother] by Dorothea Lange

wipe away the tears on her mother's face. Crowley's decisions regarding *Isabel's* composition create an image that is highly disturbing.

6   In contrast to Crowley's (2010) photograph, Lange's (1936) *Migrant Mother*—through its content, focus, frame, rhythm, and angle—conveys long-standing poverty. Yet through this image of inescapable poverty pressing upon its subjects, it evokes admiration for this mother.

7   Lange's (1936) frame and focus generate much of the intensity of *Migrant Mother.* This photo is also a medium close up, but Lange's frame is tight with no open space. The lack of this openness cramps Lange's subjects and creates a claustrophobic feel intensified by the number of subjects shown—four to *Isabel's* two. There is almost no background. The subjects filling the foreground are crowded and sharply focused. The contrast between crowded foreground and empty background exaggerates the former and adds a touch of loneliness to *Migrant Mother;* this mother has no resources besides herself. Additionally, the subjects of *Migrant Mother* almost epitomize poverty: their hair is messy and uncombed, their skin dirt-stained. Even their clothes are worn—from the hem of Thompson's frayed sleeve to the smudges on her baby's blanket, Lange's photograph shows that Thompson can barely afford functional items.

8   *Migrant Mother's* circular lines also create a sense of sameness, stagnation, and hopelessness. Thompson's face draws viewers' eyes as the dominant feature, and Lange (1936) has ringed it with several arcs. The parentheses of her standing children's bodies, the angle of her baby in its blanket, and the arc of her dark hair form a ring that hems Thompson in and creates a circular path for the eyes of viewers. Seen with the obvious destitution of Lange's subjects, this repetition is threatening and grimly promises that it will be difficult, if not impossible, for this family to escape its poverty.

9   Like Crowley's (2010) *Isabel,* the impact of Lange's (1936) *Migrant Mother* derives from both the tragedy of her subjects' situation and their reactions. Lange uses angle and scale to generate sympathy and admiration for Thompson's strength. Once again we see a slightly high angle highlighting the subjects' vulnerability, which Lange reinforces with the slender necks of Thompson's children and a glimpse of her brassiere. However, Lange then contrasts this vulnerability with Thompson's strength, fostering viewers' admiration rather than compassion. *Migrant Mother's* scale, for example, exaggerates rather than diminishes Thompson's size: the photograph's frame focuses viewers' attention on the mother, who looks large, compared to her children. Additionally, Lange's subject literally supports the bodies of the children surrounding her. Unlike Bermudez, Thompson sits tall as a pillar of strength for her vulnerable children. Even her expression—worried but dry eyed—fosters admiration and respect in viewers. By juxtaposing Thompson's vulnerability with her strength, Lange creates a photograph that conveys both its subjects' poverty and their stoicism in facing the Great Depression.

10   Lange (1936) and Crowley (2010) guide viewer's reactions to their photographs through careful control of the elements that influence our emotional responses to their work. Though they both show women in

economic crises, these artists are able to convey the distinct realities of their subjects' situations and consequently send viewers away in different emotional states: one of compassion, one of admiration. The fame and veneration of Lange's *Migrant Mother* is a testament to her ability to evoke desired emotions. The photograph was exhibited at the Museum of Modern Art in 1941 and again in 1955, and was co-opted by countless movements since it was first published. Whether Crowley's *Isabel* will achieve similar fame for epitomizing this generation's economic crisis remains to be seen, but both photographs certainly succeed in delivering strong, lasting emotional statements.

References

Crowley, S. (2004). (Photograph). Retrieved from www.chron.com/news/nation-world/article/As-recession-lingers-more-Americans-living-on 1615172.php

Lange, D. (2004). *Migrant mother*. Retrieved from www.eyewitnesstohistory .com/migrantmother.htm

PRACTICE

Face to Face with Tragedy, p. 479

1 According to Clark Hoyt, what are the ethical and rhetorical problems that photojournalists face in photographing disasters like the Haiti earthquake? Who are the different stakeholders in this controversy?

a. On page 453 in this chapter, we discussed the importance of the photographer's purpose and of the cultural, social, historical and political context of the photograph. What claims does Hoyt make for the purpose and context of the published images of human suffering in Haiti?

b. Research the coverage of the Haiti earthquake in one of the prominent general news commentary sources such as *Newsweek, Time, USA Today* or a leading newspaper's or online news site's archives. What images appear the most often? How did the captions for these images shape your impression of them?

c. What intellectual and emotional impact did these images have on you?

Disturbing Images of Haiti Earthquake Aftermath, p. 481

2 In her criticism of the media's use of "graphic and emotionally charged images," how does Manoucheka Celeste argue against the main perspective that Hoyt endorses?

a. Celeste's op-ed piece examines the role of viewers' knowledge, values, and assumptions in interpreting photos in news stories. What historical, political, and racial elements does Celeste underscore?

b. For the photographs of the Haiti disaster that you located and viewed, argue that they either simplified and distorted the issues or pushed them toward complexity and depth. In your mind, what does it mean to treat the human subjects of photographs with "dignity?"

Port Sanilac
Port Sanilac, MI

How Do I Work with Multiple Sources?

12

A S A COLLEGE WRITER, YOU WILL OFTEN COMPOSE PAPERS THAT DRAW ON MULTIPLE READING SOURCES. YOU MIGHT WRITE AN ESSAY COMPARING AND CONTRASTING TWO TEXTS OR A PAPER BASED ON SEVERAL JOURNAL ARTICLES, A CHAPTER FROM A book, and a piece from a newspaper. Working with multiple sources is complex because you have to identify consistencies among the texts and then integrate these bits of relevant information with your own ideas. The amount of information you draw from the sources will depend on the topic and the assignment.

Comparing and Contrasting Sources

How many times have you received a writing assignment that began "Compare and contrast . . ."? Your social studies teacher may have asked you to contrast the abolitionists' view of slavery with the pro-slavery view, or your English teacher may have told you to compare two characters in a short story. In primary school, you probably wrote reports comparing two types of animals or showing the difference between two countries or states. We use comparison and contrast every day. Asked to describe a new song on the radio, we say, "It has a rap beat, but the lyrics sound more like pop music." We frequently view things in terms of what they are like and unlike.

USES OF COMPARISON AND CONTRAST

Writers use comparison and contrast to describe, explain, and argue. Let us look first at a descriptive paragraph from Leslie Heywood's memoir, *Pretty Good for a Girl.* The setting is the weight room where Heywood works out with the boys on the distance running team. She is describing a confrontation with the coach of the sprinters' team. Identify the comparisons.

> I sit up and there he is: the sprinters' coach. He looks just like—*just like*—Luke Spencer on *General Hospital,* and this is Luke Spencer's year. A few months from now he will rape Laura [and] then marry her, and the whole country will tune in, whether they usually watch the soaps or not, the hype in the papers approaching that reserved for Prince Charles and Princess Di, whose wedding will also happen that month. Like Luke on TV, Coach Luke is gaunt and thin, skin really white, with unruly threads of albino-red hair fanning the air behind him, thinning a bit right on top. He moves quickly, and is sarcastic a lot like he's sarcastic right now, twisting that smile that says he knows it all and knows it right, your place in the universe nothing like his. I look up at him, ready for a fight. He looks at me like you'd look at a rooster who's strutting his stuff just before he's going to get cooked. Not this rooster, mister, not me. I look at him with his own look that says you don't even exist and you'd better get out of my way. His mouth turns up at one corner and he laughs, "Hey, my guys need this bench and you all should go do something else." I don't move.

Did you find the following comparisons between

- Coach Luke and Luke Spencer on *General Hospital?*
- media hype over *General Hospital* and media coverage of the royal wedding?
- Heywood herself and a rooster who's strutting his stuff before he's about to be cooked?

Comparisons add depth to descriptive writing and leave the reader with rich, memorable images.

Next, consider how comparison is used for the purpose of explanation. In the following paragraph, philosophy professor David Rothenberg explains the difference between university students in Finland and in the United States. The passage is from "Learning in Finland: No Grades, No Criticism," an article published in *The Chronicle of Higher Education.*

> The Finnish view is that simply doing the work on one's own time is the point of education. My students always claimed to be too busy, but they rarely seemed stressed or burned out. Students must think, they must write. In Europe, they often save all their thinking for the final project

and the final exam at the end of the single course they typically take each semester. In the United States, students and professors communicate all the time—discussing, chatting, bouncing ideas back and forth, at least in small classes. The Finns put more of a boundary between the learned and the learner. Professors are encouraged to pontificate, to put forth information, and the student to sit silently and take it all down.

Last, let us examine how Professor Pat Griffin makes an argument on the basis of similarity. The paragraph is from Griffin's book, *Strong Women, Deep Closets: Lesbians and Homophobia in Sport.* Griffin argues that women athletes possess qualities, talents, and characteristics that are attributed only to male athletes.

Women's serious participation in sport brings into question the "natural" and mutually exclusive nature of gender and gender roles. If women in sport can be tough minded, competitive, and muscular too, then sport loses its special place in the development of masculinity for men. If women can so easily develop these so-called masculine qualities, then what are the meanings of femininity and masculinity? What does it mean to be a man or a woman? These challenges threaten an acceptance of the traditional order in which men are privileged and women are subordinate.

In "A Young Person's Guide to the Grading System" (p. 184), Jerry Farber argues that students don't need grades even though they may think otherwise. Farber (1969) compares students to addicts:

We're like those sleeping pill addicts who have reached the point where they need strong artificial inducement to do what comes naturally. We're grade junkies—convinced that we'd never learn without the A's and F's to keep us going. (p. 204)

Notice that the quoted passages show writers using comparison and contrast for a precise purpose. Heywood is describing Coach Luke, Rothenberg is explaining the differences between Finnish and American views of higher education, Griffin is making a case for gender equality, and Farber is arguing against grades. Writers may use comparison and contrast simply to explore interesting points of similarity between two subjects or to demonstrate that grounds for comparison actually exist, but more often they describe, explain, or argue.

RHETORICAL PURPOSE FOR COMPARISON-AND-CONTRAST

As a college writer, you will occasionally be asked to compare your own experience with information from reading sources, but more typically you will be required to compare and contrast the views expressed in various texts. Here is a typical assignment.

Compare and contrast two authors' views on assisted suicide: those of Ernest van den Haag in his *National Review* article, "Make Mine Hemlock," and those of Rand Richards Cooper in his *Commonweal* article, "The Dignity of Helplessness: What Sort of Society Would Euthanasia Create?"

Since this is a loosely defined assignment, there are a number of ways you can approach it. The most rudimentary approach is simply to list the similarities and differences in the two authors' views and use the list to compose your essay.

SIMILARITIES

- Neither author is questioning assisted suicide per se.
- Both authors offer some of the same examples.

DIFFERENCES

- Van den Haag is in favor of institutionalizing assisted suicide; Cooper is against it.
- Van den Haag bases his argument on the notion of rights; Cooper claims that this notion is too narrow a framework.
- Van den Haag finds fault with the argument that life is a social duty that no one should shirk; Cooper bases his argument on the "texture of civic life."
- Van den Haag discusses abled individuals' right to commit suicide and also goes into detail about assisted suicide for disabled individuals; Cooper focuses on the elderly.
- Van den Haag goes into detail about the competence of individuals who wish to shorten their life; Cooper does not treat this issue.
- Van den Haag goes into detail about safeguarding the disinterestedness of people who assist with suicides; Cooper predicts that people may act out of self-interest.
- Van den Haag dismisses "slippery slope" arguments; Cooper dwells on the long-range negative consequences of euthanasia.
- Van den Haag says that today people hold the view that "individuals collectively own society, rather than vice versa"; Cooper claims that contemporary society is moving toward communitarianism and interest in togetherness rather than separateness.
- Van den Haag thinks Dr. Kevorkian is courageous; Cooper questions everything Kevorkian has done.
- Van den Haag claims that there are safeguards to ensure that no one is pressured to end his or her life; Cooper claims that the elderly do not have "absolute autonomy" in this matter.

You could easily construct an essay from this list by using a block presentational pattern, allocating a small block to similarities and a large one to differences. The resulting essay would be rather flat because it would simply catalog the similarities and differences. There is nothing intrinsically wrong with this goal, but when it is the only end in mind, it is easy to fall into the trap of doing too much summarizing and too little discussion of similarities and differences. We recommend that you take the process a step further. After you identify similarities and differences, step back and ask yourself what they represent, reveal, or demonstrate. Reflect on the list, select from it, shape it, or expand it. Ask yourself the following questions.

QUESTIONS ABOUT SIMILARITIES AND DIFFERENCES

- Can you select from among the similarities and differences and categorize them in a way that will make your essay more interesting, relevant, eventful, or meaningful?
- Is there a new angle or point of view you can take?
- Can you make the essay functional? Can you create a "rhetorical imperative," that is, write to move or influence a certain group of readers for a specific reason?
- Can you address a more definite audience?
- How can you engage the reader best?
- Can you fashion a richer rhetorical situation?

To illustrate, let us examine a student essay written in response to the assignment on page 494.

THE CONTROVERSY OVER ASSISTED SUICIDE   2

The Controversy over Assisted Suicide

1   Should competent people, particularly those who are terminally ill or handicapped, have the right to end their lives? Or should they be forced to go on living even if they do not wish to do so? What it comes down to is the question of who owns life: God, the individual, or the larger society? Many people believe that suicide is a sin and a transgression against God and nature. End of discussion. But Ernest van den Haag (1995) and Rand Richards Cooper (1996) wish to pursue the matter further. Van den Haag presents his argument in "Make Mine Hemlock," and Cooper makes his case in "The Dignity of

Paper opener: rhetorical questions

Background, titles, and authors

Helplessness: What Sort of Society Would Euthanasia Create?" Van den Haag

claims that no one "owns" us. We own ourselves and control our own destinies.

Therefore, any able-bodied person should be permitted to end his or her life.

And disabled people who wish to end their lives should be given assistance.

Cooper disagrees. He thinks it is wrong to eliminate the stage of life when

people become sick and helpless, and he questions whether we will "be a

better, richer, more humane society for having done so" (p. 14). He also warns

Thesis

that widespread practice of assisted suicide will present a dire threat to society.

Ernest van den Haag and Rand Richards Cooper have very little in common.

They base their arguments on different assumptions, and they have very

different views of the consequences of assisted suicide.

2   Both van den Haag (1995) and Cooper (1996) agree on one point. Dying

Points of similarity

patients have the right to refuse treatment, and physicians may choose to

respect the decision and even help them die. Van den Haag thinks physicians

are obligated to assist terminally ill patients. Cooper does not go that far, but he

does accept the idea of physicians relieving unnecessary pain. He remarks:

> In fact, it's not assisted suicide per se I'm questioning, which in other

Support from the article: quotation

> forms has long been practiced unofficially by physicians informing the

> gravely ill about lethal doses, turning off ventilators to "let nature

> take its course," and so on. It's the institutionalizing of the practice

> I'm wondering about, and its effect on our relation to the idea of

> suffering. (p. 14)

Even though they don't really see eye to eye, this seems to be the only point on

which van den Haag and Cooper share any common ground.

First point of difference   3   Very different assumptions underlie Van den Haag's (1995) and Cooper's

(1996) arguments. Van den Haag bases his argument on individual rights,

whereas Cooper maintains that the notion of individual rights is too narrow a

Van den Haag

framework. Van den Haag says that neither God nor society "owns" people. They "are thought to own themselves" (p. 60). He explains: "Owners can dispose of what they own as they see fit. We thus become entitled to control life, including its duration, to the extent nature permits, provided that this control does not harm others in ways proscribed by law" (p. 60). Van den Haag believes that our obligations to ourselves are more important than our obligations to society. He finds fault with the argument that life is a social duty that no one should shirk.

Support from the article: quotation

4   Cooper (1996) moves his argument outside the framework of the "right" to die. He feels that Americans are obsessed with individual rights: "The appeal of rights is so compelling that it leaves scant room for realities and interests not easily expressed as rights" (p. 12). For Cooper, "our deaths are both solo journeys toward an ultimate mystery and strands in the tapestries of each other's lives" (p. 14). We are interconnected, and this connectedness to one another, the effect that each individual has on "the texture of civic life" (p. 13), is more important than individual rights. In other words, our duty to society outweighs our duty to ourselves.

Cooper

Support from the article: quotation and paraphrase

5   Van den Haag (1995) and Cooper (1996) also have different opinions about the ramifications of institutionalizing assisted suicide. Cooper points out that if the practice is sanctioned, it will lead unavoidably to undesirable attitudes. He predicts a "creep toward an increased sense of burdensomeness" (p. 12) on the part of the elderly. Viewing themselves as burdens to their loved ones, they will end their lives. Cooper also claims that the ready availability of assisted suicide will transform the way we regard aging. "How often in the assisted-suicide future," he asks, "will someone look at an elderly person and think, consciously or semiconsciously, 'Gee, guess it's about time, huh?'" (p. 13). Cooper sees other negative consequences. He predicts that if we legalize assisted suicide and thus follow what he calls "the quality-of-life, take-me-out-and-shoot-me principle," we will "preempt the infirmities of old age and terminal illness" (p. 13). Eventually, we will look

Second point of difference

Cooper

Support from the article: quotation and paraphrase

askance at disabled and handicapped people of all ages. We will end up thinking, "as Germany did under the Nazis, . . . of the handicapped as a drain or drag on the healthy body of the rest of us: a pointless deformity; an un-luck; an un-person" (p. 13).

Van den Haag   6

Van den Haag (1995) would accuse Cooper (1996) of committing the slippery slope fallacy. Slippery slope arguers predict that one thing will inevitably lead to another more undesirable thing. They also warn of dangerous precedents. Van den Haag says the suggestion that doctors, or anyone else, "would wantonly kill burdensome patients who do not want to die" (p. 62) is unjustified. He also thinks the analogy to Nazi Germany is unsound. He argues, "But Nazi practices were imposed on physicians and hospitals by political directives which did not evolve from any prior authority given physicians to assist in suicide. There was no 'slippery slope'" (p. 62). To van den Haag, the slippery slope argument is an "unrealistic nightmare" (p. 62).

Support from the article: quotation

7

Cooper (1996) speaks of the importance of accompanying people through terminal illnesses and asks if this is not "one of the core experiences we need to have" (p. 14). Toward the end of his article, he asks, "Whose death is it anyway?" (p. 14), implying that the duty to die, as well as the duty to live, is owed to society. Van den Haag (1995) could not disagree more. "Society cannot be shown to have a compelling interest in forcing persons to live against their will," he says. "Moreover, such an interest would hardly justify the cruelty involved" (p. 62).

Conclusion

References

Cooper, R. R. (1996). The dignity of helplessness: What sort of society would euthanasia create? *Commonweal*, 12–14.

van den Haag, E. (1995). Make mine hemlock. *National Review*, 60–62.

Anna does more than list the multitude of differences between van den Haag and Cooper. She describes one area of agreement, and then she selects two points of difference and makes them the focus of her essay: the different assumptions that underlie each author's argument and the views each holds about the consequences of permitting assisted suicide. In paragraph 2, she explains that both van den Haag and Cooper acknowledge that dying patients have the right to refuse treatment and that physicians may choose to respect the decision and even help them die. Next, in paragraphs 3 and 4, she investigates the bases of each author's argument: van den Haag's claims about individual rights and Cooper's claims about civic duty and the needs of society. Then, in paragraphs 5 and 6, Anna discusses Cooper's predictions about the dangers inherent in the legalization of assisted suicide and van den Haag's dismissal of this chain of events.

Writing That Compares and Contrasts Sources

PREWRITING

Before you sit down to compose a preliminary draft, read and reread the sources, annotate them, take notes, and plan your essay. The effort you put into these prewriting activities will save time and ensure you of more success than if you move directly from reading the sources to writing your essay. To begin, tailor your reading goal and strategies to the task at hand.

For illustration, we take you through the process Anna Robles followed to address the assignment you just read:

> Compare and contrast two authors' views on assisted suicide: those of Ernest van den Haag in his *National Review* article, "Make Mine Hemlock," and those of Rand Richards Cooper in his *Commonweal* article, "The Dignity of Helplessness: What Sort of Society Would Euthanasia Create?"

● **DO A FIRST READING TO GET A GENERAL IMPRESSION OF THE SOURCE** Since the assignment asks her to compare and contrast van den Haag's and Cooper's views on assisted suicide, Anna's first step is to read the articles to determine how the two authors' views are similar and how they are different. She reads with two questions in mind:

- How are Cooper's and van den Haag's views on assisted suicide similar?
- How are Cooper's and van den Haag's views on assisted suicide different?

After the first reading of the texts, Anna freewrites her reactions, writing nonstop for ten minutes, jotting down whatever comes to her mind.

● **REREAD, ELABORATE, AND MAP CORRESPONDENCES** Next, she rereads the two articles. The second reading allows her to do two things:

- Tap memory and make associations between previous knowledge and experiences and the reading sources.
- Identify and map correspondences between the two sources.

As Anna performs these activities, she annotates the texts or takes separate notes. As she rereads the selection by van den Haag, she elaborates and identifies places where he agrees or disagrees with Cooper.

van den Haag

Paragraph 11

Elaborations

It is not clear to whom the duty to live could be owed. Once the government no longer legally recognizes God as the authority to which duties are owed, nature cannot have prescriptive authority to force unwilling persons to live, since such authority would have to come from God. Only society is left as the source of this alleged duty. But society cannot be shown to have a compelling interest in forcing persons to live against their will. Moreover, such an interest would hardly justify the cruelty involved. . . .

Cooper disagrees. He claims that society should have a compelling interest in keeping people alive because we are all interconnected. He doesn't think society is forcing elderly people to stay alive. He claims that they really don't want to die; they consent to assisted suicide because they feel helpless and they are convinced they are a burden to society. I don't know what he'd say about cruelty. He seems to think that it is important for people to suffer.

As she rereads the two sources, she elaborates fully and identifies as many similarities and differences as she can. A rich store of prewriting notes and annotations will be a great help when she writes her essay. Here are some strategies that will help you compare the two reading sources.

ELABORATING TO UNCOVER COMPARISONS AND CONTRASTS

- Identify points where one source author (1) agrees or disagrees with the other author, (2) says something relevant about the topic that the other author has neglected to say, (3) qualifies ideas stated by the other author, and (4) extends a proposition made by the other author.
- Validate one author's assertion with information provided by the other author.
- Subsume similarities and differences between the sources under subordinate categories.
- Create hierarchies of importance among ideas that are similar or different.
- Make judgments about the relevance of one author's view in relation to the other's view.

As you identify correspondences between the two reading sources, create a *web*. Webbing enables you to link points of similarity and difference. Identify a point of similarity or difference, summarize it in a short phrase, and write it in a box on a sheet of paper. Next, spin out the web by placing each author's ideas around this key idea node. Circle each idea, and draw lines connecting it to the key idea. Where appropriate, connect the circles to each other. When you are finished webbing, you will have a visual display of the points of similarity and difference.

● **PLAN YOUR ESSAY**   Once you have generated a series of elaborations, you are ready to select and organize your ideas and sketch out a blueprint for your essay. Keep in mind that your purpose is to compare and contrast the views expressed by the two authors. As you review your elaborations, separate the ones dealing with similarities from the ones dealing with differences. Mark the text wherever you discover similarities or differences (use symbols: = or ✓ for similarities, ≠ or × for differences), and create two lists.

Next, analyze the similarities and differences to discover the points you will discuss. They can be aspects of the subject, major topics, or prominent themes. Categorize the similarities and differences accordingly. See if you can form one or two generalizations. Even if your generalizations have exceptions, they will still be useful.

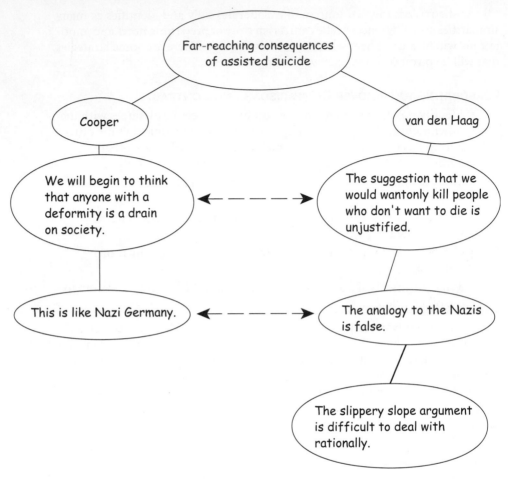

Figure 12.1 Beginning of a Web for Comparison and Contrast

Usually, writers compare reading sources in order to draw certain conclusions and make particular points clearer to the reader. As we said earlier, you could simply catalog the similarities and differences, but this limited rhetorical purpose leaves little room for you to exercise judgment or analytical skill. The more powerful purpose requires you to select, categorize, and focus.

Limited Goal

Catalog all the similarities and differences.

More Powerful Goal

Select from among the similarities and differences, categorize them, and focus the essay on generalizations.

Observe how Anna selected from among the long list of differences between van den Haag and Cooper. She pinpoints two major areas of difference: the assumptions underlying their arguments and their views on the consequences of assisted suicide.

ASSUMPTIONS FOR ARGUMENTS

- Van den Haag says that today we believe that "individuals collectively own society, rather than vice versa." He bases his argument on the notion of rights. He finds fault with the argument that life is a social duty that no one should shirk.
- Cooper argues that the notion of individual rights is too narrow a framework. He claims that we're moving toward communitarianism and togetherness rather than separateness. He bases his argument on the "texture of civic life."

VIEWS ON CONSEQUENCES OF ASSISTED SUICIDE

- Cooper emphasizes long-range negative consequences of euthanasia. Van den Haag dismisses Cooper's "slippery slope" arguments.
- Van den Haag claims there are safeguards to ensure that no one is pressured to end his or her life; Cooper contends that the elderly do not have "absolute autonomy" in this matter.

Once you have decided on your areas of focus, return to the reading sources and search for any relevant material you may have overlooked.

Comparison-and-contrast essays are usually organized in one of two formats: point-by-point or block. Point-by-point arrangement identifies key aspects or facets of the subject that is being compared and contrasted. For the assignment we are working on, that means we would move back and forth between van den Haag and Cooper, comparing and contrasting them on the basis of key points or features of their arguments. Block arrangement presents one side at a time. We would discuss everything van den Haag has to say about the topic before moving on to Cooper. To see how professional writers use these arrangements, read the following passages from an article in which Nancy Henley, Mykol Hamilton, and Barrie Thorne discuss sex differences and sexism in communication.

Point-by-Point Arrangement

There are other sex differences in speech sounds. For boys in our culture, masculinity and toughness are projected by a slightly nasal speech; girls and "gentlemanly" boys have oral, or non-nasal, speech. Males also speak with greater intensity than females. There are differences in the intonation patterns used by each sex: Women have more variable intonations (contrasting levels) than men do; women are said to have

Table 12.1 Point-by-Point Presentation

Subject	Males	Females	Points of Comparison
Sex differences in speech sounds	Projects masculinity and toughness for boys; oral non-nasal speech for gentlemen	Have oral, non-nasal speech	Nasal quality
	More intensity than females	Less intensity than males	Intensity
	Glides absent	More variable; more extremes of high and low; speak with long, rapid glides	Intonation

more extremes of high and low intonation than men, and to speak with long rapid glides that are absent in men's speech. (2006, p. 174)

Table 12.1 depicts the point-by-point arrangement. Henley, Hamilton, and Thorne explain sex differences in speech sounds by comparing the speech of males and females on the basis of three features: nasality, intensity, and intonation.

Block Arrangement

Self-disclosure is another variable that involves language but goes beyond it. Research studies have found that women disclose more personal information to others than men do. Subordinates (in work situations) are also more likely to self-disclose than superiors. People in positions of power are required to reveal little about themselves, yet typically know much about the lives of others—perhaps the ultimate exemplar of this principle is the fictional Big Brother.

According to the research of Jack Sattel (2006), men exercise and maintain power over women by withholding self-disclosure. An institutional example of this use of power is the psychiatrist (usually male), to whom much is disclosed (by a predominantly female clientele), but who classically maintains a reserved and detached attitude, revealing little or nothing of himself. Nonemotionality is the "cool" of the professional, the executive, the poker player, the street-wise operator. Smart men—those who manipulate others—maintain unruffled exteriors.

	Table 12.2 Writing Multiple-Source Essays	
Sex	Behavior	Points of Comparison
Males	1. Exercise and maintain power over women by withholding personal information.	Self-disclosure
	2. Are "cool," nonemotional, unruffled.	emotionality
Females	1. Display personal information to people in power.	Self-disclosure
	2. Appear to be more emotional because they display emotion.	emotionality

Women who obtain authoritative positions may do likewise, but most women have been socialized to display their emotions, thoughts, and ideas. Giving out this information about themselves, especially in a context of inequality, is giving others power over them. Women may not be more emotionally variable than men, but their emotional variability is more visible. This display of emotional variability, like that of variability of intonation, contributes to the stereotype of instability in women. Self-disclosure is not in itself a weakness or negative behavior trait; like other gestures of intimacy, it has positive aspects—such as sharing of oneself and allowing others to open up—when it is voluntary and reciprocal.

Table 12.2 depicts the block arrangement. Discussing sex differences in self-disclosure and emotionality, Henley, Hamilton, and Thorne first describe the behavior of males and then describe the behavior of females.

Notice that Anna Robles organizes the body paragraphs of her essay in a point-by-point arrangement. She covers three points: one point on which van den Haag and Cooper agree and two points on which they disagree. You can visualize this arrangement in a chart or tree diagram. It is beneficial to use some type of graphic organizer as a preliminary outline.

If Anna had used the block comparison pattern, then instead of taking up each of the three points of comparison and alternating between van den Haag and Cooper, she would have presented one side at a time and contrasted the two authors in blocks, one block devoted to van den Haag and the other to Cooper.

READINGS

Laws Limit Schools Even After Alarms*

Jeff Gammage and Stacey Burling

This article first appeared in the Philadelphia Inquirer *on April 19, 2007, just three days after the Virginia Tech shootings.* Inquirer *staff writer Paul Nussbaum contributed to the article.*

If Cho Seung-Hui had been a warning light, he would have been blinking bright red.

Two female students complained to campus police that he was stalking them. His poetry was so twisted that his writing professor said she would quit if he weren't removed from her room. Some students found him so menacing that they refused to attend class with him.

Yet Virginia Tech, like other colleges trying to help emotionally troubled students, had little power to force Cho off campus and into treatment.

"We can't even pick up the phone and call their family. They're adults. You have to respect their privacy," said Brenda Ingram-Wallace, director of counseling and chair of the psychology department at Albright College in Reading.

5   In the aftermath of the deadliest shooting in U.S. history, counselors, police authorities, and mental-health professionals say privacy laws prevent colleges from taking strong action regarding students who might be dangerous.

Many at Tech saw Cho as a threat—and shared those fears with authorities. In 2005, after the second stalking complaint, the school obtained a temporary detention order that resulted in Cho undergoing a psychiatric evaluation. But the 23-year-old remained enrolled at the university until the moment he shot himself to death.

Federal laws such as the 1974 Family Educational Rights and Privacy Act (FERPA) and the 1996 Health Insurance Portability and Accountability Act (HIPAA) protect students' right to privacy by banning disclosure of any mental-health problems—even to family members—without a signed waiver.

Patient-therapist confidentiality is crucial, privacy advocates say. Students may shy from treatment for fear of exposure.

FERPA does allow colleges to release information without permission in cases of "health and safety emergencies." But the criteria are so

**Philadelphia Inquirer* 19 Apr. 2007: A01.

vague, and the potential liability so severe, that administrators say they hesitate to act in any but the most dire circumstances.

10   "The law tends to be protective of individual autonomy rather than getting in there and forcing people to get treatment," said Anthony Rostain, associate professor of psychiatry at the University of Pennsylvania School of Medicine.

Lots of students write violent stories, he noted. How do you distinguish between a future Cho Seung-Hui and a future Quentin Tarantino?*

"This kind of problem happens all the time across college campuses," Rostain said.

The law puts colleges in a tough position, said Dana Fleming, a lawyer with the college and university practice group at Nelson, Kinder, Mousseau & Saturley in Manchester, N.H. Schools may face legal trouble if they try to keep ill students out, if they try to send them home, or if they let them stay.

"No matter which decision they make," she said, "they can find liability on the other end."

15   Colleges can't screen students for mental illnesses during the admissions process because that violates the Americans With Disabilities Act. As a result, schools know which students will need tutoring or want to play soccer, but have no idea who is likely to need mental-health care, Fleming said.

Virginia Tech and most other universities cannot summarily suspend a student. Formal disciplinary charges must be filed and hearings held. Students who initiate a complaint often end up dropping the matter.

Nor can schools expect courts to hospitalize a student involuntarily without solid evidence that he poses a danger to himself or others.

That has left many colleges trying to find creative ways to identify and help troubled students.

At Albright College, administrators recently updated a program where anyone concerned about a student's behavior—a work supervisor, a professor or another student—can fill out a "student alert form."

20   Perhaps friends notice a student has become withdrawn or has stopped showing up for class. If multiple forms arrive concerning the same person, counseling director Ingram-Wallace said, the counseling center investigates by contacting housing officials or by reaching the student via phone or e-mail.

But the choice to speak with a psychological counselor stays with the student. The center can't send a therapist to knock on the student's door, she said.

"On the surface, it sounds like a caring thing to do," she said, but "if they haven't been dangerous to themselves or others, there's no reason to mandate them into any kind of services."

---

*Director, screenwriter, and producer of frequently violent films such as *Reservoir Dogs* (1992), *Pulp Fiction* (1994), and *Kill Bill* (vol. 1, 2003; vol. 2, 2004).

...continued Laws Limit Schools Even After Alarms, **Jeff Gammage and Stacey Burling**

Among students who have been referred to the counseling center, "the responses are mixed," she said. "Some people felt imposed upon."

At St. Lawrence University in Canton, N.Y., every student who visits the health center—even for a head cold—is screened for depression and signs of other mental illness. The effort follows a national study that showed depression rising among college students.

25   If a screening shows someone needs help from the health center, "we literally walk them over there," said Patricia Ellis, director of counseling services.

More than a year before Monday's massacre of 32 students and staff members, Cho was twice accused of stalking female students and taken to a mental-health facility amid fears he was suicidal, police said yesterday.

After the first incident, in November 2005, police referred him to the university disciplinary system. Ed Spencer, Tech's assistant vice president of student affairs, said he could not comment on any proceedings against the gunman because federal law protects students' medical privacy even after death.

The university obtained the detention order after the second stalking complaint, in December 2005. "His insight and judgment are normal," an examiner at the psychiatric hospital concluded.

Yet poet Nikki Giovanni, one of his professors, told CNN that students were so unnerved by Cho's behavior, which included taking cell-phone photos of them in class, that most stopped attending the course. She insisted that he be removed.

30   Lucinda Roy, a codirector of the creative writing program, tutored Cho after that, and tried to get him into counseling. He always refused. Roy sent samples of Cho's writing, with its images of people attacking each other with chain saws, to the campus police, student-affairs office, and other agencies.

Perilous Privacy at Virginia Tech

This editorial appeared in the Christian Science Monitor *on September 4, 2007.*

Colleges didn't need last week's report on the Virginia Tech shootings to address a key finding: a faster alert during the crisis may have saved lives. Many colleges have already set blast-notice plans. But here's what needs careful study: the report's conclusions about privacy.

Privacy is a huge issue on campuses. Colleges and universities are dealing with young people who have just become legal adults, but who may still require supervision and even intervention.

That was the case with Seung-Hui Cho, the student who killed 32 people and then himself on April 16. According to the report, which was commissioned by Virginia Gov. Timothy Kaine, this troubled student's behavior raised serious questions about his mental stability while he was at VT, yet no one contacted his parents, and communication about his case broke down among school, law-enforcement, and mental-health officials.

A big reason? A "widespread perception" that privacy laws make it difficult to respond to troubled students, according to the report. But this is "only partly correct."

Lack of understanding about federal and state laws is a major obstacle to helping such students, according to the report. The legal complexity, as well as concerns about liability, can easily push teachers, administrators, police, and mental-health workers into a "default" position of withholding information, the report found.

There's no evidence that VT officials consciously decided not to inform Mr. Cho's parents. But the university's lawyer told the panel investigating Cho's case that privacy laws prevent sharing information such as that relating to Cho.

That's simply not true. The report listed several steps that could quite legally have been taken:

The Virginia Tech police, for instance, could have shared with Cho's parents that he was temporarily detained, pending a hearing to commit him involuntarily to a mental-health institution, because that information was public.

And teachers and administrators could have called Cho's parents to notify them of his difficulties, because only student records—not personal observations or conversations—are shielded by the federal privacy law that covers most secondary schools.

Notifying Cho's parents was intuitively the right course. Indeed, his middle school contacted his parents to get him help, and they cooperated. His high school also made special arrangements. He improved.

The report points out that the main federal privacy laws that apply to a college student's health and campus records recognize exceptions for information sharing in emergencies that affect public health and safety.

Privacy is a bedrock of American law and values. In a mental-health case, it gives a patient the security to express innermost thoughts, and protects that person from discrimination. But the federal law, at least, does recognize a balance between privacy and public safety, even when colleges can't, or won't.

...continued Perilous Privacy at Virginia Tech

The report is to be commended for pointing out this disconnect, and for calling for greater clarification of privacy laws and school policies.

Perhaps now, common sense can match up with legal obligations so both privacy and public safety can be served.

Colleges Are Watching Troubled Students

Jeffrey McMurray

During the year following the Virginia Tech shootings, many colleges and universities took a hard look at their policies on student privacy and their procedures for monitoring and sharing information about troubled students. This article, by the Associated Press, was first published on March 28, 2008. AP writer Sue Lindsay contributed to this report.

On the agenda: A student who got into a shouting match with a faculty member. Another who harassed a female classmate. Someone found sleeping in a car. And a student who posted a threat against a professor on Facebook.

In a practice adopted at one college after another since the massacre at Virginia Tech, a University of Kentucky committee of deans, administrators, campus police and mental health officials has begun meeting regularly to discuss a watch list of troubled students and decide whether they need professional help or should be sent packing.

These "threat assessment groups" are aimed at heading off the kind of bloodshed seen at Virginia Tech a year ago and at Northern Illinois University last month.

"You've got to be way ahead of the game, so to speak, expect what may be coming. If you're able to identify behaviors early on and get these people assistance, it avoids disruptions in the classrooms and potential violence," said Maj. Joe Monroe, interim police chief at Kentucky.

5   The Kentucky panel, called Students of Concern, held its first meeting last week and will convene at least twice a month to talk about students whose strange or disturbing behavior has come to their attention.

Such committees represent a change in thinking among U.S. college officials, who for a long time were reluctant to share information about students' mental health for fear of violating privacy laws.

"If a student is a danger to himself or others, all the privacy concerns go out the window," said Patricia Terrell, vice president of student affairs, who created the panel.

Terrell shared details of the four discussed cases with The Associated Press on the condition that all names and other identifying information be left out.

Among other things, the panel can order a student into counseling or bar him or her from entering a particular building or talking to a certain person. It can also order a judicial hearing that can lead to suspension or expulsion if the student's offense was a violation of the law or school policy.

10   Although the four cases discussed last week were the ones administrators deemed as needing the most urgent attention, a database listing 26 other student cases has been created, providing fodder for future meetings.

Students are encouraged during their freshman orientation to report suspicious behavior to the dean of students, and university employees all the way down to janitors and cafeteria workers are instructed to tell their supervisors if they see anything.

Virtually every corner of campus is represented in the group's closed-door meetings, including dorm life, academics, counseling, mental health and police.

"If you look back at the Virginia Tech situation, the aftermath, there were several people who knew that student had problems, but because of privacy and different issues, they didn't talk to others about it," said Lee Todd, UK president.

High schools have been doing this sort of thing for years because of shootings, but only since Virginia Tech, when a disturbed student gunman killed 32 people and committed suicide, have colleges begun to follow suit, said Mike Dorn, executive director of Safe Havens International, a leading campus safety firm.

15   "They didn't think it was a real threat to them," Dorn said.

Virginia Tech has added a threat assessment team since the massacre there. Boston University, the University of Utah, the University of Illinois–Chicago and numerous others also have such groups, said Gwendolyn Dungy, executive director of the National Association of Student Personnel Administrators.

Bryan Cloyd, a Virginia Tech accounting professor whose daughter Austin was killed in the rampage, welcomed the stepped-up efforts to monitor troubled students but stressed he doesn't want to turn every college campus into a "police state."

"We can't afford to overreact," Cloyd said, but "we also can't afford to underreact."

Seung-Hui Cho, the Virginia Tech gunman, was ruled a danger to himself in a court hearing in 2005 that resulted from a roommate's call to police after Cho mentioned suicide in an e-mail. He was held overnight at a mental health center off campus and was ordered into outpatient treatment, but he received no follow-up services, despite his sullen, withdrawn behavior and his twisted, violence-filled writings.

...*continued* Colleges Are Watching Troubled Students, **Jeffrey McMurray**

20   Mary Bolin-Reece, director of counseling and testing at Kentucky, attends the threat assessment group's meetings but cannot share what she knows or, in most cases, even whether a student has been undergoing counseling. But participants can share information on other possible red flags.

"We always look at, 'Is there a change in the baseline?'" Bolin-Reece said. "The student had previously gotten very good grades, and then there was a drop-off. Something has happened. Is there some shift in their ability to function? If a student is coming to the attention of various parties around the university, we begin to be able to connect the dots."

The University of Kentucky has not had a murder on campus since 1984. Still, the threat-assessment effort has the strong backing of Carol Graham of Fort Carson, Colo., whose son Kevin was a Kentucky student when he committed suicide before leaving for an ROTC summer camp in 2003.

"UK is such a huge university," Graham said. "It's important to know there's a safety net—that people are looking out for each other. With Kevin, his professors thought he was perfect. He'd be an A student. But the people around him were noticing differences."

As for the four cases taken up by the committee: The student who got into an argument with a faculty member—and had also seen a major dip in grades and exhibited poor hygiene—was ordered to meet with the dean of students.

25   The one accused of harassment was referred to a judicial hearing, during which he was expelled from university housing. The student who made the Facebook threat was given a warning. In the case of the student sleeping in a car, a committee member was dispatched to check on the person. No further details were released.

Virginia Tech Massacre Has Altered Campus Mental Health Systems

This article, prepared by the Associated Press, is representative of numerous reports of how college administrators across the nation responded to the Virginia Tech killings. Many schools reviewed their existing policies on student privacy and communication and instituted new procedures. The article appeared in the Los Angeles Times *on April 14, 2008.*

The rampage carried out nearly a year ago by a Virginia Tech student who slipped through the mental health system has changed how American colleges reach out to troubled students.

Administrators are pushing students harder to get help, looking more aggressively for signs of trouble and urging faculty to speak up when they have concerns. Counselors say the changes are sending even more students their way, which is both welcome and a challenge, given that many still lack the resources to handle their growing workloads.

Behind those changes, colleges have edged away in the last year from decades-old practices that made student privacy paramount. Now, they are more likely to err on the side of sharing information—with the police, for instance, and parents—if there is any possible threat to community safety. But even some who say the changes are appropriate worry it could discourage students from seeking treatment.

Concerns also linger that the response to shooters like Seung-hui Cho at Virginia Tech and Steven Kazmierczak, who killed five others at Northern Illinois University, has focused excessively on boosting the capacity of campus police to respond to rare events. Such reforms may be worthwhile, but they don't address how to prevent such a tragedy in the first place.

5   It was last April 16, just after 7 a.m., that Cho killed two students in a Virginia Tech dormitory, the start of a shooting spree that continued in a classroom building and eventually claimed 33 lives, including his own.

Cho's behavior and writing had alarmed professors and administrators, as well as the campus police, and he had been put through a commitment hearing where he was found to be potentially dangerous. But when an off-campus psychiatrist sent him back to the school for outpatient treatment, there was no follow-up to ensure that he got it.

People who work every day in the campus mental health field—counselors, lawyers, advocates and students at colleges around the country—say they have seen three major types of change since the Cho shootings:

Faculty are speaking up more about students who worry them. That's accelerating a trend of more demand for mental health services that was already under way before the Virginia Tech shootings.

Professors "have a really heightened level of fear and concern from the behavior that goes on around them," said Ben Locke, assistant director of the counseling center at Penn State University.

10   David Wallace, director of counseling at the University of Central Florida, said teachers are paying closer attention to violent material in writing assignments—warning bells that had worried Cho's professors.

"Now people are wondering, 'Is this something that could be more ominous?'" he said. "Are we talking about the Stephen Kings of the future or about somebody who's seriously thinking about doing something harmful?"

The downside is officials may be hypersensitive to any eccentricity. Says Susan Davis, an attorney who works in student affairs at the University of Virginia: "There's no question there's some hysteria and there's some things we don't need to see."

...continued Virginia Tech Massacre Has Altered Campus Mental Health Systems

Changes are being made to privacy policies. In Virginia, a measure signed into law Wednesday by Gov. Tim Kaine requires colleges to bring parents into the loop when dependent students may be a danger to themselves or others.

Even before Virginia Tech, Cornell University had begun treating students as dependents of their parents unless told otherwise—an aggressive legal strategy that gives the school more leeway to contact parents with concerns without students' permission.

15   In Washington, meanwhile, federal officials are trying to clarify privacy guidelines so faculty won't hesitate to report potential threats.

"Nobody's throwing privacy out the window, but we are coming out of an era when individual rights were paramount on college campuses," said Brett Sokolow, who advises colleges on risk management. "What colleges are struggling with now is a better balance of those individual rights and community protections."

The big change since the Virginia Tech shootings, legal experts say, is colleges have shed some of their fear of violating the federal Family Educational Rights and Privacy Act.

Many faculty hadn't realized that the law applies only to educational records, not observations of classroom behavior, or that it contains numerous exceptions.

The stigma of mental illness, in some cases, has grown. "In general, the attention to campus mental health was desperately needed," said Alison Malmon, founder of the national Active Minds group. But some of the debate, she added, "has turned in a direction that does not necessarily support students."

20   All the talk of "threat assessments" and better-trained campus SWAT teams, she said, has distracted the public from the fact that the mentally ill rarely commit violence—especially against others.

"I know that, for many students, it made them feel more stigmatized," Malmon said. "It made them more likely to keep their mental health history silent."

Sokolow, the risk consultant for colleges, estimated in the aftermath of the Virginia Tech and NIU shootings, the schools he works with spent $25 on police and communications for every $1 on mental health. Only recently has he seen a shift.

"Campuses come to me, they want me to help them start behavioral intervention systems," Sokolow said. "Then they go to the president to get the money and, oh, well, the money went into the door locks."

Phone messaging systems and security are nice, he said, but "there is nothing about text-messaging that is going to prevent violence."

The Family Educational Rights and Privacy Act

United States Code
Title 20. Education
CHAPTER 31. General Provisions Concerning Education
§ 1232g. Family Educational and Privacy Rights

Following are excerpts from the Family Educational Rights and
Privacy Act (FERPA), *the federal law enacted in 1974 that governs
restrictions on the release of student educational records. FERPA
provides for the withholding of federal funds to educational
institutions that violate its provisions, and it is the federal guarantor
of the privacy rights of post-secondary students.*

(1)(A) No funds shall be made available under any applicable program to
any educational agency or institution which has a policy of denying, or
which effectively prevents, the parents of students who are or have been
in attendance at a school of such agency or at such institution, as the case
may be, the right to inspect and review the education records of their children. If any material or document in the education record of a student
includes information on more than one student, the parents of one of
such students shall have the right to inspect and review only such part of
such material or document as relates to such student or to be informed of
the specific information contained in such part of such material. Each
educational agency or institution shall establish appropriate procedures
for the granting of a request by parents for access to the education records
of their children within a reasonable period of time, but in no case more
than forty-five days after the request has been made, . . .

(C) The first sentence of subparagraph (A) shall not operate to make
available to students in institutions of postsecondary education the following materials:

  (i) financial records of the parents of the student or any informa-
      tion contained therein;

 (ii) confidential letters and statements of recommendation, which
      were placed in the education records prior to January 1, 1975,
      if such letters or statements are not used for purposes other
      than those for which they were specifically intended;

(iii) if the student has signed a waiver of the student's right of access
      under this subsection in accordance with subparagraph (D),
      confidential recommendations—

    (I) respecting admission to any educational agency or
        institution,

   (II) respecting an application for employment, and

  (III) respecting the receipt of an honor or honorary recognition.

...continued The Family Educational Rights and Privacy Act

(B) The term "education records" does not include—

(i) records of instructional, supervisory, and administrative personnel and educational personnel ancillary thereto which are in the sole possession of the maker thereof and which are not accessible or revealed to any other person except a substitute;

(ii) records maintained by a law enforcement unit of the educational agency or institution that were created by that law enforcement unit for the purpose of law enforcement;

(iii) in the case of persons who are employed by an educational agency or institution but who are not in attendance at such agency or institution, records made and maintained in the normal course of business which relate exclusively to such person in that person's capacity as an employee and are not available for use for any other purpose; or

(iv) records on a student who is eighteen years of age or older, or is attending an institution of postsecondary education, which are made or maintained by a physician, psychiatrist, psychologist, or other recognized professional or paraprofessional acting in his professional or paraprofessional capacity, or assisting in that capacity, and which are made, maintained, or used only in connection with the provision of treatment to the student, and are not available to anyone other than persons providing such treatment, except that such records can be personally reviewed by a physician or other appropriate professional of the student's choice. . . .

(h) Certain disciplinary action information allowable. Nothing in this section shall prohibit an educational agency or institution from—

(1) including appropriate information in the education record of any student concerning disciplinary action taken against such student for conduct that posed a significant risk to the safety or well-being of that student, other students, or other members of the school community; or

(2) disclosing such information to teachers and school officials, including teachers and school officials in other schools, who have legitimate educational interests in the behavior of the student.

STUDENT MODELS

Running head: BALANCING PRIVACY AND SAFETY   1

Balancing Privacy and Safety

in the Wake

of Virginia Tech

David Harrison

Professor Shanker

Law and Society—February 14, 2009

Taken from: *Writing and Reading Across the Curriculum*, Eleventh Edition by Laurence Behrens and Leonard J. Rosen.

Balancing Privacy and Safety in the Wake of Virginia Tech

1   On April 16, 2007, Seung Hui Cho, a mentally ill student at Virginia Polytechnic Institute, shot to death 32 fellow students and faculty members, and injured 17 others, before killing himself. It was the worst mass shooting in U.S. history, and the fact that it took place on a college campus lent a special horror to the event. In the days after the tragedy, several facts about Seung Hui Cho came to light. According to the official Virginia State Panel report on the killings, Cho had exhibited signs of mental disturbance, including "suicidal and homicidal ideations" dating back to high school. And during Cho's junior year at Virginia Tech, numerous incidents occurred that provided clear warnings of Cho's mental instability and violent impulses (Virginia Tech Review, 2007). University administrators, faculty, and officials were aware of these incidents but failed to intervene to prevent the impending tragedy.

2   In the search for answers, attention quickly focused on federal rules governing student privacy that Virginia Tech officials said prevented them from communicating effectively with each other or with Cho's parents regarding his troubles. These rules, the officials argued, prohibit the sharing of information concerning students' mental health with parents or other students. The publicity about such restrictions revived an ongoing debate over university policies that balance student privacy against campus safety. In the wake of the Virginia Tech tragedy, the pendulum seems to have swung in favor of safety. In April 2008, Virginia Governor Tim Kaine signed into law a measure requiring colleges to alert parents when dependent students may be a danger to themselves or to others ("Virginia Tech Massacre," 2008). Peter Lake, an educator at Stetson University College of Law, predicted that in the wake of Virginia Tech, "people will go in a direction of safety over privacy" (as cited in Bernstein, "Mother," 2007, p. A1).

3   The shootings at Virginia Tech demonstrate, in the most horrifying way, the need for secure college campuses. Nevertheless, privacy remains a crucial

right to most Americans—including college students, many of whom for the first time are exercising their prerogatives as adults. Many students who pose no threat to anyone will, and should, object strenuously to university administrators peering into and making judgments about their private lives. Some might be unwilling to seek professional therapy if they know that the records of their counseling sessions might be released to their parents or to other students. In responding to the Virginia Tech killings, we should resist rolling back federal rules protecting student privacy; for as long as college officials effectively respond to signs of trouble, these rules already provide a workable balance between privacy and public safety.

4   In these days of *Facebook* and reality TV, the notion of privacy rights, particularly for young people, may seem quaint. In fact, recently a top lawyer for the search engine *Google* claimed that in the Internet age, young people just don't care about privacy the way they once did (Cohen, 2008). Whatever the changing views of privacy in a wired world, the issue of student privacy rights is a serious legal matter that must be seen in the context of the student-college relationship, which has its historical roots in the doctrine of in *loco parentis,* Latin for "in the place of the parents." Generally, this doctrine is understood to mean that the college stands in place as the student's parent or guardian. The college therefore has "a duty to protect the safety, morals, and welfare of their students, just as parents are expected to protect their children" (Pollet, 2002, p. 288).

5   Writing of life at the University of Michigan before the 1960s, one historian observes that "*in loco parentis* comprised an elaborate structure of written rules and quiet understandings enforced in the trenches by housemothers [who] governed much of the what, where, when, and whom of students' lives, especially women: what to wear to dinner, what time to be home, where, when, and for how long they might receive visitors" (Tobin, 2007, p. 21).

6   During the 1960s court decisions began to chip away at the doctrine of *in loco parentis.* These rulings illustrate that the students' rights movement during

that era was an integral part of a broader contemporary social movement for civil rights and liberties. In *Dixon v. Alabama State Board of Education*, Alabama State College invoked *in loco parentis* to defend its decision to expel six African-American students without due process for participating in a lunchroom counter sit-in. Eventually, a federal appeals court rejected the school's claim to unrestrained power, ruling that students' constitutional rights did not end once they stepped onto campus (Weigel, 2004).

7   Students were not just fighting for the right to hold hands in dorm rooms; they were also asserting their rights as the vanguard of a social revolution. As Stetson law professor Robert Bickel notes: "The fall of *in loco parentis* in the 1960s correlated exactly with the rise of student economic power and the rise of student civil rights" (as cited in Weigel, 2004, p. 36).

8   The students' rights movement received a further boost with the Family Educational Rights and Privacy Act (FERPA, 2006), signed into law by President Ford in 1974. FERPA barred schools from releasing educational records—including mental health records—without the student's permission. The Act provides some important exceptions: educational records *can* be released in the case of health and safety emergencies or if the student is declared a dependent on his or her parents' tax returns (Federal, 2006).

9   In the wake of Virginia Tech, however, many observers pointed the finger of blame at federal restrictions on sharing available mental health information. Also held responsible were the school's officials, who admitted knowing of Cho's mental instability but claimed that FERPA (2006) prevented them from doing anything about it. The State of Virginia official report on the killings notes as follows:

"University officials . . . explained their failures to communicate with one another or with Cho's parents by noting their belief that such communications are prohibited by the federal laws governing the privacy of health and education records" (Virginia Tech Review, 2007, p. 2).

10   Observers were quick to declare the system broken. "Laws Limit Schools Even after Alarms," trumpeted a headline in the *Philadelphia Inquirer* (Gammage and Burling, 2007, p. A1). Commentators attacked federal privacy law, charging that the pendulum had swung too far away from campus safety. Judging from this letter to the editor of the *Wall Street Journal*, many agreed wholeheartedly: "Parents have a right to know if their child has a serious problem, and they need to know the progress of their child's schoolwork, especially if they are paying the cost of the education. Anything less than this is criminal" (Guerriero, 2008, p. 21).

11   As part of this public clamor, some schools have enacted policies that effectively curtail student privacy in favor of campus safety. For example: after Virginia Tech, Cornell University began assuming that students were dependents of their parents. Exploiting what the *Wall Street Journal* termed a "rarely used legal exception" in FERPA allows Cornell to provide parents with confidential information without students' permission (Bernstein, "Bucking," 2007).

12   Conversely, the Massachusetts Institute of Technology lies at the opposite end of the spectrum from Cornell in its staunch defense of student privacy. M.I.T. has stuck to its position even in the wake of Virginia Tech, recently demanding that the mother of a missing M.I.T. student obtain a subpoena in order to access his dorm room and e-mail records. That student was later found dead, an apparent suicide (Bernstein, "Mother," 2007). Even in the face of lawsuits, M.I.T. remains committed to its stance. Its Chancellor explained the school's position this way:

> Privacy is important. . . . Different students will do different things they absolutely don't want their parents to know about. . . . Students expect this kind of safe place where they can address their difficulties, try out lifestyles, and be independent of their parents. (as cited in Bernstein, "Mother," 2007, p. A2)

13   One can easily understand how parents would be outraged by the M.I.T. position. No parent would willingly let his or her child enter an environment where that child's safety cannot be assured. Just as the first priority for any government is to protect its citizens, the first priority of an educational institution must be to keep its students safe. But does this responsibility justify rolling back student privacy rights or returning to a more traditional interpretation of *in loco parentis* in the relationship between a university and its students? No, for the simple reason that the choice is a false one.

14   As long as federal privacy laws are properly interpreted and implemented, they do nothing to endanger campus safety. The problem at Virginia Tech was not the federal government's policy; it was the university's own practices based on a faulty interpretation of that policy. The breakdown began with the failure of Virginia Tech officials to understand federal privacy laws. Interpreted correctly, these laws would *not* have prohibited officials from notifying appropriate authorities of Cho's problems. The Virginia Tech Review Panel (2007) report was very clear on this point: "[F]ederal laws and their state counterparts afford ample leeway to share information in potentially dangerous situations" (p. 2). FERPA (2006) does, in fact, provide for a "health and safety emergencies" exception; educational records *can* be released without the student's consent "in connection with an emergency, [to] appropriate persons if the knowledge of such information is necessary to protect the health or safety of the student or other person . . . " (232g (b) (1) (g-h)). But Virginia Tech administrators did not invoke this important exception to FERPA's privacy rules.

15   An editorial in the *Christian Science Monitor* suggested several other steps that the university could legally have taken, including informing Cho's parents that he had been briefly committed to a mental health facility, a fact that was public information. The editorial concluded, scornfully, that "federal law, at least, does recognize a balance between privacy and public safety, even when colleges can't, or won't" ("Perilous," 2007, p. 1).

16   To be fair, such confusion about FERPA's contingencies appears widespread among college officials. For this reason, the U.S. Department of Education's revised privacy regulations, announced in March 2008 and intended to "clarify" when schools may release student records, are welcome and necessary. But simply reassuring anxious university officials that they won't lose federal funds for revealing confidential student records won't be enough to ensure campus safety. We need far more effective intervention for troubled students than the kind provided by Virginia Tech, which the Virginia Tech Review Panel (2008) blasted for its "lack of resources" and "passivity" (p. 2).

17   Schools like the University of Kentucky offer a positive example of such intervention, demonstrating that colleges can adopt a robust approach to student mental health without infringing on privacy rights. At Kentucky, "threat assessment groups" meet regularly to discuss a "watch list" of troubled students and decide what to do about them (McMurray, 2008). These committees emphasize proactiveness and communication--elements that were sorely missing at Virginia Tech. The approach represents a prudent middle ground between the extreme positions of M.I.T. and Cornell.

18   Schools such as Kentucky carry out their policies with a firm eye toward student privacy rights. For example, the University of Kentucky's director of counseling attends the threat assessment group's meetings but draws a clear line at what information she can share—for instance, whether or not a student has been undergoing counseling. Instead, the group looks for other potential red flags, such as a sharp drop-off in grades or difficulty functioning in the campus environment (McMurray, 2008). This open communication between university officials will presumably also help with delicate judgments—whether, for example, a student's violent story written for a creative writing class is an indication of mental instability or simply an early work by the next Stephen King ("Virginia Tech Massacre," 2008, p. 1).

BALANCING PRIVACY AND SAFETY   8

19   What happened at Virginia Tech was a tragedy. Few of us can appreciate

the grief of the parents of the shooting victims at Virginia Tech, parents who

trusted that their children would be safe and who were devastated when that faith

was betrayed. To these parents, the words of the MIT chancellor quoted earlier—

platitudes about students "try[ing] out lifestyles" or "address[ing] their

difficulties"—must sound hollow. But we must guard against allowing a few

isolated incidents, however tragic, to restrict the rights of millions of students, the

vast majority of whom graduate college safely and without incident. Schools must

not use Virginia Tech as a pretext to bring back the bad old days of resident

assistants snooping on the private lives of students and infringing on their privacy.

That step is the first down a slippery slope of dictating morality. Both the federal

courts and Congress have rejected that approach and for good reason have

established the importance of privacy rights on campus. These rights must be

preserved.

20   The Virginia Tech shooting does not demonstrate a failure of current policy,

but rather a breakdown in the enforcement of policy. In its wake, universities have

undertaken important modifications to their procedures. We should support

changes that involve a more proactive approach to student mental health and

improvements in communication between departments, such as those at the

University of Kentucky. Such measures will not only bring confidential help to the

troubled students who need it, they will also improve the safety of the larger

college community. At the same time, these measures will preserve hard-won

privacy rights on campus.

BALANCING PRIVACY AND SAFETY   9

References

Bernstein, E. (2007). Bucking privacy concerns, Cornell acts as watchdog. *Wall*

Street Journal 27, A1–A3. Retrieved from http://www.lexisnexis.com/

hottopics/Inacademic/?

——. A mother takes on MIT. (2007, September). *Wall Street Journal,* A1.

    Retrieved from LexisNexis.

Cohen, A. (2008, February). One friend facebook hasn't made yet: Privacy rights.

    New York Times, A1. Retrieved from Academic Search Complete.

Federal Educational Rights and Privacy Act (FERPA). (2006). 20 U.S.C. 1232g (b)

    (1) (g–h).

Gammage, J., & Burling S. (2007, April). Laws limit schools even after

    alarms. *Philadelphia Inquirer,* A1. Retrieved from Academic Search

    Complete.

Guerriero, D. (2008, January). (Letter). *Wall Street Journal.* Retrieved from

    LexisNexis.

McMurray, J. (2008, March). Colleges are watching troubled students. *Associ-*

    ated Press. Retrieved from AP Online.

Perilous privacy at Virginia Tech. (2007, September). (Editorial). *Christian Science*

    Monitor. Retrieved from Academic Search Complete.

Pollet, S. J. (2002). Is "in loco parentis" at the college level a dead doctrine? *New*

    York Law Journal, 288.

Tobin, J. (2007, November). The day "in loco parentis" died. *Michigan Today.*

    Retrieved from michigantoday.umich.edu/2007/11/dorms.php

Virginia Tech massacre has altered campus mental health systems. (2008, April).

    Los Angeles Times, A1. Retrieved from LexisNexis.

Virginia Tech Review Panel. (2007). Mass shootings at Virginia Tech,

    April 16, 2007: Report of the Virginia Tech review panel presented

    to Timothy M. Kaine, Governor, Commonwealth of Virginia.

    Arlington, VA.

Weigel, D. (2004, October). Welcome to the fun-free university: The return of *in*

    loco parentis is killing student freedom. *Reason Magazine.* Retrieved from

    Reasononline.

PRACTICE

1 Having read the selections relating to privacy and safety, pages 506–516, write a one-sentence summary of each. On the same page, list two or three topics that you think are common to several of the selections. Beneath each topic, list the authors who have something to say and briefly note what they have to say. Finally, for each topic, jot down what *you* have to say. Now regard your effort: With each topic you have created a discussion point suitable for inclusion in a paper. (Of course, until you determine the claim of such a paper, you won't know to what end you would put the discussion.) Write a paragraph or two in which you introduce the topic and then conduct a brief conversation among the interested parties (including yourself).

2 Review the model argument synthesis (pages 517–525) for elements of comparison-and-contrast—specifically those paragraphs concerning how Cornell University, M.I.T. and the University of Kentucky balance student privacy with the parental right to know about the health and welfare of their children.

3 From these paragraphs in the model paper, extract raw information concerning the positions of the three schools on the issue of student privacy and then craft your own brief comparison-and-contrast synthesis. Identify criteria for comparison and contrast, and discuss the positions of each school in relation to these criteria. *Note:* For this exercise, do not concern yourself with parenthetical citation (that is, with identifying your source materials).

4 Write a paragraph or two that traces the development of comparison-and-contrast throughout the model paper. Having discussed the *how* and *where* of this development, discuss the *why*. Answer this question: Why has the writer used comparison-and-contrast? (Hint: it is not an end in itself.) To what use is it put?

Baker College
Muskegon

How Do I Write to Inform?

13

As a reader, you regularly encounter writing with an informative aim, ranging from the instruction booklet for a smart phone to a newspaper feature story on the South African Aids crisis. Informative documents include encyclopedias, cookbooks, voters' pamphlets, and various kinds of reports, as well as informative Web sites and magazine articles. In some informative prose, visual representations of information such as diagrams, photographs, maps, tables, and graphs can be as important as the prose itself.

A useful way to begin thinking about informative writing is to classify it according to the reader's motivation for reading. From this perspective, we can place informative prose in two categories.

In the first category, readers are motivated by an immediate need for information (setting the clock on a new microwave) or by curiosity about a subject (the impressionist movement in painting or new developments in rooftop solar panels). Informative writing in this category does not necessarily contain a contestable thesis. Documents are organized effectively, of course, but they often follow a chronological, step-by-step organization (as in a set of instructions) or an "all-about" topic-by-topic organization (as in an encyclopedia article on, say, Pakistan, divided into "Geography," "Climate," "Population," "History," and so forth). The writer provides factual information about a subject without necessarily shaping the information specifically to support a thesis.

In contrast, the second category of informative writing *is* thesis-based and is therefore aligned with other kinds of thesis-based prose. The thesis brings new or surprising information to readers who may not be initially motivated by a need-to-know occasion or by their own curiosity. In fact, readers might not be initially interested in the writer's topic at all, so the writer's first task is to hook readers' interest and motivate their desire to learn something new or surprising about a topic. An excellent strategy for creating this motivation is the technique of "surprising reversal," which we explain later.

Exploring Informative (and Surprising) Writing

Let's say that you have just watched an old James Bond movie featuring a tarantula in Bond's bathroom. Curious about tarantulas, you do a quick Web search and retrieve the following short informative pieces. Read each one, and then proceed to the questions that follow.

Our first mini-article comes from the Web site EnchantedLearning.com, a commercial site aimed at providing interesting, fact-filled learning lessons for children.

Tarantulas

EnchantedLearning.com

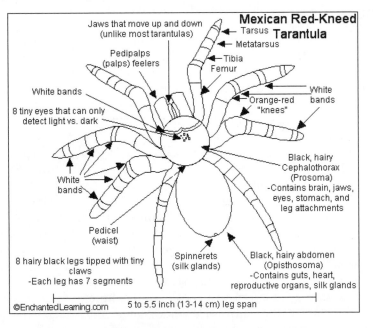

1   Tarantulas are large hairy spiders that live in warm areas around the world, including South America, southern North America, southern Europe, Africa, southern Asia, and Australia. The greatest concentration of tarantulas is in South America. There are about 300 species of tarantulas. The biggest tarantula is *Pseudotherathosa apophysis,* which has a leg

span of about 13 inches (33 cm). These arachnids have a very long life span; some species can live over 30 years.

2   **Habitat:** Some tarantulas live in underground burrows; some live on the ground, and others live in trees. They live in rain forests, deserts, and other habitats.

3   **Diet:** Tarantulas are carnivores (meat-eaters). They eat insects (like grasshoppers and beetles), other arachnids, small reptiles (like lizards and snakes), amphibians (like frogs), and some even eat small birds. Tarantulas kill their prey using venomous fangs; they also inject a chemical into the prey that dissolves the flesh. Tarantulas can crush their prey using powerful mouthparts. No person has ever died of a tarantula bite.

4   **Anatomy:** Tarantulas have a hairy two-part body and very strong jaws (with venomous fangs). They have eight hairy legs; each leg has 2 tiny claws at the end and a cushioning pad behind the claws. The hairs on the body and legs are sensitive to touch, temperature, and smell. Tarantulas have a hard exoskeleton and not an internal skeleton.
© Copyright EnchantedLearning.com. Used by permission.

The second mini article comes from the Web site of the University of Washington's Burke Museum. The author of this piece is the curator of arachnids at the Burke Museum.

Myths about "Dangerous" Spiders

Rod Crawford

1   **Myth:** Tarantulas are dangerous or deadly to humans.

2   **Fact:** Outside of southern Europe (where the name is used for a wolf spider, famous in medieval superstition as the alleged cause of "tarantella" dancing), the word tarantula is most often used for the very large, furry spiders of the family Theraphosidae.

3   Hollywood is squarely to blame for these spiders' toxic-to-humans reputation. Tarantulas are large, photogenic and easily handled, and therefore have been very widely used in horror and action-adventure movies. When some "venomous" creature is needed to menace James Bond or Indiana Jones, to invade a small town in enormous numbers, or to grow to gigantic size and prowl the Arizona desert for human prey, the special-effects team calls out the tarantulas!

4   In reality, the venom of these largest-of-all-spiders generally has **very low toxicity to humans**. I myself was once bitten by a Texan species and hardly even felt it. None of the North American species or those commonly kept as pets are considered to pose even a mild bite hazard. There are some reports that a few tropical species may have venom more toxic to vertebrates, but human bite cases haven't been reported, so we can't know for sure.

European tarantula
Lycosa Tarentula
Southern Europe; body length 2–3 cm
(photo courtesy of Manuel J. Cabrero)
Click image to enlarge

Pink toe tarantula
Avicularia avicularia
Brazil to Trinidad; body length 6–7 cm
(photo courtesy of Ron Taylor)
Click image to enlarge

Both the *European wolf spiders* (**left**) originally called tarantulas, and the *theraphosid spiders* (**right**), often kept as pets and called tarantulas now, have been reputed dangerous to humans. They aren't.

5   The only health hazard posed by keeping pet tarantulas comes from the irritating chemicals on the hairs of the abdomen, which can cause skin rashes or inflammation of eyes and nasal passages. To prevent such problems, simply keep tarantulas away from your face and wash your hands after handling one.

6   Compared to common pets such as dogs, tarantulas are not dangerous at all. (For more information see the American Tarantula Society.)

THINKING CRITICALLY
about "Tarantulas" and "Myths about 'Dangerous' Spiders"

1. Why do you think the reading from EnchantedLearning.com uses a diagram of a tarantula while the Burke Museum Web site uses photographs? How is each choice connected to the piece's targeted audience and purpose?

2. How would you describe the difference in organizational strategies for each of the readings?

3. One might suppose that informational writing would be unaffected by the writer's angle of vision—that facts would simply be facts and that informational pieces on the same topic would contain the same basic information. Yet these two short pieces give somewhat different impressions of the tarantula. For example, how do these readings differ in the way they portray the bite of the tarantula? How else do they differ in overall effect?

Understanding Informative Writing

In informative writing, the writer is assumed to have more expertise than the reader on a given subject. The writer's aim is to enlarge the reader's view of the subject by bringing the reader new information. The writer's information can come from a variety of sources:

- From the writer's preexisting expertise in a subject
- From the writer's own personal experiences
- From field research such as observations, interviews, questionnaires, and so forth
- From library or Internet research

INFORMATIVE ESSAY USING THE SURPRISING-REVERSAL STRATEGY

A commonly encountered genre is an informative article with surprising information, often found in magazines or newspapers. In this section, we focus on a specific version of this kind of essay—a thesis-based informative article aimed at general audiences. Because readers are assumed to be browsing through the pages of a magazine, the writer's rhetorical challenge is to arouse the reader's curiosity and then to keep the reader reading by providing interesting new information. The writer's first task is to hook the reader on a question and then to provide a surprising thesis that gives shape and purpose to the information. A good way to focus and sharpen the thesis, as we will show, is to use the "surprising-reversal" strategy.

● "ALL-ABOUT" VERSUS "THESIS-GOVERNED" INFORMATIVE PROSE

Let's begin by revisiting the difference between an encyclopedic (or "all-about") informative piece and a thesis-based piece. To appreciate this distinction, consider again the difference between the EnchantedLearning.com Web site on tarantulas and the Burke Museum piece "Myths about 'Dangerous' Spiders." The EnchantedLearning.com piece is a short "all-about" report organized under the topic headings "Habitat," "Diet," and "Anatomy." The Web writer may simply have adapted an encyclopedia article on tarantulas into a format for children. In contrast, the Burke Museum piece by Rod Crawford is thesis-based. Crawford wishes to refute the myth that "[t]arantulas are dangerous or deadly to humans." He does so by providing information on the low toxicity of tarantula venom to humans and the relative painlessness of tarantula bites. All of Crawford's data focus on the danger potential of tarantulas. There are no data about habitat, diet, or other aspects of tarantula life—material that would be included if this were an all-about report. Because the piece also includes data about misconceptions of tarantulas, it follows the basic pattern of surprising reversal: "Many people believe that tarantulas are toxic to humans, but I will show that tarantulas are not dangerous at all."

● **SURPRISING-REVERSAL PATTERN**   **Surprising reversal** is a strategy in which the writer's thesis pushes sharply against a counterthesis. This structure automatically creates a thesis with tension focused on a question or problem. Because of its power to hook and sustain readers, surprising-reversal essays can be found in many publications, ranging from easy-reading magazines to scholarly journals. Here, for example, is an abstract of an article from *Atlantic Monthly*.

"Reefer Madness" By Eric Schlosser

Marijuana has been pushed so far out of the public imagination by other drugs, and its use is so casually taken for granted in some quarters of society, that one might assume it had been effectively decriminalized. In truth, the government has never been tougher on marijuana offenders than it is today. In an era when violent criminals frequently walk free or receive modest jail terms, tens of thousands of people are serving long sentences for breaking marijuana laws.

This article asserts a surprising, new position ("the government has never been tougher on marijuana offenders than it is today") that counters a commonly held view (marijuana laws are no longer enforced). Here are additional examples of the surprising-reversal pattern:

Commonly Held, Narrow, or Inaccurate View	New, Surprising Information
Native Americans used to live in simple harmony with the earth.	Many American Indians used to "control" nature by setting fire to forests to make farming easier or to improve hunting.
Having fathers present in the delivery room helps the mother relax and have an easier birth.	Having fathers present in delivery rooms may reduce the amount of oxytocin produced by the mother and lead to more caesarean sections.

A similar pattern is often found in scholarly academic writing, which typically has the following underlying shape:

Whereas some scholars say X, I am going to argue Y.

Because the purpose of academic research is to advance knowledge, an academic article almost always shows the writer's new view against a background of prevailing views (what other scholars have said). This kind of tension is what often makes thesis-based writing memorable and provocative.

The writer's surprising information can come from personal experience, field research, or library/Internet research. If a college writer bases an informative piece on research sources and documents them according to academic conventions, the magazine genre doubles as an effective college research paper by combining academic citations with a tone and style suitable for general readers. Shannon King's article on hydrogen cars (p. 575) is an example of a student research paper written in magazine article style.

● **"SURPRISE" AS A RELATIVE TERM** When using the surprising-reversal strategy, keep in mind that *surprise* is a relative term based on the relationship between you and your intended audience. You don't have to surprise everyone in the world, just those who hold a mistaken or narrow view of your topic. The key is to imagine an audience less informed about your topic than you are. Suppose, as an illustration, that you have just completed an introductory economics course. You are less informed about economics than your professor, but more informed about economics than persons who have never had an econ class. You might therefore bring surprising information to the less informed audience:

> The average airplane traveler thinks that the widely varying ticket pricing for the same flight is chaotic and silly, but I can show how this pricing scheme makes perfect sense economically. [written to the "average airplane traveler," who hasn't taken an economics course]

This paper would be surprising to your intended audience, but not to the economics professor. From a different perspective, however, you could also write about economics to your professor because you might know more than your professor about, say, how students struggle with some concepts:

> Many economics professors assume that students can easily learn the concept of "elasticity of demand," but I can show why this concept was particularly confusing for me and my classmates. [written to economics professors who aren't aware of student difficulties with particular concepts]

Additionally, your surprising view doesn't necessarily have to be diametrically opposed to the common view. Perhaps you think the common view is *incomplete* or *insufficient* rather than *dead wrong*. Instead of saying, "View X is wrong, whereas my view, Y, is correct," you can say, "View X is correct and good as far as it goes, but my view, Y, adds a new perspective." In other words, you can also create surprise by going a step beyond the common view to show readers something new.

Depending on the wishes of your instructor, this assignment can draw either on personal experience or on research. Shannon King's "How Clean and Green Are Hydrogen Fuel-Cell Cars?" (pp. 575–578) is an example of a researched essay that enlarges the targeted audience's view of a subject in a surprising way. Although it is an example of a short academic research article, it is written in a relaxed style suitable for magazine publication.

For this assignment, try to avoid issues calling for persuasive rather than informative writing. With persuasive prose, you imagine a resistant reader who may argue back. With informative prose, you imagine a more trusting reader, one willing to learn from your experience or research. Although you hope to enlarge your reader's view of a topic, you aren't necessarily saying that your audience's original view is wrong, nor are you initiating a debate. For example, suppose a writer wanted to develop the following claim: "Many of my friends think that having an alcoholic mother would be the worst thing that could happen to you, but I will show that my mother's disease forced our family closer together." In this case the writer isn't arguing that alcoholic mothers are good or that everyone should have an alcoholic mother. Rather, the writer is simply offering readers a new, unexpected, and expanded view of what it might be like to have an alcoholic mother.

Generating and Exploring Ideas

If you do field research or library/Internet research for your article, start by posing a research question. As you begin doing initial research on your topic area, you will soon know more about your topic than most members of the general public. Ask yourself, "What has surprised me about my research so far? What have I learned that I didn't know before?" Your answers to these questions can suggest possible approaches to your paper. For example, Shannon King began her research believing that fuel-cell technology produced totally pollution-free energy. She didn't realize that one needs to burn fossil fuels in order to produce the hydrogen. This initial surprise shaped her paper. She decided that if this information surprised her, it should surprise others also.

Shaping, Drafting, and Revising

A surprising-reversal informative essay has the features and organization shown in Figure 13.1.

To create the "surprising-reversal" feel, it's important to delay your thesis until after you have explained your audience's common, expected answer to your opening question. This delay in presenting the thesis creates an open-form

Introduction (one to several paragraphs)	• Engages readers' interest in the writer's question • Provides background and context
Body section 1 (brief)	• Explains the common or popular answer to the writer's question
Body section 2 (major)	• Provides a delayed thesis—the writer's surprising answer to the question • Supports the thesis with information from personal experience or research • Displays numeric data in graphs or tables referenced in the text
Conclusion	• Suggests the significance of the writer's new perspective on the question

Figure 13.1   Framework for an Informative Essay Using the Surprising-Reversal Strategy

feel that readers often find engaging. Shannon King's research paper on hydrogen cars (pp. 575–578) has this surprising-reversal shape.

As a way of helping you generate ideas, we offer the following five questions. Following each question, we speculate about what King might have written if she had used the same questions to help her get started on her essay.

1. *What question does your essay address?* (King might have asked, "Will hydrogen fuel-cell automobiles solve our nation's energy and pollution crises?")

2. *What is the common, expected, or popular answer to this question held by your imagined audience?* (King might have said, "Most people believe that hydrogen fuel-cell cars will solve our country's pollution and energy crises.")

3. *What examples and details support your audience's view?* Expand on these views by developing them with supporting examples and details. (King might have noted her research examples praising fuel-cell technology such as the Bush/Cheney National Energy Report or California Governor Arnold Schwarzenegger's desire to build hydrogen fuel stations across the state.)

4. *What is your own surprising view?* (King might have said, "Although hydrogen fuel-cell cars are pollution free, getting the hydrogen in the first place requires burning fossil fuels.")

5. *What examples and details support this view? Why do you hold this view? Why should a reader believe you?* Writing rapidly, spell out the evidence that supports your point. (King would have done a freewrite about her research discoveries that hydrogen has to be recovered from carbon-based fossils or from electrolysis of water—all of which means continued use of pollution-causing fossil fuels.)

After you finish exploring your responses to these five trigger questions, you will be well on your way to composing a first draft of your article. Now finish writing your draft fairly rapidly without worrying about perfection.

Once you have your first draft on paper, the goal is to make it work better, first for yourself and then for your readers. If you discovered ideas as you wrote, you may need to do some major restructuring. Check to see that the question you are addressing is clear. If you are using the surprising-reversal strategy, make sure that you distinguish between your audience's common view and your own surprising view.

How to Write to Inform

These steps for the process of informative writing may not progress as neatly as this chart might suggest. Writing is not an assembly-line process. As you write, you are constantly reading what you have written and rethinking.

Keep your readers in mind while you are writing, and if you don't know who your readers might be, imagine someone. What questions might that person have? Where would they appreciate a more detailed explanation?

Assess the Writing Task

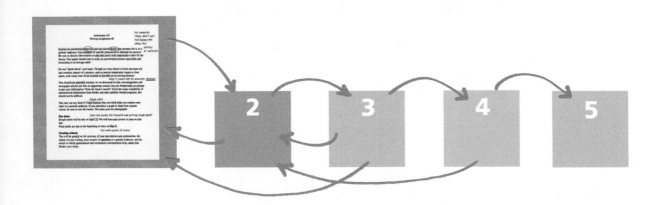

ANALYZE THE ASSIGNMENT

Read your assignment slowly and carefully. Mark off any information about the length specified, date due, formatting, and other requirements. You can attend to this information later. At this point you want to zero in on the subject you will write about and how you will approach that subject.

WHAT KIND OF WRITING IS REQUIRED?

Look for key words such as *analyze, compare* and *contrast, define, discuss,* or *explain.* Often these key words will help you in determining what direction to take. Highlight key words in all questions and commands.

Analyze	Find connections among a set of facts, events, or things, and make them meaningful.
Compare and contrast	Examine how two or more things are alike and how they differ.
Define	Make a claim about how something should be defined, according to features that you set out.
Discuss	Summarize what is known about a particular subject or issue, including research findings.
Explain	Go into detail about how something works or make an unfamiliar subject comprehensible.

IS THE AUDIENCE SPECIFIED?

If the audience is mentioned in the assignment, how much will they know about your subject? How much background will you need to provide? What attitudes are they likely to have about your subject?

FIND A TOPIC

Sometimes you know immediately what you want to write about, but most often, it takes some time to find the right topic. Think first about what is most interesting to you.

What do you know about the general topic?	A good first step is to make an inventory of what you know. Make a list of possible ideas. After you write down as many ideas as you can, go back through the list and place a star beside the ideas that seem most promising.
What ideas can you find your course notes, class discussions, and your textbooks?	Often you need to look no further than your course in materials for possible topics. Think about subjects raised in lectures, in class discussions, or in your textbooks for potential ideas.
What can you find in a database or online library catalog?	Subject directories on databases and your library's online catalog can be valuable sources of potential topics.

What might you find on the Web? Google searches and other search engines often turn up promising ideas to pursue. Yahoo has a subject directory that breaks down large topics into subtopics.

What might you find doing field research? Sometimes the information you need cannot be found in libraries or on the Web, and you have to collect the information firsthand through interviews, surveys, or observations.

EXPLORE POSSIBLE TOPICS

1. Make a list of concepts in your courses. Textbooks usually highlight key concepts, so use them and your course notes to develop your list.

2. Put a check beside the concepts that look most interesting to write about or the ones that mean the most to you.

3. Put a question mark beside the concepts that you don't know much about. If you choose one of these concepts, you will probably have to do in-depth research—by talking to people, by using the Internet, or by going to the library.

4. Select a possible concept. Write nonstop for five minutes about why this concept is interesting to you and how it affects you and other people.

Choose a Topic and Write a Thesis

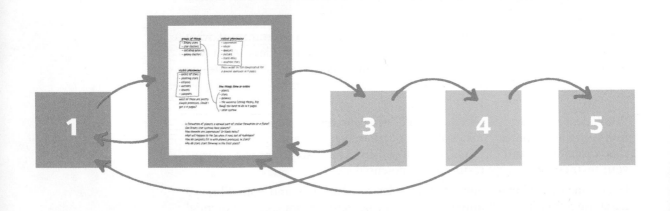

CONNECT YOUR IDEAS

After you have done preliminary research and collected ideas, it's time to list possible topics and begin making connections. Circle the most interesting possibilities.

Choose a topic you will enjoy writing about

Writing is fun when you discover new things along the way. Choose a topic you want to explore. If your topic isn't interesting for you, it likely won't be for your readers either.

Choose a topic that your readers will enjoy reading about

Readers may ask, "Why are you telling me this?" Your subject should be interesting to your readers. If the subject isn't one that is immediately interesting, think about ways you can make it so

Choose a topic that either you know something about or for which you can find the information you need

A central difficulty with writing to inform is determining where to stop. The key to success is to limit the topic. Choose a topic for which you can find the information you need and which you can cover thoroughly in the space you have. If you choose an unfamiliar topic, you must be strongly committed to learning much about it in a short time.

Narrow your topic and write a thesis

Look for ways of dividing large topics into smaller categories, and select one that is promising.

1. What is your topic exactly? (Try to state your answer in specific terms.)
2. What points do you want to make about your topic?
3. What exactly is your purpose in this project? To inform? explain? compare?
4. Develop a working thesis that draws on your answers to questions 1 and 2 and that reflects the purpose you described in your answer to question 3.

EVALUATE YOUR THESIS

Your thesis should fulfill the assignment

If your assignment is informative, your purpose is not to argue something is good or bad, not to argue for a position, and not to argue for change.

OFF TRACK

"The electoral college is an antiquated system that results in unfair election results." *(evaluates rather than informs)*

ON TRACK

"Considering the huge impact the electoral college system has on American presidential elections, it is surprising that few people understand how it actually works."

Your thesis should be interesting

If your readers already know everything that you have to say, you will bore them. Likewise, your thesis should be significant. Readers will care little about what you have to say if they find your subject trivial.

OFF TRACK

"There are many steps involved before a bill becomes a law." *(vague, bland)*

ON TRACK

"Only a tiny fraction of the bills proposed in Congress will ever become laws, and of those, most will accrue so many bizarre amendments and riders that they will barely resemble the original document."

Your thesis should be focused

You cannot tell the story of the Cold War in five pages. Narrow your thesis to a topic you can treat in depth.

OFF TRACK

"Many new products were developed in the 1950s to support the boom in housing construction." *(possibly interesting if particular products are described)*

ON TRACK

"The rush to create new housing for returning WWII veterans in the 1950s resulted in many houses that are now extremely hazardous to live in."

Write a Draft

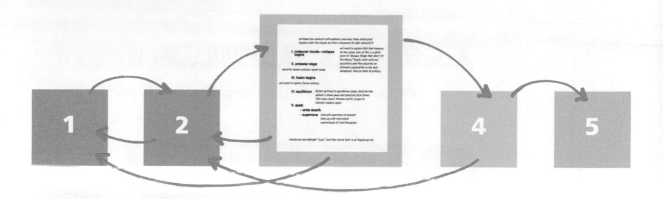

ORGANIZE YOUR INFORMATION

Gather your notes and other materials. Think about how you want to convey the information to your readers.

- If your subject matter occurs over time, you might want to use a chronological order.
- If you need to discuss several aspects, you likely will need to identify key concepts and think about how they relate to each other. An idea map can help you to determine these relationships.
- If you are comparing two or more things, you will want to think about how these things are similar and how they are different.

MAKE A WORKING OUTLINE

A working outline is a tool that you can use as you write your first draft. The more detailed it is, the better. (If you would prefer to write a complete, formal outline before drafting your essay, by all means do so.) To make your outline, follow these steps:

1. List the sections of your essay, in the order that you expect them to appear.
2. Write two or three complete sentences describing the content and purpose of each section.
3. Now, review your outline. Does the project as you have described it here achieve the purpose you intend it to?

THINK ABOUT A TITLE

An effective title motivates your readers to want to read what you have written. Be as specific as you can.

CONSIDER THE USE OF VISUALS

Would a table or chart be helpful? photographs? a map? Do you need headings and subheadings?

WRITE AN EFFECTIVE INTRODUCTION AND CONCLUSION

Write an effective introduction

Get off to a fast start. Cut to the chase: no empty sentences or big generalizations at the beginning.

OFF TRACK

"Because we all live such busy, hectic lives in these modern times, everyone wants to know why we must wait for hours and hours at the airport before boarding a flight."
(boring, predictable beginning—a signal that the paper will be dull)

ON TRACK

"It's a traveler's worst nightmare: the long line of people at the security gate, snaking back and forth across the waiting area. What exactly goes on in an airport screening area, and how does it help to keep us safe?"

Write an effective conclusion

Remember that a summary of what you have just written is the weakest way to conclude. Think of something interesting for your reader to take away such as an unexpected implication or a provocative example.

OFF TRACK

"In conclusion, we have seen how peer-to-peer file sharing works."
(ineffective; says only that the paper is finished)

ON TRACK

"The peer-to-peer file sharing process is relatively simple.
Unfortunately, in many cases it is also illegal. It is ironic that a technology intended to help people has resulted in turning many of them into *de facto* criminals."
(ends with a significant point, which helps readers remember the paper)

Revise, Revise, Revise

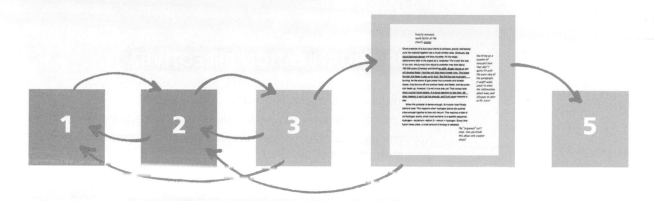

Skilled writers know that the secret to writing well is rewriting. Even the best writers often have to revise several times to get the result they want. You also must have effective strategies for revising if you're going to be successful. The biggest trap you can fall into is starting off with the little stuff first. Leave the small stuff for last.

DOES YOUR PAPER OR PROJECT MEET THE ASSIGNMENT?

- Look again at your assignment. Does your paper or project do what the assignment asks?
- Look again at the assignment for specific guidelines, including length, format, and amount of research. Does your work meet these guidelines?

IS YOUR TITLE SPECIFIC?

- Vague titles suggest dull treatment of the topic. Can you make your title more accurate?

DOES YOUR WRITING HAVE A CLEAR FOCUS?

- Does your project have an explicitly stated thesis? If not, is your thesis clearly implied?
- Is each paragraph related to your thesis?
- Do you get off the track at any point by introducing other topics?

- Are your main points adequately developed?
- Do you support your main points with reasons and evidence?
- Can you add more examples and details that would help to explain your main points?

IS YOUR ORGANIZATION EFFECTIVE?

- Is the order of your main points clear to your reader?
- Are there any places where you find abrupt shifts or gaps?
- Are there sections or paragraphs that could be rearranged to make your draft more effective?

IS YOUR INTRODUCTION EFFECTIVE?

- Do you have any general statements that you might cut to get off to a faster start?
- Can you think of a vivid example that might draw in readers?
- Can you use a striking fact to get readers interested?
- Does your introduction make clear where you are headed?

IS YOUR CONCLUSION EFFECTIVE?

- Conclusions that only summarize tend to bore readers. Does your conclusion add anything new to what you've said already?
- Can you use the conclusion to discuss further implications?
- Have you left your audience with a final provocative idea that might invite further discussion?

DO YOU REPRESENT YOURSELF EFFECTIVELY?

- To the extent you can, forget for a moment that you wrote what you are reading. What impression do you have of you, the writer?
- Does "the writer" create an appropriate tone?
- Has "the writer" done his or her homework?

IS THE WRITING PROJECT VISUALLY EFFECTIVE?

- Is the font attractive and readable?
- Are the headings and visuals effective?

SAVE THE EDITING FOR LAST

When you have finished revising, edit and proofread carefully.

REVIEWING YOUR DRAFT

Give yourself plenty of time for reviewing your draft.

Some good questions to ask yourself when reviewing informative writing

- Are the explanations in the essay easy to follow?
- Are there gaps or places where you feel you need more information?
- Are any unusual or discipline-specific words defined for readers?
- Can the reader construct a clear picture of what the essay describes?
- Is the essay interesting enough to catch readers' attention and keep them reading?

Questions for Peer Review

Ask your peer reviewers to address these questions:

1. What is the question the paper addresses? How effective is the paper at hooking the reader's interest in the question?
2. Where does the writer explain the common or popular view of the topic? Do you agree that this is the common view? How does the writer develop or support this view? What additional supporting examples, illustrations, or details might make the common view more vivid or compelling?

3. What is the writer's surprising view? Were you surprised? What details does the writer use to develop the surprising view? What additional supporting examples, illustrations, or details might help make the surprising view more vivid and compelling?

4. Is the draft clear and easy to follow? Is the draft interesting? How might the writer improve the style, clarity, or interest level of the draft?

5. If the draft includes graphics, are they effective? Do the words and the visuals tell the same story? Are the visuals properly titled and labeled? How might the use of visuals be improved?

READINGS

Affairs of the Lips: Why We Kiss
(Essay)
Chip Walter

Chip Walter is a former CNN bureau chief, filmmaker, science journalist, and author. His science books, written for a mainstream audience, cover subjects as diverse as astrophysics, cognitive psychology, and evolution and are devoted to exploring why humans do what we do. "Affairs of the Lips: Why We Kiss" was the cover story of the February 2008 edition of Scientific American Mind. In this article, Walters explores why humans kiss and the wealth of information transmitted in this small act.

When passion takes a grip, a kiss locks two humans together in an exchange of scents, tastes, textures, secrets and emotions. We kiss furtively, lasciviously, gently, shyly, hungrily and exuberantly. We kiss in broad daylight and in the dead of night. We give ceremonial kisses, affectionate kisses, Hollywood air kisses, kisses of death and, at least in fairytales, pecks that revive princesses.

Lips may have evolved first for food and later applied themselves to speech, but in kissing they satisfy different kinds of hungers. In the body, a kiss triggers a cascade of neural messages and chemicals that transmit tactile sensations, sexual excitement, feelings of closeness, motivation and even euphoria.

Not all the messages are internal. After all, kissing is a communal affair. The fusion of two bodies dispatches communiqués to your partner as powerful as the data you stream to yourself. Kisses can convey important information about the status and future of a relationship. So much, in fact, that, according to recent research, if a first kiss goes bad, it can stop an otherwise promising relationship dead in its tracks.

Some scientists believe that the fusing of lips evolved because it facilitates mate selection. "Kissing," said evolutionary psychologist Gordon G. Gallup of the University at Albany, State University of New York, last September in an interview with the BBC, "involves a very complicated exchange of information—olfactory information, tactile information and postural types of adjustments that may tap into underlying evolved and unconscious mechanisms that enable people to make determinations . . . about the degree to which they are genetically incompatible." Kissing may even reveal the extent to which a partner is willing to commit to raising children, a central issue in long-term relationships and crucial to the survival of our species.

SATISFYING HUNGER

Whatever else is going on when we kiss, our evolutionary history is embedded within this tender, tempestuous act. In the 1960s British zoologist and author Desmond Morris first proposed that kissing might have evolved from the practice in which primate mothers chewed food for their young and then fed them mouth-to-mouth, lips puckered. Chimpanzees feed in this manner, so our hominid ancestors probably did, too. Pressing outturned lips against lips may have then later developed as a way to comfort hungry children when food was scarce and, in time, to express love and affection in general. The human species might eventually have taken these proto-parental kisses down other roads until we came up with the more passionate varieties we have today.

Silent chemical messengers called pheromones could have sped the evolution of the intimate kiss. Many animals and plants use pheromones to communicate with other members of the same species. Insects, in particular, are known to emit pheromones to signal alarm, for example, the presence of a food trail, or sexual attraction.

Whether humans sense pheromones is controversial. Unlike rats and pigs, people are not known to have a specialized pheromone detector, or vomeronasal organ, between their nose and mouth [see "Sex and the Secret Nerve," by R. Douglas Fields; *Scientific American Mind,* February/March 2007]. Nevertheless, biologist Sarah Woodley of Duquesne University suggests that we might be able to sense pheromones with our nose. And chemical communication could explain such curious findings as a tendency of the menstrual cycles of female dormitory mates to synchronize or the attraction of women to the scents of T-shirts worn by men whose immune systems are genetically compatible with theirs. Human pheromones could include androstenol, a chemical component of male sweat that may boost sexual arousal in women, and female vaginal hormones called copulins that some researchers have found raise testosterone levels and increase sexual appetite in men.

If pheromones do play a role in human courtship and procreation, then kissing would be an extremely effective way to pass them from one person to another. The behavior may have evolved because it helps humans find a suitable mate—making love, or at least attraction, quite literally blind.

We might also have inherited the intimate kiss from our primate ancestors. Bonobos, which are genetically very similar to us (although we are not their direct descendants), are a particularly passionate bunch, for example. Emory University primatologist Frans B. M. de Waal recalls a zookeeper who accepted what he thought would be a friendly kiss from one of the bonobos, until he felt the ape's tongue in his mouth!

GOOD CHEMISTRY

Since kissing evolved, the act seems to have become addictive. Human lips enjoy the slimmest layer of skin on the human body, and the lips are among the most densely populated with sensory neurons of any body region. When we kiss, these neurons, along with those in the tongue and mouth, rocket messages to the brain and body, setting off delightful sensations, intense emotions and physical reactions.

Of the 12 or 13 cranial nerves that affect cerebral function, five are at work when we kiss, shuttling messages from our lips, tongue, cheeks and nose to a brain that snatches information about the temperature, taste, smell and movements of the entire affair. Some of that information arrives in the somatosensory cortex, a swath of tissue on the surface of the brain that represents tactile information in a map of the body. In that map, the lips loom large because the size of each represented body region is proportional to the density of its nerve endings.

Kissing unleashes a cocktail of chemicals that govern human stress, motivation, social bonding and sexual stimulation. In a new study, psychologist Wendy L. Hill and her student Carey A. Wilson of Lafayette College compared the levels of two key hormones in 15 college male-female couples before and after they kissed and before and after they talked to each other while holding hands. One hormone, oxytocin, is involved in social bonding, and the other, cortisol, plays a role in stress. Hill and Wilson predicted that kissing would boost levels of oxytocin, which also influences social recognition, male and female orgasm, and childbirth. They expected this effect to be particularly pronounced in the study's females, who reported higher levels of intimacy in their relationships. They also forecast a dip in cortisol, because kissing is presumably a stress reliever.

But the researchers were surprised to find that oxytocin levels rose only in the males, whereas it decreased in the females, after either kissing or talking while holding hands. They concluded that females must require more than a kiss to feel emotionally connected or sexually excited during physical contact. Females might, for example, need a more romantic atmosphere than the experimental setting provided, the authors speculate. The study, which Hill and Wilson reported in November 2007 at the annual meeting of the Society for Neuroscience, revealed that cortisol levels dropped for both sexes no matter the form of intimacy, a hint that kissing does in fact reduce stress.

To the extent that kissing is linked to love, the act may similarly boost brain chemicals associated with pleasure, euphoria and a motivation to connect with a certain someone. In 2005 anthropologist Helen Fisher of Rutgers University and her colleagues reported scanning the brains of 17 individuals as they gazed at pictures of people with whom they were deeply in love. The researchers found an unusual flurry of activity in two brain regions that govern pleasure, motivation and reward: the right ventral tegmental area and the right caudate nucleus. Addictive drugs such as cocaine similarly stimulate these reward centers, through the release of the neurotransmitter dopamine. Love, it seems, is a kind of drug for us humans.

Kissing has other primal effects on us as well. Visceral marching orders boost pulse and blood pressure. The pupils dilate, breathing deepens and rational thought retreats, as desire suppresses both prudence and self-consciousness. For their part, the participants are probably too enthralled to care. As poet e. e. cummings once observed: "Kisses are a better fate / than wisdom."

LITMUS TEST

Although a kiss may not be wise, it can be pivotal to a relationship. "One dance," Alex "Hitch" Hitchens says to his client and friend in the 2005 movie *Hitch,* "one look, one kiss, that's all we get . . . one shot, to make the difference between 'happily ever after' and, 'Oh? He's just some guy I went to some thing with once.' "

Can a kiss be that powerful? Some research indicates it can be. In a recent survey Gallup and his colleagues found that 59 percent of 58 men and 66 percent of 122 women admitted there had been times when they were attracted to someone only to find that their interest evaporated after their first kiss. The "bad" kisses had no particular flaws; they simply did not feel right—and they ended the romantic relationship then and there—a kiss of death for that coupling.

The reason a kiss carries such weight, Gallup theorizes, is that it conveys subconscious information about the genetic compatibility of a prospective mate. His hypothesis is consistent with the idea that kissing evolved as a courtship strategy because it helps us rate potential partners.

From a Darwinian perspective, sexual selection is the key to passing on your genes. For us humans, mate choice often involves falling in love. Fisher wrote in her 2005 paper that this "attraction mechanism" in humans "evolved to enable individuals to focus their mating energy on specific others, thereby conserving energy and facilitating mate choice— a primary aspect of reproduction."

According to Gallup's new findings, kissing may play a crucial role in the progression of a partnership but one that differs between men and women. In a study published in September 2007 Gallup and his colleagues surveyed 1,041 college undergraduates of both sexes about kissing. For most of the men, a deep kiss was largely a way of advancing to the next level sexually. But women were generally looking to take the relationship to the next stage emotionally, assessing not simply whether the other person would make a first-rate source of DNA but also whether he would be a good long-term partner.

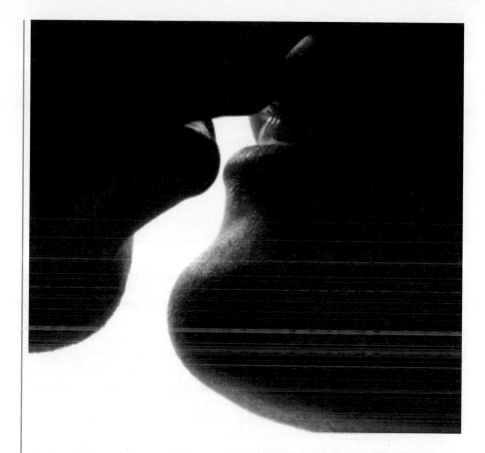

"Females use [kissing] . . . to provide information about the level of commitment if they happen to be in a continuing relationship," Gallup told the BBC in September. The locking of lips is thus a kind of emotional barometer: the more enthusiastic it is, the healthier the relationship.

Because women need to invest more energy in producing children and have a shorter biological window in which to reproduce, they need to be pickier about whom they choose for a partner—and they cannot afford to get it wrong. So, at least for women, a passionate kiss may help them choose a mate who is not only good at fathering children but also committed enough to stick around and raise them.

That said, kissing is probably not strictly necessary from an evolutionary point of view. Most other animals do not neck and still manage to produce plenty of offspring. Not even all humans kiss. At the turn of the 20th century Danish scientist Kristoffer Nyrop described Finnish tribes whose members bathed together but considered kissing indecent. In 1897 French anthropologist Paul d'Enjoy reported that the Chinese regard mouth-to-mouth kissing to be as horrifying as many people deem cannibalism to be. In Mongolia some fathers do not kiss their sons. (They smell their heads instead.)

...continued Affairs of the Lips: Why We Kiss, **Chip Walter**

In fact, up to 10 percent of humanity does not touch lips, according to human ethology pioneer Irenäus Eibl-Eibesfeldt, now head of the Max-Planck-Society Film Archive of Human Ethology in Andechs, Germany, writing in his 1970 book, *Love and Hate: The Natural History of Behavior Patterns*. Fisher published a similar figure in 1992. Their findings suggest that some 650 million members of the human species have not mastered the art of osculation, the scientific term for kissing; that is more than the population of any nation on earth except for China and India.

LOPSIDED LOVE

For those cultures that do kiss, however, osculation conveys additional hidden messages. Psychologist Onur Güntürkün of the Ruhr-University of Bochum in Germany recently surveyed 124 couples kissing in public places in the U.S., Germany and Turkey and found that they tilted their heads to the right twice as often as to the left before their lips touched. Right-handedness cannot explain this tendency, because being right-handed is four times more common than is the act of kissing on the right. Instead Güntürkün suspects that right-tilted kissing results from a general preference that develops at the end of gestation and in infancy. This "behavioral asymmetry" is related to the lateralization of brain functions such as speech and spatial awareness.

Nurture may also influence our tendency to tilt to the right. Studies show that as many as 80 percent of mothers, whether right-handed or left-handed, cradle their infants on their left side. Infants cradled, face up, on the left must turn to the right to nurse or nuzzle. As a result, most of us may have learned to associate warmth and security with turning to the right.

Some scientists have proposed that those who tilt their heads to the left when they kiss may be showing less warmth and love than those who tilt to the right. In one theory, tilting right exposes the left cheek, which is controlled by the right, more emotional half of the brain. But a 2006 study by naturalist Julian Greenwood and his colleagues at Stranmillis University College in Belfast, Northern Ireland, counters this notion. The researchers found that 77 percent of 240 undergraduate students leaned right when kissing a doll on the cheek or lips. Tilting to the right with the doll, an impassive act, was nearly as prevalent among subjects as it was among 125 couples observed osculating in Belfast; they tilted right 80 percent of the time. The conclusion: right-kissing probably results from a motor preference, as Güntürkün hypothesized, rather than an emotional one.

Despite all these observations, a kiss continues to resist complete scientific dissection. Close scrutiny of couples has illuminated new complexities woven throughout this simplest and most natural of acts—and the quest to unmask the secrets of passion and love is not likely to end soon. But romance gives up its mysteries grudgingly. And in some ways, we like it like that.

The Stanford Prison Experiment

Philip G. Zimbardo

As well known—and as controversial—as the Milgram obedience experiments, the Stanford Prison Experiment (1973) raises troubling questions about the ability of individuals to resist authoritarian or obedient roles, if the social setting requires these roles. Philip G. Zimbardo, professor of psychology at Stanford University, set out to study the process by which prisoners and guards "learn" to become compliant and authoritarian, respectively. To find subjects for the experiment, Zimbardo placed an advertisement in a local newspaper:

Male college students needed for psychological study of prison life. $15 per day for 1–2 weeks beginning Aug. 14. For further information & applications, come to Room 248, Jordan Hall, Stanford U.

The ad drew 75 responses. From these Zimbardo and his colleagues selected 21 college-age men, half of whom would become "prisoners" in the experiment, the other half "guards." The elaborate role-playing scenario, planned for two weeks, had to be cut short due to the intensity of subjects' responses. This article first appeared in the New York Times Magazine *on April 8, 1973.**

In prison, those things withheld from and denied to the prisoner become precisely what he wants most of all.

—Eldridge Cleaver, "Soul on Ice"

Our sense of power is more vivid when we break a man's spirit than when we win his heart.

—Eric Hoffer, "The Passionate State of Mind"

*"The Mind Is a Formidable Jailer" ["The Stanford Prison Experiment"] by Philip G. Zimbardo as published in the *New York Times Magazine*, 8 April 1973. Copyright © 1973 by the New York Times. Reprinted with permission from the New York Times.

...continued The Stanford Prison Experiment, **Philip G. Zimbardo**

Every prison that men build / Is built with bricks of shame, / And bound with bars lest Christ should see / How men their brothers maim.

—Oscar Wilde, "The Ballad of Reading Gaol"

Wherever anyone is against his will that is to him a prison.

—Epictetus, "Discourses"

The quiet of a summer morning in Palo Alto, Calif., was shattered by a screeching squad car siren as police swept through the city picking up college students in a surprise mass arrest. Each suspect was charged with a felony, warned of his constitutional rights, spread-eagled against the car, searched, handcuffed, and carted off in the back seat of the squad car to the police station for booking.

After fingerprinting and the preparation of identification forms for his "jacket" (central information file), each prisoner was left isolated in a detention cell to wonder what he had done to get himself into this mess. After a while, he was blindfolded and transported to the "Stanford County Prison." Here he began the process of becoming a prisoner— stripped naked, skin-searched, deloused, and issued a uniform, bedding, soap, and towel.

The warden offered an impromptu welcome:

"As you probably know, I'm your warden. All of you have shown that you are unable to function outside in the real world for one reason or another—that somehow you lack the responsibility of good citizens of this great country. We of this prison, your correctional staff, are going to help you learn what your responsibilities as citizens of this country are. Here are the rules. Sometime in the near future there will be a copy of the rules posted in each of the cells. We expect you to know them and to be able to recite them by number. If you follow all of these rules and keep your hands clean, repent for your misdeeds, and show a proper attitude of penitence, you and I will get along just fine."

5   There followed a reading of the 16 basic rules of prisoner conduct, "Rule Number One: Prisoners must remain silent during rest periods, after lights are out, during meals, and whenever they are outside the prison yard. Two: Prisoners must eat at mealtimes and only at mealtimes. Three: Prisoners must not move, tamper, deface, or damage walls, ceilings, windows, doors, or other prison property. . . . Seven: Prisoners must address each other by their ID number only. Eight: Prisoners must address the guards as 'Mr. Correctional Officer.' . . . Sixteen: Failure to obey any of the above rules may result in punishment."

By late afternoon these youthful "first offenders" sat in dazed silence on the cots in their barren cells trying to make sense of the events that had transformed their lives so dramatically.

If the police arrests and processing were executed with customary detachment, however, there were some things that didn't fit. For these men were now part of a very unusual kind of prison, an experimental mock prison, created by social psychologists to study the effects of imprisonment upon volunteer research subjects. When we planned our two-week-long simulation of prison life, we sought to understand more about the process by which people called "prisoners" lose their liberty, civil rights, independence, and privacy, while those called "guards" gain social power by accepting the responsibility for controlling and managing the lives of their dependent charges.

Why didn't we pursue this research in a real prison? First, prison systems are fortresses of secrecy, closed to impartial observation, and thereby immune to critical analysis from anyone not already part of the correctional authority. Second, in any real prison, it is impossible to separate what each individual brings into the prison from what the prison brings out in each person.

We populated our mock prison with a homogeneous group of people who could be considered "normal-average" on the basis of clinical interviews and personality tests. Our participants (10 prisoners and 11 guards) were selected from more than 75 volunteers recruited through ads in the city and campus newspapers. The applicants were mostly college students from all over the United States and Canada who happened to be in the Stanford area during the summer and were attracted by the lure of earning $15 a day for participating in a study of prison life. We selected only those judged to be emotionally stable, physically healthy, mature, law-abiding citizens.

10   The sample of average, middle-class, Caucasian, college-age males (plus one Oriental student) was arbitrarily divided by the flip of a coin. Half were randomly assigned to play the role of guards, the others of prisoners. There were no measurable differences between the guards and the prisoners at the start of the experiment. Although initially warned that as prisoners their privacy and other civil rights would be violated and that they might be subjected to harassment, every subject was completely confident of his ability to endure whatever the prison had to offer for the full two-week experimental period. Each subject unhesitatingly agreed to give his "informed consent" to participate.

The prison was constructed in the basement of Stanford University's psychology building, which was deserted after the end of the summer-school session. A long corridor was converted into the prison "yard" by partitioning off both ends. Three small laboratory rooms opening onto this corridor were made into cells by installing metal barred doors and replacing existing furniture with cots, three to a cell. Adjacent offices were refurnished as guards' quarters, interview-testing rooms, and bedrooms for the "warden" (Jaffe) and the "superintendent" (Zimbardo). A

...*continued* The Stanford Prison Experiment, **Philip G. Zimbardo**

concealed video camera and hidden microphones recorded much of the activity and conversation of guards and prisoners. The physical environment was one in which prisoners could always be observed by the staff, the only exception being when they were secluded in solitary confinement (a small, dark storage closet, labeled "The Hole").

Our mock prison represented an attempt to simulate the psychological state of imprisonment in certain ways. We based our experiment on an in-depth analysis of the prison situation, developed after hundreds of hours of discussion with Carlo Prescott (our ex-con consultant), parole officers, and correctional personnel, and after reviewing much of the existing literature on prisons and concentration camps.

"Real" prisoners typically report feeling powerless, arbitrarily controlled, dependent, frustrated, hopeless, anonymous, dehumanized, and emasculated. It was not possible, pragmatically or ethically, to create such chronic states in volunteer subjects who realize that they are in an experiment for only a short time. Racism, physical brutality, indefinite confinement, and enforced homosexuality were not features of our mock prison. But we did try to reproduce those elements of the prison experience that seemed most fundamental.

We promoted anonymity by seeking to minimize each prisoner's sense of uniqueness and prior identity. The prisoners wore smocks and nylon stocking caps; they had to use their ID numbers; their personal effects were removed and they were housed in barren cells. All of this made them appear similar to each other and indistinguishable to observers. Their smocks, which were like dresses, were worn without undergarments, causing the prisoners to be restrained in their physical actions and to move in ways that were more feminine than masculine. The prisoners were forced to obtain permission from the guard for routine and simple activities such as writing letters, smoking a cigarette, or even going to the toilet; this elicited from them a childlike dependency.

15

Their quarters, though clean and neat, were small, stark, and without esthetic appeal. The lack of windows resulted in poor air circulation, and persistent odors arose from the unwashed bodies of the prisoners. After 10 P.M. lockup, toilet privileges were denied, so prisoners who had to relieve themselves would have to urinate and defecate in buckets provided by the guards. Sometimes the guards refused permission to have them cleaned out, and this made the prison smell.

Above all, "real" prisons are machines for playing tricks with the human conception of time. In our windowless prison, the prisoners often did not even know whether it was day or night. A few hours after falling asleep, they were roused by shrill whistles for their "count." The ostensible purpose of the count was to provide a public test of the prisoners' knowledge of the rules and of their ID numbers. But more important, the count, which occurred at least once on each of the three different guard shifts, provided a regular occasion for the guards to relate to the prisoners. Over the course of the study, the duration of the counts was spontaneously increased by the guards from their initial perfunctory 10 minutes to a seemingly interminable several hours. During these confrontations, guards who were bored could find ways to amuse themselves, ridiculing recalcitrant prisoners, enforcing arbitrary rules, and openly exaggerating any dissension among the prisoners.

The guards were also "deindividualized": They wore identical khaki uniforms and silver reflector sunglasses that made eye contact with them impossible. Their symbols of power were billy clubs, whistles, handcuffs, and the keys to the cells and the "main gate." Although our guards received no formal training from us in how to be guards, for the most part they moved with apparent ease into their roles. The media had already provided them with ample models of prison guards to emulate.

Because we were as interested in the guards' behavior as in the prisoners', they were given considerable latitude to improvise and to develop strategies and tactics of prisoner management. Our guards were told that they must maintain "law and order" in this prison, that they were responsible for handling any trouble that might break out, and they were cautioned about the seriousness and potential dangers of the situation they were about to enter. Surprisingly, in most prison systems, "real" guards are not given much more psychological preparation or adequate training than this for what is one of the most complex, demanding, and dangerous jobs our society has to offer. They are expected to learn how to adjust to their new employment mostly from on-the-job experience, and from contacts with the "old bulls" during a survival-of-the-fittest orientation period. According to an orientation manual for correctional officers at San Quentin, "the only way you really get to know San Quentin is through experience and time. Some of us take more time and must go through more experiences than others to accomplish this; some really never do get there."

You cannot be a prisoner if no one will be your guard, and you cannot be a prison guard if no one takes you or your prison seriously. Therefore, over time a perverted symbiotic relationship developed. As the guards became more aggressive, prisoners became more passive; assertion by the guards led to dependency in the prisoners; self-aggrandizement was met with self-deprecation, authority with helplessness, and the counterpart of the guards' sense of mastery and control was the depression and hopelessness witnessed in the prisoners. As these differences in behavior, mood, and perception became more evident to all, the need for the now "righteously" powerful guards to rule the obviously inferior and powerless inmates became a sufficient reason to support almost any further indignity of man against man:

20   Guard K: "During the inspection, I went to cell 2 to mess up a bed which the prisoner had made and he grabbed me, screaming that he had just made it, and he wasn't going to let me mess it up. He grabbed my

throat, and although he was laughing I was pretty scared. . . . I lashed out with my stick and hit him in the chin (although not very hard), and when I freed myself I became angry. I wanted to get back in the cell and have a go with him, since he attacked me when I was not ready."

Guard M: "I was surprised at myself . . . I made them call each other names and clean the toilets out with their bare hands. I practically considered the prisoners cattle, and I kept thinking: 'I have to watch out for them in case they try something.'"

Guard A: "I was tired of seeing the prisoners in their rags and smelling the strong odors of their bodies that filled the cells. I watched them tear at each other on orders given by us. They didn't see it as an experiment. It was real and they were fighting to keep their identity. But we were always there to show them who was boss."

Because the first day passed without incident, we were surprised and totally unprepared for the rebellion that broke out on the morning of the second day. The prisoners removed their stocking caps, ripped off their numbers, and barricaded themselves inside the cells by putting their beds against the doors. What should we do? The guards were very much upset because the prisoners also began to taunt and curse them to their faces. When the morning shift of guards came on, they were upset at the night shift who, they felt, must have been too permissive and too lenient. The guards had to handle the rebellion themselves, and what they did was startling to behold.

At first they insisted that reinforcements be called in. The two guards who were waiting on stand-by call at home came in, and the night shift of guards voluntarily remained on duty (without extra pay) to bolster the morning shift. The guards met and decided to treat force with force. They got a fire extinguisher that shot a stream of skin-chilling carbon dioxide and forced the prisoners away from the doors; they broke into each cell, stripped the prisoners naked, took the beds out, forced the prisoners who were the ringleaders into solitary confinement, and generally began to harass and intimidate the prisoners.

25

After crushing the riot, the guards decided to head off further unrest by creating a privileged cell for those who were "good prisoners" and then, without explanation, switching some of the troublemakers into it and some of the good prisoners out into the other cells. The prisoner ringleaders could not trust these new cellmates because they had not joined in the riot and might even be "snitches." The prisoners never again acted in unity against the system. One of the leaders of the prisoner revolt later confided:

"If we had gotten together then, I think we could have taken over the place. But when I saw the revolt wasn't working, I decided to toe the line. Everyone settled into the same pattern. From then on, we were really controlled by the guards."

It was after this episode that the guards really began to demonstrate their inventiveness in the application of arbitrary power. They made the prisoners obey petty, meaningless, and often inconsistent rules, forced them to engage in tedious, useless work, such as moving cartons back and forth between closets and picking thorns out of their blankets for hours on end. (The guards had previously dragged the blankets through thorny bushes to create this disagreeable task.) Not only did the prisoners have to sing songs or laugh or refrain from smiling on command; they were also encouraged to curse and vilify each other publicly during some of the counts. They sounded off their numbers endlessly and were repeatedly made to do pushups, on occasion with a guard stepping on them or a prisoner sitting on them.

Slowly the prisoners became resigned to their fate and even behaved in ways that actually helped to justify their dehumanizing treatment at the hands of the guards. Analysis of the tape-recorded private conversations between prisoners and of remarks made by them to interviewers revealed that fully half could be classified as nonsupportive of other prisoners. More dramatic, 85 percent of the evaluative statements by prisoners about their fellow prisoners were uncomplimentary and deprecating.

This should be taken in the context of an even more surprising result. What do you imagine the prisoners talked about when they were alone in their cells with each other, given a temporary respite from the continual harassment and surveillance by the guards? Girl friends, career plans, hobbies or politics?

No, their concerns were almost exclusively riveted to prison topics. Their monitored conversations revealed that only 10 percent of the time was devoted to "outside" topics, while 90 percent of the time they discussed escape plans, the awful food, grievances or ingratiating tactics to use with specific guards in order to get a cigarette, permission to go to the toilet, or some other favor. Their obsession with these immediate survival concerns made talk about the past and future an idle luxury.

And this was not a minor point. So long as the prisoners did not get to know each other as people, they only extended the oppressiveness and reality of their life as prisoners. For the most part, each prisoner observed his fellow prisoners allowing the guards to humiliate them, acting like compliant sheep, carrying out mindless orders with total obedience, and even being cursed by fellow prisoners (at a guard's command). Under such circumstances, how could a prisoner have respect for his fellows, or any self-respect for what *he* obviously was becoming in the eyes of all those evaluating him?

The combination of realism and symbolism in this experiment had fused to create a vivid illusion of imprisonment. The illusion merged inextricably with reality for at least some of the time for every individual in the situation. It was remarkable how readily we all slipped into our roles, temporarily gave up our identities, and allowed these assigned roles and the social forces in the situation to guide, shape, and eventually to control our freedom of thought and action.

...*continued* The Stanford Prison Experiment, **Philip G. Zimbardo**

But precisely where does one's "identity" end and one's "role" begin? When the private self and the public role behavior clash, what direction will attempts to impose consistency take? Consider the reactions of the parents, relatives, and friends of the prisoners who visited their forlorn sons, brothers, and lovers during two scheduled visitors' hours. They were taught in short order that they were our guests, allowed the privilege of visiting only by complying with the regulations of the institution. They had to register, were made to wait half an hour, were told that only two visitors could see any one prisoner; the total visiting time was cut from an hour to only 10 minutes, they had to be under the surveillance of a guard, and before any parents could enter the visiting area, they had to discuss their son's case with the warden. Of course they complained about these arbitrary rules, but their conditioned, middle-class reaction was to work within the system to appeal privately to the superintendent to make conditions better for their prisoners.

In less than 36 hours, we were forced to release prisoner 8612 because of extreme depression, disorganized thinking, uncontrollable crying, and fits of rage. We did so reluctantly because we believed he was trying to "con" us—it was unimaginable that a volunteer prisoner in a mock prison could legitimately be suffering and disturbed to that extent. But then on each of the next three days another prisoner reacted with similar anxiety symptoms, and we were forced to terminate them, too. In a fifth case, a prisoner was released after developing a psychosomatic rash over his entire body (triggered by rejection of his parole appeal by the mock parole board). These men were simply unable to make an adequate adjustment to prison life. Those who endured the prison experience to the end could be distinguished from those who broke down and were released early in only one dimension—authoritarianism. On a psychological test designed to reveal a person's authoritarianism, those prisoners who had the highest scores were best able to function in this authoritarian prison environment.

35   If the authoritarian situation became a serious matter for the prisoners, it became even more serious—and sinister—for the guards. Typically, the guards insulted the prisoners, threatened them, were physically aggressive, used instruments (night sticks, fire extinguishers, etc.) to keep the prisoners in line, and referred to them in impersonal, anonymous, deprecating ways: "Hey, you," or "You [obscenity], 5401, come here." From the first to the last day, there was a significant increase in the guards' use of most of these domineering, abusive tactics.

Everyone and everything in the prison was defined by power. To be a guard who did not take advantage of this institutionally sanctioned use of power was to appear "weak," "out of it," "wired up by the prisoners," or simply a deviant from the established norms of appropriate guard behavior. Using Erich Fromm's definition of sadism, as "the wish for absolute control over another living being," all of the mock guards at one time or another during this study behaved sadistically toward the prisoners. Many of them reported—in their diaries, on critical-incident report forms, and during post-experimental interviews—being delighted in the new-found power and control they exercised and sorry to see it relinquished at the end of the study.

Some of the guards reacted to the situation in the extreme and behaved with great hostility and cruelty in the forms of degradation they invented for the prisoners. But others were kinder; they occasionally did little favors for the prisoners, were reluctant to punish them, and avoided situations where prisoners were being harassed. The torment experienced by one of these good guards is obvious in his perceptive analysis of what it felt like to be responded to as a "guard":

"What made the experience most depressing for me was the fact that we were continually called upon to act in a way that just was contrary to what I really feel inside. I don't feel like I'm the type of person that would be a guard, just constantly giving out [orders] . . . and forcing people to do things, and pushing and lying—it just didn't seem like me, and to continually keep up and put on a face like that is just really one of the most oppressive things you can do. It's almost like a prison that you create yourself—you get into it, and it becomes almost the definition you make of yourself, it almost becomes like walls, and you want to break out and you want just to be able to tell everyone that 'this isn't really me at all, and I'm not the person that's confined in there—I'm a person who wants to get out and show you that I am free, and I do have my own will, and I'm not the sadistic type of person that enjoys this kind of thing.'"

Still, the behavior of these good guards seemed more motivated by a desire to be liked by everyone in the system than by a concern for the inmates' welfare. No guard ever intervened in any direct way on behalf of the prisoners, ever interfered with the orders of the cruelest guards, or ever openly complained about the subhuman quality of life that characterized this prison.

40   Perhaps the most devastating impact of the more hostile guards was their creation of a capricious, arbitrary environment. Over time the prisoners began to react passively. When our mock prisoners asked questions, they got answers about half the time, but the rest of the time they were insulted and punished—and it was not possible for them to predict which would be the outcome. As they began to "toe the line," they stopped resisting, questioning and, indeed, almost ceased responding altogether. There was a general decrease in all categories of response as they learned the safest strategy to use in an unpredictable, threatening environment from which there is no physical escape—do nothing, except what is required. Act not, want not, feel not, and you will not get into trouble in prisonlike situations.

Can it really be, you wonder, that intelligent, educated volunteers could have lost sight of the reality that they were merely acting a part in an elaborate game that would eventually end? There are many indications not only that they did, but that, in addition, so did we and so did other apparently sensible, responsible adults.

Prisoner 819, who had gone into an uncontrollable crying fit, was about to be prematurely released from the prison when a guard lined up the prisoners and had them chant in unison, "819 is a bad prisoner. Because of what 819 did to prison property we all must suffer. 819 is a bad prisoner." Over and over again. When we realized 819 might be overhearing this, we rushed into the room where 819 was supposed to be resting, only to find him in tears, prepared to go back into the prison because he could not leave as long as the others thought he was a "bad prisoner." Sick as he felt, he had to prove to them he was not a "bad" prisoner. He had to be persuaded that he was not a prisoner at all, that the others were also just students, that this was just an experiment and not a prison and the prison staff were only research psychologists. A report from the warden notes, "While I believe that it was necessary for *staff* [me] to enact the warden role, at least some of the time, I am startled by the ease with which I could turn off my sensitivity and concern for others for 'a good cause.'"

Consider our overreaction to the rumor of a mass escape plot that one of the guards claimed to have overheard. It went as follows: Prisoner 8612, previously released for emotional disturbance, was only faking. He was going to round up a bunch of his friends, and they would storm the prison right after visiting hours. Instead of collecting data on the pattern of rumor transmission, we made plans to maintain the security of our institution. After putting a confederate informer into the cell 8612 had occupied to get specific information about the escape plans, the superintendent went back to the Palo Alto Police Department to request transfer of our prisoners to the old city jail. His impassioned plea was only turned down at the last minute when the problem of insurance and city liability for our prisoners was raised by a city official. Angered at this lack of cooperation, the staff formulated another plan. Our jail was dismantled, the prisoners, chained and blindfolded, were carted off to a remote storage room. When the conspirators arrived, they would be told the study was over, their friends had been sent home, there was nothing left to liberate. After they left, we would redouble the security features of our prison making any future escape attempts futile. We even planned to lure ex-prisoner 8612 back on some pretext and imprison him again, because he had been released on false pretenses! The rumor turned out to be just that— a full day had passed in which we collected little or no data, worked incredibly hard to tear down and then rebuild our prison. Our reaction, however, was as much one of relief and joy as of exhaustion and frustration.

When a former prison chaplain was invited to talk with the prisoners (the grievance committee had requested church services), he puzzled everyone by disparaging each inmate for not having taken any constructive action in order to get released. "Don't you know you must have a lawyer in order to get bail, or to appeal the charges against you?" Several of them accepted his invitation to contact their parents in order to secure the services of an attorney. The next night one of the parents stopped at the superintendent's office before visiting time and handed him the name and phone number of her cousin who was a public defender. She said that a priest had called her and suggested the need for a lawyer's services! We called the lawyer. He came, interviewed the prisoners, discussed sources of bail money, and promised to return again after the weekend.

45   But perhaps the most telling account of the insidious development of this new reality, of the gradual Kafkaesque metamorphosis of good into evil, appears in excerpts from the diary of one of the guards, Guard A:

Prior to start of experiment: "As I am a pacifist and nonaggressive individual, I cannot see a time when I might guard and/or maltreat other living things."

After an orientation meeting: "Buying uniforms at the end of the meeting confirms the gamelike atmosphere of this thing. I doubt whether many of us share the expectations of 'seriousness' that the experimenters seem to have."

First Day: "Feel sure that the prisoners will make fun of my appearance and I evolve my first basic strategy—mainly not to smile at anything they say or do which would be admitting it's all only a game. . . . At cell 3 I stop and setting my voice hard and low say to 5486, 'What are you smiling at?' 'Nothing, Mr. Correctional Officer.' 'Well, see that you don't.' (As I walk off I feel stupid.)"

Second Day: "5704 asked for a cigarette and I ignored him—because I am a non-smoker and could not empathize. . . . Meanwhile since I was feeling empathetic towards 1037, I determined not to talk with him. . . . After we had count and lights out [Guard D] and I held a loud conversation about going home to our girl friends and what we were going to do to them."

50   *Third Day (preparing for the first visitors' night):* "After warning the prisoners not to make any complaints unless they wanted the visit terminated fast, we finally brought in the first parents. I made sure I was one of the guards on the yard, because this was my first chance for the type of manipulative power that I really like—being a very noticed figure with almost complete control over what is said or not. While the parents and prisoners sat in chairs, I sat on the end of the table dangling my feet and contradicting anything I felt like. This was the first part of the experiment I was really enjoying. . . . 817 is being obnoxious and bears watching."

Fourth Day: " . . . The psychologist rebukes me for handcuffing and blindfolding a prisoner before leaving the [counseling] office, and I resentfully reply that it is both necessary security and my business anyway."

Fifth Day: "I harass 'Sarge' who continues to stubbornly overrespond to all commands. I have singled him out for the special abuse both because he begs for it and because I simply don't like him. The real trouble starts at dinner. The new prisoner (416) refuses to eat his sausage . . . we throw him into the Hole ordering him to hold sausages in each hand. We have a crisis of authority; this rebellious conduct potentially undermines the complete control we have over the others. We decide to play upon prisoner solidarity and tell the new one that all the others will be deprived of visitors if he does not eat his dinner. . . . I walk by and slam my stick into the Hole door. . . . I am very angry at this prisoner for causing discomfort and trouble for the others. I decided to force-feed him, but he wouldn't eat. I let the food slide down his face. I didn't believe it was me doing it. I hated myself for making him eat but I hated him more for not eating."

Sixth Day: "The experiment is over. I feel elated but am shocked to find some other guards disappointed somewhat because of the loss of money and some because they are enjoying themselves."

We were no longer dealing with an intellectual exercise in which a hypothesis was being evaluated in the dispassionate manner dictated by the canons of the scientific method. We were caught up in the passion of the present, the suffering, the need to control people, not variables, the escalation of power, and all the unexpected things that were erupting around and within us. We had to end this experiment: So our planned two-week simulation was aborted after only six (was it only six?) days and nights.

55   Was it worth all the suffering just to prove what everybody knows—that some people are sadistic, others weak, and prisons are not beds of roses? If that is all we demonstrated in this research, then it was certainly not worth the anguish. We believe there are many significant implications to be derived from this experience, only a few of which can be suggested here.

The potential social value of this study derives precisely from the fact that normal, healthy, educated young men could be so radically transformed under the institutional pressures of a "prison environment." If this could happen in so short a time, without the excesses that are possible in real prisons, and if it could happen to the "cream-of-the-crop of American youth," then one can only shudder to imagine what society is doing both to the actual guards and prisoners who are at this very moment participating in that unnatural "social experiment."

The pathology observed in this study cannot be reasonably attributed in preexisting personality differences of the subjects, that option being eliminated by our selection procedures and random assignment. Rather, the subjects' abnormal social and personal reactions are best seen as a product of their transaction with an environment that supported the behavior that would be pathological in other settings, but was "appropriate" in this prison. Had we observed comparable reactions in a real prison, the psychiatrist undoubtedly would have been able to attribute any prisoner's behavior to character defects or personality maladjustment, while critics of the prison system would have been quick to label the guards as "psychopathic." This tendency to locate the source of behavior disorders inside a particular person or group underestimates the power of situational forces.

Our colleague, David Rosenhan, has very convincingly shown that once a sane person (pretending to be insane) gets labeled as insane and committed to a mental hospital, it is the label that is the reality which is treated and not the person. This dehumanizing tendency to respond to other people according to socially determined labels and often arbitrarily assigned roles is also apparent in a recent "mock hospital" study designed by Norma Jean Orlando to extend the ideas in our research.

Personnel from the staff of Elgin State Hospital in Illinois role-played either mental patients or staff in a weekend simulation on a ward in the hospital. The mock mental patients soon displayed behavior indistinguishable from that we usually associate with the chronic pathological syndromes of acute mental patients: Incessant pacing, uncontrollable weeping, depression, hostility, fights, stealing from each other, complaining. Many of the "mock staff" took advantage of their power to act in ways comparable to our mock guards by dehumanizing their powerless victims.

60 During a series of encounter debriefing sessions immediately after our experiment, we all had an opportunity to vent our strong feelings and to reflect upon the moral and ethical issues each of us faced, and we considered how we might react more morally in future "real-life" analogues to this situation. Year-long follow-ups with our subjects via questionnaires, personal interviews, and group reunions indicate that their mental anguish was transient and situationally specific, but the self-knowledge gained has persisted.

By far the most disturbing implication of our research comes from the parallels between what occurred in that basement mock prison and daily experiences in our own lives—and we presume yours. The physical institution of prison is but a concrete and steel metaphor for the existence of more pervasive, albeit less obvious, prisons of the mind that all of us daily create, populate, and perpetuate. We speak here of the prisons of racism, sexism, despair, shyness, "neurotic hang-ups," and the like. The social convention of marriage, as one example, becomes for many couples a state of imprisonment in which one partner agrees to be prisoner or guard, forcing or allowing the other to play the reciprocal role—invariably without making the contract explicit.

...continued The Stanford Prison Experiment, **Philip G. Zimbardo**

To what extent do we allow ourselves to become imprisoned by docilely accepting the roles others assign us or, indeed, choose to remain prisoners because being passive and dependent frees us from the need to act and be responsible for our actions? The prison of fear constructed in the delusions of the paranoid is no less confining or less real than the cell that every shy person erects to limit his own freedom in anxious anticipation of being ridiculed and rejected by his guards—often guards of his own making.

STUDENT MODELS

The Life Cycle of Stars

Lakshmi Kotra

Professor Jenson

Astronomy 101—May 6, 2008

The Life Cycle of Stars

"Twinkle, twinkle, little star; how I wonder what you are." This old nursery rhyme may not seem profound, but it echoes some of the biggest questions astronomers puzzle over: What are stars made of? How do they form? How are they born and how do they die? Current theories of star formation answer some of these questions, but not all of them. We do know that, even though stars are separated from one another by vast amounts of space, their life cycles are intertwined.

Twinkling stars are born in dark, cold clouds of dust and gas called nebulae. These clouds consist mainly of hydrogen, and may be as cold as 10 degrees Kelvin (Chaisson and McMillan, 2008). Nebulae are very dense compared to the near-vacuum of interstellar space. But something must concentrate this dust and gas even more if a star is to form. This first part of the star-forming process is not fully understood. Some force has to cause a portion of the nebula to begin collapsing. Magnetism and rotation are two forces already at work in most clouds, but astronomers have long thought that these forces are more likely to counteract the collapsing force of gravity. However, new research may have found a solution to this problem. In some clouds, magnetic fields may cancel out some or all of the rotational force. This reorganization would allow gravity to begin collapsing the star (Farivar, 2002).

Another theory is that a shock wave from some outside event or object might trigger the collapse of a cloud. The Eagle Nebula provides a good illustration of this theory. Ultraviolet radiation from super-hot stars in the nebula has been observed bombarding the surrounding dust and gas. The radiation has stripped away a lot of dust but left dense columns of cloud where stars are believed to be forming. The impact of this "stellar wind" may have also triggered the star formation. Smaller clumps of denser gas are contracting within the columns, taking their first step on the journey to stardom (see Figure 1).

Figure 1   Eagle Nebula
The columns of interstellar gas in the Eagle Nebula are incubators for new stars
(US, NASA, "Eagle," 1995).

Once a section of a dust cloud starts to collapse, gravity relentlessly pulls
the material together into a much smaller area. Gradually, the center of the
cloud becomes denser and less cloudlike. At this stage, astronomers refer to the
object as a "protostar." For a star the size of our sun, the journey from cloud to
protostar may take about 100,000 years (Chaisson & McMillan, 2008). As the
atoms of gas crowd into a smaller and smaller space, they bounce off one
another faster and faster, and the protostar heats up. However, it is not a true
star yet. That comes later, when nuclear fusion begins. For now, the developing
protostar is still surrounded by a shroud of dust that hides it from view. This
dust mantle is called a cocoon nebula. Some protostars can be detected by the
infrared glow of their cocoon nebulae.

Over millions of years, the protostar continues to grow and change, like a
butterfly in its cocoon. Gravity keeps compacting it, making it smaller in size and
denser. When the protostar is dense enough, its nuclear heart finally starts to
beat. This happens when hydrogen atoms are pushed close enough together to

fuse into helium. The fusion process involves several steps. First, two hydrogen atoms will fuse to form an atom of deuterium, or heavy hydrogen. When a third hydrogen atom joins the deuterium atom, an isotope called helium 3 results. Finally, when two helium 3 atoms fuse together, an atom of regular helium plus two of hydrogen are created. But the crucial part of this process is that, every time fusion takes place, a small amount of energy is released. The radiation emitted from the fusion of hydrogen into helium is what makes the majority of stars shine. Fusion radiation from the Sun lights our planet in the daytime, makes the moon shine at night—and gives you sunburn.

Hydrogen atoms must be moving at extremely high speeds in order to fuse. Another way to say this is that the temperature in the core of a protostar must be very high for fusion to take place: at least 10 million degrees Kelvin (Chaisson and McMillan, 2008). Now nuclear forces, not just gravity's grip, are controlling the star's development. In fact, these two forces will compete throughout the star's life. Gravity tries to collapse the star, while the pressure of its fast-moving, superheated atoms pushes it outward. As long as the two forces balance each other, the star will remain stable. Astronomers call this state "equilibrium."

During the intense heating at the end of the protostar stage, and when hydrogen fusion is beginning, intense radiation streams off the young star. The dust and gas that have surrounded the protostar are swept away by this energy bombardment, and the star emerges from its cocoon. This phenomenon can be observed visually in NGC 4214. Young stars in this nebula are pouring out radiation that has created "bubbles" in the surrounding gas. Brighter and older stars have pushed away more of the dust and gas. The bubbles around these stars are bigger than those around younger or cooler stars in the nebula (see Figure 2).

Sometimes, not all of a protostar's dust cocoon blows away. According to one theory, you can look around our own solar system and see the remnants of

Figure 2   Star Formation
Clusters of new stars form from interstellar gas and dust in galaxy NGC 4214 (US, NASA, "Star," 2000).

the dust that once surrounded our Sun. In fact, you are standing on some of it. The Earth and the rest of the planets in our solar system are believed to have formed from a disk of dust and gas left over after the sun formed. The reasons this happens are not entirely clear, but astronomers now think that many stellar systems have planetary disks around them. The Orion Nebula provides some confirmation of this theory. There, astronomers have observed many glowing disks of dust, called "proplyds." They think these disks are actually young stars surrounded by material that will eventually form a system of orbiting planets (see Figure 3).

The size of the original dust cloud a star is born from will also determine how it dies. Some protostars don't quite have what it takes to become a star. Clumps of dust and gas that are smaller than .08 solar masses never get hot enough to begin fusing hydrogen (Chaisson & McMillan, 2008). These "brown dwarfs" produce infrared radiation, but they never shine visibly.

THE LIFE CYCLE OF STARS   6

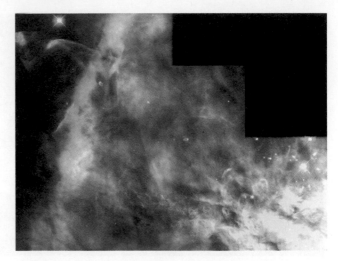

Figure 3   Orion Nebula
This composite photo of the Orion nebula assembled from images taken by the
Hubble Space Telescope shows the beginnings of new solar systems surround-
ing young stars (US, NASA, "Orion," 1995).

True stars burn through their nuclear fuel at different rates. The larger the
star, the faster its fuel is fused. Smaller stars, like our Sun, are called "dwarf
stars." If they began life with less than eight times the mass of our Sun, they
will quietly burn hydrogen for perhaps ten billion years. Toward the end of their
lives, as they begin to run out of fuel, they will swell briefly into red giant stars,
fusing their helium into carbon, and cooling substantially. Finally, they will
subside into "white dwarf" stars, about the size of the planet earth. Provided
they do not have nearby neighboring stars that might interact with them, white
dwarfs gradually dim and cool, until they go dark altogether (Chaisson &
McMillan, 2008). This cooling process is what astronomers predict will some day
happen to our Sun.

A star of more than about eight solar masses has a shorter but much more
spectacular life. It will fuse all its available fuel in well under one billion years—
perhaps in as little as one million years. When a giant star has run through all its

available nuclear fuel, it develops a core of iron atoms, which cannot be fused into anything else. When this core has grown to about 1.4 solar masses, the star will explode in a supernova. All that will be left of the original star is a dark neutron star or black hole (Chaisson and McMillan, 2008). But the shock wave from the supernova may go on to trigger new star formation in dust clouds nearby. In this way, dying stars contribute to the birth of new ones, and the life cycle of stars continues.

References

Chaisson, E., & McMillan, S. (2008). *Astronomy today*. 6th ed. Saddle River: Prentice.

Farivar, C. (2002, January). Galactic map aids stellar formation theory. *Daily Californian*. Retrieved from http://archive.dailycal.org/article/7441/ galactic_map_aids_stellar_formation_theory

United States. National Aeronautics and Space Adm. (1995, April). The Eagle nebula. Photograph retrieved from http://grin.hq.nasa.gov/UTILS/search.cgi

———. Fireworks of star formation light up a galaxy. (2000, January). Photograph retrieved from http://grin.hq.nasa.gov/UTILS/search.cgi

———. The Orion nebula (1995, November). Photograph retrieved from http://grin.hq.nasa.gov/UTILS/search.cgi

---

How Clean and Green Are Hydrogen Fuel-Cell Cars?

Shannon King (student)

1   The United States is embroiled in a controversy over energy and pollution. We are rapidly using up the earth's total supply of fossil fuels, and many experts think that children being born today will experience the end of affordable oil. One energy expert, Paul Roberts (2004), believes that serious oil shortages will start occurring by 2015 when the world's demand for oil will outstrip the world's capacity for further oil production. An equally

serious problem is that the burning of fossil fuels spews carbon dioxide into the atmosphere, which increases the rate of global warming.

2   One hopeful way of addressing these problems is to develop hydrogen fuel cell cars. According to Karim Nice (2000), the author of the fuel cell pages on the *HowStuffWorks* Web site, a fuel cell is "an electrochemical energy conversion device that converts hydrogen and oxygen into water, producing electricity and heat in the process" (p. 34). A hydrogen-fueled car is therefore an electric car, powered by an electric motor. The car's electricity is generated by a stack of fuel cells that act like a battery. In the hydrogen fuel cell, the chemicals that produce the electricity are hydrogen from the car's pressurized fuel tank, oxygen from the air, and special catalysts inside the fuel cell. The fuel cell releases no pollutants or greenhouse gases. The only waste product is pure water.

3   To what extent will these pollution-free fuel cells be our energy salvation? Are they really clean and green?

4   Many people think so. The development of hydrogen fuel cells has caused much excitement. I know people who say we don't need to worry about running out of oil because cars of the future will run on water. One recent *New York Times* advertisement produced by General Motors (2004) has as its headline, "Who's driving the hydrogen economy?" (p. A19). The text of the ad begins by saying "The hydrogen economy isn't a pipe dream. . . . The hydrogen economy is the endgame of a multifaceted strategy General Motors set in motion years ago, with steps that are real, progressive, and well-underway" (p. A19). The Web site for the Hydrogen Fuel Cell Institute (2001) includes a picture of a crystal clear blue sky landscape with a large letter headline proclaiming "At long last, a technology too long overlooked promises to transform society" (p. 18). At the bottom of the picture are the words, "Offering clean & abundant power, hydrogen-based fuel cells could soon end our reliance on oil and minimize emissions of pollution and global-warming gases" (p. 1). According to CNN News (2004), the Bush administration proposed devoting 1.7 billion dollars of federal funds to developing hydrogen fuel cells. The biggest nationally known proponent of hydrogen fuel cells is California Governor Arnold Schwarzenegger, who signed an Executive Order (2004) that California's "21 interstate freeways shall be designated as the 'California Hydrogen Highway Network'" (p. 2). In this executive order, Schwarzenegger envisioned

> a network of hydrogen fueling stations along these roadways and in the urban centers that they connect, so that by 2010, every Californian will have access to hydrogen fuel, with a significant and increasing percentage produced from clean, renewable sources. (p. 2)

Schwarzenegger's optimism about the hydrogen highway sums up the common view that hydrogen is a clean alternative energy source that is abundant throughout nature. All we have to do is bottle it up, compress it, and transport it to a network of new "gas stations" where the gas being pumped is hydrogen.

5   But what I discovered in my research is that hydrogen is not as green as most people think. Although hydrogen fuel cells appear to be an environmentally friendly alternative to fossil fuels, the processes for producing hydrogen actually require the use of fossil fuels. The problem is that pure hydrogen doesn't occur naturally on earth. It has to be separated out from chemical compounds containing hydrogen, and that process requires other forms of energy. What I discovered is that there are only two major ways to produce hydrogen. The first is to produce it from fossil fuels by unlocking the hydrogen that is bonded to the carbon in coal, oil, or natural gas. The second is to produce it from water through electrolysis, but the power required for electrolysis would also come mainly from burning fossil fuels. These problems make hydrogen fuel cell cars look less clean and green than they first appear.

6   One approach to creating hydrogen from fossil fuels is to use natural gas. According to Matthew L. Wald (2003), writing in a *New York Times* article, natural gas is converted to hydrogen in a process called "steam reforming." Natural gas (made of hydrogen and carbon atoms) is mixed with steam (which contains hydrogen and oxygen atoms) to cause a chemical reaction that produces pure hydrogen. But it also produces carbon dioxide, which contributes to global warming. According to Wald, if fuel cell cars used hydrogen from steam reforming, they would emit 145 grams of global warming gases per mile compared to 374 grams an ordinary gas-powered car would emit. The good news is that using hydrogen power would cut carbon emissions by more than half. The bad news is that these cars would still contribute to global warming and consume natural gas. Moreover, Wald suggests that the natural gas supply is limited and that natural gas has many better, more efficient uses than converting it to hydrogen.

7   Another method for producing hydrogen would come from coal, which is the cheapest and most abundant source of energy. However, the current method of generating electricity by burning coal is the leading source of carbon dioxide emission. At Ohio University, engineers state we still have enough coal to last us two hundred and fifty years and that we should find some better uses for coal. The engineers have received a 4 million dollar federal grant to investigate the production of hydrogen from coal. They plan on mixing coal with steam, air, and oxygen under high temperatures and pressure to produce hydrogen and carbon monoxide (2003). But this too would generate greenhouse gases and is a long way off from producing results.

8   The next likely source of hydrogen is to produce it directly from water using an electrolyzer. Wald (2003) explains that the electrolyzer

uses an electrical current to break down water molecules into hydrogen and oxygen atoms. Creating hydrogen through electrolysis sounds like a good idea because its only waste product is oxygen. But the hazardous environmental impact is not in the electrolysis reaction, but in the need to generate electricity to run the electrolyzer. Wald claims that if the electricity to run the electrolyzer came from a typical coal-fired electrical plant, the carbon dioxide emissions for a fuel cell car would be 17 percent worse than for today's gasoline powered cars. One solution would be to run the electrolyzer with wind-generated or nuclear-powered electricity. But wind power would be able to produce only a small fraction of what would be needed, and nuclear power brings with it a whole new set of problems including disposal of nuclear waste.

9   Although there seem to be various methods of producing hydrogen, the current sources being considered do not fulfill the claim that hydrogen fuel cell technology will end the use of fossil fuels or eliminate greenhouse gases. The problem is not with the fuel cells themselves but with the processes needed to produce hydrogen fuel. I am not arguing that research and development should be abandoned, and I hope some day that the hydrogen economy will take off. But what I have discovered in my research is that hydrogen power is not as clean and green as I thought.

References

Executive Order S-7-04. (2004, April). Retrieved from http://www.dot.ca.gov/hq/energy/ExecOrderS-7-04.htm

The issues/George Bush. (2004). CNN. Retrieved from http://www.cnn.com/ELECTION/2004/special/president/issues/index.bush.new.html

General Motors. (2004). Advertisement. *New York Times*, A19.

Hydrogen Fuel Cell Institute. (2001). Retrieved from http://h2fuelcells.org/

Nice, K., & Strickland, J. (2000, September). How fuel cells work. Retrieved from http://auto.howstuffworks.com/fuel-efficiency/alternative-fuels/fuel-cell.htm

Ohio University aims to use coal to power fuel cells. (2003, November). Retrieved from http://h2fuelcells.org/

Roberts, P. (2004, March). Running out of oil—and time. *Los Angeles Times.* Retrieved from http://www.commondreams.org/views04/0307-02.htm

Wald, M. L. (2003). Will hydrogen clear the air? Maybe not, some say. *New York Times,* C1.

PRACTICE

1 Explain Shannon King's use of the surprising-reversal strategy. What question does she pose? What is the common answer? What is her surprising answer? How effectively does she use research data to support her surprising answer?

The line between information and persuasion is often blurred. Some might argue that Shannon's essay has a persuasive aim that argues against hydrogen fuel-cell cars rather than an informative aim that simply presents surprising information about hydrogen production. To what extent do you agree with our classification of Shannon's aim as primarily informative rather than persuasive? Can it be both?

2 Walter cites a variety of sources on the subject of kissing, from scientists and psychologists to the poet e. e. cummings and a character from the movie *Hitch*. Why do you think he uses such a range of sources?

Informative writing assumes that its audience has a certain amount of information about the subject already and then provides new information on that subject. What information does Walter assume his audience has about his subject? What new information is he presenting?

Walter ends the essay with the sentence: "But romance gives up its mysteries grudgingly. And in some ways, we like it like that." Why does he end the essay in this way?

Most people think humans kiss just because it is pleasurable. With so many different opinions, why is it important to study behaviors such as kissing?

3 What was Zimbardo's primary goal in undertaking the prison experiment?

What was the profile of the subjects in the experiment? Why is this profile significant?

Zimbardo claims that there is a "process" (paragraphs 2, 7) of becoming a prisoner. What is this process?

What inverse psychological relationships developed between prisoners and guards?

What was the result of the prison "riot"?

Why did prisoners have no respect for each other or for themselves?

How does the journal of Guard A illustrate what Zimbardo calls the "gradual Kafkaesque metamorphosis of good into evil"? (See paragraphs 45–54.)

What are the reasons people would voluntarily become prisoners?

How can the mind keep people in jail?

Reread the four epigraphs to this article. Write a paragraph of response to any one of them, in light of Zimbardo's discussion of the prison experiment.

You may have thought, before reading this article, that being a prisoner is a physical fact, not a psychological state. What are the differences between these two views?

In paragraph 8, Zimbardo explains his reasons for not pursuing his research in a real prison. He writes that "it is impossible to separate what each individual brings into the prison from what the prison brings out in each person." What does he mean? And how does this distinction prove important later in the article? (See paragraph 58.)

Zimbardo reports that at the beginning of the experiment each of the "prisoner" subjects "was completely confident of his ability to endure whatever the prison had to offer for the full two-week experimental period" (paragraph 10). Had you been a subject, would you have been so confident, prior to the experiment? Given what you've learned of the experiment, do you think you would have psychologically "become" a prisoner or guard if you had been selected for these roles? (And if not, what makes you so sure?)

Identify two passages in this article: one that surprised you relating to the prisoners and one that surprised you relating to the guards. Write a paragraph explaining your response to each. Now read the two passages in light of each other. Do you see any patterns underlying your responses?

Zimbardo claims that the implications of his research matter deeply—that the mock prison he created is a metaphor for prisons of the mind "that all of us daily create, populate, and perpetuate" (paragraph 61). Zimbardo mentions the prisons of "racism, sexism, despair, [and] shyness." Choose any one of these and discuss how it might be viewed as a mental prison.

Reread paragraphs 61 and 62. Zimbardo makes a metaphorical jump from his experiment to the psychological realities of your daily life. Prisons—the artificial one he created and actual prisons—stand for something: social systems in which there are those who give orders and those who obey. All metaphors break down at some point. Where does this one break down?

Zimbardo suggests that we might "choose to remain prisoners because being passive and dependent frees us from the need to act and be responsible for our actions" (paragraph 62). Do you agree? What are the burdens of being disobedient?

❹ Individual Task to Generate Ideas

Here is a template that can help you generate ideas by asking you to think specifically about differences in knowledge levels between you and various audiences.

> I know more about X [topic area] than [specific person or persons].

For example, you might say, "I know more about [computer games/gospel music/the energy crisis] than [my roommate/my high school friends/my parents]." This exercise helps you discover subjects about which you already have expertise compared to other audiences. Likewise, you can identify a subject that interests you, do a couple of hours of research on it, and then say: "Based on just this little amount of research, I know more about X than my roommate." Thinking in this way, you might be able to create an intriguing question that you could answer through your research.

⑤ Small-Group Task to Generate Ideas

Form small groups. Assign a group recorder to make a two-column list, with the left column titled "Mistaken or Narrow View of X" and the right column titled "Groupmate's Surprising View." Using the surprising-reversal strategy, brainstorm ideas for article topics until every group member has generated at least one entry for the right-hand column. Here are several examples:

Mistaken or Narrow View of X	Groupmate's Surprising View
Being an offensive lineman in football is a no-brain, repetitive job requiring size and strength, but only enough intelligence and athletic ability to push people out of the way.	Jeff can show that being an offensive lineman is a complex job that requires mental smarts as well as size, strength, and athletic ability.
Pawnshops are disreputable places.	Samantha's uncle owns a pawnshop that is a wholesome family business that serves an important social function.
To most straight people, *Frankenstein* is a monster movie about science gone amuck.	Cody can show how to the gay community, *Frankenstein* holds a special and quite different meaning.

a. To help stimulate ideas, you might consider topic areas such as the following:

   - *People:* computer programmers, homeless people, cheerleaders, skateboarders, gang members, priests or rabbis, reality show stars, feminists, mentally ill or developmentally disabled persons.
   - *Activities:* washing dishes, climbing mountains, wrestling, modeling, gardening, living with a chronic disease or disability, owning a certain breed of dog, riding a subway at night, posting status updates on Facebook, entering a dangerous part of a city.
   - *Places:* particular neighborhoods, specific buildings or parts of buildings, local attractions, junkyards, college campuses, places of entertainment, summer camps.
   - *Other similar categories:* groups, events, animals and plants, gadgets, and so forth; the list is endless.

b. Next, go around the room, sharing with the entire class the topics you have generated. Remember that you are not yet committed to writing about any of these topics.

Sleeping Bear Dunes
Glen Arbor, MI

How Do I Compose a Research Essay?

14

THE RESEARCH PAPER IS, BY ITS VERY NATURE, A SYNTHESIS. THE POWER OF RESEARCH IS ITS ABILITY TO BRING TOGETHER INFORMATION FROM VARIOUS SOURCES TO ILLUMINATE AN ISSUE, POSSIBLY IN WAYS THAT THE SOURCE AUTHORS DID NOT ANTICIPATE. The researcher can be creative at all stages of the research process, but it is the act of synthesis that offers special opportunities for originality. You may be able to make connections among sources that have previously gone unnoticed or to structure information in new ways. Through synthesis, you give shape to the information. This is the ultimate goal of the research process.

It is common for long research papers to include more than one type of synthesis. Argument, analysis, and evaluation may also be important elements in a research paper.

DRAFT A THESIS

You may have a working thesis in mind when you begin researching. If not, one may emerge as you collect information. The following procedure will help you generate a working thesis from your research notes.

GENERATING A THESIS

1. Scan your research notes quickly, noting any general trends, main concepts, or overall patterns.
2. Freewrite for ten minutes on what you think your research might tell your reader.
3. Reduce your freewriting to several sentences that explain what you want to say to your reader.

After scanning her research notes, Kristen freewrites the following paragraph:

> From the sources I read, it seems as if a lot of the current attention to the American family comes from political debates about "family values." One thing that the politicians seem to agree on is that the traditional nuclear family is declining. Some politicians think that this change means that family values are also declining, but others think that a new set of family values is developing that is positive in its own way. Whatever their viewpoint, politicians often use the expression "family values" in a vague way. It's hard to pin down what they have in mind. However, the articles I read that were written by sociologists were much clearer on exactly how family values are changing and what the advantages and disadvantages of those changes might be. I can use the observations of the sociologists to make better sense of what the politicians are talking about in the political debate over family values.

Kristen rereads her freewriting and condenses it into a preliminary thesis:

> The political debate over family values has to do with the fact that the traditional nuclear family is declining. But the politicians use expressions like "family values" in a vague way and do not always explain exactly what they are thinking. The writings of sociologists on the family are more objective; the issues are clearer. I will try to use sociology to explain the issues that are at the base of politicians' positions on family values.

This is still a preliminary thesis. Compare it with the thesis excerpted from the final version of Kristen's research paper:

> To a large extent, the debate over family values revolves around whether this transformation represents the decline of the American family or an opportunity to strengthen and improve families. The sociological literature on the evolution and current status of the American family helps clarify the issues that are at the core of this political debate. I will use the findings of sociologists who study the American family to analyze issues that lie at the core of the political controversy over family values.

Notice that Kristen's final thesis is refined, more fully developed, and more coherent. The main purpose of a preliminary thesis is to focus your research activities, but sometimes you may need to depart from the initial thesis as you understand more about the topic.

DERIVE A PLAN

A research paper can follow one organizational plan or a combination of plans.

A plan may occur to you as you conduct research. You may see that the information you collect from various sources fits into an obvious pattern, or you may borrow a plan from one of your sources. You might also consider how you might use the source information to support your thesis.

If no obvious pattern emerges from the information you collected, systematically examine your research notes. Derive one or more possible plans by categorizing the notes. If you use note cards, sort them into piles, grouping related information, to see what patterns appear. Try several grouping schemes to find what works best.

As Kristen sorts her note cards into piles, she fits them into five main categories:

1. Facts about how the traditional American nuclear family is fading and the new structures that are taking its place
2. Evidence that shifting cultural values caused changes in family structure
3. Evidence economic factors caused changes in family structure
4. Evidence that nontraditional family structures are harmful to children
5. Evidence that nontraditional family structures do not harm children

Kristen thinks about these five categories, reconsiders her preliminary thesis, and comes up with the following plan.

> – Thesis: The political debate over family values has to do with the fact that the traditional nuclear family is declining. But the politicians use expressions like "family values" in a vague way and do not always explain exactly what they are thinking. The writings of sociologists on the family are more objective; the issues are clearer. I will try to use sociology to explain the issues that are at the base of politicians' positions on family values.
>
> – First, I need to explain how the American family has changed over time. In particular, I need to trace the decline of the traditional nuclear family and the rise of alternative family structures.
>
> – Next, I will explain the sociological evidence that decline of the traditional nuclear family results from a shift in cultural values.
>
> – Then I will explain the evidence that economic conditions, not cultural values, have led to the increase in nontraditional families.
>
> – Next, I will give the evidence that nontraditional families are harmful to children.
>
> – Finally, I will examine the evidence that nontraditional families are viable structures for raising children.

CREATE AN OUTLINE

Detailed outlines are required for research projects. Because research writers must juggle many sources and deal with issues in depth, they need an outline that will keep them on task and provide a unifying framework for information from various sources. A pitfall of research paper writing is becoming bogged down in the details from sources and failing to clarify the relationships among ideas. If you draft your research paper working from a detailed outline, it will be easier to write, and in the end, your train of thought will be more evident to your audience.

Some instructors call for a traditional outline based on the following structure. Note that such an outline requires at least two entries at each successive level.

I.
   A.
      1.
         a.
            i.
            ii.
         b.
      2.
   B.
II.

The formal outline provides a clear hierarchical structure that is useful for imposing order on a complicated topic with a number of discrete subtopics. Here is a portion of a formal outline for a paper on contemporary family structure.

IV. Advantages of families in which both parents work
   A. Financial security
      1. The majority of families need two incomes to survive.
      2. Welfare reform is based on the premise that both parents are capable of earning money.
      3. Children derive significant benefits from the family's financial security.
   B. Gender role equality
      1. Home responsibilities are shared.
         a. Housecleaning and maintenance
         b. Food preparation
         c. Child rearing

2. Men and women retain economic autonomy.

3. Men and women hold equal authority over and responsibility for the fate of the family.

V. Disadvantages of having two working parents

With some topics or certain collections of sources, however, you may feel constrained if you have to force the material into this hierarchy. In these cases, free-form outlining, which allows the writer to determine his or her own structure, may come closer to reflecting your actual thinking. Here is a draft of Kristen's free-form outline based on the organization plan shown earlier. Notice that she expands on the organizational plan as she begins to plug in ideas from some of her sources.

Thesis: The political debate over family values has to do with the fact that the traditional nuclear family is declining. But the politicians use expressions like "family values" in a vague way and do not always explain exactly what they are thinking. The writings of sociologists on the family are more objective; the issues are clearer. I will try to use sociology to explain the issues that are at the base of politicians' positions on family values.

Changes in the American family in the 20th century
    Katz and Stern (2007)
        - nuclear families: 55% in 1900, 25% in 2000 (p. 91)
        - rates of out-of-wedlock birth increased since 1970 (p. 91)
        - 30% of households, single woman is head (p. 91)

    Trimberger (2007)
        - current out-of-wedlock birth rate at 25% (p. 83)
        - more Americans currently living alone than in families with children (p. 82)

    Bouchey (2007)
        - 1/3 American children raised by single parent

    Popenoe (1997)
        - half of American marriages now end in divorce

Evidence that changes in "family values" led to structural changes in the family
    Popenoe (1999)
        - "highly expressive or self-focused individualism" (p. 30)
        - "Playboy-style sexual opportunism and rejection of responsibilities" (p. 30)
        - women see the nuclear family as an "oppressive institution" (p. 30)

– sexual revolution led to sex outside marriage and divorce
– must restore "cultural importance of voluntary, lifelong monogamy" (p. 30)

Whitehead (1997)
– divorce comes to be viewed as an issue of what is best for adults, not for children

Elshtain (2000)
– children who grow up without "experience of seeing married life" do not develop family values

Evidence that American family has changed in response to economic conditions

Skolnick (1997)
– Since 1965, economy has not favored the "family-sustaining career opportunities"

Boushey (2007)
– Women entered workforce out of economic necessity even though the women's movement did open up career opportunities and reproductive options

Skolnick (2006)
– Homemaking no longer a viable career for women, so traditional family had to give way to other forms

Stacey (1994) and Skolnick (2004, p. 46)
– provide list of economic factors that changed family structure
– "Talk about family change is almost totally disconnected from the discussion of technology and economy" (Skolnick, 2006, p. 47).

Evidence that children are harmed by being raised in nontraditional families

Whitehead (2007)
– Single mothers lack access to "two of the most effective sources of self-sufficiency—professional jobs and marriage" (p. 6)

Gallagher and Blankenhorn (1997)
– List drugs, psychological problems, violence, and abuse as risks of nontraditional families (p. 13)

Elshtain (2000) and Popenoe (1997)
– Children who don't live with both parents are two to three times more likely to develop psychological and behavioral problems

Whitehead (1997)

– Intact families allow parents to invest more time in their children

Evidence that children are not harmed by being raised in nontraditional families

Skolnick (1997), Stacey (1994), and Ehrenreich (1996)

– Impact of divorce on children is exaggerated

– Stacey (p. 120) and Ehrenreich show weaknesses in research by Wallerstein that is most often cited to show that divorce is harmful to children

Ehrenreich (1996)

– Media distorts the impact of divorce and typically depicts divorce as bad

Stacey (1994)

– Social scientists think that the quality of relationships within families is more important than family structure (p. 120)

Evidence that homosexual parenting is not harmful

Many politicians are opposed to gay marriage and gay parenting on moral/religious grounds

Perrin (2002)

– Review of the literature shows that children of gay and lesbian parents are not substantially different from their peers raised by straight parents. "Apparently parents' sexual orientation has no measurable effect on the quality of parent-child relations or on children's health or social adjustment" (p. 129)

Advantages of postmodern families

Sherer (1996)

– Postmodern families more flexible and can adapt to the times.

Mack-Canty and Wright (2004)

– Research shows feminist parents led to happier families and personal growth

Bouchey (2007)

– Research shows that working mothers actually spend more time with their children than stay-at-home moms

Conclusion: Comment on current election year and the continuing family values debate

WRITE FROM YOUR OUTLINE

Use your outline as a guide for drafting. Group your notes or note cards according to the points in your outline, and draft the essay paragraph by paragraph. Be sure to include complete references for all source information. It is easy to lose track of where information came from if you do not record this information in the first draft.

As you draft your essay, you may find that you need to depart from your outline. The outline is intended to serve as a guide, not a straitjacket. If you discover new patterns or ideas in the process of writing, don't hesitate to include them in your essay.

Revising

REVISE BASED ON READERS' COMMENTS

One result of going through the research process is that you become engrossed in the material; that makes it difficult for you to view your writing objectively. It is important to get feedback on your draft to see if your message gets through to the audience. You may ask your reader to use the following checklist as a feedback guide, or you may work alone and apply the checklist to the draft yourself.

✓ *Checklist for Revising a Research Paper*

_____ 1. Is the paper written on a sufficiently narrow topic?

_____ 2. Can you understand the writer's research goals?

_____ 3. Does the writer present a clear thesis?

_____ 4. Does the writer make sense of the information from sources?

_____ 5. Can you discern the research paper's form (multisource comparison and contrast, summary of multiple sources, objective synthesis, essay of response to multiple sources, synthesis with a specific purpose, argument, analysis, or evaluation)?

_____ 6. Is the information from sources organized according to a clear plan?

_____ 7. Does the writer use information from sources convincingly?

_____ 8. Are the writer's assertions substantiated with material from sources?

_____ 9. Does the writer provide transitions among sources and among pieces of information?

_____ 10. Is the writer's voice appropriate for this type of essay? Why or why not?

_____ 11. Is the opening satisfactory? Why or why not?

_____ 12. Does the essay have an appropriate conclusion?

_____ 13. Is the title suitable for the piece?

_____ 14. Can you identify the source for each piece of information?

_____ 15. Does the paper end with a list of references that includes all sources referred to in the text of the paper?

Editing

When you are satisfied with your revision, read your paper aloud. Then reread it line by line and sentence by sentence. Check for correct usage, punctuation, spelling, mechanics, manuscript form, and typographical errors. If your editing skills are not strong, get a friend to read over your work. Keep in mind the following concerns:

✓ Checklist for Editing a Research Paper

_____ 1. Are all your sentences complete?

_____ 2. Have you avoided run-on sentences, both fused sentences and comma splices?

_____ 3. Do pronouns have clear antecedents, and do they agree in number, gender, and case with the words for which they stand?

_____ 4. Do all subjects and verbs agree in person and number?

_____ 5. Is the verb tense consistent and correct?

_____ 6. Have you used modifiers (words, phrases, subordinate clauses) correctly and placed them where they belong?

_____ 7. Have you used matching elements in parallel constructions?

_____ 8. Are punctuation marks used correctly?

_____ 9. Are spelling, capitalization, and other mechanics (abbreviations, numbers, italics) correct?

As Kristen drafts her essay, she uses the American Psychological Society (APA) manuscript and documentation style. The APA style is commonly used in the social sciences, and Kristen's instructor suggested that APA format might be appropriate for her topic.

FAMILY VALUES   2

Family Values in an Election Year

1   It seems that each election year, conservative, moderate, and liberal

candidates go to considerable lengths to express their strong support for "family

values." Since 1976, the phrase "family values" has been used in every

Republican Party national platform (Quindlen, 2007). "Strong families, blessed

with opportunity, guided by faith, and filled with dreams are the heart of a

strong America" ("Strong at home," 2004) read the 2004 Democratic Party

platform. In a speech given on Father's Day 2008, Barack Obama identified

absent fathers as a major cause of problems in black communities, an argument

that sociologist Michael Eric Dyson (2008) claimed was calculated to sway "those

whites still on the fence about whom to send to the White House" (p. 38). In an

election year, everyone seems anxious to play the family values card, and with

good reason. In a 2007 USA Today/Gallup poll, 75% of Americans said that the

candidates' positions on "family values" would have an important influence on

their votes in the next presidential election (Carroll, 2007).

2   The assumption underneath this dialogue is that the American family is

endangered and needs reinforcement. Unfortunately, the political rhetoric

around family values often degenerates to posturing that lacks precision and

clarity. What exactly are "family values," and how are they in peril? Without a

doubt, American families have changed significantly in recent years. The

traditional nuclear family, with a breadwinner father, homemaker mother, and

children, has been on the decline, and it is being replaced by what sociologist

David Elkind calls the "postmodern family," a term that encompasses various

types of domestic units such as single-parent families, dual-income families, and

remarried families (as cited in Scherer, 1996). To a large extent, the debate over

family values revolves around whether this transformation represents the

decline of the American family or an opportunity to strengthen and improve

families. The sociological literature on the evolution and current status of the

American family helps clarify the issues that are at the core of this political debate. I will use the findings of sociologists who study the American family to analyze issues that lie at the core of the political controversy over family values.

3   Social scientists agree that Americans are now living less frequently in traditional nuclear families than they did in the past. In 1900, 55% of households were traditional nuclear families (two married parents and children) as opposed to 25% in 2000 (Katz & Stern, 2007). Twenty-five percent of children are currently born out of wedlock (Trimberger, 2007) and the rates of out-of-wedlock birth increased 404% for white women and 82% for black women between 1970 and 2000 (Katz & Stern, 2007). Around a third of all American children are being raised by a single parent, who in most cases is employed (Boushey, 2007). In 1900, almost all single mothers were widows, whereas in 2000, "most were either divorced, separated, or never married" (Katz & Stern, 2007, p. 91). There are currently more Americans living alone than there are households with a married couple and one or more children (Trimberger, 2007) and in 30 percent of families, the head of household is a single woman (Katz & Stern, 2007). Fifty percent of American marriages end in divorce (Popenoe, 1997). Politicians who refer to dramatic structural changes in the American family could certainly find support in social science research. Without a doubt, the American family has changed during the latter part of the twentieth century.

4   When politicians call for a return to "family values," they often seem to imply that Americans merely have to recommit themselves to the traditional nuclear family, which will then change the larger society. This suggests that family structure is largely a function of Americans' belief systems, and that it will shift along with those beliefs. Some social scientists do support the notion that values determine social structure. David Popenoe (1999) believes that the shift in family structure resulted from social movements of the 1960s and 1970s, particularly "highly expressive or self-focused individualism" (p. 30), feminism, "female economic pursuit" (p. 30), and the sexual revolution. According to Popenoe, the modern nuclear family was a key to American and European social stability, but this social structure was threatened by cultural changes that

placed more emphasis on personal liberation than on family unity. The impact on males was to encourage "Playboy-style sexual opportunism and rejection of responsibilities" and on females to view "the modern nuclear family as an oppressive institution" (Popenoe, 1999, p. 30). The sexual revolution undermined the idea that sex should take place only within a marriage and made divorce more acceptable. Whitehead (1997) points out that attitudes toward divorce changed so that "society no longer defined divorce as a social or family event, with multiple stakeholders, notably the children whose interests must be represented and served. Instead, it saw divorce as an individual and psychological event with a single stakeholder, the initiating adult" (p. 6). According to Elshtain (2000), the situation worsens as antifamily cultural values are passed on to children:

> We see that more and more children are growing up with little or no experience of seeing married life, hence no living examples of what it means for two people to commit themselves to one another over time.... Over the past three or four decades, the message American children receive from the wider culture is one that is high on romance and sex but hostile or, at best, indifferent to marriage... [;consequently,] we have not been imparting to the next generation a set of fundamental norms and beliefs about the meaning and purposes, responsibilities and freedom, of marriage and family life. (p. 312)

5   Popenoe (1999) maintains that we Americans need to reexamine our cultural values with regard to the family: "If the nuclear family is to be revived, *we must restore the cultural importance of voluntary, lifelong monogamy*" (p. 30). Many politicians echo Popenoe's explanation for the collapse of the American family and call for a return to traditional family values in order to resurrect the nuclear family.

6   Other social scientists, however, believe that American family structure has changed largely in response to economic conditions rather than shifting cultural values.

Since 1965, two major developments have had a profound impact on

families. One was the shift at the end of the postwar boom to a lean-

and-mean postindustrial economy that stripped family-sustaining career

opportunities from many blacks and noncollege-educated adults of all

demographic groups. Young adults in the family-forming stage of life

have been hit especially hard by an insecure and uncertain job market.

(Skolnick, 1997, p. 81)

7   While some conservative politicians and certain social scientists point to

feminism as a reason that fewer women stay home with young children,

sociologists more often cite economic pressures. Boushey (2007) points out that

while the women's movement made it possible for more females to obtain better

jobs, most women enter the workforce out of economic necessity:

Mothers work because they can and also because they have to. The

feminist revolution opened up job opportunities and the Pill allowed

women to choose when to have a family. But for most families, if Mom's

at work it's because she has to be. Who can raise a family on just one

income? How can a single mother even contemplate not working now

that we've closed the welfare offices? . . . And the higher the family

income, the more likely it is that Mom has a job and works full time. In

recent decades, the families that were upwardly mobile were those who

had a working wife. (p. A3)

8   From this perspective, women's participation in the workforce is a response

to economic conditions rather than a voluntary assertion of feminist values. In

this day and age, demographic and economic changes make it unnecessary

and impractical for homemaking to be a lifetime career (Skolnick, 2006). When

both parents work, the economic pressures on the family lessen. Just as the

rise of the traditional nuclear family was a response to industrialization, the

current shift away from the traditional family has the same driving force: a

changing economic reality (Skolnick, 2006). As this example indicates,

FAMILY VALUES   6

Americans are not entirely free to choose their "family values," but often must organize their family life to accommodate social conditions in the larger society.

> The [revisionist social scientists] . . . have it backwards when they argue that the collapse of traditional family values is at the heart of our social decay. The losses in real earnings and in breadwinner jobs, the persistence of low-wage work for women and the corporate greed that has accompanied global economic restructuring have wreaked far more havoc on Ozzie and Harriet Land than the combined effects of feminism, sexual revolution, gay liberation, the counterculture, narcissism, and every other value flip of the past half-century. (Stacey, 1994, pp. 120–121)

9   Skolnick (2004) adds to Stacey's (1994) list of factors responsible for social problems

> . . . growing inequality; a new economic insecurity that reaches far up into the middle class; a mismatch between the needs of families and the demands of employers for longer hours and lower labor costs; declining public services; rising costs for housing, healthcare and education; and on and on. (p. 46)

According to Skolnick (2004), Americans understand that family life has changed and that the world in general has changed, but they don't perceive the relationship between the two. "Talk about family change is almost totally disconnected from the discussion of technology and economy" (Skolnick, 2004, p. 47). According to this perspective, politicians tend to blame declining moral values for social problems because it absolves them, to some extent, from addressing the complex causes of those problems.

10   A common assumption in political rhetoric is that children are better off in traditional nuclear families than in other household types. One might think that candidates for office cannot afford to alienate the huge and growing population of single parents, but much political rhetoric implies that single-parent families are unacceptable structures in which to raise children. This notion receives some support from social scientists such as Barbara Defoe Whitehead (2007),

who argues that single motherhood is detrimental to the mothers themselves and their children. Single mothers typically lack access to "two of the most effective sources of self-sufficiency—professional jobs and marriage" and as as result their children often begin life "at the bottom of the [economic] ladder" (p. 6). Based on their review of "large-scale studies," Gallagher and Blankenhorn (1997) paint a dire picture of the consequences for children growing up in single parent families: "Children raised outside of intact marriages are more likely to be poor, to have trouble in school, to report psychological problems, to commit violence against themselves and others, to use drugs, and to experience sexual and physical abuse" (p. 13). Research studies indicate that the rate of mental and behavioral problems is two to three times higher for children who are not living with both parents (Elshtain, 2000; Popenoe, 1997). According to Whitehead (1997), "Nondisrupted two-parent households simply have a greater capacity to make higher and often longer-term investments of time and money in their children than the fast-growing alternatives: one-parent, stepparent, and foster-parent families" (p. 16).

11   However, many social scientists maintain that the breakup of a marriage does not stop effective parenting and that effects of divorce on children are often exaggerated (Skolnick, 1997). A study by California therapist Judith Wallerstein is most commonly cited when measuring these effects (Ehrenreich, 1996). According to Ehrenreich (1996), Wallerstein found that 41% of children whose parents are divorced are "doing poorly, worried, underachieving, deprecating, and often angry" (as cited on p. 80) years after the split. Ehrenreich, however, points out that this report lacks credibility because it focused on just sixty couples. More important, two-thirds of them were without "adequate psychological functioning" previous to the divorce (p.80). Stacey (1994) points out that Wallenstein's research compares the children of divorce with all other children, but not specifically with children living in families with problematic marriages but no divorce. Without that comparison, Stacey (1994) says that the research tells us nothing about the real impact of divorce.

12   Divorce is typically portrayed on television and in films as devastating for all involved, but "just as there are bad divorces, there are good divorces too" (p. 80), Constance Ahron points out (as cited in Ehrenreich, 1996). Both parents do, in many cases, remain financially and emotionally responsible for their children. The situation after divorce sometimes even improves when families are relieved of constant fighting and abuse. As divorce has become more acceptable, its effects have become less harsh. Stacey (1994) maintains that "most social scientists do not agree that a family's structure is more important than the quality of the relationships" (p. 120). She agrees that children of divorced parents do have more social difficulties, in general, than children of parents who stay together, but she points out that it may be the hostility within the home, not the divorce itself, that is responsible for the children's problems.

13   Homosexual parenting is more often opposed by conservative politicians than by moderates or liberals. Currently, states and municipalities recognize the rights of same-sex couples to varying degrees, with liberals generally supporting those rights and conservatives challenging them. Of all the political debates over the American family, this one is perhaps the least informed by sociological research. However, such research does exist. Perrin (2002) reviewed the sociological literature on gay and lesbian parenting and concluded that children of gays or lesbians are not significantly different from their peers raised by straight parents. "It appears that the psychosocial adjustment of children is influenced more strongly by family processes and interactions than by the number and sexual orientation of their parents" (p. 125). Overall, the strength of attachment to their parents is comparable in families with gay, lesbian and straight parents. Some of these children do have difficulty coming to grips with their parents' sexual orientation, but others not only accept their gay and lesbian parents but also develop closer relationships with them than is typical in straight families. The sociological research provides no support for the view expressed by some politicians that gay and lesbian parenting is incompatible

with good family values. As Perrin (2002) states, "Apparently parents' sexual orientation has no measurable effect on the quality of parent-child relationships or on children's mental health or social adjustment" (p. 129).

14   A number of social scientists embrace the postmodern family and argue that politicians should do more to support it rather than pine for the traditional nuclear family. David Elkind says that the postmodern family "is more fluid and more flexible. . . .It mirrors the openness, complexity, and diversity of our contemporary lifestyle" (as cited in Scherer, 1996, p. 4). In their literature review, Mack, Canty, and Wright (2004) cite research showing that personal growth and family happiness are enhanced in families where "parents identify with feminist principles and parent from feminist perspectives" (p. 860). Boushey (2007) points out that working mothers actually spend more time with their children but less on housework. It seems possible that postmodern families will be more responsive than traditional nuclear families to the new economic, technological, and cultural changes facing American families today. We are presented with new challenges and opportunities to which postmodern families are highly responsive.

15   As the current election year unfolds, we will undoubtedly witness more political battles over what is best for the American family: a return to traditional family values and structures, or an effort to improve the success of the various postmodern family forms. What is the reality beneath the political rhetoric? Are we weakening the most basic social element of our society, or are we gaining a flexibility that the family will need to survive in the twenty-first century? The sociological literature does not provide definite answers to these questions even though it may clarify the underlying issues. When seeking answers to these questions, it is essential to consider which structure is most suitable for raising children so that they grow up to be both autonomous and socially responsible. Children must feel like an important part of their parents' lives and need to be embraced with love, care, and guidance. When these qualities are provided, both individual happiness and social harmony will follow.

References

Boushey, H. (2007, March). Values begin at home, but who's home? *The American Prospect, 18,* A2–4. Retrieved from Proquest Research Library database.

Carroll, J. (2007, December). Public: "Family values" important to presidential vote. *The Gallup Poll Briefing, 97.* Abstract retrieved from Proquest Research Library database.

Dyson, M. E. (2008, June 30). The blame game. *Time, 171,* 38.

Ehrenreich, B. (1996, April 8). In defense of splitting up: The growing anti-divorce movement is blind to the costs of bad marriage. *Time, 147,* 80. Retrieved from Proquest Research Library database.

Elshtain, J. B. (2000, March). Philosophic reflections on the family at millennium's beginning. *World and I, 15,* 312. Retrieved from General OneFile database.

Gallagher, M., & Blankenhorn, D. (1997, July/August). Family feud. *The American Prospect,* 12–16. Retrieved from Proquest Research Library database.

Katz, M.B., & Stern, M. J. (2007, Fall). American families: Changes in the twentieth century. *Dissent, 54,* 90–92. Retrieved from Proquest Research Library database.

Mack-Canty, C., & Wright, S. (2004, October) Family values as practiced by feminist parents. *Journal of Family Issues, 25,* 851–880. Retrieved from Sociology: A Sage Full Text Collection database.

Perrin, E. (2002). *Sexual orientation in child adolescent health care.* New York: Kluwer. Retrieved from SocINDEX database.

Popenoe, D. (1997, September–October). Family trouble (divorce). *American Prospect,* 16. Retrieved from General OneFile database.

Popenoe, D. (1999, July–August). Can the nuclear family be revived? *Society, 36,* 28–30. Retrieved from SocINDEX database.

FAMILY VALUES   11

Quindlen, A. (2007, September). Disinvited to the party. *Newsweek,* 68.

    Retrieved from General OneFile database.

Scherer, M. (1996). On our changing family values: A conversation with David

    Elkind. *Educational Leadership, 53,* 4–9.

Skolnick, A. (1997, September–October). Family trouble (divorce). *American*

    Prospect, 16. Retrieved from General OneFile database.

Skolnick, A. (2004, Fall). Special series: Rethinking the politics of the family.

    Dissent, 51, 45–47. Retrieved from Proquest Research Library database.

Skolnick, A. (2006, Fall). Beyond the "M" word. *Dissent, 53,* 81–87. Retrieved

    from Academic Search Premier database.

Stacey, J. (1994, July 25–August 1). The new family values crusaders. *The*

    Nation, 259, 119–122. Retrieved from General OneFile database.

Strong at home, respected in the world: The 2004 Democratic national platform

    for America. (n.d.). Retrieved from http://www.democrats.org/pdfs/

    2004platform.pdf

Trimberger, E. K. (2007, Spring). Further beyond the "M" word. *Dissent, 54,*

    82–84. Retrieved from Proquest Research Library database.

Whitehead, B. D. (1997, September/October). Family trouble (divorce). *American*

    Prospect, 16. Retrieved from Proquest Research Library database.

Whitehead, B. D. (2007, January 26). Single mothers: The costs of going it alone.

    Commonweal 134, 6. Retrieved from Proquest Research Library database.

Composition II

Baker College
Online

What Is Argument?

O NE OF THE BEST-KNOWN CELEBRITIES ON YOUTUBE IS AN ANONYMOUS
VIDEO DIRECTOR WHO WEARS A GUY FAWKES MASK AND USES THE NAME
MADV. IN NOVEMBER 2006 HE POSTED A SHORT VIDEO IN WHICH HE
HELD UP HIS HAND WITH THE WORDS "ONE WORLD" WRITTEN
on his palm and invited viewers to take a stand by uploading a video to
YouTube. They responded by the thousands, writing short messages written
on their palms. MadV then compiled many of the responses in a 4-minute video
titled The Message and posted it on YouTube.

MadV's project has been praised as a celebration of the values of the
YouTube community. The common theme that we all should try to love and
better understand other people is one that few oppose. Yet the video also
raises the question of how any of the goals might be achieved. One hand
reads "Stop Bigotry." We see a great deal of hatred in written responses to
many YouTube videos. Slogans like "Open Mind," "Be Colorblind," "Love Is
Stronger," "No more racism," and "Yup One World" seem inadequate for the
scope of the problem.

Like the ink-on-hand messages, bumper stickers usually consist of unilateral statements ("Be Green," "Save the Whales," or "Share the Road") but
provide no supporting evidence or reasons for why anyone should do what
they say. People committed to a particular cause or belief often assume that
their reasons are self-evident, and that everyone thinks the same way. These
writers know they can count on certain words and phrases to produce predictable responses.

In college courses, in public life, and in professional careers, however,
written arguments cannot be reduced to signs or slogans. Writers of effective
arguments do not assume that everyone thinks the same way or holds the
same beliefs. They attempt to change people's minds by convincing them of
the validity of new ideas or the superiority of a particular course of action.
Writers of such arguments not only offer evidence and reasons to support
their position but also examine the assumptions on which an argument is
based, address opposing arguments, and anticipate their readers' objections.

MadV's *The Message* consists of a series of extremely short videos from YouTube members of words written on hands.

Extended written arguments make more demands on their readers than most other kinds of writing. Like bumper stickers, these arguments often appeal to our emotions. But they typically do much more.

- They expand our knowledge with the depth of their analysis.
- They lead us through a complex set of claims by providing networks of logical relationships and appropriate evidence.
- They build on what has been written previously by providing trails of sources.

Finally, they cause us to reflect on what we read, in a process that we will shortly describe as critical reading.

The Defining Features of Argument

We turn now to examine arguments in more detail. (Unless we say otherwise, by *argument* we mean explicit arguments that attempt to supply reasons and evidence to support their claims.) This section examines three defining features of such arguments.

ARGUMENT REQUIRES JUSTIFICATION OF ITS CLAIMS

To begin defining argument, let's turn to a humble but universal site of disagreement: the conflict between a parent and a teenager over rules. In what way and in what circumstances do such conflicts constitute arguments?

Consider the following dialogue:

YOUNG PERSON (*racing for the front door while putting coat on*): Bye. See you later.

PARENT: Whoa! What time are you planning on coming home?

YOUNG PERSON (*coolly, hand still on doorknob*): I'm sure we discussed this earlier. I'll be home around 2 A.M. (*The second sentence, spoken very rapidly, is barely audible.*)

PARENT (*mouth tightening*): We did *not* discuss this earlier and you're *not* staying out till two in the morning. You'll be home at twelve.

At this point in the exchange, we have a quarrel, not an argument. Quarrelers exchange antagonistic assertions without any attempt to support them rationally. If the dialogue never gets past the "Yes-you-will/No-I-won't" stage, it either remains a quarrel or degenerates into a fight.

Let us say, however, that the dialogue takes the following turn:

YOUNG PERSON (*tragically*): But I'm *sixteen years old!*

Now we're moving toward argument. Not, to be sure, a particularly well-developed or cogent one, but an argument all the same. It's now an argument because one of the quarrelers has offered a reason for her assertion. Her choice of curfew is satisfactory, she says, *because* she is sixteen years old, an argument that depends on the unstated assumption that sixteen-year-olds are old enough to make decisions about such matters.

The parent can now respond in one of several ways that will either advance the argument or turn it back into a quarrel. The parent can simply invoke parental authority ("I don't care—you're still coming home at twelve"), in which case argument ceases. Or the parent can provide a reason for his or her view ("You will be home at twelve because your dad and I pay the bills around here!"), in which case the argument takes a new turn.

So far we've established two necessary conditions that must be met before we're willing to call something an argument: (1) a set of two or more conflicting assertions and (2) the attempt to resolve the conflict through an appeal to reason.

But good argument demands more than meeting these two formal requirements. For the argument to be effective, an arguer is obligated to clarify and support the reasons presented. For example, "But I'm sixteen years old!" is not yet a clear support for the assertion "I should be allowed to set my own curfew." On the surface, Young Person's argument seems absurd. Her parent, of all people, knows precisely how old she is. What makes it an argument is that behind her claim lies an unstated assumption—all sixteen-year-olds are old enough to set their own curfews. What Young Person needs to do now is to support that assumption. In doing so, she must anticipate the sorts of questions the assumption will raise in the minds of her parent: What is the legal status of sixteen-year-olds? How psychologically mature, as opposed to chronologically mature, is Young Person? What is the actual track record of Young Person in being responsible? and so forth. Each of these questions will force Young Person to reexamine and clarify her assumptions about the proper degree of autonomy for sixteen-year-olds. And her response to those questions should in turn force the parents to reexamine their assumptions about the dependence of sixteen-year-olds on parental guidance and wisdom. (Likewise, the parents will need to show why "paying the bills around here" automatically gives them the right to set Young Person's curfew.)

As the argument continues, Young Person and Parent may shift to a different line of reasoning. For example, Young Person might say: "I should be allowed to stay out until 2 A.M. because all my friends get to stay out that late." (Here the unstated assumption is that the rules in this family ought to be based on the rules in other families.) The parent might in turn respond, "But I certainly never stayed out that late when I was your age"—an argument assuming that the rules in this family should follow the rules of an earlier generation.

As Young Person and Parent listen to each other's points of view (and begin realizing why their initial arguments have not persuaded their intended audience), both parties find themselves in the uncomfortable position of having to examine their own beliefs and to justify assumptions that they have taken for granted. Here we encounter one of the earliest senses of the term *to argue,* which is "to clarify." As an arguer begins to clarify her own position on an issue, she also begins to clarify her audience's position. Such clarification helps the arguer see how she might accommodate her audience's views, perhaps by adjusting her own position or by developing reasons that appeal to her audience's values. Thus Young Person might suggest an argument like this:

> I should be allowed to stay out until two on a trial basis because I need enough space to demonstrate my maturity and show you I won't get into trouble.

The assumption underlying this argument is that it is good to give teenagers freedom to demonstrate their maturity. Because this reason is likely to appeal to her parent's own values (the parent wants to see his or her daughter grow in maturity) and because it is tempered by the qualifier "on a trial basis" (which reduces some of the threat of Young Person's initial demands), it may prompt productive discussion.

Whether or not Young Person and Parent can work out a best solution, the preceding scenario illustrates how argument leads people to clarify their reasons and provide justifications that can be examined rationally. The scenario also illustrates two specific aspects of argument that we will explore in detail in the next sections: (1) Argument is both a process and a product. (2) Argument combines truth seeking and persuasion.

ARGUMENT IS BOTH A PROCESS AND A PRODUCT

As the preceding scenario revealed, argument can be viewed as a *process* in which two or more parties seek the best solution to a question or problem. Argument can also be viewed as a *product*, each product being any person's contribution to the conversation at a given moment. In an informal discussion, the products are usually short, whatever time a person uses during his or her turns in the conversation. Under more formal settings, an orally delivered product might be a short impromptu speech (say, during an open-mike discussion of a campus issue) or a longer, carefully prepared formal speech (as in a PowerPoint presentation at a business meeting or an argument at a public hearing for or against a proposed city project).

Similar conversations occur in writing. Roughly analogous to a small-group discussion is an exchange of the kind that occurs regularly through informal chat groups or professional e-mail discussion lists. In an online discussion, participants have more thinking time to shape their messages than they do in a real-time oral discussion. Nevertheless, messages are usually short and informal, making it possible over the course of several days to see participants' ideas shift and evolve as conversants modify their initial views in response to others' views.

Roughly equivalent to a formal speech would be a formal written argument, which may take the form of an academic argument for a college course; a grant proposal; a guest column for the op-ed* section of a newspaper; a legal

Op-ed stands for "opposite-editorial." It is the generic name in journalism for a signed argument that voices the writer's opinion on an issue, as opposed to a news story that is supposed to report events objectively, uncolored by the writer's personal views. Op-ed pieces appear in the editorial-opinion section of newspapers, which generally features editorials by the resident staff, opinion pieces by syndicated columnists, and letters to the editor from readers. The term *op-ed* is often extended to syndicated columns appearing in newsmagazines, advocacy Web sites, and online news services.

brief; a letter to a member of Congress; or an article for an organizational newsletter, popular magazine, or professional journal. In each of these instances, the written argument (a product) enters a conversation (a process)—in this case, a conversation of readers, many of whom will carry on the conversation by writing their own responses or by discussing the writer's views with others. The goal of the community of writers and readers is to find the best solution to the problem or issue under discussion.

ARGUMENT COMBINES TRUTH SEEKING AND PERSUASION

In thinking about argument as a product, the writer will find herself continually moving back and forth between truth seeking and persuasion—that is, between questions about the subject matter (What is the best solution to this problem?) and about audience (What do my readers already believe or value? What reasons and evidence will most persuade them?). Back and forth she'll weave, alternately absorbed in the subject of her argument and in the audience for that argument.

Neither of the two focuses is ever completely out of mind, but their relative importance shifts during different phases of the development of a paper. Moreover, different rhetorical situations place different emphases on truth seeking versus persuasion. We could thus place arguments on a kind of continuum that measures the degree of attention a writer gives to subject matter versus audience. (See Figure 15.1.) At the far truth-seeking end of the continuum might be an exploratory piece that lays out several alternative approaches to a problem and weighs the strengths and weaknesses of each with no concern for persuasion. At the other end of the continuum would be outright propaganda, such as a political campaign advertisement that reduces a complex issue to sound bites and distorts an opponent's position through out-of-context quotations or misleading use of data. (At its most blatant, propaganda obliterates truth seeking; it will do anything, including the knowing use of bogus evidence, distorted assertions, and outright lies, to win over an audience.) In the middle ranges of the continuum, writers shift their focuses back and forth between truth seeking and persuasion but with varying degrees of emphasis.

As an example of a writer focusing primarily on truth seeking, consider the case of Kathleen, who, in her college argument course, addressed the definitional question "Is American Sign Language (ASL) a 'foreign language' for purposes of meeting the university's foreign language requirement?" Kathleen had taken two years of ASL at a community college. When she transferred to a four-year college, the chair of the foreign languages department at her new college would not allow her ASL proficiency to count for the foreign language requirement. ASL isn't a "language," the chair said summarily. "It's not equivalent to learning French, German, or Japanese."

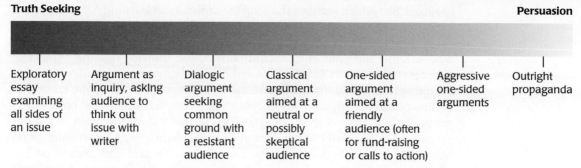

Figure 15.1   Continuum of Arguments from Truth Seeking to Persuasion

Kathleen disagreed, so she immersed herself in developing her argument. While doing research, she focused almost entirely on subject matter, searching for what linguists, neurologists, cognitive psychologists, and sociologists had said about the language of deaf people. Immersed in her subject matter, she was only tacitly concerned with her audience, whom she thought of primarily as her classmates and the professor of her argument class—people who were friendly to her views and interested in her experiences with the deaf community. She wrote a well-documented paper, citing several scholarly articles, that made a good case to her classmates (and the professor) that ASL is indeed a distinct language.

Proud of the big red A the professor had placed on her paper, Kathleen decided for a subsequent assignment to write a second paper on ASL—but this time aiming it directly at the chair of foreign languages and petitioning him to accept her ASL proficiency for the foreign language requirement. Now her writing task falls closer to the persuasive end of our continuum. Kathleen once again immersed herself in research, but this time focused not on subject matter (whether ASL is a distinct language) but on audience. She researched the history of the foreign language requirement at her college and discovered some of the politics behind it (an old foreign language requirement had been dropped in the 1970s and reinstituted in the 1990s, partly—a math professor told her—to boost enrollments in foreign language courses). She also interviewed foreign language teachers to find out what they knew and didn't know about ASL. She discovered that many teachers thought ASL was "easy to learn," so that accepting ASL would allow students a Mickey Mouse way to avoid the rigors of a "real" foreign language class. Additionally, she learned that foreign language teachers valued immersing students in a foreign culture; in fact, the foreign language requirement was part of her college's effort to create a multicultural curriculum.

This new understanding of her target audience helped Kathleen reconceptualize her argument. Her claim that ASL was a real language (the subject of her first paper) became only one section of her second paper, much condensed and abridged. She added sections showing the difficulty of learning ASL (to counter her audience's belief that learning ASL was easy), showing how the deaf community formed a distinct culture with its own customs and literature (to show how ASL met the goals of multiculturalism), and showing that the number of transfer students with ASL credits would be negligibly small (to allay fears that accepting ASL would threaten enrollments in language classes). She ended her argument with an appeal to her college's public emphasis (declared boldly in its mission statement) on eradicating social injustice and reaching out to the oppressed. She described the isolation of deaf people in a world where almost no hearing people learn ASL, and she argued that the deaf community on her campus could be integrated more fully into campus life if more students could "talk" with them. Thus the ideas included in her new argument—the reasons selected, the evidence used, the arrangement and tone—all were determined by her primary focus on persuasion.

Our point, then, is that all along the continuum writers attempt both to seek truth and to persuade, but not necessarily with equal balance. Kathleen could not have written her second paper, aimed specifically at persuading the chair of foreign languages, if she hadn't first immersed herself in truth-seeking research that convinced her that ASL is indeed a distinct language. Nor are we saying that her second argument was better than her first. Both fulfilled their purposes and met the needs of their intended audiences. Both involved truth seeking and persuasion, but the first focused primarily on subject matter whereas the second focused primarily on audience.

Argument and the Problem of Truth

The tension that we have just examined between truth seeking and persuasion raises an ancient issue in the field of argument: Is the arguer's first obligation to truth or to winning the argument? And just what is the nature of the truth to which arguers are supposed to be obligated?

In Plato's famous dialogues from ancient Greek philosophy, these questions were at the heart of Socrates' disagreement with the Sophists. The Sophists were professional rhetoricians who specialized in training orators to win arguments. Socrates, who valued truth seeking over persuasion and believed that truth could be discovered through philosophic inquiry, opposed the Sophists. For Socrates, Truth resided in the ideal world of forms, and through philosophic rigor humans could transcend the changing, shadowlike world of everyday reality to perceive the world of universals where Truth, Beauty, and Goodness resided. Through his method of questioning his interlocutors, Socrates would gradually peel away layer after layer of false views until Truth was revealed. The good person's duty, Socrates believed, was not to win an argument but to pursue this higher Truth. Socrates distrusted rhetoricians because they were interested only in the temporal power and wealth that came from persuading audiences to the orator's views.

Let's apply Socrates' disagreement with the Sophists to a modern instance. Suppose your community is divided over the issue of raising environmental standards versus keeping open a job-producing factory that doesn't meet new guidelines for waste discharge. The Sophists would train you to argue any side of this issue on behalf of any lobbying group willing to pay for your services. If, however, you followed the spirit of Socrates, you would be inspired to listen to all sides of the dispute, peel away false arguments, discover the Truth through reasonable inquiry, and commit yourself to a Right Course of Action.

But what is the nature of Truth or Right Action in a dispute between jobs and the environment? The Sophists believed that truth was determined by those in power; thus they could enter an argument unconstrained by any transcendent beliefs or assumptions. When Socrates talked about justice and virtue, the Sophists could reply contemptuously that these were fictitious concepts invented by the weak to protect themselves from the strong. Over the years, the Sophists' relativist beliefs became so repugnant to people that the term *sophistry* became synonymous with trickery in argument.

However, in recent years the Sophists' critique of a transcendent Universal Truth has been taken seriously by many philosophers, sociologists, and other thinkers who doubt Socrates' confident belief that arguments, properly conducted, necessarily arrive at a single Truth. For these thinkers, as for the Sophists, there are often different degrees of truth and different kinds of truths for different situations or cultures. From this perspective, when we consider questions of interpretation or value, we can never demonstrate that a belief or assumption is true—not through scientific observation, not through reason, and not through religious revelation. We get our beliefs, according to these contemporary thinkers, from the shared assumptions of our particular cultures. We are condemned (or liberated) to live in a pluralistic, multicultural world with competing visions of truth.

If we accept this pluralistic view of the world, do we then endorse the Sophists' radical relativism, freeing us to argue any side of any issue? Or do we doggedly pursue some modern equivalent of Socrates' truth?

Our own sympathies are with Socrates, but we admit to a view of truth that is more tentative, cautious, and conflicted than his. For us, truth seeking does not mean finding the "Right Answer" to a disputed question, but neither does it mean a valueless relativism in which all answers are equally good. For us, truth seeking means taking responsibility for determining the "best answer" or "best solution" to the question for the good of the whole community when taking into consideration the interests of all stakeholders. It means making hard decisions in the face of uncertainty. This more tentative view of truth means that you cannot use argument to "prove" your claim, but only to make a reasonable case for your claim. One contemporary philosopher says that argument can hope only to "increase adherence" to ideas, not absolutely convince an audience of the necessary truth of ideas. Even though you can't be certain, in a Socratic sense, that your solution to the problem is the best one available, you must ethically take responsibility for the consequences of your claim and you must seek justice for stakeholders beyond yourself. You must, in other words, forge a personal stance based on your examination of all the evidence and your articulation of values that you can make public and defend.

To seek truth, then, means to seek the best or most just solution to a problem while observing all available evidence, listening with an open mind to the views of all stakeholders, clarifying and attempting to justify your own values and assumptions, and taking responsibility for your argument. It follows that truth seeking often means delaying closure on an issue, acknowledging the pressure of alternative views, and being willing to change one's mind. Seen in this way, learning to argue effectively has the deepest sort of social value: It helps communities settle conflicts in a rational and humane way by finding, through the dialectic exchange of ideas, the best solutions to problems without resorting to violence or to other assertions of raw power.

Writing Arguments in College

Writing in college varies considerably from course to course. A lab report for a biology course looks quite different from a paper in your English class, just as a classroom observation in an education course differs from a case study report in an accounting class.

Nevertheless, much of the writing you will do in college will consist of arguments. Some common expectations about arguments in college writing extend across disciplines. For example, you could be assigned to write a proposal for a downtown light-rail system in a number of different classes—civil engineering, urban planning, government, or management. The emphasis of such a proposal would change depending on the course. In all cases, however, the proposal would require a complex argument in which you describe the problem that the light-rail system would improve, make a specific proposal that addresses the problem, explain the benefits of the system, estimate the cost, identify funding sources, assess alternatives to your plan, and anticipate possible opposition. It's a lot to think about.

Setting out a specific proposal or claim supported by reasons and evidence is at the heart of most college writing, no matter what the course. Some expectations of arguments (such as including a thesis statement) may be familiar to you, but others (such as the emphasis on finding alternative ways of thinking about a subject and finding facts that might run counter to your conclusions) may be unfamiliar.

Written Arguments...	Writers Are Expected to...
State explicit claims	Make a claim that isn't obvious. The main claim is often called a **thesis.**
Support claims with reasons	Express reasons in a **because clause** after the claim (We should do something *because* _____).
Base reasons on evidence	Provide evidence for reasons in the form of facts, statistics, testimony from reliable sources, and direct observations.
Consider opposing positions	Help readers understand why there are disagreements about issues by accurately representing differing views.
Analyze with insight	Provide in-depth analysis of what they read and view.
Investigate complexity	Explore the complexity of a subject by asking "Have you thought about this?" or "What if you discard the usual way of thinking about a subject and take the opposite point of view?"
Organize information clearly	Make the main ideas evident to readers and to indicate which parts are subordinate to others.
Signal relationships of parts	Indicate logical relationships clearly so that readers can follow an argument without getting lost.
Document sources carefully	Provide the sources of information so that readers can consult the same sources the writer used.

HOW CAN YOU ARGUE RESPONSIBLY?

In Washington, D.C., cars with diplomatic license plates are often parked illegally. Their drivers know they will not be towed or ticketed. People who abuse the diplomatic privilege are announcing, "I'm not playing by the rules."

When you begin an argument by saying "in my opinion," you are making a similar announcement. First, the phrase is redundant. A reader assumes that if you make a claim in writing, you believe that claim. More important, a claim is rarely *only* your opinion. Most beliefs and assumptions are shared by many people. If a claim truly is only your opinion, it can be easily dismissed. If your position is likely to be held by at least a few other people, however, then a responsible reader must consider your position seriously. You argue responsibly when you set out the reasons for making a claim and offer facts to support those reasons. You argue responsibly when you allow readers to examine your evidence by documenting the sources you have consulted. Finally, you argue responsibly when you acknowledge that other people may have positions different from yours.

HOW CAN YOU ARGUE RESPECTFULLY?

Our culture is competitive, and our goal often is to win. Professional athletes, top trial lawyers, or candidates for president of the United States either win big or lose. But most of us live in a world in which our opponents don't go away when the game is over.

Most of us have to deal with people who disagree with us at times but continue to work and live in our communities. The idea of winning in such situations can only be temporary. Soon enough, we will need the support of those who were on the other side of the most recent issue. You can probably think of times when a friendly argument resulted in a better understanding of all peoples' views. And probably you can think of a time when an argument created hard feelings that lasted for years.

Usually, listeners and readers are more willing to consider your argument seriously if you cast yourself as a respectful partner rather than as a competitor. Put forth your arguments in the spirit of mutual support and negotiation—in the interest of finding the *best* way, not "my way." How can you be the person that your reader will want to join rather than resist? Here are a few suggestions for both your written arguments and for discussing controversial issues.

- **Try to think of yourself as engaged not so much in winning over your audience as in courting your audience's cooperation.** Argue vigorously, but not so vigorously that opposing views are vanquished or silenced. Remember that your goal is to invite a response that creates a dialogue.

- **Show that you understand and genuinely respect your listener's or reader's position even if you think the position is ultimately wrong.** Remember to argue against opponents' positions, not against the opponents themselves. Arguing respectfully often means representing an opponent's position in terms that he or she would accept. Look for ground that you already share with your opponent, and search for even more. See yourself as a mediator. Consider that neither you nor the other person has arrived at a best solution. Then carry on in the hope that dialogue will lead to an even better course of action than the one you now recommend. Expect and assume the best of your listener or reader, and deliver your best.

- **Cultivate a sense of humor and a distinctive voice.** Many textbooks about argument emphasize using a reasonable voice. But a reasonable voice doesn't have to be a dull one. Humor is a legitimate tool of argument. Although playing an issue strictly for laughs risks not being taken seriously, nothing creates a sense of goodwill quite as much as tasteful humor. A sense of humor can be especially welcome when the stakes are high, the sides have been chosen, and tempers are flaring.

Arguments as Turns in a Conversation

Consider your argument as just one move in a larger process that might end up helping you. Most times we argue because we think we have something to offer. In the process of researching what has been said and written on a particular issue, however, often your own view is expanded and you find an opportunity to add your voice to the ongoing conversation.

A CASE STUDY: THE MICROCREDIT DEBATE

World Bank researchers reported in 2009 that 1.4 billion people—over 20 percent of the 6.7 billion people on earth—live below the extreme poverty line of $1.25 a day, with 6 million children starving to death every year. One cause of continuing extreme poverty is the inability of poor people to borrow money because they have no cash income or assets. Banks have seldom made loans to very poor people, who have had to turn to moneylenders that charge high interest rates sometimes exceeding 100 percent a month.

In 1976, Muhammad Yunus observed that poor women in Bangladesh who made bamboo furniture could not profit from their labor because they had to borrow money at high interest rates to buy bamboo. Yunus loaned $27 to forty-two women out of his pocket. They repaid him at an interest rate of two cents per loan. The success of the experiment eventually led to Yunus securing a loan from the government to create a bank to make loans to poor people. The Grameen Bank (Village Bank) became a model for other microfinancing projects in Bangladesh, serving 7 million people, 94 percent of whom are women. For his work with the Grameen initiative, Yunus received the Nobel Peace Prize in 2006.

(continued)

Two women financed by microcredit sell scarves in Quito, Ecuador.

Microcredit now has many supporters, including Hollywood stars like Natalie Portman and Michael Douglas, companies like Benetton and Sam's Club, and former President Bill Clinton. But the success in Bangladesh has not been replicated in many other poor countries. Many critics point to the shortcomings of microcredit. This debate can be better understood if you consider the different points of view on microcredit to be different voices in a conversation.

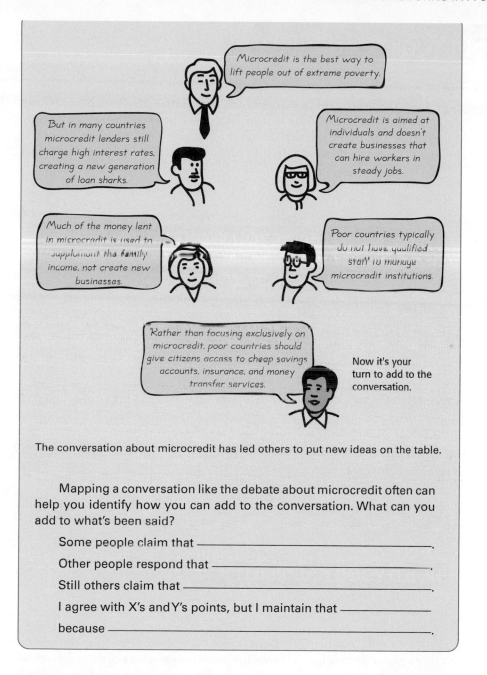

The conversation about microcredit has led others to put new ideas on the table.

Mapping a conversation like the debate about microcredit often can help you identify how you can add to the conversation. What can you add to what's been said?

Some people claim that ————————————————.

Other people respond that ————————————————.

Still others claim that ————————————————.

I agree with X's and Y's points, but I maintain that ——————

because ————————————————.

Think About Your Credibility

A few writers begin with instant credibility because of what they have accomplished. If you're a tennis player, likely you will pay attention to advice from Serena Williams. If you're interested in future trends in computers and entertainment, you have listened to the forecasts of the late Steve Jobs, the cofounder and former CEO of Apple. But if you are like most of the rest of us, you don't have instant credibility.

THINK ABOUT HOW YOU WANT YOUR READERS TO SEE YOU

To get your readers to take you seriously, you must convince them that they can trust you. You need to get them to see you as

Concerned. Readers want you to be committed to what you are writing about. They also expect you to be concerned with them as readers. After all, if you don't care about them, why should they read what you write?

Well informed. Many people ramble on about any subject without knowing anything about it. If they are family members, you have to suffer their opinions, but it is not enjoyable. College writing requires that you do your homework on a subject.

Fair. Many writers look at only one side of an issue. Readers respect objectivity and an unbiased approach.

Ethical. Many writers use only the facts that support their positions and often distort facts and sources. Critical readers often notice what is being left out. Don't try to conceal what doesn't support your position.

BUILD YOUR CREDIBILITY

Know what's at stake. What you are writing about should matter to your readers. If its importance is not evident, it's your job to explain why your readers should consider it important.

Less Effective:

We should be concerned about two-thirds of Central and South America's 110 brightly colored harlequin frog species becoming extinct in the last twenty years. (*The loss of any species is unfortunate, but the writer gives us no other reason for concern.*)

More Effective:
The rapid decline of amphibians worldwide due to global warming may be the advance warning of the loss of cold-weather species such as polar bears, penguins, and reindeer.

Have your readers in mind. If you are writing about a specialized subject that your readers don't know much about, take the time to explain key concepts.

Less Effective:
Reduction in the value of a debt security, especially a bond, results from a rise in interest rates. Conversely, a decline in interest rates results in an increase in the value of a debt security, especially bonds. (*The basic idea is here, but it is not expressed clearly, especially if the reader is not familiar with investing.*)

More Effective:
Bond prices move inversely to interest rates. When interest rates go up, bond prices go down, and when interest rates go down, bond prices go up.

Think about alternative solutions and points of view. Readers appreciate a writer's ability to see a subject from multiple perspectives.

Less Effective:
We will reduce greenhouse gas and global warming only if we greatly increase wind-generated electricity. (*Wind power is an alternative energy source, but it is expensive and many people don't want windmills in scenic areas. The writer also doesn't mention using energy more efficiently.*)

More Effective:
If the world is serious about limiting carbon emissions to reduce global warming, then along with increasing efficient energy use, all non-carbon-emitting energy sources must be considered, including nuclear power. Nuclear power now produces about 20 percent of U.S. electricity with no emissions—the equivalent of taking 58 million passenger cars off the road.

Be honest. Readers also appreciate writers who admit what they aren't sure about. Leaving readers with unanswered questions can lead them to think further about your subject.

Less Effective:
The decline in violent crime during the 1990s was due to putting more people in jail with longer sentences.

More Effective:
Exactly what caused the decline in violent crime during the 1990s remains uncertain.

Politicians point to longer sentences for criminals, but the decrease in the population most likely to commit crimes—the 16-to-35 age group—may have been a contributing factor.

Write well. Nothing impresses readers more than graceful, fluent writing that is clear, direct, and forceful. Even if readers don't agree with you in the end, they still will appreciate your writing ability.

Less Effective:

Nobody can live today without taking some risks, even very rich people. After all, we don't know what we're breathing in the air. A lot of food has chemicals and hormones in it. There's a big hole in the ozone, so more people will get skin cancer. And a lot of people have sexually transmitted diseases these days. (*The impact of the point is lost with unfocused writing.*)

More Effective:

We live in a world of risks beyond our control to the extent that it difficult to think of anything that is risk free down to the most basic human acts—sex in an era of AIDS, eating in an era of genetically altered food, walking outside in an ozone-depleted atmosphere, drinking water and breathing air laden with chemicals whose effects we do not understand.

Explore Controversies

People in general agree on broad goals for their society: clean water, abundant healthy food, efficient transportation, good schools, full employment, affordable health care, safe cities and neighborhoods, and peace with others near and far. People in general, however, often disagree on how to define and achieve these goals. Controversies surround major issues and causes.

Often controversies are portrayed in the media as pro and con or even take on political labels. But if you read and listen carefully to what people have to say about a particular issue, you usually find a range of different positions on the issue, and you often discover nuances and complexities in the reasons people offer for their positions.

FIND CONTROVERSIES

Online subject directories can help you identify the differing views on a large, general topic. Try the subject index of your library's online catalog. You'll likely

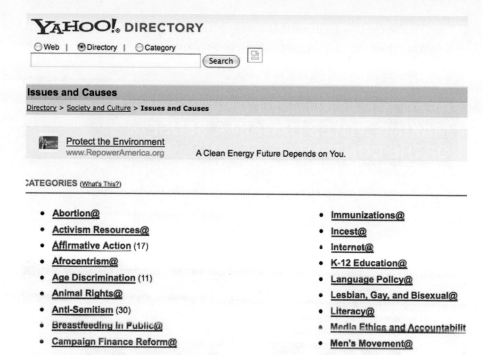

Yahoo! Issues and Causes directory (dir.yahoo.com/Society_and_Culture/
Issues_and_Causes/)

find subtopics listed under large topics. Also, your library's Web site may have a
link to the *Opposing Viewpoints* database.

One of the best Web subject directories for finding arguments is Yahoo's
Issues and Causes directory. This directory provides subtopics for major issues
and provides links to the Web sites of organizations interested in particular issues.

Read Critically

After you survey the landscape of a particular issue, turn to careful reading of
individual arguments, one at a time.

BEFORE YOU BEGIN READING, ASK THESE QUESTIONS

- Where did the argument first appear? Was it published in a book,
  newspaper, magazine, or electronic source? Many items in library
  databases and on the Web were published somewhere else first.

- Who wrote this argument? What do you know about the author?
- What does the title suggest argument be about?

READ THE ARGUMENT ONCE WITHOUT MAKING NOTES TO GAIN A SENSE OF THE CONTENT

- When you finish, write one sentence that sums up the argument.

HAS THE INTERNET MADE EVERYONE WRITERS?

Video blogs, known as vlogs, became a popular genre on YouTube.

Before the Internet was invented, readers had to make some effort to respond to writers by writing to them directly, sending a letter to the editor, or even scribbling or spray-painting a response. The Internet has changed the interaction between writers and readers by allowing readers to respond easily to writers and, in turn, turning readers into writers. Look, for example, at Amazon.com. An incredible amount of writing surrounds any best-selling book—often an author's Web site and blog, newspaper reviews, and over a hundred readers' reviews. Or read a political, sports, culture, fashion, or parenting blog and the comments by readers of those blogs. Think about how the Internet has changed the relationship between readers and writers.

To find a blog that interests you, use a blog search engine such as Bloglines (www. bloglines. com), Google Blog Search (blogsearch .google.com), IceRocket (blogs.icerocket.com), or Technorati (www . technorati. com).

READ THE ARGUMENT A SECOND AND THIRD TIME AND MAKE NOTES

- Go back through the text and underline the author's thesis.
- Does your sentence and the author's thesis match? If not, look at the text again and either adjust your sentence or check if you underlined the correct sentence.
- How is the argument organized? How are the major points arranged?
- What reasons or evidence does the writer offer in support of the thesis?
- How does the writer conclude the argument? Does the conclusion follow from the evidence presented?
- Who is the intended audience? What does the writer assume the readers know and believe?
- Do you detect a bias in the writer's position?
- Where do the writer's facts come from? Does the writer give the sources? Are the sources reliable?
- Does the writer acknowledge other views and unfavorable evidence? Does the writer deal fairly with the views of others?
- If there are images or graphics, are they well integrated and clearly labeled?

ANNOTATE WHAT YOU READ

- **Mark major points and key concepts.** Sometimes major points are indicated by headings, but often you will need to locate them.
- **Connect with your experience.** Think about your own experiences and how they match up or don't match up with what you are reading.

- **Connect passages.** Notice how ideas connect to each other. Draw lines and arrows. If an idea connects to something from a few pages earlier, write a note in the margin with the page number.
- **Ask questions.** Note anything that puzzles you, including words you don't know and need to look up.

MAP A CONTROVERSY

Read broadly about an issue and identify three or more sources that offer different points of view on that issue. The sources may approach the issue from different angles or raise different questions instead of simply stating differing positions on the issue. Draw a map that represents the different views. The map below shows some of the different positions on sustainable agriculture.

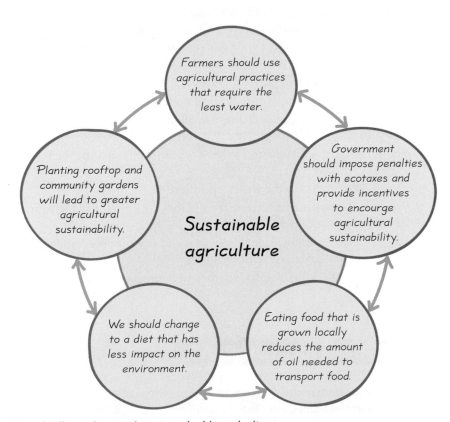

Map of different issues about sustainable agriculture

Map and Summarize Arguments

When you finish annotating a reading, you might want to map it.

DRAW A MAP

Marta Ramos drew a map of James McWilliams's argument.

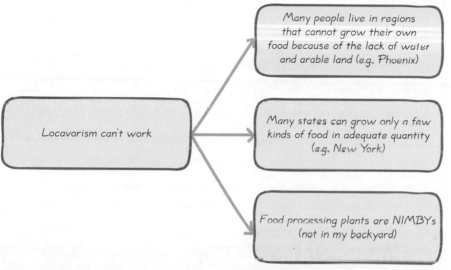

Map of the argument in James McWilliams's "On Locavorism"

WRITE A SUMMARY

A summary should be concise but thorough representation of the source.

- Begin your summary with the writer's name, the title of the argument, and the main point.
- Then report the key ideas. Represent the author's argument in condensed form as accurately as you can, quoting exact words for key points.

- Your aim is to give your readers an understanding of what the author is arguing for. Withhold judgment even if you think the author is dead wrong. Do not insert your opinions and comments. Stick to what the author is saying and what position the author is advocating.
- Usually summaries are no longer than 150 words. If your summary is longer than 150 words, delete excess words without eliminating key ideas.

McWilliams, J. (2008, August). On locavorism. *New York Times*. Retrieved from

  http://www.nytimes.com

Summary

In "On Locavorism," James McWilliams (2008) argues that locavorism—the develop of local food-supply systems—is an impractical goal. He offers three reasons why locavorism is not achievable. First, many people live in regions where they cannot grow their own food because of lack of water and arable land (for example, Phoenix). Second many states can grow only a few kinds of food in adequate quantity (for example, New York), thus restricting food choices and limiting consumption to processed fruits and vegetables for much of the year. Third, many people will not like food processing plants near their homes.

FOCUSING YOUR THESIS

The thesis can make or break your paper. If the thesis is too broad, you cannot do justice to the argument. Who wouldn't wish for fewer traffic accidents, better medical care, more effective schools, or a cleaner environment? Simple solutions for these complex problems are unlikely.

Stating something that is obvious to everyone isn't an arguable thesis. Don't settle for easy answers. When a topic is too broad, a predictable thesis often results. Narrow your focus and concentrate on the areas where you have the most questions. Those are likely the areas where your readers will have the most questions too.

The opposite problem is less common: a thesis that is too narrow. If your thesis simply states a commonly known fact, then it is too narrow. For example, the growth rate of the population in the United States has doubled since 1970 because of increased immigration. The U.S. Census Bureau provides reasonably

People frequently revise things that they own. What objects have you revised?

accurate statistical information, so this claim is not arguable. But the policies that allow increased immigration and the effects of a larger population—more crowding and higher costs of health care, education, and transportation—are arguable.

Not arguable: The population of the United States grew faster in the 1990s than in any previous decade because Congress increased the rate of legal immigration and the government stopped enforcing most laws against illegal immigration in the interior of the country.

Arguable: Allowing a high rate of immigration helps the United States deal with the problems of an increasingly aging society and helps provide funding for millions of Social Security recipients.

Arguable: The increase in the number of visas to foreign workers in technology industries is the major cause of unemployment in those industries.

EVALUATING YOUR THESIS

Once you have a working thesis, ask these questions.

- Is it arguable?
- Is it specific?
- Is it manageable given your length and time requirements?
- Is it interesting to your intended readers?

● **EXAMPLE 1**

Sample Thesis

We should take action to resolve the serious traffic problem in our city.

Is it arguable? The thesis is arguable, but it lacks a focus.

Is it specific? The thesis is too broad.

Is it manageable? Transportation is a complex issue. New highways and rail systems are expensive and take many years to build. Furthermore, citizens don't want new roads running through their neighborhoods.

Is it interesting? The topic has the potential to be interesting if the writer can propose a specific solution to a problem that everyone in the city recognizes.

When a thesis is too broad, it needs to be revised to address a specific aspect of an issue. Make the big topic smaller.

Revised Thesis

The existing freight railway that runs through the center of the city should be converted to a passenger railway because this is the cheapest and quickest way to decrease traffic congestion downtown.

● **EXAMPLE 2**

Sample Thesis

Over 60 percent of Americans play computer games on a regular basis.

Is it arguable? The thesis states a commonly acknowledged fact. It is not arguable.

Is it specific? The thesis is too narrow.

Is it manageable? A known fact is stated in the thesis, so there is little to research. Several surveys report this finding.

Is it interesting? The popularity of video games is well established. Nearly everyone is aware of the trend.

There's nothing original or interesting about stating that Americans love computer games. Think about what is controversial. One debatable topic is how computer games affect children.

Revised Thesis

Computer games are valuable because they improve children's visual attention skills, literacy skills, and computer literacy skills.

Evaluate Your Draft

To review and evaluate your draft, pretend you are someone who is either uninformed about your subject or informed but likely to disagree with you. If possible, think of an actual person and imagine yourself as that person.

Read your draft aloud all the way through. When you read aloud, you often hear clunky phrases and catch errors, but just put checks in the margins so you can return to them later. You don't want to get bogged down with the little stuff. What you are after in this stage is an overall sense of how well you accomplished what you set out to do.

Use the questions in the checklist on the next two pages to evaluate your draft. Note any places where you might make improvements. When you finish, make a list of your goals for the revision. You may have to write another draft before you move to the next stage.

✓ Checklist for Evaluating Your Draft

Does your paper or project meet the assignment?

- Look again at your assignment, especially at key words such as *define, analyze causes, evaluate,* and *propose.* Does your paper or project do what the assignment requires? If not, how can you change it?
- Look again at the assignment for specific guidelines including length, format, and amount of research. Does your work meet these guidelines?

Can you better focus your thesis and your supporting reasons?

- You may have started out with a large topic and ended up writing about one aspect of it. Can you make your thesis even more precise?
- Can you find the exact location where you link each reason to your thesis?

Are your main points adequately developed?

- Can you explain your reasons in more detail?
- Can you add evidence to better support your main points?
- Do you provide enough background on your topic?

Is your organization effective?

- Is the order of your main points clear? (You may want to make a quick outline of your draft if you have not done so already.)
- Are there any abrupt shifts or gaps?
- Are there sections or paragraphs that should be rearranged?

Are your key terms adequately defined?

- What are your key terms?
- Can you define these terms more precisely?

Do you consider other points of view?

- Where do you acknowledge views besides your own? If you don't acknowledge other views, where can you add them?
- How can you make your discussion of opposing views more acceptable to readers who hold those views?

Do you represent yourself effectively?

- Forget for the moment that you wrote what you are reading. What is your impression of the writer?
- Is the tone of the writing appropriate for the subject?

Can you improve your title and introduction?

- Can you make your title more specific and indicate your stance?
- Can you think of a way to start faster and to get your readers interested in what you have to say?

Can you improve your conclusion?

- Can you think of an example that sums up your position?
- Can you discuss an implication of your argument that will make your readers think more about the subject?
- If you are writing a proposal, can you end with a call for action?

Can you improve your visual presentation?

- Is the type style easy to read and consistent?
- Would headings and subheadings help to mark the major sections of your argument?
- If you have statistical data, do you use charts?
- Would illustrations, maps, or other graphics help to explain your main points?

Table 15.1   Twelve Tests of an Arguable Issue

Do You Have an Arguable Issue?

If you cannot answer yes to all of these questions, change or modify your issue.

Your issue (phrased as a question): _____

Yes _____   No _____   1. Is this an issue that has not been resolved or settled?

Yes _____   No _____   2. Does this issue potentially inspire two or more views?

Yes _____   No _____   3. Are you willing to consider a position different from your own and, perhaps, even modify your views on this issue?

Yes _____   No _____   4. Are you sufficiently interested and engaged with this issue to inspire your audience also to become interested?

Yes _____   No _____   5. Do other people perceive this as an issue?

Yes _____   No _____   6. Is this issue significant enough to be worth your time?

Yes _____   No _____   7. Is this a safe issue for you? Not too risky? Scary? Will you be willing to express your ideas?

Yes _____   No _____   8. Can you establish common ground with your audience on this issue—common terms, common background, and related values?

Yes _____   No _____   9. Will you be able to get information and come up with convincing insights on this issue?

Yes _____   No _____   10. Can you eventually get a clear and limited focus on this issue, even if it is a complicated one?

Yes _____   No _____   11. Is it an enduring issue, or can you build perspective by linking it to an enduring issue?

Yes _____   No _____   12. Can you predict one or more audience outcomes? (Think of your classmates as the audience. Will they be convinced? Hostile? Neutral? Attentive? Remember that any outcomes at all can be regarded as significant in argument.)

READINGS

The Argument Culture

Deborah Tannen

A professor of linguistics at Georgetown University, Deborah Tannen is also a best-selling author of many books on discourse and gender, including You Just Don't Understand: Women and Men in Conversation *(1990),* Talking from 9 to 5 *(1994),* The Argument Culture: Moving from Debate to Dialogue *(1998), and* I Only Say This Because I Love You *(2001). Throughout her career, Tannen has focused on how men and women have different conversational habits and assumptions, whether they talk on the job or at home. In the following essay, taken from* The Argument Culture, *Tannen tries to convince her readers that adversarial debates—which typically represent only two sides of an issue and thus promote antagonism—create problems in communication. As a culture, Tannen believes, we would be much more successful if we didn't always think of argument as a war or a fight but as a dialogue among a variety of different positions. As you read her essay, does Tannen persuade you that our "argument culture" really is a problem and that her solutions will help solve that problem?*

1   Balance. Debate. Listening to both sides. Who could question these noble American traditions? Yet today, these principles have been distorted. Without thinking, we have plunged headfirst into what I call the "argument culture."

2   The argument culture urges us to approach the world, and the people in it, in an adversarial frame of mind. It rests on the assumption that opposition is the best way to get anything done: The best way to discuss an idea is to set up a debate; the best way to cover news is to find spokespeople who express the most extreme, polarized views and present them as "both sides"; the best way to settle disputes is litigation that pits one party against the other; the best way to begin an essay is to attack someone; and the best way to show you're really thinking is to criticize.

3   More and more, our public interactions have become like arguing with a spouse. Conflict can't be avoided in our public lives any more than we can avoid conflict with people we love. One of the great strengths of our society is that we can express these conflicts openly. But just as spouses have to learn ways of settling their differences without inflicting

"What about here? This looks like a good spot for an argument."

real damage, so we, as a society, have to find constructive ways of resolving disputes and differences.

4. The war on drugs, the war on cancer, the battle of the sexes, politicians' turf battles—in the argument culture, war metaphors pervade our talk and shape our thinking. The cover headlines of both *Time* and *Newsweek* one recent week are a case in point: "The Secret Sex Wars," proclaims *Newsweek*. "Starr at War," declares *Time*. Nearly everything is framed as a battle or game in which winning or losing is the main concern.

5. The argument culture pervades every aspect of our lives today. Issues from global warming to abortion are depicted as two-sided arguments, when in fact most Americans' views lie somewhere in the middle. Partisanship makes gridlock in Washington the norm. Even in our personal relationships, a "let it all hang out" philosophy emphasizes people expressing their anger without giving them constructive ways of settling differences.

SOMETIMES YOU HAVE TO FIGHT

6. There are times when it is necessary and right to fight—to defend your country or yourself, to argue for your rights or against offensive or dangerous ideas or actions. What's wrong with the argument culture is the ubiquity, the knee-jerk nature of approaching any issue, problem or public person in an adversarial way.

7. Our determination to pursue truth by setting up a fight between two sides leads us to assume that every issue has two sides—no more, no less.

But if you always assume there must be an "other side," you may end up scouring the margins of science or the fringes of lunacy to find it.

8   This accounts, in part, for the bizarre phenomenon of Holocaust denial. Deniers, as Emory University professor Deborah Lipstadt shows, have been successful in gaining TV air time and campus newspaper coverage by masquerading as "the other side" in a "debate." Continual reference to "the other side" results in a conviction that everything has another side—and people begin to doubt the existence of any facts at all.

9   The power of words to shape perception has been proved by researchers in controlled experiments. Psychologists Elizabeth Loftus and John Palmer, for example, found that the terms in which people are asked to recall something affect what they recall. The researchers showed subjects a film of two cars colliding, then asked how fast the cars were going; one week later they asked whether there had been any broken glass. Some subjects were asked, "How fast were the cars going when they bumped into each other?" Others were asked, "How fast were the cars going when they smashed into each other?"

10   Those who read the question with "smashed" tended to "remember" that the cars were going faster. They were also more likely to "remember" having seen broken glass. (There wasn't any.) This is how language works. It invisibly molds our way of thinking about people, actions and the world around us.

11   In the argument culture, "critical" thinking is synonymous with criticizing. In many classrooms, students are encouraged to read someone's life work, then rip it to shreds.

12   When debates and fighting predominate, those who enjoy verbal sparring are likely to take part—by calling in to talk shows or writing letters to the editor. Those who aren't comfortable with oppositional discourse are likely to opt out.

HOW HIGH-TECH COMMUNICATION PULLS US APART

13   One of the most effective ways to defuse antagonism between two groups is to provide a forum for individuals from those groups to get to know each other personally. What is happening in our lives, however, is just the opposite. More and more of our communication is not face to face, and not with people we know. The proliferation and increasing portability of technology isolates people in a bubble.

14   Along with the voices of family members and friends, phone lines bring into our homes the annoying voices of solicitors who want to sell something—generally at dinnertime. (My father-in-law startles phone solicitors by saying, "We're eating dinner, but I'll call you back. What's

your home phone number?" To the nonplused caller, he explains, "Well, you're calling me at home; I thought I'd call you at home, too.")

15   It is common for families to have more than one TV, so the adults can watch what they like in one room and the kids can watch their choice in another—or maybe each child has a private TV.

16   E-mail, and now the Internet, are creating networks of human connection unthinkable even a few years ago. Though e-mail has enhanced communication with family and friends, it also ratchets up the anonymity of both sender and receiver, resulting in stranger-to-stranger "flaming."

17   "Road rage" shows how dangerous the argument culture—and especially today's technologically enhanced aggression—can be. Two men who engage in a shouting match may not come to blows, but if they express their anger while driving down a public highway, the risk to themselves and others soars.

THE ARGUMENT CULTURE SHAPES WHO WE ARE

18   The argument culture has a defining impact on our lives and on our culture

- **It makes us distort facts,** as in the Nancy Kerrigan-Tonya Harding story. After the original attack on Kerrigan's knee, news stories focused on the rivalry between the two skaters instead of portraying Kerrigan as the victim of an attack. Just last month, *Time* magazine called the event a "contretemps" between Kerrigan and Harding. And a recent joint TV interview of the two skaters reinforced that skewed image by putting the two on equal footing, rather than as victim and accused.
- **It makes us waste valuable time,** as in the case of scientist Robert Gallo, who co-discovered the AIDS virus. Gallo was the object of a groundless four-year investigation into allegations he had stolen the virus from another scientist. He was ultimately exonerated, but the toll was enormous. Never mind that, in his words, "These were the most painful and horrible years of my life." Gallo spent four years fighting accusations instead of fighting AIDS.
- **It limits our thinking.** Headlines are intentionally devised to attract attention, but the language of extremes actually shapes, and misshapes, the way we think about things. Military metaphors train us to think about, and see, everything in terms of fighting, conflict and war. Adversarial rhetoric is a kind of verbal inflation—a rhetorical boy-who-cried-wolf.
- **It encourages us to lie.** If you fight to win, the temptation is great to deny facts that support your opponent's views and say only what supports your side. It encourages people to misrepresent and, in the extreme, to lie.

...*continued* The Argument Culture, **Deborah Tannen**

END THE ARGUMENT CULTURE BY LOOKING AT ALL SIDES

19   How can we overcome our classically American habit of seeing issues in absolutes? We must expand our notion of "debate" to include more dialogue. To do this, we can make special efforts not to think in twos. Mary Catherine Bateson, an anthropologist at Virginia's George Mason University, makes a point of having her class compare three cultures, not two. Then, students are more likely to think about each on its own terms, rather than as opposites.

20   In the public arena, television and radio producers can try to avoid, whenever possible, structuring public discussions as debates. This means avoiding the format of having two guests discuss an issue. Invite three guests—or one. Perhaps it is time to re-examine the assumption that audiences always prefer a fight.

21   Instead of asking, "What's the other side?" we might ask, "What are the other sides?" Instead of insisting on hearing "both sides," let's insist on hearing "all sides."

22   We need to find metaphors other than sports and war. Smashing heads does not open minds. We need to use our imaginations and ingenuity to find different ways to seek truth and gain knowledge through intellectual interchange, and add them to our arsenal—or, should I say, to the ingredients for our stew. It will take creativity for each of us to find ways to change the argument culture to a dialogue culture. It's an effort we have to make, because our public and private lives are at stake.

Homophobic? Read Your Bible

Peter J. Gomes

Peter J. Gomes (1942–) is an American Baptist minister. Widely regarded as one of the most distinguished preachers in the nation, he has served since 1970 in the Memorial Church at Harvard University. Since 1974 he has been Plummer Professor of Christian Morals at Harvard Divinity School as well. On September 15, 2008, he appeared on The Colbert Report *to promote his most recent book,* The Scandalous Gospel of Jesus, *and that same year he was featured by Henry Louis Gates on the PBS documentary* African American Lives. *He wrote the following essay for the* New York Times *in 1992.*

1   Opposition to gays' civil rights has become one of the most visible symbols of American civic conflict this year, and religion has become the weapon of choice. The army of the discontented, eager for clear villains and simple solutions and ready for a crusade in which political self-

The Reverend Peter J. Gomes

interest and social anxiety can be cloaked in morality, has found hatred of homosexuality to be the last respectable prejudice of the century.

2   Ballot initiatives in Oregon and Maine would deny homosexuals the protection of civil rights laws. The Pentagon has steadfastly refused to allow gays into the armed forces. Vice President Dan Quayle is crusading for "traditional family values." And Pat Buchanan, who is scheduled to speak at the Republican National Convention this evening, regards homosexuality as a litmus test of moral purity.

3   Nothing has illuminated this crusade more effectively than a work of fiction, *The Drowning of Stephan Jones*, by Bette Greene. Preparing for her novel, Ms. Greene interviewed more than 400 young men incarcerated for gay-bashing, and scrutinized their case studies. In an interview published in *The Boston Globe* this spring, she said she found that the gay-bashers generally saw nothing wrong in what they did, and, more often than not, said their religious leaders and traditions sanctioned their behavior. One convicted teen-age gay-basher told her that the pastor of his church had said, "Homosexuals represent the devil, Satan," and that the Rev. Jerry Falwell had echoed that charge.

4   Christians opposed to political and social equality for homosexuals nearly always appeal to the moral injunctions of the Bible, claiming that Scripture is very clear on the matter and citing verses that support their

opinion. They accuse others of perverting and distorting texts contrary to their "clear" meaning. They do not, however, necessarily see quite as clear a meaning in biblical passages on economic conduct, the burdens of wealth, and the sin of greed.

5   Nine biblical citations are customarily invoked as relating to homosexuality. Four (Deuteronomy 23:17, I Kings 14:24, I Kings 22:46, and II Kings 23:7) simply forbid prostitution, by men and women.

6   Two others (Leviticus 18:19–23 and Leviticus 20:10–16) are part of what biblical scholars call the Holiness Code. The code explicitly bans homosexual acts. But it also prohibits eating raw meat, planting two different kinds of seed in the same field, and wearing garments with two different kinds of yarn. Tattoos, adultery, and sexual intercourse during a woman's menstrual period are similarly outlawed.

7   There is no mention of homosexuality in the four Gospels of the New Testament. The moral teachings of Jesus are not concerned with the subject.

8   Three references from St. Paul are frequently cited (Romans 1:26–2:1, I Corinthians 6:9–11, and I Timothy 1:10). But St. Paul was concerned with homosexuality only because in Greco-Roman culture it represented a secular sensuality that was contrary to his Jewish-Christian spiritual idealism. He was against lust and sensuality in anyone, including heterosexuals. To say that homosexuality is bad because homosexuals are tempted to do morally doubtful things is to say that heterosexuality is bad because heterosexuals are likewise tempted. For St. Paul, anyone who puts his or her interest ahead of God's is condemned, a verdict that falls equally upon everyone.

9   And lest we forget Sodom and Gomorrah, recall that the story is not about sexual perversion and homosexual practice. It is about inhospitality, according to Luke 10:10–13, and failure to care for the poor, according to Ezekiel 16:49–50: "Behold, this was the iniquity of thy sister Sodom, pride, fullness of bread, and abundance of idleness was in her and in her daughters, neither did she strengthen the hand of the poor and needy." To suggest that Sodom and Gomorrah is about homosexual sex is an analysis of about as much worth as suggesting that the story of Jonah and the whale is a treatise on fishing.

10   Part of the problem is a question of interpretation. Fundamentalists and literalists, the storm troopers of the religious right, are terrified that Scripture, "wrongly interpreted," may separate them from their values. That fear stems from their own recognition that their "values" are not derived from Scripture, as they publicly claim. Indeed, it is through the lens of their own prejudices that they "read" Scripture and cloak their own views in its authority. We all interpret Scripture: Make no mistake. And no one truly is a literalist, despite the pious temptation. The ques-

tions are, By what principle of interpretation do we proceed, and by what means do we reconcile "what it meant then" to "what it means now"?

11   These matters are far too important to be left to scholars and seminarians alone. Our ability to judge ourselves and others rests on our ability to interpret Scripture intelligently. The right use of the Bible, an exercise as old as the church itself, means that we confront our prejudices rather than merely confirm them.

12   For Christians, the principle by which Scripture is read is nothing less than an appreciation of the work and will of God as revealed in that of Jesus. To recover a liberating and inclusive Christ is to be freed from the semantic bondage that makes us curators of a dead culture rather than creatures of a new creation.

13   Religious fundamentalism is dangerous because it cannot accept ambiguity and diversity and is therefore inherently intolerant. Such intolerance, in the name of virtue, is ruthless and uses political power to destroy what it cannot convert. It is dangerous, especially in America, because it is antidemocratic and is suspicious of "the other," in whatever form that "other" might appear. To maintain itself, fundamentalism must always define "the other" as deviant.

14   But the chief reason that fundamentalism is dangerous is that, at the hands of the Rev. Pat Robertson, the Rev. Jerry Falwell, and hundreds of lesser-known but equally worrisome clerics, preachers, and pundits, it uses Scripture and the Christian practice to encourage ordinarily good people to act upon their fears rather than their virtues. Fortunately, those who speak for the religious right do not speak for all American Christians, and the Bible is not theirs alone to interpret. The same Bible that the advocates of slavery used to protect their wicked self-interests is the Bible that inspired slaves to revolt and their liberators to action. The same Bible that the predecessors of Mr. Falwell and Mr. Robertson used to keep white churches white is the source of the inspiration of the Rev. Martin Luther King, Jr., and the social reformation of the 1960's. The same Bible that antifeminists use to keep women silent in the churches is the Bible that preaches liberation to captives and says that in Christ there is neither male nor female, slave nor free.

15   And the same Bible that on the basis of an archaic social code of ancient Israel and a tortured reading of Paul is used to condemn all homosexuals and homosexual behavior includes metaphors of redemption, renewal, inclusion, and love—principles that invite homosexuals to accept their freedom and responsibility in Christ and demands that their fellow Christians accept them as well.

16   The political piety of the fundamentalist religious right must not be exercised at the expense of our precious freedoms. And in this summer of our discontent, one of the most precious freedoms for which we must all fight is freedom from this last prejudice.

Proposed Amendment to the U.S. Constitution

U.S. Congress

108th CONGRESS, 1st Session

RESOLUTION 56 Proposing an amendment to the Constitution of the United States relating to marriage.

Resolved by the Senate and House of Representatives of the United States of America in Congress assembled (two-thirds of each House concurring therein). That the following article is proposed as an amendment to the Constitution of the United States, which shall be valid to all intents and purposes as part of the Constitution when ratified by the legislatures of three-fourths of the several States within seven years after the date of its submission for ratification:

"Article—

"SECTION 1. Marriage in the United States shall consist only of the union of a man and a woman. Neither this Constitution or the constitution of any State, nor state or federal law, shall be construed to require that marital status or the legal incidents thereof be conferred upon unmarried couples or groups."

The Defense of Marriage Act

House of Representatives

Congress of the United States
House of Representatives
AS INTRODUCED ON MAY 7, 1996

SUMMARY OF THE ACT

1   The Defense of Marriage Act (DOMA) does two things. First, it provides that no State shall be required to give effect to a law of any other State with respect to a same-sex "marriage." Second, it defines the words "marriage" and "spouse" for purposes of Federal law.

2   The first substantive section of the bill is an exercise of Congress' power under the "Effect" clause of Article IV, section I of the Constitution (the Full Faith and Credit Clause) to allow each State (or other political jurisdiction) to decide for itself whether it wants to grant legal status to same-sex "marriage." This provision is necessary in light of the possibility of Hawaii giving sanction to same-sex "marriage" under its state

law, as interpreted by its state courts, and other states being placed in the position of having to give "full faith and credit" to Hawaii's interpretation of what constitutes "marriage." Although so-called "conflicts of law" principles do not necessarily compel such a result, approximately 30 states of the union are sufficiently alarmed by such a prospect to have initiated legislative efforts to defend themselves against any compulsion to acknowledge same sex "marriage."

3   This is a problem most properly resolved by invoking Congress' authority under the Constitution to declare what "effect" one State's acts, records, and judicial proceedings shall have in another State. Congress has invoked this authority recently on two other occasions: in the Parental Kidnapping Prevention Act of 1980, which required each State to enforce child custody determinations made by the home State if made consistently with the provisions of the Act; and in the Full Faith and Credit for Child Support Order Act of 1994, which required each State to enforce child support orders made by the child's State if made consistently with the provisions of the Act.

4   The second substantive section of the bill amends the U.S. Code to make explicit what has been understood under federal law for over 200 years: that a marriage is the legal union of a man and a woman as husband and wife, and a spouse is a husband or wife of the opposite sex. The DOMA definition of marriage is derived most immediately from a Washington state case from 1974, Singer v. Hara, which is included in the 1990 edition of Black's Law Dictionary. More than a century ago, the U.S. Supreme Court spoke of the "union for life of one man and one woman in the holy estate of matrimony." Murphy v. Ramsey, 114 U.S. 15, 45 (1885).

5   DOMA is not meant to affect the definition of "spouse" (which under the Social Security law, for example, runs to dozens of lines). It ensures that whatever definition of "spouse" may be used in Federal law, the word refers only to a person of the opposite sex.

PROVISIONS OF THE ACT

4th CONGRESS 2D SESSION
H.R. 3396

IN THE HOUSE OF REPRESENTATIVES

Mr. BARR of Georgia (for himself, Mr. LARGENT, Mr. SENSENBRENNER, Ms. MYRICK, Mr. VOLKMER, Mr. SKELTON, Mr. BRYANT, and Mr. EMERSON) introduced the following bill, which was referred to the Committee

A BILL To define and protect the institution of marriage.

Be it enacted by the Senate and House of Representatives of the United States of America in Congress assembled,

...*continued* The Defense of Marriage Act, **House of Representatives**

SECTION 1. SHORT TITLE.

This Act may be cited as the "Defense of Marriage Act."

SECTION 2. POWERS RESERVED TO THE STATES.

(a) IN GENERAL.—Chapter 115 of title 28, United States Code, is amended by adding after section 1738B the following:

Section 1738C. Certain acts, records, and proceedings and the effect thereof "No State, territory, or possession of the United States, or Indian tribe, shall be required to give effect to any public act, record, or judicial proceeding of any other State, territory, possession, or tribe respecting a relationship between persons of the same sex that is treated as a marriage under the laws of such other State, territory, possession, or tribe, or a right or claim arising from such relationship."

(b) CLERICAL AMENDMENT.—The table of sections at the beginning of Chapter 115 of title 28, United States Code, is amended by inserting after the item relating to section 1738B the following new item: "1738C. Certain acts, records, and proceedings and the effect thereof."

SECTION 3. DEFINITION OF MARRIAGE.

(a) IN GENERAL.—Chapter 1 of title 1, United States Code, is amended by adding at the end the following:

"Section 7. Definition of 'marriage' and 'spouse'

"In determining the meaning of any Act of Congress, or of any ruling, regulation, or interpretation of the various administrative bureaus and agencies of the United States, the word 'marriage' means only a legal union between one man and one woman as husband and wife, and the word 'spouse' refers only to a person of the opposite sex who is a husband or a wife."

The Conservative Case for Gay Marriage

Theodore Olson

1   Together with my good friend and occasional courtroom adversary David Boies, I am attempting to persuade a federal court to invalidate California's Proposition 8—the voter-approved measure that over-turned California's constitutional right to marry a person of the same sex.

2   My involvement in this case has generated a certain degree of consternation among conservatives. How could a politically active, lifelong Republican, a veteran of the Ronald Reagan and George W. Bush administrations, challenge the "traditional" definition of marriage and press for an "activist" interpretation of the Constitution to create another "new" constitutional right?

3   My answer to this seeming conundrum rests on a lifetime of exposure to persons of different backgrounds, histories, viewpoints, and intrinsic characteristics, and on my rejection of what I see as superficially appealing but ultimately false perceptions about our Constitution and its protection of equality and fundamental rights.

4   Many of my fellow conservatives have an almost knee-jerk hostility toward gay marriage. This does not make sense, because same-sex unions promote the values conservatives prize. Marriage is one of the basic building blocks of our neighborhoods and our nation. At its best, it is a stable bond between two individuals who work to create a loving household and a social and economic partnership. We encourage couples to marry because the commitments they make to one another provide benefits not only to themselves but also to their families and communities. Marriage requires thinking beyond one's own needs. It transforms two individuals into a union based on shared aspirations, and in doing so establishes a formal investment in the well-being of society. The fact that individuals who happen to be gay want to share in this vital social institution is evidence that conservative ideals enjoy widespread acceptance. Conservatives should celebrate this, rather than lament it.

5   Legalizing same-sex marriage would also be a recognition of basic American principles, and would represent the culmination of our nation's commitment to equal rights. It is, some have said, the last major civil-rights milestone yet to be surpassed in our two-century struggle to attain the goals we set for this nation at its formation.

6   This bedrock American principle of equality is central to the political and legal convictions of Republicans, Democrats, liberals, and conservatives alike. The dream that became America began with the revolutionary concept expressed in the Declaration of Independence in words that are among the most noble and elegant ever written: "We hold these truths to be self-evident, that all men are created equal, that they are endowed by their Creator with certain unalienable Rights, that among these are Life, Liberty and the pursuit of Happiness."

7   Sadly, our nation has taken a long time to live up to the promise of equality. In 1857, the Supreme Court held that an African-American could not be a citizen. During the ensuing Civil War, Abraham Lincoln eloquently reminded the nation of its founding principle: "our fathers brought forth on this continent, a new nation, conceived in liberty and dedicated to the proposition that all men are created equal." At the end of the Civil War, to make the elusive promise of equality a reality, the 14th

Amendment to the Constitution added the command that "no State shall deprive any person of life, liberty or property, without due process of law; nor deny to any person the equal protection of the laws."

8   Subsequent laws and court decisions have made clear that equality under the law extends to persons of all races, religions, and places of origin. What better way to make this national aspiration complete than to apply the same protection to men and women who differ from others only on the basis of their sexual orientation? I cannot think of a single reason—and have not heard one since I undertook this venture—for continued discrimination against decent, hardworking members of our society on that basis.

9   Various federal and state laws have accorded certain rights and privileges to gay and lesbian couples, but these protections vary dramatically at the state level, and nearly universally deny true equality to gays and lesbians who wish to marry. The very idea of marriage is basic to recognition as equals in our society; any status short of that is inferior, unjust, and unconstitutional.

10   The United States Supreme Court has repeatedly held that marriage is one of the most fundamental rights that we have as Americans under our Constitution. It is an expression of our desire to create a social partnership, to live and share life's joys and burdens with the person we love, and to form a lasting bond and a social identity. The Supreme Court has said that marriage is a part of the Constitution's protections of liberty, privacy, freedom of association, and spiritual identification. In short, the right to marry helps us to define ourselves and our place in a community. Without it, there can be no true equality under the law.

11   It is true that marriage in this nation traditionally has been regarded as a relationship exclusively between a man and a woman, and many of our nation's multiple religions define marriage in precisely those terms. But while the Supreme Court has always previously considered marriage in that context, the underlying rights and liberties that marriage embodies are not in any way confined to heterosexuals.

12   Marriage is a civil bond in this country as well as, in some (but hardly all) cases, a religious sacrament. It is a relationship recognized by governments as providing a privileged and respected status, entitled to the state's support and benefits. The California Supreme Court described marriage as a "union unreservedly approved and favored by the community." Where the state has accorded official sanction to a relationship and provided special benefits to those who enter into that relationship, our courts have insisted that withholding that status requires powerful justifications and may not be arbitrarily denied.

13 What, then, are the justifications for California's decision in Proposition 8 to withdraw access to the institution of marriage for some of its citizens on the basis of their sexual orientation? The reasons I have heard are not very persuasive.

14 The explanation mentioned most often is tradition. But simply because something has always been done a certain way does not mean that it must always remain that way. Otherwise we would still have segregated schools and debtors' prisons. Gays and lesbians have always been among us, forming a part of our society, and they have lived as couples in our neighborhoods and communities. For a long time, they have experienced discrimination and even persecution; but we, as a society, are starting to become more tolerant, accepting, and understanding. California and many other states have allowed gays and lesbians to form domestic partnerships (or civil unions) with most of the rights of married heterosexuals. Thus, gay and lesbian individuals are now permitted to live together in state-sanctioned relationships. It therefore seems anomalous to cite "tradition" as a justification for withholding the status of marriage and thus to continue to label those relationships as less worthy, less sanctioned, or less legitimate.

15 The second argument I often hear is that traditional marriage furthers the state's interest in procreation—and that opening marriage to same-sex couples would dilute, diminish, and devalue this goal. But that is plainly not the case. Preventing lesbians and gays from marrying does not cause more heterosexuals to marry and conceive more children. Likewise, allowing gays and lesbians to marry someone of the same sex will not discourage heterosexuals from marrying a person of the opposite sex. How, then, would allowing same-sex marriages reduce the number of children that heterosexual couples conceive? This procreation argument cannot be taken seriously. We do not inquire whether heterosexual couples intend to bear children, or have the capacity to have children, before we allow them to marry. We permit marriage by the elderly, by prison inmates, and by persons who have no intention of having children. What's more, it is pernicious to think marriage should be limited to heterosexuals because of the state's desire to promote procreation. We would surely not accept as constitutional a ban on marriage if a state were to decide, as China has done, to discourage procreation.

16 Another argument, vaguer and even less persuasive, is that gay marriage somehow does harm to heterosexual marriage. I have yet to meet anyone who can explain to me what this means. In what way would allowing same-sex partners to marry diminish the marriages of heterosexual couples? Tellingly, when the judge in our case asked our opponent to identify the ways in which same-sex marriage would harm heterosexual marriage, to his credit he answered honestly: he could not think of any.

...*continued* The Conservative Case for Gay Marriage, **Theodore Olson**

17   The simple fact is that there is no good reason why we should deny marriage to same-sex partners. On the other hand, there are many reasons why we should formally recognize these relationships and embrace the rights of gays and lesbians to marry and become full and equal members of our society.

18   No matter what you think of homosexuality, it is a fact that gays and lesbians are members of our families, clubs, and workplaces. They are our doctors, our teachers, our soldiers (whether we admit it or not), and our friends. They yearn for acceptance, stable relationships, and success in their lives, just like the rest of us.

19   Conservatives and liberals alike need to come together on principles that surely unite us. Certainly, we can agree on the value of strong families, lasting domestic relationships, and communities populated by persons with recognized and sanctioned bonds to one another. Confining some of our neighbors and friends who share these same values to an outlaw or second-class status undermines their sense of belonging and weakens their ties with the rest of us and what should be our common aspirations. Even those whose religious convictions preclude endorsement of what they may perceive as an unacceptable "lifestyle" should recognize that disapproval should not warrant stigmatization and unequal treatment.

20   When we refuse to accord this status to gays and lesbians, we discourage them from forming the same relationships we encourage for others. And we are also telling them, those who love them, and society as a whole that their relationships are less worthy, less legitimate, less permanent, and less valued. We demean their relationships and we demean them as individuals. I cannot imagine how we benefit as a society by doing so.

21   I understand, but reject, certain religious teachings that denounce homosexuality as morally wrong, illegitimate, or unnatural; and I take strong exception to those who argue that same-sex relationships should be discouraged by society and law. Science has taught us, even if history has not, that gays and lesbians do not choose to be homosexual any more than the rest of us choose to be heterosexual. To a very large extent, these characteristics are immutable, like being left-handed. And, while our Constitution guarantees the freedom to exercise our individual religious convictions, it equally prohibits us from forcing our beliefs on others. I do not believe that our society can ever live up to the promise of equality, and the fundamental rights to life, liberty, and the pursuit of happiness, until we stop invidious discrimination on the basis of sexual orientation.

22   If we are born heterosexual, it is not unusual for us to perceive those who are born homosexual as aberrational and threatening. Many religions and much of our social culture have reinforced those impulses. Too often, that has led to prejudice, hostility, and discrimination. The antidote is understanding, and reason. We once tolerated laws throughout this nation that prohibited marriage between persons of different races. California's Supreme Court was the first to find that discrimination unconstitutional. The U.S. Supreme Court unanimously agreed 20 years later, in 1967, in a case called *Loving v. Virginia*. It seems inconceivable today that only 40 years ago there were places in this country where a black woman could not legally marry a white man. And it was only 50 years ago that 17 states mandated segregated public education—until the Supreme Court unanimously struck down that practice in *Brown v. Board of Education.* Most Americans are proud of these decisions and the fact that the discriminatory state laws that spawned them have been discredited. I am convinced that Americans will be equally proud when we no longer discriminate against gays and lesbians and welcome them into our society.

Evan's Two Moms

Anna Quindlen

1   Evan has two moms. This is no big thing. Evan has always had two moms in his school file, on his emergency forms, with his friends. "Ooooh, Evan, you're lucky," they sometimes say. "You have two moms." It sounds like a sitcom, but until last week it was emotional truth without legal bulwark. That was when a judge in New York approved the adoption of a six-year-old boy by his biological mother's lesbian partner. Evan. Evan's mom. Evan's other mom. A kid, a psychologist, a pediatrician. A family.

2   The matter of Evan's two moms is one in a series of events over the last year that led to certain conclusions. A Minnesota appeals court granted guardianship of a woman left a quadriplegic in a car accident to her lesbian lover, the culmination of a seven-year battle in which the injured woman's parents did everything possible to negate the partnership between the two. A lawyer in Georgia had her job offer withdrawn after the state attorney general found out that she and her lesbian lover were planning a marriage ceremony: she's brought suit. The computer

...*continued* Evan's Two Moms, **Anna Quindlen**

company Lotus announced that the gay partners of employees would be eligible for the same benefits as spouses.

3   Add to these public events the private struggles, the couples who go from lawyer to lawyer to approximate legal protections their straight counterparts take for granted, the AIDS survivors who find themselves shut out of their partners' dying days by biological family members and shut out of their apartments by leases with a single name on the dotted line, and one solution is obvious.

4   Gay marriage is a radical notion for straight people and a conservative notion for gay ones. After years of being sledge-hammered by society, some gay men and lesbian women are deeply suspicious of participating in an institution that seems to have "straight world" written all over it.

5   But the rads of twenty years ago, straight and gay alike, have other things on their minds today. Family is one, and the linchpin of family has commonly been a loving commitment between two adults. When same-sex couples set out to make that commitment, they discover that they are at a disadvantage: No joint tax returns. No health insurance coverage for an uninsured partner. No survivor's benefits from Social Security. None of the automatic rights, privileges, and responsibilities society attaches to a marriage contract. In Madison, Wisconsin, a couple who applied at the Y with their kids for a family membership were turned down because both were women. It's one of those small things that can make you feel small.

6   Some took marriage statutes that refer to "two persons" at their word and applied for a license. The results were court decisions that quoted the Bible and embraced circular argument: marriage is by definition the union of a man and a woman because that is how we've defined it.

7   No religion should be forced to marry anyone in violation of its tenets, although ironically it is now only in religious ceremonies that gay people can marry, performed by clergy who find the blessing of two who love each other no sin. But there is no secular reason that we should take a patchwork approach of corporate, governmental, and legal steps to guarantee what can be done simply, economically, conclusively, and inclusively with the words "I do."

8   "Fran and I chose to get married for the same reasons that any two people do," said the lawyer who was fired in Georgia. "We fell in love; we wanted to spend our lives together." Pretty simple.

9   Consider the case of *Loving v. Virginia*, aptly named. At the time, sixteen states had laws that barred interracial marriage, relying on natural

law, that amorphous grab bag for justifying prejudice. Sounding a little like God throwing Adam and Eve out of paradise, the trial judge suspended the one-year sentence of Richard Loving, who was white, and his wife, Mildred, who was black, provided they got out of the State of Virginia.

10   In 1967 the Supreme Court found such laws to be unconstitutional. Only twenty-five years ago it was a crime for a black woman to marry a white man. Perhaps twenty-five years from now we will find it just as incredible that two people of the same sex were not entitled to legally commit themselves to each other. Love and commitment are rare enough; it seems absurd to thwart them in any guise.

A Gay-Marriage Solution: End Marriage?

Michael Lindenberger

1   When a Jewish boy turns 13, he heads to a temple for a deeply meaningful rite of passage, his bar mitzvah. When a Catholic girl reaches about the same age, she stands in front of the local bishop, who touches her forehead with holy oil as she is confirmed into a 2,000-year-old faith tradition. But missing in each of those cases—and in countless others of equal religious importance—is any role for government. There is no baptism certificate issued by the local courthouse and no federal tax benefit attached to the confessional booth, the into-the-water-and-out born-again ceremony, or any of the other sacraments that believers hold sacred.

2   Only marriage gets that treatment, and it's a tradition that some legal scholars have been arguing should be abandoned. In a paper published March 2 in the San Francisco *Chronicle*, two law professors from Pepperdine University issued a call to re-examine the role the government plays in marriage. The authors—one of whom voted for and one against Proposition 8, which ended gay marriage in California—say the best way out of the intractable legal wars over gay marriage is to take marriage out of the hands of the government altogether.

3   Instead, give gay and straight couples alike the same license, a certificate confirming them as a family, and call it a civil union—anything, really, other than marriage. For people who feel the word *marriage* is important, the next stop after the courthouse could be the church, where they could bless their union with all the religious ceremony they wanted.

...continued A Gay-Marriage Solution: End Marriage?, **Michael Lindenberger**

Religions would lose nothing of their role in sanctioning the kinds of unions that they find in keeping with their tenets. And for nonbelievers and those who find the word *marriage* less important, the civil-union license issued by the state would be all they needed to unlock the benefits reserved in most states and in federal law for married couples.

4   "While new terminology for all may at first seem awkward—mostly in greeting-card shops—[it] dovetails with the court's important responsibility to reaffirm the unfettered freedom of all faiths to extend the nomenclature of marriage as their traditions allow," wrote Douglas W. Kmiec and Shelley Ross Saxer. Kmiec voted for Prop 8 because of his belief in the teachings of the Catholic Church and his notion of religious liberty but has since said he thinks the courts should not allow one group of Californians to marry while denying the privilege to others.

5   Their idea got a big boost three days later, during the March 5 oral arguments before the California Supreme Court, which is expected to issue a ruling soon in the case brought by gay couples and others who argue the constitutional amendment passed by voters last fall should be invalidated. Justice Ming Chin asked attorneys for each side whether the idea would solve the legal issues connected to gay marriage—issues that at their core revolve around the question of whether allowing some couples to marry but not others violates constitutional guarantees of equal protection under the law.

6   Both sets of lawyers agreed that the idea would resolve the equal-protection issue. Take the state out of the marriage business, and then both kinds of couples—straight and gay—would be treated the same. Even Ken Starr, the Pepperdine law dean and former Whitewater independent counsel who argued in favor of Prop 8, agreed that the idea would solve the legal issues, though he said it was a solution that lies outside the legal authority of the court. An attorney for the other side, Michael Maroko, didn't expressly endorse the idea, but he told Chin, "If you're in the marriage business, do it equally. And if you're not going to do it equally, get out of the business."

7   The two Pepperdine professors are arguing that the court should use that line of thinking in crafting its decision in the case before it, short-circuiting the need for a new referendum. Their proposal is aimed at helping speed a resolution on the issue in other states—gay marriage is heating up in Iowa, Connecticut, Vermont and elsewhere—and at the federal level. All sides on the debate expect the issues bubbling up out of the state courts and legislatures to eventually gain traction in federal courts too, ultimately leading to a case before the Supreme Court or efforts to amend the U.S. Constitution or both.

8   But as Solomonic as the compromise seems, giving up the word *marriage* may be impossible. For many couples joined in matrimony,

having the state no longer call them married may make them feel as if something important had been taken away—even if it's hard to define just what was lost. And for many others—the folks who feel most strongly about marriage and most passionately supported the expensive campaign to defeat gay marriage—the issue of nomenclature is only the beginning. They are against not just gay marriage but also gay couples—and especially against government sanctioning of those relationships, no matter what they are called.

9   And as Chin considers whether he can craft a compromise with his fellow justices that would both uphold Prop 8—and therefore the right of the people to amend the state constitution—and assert the right of gay people to be treated equally, he may find that the folks who cling hardest to *marriage* are gay couples. After all, what was the most sweeping part of the May 2008 decision Ming and his colleagues issued that granted gays the right to marry? It was the idea that the word *marriage* is so strong that denying it to gay couples violates the most sacred right enshrined in the state constitution: the right for all people to be treated with dignity and fairness. Just 10 months later, gay couples—whether or not they are among the 18,000 who married in the state before Prop 8 stopped the ceremonies—are loath to lose a word for which so many fought so hard and so long to have apply to themselves.

10   But the Pepperdine idea puts into a play a new way of thinking—and whether it's part of the court's decision in the Prop 8 case or whether it makes its way into a new referendum, the idea of getting governments out of the marriage business offers a creative way of thinking about a problem that is otherwise likely to be around for a long, long time.

A Robot in Every Home

Bill Gates

From 1995 to 2009, Bill Gates had been ranked by Forbes *magazine as the richest person in the world (he has now "fallen" to number 2). Best known for his role with Microsoft, the company he cofounded with Paul Allen, Gates now serves as the primary stockholder for that corporation. He spends most of his time doing philanthropic work with the Gates Foundation, which he and his wife, Melinda, founded in 2000. In "A Robot in Every Home," which first appeared in the December 2006 issue of* Scientific American, *Gates waxes enthusiastic and optimistic about the prospect of bringing robotics into every American household—much as Microsoft did with personal computers.*

...continued A Robot in Every Home, **Bill Gates**

1   Imagine being present at the birth of a new industry. It is an industry based on groundbreaking new technologies, wherein a handful of well-established corporations sell highly specialized devices for business use and a fast-growing number of start-up companies produce innovative toys, gadgets for hobbyists and other interesting niche products. But it is also a highly fragmented industry with few common standards or platforms. Projects are complex, progress is slow, and practical applications are relatively rare. In fact, for all the excitement and promise, no one can say with any certainty when—or even if—this industry will achieve critical mass. If it does, though, it may well change the world.

2   Of course, the paragraph above could be a description of the computer industry during the mid-1970s, around the time that Paul Allen and I launched Microsoft. Back then, big, expensive mainframe computers ran the back-office operations for major companies, governmental departments and other institutions. Researchers at leading universities and industrial laboratories were creating the basic building blocks that would make the information age possible. Intel had just introduced the 8080 microprocessor, and Atari was selling the popular electronic game Pong. At homegrown computer clubs, enthusiasts struggled to figure out exactly what this new technology was good for.

3   But what I really have in mind is something much more contemporary: the emergence of the robotics industry, which is developing in much the same way that the computer business did 30 years ago. Think of the manufacturing robots currently used on automobile assembly lines as the equivalent of yesterday's mainframes. The industry's niche products include robotic arms that perform surgery, surveillance robots deployed in Iraq and Afghanistan that dispose of roadside bombs, and domestic robots that vacuum the floor. Electronics companies have made robotic toys that can imitate people or dogs or dinosaurs, and hobbyists are anxious to get their hands on the latest version of the Lego robotics system.

4   Meanwhile some of the world's best minds are trying to solve the toughest problems of robotics, such as visual recognition, navigation and machine learning. And they are succeeding. At the 2004 Defense Advanced Research Projects Agency (DARPA) Grand Challenge, a competition to produce the first robotic vehicle capable of navigating autonomously over a rugged 142-mile course through the Mojave Desert, the top competitor managed to travel just 7.4 miles before breaking down. In 2005, though, five vehicles covered the complete distance, and the race's winner did it at an average speed of 19.1 miles an hour. (In another intriguing parallel between the robotics and computer industries, DARPA also funded the work that led to the creation of Arpanet, the precursor to the Internet.)

5   What is more, the challenges facing the robotics industry are similar to those we tackled in computing three decades ago. Robotics companies have no standard operating software that could allow popular application programs to run in a variety of devices. The standardization of robotic processors and other hardware is limited, and very little of the programming code used in one machine can be applied to another. Whenever somebody wants to build a new robot, they usually have to start from square one.

6   Despite these difficulties, when I talk to people involved in robotics—from university researchers to entrepreneurs, hobbyists and high school students—the level of excitement and expectation reminds me so much of that time when Paul Allen and I looked at the convergence of new technologies and dreamed of the day when a computer would be on every desk and in every home. And as I look at the trends that are now starting to converge, I can envision a future in which robotic devices will become a nearly ubiquitous part of our day-to-day lives. I believe that technologies such as distributed computing, voice and visual recognition, and wireless broadband connectivity will open the door to a new generation of autonomous devices that enable computers to perform tasks in the physical world on our behalf. We may be on the verge of a new era, when the PC will get up off the desktop and allow us to see, hear, touch and manipulate objects in places where we are not physically present.

FROM SCIENCE FICTION TO REALITY

7   The word "robot" was popularized in 1921 by Czech playwright Karel Capek, but people have envisioned creating robot-like devices for thousands of years. In Greek and Roman mythology, the gods of metalwork built mechanical servants made from gold. In the first century A.D., Heron of Alexandria—the great engineer credited with inventing the first steam engine—designed intriguing automatons, including one said to have the ability to talk. Leonardo da Vinci's 1495 sketch of a mechanical knight, which could sit up and move its arms and legs, is considered to be the first plan for a humanoid robot.

8   Over the past century, anthropomorphic machines have become familiar figures in popular culture through books such as Isaac Asimov's *I, Robot*, movies such as *Star Wars* and television shows such as *Star Trek*. The popularity of robots in fiction indicates that people are receptive to the idea that these machines will one day walk among us as helpers and even as companions. Nevertheless, although robots play a vital role in industries such as automobile manufacturing—where there is about one robot for every 10 workers—the fact is that we have a long way to go before real robots catch up with their science-fiction counterparts.

9   One reason for this gap is that it has been much harder than expected to enable computers and robots to sense their surrounding environment

---

...*continued* A Robot in Every Home, **Bill Gates**

---

and to react quickly and accurately. It has proved extremely difficult to give robots the capabilities that humans take for granted—for example, the abilities to orient themselves with respect to the objects in a room, to respond to sounds and interpret speech, and to grasp objects of varying sizes, textures and fragility. Even something as simple as telling the difference between an open door and a window can be devilishly tricky for a robot.

10   But researchers are starting to find the answers. One trend that has helped them is the increasing availability of tremendous amounts of computer power. One megahertz of processing power, which cost more than $7,000 in 1970, can now be purchased for just pennies. The price of a megabit of storage has seen a similar decline. The access to cheap computing power has permitted scientists to work on many of the hard problems that are fundamental to making robots practical. Today, for example, voice-recognition programs can identify words quite well, but a far greater challenge will be building machines that can understand what those words mean in context. As computing capacity continues to expand, robot designers will have the processing power they need to tackle issues of ever greater complexity.

11   Another barrier to the development of robots has been the high cost of hardware, such as sensors that enable a robot to determine the distance to an object as well as motors and servos that allow the robot to manipulate an object with both strength and delicacy. But prices are dropping fast. Laser range finders that are used in robotics to measure distance with precision cost about $10,000 a few years ago; today they can be purchased for about $2,000. And new, more accurate sensors based on ultrawideband radar are available for even less.

12   Now robot builders can also add Global Positioning System chips, video cameras, array microphones (which are better than conventional microphones at distinguishing a voice from background noise) and a host of additional sensors for a reasonable expense. The resulting enhancement of capabilities, combined with expanded processing power and storage, allows today's robots to do things such as vacuum a room or help to defuse a roadside bomb—tasks that would have been impossible for commercially produced machines just a few years ago.

A BASIC APPROACH

13   In February 2004 I visited a number of leading universities, including Carnegie Mellon University, the Massachusetts Institute of Technology, Harvard University, Cornell University and the University of Illinois, to talk about the powerful role that computers can play in solving some of society's most pressing problems. My goal was to help students understand how exciting and important computer science can be, and I hoped

to encourage a few of them to think about careers in technology. At each university, after delivering my speech, I had the opportunity to get a first-hand look at some of the most interesting research projects in the school's computer science department. Almost without exception, I was shown at least one project that involved robotics.

14   At that time, my colleagues at Microsoft were also hearing from people in academia and at commercial robotics firms who wondered if our company was doing any work in robotics that might help them with their own development efforts. We were not, so we decided to take a closer look. I asked Tandy Trower, a member of my strategic staff and a 25-year Microsoft veteran, to go on an extended fact-finding mission and to speak with people across the robotics community. What he found was universal enthusiasm for the potential of robotics, along with an industry-wide desire for tools that would make development easier. "Many see the robotics industry at a technological turning point where a move to PC architecture makes more and more sense," Tandy wrote in his report to me after his fact-finding mission. "As Red Whittaker, leader of [Carnegie Mellon's] entry in the DARPA Grand Challenge, recently indicated, the hardware capability is mostly there; now the issue is getting the software right."

15   Back in the early days of the personal computer, we realized that we needed an ingredient that would allow all of the pioneering work to achieve critical mass, to coalesce into a real industry capable of producing truly useful products on a commercial scale. What was needed, it turned out, was Microsoft BASIC. When we created this programming language in the 1970s, we provided the common foundation that enabled programs developed for one set of hardware to run on another. BASIC also made computer programming much easier, which brought more and more people into the industry. Although a great many individuals made essential contributions to the development of the personal computer, Microsoft BASIC was one of the key catalysts for the software and hardware innovations that made the PC revolution possible.

16   After reading Tandy's report, it seemed clear to me that before the robotics industry could make the same kind of quantum leap that the PC industry made 30 years ago, it, too, needed to find that missing ingredient. So I asked him to assemble a small team that would work with people in the robotics field to create a set of programming tools that would provide the essential plumbing so that anybody interested in robots with even the most basic understanding of computer programming could easily write robotic applications that would work with different kinds of hardware. The goal was to see if it was possible to provide the same kind of common, low-level foundation for integrating hardware and software into robot designs that Microsoft BASIC provided for computer programmers.

...*continued* A Robot in Every Home, **Bill Gates**

17   Tandy's robotics group has been able to draw on a number of advanced technologies developed by a team working under the direction of Craig Mundie, Microsoft's chief research and strategy officer. One such technology will help solve one of the most difficult problems facing robot designers: how to simultaneously handle all the data coming in from multiple sensors and send the appropriate commands to the robot's motors, a challenge known as concurrency. A conventional approach is to write a traditional, single-threaded program—a long loop that first reads all the data from the sensors, then processes this input and finally delivers output that determines the robot's behavior, before starting the loop all over again. The shortcomings are obvious: if your robot has fresh sensor data indicating that the machine is at the edge of a precipice, but the program is still at the bottom of the loop calculating trajectory and telling the wheels to turn faster based on previous sensor input, there is a good chance the robot will fall down the stairs before it can process the new information.

18   Concurrency is a challenge that extends beyond robotics. Today as more and more applications are written for distributed networks of computers, programmers have struggled to figure out how to efficiently orchestrate code running on many different servers at the same time. And as computers with a single processor are replaced by machines with multiple processors and "multicore" processors—integrated circuits with two or more processors joined together for enhanced performance—software designers will need a new way to program desktop applications and operating systems. To fully exploit the power of processors working in parallel, the new software must deal with the problem of concurrency.

19   One approach to handling concurrency is to write multi-threaded programs that allow data to travel along many paths. But as any developer who has written multithreaded code can tell you, this is one of the hardest tasks in programming. The answer that Craig's team has devised to the concurrency problem is something called the concurrency and coordination runtime (CCR). The CCR is a library of functions—sequences of software code that perform specific tasks—that makes it easy to write multithreaded applications that can coordinate a number of simultaneous activities. Designed to help programmers take advantage of the power of multicore and multiprocessor systems, the CCR turns out to be ideal for robotics as well. By drawing on this library to write their programs, robot designers can dramatically reduce the chances that one of their creations will run into a wall because its software is too busy sending output to its wheels to read input from its sensors.

20 In addition to tackling the problem of concurrency, the work that Craig's team has done will also simplify the writing of distributed robotic applications through a technology called decentralized software services (DSS). DSS enables developers to create applications in which the services—the parts of the program that read a sensor, say, or control a motor—operate as separate processes that can be orchestrated in much the same way that text, images and information from several servers are aggregated on a Web page. Because DSS allows software components to run in isolation from one another, if an individual component of a robot fails, it can be shut down and restarted—or even replaced—without having to reboot the machine. Combined with broadband wireless technology, this architecture makes it easy to monitor and adjust a robot from a remote location using a Web browser.

21 What is more, a DSS application controlling a robotic device does not have to reside entirely on the robot itself but can be distributed across more than one computer. As a result, the robot can be a relatively inexpensive device that delegates complex processing tasks to the high-performance hardware found on today's home PCs. I believe this advance will pave the way for an entirely new class of robots that are essentially mobile, wireless peripheral devices that tap into the power of desktop PCs to handle processing-intensive tasks such as visual recognition and navigation. And because these devices can be networked together, we can expect to see the emergence of groups of robots that can work in concert to achieve goals such as mapping the seafloor or planting crops.

22 These technologies are a key part of Microsoft Robotics Studio, a new software development kit built by Tandy's team. Microsoft Robotics Studio also includes tools that make it easier to create robotic applications using a wide range of programming languages. One example is a simulation tool that lets robot builders test their applications in a three-dimensional virtual environment before trying them out in the real world. Our goal for this release is to create an affordable, open platform that allows robot developers to readily integrate hardware and software into their designs.

SHOULD WE CALL THEM ROBOTS?

23 How soon will robots become part of our day-to-day lives? According to the International Federation of Robotics, about two million personal robots were in use around the world in 2004, and another seven million will be installed by 2008. In South Korea the Ministry of Information and Communication hopes to put a robot in every home there by 2013. The Japanese Robot Association predicts that by 2025, the personal robot industry will be worth more than $50 billion a year worldwide, compared with about $5 billion today.

...continued A Robot in Every Home, **Bill Gates**

Robots like this vacuum by IRobot are already in use in households around the world.

24   As with the PC industry in the 1970s, it is impossible to predict exactly what applications will drive this new industry. It seems quite likely, however, that robots will play an important role in providing physical assistance and even companionship for the elderly. Robotic devices will probably help people with disabilities get around and extend the strength and endurance of soldiers, construction workers and medical professionals. Robots will maintain dangerous industrial machines, handle hazardous materials and monitor remote oil pipelines. They will enable health care workers to diagnose and treat patients who may be thousands of miles away, and they will be a central feature of security systems and search-and-rescue operations.

25   Although a few of the robots of tomorrow may resemble the anthropomorphic devices seen in *Star Wars*, most will look nothing like the humanoid C-3PO. In fact, as mobile peripheral devices become more and more common, it may be increasingly difficult to say exactly what a robot is. Because the new machines will be so specialized and ubiquitous—and look so little like the two-legged automatons of science fiction—we probably will not even call them robots. But as these devices become affordable to consumers, they could have just as profound an impact on the way we work, communicate, learn and entertain ourselves as the PC has had over the past 30 years.

Armchair Warlords and Robot Hordes

Paul Marks

Paul Marks is a technology correspondent for New Scientist, *an international weekly science magazine and Web site that covers issues in science and technology. In 2007, Marks won the BT IT Security Journalist of the Year Award. His portfolio included the article below, published in* New Scientist *on October 28, 2006, which examines the development of lethal robot soldiers and the risks attached to their use.*

1   It sounds like every general's dream: technology that allows a nation to fight a war with little or no loss of life on its side. It is also a peace-seeking citizen's nightmare. Without the politically embarrassing threat of soldiers returning home in flag-wrapped coffins, governments would find it far easier to commit to military action. The consequences for countries on the receiving end—and for world peace—would be immense.

2   This is not a fantasy scenario. Over the coming years, the world's most powerful military machine, the U.S. Department of Defense, aims to replace a large proportion of its armed vehicles and weaponry with robotized technologies. By 2010, a third of its "deep-strike" aircraft will be unmanned aerial vehicles (UAVs), according to a Congressional Research Service report issued in July (http://tinyurl.com/yafoht). In a further five years a similar proportion of the U.S. army's ground combat vehicles will be remote-controlled robots varying in size from supermarket carts to trucks. The U.S. navy, too, will have fleets of uncrewed boats and submarines.

3   The U.S. military is already using robots in various roles. In November 2002, for example, an armed UAV destroyed a car in Yemen carrying the suspected chief of Al-Qaida in that country, killing him and five others. In Iraq and Afghanistan, robots are proving highly successful in neutralizing roadside bombs and other small-scale explosives.

4   This is only the start. One of the next steps is to give robotic ground vehicles the attack power of UAVs, arming them with weapons such as machine guns, grenade launchers and anti-tank rockets (*New Scientist*, 21 September, p. 28). They could then be sent into places that were particularly dangerous for troops, such as booby-trapped or ambush-vulnerable buildings.

5   After that the plan is to take things to a whole new level, with unmanned planes and ground robots able to communicate with each other and act in concert. A reconnaissance UAV could signal swarms of robots to attack an enemy position, for example, or an unmanned ground vehicle might call in an air strike from UAVs.

...continued Armchair Warlords and Robot Hordes, **Paul Marks**

---

6   All uncrewed vehicles are remote-controlled at present, but the Pentagon's Office of Naval Research is planning to develop technology that it hopes will enable a robot to determine whether a person it comes across is a threat, using measures such as the remote sensing of their heartbeat—though whether these kinds of methods can be made reliable is highly questionable.

7   "Teleoperation [remote control] is the norm, but semi-autonomous enhancements are being added all the time," says Bob Quinn of Foster-Miller, a technology firm in Waltham, Massachusetts, owned by the UK defense research company Qinetiq. Foster-Miller, like its main rival iRobot, was set up by roboticists from the Massachusetts Institute of Technology. The company's armed robot, dubbed Swords, has just received U.S. army safety certification. Nevertheless, doubts remain over how reliable armed robotic devices will be, especially if they end up operating autonomously. What happens when the software fails?

8   Such fears have persuaded the military to go slow on the use of autonomous weaponry. An early version of one of Foster-Miller's robots was designed to de-mine beaches autonomously but was later converted to remote control at the navy's request. It is feasible that as safety concerns are addressed, autonomous devices will become increasingly popular, though experts in robotics point out that might be a long time away. An armed robot will not only need to be fail-safe, it must also be able to identify friend and foe just as well as a soldier.

9   Despite these fears, the rise of armed robots seems inevitable. Quinn tells the story of a group of U.S. marines impressed by a Swords robot armed with a machine gun being tested at a U.S. army base. "If they could have, they would have put that robot in their trunk, because they were off to Ramadi, Iraq, and they wanted that robot to [help them] stay alive. When you see that passion, I have no philosophical problems about this technology whatsoever," he says.

10   Outside the military, however, plenty of people beg to differ. Ultimately, these developments will allow the U.S., as well as several NATO countries that are also keen on the technology, to fight wars without suffering anywhere near as many casualties. The idea that warfare can be "clinical" has been found wanting time and again in recent years—think of the current conflicts in Iraq and Afghanistan, and Israel's recent bombardment of Lebanon—but there's no question that reliable autonomous robots deployed on a large scale could make fighting wars a great deal less risky for those that own them.

11   And therein lies the great danger. What are the chances of a less violent world when the powerful nations can make their mark on the less powerful at the flick of a switch? As Quinn puts it: "We are not trying to create a level battlefield here, we are trying to do the opposite: create a very un-level battlefield."

Speech at the Democratic National Convention, July 27, 2004

Ron Reagan

Ron Reagan is the son of the fortieth president of the United States. In August 1994, at the age of 83, President Reagan was diagnosed with Alzheimer's disease, an incurable neurological disorder that destroys brain cells, and he died of the disease in June 2004. A few months later, on July 27, Ron Reagan offered the following speech to the delegates to the Democratic National Convention and to the millions of Americans watching on television. It was countered the next day by Richard Doerflinger, whose piece follows this one.

1   Good evening, ladies and gentlemen.

2   A few of you may be surprised to see someone with my last name showing up to speak at a Democratic Convention. Apparently some of you are not. Let me assure you, I am not here to make a political speech and the topic at hand should not—must not—have anything to do with partisanship.

3   I am here tonight to talk about the issue of research into what may be the greatest medical breakthrough in our or any lifetime: the use of embryonic stem cells—cells created using the material of our own bodies—to cure a wide range of fatal and debilitating illnesses: Parkinson's disease, multiple sclerosis, diabetes, lymphoma, spinal cord injuries, and much more.

4   Millions are afflicted. And every year, every day, tragedy is visited upon families across the country, around the world. Now, it may be within our power to put an end to this suffering. We only need to try.

5   Some of you already know what I'm talking about when I say embryonic stem cell research. Others of you are probably thinking, that's quite a mouthful. Maybe this is a good time to go for a tall cold one. Well, wait a minute, wait a minute.

6   Let me try and paint as simple a picture as I can while still doing justice to the science, the incredible science involved. Let's say that ten or so years from now you are diagnosed with Parkinson's disease. There is currently no cure, and drug therapy, with its attendant side-effects, can only temporarily relieve the symptoms.

7   Now, imagine going to a doctor who, instead of prescribing drugs, takes a few skin cells from your arm. The nucleus of one of your cells is placed into a donor egg whose own nucleus has been removed. A bit of chemical or electrical stimulation will encourage your cell's nucleus to begin dividing, creating new cells which will then be placed into a tissue

culture. Those cells will generate embryonic stem cells containing only your DNA, thereby eliminating the risk of tissue rejection. These stem cells are then driven to become the very neural cells that are defective in Parkinson's patients. And finally, those cells—with your DNA—are injected into your brain where they will replace the faulty cells whose failure to produce adequate dopamine led to the Parkinson's disease in the first place.

8   In other words, you're cured.

9   And another thing, these embryonic stem cells, they could continue to replicate indefinitely and, theoretically, can be induced to recreate virtually any tissue in your body.

10   How'd you like to have your own personal biological repair kit standing by at the hospital? Sound like magic? Welcome to the future of medicine.

11   Now by the way, no fetal tissue is involved in this process. No fetuses are created, none destroyed. This all happens in the laboratory at the cellular level.

12   Now, there are those who would stand in the way of this remarkable future, who would deny the federal funding so crucial to basic research. They argue that interfering with the development of even the earliest stage embryo, even one that will never be implanted in a womb and will never develop into an actual fetus, is tantamount to murder.

13   A few of these folks, needless to say, are just grinding a political axe and they should be ashamed of themselves. But many are well-meaning and sincere. Their belief is just that, an article of faith, and they are entitled to it. But it does not follow that the theology of a few should be allowed to forestall the health and well-being of the many.

14   And how can we affirm life if we abandon those whose own lives are so desperately at risk? It is a hallmark of human intelligence that we are able to make distinctions.

15   Yes, these cells could theoretically have the potential, under very different circumstances, to develop into human beings—that potential is where their magic lies. But they are not, in and of themselves, human beings. They have no fingers and toes, no brain or spinal cord. They have no thoughts, no fears. They feel no pain.

16   Surely we can distinguish between these undifferentiated cells multiplying in a tissue culture and a living, breathing person—a parent, a spouse, a child.

17   I know a child—well, she must be 13 now so I guess I'd better call her a young woman. She has fingers and toes. She has a mind. She has memories. She has hopes. She has juvenile diabetes. Like so many kids with this disease, she's adjusted amazingly well. The insulin pump she wears—she's decorated hers with rhinestones. She can handle her own catheter

Actor Michael J. Fox, who was diagnosed in 1991 with Parkinson's disease, spoke at the Bio International Convention in 2007. Fox appealed to scientists and investors to aggressively translate scientific research into creative treatments for debilitating diseases, including Parkinson's.

needle. She's learned to sleep through the blood drawings in the wee hours of the morning.

18   She's very brave. She is also quite bright and understands full well the progress of her disease and what that might ultimately mean: blindness, amputation, diabetic coma. Every day, she fights to have a future.

19   What excuse will we offer this young woman should we fail her now? What might we tell her children? Or the millions of others who suffer? That when given an opportunity to help, we turned away? That facing political opposition, we lost our nerve? That even though we knew better, we did nothing?

20   And, should we fail, how will we feel if, a few years from now, a more enlightened generation should fulfill the promise of embryonic stem cell therapy? Imagine what they would say of us who lacked the will.

21   No, we owe this young woman and all those who suffer—we owe ourselves—better than that. We are better than that. We are a wiser people, a finer nation.

22   And for all of us in this fight, let me say: we will prevail. The tide of history is with us. Like all generations who have come before ours, we are motivated by a thirst for knowledge and compelled to see others in need as fellow angels on an often difficult path, deserving of our compassion.

23   In a few months, we will face a choice. Yes, between two candidates and two parties, but more than that. We have a chance to take a giant stride forward for the good of all humanity. We can choose between the

...*continued* Speech at the Democratic National Convention, July 27, 2004, **Ron Reagan**

future and the past, between reason and ignorance, between true compassion and mere ideology.

24   This—this is our moment, and we must not falter.

25   Whatever else you do come November 2, I urge you, please, cast a vote for embryonic stem cell research.

26   Thank you for your time.

Don't Clone Ron Reagan's Agenda

Richard M. Doerflinger

Richard M. Doerflinger is the Secretariat on Pro-life Activities for the United States Conference of Catholic Bishops. In 2009 Doerflinger was awarded an inaugural Life Prize by the Gerard Health Foundation for his work in "preserving and upholding the sanctity of human life" in areas such as public advocacy, legal action, and outreach. A specialist in bioethics, biotechnology, and public policy, he wrote the essay that follows on July 28, 2004, in response to the previous essay by Ron Reagan.

1   Ron Reagan's speech at the Democratic convention last night was expected to urge expanded funding for stem cell research using so-called "spare" embryos—and to highlight these cells' potential for treating the Alzheimer's disease that took his father's life.

2   He did neither. He didn't even mention Alzheimer's, perhaps because even strong supporters of embryonic stem cell research say it is unlikely to be of use for that disease. (Reagan himself admitted this on a July 12 segment of MSNBC's *Hardball*.) And he didn't talk about current debates on funding research using existing embryos. Instead he endorsed the more radical agenda of human cloning—mass-producing one's own identical twins in the laboratory so they can be exploited as (in his words) "your own personal biological repair kit" when disease or injury strikes.

3   Politically this was, to say the least, a gamble. Americans may be tempted to make use of embryos left over from fertility clinics, but most polls show them to be against human cloning for any purpose. Other advanced nations—Canada, Australia, France, Germany, Norway—have banned the practice completely, and the United Nations may approve an international covenant against it this fall. Many groups and individuals

who are "pro-choice" on abortion oppose research cloning, not least because it would require the mass exploitation of women to provide what Ron Reagan casually calls "donor eggs." And the potential "therapeutic" benefits of cloning are even more speculative than those of embryonic stem cell research—the worldwide effort even to obtain viable stem cells from cloned embryos has already killed hundreds of embryos and produced exactly one stem cell line, in South Korea.

4   But precisely for these reasons, Ron Reagan should be praised for his candor. The scientists and patient groups promoting embryonic stem cell research know that the current debate on funding is a mere transitional step. For years they have supported the mass manufacture of human embryos through cloning, as the logical and necessary goal of their agenda, but lately they have been coy about this as they fight for the more popular slogan of "stem cell research." With his speech Reagan has removed the mask, and allowed us to debate what is really at stake.

5   He claimed in his speech, of course, that what is at stake in this debate is the lives of millions of patients with devastating diseases. But by highlighting Parkinson's disease and juvenile diabetes as two diseases most clearly justifying the move to human cloning, he failed to do his homework. These are two of the diseases that pro-cloning scientists now admit will probably *not* be helped by research cloning.

6   Scottish cloning expert Ian Wilmut, for example, wrote in the *British Medical Journal* in February that producing genetically matched stem cells through cloning is probably quite unnecessary for treating any neurological disease. Recent findings suggest that the nervous system is "immune privileged," and will not generally reject stem cells from a human who is genetically different. He added that cloning is probably useless for auto-immune diseases like juvenile diabetes, where the body mistakenly rejects its own insulin-producing cells as though they were foreign. "In such cases," he wrote, "transfer of immunologically identical cells to a patient is expected to induce the same rejection."

7   Wilmut's observations cut the ground out from under Ron Reagan's simple-minded claim that cloning is needed to avoid tissue rejection. For some diseases, genetically matched cells are unnecessary; for others, they are useless, because they only replicate the genetic profile that is part of the problem. (Ironically, for Alzheimer's both may be true—cloning may be unnecessary to avoid tissue rejection in the brain, and useless because the cloned cells would have the same genetic defect that may lead to Alzheimer's.) Reagan declared that this debate requires us to "choose between . . . reason and ignorance," but he did not realize which side has the monopoly on ignorance.

8   That ignorance poses an obstacle to real advances that are right before our eyes. Two weeks before Ron Reagan declared that a treatment for Parkinson's may arrive "ten or so years from now," using "the material of our own bodies," a Parkinson's patient and his doctor quietly

...*continued* Don't Clone Ron Reagan's Agenda, **Richard M. Doerflinger**

Is stem cell research ethical?

appeared before Congress to point out that this has already been done. Dennis Turner was treated in 1999 by Dr. Michel Levesque of Cedars-Sinai Medical Center in Los Angeles, using his own adult neural stem cells. Dr. Levesque did not use the Rube Goldberg method of trying to turn those cells into a cloned embryo and then killing the embryo to get stem cells—he just grew Turner's own adult stem cells in the lab, and turned them directly into dopamine-producing cells. And with just one injection, on one side of Turner's brain, he produced an almost complete reversal of Parkinson's symptoms over four years.

9   Turner stopped shaking, could eat without difficulty, could put in his own contact lenses again, and resumed his avocation of big-game photography—on one occasion scrambling up a tree in Africa to escape a charging rhinoceros.

10   Amazingly, while this advance has been presented at national and international scientific conferences and featured on ABC-TV in Chicago, the scientific establishment supporting embryonic stem cell research has almost completely ignored it, and most news media have obediently imposed a virtual news blackout on it. That did not change even after the

results were presented to the Senate Commerce Subcommittee on Science, Technology and Space this month. Pro-cloning Senators on the panel actually seemed angry at the witnesses, for trying to distract them from their fixation on destroying embryos.

11   Turner also testified that his symptoms have begun to return, especially arising from the side of his brain that was left untreated, and he would like to get a second treatment. For that he will have to wait. Dr. Levesque has received insufficient appreciation and funding for his technique, and is still trying to put together the funds for broader clinical trials—as most Parkinson's foundations and NIH peer reviewers look into the starry distance of Ron Reagan's dreams about embryonic stem cells.

12   But hey, who cares about real Parkinson's patients when there's a Brave New World to sell?

Pay Your Own Way! (Then Thank Mom)*

Audrey Rock-Richardson

The author, who lives in Utah, wrote this essay in 2000 after she had completed her college education. She wonders why more students do not do what she did.

1   Is it me, or are students these days lazy? I'm not talking about tweens who don't want to do their homework or make their bed. I'm referring to people in legal adulthood who are in the process of making hugely consequential life decisions. And collectively, their attitude is that they simply cannot pay for college.

2   Don't get me wrong. I realize that there are people out there who pay their own tuition. I know that some cannot put themselves through school because of disabilities or extenuating circumstances. But I have to say: the notion that parents must finance their children's education is ridiculous.

3   During college I consistently endured comments from peers with scholarships and loans, peers who had new Jeeps and expensive apartments, all who would say to me, eyes bulging, "You mean your parents didn't help you at *all*?"

4   I resented my fellow students for asking this, first because they made it sound like my parents were demons, and second because they were

...continued Pay Your Own Way!, **Audrey Rock-Richardson**

insinuating that I wasn't capable of paying my own way. "How did you pay tuition?" they'd ask. My response was simple: "I worked." They would look at me blankly, as though I had told them I'd gone to the moon.

5   As an undergrad (University of Utah, 1998), I put myself through two solid years of full-tuition college by working as a day-care provider for $4.75 an hour. I then married and finished out seven more quarters by working as an interpreter for the deaf and a tutor in a private school.

6   I didn't work during high school or save for years. I simply got a job the summer following graduation and worked 40 hours a week. I didn't eat out every weekend, shop a lot or own a car. I sacrificed. I was striving for something bigger and longer-lasting than the next kegger.

7   Looking at the numbers now, I'm not sure how I managed to cover all the costs of my education. But I did. And I bought every single textbook and pencil myself, too.

8   I remember sitting in a classroom one afternoon during my senior year, listening to everyone introduce themselves. Many students mentioned their part-time jobs. There were several members of a sorority in the class. When it came to the first girl, she told us her name and that she was a sophomore. "Oh," she added, "I major in communications." After an awkward silence, the teacher asked, "Do you work?"

9   "Oh, no," she said emphatically, "I go to school full time." (As if those of us who were employed weren't really serious about our classes.)

10   The girl went on to explain that her parents were paying tuition and for her to live in a sorority house (complete with a cook, I later found out). She was taking roughly 13 credit hours. And she was too busy to work.

11   I, on the other hand, was taking 18, count 'em, 18 credit hours so I could graduate within four years. I worked 25 hours a week so my husband and I could pay tuition without future loan debt. And here's the kicker: I pulled straight A's.

12   I caught a glimpse of that same girl's report card at the end of the quarter, and she pulled C's and a few B's, which didn't surprise me. Having to juggle tasks forces you to prioritize, a skill she hadn't learned.

13   I'm weary of hearing kids talk about getting financial help from their parents as though they're entitled to it. I am equally tired of hearing stressed-out parents groaning, "How are we going to pay for his/her college?" Why do they feel obligated?

14   I do not feel responsible for my daughter's education. She'll find a way to put herself through if she wants to go badly enough. And (I'm risking sounding like my mom here), she'll thank me later. I can say this because I honestly, wholeheartedly thank my parents for giving me that experience.

15   I'm not saying that it's fun. It's not. I spent the first two years of school cleaning up after 4-year-olds for the aforementioned $4.75 an hour and taking a public bus to campus. My husband and I spent the second two struggling to pay out our tuition. We lived in a cinder-block apartment with little privacy and no dishwasher.

16   Lest I sound like a hypocrite, yes, I would have taken free college money had the opportunity presented itself. However, because my parents put themselves through school they expected me to do the same. And, frankly, I'm proud of myself. I feel a sense of accomplishment that I believe I couldn't have gained from 50 college degrees all paid for by someone else.

17   Getting through school on our own paid off in every way. My husband runs his own business, a demanding but profitable job. I write part time and work as a mother full time. I believe the fact that we are happy and financially stable is a direct result of our learning how to manage time and money in college.

18   So, kids, give your parents a break. Contrary to popular belief, you can pay tuition by yourself. And you might just thank your mother for it, too.

Why You Can't Cite Wikipedia in My Class

Neil L. Waters

1   The case for an online opensource encyclopedia is enormously appealing. What's not to like? It gives the originators of entries a means to publish, albeit anonymously, in fields they care deeply about and provides editors the opportunity to improve, add to, and polish them, a capacity not afforded to in-print articles. Above all, open sourcing marshals legions of unpaid, eager, frequently knowledgeable volunteers, whose enormous aggregate labor and energy makes possible the creation of an entity—Wikipedia, which today boasts more than 1.6 million entries in its English edition alone—that would otherwise be far too costly and labor-intensive to see the light of day. In a sense it would have been technologically impossible just a few years ago; open sourcing is democracy in action, and Wikipedia is its most ubiquitous and accessible creation.

2   Yet I am a historian, schooled in the concept that scholarship requires accountability and trained in a discipline in which collaborative research is rare. The idea that the vector-sum products of tens or hundreds of anonymous collaborators could have much value is, to say the least, counterintuitive for most of us in my profession. We don't allow

our students to cite printed general encyclopedias, much less open-source ones. Further, while Wikipedia compares favorably with other tertiary sources for articles in the sciences, approximately half of all entries are in some sense historical. Here the qualitative record is much spottier, with reliability decreasing in approximate proportion to distance from "hot topics" in American history [1]. For a Japan historian like me to perceive the positive side of Wikipedia requires an effort of will.

3   I made that effort after an innocuous series of events briefly and improbably propelled me and the history department at Middlebury College into the national, even international, spotlight. While grading a set of final examinations from my "History of Early Japan" class, I noticed that a half-dozen students had provided incorrect information about two topics—the Shimabara Rebellion of 1637–1638 and the Confucian thinker Ogyu Sorai—on which they were to write brief essays. Moreover, they used virtually identical language in doing so. A quick check on Google propelled me via popularity-driven algorithms to the Wikipedia entries on them, and there, quite plainly, was the erroneous information. To head off similar events in the future, I proposed a policy to the history department it promptly adopted: "(1) Students are responsible for the accuracy of information they provide, and they cannot point to Wikipedia or any similar source that may appear in the future to escape the consequences of errors. (2) Wikipedia is not an acceptable citation, even though it may lead one to a citable source."

4   The rest, as they say, is history. The Middlebury student newspaper ran a story on the new policy. That story was picked up online by *The Burlington Free Press,* a Vermont newspaper, which ran its own story. I was interviewed, first by Vermont radio and TV stations and newspapers, then by *The New York Times,* the *Asahi Shimbun* in Tokyo, and by radio and TV stations in Australia and throughout the U.S., culminating in a story on NBC Nightly News. Hundreds of other newspapers ran stories without interviews, based primarily on the *Times* article. I received dozens of phone calls, ranging from laudatory to actionably defamatory. A representative of the Wikimedia Foundation (www.wikipedia.org), the board that controls Wikipedia, stated that he agreed with the position taken by the Middlebury history department, noting that Wikipedia states in its guidelines that its contents are not suitable for academic citation, because Wikipedia is, like a print encyclopedia, a tertiary source. I repeated this information in all my subsequent interviews, but clearly the publication of the department's policy had hit a nerve, and many news outlets implied, erroneously, that the department was at war with Wikipedia itself, rather than with the uses to which students were putting it.

5   In the wake of my allotted 15 minutes of Andy Warhol-promised fame I have tried to figure out what all the fuss was about. There is a great deal of uneasiness about Wikipedia in the U.S., as well as in the rest of the computerized world, and a great deal of passion and energy have been spent in its defense. It is clear to me that the good stuff is related to the bad stuff. Wikipedia owes its incredible growth to open-source editing, which is also the root of its greatest weakness. Dedicated and knowledgeable editors can and do effectively reverse the process of entropy by making entries better over time. Other editors, through ignorance, sloppy research, or, on occasion, malice or zeal, can and do introduce or perpetuate errors in fact or interpretation. The reader never knows whether the last editor was one of this latter group; most editors leave no trace save a whimsical cyber-handle.

6   Popular entries are less subject to enduring errors, innocent or otherwise, than the seldom-visited ones, because, as I understand it, the frequency of visits by a Wikipedia "policeman" is largely determined, once again, by algorithms that trace the number of hits and move the most popular sites to a higher priority. The same principle, I have come to realize, props up the whole of the Wiki-world. Once a critical mass of hits is reached, Google begins to guide those who consulted it to Wikipedia before all else. A new button on my version of Firefox goes directly to Wikipedia. Preferential access leads to yet more hits, generating a still higher priority in an endless loop of mutual reinforcement.

7   It seems to me that there is a major downside to the self-reinforcing cycle of popularity. Popularity begets ease of use, and ease of use begets the "democratization" of access to information. But all too often, democratization of access to information is equated with the democratization of the information itself, in the sense that it is subject to a vote. That last mental conflation may have origins that predate Wikipedia and indeed the whole of the Internet.

8   The quiz show "Family Feud" has been a fixture of daytime television for decades and is worth a quick look. Contestants are not rewarded for guessing the correct answer but rather for guessing the answer that the largest number of people have chosen as the correct answer. The show must tap into some sort of popular desire to democratize information. Validation is not conformity to verifiable facts or weighing of interpretations and evidence but conformity to popular opinion. Expertise plays practically no role at all.

9   Here is where all but the most hopelessly postmodernist scholars bridle. "Family Feud" is harmless enough, but most of us believe in a real, external world in which facts exist independently of popular opinion, and some interpretations of events, thoroughly grounded in disciplinary rigor and the weight of evidence, are at least more likely to be right than

...*continued* Why You Can't Cite Wikipedia in My Class, **Neil L. Waters**

others that are not. I tell my students that Wikipedia is a fine place to search for a paper topic or begin the research process, but it absolutely cannot serve subsequent stages of research. Wikipedia is not the direct heir to "Family Feud," but both seem to share an element of faith—that if enough people agree on something, it is most likely so.

10   What can be done? The answer depends on the goal. If it is to make Wikipedia a truly authoritative source, suitable for citation, it cannot be done for any general tertiary source, including the *Encyclopaedia Britannica.* For an anonymous open-source encyclopedia, that goal is theoretically, as well as practically, impossible. If the goal is more modest—to make Wikipedia more reliable than it is—then it seems to me that any changes must come at the expense of its open-source nature. Some sort of accountability for editors, as well as for the originators of entries, would be a first step, and that, I think, means that editors must leave a record of their real names. A more rigorous fact-checking system might help, but are there enough volunteers to cover 1.6 million entries, or would checking be in effect reserved for popular entries?

11   Can one move beyond the world of cut-and-dried facts to check for logical consistency and reasonableness of interpretations in light of what is known about a particular society in a particular historical period? Can it be done without experts? If you rely on experts, do you pay them or depend on their voluntarism?

12   I suppose I should now go fix the Wikipedia entry for Ogyu Sorai (en.wikipedia.org/wiki/Ogyu_Sorai). I have been waiting since January to see how long it might take for the system to correct it, which has indeed been altered slightly and is rather good overall. But the statement that Ogyu opposed the Tokugawa order is still there and still highly misleading [2]. Somehow the statement that equates the samurai with the lower class in Tokugawa Japan has escaped the editors' attention, though anyone with the slightest contact with Japanese history knows it is wrong. One down, 1.6 million to go.

References

1. Rosenzweig, R. Can history be open source? *Journal of American History 93,* 1 (June 2006), 117–146.

2. Tucker, J. (editor and translator). *Ogyu Sorai's Philosophical Masterworks.* Association for Asian Studies and University of Hawaii Press, Honolulu, 2006, 12–13, 48–51; while Ogyu sought to redefine the sources of Tokugawa legitimacy, his purpose was clearly to strengthen the authority of the Tokugawa shogunate.

Professors Should Embrace Wikipedia

Mark A. Wilson

1   When the online, anyone-can-edit Wikipedia appeared in 2001, teachers, especially college professors, were appalled. The Internet was already an apparently limitless source of nonsense for their students to eagerly consume–now there was a Web site with the appearance of legitimacy and a dead-easy interface that would complete the seduction until all sense of fact, fiction, myth and propaganda blended into a popular culture of pseudointelligence masking the basest ignorance. An *Inside Higher Ed* article just last year on Wikipedia use in the academy drew a huge and passionate response, much of it negative.

2   Now the English version of Wikipedia has over 2 million articles, and it has been translated into over 250 languages. It has become so massive that you can type virtually any noun into a search engine and the first link will be to a Wikipedia page. After seven years and this exponential growth, Wikipedia can still be edited by anyone at any time. A generation of students was warned away from this information siren, but we know as professors that it is the first place they go to start a research project, look up an unfamiliar term from lecture, or find something disturbing to ask about during the next lecture. In fact, we learned too that Wikipedia is indeed the most convenient repository of information ever invented, and we go there often—if a bit covertly—to get a few questions answered. Its accuracy, at least for science articles, is actually as high as the revered *Encyclopedia Britannica,* as shown by a test published in the journal *Nature.*

3   It is time for the academic world to recognize Wikipedia for what it has become: a global library open to anyone with an Internet connection and a pressing curiosity. The vision of its founders, Jimmy Wales and Larry Sanger, has become reality, and the librarians were right: the world has not been the same since. If the Web is the greatest information delivery device ever, and Wikipedia is the largest coherent store of information and ideas, then we as teachers and scholars should have been on this train years ago for the benefit of our students, our professions, and that mystical pool of human knowledge.

4   What Wikipedia too often lacks is academic authority, or at least the perception of it. Most of its thousands of editors are anonymous, sometimes known only by an IP address or a cryptic username. Every article has a "talk" page for discussions of content, bias, and organization. "Revert" wars can rage out of control as one faction battles another over

a few words in an article. Sometimes administrators have to step in and lock a page down until tempers cool and the main protagonists lose interest. The very anonymity of the editors is often the source of the problem: how do we know who has an authoritative grasp of the topic?

5   That is what academics do best. We can quickly sort out scholarly authority into complex hierarchies with a quick glance at a vita and a sniff at a publication list. We make many mistakes doing this, of course, but at least our debates are supported with citations and a modicum of civility because we are identifiable and we have our reputations to maintain and friends to keep. Maybe this academic culture can be added to the Wild West of Wikipedia to make it more useful for everyone?

6   I propose that all academics with research specialties, no matter how arcane (and nothing is too obscure for Wikipedia), enroll as identifiable editors of Wikipedia. We then watch over a few wikipages of our choosing, adding to them when appropriate, stepping in to resolve disputes when we know something useful. We can add new articles on topics which should be covered, and argue that others should be removed or combined. This is not to displace anonymous editors, many of whom possess vast amounts of valuable information and innovative ideas, but to add our authority and hard-won knowledge to this growing universal library.

7   The advantages should be obvious. First, it is another outlet for our scholarship, one that may be more likely to be read than many of our journals. Second, we are directly serving our students by improving the source they go to first for information. Third, by identifying ourselves, we can connect with other scholars and interested parties who stumble across our edits and new articles. Everyone wins.

8   I have been an open Wikipedia editor now for several months. I have enjoyed it immensely. In my teaching I use a "living syllabus" for each course, which is a kind of academic blog. (For example, see my History of Life course online syllabus.) I connect students through links to outside sources of information. Quite often I refer students to Wikipedia articles that are well-sourced and well written. Wikipages that are not so good are easily fixed with a judicious edit or two, and many pages become more useful with the addition of an image from my collection (all donated to the public domain). Since I am open in my editorial identity, I often get questions from around the world about the topics I find most fascinating. I've even made important new connections through my edits to new collaborators and reporters who want more background for a story.

9   For example, this year I met online a biology professor from Centre College who is interested in the ecology of fish on Great Inagua Island in the Bahamas. He saw my additions and images on that Wikipedia page and had several questions about the island. He invited me to speak at Centre next year about evolution–creation controversies, which is unrelated to the original contact but flowed from our academic conversations. I in turn have been learning much about the island's living ecology I did not know. I've also learned much about the kind of prose that is most effective for a general audience, and I've in turn taught some people how to properly reference ideas and information. In short, I've expanded my teaching.

10   Wikipedia as we know it will undoubtedly change in the coming years as all technologies do. By involving ourselves directly and in large numbers now, we can help direct that change into ever more useful ways for our students and the public. This is, after all, our sacred charge as teacher-scholars: to educate when and where we can to the greatest effect.

PRACTICE

1 Test the idea that argument can be found everywhere. Each member of the class should bring in an example of an argument and explain why it can be defined as argument. Each example should focus on an issue that people are still arguing about and on which there is no general agreement. Each student should also define a position on the issue, and the position should be supported with reasons and evidence. Look for examples in a variety of contexts: newspapers, magazines, the Internet, television, motion pictures, music, sermons, other college classes, conversations, and printed material you find at work, at school, and at home.

   a. Bring in actual examples of articles, images, letters to the editor, bumper stickers, advertisements, or other easily transportable argument formats, or provide clear and complete descriptions and explanations of argument sources you cannot bring to class, such as lectures, television shows, or billboards. Students should give two- to three-minute oral reports on the example of argument they have selected, including a description of the issue and some of the reasons and evidence offered. This is most easily achieved by completing the statement "This arguer wants us to believe . . . , because. . . ." The class should decide whether all examples described in this activity are indeed examples of argument.

2 Write an essay defining the ideal marriage in order to support or undermine the concept of same-sex marriage. Just what is marriage, anyway?

   a. Just as Anna Quindlen did, write an essay that describes a particular, monogamous, same-sex couple that you know. In your essay, support or undermine the notion of legal same-sex unions.

   b. Write a proposal argument that is based on the positive or negative consequences that would follow from legalizing same-sex unions.

   c. Do a rhetorical analysis of an essay or image associated with same-sex marriage. You might use an argument, photo, or cartoon reprinted here; or, you could use another argument with which you are familiar. Consider how the author uses good reasons to support his or her perspective, as well as the completeness of the argument and the credibility of the arguer.

   d. Evaluate the Defense of Marriage Act or the proposed constitutional amendment banning same-sex marriage. Based on aesthetic, ethical, and practical criteria, are these good laws or not? Why?

   e. What alternatives to marriage might make sense? Would civil unions satisfy the political, legal, and moral issues in a way that would lead to a national consensus on the issue?

   f. Do some research into the views within the gay, lesbian, bisexual, and transgender community regarding marriage. Does everyone agree that it's a good idea? After you complete your research, write an essay characterizing the views of various constituencies within the community that is fair and balanced.

3 In his essay, Bill Gates writes glowingly of the potential for robots to benefit human society. Yet, as you have also seen (in the arguments put forth by Joy and Marks), robots are not without their critics. Exactly what is a robot, anyway? What differentiates robots from other machines? Write an essay that shows your attitude toward robots by defining them in a particular way.

4 Conduct a rhetorical analysis of the arguments of Ron Reagan. How is his speech a product of the particular rhetorical situation that he found himself in: in front of the Democratic National Convention, a few weeks after the death of his Republican father, and before a national television audience? How might he have presented his argument if he had appeared before Republicans, or if his speech had not been televised? Do you agree with Reagan's assertion that his speech is not political?

5 In this next group task, your problem is to define and identify "good argumentative writing" by creating criteria for evaluating an argument. This is a particularly crucial problem for developing writers insofar as you can't begin to measure your growth as a writer until you have some notion of what you're aiming for. For this task you will rank-order five student essays from best to worst according to criteria you establish within your small groups. College professors use this process regularly (often known as a "norming session") to determine criteria for grading student essays for large-scale assessment projects.

Task 1 (Homework): Preparing for the Group Discussion   Read the five student essays on pages 680–687. These essays were written early in an argument course. Students were asked to develop two or three reasons in support of a claim. Students had studied the argumentative concepts but had not yet studied refutation strategies. Although the students were familiar with classical argument structure, this introductory assignment did not ask them to summarize and respond to opposing views. The instructor's focus was only on students' developing some good reasons in support of a contestable claim.

After you have looked over the five student essays, concentrate for this task on "Bloody Ice" and "Legalization of Prostitution." Which of these two arguments is the better one? Freewrite your reasons for selecting the better argument, focusing on specific details of what you liked in the better essay and what you saw as problems in the weaker essay. (Note: Both essays have strengths and weaknesses, so you aren't trying to argue that one is excellent and the other is totally awful; you are just trying to determine which of the two more nearly meets the criteria for "good argumentative writing.") When you have finished your freewrite, develop a list of the criteria you used to make your judgment. You will be sharing this list with your classmates.

Task 2 (In-Class Group Work): Developing a Master List of Criteria   As a group, share your evaluations of "Bloody Ice" and "Legalization of Prostitution." Then try to reach group consensus on which of these two is the better essay and why. As a group, justify your evaluation by making a list of criteria you used and a rationale for rating some criteria more important than others. For example, does "quality of reasons" rank higher than "organization and development"? Does "use of evidence" rank higher than "lively style"? Your instructor may then ask each group to report its rankings to the whole class. The goal in this case is to create a class consensus about the two essays along with a master list of criteria.

Task 3 (Homework or Individual In-Class Time): Applying the Criteria to All Five Essays   Read again all five of the essays and rank-order them 1 to 5, best to worst, using the criteria developed during the previous discussions. Freewrite your rationale for ranking each essay as you did.

Task 4 (In-Class Group Work): Reaching Consensus on Ranking of Essays   Your goal now is to reach consensus on how you rank the essays and why you rank them the way you do. Feel free to change the criteria you established earlier if they seem to need some modification. Be careful in your discussions to distinguish between evaluation of the writer's written product and your own personal position on the writer's issue. In other words, there is a crucial difference between saying, "I don't like LeShawn's essay because I disagree with his claim" versus saying, "I don't like LeShawn's essay because he didn't provide adequate evidence to support several of his reasons." As each group reports the results of its deliberations to the whole class, the instructor will highlight discrepancies among the groups' decisions and collate the criteria as they emerge. If the instructor disagrees with the class consensus or wants to add items to the criteria, he or she may choose to make these things known at this time. By the end of this stage, everyone should have a list of criteria for good argumentative writing established by the class.

Bloody Ice

It is March in Alaska. The ocean-side environment is full of life and death. Man and animal share this domain but not in peace. The surrounding iceflows, instead of being cold and white, are steaming from the remains of gutted carcasses and stained red. The men are hunters and the animals are barely six weeks old. A slaughter has just taken place. Thousands of baby harp seals lie dead on the ice and thousands more adult mothers lie groaning over the death of their babies. Every year a total limit of 180,000 seals set by the U.S. Seal Protection Act is filled in a terrifying bloodbath. But Alaska with its limit of 30,000 is not alone. Canadians who hunt seals off the coast of Northern Newfoundland and

Quebec are allowed 150,000 seals. The Norwegians are allowed 20,000 and native Eskimos of Canada and Greenland are allowed 10,000 seals per year. Although this act appears heartless and cruel, the men who hunt have done this for 200 years as a tradition for survival. They make many good arguments supporting their traditions. They feel the seals are in no immediate danger of extinction. Also seal furs can be used to line boots and gloves or merely traded for money and turned into robes or fur coats. Sometimes the meat is even used for food in the off hunting months when money is scarce. But are these valid justifications for the unmerciful killings? No, the present limit on harp seal killings should be better regulated because the continued hunting of the seals will lead to eventual extinction and because the method of slaughter is so cruel and inhumane.

The harp seal killing should be better regulated first because eventual extinction is inevitable. According to *Oceans* magazine, before the limit of 180,000 seals was established in 1950, the number of seals had dwindled from 3,300,000 to 1,250,000. Without these limitations hundreds of thousands were killed within weeks of birth. Now, even with this allotment, the seals are being killed off at an almost greater rate than they can remultiply. Adult female seals give birth once every year but due to pollution, disease, predation, whelping success, and malnutrition they are already slowly dying on their own without being hunted. Eighty percent of the seals slaughtered are pups and the remaining twenty percent are adult seals and even sometimes mothers who try attacking the hunters after seeing their babies killed. The hunters, according to the Seal Protection Act, have this right.

Second, I feel the killing should be better regulated because of the inhumane method used. In order to protect the fur value of the seals, guns are not used. Instead, the sealers use metal clubs to bludgeon the seal to death. Almost immediately after being delivered a direct blow, the seals are gutted open and skinned. Although at this stage of life the seal's skull is very fragile, sometimes the seals are not killed by the blows but merely stunned; thus hundreds are skinned alive. Still others are caught in nets and drowned, which, according to *America* magazine, the Canadian government continues to deny. But the worst of the methods used is when a hunter gets tired of swinging his club and uses the heel of his boot to kick the seal's skull in. Better regulation is the only way to solve this problem because other attempts seem futile. For example, volunteers who have traveled to hunting sites trying to dye the seals to ruin their fur value have been caught and fined heavily.

The plight of the harp seals has been long and controversial. With the Canadian hunters feeling they have the right to kill the seals because it has been their industry for over two centuries, and on the other hand with humane organizations fearing extinction and strongly opposing the method of slaughter, a compromise must be met among both sides. As I

...continued Bloody Ice

see it, the solution to the problem is simple. Since the Canadians do occasionally use the whole seal and have been sealing for so long they could be allowed to continue but at a more heavily regulated rate. Instead of filling the limit of 180,000 every year and letting the numbers of seals decrease, Canadians could learn to ranch the seals as Montanans do cattle or sheep. The United States has also offered to help them begin farming their land for a new livelihood. The land is adequate for crops and would provide work all year round instead of only once a month every year. As a result of farming, the number of seals killed would be drastically cut down because Canadians would not be so dependent on the seal industry as before. This would in turn lead back to the ranching aspect of sealing and allow the numbers to grow back and keeping the tradition alive for future generations and one more of nature's creatures to enjoy.

RSS Should Not Provide Dorm Room Carpets

Tricia, a University student, came home exhausted from her work-study job. She took a blueberry pie from the refrigerator to satisfy her hunger and a tall glass of milk to quench her thirst. While trying to get comfortable on her bed, she tipped her snack over onto the floor. She cleaned the mess, but the blueberry and milk stains on her brand new carpet could not be removed. She didn't realize that maintaining a clean carpet would be difficult and costly. Tricia bought her own carpet. Some students living in dorm rooms want carpeted rooms provided for them at the expense of the University. They insist that since they pay to live on campus, the rooms should reflect a comfortable home atmosphere. However, Resident Student Services (RSS) should not be required to furnish the carpet because other students do not want carpets. Furthermore, carpeting all the rooms totals into a very expensive project. And lastly, RSS should not have to provide the carpet because many students show lack of respect and responsibility for school property.

Although RSS considers the carpeting of all rooms a strong possibility, students like Tricia oppose the idea. They feel the students should buy their own carpets. Others claim the permanent carpeting would make dorm life more comfortable. The carpet will act as insulation and as a soundproofing system. These are valid arguments, but they should not be the basis for changing the entire residence hall structure. Those students with "cold feet" can purchase house footwear, which cost less than carpet. Unfortunately carpeting doesn't muffle all the noise; therefore, some students will be disturbed. Reasonable quietness should be a matter of respect for other students' privacy and comfort. Those opposed to the idea reason out the fact that students constantly change rooms or move out. The next person may not want carpet. Also, if RSS carpets the rooms, the students will lose the privilege they have of painting their rooms any color. Paint stains cannot be removed. Some students can't afford to replace the carpet. Still another factor, carpet color, may not please everyone. RSS would provide a neutral color like brown or gray. With tile floors, the students can choose and purchase their own carpets to match their taste.

Finally, another reason not to have carpet exists in the fact that the project can be expensive due to material costs, installation cost, and the maintenance cost caused mainly by the irresponsibility of many students. According to Rick Jones, Asst. Director of Housing Services, the cost will be $300 per room for the carpet and installation. RSS would also have to purchase more vacuum cleaners for the students' use. RSS will incur more expense in order to maintain the vacuums. Also, he claims that many accidents resulting from shaving cream fights, food fights, beverage parties, and smoking may damage the carpet permanently. With floor tiles, accidents such as food spills can be cleaned up easier than carpet. The student's behavior plays an important role in deciding against carpeting. Many students don't follow the rules of maintaining their rooms. They drill holes into the walls, break mirrors, beds, and closet doors, and leave their food trays all over the floor. How could they be trusted to take care of school carpet when they violate the current rules? Many students feel they have the "right" to do as they please. This irresponsible and disrespectful behavior reflects their future attitude about carpet care.

In conclusion, the university may be able to afford to supply the carpets in each room, but maintaining them would be difficult. If the students want carpets, they should pay and care for the carpets themselves. Hopefully, they will be more cautious and value it more. They should take the initiative to fundraise or find other financial means of providing this "luxury." They should not rely on the school to provide unnecessary room fixtures such as carpets. Also, they must remember that if RSS provides the carpet and they don't pay for the damages, they and future students will endure the consequences. What will happen???? Room rates will skyrocket!!!!!

Sterling Hall Dorm Food

The quality of Sterling Hall dorm food does not meet the standard needed to justify the high prices University students pay. As I watched a tall, medium-built University student pick up his Mexican burrito from the counter it didn't surprise me to see him turn up his nose. Johnny, our typical University student, waited five minutes before he managed to make it through the line. After he received his bill of $8.50 he turned his back to the cash register and walked away displeased with his meal.

As our neatly groomed University student placed his ValiDine eating card back into his Giorgio wallet, he thought back to the balance left on his account. Johnny had $24 left on his account and six more weeks left of school. He had been eating the cheapest meals he could and still receive a balanced meal, but the money just seemed to disappear. No student, not even a thrifty boy like Johnny, could possibly afford to live healthfully according to the University meal plan system.

Johnny then sat down at a dirty table to find his burrito only halfway cooked. Thinking back to the long-haired cook who served him the burrito, he bit into the burrito and noticed a long hair dangling from his lips. He realized the cook's lack of preparation when preparing his burrito.

Since the food costs so much, yet the quality of the food remains low, University students do not get the quality they deserve. From the information stated I can conclude that using the ValiDine service system University students would be jeopardizing their health and wasting their hard-earned money. University students deserve something more than what they have now.

ROTC Courses Should Not Get College Credit

One of the most lucrative scholarships a student can receive is a four-year ROTC scholarship that pays tuition and books along with a living allowance. It was such a scholarship that allowed me to attend an expensive liberal arts college and to pursue the kind of well-rounded education that matters to me. Of course, I am obligated to spend four years on active duty—an obligation that I accept and look forward to. What I am disappointed in, however, is the necessity to enroll in Military Science classes. Strong ROTC advocates argue that Military Science classes are essential because they produce good citizens, teach leadership skills, and provide practical experience for young cadets. Maybe so. But we could get the same benefits without having to take these courses for credit. Colleges should make ROTC training an extracurricular activity, not a series of academic courses taken for academic credit.

First of all, ROTC courses, unlike other college courses, do not stress inquiry and true questioning. The ROTC program has as its objective the preparation of future officers committed to the ideals and structure of the military. The structure of the military is based upon obediently following the orders of military superiors. Whereas all my other teachers stress critical thinking and doing independent analysis, my ROTC instructors avoid political or social questions saying it is the job of civilian leaders to debate policies and the job of the military to carry them out. We don't even debate what role the military should play in our country. My uncle, who was an ROTC cadet during the Vietnam war, remembers that not only did ROTC classes never discuss the ethics of the war but that cadets were not allowed to protest the war outside of their ROTC courses. This same obedience is demanded in my own ROTC courses, where we are not able to question administration policies and examine openly the complexity of the situation in Iraq and Afghanistan.

A second reason that Army ROTC courses do not deserve academic credit is that the classes are not academically strenuous, thus giving cadets a higher GPA and an unfair advantage over their peers. Much of what a cadet does for academic credit involves nonacademic activities such as physical training for an hour three days a week so that at least some of a cadet's grade is based on physical activity, not mental activity. In conducting an informal survey of 10 upperclassmen, I found out that none of them has ever gotten anything lower than an A in a Military Science class and they do not know of anyone who got anything lower than an A. One third-year cadet stated that "the classes are basic. A monkey coming out of the zoo could get college credit for a Military Science class." He went on to say that most of the information given in his current class is a brush-up to 8th grade U.S. history. In contrast, a typical liberal arts college class requires much thought, questioning, and analysis. The ROTC Military Science class is taught on the basis of "regurgitated knowledge," meaning that once you are given a piece of information you are required to know it and reproduce it at any time without thought or question. A good example is in my class Basic Officership. Our first assignment is to memorize and recite in front of the class the Preamble to the Constitution of the United States. The purpose of doing so doesn't seem to be to understand or analyze the Constitution because we never talk about that. In fact, I don't know what the purpose is. I just do it because I am told to. Because the "A" is so easy to get in my ROTC class, I spend all my time studying for my other classes. I am a step ahead of my peers in the competition for a high GPA, even though I am not getting as good an education.

Finally, having to take ROTC classes means that I can't take other liberal arts courses which would be more valuable. One of the main purposes

...continued ROTC Courses Should Not Get College Credit

for ROTC is to give potential officers a liberal education. Many cadets have the credentials to get into an armed forces academy, but they chose ROTC programs because they could combine military training with a well-rounded curriculum. Unfortunately, by taking Military Science classes each quarter, cadets find that their electives are all but eaten up by the time they are seniors. If ROTC classes were valuable in themselves, I wouldn't complain. But they aren't, and they keep me from taking upper division electives in philosophy, literature, and the humanities.

All of these reasons lead me to believe that Army ROTC cadets are getting shortchanged when they enroll for Military Science classes. Because cadets receive a lucrative scholarship, they should have to take the required military science courses. But these courses should be treated as extracurricular activities, like a work-study job or like athletics. Just as a student on a full-ride athletic scholarship does not receive academic credit for football practices and games, so should a student on a full-ride ROTC scholarship have to participate in the military education program without getting academic credit. By treating ROTC courses as a type of extracurricular activity like athletics, students can take more elective credits that will expand their minds, better enabling them to have the knowledge to make moral decisions and to enjoy their world more fully.

Legalization of Prostitution

Prostitution . . . It is the world's oldest profession. It is by definition the act of offering or soliciting sex for payment. It is, to some, evil. Yet the fact is it exists.

Arguments are not necessary to prove the existence of prostitution. Rather, the argument arises when trying to prove something must be done to reduce the problems of this profession. The problems which exist are in the area of crime, of health, and of environment. Crime rates are soaring, diseases are spreading wildly, and the environment on the streets is rapidly decaying. Still, it has been generally conceded that these problems cannot be suppressed. However, they can be reduced. Prostitution should be legalized because it would reduce the wave of epidemics, decrease high crime rates, provide good revenue by treating it like other businesses, and get girls off the streets where sexual crimes often occur.

Of course, there are those who would oppose the legalization of prostitution stating that it is one of the main causes for the spread of venereal diseases. Many argue that it is interrelated with drug trafficking and other organized crimes. And probably the most controversial is the moral aspect of the subject; it is morally wrong, and legalizing it would be enforcing, or even justifying, such an existence.

These points propose good arguments, but I shall counter each point and explain the benefits and advantages of legalizing prostitution. In the case of prostitution being the main cause for the spread of epidemics, I disagree. By legalizing it, houses would be set up which would solve the problem of girls working on the streets and being victims of sexual crimes. It would also provide regular health checks, as is successfully done in Nevada, Germany, and other parts of the United States and Europe, which will therefore cut down on diseases spreading unknowingly.

As for the increase of organized crime if prostitution is legalized, I disagree again. Firstly, by treating it like businesses, then that would make good state revenue. Secondly, like all businesses have regulations, so shall these houses. That would put closer and better control in policing the profession, which is presently a problem. Obviously, if the business of prostitution is more closely supervised, that would decrease the crime rates.

Now, I come to one of the most arguable aspects of legalizing prostitution: the moral issue. Is it morally wrong to legalize prostitution? That is up to the individual. To determine whether anything is "right or wrong" in our society is nearly impossible to do since there are various opinions. If a person were to say that prostitution is the root of all evil, that will not make it go away. It exists. Society must begin to realize that fear or denial will not make the "ugliness" disappear. It still exists.

Prostitution can no longer go ignored because of our societal attitudes. Legalizing it is beneficial to our society, and I feel in time people may begin to form an accepting attitude. It would be the beginning of a more open-minded view of what is reality. Prostitution . . . it is the world's oldest profession. It exists. It is a reality.

6 Read "Pay Your Own Way" (p. 669). Then, in small groups, answer the questions listed below for each of them.

a. What is the issue?

b. What is the author's position on the issue?

c. What reasons and evidence are given to support the author's position?

d. What makes each of these arguments successful?

e. What are the weaknesses in the arguments, if any?

7 Finally, in class discussion, compile a list of the best as well as the weakest features of argumentation in each essay. Keep a copy of this list. It is a starting point. You will add to it as you learn more about what it takes to make a good argument.

Lake Superior
Marquette, MI

Courtesy of aaronpeterson.net/Alamy.

How Do I Assess My Audience?

16

I N THIS CHAPTER WE EXAMINE STRATEGIES FOR ADDRESSING OPPOSING OR ALTERNATIVE VIEWS—WHETHER TO OMIT THEM, REFUTE THEM, CONCEDE TO THEM, OR INCORPORATE THEM THROUGH COMPROMISE AND CONCILIATION. WE SHOW YOU HOW YOUR CHOICES ABOUT STRUCTURE, content, and tone may differ depending on whether your audience is sympathetic, neutral, or resistant to your views. The strategies explained in this chapter will increase your flexibility as an arguer and enhance your chance of persuading a wide variety of audiences.

One-Sided, Multisided, and Dialogic Arguments

Arguments are said to be one-sided, multisided, or dialogic:

- *A one-sided argument* presents only the writer's position on the issue without summarizing and responding to alternative viewpoints.
- *A multisided argument* presents the writer's position, but also summarizes and responds to possible objections and alternative views.
- *A dialogic argument* has a much stronger component of inquiry, in which the writer presents himself as uncertain or searching, the audience is considered a partner in the dialogue, and the writer's purpose is to seek common ground perhaps leading to a consensual solution to a problem.

One-sided and *multisided* arguments often take an adversarial stance in that the writer regards alternative views as flawed or wrong and supports his own claim with a strongly persuasive intent. Although multisided arguments can be adversarial, they can also be made to feel dialogic, depending on the way the writer introduces and responds to alternative views.

At issue, then, is the writer's treatment of alternative views. Does the writer omit them (a one-sided argument), summarize them in order to rebut them (an adversarial kind of multisided argument), or summarize them in order to acknowledge their validity, value, and force (a more dialogic kind of multisided argument)? Each of these approaches can be appropriate for certain occasions, depending on your purpose, your confidence in your own stance, and your audience's resistance to your views.

How can one determine the kind of argument that would be most effective in a given case? As a general rule, one-sided arguments occur commonly when an issue is not highly contested. If the issue is highly contested, then one-sided arguments tend to strengthen the convictions of those who are already in the writer's camp, but alienate those who aren't. In contrast, for those initially opposed to a writer's claim, a multisided argument shows that the writer has considered other views and thus reduces some initial hostility. An especially interesting effect can occur with neutral or undecided audiences. In the short run, one-sided arguments are often persuasive to a neutral audience, but in the long run multisided arguments have more staying power. Neutral audiences who have heard only one side of an issue tend to change their minds when they hear alternative arguments. By anticipating and rebutting opposing views, a multisided argument diminishes the surprise and force of subsequent counterarguments. If we move from neutral to highly resistant audiences, adversarial approaches—even multisided ones—are seldom effective because they increase hostility and harden the differences between writer and reader. In such cases, more dialogic approaches have the best chance of establishing common ground for inquiry and consensus.

In the rest of this chapter we will show you how your choice of writing one-sided, multisided, or dialogic arguments is a function of how you perceive your audience's resistance to your views as well as your level of confidence in your own views.

Determining Your Audience's Resistance to Your Views

When you write an argument, you must always consider your audience's point of view. One way to imagine your relationship to your audience is to place it on a scale of resistance ranging from strong support of your position to strong opposition (see Figure 16.1). At the "Accord" end of this scale are like-minded people who basically agree with your position on the issue. At the "Resistance" end are those who strongly disagree with you, perhaps unconditionally, because their values, beliefs, or assumptions sharply differ from your own. Between "Accord" and "Resistance" lies a range of opinions. Close to your position will be those leaning in your direction but with less conviction than you have. Close to the resistance position will be those basically opposed to your view but willing

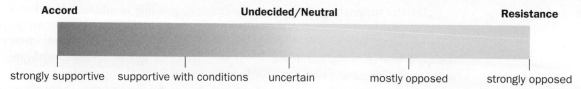

Figure 16.1   Scale of Resistance

to listen to your argument and perhaps willing to acknowledge some of its strengths. In the middle are those undecided people who are still sorting out their feelings, seeking additional information, and weighing the strengths and weaknesses of alternative views.

Seldom, however, will you encounter an issue in which the range of disagreement follows a simple line from accord to resistance. Often resistant views fall into different categories so that no single line of argument appeals to all those whose views are different from your own. You have to identify not only your audience's resistance to your ideas but also the causes of that resistance.

Consider, for example, the issues surrounding publicly financed sports stadiums. In one city, a ballot initiative asked citizens to raise sales taxes to build a new retractable-roof stadium for its baseball team. Supporters of the initiative faced a complex array of resisting views (see Figure 16.2). Opponents of the initiative could be placed into four categories. Some simply had no interest in sports, cared nothing about baseball, and saw no benefit in building a huge publicly financed sports facility. Another group loved baseball and followed the home team passionately, but was philosophically opposed to subsidizing rich players and owners with taxpayer money. This group argued that the whole sports industry needed to be restructured so that stadiums were paid for out of sports revenues. Still another group was opposed to tax hikes in general. It focused on the principle of reducing the size of government and of using tax revenues only for essential services. Finally, another powerful group supported baseball and supported the notion of public funding of a new stadium but opposed the kind of retractable-roof stadium specified in the initiative. This group wanted an old-fashioned, open-air stadium like Baltimore's Camden Yards or Cleveland's Jacobs Field.

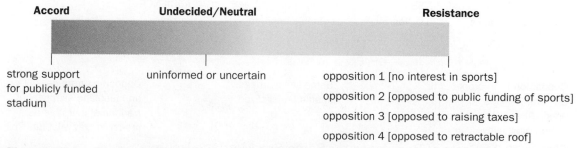

Figure 16.2   Scale of Resistance, Baseball Stadium Issue

Writers supporting the initiative found it impossible to address all of these resisting audiences at once. If a supporter of the initiative wanted to aim an argument at sports haters, he or she could stress the spinoff benefits of a new ballpark (for example, the new ballpark would attract tourist revenue, renovate a deteriorating downtown neighborhood, create jobs, make sports lovers more likely to vote for public subsidies of the arts, and so forth). But these arguments were irrelevant to those who wanted an open-air stadium, who opposed tax hikes categorically, or who objected to public subsidy of millionaires.

Another kind of complexity occurs when a writer is positioned between two kinds of resisting views. Consider the position of student writer Sam, a gay man who wished to argue that gay and lesbian people should actively support legislation to legalize same-sex marriage (see Figure 16.3). Most arguments that support same-sex marriage hope to persuade conservative heterosexual audiences who tend to disapprove of homosexuality and stress traditional family values. But Sam imagined writing for a gay magazine such as the *Harvard Gay and Lesbian Review* or *The Advocate,* and he wished to aim his argument at liberal gay and lesbian activists who opposed traditional marriage on different grounds. These thinkers, critiquing traditional marriage for the way it stereotypes gender roles and limits the freedom of partners, argued that heterosexual marriage is not a good model for relationships in the gay community. These people constituted an audience 180 degrees removed from the conservative proponents of family values who oppose same-sex marriage on moral and religious grounds.

In writing his early drafts, Sam was stymied by his attempt to address both audiences at once. Only after he blocked out the conservative "family values" audience and imagined an audience of what he called "liberationist" gays and lesbians was he able to develop a consistent argument.

The baseball stadium example and the same-sex marriage example illustrate the difficulty of adapting your argument to your audience's position on the scale of resistance. Yet doing so is important because you need a stable vision of your audience before you can determine an effective content, structure, and tone for your argument. An effective content derives from choosing audience-based reasons that appeal to your audience's values, assumptions, and beliefs. As we show in the rest of this chapter, an effective structure and tone are often a function of

Figure 16.3 Scale of Resistance for Same-Sex Marriage Issue

where your audience falls on the scale of resistance. The next sections show how you can adjust your arguing strategy depending on whether your audience is supportive, neutral, or hostile.

Appealing to a Supportive Audience: One-Sided Argument

One-sided arguments commonly occur when an issue isn't highly contested and the writer's aim is merely to put forth a new or different point of view. When an issue is contested, however, one-sided arguments are used mainly to stir the passions of supporters—to convert belief into action by inspiring a party member to contribute to a senator's campaign or a bored office worker to sign up for a change-your-life weekend seminar.

Typically, appeals to a supportive audience are structured as one-sided arguments that either ignore opposing views or reduce them to "enemy" stereotypes. Filled with motivational language, these arguments list the benefits that will ensue from your donations to the cause and the horrors just around the corner if the other side wins. One of the authors of this text recently received a fund-raising letter from an environmental lobbying group declaring, "It's crunch time for the polluters and their pals on Capitol Hill." The "corporate polluters" and "anti-environment politicians," the letter continues, have "stepped up efforts to roll back our environmental protections—relying on large campaign contributions, slick PR firms and well-heeled lobbyists to get the job done before November's election." This letter makes the reader feel part of an in-group of good guys fighting the big business "polluters." Nothing in the letter examines environmental issues from business's perspective or attempts to examine alternative views fairly. Because the intended audience already believes in the cause, nothing in the letter invites readers to consider the issues more thoroughly. Rather, the goal is to solidify support, increase the fervor of belief, and inspire action. Most appeal arguments make it easy to act, ending with an 800 phone number to call, a Web site to visit, a tear-out postcard to send in, or a congressperson's address to write to.

Appealing to a Neutral or Undecided Audience: Classical Argument

The in-group appeals that motivate an already supportive audience can repel a neutral or undecided audience. Because undecided audiences are like jurors weighing all sides of an issue, they distrust one-sided arguments that caricature other views. Generally the best strategy for appealing to undecided audiences is the classically structured argument.

What characterizes the classical argument is the writer's willingness to summarize opposing views fairly and to respond to them openly—either by trying to refute them or by conceding to their strengths and then shifting to a different field of values. Let's look at these strategies in more depth.

SUMMARIZING OPPOSING VIEWS

The first step toward responding to opposing views in a classical argument is to summarize them fairly. Follow the *principle of charity,* which obliges you to avoid loaded, biased, or "straw man" summaries that oversimplify or distort opposing arguments, making them easy to knock over.

Consider the difference between an unfair and a fair summary of an argument. In the following example, a hypothetical supporter of genetically engineered foods intends to refute the argument of organic-food advocate Lisa Turner, who opposes all forms of biotechnology.

Unfair Summary of Turner's Argument

In a biased article lacking scientific understanding of biotechnology, natural-foods huckster Lisa Turner parrots the health food industry's party line that genetically altered crops are Frankenstein's monsters run amok. She ignorantly claims that consumption of biotech foods will lead to worldwide destruction, disease, and death, ignoring the wealth of scientific literature showing that genetically modified foods are safe. Her misinformed attacks are scare tactics aimed at selling consumers on overpriced "health food" products to be purchased at boutique organic-food stores.

Fair Summary of Turner's Argument

In an article appearing in a nutrition magazine, health food advocate Lisa Turner warns readers that much of our food today is genetically modified using gene-level techniques that differ completely from ordinary crossbreeding. She argues that the potential, unforeseen, harmful consequences of genetic engineering offset the possible benefits of increasing the food supply, reducing the use of pesticides, and boosting the nutritional value of foods. Turner asserts that genetic engineering is imprecise, untested, unpredictable, irreversible, and also uncontrollable because of animals, insects, and winds.

In the unfair summary, the writer distorts and oversimplifies Turner's argument, creating a straw man argument that is easy to knock over because it doesn't make the opponent's best case. In contrast, a fair summary follows the "principle of charity," allowing the strength of the opposing view to come through clearly.

REFUTING OPPOSING VIEWS

Once you have summarized opposing views, you can either refute them or concede to their strengths. In refuting an opposing view, you attempt to convince
readers that its argument is logically flawed, inadequately supported, or based
on erroneous assumptions. In refuting an argument, you can rebut (1) the
writer's stated reason and grounds, (2) the writer's warrant and backing, or
(3) both. Put in less specialized language, you can rebut a writer's reasons and
evidence or the writer's underlying assumptions. Suppose, for example, that you
wanted to refute this argument:

We shouldn't elect Joe as committee chair because he is too bossy.

One way to refute this argument is to rebut the stated reason that Joe is too
bossy. Your rebuttal might go something like this:

I disagree that Joe is bossy. In fact, Joe is very unbossy. He's a good listener who's willing to compromise, and he involves others in decisions.
The example you cite for his being bossy wasn't typical. It was a one-
time circumstance that doesn't reflect his normal behavior. [The writer
could then provide examples of Joe's cooperative nature.]

Or you could concede that Joe is bossy but rebut the argument's warrant
that bossiness is a bad trait for committee chairs:

I agree that Joe is bossy, but in this circumstance bossiness is just the
trait we need. This committee hasn't gotten anything done for six
months and time is running out. We need a decisive person who can
come in, get the committee organized, assign tasks, and get the job
done.

Let's now illustrate these strategies in a more complex situation. Consider
the controversy inspired by a *New York Times Magazine* article titled "Recycling
Is Garbage." Its author, John Tierney, argued that recycling is not environmentally sound and that it is cheaper to bury garbage in a landfill than to recycle it.
In criticizing recycling, Tierney argued that recycling wastes money; he provided
evidence that "every time a sanitation department crew picks up a load of bottles and cans from the curb, New York City loses money."

A number of environmentalists responded angrily to Tierney's argument,
challenging either his reason, his warrant, or both. Those refuting the reason
offered counterevidence showing that recycling isn't as expensive as Tierney
claimed. Those refuting the warrant said that even if the costs of recycling are
higher than burying wastes in a landfill, recycling still benefits the environment
by reducing the amount of virgin materials taken from nature. These critics, in
effect, offered a new warrant: We should dispose of garbage in the way that most
saves the world's resources.

STRATEGIES FOR REBUTTING EVIDENCE

Whether you are rebutting an argument's reasons or its warrant, you will frequently need to question a writer's use of evidence. Here are some strategies you can use:

- *Deny the truth of the data.* Arguers can disagree about the facts of a case. If you have reasons to doubt a writer's facts, call them into question.

- *Cite counterexamples and countertestimony.* You can often rebut an argument based on examples or testimony by citing counterexamples or countertestimony that denies the conclusiveness of the original data.

- *Cast doubt on the representativeness or sufficiency of examples.* Examples are powerful only if the audience feels them to be representative and sufficient. Many environmentalists complained that John Tierney's attack on recycling was based too largely on data from New York City and that it didn't accurately take into account the more positive experiences of other cities and states. When data from outside New York City were examined, the cost-effectiveness and positive environmental impact of recycling seemed more apparent.

- *Cast doubt on the relevance or recency of the examples, statistics, or testimony.* The best evidence is up-to-date. In a rapidly changing universe, data that are even a few years out-of-date are often ineffective. For example, as the demand for recycled goods increases, the cost of recycling will be reduced. Out-of-date statistics will skew any argument about the cost of recycling.

- *Call into question the credibility of an authority.* If an opposing argument is based on testimony, you can undermine its persuasiveness if you show that a person being cited lacks up-to-date or relevant expertise in the field. (This procedure is different from the *ad hominem* fallacy because it doesn't attack the personal character of the authority but only the authority's expertise on a specific matter.)

- *Question the accuracy or context of quotations.* Evidence based on testimony is frequently distorted by being either misquoted or taken out of context. Often scientists qualify their findings heavily, but these qualifications are omitted by the popular media. You can thus attack the use of a quotation by putting it in its original context or by restoring the qualifications accompanying the quotation in its original source.

- *Question the way statistical data were produced or interpreted.* In general, you can rebut statistical evidence by calling into account how the data were gathered, treated mathematically, or interpreted. It can make a big difference, for example, whether you cite raw numbers or percentages or whether you choose large or small increments for the axes of graphs.

CONCEDING TO OPPOSING VIEWS

In writing a classical argument, a writer must sometimes concede to an opposing argument rather than refute it. Sometimes you encounter portions of an argument that you simply can't refute. For example, suppose you support the legalization of hard drugs such as cocaine and heroin. Adversaries argue that legalizing hard drugs will increase the number of drug users and addicts. You might dispute the size of their numbers, but you reluctantly agree that they are right. Your strategy in this case is not to refute the opposing argument but to concede to it by admitting that legalization of hard drugs will promote heroin and cocaine addiction. Having made that concession, your task is then to show that the benefits of drug legalization still outweigh the costs you've just conceded.

As this example shows, the strategy of a concession argument is to switch from the field of values employed by the writer you disagree with to a different field of values more favorable to your position. You don't try to refute the writer's stated reason and grounds (by arguing that legalization will *not* lead to increased drug usage and addiction) or the writer's warrant (by arguing that increased drug use and addiction is not a problem). Rather, you shift the argument to a new field of values by introducing a new warrant, one that you think your audience can share (that the benefits of legalization—eliminating the black market and ending the crime, violence, and prison costs associated with procurement of drugs—outweigh the costs of increased addiction). To the extent that opponents of legalization share your desire to stop drug-related crime, shifting to this new field of values is a good strategy. Although it may seem that you weaken your own position by conceding to an opposing argument, you may actually strengthen it by increasing your credibility and gaining your audience's goodwill. Moreover, conceding to one part of an opposing argument doesn't mean that you won't refute other parts of that argument.

READINGS

The Characteristics of Youth*

Aristotle

In the second book of the Rhetoric, *written between 360 and 334 B.C., Aristotle characterizes different types of audiences to help the orator with audience analysis. By understanding a particular audience, the orator could more easily persuade them. No young women are mentioned in the* Rhetoric, *but you may want to apply relevant parts of this description of youth to them as well. Compare this description of the young with modern perceptions of the young reflected in the other essays in this section. How would you describe the characteristics of youth?*

1   We shall begin with the characteristics of youth. Young men have strong desires, and whatever they desire they are prone to do. Of the bodily desires the one they let govern them most is the sexual; here they lack self-control. They are shifting and unsteady in their desires, which are vehement for a time, but soon relinquished; for the longings of youth are keen rather than deep—are like sick people's fits of hunger and thirst. The young are passionate, quick to anger, and apt to give way to it. And their angry passions get the better of them; for, since they wish to be honored, young men cannot put up with a slight; they are resentful if they only imagine that they are unfairly treated. Fond of honor, they are even fonder of victory, for youth likes to be superior, and winning evinces superiority. They love both honor and victory more than they love money. Indeed, they care next to nothing about money, for they have not yet learned what the want of it means. . . . The young think no evil [are not cynical], but believe in human goodness, for as yet they have not seen many examples of vice. They are trustful, for as yet they have not been often deceived. And they are sanguine; for young men glow with a natural heat as drinkers are heated with wine, while as yet their failures have not been many. They live their lives for the most part in hope [anticipation], as hope is of the future and memory of the past; and for young men the future is long, the past but short; on the first day of life there is nothing to remember, everything to expect. They are easily deceived, and for the same reason, since they are quick to hope. Being passionate as well as hopeful, they are relatively brave; the passion excludes fear, and the hope

*"Types of Character," *The Rhetoric of Aristotle.* 2.12. Lane Cooper, ed. and trans. (New York: Appleton-Century-Crofts, 1932), 32–34.

inspires confidence—no one is afraid when he is angry, and an anticipation of good makes one confident. And they are shy; for as yet they have no independent standard of good conduct, but only the conventional standards in which they were reared. They are high-minded [have lofty aspirations]; first, because they have not yet been humbled by life, nor come to know the force of circumstances; and secondly, because high-mindedness means thinking oneself fitted for great things, and this again is characteristic of the hopeful. In their actions they prefer honor to expediency; for their lives are rather lives of good impulse [moral instinct or feeling] than of calculation [reason]; and calculation aims at the expedient, virtue at the honorable. They are fond of their friends, intimates, and associates—more so than are men in the other two periods of life; this comes from their love of company, and from the fact that as yet they judge nothing, and hence do not judge their friends, by the standard of expediency. All their mistakes are on the side of intensity and excess, running counter to the maxim of Chilon ['Moderation in all things']. They carry everything too far: they love to excess, they hate to excess—and so in all else. They think they know everything, and are positive about everything; indeed, this is why they always carry their doings too far. When they wrong other people, the injuries are wanton [insolent], not malicious. The young are prone to pity, because they think every one good, or at all events better than people really are. That is, they judge their fellow man by their own guilelessness, and hence assume that his sufferings are undeserved. . . . They are fond of laughter, and therefore facetious, facetiousness being a subdued insolence.

From "First Place: A Healing School for Homeless Children"

Marybeth Hamilton (Student)

. . . As stated earlier, the goal of First Place is to prepare students for returning to mainstream public schools. Although there are many reasons to continue operating an agency like First Place, there are some who would argue against it. One argument is that the school is too expensive, costing many more taxpayer dollars per child than a mainstream school. I can understand this objection to cost, but one way to look at First Place is as a preventative action by the city to reduce the future costs of crime and welfare. Because all the students at First Place are at risk for educational failure, drug and alcohol abuse, or numerous other long-term problems, a program like First Place attempts to stop the problems before they start. In the long run, the city could be saving money in areas such as drug rehabilitation, welfare payments, or jail costs.

...continued From "First Place: A Healing School for Homeless Children," **Marybeth Hamilton**

Others might criticize First Place for spending some of its funding on social services for the students and their families instead of spending it all on educational needs. When the city is already making welfare payments and providing a shelter for the families, why do they deserve anything more? Basically, the job of any school is to help a child become educated and have social skills. At First Place, students' needs run deep, and their entire families are in crisis. What good is it to help just the child when the rest of the family is still suffering? The education of only the child will not help the family out of poverty. Therefore, First Place helps parents look for jobs by providing job search help including assistance with résumés. They even supply clothes to wear to an interview. First Place also provides a parent support group for expressing anxieties and learning coping skills. This therapy helps parents deal with their struggles in a productive way, reducing the chance that they will take out their frustration on their child. All these "extras" are an attempt to help the family get back on its feet and become self-supporting.

Another objection to an agency like First Place is that the short-term stay at First Place does no long-term good for the student. However, in talking with Michael Siptroth, a teacher at First Place, I learned that the individual attention the students receive helps many of them catch up in school quite quickly. He reported that some students actually made a three-grade-level improvement in one year. This improvement definitely contributes to the long-term good of the student, especially in the area of self-esteem. Also, the students at First Place are in desperate situations. For most, any help is better than no help. Thus First Place provides extended day care for the children so they won't have to be unsupervised at home while their parents are working or looking for work. For example, some homeless children live in motels on Aurora Avenue, a major highway that is overrun with fast cars, prostitutes, and drugs. Aurora Avenue is not a safe place for children to play, so the extended day care is important for many of First Place's students.

Finally, opponents might question the value of removing students from mainstream classrooms. Some might argue that separating children from regular classrooms is not good because it further highlights their differences from the mainstream children. Also, the separation period might cause additional alienation when the First Place child does return to a mainstream school. In reality, though, the effects are quite different. Children at First Place are sympathetic to each other. Perhaps for the first time in their lives, they do not have to be on the defensive because no one is going to make fun of them for being homeless; they are all homeless. The time spent at First Place is usually a time for catching up to the students in mainstream schools. When students catch up, they have one fewer reason to be seen as different from mainstream students. If the students stayed in the mainstream school and continued to fall behind, they would only get teased more.

5   First Place is a program that merits the community's ongoing moral and financial support. With more funding, First Place could help many more homeless children and their families along the path toward self-sufficiency. While this school is not the ultimate answer to the problem of homelessness, it is a beginning. These children deserve a chance to build their own lives, free from the stigma of homelessness, and I, as a responsible citizen, feel a civic and moral duty to do all I can to help them.

PRACTICE

1 Magazines sell advertising by targeting specific readers. Bring to class a magazine that you read regularly or one that you find interesting. Organize in groups of three or four students and exchange magazines with each other. Look at the articles and the advertising in the magazine.

Analyze your classmate's magazine for these criteria.

a. What is the target age group?

b. What percentages of men and women are likely to read the magazine?

c. What income level is targeted?

d. Is a particular ethnicity being targeted?

e. What else is being assumed about the audience? For magazines that cover a specific subject or activity (for example, backpacking, beauty, snowboarding, parenting, fitness, cats, and so on), what other products and services do you find being advertised?

Share your analysis with other members of your group. Ask the person who brought the magazine you analyzed if he or she agrees with your description of the target audience.

2 Before you read further, get a pen or pencil and several sheets of paper and do the following exercise.

a. For your eyes only, write about what you did at a recent party. Write for four minutes.

b. On a second sheet of paper, describe for the members of your writing class what you did at this party; you will read this aloud to the class. Stop after four minutes.

c. On a third sheet of paper, write a letter to one of your parents or a relative describing what you did at the party. Stop after four minutes.

❸ Writing Assignment: Writing a Letter to a Specific Audience
Read the following rhetorical situation and write a letter in response to one of the four individuals in the prompts that appear immediately after it. Do not confer with other members of the class. Make sure at least some students write in response to each of the four prompts.

The Rhetorical Situation

You are enrolled in a freshman English class and your teacher allows you to be absent five times before she gives you an F for the course. If you are tardy to class three times, it counts as an absence. You have been absent five times and tardy to class twice. Your parents are angry at you for missing class so much, and they say that if you fail English you will have to get a job and start paying rent to live at home. Your teacher has explained that if you are tardy or absent from class one more time, she is going to fail you. You really want to do better; you are determined to change your ways.

   On the way to class you have a blowout on the freeway. You pull over to change the tire and when you get the spare from the trunk, it is flat. This is not your fault, as you have just had your car serviced and the tires checked. A fellow motorist pulls over and helps you, but by the time you get a good tire on your car and drive to class, you are forty-five minutes late. You enter the classroom as quietly as you can. Your best friend raises her eyebrows. Your teacher gives you a stern look. You feel terrible.

The Writing Prompts

   a. You are too embarrassed to talk to your teacher. Write her a letter to explain what happened and ask her for another chance.

   b. Your parents are too angry to talk to you. Write them a letter to explain what happened and to ask their forgiveness.

   c. You are very upset with the tire company. Write them a letter to explain what happened and ask for a reimbursement.

   d. You don't have time to talk to your best friend after class. Write her a note to explain what happened and tell her what you intend to do about it.*

*I am indebted to Samantha Masterton for this assignment.

You and your classmates should now read some of these letters aloud. When you read them, do not divulge who the intended audience is. Ask the other students to guess who the intended reader of the letter is. Continue doing this until you have a sampling of all four letters and the class has guessed to whom each has been written.

Discuss the Results

What clues helped you surmise the audience for each letter? How are the letters different from each other? In your discussion, consider how each audience influenced the purpose for writing each letter, the tone of each letter, and the type and level of vocabulary used in each letter.

4 Class Discussion and Writing Assignment: Analyzing Your Class as an Audience

Learn more about your class as an audience by answering the questions listed here.

a. How many students are in your class? What are some of the qualities and features you have in common?

b. Consider some of the demographics of your class (ask for a show of hands to answer some of these): How many are traditional college-age students (18–22 years old); and how many are older, new, or returning students? Count the number of men and the number of women. How many are international students, and what countries do they represent? How would you describe the cultural diversity in the class? How many in the class agree that their heritage or native culture influences their personal life? How many are first-years and sophomores? How many are juniors and seniors? How many work part-time? How many work full-time? What are some of the types of work represented in class?

c. What college majors are represented in your class?

d. What are some of the groups class members belong to that are important to them? Consider political, religious, social, and living groups. Ask for students to volunteer this information.

e. What are some of the special interests and hobbies of class members? Make a list.

Using this class survey data, write as full a description of your classroom audience as you can. Which of the issues that you have considered writing about would immediately interest them? Why? Which would they find less interesting? Why? What could you provide in your paper to increase their interest?

Baker College
Owosso

How Do I Write an Argument?

17

F OR THE MOST PART, ARGUMENTS SHOULD BE CONSTRUCTED LOGI-
CALLY SO THAT ASSUMPTIONS LINK EVIDENCE (SUPPORTING FACTS
AND EXPERT OPINIONS) TO CLAIMS. AS WE'LL SEE, HOWEVER, LOGIC
IS ONLY ONE COMPONENT OF EFFECTIVE ARGUMENTS.

THE THREE APPEALS OF ARGUMENT: LOGOS, ETHOS, PATHOS

Speakers and writers have never relied on logic alone in advancing and supporting their claims. More than 2000 years ago, the Athenian philosopher
and rhetorician Aristotle explained how speakers attempting to persuade
others to their point of view could achieve their purpose by relying on one
or more *appeals*, which he called *logos*, *ethos*, and *pathos*.

Since we frequently find these three appeals employed in political argument, we'll use political examples in the following discussion. But keep in
mind that these appeals are also used extensively in advertising, legal cases,
business documents, and many other types of argument.

● **LOGOS** *Logos* is the rational appeal, the appeal to reason. If speakers
expect to persuade their audiences, they must argue logically and must supply appropriate evidence to support their case. Logical arguments are commonly of two types (often combined): deductive and inductive. The
deductive argument begins with a generalization, then cites a specific case
related to that generalization, from which follows a conclusion.

An example of a deductive argument may be seen in President John F.
Kennedy's address to the nation in June 1963 on the need for sweeping civil
rights legislation. Kennedy begins with the generalizations that it "ought to
be possible . . . for American students of any color to attend any public institution they select without having to be backed up by troops" and that "it
ought to be possible for American citizens of any color to register and vote
in a free election without interference or fear of reprisal." Kennedy then

provides several specific examples (primarily recent events in Birmingham, Alabama) and statistics to show that this was not the case. He concludes:

> We face, therefore, a moral crisis as a country and a people. It cannot be met by repressive police action. It cannot be left to increased demonstrations in the streets. It cannot be quieted by token moves or talk. It is time to act in the Congress, in your state and local legislative body, and, above all, in all of our daily lives.

Underlying Kennedy's argument is this reasoning:

> All Americans should enjoy certain rights. (*assumption*)
> Some Americans do not enjoy these rights. (*support*)
> We must take action to ensure that all Americans enjoy these rights. (*claim*)

Another form of logical argumentation is *inductive* reasoning. A speaker or writer who argues inductively begins not with a generalization, but with several pieces of specific evidence. The speaker then draws a conclusion from this evidence. For example, in a 1990 debate on gun control, Senator Robert C. Byrd cited specific examples of rampant crime involving guns: "I read of young men being viciously murdered for a pair of sneakers, a leather jacket, or $20." He also offered statistical evidence of the increasing crime rate: "in 1951, there were 3.2 policemen for every felony committed in the United States; this year nearly 3.2 felonies will be committed per every police officer." He concluded, "Something has to change. We have to stop the crimes that are distorting and disrupting the way of life for so many innocent, law-respecting Americans. The bill that we are debating today attempts to do just that."

Senator Edward M. Kennedy also used statistical evidence in arguing for passage of the Racial Justice Act of 1990, which was designed to ensure that minorities were not disproportionately singled out for the death penalty. Kennedy pointed out that between 1973 and 1980, 17 defendants in Fulton County, Georgia, were charged with killing police officers, but the only defendant who received the death sentence was a black man. Kennedy also cited statistics to show that "those who killed whites were 4.3 times more likely to receive the death penalty than were killers of blacks," and that "in Georgia, blacks who killed whites received the death penalty 16.7 percent of the time, while whites who killed received the death penalty only 4.2 percent of the time."

Of course, the mere piling up of evidence does not in itself make the speaker's case. As Donna Cross explains in "Politics: The Art of Bamboozling,"* politicians are very adept at "card-stacking." And statistics can be selected and manipulated to prove anything, as demonstrated in Darrell Huff's landmark book *How to Lie with Statistics* (1954). Moreover, what appears to be a logical argument may in fact be fundamentally flawed. On the other hand, the fact that evidence can be distorted, statistics misused, and logic fractured does not mean

*Donna Cross, *Word Abuse: How the Words We Use Use Us* (New York: Coward, 1979).

that these tools of reason can be dispensed with or should be dismissed. It means only that audiences have to listen and read critically—perceptively, knowledgeably, and skeptically (though not necessarily cynically).

Sometimes in political disagreements, people can turn their opponents' faulty logic against them. For example, in the wake of the meltdown in 2008 of the mortgage loan industry, with more than 1.2 million homes in foreclosure, some argued that it would be bad policy to help homeowners who had lost their homes as a consequence of no longer being able to make mortgage payments. Their argument worked like this:

> Financially irresponsible behavior should not be rewarded with government bailouts. (*assumption*)
>
> Taking on a mortgage that one cannot afford is financially irresponsible behavior. (*support*)
>
> Taking on a mortgage that one cannot afford should not be rewarded with government bailouts. (*claim*)

But this argument was made to work for the opposite position by those who favored government assistance. Their strategy was simply to change the middle term—the *support*. In light of the almost immediate massive financial support provided by the Federal Reserve to assist the large investment banking house Bear Stearns when it was threatened with bankruptcy, the middle term was switched to:

> Large-scale investing in subprime mortgages is financially irresponsible behavior.

Thus, the inescapable conclusion—the *claim*—of this argument inevitably became:

> Banks threatened with bankruptcy as a result of having made poor investments in subprime mortgages should not be rewarded with government bailouts.

The inconsistency of helping out investment banks while not helping out homeowners was illogical enough that Congress rushed to consider legislation that would also help out homeowners. But beyond being illogical, the initial decision not to help out individual homeowners created a powerful appeal to *pathos*: Legislators did not want to be seen as unsympathetic to families who, because of large-scale economic factors beyond their control, would lose their homes and, in effect, be thrown out on the streets.

● **ETHOS**   *Ethos*, or the ethical appeal, is based not on the ethical rationale for the subject under discussion, but rather on the ethical status of the person making the appeal. A person making an argument must have a certain degree of credibility: That person must be of good character, have sound sense, and be qualified to hold the office or recommend policy.

For example, Elizabeth Cervantes Barrón, running for senator as the Peace and Freedom candidate, begins her statement with "I was born and raised in central Los

Angeles. I grew up in a multiethnic, multicultural environment where I learned to respect those who were different from me. . . . I am a teacher and am aware of how cutbacks in education have affected our children and our communities."

On the other end of the political spectrum, the American Independent gubernatorial candidate Jerry McCready also begins with an ethical appeal: "As a self-employed businessman, I have learned firsthand what it is like to try to make ends meet in an unstable economy being manipulated by out-of-touch politicians." Both candidates are making an appeal to *ethos*, an appeal based on the strength of their personal qualities for the office they seek.

L. A. Kauffman is not running for office but writing an article arguing against socialism as a viable ideology for the future ("Socialism: No," *Progressive*, April 1, 1993). To defuse objections that he is simply a tool of capitalism, Kauffman begins with an appeal to *ethos:* "Until recently, I was executive editor of the journal *Socialist Review*. Before that I worked for the Marxist magazine, *Monthly Review*. My bookshelves are filled with books of Marxist theory, and I even have a picture of Karl Marx up on my wall." Thus, Kauffman establishes his credentials to argue knowledgeably about Marxist ideology.

The conservative commentator Rush Limbaugh frequently makes use of the ethical appeal by linking himself with the kind of Americans he assumes his audiences to be (the writer Donna Cross calls this "glory by association"):

> In their attacks [on me], my critics misjudge and insult the American people. If I were really what liberals claim—racist, hatemonger, blowhard—I would years ago have deservedly gone into oblivion. The truth is, I provide information and analysis the media refuses to disseminate, information and analysis the public craves. People listen to me for one reason: I am effective. And my credibility is judged in the marketplace every day. . . . I represent America's rejection of liberal elites. . . . I validate the convictions of ordinary people.*

● **PATHOS**   Finally, speakers and writers appeal to their audiences by using *pathos*, the appeal to the emotions. Nothing is inherently wrong with using an emotional appeal. Indeed, because emotions often move people far more powerfully than reason alone, speakers and writers would be foolish not to use emotion. And it would be a drab, humorless world if human beings were not subject to the sway of feeling as well as reason. The emotional appeal becomes problematic only when it is the *sole* or *primary* basis of the argument. This imbalance of emotion over logic is the kind of situation that led, for example, to the internment of Japanese Americans during World War II or that leads to periodic political spasms that call for enacting anti-flag-burning legislation.

President Ronald Reagan was a master of emotional appeal. He closed his first Inaugural Address with a reference to the view from the Capitol to the Arlington National Cemetery, where lie thousands of markers of "heroes":

> Under one such marker lies a young man, Martin Treptow, who left his job in a small-town barbershop in 1917 to go to France with the famed

*Rush Limbaugh, "Why I Am a Threat to the Left," *Los Angeles Times*, 9 Oct. 1994.

Rainbow Division. There, on the western front, he was killed trying to carry a message between battalions under heavy artillery fire. We're told that on his body was found a diary. On the flyleaf under the heading, "My Pledge," he had written these words: "America must win this war. Therefore, I will work, I will save, I will sacrifice, I will endure, I will fight cheerfully and do my utmost, as if the issue of the whole struggle depended on me alone." The crisis we are facing today does not require of us the kind of sacrifice that Martin Treptow and so many thousands of others were called upon to make. It does require, however, our best effort and our willingness to believe in ourselves and to believe in our capacity to perform great deeds, to believe that together with God's help we can and will resolve the problems which now confront us.

Surely, Reagan implies, if Martin Treptow can act so courageously and so selflessly, we can do the same. His logic is somewhat unclear because the connection between Martin Treptow and ordinary Americans of 1981 was rather tenuous (as Reagan concedes); but the emotional power of Martin Treptow, whom reporters were sent scurrying to research, carried the argument.

President Bill Clinton also used *pathos*. Addressing an audience of the nation's governors about his welfare plan, Clinton closed his remarks by referring to a conversation he had had with a welfare mother who had gone through the kind of training program Clinton was advocating. Asked by Clinton whether she thought that such training programs should be mandatory, the mother said, "I sure do." Clinton in his remarks explained what she said when he asked her why:

> "Well, because if it wasn't, there would be a lot of people like me home watching the soaps because we don't believe we can make anything of ourselves anymore. So you've got to make it mandatory." And I said, "What's the best thing about having a job?" She said, "When my boy goes to school, and they say, 'What does your mama do for a living?' he can give an answer."

Clinton uses the emotional power he counts on in that anecdote to set up his conclusion: "We must end poverty for Americans who want to work. And we must do it on terms that dignify all of the rest of us, as well as help our country to work better. I need your help, and I think we can do it."

THE LIMITS OF ARGUMENT

Our discussion of *ethos* and *pathos* indicates a potentially troubling but undeniable reality: Arguments are not won on the basis of logic and evidence alone. In the real world, arguments don't operate like academic debates. If the purpose of argument is to get people to change their minds or to agree that the writer's or speaker's position on a particular topic is the best available, then the person making the argument must be aware that factors other than evidence and good reasoning come into play when readers or listeners are considering the matter.

These factors involve deep-seated cultural, religious, ethnic, racial, and gender identities, moral predilections, and the effects of personal experiences (either pleasant or unpleasant) that are generally impervious to the weight of reasoning, however well-framed. Try—using the best available arguments—to convince someone who is pro-life to agree with the pro-choice position (or vice versa). Try to persuade someone who opposes capital punishment to believe that state-endorsed executions are necessary for deterrence (or for any other reason). Marshall your evidence and logic to persuade someone whose family members have had run-ins with the law that police efforts are directed at protecting the law-abiding. On such emotionally loaded topics, it is extremely difficult, if not impossible, to get people to change their minds because they are so personally invested in their beliefs. It is not just a matter of their forming or choosing an opinion on a particular topic; it is a matter of an opinion's emerging naturally from an often long-established component of the person's psyche. Someone who believes that all life is sacred is not likely to be swayed by an argument that abortion or stem-cell research that involves the destruction of a fetus is acceptable. As Susan Jacoby, author of *The Age of American Unreason,* notes, "Whether watching television news, consulting political blogs, or (more rarely) reading books, Americans today have become a people in search of validation for opinions that they already hold."*

The tenacity with which people hold on to longtime beliefs does not mean, however, that they cannot change their minds or that subjects like abortion, capital punishment, gun control, and gay marriage should be off-limits to reasoned debate. It means only that you should be aware of the limits of argument. The world is not populated by Mr. and Ms. Spocks of *Star Trek* fame, whose brains function by reason alone. Even those who claim to be open-minded on a given topic are often captive to deeply held beliefs and, so, deceive themselves concerning their willingness to respond rationally to arguments. As one letter writer to the *New York Times Book Review* observed, "[P]eople often fail to identify their own biases because of a compelling human desire to believe they are fair-minded and decent."†

The most fruitful topics for argument in a freshman setting, therefore, tend to be those on which most people are persuadable, either because they know relatively little about the topic or because deep-rooted cultural, religious, or moral beliefs are not involved. At least initially in your career as a writer of academic papers, it's probably best to avoid "hot button" topics that are the focus of broader cultural debates, and to focus instead on topics in which *pathos* plays less of a part. Most people are not heavily invested in plug-in hybrid or hydrogen-powered vehicles, so an argument on behalf of the more promising technology for the coming decades will not be complicated by deep-seated beliefs. Similarly, most people don't know enough about the mechanics of sleep to have strong opinions on how to deal with sleep deprivation. Your arguments

---

*Susan Jacoby, "Talking to Ourselves: Americans Are Increasingly Close-Minded and Unwilling to Listen to Opposing Views," *Los Angeles Times* 20 Apr. 2008: M10.
†Susan Abendroth, letter in *New York Times Book Review,* 30 Mar. 2008: 12.

Message
LOGOS: *How can I make the argument internally consistent and logical? How can I find the best reasons and support them with the best evidence?*

Figure 17.1   The Rhetorical Triangle

Audience
PATHOS: *How can I make the reader open to my message? How can I best appeal to my reader's values and interests? How can I engage my reader emotionally and imaginatively?*

Writer or Speaker
ETHOS: *How can I present myself effectively? How can I enhance my credibility and trustworthiness?*

on such topics, therefore, will provide opportunities both to inform your readers or listeners and to persuade them that your arguments, if well reasoned and supported by sound evidence, are at least plausible if not entirely convincing.

How to Create an Effective *Ethos:* The Appeal to Credibility

The ancient Greek and Roman rhetoricians recognized that an argument would be more persuasive if the audience trusted the speaker. Aristotle argued that such trust resides within the speech itself, not in the prior reputation of the speaker. In the speaker's manner and delivery, tone, word choice, and arrangement of reasons, in the sympathy with which he or she treats alternative views, the speaker creates a trustworthy persona. Aristotle called the impact of the speaker's credibility the appeal from *ethos.* How does a writer create credibility? We suggest three ways:

- **Be Knowledgeable about Your Issue.** The first way to gain credibility is to *be* credible—that is, to argue from a strong base of knowledge, to have at hand the examples, personal experiences, statistics, and other empirical data needed to make a sound case. If you have done your homework, you will command the attention of most audiences.

- **Be Fair.** Besides being knowledgeable about your issue, you need to demonstrate fairness and courtesy to alternative views. Because true argument can occur only where people may reasonably disagree with one another, your *ethos* will be strengthened if you demonstrate that you understand and empathize with other points of view. There are times, of course, when you may appropriately scorn an opposing view. But these times are rare, and they mostly occur when you address audiences predisposed to your view. Demonstrating empathy to alternative views is generally the best strategy.

- **Build a Bridge to Your Audience.** A third means of establishing credibility—building a bridge to your audience—has been treated at length in our earlier discussions of audience-based reasons. By grounding your argument in shared values and assumptions, you demonstrate your goodwill and enhance your image as a trustworthy person respectful of your audience's views. We mention audience-based reasons here to show how this aspect of *logos*—finding the reasons that are most rooted in the audience's values—also affects your *ethos* as a person respectful of your readers' views.

How to Create *Pathos:* The Appeal to Beliefs and Emotions

Before the federal government outlawed unsolicited telephone marketing, newspapers published flurries of articles complaining about annoying telemarketers. Within this context, a United Parcel Service worker, Bobbi Buchanan, wanted to create sympathy for telemarketers. She wrote a *New York Times* op-ed piece entitled "Don't Hang Up, That's My Mom Calling," which begins as follows:

> The next time an annoying sales call interrupts your dinner, think of my 71-year-old mother, LaVerne, who works as a part-time telemarketer to supplement her social security income. To those Americans who have signed up for the new national do-not-call list, my mother is a pest, a nuisance, an invader of privacy. To others, she's just another anonymous voice on the other end of the line. But to those who know her, she's someone struggling to make a buck, to feed herself and pay her utilities—someone who personifies the great American way.

The editorial continues with a heartwarming description of LaVerne. Buchanan's rhetorical aim is to transform the reader's anonymous, depersonalized image of telemarketers into the concrete image of her mother: a "hardworking, first generation American; the daughter of a Pittsburgh steelworker;

survivor of the Great Depression; the widow of a World War II veteran; a mother of seven, grandmother of eight, great-grandmother of three. . . ." The intended effect is to alter our view of telemarketers through the positive emotions triggered by our identification with LaVerne.

By urging readers to think of "my mother, LaVerne" instead of an anonymous telemarketer, Buchanan illustrates the power of *pathos,* an appeal to the reader's emotions. Arguers create pathetic appeals whenever they connect their claims to readers' values, thus triggering positive or negative emotions depending on whether these values are affirmed or transgressed. Pro-life proponents appeal to *pathos* when they graphically describe the dismemberment of a fetus during an abortion. Proponents of improved women's health and status in Africa do so when they describe the helplessness of wives forced to have unprotected sex with husbands likely infected with HIV. Opponents of oil exploration in the Arctic National Wildlife Refuge (ANWR) do so when they lovingly describe the calving grounds of caribou.

Are such appeals legitimate? Our answer is yes, if they intensify and deepen our response to an issue rather than divert our attention from it. Because understanding is a matter of feeling as well as perceiving, *pathos* can give access to nonlogical, but not necessarily nonrational, ways of knowing. *Pathos* helps us see what is deeply at stake in an issue, what matters to the whole person. Appeals to *pathos* help readers walk in the writer's shoes. That is why arguments are often improved through the use of stories that make issues come alive or sensory details that allow us to see, feel, and taste the reality of a problem.

Appeals to *pathos* become illegitimate, we believe, when they confuse an issue rather than clarify it. Consider the case of a student who argues that Professor Jones ought to raise his grade from a D to a C, lest he lose his scholarship and leave college, shattering the dreams of his dear old grandmother. To the extent that students' grades should be based on performance or effort, the student's image of the dear old grandmother is an illegitimate appeal to *pathos* because it diverts the reader from rational to irrational criteria. The weeping grandmother may provide a legitimate motive for the student to study harder but not for the professor to change a grade.

Although it is difficult to classify all the ways that writers can create appeals from *pathos,* we will focus on four strategies: concrete language; specific examples and illustrations; narratives; and connotations of words, metaphors, and analogies. Each of these strategies lends "presence" to an argument by creating immediacy and emotional impact.

USE CONCRETE LANGUAGE

Concrete language—one of the chief ways that writers achieve voice—can increase the liveliness, interest level, and personality of a writer's prose. When used in argument, concrete language typically heightens *pathos.* For example, consider the differences between the first and second drafts of the following student argument:

First Draft

People who prefer driving a car to taking a bus think that taking the bus will increase the stress of the daily commute. Just the opposite is true. Not being able to find a parking spot when in a hurry to be at work or school can cause a person stress. Taking the bus gives a person time to read or sleep, etc. It could be used as a mental break.

Second Draft (Concrete Language Added)

Taking the bus can be more relaxing than driving a car. Having some-one else behind the wheel gives people time to chat with friends or cram for an exam. They can balance their checkbooks, do homework, doze off, read the daily newspaper, or get lost in a novel rather than foam at the mouth looking for a parking space.

In this revision, specific details enliven the prose by creating images that trigger positive feelings. Who wouldn't want some free time to doze off or to get lost in a novel?

USE SPECIFIC EXAMPLES AND ILLUSTRATIONS

Specific examples and illustrations serve two purposes in an argument. They provide evidence that supports your reasons; simultaneously, they give your argument presence and emotional resonance. Note the flatness of the following draft arguing for the value of multicultural studies in a university core curriculum:

First Draft

Another advantage of a multicultural education is that it will help us see our own culture in a broader perspective. If all we know is our own heritage, we might not be inclined to see anything bad about this heritage because we won't know anything else. But if we study other heritages, we can see the costs and benefits of our own heritage.

Now note the increase in "presence" when the writer adds a specific example:

Second Draft (Example Added)

Another advantage of multicultural education is that it raises questions about traditional Western values. For example, owning private prop-erty (such as buying your own home) is part of the American dream. However, in studying the beliefs of American Indians, students are confronted with a very different view of private property. When the U.S. government sought to buy land in the Pacific Northwest from Chief Sealth, he is alleged to have replied:

> The president in Washington sends words that he wishes to buy our land. But how can you buy or sell the sky? The land? The idea is strange to us. If we do not own the freshness of the air and the sparkle of the water, how can you buy them?[. . .]We are part of the earth and it is part of us.[. . .]This we know: The earth does not belong to man, man belongs to the earth.

Our class was shocked by the contrast between traditional Western views of property and Chief Sealth's views. One of our best class discussions was initiated by this quotation from Chief Sealth. Had we not been exposed to a view from another culture, we would have never been led to question the "rightness" of Western values.

The writer begins his revision by evoking a traditional Western view of private property, which he then questions by shifting to Chief Sealth's vision of land as open, endless, and unobtainable as the sky. Through the use of a specific example, the writer brings to life his previously abstract point about the benefit of multicultural education.

USE NARRATIVES

A particularly powerful way to evoke *pathos* is to tell a story that either leads into your claim or embodies it implicitly and that appeals to your readers' feelings and imagination. Brief narratives—whether true or hypothetical—are particularly effective as opening attention grabbers for an argument. To illustrate how an introductory narrative (either a story or a brief scene) can create pathetic appeals, consider the following first paragraph to an argument opposing jet skis:

> I dove off the dock into the lake, and as I approached the surface I could see the sun shining through the water. As my head popped out, I located my cousin a few feet away in a rowboat waiting to escort me as I, a twelve-year-old girl, attempted to swim across the mile-wide, pristine lake and back to our dock. I made it, and that glorious summer day is one of my most precious memories. Today, however, no one would dare attempt that swim. Jet skis have taken over this small lake where I spent many summers with my grandparents. Dozens of whining jet skis crisscross the lake, ruining it for swimming, fishing, canoeing, rowboating, and even waterskiing. More stringent state laws are needed to control jet skiing because it interferes with other uses of lakes and is currently very dangerous.

This narrative makes a case for a particular point of view toward jet skis by winning our identification with the writer's experience. She invites us to relive that experience with her while she also taps into our own treasured memories of summer experiences that have been destroyed by change.

Opening narratives to evoke *pathos* can be powerfully effective, but they are also risky. If they are too private, too self-indulgent, too sentimental, or even too dramatic and forceful, they can backfire on you. If you have doubts about an opening narrative, read it to a sample audience before using it in your final draft.

USE WORDS, METAPHORS, AND ANALOGIES WITH APPROPRIATE CONNOTATIONS

Another way of appealing to *pathos* is to select words, metaphors, or analogies with connotations that match your aim. By using words with particular connotations, a writer guides readers to see the issue through the writer's angle of vision. Thus if you want to create positive feelings about a recent city council decision, you can call it "bold and decisive"; if you want to create negative feelings, you can call it "haughty and autocratic." Similarly, writers can use favorable or unfavorable metaphors and analogies to evoke different imaginative or emotional responses. A tax bill might be viewed as a "potentially fatal poison pill" or as "unpleasant but necessary economic medicine." In each of these cases, the words create an emotional as well as intellectual response.

Logos, Ethos, and *Pathos* Communicated through Language and Style

You can learn to recognize logic, *ethos,* and emotion in argument not only by the use of proofs but also by the language and style associated with each of these types of appeal. Actually, you will not often encounter pure examples of one of these styles, but instead you will encounter a mix, with one of the styles predominating. The same is true of writing. You may plan to write in a logical style, but emotion and *ethos* seep in and actually help you create a richer and more varied style for your argument.

LANGUAGE THAT APPEALS TO LOGIC

The language of logical argument, which is the language associated with reason, is sometimes called rational style. Words that carry mainly denotative meaning are favored in rational style over connotative and emotionally loaded language.

The denotative meaning of a word is the commonly held meaning found in the dictionary. It is the meaning most people would agree on because to denote is to name or indicate specifically. Examples of words that have predominantly denotative meanings and that are emotionally neutral include *introduction, fact, information, question*, and *literal meaning*. Most people would agree on the meanings of those words and could produce synonyms. Words with strong connotative meaning may have many extra, unique, symbolic, or personal meanings and associations attached to them that vary from person to person. Examples of words with connotative meaning include *rock star, politician, mugger, family values,* and *human rights*. Asked to define such words, different people would provide meanings and examples that would not be exactly alike or match the denotative meanings of these words in a dictionary.

For support, rational style relies on opinion in the form of reasons, literal or historical analogies, explanations, and definitions and also on factual data, quotations, and citations from experts and authorities. Furthermore, the reader is usually not required to make as many inferences as for other, less formal styles of writing. Most parts of the argument are spelled out explicitly for the sake of agreement and better adherence of minds.

Slogans that elicit emotional responses, such as "America is the greatest country," "The American people want change," or "Now is the time for healing," are generally omitted in rational style. Slogans of this type substitute for logical thinking. Readers think better and draw better conclusions when provided with well-reasoned opinion, quotations from authorities, and facts.

For example, in the opening paragraph of an essay titled "The Lost Art of Political Argument," Christopher Lasch uses rational style to argue in favor of argument and debate.

> Let us begin with a simple proposition: What democracy requires is public debate, not information. Of course it needs information too, but the kind of information it needs can be generated only by vigorous popular debate. We do not know what we need to know until we ask the right questions, and we can identify the right questions only by subjecting our own ideas about the world to the test of public controversy. Information, usually seen as the precondition of debate, is better understood as its by-product. When we get into arguments that focus and fully engage our attention, we become avid seekers of relevant information. Otherwise, we take in information passively—if we take it in at all.*

Rational style, as you can see in this excerpt, evokes mainly a cognitive, rational response from its readers.

*Christopher Lasch, "The Lost Art of Political Argument," *Harper's,* September 1990, 17.

LANGUAGE THAT DEVELOPS *ETHOS*

Authors who seek to establish their own credentials and good character use language to provide a fair-minded view of reality that is restrained and accurate rather than exaggerated or overly opinionated. When language is used to create positive *ethos,* an audience will trust the author as a credible source of information and opinion.

Language that develops *ethos* has several specific characteristics. To begin with, the writer exhibits a consistent awareness of the audience's background and values by adopting a vocabulary level that is appropriate for the topic and the audience. The writer does not either talk down to or overwhelm the audience, use technical jargon for an audience unfamiliar with it, or use slang or colloquial language unless the context specifically calls for that. Rap music, for example, invites a different vocabulary level than a scholarly paper does.

Writers intent on establishing *ethos* are sensitive to different audiences and what they will admire, trust, and accept. They try to use language precisely and to say exactly what they mean. They project an honest desire to communicate by avoiding ranting, filler material that gets off the subject, or anything that the audience would perceive as offensive or repugnant.

As you have probably already realized, an author can destroy *ethos* and alter an audience's favorable impression by changing the language. A student who uses colloquial, everyday expressions in a formal essay written for a professor, a commencement speaker who shouts obscenities at the audience, a father who uses formal, abstract language to talk to his five-year-old—all have made inappropriate language choices for their particular audiences, thereby damaging their *ethos* with those audiences.

When you read argument, notice how an author uses language to build connections and trust as well as to establish reliability with the audience. When you write argument, use language that will help the audience regard you as sincere and trustworthy. Appropriate language is essential when you write a college paper. The use of slang, slogans, and street language and expressions in otherwise formal writing damages your credibility as a serious thinker. Writing errors, including mistakes in spelling, punctuation, and grammar, also destroy *ethos* because they indicate a lack of concern and goodwill for your readers.

Here is an example of language that builds effective *ethos* with an audience. These excerpts come from Martin Luther King Jr.'s "Letter from Birmingham Jail." King was jailed because of his involvement in the civil rights movement in Birmingham, Alabama, and he had been criticized publicly for his participation by eight fellow clergymen of that city. He wrote this letter to those clergymen. Notice that he deliberately uses language that is sincere and honest and that establishes his credibility as a trustworthy and responsible human being with values his audience is likely to share. He does not come across as a troublemaker or a man who is angry at the system, as one might find with someone who has been jailed for participating in civil rights demonstrations. Rather, he comes across as thoughtfully conscious of his actions and ethically bound to participate as he is.

> My Dear Fellow Clergymen:
>
> While confined here in the Birmingham city jail, I came across your recent statement calling my present activities "unwise and untimely." . . . Since I feel that you are men of genuine good will and that your criticisms are sincerely set forth, I want to try to answer your statement in what I hope will be patient and reasonable terms.
>
> I think I should indicate why I am here in Birmingham, since you have been influenced by the view which argues against "outsiders coming in." . . . I, along with several members of my staff, am here because I was invited here. I am here because I have organizational ties here.
>
> But more basically, I am in Birmingham because injustice is here. Just as the prophets of the eighth century B.C. left their villages and carried their "thus saith the Lord" far beyond the boundaries of their home towns, and just as the Apostle Paul left his village of Tarsus and carried the gospel of Jesus Christ to the far corners of the Greco-Roman world, so am I compelled to carry the gospel of freedom beyond my own home town. Like Paul, I must constantly respond to the Macedonian call for aid.
>
> Moreover, I am cognizant of the interrelatedness of all communities and states. I cannot sit idly by in Atlanta and not be concerned about what happens in Birmingham. Injustice anywhere is a threat to justice everywhere. We are caught in an inescapable network of mutuality, tied in a single garment of destiny. Whatever affects one directly, affects all indirectly. Never again can we afford to live with the narrow, provincial "outside agitator" idea. Anyone who lives inside the United States can never be considered an outsider anywhere within its bounds.

Highlight the language in these passages that you think King used to establish good *ethos* with the eight clergymen. Notice how King deliberately uses language to project sincerity and goodwill toward this audience. He also selects examples and appeals to values that are compatible with their interests and values. King's letter is a classic example of argument that establishes effective *ethos* with a particular audience.

LANGUAGE THAT APPEALS TO EMOTION

References to values and motives summon feelings about what people regard as good and bad and about what they want, and authors use the language associated with emotional style in a variety of ways to express and evoke feelings about these matters. The following paragraphs describe a few special techniques that are characteristic of emotional style.

Emotionally loaded language evokes connotative meanings and causes the audience to experience feelings and associations at a personal level that are not described in dictionaries. Here is an example: "It's hard to feel like a Master of the Universe when you're sleeping in your old twin bed." Underline the words and phrases in the sentence that draw forth your emotions.

Emotional examples engage the emotions, as in this example: "When Silvia Geraci goes out to dinner with friends, she has a flash of anxiety when the check comes. She can pay her share—her parents give her enough money to cover all her expenses. It's just that others in her circle make their own money now." Most readers can share this type of anxiety.

Vivid description of an emotional scene creates an emotional reader response, as in this example: "Jimmy Finn, 24, a paralegal at the Manhattan-based law firm of Sullivan & Cromwell, made the most of his $66,000 annual income by moving back to his childhood home in nearby Staten Island. While his other friends paid exorbitant rents, Finn bought a new car and plane tickets to Florida so he could see his girlfriend on the weekends. He had ample spending money for restaurants and cabs, and began paying down his student loans." Notice how this description brings you into the scene, causing you to imagine the daily life of Jimmy Finn.

Narratives of emotional events draw readers into a scene just as vivid description does. Here is a story about a mother and her daughter: "A few years ago, Janice Charlton of Philadelphia pressured her daughter, Mary, then 26, to get a master's degree, even agreeing to cosign two $17,000 school loans if she did. Mary dropped out, Janice says, and the loans went into default. 'I'm sorry I ever suggested it,' says Janice. 'We're still close but it's a sticky issue between us.'" By describing the emotions of the mother, the author invites the reader to share them.

Emotional tone, created by emotional language and examples, indicates that the author has a strong feeling about the subject and wants the audience to share that feeling. Here is an example: "No matter how loving the parent-child bond, parents inevitably heave a sigh of relief when their adult kids finally start paying their own way. Seven months ago, when Finn's paralegal job moved to Washington, DC, he left home and got an apartment there. The transition, he said, was hard on his mother, Margie. Mom, though, reports that she's doing just fine." Also, irony and sarcasm should always be viewed as examples of emotional tone. They indicate strong feeling and a desire for change.

Figurative analogies contribute to emotion in an argument, particularly when two emotional subjects are compared and the resulting effect appeals more to emotion than to reason. For example, a researcher who is studying the adultolescent phenomenon states, "The conveyor belt that transported adolescents into adulthood has broken down." The comparison of an operational and a broken conveyor belt, particularly in their relationship to moving students toward adulthood, is supposed to have an emotional effect on the reader.

Table 17.1 A Summary of Language and Style in Argument

How Do You Make Appeals in Argument?		
To Appeal to Logic	To Develop *Ethos*	To Appeal to Emotion
Style		
Theoretical abstract language Denotative meanings Reasons Literal and historical analogies Explanations Definitions Factual data and statistics Quotations Citations from experts and authorities Informed opinion	Language appropriate to audience and subject Restrained, sincere, fair-minded presentation Appropriate level of vocabulary Correct grammar	Vivid, concrete language Emotionally loaded language Connotative meanings Emotional examples Vivid descriptions Narratives of emotional events Emotional tone Figurative analogies
Effect		
Evokes a cognitive, rational	Demonstrates author's reliability, competence, and respect for the audience's ideas and values through reliable and appropriate use of support and general accuracy	Evokes an emotional response

Emotional style is the easiest of all the styles to recognize because it uses charged language and is often close to our own experiences. Do not become distracted by emotional material or use it excessively in your own arguments. Remember, in argument, logic is the plot and emotion and *ethos* add support. Table 17.1 provides a summary of the characteristics of language used to appeal to reason, to establish *ethos,* and to appeal to emotion.

An Overview of Informal Fallacies

The study of informal fallacies remains the murkiest of all logical endeavors. It's murky because informal fallacies are as unsystematic as formal fallacies are rigid and systematized. Whereas formal fallacies of logic have the force of laws, informal fallacies have little more than explanatory power. Informal fallacies are quirky; they identify classes of less conclusive arguments that recur with some frequency, but they do not contain formal flaws that make their conclusions illegitimate no matter what the terms may say. Informal fallacies require us to look at the meaning of the terms to determine how much we should trust or distrust the conclusion. In evaluating arguments with informal fallacies, we usually find that arguments are "more or less" fallacious, and determining the degree of fallaciousness is a matter of judgment.

Knowledge of informal fallacies is most useful when we run across arguments that we "know" are wrong, but we can't quite say why. They just don't "sound right." They look reasonable enough, but they remain unacceptable to us. Informal fallacies are a sort of compendium of symptoms for arguments flawed in this way. We must be careful, however, to make sure that the particular case before us "fits" the descriptors for the fallacy that seems to explain its problem. It's much easier, for example, to find informal fallacies in a hostile argument than in a friendly one simply because we are more likely to expand the limits of the fallacy to make the disputed case fit.

In arranging the fallacies, we have, for convenience, put them into three categories derived from classical rhetoric: *pathos, ethos,* and *logos.* Fallacies of *pathos* rest on flaws in the way an argument appeals to the audience's emotions and values. Fallacies of *ethos* rest on flaws in the way the argument appeals to the character of opponents or of sources and witnesses within an argument. Fallacies of *logos* rest on flaws in the relationship among statements in an argument.

FALLACIES OF *PATHOS*

● **ARGUMENT TO THE PEOPLE (APPEALING TO STIRRING SYMBOLS)**
This is perhaps the most generic example of a *pathos* fallacy. Arguments to the people appeal to the fundamental beliefs, biases, and prejudices of the audience in order to sway opinion through a feeling of solidarity among those of the group. Thus a "Support Our Troops" bumper sticker, often including the American flag, creates an initial feeling of solidarity among almost all citizens of goodwill. But the car owner may have the deeper intention of actually meaning "support our president" or "support the war in _____." The stirring symbol of

the flag and the desire shared by most people to support our troops is used fallaciously to urge support of a particular political act. Arguments to the people often use visual rhetoric, as in the soaring eagle used in Wal-Mart corporate ads or images of happy families in marketing advertisements.

● **APPEAL TO IGNORANCE**   This fallacy persuades an audience to accept as true a claim that hasn't been proved false or vice versa. "Jones must have used steroids to get those bulging biceps because he can't prove that he hasn't used steroids." Appeals to ignorance are particularly common in the murky field of pseudoscience. "UFOs (ghosts, abominable snowmen) do exist because science hasn't proved that they don't exist." Sometimes, however, it is hard to draw a line between a fallacious appeal to ignorance and a legitimate appeal to precaution: "Genetically modified organisms must be dangerous to our health because science hasn't proved that they are safe."

● **APPEAL TO POPULARITY—BANDWAGON**   To board the bandwagon means (to use a more contemporary metaphor) to board the bus or train of what's popular. Appeals to popularity are fallacious because the popularity of something is irrelevant to its actual merits. "Living together before marriage is the right thing to do because most couples are now doing it." Bandwagon appeals are common in advertising where the claim that a product is popular substitutes for evidence of the product's excellence. There are times, however, when popularity may indeed be relevant: "Global warming is probably caused by human activity because a preponderance of scientists now hold this position." (Here we assume that scientists haven't simply climbed on a bandwagon themselves, but have formed their opinions based on research data and well-vetted, peer-reviewed papers.)

● **APPEAL TO PITY**   Here the arguer appeals to the audience's sympathetic feelings in order to support a claim that should be decided on more relevant or objective grounds. "Honorable judge, I should not be fined $200 for speeding because I was distraught from hearing news of my brother's illness and was rushing to see him in the hospital." Here the argument is fallacious because the arguer's reason, while evoking sympathy, is not a relevant justification for speeding (as it might have been, for instance, if the arguer had been rushing an injured person to the emergency room). In many cases, however, an arguer can legitimately appeal to pity, as in the case of fund-raising for victims of a tsunami or other disaster.

● **RED HERRING**   This fallacy's funny name derives from the practice of using a red herring (a highly odiferous fish) to throw dogs off a scent that they are supposed to be tracking. It refers to the practice of throwing an audience off track by raising an unrelated or irrelevant point. "Debating a gas tax increase is valuable, but I really think there should be an extra tax on SUVs." Here the arguer, apparently uncomfortable with the gas tax issue, diverts the conversation to the emotional issue of SUVs. A conversant who noted how the argument has gotten off track might say, "Stop talking, everyone. The SUV question is a red herring; let's get back to the topic of a gas tax increase."

FALLACIES OF *ETHOS*

● **APPEAL TO FALSE AUTHORITY** Arguers appeal to false authority when they use famous people (often movie stars or other celebrities) to testify on issues about which these persons have no special competence. "Joe Quarterback says Gooey Oil keeps his old tractor running sharp; therefore, Gooey Oil is a good oil." Real evidence about the quality of Gooey Oil would include technical data about the product rather than testimony from an actor or hired celebrity. However, the distinction between a "false authority" and a legitimate authority can become blurred. Consider the Viagra ads by former senator Bob Dole during the first marketing years of this impotence drug. As a famous person rather than a doctor, Dole would seem to be a false authority. But Dole was also widely known to have survived prostate cancer, and he may well have used Viagra. To the extent a person is an expert in a field, he or she is no longer a "false authority."

● **AD HOMINEM** Literally, *ad hominem* means "to the person." An *ad hominem* argument is directed at the character of an opponent rather than at the quality of the opponent's reasoning. Ideally, arguments are supposed to be *ad rem* ("to the thing"), that is, addressed to the specifics of the case itself. Thus an *ad rem* critique of a politician would focus on her voting record, the consistency and cogency of her public statements, her responsiveness to constituents, and so forth. An *ad hominem* argument would shift attention from her record to features of her personality, life circumstances, or the company she keeps. "Senator Sweetwater's views on the gas tax should be discounted because her husband works for a huge oil company" or "Senator Sweetwater supports tax cuts for the wealthy because she is very wealthy herself and stands to gain." But not all *ad hominem* arguments are *ad hominem* fallacies. Lawyers, for example, when questioning expert witnesses who give damaging testimony, often make an issue of their honesty, credibility, or personal investment in an outcome.

● **POISONING THE WELL** This fallacy is closely related to *ad hominem*. Arguers poison the well when they discredit an opponent or an opposing view in advance. "Before I yield the floor to the next speaker, I must remind you that those who oppose my plan do not have the best interests of working people in their hearts."

● **STRAW MAN** The straw man fallacy occurs when you oversimplify an opponent's argument to make it easier to refute or ridicule. Rather than summarizing an opposing view fairly and completely, you basically make up the argument you wish your opponent had made because it is so much easier to knock over, like knocking over a straw man or scarecrow in a corn field.

FALLACIES OF *LOGOS*

● **HASTY GENERALIZATION**   This fallacy occurs when someone makes a broad generalization on the basis of too little evidence. But what constitutes a sufficient amount of evidence? The generally accepted standards of sufficiency in any given field are difficult to determine. The Food and Drug Administration (FDA), for example, generally proceeds cautiously before certifying a drug as "safe." However, if people are harmed by the side effects of an FDA-approved drug, critics often accuse the FDA of having made a hasty generalization. At the same time, patients eager to have access to a new drug and manufacturers eager to sell a new product may lobby the FDA to quit "dragging its feet" and get the drug to market. Hence, the point at which a hasty generalization passes over into the realm of a prudent generalization is nearly always uncertain and contested.

● **PART FOR THE WHOLE**   Sometimes called by its Latin name *pars pro toto*, this fallacy is closely related to hasty generalization. In this fallacy, arguers pick out a part of the whole or a sample of the whole (often not a typical or representative part or sample) and then claim that what is true of the part is true for the whole. If, say, individuals wanted to get rid of the National Endowment for the Arts (NEA), they might focus on several controversial programs funded by the NEA and use them as justification for wiping out all NEA programs. The flip side of this fallacy occurs when an arguer picks only the best examples to make a case and conveniently forgets about other examples that may weaken the case.

● *Post Hoc, Ergo Propter Hoc*   The Latin name of this fallacy means "after this, therefore because of this." The fallacy occurs when a sequential relationship is mistaken for a causal relationship. For example, you may be guilty of this fallacy if you say, "Cramming for a test really helps because last week I crammed for my psychology test and I got an A on it." When two events occur frequently in conjunction with each other, we've got a good case for a causal relationship. But until we can show how one causes the other and until we have ruled out other causes, we cannot be certain that a causal relationship is occurring. For example, the A on your psych test may be caused by something other than your cramming. Maybe the exam was easier, or perhaps you were luckier or more mentally alert. It is often difficult to tell when a *post hoc* fallacy occurs. When the New York police department changed its policing tactics in the early 1990s, the crime rate plummeted. Many experts attributed the declining crime rate to the new policing tactics, but some critics proposed other explanations.

● **BEGGING THE QUESTION — CIRCULAR REASONING**   Arguers beg the question when they provide a reason that simply restates the claim in different words. Here is an example: "Abortion is murder because it is the intentional taking of the life of a human being." Because "murder" is defined as "the intentional taking of the life of a human being," the argument is circular. It is tantamount to saying, "Abortion is murder because it is murder." In the abortion debate, the crucial issue is whether a fetus is a "human being" in the legal sense. So in this case the arguer has fallaciously "begged the question" by assuming from the start that the fetus is a legal human being. The argument is similar to saying, "That person is obese because he is too fat."

● **FALSE DILEMMA—EITHER/OR**   This fallacy occurs when an arguer oversimplifies a complex issue so that only two choices appear possible. Often one of the choices is made to seem unacceptable, so the only remaining option is the other choice. "It's my way or the highway" is a typical example of a false dilemma. Here is a more subtle one: "Either we allow embryonic stem cell research, or we condemn people with diabetes, Parkinson's disease, or spinal injuries to a life without a cure." Clearly, there may be other options, including other approaches to curing these diseases. A good extended example of the false dilemma fallacy is found in sociologist Kai Erikson's analysis of President Truman's decision to drop the A-bomb on Hiroshima. His analysis suggests that the Truman administration prematurely reduced numerous options to just two: either drop the bomb on a major city, or sustain unacceptable losses in a land invasion of Japan. Erikson, however, shows there were other alternatives.

● **SLIPPERY SLOPE**   The slippery slope fallacy is based on the fear that once we put a foot on a slippery slope heading in the wrong direction, we're doomed to slide right out of sight. The controlling metaphor is of a slick mountainside without places to hold on rather than of a staircase with numerous stopping places. Here is an example of a slippery slope: "Once we allow medical use of marijuana, we'll eventually legalize it for everyone, after which we're on a slippery slope toward social acceptance of cocaine and heroin." Slippery slope arguments are frequently encountered when individuals request exceptions to bureaucratic rules: "Look, Blotnik, no one feels worse about your need for open-heart surgery than I do. But I still can't let you turn this paper in late. If I were to let you do it, then I'd have to let everyone turn in papers late." Slippery slope arguments can be very persuasive—and often rightfully so because every slippery slope argument isn't necessarily a slippery slope fallacy. Some slopes really are slippery. The slippery slope becomes a fallacy when we forget that we can often dig a foothold into the slope and stop. For example, we can define procedures for exceptions to rules so that Blotnik can turn in his paper late without allowing everyone to turn in a paper late. Likewise, a state could legalize medical use of marijuana without legalizing it for everyone.

● **FALSE ANALOGY**   Any two things being compared are similar in some ways and different in other ways. Whether an analogy is persuasive or false often depends on the audience's initial degree of skepticism. For example, people opposed to gun control may find the following argument persuasive: "Banning guns on the basis that guns accidentally kill people is like banning cars on the basis that cars accidentally kill people." In contrast, supporters of gun control are likely to call this argument a false analogy on the basis of dissimilarities between cars and guns. (For example, they might say that banning cars would be far more disruptive on our society than would be banning guns.) Just when a persuasive analogy turns into a false analogy is difficult to say.

● *NON SEQUITUR*   The name of this fallacy means "it does not follow." *Non sequitur* is a catchall term for any claim that doesn't follow from its premises or is supported by irrelevant premises. Sometimes the arguer seems to make an inexplicably illogical leap: "Genetically modified foods should be outlawed because they are not natural." (Should anything that is not natural be outlawed? In what way are they not natural?) At other times there may be a gap in the chain of reasons: "Violent video games have some social value because the army uses them for recruiting." (There may be an important idea emerging here, but too many logical steps are missing.) At still other times an arguer may support a claim with irrelevant reasons: "I should not receive a C in this course because I currently have a 3.8 GPA." In effect, almost any fallacy could be called a *non sequitur* because fallacious reasoning always indicates some kind of disconnect between the reasons and the claim.

● LOADED LABEL OR DEFINITION   Sometimes arguers try to influence their audience's view of something by creating a loaded label or definition. For example, people who oppose the "estate tax" (which calls to mind rich people with estates) have relabeled it the "death tax" in order to give it a negative connotation without any markers of class or wealth. Or to take another example, proponents of organic foods could create definitions like the following: "Organic foods are safe and healthy foods grown without any pesticides, herbicides, or other unhealthy additives." "Safe" and "healthy" are evaluative terms used fallaciously in what purports to be a definition. The intended implication is that nonorganic foods are not safe and healthy.

READINGS

Excerpt from "Immigration Policy Must Help Economy While Preserving Ideals"

Senator Mike Crapo

http://blog.thehill.com/2007/07/07/
immigration-policy-must-help-economy-while-preserving-ideals-sen-
mike-crapo/

A robust economy hinges on having a temporary guest worker program to fill jobs that are not filled by American citizens. U.S.-based businesses need economic incentives to keep operations stateside. If they have a dependable labor pool at all skill levels, incentives to move operations overseas are greatly decreased. We appreciate consumer goods and agriculture products "Made in America." We can keep things that way by approaching immigration rationally and sensibly. Whatever the skill level, any temporary guest worker system must be enforceable and reliable for the worker and employer. Once Americans have been given "first right" to jobs, employers such as the agriculture industry must have access to a system that's cost-effective, not bureaucratic, and doesn't carry the risk of prosecution while employers are trying to comply with the law. Congress understands the urgency of reaching a workable solution and is moving in the right direction.

What to the Slave Is the Fourth of July?
(Speech)
Frederick Douglass

On the fifth of July, 1852, former slave Frederick Douglass spoke at a meeting of the Ladies' Anti-Slavery Society in Rochester, New York. In this series of excerpts from his lengthy oration (published shortly thereafter as a pamphlet), Douglass reminds his audience of the irony of celebrating freedom and liberty in a land where much of the population was enslaved.

Fellow-citizens, pardon me, allow me to ask, why am I called upon to speak here to-day? What have I, or those I represent, to do with your national independence? Are the great principles of political freedom and of natural

justice, embodied in that Declaration of Independence, extended to us? And am I, therefore, called upon to bring our humble offering to the national altar, and to confess the benefits and express devout gratitude for the blessings resulting from your independence to us?

But, such is not the state of the case. I say it with a sad sense of the disparity between us. I am not included within the pale of this glorious anniversary! Your high independence only reveals the immeasurable distance between us. The blessings in which you, this day, rejoice, are not enjoyed in common. The rich inheritance of justice, liberty, prosperity, and independence, bequeathed by your fathers, is shared by you, not by me. The sunlight that brought life and healing to you has brought stripes and death to me. This Fourth [of] July is yours, not mine. You may rejoice, I must mourn. To drag a man in fetters into the grand illuminated temple of liberty, and call upon him to join you in joyous anthems is inhuman mockery and sacrilegious irony. Do you mean, citizens, to mock me, by asking me to speak to-day?

Fellow-citizens, above your national, tumultuous joy, I hear the mournful wail of millions whose chains, heavy and grievous yesterday, are, to-day, rendered more intolerable by the jubilee shouts that reach them. To forget them, to pass lightly over their wrongs, and to chime in with the popular theme, would be treason most scandalous and shocking, and would make me a reproach before God and the world. My subject, then fellow citizens, is AMERICAN SLAVERY. I shall see, this day, and its popular characteristics, from the slave's point of view. Standing, there, identified with the American bondman, making his wrongs mine, I do not hesitate to declare, with all my soul, that the character and conduct of this nation never looked blacker to me than on this 4th of July! Whether we turn to the declarations of the past, or to the professions of the present, the conduct of the nation seems equally hideous and revolting. America is false to the past, false to the present, and solemnly binds herself to be false to the future. Standing with God and the crushed and bleeding slave on this occasion, I will, in the name of humanity which is outraged, in the name of liberty which is fettered, in the name of the constitution and the Bible, which are disregarded and trampled upon, dare to call in question and to denounce, with all the emphasis I can command, everything that serves to perpetuate slavery—the great sin and shame of America! "I will not equivocate; I will not excuse"; I will use the severest language I can command; and yet not one word shall escape me that any man, whose judgment is not blinded by prejudice, or who is not at heart a slaveholder, shall not confess to be right and just.

But I fancy I hear some one of my audience say, it is just in this circumstance that you and your brother abolitionists fail to make a favorable impression on the public mind. Would you argue more, and denounce less, would you persuade more, and rebuke less, your cause would be much more likely to succeed. But, I submit, where all is plain there is nothing to be argued. What point in the anti-slavery creed would you have me argue? On what branch of the subject do the people of this country need light? Must I undertake to prove that the slave is a man? That point is conceded already. Nobody doubts it. The slaveholders themselves acknowledge it in the enactment of laws for their government. They acknowledge it when they punish disobedience on the part of the slave. There are seventy-two crimes in the State of Virginia, which, if committed by a black man, (no matter how ignorant he be), subject him to the punishment of death; while only two of the same crimes will subject a white man to the like punishment. What is this but the acknowledgement that the slave is a moral, intellectual and responsible being? The manhood of the slave is conceded. It is admitted in the fact that Southern statute books are covered with enactments forbidding, under severe fines and penalties, the teaching of the slave to read or to write. When you can point to any such laws, in reference to the beasts of the field, then I may consent to argue the manhood of the slave. When the dogs in your streets, when the fowls of the air, when the cattle on your hills, when the fish of the sea, and the reptiles that crawl, shall be unable to distinguish the slave from a brute, there will I argue with you that the slave is a man!

For the present, it is enough to affirm the equal manhood of the negro race. Is it not astonishing that, while we are ploughing, planting and reaping, using all kinds of mechanical tools, erecting houses, constructing bridges, building ships, working in metals of brass, iron, copper, silver and gold; that, while we are reading, writing and ciphering, acting as clerks, merchants and secretaries, having among us lawyers, doctors, ministers, poets, authors, editors, orators and teachers; that, while we are engaged in all manner of enterprises common to other men, digging gold in California, capturing the whale in the Pacific, feeding sheep and cattle on the hillside, living, moving, acting, thinking, planning, living in families as husbands, wives and children, and, above all, confessing and worshipping the Christian's God, and looking hopefully for life and immortality beyond the grave, we are called upon to prove that we are men!

Would you have me argue that man is entitled to liberty? That he is the rightful owner of his own body? You have already declared it. Must I argue the wrongfulness of slavery? Is it to be settled by the rules of logic and argumentation, as a matter beset with great difficulty, involving a doubtful application of the principle of justice, hard to be understood?

How should I look to-day, in the presence of Americans, dividing, and subdividing a discourse, to show that men have a natural right to freedom? speaking of it relatively, and positively, negatively, and affirmatively. To do so would be to make myself ridiculous and offer an insult to your understanding. There is not a man beneath the canopy of heaven that does not know that slavery is wrong for him.

What, am I to argue that it is wrong to make men brutes, to rob them of their liberty, to work them without wages, to keep them ignorant of their relations to their fellow men, to beat them with sticks, to flay their flesh with the lash, to load their limbs with irons, to hunt them with dogs, to sell them at auction, to sunder their families, to knock out their teeth, to burn their flesh, to starve them into obedience and submission to their masters? Must I argue that a system thus marked with blood, and stained with pollution, is wrong? No! I will not. I have better employments for my time and strength, than such arguments would imply.

What, then, remains to be argued? Is it that slavery is not divine; that God did not establish it; that our doctors of divinity are mistaken? There is blasphemy in the thought. That which is inhuman, cannot be divine! Who can reason on such a proposition? They that can, may; I cannot. The time for such argument is past.

What, to the American slave, is your 4th of July? I answer: a day that reveals to him, more than all other days in the year, the gross injustice and cruelty to which he is the constant victim. To him, your celebration is a sham; your boasted liberty, an unholy license; your national greatness, swelling vanity; your sounds of rejoicing are empty and heartless; your denunciations of tyrants, brass fronted impudence; your shouts of liberty and equality, hollow mockery; your prayers and hymns, your sermons and thanksgivings, with all your religious parade, and solemnity, are, to him, mere bombast, fraud, deception, impiety, and hypocrisy—a thin veil to cover up crimes which would disgrace a nation of savages. There is not a nation on the earth guilty of practices, more shocking and bloody, than are the people of these United States, at this very hour.

Go where you may, search where you will, roam through all the monarchies and despotisms of the old world, travel through South America, search out every abuse, and when you have found the last, lay your facts by the side of the everyday practices of this nation, and you will say with me, that, for revolting barbarity and shameless hypocrisy, America reigns without a rival. Take the American slave-trade, which we are told by the papers, is especially prosperous just now. Ex-Senator Benton tells us that the price of men was never higher than now. He mentions the fact to show that slavery is in no danger. This trade is one of the peculiarities of American institutions. It is carried on in all the large towns and cities in one-half of this confederacy; and millions are pocketed every year, by dealers in this horrid traffic. In several states, this trade is a chief source of wealth. It is called (in contradistinction to the foreign slave-trade) "the internal slave trade." It is, probably, called so, too, in order to

...*continued* What to the Slave Is the Fourth of July?, **Frederick Douglass**

divert from it the horror with which the foreign slave-trade is contemplated. That trade has long since been denounced by this government, as piracy. It has been denounced with burning words, from the high places of the nation, as an execrable traffic. To arrest it, to put an end to it, this nation keeps a squadron, at immense cost, on the coast of Africa. Everywhere, in this country, it is safe to speak of this foreign slave-trade, as a most inhuman traffic, opposed alike to the laws of God and of man. The duty to extirpate and destroy it is admitted even by our DOCTORS OF DIVINITY. In order to put an end to it, some of these last have consented that their colored brethren (nominally free) should leave this country, and establish themselves on the western coast of Africa! It is, however, a notable fact that, while so much execration is poured out by Americans upon those engaged in the foreign slave-trade, the men engaged in the slave-trade between the states pass without condemnation, and their business is deemed honorable.

Behold the practical operation of this internal slave-trade, the American slave-trade, sustained by American politics and American religion. Here you will see men and women reared like swine for the market. You know what is a swine-drover? I will show you a man-drover. They inhabit all our Southern States. They perambulate the country and crowd the highways of the nation, with droves of human stock. You will see one of these human flesh-jobbers, armed with pistol, whip and Bowie-knife, driving a company of a hundred men, women, and children from the Potomac to the slave market at New Orleans. These wretched people are to be sold singly, or in lots, to suit purchasers. They are food for the cotton-field, and the deadly sugar-mill. Mark the sad procession, as it moves wearily along, and the inhuman wretch who drives them. Hear his savage yells and his blood-chilling oaths, as he hurries on his affrighted captives! There, see the old man, with locks thinned and gray. Cast one glance, if you please, upon that young mother, whose shoulders are bare to the scorching sun, her briny tears falling on the brow of the babe in her arms. See, too, that girl of thirteen, weeping, yes! weeping, as she thinks of the mother from whom she has been torn! The drove moves tardily. Heat and sorrow have nearly consumed their strength; suddenly you hear a quick snap, like the discharge of a rifle; the fetters clank, and the chain rattles simultaneously; your ears are saluted with a scream, that seems to have torn its way to the centre of your soul! The crack you heard, was the sound of the slave-whip; the scream you heard, was from the woman you saw with the babe. Her speed had faltered under the weight of her child and her chains! that gash on her shoulder tells her to move on. Follow this drove to New Orleans. Attend the auction; see men examined like horses; see the forms of women rudely and brutally exposed to the shocking gaze of American slave-buyers. See this drove sold and separated forever; and never forget the deep, sad sobs that arose from that scattered multitude. Tell me citizens, WHERE, under the sun, you can witness a spectacle more fiendish and shocking. Yet this is but a glance at the American slave-trade, as it exists, at this moment, in the ruling part of the United States.

I was born amid such sights and scenes. To me the American slave-trade is a terrible reality. When a child, my soul was often pierced with a sense of its horrors. I lived on Philpot Street, Fell's Point, Baltimore, and have watched from the wharves, the slave ships in the Basin, anchored from the shore, with their cargoes of human flesh, waiting for favorable winds to waft them down the Chesapeake. There was, at that time, a grand slave mart kept at the head of Pratt Street, by Austin Woldfolk. His agents were sent into every town and county in Maryland, announcing their arrival, through the papers, and on flaming "hand-bills," headed CASH FOR NEGROES. These men were generally well dressed men, and very captivating in their manners. Ever ready to drink, to treat, and to gamble. The fate of many a slave has depended upon the turn of a single card; and many a child has been snatched from the arms of its mother by bargains arranged in a state of brutal drunkenness.

Allow me to say, in conclusion, notwithstanding the dark picture I have this day presented of the state of the nation, I do not despair of this country. There are forces in operation, which must inevitably work the downfall of slavery. "The arm of the Lord is not shortened," and the doom of slavery is certain. I, therefore, leave off where I began, with hope. While drawing encouragement from the Declaration of Independence, the great principles it contains, and the genius of American Institutions, my spirit is also cheered by the obvious tendencies of the age. Nations do not now stand in the same relation to each other that they did ages ago. No nation can now shut itself up from the surrounding world, and trot round in the same old path of its fathers without interference. The time was when such could be done. Long established customs of hurtful character could formerly fence themselves in, and do their evil work with social impunity. Knowledge was then confined and enjoyed by the privileged few, and the multitude walked on in mental darkness. But a change has now come over the affairs of mankind. Walled cities and empires have become unfashionable. The arm of commerce has borne away the gates of the strong city. Intelligence is penetrating the darkest corners of the globe. It makes its pathway over and under the sea, as well as on the earth. Wind, steam, and lightning are its chartered agents. Oceans no longer divide, but link nations together. From Boston to London is now a holiday excursion. Space is comparatively annihilated. Thoughts expressed on one side of the Atlantic are distinctly heard on the other. The far off and almost fabulous Pacific rolls in grandeur at our feet. The Celestial Empire, the mystery of ages, is being solved. The fiat of the Almighty, "Let there be Light," has not yet spent its force. No abuse, no outrage whether in taste, sport or avarice, can now hide itself from the all-pervading light.

Kate Winslet, Please Save Us!

Terrence Rafferty

Brooklyn native Terrence Rafferty is a film critic whose articles have appeared in the Atlantic, *the* Village Voice, Film Quarterly, *the* New York Times, *and many other publications. He also has been the "critic-at-large" for* GQ *(short for* Gentleman's Quarterly*), a fashion and culture magazine geared to young professional men.* GQ *carried the following argument in May 2001. Do you think the argument would have been constructed differently if it had been published elsewhere?*

When I go to the movies these days, I sometimes find myself gripped by a very peculiar sort of nostalgia: I miss flesh. I see skin, I see bones, I see many rocklike outcroppings of muscle, but I rarely see, in the angular bodies up there on the screen—either the hard, sculpted ones or the brittle, anorexic ones—anything extra, not even a hint of the soft layer of fatty tissue that was once an essential component of the movies' romantic fantasy, the cushion that made encounters between the sexes seem like pleasant, sensual experiences rather than teeth-rattling head-on collisions. The sleek form-follows-function physiques of today's film stars suggest a world in which power and brutal efficiency are all that matter, in the bedroom no less than in the pitiless, sun-seared arena of Gladiator. This may well be an accurate reflection of our anxious time, but it's also mighty depressing. When I come out of the multiplex now, I often feel like the archetypal ninety-eight-pound weakling in the old Charles Atlas ads—like big bullies have been kicking sand in my face for two hours. And that's just the women.

2   This is a touchy area, I realize. Where body type is concerned, an amazingly high percentage of social and cultural commentary is fueled by simple envy, resentment of the young and the buff. A few years ago, when Calvin Klein ads featuring the stunning, waiflike Kate Moss appeared on the sides of New York City buses, they were routinely defaced with bitter-sounding graffiti—FEED ME was the most popular—which was, you had to suspect, largely the product of women who were enraged by her distinctive beauty. (Men, to my knowledge, had few complaints about having to see Moss in her underwear whiz past them on Madison Avenue.) Protesters insisted that images such as those in the Klein ads promote eating disorders in impressionable teenage girls. Maybe that's so—I don't have the statistics—but the sheer violence of the attacks on Moss, along with the fact that they seemed to be directed more at the model herself than at the marketing wizards who exploited

her, strongly suggested another, less virtuous agenda. The taste of sour grapes was
unmistakable.

3   I happened to think Moss looked
great—small, but well-proportioned, and
mercifully lacking the ropy musculature
that had begun to creep into pop-culture
images of femininity, in the cunning guise
of "empowerment." The Bionic Woman
could only dream of the bulging biceps
sported by Linda Hamilton in *Terminator 2:
Judgment Day* (1991); and Ginger Rogers,
even when she was struggling to match
steps with Astaire, never had the calf muscles of the mighty Madonna. (Nor would
she have wanted them: She was a dancer
and not, like Mrs. Ritchie or any of her
brood of MTV chicks, a kinky aerobics

Kate Moss, waiflike

instructor.) It's understandable, I suppose, that women might have felt
the impulse to bulk up during the might-makes-right regimes of Ronald
Reagan and George Herbert Walker Bush, when the rippling behemoths
of machismo, Arnold and Sly, ruled the screen; in that context, working
on one's abs and pecs could be considered a prudent strategy of self-
defense. But the arms buildup in the Cold War between the sexes was not
a pretty sight. Applied to sex, the doctrine of Mutually Assured Destruction is kind of a bummer. The wages of sinew is the death of romance.

4   At least that's how it looks to people of my generation, whose form-
ative years were the '60s, and to many of Moss's generation (the one commonly designated "X"), who in their youth embraced, for a while, the
antipower aesthetic of grunge. What we oversaturated pop-culture consumers consider attractive— i.e., what's sexy in the opposite gender and
worth aspiring to in one's own—usually develops in adolescence, as the
relevant body parts do, and doesn't change much thereafter. For men
older than I am, the perfect woman might have been Sophia Loren or
Elizabeth Taylor or Marilyn Monroe or Rita Hayworth or the wartime
pinup Betty Grable or (reaching back to the hugely eroticized flapper
era) the original It girl, Clara Bow. And for them, the image of the ideal
masculine self might have been Cary Grant or Clark Gable or Henry
Fonda or Gary Cooper or even, for the less physically prepossessing—
OK, shorter—guys, Cagney or Bogart or Tracy. By the time the '60s
rocked and rolled into history, some subtle transformations had
occurred, primarily in female sexual iconography. While the male stars of
that decade remained more or less within the range of body types of their

...*continued* Kate Winslet, Please Save Us!, **Terrence Rafferty**

predecessors—Steve McQueen and Sean Connery might have looked a bit more athletic than the old norms demanded, but they wouldn't qualify as hard-bodies by today's standards—the shape of desirability in women distinctly altered, to something less voluptuous and more elongated. The fashions of the era tended to shift the erotic focus southward, from the breasts and the hips down to the legs, which, in a miniskirt, did rather overwhelm all other possible indicators of a woman's sexual allure. Although smaller-chested, leaner-hipped women, such as Julie Christie, stole some thunder from the conspicuously curvaceous, a certain amount of flesh was still required. Minis didn't flatter skinny legs any more than they did chubby ones.

5   So there was, to the avid eyes of teenage boys like me, a fine balance struck in the body aesthetic of the '60s, between, so to speak, length and width, Giacometti and Rubens. And muscles weren't part of the equation. He-men such as Steve Reeves—whose 1959 *Hercules*, a cheap Italian import initiated a spate of "sword and sandal" epics—seemed, to both sexes, ridiculous, vain rather than truly manly. (It's worth noting that in those days it was widely perceived that the primary market for body-building magazines was gay men.) And women? Forget it. The epitome of the muscular gal was the Russian or East German Olympic athlete, an Olga or a Helga, whose gender identity was frequently, and often justly, a matter of some dispute. There's an echo of that attitude in Ridley Scott's 1997 *G.I. Jane,* in which a feminist senator played by Anne Bancroft, trying to select a candidate for the first woman to undergo Navy SEAL training, summarily dismisses several of the beefier applicants on the grounds of ambiguous sexuality. She settles on Demi Moore, who is slender and pretty and, on the evidence of a spectacularly obvious boob job, unquestionably straight.

6   But bodies like Moore's puzzle me. What, exactly, is the empowering element here—the iron she's pumped or the silicone that's been pumped into her chest? My number one teenage crush, Diana Rigg, didn't need either in order to be wholly convincing as kick-ass secret agent Emma Peel in the TV series *The Avengers.* Paired with a dapper male partner, John Steed (played by Patrick Macnee), Mrs. Peel was not only fully empowered but was also by far the more physically active of the two. In her mod pantsuits and go-go boots, she did most of the actual fighting in the kung fu-ish battles that climaxed virtually every episode, while Steed, perhaps mindful of potential damage to his impeccably cut Pierre Cardin suits, generally limited his martial activity to an occasional deft thrust with the umbrella.

7   Maybe if I'd come of age with visions of Madonna dancing in my head, I might find GI Demi devastatingly sexy rather than grotesque, but, objectively, I think the idea that women's power depends on either

sculpted muscles or gigantic, orblike breasts (much less both) smacks of desperation. Mrs. Peel wielded her power so coolly, so confidently, and clearly never felt the need to enhance it by strenuous training or expensive medical procedures. Comfort in one's own skin is always appealing, which is probably why, in this sweating, striving, aggressively self-improving era, I find bodies as diverse as Kate Moss's and Kate Winslet's mighty attractive. It's not the body type per se—neither the frail Kate nor the ampler one precisely conforms to my Riggian ideal—but a woman's attitude toward her body that makes her sexy.

Kate Winslet from *Titanic* days

8 What's unnerving about today's pop-culture images of women is how extreme they are—and how much emphasis they place on the *effort* required to correct nature, to retard the aging process, to be all that you can be (and not, God forbid, simply what you are). The ethic of progress through hard work and technology is deeply ingrained in our society, as is the democratic notion that everyone should be whatever he or she wants to be—a noble idea that gets a tad problematic when what everyone wants to be is a star. And every star wants to be a bigger star. As a result, we're seeing, in the movies and on television and in the pages of fashion magazines, increasingly bizarre manifestations of our paradoxical collective need to feel unique and, more, admired. Being really fat, for example, can confer on a person a certain distinction, but not the kind most of us yearn for. (In the old days, for men, a degree of heft often indicated prosperity; the movies embodied their image of financial success in portly figures such as Eugene Pallette and Edward Arnold. No more.) To stand out on the runway these days, a model has to be significantly gaunter—and younger—than even the FEED ME–era Moss. And to make her mark on the screen, an actress has several equally grueling options: starve herself skeletal, go to the gym and get muscular, or—sometimes in perverse combination with one of the previous—have her breasts inflated surgically. In each case, the result is a wild exaggeration of what would be, in moderation, a desirable quality: slimness, fitness or voluptuousness. When I look at women in the movies now, I often feel as if I were gazing not at real people but at cartoon characters—Olive Oyl, Popeye (in drag) and Jessica Rabbit.

...*continued* Kate Winslet, Please Save Us!, **Terrence Rafferty**

9   Of course, there are exceptions: the spectacular Winslet; the cherubic and blissfully unself-conscious Drew Barrymore; the graceful, athletic Asian stars Michelle Yeoh and Maggie Cheung; and (no epithet necessary) Julia Roberts. But too many of the screen's great beauties have been developing a lean and hungry look in recent years. They've felt the burn, and something more than body fat appears to have been eliminated—a certain amount of joy seems to have melted away at the same time. Clearly, we live in extraordinarily ruthless and competitive times; and popular culture is bound to reflect that condition, but I can't think of another age in which the competitive anxieties of the performers themselves were so mercilessly exposed to the public's view. When tough, chunky guys like Cagney squared off against one another in a boxing ring or on the mean streets of New York or Chicago, you sensed that the survival of an entire community of immigrants was at stake; you could see it in every movement of their squat brawler's bodies. And when the Depression was over, those fierce small men just about vanished from the movies, giving way to their larger, better-nourished children, who left the field, in turn, to generations who would be conscious of their bodies without having nearly as much use for them as their ancestors had had. What's at stake for today's action heroes and heroines, all pumped up with no place to go except to the "explosive" climax of a fanciful plot? The steroidal action pictures of the '80s and '90s created a race of pointless Supermen. Everyone in the audience was in on the joke: Bruce Willis and Tom Cruise and Nicolas Cage and Keanu Reeves didn't bulk up to save the world or any recognizable part of it; they did it because starring in an action franchise was, and remains, a surefire means of moving up the Hollywood ladder.

10   As the historian Lynne Luciano points out in her useful new book, *Looking Good: Male Body Image in America,* in a white-collar, service economy all most of us do with our bodies is compare them with everybody else's. We look, we admire, we envy, we check the mirror, we get dissatisfied, we go back to the old drawing board (the gym, the plastic surgeon, Jenny Craig, whatever). And this strikes many as perfectly reasonable and natural: You have to keep an edge, and you have to *work* on it. Constant vigilance is required for both men and women, and folks are starting to look a little haggard. This applies even to the beautiful people of the silver screen. We can see the strain as they try to hang on to their precarious positions, like Tom Cruise at the beginning of *M.I.2.* And who, aside from the stars themselves, their families and their agents, could possibly care?

11   I haven't used the word *narcissism* yet, and it's long overdue. The unseemly vanity once ascribed to poor Steve Reeves has become the norm in Hollywood, which, kind of hilariously, apparently believes that

we're so vain we probably think their movies are about us. I can't come up with another explanation for berserk pictures like David Fincher's *Fight Club* (1999), in which Edward Norton, as a harried white collar Everyman, takes as his guru and alter ego an alarmingly buff *Übermensch* played by Brad Pitt. If the weak box-office returns are any indication, *Fight Club* did not strike the deep chord in the hearts of American men that its makers evidently thought it would, and, to add insult to injury, the picture didn't even provoke the "controversy" that might have validated the artists' sense of their own fearlessness and edginess. The whole spectacle was simply self-important and silly—as silly as *Hercules* and, because no one involved seemed to recognize it, then some.

12   It's time to stop the madness. Sure, we viewers are stressed-out and perhaps slightly self-absorbed, but more of us than Hollywood thinks have some perspective on the absurdities of our lives and the insanities of our culture. Fewer of us than the studios imagine actually believe that a diet or a set of weights or silicone implants will change our lives, even if every movie star worth his or her (pardon the expression) salt apparently does believe it. That's their business, and, as we know—though Hollywood has obviously forgotten—there's *no business like show business*. The feral, predatory creatures prowling across the screen for our amusement are in a world of their own. And although they carry themselves as if they were wolves, magnificent in their power, they're really just coyotes, roaming the hills restlessly for scraps and deluding themselves even more doggedly than Chuck Jones's indefatigable Wile E. At least he knew what he was.

13   In a sense, body image represents the final frontier of postmodernism, the only area as yet untouched by our culture's pervasive irony. It would be useful, I think, for moviemakers to drop the pretense that entertainment is a life-and-death struggle, which only the strong survive. The stars of earlier eras, with their variety of unapologetically eccentric physiques, understood it was all a lovely con, a game played for pleasure: That's what those discreet little layers of flesh ultimately meant. But what would it take, I wonder, to make today's hardbodies lighten up and laugh at their own desperate exertions or, failing that, merely stop gazing out at us cowed viewers as if they were dying to beat the crap out of us? I don't know, but I suspect that cranky magazine columns won't do the job. A higher power will have to be invoked. Mrs. Peel, you're needed.

"Real Beauty"—Or Really Smart Marketing?

Rebecca Traister

Traister is staff writer for the "Life" section of Salon, the online news and culture journal which carried the following article in 2005. Her work typically considers issues related to women, gender, and power and has been published in a variety of publications, including ELLE, the New York Times, Vogue, and The Nation.

The words appear slowly, against the familiar powder-blue shape of the bird in flight—the Dove soap symbol—like soothing, watery poetry:

> *For too long*
> *beauty has been defined by narrow, stifling sterotypes [sic].*
> *You've told us it's time to change all that. We agree.*
> *Because we believe real beauty comes*
> *In many shapes, sizes and ages.*
> *It is why we started the Campaign for Real Beauty.*
> *And why we hope you'll take part.*

2   This is the lilting intro to the Web site that Dove has dedicated to its "Real Beauty" advertising campaign, for which it has picked six women who are not professional models—each beautiful, but broader than Bundchen, heftier than an Olsen twin—to model in bras and panties.

3   The campaign is massive; these six broads are currently featured in national television and magazine ads, as well as on billboards and the sides of buses in urban markets like Boston, Chicago, Washington, Dallas, Los Angeles, Miami, New York, and San Francisco. And they've made quite an impact. Apparently, this public display of non-liposuctioned thighs is so jaw-droppingly revelatory that recent weeks have seen the Real Beauty models booked on everything from "The Today Show" to "The View" to CNN.

4   All the hoopla is precisely what Dove expected. According to a press release, Dove wants "to make women feel more beautiful every day by challenging today's stereotypical view of beauty and inspiring women to take great care of themselves." The use of "real women" (don't think too hard about the Kate Mosses of the world losing their status as biological females here) "of various ages, shapes and sizes" is designed "to provoke discussion and debate about today's typecast beauty images."

5   It's a great idea—a worthy follow-up to Dove's 2004 campaign, which featured women with lined faces, silver hair and heavy freckles, and asked questions like, "Wrinkled? Or Wonderful?" and also got a lot of attention, including a shout-out on the "Ellen DeGeneres Show."

6   As Stacy Nadeau, one of the Real Beauty models and a full-time student from Ann Arbor, Mich., says on the campaign Web site, "I have always been a curvier girl and always will be. I am proud of my body and think all women should be proud of theirs too. This is my time to encourage and help women feel great about themselves, no matter what they weigh or look like. Women have surrendered to diets and insane eating habits to live up to social stereotypes for too long. It's time that all women felt beautiful in their own skin."

7   But let's hope that skin doesn't have any cellulite. Because no one wants to look at a cottage-cheesy ass.

8   That's right. The one little wrinkle—so to speak—in this you-go-girl stick-it-to-the-media-man empowerment campaign is that the set of Dove products that these real women are shilling for is *cellulite firming cream*. Specifically, Dove's new "Intensive Firming Cream," described as "a highly effective blend of glycerin, plus seaweed extract and elastin peptides known for their skin-firming properties." It's supposed "to work on problem areas to help skin feel firmer and reduce the appearance of cellulite in two weeks." There are also the Intensive Firming Lotion and the Firming Moisturizing Body Wash, which do pretty much the same thing.

9   The ad copy on the posters—in which the women stand alone, often looking over their rounded backsides—is composed of sing-it-sister lines like "Let's face it, firming the thighs of a size 2 supermodel is no challenge" and "New Dove Firming. As tested on real curves."

10   Meanwhile, on its Web site, Dove encourages us to get behind something called "The Dove Self-Esteem Fund," which involves a partnership with the Girl Scouts (and a program called *uniquely ME!*). It is supposed to help "girls to overcome life damaging hang-ups by putting beauty into perspective." Yes, when I think of putting beauty in perspective for girls, mostly I think of suggesting that they shell out for three separately sold products that will temporarily make it appear that they have less cellulite.

11   It's not that I have anything against firming cream. By all means, sell firming cream! Go ahead! I'm even prepared to believe that it may be a useful tool for women who truly are plagued by their cellulite and are thankful to have a product that can help them combat it. I also understand that companies sell stuff. They advertise, they flog product; thus is life and business.

12   But as long as you're patting yourself on the back for hiring real-life models with imperfect bodies, thereby "challenging today's stereotypical view of beauty and inspiring women to take great care of themselves," why ask those models to flog a cream that has zero health value and is just an expensive and temporary Band-Aid for a "problem" that the media has told us we have with our bodies. Incidentally, cellulite isn't even a result of being overweight! It's the result of cellular changes in the skin. Skinny people have cellulite. Old people have cellulite. Young people have cellulite. Gwyneth Paltrow has cellulite. All God's children have cellulite.

13   Why not run an ad that proclaims, "Cellulite: Uniquely MINE!"

14   Or, more realistically, why aren't these women selling shampoo? Or soap? Or moisturizer?

15   Stacie Bright, a spokeswoman for Unilever, Dove's parent company, emphasized that this campaign "is for women of all shapes and sizes, and a lot of women want firming products. It's about feeling good about yourself. And that's about bringing products that matter to women." Pressed on the inconsistency of having women who feel good about themselves sell a product that makes a lot of us feel bad about ourselves, Bright replied, "Let's face it, if you had a firming product, and you had a size 2 woman selling it, that would really be the contradiction."

16   Clearly the idea behind the campaign is a smart, worthwhile and rational one. It does feel refreshingly non-self-loathing to log on to the Dove site and hear the models saying things like "I love these big ol' hips" and "I don't think about being slim." It's a little ray of sanity in this anorexic world. But it's also a business proposition and an advertising campaign. And doing something radically different—like presenting female consumers with models who actually resemble human beings they've met—is getting these products a lot of coveted attention. In fact, Dove may have tapped a zeitgeist vein, since the sport of lashing out at manipulated images of female beauty seems to be enjoying a bit of a vogue right now.

17   This spring, Oscar-winning actress Cate Blanchett spoke in interviews about her horror at the Botox craze. "I look at people sort of entombing themselves and all you see is their little pinholes of terror," said the actress. "And you think, Just live your life—death is not going to be any easier just because your face can't move." Blanchett also said that she thinks "that women and their vulnerabilities are played on in the cosmetic industry. . . . Women are encouraged to be terrified of aging." In this month's *Vogue*, Kate Winslet says of her battle with the press over her normal weight, "I'm relatively slim, I eat healthily, I keep fit. . . . I couldn't be 105 pounds even if I tried, and I really don't want to be 105 pounds."

18   And in just over a week, Bath and Body Works in association with American Girl dolls, will launch a line of "Real Beauty Inside and Out" personal care products "designed to help girls ages 8 to 12 feel—and be—their best." The line will include body lotions, splashes, soaps and lip balms, all dressed up in girl-friendly "hues of berry" and each arriving with an inspirational message like "Real beauty means no one's smile shines exactly like yours," "Real beauty is helping a friend," or "Real beauty is trusting in yourself."

19 It's a great gimmick—one that few of us can take issue with. But just like Dove's "love your ass but not the fat on it" campaign, much of this stuff prompts grim questions about whether it's even possible to break the feel-bad cycle of the beauty industry. Blanchett, after all, recently signed on as spokeswoman for SK-II line of cosmetics. And while it's all well and good to tell 8-year-old girls that real beauty is about trust, it's sort of funny to think about doing it while selling them minty lip shine or fruit-scented "My Way Styling Gel" for eight bucks a pop.

20 Let them be. After all, they have decades ahead of them in which to worry about eradicating the cellulite from their really beautiful curves.

STUDENT MODELS

"Half-Criminals" or Urban Athletes?
A Plea for Fair Treatment of Skateboarders

David Langley (Student)

For skateboarders, the campus of the University of California at San Diego is a wide-open, huge, geometric, obstacle-filled, stair-scattered cement paradise. The signs posted all over campus read, "No skateboarding, biking, or rollerblading on campus except on Saturday, Sunday, and holidays." I have always respected these signs at my local skateboarding spot. On the first day of 1999, I was skateboarding here with my hometown skate buddies and had just landed a trick when a police officer rushed out from behind a pillar, grabbed me, and yanked me off my board. Because I didn't have my I.D. (I had emptied my pockets so I wouldn't bruise my legs if I fell—a little trick of the trade), the officer started treating me like a criminal. She told me to spread my legs and put my hands on my head. She frisked me and then called in my name to police headquarters.

"What's the deal?" I asked. "The sign said skateboarding was legal on holidays."

"The sign means that you can only *roll* on campus," she said.

But that's *not* what the sign said. The police officer gave one friend and me a warning. Our third friend received a fifty-dollar ticket because it was his second citation in the last twelve months.

5   Like other skateboarders throughout cities, we have been bombarded with unfair treatment. We have been forced out of known skate spots in the city by storeowners and police, kicked out of every parking garage in downtown, compelled to skate at strange times of day and night, and herded into crowded skateboard parks. However, after I was searched by the police and detained for over twenty minutes in my own skating sanctuary, the unreasonableness of the treatment of skateboarders struck me. Where are skateboarders supposed to go? Cities need to change their unfair treatment of skateboarders because skateboarders are not antisocial misfits as popularly believed, because the laws regulating skateboarding are ambiguous, and because skateboarders are not given enough legitimate space to practice their sport.

Possibly because to the average eye most skateboarders look like misfits or delinquents, adults think of us as criminal types and associate our skateboards with antisocial behavior. But this view is unfair. City dwellers should recognize that skateboards are a natural reaction to the urban environment. If people are surrounded by cement, they are going to figure out a way to ride it. People's different environments have always produced transportation and sports to suit the conditions: bikes, cars, skis, ice skates, boats, canoes, surfboards. If we live on snow, we are going to develop skis or snowshoes to move around. If we live in an environment that has flat panels of cement for ground with lots of curbs and stairs, we are going to invent an ingeniously designed flat board with wheels. Skateboards are as natural to cement as surfboards are to water or skis to snow. Moreover, the resulting sport is as healthful, graceful, and athletic. A fair assessment of skateboarders should respect our elegant, nonpolluting means of transportation and sport, and not consider us hoodlums.

A second way that skateboarders are treated unfairly is that the laws that regulate skateboarding in public places are highly restrictive, ambiguous, and open to abusive application by police officers. My being frisked on the UCSD campus is just one example. When I moved to Seattle to go to college, I found the laws in Washington to be equally unclear. When a sign says "No Skateboarding," that generally means you will get ticketed if you are caught skateboarding in the area. But most areas aren't posted. The general rule then is that you can skateboard so long as you do so safely without being reckless. But the definition of "reckless" is up to the whim of the police officer. I visited the front desk of the Seattle East Precinct and asked them exactly what the laws against reckless skateboarding meant. They said that skaters are allowed on the sidewalk as long as they travel at reasonable speed and the sidewalks aren't crowded. One of the officers explained that if he saw a skater sliding down a handrail with people all around, he would definitely arrest the skater. What if there were no people around, I asked? The officer admitted that he might arrest the lone skater anyway and not be questioned by his superiors. No wonder skateboarders feel unfairly treated.

One way that cities have tried to treat skateboarders fairly is to build skateboard parks. Unfortunately, for the most part these parks are no solution at all. Most parks were designed by nonskaters who don't understand the momentum or gravity pull associated with the movement of skateboards. For example, City Skate, a park below the Space Needle in Seattle, is very appealing to the eye, but once you start to ride it you realize that the transitions and the verticals are all off, making it unpleasant and even dangerous to skate there. The Skate Park in Issaquah, Washington, hosts about thirty to fifty skaters at a time. Collisions are frequent and close calls, many. There are simply too many people in a small area. The people who built the park in Redmond, Washington, decided to make a huge wall in it for graffiti artists "to tag on" legally. They apparently thought they ought to throw all us teenage "half-criminals" in together. At this park, young teens are nervous about skating near a gangster "throwing up his piece," and skaters become dizzy as they take deep breaths from their workouts right next to four or five cans of spray paint expelling toxins in the air.

Of course, many adults probably don't think skateboarders deserve to be treated fairly. I have heard the arguments against skateboarders for years from parents, storeowners, friends, police officers, and security guards. For one thing, skateboarding tears up public and private property, people say. I can't deny that skating leaves marks on handrails and benches, and it does chip cement and granite. But in general skateboarders help the environment more than they hurt it. Skateboarding places are not littered or tagged up by skaters. Because skaters need smooth surfaces and because any small object of litter can lead to painful accidents, skaters actually keep the environment cleaner than the average citizen does. As for the population as a whole, skateboarders are keeping the air a lot cleaner than many other commuters and athletes such as boat drivers, car drivers, and skiers on ski lifts. In the bigger picture, infrequent repair of curbs and benches is cheaper than attempts to heal the ozone.

10   We skateboarders aren't going away, so cities are going to have to make room for us somewhere. Here is how cities can treat us fairly. We should be allowed to skate when others are present as long as we skate safely on the sidewalks. The rules and laws should be clearer so that skaters don't get put into vulnerable positions that make them easy targets for tickets. I do support the opening of skate parks, but cities need to build more of them, need to situate them closer to where skateboarders live, and need to make them relatively wholesome environments. They should also be designed by skateboarders so that they are skater-friendly and safe to ride. Instead of being treated as "half-criminals," skaters should be accepted as urban citizens and admired as athletes; we are a clean population, and we are executing a challenging and graceful sport. As human beings grow, we go from crawling to walking; some of us grow from strollers to skateboards.

"The Credit Card Company Made Me Do It"—
The Credit Card Industry's Role in Causing Student Debt

Carlos Macias

One day on spring break this year, I strolled into a Gap store. I found several items that I decided to buy. As I was checking out, the cute female clerk around my age, with perfect hair and makeup, asked if I wanted to open a GapCard to save 10 percent on all purchases I made at Gap, Banana Republic, and Old Navy that day. She said I would also earn points toward Gap gift certificates in the future. Since I shop at the Gap often enough, I decided to take her up on her offer. I filled out the form she handed me, and within seconds I—a jobless, indebted-from-student-loans, full-time college student with no substantial assets or income what-soever—was offered a card with a $1000 credit line. Surprised by the speed in which I was approved and the amount that I was approved for, I decided to proceed to both Banana Republic and Old Navy that day to see if there was anything else I might be interested in getting (there was). By the end of the day, I had rung up nearly $200 in purchases.

I know my $200 shopping spree on credit is nothing compared to some of the horror stories I have heard from friends. One of my friends, a college sophomore, is carrying $2000 on a couple of different cards, a situation that is not unusual at all. According to a May 2005 study, students with credit cards carry average balances of just under $3000 by the time they are seniors (Mae, 2005). The problem is that most students don't have the income to pay off their balances, so they become hooked into paying high interest rates and fees that enrich banks while exploiting students who have not yet learned how to exercise control on their spending habits.

Who is to blame for this situation? Many people might blame the students themselves, citing the importance of individual responsibility and proclaiming that no one forces students to use credit cards. But I put most of the blame directly on the credit card companies. Credit cards are enormously profitable; according to a *New York Times* article, the industry made $30 billion in pretax profits in 2003 alone (McGeehan, 2004). Hooking college students on credit cards is essential for this profit, not only because companies make a lot of money off the students themselves, but because hooking students on cards creates a habit that lasts a lifetime. Credit card companies' predatory lending practices—such as using exploitive advertising, using credit scoring to determine creditworthiness, disguising the real cost of credit, and taking advantage of U.S. government deregulation—are causing many unwitting college students to accumulate high levels of credit card debt.

First of all, credit card companies bombard students with highly sophisticated advertising. College students, typically, are in an odd "in-between" stage where they are not necessarily teens anymore, provided for by their parents, but neither are they fully adults, able to provide entirely for themselves. Many students feel the pressures from family, peers and themselves to assume adult roles in terms of their dress and jobs, not relying on Mom or Dad for help. Card companies know about these pressures. Moreover, college students are easy to target because they are concentrated on campuses and generally consume the same media. I probably get several mailings a month offering me a preapproved credit card. These advertisements are filled with happy campus scenes featuring students wearing just the right clothes, carrying their books in just the right backpack, playing music on their iPods or opening their laptop computers. They also appeal to students' desire to feel like responsible adults by emphasizing little emergencies that college students can relate to such as car breakdowns on a road trip. These advertisements illustrate a point made by a team of researchers in an article entitled "Credit Cards as Lifestyle Facilitators": The authors explain how credit card companies want consumers to view credit cards as "lifestyle facilitators" that enable "lifestyle building" and "lifestyle signaling" (Bernthal, Crockett, & Rose, 2005). Credit cards make it easy for students to live the lifestyle pictured in the credit card ads.

5   Another contributing cause of high credit card debt for college students is the method that credit card companies use to grant credit—through credit scoring that does not consider income. It was credit scoring that allowed me to get that quadruple-digit credit line at the Gap while already living in the red. The application I filled out never asked my income. Instead, the personal information I listed was used to pull up my credit score, which is based on records of outstanding debts and payment history. Credit scoring allows banks to grant credit cards based on a person's record of responsibility in paying bills rather than on income. According to finance guru Suze Orman (2005), "Your FICO (credit) score is a great tool to size up how good you will be handling a new loan or credit card" (p. 21). Admittedly, credit scoring has made the lending process as a whole much fairer, giving individuals such as minorities and women the chance to qualify for credit even if they have minimal incomes. But when credit card companies use credit scoring to determine college students' creditworthiness, many students are unprepared to handle a credit line that greatly exceeds their ability to pay based on income. In fact, the Center for Responsible Lending, a consumer advocacy organization in North Carolina, lobbied Congress in September 2003 to require credit card companies to secure proof of adequate income for college-age customers before approving credit card applications ("Credit Card Policy Recommendations," 2003). If Congress passed such legislation, credit card companies would not be able to as easily take advantage of college students who have not yet learned how to exercise control on their spending habits. They would have to offer students credit lines commensurate to their incomes. No wonder these companies vehemently opposed this legislation.

Yet another contributing cause of high levels of credit card debt is the high cost of having this debt, which credit card companies are especially talented at disguising. As credit card debt increases, card companies compound unpaid interest, adding it to the balance that must be repaid. If this balance is not repaid, they charge interest on unpaid interest. They add exorbitant fees for small slip-ups like making a late payment or exceeding the credit limit. While these costs are listed on statements when first added to the balance, they quickly vanish into the "New Balance" number on all subsequent statements, as if these fees were simply past purchases that have yet to be repaid. As the balance continues to grow, banks spike interest rates even higher. In his 2004 article "Soaring Interest Is Compounding Credit Card Pain for Millions," Patrick McGeehan describes a "new era of consumer credit, in which thousands of Americans are paying millions of dollars each month in fees that they did not expect . . . lenders are doubling or tripling interest rates with little warning or explanation." These rate hikes are usually tucked into the pages of fine print that come with credit cards, which many consumers are unable to fully read, let alone understand. Usually, a credit card company will offer a very low "teaser rate" that expires after several months. While this industry practice is commonly understood by consumers, many do not understand that credit card companies usually reserve the right to raise the rate at any time for almost any reason, causing debt levels to rise further.

Admittedly, while individual consumers must be held accountable for any debt they accumulate and should understand compound and variable interest and fees, students' ignorance is welcomed by the credit card industry. In order to completely understand how the credit card industry has caused college students to amass high amounts of credit card debt, it is necessary to explain how this vicious monster was let loose during banking deregulation over the past 30 years. In 1978, the Supreme Court opened the floodgates by ruling that the federal government could not set a cap on interest rates that banks charged for credit cards; that was to be left to the states. With Uncle Sam no longer protecting consumers, Delaware and South Dakota passed laws that removed caps on interest rates, in order to woo credit card companies to conduct nationwide business there (McGeehan, 2004). Since then, the credit card industry has become one of the most profitable industries ever. Credit card companies were given another sweet deal from the U.S. Supreme Court in 1996, when the Court deregulated fees. Since then, the average late fee has risen from $10 or less, to $39 (McGeehan). While a lot of these fees and finance charges are avoidable if the student pays the balance in full, on time, every month, for college students who carry balances for whatever reason, these charges are tacked on, further adding to the principal on which they pay a high rate of compounded interest. (79% of the students surveyed in the Nellie Mae [2005] study said that they regularly carried a balance on their cards.) Moreover, the U.S. government has refused to step in to regulate the practice of universal default, where a credit card company can raise the rate they charge if a consumer is late on an unrelated bill, like a utility payment. Even for someone who pays his or her bills in full, on time, 99% of the time, one bill-paying slip-up can cause an avalanche of fees and frustration, thanks to the credit card industry.

Credit card companies exploit college students' lack of financial savvy and security. It is no secret that most full-time college students are not independently wealthy; many have limited means. So why are these companies so willing to issue cards to poor college students? Profits, of course! If they made credit cards less available to struggling consumers such as college students, consumers would have a more difficult time racking up huge balances, plain and simple. It's funny that Citibank, one of the largest, most profitable credit card companies in the world, proudly exclaims "Live richly" in its advertisements. At the rate that it and other card companies collect interest and fees from their customers, a more appropriate slogan would be "Live poorly."

References

Bernthal, M. J., Crockett, D., & Rose, R. L. (2005). Credit cards as lifestyle facilitators. *Journal of Consumer Research 32*(1). Retrieved from http://www.jstor.org/stable/10.1086/jcr.2005.32.issue-1

Credit card policy recommendations. (2003, September). *Center for Responsible Lending.* Retrieved from http://www.responsiblelending.org/

McGeehan, P. (2004, November). Soaring interest is compounding credit card pain for millions. *New York Times.* Retrieved from http://www.nytimes.com

Nellie Mae. (2005, May). Undergraduate students and credit cards in 2004: An analysis of usage rates and trends. *Nellie Mae.* Retrieved from http://www.nelliemae.com/library/research_12.html

Orman, S. (2005). *The money book for the young, fabulous and broke.* New York: Riverhead.

Disassemble the Hoops

Fiana Muhlberger

Professor Smith

Academic Writing—September 25, 2008

Disassemble the Hoops

The lead compares grades to a jail cell

Grades are nothing more than a jail cell for students' ambition and a cage for students' drive to learn. Students are taught at an early age that grades give them value, worth, and status. A's will get you rewards, honors programs, scholarships, and the title of "straight A student." C's mean you're average, nothing special. F's mean you're out of luck: low achieving students are likely to be overlooked in the classroom, skipped over to answer questions, praised for wrong answers, and given little to no help even though they need it the most (Woolfolk, 2007). Grades move students to do the bare minimum to receive an A. Once they receive the grade, course content ceases to be important and is more often than not completely forgotten. So what have they actually learned? If anything, it is that education is about grades, not a love of learning nor a desire to acquire knowledge. Despite the fact that teachers will argue that they need grades to motivate, discipline, and evaluate students, the current grading system must be weeded out from our classrooms and replaced with a new method of evaluation that will encourage active and long term student learning.

Uses source to support position

Writer's central claim acknowledges opposing view

2

Gives background

Why do professors give A, B, C, D, and F grades? According to Barbara Gross Davis (1993) in her book, *Tools for Teaching,* grades reveal how much students are learning. They are also valuable because they stimulate and motivate students, show them the worth of the work they have done, help them to identify high quality work as compared to unsatisfactory work, make them eligible to receive awards and honors, and communicate their teachers' estimation of their progress. Because teachers place such a high value on evaluation, grades are an integral part of the educational system. Colleges did not always use A, B, C, D, and F grading. Mark Durm (1993) explains that throughout the nineteenth century, many colleges used descriptive adjectives to evaluate students. It wasn't until 1897 that Mount Holyoke created the letter grade system that is still used today.

3   Granted, grades are meant to evaluate students' work and understanding of

subject material, but what is the real distinction between an A and an A-, and an

A- and a B+? It's indefinable. Does assigning such trivial insignia to the quality of a

student's work really measure how much the student has learned? These letters

have meaning only because we have attached so much significance to them. A's

are worth thousands of dollars in scholarships, acceptance to college and graduate

programs, coveted internships, and prestigious jobs. Professor of philosophy

Stephen Vogel (1997) puts it well: "Grades are money, a currency around which

everything revolves" (p. 446). The pressures grades put on students are abundant.

It is no wonder that when Cornell University decided to post course listings with

median grade averages for the class, the students began to pick gut courses "to

pump their GPA's" (Douthat, Ross, Henry, and Poe, 2005). This isn't a surprise,

because our current educational system demands high GPA's of its students in

order for them to achieve a bright future. A statement that psychologist Isidor

Finkelstein made in 1913 is still true today:

> The evidence is clear that marks constitute a very real and a very strong
>
> inducement to work, that they are accepted as real and fairly exact
>
> measurements of ability or of performance. Moreover, they not infrequently
>
> are determiners of a student's career. (as cited in Durm, 1993, p. 1)

4   The claim that the grading system motivates students to better themselves

by striving for higher grades has some merit. It may be true that students are

motivated, but most students find themselves obsessing over the letter on their

report card or transcript, rather than focusing on what they actually learn and can

take away from the class. In an article in *The Chronicle of Higher Education*,

James Lang (2004), describes the first time grades "motivated him":

> I was so incensed about the grades that I disengaged from that course
>
> completely. I was a trained seal jumping through hoops. . . . But I
>
> learned nothing. I remember nothing from the course. In fact, I don't
>
> even remember what the course was about. (p. C2)

Conciliatory expression

*Acknowledges opposing
view and refutes it*

Conciliatory expression

*Acknowledgment
and rebuttal*

Being obsessed with letter grades often causes students to work just hard enough to boost their GPAs. It doesn't matter if they will not remember any of the material after the course is completed and the final is over. Lang, who is now a professor of English, cites another case of using grades as a motivation, this time in his own classroom. He gave a student a D in hopes that she would start trying harder in his class but the experiment failed and the grade "discouraged the student and caused her to further disengage from the class" (p. C4) by being absent the next class and never attempting to get help for the next assignment as Professor Lang suggested. Grades may increase motivation, but, unfortunately, this is motivation for the wrong reasons.

5   Professors should motivate students to learn, not motivate them to become "trained seals," as Lang (2004) suggests, doing just what's required of them to get an A and never fully engaging with their own learning. Research has shown that the type of motivation students want is motivation to learn. In 2000, Howard Pollio and Hall Beck (2000) conducted a study that assessed college students' and instructors' views on grades. They distinguished between those who were learning-oriented and those who were grade-oriented. In the conclusion to the study, they write: "Most students wanted to be more learning and less grade oriented in their personal orientation and for their instructors to afford greater emphasis to learning orientation in teaching their classes" (p. 5). Pollio and Beck (2000) go on to say, "Most instructors believed that a strict orientation toward grades yields an undesirable learning environment; despite this, they rely on grades to promote the learning of course material" (p. 4). This is a contradiction. Instructors need to create a favorable learning environment in which students can enrich their minds. Grades will not do this. As English professor Jerry Farber (1970) points out, "Grades don't make us want to enrich our minds, they make us want to please our teachers" (p. 441). Instructors should act on their convictions and stop requiring their students to jump through Lang's proverbial hoops.

Additional support for writer's position

6   Proponents of grades will argue that they are necessary for self-discipline. *Acknowledges*
My English professor gives daily quiz grades in order to ensure that we have   *opposition*

done the assigned reading. But is this instilling self-discipline? Farber (1970)

notes that true self-discipline "is nothing more than a certain way of pleasing

yourself" (p. 442), a true desire to make yourself better like revising the same

paragraph a thousand times until you're happy with it, by learning the science

of cooking because you enjoy it, or by learning how to drive because you want to

do it. When I was younger, I spent countless hours practicing gymnastics   *Gives rebuttal*

routines until I had perfected them. I did this because I wanted to excel at

gymnastics. I think I would have been less motivated if I was receiving A, B, and

C grades for my routines. As Farber says, "Learning, actual learning, happens

when you want to know" (p. 441) and the self-discipline needed to do so "is the

last thing anyone is likely to learn for a grade" (p. 442).

7   When looked at closely, grades actually fail to motivate or teach self-
discipline. If grades teach students anything, it is a dislike of learning. Students

are forced to write, speak, calculate, evaluate, scientifically prove, and/or   *Recap of argument*

mathematically prove some kind of objective by a certain due date to be marked

with a grade that will seemingly affect their future. No wonder students hate

learning. There's so much pressure on that one little letter.

8   Grades fail to motivate and discipline students properly, but what's worse
is they completely fall short of their most important objective: indicating the

degree to which students have learned what they need for success in later life.

Vogel (1997) points out that many colleges have an average grade of an A–. Yet

most "employers and professors deem many students' academic preparation as   *Additional support for*

lacking . . . saying they're unprepared for the real challenges they are now   *position*

facing in college and the work world" ("Students Want," 2005). Similarly,

McMurtrie (2001), writing in *The Chronicle of Higher Education,* reports, "The

traditional measure of grades doesn't seem to satisfy employers, lawmakers, or

the public anymore" (p. A29). The reason college and high school graduates are "deemed unprepared and unsatisfactory" is because grades have condemned our students to the fate of hoop-jumping seals, studying only what will be on the test and trying to beat the system, when they should and need to be active learners engaging their minds in order to better themselves, their community, and our society.

9

Offers plan for action

The current grading system needs a complete overhaul. However, it is irrational to suggest that we immediately abolish grades in all colleges, high schools, middle schools, and elementary schools. Students are already conditioned to and invested in our current grading system. Change needs to begin in elementary schools. The primary grades are crucial years when students will either fall in love with learning or just work for the A so mom can put a "Proud Parent of an Honor Student" sticker on her bumper. If grades are abolished at this level, we can weed them out at every subsequent grade level as these first classes advance through the system. Once the first class makes it through the educational system, grades wouldn't be a necessary constraint on students and actual learning will take place.

10

Gives alternative

How should students be evaluated under the new system? There are many different ways this could be accomplished. Students could create portfolios of work: essays, papers, science labs, math projects and problems saved throughout the year that demonstrate they have learned the objectives their teachers required of them. Students could give presentations portraying what they have learned to a panel of educators that would allow for advancement into the next grade. Students could have interviews with a teacher during which the student has to demonstrate an understanding of the course work in order to carry on the conversation.

11

None of the alternative methods of assessment need to be linked to letter grades. Teachers could use narrative evaluations to report on students' progress. They could also use descriptions such as Satisfactory, Unsatisfactory, and Incomplete. Some colleges and universities already do this. Faculty at prestigious law schools, for example, Yale and Berkeley, have replaced letter *Alternative*

grades with broad categories. Yale uses Honors, Pass, Low Pass, and Fail.

Recently Stanford Law abolished grades. Those who advocated the change at

Stanford argued that "shifting from the precision of letter grades to broader

categories will reduce some pressure and refocus students' and professors'

energies on classroom learning" (Guess, 2008, p. 10).

12   Professors of the Ithaca College Sports Psychology courses do not believe

in giving letter grades. Their methods of evaluation include some of the

elements listed above but also journals that the students keep to log what they

have learned. More importantly, students grade the journals themselves.

Skeptics might ask, "Don't all the students just give themselves A's?" Not *Alternative*

necessarily. The students enrolled in these classes have to justify the grade

they're giving themselves by citing their own work in the class and proving that

they know the material. Students have a tendency to be honest when they're

forced to confront how much they have actually engaged in a course.

13   Grade reform needs to become a priority. Much can be done to change the

current grading system. There are even more possibilities than I have described. *Exhortation to readers*

The major goal of all teachers should be to allow students the opportunity to

focus on genuine learning instead of on "making the grade." To do so, teachers

everywhere need to disassemble the hoops.

References

Davis, B. G. (1993). *Tools for teaching,* San Francisco: Jossey.

Douthat, R., Henry, T., & Poe, M. (2005, June). Gut check. *The Atlantic Monthly, 44.* Retrieved from General One File.

Durm, M. (1993). An A is not an A is not an A: A history of grading. *The Educational Forum 57,* 1–4. Retrieved from <http://www.indiana.edu/ ~educy520/sec6342/week_07/durm93.pdf>.

Farber, J. (1970). A young person's guide to the grading system. In *The Student as Nigger*. New York: Pocket. In *Reading and Writing in the Academic Community* (3rd ed.). In Kennedy, M. L. & Smith, H. M. (Eds.) Upper Saddle River: Prentice Hall. (pp. 441–44).

Guess, A. (2008, June). Stanford law drops letter grades. *Inside Higher Ed.*

Lang, J. M. (2004, December). Failing to motivate. *The Chronicle of Higher Education,* C2.

McMurtie, B. (2001, February). Colleges urged to find ways to gauge learning. *The Chronicle of Higher Education,* A29. Retrieved from Proquest Research Library.

Pollio, H. R., & Beck, H. P. (2000, Jan/Feb). When the tail wags the dog. *The Journal of Higher Education, 71*(1). Retrieved from Proquest Research Library.

Students Want to be Challenged. (2005, April). *American Teacher 5.* Retrieved from Proquest Research Library.

Vogel, S. (1997, Fall). Grades and money. *Reading and Writing in the Academic Community* (3rd ed.). In M. L. Kennedy, & H. M. Smith, (Eds.). Upper Saddle River: Prentice Hall. (pp. 445–48).

Woolfolk, A. (2007). *Education Psychology.* New York: Pearson.

PRACTICE

1 Douglass spends considerable time telling his audience what points do *not* need to be argued: that a slave is human, that man is entitled to liberty, and so on. If in fact these points are agreed upon by all, why do you think Douglass spends so much time talking about them?

    a. Douglass was speaking in the last few years before the American Civil War began. How did the vivid imagery in this speech likely affect listeners? Read carefully through Douglass's descriptions of the slave trade and its impact on individuals and families. What values is he appealing to?

    b. What impact does Douglass's personal history have on his credibility? Would the argument in this speech have been as compelling if it had been made by someone who had never experienced slavery firsthand?

    c. What words would you use to describe the overall tone of Douglass's speech? Is it angry? threatening? hopeful? pessimistic? Why do you think Douglass chose the tone he used in this argument?

    d. Imagine you were at Douglass's speech. Write a brief newspaper article describing the event and summarizing Douglass's argument. Make sure to also describe how the audience might have reacted to Douglass as a speaker and particular passages, especially the last paragraph. What appeals was he using and how did the audience respond?

2 How effective is Macias's argument that the predatory practices of banks and credit card companies are the primary cause of credit card debt among college students?

    Suppose that you wanted to join this conversation by offering a counterview with a thesis something like this: "Although Macias is partially correct that banks and credit card companies play a role in producing credit card debt among college students, he underestimates other important factors." What would you emphasize as the causes of credit card debt? How would you make your case?

3 After reading Fiana Muhlberger's essay, break into small groups, and select a recorder and a reporter. Each member reads to the group his or her answers to the following questions: Does the writer convince you of her position on the issue? Why or why not? Which features of the essay account for its impact? Come up with a group response, and report it to the rest of the class.

Streets of Mackinac
Mackinac Island, MI

How Do I Present My Position?

18

THE STUDY OF ARGUMENTATION INVOLVES TWO COMPONENTS: TRUTH SEEKING AND PERSUASION:

- By *truth seeking*, we mean a diligent, open-minded, and responsible search for the best course of action or solution to a problem, taking into account all the available information and alternative points of view.
- By *persuasion*, we mean the art of making a claim* on an issue and justifying it convincingly so that the audience's initial resistance to your position is overcome and they are moved toward your position.

These two components of argument seem paradoxically at odds: Truth seeking asks us to relax our certainties and be willing to change our views; persuasion asks us to be certain, to be committed to our claims, and to get others to change their views. We can overcome this paradox if we dispel two common but misleading views of argument. The most common view is that argument is a fight as in "I just got into a horrible argument with my roommate." This view of argument as a fist-waving, shouting match in which you ridicule anyone who disagrees with you (popularized by radio and television talk shows and the Internet) entirely disregards argument as truth seeking, but it also misrepresents argument as persuasion because it polarizes people, rather than promoting understanding, new ways of seeing, and change.

Another common but misleading view is that argument is a pro/con debate modeled after high school or college debate matches. Although debating can be an excellent way to develop critical thinking skills, it misrepresents argument as a two-sided contest with winners and losers.

---

*By long-standing tradition, the thesis statement of an argument is often called its "claim."

Because controversial issues involve many different points of view, not just two, reducing an issue to pro/con positions distorts the complexity of the disagreement. Instead of thinking of *both* sides of an issue, we need to think of *all* sides. Equally troublesome, the debate image invites us to ask, "Who won the debate?" rather than "What is the best solution to the question that divides us?" The best solution might be a compromise between the two debaters or an undiscovered third position. The debate image tends to privilege the confident extremes in a controversy rather than the complex and muddled middle.

From our perspective, the best image for understanding argument is neither "fight" nor "debate" but the deliberations of a committee representing a wide spectrum of community voices charged with finding the best solution to a problem. From this perspective, argument is both a *process* and a *product*. As a process, argument is an act of inquiry characterized by fact-finding, information gathering, and consideration of alternative points of view. As a product, it is someone's contribution to the conversation at any one moment—a turn taking in a conversation, a formal speech, or a written position paper such as the one you will write for this chapter. The goal of argument as process is truth seeking; the goal of argument as product is persuasion. When members of a diverse committee are willing to argue persuasively for their respective points of view but are simultaneously willing to listen to other points of view and to change or modify their positions in light of new information or better arguments, then both components of argument are fully in play.

We cannot overemphasize the importance of both truth seeking and persuasion to your professional and civic life. Truth seeking makes you an informed and judicious employee and a citizen who delays decisions until a full range of evidence and alternative views are aired and examined. Persuasion gives you the power to influence the world around you, whether through letters to the editor or blogs on political issues or through convincing position papers for professional life. Whenever an organization needs to make a major decision, those who can think flexibly and write persuasively can wield great influence.

Exploring Classical Argument

An effective way to appreciate argument as both truth seeking and persuasion is to address an issue that is new to you and then watch how your own views evolve. Your initial position will probably reflect what social scientists sometimes call your personal *ideology*—that is, a network of basic values, beliefs, and assumptions that tend to guide your view of the world. However, if you adopt a truth-seeking attitude, your initial position may evolve as the conversation progresses. In fact, the conversation may even cause changes in some of your basic beliefs, since ideologies aren't set in stone and since many of us have unresolved allegiance to competing ideologies that may be logically inconsistent (for example, a belief in freedom of speech combined with a belief that hate speech should be banned). In this exercise we ask you to keep track of how your views change and to note what causes the change.

The case we present for discussion involves ethical treatment of animals.

Situation: A bunch of starlings build nests in the attic of a family's house, gaining access to the attic through a torn vent screen. Soon the eggs hatch, and every morning at sunrise the family is awakened by the sound of birds squawking and wings beating against rafters as the starlings fly in and out of the house to feed the hatchlings. After losing considerable early morning sleep, the family repairs the screen. Unable to get in and out, the parent birds are unable to feed their young. The birds die within a day. Is this cruelty to animals?

1. Freewrite your initial response to this question. Was the family's act an instance of cruelty to animals (that is, was their act ethically justifiable or not)?

2. Working in small groups or as a whole class, share your freewrites and then try to reach a group consensus on the issue. During this conversation (argument as process), listen carefully to your classmates' views and note places where your own initial views begin to evolve.

3. So far we have framed this issue as an after-the-fact yes/no question: Is the family guilty of cruelty to animals? But we can also frame it as an open-ended, before-the-fact question: "What should the family have done about the starlings in the attic?" Suppose you are a family member discussing the starlings at dinner, prior to the decision to fix the vent screen. Make a list of your family's other options and try to reach class consensus on the two or three best alternative solutions.

4. At the end of the discussion, do another freewrite exploring how your ideas evolved during the discussion. What insights did you get about the twin components of argument, truth seeking and persuasion?

Understanding Classical Argument

Having introduced you to argument as both process and product, we now turn to the details of effective argumentation. To help orient you, we begin by describing the typical stages that mark students' growth as arguers.

STAGES OF DEVELOPMENT: YOUR GROWTH AS AN ARGUER

We have found that when we teach argument in our classes, students typically proceed through identifiable stages as their argumentative skills increase. While these stages may or may not describe your own development, they suggest the skills you should strive to acquire.

- **Stage 1: Argument as personal opinion.** At the beginning of instruction in argument, students typically express strong personal opinions but have trouble justifying their opinions with reasons and evidence and often create short, undeveloped arguments that are circular, lacking in evidence, and insulting to those who disagree. The following freewrite, written by a student first confronting the starling case, illustrates this stage:

  > The family shouldn't have killed the starlings because that is really wrong! I mean that act was disgusting. It makes me sick to think how so many people are just willing to kill something for no reason at all. How are these parents going to teach their children values if they just go out and kill little birds for no good reason?!! This whole family is what's wrong with America!

  This writer's opinion is passionate and heartfelt, but it provides neither reasons nor evidence why someone else should hold the same opinion.

- **Stage 2: Argument structured as claim supported by one or more reasons.** This stage represents a quantum leap in argumentative skill because the writer can now produce a rational plan containing point sentences (the reasons) and particulars (the evidence). The writer who produced the previous freewrite later developed a structure like this:

  The family's act constituted cruelty to animals
  - because the starlings were doing minimal harm.
  - because other options were available.
  - because the way they killed the birds caused needless suffering.

- **Stage 3: Increased attention to truth seeking.** In stage 3 students become increasingly engaged with the complexity of the issue as they listen to their classmates' views, conduct research, and evaluate alternative perspectives and stances. They are often willing to change their positions when they see the power of other arguments.

- **Stage 4: Ability to articulate the unstated assumptions underlying their arguments.** As we show later in this chapter, each reason in a writer's argument is based on an assumption, value, or belief (often unstated) that the audience must accept if the argument is to be persuasive. Often the writer needs to state these assumptions explicitly and support them. At this stage students identify and analyze their own assumptions and those of their intended audiences. Students gain increased skill at accommodating alternative views through refutation or concession.

• **Stage 5: Ability to link an argument to the values and beliefs of the intended audience.** In this stage students are increasingly able to link their arguments to their audience's values and beliefs and to adapt structure and tone to the resistance level of their audience. Students also appreciate how delayed-thesis arguments or other psychological strategies can be more effective than closed-form arguments when addressing hostile audiences.

The rest of this chapter helps you progress through these stages. Although you can read the remainder in one sitting, we recommend that you break your reading into sections, going over the material slowly and applying it to your own ideas in progress. Let the chapter's concepts and explanations sink in gradually, and return to them periodically for review. This section on "Understanding Classical Argument" comprises a compact but comprehensive course in argumentation.

CREATING AN ARGUMENT FRAME: A CLAIM WITH REASONS

Somewhere in the writing process, whether early or late, you need to create a frame for your argument. This frame includes a clear question that focuses the argument, your claim, and one or more supporting reasons. Often your reasons, stated as *because* clauses, can be attached to your claim to provide a working thesis statement.

● **FINDING AN ARGUABLE ISSUE**   At the heart of any argument is an **issue,** which we can define as a question that invites more than one reasonable answer and thus leads to perplexity or disagreement. This requirement excludes disagreements based on personal tastes, where no shared criteria can be developed ("Baseball is more fun than soccer"). It also excludes purely private questions because issues arise out of disagreements in communities.

Issue questions are often framed as yes/no choices, especially when they appear on ballots or in courtrooms: Should gay marriage be legalized? Should the federal government place a substantial tax on gasoline to elevate its price? Is this defendant guilty of armed robbery? Just as frequently, they can be framed openly, inviting many different possible answers: What should our city do about skateboarders in downtown pedestrian areas? How can we best solve the energy crisis?

It is important to remember that framing an issue as a yes/no question does not mean that all points of view fall neatly into pro/con categories. Although citizens may be forced to vote yes or no on a proposed ballot initiative, they can support or oppose the initiative for a variety of reasons. Some may vote happily for the initiative, others vote for it only by holding their noses, and still others oppose it vehemently but for entirely different reasons. To argue effectively, you need to appreciate the wide range of perspectives from which people approach the yes/no choice.

How you frame your question necessarily affects the scope and shape of your argument itself. In our exploratory exercise we framed the starling question in two ways: (1) Was the family guilty of cruelty to animals? and (2) What should the family have done about the starlings? Framed in the first way, your argument would have to develop criteria for "cruelty to animals" and then argue whether the family's actions met those criteria. Framed in the second way, you could argue for your own solution to the problem, ranging from doing nothing (waiting for the birds to grow up and leave, then fixing the screen) to climbing into the attic and drowning the birds so that their deaths are quick and painless. Or you could word the question in a broader, more philosophical way: When are humans justified in killing animals? Or you could focus on a subissue: When can an animal be labeled a "pest"?

● **STATING A CLAIM**   Your **claim** is the position you want to take on the issue. It is your brief, one-sentence answer to your issue question:

> The family was not ethically justified in killing the starlings.
> The city should build skateboarding areas with ramps in all city parks.
> The federal government should substantially increase its taxes on gasoline.

You will appreciate argument as truth seeking if you find that your claim evolves as you think more deeply about your issue and listen to alternative views. Be willing to rephrase your claim to soften it or refocus it or even to reverse it as you progress through the writing process.

ARTICULATING REASONS

Your claim, which is the position you take on an issue, needs to be supported by reasons and evidence. A **reason** (sometimes called a "premise") is a subclaim that supports your main claim. In speaking or writing, a reason is usually linked to the claim with such connecting words as *because, therefore, so, consequently,* and *thus*. In planning your argument, a powerful strategy for developing reasons is to harness the grammatical power of the conjunction *because;* think of your reasons as *because* clauses attached to your claim. Formulating your reasons in this way allows you to create a thesis statement that breaks your argument into smaller parts, each part devoted to one of the reasons.

Suppose, for example, that you are examining the issue "Should the government legalize hard drugs such as heroin and cocaine?" Here are several different points of view on this issue, each expressed as a claim with *because* clauses:

One View

Cocaine and heroin should be legalized
- because legalizing drugs will keep the government out of people's private lives.
- because keeping these drugs illegal has the same negative effects on our society that alcohol prohibition did in the 1920s.

Another View

Cocaine and heroin should be legalized
- because taking drug sales out of the hands of drug dealers would reduce street violence.
- because decriminalization would cut down on prison overcrowding and free police to concentrate on dangerous crime rather than on finding drug dealers.
- because elimination of underworld profits would change the economic structure of the underclass and promote shifts to socially productive jobs and careers.

Still Another View

The government should not legalize heroin and cocaine
- because doing so will lead to an increase in drug users and addicts.
- because doing so will send the message that it is okay to use hard drugs.

Although the yes/no framing of this question seems to reduce the issue to a two-position debate, many different value systems are at work here. The first pro-legalization argument, libertarian in perspective, values maximum individual freedom. The second argument—although it too supports legalization—takes a community perspective valuing the social benefits of eliminating the black market drug-dealing culture. In the same way, individuals could oppose legalization for a variety of reasons.

ARTICULATING UNDERLYING ASSUMPTIONS

So far, we have focused on the frame of an argument as a claim supported with one or more reasons. Shortly, we will proceed to the flesh and muscle of an argument, which is the evidence you use to support your reasons. But before turning to evidence, we need to look at another crucial part of an argument's frame: its *underlying assumptions.*

● **WHAT DO WE MEAN BY AN UNDERLYING ASSUMPTION?** Every time you link a claim with a reason, you make a silent assumption that may need to be articulated and examined. Consider this argument:

> The family was justified in killing the starlings because starlings are pests.

To support this argument, the writer would first need to provide evidence that starlings are pests (examples of the damage they do and so forth). But the persuasiveness of the argument rests on the underlying assumption that it is okay to kill pests. If an audience doesn't agree with that assumption, then the argument flounders unless the writer articulates the assumption and defends it. The complete frame of the argument must therefore include the underlying assumption.

Claim: The family was justified in killing the starlings.
Reason: Because starlings are pests.
Underlying assumption: It is ethically justifiable to kill pests.

It is important to examine the underlying assumption that connects any reason to its claim *because you must determine whether your audience will accept that assumption. If not, you need to make it explicit and support it.* Think of the underlying assumption as a general principle, rule, belief, or value that connects the reason to the claim. It answers your reader's question, "Why, if I accept your reason, should I accept your claim?"*

Here are a few more examples:

Claim with reason: Women should be allowed to join combat units because the image of women as combat soldiers would help society overcome gender stereotyping.
Underlying assumption: It is good to overcome gender stereotyping.

Claim with reason: The government should not legalize heroin and cocaine because doing so will lead to an increase in drug users.
Underlying assumption: It is bad to increase the number of drug users.

Claim with reason: The family was guilty of cruelty to animals in the starling case because less drastic means of solving the problem were available.
Underlying assumption: A person should choose the least drastic means to solve a problem.

---

*Our explanation of argument structure is influenced by the work of philosopher Stephen Toulmin, who viewed argument as a dynamic courtroom drama where opposing attorneys exchange arguments and cross-examinations before a judge and jury. Although we use Toulmin's strategies for analyzing an argument structure, we have chosen not to use his specialized terms, which include *warrant* (the underlying assumption connecting a reason to a claim), *grounds* (the evidence that supports the claim), *backing* (the evidence and subarguments that support the warrant), *conditions of rebuttal* (all the ways that skeptics could attack an argument or all the conditions under which the argument wouldn't hold), and finally *qualifier* (an indication of the strength of the claim). However, your instructor may prefer to use these terms and in that case may provide you with more explanation and examples.

USING EVIDENCE EFFECTIVELY

Inside your arguments, each of your reasons (as well as any underlying assumptions that you decide to state explicitly and defend) needs to be supported either by subarguments or by evidence. By "evidence" we mean facts, examples, summaries of research articles, statistics, testimony, or other relevant data that will persuade your readers to accept your reasons. Note that evidence always exists within a rhetorical context; as a writer you select and shape the evidence that will best support your position, knowing that skeptics may point to evidence that you did not select. Evidence is thus not the same as "proof"; used ethically, evidence presents the best case for your claim without purporting to be the whole truth.

Evidence can sometimes come from personal experience, but in most cases it comes from your own field or library research. The kinds of evidence most often used in argument are the following:

- **FACTUAL DATA** Factual data can provide persuasive support for your arguments. (Keep in mind that writers always select their facts through an angle of vision, so the use of facts doesn't preclude skeptics from bringing in counterfacts.) Here is how evolutionary biologist Olivia Judson used factual data to support her point that malaria-carrying mosquitoes cause unacceptable harm to human lives and wealth.

> Each year, malaria kills at least one million people and causes more than 300 million cases of acute illness. For children worldwide, it's one of the leading causes of death. The economic burden is significant too: malaria costs Africa more than $12 billion in lost growth each year. In the United States, hundreds of millions of dollars are spent every year on mosquito control.

- **EXAMPLES** An example from personal experience can often be used to support a reason. Here is how student writer Ross Taylor used personal experience to argue that paintball is safe even though accidents can happen.

> I admit that paintball can be dangerous and that accidents do happen. I personally had a friend lose an eye after inadvertently shooting himself in the eye from a very close range. The fact of the matter is that he made a mistake by looking down the barrel of a loaded gun and the trigger malfunctioned. Had he been more careful or worn the proper equipment, he most likely would have been fine. During my first organized paintball experience I was hit in the goggles by a very powerful gun and felt no pain. The only discomfort came from having to clean all the paint off my goggles after the game. When played properly, paintball is an incredibly safe sport.

Besides specific examples like this, writers sometimes invent hypothetical examples, or *scenarios,* to illustrate an issue or hypothesize about the consequences of an event. (Of course, you must tell your reader that the example or scenario is hypothetical.)

● **SUMMARIES OF RESEARCH**   Another common way to support an argument is to summarize research articles. Here is how a student writer, investigating whether menopausal women should use hormone replacement therapy to combat menopausal symptoms, used one of several research articles in her paper. The student began by summarizing research studies showing possible dangers of hormone replacement therapy. She then made the following argument:

> Another reason not to use hormone replacement therapy is that other means are available to ease menopausal symptoms such as hot flashes, irritability, mood changes, and sleep disturbance. One possible alternative treatment is acupuncture. One study (Cohen, Rousseau, and Carey) revealed that a randomly selected group of menopausal women receiving specially designed acupuncture treatment showed substantial decreases in menopausal symptoms as compared to a control group. What was particularly persuasive about this study was that both the experimental group and the control group received acupuncture, but the needle insertion sites for the experimental group were specifically targeted to relieve menopausal symptoms whereas the control group received acupuncture at sites used to promote general well-being. The researchers concluded that "acupuncture may be recommended as a safe and effective therapy for reducing menopausal hot flushes as well as contributing to the reduction in sleep disruptions" (299).

● **STATISTICS**   Another common form of evidence is statistics. Here is how one writer used statistics to argue that the federal government should raise fuel-efficiency standards placed on auto manufacturers:

> There is very little need for most Americans to drive huge SUVs. One recent survey found that 87 percent of four-wheel-drive SUV owners had never taken their SUVs off-road (Yacobucci). . . . By raising fuel-efficiency standards, the government would force vehicle manufacturers to find a way to create more earth-friendly vehicles that would lower vehicle emissions and pollution. An article entitled "Update: What You Should Know Before Purchasing a New Vehicle" states that for every gallon of gasoline used by a vehicle, 20 to 28 pounds of carbon dioxide are released into the environment. This article further states that carbon dioxide emissions from automobiles are responsible for 20 percent of all carbon dioxide released into the atmosphere from human causes.

Just as writers select facts, examples, and research studies according to their angle of vision, so do they select and shape numerical data. In the above example, the writer focuses on the environmental harm caused by vehicles, especially SUVs. But you must always read statistics rhetorically. For example, the same statistical "fact" can be framed in different ways. There is a difference in focus and feel between these two ways of using the same data:

- "20 percent of human-caused CO_2 emissions come from automobiles" [puts automobiles in the foreground]
- "Although cars do cause some pollution, a full 80 percent of human-caused CO_2 emissions come from sources other than cars." [puts automobiles in the background]

● **TESTIMONY**   Writers can also use expert testimony to bolster a case. The following passage from a student essay arguing in favor of therapeutic cloning uses testimony from a prominent physician and medical researcher. Part of the paragraph quotes this expert directly; another part paraphrases the expert's argument:

> As Dr. Gerald Fischbach, Executive Vice President for Health and Biomedical Sciences and Dean of Medicine at Columbia University, said in front of a United States Senate subcommittee: "New embryonic stem cell procedures could be vital in solving the persistent problem of a lack of genetically matched, qualified donors of organs and tissues that we face today." Fischbach goes on to say that this type of cloning could also lead to the discovery of cures for diseases such as ALS, Parkinson's disease, Alzheimer's disease, diabetes, heart disease, cancer, and possibly others.

Rather than provide direct research evidence that stem cell cloning might one day lead to cures for diseases, the writer draws on testimony from the dean of a prestigious medical school. Opponents of stem cell research might draw on other experts, selecting those who are skeptical of this claim.

● **SUBARGUMENTS**   Sometimes writers support reasons not directly through data but through sequences of subarguments. Sometimes these subarguments develop a persuasive analogy, hypothesize about consequences, or simply advance the argument through a chain of connected points. In the following passage, taken from a philosophic article justifying torture under certain conditions, the author uses a subargument to support one of his main points—that a terrorist holding victims hostage has no "rights":

> There is an important difference between terrorists and their victims that should mute talk of the terrorist's "rights." The terrorist's victims are at risk unintentionally, not having asked to be endangered. But the terrorist knowingly initiated his actions. Unlike his victims, he volunteered for the risks of his deed. By threatening to kill for profit or idealism, he renounces civilized standards, and he can have no complaint if civilization tries to thwart him by whatever means necessary.

Rather than using direct empirical evidence, the author supports his point with a subargument showing how terrorists differ from victims and thus relinquish their claim to rights.

EVALUATING EVIDENCE: THE STAR CRITERIA

To make your arguments as persuasive as possible, apply to your evidence what rhetorician Richard Fulkerson calls the STAR criteria (**S**ufficiency, **T**ypicality, **A**ccuracy, and **R**elevance),* as shown in the chart on this page.

It is often difficult to create arguments in which all your evidence fully meets the STAR criteria. Sometimes you need to proceed on evidence that might not be typical, verifiable, or as up-to-date as you would like. In such cases, you can often increase the effectiveness of your argument by qualifying your claim. Consider the difference between these two claims:

- **Strong claim:** Watching violent TV cartoons increases aggressive play behavior in boys.
- **Qualified claim:** Watching violent TV cartoons can increase aggressive play behavior in some boys.

To be made persuasive, the strong claim requires substantial evidence meeting the STAR criteria. In contrast, the qualified claim requires less rigorous evidence, perhaps only an example or two combined with the results of one study.

The STAR Criteria for Evaluating Evidence

STAR Criteria	Implied Question	Comments
Sufficiency	Is there enough evidence?	If you don't provide enough evidence, skeptical audiences can dismiss your claim as a "hasty generalization." To argue that marijuana is not a harmful drug, you would probably need more evidence than the results of one study or the testimony of a healthy pot smoker.
Typicality	Are the chosen data representative and typical?	If you choose extreme or rare-case examples, rather than typical and representative ones, your audience might accuse you of cherry-picking your data. Testimony from persons whose back pain was cured by yoga may not support the general claim that yoga is good for back pain.
Accuracy	Are the data accurate and up-to-date?	Providing recent, accurate data is essential for your own *ethos* as a writer. Data from 1998 on homelessness or inaccurately gathered data may be ineffective for a current policy argument.

*Richard Fulkerson, *Teaching the Argument in Writing,* Urbana: National Council of Teachers of English, 1996, pp. 44–53. In this section we are indebted to Fulkerson's discussion.

STAR Criteria	Implied Question	Comments
Relevance	Are the data relevant to the claim?	Even though your evidence is accurate, up-to-date, and representative, if it's not pertinent to the claim, it will be ineffective. For example, evidence that nuclear waste is dangerous is not relevant to the issue of whether it can be stored securely in Yucca Mountain.

As you gather evidence, consider also its source and the extent to which your audience will trust that source. While all data must be interpreted and hence are never completely impartial, careful readers are aware of how easily data can be skewed. Newspapers, magazines, blogs, and journals often have political biases and different levels of respectability. Generally, evidence from peer-reviewed scholarly journals is more highly regarded than evidence from secondhand sources. Particularly problematic is information gathered from Internet Web sites, which can vary widely in reliability and degree of bias.

ADDRESSING OBJECTIONS AND COUNTERARGUMENTS

Having looked at the frame of an argument (claim, reasons, and underlying assumptions) and at the kinds of evidence used to flesh out the frame, let's turn now to the important concern of anticipating and responding to objections and counterarguments. In this section, we show you an extended example of a student's anticipating and responding to a reader's objection. We then describe a planning schema that can help you anticipate objections and show you how to respond to counterarguments, either through refutation or concession. Finally, we show how your active imagining of alternative views can lead you to qualify your claim.

● **ANTICIPATING OBJECTIONS: AN EXTENDED EXAMPLE**   In our earlier discussions of the starling case, we saw how readers might object to the argument "The family was justified in killing the starlings because starlings are pests." What rankles these readers is the underlying assumption that it is okay to kill pests. Imagine an objecting reader saying something like this:

> It is *not* okay to get annoyed with a living creature, label it a "pest," and then kill it. This whole use of the term pest suggests that humans have the right to dominate nature. We need to have more reverence for nature. The ease with which the family solved their problem by killing living things sets a bad example for children. The family could have waited until fall and then fixed the screen.

Imagining such an objection might lead a writer to modify his or her claim. But if the writer remains committed to that claim, then he or she must develop a response. In the following example in which a student writer argues that it is okay to kill the starlings, note (1) how the writer uses evidence to show that starlings are pests; (2) how he summarizes a possible objection to his underlying assumption that killing pests is morally justified; and (3) how he supports his assumption with further arguments.

Student Argument Defending Reason and Underlying Assumption

Claim with reason

Evidence that starlings are pests

The family was justified in killing the starlings because starlings are pests. Starlings are nonindigenous birds that drive out native species and multiply rapidly. When I searched "starlings pests" on Google, I discovered thousands of Web sites dealing with starlings as pests. Starlings are hated by farmers and gardeners because huge flocks of them devour newly planted seeds in spring as well as fruits and berries at harvest. A flock of starlings can devastate a cherry orchard in a few days. As invasive nesters, starlings can also damage attics by tearing up insulation and defecating on stored items. Many of the Web site articles focused on ways to kill off starling populations. In killing the starlings, the family was protecting its own property and reducing the population of these pests.

Summary of a possible objection

Response to the objection

Many readers might object to my argument, saying that humans should have a reverence for nature and not quickly try to kill off any creature they label a pest. Further, these readers might say that even if starlings are pests, the family could have waited until fall to repair the attic or found some other means of protecting their property without having to kill the baby starlings. I too would have waited until fall if the birds in the attic had been swallows or some other native species without starlings' destructiveness and propensity for unchecked population growth. But starlings should be compared to rats or mice. We set traps for rodents because we know the damage they cause when they nest in walls and attics. We don't get sentimental trying to save the orphaned rat babies. In the same way, we are justified in eliminating starlings as soon as they begin infesting our houses.

In the preceding example, we see how the writer uses evidence to support his reason and then, anticipating readers' objection to his underlying assumption, summarizes that objection and provides a response to it. One might not be convinced by the argument, but the writer has done a good job of trying to support both his reason (starlings are pests) and his underlying assumption (it is morally justifiable to kill at least some pests).

● **USING A PLANNING SCHEMA TO ANTICIPATE OBJECTIONS**   In the previous example, the student's arguing strategy was triggered by his anticipation of reader objections. Note that a skeptical audience can attack an argument by attacking either a writer's reasons or a writer's underlying assumptions. This knowledge allows us to create a planning schema that can help writers develop a persuasive argument. This schema encourages writers to articulate their argument frame (claim, reason, and underlying assumption) and then to imagine what kinds of evidence or arguments could be used to support both the reason and the underlying assumption. Equally important, the schema encourages writers to anticipate counterarguments by imagining how skeptical readers might object to the writer's reason or underlying assumption or both. To create the schema, simply make a chart with slots for each of these elements. Here is how another student writer used this schema to plan an argument on the starling case:

Claim with Reason

The family showed cruelty to animals because the way they killed the birds caused needless suffering.

Underlying Assumption

If it is necessary to kill an animal, then the killing should be done in the least painful way possible.

Evidence to Support Reason

First I've got to show how the way of killing the birds (starving them slowly) caused the birds to suffer. I've also got to show that this way of killing was needless since other means were available such as calling an exterminator who would remove the birds and either relocate them or kill them painlessly. If no other alternative was available, someone should have crawled into the attic and found a painless way to kill the birds.

Evidence/Arguments to Support Underlying Assumptions

I've got to convince readers it is wrong to make an animal suffer if you don't have to. Humans have a natural antipathy to needless suffering— our feeling of unease if we imagine cattle or chickens caused to suffer for our food rather than being cleanly and quickly killed. If a horse is incurably wounded, we put it to sleep rather then let it suffer. We are morally obligated to cause the least pain possible.

Ways Skeptics Might Object

How could a reader object to my reason? A reader might say that the starlings didn't suffer much (baby birds don't feel pain). A reader might also object to my claim that other means were available: They might say there was no other way to kill the starlings. Poison may cause just as much suffering. Cost of exterminator is prohibitive.

How could a reader object to my underlying assumption? Perhaps the reader would say that my rule to cause the least pain possible does not apply to animal pests. In class, someone said that we shouldn't worry about the baby starlings any more than we would worry about killing baby rats. Laws of nature condemn millions of animals each year to death by starvation or by being eaten alive by other animals. Humans occasionally have to take their place within this tooth-and-claw natural system.

How many of the ideas from this schema would the writer use in her actual paper? That is a judgment call based on the writer's analysis of the audience. If this student's target audience includes classmates who think it is morally okay to kill pests by the most efficient means possible, then she should summarize her classmates' argument fairly and then try to convince them that humans are ethically called to rise above tooth-and-claw nature.

RESPONDING TO OBJECTIONS, COUNTERARGUMENTS, AND ALTERNATIVE VIEWS

We have seen how a writer needs to anticipate alternative views that give rise to objections and counterarguments. Surprisingly, one of the best ways to approach counterarguments is to summarize them fairly. Make your imagined reader's best case against your argument. By resisting the temptation to distort a counterargument, you demonstrate a willingness to consider the issue from all sides. Moreover, summarizing a counterargument reduces your reader's tendency to say, "Yes, but have you thought of . . . ?" After you have summarized an objection or counterargument fairly and charitably, you must then decide how to respond to it. Your two main choices are to rebut it or concede to it.

● **REBUTTING OPPOSING VIEWS**   When rebutting or refuting an argument, you can question the argument's reasons and supporting evidence or the underlying assumptions or both. In the following student example, the writer summarizes her classmates' objections to abstract art and then analyzes shortcomings in their argument.

Some of my classmates object to abstract art because it apparently takes no technical drawing talent. They feel that historically artists turned to abstract art because they lacked the technical drafting skills exhibited by Remington, Russell, and Rockwell. Therefore these abstract artists created an art form that anyone was capable of and that was less time consuming, and then they paraded it as artistic progress. But I object to the notion that these artists turned to abstraction because they could not do representative drawing. Many abstract artists, such as Picasso, were excellent draftsmen, and their early pieces show very realistic drawing skill. As his work matured, Picasso became more abstract in order to increase the expressive quality of his work. *Guernica* was meant as a protest against the bombing of that city by the Germans. To express the terror and suffering of the victims more vividly, he distorted the figures and presented them in a black and white journalistic manner. If he had used representational images and color—which he had the skill to do—much of the emotional content would have been lost and the piece probably would not have caused the demand for justice that it did.

● **CONCEDING TO OPPOSING VIEWS**   In some cases, an alternative view can be very strong. If so, don't hide that view from your readers; summarize it and concede to it.

Making concessions to opposing views is not necessarily a sign of weakness; in many cases, a concession simply acknowledges that the issue is complex and that your position is tentative. In turn, a concession can enhance a reader's respect for you and invite the reader to follow your example and weigh the strengths of your own argument charitably. Writers typically concede to opposing views with transitional expressions such as the following:

admittedly	I must admit that	I agree that	granted
even though	I concede that	while it is true that	

After conceding to an opposing view, you should shift to a different field of values where your position is strong and then argue for those new values. For example, adversaries of drug legalization argue plausibly that legalizing drugs would increase the number of users and addicts. If you support legalization, here is how you might deal with this point without fatally damaging your own argument:

> Opponents of legalization claim—and rightly so—that legalization will lead to an increase in drug users and addicts. I wish this weren't so, but it is. Nevertheless, the other benefits of legalizing drugs—eliminating the black market, reducing street crime, and freeing up thousands of police from fighting the war on drugs—more than outweigh the social costs of increased drug use and addiction, especially if tax revenues from drug sales are plowed back into drug education and rehabilitation programs.

The writer concedes that legalization will increase addiction (one reason for opposing legalization) and that drug addiction is bad (the underlying assumption for that reason). But then the writer redeems the case for legalization by shifting the argument to another field of values (the benefits of eliminating the black market, reducing crime, and so forth).

● **QUALIFYING YOUR CLAIM** The need to summarize and respond to alternative views lets the writer see an issue's complexity and appreciate that no one position has a total monopoly on the truth. Consequently, writers often need to qualify their claims—that is, limit the scope or force of a claim to make it less sweeping and therefore less vulnerable. Consider the difference between the sentences "After-school jobs are bad for teenagers" and "After-school jobs are often bad for teenagers." The first claim can be refuted by one counterexample of a teenager who benefited from an after-school job. Because the second claim admits exceptions, it is much harder to refute. Unless your argument is airtight, you will want to limit your claim with qualifiers such as the following:

perhaps	maybe
in many cases	generally
tentatively	sometimes
often	usually
probably	likely

may *or* might (*rather than* is)

You can also qualify a claim with an opening *unless* clause ("*Unless* your apartment is well soundproofed, you should not buy such a powerful stereo system").

SEEKING AUDIENCE-BASED REASONS

Much of the advice that we have presented so far can be consolidated into a single principle: Seek "audience-based reasons." By **audience-based reasons,** we mean reasons that depend on underlying assumptions, values, or beliefs that your targeted audience already holds. In such cases, you won't need to state and defend your underlying assumptions because the audience already accepts them.

When you plan your argument, seek audience-based reasons whenever possible. Suppose, for example, that you are advocating the legalization of heroin and cocaine. If you know that your audience is concerned about street crime, then you can argue that legalization of drugs will make the streets safer.

We should legalize drugs *because doing so will make our streets safer*: It will cut down radically on street criminals seeking drug money, and it will free up narcotics police to focus on other kinds of crime.	Audience-based reason: Underlying assumption is that making our streets safer is a good thing—a value the audience already holds.

For another group of readers—those concerned about improving the quality of life for youths in inner cities—you might argue that legalization of drugs will lead to better lives for people in poor neighborhoods.

We should legalize drugs *because doing so will improve the lives of inner-city youth* by eliminating the lure of drug trafficking that tempts so many inner-city youth into crime.	Audience-based reason: Its underlying assumption is that it is good to improve the lives of inner-city youth.

Or if your audience is concerned about high taxes and government debt, you might say:

We should legalize drugs *because doing so will help us balance federal and state budgets*: It will decrease police and prison costs by decriminalizing narcotics; and it will eliminate the black market in drugs, allowing us to collect taxes on drug sales.	Audience-based reason: Assumes that it is a good thing to balance federal and state budgets.

In contrast, if you oppose legalizing drugs, you could appeal to those concerned about drug addiction and public health by using the following audience-based reason:

We should not legalize drugs *because doing so will increase the number of drug addicts and make drug use seem socially acceptable.*	Audience-based reason: Appeals to the underlying assumption that increasing the number of drug addicts and making drugs socially acceptable are bad things.

In each case, you move people toward your position by connecting your argument to their beliefs and values.

Read About Your Topic

Much college writing draws on and responds to sources—books, articles, reports, and other material written by other people. Every significant issue discussed in today's world has an extensive history of discussion involving many people and various points of view. Before you formulate a claim about a significant issue, you need to become familiar with the conversation that's already happening by reading widely about it.

One of the most controversial and talked-about subjects in recent years is the outsourcing of white-collar and manufacturing jobs to low-wage nations. Since 2000 an estimated 400,000 to 500,000 American jobs each year have gone to cheap overseas labor markets. The Internet has made this migration of jobs possible, allowing companies to outsource not only low-skilled jobs but highly skilled jobs in fields such as software development, data storage, and even examining X-rays and MRI scans.

You may have read about this or another complex and controversial topic in one of your courses. Just as in a conversation with several people who hold different views, you may agree with some people, disagree with some, and with others agree with some of their ideas up to a point but then disagree.

CNN commentator Lou Dobbs has been sharply critical of outsourcing. In *Exporting America: Why Corporate Greed Is Shipping American Jobs Overseas* (2006), Dobbs blames large corporations for putting profits ahead of the good of the nation. He accuses both Republicans and Democrats of ignoring the effects of a massive trade deficit and the largest national debt in American history, which Dobbs claims will eventually destroy the American way of life.

Thomas Friedman, columnist for the *New York Times*, takes a different viewpoint on outsourcing in *The World Is Flat: A Brief History of the Twenty-first Century* (2006). By *flat*, Friedman means that the nations of the world are connected like never before through the Internet and the lowering of trade barriers, putting every nation in direct competition with all the others. Friedman believes that outsourcing is not only unstoppable, but also desirable. He argues that Americans need to adapt to the new reality and rethink our system of education, or else we will be left hopelessly behind.

If you decide to write an argument about the issue of outsourcing, you might use either Dobbs's or Friedman's book as your starting point in making a claim. You could begin by taking on the role of **skeptic,** disagreeing with the author; the role of **contributor,** agreeing with the author and adding another point; or the role of the **analyst,** finding some points to agree with while disagreeing with others.

THE SKEPTIC: DISAGREEING WITH A SOURCE

It's easy to disagree by simply saying an idea is dumb, but readers expect you to be persuasive about why you disagree and to offer reasons to support your views.

X claims that _____, but this view is mistaken because _____.

Example claim: Arguing against outsourcing resulting from free trade policies

Thomas Friedman claims that the world is "flat," giving a sense of a level playing field for all, but it is absurd to think that the millions of starving children in the world have opportunities similar to those in affluent countries who pay $100.00 for basketball shoes made by the starving children.

Example claim: Arguing in favor of outsourcing resulting from free trade policies

Lou Dobbs is a patriotic American who recognizes the suffering of manufacturing workers in industries like steel and automobiles, but he neglects that the major cause of the loss of manufacturing jobs in the United States and China alike is increased productivity—the 40 hours of labor necessary to produce a car just a few years ago has now been reduced to 15.

THE CONTRIBUTOR: AGREEING WITH A SOURCE WITH AN ADDITIONAL POINT

Sources should not make your argument for you. With sources that support your position, indicate exactly how they fit into your argument with an additional point.

I agree with _____ and will make the additional point that _____.

Example claim: Arguing against outsourcing resulting from free trade policies

Lou Dobbs's outcry against the outsourcing of American jobs also has a related argument: We are dependent not only on foreign oil, but also on foreign clothing, foreign electronics, foreign tools, foreign toys, foreign cars and trucks—indeed, just about everything—which is quickly eroding the world leadership of the United States.

Example claim: Arguing in favor of outsourcing resulting from free trade policies

Thomas Friedman's claim that the Internet enables everyone to become an entrepreneur is demonstrated by thousands of Americans, including my aunt, who could retire early because she developed an income stream by buying jeans and children's clothes at garage sales and selling them to people around the world on eBay.

THE ANALYST: AGREEING AND DISAGREEING SIMULTANEOUSLY WITH A SOURCE

Incorporating sources is not a matter of simply agreeing or disagreeing with them. Often you will agree with a source up to a point, but you will come to a different conclusion. Or you may agree with the conclusions, but not agree with the reasons put forth.

I agree with ———————— up to a point, but I disagree with the conclusion ———————— because ————————.

Example claim: Qualifying the argument against outsourcing resulting from free-trade policies

Lou Dobbs accurately blames our government for giving multinational corporations tax breaks for exporting jobs rather than regulating the loss of millions of jobs, but the real problem lies in the enormous appetite of Americans for inexpensive consumer products like HD televisions that is supported by borrowing money from overseas to the point that our dollar has plummeted in value.

Example claim: Qualifying the argument in favor of outsourcing resulting from free-trade policies

Thomas Friedman's central claim that the world is being "flattened" by globalization and there is not much we can do to stop it is essentially correct, but he neglects the social costs of globalization around the world, where the banner of free trade has been the justification for devastating the environment, destroying workers' rights and the rights of indigenous peoples, and ignoring laws passed by representative governments.

Find Good Reasons

Get in the habit of asking these questions every time you are asked to write an argument.

CAN YOU ARGUE BY DEFINITION?

Probably the most powerful kind of good reason is an argument from definition. You can think of a definition as a simple statement: ———————— *is a*

_____. You use these statements all the time. When you need a course to fulfill your social-science requirement, you look at the list of courses that are defined as social-science courses. You find out that the anthropology class you want to take is one of them. It's just as important when _____ *is not a* _____. Suppose you are taking College Algebra, which is a math course taught by the math department, yet it doesn't count for the math requirement. The reason it doesn't count is because College Algebra is not defined as a college-level math class. So you have to enroll next semester in Calculus I.

Many definitions are not nearly as clear-cut as the math requirement. If you want to argue that figure skaters are athletes, you will need to define what an athlete is. You start thinking. An athlete competes in an activity, but that definition alone is too broad, since many competitions do not require physical activity. Thus, an athlete must participate in a competitive physical activity and must train for it. But that definition is still not quite narrow enough, because soldiers also train for competitive physical activity. You decide to add that the activity must be a sport and that it must require special competence and precision. Your because clause turns out as follows: *Figure skaters are athletes because true athletes train for and compete in physical sporting competitions that require special competence and precision.*

If you can get your audience to accept your definitions, you've gone a long way toward convincing them of the validity of your claim. That is why the most controversial issues in our culture—abortion, affirmative action, gay rights, pornography, women's rights, privacy rights, gun control, the death penalty—are argued from definition. Is abortion a crime or a medical procedure? Is pornography protected by the First Amendment, or is it a violation of women's rights? Is the death penalty just or cruel and inhuman? You can see from these examples that definitions often rely on deeply held beliefs.

Because people have strong beliefs about controversial issues, they often don't care about the practical consequences. Arguing that it is much cheaper to execute prisoners who have been convicted of first-degree murder than to keep them in prison for life does not convince those who believe that it is morally wrong to kill.

CAN YOU ARGUE FROM VALUE?

A special kind of argument from definition, one that often implies consequences, is the argument from value. You can support your claim with a "because clause" (or several of them) that includes a sense of evaluation. Arguments from value follow from claims like _____ *is a good* _____, or _____ *is not a good* _____.

Evaluation arguments usually proceed from the presentation of certain criteria. These criteria come from the definitions of good and bad, of poor and not so poor, that prevail in a given case. A great burger fulfills certain criteria; so does an outstanding movie, an excellent class, or the best laptop in your price range. Sometimes the criteria are straightforward, as in the burger example. A great burger has to have tasty meat—tender and without gristle, fresh, never frozen— a fresh bun that is the right size, and your favorite condiments.

But if you are buying a laptop computer and want to play the latest games along with your school tasks, you need to do some homework. For realistic graphics the best laptop will have a fast chip, preferably a dual core system. It will be equipped with a wireless modem, so you have access to the Internet at wireless hot spots. The battery life should be at least two hours, the hard drive should be large enough for your needs, the construction should be sturdy, and the warranty should cover the computer for at least three years. The keys for evaluation arguments are finding the appropriate criteria and convincing your readers that those criteria are the right criteria.

CAN YOU ARGUE FROM CONSEQUENCE?

Another powerful source of good reasons comes from considering the possible consequences of your position: Can you sketch out the good things that will follow from your position? Can you establish that certain bad things will be avoided if your position is adopted? If so, you will have other good reasons to use.

Causal arguments take the basic form of _____ *causes* _____ (or _____ *does not cause* _____). Very often, causal arguments are more complicated, taking the form _____ *causes* _____ *which, in turn, causes* _____ and so on. In one famous example, environmentalist Rachel Carson in *Silent Spring* makes powerful arguments from consequence. Rachel Carson's primary claim is that *DDT should not be sprayed on a massive scale because it will poison animals and people.* The key to her argument is the causal chain that explains how animals and people are poisoned. Carson describes how nothing exists alone in nature. When a potato field is sprayed with DDT, some of that poison is absorbed by the skin of the potatoes and some washes into the groundwater, where it contaminates drinking water. Other poisonous residue is absorbed into streams, where it is ingested by insect larvae, which in turn are eaten by fish. Fish are eaten by other fish, which are then eaten by waterfowl and people. At each stage, the poisons become more concentrated.

Proposal arguments are future-oriented arguments from consequence. In a proposal argument, you cannot stop with naming good reasons; you also have to show that these consequences would follow from the idea or course of action that you are arguing. For example, if you are proposing designated lanes for bicycles on the streets of your city, you must argue that they will encourage more people to ride bicycles to work and school, reducing air pollution and traffic congestion for everyone.

CAN YOU COUNTER OBJECTIONS TO YOUR POSITION?

Another good way to find convincing good reasons is to think about possible objections to your position. If you can imagine how your audience might counter or respond to your argument, you will probably include in your argument precisely the points that will address your readers' particular needs and objections. If you are successful, your readers will be convinced that you are right. You've no doubt had the experience of mentally saying to a writer in the course of your reading, "Yeah, but what about this other idea?"—only to have the writer address precisely this objection.

You can impress your readers if you've thought about why anyone would oppose your position and exactly how that opposition would be expressed. If you are writing a proposal argument for a computer literacy requirement for all high school graduates, you might think about why anyone would object, since computers are critical for our jobs and lives. What will the practical objections be? What about philosophical ones? Why hasn't such a requirement been put in place already? By asking such questions in your own arguments, you are likely to develop robust because clauses.

Sometimes, writers pose rhetorical questions. You might ask, "But won't paying for computers for all students make my taxes go up?" Stating objections explicitly can be effective if you make the objections as those of a reasonable person with an alternative point of view. But if the objections you state are ridiculous ones, then you risk being accused of setting up a **straw man**—that is, making the position opposing your own so simplistic that no one would likely identify with it.

UNDERSTAND HOW POSITION ARGUMENTS WORK

Position arguments often take two forms—definition arguments and rebuttal arguments.

● **DEFINITION ARGUMENTS**   The continuing controversies about what art is, free speech, pornography, and hate crimes (to name just a few) illustrate why definitions often matter more than we might think. People argue about definitions because of the consequences of something being defined in a certain way.

People make definitions that benefit their interests. Early in life you learned the importance of defining actions as "accidents." Windows can be broken through carelessness, especially when you are tossing a ball against the side of the house, but if it's an accident, well, accidents just happen (and don't require punishment). Your mother or father probably didn't think breaking the window was an accident, so you had to convince Mom or Dad that you were really being careful, and the ball just slipped out of your hand. If you can get your audience to accept your definition, then usually you succeed. For this reason, definition arguments are the most powerful arguments.

For example, is graffiti vandalism? Or is it art? If you claim at least some forms of graffiti should be considered art, you need to set out criteria to define art and argue that graffiti meets those criteria.

Something = or ≠ _____
Criteria A
Criteria B
Criteria C

Example

Graffiti **is** art **because** it is a means of self expression, it shows an understanding of design principles, **and** it stimulates both the senses and the mind.

● **REBUTTAL ARGUMENTS**   Rebuttal arguments take the opposite position. You can challenge the criteria a writer uses to make a definition or you can challenge the evidence that supports a claim. Sometimes the evidence presented is incomplete or simply wrong. Sometimes you can find counterevidence. Often when you rebut an argument, you identify one or more fallacies in that argument.

Opposing claim
Bad reason 1
Bad reason 2

Example

The great white shark gained a reputation as a "man eater" from the 1975 movie *Jaws,* **but in fact** attacks on humans are rare **and** most bites have been "test bites," which is a common shark behavior with unfamiliar objects.

KEYS TO POSITION ARGUMENTS

- **UNDERSTAND YOUR GOAL**   A well-written and well-reasoned position argument may not change minds entirely, but it can convince readers that a reasonable person can hold this point of view. Position arguments do not necessarily have winners and losers. Your goal is to invite a response that creates a dialogue.

- **BE SENSITIVE TO THE CONTEXT**   Even position arguments that have become classics and in a sense "timeless" frequently were written in response to a historical event; for example, Martin Luther King, Jr. wrote his powerful argument for civil disobedience, "Letter from Birmingham Jail," in response to a published statement by eight Birmingham clergymen. A careful analysis of a recent or historical event often provides your argument with a sense of immediacy.

- **RELY ON CAREFUL DEFINITIONS**   What exactly does *freedom of speech* mean? What exactly does *privacy* mean? What exactly does *animal rights* mean? Getting readers to accept a definition is often the key to a position argument. For example, torturing animals is against the law. Animal rights activists argue that raising and slaughtering animals for food is torture and thus would extend the definition. If you can get readers to accept your definition, then they will agree with your position.

- **USE QUALITY SOURCES**   Find the highest-quality sources for citing evidence. Recent sources are critical for current topics, such as the relationship of certain diets to disease.

- **CREATE CREDIBILITY**   You have probably noticed that many times in the course of reading, you get a strong sense of the writer's character, even if you know nothing about the person. Be honest about strengths and weaknesses and about what you don't know, and avoid easy labels. If readers trust you are sincere, they will take you seriously.

- **CULTIVATE A SENSE OF HUMOR AND A DISTINCTIVE VOICE**   A reasonable voice doesn't have to be a dull one. Humor is a legitimate tool of argument, especially when the stakes are high and tempers are flaring.

- **ARGUE RESPONSIBLY**   When you begin an argument by stating "in my opinion," you are not arguing responsibly. If you don't like broccoli, it is a matter of personal taste. But if you are for or against universal health care, then it is not just your opinion. Millions of other Americans hold views similar to yours on this contested issue.

READINGS

Take My Privacy, Please!

Ted Koppel

Ted Koppel joined ABC News in 1963 and served from 1980 until 2005 as the anchor and managing editor of Nightline, *the first late-night network news program. He has had a major reporting role in every presidential campaign since 1964. "Take My Privacy, Please!" which appeared in June 2005 in the New York Times, is an example of a position argument that doesn't begin with a thesis but first gives a series of examples.*

Koppel announces his stance and his subject in the first two paragraphs. He questions the Patriot Act and then suggests that there may be bigger threats to privacy.

The Patriot Act—brilliant! Its critics would have preferred a less stirring title, perhaps something along the lines of the Enhanced Snooping, Library and Hospital Database Seizure Act. But then who, even right after 9/11, would have voted for that?

Precisely. He who names it and frames it, claims it. The Patriot Act, however, may turn out to be among the lesser threats to our individual and collective privacy.

There is no end to what we will endure, support, pay for and promote if only it makes our lives easier, promises to save us money, appears to enhance our security and comes to us in a warm, cuddly and altogether nonthreatening package. To wit: OnStar, the subscription vehicle tracking and assistance system. Part of its mission statement, as found on the OnStar Web site, is the creation of "safety, security and peace of mind for drivers and passengers with thoughtful wireless services that are always there, always ready." You've surely seen or heard their commercials, one of which goes like this:

The OnStar commercial provides a concrete example.

ANNOUNCER: The following is an OnStar conversation. (Ring)

ONSTAR: OnStar emergency, this is Dwight.

DRIVER: (crying) Yes, yes??!

ONSTAR: Are there any injuries, ma'am?

DRIVER: My leg hurts, my arm hurts.

ONSTAR: O.K. I do understand. I will be contacting emergency services.

ANNOUNCER: If your airbags deploy, OnStar receives a signal and calls to check on you. (Ring)

EMERGENCY SERVICES: Police.

ONSTAR: This is Dwight with OnStar. I'd like to report a vehicle crash with airbag deployment on West 106th Street.

EMERGENCY SERVICES: We'll send police and E.M.S. out there.

DRIVER: (crying) I'm so scared!

ONSTAR: O.K., I'm here with you, ma'am; you needn't be scared.

In the ad, OnStar is portrayed as a technology that can save lives.

Well, maybe just a little scared. Tell us again how Dwight knows just where the accident took place. Oh, right! It's those thoughtful wireless services that are always there. Always, as in any time a driver gets into an OnStar-equipped vehicle. OnStar insists that it would disclose the whereabouts of a subscriber's vehicle only after being presented with a criminal court order or after the vehicle has been reported stolen. That's certainly a relief. I wouldn't want to think that anyone but Dwight knows where I am whenever I'm traveling in my car.

Koppel uses critical thinking to question the main assumption of the ad: Is it necessarily good that OnStar always knows where you are while driving?

Of course, E-ZPass and most other toll-collecting systems already know whenever a customer passes through one of their scanners. That's because of radio frequency identification technology. In return for the convenience of zipping through toll booths, you need to have in your car a wireless device. This tag contains information about your account, permitting E-ZPass to deduct the necessary toll—and to note when your car whisked through that particular toll booth. They wouldn't share that information with anyone, either; that is, unless they had to.

Convenient technologies also keep track of our movements. Koppel gets his readers to think about what happens to personal information that is passively collected.

Radio frequency identification technology has been used for about 15 years now to reunite lost pets with their owners. Applied Digital Solutions, for example, manufactures the VeriChip, a tiny, implantable device that holds a small amount of data. Animal shelters can scan the chip for the name and phone number of the lost pet's owner. The product is now referred to as the HomeAgain Microchip Identification System.

Useful? Sure. Indeed, it's not much of a leap to suggest that one day, the VeriChip might be routinely implanted under the skin of, let's say, an Alzheimer's patient. The Food and Drug Administration approved the VeriChip for use in people last October. An Applied Digital Solutions spokesman estimates that about 1,000 people have already had a VeriChip implanted, usually in the right triceps. At the moment, it doesn't carry much information, just an identification number that health care providers can use to tap into a patient's medical history. A Barcelona nightclub also uses it to admit customers with a qualifying code to enter a V.I.P. room where drinks are automatically put on their bill. Possible variations on the theme are staggering.

Technologies used to track pets can also track people.

And how about all the information collected by popular devices like TiVo, the digital video recorder that enables you to watch and store an entire season's worth of favorite programs at your own convenience? It also lets you electronically mark the programs you favor, allowing TiVo to suggest similar programs for your viewing pleasure. In February, TiVo announced the most frequently played and replayed commercial moment during the Super Bowl (it involves a wardrobe malfunction, but believe me, you don't want to know), drawing on aggregated data from a sample of 10,000 anonymous TiVo households. No one is suggesting that TiVo tracks what each subscriber records and replays. But could they, if they needed to? That's unclear, although TiVo does have a privacy policy. "Your privacy," it says in part, "is very important to us. Due to factors beyond our control, however, we cannot fully ensure that your user information will not be disclosed to third parties."

The popular TiVo service admits that it does not fully protect the privacy of its subscribers.

Unexpected and unfortunate things happen, of course, even to the most reputable and best-run organizations. Only last February, the Bank of America Corporation notified federal investigators that it had lost computer backup tapes containing personal information about 1.2 million federal government employees, including some senators. In April, LexisNexis unintentionally gave outsiders access to the personal files (addresses, Social Security numbers, drivers license information) of as many as 310,000 people. In May, Time Warner revealed that an outside storage company had misplaced data stored on computer backup tapes on 600,000 current and former employees. That same month, United Parcel Service picked up a box of computer tapes in New Jersey from CitiFinancial, the consumer finance subsidiary of Citigroup, that contained the names, addresses, Social Security numbers, account numbers, payment histories and other details on small personal loans made to an estimated 3.9 million customers. The box is still missing.

Numerous accidents and data thefts have given private information to unauthorized people.

Whoops!

CitiFinancial correctly informed its own customers and, inevitably, the rest of the world about the security breach. Would they have done so entirely on their own? That is less clear. In July 2003, California started requiring companies to inform customers living in the state of any breach in security that compromises personally identifiable information. Six other states have passed similar legislation.

No such legislation exists on the federal stage, however—only discretionary guidelines for financial institutions about whether and how they should inform their customers with respect to breaches in the security of their personal information.

Both the House and Senate are now considering federal legislation similar to the California law. It's a start but not nearly enough. We need mandatory clarity and transparency; not just with regard to the services that these miracles of microchip and satellite technology offer but also the degree to which companies share and exchange their harvest of private data.

We cannot even begin to control the growing army of businesses and ◄── industries that monitor what we buy, what we watch on television, where we drive, the debts we pay or fail to pay, our marriages and divorces, our litigations, our health and tax records and all else that may or may not yet exist on some computer tape, if we don't fully understand everything we're signing up for when we avail ourselves of one of these services.

Koppel hopes by this point he has raised concerns about privacy for his readers. He now gives his thesis: The public has the right to know what is being done with private information they give to companies and services.

Reflections from a Life Behind Bars: Build Colleges, Not Prisons*

James Gilligan

James Gilligan is the former director of mental health for the Massachusetts prison system. He is also a clinical instructor in psychiatry at Harvard Medical School who has twenty-five years of experience as a prison psychiatrist. He believes that education is the key to preventing recidivism.

1   Neither words nor pictures, no matter how vivid, can do more than give a faint suggestion of the horror, brutalization, and degradation of the prisons of this country. I speak from extensive personal knowledge of this subject, for I have spent 25 years of my professional life behind bars—not as an inmate, but as a prison psychiatrist.

2   I am a physician, and I see violence (whether it is legal or illegal, homicidal or suicidal, intentional or careless) as a public-health problem— indeed, the most important and dangerous threat to public health in our time. Because it affects mostly the young, violence kills more people under the age of 65 in this country than do cancer and heart disease, the two illnesses that are often (and mistakenly) thought to be the most significant causes of death.

3   So I cannot emphasize too strongly how seriously I take the problem of violence. Far from being tolerant or permissive toward it, I am far more strongly opposed to violence in all its forms and in all its legal statuses, and far less tolerant and permissive toward it than are those who believe that our salvation lies in building more and more punitive (i.e., violent) prisons.

*Chronicle of Higher Education, October 16, 1998, B7–B9.

4   There is a widespread misimpression that punishment deters violence—in other words, that punishment is one means of preventing violence. However, the overwhelming weight of empirical evidence suggests that exactly the opposite is true—namely, that punishment, far from inhibiting or preventing violence, is the most potent stimulus or cause of violence that we have yet discovered. Several different lines of evidence, from several different populations and stages of the life cycle, converge in supporting that conclusion.

5   For example, child-rearing is such an inherently and inescapably complicated subject that there are relatively few findings from the past several decades of research on it that are so clear, so unmistakable, and so consistently replicated that they are virtually universally agreed on. But among those few is this: The more severely punished children are, the more violent they become, both as children and as adults. This is especially true of violent punishments. For example, children who are subjected to corporal discipline are significantly more likely to subject other people to physical punishments (i.e., inflict violence on them), both while they are still children and after they have reached adulthood. That is hardly surprising, of course, for corporal discipline is simply another name for physical violence; it would be called assault and battery if committed against an adult.

6   In fact, even with respect to nonviolent behavior, such as bed-wetting or excessive dependency or passivity ("laziness"), punishment has a counterproductive effect; that is, the more severely children are punished for a given behavior, the more strongly they persist in repeating it. To put it the other way around: If we want to produce as violent a generation of children and adults as possible, the most effective thing we can do is to punish our children and adults as severely as possible.

7   While the research just referred to can be found in the literature on child development and child abuse, there is no reason to think that the psychology of adults differs in this respect from that of children, and every reason to think that it is the same. In fact, I have been able to confirm those findings on children from my own clinical experience of over 25 years with violent adult criminals and the violent mentally ill. The degree of violent child abuse to which this population had been subjected was so extreme that the only way to summarize it is to say that the most violent people in our society—those who murder others—are disproportionately the survivors of attempted murder themselves, or of the completed murders of their closest relatives, siblings, or parents.

8   Thus, if punishment could prevent violence, these men would never have become violent in the first place, for they were already punished, even before they became violent, as severely as it is possible to punish a person without actually killing him. Many were beaten nearly to death as children, so when they became adults, they did beat someone else to death.

9   Fortunately, we not only know what stimulates violence (punishment, humiliation), we also know what prevents violence, both in society in general and in the criminal-justice and prison systems in particular. Unfortunately, we Americans have been dismantling the conditions that do prevent violence as rapidly as we could over the past 25 years, with the entirely predictable result that the levels of violent crimes, such as murder, have repeatedly reached the highest recorded levels in our history. For example, for the last quarter of a century our murder rates have been twice as high as they were 40 years ago, and five to ten times as high as they currently are in any other democracy and developed economy on earth.

10   What are the conditions that prevent violence? Among general social conditions, there are several, but space permits mentioning only the most powerful one: a relatively classless society, with an equitable social and economic system in which there are minimal discrepancies in wealth, income, and standard of living between the poorest and the wealthiest factions of the population (people are vulnerable to feelings of shame and inferiority if they are poor, or economically inferior, while other people are rich, or economically superior).

11   Around the world, the nations with the most equitable economic systems, such as Sweden and Japan, are significantly more likely to have the lowest murder rates. And those with the greatest economic discrepancies between the rich and the poor (of which the United States is the world leader among developed democracies) have the highest murder rates (a statistic in which the United States is also the world leader). Even within the United States, the most equitable or "classless" states have the lowest murder rates, and those with the most inequitable degrees of class stratification have the highest. Yet the last Congress dismantled one of the few programs we had that tended to equalize income in this country—the earned-income tax credit.

12   Among the conditions in the prison system that prevent violent behavior (both during imprisonment and after release to the community), the most powerful is education. In Massachusetts, for example, when I headed the prison mental-health service, we did a study to see what programs within the prison had been most effective in preventing recidivism among prison inmates after they had been released from prison and returned to the community. While several programs had worked, the most successful of all, and the only one that had been 100 percent effective in preventing recidivism, was the program that allowed inmates to receive a college degree while in prison. Several hundred prisoners in Massachusetts had completed at least a bachelor's degree while in prison over a 25-year period, and not one of them had been returned to prison for a new crime.

13   Immediately after I announced this finding in a public lecture at Harvard, and it made its way into the newspaper, our new governor, William Weld, who had not previously been aware that prison inmates

could take college courses, gave a press conference on television in which he declared that Massachusetts should rescind that "privilege," or else the poor would start committing crimes in order to be sent to prison so they could get a free college education! And lest one think that that was merely the rather bizarre response of one particularly cynical demagogue, it is worth noting that the U.S. Congress responded the same way. The last Congress declared that inmates throughout the federal prison system would no longer be eligible to receive Pell grants.

14   It is too late now to even begin to attempt to "reform" prisons. The only thing that can be done with them is to tear them all down, for their architecture alone renders them unfit for human beings. Or even animals: No humane society permits animals in zoos to be housed in conditions as intolerable as those in which we cage humans. The reason for the difference, of course, is clear: Zoos are not intended for punishment; prisons are. That is why it would benefit every man, woman, and child in this country, and it would hurt no one, to demolish the prisons and replace them with much smaller, locked, secure residential schools and colleges in which the residents could acquire as much education as their intelligence and curiosity would permit.

15   Such institutions would of course be most effective in their only rational purpose, which would be to prevent crime and violence, if they were designed to be as humane and homelike as possible, and as near the prisoners' own homes as possible, so that their families could visit as freely as possible (including frequent conjugal visits), and so they could visit their families as freely as possible. (For conjugal and home visits have repeatedly been shown, in this country and around the world, to be associated with lowered rates of violence, both during incarceration and after release into the community—which is probably why both have been effectively abolished in this country.)

16   Since there is no reason to isolate anyone from the community against his will unless he poses a danger of physically harming others, these residential schools would need to be limited to those who have been, or have threatened or attempted to be, violent. (Very few, if any, nonviolent "criminals" need to be removed from the community at all. Nor should those who have committed only nonviolent crimes ever have to be housed with those who have been seriously violent; and there are many reasons why they should not be.)

17   Thus one of the most constructive responses I can think of . . . would be the designing of an "anti-prison"—not prison reform, but prison replacement; not prison construction, but prison deconstruction. If we replaced prisons with a boarding-school "home away from home" for many people who are literally homeless in the so-called community, and provided them with the tools they need in order to acquire knowledge

and skill, self-esteem and self-respect, and the esteem and respect of others, these new facilities could actually reduce the rates of crime and violence in our society, instead of feeding them, as our current prisons do.

18   Of course, before we could do that, we would need to overcome our own irrational need to inflict revenge (i.e., punishment) on those who are weaker than we. Nothing corrodes the soul of the vengeful person as thoroughly as his own vengeful impulses. Thus the main reason we need to abolish [prisons] is not only, or even primarily, for the sake of those who get imprisoned in them, but in order to heal our own souls—and indeed, our whole society, which is sick with an epidemic of violence, both legal and illegal.

When Handouts Keep Coming, the Food Line Never Ends (Opinion)

Mark Winne

Mark Winne was the director of Connecticut's Hartford Food System from 1979 to 2003. He is the author of Closing the Food Gap: Resetting the Table in the Land of Plenty *(2008), which examines how people from all classes obtain food: from lower income people at food pantries and convenience stores to more affluent people who tend to seek out organic and local products. Instead of the term* hunger, *Winne uses the phrase* food insecure, *which refers to a lack of access at all times to enough food for an active, healthy life. According to the USDA, 10.9% of households in the United States were food insecure at least some time during 2006. "When Handouts Keep Coming, the Food Line Never Ends" was published in the* Washington Post *on November 18, 2007.*

How can anyone not get caught up in the annual Thanksgiving turkey frenzy? At the food bank I co-founded in Hartford, Conn., November always meant cheering the caravans of fowl-laden trucks that roared into our parking lot. They came on the heels of the public appeals for "A bird in every pot," "No family left without a turkey" and our bank's own version—"A turkey and a 20 [dollar bill]."

Like pompom girls leading a high school pep rally, we revved up the community's charitable impulse to a fever pitch with radio interviews, newspaper stories and dramatic television footage to extract the last gobbler from the stingiest citizen. After all, our nation's one great day of social equity was upon us. In skid row soup kitchens and the gated communities of hedge-fund billionaires alike, everyone was entitled, indeed expected, to sit down to a meal of turkey with all the fixings.

And here we are, putting on the same play again this year. But come Friday, as most of us stuff more leftovers into our bulging refrigerators, 35 million Americans will take their place in line again at soup kitchens, food banks and food stamp offices nationwide. The good souls who staff America's tens of thousands of emergency food sites will renew their pleas to donors fatigued by their burst of holiday philanthropy. Food stamp workers will return to their desks and try to convince mothers that they can feed their families on the $3 per person per day that the government allots them. The cycle of need—always present, rarely sated, never resolved—will continue.

Unless we rethink our devotion to food donation.

America's far-flung network of emergency food programs—from Second Harvest to tens of thousands of neighborhood food pantries—constitutes one of the largest charitable institutions in the nation. Its vast base of volunteers and donors and its ever-expanding distribution infrastructure have made it a powerful force in shaping popular perceptions of domestic hunger and other forms of need. But in the end, one of its most lasting effects has been to sidetrack efforts to eradicate hunger and its root cause, poverty.

As sociologist Janet Poppendieck made clear in her book *Sweet Charity,* there is something in the food-banking culture and its relationship with donors that dampens the desire to empower the poor and take a more muscular, public stand against hunger.

It used to be my job to scour every nook and cranny of Hartford for food resources, and I've known the desperation of workers who saw the lines of the poor grow longer while the food bank's inventory shrank. The cutback in federal support for social welfare programs triggered by the Reagan administration in the 1980s unleashed a wave of charitable innovation and growth not seen since the Great Depression. As demand for food rose unabated—as it does to this day—our food bank's staff became increasingly adept at securing sustenance from previously unimaginable sources.

No food donation was too small, too strange or too nutritionally unsound to be refused.

I remember the load of nearly rotten potatoes that we "gratefully" accepted at the warehouse loading dock and then promptly shoveled into the dumpster once the donor was safely out of sight. One of our early food bank meetings included a cooking demonstration by a group of local entrepreneurs who were trying to develop a market for horse meat. The product's name was Cheva-lean, taken from "cheval," the French word for horse. The promoters reminded us that the French, the world's leading authorities on food, ate horse meat, implying that therefore our poor clients could certainly do the same. The only thing that topped that was when we had to secure recipes from the University of Maine to help us use the moose parts proudly presented by representatives of the Connecticut Fish and Game Division who'd been forced to put down the disoriented Bullwinkle found wandering through suburban back yards.

We did our job well, and everything grew: Over 25 years, the food bank leapfrogged five times from warehouse to ever-vaster warehouse, finally landing in a state-of-the-art facility that's the equal of most commercial food distribution centers in the country. The volunteers multiplied to 3,000 because the donations of food, much of it unfit for human consumption, required many hands for sorting and discarding. The number of food distribution sites skyrocketed from five in 1982 to 360 today.

But in spite of all the outward signs of progress, more than 275,000 Connecticut residents—slightly less than 8.6 percent of the state's residents—remain hungry or what we call "food insecure." The Department of Agriculture puts 11 percent of the U.S. population in this category. (The department also provides state-by-state breakdowns.)

The overall futility of the effort became evident to me one summer day in 2003 when I observed a food bank truck pull up to a low-income housing project in Hartford. The residents had known when and where the truck would arrive, and they were already lined up at the edge of the parking lot to receive handouts. Staff members and volunteers set up folding tables and proceeded to stack them with produce, boxed cereal and other food items. People stood quietly in line until it was their turn to receive a bag of pre-selected food.

No one made any attempt to determine whether the recipients actually needed the food, nor to encourage the recipients to seek other forms of assistance, such as food stamps. The food distribution was an unequivocal act of faith based on generally accepted knowledge that this was a known area of need. The recipients seemed reasonably grateful, but the staff members and volunteers seemed even happier, having been fortified by the belief that their act of benevolence was at least mildly appreciated.

As word spread, the lines got longer until finally the truck was empty. The following week, it returned at the same time, and once again the people were waiting. Only this time there were more of them. It may have been that a donor-recipient co-dependency had developed. Both parties were trapped in an ever-expanding web of immediate gratification that offered the recipients no long-term hope of eventually achieving independence and self-reliance. As the food bank's director told me later, "The more you provide, the more demand there is."

My experience of 25 years in food banking has led me to conclude that co-dependency within the system is multifaceted and frankly

...continued When the Handouts Keep Coming, the Food Line Never Ends, **Mark Winne**

troubling. As a system that depends on donated goods, it must curry favor with the nation's food industry, which often regards food banks as a waste-management tool. As an operation that must sort through billions of pounds of damaged and partially salvageable food, it requires an army of volunteers who themselves are dependent on the carefully nurtured belief that they are "doing good" by "feeding the hungry." And as a charity that lives from one multimillion-dollar capital campaign to the next (most recently, the Hartford food bank raised $4.5 million), it must maintain a ready supply of well-heeled philanthropists and captains of industry to raise the dollars and public awareness necessary to make the next warehouse expansion possible.

Food banks are a dominant institution in this country, and they assert their power at the local and state levels by commanding the attention of people of good will who want to address hunger. Their ability to attract volunteers and to raise money approaches that of major hospitals and universities. While none of this is inherently wrong, it does distract the public and policymakers from the task of harnessing the political will needed to end hunger in the United States.

The risk is that the multibillion-dollar system of food banking has become such a pervasive force in the anti-hunger world, and so tied to its donors and its volunteers, that it cannot step back and ask if this is the best way to end hunger, food insecurity and their root cause, poverty.

During my tenure in Hartford, I often wondered what would happen if the collective energy that went into soliciting and distributing food were put into ending hunger and poverty instead. Surely it would have a sizable impact if 3,000 Hartford-area volunteers, led by some of Connecticut's most privileged and respected citizens, showed up one day at the state legislature, demanding enough resources to end hunger and poverty. Multiply those volunteers by three or four—the number of volunteers in the state's other food banks and hundreds of emergency food sites—and you would have enough people to dismantle the Connecticut state capitol brick by brick. Put all the emergency food volunteers and staff and board members from across the country on buses to Washington, to tell Congress to mandate a living wage, health care for all and adequate employment and child-care programs, and you would have a convoy that might stretch from New York City to our nation's capital.

But what we have done instead is to continue down a road that never comes to an end. Like transportation planners who add more lanes to already clogged highways, we add more space to our food banks in the futile hope of relieving the congestion.

We know hunger's cause—poverty. We know its solution—end poverty. Let this Thanksgiving remind us of that task.

Should Educators Use Commercial Services to Combat Plagiarism?

The following is a summary of John Barrie's argument, which appeared in the CQ Researcher *in 2003. (Mr. Barrie declined to give permission to reproduce his remarks as they appear there.) The entire article can be read on the* CQ Researcher *Web site (http://library.cqpress.com/cqresearcher).*

Mr. Barrie believes that because we all "draw from the past to create the present," our writing and learning in schools and colleges should take advantage of the power of collaboration. Students should, Barrie believes, be able to "share ideas and criticism" as they work to prepare a high school report about a Shakespeare play or a college level paper about Nietzsche's philosophy. "The problem begins," Barrie acknowledges, "when faculty cannot determine whether a student wrote a term paper or plagiarized it from other sources." Barrie cites a recent study by Rutgers University Professor Donald McCabe that concludes that "nearly 40% of college undergraduates admitted to plagiarizing term papers" by lifting information directly from Internet sources. Solving this growing problem of plagiarism, Barrie argues, requires a solution that goes beyond the "status quo" of campus honor codes, detective work by faculty, and punishments for plagiarism. "Digital plagiarism," Barrie says, "is a digital problem [that] demands a digital solution." According to Barrie, TurnItIn is an important part of that solution. It receives thousands of essays to check each day and finds that "30 percent of those papers are less than original." Barrie concludes by arguing that educators and administrators should not "shirk their responsibility" as educators and should "demand original work" from all students by using plagiarism detection programs such as TurnItIn.

Rebecca Moore Howard

Associate Professor of Writing and Rhetoric, Syracuse University

Teaching, not software, is the key to preventing plagiarism. Today's students can access an array of electronic texts and images unimaginable just 20 years ago, and students' relationship to the practice of information-sharing has changed along with the technology.

But today's students lack extensive training and experience in working carefully from print sources, and they may not understand that they need to learn this skill. They may also find it difficult to differentiate between kinds of sources on the Internet. With information arriving as a cacophony of electronic voices, even well-intentioned students have difficulty keeping track of—much less citing—who said what.

Moreover, the sheer volume of available information frequently leaves student writers feeling that they have nothing new to say about an issue. Hence too many students—one in three, according to a recent survey conducted by Rutgers University Professor Donald McCabe—may fulfill assignments by submitting work they have not written.

Were we in the throes of widespread moral decay, capture-and-punishment might provide an appropriate deterrent. We are, however, in the midst of a revolution in literacy, and teachers' responses must be more complex. They must address the underlying issues: students' ability to conduct research, comprehend extended written arguments, evaluate sources and produce their own persuasive written texts, in explicit dialogue with their sources.

Classrooms must engage students in text and in learning—communicating a value to these activities that extends beyond grades earned and credentials accrued. McCabe, who is a founder of the renowned Center for Academic Integrity at Duke University, recommends pedagogy and policies that speak to the causes of plagiarism, rather than buying software for detection and punishment. In a 2003 position statement, the Council of Writing Program Administrators urges, "Students should understand research assignments as opportunities for genuine and rigorous inquiry and learning." The statement offers extensive classroom suggestions for teachers and cautions that using plagiarism-catching software may "justify the avoidance of responsible teaching methods."

Buying software instead of revitalizing one's teaching means that teachers, like students, have allowed the electronic environment to encourage a reductive, automated vision of the educational experience. As one of my colleagues recently remarked, "The 'world's leading plagiarism-prevention system' is not TurnItIn.com—it's careful pedagogy."

The Perils of Obedience

Stanley Milgram

In 1963, a Yale psychologist conducted one of the classic studies on obedience. Stanley Milgram designed an experiment that forced participants either to violate their conscience by obeying the immoral demands of an authority figure or to refuse those demands. Surprisingly, Milgram found that few participants could resist the authority's orders, even when the participants knew that following these orders would result in another person's pain. Were the participants in these experiments incipient mass murderers? No, said Milgram. They were "ordinary people, simply doing their jobs." The implications of Milgram's conclusions are immense.

Consider these questions: Where does evil reside? What sort of people were responsible for the Holocaust, and for the long list of other atrocities that seem to blight the human record in every generation? Is it a lunatic fringe, a few sick but powerful people who are responsible for atrocities? If so, then we decent folk needn't ever look inside ourselves to understand evil since (by our definition) evil lurks out there, in "those sick ones." Milgram's study suggested otherwise: that under a special set of circumstances the obedience we naturally show authority figures can transform us into agents of terror.

The article that follows is one of the longest in this book, and it may help you to know in advance the author's organization. In paragraphs 1–11, Milgram discusses the larger significance and the history of dilemmas involving obedience to authority; he then summarizes his basic experimental design and follows with a report of one experiment. Milgram organizes the remainder of his article into sections, which he has subtitled "An Unexpected Outcome," "Peculiar Reactions," "The Etiquette of Submission," and "Duty Without Conflict." He begins his conclusion in paragraph 108. If you find the article too long or complex to complete in a single sitting, then plan to read sections at a time, taking notes on each until you're done. Anticipate the article that immediately follows this one: It reviews Milgram's work and largely concerns the ethics of his experimental design. Consider these ethics as you read so that you, in turn, can respond to Milgram's critics.

Stanley Milgram (1933–1984) taught and conducted research at Yale and Harvard Universities and at the Graduate Center, City University of New York. He was named Guggenheim Fellow in 1972–1973 and a year later was nominated for the National Book Award for Obedience to Authority. *His other books include* Television and Antisocial Behavior *(1973),* The City and the Self *(1974),* Human Aggression *(1976), and* The Individual in the Social World *(1977).*

Obedience is as basic an element in the structure of social life as one can point to. Some system of authority is a requirement of all communal living, and it is only the person dwelling in isolation who is not forced to respond, with defiance or submission, to the commands of others. For many people, obedience is a deeply ingrained behavior tendency, indeed a potent impulse overriding training in ethics, sympathy, and moral conduct.

...*continued* The Perils of Obedience, **Stanley Milgram**

The dilemma inherent in submission to authority is ancient, as old as the story of Abraham, and the question of whether one should obey when commands conflict with conscience has been argued by Plato, dramatized in *Antigone,* and treated to philosophic analysis in almost every historical epoch. Conservative philosophers argue that the very fabric of society is threatened by disobedience, while humanists stress the primacy of the individual conscience.

The legal and philosophic aspects of obedience are of enormous import, but they say very little about how most people behave in concrete situations. I set up a simple experiment at Yale University to test how much pain an ordinary citizen would inflict on another person simply because he was ordered to by an experimental scientist. Stark authority was pitted against the subjects' strongest moral imperatives against hurting others, and with the subjects' ears ringing with the screams of the victims, authority won more often than not. The extreme willingness of adults to go to almost any lengths on the command of an authority constitutes the chief finding of the study and the fact most urgently demanding explanation.

In the basic experimental design, two people come to a psychology laboratory to take part in a study of memory and learning. One of them is designated as a "teacher" and the other a "learner." The experimenter explains that the study is concerned with the effects of punishment on learning. The learner is conducted into a room, seated in a kind of miniature electric chair; his arms are strapped to prevent excessive movement, and an electrode is attached to his wrist. He is told that he will be read lists of simple word pairs, and that he will then be tested on his ability to remember the second word of a pair when he hears the first one again. Whenever he makes an error, he will receive electric shocks of increasing intensity.

5   The real focus of the experiment is the teacher. After watching the learner being strapped into place, he is seated before an impressive shock generator. The instrument panel consists of thirty level switches set in a horizontal line. Each switch is clearly labeled with a voltage designation ranging from 15 to 450 volts. The following designations are clearly indicated for groups of four switches, going from left to right: Slight Shock, Moderate Shock, Strong Shock, Very Strong Shock, Intense Shock, Extreme Intensity Shock, Danger: Severe Shock. (Two switches after this last designation are simply marked XXX.)

When a switch is depressed, a pilot light corresponding to each switch is illuminated in bright red; an electric buzzing is heard; a blue light, labeled "voltage energizer," flashes; the dial on the voltage meter swings to the right; and various relay clicks sound off.

The upper left-hand corner of the generator is labeled SHOCK GENERATOR, TYPE ZLB, DYSON INSTRUMENT COMPANY, WALTHAM, MASS. OUTPUT 15 VOLTS—450 VOLTS.

A subject in Stanley Milgram's study of obedience, seated at the "Shock Generator."

Each subject is given a sample 45-volt shock from the generator before his run as teacher, and the jolt strengthens his belief in the authenticity of the machine.

The teacher is a genuinely naive subject who has come to the laboratory for the experiment. The learner, or victim, is actually an actor who receives no shock at all. The point of the experiment is to see how far a person will proceed in a concrete and measurable situation in which he is ordered to inflict increasing pain on a protesting victim.

Conflict arises when the man receiving the shock begins to show that he is experiencing discomfort. At 75 volts, he grunts; at 120 volts, he complains loudly; at 150, he demands to be released from the experiment. As the voltage increases, his protests become more vehement and emotional. At 285 volts, his response can be described only as an agonized scream. Soon thereafter, he makes no sound at all.

For the teacher, the situation quickly becomes one of gripping tension. It is not a game for him; conflict is intense and obvious. The manifest suffering of the learner presses him to quit; but each time he hesitates to administer a shock, the experimenter orders him to continue. To extricate himself from this plight, the subject must make a clear break with authority.*

*The ethical problems of carrying out an experiment of this sort are too complex to be dealt with here, but they receive extended treatment in the book from which this article is adapted.

...*continued* The Perils of Obedience, **Stanley Milgram**

The subject, Gretchen Brandt,[†] is an attractive thirty-one-year-old medical technician who works at the Yale Medical School. She had emigrated from Germany five years before.

On several occasions when the learner complains, she turns to the experimenter coolly and inquires, "Shall I continue?" She promptly returns to her task when the experimenter asks her to do so. At the administration of 210 volts, she turns to the experimenter, remarking firmly, "Well, I'm sorry, I don't think we should continue."

EXPERIMENTER: The experiment requires that you go on until he has learned all the word pairs correctly.

15 BRANDT: He has a heart condition. I'm sorry. He told you that before.

EXPERIMENTER: The shocks may be painful but they are not dangerous.

BRANDT: Well, I'm sorry, I think when shocks continue like this, they *are* dangerous. You ask him if he wants to get out. It's his free will.

EXPERIMENTER: It is absolutely essential that we continue. . . .

BRANDT: I'd like you to ask him. We came here of our free will. If he wants to continue I'll go ahead. He told you he had a heart condition. I'm sorry. I don't want to be responsible for anything happening to him. I wouldn't like it for me either.

20 EXPERIMENTER: You have no other choice.

BRANDT: I think we are here on our own free will. I don't want to be responsible if anything happens to him. Please understand that.

She refuses to go further and the experiment is terminated.

The woman is firm and resolute throughout. She indicates in the interview that she was in no way tense or nervous, and this corresponds to her controlled appearance during the experiment. She feels that the last shock she administered to the learner was extremely painful and reiterates that she "did not want to be responsible for any harm to him."

The woman's straightforward, courteous behavior in the experiment, lack of tension, and total control of her own action seem to make disobedience a simple and rational deed. Her behavior is the very embodiment of what I envisioned would be true for almost all subjects.

AN UNEXPECTED OUTCOME

25 Before the experiments, I sought predictions about the outcome from various kinds of people—psychiatrists, college sophomores, middle-class adults, graduate students, and faculty in the behavioral sciences.

†Names of subjects described in this piece have been changed.

With remarkable similarity, they predicted that virtually all subjects would refuse to obey the experimenter. The psychiatrists, specifically, predicted that most subjects would not go beyond 150 volts, when the victim makes his first explicit demand to be freed. They expected that only 4 percent would reach 300 volts, and that only a pathological fringe of about one in a thousand would administer the highest shock on the board.

These predictions were unequivocally wrong. Of the forty subjects in the first experiment, twenty-five obeyed the orders of the experimenter to the end, punishing the victim until they reached the most potent shock available on the generator. After 450 volts were administered three times, the experimenter called a halt to the session. Many obedient subjects then heaved sighs of relief, mopped their brows, rubbed their fingers over their eyes, or nervously fumbled cigarettes. Others displayed only minimal signs of tension from beginning to end.

When the very first experiments were carried out, Yale undergraduates were used as subjects, and about 60 percent of them were fully obedient. A colleague of mine immediately dismissed these findings as having no relevance to "ordinary" people, asserting that Yale undergraduates are a highly aggressive, competitive bunch who step on each other's necks on the slightest provocation. He assured me that when "ordinary" people were tested, the results would be quite different. As we moved from the pilot studies to the regular experimental series, people drawn from every stratum of New Haven life came to be employed in the experiment: professionals, white-collar workers, unemployed persons, and industrial workers. *The experiment's total outcome was the same as we had observed among the students.*

Moreover, when the experiments were repeated in Princeton, Munich, Rome, South Africa, and Australia, the level of obedience was invariably somewhat *higher* than found in the investigation reported in this article. Thus one scientist in Munich found 85 percent of his subjects to be obedient.

Fred Prozi's reactions, if more dramatic than most, illuminate the conflicts experienced by others in less visible form. About fifty years old and unemployed at the time of the experiment, he has a good-natured, if slightly dissolute, appearance, and he strikes people as a rather ordinary fellow. He begins the session calmly but becomes tense as it proceeds. After delivering the 180-volt shock, he pivots around in his chair and, shaking his head, addresses the experimenter in agitated tones:

30   PROZI: I can't stand it. I'm not going to kill that man in there. You hear him hollering?

EXPERIMENTER: As I told you before, the shocks may be painful, but . . .

...continued The Perils of Obedience, **Stanley Milgram**

PROZI: But he's hollering. He can't stand it. What's going to happen to him?

EXPERIMENTER (*HIS VOICE PATIENT, MATTER-OF-FACT*):   The experiment requires that you continue, Teacher.

PROZI: Aaah, but unh, I'm not going to get that man sick in there—know what I mean?

35   EXPERIMENTER: Whether the learner likes it or not, we must go on, through all the word pairs.

PROZI: I refuse to take the responsibility. He's in there hollering!

EXPERIMENTER: It's absolutely essential that you continue, Prozi.

PROZI (*INDICATING THE UNUSED QUESTIONS*):   There's too many left here. I mean, Jeez, if he gets them wrong, there's too many of them left. I mean, who's going to take the responsibility if anything happens to that gentleman?

EXPERIMENTER: I'm responsible for anything that happens to him. Continue, please.

40   PROZI: All right. (*Consults list of words.*) The next one's "Slow—walk, truck, dance, music." Answer, please (*A buzzing sound indicates the learner has signaled his answer.*) Wrong. A hundred and ninety-five volts. "Dance." (*Zzumph!*)

LEARNER (*YELLING*):   Let me out of here! My heart's bothering me! (*Teacher looks at experimenter.*)

EXPERIMENTER: Continue, please.

LEARNER (*SCREAMING*):   Let me out of here! You have no right to keep me here! Let me out of here, my heart's bothering me, let me out!

PROZI: (*SHAKES HEAD, PATS THE TABLE NERVOUSLY*):   You see, he's hollering. Hear that? Gee, I don't know.

45   EXPERIMENTER: The experiment requires . . .

PROZI (*INTERRUPTING*):   I know it does, sir, but I mean—hunh! He don't know what he's getting in for. He's up to 195 volts! (*Experiment continues, through 210 volts, 225 volts, 240 volts, 255 volts, 270 volts, at which point Prozi, with evident relief, runs out of word-pair questions.*)

EXPERIMENTER: You'll have to go back to the beginning of that page and go through them again until he's learned them all correctly.

PROZI: Aw, no. I'm not going to kill that man. You mean I've got to keep going up with the scale? No sir. He's hollering in there. I'm not going to give him 450 volts.

EXPERIMENTER: The experiment requires that you go on.

50 LEARNER: Ohhh. I absolutely refuse to answer anymore. (*Shouting urgently now.*) Let me out of here! You can't hold me here! Get me out. Get-me-out-of-here!

EXPERIMENTER: Continue. The next word is "Green," please.

PROZI: "Green—grass, hat, ink, apple." (*Nothing happens. No answering buzz. Just gloomy silence.*)

PROZI: I don't think he is going to answer.

EXPERIMENTER: If the learner doesn't answer in a reasonable time, about four or five seconds, consider the answer wrong. And follow the same procedures you have been doing for wrong answers. Say, "Wrong," tell him the number of volts, give him the punishment, read him the correct answer. Continue, please.

55 PROZI: "Green—grass, hat, ink, apple." Answer, please. (*More silence. Subject just sits there.*)

EXPERIMENTER: Go on with the procedure, please.

PROZI: Three hundred and fifteen volts. The answer is "ink." (*Zzumph!*)

LEARNER: Ohh. Ooohh.

PROZI (*RELIEVED TO HEAR RESPONSE*):   Next one . . .

60 LEARNER: I absolutely refuse to answer.

PROZI: You got to. You get a shock if you don't answer. (*Experiment continues with learner refusing to answer, and finally, failing even to grunt or groan. At 375 volts, the subject stands up.*)

PROZI: I think something's happened to that fellow in there. I don't get no answer. He was hollering at less voltage. Can't you check in and see if he's all right, please?

EXPERIMENTER (*WITH SAME DETACHED CALM*):   Not once we've started. Please continue, Teacher.

PROZI (*SITS DOWN, SIGHS DEEPLY*):   "Cool—day, shade, water, paint." Answer, please. Are you all right in there? Are you all right?

65 EXPERIMENTER: Please continue, Teacher. Continue, please. (*Subject pushes lever. Zzumph!*)

PROZI (*SWIVELING AROUND IN HIS CHAIR*):   Something's happened to that man in there. (*Swiveling back.*) Next one. "Low—dollar, necklace, moon, paint." (*Turning around again.*) Something's happened to that man in there. You better check on him, sir. He won't answer or nothing.

EXPERIMENTER: Continue. Go on, please.

...continued The Perils of Obedience, **Stanley Milgram**

PROZI: You accept all responsibility?

EXPERIMENTER: The responsibility is mine. Correct. Please go on. (*Subject returns to his list, starts running through words as rapidly as he can read them, works through to 450 volts.*)

70   PROZI: That's that.

EXPERIMENTER: Continue using the 450 switch for each wrong answer. Continue, please.

PROZI: But I don't get anything!

EXPERIMENTER: Please continue. The next word is "white."

PROZI: Don't you think you should look in on him, please?

75   EXPERIMENTER: Not once we've started the experiment.

PROZI: What if he's dead in there? (*Gestures toward the room with the electric chair.*) I mean, he told me he can't stand the shock, sir. I don't mean to be rude, but I think you should look in on him. All you have to do is look in on him. All you have to do is look in the door. I don't get no answer, no noise. Something might have happened to the gentleman in there, sir.

EXPERIMENTER: We must continue. Go on, please.

PROZI: You mean keep giving him what? Four-hundred-fifty volts, what he's got now?

EXPERIMENTER: That's correct. Continue. The next word is "white."

80   PROZI (*NOW AT A FURIOUS PACE*):   "White—cloud, horse, rock, house." Answer, please. The answer is "horse." Four hundred and fifty volts. (*Zzumph!*) Next word, "Bag—paint, music, clown, girl." The answer is "paint." Four hundred and fifty volts. (*Zzumph!*) Next word is "Short—sentence, movie . . . "

EXPERIMENTER: Excuse me, Teacher. We'll have to discontinue the experiment.

PECULIAR REACTIONS

Morris Braverman, another subject, is a thirty-nine-year-old social worker. He looks older than his years because of his bald head and serious demeanor. His brow is furrowed, as if all the world's burdens were carried on his face. He appears intelligent and concerned.

When the learner refuses to answer and the experimenter instructs Braverman to treat the absence of an answer as equivalent to a wrong answer, he takes his instruction to heart. Before administering 300 volts he asserts officiously to the victim, "Mr. Wallace, your silence has to be considered as a wrong answer." Then he administers the shock. He offers half-heartedly to change places with the learner, then asks the experimenter, "Do I have to follow these instructions literally?" He is satisfied with the experimenter's answer that he does. His very refined and authoritative manner of speaking is increasingly broken up by wheezing laughter.

The experimenter's notes on Mr. Braverman at the last few shocks are:

> Almost breaking up now each time gives shock. Rubbing face to hide laughter. Squinting, trying to hide face with hand, still laughing. Cannot control his laughter at this point no matter what he does. Clenching fist, pushing it onto table.

85   In an interview after the session, Mr. Braverman summarizes the experiment with impressive fluency and intelligence. He feels the experiment may have been designed also to "test the effects on the teacher of being in an essentially sadistic role, as well as the reactions of a student to a learning situation that was authoritative and punitive." When asked how painful the last few shocks administered to the learner were, he indicates that the most extreme category on the scale is not adequate (it read EXTREMELY PAINFUL) and places his mark at the edge of the scale with an arrow carrying it beyond the scale.

It is almost impossible to convey the greatly relaxed, sedate quality of his conversation in the interview. In the most relaxed terms, he speaks about his severe inner tension.

EXPERIMENTER: At what point were you most tense or nervous?

MR. BRAVERMAN: Well, when he first began to cry out in pain, and I realized this was hurting him. This got worse when he just blocked and refused to answer. There was I. I'm a nice person, I think, hurting somebody, and caught up in what seemed a mad situation . . . and in the interest of science, one goes through with it.

When the interviewer pursues the general question of tension, Mr. Braverman spontaneously mentions his laughter.

90   "My reactions were awfully peculiar. I don't know if you were watching me, but my reactions were giggly, and trying to stifle laughter. This isn't the way I usually am. This was a sheer reaction to a totally impossible situation. And my reaction was to the situation of having to hurt somebody. And being totally helpless and caught up in a set of circumstances where I just couldn't deviate and I couldn't try to help. This is what got me."

Mr. Braverman, like all subjects, was told the actual nature and purpose of the experiment, and a year later he affirmed in a questionnaire that he had learned something of personal importance: "What appalled me was that I could possess this capacity for obedience and compliance to a central

---

...continued The Perils of Obedience, **Stanley Milgram**

---

idea, i.e., the value of a memory experiment, even after it became clear that continued adherence to this value was at the expense of violation of another value, i.e., don't hurt someone who is helpless and not hurting you. As my wife said, 'You can call yourself Eichmann.'* I hope I deal more effectively with any future conflicts of values I encounter."

THE ETIQUETTE OF SUBMISSION

One theoretical interpretation of this behavior holds that all people harbor deeply aggressive instincts continually pressing for expression, and that the experiment provides institutional justification for the release of these impulses. According to this view, if a person is placed in a situation in which he has complete power over another individual, whom he may punish as much as he likes, all that is sadistic and bestial in man comes to the fore. The impulse to shock the victim is seen to flow from the potent aggressive tendencies, which are part of the motivational life of the individual, and the experiment, because it provides social legitimacy, simply opens the door to their expression.

It becomes vital, therefore, to compare the subject's performance when he is under orders and when he is allowed to choose the shock level.

The procedure was identical to our standard experiment, except that the teacher was told that he was free to select any shock level on any of the trials. (The experimenter took pains to point out that the teacher could use the highest levels on the generator, the lowest, any in between, or any combination of levels.) Each subject proceeded for thirty critical trials. The learner's protests were coordinated to standard shock levels, his first grunt coming at 75 volts, his first vehement protest at 150 volts.

95

The average shock used during the thirty critical trials was less than 60 volts—lower than the point at which the victim showed the first signs of discomfort. Three of the forty subjects did not go beyond the very lowest level on the board, twenty-eight went no higher than 75 volts, and thirty-eight did not go beyond the first loud protest at 150 volts. Two subjects provided the exception, administering up to 325 and 450 volts, but the overall result was that the great majority of people delivered very low, usually painless, shocks when the choice was explicitly up to them.

---

*Adolf Eichmann (1906–1962), the Nazi official responsible for implementing Hitler's "Final Solution" to exterminate the Jews, escaped to Argentina after World War II. In 1960, Israeli agents captured him and brought him to Israel, where he was tried as a war criminal and sentenced to death. At his trial, Eichmann maintained that he was merely following orders in arranging murders of his victims.

This condition of the experiment undermines another commonly offered explanation of the subjects' behavior—that those who shocked the victim at the most severe levels came only from the sadistic fringe of society. If one considers that almost two-thirds of the participants fall into the category of "obedient" subjects, and that they represented ordinary people drawn from working, managerial, and professional classes, the argument becomes very shaky. Indeed, it is highly reminiscent of the issue that arose in connection with Hannah Arendt's 1963 book, *Eichmann in Jerusalem*. Arendt contended that the prosecution's efforts to depict Eichmann as a sadistic monster was fundamentally wrong, that he came closer to being an uninspired bureaucrat who simply sat at his desk and did his job. For asserting her views, Arendt became the object of considerable scorn, even calumny. Somehow, it was felt that the monstrous deeds carried out by Eichmann required a brutal, twisted personality, evil incarnate. After witnessing hundreds of ordinary persons submit to the authority in our own experiments, I must conclude that Arendt's conception of the banality of evil comes closer to the truth than one might dare imagine. The ordinary person who shocked the victim did so out of a sense of obligation—an impression of his duties as a subject—and not from any peculiarly aggressive tendencies.

This is, perhaps, the most fundamental lesson of our study: ordinary people, simply doing their jobs, and without any particular hostility on their part, can become agents in a terrible destructive process. Moreover, even when the destructive effects of their work become patently clear, and they are asked to carry out actions incompatible with fundamental standards of morality, relatively few people have the resources needed to resist authority.

Many of the people were in some sense against what they did to the learner, and many protested even while they obeyed. Some were totally convinced of the wrongness of their actions but could not bring themselves to make an open break with authority. They often derived satisfaction from their thoughts and felt that—within themselves, at least—they had been on the side of the angels. They tried to reduce strain by obeying the experimenter but "only slightly," encouraging the learner, touching the generator switches gingerly. When interviewed, such a subject would stress that he had "asserted my humanity" by administering the briefest shock possible. Handling the conflict in this manner was easier than defiance.

The situation is constructed so that there is no way the subject can stop shocking the learner without violating the experimenter's definitions of his own competence. The subject fears that he will appear arrogant, untoward, and rude if he breaks off. Although these inhibiting emotions appear small in scope alongside the violence being done to the learner, they suffuse the mind and feelings of the subject, who is miserable at the prospect of having to repudiate the authority to his face. (When the experiment was altered so that the experimenter gave his instructions by telephone instead of in person, only a third as many people were fully obedient through 450 volts.) It is a curious thing that a measure of compassion on the part of the subject—an unwillingness to "hurt" the experimenter's feelings—is part of those binding forces inhibiting his disobedience. The withdrawal of such deference may be as painful to the subject as to the authority he defies.

DUTY WITHOUT CONFLICT

100

The subjects do not derive satisfaction from inflicting pain, but they often like the feeling they get from pleasing the experimenter. They are proud of doing a good job, obeying the experimenter under difficult circumstances. While the subjects administered only mild shocks on their own initiative, one experimental variation showed that, under orders, 30 percent of them were willing to deliver 450 volts even when they had to forcibly push the learner's hand down on the electrode.

Bruno Batta is a thirty-seven-year-old welder who took part in the variation requiring the use of force. He was born in New Haven, his parents in Italy. He has a rough-hewn face that conveys a conspicuous lack of alertness. He has some difficulty in mastering the experimental procedure and needs to be corrected by the experimenter several times. He shows appreciation for the help and willingness to do what is required. After the 150-volt level, Batta has to force the learner's hand down on the shock plate, since the learner himself refuses to touch it.

When the learner first complains, Mr. Batta pays no attention to him. His face remains impassive, as if to dissociate himself from the learner's disruptive behavior. When the experimenter instructs him to force the learner's hand down, he adopts a rigid, mechanical procedure. He tests the generator switch. When it fails to function, he immediately forces the learner's hand onto the shock plate. All the while he maintains the same rigid mask. The learner, seated alongside him, begs him to stop, but with robotic impassivity he continues the procedure.

What is extraordinary is his apparent total indifference to the learner; he hardly takes cognizance of him as a human being. Meanwhile, he relates to the experimenter in a submissive and courteous fashion.

At the 330-volt level, the learner refuses not only to touch the shock plate but also to provide any answers. Annoyed, Batta turns to him, and chastises him: "You better answer and get it over with. We can't stay here all night." These are the only words he directs to the learner in the course of an hour. Never again does he speak to him. The scene is brutal and depressing, his hard, impassive face showing total indifference as he subdues the screaming learner and gives him shocks. He seems to derive no pleasure from the act itself, only quiet satisfaction at doing his job properly.

When he administers 450 volts, he turns to the experimenter and asks, "Where do we go from here, Professor?" His tone is deferential and expresses his willingness to be a cooperative subject, in contrast to the learner's obstinacy.

At the end of the session he tells the experimenter how honored he has been to help him, and in a moment of contrition, remarks, "Sir, sorry it couldn't have been a full experiment."

He has done his honest best. It is only the deficient behavior of the learner that has denied the experimenter full satisfaction.

The essence of obedience is that a person comes to view himself as the instrument for carrying out another person's wishes, and he therefore no longer regards himself as responsible for his actions. Once this critical shift of viewpoint has occurred, all of the essential features of obedience follow. The most far-reaching consequence is that the person feels responsible to the authority directing him but feels no responsibility *for* the content of the actions that the authority prescribes. Morality does not disappear—it acquires a radically different focus: the subordinate person feels shame or pride depending on how adequately he has performed the actions called for by authority.

Language provides numerous terms to pinpoint this type of morality: *loyalty*, *duty*, *discipline* all are terms heavily saturated with moral meaning and refer to the degree to which a person fulfills his obligations to authority. They refer not to the "goodness" of the person per se but to the adequacy with which a subordinate fulfills his socially defined role. The most frequent defense of the individual who has performed a heinous act under command of authority is that he has simply done his duty. In asserting this defense, the individual is not introducing an alibi concocted for the moment but is reporting honestly on the psychological attitude induced by submission to authority.

For a person to feel responsible for his actions, he must sense that the behavior has flowed from "the self." In the situation we have studied, subjects have precisely the opposite view of their actions—namely, they see them as originating in the motives of some other person. Subjects in the experiment frequently said, "If it were up to me, I would not have administered shocks to the learner."

Once authority has been isolated as the cause of the subject's behavior, it is legitimate to inquire into the necessary elements of authority and how it must be perceived in order to gain compliance. We conducted some investigations into the kinds of changes that would cause the experimenter to lose his power and to be disobeyed by the subject. Some of the variations revealed that:

- *The experimenter's physical presence has a marked impact on his authority.* As cited earlier, obedience dropped off sharply when orders

were given by telephone. The experimenter could often induce a disobedient subject to go on by returning to the laboratory.

- *Conflicting authority severely paralyzes action.* When two experimenters of equal status, both seated at the command desk, gave
incompatible orders, no shocks were delivered past the point of their
disagreement.

- *The rebellious action of others severely undermines authority.* In one
variation, three teachers (two actors and a real subject) administered
a test and shocks. When the two actors disobeyed the experimenter
and refused to go beyond a certain shock level, thirty-six of the forty
subjects joined their disobedient peers and refused as well.

Although the experimenter's authority was fragile in some respects,
it is also true that he had almost none of the tools used in ordinary command structures. For example, the experimenter did not threaten the
subjects with punishment—such as loss of income, community
ostracism, or jail—for failure to obey. Neither could he offer incentives.
Indeed, we should expect the experimenter's authority to be much less
than that of someone like a general, since the experimenter has no power
to enforce his imperatives, and since participation in a psychological
experiment scarcely evokes the sense of urgency and dedication found in
warfare. Despite these limitations, he still managed to command a dismaying degree of obedience.

I will cite one final variation of the experiment that depicts a
dilemma that is more common in everyday life. The subject was not
ordered to pull the lever that shocked the victim, but merely to perform
a subsidiary task (administering the word-pair test) while another person administered the shock. In this situation, thirty-seven of forty adults
continued to the highest level on the shock generator. Predictably, they
excused their behavior by saying that the responsibility belonged to the
man who actually pulled the switch. This may illustrate a dangerously
typical arrangement in a complex society: it is easy to ignore responsibility when one is only an intermediate link in a chain of action.

The problem of obedience is not wholly psychological. The form
and shape of society and the way it is developing have much to do with
it. There was a time, perhaps, when people were able to give a fully
human response to any situation because they were fully absorbed in it
as human beings. But as soon as there was a division of labor things
changed. Beyond a certain point, the breaking up of society into people
carrying out narrow and very special jobs takes away from the human
quality of work and life. A person does not get to see the whole situation
but only a small part of it, and is thus unable to act without some kind of
overall direction. He yields to authority but in doing so is alienated from
his own actions.

Even Eichmann was sickened when he toured the concentration camps, but he had only to sit at a desk and shuffle papers. At the same time the man in the camp who actually dropped Cyclon-b into the gas chambers was able to justify *his* behavior on the ground that he was only following orders from above. Thus there is a fragmentation of the total human act; no one is confronted with the consequences of his decision to carry out the evil act. The person who assumes responsibility has evaporated. Perhaps this is the most common characteristic of socially organized evil in modern society.

Facebook: Why I Love It . . .*

Kurt Soller

Kurt Soller is a staff writer for Newsweek.

1   I have three fond memories from my senior year of high school: the day I got my college acceptance letter, the day I graduated, and the day I joined Facebook. The latter happened on a May afternoon before graduation, when a college friend e-mailed me an invitation to join. I was 17, and anything the older kids were doing was automatically cool. All I needed was an attractive profile photo (easier said than done) and a well-curated list of interests to meet the friends I always dreamed I'd have in college: people who preferred Faulkner over Hemingway, liked thrift shopping, and wanted to sneak into Chicago jazz clubs. Facebook became my dry-erase tabula rasa. Under favorite quote, I wrote "True friends stab you in the front," as Oscar Wilde said. For the section titled "About Me," I said, "I like to write, but writing 'about me' is difficult."

2   As summer days passed and friend requests poured in, it didn't matter that I'd never met these people, because soon we'd be on campus together at Northwestern. When I landed at O'Hare that September, I met a girl who had seen my profile and wanted to introduce herself. Later, when I walked in on her in bed with a dormmate, she told me, "Don't be awkward." After all, we'd already met on Facebook.

3   As Facebook grew up alongside us, it improved our collective social lives—all 1,042 friends of mine and counting. I can't go to a sorority formal or football game without photos from the event winding up on Facebook, uploaded by me or a friend. Sure, it may be overly indulgent, and some of the pictures are unflattering, but this constant chronicling of life

*Kurt Soller, "Facebook: Why I Love It . . . ," *Newsweek*, August 14, 2007, 44.

...continued Facebook: Why I Love It . . . , **Kurt Soller**

eliminates the secret diary or crafty scrapbook. Before Facebook, I may have written some words in my journal about a wild night in Chicago; now my friends and I are building each other's collective stories—one photo, caption, and poke at a time.

4   Facebook is my personal assistant, allowing me to catch up on my social life without telephone tag, awkward lunches, and 5-, 10-, 15-year reunions. We write on each other's Wall, a message board, when we want to say happy birthday without singing into an answering machine. When I'm having a hectic week at my internship, I can change my status so that people know why I haven't returned their telephone calls—much better than wasting time calling people to tell them you're too busy to talk.

5   It may seem artificial that I don't have to go out of my way to get in touch. But in the end, I've beaten the system. I have more time for my closest friends, those whose relationships transcend computers. And Facebook enriches those close friendships: when a best friend changed her dating status from "In a Relationship" to "Single," I brought over a movie, one that she had listed as a fave.

6   You've heard criticism that Facebook makes us robotic, but history shows we've always feared new communication tools. In 360 B.C., Plato criticized writing, saying that it would induce forgetfulness; 2,200 years later, the telephone was seen as invasive and unnecessary. Mark Zuckerberg is no more, or no less, than the next Samuel Morse or Alexander Graham Bell.[1] We all want to interact as best we can, and Facebook allows us to do that. That said, if you're thinking of friending me after reading this, you should know: I'm not in the market for any more friends.

Editor's Note

1. Mark Zuckerberg invented Facebook when he was just nineteen years old. Samuel Morse invented the telegraph, and Alexander Graham Bell invented the telephone.

Facebook: Why I Hate It . . .*

Sarah Kliff

Sarah Kliff is a staff writer for Newsweek.

1   I have no idea how many hours of my life I've wasted on Facebook. When I wake up each morning, with my laptop sitting on the edge of my futon, I check it. Before I've thought about brushing my teeth, I have already seen the photographs of my brother's new apartment in San Francisco and discovered the evidence of my friend's tumultuous breakup: she changed her relationship status from "In a Relationship" to "Single" to "It's Complicated," all while I was sleeping. As best I can figure, since joining the site in 2004 when I was a freshman at Washington University in St. Louis, I've been logging on a dozen times a day. When I should have been studying or working, I found myself instead doing tasks like flipping through 400 photos of myself online, debating whether I wanted the picture where I have food in my hair to be on display to the world. (I decided to leave it: while it's not the most attractive pose, I think it indicates that I am a laid-back, good-humored person.)

2   I spend an inordinate amount of time like this, worrying about what's in my online profile. When I graduated from college this May, I decided it was time for a Facebook makeover. Looking to present a more "professional" image, I stripped my profile of many of my collegiate interests—you'll no longer know from Facebook that I'm obsessed with penguins—and I purged my membership in questionable Facebook groups such as "Scotland? Sounds more like Hotland" (tamer than it sounds). I know I'm not the only one constantly revamping my cyber-image: according to my Facebook account, 109 of my friends have changed something over the past two days. One friend added "goofy dads" to her interests, and another let it be known that he "falls asleep easily" and "loses things all the time."

3   What is with all this time we've spent, thinking about ourselves and creating well-planned lists of our interests? Facebook is much worse than e-mail, cell phones, instant messaging and the other devices that keep me constantly connected. It nurses every self-indulgent urge I could possibly have. I hate that Facebook encourages me to home in on each of my idiosyncrasies—that I like running in Central Park, for example, or that my favorite forms of punctuation are the dash and semicolon—and broadcast them to a largely uninterested world. I have a sneaking suspicion that very few people want to know that I am particularly fond of bagels. And no one really cares when I change my Facebook status, a fill-in-the-blank

*Sarah Kliff, "Facebook: Why I Hate It . . . ," *Newsweek*, August 14, 2007, 45.

feature where users can let people know what they're up to at any moment. Mine is currently set to "Sarah is trying to write an article about Facebook . . . but is ironically too distracted by Facebook." The network is as much about obsessing over the dull details of my life as it as about connecting with others.

4   As a recent college graduate, with my friends scattered across the globe, I understand the communicative value of Facebook. Right now, I have 469 "friends"—though I admit many of these virtual relationships are tenuous at best. Still, I would be hard-pressed to give up my four-year-long membership or leave Facebook out of my early morning routine. But who knows what I'm missing out on in the real world while sitting at my laptop, debating whether penguins or bagels are more respectable?

Teach Diversity—with a Smile

Barbara Ehrenreich

Barbara Ehrenreich was born in Butte, Montana, in 1941 and received a B.A. degree from Reed College and a Ph.D. from Rockefeller University. She has been a health policy adviser and a professor of health sciences, but since 1974, she has spent most of her time writing books and articles about socialist and feminist issues. She has received a Ford Foundation Award and a Guggenheim Fellowship for her writings, which include The Worst Years of Our Lives: Irreverent Notes from a Decade of Greed *(1990),* The Snarling Citizen: Essays *(1995),* Nickel and Dimed: On (Not) Getting by in America *(2001), and* This Land Is Their Land: Reports from a Divided Nation *(2008). Her articles and essays have appeared in* Esquire, Mother Jones, Ms., New Republic, The New York Times Magazine, *and* Time. *The following essay on cultural diversity appeared in* Time *magazine.*

1   Something had to replace the threat of communism, and at last a workable substitute is at hand. "Multiculturalism," as the new menace is known, has been denounced in the media recently as the new McCarthyism, the new fundamentalism, even the new totalitarianism—take your choice. According to its critics, who include a flock of tenured conservative scholars, multiculturalism aims to toss out what it sees as the Euro-

centric bias in education and replace Plato with Ntozake Shange and traditional math with the Yoruba number system. And that's just the beginning. The Jacobins of the multiculturalist movement, who are described derisively as P.C., or politically correct, are said to have launched a campus reign of terror against those who slip and innocently say "freshman" instead of "freshperson," "Indian" instead of "Native American" or, may the Goddess forgive them, "disabled" instead of "differently abled."

2   So you can see what is at stake here: freedom of speech, freedom of thought, Western civilization and a great many professorial egos. But before we get carried away by the mounting backlash against multiculturalism, we ought to reflect for a moment on the system that the P.C. people aim to replace. I know all about it; in fact it's just about all I do know, since I—along with so many educated white people of my generation—was a victim of monoculturalism.

3   American history, as it was taught to us, began with Columbus's "discovery" of an apparently unnamed, unpeopled America, and moved on to the Pilgrims serving pumpkin pie to a handful of grateful red-skinned folks. College expanded our horizons with courses called Humanities or sometimes Civ, which introduced us to a line of thought that started with Homer, worked its way through Rabelais and reached a poignant climax in the pensées of Matthew Arnold. Graduate students wrote dissertations on what long-dead men had thought of Chaucer's verse or Shakespeare's dramas; foreign languages meant French or German. If there had been high technology in ancient China, kingdoms in black Africa or women anywhere, at any time, doing anything worth noticing, we did not know it, nor did anyone think to tell us.

4   Our families and neighborhoods reinforced the dogma of monoculturalism. In our heads, most of us '50s teenagers carried around a social map that was about as useful as the chart that guided Columbus to the "Indies." There were "Negroes," "whites" and "Orientals," the latter meaning Chinese and "Japs." Of religions, only three were known—Protestant, Catholic and Jewish—and not much was known about the last two types. The only remaining human categories were husbands and wives, and that was all the diversity the monocultural world could handle. Gays, lesbians, Buddhists, Muslims, Malaysians, Mormons, etc. were simply off the map.

5   So I applaud—with one hand, anyway—the multiculturalist goal of preparing us all for a wider world. The other hand is tapping its fingers impatiently, because the critics are right about one thing: when advocates of multiculturalism adopt the haughty stance of political correctness, they quickly descend to silliness or worse. It's obnoxious, for example, to rely on university administrations to enforce P.C. standards of verbal inoffensiveness. Racist, sexist and homophobic thoughts cannot, alas, be abolished by fiat but only by the time-honored methods of persuasion,

...*continued* Teach Diversity—with a Smile, **Barbara Ehrenreich**

education and exposure to the other guy's—or, excuse me, woman's—point of view.

6   And it's silly to mistake verbal purification for genuine social reform. Even after all women are "Ms." and all people are "he or she," women will still earn only 65¢ for every dollar earned by men. Minorities by any other name, such as "people of color," will still bear a hugely disproportionate burden of poverty and discrimination. Disabilities are not just "different abilities" when there are not enough ramps for wheelchairs, signers for the deaf or special classes for the "specially" endowed. With all due respect for the new politesse, actions still speak louder than fashionable phrases.

7   But the worst thing about the P.C. people is that they are such poor advocates for the multicultural cause. No one was ever won over to a broader, more inclusive view of life by being bullied or relentlessly "corrected." Tell a 19-year-old white male that he can't say "girl" when he means "teen-age woman," and he will most likely snicker. This may be the reason why, despite the conservative alarms, P.C.-ness remains a relatively tiny trend. Most campuses have more serious and ancient problems: faculties still top-heavy with white males of the monocultural persuasion; fraternities that harass minorities and women; date rape; alcohol abuse; and tuition that excludes all but the upper fringe of the middle class.

8   So both sides would be well advised to lighten up. The conservatives ought to realize that criticisms of the great books approach to learning do not amount to totalitarianism. And the advocates of multiculturalism need to regain the sense of humor that enabled their predecessors in the struggle to coin the term P.C. years ago—not in arrogance but in self-mockery.

9   Beyond that, both sides should realize that the beneficiaries of multiculturalism are not only the "oppressed peoples" on the standard P.C. list (minorities, gays, etc.). The "unenlightened"—the victims of monoculturalism—are oppressed too, or at least deprived. Our educations, whether at Yale or at State U, were narrow and parochial and left us ill-equipped to navigate a society that truly is multicultural and is becoming more so every day. The culture that we studied was, in fact, *one* culture and, from a world perspective, all too limited and ingrown. Diversity is challenging, but those of us who have seen the alternative know it is also richer, livelier and ultimately more fun.

What Defines a Sport?

David Andriesen

Search for "cup stacking" on YouTube, and you can watch more than 1,000 videos of people taking nested stacks of plastic cups and arranging them into pyramids and back again so quickly the whole thing is almost a blur.

It's impressive. It takes skill and agility. But is it a sport?

Stacking supporters think so. In 2005, the governing body changed the name officially to "sport stacking."

"When people challenge me on whether it's a sport, I usually turn it around on them," said Matt Reed, executive director of the World Sport Stacking Association. "I ask them, 'What's your definition of sport?' Invariably many of the things they mention are involved in our sport."

5 ESPN shows poker, cheerleading, arm wrestling, and, yes, sport stacking.

Bass fishing events offer million-dollar purses.

Mainstream newspaper sports sections report on hot dog–eating world records.

The Olympics offer medals for kayaking and bobsled, but not for golf or football (at least not the American kind).

Some school districts classify chess as a sport.

10 So how, in this age of media saturation and fringe activities clamoring for legitimacy, can we define "sport"?

It's one of the great barroom debates, usually triggered by the sight of billiards or the X Games on TV at a watering hole. But while fans have argued over it for decades, there hasn't really been any official effort to define sport.

Rodney Fort, a professor of sport management at the University of Michigan who taught for more than two decades at Washington State University, uses a discussion about the definition of sport as an exercise to get students thinking about the field.

Fort has narrowed his definition to three parameters:

- It must use a "large motor skill."
- It must have an objective scoring system.
- It must use nothing more complicated than a "simple machine," such as a baseball bat or vaulting pole.

"That's just me talking, my personal opinion," Fort said. "You'll never find a group of people who will reach total agreement."

15 There are many factors to consider, but most arguments end up centering on a few common factors.

...continued What Defines a Sport?, **David Andriesen**

Takeru Kobayashi won Nathan's Famous Hot Dog Eating Competition six years in a row. But is the event an actual sport?

WHO'S GOT THE BALL?

A ball helps a lot. Most things with a ball (or ball-like object, such as a puck) are generally considered to be sports. Heck, America's three top pro sports have "ball" right in the name.

If there are two people or teams on a playing surface at the same time competing with a ball, particularly the same ball, it's almost certainly a sport. Dozens of sports fit under this umbrella.

WHO'S RACING?

A footrace is the simplest form of sport, and most racing under human power is inarguably a sport. Whether people are racing over hurdles, through the woods, or in a pool, they're engaged in sport.

The question becomes what level of human power you require, and what other implements you accept.

For instance, horse racing might be "the sport of kings," but is it a sport?

"It's a sport for the horse," Fort said. "They're the ones doing the racing. Certainly the jockey has something to do with it, but it's hard to conclude that that's a sport in the same way, say, the 100-meter dash is."

And in horse racing, at least it's the horse that gets the glory. Most people can name horses that have won the Triple Crown, but not jockeys who have done it.

But what about auto racing? NASCAR is one of the most popular sports in America, but it's the cars that are providing the power, and the fastest car usually wins, even if it's not driven by the most skilled driver on a particular day. Purists would reject all motorized racing, though they'd get a powerful argument south of the Mason-Dixon line.

What about human-powered racing in disciplines where differences in the equipment can affect the outcome, such as cycling and crew? Fort rejects these under his "simple machines" provision, but if you set the standard at the conveyance being primarily human powered, pedaling and rowing qualify.

WHOSE TURN IS IT?

25

Then there is the question of whether participants must compete head-to-head. In a footrace, first one to the finish wins. But what about races like downhill skiing, in which competitors are theoretically racing each other but really just racing a clock?

Golf and bowling also are turn-based. In the case of bowling, it's to assure two competitors have the same lane conditions, but in golf a field of 144 can experience vastly different conditions on the same course— some might play a hole early or late, with or without wind or rain. People often complete the same round on different days.

Are the golfers truly competing against each other? And if you could get the same results by having golfers drop by and play four rounds at a certain course at their leisure, and then comparing scores to determine a winner, can a golf tournament be said to be a sporting event?

WHAT'S THE SCORE?

When the results of a competition are a matter of opinion, it's tough for many to accept it as a sport.

If a judge scores an athlete higher or lower based on politics, or loving or hating a certain move, or, heaven forbid, whether he likes his outfit, the notion of competition goes down the drain quickly.

30   We like to know for certain whether someone won a contest. The ball went in the net or it didn't. The runner beat the throw to the plate or he didn't. Our most popular sports have this in common, even though human error is sometimes a factor.

"We have to all know what constitutes you getting a point," Fort said. "This causes a problem for some people, because they confuse the existence of an objective scoring definition with the human fallibility of recognizing it when they see it."

"They say, 'Well, what about when a ref blows a call in the end zone?' But that's not the point. We all know what constitutes a touchdown. We're just arguing about whether the ref saw it correctly or not."

Women often argue against the insistence on objective scoring, because it eliminates several sports most closely identified with women, or most popular when women are competing: figure skating, gymnastics, cheer.

But its sweep is much wider than that. Diving, out. Most extreme sports, out. Many rodeo events, out.

35   Even boxing, considered one of the most basic and pure sports, goes by the wayside if we insist on objective scoring. Are you ready to throw out boxing?

If you want boxing, you pretty much have to accept figure skating.

GETTING PHYSICAL?

Even if you insist on humans doing the competing, head-to-head competition and objective scoring, you're still left with a lot of things that don't pass muster. Pinball. Poker. Darts. Which of your frat brothers can eat the most jalapeno poppers.

There has to be some level of physical effort. But where do you draw the line?

Golf looks pretty easy, but the average person might change his mind on that after playing 18 holes on foot carrying his own bag.

40   You could argue that throwing a 15-pound bowling ball for a few hours requires more physical strength than swinging a golf club, but a trip to the local bowling alley doesn't exactly turn up a lot of world-class athletes.

Tennis is a sport, but how about table tennis? It's pretty much the same thing, only on a smaller scale—and if you watch an international match you see that there's some physical effort involved.

Curling is an Olympic medal sport, but requires about the same level of effort as sweeping the back porch.

The question of what is or is not a sport will continue to be argued, and the only point of agreement likely to be reached is that we'll never agree.

What combination of factors must exist to make something a sport is up to you. Or maybe it's like the famous definition of art: You know it when you see it.

45   "Are we going to be in the Olympics? I don't know about that," cup stacking, er, *sport stacking* chief Reed said. "We're never going to be one of the major sports, but we feel like we're legit."

For Reed, whether sport stacking is classified as a sport is less important than people having fun doing it.

After all, that's the point, isn't it?

Running head: WHY FACEBOOK MIGHT NOT BE GOOD FOR YOU   1

Why Facebook Might Not Be Good for You:

Some Dangers of Online Social Networks

James Gardiner

Professor Johnson

Writing Seminar: Inquiry and Argument—May 15, 2007

Include the title and page number on each page.

Center title.

Indent paragraphs 5 spaces or 1/2 inch.

Double-space all text.

Use 1-inch margins.

Italicize book and periodical titles and Web site names.

Use quotation marks for article titles.

Why Facebook Might Not Be Good for You:

Some Dangers of Online Social Networks

Walk into any computer lab located at any college campus across the country and you'll see dozens of students logged onto an online social network (OSN). In the last few years, the use of these networks has skyrocketed among Internet users, especially young adults. These new virtual communities are significantly influencing the way young people communicate and interact with one another. A report titled "E-Expectations: The Class of 2007" went so far as to label upcoming college freshmen "the Social-Networking Generation" (as cited in Joly, 2007).

In late 2006, the Pew Internet Project, a nonpartisan, nonprofit research group that examines the social impact of the Internet, reported that 55 percent of online teens have created a personal profile on OSNs and that 48 percent of teens visit social networking Web sites daily, with 22 percent visiting several times a day (Lenhart & Madden, 2007). The two most popular OSNs are MySpace and Facebook. MySpace is a general networking site that allows anyone to join, develop a profile, and display personal information. In less than four years of existence, MySpace has exploded to become the third most visited Web site on the Internet behind only Google and Yahoo ("Top Sites," 2007) with more than 100 million members (Joly, 2007). Facebook is geared more toward college students (until recently it required that a person attend a university to join the network) and is the number one site accessed by 18- to 24-year-olds. According to research studies cited in an article in the *Toronto Star,* 90 percent of all undergraduates log on to Facebook and 60 percent log on daily (George-Cosh, 2007). Facebook has also experienced unprecedented growth in its relatively short existence and now ranks as the seventh most visited site on the Internet ("Top Sites") and has a member base of more than 19 million (Joly, 2007).

With the use of OSNs increasing among young people, the term "Facebook trance" has emerged to describe a person who loses track of all time and stares at

WHY FACEBOOK MIGHT NOT BE GOOD   3

the screen for hours (Copeland, 2004). While "Facebook trance" might describe only an occasional and therefore harmless phenomenon, it gives rise to important questions: What are the possible negative consequences of OSNs? What should youthful users be watchful for and guard against? The purpose of this paper is to identify the possible harms of OSNs. I will suggest that overuse of OSNs can be a contributing factor to a decline in grades as well as to other problems such as a superficial view of relationships, an increase in narcissism, and possible future embarrassment.

I don't mean to deny that OSNs have positive consequences for young people. For one thing, they provide a "virtual hangout" that acts as a convenient and cost-effective way to stay in close contact with friends and family. According to the Pew survey, 91 percent of users use OSNs to keep in touch with their regularly seen friends, while 82 percent use the sites to stay in touch with distant friends (Lenhart & Madden, 2007). OSNs let young people regularly view their friends' profiles, leave short messages or comments, and share personal information. OSN researcher Danah Boyd also claims that these sites give young people a platform on which to experiment with identities, voice their opinions, and practice how they present themselves through personal data, pictures, and music placed in their profiles (Bowley, 2006). OSNs also assist them in learning more about people they've met offline. Used as an investigative tool, OSNs offer quick ways to get additional background information on someone. For example, a student could use an OSN to decide whom to partner with for a class project, to learn more about a new roommate, or to find out more about someone he or she just met at a party, all by browsing classmates' profiles.

Despite these benefits, OSNs have a downside. One potential harm is that OSNs could have a negative effect on grades. One study shows a direct connection between the amount of time spent on the networks and declining grades in school. A college newspaper article entitled "Research Links MySpace Use to Drop in Grades"

(2007) reports a survey of high school students conducted by Fresno State University

professor Tamyra Pierce. Pierce found that students with MySpace accounts were

significantly more likely than students without MySpace accounts to report a decline

in grades since the previous year. According to Pierce, "We can't know for sure that

MySpace caused the lower grades, but when compared to other after-school

activities (work, sports, video games, etc.), only MySpace showed significance"

Use "as cited in" for an author quoted in another source.

(as cited in "Research Links," 2007, p. 24). Pierce's research also revealed that 42

percent of polled students said they often had MySpace open while doing homework,

and 34 percent stated that they would delay homework to spend time on social

networking sites. Pierce adds that 59 percent of students reported spending

"between 30 minutes and six hours daily on MySpace." Such heavy usage

significantly takes time away from school work, extracurricular activities, and sleep.

Although this specific study focused on high school students, it would be safe to

assume that the results would be generally similar for college students. In fact, the

results of the Fresno State study were reported in other college newspapers (Scrabis,

2007; Jimenez, 2007); the writers for these college newspapers usually included

anecdotes from their own campuses about college students obsessed with OSNs.

One Penn State student said of MySpace, "I keep getting rid of it and then getting it

back again because I'm addicted. It's like cocaine" (as cited in Scrabis, 2007, p. 23).

Another potential problem with OSNs is their tendency to promote superficial

or unsatisfying relationships. According to Chou, Condron, and Belland (2005), for

some users "over-dependence on online relationships may result in significant

problems with real-life interpersonal and occupational functioning" (p. 381). When

logged on to the network, students may believe that they are "in touch" with people,

when actually they are physically alone with their computers. In a controversial 1998

article cited by Matsuba (2006), Kraut and his colleagues suggested that extensive

Internet use "was associated with declines in participants' communication with family members in the household, declines in the size of their social circle, and increases in their depression and loneliness" (as cited in Matsuba, 2006 p. 275). Matsuba conducted an extensive study to test Kraut's conclusions. Matsuba found that persons who scored high on measures of loneliness spent more time on the Internet than persons who scored low on the loneliness measures. In another facet of his study, Matsuba found that for persons who established online friendships, these friendships did not seem "as rich and diverse in quality compared to face to face friendships" (p. 283). Matsuba concludes that while online communication can be used to enhance relationships, it can become a problem when it begins to replace offline interaction. He found that face-to-face friendships scored higher for both positive and negative aspects of relationships than did online friendships. He then speculates, "While it is possible that the internet is helping |lonely| people in their search, the possibility remains that the internet is hindering them in facing life in the 'real' world and thus preventing them from developing an adult identity" (p. 283).

Matsuba's (2006) finding that face-to-face friendships are more "rich and diverse in quality" than online friendships has led me to speculate that a possible problem with OSNs is the complete lack of nonverbal communication exchanged between users. According to communications professor Julia T. Woods (2007), "Scholars estimate that nonverbal behaviors account for 65 percent to 93 percent of the total meaning of communication" (p. 132). Since the people interacting on OSNs are unable to view each other, they are unable to gauge the other's subtle body language, facial expressions, and voice tones that are such vital ingredients of effective communication. Part of achieving the "adult identity" called for by Matsuba is learning to communicate nonverbally as well as verbally in an environment requiring real contact.

For me, a particularly interesting yet subtle danger of OSNs is their contribution to a rise in narcissism. In an article with the subtitle "Study Says Many Students Are

Narcissists," journalist E. Hoover (2007) reports on the unpublished research of
Jean M. Twenge, a psychology professor at San Diego State University, who says that
new technology such as OSNs have "stoked the self-loving tendencies of modern
students" (as cited in Hoover, p. A41). Twenge's recent research shows that college
kids today are more narcissistic than college kids were in the 1980s; she labels the
current generation of youth as "the most narcissistic in recent history" (Hoover).
According to Hoover, Twenge defines narcissism as "excessive vanity and a sense of
entitlement." Narcissists, Hoover reports, "tend to lack empathy for others, behave
aggressively when insulted, and ignore the needs of those around them" (p. A41).

     According to Twenge, narcissism finds expression on OSNs in the way that
young people on MySpace and Facebook compete with each other to be heard. In
another article reporting Twenge's research, Melissa Ludwig (2007) states that OSNs
have "gone beyond touching base with friends to an arena where people vie for the
most digital friends, the best videos, the coolest sites, and the biggest audience"
(p. A15). She then quotes Twenge: "Now it all becomes a competition, seeking
attention and seeking status rather than a true connection between people, or a
meaningful connection" (p. A15). The work of Twenge and others suggests that the
popularity of OSNs is partly the result of young people's finding an online way to
express their narcissistic tendencies. The sites may contribute to self-expression
more than to connection and friendship.

     A final danger of OSNs is that persons will place on their sites material that
they will later regret. Young people tend to think that their audiences are only their
like-minded friends and classmates. They often don't imagine their professors, their
potential employers, or even their parents reading their sites. One journalist
describes a MySpace profile in which a college student has posted photos of herself
in "a skin-tight black leather Catwoman costume, two triangles of vinyl struggling to
cover her silicone-enhanced breasts" (Ludwig, 2007, p. A15). Ludwig continues:

WHY FACEBOOK MIGHT NOT BE GOOD   7

> Much of the stuff floating around in cyberspace is tame, mundane even.
>
> But there also is plenty that's racy, embarrassing or squeamishly intimate.
>
> Bad or good, Generation Next is living out loud and doing it online, before
>
> a global audience, in a medium where digital archives may linger for a
>
> long, long time. . . . [Generation Nexters] still are too young to fully grasp
>
> the permanence of their online actions, and the possible consequences
>
> down the road. (p. A15)

One indication of this danger has already surfaced in the case of some sports teams. The University of Minnesota Duluth recently barred all athletes from creating profiles on MySpace, Facebook, and similar sites, a policy that, according to journalist Chao Xiong (2007), aims to shield students and the school from bad press that might occur from the posting of inappropriate material. Xiong reports that athletic departments across the country are considering similar bans. One coach at the UM–Duluth campus said, "It was amazing to me how revealing people are with their lives on the Internet" (as cited in Xiong, p. 1A). (This coach had established her own Facebook profile in order to police the activities of her team members.) Xiong reports that across the country athletes have embarrassed their programs by posting pictures of themselves drinking blindfolded at parties or making disparaging comments about coaches or teammates. It is unclear whether coaches have the legal right to forbid their team members to place profiles on OSNs (some students are claiming violation of free speech rights). However, the fact that athletic programs are concerned about the impact of these social networks shows the potential negative consequence of posting embarrassing material on OSNs.

Although I don't support the banning of Facebook or MySpace profiles for athletes or other students, I do think that young people should be aware of some of the problems associated with them. Two of the problems I have noted here—decline in grades and narcissistic competition for the coolest sites—could be avoided by

Indent longer quotations 10 spaces or 1 inch.

Use ellipsis to show omitted words.

Use brackets when inserting explanatory words in quotation.

students' simply limiting their time online. Knowing that OSNs can promote a superficial view of friendships might encourage people to use OSNs to stay in touch face-to-face with friends rather than try to find online substitutes for real friendships. Finally, young people should be aware that the materials they post on their profiles might one day come back to haunt them. To gain the maximum benefits of online social networks and avoid the pitfalls associated with them, my advice to today's students would be to use them as an advanced e-mail-type communication tool rather than as a place to loiter and waste valuable hours that they will never get back.

WHY FACEBOOK MIGHT NOT BE GOOD   9

References

Bowley, G. (2006, October). The high priestess of internet friendship. *Financial Times Weekend Magazine*. Retrieved from http://www.lexisnexis.com/hottopics/ Inacademic/?

Chou, C., Condron, L., & Belland, J.C. (2005). A review of the research on internet addiction. *Educational Psychology Review 17*(4), 363–389. Retrieved from http://web.ebscohost.com

Copeland, L. (2004, December). Click clique: *Facebook's* online college community. *Washington Post*. Retrieved from http://www.washingtonpost.com/ wp-dyn/articles/A30002-2004Dec27.html

George-Cosh, D. (2007, January). Social net: Thousands of students build friendships on *Facebook*. *Toronto Star*. Retrieved from http://www.strangehold.com/2007/ 01/20/social-net-thousands-of-local-students-build-friendships-on-facebook

Hoover, E. (2007, March). Here's you looking at you, kid: Study says many students are narcissists. *Chronicle of Higher Education 53*(29), A41. Retrieved from http://web.ebscohost.com

Jimenez, E. (2007, March). *MySpace* adds to overload for teens. Retrieved from http://www.ebscohost.com/academic/newspaper-source

Joly, K. (2007, April). *Facebook, MySpace* and co. *University Business*. Retrieved from http://www.universitybusiness.com/viewarticle.aspx?articleid=735

Lenhart, A. & Madden, M. (2007). Social networking websites and teens: An overview. *Pew Internet & American Life Project*. Retrieved from http://www.pewinternet .org/Reports/2007/Social-Networking-Websites-and-Teens.aspx

Ludwig, M. (2007, March). LOOK@ME: Generation next is living out loud and online. *San Antonio Express News*. Retrieved from http://www.mysanantonio.com/

Matsuba, K.M. (2006). Searching for self and relationships online. *Cyber Psychology & Behavior* 9.3. Retrieved from http://web.ebscohost.com

Research Links *MySpace* Use to Drop in Grades. (2007, March). California State U. Retrieved from http://www.fresnostatenews.com

Start References list on a new page.

Center heading.

List sources alpha-betically.

Use month-day-year format for dates.

Italicize periodical titles.

Scrabis, J. (2007, March). *MySpace* usage may lower grades in both high school, col-

lege students. *Daily Collegian.* Retrieved from http://www.google.com/

search?q=Daily+Collegian

Top Sites for United States. *alexia.com.* Retrieved from http//www.alexia.com/site/

ds/top_sites? cc=US&ts_mode+country&lang=none

Woods, J.T. (2007). *Interpersonal communication: Everyday encounters* (5th ed.). New

York: Wadsworth.

Xiong, C. (2007, April). Not their space. *Minneapolis Star Tribune.* Retrieved from

http://www.lexisnexis.com/hottopics/Inacademic/?

Italicize book titles.

Check that everything cited in paper is in References list.

1 INCH

1/2 INCH
PAGE NUMBER ➜ 2

Alaskan Wolf Management

Whether or not to control the wolf population by aerial shooting when wolves become

DOUBLE-SPACE

Introduction and background of problem

plentiful enough to threaten other animal populations has been a contested issue in

Alaska for more than fifty years (see Figure 1). The Alaska Department of Fish and Game

has the responsibility for conserving wildlife in Alaska. When they determine caribou and

moose are endangered by a growing wolf population, they periodically recommend that

the wolf population be reduced, usually by hunters who shoot the wolves from airplanes

and helicopters or who land their planes and shoot the wolves when they are exhausted

from running. The position of the Department of Fish and Game (2003) is that the wolf

population must be reduced at times in Alaska when the caribou and moose populations

become endangered because predators, like wolves, "kill 80 percent of the moose and

caribou that die during an average year, while humans kill less than 10 percent" (p. 10).

1 INCH

Even when many wolves are killed, the wolf population is only temporarily reduced, and

Two main positions

it soon recovers ("Wolf Control," 2008). The animal rights advocates, many of whom are

members of the Defenders of Wildlife organization in Alaska, passionately oppose this

1 INCH

Figure 1   Wolf population threatening other wildlife is a persistent issue in Alaska.
From www.shutterstock.com

1 INCH

ALASKAN WOLF   1 INCH   3   1/2 INCH

practice, arguing that shooting wolves from airplanes is unsporting and unethical and that it upsets the natural ecology of the region ("History," 2008).

Quotation from authority to show difficulty of problem

According to Wayne L. Regelin (2002), past director of Wildlife Conservation for the Alaska Department of Fish and Game, public attitudes "are based on deeply held values" (p. 8), and that makes it extremely difficult to set wildlife policy in Alaska.

History of problem

Regelin, Valkenburg, and Boertje (2005) detail some of the history of aerial shooting of wolves in Alaska. It began officially in 1948 and was conducted by federal agents until the late 1950s. When Alaska became a state in 1959, legislation was passed to protect the wolf population. The issue did not go away, however. Aerial shooting resumed in the 1960s, and periodic efforts to control the wolf population in Alaska in this manner continued through the early 1980s.

1 INCH

Since 1986, the policy on wolf control in Alaska seems to change with the election of each new governor. Governor Steve Cooper (1986–1990) opposed wolf control and suspended the aerial shooting of wolves while he was governor. Cooper was followed by Governor Walter Hickel (1990–1994), who reinstated the practice. Public reaction against killing wolves was so strong during Governor Hickel's term that the governor commissioned "The Wolf Conservation and Management Policy for Alaska," in 1993, to set an official state policy on wolf control. This document is still the guiding policy for the state (Regelin, 2005).

1 INCH

Governor Tony Knowles (1994–2002) followed Hickel. Under Knowles, voters showed their support of animal rights groups by voting in 1996 and 2000 to ban the aerial shooting of wolves ("History," 2008). Governor Knowles not only suspended the wolf control program, he also assigned it to the U.S. National Academy of Sciences to study for a year. That group concluded that wolf control could be effective in Alaska and that current practices were based on sound science, but cautioned that control could be costly and controversial (Regelin, 2005). Governor Frank Murkowski

1 INCH

ALASKAN WOLF   4

(2002–2006), reinstated the aerial shooting of wolves, and the controversy surrounding

this practice continued to rage throughout his term. In March 2004 *The New York*

Times published an editorial in support of the animal rights activists and warned that

the wolf population in Alaska could be wiped out if present policy is not changed. This

editorial states: "Thanks to the compliance of Gov. Frank Murkowski and the state's

official game board, the legal protections for Alaska's 7,000 to 9,000 wolves have been

seriously eroded" ("Wolf 'Control,'" 2004, p. 12). The current governor, Sarah Palin,

who took office in 2006, is continuing Murkowski's policy and has proposed legislation

to make it difficult for conservation groups, like the Defenders of Wildlife, to sue the

government for killing wolves from planes (Cockerham, 2008).

The situations in 1993 and 2008 have a lot in common. In the early 1990s

Alaska witnessed a decline in the populations of caribou and moose in the Fortymile,

Delta, and Nelchina Basin areas. This decline in the caribou and moose populations

was due mainly to the increase of the wolf populations in these three areas. Robert

Stephenson of the Alaska Department of Fish and Game claimed at that time, "Wolf

packs will kill one caribou every two days or so, and one moose every three to ten

days" (as cited in Keszler, 1993, p. 65). The Delta caribou herd alone declined from

about eleven thousand in 1989 to fewer than four thousand just four years later

("Alaska Wolf," 1993). With statistics such as these, the size of the caribou and

moose populations in Alaska was clearly a problem that needed ongoing attention.

Now, as then, a rapid decline in caribou and moose populations can be

devastating to the state. Not only are they a valuable resource for Alaska in terms of

nonresident hunting and tourist sightseeing, but for many remote residents, caribou

and moose are the main source of food.

The way of life for many Alaskans is one that the average American cannot

begin to understand. Max Peterson, the executive director of the International

Comparison

Quotations worked into text suggest the unique character of the problem in Alaska.

A long quotation of more than forty words is indented and written in block form. No quotation marks are necessary for indented quotations. The page number is indicated at the end, and the author is mentioned in the text.

Statistics and quotations from authorities to strengthen the solution preferred by this author

ALASKAN WOLF   5

Association of Wildlife Agencies, says that in Alaska, "people interact as another predator in the ecosystem," and as a result, "the interest in Alaska by people outside Alaska certainly is greater than their knowledge of Alaska" (as cited in Keszler, 1993, p. 67). Ted Williams (1993) clarifies the lifestyle that many rural Alaskans lead:

> Genuine subsistence is the most environmentally benign of all possible lifestyles. Subsisters do not—indeed cannot—deplete fish and wildlife because if they do, they will subsist no more. But even in the remotest native villages, Alaska as trackless wilderness where people blend with nature is just an old dream. Many villagers are now on social welfare programs and are therefore cash dependent. (p. 49)

Failing to protect existing caribou and moose populations can lower the subsistence level for some Alaskans, even more than it is at present.

The biologists of the state of Alaska commonly believe that wolf populations are nowhere close to being endangered, and that the current wolf control programs will sustain future wolf populations ("Wolf Control," 2008). The total wolf population in Alaska at present is estimated to be between 7,700–11,200. According to the Division of Wildlife Conservation in Alaska, the wolf population has never been endangered, and the future of the wolf in Alaska is secure ("Wolf in Alaska," 2008). In 2008 five wolf control programs are in place in about 9.4% of the total area of Alaska. Aerial shooting that is designed to protect other animal populations is permitted in these areas. "In these areas, wolf numbers will be temporarily reduced, but wolves will not be permanently eliminated from any area" ("Wolf Control," 2008, p. A12). In the past five years, gunners in airplanes who carry state permits have killed more than 700 wolves (Cockerham, 2008).

In 1993, when Governor Walter Hickel and the Alaska Department of Fish and Game announced the new "Wolf Conservation and Management Policy for Alaska" that allowed for the aerial shooting of wolves, the animal rights groups started an

ALASKAN WOLF 6

all-out war on the state. They organized widespread mailings to the governor and

threatened massive boycotts of tourism in Alaska if the plan was not repealed

(Keszler, 1993). The animal rights groups believed that other methods of

management could increase caribou and moose populations. Such methods included

reducing bag limits, shortening hunting seasons, or totally eliminating hunting in the

three main areas. This type of management was not effective, however, since

hunters were not the real cause of the problem. Pete Buist (1993), a Fairbanks,

Alaska, resident, pointed out at the time, "In control areas, hunters are taking less

than five percent of the annual production of meat animals. Predators are taking

more than seventy-five percent". Animal rights groups commonly point to hunters as

the culprits in animal conservation efforts. According to Arms (1994), however,

"Nowadays in developed countries, groups representing hunting and fishing

interests are the most active conservationists. They understand that their sport and,

sometimes, their livelihood depend on sustained or increasing populations of the

organisms they hunt or fish" (p. 347). As mentioned earlier, rural Alaskans who

depend on caribou and moose for subsistence are some of these hunters who

continue to take these animals but not in dangerously large numbers.

Another alternative management method that has been brought up by the

animal rights groups is tranquilizing and capturing the wolves and chemically

sterilizing them or using some other sort of contraception. This method was tried from

1997–2001. Alpha males and females in wolf packs in control areas were sterilized.

During these years the caribou population experienced an increase from 22,000 to

38,000. Whether or not the wolf sterilization program caused this increase in the

caribou population is still being studied. Even if it is finally judged to be the main cause

of the increase in caribou, the sterilization program has been accounted unfeasible for

implementation throughout Alaska because of its scope and cost (Regelin, 2005). In the

Refutation of the animal rights groups and their solution to the problem

1 INCH

1/2 INCH

long run, sterilization is less effective than killing wolves for another reason. It would take too long to be effective in reducing an existing wolf population. Sterilization only deals with the wolf numbers in the future, not with existing numbers, which would remain the same for the present. Existing wolves in the immediate future could devastate the caribou and moose populations in the meantime.

Refutation of other solutions and evaluation of evidence

In the U.S. Constitution, the management of fish and wildlife is left up to the individual states. When Alaska made the professional decision that the best way to control its wolf population was by aerial shootings, the animal rights groups picked only that part of a larger plan to attack. In media reports, activists "portrayed the plan simply as a mass extermination of wolves designed to increase game numbers for out-of-state hunters and wildlife watchers" (Keszler, 1993, p. 39). The Defenders of Wildlife (2008) claim now that Governor Palin's proposed bill, which makes it difficult for conservation groups to sue the government for killing wolves, will take "science and public input out of the process" (p. 10); the current wildlife director counters that people will still be able to state their views (Cockerham, 2008). After all these years, the issue of wolf population control in Alaska is still far from settled. In August 2008 the citizens of Alaska will vote for the third time on whether or not to ban aerial hunting of wolves. The 1996 and 2000 propositions of Governor Knowles's term passed by 58.5% and 53% of the votes, respectively. Each propositions either banned or limited the killing of wolves ("History," 2008).

1 INCH

Animal rights commercials in 1993 showed "visions of helicopter gunships slaughtering wolves by the hundreds" (Keszler, 1993, p.39). Since then other images of wolves in distress have been distributed to influence public opinion on this issue (Regelin, 2005). What is not always clear to the public, however, is that the aerial shooting of wolves is just one small part of the plan that also includes protecting the wolves themselves when their numbers become too low. The animal rights groups

1 INCH

ALASKAN WOLF

8

have not focused on those parts of the wolf plan that deal with restrictions to help the wolves in areas where their populations are sparse. The Alaska Department of Fish and Game, Division of Wildlife Conservation in Alaska, makes it clear that the long-term conservation of wolves is a major goal. Furthermore, when wolves are killing other important animal populations, they must be reduced ("Wolf Control," 2008).

The professional wildlife biologists at the Alaska Department of Fish and Game have taken a lot of heat from the animal rights media reports on their decision to go ahead with the original plan to manage wolf populations through aerial shootings and other methods not mentioned by the media. Governor Hickle in 1991 and Governor Palin in 2008 have both been besieged with requests from animal rights activists to discontinue aerial hunting of wolves. The biologists of the state of Alaska have devoted their lives to the preservation of wildlife. They know Alaska and Alaska's wildlife better than anyone else. After researching and trying other methods, they believe the best solution to their problem is aerial shootings. Their main concern is to protect the wildlife population as a whole, not just to wage a "war on wolves." While the animal rightists are sitting in their offices wondering which animals to save, the biologists at the Alaska Department of Fish and Game are in the field researching the range conditions and overall population conditions to manage the wildlife community as a whole.

The resolution of the Alaskan wolf management issue needs to be left to the experts. As inhumane and immoral as it might seem to many citizens, the aerial shooting of wolves is periodically the best solution for game management in Alaska.

Establishment of the ethos of conservationists in Alaska to make their plan acceptable

Author has identified a problem, evaluated several solutions, and arrived at this solution as the best possible one. This is a value argument because it claims that one of several considered solutions is the best.

Problem-solution and policy are also strong features in this argument. Value claim in last sentence

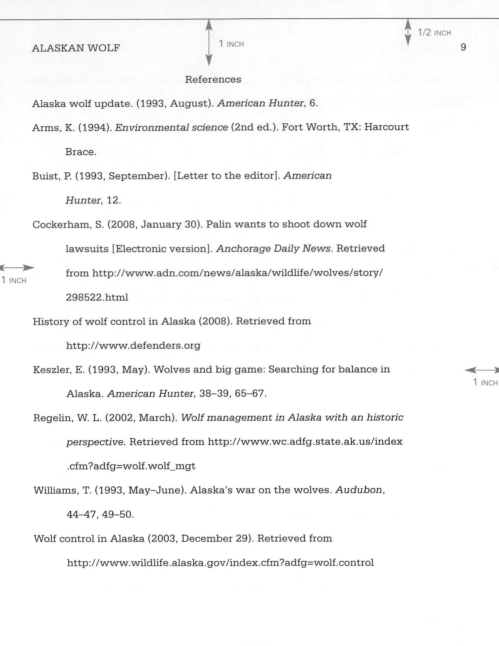

ALASKAN WOLF   9

References

Alaska wolf update. (1993, August). *American Hunter*, 6.

Arms, K. (1994). *Environmental science* (2nd ed.). Fort Worth, TX: Harcourt

Brace.

Buist, P. (1993, September). [Letter to the editor]. *American*

Hunter, 12.

Cockerham, S. (2008, January 30). Palin wants to shoot down wolf

lawsuits [Electronic version]. *Anchorage Daily News*. Retrieved

from http://www.adn.com/news/alaska/wildlife/wolves/story/

298522.html

History of wolf control in Alaska (2008). Retrieved from

http://www.defenders.org

Keszler, E. (1993, May). Wolves and big game: Searching for balance in

Alaska. *American Hunter*, 38–39, 65–67.

Regelin, W. L. (2002, March). *Wolf management in Alaska with an historic*

perspective. Retrieved from http://www.wc.adfg.state.ak.us/index

.cfm?adfg=wolf.wolf_mgt

Williams, T. (1993, May–June). Alaska's war on the wolves. *Audubon*,

44–47, 49–50.

Wolf control in Alaska (2003, December 29). Retrieved from

http://www.wildlife.alaska.gov/index.cfm?adfg=wolf.control

Wolf "control" in Alaska. (2004, March 14). [Editorial]. *The New York Times,*

    A12.

The wolf in Alaska (2008). Retrieved from http://www.wildlife.alaska.gov

In APA format, break long URLs before a period or after a slash. Never add a hyphen.

PRACTICE

Student Model, Alaskan Wolf Management, p. 837

1 Where did the author place his claim? What type of claim is it? Why do you think he placed it where he did?

a. What are the two conflicting positions on wolf management described in this paper? How much common ground would you say there is between the two positions?

b. What are some of the types of proofs and support that this student uses in his paper? Comment on the use of *logos, ethos,* and *pathos* in general, as well as on specific types of proofs, including the image of the wolf.

c. What warrants are held by the conservationists? What warrants are held by the animal rights advocates? What warrants does this author expect you to accept?

d. What major ideas does this author refute in this paper?

e. What organizational pattern do you detect in this paper?

f. Find an example of a summary of information from a document on an Internet site with no available author.

g. Find an example of a quotation that is longer than forty words.

h. Roughly what percent of this paper is made up of quotations from other people's writings and what percent is the author's own writing?

i. Read the "References" list and identify the different types of sources this author used.

Reading, What Defines a Sport?, p. 823

2 Andriesen explores some of the criteria that have been posited for an activity to be a sport. What position does he take on the issue of defining sport?

a. Under what circumstances might it be important to have accepted criteria for what constitutes a sport?

b. Develop your own definition of sport and apply it to one or more of the following cases: (1) synchronized swimming, (2) poker, (3) video game playing, (4) NASCAR racing.

Reading, Should Educators Use Commercial Services to Combat Plagiarism?, p. 801

3 The increasing use of sites such as Turnitin.com to check student papers for plagiarism has led to disagreement about how best to respond to possible cases of plagiarism. In the following passage, John Barrie, President of Turnitin.com, says that plagiarism is a "digital problem [that] demands a digital solution." Representing the point of view of many writing teachers, Rebecca Moore Howard claims that the best solution is to prevent plagiarism by teaching students how to access, use, and document sources. Read these two responses and decide which writer proposes the better overall solution.

4 Write a position paper that takes a stand on a controversial issue. Your Introduction should present your issue, provide background, and state the claim you intend to support. In constructing your claim, strive to develop audience-based reasons. The body of your argument should summarize and respond to opposing views as well as present reasons and evidence in support of your own position. You will need to choose whether to summarize and refute opposing views before or after you have made your own case. Try to end your essay with your strongest arguments. Try also to include appeals to *pathos* and to create a positive, credible *ethos*.

Baker College
Port Huron

What Is Rhetorical Argument Analysis?

19

To analyze an argument rhetorically means to examine closely how it is composed and what makes it an effective or ineffective piece of persuasion. A rhetorical analysis identifies the text under scrutiny, summarizes its main ideas, presents some key points about the text's rhetorical strategies for persuading its audience, and elaborates on these points.

Becoming skilled at analyzing arguments rhetorically will have multiple payoffs for you. Rhetorical analysis will help you develop your ability to read complex texts critically; speak back to texts from your own insights; apply the strategies of effective argumentation to your own arguments; and prepare you as a citizen to distinguish sound, ethical arguments from manipulative, unreasonable ones. By themselves, rhetorical analyses are common assignments in courses in critical thinking and argument. Rhetorical analysis also plays a major role in constructing arguments. Writers often work into their own arguments summaries and rhetorical analyses of other people's arguments—particularly in sections dealing with opposing views. This chapter focuses on the rhetorical analysis of written arguments.

Thinking Rhetorically about a Text

The suggested writing assignment for this chapter is to write your own rhetorical analysis of an argument selected by your instructor. This section will help you get started by showing you what it means to think rhetorically about a text.

Before we turn directly to rhetorical analysis, we should reconsider the key word *rhetoric*. In popular usage, *rhetoric* often means empty or deceptive language, as in, "Well, that's just rhetoric." Another related meaning of *rhetoric* is decorative or artificial language. The Greek Stoic philosopher Epictetus likened rhetoric to hairdressers fixing hair*—a view that sees

*Chaim Perelman, "The New Rhetoric: A Theory of Practical Reasoning." In *Professing the New Rhetorics: A Sourcebook,* eds. Theresa Enos and Stuart C. Brown (Englewood Cliffs, NJ: Prentice Hall, 1994), 149.

rhetoric as superficial decoration. Most contemporary rhetoricians, however, adopt the larger view of rhetoric articulated by Greek philosopher Aristotle: the art of determining what will be persuasive in every situation. Contemporary rhetorician Donald C. Bryant has described rhetoric in action as "the function of adjusting ideas to people and of people to ideas."* Focusing on this foundational meaning of rhetoric, this chapter will show you how to analyze a writer's motivation, purpose, and rhetorical choices for persuading a targeted audience.

Questions for Rhetorical Analysis

Conducting a rhetorical analysis asks you to bring to bear on an argument your knowledge of argument and your repertoire of reading strategies. The chart of questions for analysis can help you examine an argument in depth. Although a rhetorical analysis will not include answers to all of these questions, using some of these questions in your thinking stages can give you a thorough understanding of the argument while helping you generate insights for your own rhetorical analysis essay.

Questions for Rhetorical Analysis

What to Focus On	Questions to Ask	Applying These Questions
The *kairotic* moment and writer's motivating occasion	• What motivated the writer to produce this piece? • What social, cultural, political, legal, or economic conversations does this argument join?	• Is the writer responding to a bill pending in Congress, a speech by a political leader, or a local event that provoked controversy? • Is the writer addressing cultural trends such as the impact of science or technology on values?
Rhetorical context: Writer's purpose and audience	• What is the writer's purpose? • Who is the intended audience? • What assumptions, values, and beliefs would readers have to hold to find this argument persuasive? • How well does the text suit its particular audience and purpose?	• Is the writer trying to change readers' views by offering a new interpretation of a phenomenon, calling readers to action, or trying to muster votes or inspire further investigations? • Does the audience share a political or religious orientation with the writer?

*Donald C. Bryant, "Rhetoric: Its Functions and Its Scope." In *Professing the New Rhetorics: A Sourcebook,* eds. Theresa Enos and Stuart C. Brown (Englewood Cliffs, NJ: Prentice Hall, 1994), 282.

What to Focus On	Questions to Ask	Applying These Questions
Rhetorical context: Writer's identity and angle of vision	• Who is the writer and what is his or her profession, background, and expertise? • How does the writer's personal history, education, gender, ethnicity, age, class, sexual orientation, and political leaning influence the angle of vision? • What is emphasized and what is omitted in this text? • How much does the writer's angle of vision dominate the text?	• Is the writer a scholar, researcher, scientist, policy maker, politician, professional journalist, or citizen blogger? • Is the writer affiliated with conservative or liberal, religious or lay publications? • Is the writer advocating a stance or adopting a more inquiry-based mode? • What points of view and pieces of evidence are "not seen" by this writer?
Rhetorical context: Genre	• What is the argument's original genre? • What is the original medium of publication? How does the genre and its place of publication influence its content, structure, and style?	• How popular or scholarly, informal or formal is this genre? • Does the genre allow for in-depth or only sketchy coverage of an issue?
***Logos* of the argument**	• What is the argument's claim, either explicitly stated or implied? • What are the main reasons in support of the claim? Are the reasons audience-based? • How effective is the writer's use of evidence? How is the argument supported and developed? • How well has the argument recognized and responded to alternative views?	• Is the core of the argument clear and soundly developed? Or do readers have to unearth or reconstruct the argument? • Is the argument one-sided, multisided, or dialogic? • Does the argument depend on assumptions the audience may not share? • What evidence does the writer employ?
***Ethos* of the argument**	• What *ethos* does the writer project? • How does the writer try to seem credible and trustworthy to the intended audience? • How knowledgeable does the writer seem in recognizing opposing or alternative views and how fairly does the writer respond to them?	• If you are impressed or won over by this writer, what has earned your respect? • If you are filled with doubts or skepticism, what has caused you to question this writer? • How important is the character of the writer in this argument?

Questions for Rhetorical Analysis

What to Focus On	Questions to Ask	Applying These Questions
Pathos of the argument	• How effective is the writer in using audience-based reasons? • How does the writer use concrete language, word choice, narrative, examples, and analogies to tap readers' emotions, values, and imaginations?	• What examples, connotative language, and uses of narrative or analogy stand out for you in this argument? • Does this argument rely heavily on appeals to *pathos*? Or is it more brain and logical?
Writer's style	• How do the writer's language choices and sentence length and complexity contribute to the impact of the argument? • How well does the writer's tone (attitude toward the subject) suit the argument?	• How readable is this argument? • Is the argument formal, scholarly, journalistic, informal, or casual? • Is the tone serious, mocking, humorous, exhortational, confessional, urgent, or something else?
Design and visual elements	• How do design elements—layout, font sizes and styles, and use of color—influence the effect of the argument? • How do graphics and images contribute to the persuasiveness of the argument?	• Do design features contribute to the logical or the emotional/imaginative appeals of the argument? • How would this argument benefit from visuals and graphics or some different document design?
Overall persuasiveness of the argument	• What features of this argument contribute most to making it persuasive or not persuasive for its target audience and for you yourself? • How would this argument be received by different audiences? • What features contribute to the rhetorical complexity of this argument? • What is particularly memorable, disturbing, or problematic about this argument? • What does this argument contribute to its *kairotic* moment and the argumentative controversy of which it is a part?	• For example, are appeals to *pathos* legitimate and suitable? Does the quality and quantity of the evidence help build a strong case or fall short? • What specifically would count as a strength for the target audience? • If you differ from the target audience, how do you differ and where does the argument derail for you? • What gaps, contradictions, or unanswered questions are you left with? • How does this argument indicate that it is engaged in a public conversation? How does it "talk" to other arguments you have read on this issue?

An Illustration of Rhetorical Analysis

To illustrate rhetorical analysis in this section and in the student example at the end of the chapter, we will use two articles on reproductive technology, a subject that continues to generate arguments in the public sphere. By *reproductive technology* we mean scientific advances in the treatment of infertility such as egg and sperm donation, artificial insemination, in vitro fertilization, and surrogate motherhood. Our first article, from a decade ago, springs from the early and increasing popularity of these technological options. Our second article—to be used in our later student example—responds to the recent globalization of this technology.

At this point, please read the following article, "Egg Heads" by Kathryn Jean Lopez, and then proceed to the discussion questions that follow on page 883 in the Practice section. Lopez's article was originally published in the September 1, 1998, issue of the biweekly conservative news commentary magazine *National Review*.

Egg Heads

Kathryn Jean Lopez

Filling the waiting room to capacity and spilling over into a nearby conference room, a group of young women listen closely and follow the instructions: Complete the forms and return them, with the clipboard, to the receptionist. It's all just as in any medical office. Then they move downstairs, where the doctor briefs them. "Everything will be pretty much normal," she explains. "Women complain of skin irritation in the local area of injection and bloating. You also might be a little emotional. But, basically, it's really bad PMS."

This is not just another medical office. On a steamy night in July, these girls in their twenties are attending an orientation session for potential egg donors at a New Jersey fertility clinic specializing in in-vitro fertilization. Within the walls of IVF New Jersey and at least two hundred other clinics throughout the United States, young women answer the call to give "the gift of life" to infertile couples. Egg donation is a quietly expanding industry, changing the way we look at the family, young women's bodies, and human life itself.

It is not a pleasant way to make money. Unlike sperm donation, which is over in less than an hour, egg donation takes the donor some 56 hours and includes a battery of tests, ultrasound, self-administered injections, and retrieval. Once a donor is accepted into a program, she is given hormones to stimulate the ovaries, changing the number of eggs matured from the usual one per month up to as many as fifty. A doctor then surgically removes the eggs from the donor's ovary and fertilizes them with the designated sperm.

Although most programs require potential donors to undergo a series of medical tests and counseling, there is little indication that most of the young women know what they are getting themselves into. They risk bleeding, infection, and scarring. When too many eggs are matured in one cycle, it can damage the ovaries and leave the donor with weeks of abdominal pain. (At worst, complications may leave her dead.) Longer term, the possibility of early menopause raises the prospect of future regret. There is also some evidence of a connection between the fertility drugs used in the process and ovarian cancer.

5   But it's good money—and getting better. New York's Brooklyn IVF raised its "donor compensation" from $2,500 to $5,000 per cycle earlier this year in order to keep pace with St. Barnabas Medical Center in nearby Livingston, New Jersey. It's a bidding war. "It's obvious why we had to do it," says Susan Lobel, Brooklyn IVF's assistant director. Most New York–area IVF programs have followed suit.

Some infertile couples and independent brokers are offering even more for "reproductive material." The International Fertility Center in Indianapolis, Indiana, for instance, places ads in the *Daily Princetonian* offering Princeton girls as much as $35,000 per cycle. The National Fertility Registry, which, like many egg brokerages, features an online catalogue for couples to browse in, advertises $35,000 to $50,000 for Ivy League eggs. While donors are normally paid a flat fee per cycle, there have been reports of higher payments to donors who produce more eggs.

College girls are the perfect donors. Younger eggs are likelier to be healthy, and the girls themselves frequently need money—college girls have long been susceptible to classified ads offering to pay them for acting as guinea pigs in medical research. One 1998 graduate of the University of Colorado set up her own website to market her eggs. She had watched a television show on egg donation and figured it "seemed like a good thing to do"—especially since she had spent her money during the past year to help secure a country-music record deal. "Egg donation would help me with my school and music expenses while helping an infertile couple with a family." Classified ads scattered throughout cyberspace feature similar offers.

The market for "reproductive material" has been developing for a long time. It was twenty years ago this summer that the first test-tube baby, Louise Brown, was born. By 1995, when the latest tally was taken by the Centers for Disease Control, 15 percent of mothers in this country had made use of some form of assisted-reproduction technology in conceiving their children. (More recently, women past menopause have begun to make use of this technology.) In 1991 the American Society for Reproductive Medicine was aware of 63 IVF programs offering egg donation. That number had jumped to 189 by 1995 (the latest year for which numbers are available).

Defenders argue that it's only right that women are "compensated" for the inconvenience of egg donation. Brooklyn IVF's Dr. Lobel argues, "If it is unethical to accept payment for loving your neighbor, then we'll have to stop paying babysitters." As long as donors know the risks, says Glenn McGee of the University of Pennsylvania's Center for Bioethics, this transaction is only "a slightly macabre version of adoption."

10   Not everyone is enthusiastic about the "progress." Egg donation "represents another rather large step into turning procreation into manufacturing," says the University of Chicago's Leon Kass. "It's the dehumanization of procreation." And as in manufacturing, there is quality control. "People don't want to say the word any more, but there is a strong eugenics issue inherent in the notion that you can have the best eggs your money can buy," observes sociology professor Barbara Katz Rothman of the City University of New York.

The demand side of the market comes mostly from career-minded baby-boomers, the frontierswomen of feminism, who thought they could "have it all." Indeed they *can* have it all—with a little help from some younger eggs. (Ironically, feminists are also among its strongest critics; *The Nation*'s Katha Pollitt has pointed out that in egg donation and surrogacy, once you remove the "delusion that they are making babies for other women," all you have left is "reproductive prostitution.")

Unfortunately, the future looks bright for the egg market. Earlier this year, a woman in Atlanta gave birth to twins after she was implanted with frozen donor eggs. The same technology has also been successful in Italy. This is just what the egg market needed, since it avoids the necessity of coordinating donors' cycles with recipients' cycles. Soon, not only will infertile couples be able to choose from a wider variety of donor offerings, but in some cases donors won't even be needed. Young women will be able to freeze their own eggs and have them thawed and fertilized once they are ready for the intrusion of children in their lives.

There are human ovaries sitting in a freezer in Fairfax, Virginia. The Genetics and IVF Institute offers to cut out and remove young women's ovaries and cryopreserve the egg-containing tissue for future implantation. Although the technology was originally designed to give the hope of fertility to young women undergoing treatment for cancer, it is now starting to attract the healthy. "Women can wait to have children until they are well established in their careers and getting a little bored, sometime in their forties or fifties," explains Professor

Rothman. "Basically, motherhood is being reduced to a good leisure-time activity."

Early this summer, headlines were made in Britain, where the payment of egg donors is forbidden, when an infertile couple traveled to a California clinic where the woman could be inseminated with an experimental hybrid egg. The egg was a combination of the recipient's and a donor's eggs. The clinic in question gets its eggs from a Beverly Hills brokerage, the Center for Surrogate Parenting and Egg Donation, run by Karen Synesiou and Bill Handel, a radio shock-jock in Los Angeles. Miss Synesiou recently told the London *Sunday Times* that she is "interested in redefining the family. That's why I came to work here."

15   The redefinition is already well under way. Consider the case of Jaycee Buzzanca. After John and Luanne Buzzanca had tried for years to have a child, an embryo was created for them, using sperm and an egg from anonymous donors, and implanted in a surrogate mother. In March 1995, one month before the baby was born, John filed for divorce. Luanne wanted child support from John, but he refused—after all, he's not the father. Luanne argued that John is Jaycee's father legally. At this point the surrogate mother, who had agreed to carry a baby for a stable two-parent household, decided to sue for custody.

Jaycee was dubbed "Nobody's Child" by the media when a California judge ruled that John was not the legal father nor Luanne the legal mother (neither one was genetically related to Jaycee, and Luanne had not even borne her). Enter Erin Davidson, the egg donor, who claims the egg was used without her permission. Not to be left out, the sperm donor jumped into the ring, saying that his sperm was used without his permission, a claim he later dropped. In March of this year, an appeals court gave Luanne custody and decided that John is the legal father, making him responsible for child support. By contracting for a medical procedure resulting in the birth of a child, the court ruled, a couple incurs "the legal status of parenthood." (John lost an appeal in May.) For Jaycee's first three years on earth, these people have been wrangling over who her parents are.

In another case, William Kane left his girlfriend, Deborah Hect, 15 vials of sperm before he killed himself in a Las Vegas hotel in 1991. His two adult children (represented by their mother, his ex-wife) contested Miss Hect's claim of ownership. A settlement agreement on Kane's will was eventually reached, giving his children 80 percent of his estate and Miss Hect 20 percent. Hence she was allowed three vials of his sperm. When she did not succeed in conceiving on the first two tries, she filed a petition for the other 12 vials. She won, and the judge who ruled in her favor wrote, "Neither this court nor the decedent's adult children possess reason or right to prevent Hect from implementing decedent's pre-eminent interest in realizing his 'fundamental right' to procreate with the woman of his choice." One day, donors may not even have to have lived. Researchers are experimenting with using aborted female fetuses as a source of donor eggs.

And the market continues to zip along. For overseas couples looking for donor eggs, Bill Handel has the scenario worked out. The couple would mail him frozen sperm of their choice (presumably from the recipient husband); his clinic would use it to fertilize donor eggs, chosen from its catalogue of offerings, and reply back within a month with a frozen embryo ready for implantation. (Although the sperm does not yet arrive by mail, Handel has sent out embryos to at least one hundred international customers.) As for the young women at the New Jersey clinic, they are visibly upset by one aspect of the egg-donation process: they can't have sexual intercourse for several weeks after the retrieval. For making babies, of course, it's already obsolete.

A RHETORICAL ANALYSIS OF "EGG HEADS"

Now that you have identified some of the rhetorical features of "Egg Heads," we offer our own notes for a rhetorical analysis of this argument.

● **RHETORICAL CONTEXT**   As we began our analysis, we reconstructed the rhetorical context in which "Egg Heads" was published. In the late 1990s, a furious debate about egg donation rippled through college and public newspapers, popular journalism, Web sites, and scholarly commentary. This debate had been kicked off by several couples placing ads in the newspapers of the country's most prestigious colleges offering up to $50,000 for the eggs of brilliant, attractive, athletic college women. Coinciding with these consumer demands, advances in reproductive technology provided an increasing number of complex techniques to surmount the problem of infertility, including fertilizing eggs in petri dishes and implanting them into women through surgical procedures. These procedures could use either a couple's own eggs and sperm or donated eggs and sperm. All these social and medical factors created the *kairotic* moment for Lopez's article and motivated her to protest the increasing use of these procedures.

● **GENRE AND WRITER**   When we considered the genre and writer of this article and its site of publication, we noted that this article appeared in the *National Review,* which describes itself as "America's most widely read and influential magazine and Web site for Republican/conservative news, commentary, and opinion." It reaches "an affluent, educated, and highly responsive audience of corporate, financial elite, educators, journalists, community and association leaders, as well as engaged activists all across America" (http://www.nationalreview.com). According to our Internet search, Kathryn Jean Lopez is known nationally for her conservative journalistic writing on social and political issues. Currently the editor of *National Review Online,* she has also published in the *Wall Street Journal,* the *New York Post,* and the *Washington Times.* This information told us that in her article "Egg Heads," Lopez is definitely on home territory, aiming her article at a conservative audience.

● **LOGOS**   Turning to the *logos* of Lopez's argument, we decided that the logical structure of Lopez's argument is clear throughout the article. Her claim is that egg donation and its associated reproductive advances have harmful, long-reaching consequences for society. Basically, she argues that egg donation and reproductive technology represent bad scientific developments for society because they are potentially harmful to the long-range health of egg donors and because they lead to an unnatural dehumanizing of human sexuality. She states a version of this last point at the end of the second paragraph: "Egg donation is a quickly expanding industry, changing the way we look at the family, young women's bodies, and human life itself."

   The body of her article elaborates on each of these reasons. In developing her reason that egg donation endangers egg donors, Lopez lists the risks but doesn't supply supporting evidence about the frequency of these problems: damage to the ovaries, persistent pain, early menopause, possible ovarian cancer, and even death. She supports her claim about "the expanding industry" by showing how the procedures have become commercialized. To show the popularity of these procedures as well as their commercial value, she quotes a variety of experts such as directors of in vitro clinics, fertility centers, bioethicists, and the American Society for Reproductive Medicine. She also cleverly bolsters her own case by showing that even liberal cultural critics agree with her views about the big ethical questions raised by the reproductive-technology business. In addition to quoting experts, Lopez has sprinkled impressive numbers and vivid examples throughout the body of her argument, which give her argument momentum as it progresses from the potential harm to young egg donors to a number of case studies that depict increasingly disturbing ethical problems.

● **PATHOS**   Much of the impact of this argument, we noted, comes from Lopez's appeals to *pathos.* By describing in detail the waiting rooms for egg donors at fertility clinics, Lopez relies heavily on pathetic appeals to move her audience to see the physical and social dangers of egg donation. She conveys the growing commercialism of reproductive technology by giving readers an inside look at the egg donation process as these young college women embark on the multi-step process of donating their eggs. These young women, she suggests in her title, "Egg Heads," are largely unaware of the potential physical dangers to themselves and of the ethical implications and consequences of their acts. She asserts that they are driven largely by the desire for money. Lopez also appeals to *pathos* in her choice of emotionally loaded and often cynical language that creates an angle of vision opposing reproductive technology: "turning procreation into manufacturing"; "reproductive prostitution"; "the intrusion of children in their lives"; "motherhood . . . reduced to a leisure-time activity"; "aborted fe-male fetuses as a source of donor eggs"; and intercourse as an "obsolete" way to make babies.

● **AUDIENCE**   Despite Lopez's success at spotlighting serious medical and ethical questions, her lack of attention to alternative views and the alarmism of her language caused us to wonder: Who might find this argument persuasive and who would challenge it? What is noticeably missing from her argument—and apparently from her worldview—is the perspective of infertile couples hop-ing for a baby. Pursuing our question, we decided that a provocative feature of this argument—one worthy of deeper analysis—is the disparity between how well this argument is suited to its target audience and yet how unpersuasive it is for readers who do not share the assumptions, values, and beliefs of this primary audience.

To Lopez's credit, she has attuned her reasons to the values and concerns of her conservative readers of the *National Review* who believe in traditional fam-ilies, gender differences, and gender roles. Opposed to feminism as they under-stand it, this audience sanctions careers for women only if women put their families first. Lopez's choice of evidence and her orchestrating of it are intended to play to her audience's fears that science has uncontrollably fallen into the hands of those who have little regard for the sanctity of the family or traditional motherhood. For example, in playing strongly to the values of her conservative readers, Lopez belabors the physical, social, and ethical dangers of egg donation, mentioning worst-case scenarios; however, these appeals to *pathos* will most likely strike other readers who do some investigation into reproductive technology as overblown. She emphasizes the commercialism of the process as her argument moves from college girls as egg donors to a num-ber of sensationalist case studies that depict intensifying ethical ambiguity. In other words, both the *logos* and *pathos* of her argument skillfully focus on details that tap her target audience's values and beliefs and feed that audience's fears and revulsion.

● **USE OF EVIDENCE**   For a broader or skeptical audience, the alarmism of Lopez's appeals to *pathos*, her use of atypical evidence, and her distortion of the facts weaken the *logos* and *ethos* of her argument. First, Lopez's use of evidence fails to measure up to the STAR criteria (that evidence should be sufficient, typ-ical, accurate, and relevant). She characterizes all egg donors as young women seeking money. But she provides little evidence that egg donors are only out to make a buck. She also paints these young women as shortsighted, uninformed, and foolish. Lopez weakens her ethos by not considering the young women who have researched the process and who may be motivated, at least in part, by com-passion for couples who can't conceive on their own. Lopez also misrepresents the people who are using egg donation, placing them all into two groups: (1) wealthy couples eugenically seeking designer babies with preordered special traits and (2) feminist career women. She directs much of her criticism toward this latter group: "The demand side of the market comes mostly from career-minded baby-boomers, the frontierswomen of feminism, who thought they could 'have it all'." However, readers who do a little research on their own, as we did, will learn that infertility affects one in seven couples; that it is often a male and female problem, sometimes caused by an incompatibility between the husband's and wife's reproductive material; and that most couples who take the big step of investing in these expensive efforts to have a baby have been trying to get pregnant for a number of years. Rather than being casual about having children, they are often deeply desirous of children and depressed about their inability to conceive. In addition, far from being the sure thing and quick fix that Lopez suggests, reproductive technology has a success rate of only 50 percent overall and involves a huge investment of time, money, and physical discomfort for women receiving donor eggs.

Another way that Lopez violates the STAR criteria is her choice of extreme cases. For readers outside her target audience, her argument appears riddled with straw man and slippery-slope fallacies. Her examples become more bizarre as her tone becomes more hysterical. Here are some specific instance of extreme, atypical cases:

- her focus on career women casually and selfishly using the service of young egg donors
- the notorious case of Jaycee Buzzanca, dubbed "Nobody's Child" because her adoptive parents who commissioned her creation divorced before she was born
- the legal contest between a dead man's teen girlfriend and his ex-wife and adult children over his vials of sperm
- the idea of taking eggs from aborted female fetuses

By keeping invisible the vast majority of ordinary couples who come to fertility clinics out of last-hope desperation, Lopez uses extreme cases to create a "brave new world" intended to evoke a vehement rejection of these reproductive advances. These skeptical readers would offer the alternative view of the sad, ordinary couples of all ages sitting week after week in fertility clinics, hoping to conceive a child through the "miracle" of these reproductive advances and grateful to the young women who have contributed their eggs.

● **Concluding Points**   In short, we concluded that Lopez's angle of vision, although effectively in sync with her conservative readers of the *National Review*, exaggerates and distorts her case against these reproductive advances.

Lopez's traditional values and slanting of the evidence undermine her *ethos*, limit the value of this argument for a wider audience, and compel that audience to seek out alternative views for a more complete view of egg donation.

Conclusion

To analyze a text rhetorically means to determine how it works: what effect it has on readers and how it achieves or fails to achieve its persuasiveness. Assignments involving rhetorical analysis are present in courses across the curriculum, and analyzing texts rhetorically is a major step in constructing your own arguments. In this chapter, we showed you how to apply your understanding of argument concepts, such as the influence of genre and appeals to *logos, ethos,* and *pathos,* to examining the strength of verbal texts. We conclude with a student's rhetorical analysis written for the assignment in this chapter.

Writing Assignment

A RHETORICAL ANALYSIS

Write a thesis-driven rhetorical analysis essay in which you examine the rhetorical effectiveness of an argument specified by your instructor. Unless otherwise stated direct your analysis to an audience of your classmates. In your introduction, establish the argumentative conversation to which this argument is contributing. Briefly summarize the argument and present your thesis highlighting two or more rhetorical features of the argument that you find central to the effectiveness or ineffectiveness of this argument. To develop and support your own points, you will need to include textual evidence, in the form of examples or short quotations from the argument. Use attributive tags to distinguish your ideas from those of the writer of the article. Think of your rhetorical analysis as a way to shine a spotlight on important aspects of this argument and make the argument understandable and interesting for your readers.

GENERATING IDEAS FOR YOUR RHETORICAL ANALYSIS

To develop ideas for your essay, you might follow these suggested steps:

Step 1	How to Do It
Familiarize yourself with the article you are analyzing.	Read your article several times. Divide it into sections to understand its structure.
Place the article in its rhetorical context.	Use the "Questions for Rhetorical Analysis."
Summarize the article.	You may want to produce a longer summary of 150–200 words as well as a short one-sentence summary.
Reread the article identifying "hot spots."	Note hot spots in the article—points that impress you, disturb you, confuse you, or puzzle you.
Use the "Questions for Rhetorical Analysis."	Choose several of these questions and freewrite responses to them.
From your notes and freewriting, identify the focus for your analysis.	Choose several features of the article that you find particularly important and that you want to discuss in depth in your essay. Identify points that will bring something new to your readers and that will help them see this article with new understanding. You may want to list your ideas and then look for ways to group them together around main points.
Write a thesis statement for your essay.	Articulate your important points in one or two sentences, setting up these points clearly for your audience.

In finding a meaningful focus for your rhetorical analysis essay, you will need to create a focusing thesis statement that avoids wishy-washy formulas such as, "This argument has some strengths and some weaknesses." To avoid a vapid thesis statement, focus on the complexity of the argument, the writer's strategies for persuading the target audience, and the features that might impede its persuasiveness for skeptics. These thesis statements articulate how their writers see the inner workings of these arguments as well as the arguments' contribution to their public conversations.

Lopez's angle of vision, although effectively in sync with her conservative readers of the National Review, exaggerates and distorts her case against these reproductive advances, weakening her ethos and the value of her argument for a wider audience. [This is the thesis we would use if we were writing a stand-alone essay on Lopez.]

In his editorial, "Why Blame Mexico?" published in *The American Conservative*, Fred Reed's irony and hard-hitting evidence undercut his desire to contrast the United States' hypocritical and flawed immigration policies with Mexico's successful ones.

In his editorial, "Amnesty?" in the Jesuit news commentary *America*, John F. Kavanaugh makes a powerful argument for his Catholic and religious readers; however, his proposal based on ethical reasoning may fail to reach other readers.

To make your rhetorical analysis of your article persuasive, you will need to develop each of the points stated or implied in your thesis statement using textual evidence, including short quotations. Your essay should show how you have listened carefully to the argument you are analyzing, summarized it fairly, and probed it deeply.

ORGANIZING YOUR RHETORICAL ANALYSIS

A stand-alone rhetorical analysis can be organized as shown below.

Organization Plan for a Rhetorical Analysis of an Argument

Introduction

↓

- Introduce the issue and set the context for the argument you are analyzing.
- Explain your interest in the argument, if appropriate.
- State your thesis.

Summary of Argument

↓

- Provide a brief summary of the argument to help readers understand your analysis.

Rhetorical Analysis

↓

- Develop your thesis by presenting and evaluating the rhetorical strategies used by the writer to appeal to his or her target audience in light of the author's rhetorical context and purpose.

Conclusion

- Wrap up your analysis and comment on the significance of the argument, if appropriate.

READINGS

Womb for Rent—For a Price

Ellen Goodman

BOSTON—By now we all have a story about a job outsourced beyond our reach in the global economy. My own favorite is about the California publisher who hired two reporters in India to cover the Pasadena city government. Really.

There are times as well when the offshoring of jobs takes on a quite literal meaning. When the labor we are talking about is, well, labor.

In the last few months we've had a full nursery of international stories about surrogate mothers. Hundreds of couples are crossing borders in search of lower-cost ways to fill the family business. In turn, there's a new coterie of international workers who are gestating for a living.

Many of the stories about the globalization of baby production begin in India, where the government seems to regard this as, literally, a growth industry. In the little town of Anand, dubbed "The Cradle of the World," 45 women were recently on the books of a local clinic. For the production and delivery of a child, they will earn $5,000 to $7,000, a decade's worth of women's wages in rural India.

5   But even in America, some women, including Army wives, are supplementing their income by contracting out their wombs. They have become surrogate mothers for wealthy couples from European countries that ban the practice.

This globalization of baby-making comes at the peculiar intersection of a high reproductive technology and a low-tech work force. The biotech business was created in the same petri dish as Baby Louise, the first IVF baby. But since then, we've seen conception outsourced to egg donors and sperm donors. We've had motherhood divided into its parts from genetic mother to gestational mother to birth mother and now contract mother.

We've also seen the growth of an international economy. Frozen sperm is flown from one continent to another. And patients have become medical tourists, searching for cheaper health care whether it's a new hip in Thailand or an IVF treatment in South Africa that comes with a photo safari thrown in for the same price. Why not then rent a foreign womb?

I don't make light of infertility. The primal desire to have a child underlies this multinational Creation, Inc. On one side, couples who choose surrogacy want a baby with at least half their own genes. On the other side, surrogate mothers, who are rarely implanted with their own eggs, can believe that the child they bear and deliver is not really theirs.

As one woman put it, "We give them a baby and they give us much-needed money. It's good for them and for us." A surrogate in Anand used the money to buy a heart operation for her son. Another raised a dowry for her daughter. And before we talk about the "exploitation" of the pregnant woman, consider her alternative in Anand: a job crushing glass in a factory for $25 a month.

10   Nevertheless, there is—and there should be—something uncomfortable about a free market approach to baby-making. It's easier to accept surrogacy when it's a gift from one woman to another. But we rarely see a rich woman become a surrogate for a poor family. Indeed, in Third World countries, some women sign these contracts with a fingerprint because they are illiterate.

For that matter, we have not yet had stories about the contract workers for whom pregnancy was a dangerous occupation, but we will. What obligation does a family that simply contracted for a child have to its birth mother? What control do—should—contractors have over their "employees" lives while incubating "their" children? What will we tell the offspring of this international trade?

"National boundaries are coming down," says bioethicist Lori Andrews, "but we can't stop human emotions. We are expanding families and don't even have terms to deal with it."

It's the commercialism that is troubling. Some things we cannot sell no matter how good "the deal." We cannot, for example, sell ourselves into slavery. We cannot sell our children. But the surrogacy business comes perilously close to both of these deals. And international surrogacy tips the scales.

So, these borders we are crossing are not just geographic ones. They are ethical ones. Today the global economy sends everyone in search of the cheaper deal as if that were the single common good. But in the biological search, humanity is sacrificed to the economy and the person becomes the product. And, step by step, we come to a stunning place in our ancient creation story. It's called the marketplace.

Statement on the Articles of Impeachment

Barbara Jordan

Barbara Jordan (1936–1996) grew up in Houston and received a law degree from Boston University in 1959. Working on John F. Kennedy's 1960 presidential campaign stirred an interest in politics, and Jordon became the first African American woman elected to the Texas State Senate in 1966. In 1972 she was elected to the United

...continued Statement of the Articles of Impeachment, **Barbara Jordan**

States House of Representatives and thus became the first African American woman from the South ever to serve in Congress. Jordan was appointed to the House Judiciary Committee. Soon she was in the national spotlight when that committee considered articles of impeachment against President Richard Nixon, who had illegally covered up a burglary of Democratic Party headquarters during the 1972 election. When Nixon's criminal acts reached to the Judiciary Committee, Jordan's opening speech on July 24, 1974, set the tone for the debate and established her reputation as a moral beacon for the nation. Nixon resigned as president on August 9, 1974, when it was evident that he would be impeached.

Thank you, Mr. Chairman.

Mr. Chairman, I join my colleague Mr. Rangel in thanking you for giving the junior members of this committee the glorious opportunity of sharing the pain of this inquiry. Mr. Chairman, you are a strong man and it has not been easy, but we have tried as best we can to give you as much assistance as possible.

2   Earlier today, we heard the beginning of the Preamble to the Constitution of the United States: "We, the people." It's a very eloquent beginning. But when that document was completed on the seventeenth of September in 1787, I was not included in that "We, the people." I felt somehow for many years that George Washington and Alexander Hamilton just left me out by mistake. But through the process of amendment, interpretation, and court decision, I have finally been included in "We, the people."

3   Today I am an inquisitor. Any hyperbole would not be fictional and would not overstate the solemnness that I feel right now. My faith in the Constitution is whole; it is complete; it is total. And I am not going to sit here and be an idle spectator to the diminution, the subversion, the destruction, of the Constitution.

4   "Who can so properly be the inquisitors for the nation as the representatives of the nation themselves?" "The subjects of its jurisdiction are those offenses which proceed from the misconduct of public men." And that's what we're talking about. In other words, [the jurisdiction comes] from the abuse or violation of some public trust.

5   It is wrong, I suggest, it is a misreading of the Constitution for any member here to assert that for a member to vote for an article of impeachment means that that member must be convinced that the President should be removed from office. The Constitution doesn't say that. The powers relating to impeachment are an essential check in the hands of the body of the legislature against and upon the encroachments of the executive. [By creating] the division between the two branches of the legislature, the House and the Senate, assigning to the one the right to accuse and to the other the right to judge, the framers of this Constitution were very astute. They did not make the accusers and the judgers the same person.

6   We know the nature of impeachment. We've been talking about it awhile now. It is chiefly designed for the President and his high ministers to somehow be called into account. It is designed to "bridle" the executive if he engages in excesses. "It is designed as a method of national inquest into the conduct of public men." The framers confided in the Congress the power, if need be, to remove the President in order to strike a delicate balance between a President swollen with power and grown tyrannical, and preservation of the independence of the executive.

7   The nature of impeachment: [it is] a narrowly channeled exception to the separation-of-powers maxim. The Federal Convention of 1787 said that. It limited impeachment to high crimes and misdemeanors and discounted and opposed the term *maladministration*. "It is to be used only for great misdemeanors," so it was said in the North Carolina ratification convention. And in the Virginia ratification convention: "We do not trust our liberty to a particular branch. We need one branch to check the other."

8   "No one need be afraid"—the North Carolina ratification convention—"No one need be afraid that officers who commit oppression will pass with immunity." "Prosecutions of impeachments will seldom fail to agitate the passions of the whole community," said Hamilton in the Federalist Papers, number 65. "We divide into parties more or less friendly or inimical to the accused." I do not mean political parties in that sense.

9   The drawing of political lines goes to the motivation behind impeachment; but impeachment must proceed within the confines of the constitutional term "high crime[s] and misdemeanors." Of the impeachment process, it was Woodrow Wilson who said that "Nothing short of the grossest offenses against the plain law of the land will suffice to give them speed and effectiveness. Indignation so great as to overgrow party interest may secure a conviction; but nothing else can."

10 Common sense would be revolted if we engaged upon this process for petty reasons. Congress has a lot to do: Appropriations, Tax Reform, Health Insurance, Campaign Finance Reform, Housing, Environmental

...continued Statement of the Articles of Impeachment, **Barbara Jordan**

Protection, Energy Sufficiency, Mass Transportation. Pettiness cannot be allowed to stand in the face of such overwhelming problems. So today we are not being petty. We are trying to be big, because the task we have before us is a big one.

11   This morning, in a discussion of the evidence, we were told that the evidence which purports to support the allegations of misuse of the CIA by the President is thin. We're told that that evidence is insufficient. What that recital of the evidence this morning did not include is what the President did know on June the 23rd, 1972.

12   The President did know that it was Republican money, that it was money from the Committee for the Re-Election of the President, which was found in the possession of one of the burglars arrested on June the 17th. What the President did know on the 23rd of June was the prior activities of E. Howard Hunt, which included his participation in the break-in of Daniel Ellsberg's psychiatrist, which included Howard Hunt's participation in the Dita Beard ITT affair, which included Howard Hunt's fabrication of cables designed to discredit the Kennedy Administration.

13   We were further cautioned today that perhaps these proceedings ought to be delayed because certainly there would be new evidence forthcoming from the President of the United States. There has not even been an obfuscated indication that this committee would receive any additional materials from the President. The committee subpoena is outstanding, and if the President wants to supply that material, the committee sits here. The fact is that only yesterday, the American people waited with great anxiety for eight hours, not knowing whether their President would obey an order of the Supreme Court of the United States.

14   At this point, I would like to juxtapose a few of the impeachment criteria with some of the actions the President has engaged in. Impeachment criteria: James Madison, from the Virginia ratification convention: "If the President be connected in any suspicious manner with any person and there be grounds to believe that he will shelter him, he may be impeached."

15   We have heard time and time again that the evidence reflects the payment to defendants' money. The President had knowledge that these funds were being paid and these were funds collected for the 1972 presidential campaign. We know that the President met with Mr. Henry Petersen 27 times to discuss matters related to Watergate, and immediately thereafter met with the very persons who were implicated in the information Mr. Petersen was receiving. The words are: "If the President is connected in any suspicious manner with any person and there be grounds to believe that he will shelter that person, he may be impeached."

16   Justice Story: "Impeachment is intended for occasional and extraordinary cases where a superior power acting for the whole people is put into operation to protect their rights and rescue their liberties from violations." We know about the Huston plan. We know about the break-in of the psychiatrist's office. We know that there was absolute complete direction on September 3rd when the President indicated that a surreptitious entry had been made in Dr. Fielding's office, after having met with Mr. Ehrlichman and Mr. Young. "Protect their rights." "Rescue their liberties from violation."

17   The Carolina ratification convention impeachment criteria: those are impeachable "who behave amiss or betray their public trust." Beginning shortly after the Watergate break-in and continuing to the present time, the President has engaged in a series of public statements and actions designed to thwart the lawful investigation by government prosecutors. Moreover, the President has made public announcements and assertions bearing on the Watergate case, which the evidence will show he knew to be false. These assertions, false assertions, impeachable, those who misbehave. Those who "behave amiss or betray the public trust."

18   James Madison again at the Constitutional Convention: "A President is impeachable if he attempts to subvert the Constitution." The Constitution charges the President with the task of taking care that the laws be faithfully executed, and yet the President has counseled his aides to commit perjury, willfully disregard the secrecy of grand jury proceedings, conceal surreptitious entry, attempt to compromise a federal judge, while publicly displaying his cooperation with the processes of criminal justice. "A President is impeachable if he attempts to subvert the Constitution."

19   If the impeachment provision in the Constitution of the United States will not reach the offenses charged here, then perhaps that 18th-century Constitution should be abandoned to a 20th-century paper shredder.

20   Has the President committed offenses, and planned, and directed, and acquiesced in a course of conduct which the Constitution will not tolerate? That's the question. We know that. We know the question. We should now forthwith proceed to answer the question. It is reason, and not passion, which must guide our deliberations, guide our debate, and guide our decision.

21   I yield back the balance of my time, Mr. Chairman.

No Human Being Is Illegal

Mae M. Ngai

Like abortion and guns, immigration has emerged as a hot-button issue in American politics. Because immigration involves concerns in different registers, economic and cultural, it is strangely and perhaps uniquely misaligned in traditional partisan terms (Wong 2006; Zolberg 2006). President Bush cannot manage the split in his own party, between those Republicans who want to exploit immigrants and those who want to expel them. Among Democratic voters, some support cultural diversity and inclusion while others worry that cheaper immigrant labor depresses domestic wages. Political consultants, sensing a no-win situation, are advising Democrats with presidential aspirations to stay clear of the issue altogether.

2   The lack of partisan coherence, however, does not explain why immigration evokes such heated debate. There is a dimension to the debate that seems irrational, impervious to arguments involving empirical data, historical experience, or legal precedent. This was brought home to me after I wrote an op-ed in a major newspaper about how, during the first half of the twentieth century, the U.S. government legalized tens of thousands of illegal European immigrants (Ngai 2006). I received postcards with invectives like, "stupid professor!" I faced similar hostility during a live call-in show on public radio. Confronted with ranting about how immigrants are bad for the United States, I wanted to counter that immigrants are good for the United States. At one level, negative generalizations about immigrants can be refuted point by point: they do not hurt the economy, they expand it; they are more law abiding than the native-born population; they want to learn English and their children all do (Smith and Edmonston 1997; Alba and Nee 2003).

3   But this approach is risky. Generalizations reproduce stereotypes and efface the complexity and diversity of immigrant experience. As Bonnie Honig (2001) has argued, xenophilia is the flip side of xenophobia. In both cases citizens use "immigrants" as a screen onto which they project their own aspirations or frustrations about American democracy. Casting immigrants as bearers of the work ethic, family values, and consensual citizenship renews the tired citizen's faith-liberal capitalism. But when the immigrants disappoint or when conditions change, they become easy scapegoats.

4   As Honig suggests, this kind of immigration discourse is an exercise in nationalism. In an important sense, "Are immigrants good or bad for us?" is the wrong question. It takes as its premise that immigrants are not part of "us." The idea falsely posits that non-citizens are not part of

American society and leaves them out of the discussion. The mass demonstrations of Mexicans and other immigrants last spring were significant because they showed that immigrants are no longer content to be the object of discussion but have emerged as subjects with voice and agency. It was particularly noteworthy but perhaps not surprising that so many of the participants were female, from older hotel workers to high school students, giving lie to the stereotypes that the "illegal alien" is a solo male laborer or that immigrants are meek. Undocumented immigration involves men, women, and families, and they are all standing up.

5   Further, the question assumes that "we" (the United States, defined by its citizens) have a singular interest above and against the interests of "them" (all non-citizens and the foreign countries from whence they came). To be sure, while human migration is as old as human history, immigration and naturalization are modern phenomena, part of the international system based on nation-states that was consolidated in the period between the late nineteenth century and World War I. In this system, sovereign nations assert their absolute right to determine, in the first instance, who shall be admitted to territory and membership and who shall not.

6   In the United States, immigration was not regulated by the federal government until after the civil war, and not until the late 1880s and 1890s did the U.S. Supreme Court invoke the sovereign principle as the basis for immigration policy. Before that, it considered immigration part of the commerce clause of the Constitution; as laborers, immigrants were easily imagined as "articles of commerce" (Bilder 1996).

7   But Chinese exclusion, first legislated in 1882, required the Court to justify why some laborers were desired and others were not. Was the claim that Chinese were racially inassimilable an acceptable reason? The Court said yes; in fact, it said that Congress did not have to justify itself in terms of the Constitution. In the Chinese Exclusion Case (130 U.S. 518 [1889]) the Court recognized Congress's plenary, or absolute power to regulate immigration as part of its authority over foreign relations, in the same realm as declaring war and making treaties. "Aliens enter and remain in the United States only with the license, permission, and sufferance of Congress," it opined (Fong Yue Ting v. U.S., 149 U.S. 698 [1893]). To this day the plenary power doctrine over immigration stands.

8   American political culture has thoroughly normalized the primacy of national sovereignty in immigration affairs, and with important consequences. Nationalism generates the view that immigration is a zero-sum game among competitive nation-states. Americans like to believe that immigration to the United States proves the superiority of liberal capitalism, that "America" is the object of global envy; we resist examining the role that American world power has played in global structures of migration, including the gendered dimensions of migrant exploitation.

...*continued* No Human Being Is Illegal, **Mae M. Ngai**

Increasing numbers of women from the global south are leaving their families behind as they migrate to the affluent countries to work as care-takers for other people's children, as hotel-room cleaners, or as indentured sex-workers. We prefer to ignore these realities and to think, instead, that our immigration policy is generous—indeed, too generous, as we also resent the demands made upon us by others and we think we owe outsiders nothing (Ngai 2004).

9   The emphasis on national sovereignty is the basis for the alarm that we've "lost control" of the border and for the draconian proposals against unauthorized immigration: more fencing, criminalization of the undoc-umented and those who hire or assist them, mass deportations. But many liberals who are sympathetic to Mexican immigrants also want "some-thing done" to stop illegal immigration, although few would actually support turning the entire country into a police state, which is what would be necessary to truly seal the border from unauthorized entry. The cost of viewing sovereignty as the exclusive grounds for immigration policy is that we push to the margins other considerations, such as human rights and global distributive justice. The current debate over immigration policy reform reminds us that sovereignty is not just a claim to national right; it is a theory of power (Carens 1998).

10   Just two months before September 11, 2001, it will be recalled, Pres-ident Bush announced his intention to legalize undocumented Mexican immigrants and institute a guest-worker program that would offer a path to permanent residency and citizenship. In its details it was not particu-larly generous and it faced a complex process of legislative negotiation, as have all efforts to reform the immigration laws. But it did not provoke the kind of emotional controversy that we hear today.

11   However, after 9/11 the immigration issue disappeared from the Washington scene. It resurfaced a couple of years ago, with Bush's pro-posal receiving support from then-president of Mexico, Vicente Fox. But only in the last year has it become an explosive issue in national politics, with vociferous rhetoric like "stop the invasion" and "no amnesty for law-breakers." It seems no accident that immigration restriction has moved to the fore as public disaffection with the war in Iraq grows. According to Republican strategist Don Allen, immigration is an issue that "gets us talking about security and law and order" (Hulse 2006). House majority leader Dennis Hastert deploys flexible rhetoric of popular sovereignty most succinctly: "We're at war. Our borders are a sieve" (Swarns 2006). Whether mongering terrorism and illegal immigration will result in greater mass support for U.S. wars against both will succeed remains to be seen. But the very connections made between them suggest broad ground for oppositional action.

References

Alba, Richard, and Victor Nee. 2003. *Remaking the American Mainstream.* Cambridge: Harvard University Press.

Bilder, Mary Sarah. 1996. "The Struggle over Immigration: Indentured Servants, Slaves, and Articles of Commerce," *Missouri Law Review.*

Carens, Joseph. 1998. "Aliens and Citizens: The Case for Open Borders," in *The Immigration Reader: America in Multidisciplinary Perspective,* ed. David Jacobson. Malden, MA: Blackwell Publications.

STUDENT MODELS

SAMPLE STUDENT RHETORICAL ANALYSIS

Running head: AN ARGUMENT OF REASON AND PASSION 1

An Argument of Reason and Passion: Barbara Jordan's

"Statement on the Articles of Impeachment"

T. Jonathan Jackson

Dr. Netaji

English 1102—October 11, 2010

An Argument of Reason and Passion: Barbara Jordan's

"Statement on the Articles of Impeachment"

Barbara Jordan's July 24, 1974 speech before the U.S. House Judiciary

Committee helped convince the House of Representatives, and the American

public, that President Richard Nixon should be impeached. Nixon was under

investigation for his role in the cover-up of the Watergate scandal. He knew

about the burglary of Democratic Party headquarters, but denied having any

knowledge of it and illegally shielded those responsible. Jordan used her speech

to argue that the president should be impeached because his actions threatened

the Constitution and the people of the United States; however, Jordan never

explicitly states this position in her speech. Instead, she establishes her

credibility and then uses logic to set out the evidence against the president.

In one sense, the audience of Jordan's (1974) speech consisted of the

other 34 members of the House Judiciary Committee, gathered together to

decide whether or not to recommend impeachment. And yet Jordan was not

speaking just to a committee meeting; her speech was very public. The Senate

Watergate hearings had been televised during the months before her speech,

and millions of Americans watched sensational testimony by a host of

witnesses. The Senate hearings produced charges that Nixon authorized break-

ins at Democratic campaign headquarters in Washington during the 1972

election and that the White House was involved in many political dirty tricks

and improprieties.

But the accusations remained only accusations—and Americans remained

deeply divided about them—until it was discovered that Nixon had himself

collected possible hard evidence: he had taped many conversations in the Oval

Office, tapes that could support or refute the charges against the president.

Nixon engaged in a protracted legal battle to keep the tapes from being

disclosed, on the grounds that they were private conversations protected under

"executive privilege," and he released only partial and edited transcripts. Finally

on July 24, 1974, the courts ruled that Nixon had to turn all his remaining tapes

Jonathan Jackson provides background information in the first paragraph and his thesis at the end.

over. That same day, knowing that hard evidence was now at hand, the House

Judiciary Committee immediately went into session to vote whether to impeach

Nixon. Each member of the committee was given fifteen minutes for an opening

statement.

Nixon was a Republican and Jordan (1974), like the majority of the

committee, was a Democrat. Jordan had to convince her audience she was not

biased against the president simply because of her party affiliation. Jordan was

also new to Congress, relatively unknown outside of Texas, and a low-ranking

member of the committee. Consequently, she had to establish her ethos to the

committee as well as to the television audience. She had to present herself as

fair, knowledgeable, and intellectually mature.

Jackson observes that Jordan had a formidable assignment in establishing her ethos in a short speech.

At the heart of Jordan's (1974) argument is her faith in the Constitution.

She begins her speech from a personal perspective, pointing out that the

Constitution is not perfect because it originally excluded African Americans like

her. But now that the Constitution recognizes her as a citizen, Jordan says, her

faith in it "is whole, it is complete, it is total" (p. 2). She even implies that, as a

citizen, she has a moral duty to protect the Constitution, saying, "I am not going

to sit here and be an idle spectator to the diminution, the subversion, the

destruction of the Constitution" (p. 3). Jordan's emotional connection to the

Constitution shows the audience that she is motivated by a love of her country,

not by party loyalty. She establishes herself as someone fighting to defend and

protect American values.

Jackson analyzes how Jordan's fervent allegiance to the Constitution made her appear unbiased.

Jordan (1974) describes the Constitution as the accepted authority on the

laws related to impeachment. She shows the audience how the Constitution

gives her the authority to act as an "inquisitor," (p. 4) or judge. She depicts the

Constitution and the American people as potential victims, and the president as

the potential criminal. She warns of the need to remove "a President swollen

with power and grown tyrannical" (p. 2).

The appeals to pathos and ethos in the opening of the speech establishes

Jordan's (1974) motivations and credibility, allowing her to next lay out her

AN ARGUMENT OF REASON AND PASSION   4

logical arguments. Jordan proceeds to explain how the Constitution defines

impeachment, and fleshes out this brief definition with evidence from several

state Constitutional Conventions. She also quotes Supreme Court Justice Joseph

Story. Using evidence from the North Carolina and Virginia Constitutional

Conventions, Jordan shows that impeachment was intended only for "great

misdemeanors," (p. 4) and that the branches of government were intended to

act as a check upon one another.

Next Jordan (1974) uses quotations from James Madison, Justice Story,

and others to define impeachable offenses. For each offense, Jordan provides an

example of an act that President Nixon was known to have committed, and she

shows how his actions meet the definition of impeachable offenses. She

compares Nixon's meetings with Watergate suspects to Madison's statement

Jordan uses quotations from respected figures in American history to apply to Nixon's misdeeds.

that "if the President is connected in any suspicious manner with any person

and there be grounds to believe that he will shelter that person, he may be

impeached" (p. 3). She pairs Justice Story's statement that impeachment should

"protect [citizens'] rights and rescue their liberties from violation" (p. 2) with

Nixon's knowledge of the burglary of a private psychiatrist's office. She links

Nixon's attempts to bribe a judge and thwart grand jury proceedings with

Madison's statement that "a President is impeachable if he attempts to subvert

the Constitution" (p. 4).

Jordan had to confront a legal issue: Were the actions of President Nixon serious enough to justify impeachment?

Throughout this section, Jordan (1974) repeats the historical quotes

before and after her descriptions of the president's acts. This repetition makes

the connections stronger and more memorable for the audience. Jordan also

contrasts the formal, high-toned language of the Founders and the Constitution

with descriptions that make President Nixon's actions sound sordid and petty:

He knew about money "found in the possession of one of the burglars arrested

on June the 17th," about "the break-in of Daniel Ellsberg's psychiatrist," about

"the fabrication of cables designed to discredit the Kennedy Administration" (p. 5).

AN ARGUMENT OF REASON AND PASSION   5

Words like "burglars," "arrested," "break-in," and "fabrication," sound like

evidence in a criminal trial. These words are not the kind of language Americans

want to hear describing the actions of their president.

    Jordan (1974) then adds another emotional appeal, implying that the

Constitution is literally under attack. "If the impeachment provisions will not

reach the offenses charged here," she says, "then perhaps that 18th-century

Jackson notes that the
metaphor of the paper
shredder adds
emotional force.

Constitution should be abandoned to a 20th-century paper shredder" (p. 3). This

dramatic image encourages the audience to imagine President Nixon shredding

the Constitution just as he had destroyed other evidence implicating him in the

Watergate scandal. It implies that if the president is not stopped, he will commit

further abuses of power. Jordan also makes the American people responsible for

this possible outcome, saying that "we" may as well shred the Constitution if it

cannot be used to impeach Nixon. This emotional appeal has the effect of

shaming those say they can't or shouldn't vote for impeachment.

    Jordan (1974) concludes her speech not by calling for impeachment, but

by calling for an answer to the question, "Has the President committed offenses,

and planned, and directed, and acquiesced in a course of conduct which the

In his conclusion
Jackson points out how
Jordan shifts the focus
to her audience in her
conclusion.

Constitution will not tolerate?" (p. 2). It almost seems like Jordan is being

humble and trying not to judge by not stating her position outright. However,

the reverse is true: Jordan doesn't state her position because she doesn't need

to. The evidence she presented led Congress and the American public

inescapably to one conclusion: That President Nixon had committed

impeachable offenses. Just two week later, Nixon resigned from office. Jordan

had made her point.

AN ARGUMENT OF REASON AND PASSION   6

Reference

Jordan, B. (1974, July). Statement on the articles of impeachment. *American*

    Rhetoric: Top 100 Speeches. Retrieved from http://www

    .americanrhetoric.com/speeches/barbarajordanjudiciarystatement.htm

A Rhetorical Analysis of Ellen Goodman's "Womb
for Rent—For a Price"

Zachary Stumps (student)

With her op-ed piece "Womb for Rent—For a Price," published in
the *Seattle Times* on April 11, 2008 (and earlier in the *Boston Globe*), syndicated columnist Ellen Goodman enters the murky debate about reproductive technology gone global. Since Americans are outsourcing
everything else, "Why not then rent a foreign womb?" (p. B6) she asks.
Goodman, a Pulitzer Prize winning columnist for the Washington Post
Writers Group, is known for helping readers understand the "tumult of
social change and its impact on families," and for shattering "the mold of
men writing exclusively about politics" ("Ellen Goodman," 2008, p. 10).
This op-ed piece continues her tradition of examining social change
from the perspective of family issues.

    Goodman (2008) launches her short piece by asserting that one of
the most recent and consequential "jobs" to be outsourced is having
babies. She explains how the "globalization of baby production" (p. B6)
is thriving because it brings together the reproductive desires of people
in developed countries and the bodily resources of women in developing
countries like India. Briefly tracing how both reproductive technology
and medical tourism have taken advantage of global possibilities, Goodman acknowledges that the thousands of dollars Indian women earn by
carrying the babies of foreign couples represent a much larger income
than these women could earn in any other available jobs. After appearing
to legitimize this global exchange, however, Goodman shifts to her ethical concerns by raising some moral questions that she says are not being
addressed in this trade. She concludes with a full statement of her claim
that this global surrogacy is encroaching on human respect and dignity,
exploiting business-based science, and turning babies into products.

    In this piece, Goodman's (2008) delay of her thesis has several rhetor-
ical benefits: it gives Goodman space to present the perspective of poor
women, enhanced by her appeals to *pathos*, and it invites readers to join her
journey into the complex contexts of this issue; however, this strategy is
also risky because it limits the development of her own argument.

    Instead of presenting her thesis up front, Goodman (2008) devotes
much of the first part of her argument to looking at this issue from the
perspective of foreign surrogate mothers. Using the strategies of *pathos*
to evoke sympathy for these women, she creates a compassionate and
progressively minded argument that highlights the benefits to foreign

*Introduction provides
context and poses issue
to be addressed*

*Provides background
on Goodman*

*Summarizes the
op-ed piece*

Thesis paragraph

*Develops first point in
thesis: use of* pathos *in
exploring perspective of
poor women*

surrogate mothers. She cites factual evidence showing that the average job for a woman in Anand, India, yields a tiny "$25 a month" gotten through the hard work of "crushing glass in a factory," compared to the "$5,000 to $7,000" made carrying a baby to term (p. B6). To carry a baby to term for a foreign couple represents "a decade's worth of women's wages in rural India" (p. 160). Deepening readers' understanding of these women, Goodman cites one woman who used her earnings to finance her son's heart operation and another who paid for her daughter's dowry. In her fair presentation of these women, Goodman both builds her own positive *ethos* and adds a dialogic dimension to her argument by helping readers walk in the shoes of otherwise impoverished surrogate mothers.

Develops second point in thesis: the complex contexts of this issue— outsourcing and medical tourism

The second rhetorical benefit of Goodman's (2008) delayed thesis is that she invites readers to explore this complex issue of global surrogacy with her before she declares her own view. To help readers understand and think through this issue, she relates it to two other familiar global topics: outsourcing and medical tourism. First, she introduces foreign surrogacy as one of the latest forms of outsourcing: "This globalization of baby-making comes at the peculiar intersection of a high reproductive technology and a low-tech work force" (p. B6). Presenting these women as workers, she explains that women in India are getting paid for "the production and delivery of a child" (p. B6) that is analogous to the production and delivery of sneakers or bicycle parts. Goodman also sets this phenomenon in the context of global medical tourism. If people can pursue lower-cost treatment for illnesses and health conditions in other countries, why shouldn't an infertile couple seeking to start a family not also have such access to these more affordable and newly available means? This reasoning provides a foundation for readers to begin understanding the many layers of the issue.

Shows how the delayed-thesis structure creates two perspectives in conflict

The result of Goodman's (2008) delayed-thesis strategy is that the first two-thirds of this piece seem to justify outsourcing surrogate motherhood. Only after reading the whole op-ed piece can readers see clearly that Goodman has been dropping hints about her view all along through her choice of words. Although she clearly sees how outsourcing surrogacy can help poor women economically, her use of market language such as "production," "delivery," and "labor" carry a double meaning. On first reading of this op-ed piece, readers don't know if Goodman's punning is meant to be catchy and entertaining or serves another purpose. This other purpose becomes clear in the last third of the article when Goodman forthrightly asserts her criticism of the commercialism of the global marketplace that promotes worldwide searching for a "cheaper deal": "humanity is sacrificed to the economy and the person becomes the product" (p. B6). This is a bold and big claim, but does the final third of her article support it?

In the final five paragraphs of this op-ed piece, Goodman (2008) begins to develop the rational basis of her argument; however, the brevity of the op-ed genre and her choice not to state her view openly initially have left Goodman with little space to develop her own claim. The result is that she presents some profound ideas very quickly. Some of the ethically complex ideas she introduces but doesn't explore much are these:

Restates the third point in his thesis: lack of space limits development of Goodman's argument

- The idea that there are ethical limits on what can be "sold"
- The idea that surrogate motherhood might be "dangerous work"
- The idea that children born from this "international trade" may be confused about their identities.

Goodman (2008) simply has not left herself enough space to develop these issues and perhaps leaves readers with questions rather than with changed views. I am particularly struck by several questions. Why have European countries banned surrogacy in developing countries and why has the United States not banned this practice? Does Goodman intend to argue that the United States should follow Europe's lead? She could explore more how this business of finding illiterate women to bear children for the wealthy continues to exploit third-world citizens much as sex tourism exploits women in the very same countries. It seems to perpetuate a tendency for the developed world to regard developing countries as a poor place of lawlessness where practices outlawed in the rest of the world (e.g. child prostitution, slave-like working conditions) are somehow tolerable. Goodman could have developed her argument more to state explicitly that a woman who accepts payment for bearing a baby becomes an indentured servant to the family. Yet another way to think of this issue is to see that the old saying of "a bun in the oven" is more literal than metaphoric when a woman uses her womb as a factory to produce children, a body business not too dissimilar to the commercialism of prostitution. Goodman only teases readers by mentioning these complex problems without producing an argument.

Discusses examples of ideas raised by Goodman but not developed

Still, although Goodman (2008, April) does not expand her criticism of outsourced surrogate motherhood or explore the issues of human dignity and rights, this argument does introduce the debate on surrogacy in the global marketplace, raise awareness, and begin to direct the conversation toward a productive end of seeking a responsible, healthy, and ethical future. Her op-ed piece lures readers into contemplating deep, perplexing ethical and economic problems and lays a foundation for readers to create an informed view of this issue.

Conclusion

A RHETORICAL ANALYSIS OF "WOMB FOR RENT"   5

References

Ellen Goodman. (2008). Washington Post Writer's Group. Retrieved from Postwritersgroup.com.

Goodman, E. (2008, April). Womb for rent—for a price. In J. D. Ramage, J. C. Bean, & J. Johnson (Eds.). *Writing Arguments* (8th ed.). New York: Pearson Longman.

Uses APA format to list sources cited in the essay

PRACTICE

❶ Analyze the argument by Ngai, which appears on page 870, how is that argument the product of its audience and purpose? How would the argument be presented differently if it were directed to a different readership or published in a different forum? How would the argument be different if it were rewritten on this very day?

Egg Heads, p. 853

❷ Working in groups, develop responses to the following questions:

a. How does Lopez appeal to *logos*? What is her main claim and what are her reasons? What does she use for evidence? What ideas would you have to include in a short summary?

b. What appeals to *pathos* does Lopez make in this argument? How well are these suited to the conservative readers of the *National Review*?

c. How would you characterize Lopez's *ethos*? Does she seem knowledgeable and credible? Does she seem fair to stakeholders in this controversy?

d. Choose an additional focus from the "Questions for Rhetorical Analysis" to apply to "Egg Heads." How does this question expand your understanding of Lopez's argument?

e. What strikes you as problematic, memorable, or disturbing in this argument?

Reading, Womb for Rent—For a Price, p. 864

❸ What is Goodman's main claim and what are her reasons? In other words, what ideas would you have to include in a short summary?

a. What appeals to *pathos* does Goodman make in this argument? How do these appeals function in the argument?

b. Choose an additional focus from the "Questions for Rhetorical Analysis" to apply to "Womb to Rent—For a Price." How does this question affect your perspective of Goodman's argument?

c. What strikes you as problematic, memorable, or disturbing in this argument?

Detroit Skyline at Twilight
Detroit, MI

Courtesy of RoberGlusic/Alamy.

What Is a Visual Argument Analysis?

20

WE LIVE IN A WORLD FLOODED WITH IMAGES. THEY PULL ON US, COMPETE FOR OUR ATTENTION, PUSH US TO DO THINGS. BUT HOW OFTEN DO WE THINK ABOUT HOW THEY WORK?

CAN THERE BE AN ARGUMENT WITHOUT WORDS?

Arguments in written language are visual in one sense: we use our eyes to read the words on the page. But without words, can there be a visual argument? Certainly some visual symbols take on conventional meanings. Signs in airports or other public places, for example, are designed to communicate with speakers of many languages.

Some visual symbols even make explicit claims. A one-way street sign says that drivers should travel only in the one direction. But are such signs arguments? Most scholars define an argument as a claim supported by one or more reasons. A one-way sign has a claim: all drivers should go in the same direction. But is there a reason? We all know an unstated reason the sign carries: drivers who go the wrong way violate the law and risk a substantial fine (plus they risk a head-on collision with other drivers).

VISUAL ARGUMENTS REQUIRE VIEWER PARTICIPATION

The *Deepwater Horizon* oil spill (also known as the BP oil spill) was the largest offshore oil spill in the history of the United States. Caused by an explosion on April 20, 2010, the spill dumped millions of gallons of oil every day for months in spite of efforts to contain it. People around the world were reminded of the spill when they turned on their televisions and saw video of the oil gushing from the well, and nearly everyone was outraged.

People interpreted the oil flowing from the pipe quite differently, inferring multiple because clauses. Citizens were angry for different reasons.

The *Deepwater Horizon* oil spill was a disaster because

- eleven workers were killed and seventeen were injured.
- enormous harm was done to Gulf wetlands, birds, fish, turtles, marine mammals, and other animals.
- the tourism industry suffered another major blow just five years after Hurricane Katrina.
- the fishing and shrimping industries suffered huge losses.
- President Obama declared a moratorium on deep-water drilling, threatening the loss of jobs.

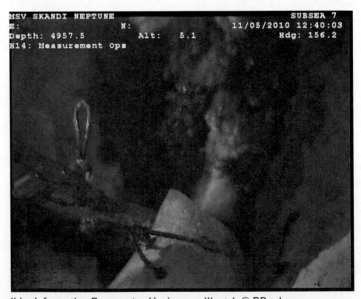

The main oil leak from the *Deepwater Horizon* wellhead. © BP p.l.c.

Photograph of a booth at the Taste of Chicago that was sent on Twitter and enraged people in New Orleans.

- BP and its partners were negligent in drilling the well.
- the spill was an unfortunate act of God like Hurricane Katrina.

Differing interpretations of visual arguments extended beyond the spill itself. A news producer in Chicago took the photo above at the Taste of Chicago festival, sent it to a friend in New Orleans, who sent it to a food writer, who posted it on Twitter. The mayor of New Orleans called it "disgraceful."

Talks shows in both Chicago and New Orleans ranted for a few days about the other city. One comment was perhaps telling about the source of the rage: a menu disclaimer would have been acceptable, but a prominent visual argument, even in text form, was hitting below the belt.

What Is a Multimedia Argument?

Multimedia describes the use of multiple content forms including text, voice and music audio, video, still images, animation, and interactivity. Multimedia goes far back in human history (texts and images were combined at the beginnings of writing), but digital technologies and the Web have made multimedia the fabric of our daily lives. But what exactly are multimedia arguments?

For example, games provide intense multimedia experiences, but are they arguments? Game designers such as Jane McGonigal believe they are arguments. McGonigal maintains that games make people more powerful because they connect them into larger wholes.

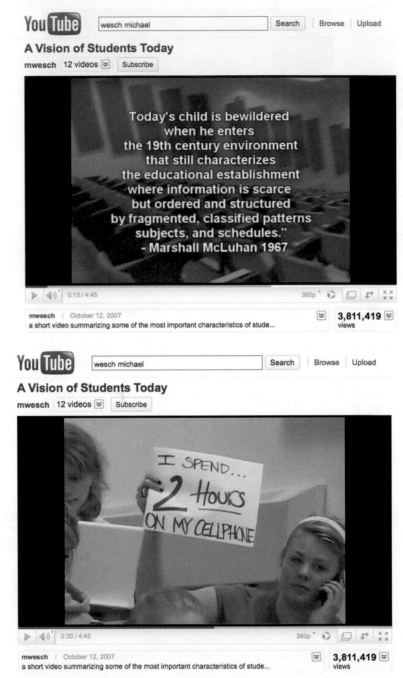

Images from Michael Wesch's *A Vision of Students Today*

Thousands of multimedia arguments have been posted on YouTube. One frequently viewed video is Michael Wesch's *A Vision of Students Today*, posted in October 2007. Wesch's point is that today's education is ill-suited for most students. He enlisted his students to make the point with text and video.

Analyze Visual Evidence

Videos without narration, images, and graphics seldom make arguments on their own, but they are frequently used to support arguments.

EVALUATE PHOTOGRAPHS AND VIDEOS AS EVIDENCE

Almost from the beginnings of photography, negatives were manipulated but realistic results required a high skill level. In the digital era anyone can alter photographs. Perhaps there's nothing wrong with using Photoshop to add absent relatives to family photographs or remove ex-boyfriends and ex-girlfriends. But where do you draw the line? Not only do many videos on YouTube use outright deception, but newsmagazines and networks have also been found guilty of these practices.

Ask questions about what you view.

- Who created the image or video? What bias might the creator have?
- Who published the image or video? What bias might the publisher have?
- Who is the intended audience? For example, political videos often assume that the viewers hold the same political views as the creators.
- What is being shown, and what is not being shown? For example, a video ad promoting tourism for the Gulf of Mexico will look very different from a video showing sources of pollution.
- Who is being represented, and who is not being represented? Who gets left out is as important as who gets included.

The ease of cropping digital photographs reveals an important truth about photography: a photograph represents reality from a particular viewpoint. A high-resolution picture of a crowd can be divided into many smaller images that each say something different about the event. The act of pointing the camera in one direction and not in another shapes how photographic evidence will be interpreted.

EVALUATE CHARTS AND GRAPHS

Statistical information is frequently used as evidence in arguments. The problem with giving many statistics in sentence form, however, is that readers shortly lose track of the numbers. Charts and graphs present statistics visually, allowing readers to take in trends and relationships at a glance.

A photographer's choices about who and what to photograph shapes how we see an event.

ASK THESE QUESTIONS WHEN YOU ARE ANALYZING CHARTS AND GRAPHS

- Is the type of chart appropriate for the information presented?

 Bar and column charts make comparisons in particular categories. If two or more charts are compared, the scales should be consistent.

 Line graphs plot variables on a vertical and a horizontal axis. They are useful for showing proportional trends over time.

 Pie charts show the proportion of parts in terms of the whole. Segments must add up to 100 percent of the whole.

- Does the chart have a clear purpose?
- Does the title indicate the purpose?
- What do the units represent (dollars, people, voters, percentages, and so on)?
- What is the source of the data?
- Is there any distortion of information?

However, charts and graphs can also be misleading. For example, a chart that compares the amounts of calories in competing brands of cereal might list one with 70 calories and another with 80 calories. If the chart begins at zero, the difference looks small. But if the chart starts at 60, the brand with 80 calories appears to have twice the calories of the brand with 70. Furthermore, the chart is worthless if the data is inaccurate or comes from an unreliable source. Creators of charts and graphs have an ethical obligation to present data as fairly and accurately as possible and to provide the sources of the data.

EVALUATE INFORMATIONAL GRAPHICS

Informational graphics more sophisticated than standard pie and bar charts have become a popular means of conveying information. Many are interactive, allowing viewers of a Web site to select the information they want displayed. These information graphics are a form of narrative argument, and the stories they tell have a rhetorical purpose.

Build a Visual Analysis

It's one thing to construct a visual argument yourself; it's another thing to analyze visual arguments that are made by someone else. Fortunately, analyzing arguments made up of images and graphics is largely a matter of following the same strategies for rhetorical analysis—except that you must analyze images instead of (or in addition to) words. To put it another way, when you analyze a visual argument, think about the image itself as well as its relationship to other images (and discourses). The arguments implied by visual images, like the arguments made through text alone, are carried both by the context and by the image.

ANALYZE CONTEXT

A critical analysis of a visual image, like the analyses of written arguments that we discuss in the previous chapter, must include a consideration of context. Consider, for example, the following advertisement for Hofstra University, on page 894. The context for the ad is not difficult to uncover through a bit of research. The ad appeared in 1989 and 1990 when Hofstra, located on Long Island 25 miles from New York City, was celebrating its fiftieth anniversary and hoping to use the occasion to enhance its esteem. At the time, Hofstra enjoyed a good reputation for its professional programs, particularly in education and business (which one-third of the 7,500 students were majoring in). However, it was not as highly regarded in the core science and humanities disciplines that are often associated with institutional prestige. In addition, Hofstra was quite well known in the New York metropolitan area—half its students were commuting to school rather than living in dormitories—but it was not attracting many students from outside the region, and its campus life was consequently regarded as mediocre. Its student body was generally well prepared, hardworking, and capable, but its most outstanding applicants were too often choosing other universities.

Feeling that its performance was exceeding its reputation and that it was capable of attracting a more diverse and talented student body, Hofstra developed a national ad campaign designed to change the opinions of prospective students and their parents, as well as the general public. It placed the ads—the ad reproduced here is one of a series—in several magazines and newspapers in order to persuade people that Hofstra was an outstanding university not just in the professions but in all fields, and that the opportunities available to its students were varied and valuable.

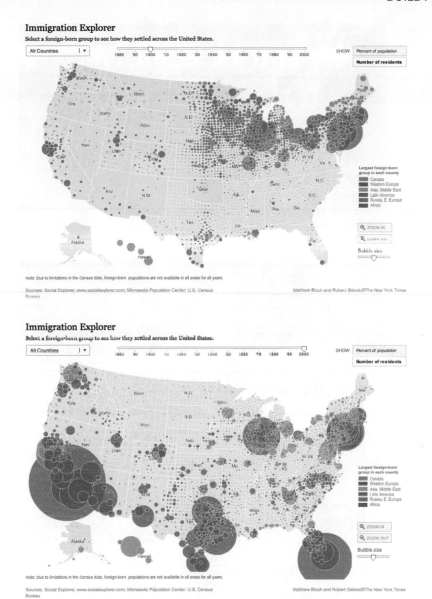

This set of information graphics on immigration tells a story. In 1900 the great majority of immigrants were from Western and Eastern Europe and Russia, and the majority settled in the Northeast and Midwest. In 2000 most immigrants came from Latin America, and they settled in Florida, Texas, and the West Coast along with the metropolitan areas of Chicago and New York City.

Ad for Hofstra University, 1989

ANALYZE VISUAL AND TEXTUAL ELEMENTS

Ads make arguments, and the message of the Hofstra ad is something like this: "Hofstra is a prestigious, high-quality institution that brings out the best in students because of its facilities, its academic reputation, its student body, and the strength of its faculty and academic programs." The text of the Hofstra ad expresses that argument specifically: "The best" and "we teach success" are prominently displayed; the size of the print visually reinforces the message; and the fine print supports the main thesis by mentioning Hofstra's facilities (the large library with "a collection [of volumes] larger than that of 95% of American universities," the "television facility . . . with broadcast quality production capability"); its reputation (its ranking in *Barron's Guide to the Most Prestigious Colleges* and its "professionally accredited programs"); and its faculty and students. The ad works by offering good reasons and supporting arguments that are based on logical reasoning and evidence, as well as appeals to our most fervently held values. By placing the ad in prestigious publications, Hofstra enhanced its credibility even further.

In this chapter, however, we are emphasizing visuals in arguments. What kind of argument is made and supported by the image of the young girl with the flute? The photo of the girl is black and white, so that it can be printed easily and inexpensively in newspapers and magazines. But the black and white format also contributes a sense of reality and truthfulness, in the manner of black and white photos or documentary films. (Color images, on the other hand, can imply flashiness or commercialism.) Even in black and white, the image is quite arresting. In the context of an ad for Hofstra, the image is particularly intriguing. The girl is young—does she seem about ten or twelve years of age?—and her readiness for distinguished performance suggests that she is a prodigy, a genius—in other words, the kind of person that Hofstra attracts and sustains. The ad implies that you might encounter her on the Hofstra campus sometime: if she is not a student at Hofstra now, she soon will be. Come to Hofstra, and you too can acquire the traits associated with excellence and success.

The girl is dressed up for some kind of musical performance, and the details of her costume imply that the performance is of a high order: it is not just any costume, but one associated with professional performances of the most rarefied kind, a concert that calls for only the best musicians. The delicacy and refinement of the girl are implied by the posture of her fingers, the highly polished flute that she holds with an upright carriage, and the meticulousness of her tie, shirt, and coat. The girl's expression suggests that she is serious, sober, disciplined, but comfortable—the kind of student (and faculty member) that Hofstra features. (The layout and consistent print style used in the ad reinforce that impression: by offering a balanced and harmonious placement of elements and by sticking to the same type style throughout, the ad stands for the values of balance, harmony, consistency, and order.) The girl is modest and unpretentious in expression, yet she looks directly at the viewer with supreme self-confidence. Her age suggests innocence, yet her face proclaims ambition; her age and the quasi-masculine costume (note that she wears neither a ring nor earrings) give her a sexual innocence that is in keeping with the contemplative life. Come to Hofstra, the image proclaims, and you will meet people who are sober and graceful, self-disciplined and confident, ambitious without being arrogant. The ad is supporting its thesis with good reasons implied by its central image—good reasons that we identified with logos and pathos in the previous chapter.

Speaking of pathos, what do you make of the fact that the girl is Asian? On one hand, the Asian girl's demeanor reinforces cultural stereotypes. Delicate, small, sober, controlled, even humorless, she embodies characteristics that re-call other Asian American icons (particularly women), especially icons of suc-cess through discipline and hard work. On the other hand, the girl speaks to the Asian community. It is as if she is on the verge of saying, "Come and join me at Hofstra, where you too can reach the highest achievement. And read the copy below me to learn more about what Hofstra has to offer." In this way the girl participates in Hofstra's ambition to attract highly qualified, highly moti-vated, and high-performing minority students—as well as any other high-performing student, regardless of ethnicity or gender, who values hard work, academic distinction, and the postponement of sensual gratification in return for long-term success.

If she is Asian, the girl is also thoroughly American. She appears not to be an international student but an American of immigrant stock. Her costume, her controlled black hair, and her unmarked face and fingers identify her as achiev-ing the American dream of material success, physical health and well being, and class advancement. If her parents or grandparents came to New York or California as immigrants, they (and she) are now naturalized—100 percent American, completely successful. The social class element to the image is unmis-takable: the entire ad speaks of Hofstra's ambition to be among the best, to achieve an elite status. When the ad appeared in 1989, Hofstra was attracting few of the nation's elite students. The girl signals a change. She displays the univer-sity's aspiration to become among the nation's elite—those who enjoy material success as well as the leisure, education, and sophistication to appreciate the finest music. That ambition is reinforced by the university's emblem in the lower right-hand corner of the ad. It resembles a coat of arms and is associated with royalty. Hofstra may be a community that is strong in the professions, but it also values the arts.

No doubt there are other aspects of the image that work to articulate and to support the complex argument of the ad. There is more to be said about this ad, and you may disagree with some of the points we have offered. But consider this: By 2009, twenty years after the ad was run, Hofstra's total enrollment had climbed above 12,000, with 7,500 undergraduates. Its admissions were more se-lective, its student body was more diverse and less regional in character, its grad-uation rate had improved, its sports teams had achieved national visibility, and its minority student population had grown. Many factors contributed to the university's advancement, but it seems likely that this ad was one of them.

Write a Visual Analysis

Like rhetorical analysis, effective visual analysis takes into account the context of the image as well as its visual elements and any surrounding text. When you an-alyze a visual image, look carefully at its details and thoroughly consider its context. What visual elements grab your attention first, and how do other details reinforce that impression—what is most important and less important? How do color and style influence impressions? How does the image direct the viewer's eyes and reinforce what is important? What is the relationship between the image and any text that might accompany it? Consider the shapes, colors, and details of the image, as well as how the elements of the image connect with different arguments and audiences.

Consider also what you know or can learn about the context of an image and the design and text that surround it. Try to determine why and when it was created, who created it, where it appeared, and the target audience. Think about how the context of its creation and publication affected its intended audience. What elements have you seen before? Which elements remind you of other visuals?

THE RHETORIC OF CLOTHING AND OTHER CONSUMER ITEMS

Not only do photographs, paintings, and drawings have rhetorical power, but so do the images projected by many of our consumer choices. Consider, for example, the rhetorical thinking that goes into our choice of clothes. We choose our clothes not only to keep ourselves covered and warm but also to project visually our identification with certain social groups and subcultures. For example, if you want to be identified as a skateboarder, a preppy socialite, a geek, a NASCAR fan, or a junior partner in a corporate law firm, you know how to select clothes and accessories that convey that identification. The way you dress is a code that communicates where you fit (or how you want to be perceived as fitting) within a class and social structure.

How do these symbolic codes get established? They can be set by fashion designers, by advertisers, or by trendy groups or individuals. The key to any new clothing code is to make it look different in some distinctive way from an earlier code or from a code of another group. Sometimes clothing codes develop to show rebellion against the values of parents or authority figures. At other times they develop to show new kinds of group identities.

Clothing codes are played on in conscious ways in fashion advertisements so that consumers become very aware of what identifications are signaled by different styles and brands. This aspect of consumer society is so ubiquitous that one of the marks of growing affluence in third world countries is people's attention to the rhetoric of consumer goods. Consider the second epigraph to this chapter, which indicates that villagers in India watching TV ads notice not only the soap or shampoo being advertised but also the brands of motorbikes and the lifestyles of the people in the ads. Buying a certain kind of consumer good projects a certain kind of status or group or class identity. Our point, from a rhetorical perspective, is that in making a consumer choice, many people are concerned not only with the quality of the item itself but also with its rhetorical symbolism. Note that the same item can send quite different messages to different groups: A Rolex watch might enhance one's credibility at a corporate board meeting while undercutting it at a barbecue for union workers.

Clothing as Visual Arguments

The rhetorical power of clothing especially comes into play in the workplace. This exercise asks to you think about workplace dress codes, which are enforced by peer pressure and peer modeling as well as by company policies. Figures 20.1 to 20.4 show four different workplace environments. Working in small groups

Figure 20.1   Engineering Firm

Figure 20.2   Warehouse

Figure 20.3   Associates, Law Firm

Figure 20.4   Espresso Bar

or as a whole class, consider the rhetoric of workplace clothing by sharing your responses to the following questions:

1. How would you describe the differences in dress codes in each of these environments?

2. If you were employed in one of these workplaces, how much do you think you could vary your style of dress without violating workplace codes?

3. Suppose that you are interviewing for a job in one of these workplaces. What clothing would be appropriate for your interview and why? (Note that how you dress for an interview might be different from how you dress once you have the job.) Share your rhetorical thinking about clothing choices aimed at making the best first impression on the people who interview you. Be as specific as possible for all items of clothing including shoes and accessories.

4. To what extent are dress codes for women more complex than those for men?

READINGS

Watergate Sue: Epilogue*

Megan Kelso

Cartoonist Megan Kelso was born in Seattle, then moved to Brooklyn, New York, with her husband. She plans to keep drawing cartoons until she is an old lady.

Context: The graphic novel *Watergate Sue* (see full novel at URL below) follows two generations of one family. During Sue's pregnancy with baby Mathilda, she and her sister, Josie, reminisce with their mother, Eve, about Sue's own conception and birth during the Watergate hearings of 1973–1974. The epilogue reveals what has happened to the family later in their lives.

For Discussion: The novel ends with an image of Eve (the grandmother in this episode) silently smoking a cigarette. Based on the conversation, what might she be thinking?

For Writing: What definition of the contemporary family is expressed in this epilogue? What holds people together as a family?

*Megan Kelso, *Watergate Sue: Epilogue, New York Times Magazine,* "The Funny Pages," September 9, 2007, http://www.nytimes.com/ref/magazine/funnypagesWatergate .html?_r=1&oref-slogin (accessed June 18, 2008).

Immigrant families on Ellis Island, 1900, waiting for a ferry to Manhattan.

FedEx
Express ®

FedEx
Express ®

Have you noticed the solid white arrow in the FedEx logo?

When Adolf Hitler became Chancellor of Germany in 1933, he declared that a centerpiece of Nazism would be the motorization of the country. He asked Ferdinand Porsche to design a car that would be affordable for everyone.

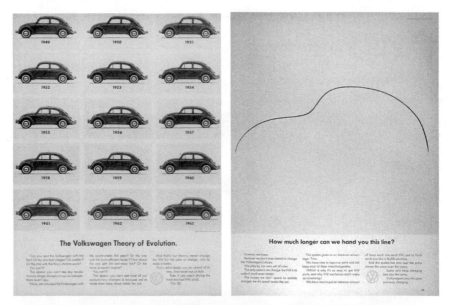

Clever advertising helped make the Beetle a hit in the 1960s. The American advertising firm Doyle Dane Bernbach (DDB) began a campaign in 1959 that emphasized the differences between the Beetle and bulky American cars that changed designs yearly.

In 1968, Walt Disney's *The Love Bug* created a new generation of Beetle fans and led to a series of *Herbie* sequels.

Beetles became part of the counterculture of the 1960s. Many were hand-painted and customized in various ways, even adding fins that mocked American cars.

Misery has enough company.
Dare to be happy.

In 1998 Volkswagen launched the New Beetle, which benefited from the lovable image of the original Beetle.

Walling Off Your Enemies: The Long View

The Chinese Perspective

The Great Wall of China, was first built between the fifth and third centuries B.C., to protect the northern borders of China. It is about 4,000 miles long at present.

The German Perspective

The Berlin Wall, which separated East Berlin from West Berlin for 28 years, fell in 1989, an event that led to the reunification of Germany in 1990.

The Israeli Perspective

This wall separates Israelis from Palestinians in the West Bank at the present time.

The Iraqi Perspective

In Baghdad, Americans are putting up walls to secure neighborhoods.

These four photographs of walls provide four different perspectives on how governments have coped with perceived enemies by building walls. What do you think about the idea of building walls for protection from enemies? How effective is this solution? What other solutions can you think of that might also work or that might even work better?

MasterCharge Ad from the 1970s

Recent "Priceless: MasterCard" Ad

Recent American Express Card Ad

Ronald Reagan at His California Ranch Home

Presidential Candidate John Kerry Windsurfing

Incumbent President Bill Clinton in a Campaign Ad

Presidential Candidate Barack Obama Making a Speech

The woman in this advertisement appears to be a successful and affluent professional based upon her attire. Many of the members of the audience for this publication are likely to be part of this elite class, since 82% of readers have a college degree. There is also an intellectual appeal in the picture: this woman is seeking to broaden her horizons even though she is already successful. Since 51% of readers for *Scientific American Mind* are women, a large number of audience members may be able to identify with her or aspire to her status and success.

The Rosetta Stone program is relatively expensive and must therefore seek to target an affluent audience. *Scientific American Mind* is a good publication to appeal to this audience because the average household income is $119,000, and average household net worth is $827,000.

THERE'S ANOTHER LANGUAGE INSIDE YOU. GIVE IT A VOICE.

Do you want to communicate a new voice to the world, to express another side of you? With Rosetta Stone® you can, in any language.

- We teach language naturally, pairing words spoken by native speakers with vivid, real-life imagery in context, activating your mind's inherent ability to learn a language.

- Speech recognition coaches you to the right pronunciation, so you'll be speaking quickly and correctly. In no time at all, you'll find that the new language you tried on is a perfect fit.

Rosetta Stone. The fastest way to learn a language. Guaranteed.

Over 30 languages available.

SAVE 10%

Level 1	$233
Level 1&2	$377
Level 1,2&3	$494

100% six-month money-back guarantee.

PICK UP A NEW LANGUAGE TODAY!
(866) 833-8301 RosettaStone.com/sas029a
Use promo code sas029a when ordering. Offer expires June 30, 2009.

RosettaStone®

The bright yellow of the Rosetta Stone logo also frames the picture and serves as a backdrop for the saying "There's another language inside you. Give it a voice." This effectively unifies the elements of the advertisement. The bright yellow is an active appeal to initiative, which is likely to draw the attention of this magazine's audience. *Scientific American Mind*'s web site says in its mission statement that it is "aimed at inquisitive adults who are passionate about knowing more about how the mind works". These same individuals who want to know more about the mind are likely to be interested in learning about other cultures and languages.

Analysis of Rosetta Stone ad by Sarah Kay Hurst

STUDENT MODELS

STUDENT MODEL #1

The Controversy behind Barbie

Prisna Virasin

1   The Barbie doll was created in 1959 by Ruth Handler, the cofounder of Mattel. Handler created the doll after seeing her daughter, whose nickname was Barbie, and her daughter's friends play with their paper dolls. According to Gaby Wood and Frances Stonor Saunders (2002), Handler realized that little girls wanted a doll "they could aspire to be like, not aspire to look after" (p. 38). This was a revolutionary idea because before the creation of Barbie, the toy store doll selection mainly consisted of baby dolls, which encouraged girls to pretend to be mothers. For Handler, according to Wood and Saunders, Barbie "has always represented the fact that a woman has choices" (p. 39). The "Barbie Dolls" entry on the *History Channel* (2008) Web site states, "ninety percent of all American girls in the last forty years have owned at least one Barbie. . . . Each week Mattel sells over 1.5 million dolls—that's two dolls per second" (p. 34).

2   The fact that Handler created Barbie as a challenge to the ideology that the proper role for women was that of a mother has become ironic in light of the present feminist protest against the Barbie doll. The Barbie protesters have stated that Barbie is responsible for the development of poor body image in girls. They believe that the Barbie's proportions create impossible images of beauty that girls will strive toward. If Barbie were a human she would be seven feet tall with a thirty-nine-inch chest measurement, twenty-two-inch waist measurement, and thirty-three-inch hip measurement ("Barbie Dolls," 2008).

3   In addition to protests of the Barbie's physical appearance, there is also the issue of the doll's intellectual image. Barbie detractors have criticized the Barbie lifestyle, which seems to center around clothes, cars, dream homes, and other material possessions. Protests followed the release of the talking Barbie that localized such expressions as "Math is hard" and "Let's go shopping." Parents feared that the first sentence would reinforce the stereotype that girls were less skilled at math than boys. The second sentence seemed to reinforce the importance of clothes, physical appearance, and material goods. In her article, "Giga-What? Barbie Gets Her Own Computer," Ophira Edut criticizes educational materials based on Barbie for the image they reinforce. Edut states that the Barbie computer is bundled with typing tutor software while the

Explain the issue.

Describe the rhetorical situation.
- *Exigence*
- *Interested parties*
- *Constraints*

What is the first perspective?

Perspectives on Argument, Sixth Edition by Nancy V. Wood.

boys' Hot Wheels computer is bundled with adventure games. Also, the Barbie Rapunzel CD-ROM is touted by Mattel to expose girls to fine art and creativity when the only creative function of the program is changing Barbie's clothes and hairstyle interactively on the computer screen.

What is the second perspective?   4

Supporters of the Barbie doll state that the toy is a fun part of growing up. They refer to the simple fun of playing with Barbie dolls. They believe that Barbie as a figure is a tool in building girls' imaginations. They also maintain that Barbie as a figure is a positive role model because she is able to do almost anything. Barbie was an astronaut before the first woman went into space. Barbie has been a veterinarian, a doctor, a businesswoman, and to top it all off, a presidential candidate.

What is the third perspective?   5

Between the anti-Barbie camp and the pro-Barbie camp, there are the Barbie moderates. The Barbie moderates do not completely agree with how Mattel chooses to portray the "ideal American woman," nor do they view the doll as all evil. They see the positive aspects of the Barbie (the many professions, the ability to foster imaginative play, and the message that girls can choose to be whomever they want) and the negative aspects of the Barbie as a figure (a materialistic nature, a focus on outward appearance, and the vapid blond stereotype). The moderates state that by banning Barbie dolls, we will not be solving the problem of poor body image. They believe that Barbie is a scapegoat—the figure (or doll) to blame for all the negative feelings that children develop about themselves. Although the moderates do not agree with the image of women that Barbie seems to sustain, they also do not believe that this doll (or figure) is the source of the problem.

What is the author's perspective? Why does she hold it?   6

As a twenty-something female who grew up in America, I am very interested in the Barbie debate. I played with Barbie dolls almost obsessively from first to third grade. I designed clothes for them out of handkerchiefs and tissues and dreamed about becoming a fashion designer. I remember envying the girls who had Barbie Ferraris and dream houses. I looked on in horror as my little sister cut Barbie's hair short and colored it hot pink with a marker. In college, when I was introduced to feminism, I tried to deny any past connection to Barbie. I was ashamed to have ever associated with this figure. I felt sorry for the girls who looked like walking Barbie dolls, always worried about looking perfect. I realize now that I cannot blame thoughts of being fat, short, or out of style on a doll or girls that look like dolls. I agree with the Barbie moderates. As simple as the Barbie looks, it seems that the Barbie issue is more complicated than "Barbie good" or "Barbie bad." The debate encompasses many interesting and controversial issues concerning how we view beauty and how we view ourselves. In my eyes, Barbie is a scapegoat. We, as an entire culture, need to look at our ideas about beauty and what we are teaching children about themselves.

References

Edut, O. (N.d.) Giga what? Barbie gets her own computer. Retrieved from http://www.adiosbarbie.com/bology/bology_computer.html

History of toys: Barbie dolls. (2008). A&E Television Networks. Retrieved from History.com.

Wood, G., & Saunders, F. S. (2002, April). Dream doll. *New Statesman*. Retrieved from Academic Search Complete.

STUDENT MODEL #2

Some Don't Like Their Blues at All

Karyn M. Lewis

Karyn Lewis decided to write an analysis of an advertisement for Fila jeans that she found in a magazine. She chose this particular advertisement because it created an image for the product that was based on stereotyped portrayals of gender roles. Instead of using its power to break down gender stereotypes, Fila deliberately used common stereotypes (men are strong and hard; women are weak and soft) to help sell their clothing. Lewis's analysis explains how Fila's images perpetuate the myth that men are "creatures of iron," while women are soft and "silly bits of fluff," leaving viewers of the advertisement without positive gender role models.

1   He strides toward us in navy and white, his body muscled and heavy-set, one arm holding his casually flung jeans jacket over his shoulder. A man in his prime, with just the right combination of macho and sartorial flair.

2   He is also black.

3   She is curled and giggling upon a chair, her hair loose and flowing around her shoulders, leaning forward innocently—the very picture of a blossoming, navy flower.

4   She is white.

5   They are each pictured on a magazine page of their own, situated opposite each other in a complementary two-page spread. They are stationed in front of a muted photograph which serves as a background for each one. They both merit their own captions: bold indigo letters presiding over them in the outer corners of each page.

6   His says: SOME LIKE THEIR BLUES HARD.

7   Hers says: SOME LIKE THEIR BLUES SOFT.

8   His background depicts a thrusting struggle between a quarterback and a leaping defender, a scene of arrested violence and high tension.

9   Her background is a lounging, bikini-clad goddess, who looks at the camera with intriguing, calm passion. She raises her hand to rest behind her head in a languid gesture as she tries to incite passion within the viewer.

10   At the bottom of the page blazes the proud emblem of the company that came up with this ad: FILA JEANS.

11   This advertisement blatantly uses stereotypes of men and women to sell its product. It caters to our need to fit into the roles that society has deemed right for the individual sexes ever since patriarchal rule rose up and replaced the primitive worship of a mother goddess and the reverence for women. These stereotypes handed down to us throughout the centuries spell out to us that men are violence and power incarnate, and that the manly attitude has no room for weakness or softness of nature. And we find our role model of women in the compliant and eager female who obeys her man in all things, who must not say no to a male, and who is not very bright—someone who flutters her eyelashes, giggles a lot, and uses tears to get her way.

12   This ad tells us, by offering the image of a hard, masculine male, who is deified in violence, that he is the role model men should aspire to, and that for women, their ideal is weak but sexual, innocent and at the same time old enough to have sex. In viewing this ad, we see our aspirations clothed in Fila jeans, and to be like them, we must buy the clothes pictured here. This ad also suggests that a man can become hard and powerful (or at least look it) dressed in these jeans; a woman can become sexually intense and desirable dressed in Fila's clothing.

13   The words of the captions tantalize with their sexual innuendo. The phrase "Some like their blues hard" hints at male sexual prowess. Most men and women in this country are obsessed with males' need to prove their virility, and Fila plays on this obsession. Females too have their own stereotype of what constitutes their sexuality. "Some like their blues soft" exemplifies this ideal: A woman should be soft and yielding. Her soft, sensuous body parts, which so excite her partners, have been transformed into her personal qualities. By using the term *soft*, Fila immediately links the girl with her sexuality and sexual organs.

14   We are shown by the models' postures that men and women are (according to Fila) fundamentally different and total antonyms of one another. He is standing and walking with purpose; she sits, laughing trivially at the camera. Even the background hints at separation of the sexes.

15   The football players on the man's page are arranged in a diagonal line which starts at the upper left-hand corner and runs to the opposite

corner, which is the center of the ad. On her page, the enchanting nymph in the bathing suit runs on a diagonal; beginning where his ends, and traveling up to the upper right-hand corner of her page. These two photos in effect create a *V*, which both links the two models and suggests movement away from one another. Another good example of their autonomy from one another is their skin color. He is a black man, she's white. Black is the opposite color of white on an artist's color wheel and palette and symbolizes dynamically opposed forces: good and evil, night and day, man and woman. This ad hits us with the idea that men and women are not parallel in nature to one another but are fundamentally different in all things. It alienates the sexes from each other. Opposites may attract, but there is no room for understanding a nature completely alien to your own.

16   So in viewing this ad, and reading its captions, the consumer is left with the view that a woman must be "soft" and sensual, a male's sexual dream, and must somehow still retain her innocence after having sex. She must be weak, the opposite of the violence which contrasts with her on the opposite page. The men looking at this ad read the message that they are supposed to be well dressed and powerful and possess a strength that borders on violence. As we are told by the caption, men should be "hard." Furthermore, men and women are opposite creatures, as different as two sides of a coin.

17   This ad is supposed to cause us to want to meet these requirements, but it fills me with a deep-rooted disgust that we perpetuate the myth that men are unyielding creatures of iron and women are silly bits of fluff. The ad generates no good role models to aspire to, where men and women are equal beings, and both can show compassion and still be strong. Fila may like their blues hard and soft, but I don't like their blues at all.

PRACTICE

❶ FEDERAL EXPRESS LOGO
(Corporate Logo)
Landor Associates

Federal Express, founded in 1973, created a new market for rapid delivery of packages and documents. By 1993 the company had greatly expanded and operated around the world. Federal Express hired the design firm, Landor Associates, to create a new logo. By this time Federal Express had become universally known as FedEx, which Landor chose to use for the new logo. The FedEx logo quickly became one of the most recognizable in the world.

   a. Make a list of all the logos you can think of. What makes these logos memorable?

   b. Logos were originally designed to distinguish products and companies. Notice how many now look similar. Why do you think so many logos look alike?

   c. Which logos suggest what a company actually does?

   d. Your school probably has a logo. How frequently do you see the logo? What message does the logo convey about your school?

   e. Knowing what you do about the company FedEx, what values are being promoted with the design elements of its logo? Pretend you are a representative for Landor Associates. Write a memo to FedEx executives explaining how the logo reflects these values.

❷ VOLKSWAGEN BEETLE
(Product Design)

The Volkswagen Type 1, better known as the Beetle or Bug, is the most produced car in history. From 1938 until the last original Beetle came off an assembly line in Puebla, Mexico, over twenty-one million were built. The Beetle began in Nazi Germany, when Adolf Hitler commissioned Ferdinand Porsche to produce a car for common people. Only a handful were produced before World War II started in 1939. Volkswagen was soon back in production after the war, and by 1954, the number of Beetles passed a million. Volkswagen began shipping cars to the United States at a time when American cars were big and boxy. The VW Beetle was just the opposite—small and rounded, inexpensive, and three times as fuel efficient. Beetles dominated the small-car market until Japanese imports showed up in large numbers in the mid-1970s.

More than the story of a car, however, the Beetle demonstrates how what we buy reflects cultural attitudes and values.

a. Volkswagen ads in the United States in the 1960s appealed to simplicity—simple shape, simple technology—which grew out of long-standing American values of honesty, economy, and lack of pretense. Look at automobile ads today, both in print and on television. What values do they appeal to?

b. Your campus may have a building that is better known by a nickname than its official name. Is the building liked or disliked by students? How does the nickname change the image of the building? For example, is it more friendly or less friendly?

c. Look up the word *bug* in the *Oxford English Dictionary*, which traces the histories of words. Your library has the print OED and may allow access through the library's Web site. How has the meaning of *bug* changed over time? Think about how *bug* is used today. For example, a common saying among computer programmers is "It's not a bug, it's a feature." Identify examples of other words such as *pimp* that have changed meanings in recent years.

d. Think of other products that we find cute and lovable. What makes them cute and lovable? Does advertising promote these associations?

e. The Volkswagen Beetle has a complicated and dark history. What values from the car's conceptualization were carried over into the advertising you see here? How were the negative historical associations downplayed or erased? How do today's advertisements for Volkswagen cars compare? Write a paragraph describing the associations the brand has now, and how these relate (or not relate) to the car's history.

③ *Credit Card Campaigns:* Credit card companies have always faced a challenge: persuading consumers to buy with credit cards rather than cash and checks (with the expectation that many customers will not pay off the balance each month and thus pay substantial interest charges). Currently, banks and credit card companies must also overcome consumers' anger and distrust in this age of the banking crisis, overextended consumer debt, and high credit card interest.

a. Choose one or more of the magazine ads for credit cards on pages 905–906, and analyze them, using the ideas presented throughout this section (target audience, choice of medium, brand building, mirror and window strategy, and compositional features).

Cultural Criticism

b. Reexamine the same credit card ads from the perspectives of gender, class, and ethnicity. To what extent do these ads break or reinforce traditional notions of gender, race, and class?

4 The techniques for constructing photos come into play prominently in news photography. In this exercise, we ask you to examine four photographs of American presidential campaigns. Working individually or in groups, study the four photos on page 907 and then answer the following questions:

a. What do you think is the dominant impression of each photo? In other words, what is each photo's implicit argument?

b. What camera techniques and compositional features do you see in each photo?

c. What image of the candidates do these photographs attempt to create for citizens and voters?

5 Three of these photographs (of Reagan, Clinton, and Obama) are mostly successful in promoting the image intended by their campaigns. But one of the photographs (of Democratic candidate John Kerry in 1994, running against George W. Bush) is an example of a photograph that "backfired." Republicans reversed the intended impact of the photograph and used it to ridicule Kerry.

a. What is the intended effect of the Kerry photograph, which is from a windsurfing video showing Kerry zigzagging across the water?

b. How might the Kerry photograph (and the windsurfing video) produce an unintended effect that opens the candidate to ridicule from the opposing party? (Suggestion: Enter "Kerry windsurfing photo" into your Web search engine. For another example of a campaign photograph that backfired, search for "Michael Dukakis tank photo.")

6 The poster shown on the next page is for the documentary film "Wal-Mart: The High Cost of Low Prices," produced in 2005 by filmmaker and political activist Robert Greenwald. According to its Web site, the movie features "the deeply personal stories and everyday lives of families and communities struggling to survive in a Wal-Mart world."

Working individually or in groups, answer the following questions:

a. What compositional features and drawing techniques do you see in this image? What is striking or memorable about the visual features?

b. How would you state the argument made by this image?

c. This effect of this image derives partly from what cultural analysts call "intertextuality." By this term, analysts mean the way that a viewer's reading of an image depends on familiarity with a network of

Poster for "Wal-Mart: The High Cost of Low Prices"

Urban Assault Scene, America's Army Video Game

Village Scene, America's Army Video Game

"connected" images—in this case, familiarity with posters for Godzilla films from the 1950s as well as with Wal-Mart's conventional use of the smiley face. How does this drawing use viewers' cultural knowledge of Godzilla and of smiley-faces to create an image of Wal-Mart? Why is this monster wearing a suit? Why does it have five or more arms? Why is this monster destroying a suburb or housing area rather than a city of skyscrapers? In short, what does it retain of conventional Godzilla images, what does it change, and why? Similarly, how is the monster's smiley face similar to and different from the traditional Wal-Mart smiley face?

7 The images on the previous page are screen captures from the very popular and controversial PC action game *America's Army*, created by the U.S. Army. This "virtual soldiering" game, free to download from the Web site http://www.americasarmy.com, claims to "provide players with the most authentic military experience available."

a. In these screen captures from the game, what is the effect of the camera's distance from the subject and the camera's point of view on the viewer/player?

b. How do color and composition affect the visual appeal of these images?

c. What impressions do settings, characters, and roles convey?

d. Based on these two scenes from the game, why do you think this game has provoked heated public discussion? How effective do you think this game is as a recruitment device?

8 The three images reprinted on pages 920 and 923 are visual arguments that memorialize historic events. They may not appear at first to be visual arguments until you learn something about the history and original rhetorical situations in which they were situated. All three are photographs, and they are accompanied by enough explanation to help you understand the rhetorical situations in which they occurred. This will allow you to evaluate their effectiveness as visual arguments, both now and when they first appeared.

Form small groups, view each image, read the written commentary and essays that provide information about the photos, and answer the questions that follow them. Then answer the following questions about their rhetorical situations.

a. *Image.* What type of image is it? What are its qualities and features? What is it about?

b. *Viewer or audience:* Who do you think was targeted as the most appropriate audience at the time each photo was taken? Who might still regard each of these photos as a compelling visual argument?

c. *Photographer:* What do you know about the photographer, and what may have motivated that individual to take the photo? What might have been the intended result?

d. *Constraints:* What constraints influenced the photographer? Consider the influential events, circumstances, and traditions already in place at the time each photo was taken. Consider, also, the possible beliefs, attitudes, motives, and prejudices of the photographer. How about your constraints? Do any of your beliefs, attitudes, or prejudices seem to match those of the photographer, or are they different? Do the possible constraints you have identified create common ground between you and the photographer, or do they drive you apart?

e. *Exigence:* What motivated the photographer to take each of these photos? What happened? Was it perceived as a defect or problem? If yes, why? Was it new or recurring?

Figure 1: This photograph was taken in 1956 early in the civil rights movement in Alabama when the issue was segregation in public facilities. Until this time, African American people were required to sit only at the back of public buses. A new national ruling gave them the right to sit wherever they wanted to sit. In the photograph, Rosa Parks, an African American civil rights activist, tests this new ruling by taking a seat in the front of the bus with a white man seated behind her. This is a famous photograph. It appears on the walls of buses in New York City and has come to symbolize change brought about by the movement for civil rights that continued into the next decades.

**Figure 1
Rosa Parks Rides in the
Front of the Bus**
Look at the image and read the essay that follows. It explains the history of this photograph and will provide you with the information you need to analyze the rhetorical situation.

Rosa Parks riding a Montgomery, Ala., bus in December 1956, after the Supreme Court outlawed segregation on buses.

The Man behind Rosa Parks[*]

Peter Applebome

The author has been a reporter and editor at the New York Times *newspaper since 1987 where he is now the deputy metropolitan editor. His work has appeared in many other publications as well. He often writes about education and culture.*

1   Almost everyone has seen the famous study in black and white, one of those rare photographs that enters the collective memory as a snapshot not of a moment but of an era and maybe something more. It's now on almost any bus in New York City and many of its suburbs, an invitation not just to remember but to reflect.

2   At the front of a bus, previously reserved for white riders, is Rosa Parks, head slightly bowed, face turned to the window to her left, seemingly lost in thought as she rides through Montgomery, Ala. In the seat behind her, is a young white man looking to his right, his face hard, almost expressionless. The two, the only figures visible on the bus, seem a few inches and a universe apart, each seemingly looking at and for something utterly different.

3   Everyone knows her. No one knows him.

4   Except for Catherine Chriss, his daughter. And, like his identity, hidden in plain sight, unknown even to the veterans of that era still living, what's most telling about the real story of the black woman and the white man is how much of what we think we know is what we read into the picture, not what's there.

5   The man on the bus, Nicholas C. Chriss, was not some irritated Alabama segregationist preserved for history but a reporter working at the time for United Press International out of Atlanta. . . .

6   Mr. Chriss, who also worked for *The Los Angeles Times* and *The Houston Chronicle*, publicly disclosed his role in the picture just once. It was three paragraphs in the middle of a 2,183-word article he wrote for *The Chronicle* in 1986 about his experiences covering the civil rights movement.

7   He explained that the picture was taken on Dec. 21, 1956, the day after the United States Supreme Court ruled Montgomery's segregated bus system illegal. (Actually, the ruling had come a month earlier, but it was not until Dec. 20 that the district court entered the order putting it into effect.) He said that he boarded the bus in downtown Montgomery and that he and Mrs. Parks were the only riders up front.

8   He wrote: "It was a historic occasion. I was then with the United Press International wire service. A UPI photographer took a picture of Mrs. Parks on the bus. It shows a somber Mrs. Parks seated on the bus

[1] *New York Times,* December 7, 2005, A1 and A33.

...*continued* The Man behind Rosa Parks, **Peter Applebome**

looking calmly out the window. Seated just behind her is a hard-eyed white man.

9   "Each anniversary of that day, this photograph is brought out of musty files and used in various publications around the world. But to this day no one has ever made clear that it was a reporter, I, covering this event and sitting behind Mrs. Parks, not some sullen white segregationist! It was a great scoop for me, but Mrs. Parks had little to say. She seemed to want to savor the event alone." . . .

10   Still, if little known, the history of the picture is explored in at least one source, the biography of Rosa Parks by Douglas Brinkley, first published in 2000 as part of the Penguin Lives series of biographies.

11   Mr. Brinkley said Mrs. Parks, in interviews with him, said she left her home at the Cleveland Courts housing project specifically for a picture of her on a bus and that the idea was for her to be seated in the front of the bus with a white man behind. Similar photo opportunities were arranged for the Rev. Dr. Martin Luther King Jr. and others during the day, he said.

12   Mr. Chriss then agreed to sit behind her for the purpose of the picture. Mr. Brinkley does not identify Mr. Chriss in the book and says that a reporter and two photographers from *Look* magazine arranged for the picture. He said Mrs. Parks told him she was reluctant to take part in the picture, but both the journalists and members of the civil rights community wanted an image that would dramatize what had occurred.

13   "It was completely a 100 percent staged event," Mr. Brinkley said. "There was nothing random about it." . . .

14   None of that diminishes the achievement or her life, just as, perhaps, the true story of the picture need not detract from its power. It's just a reminder that history is almost always more complicated and surprising than the images that most effectively tell its story.

Figures 2 and 3: The next two images are Holocaust photographs taken in the early 1940s during the Second World War at the Auschwitz concentration and death camp in Poland. The issues were anti-Semitism, genocide, and the desire on the part of the Nazis, who ran this camp, to create a so-called master race. More than a million Jews died in the gas chambers at Auschwitz, were the victims of deadly medical experiments, or died of other causes such as starvation. Answer the questions that follow the next reading and then analyze the rhetorical situation for Figures 2 and 3 separately.

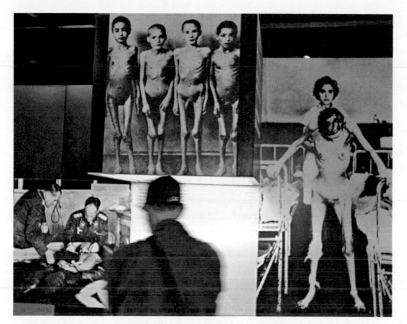

Figure 2
Auschwitz Victims of Medical Experiments

This is a photograph of an Israeli soldier in Jerusalem, Israel, who is viewing historical photographs at the Yad Vashem Holocaust Memorial Museum of Jewish victims from Auschwitz. Photojournalist David Silverman, who works for Getty Images and has been based in Israel and the West Bank since 1991, took this photo the week before the 60th anniversary of the liberation of Auschwitz.

Auschwitz Exhibit at Jerusalem's Yad Vashem Holocaust Memorial

Figure 3
Camp Officials at Leisure

This is a photograph of some of the Nazi SS who ran the Auschwitz concentration and death camp in the 1940s in Poland. Approximately 6,000 individuals worked at Auschwitz. Look at the image, read the following essay, and analyze the rhetorical situation.

An SS Officer's Auschwitz Photo Album
SS officers and death camp staff at leisure near Auschwitz, one of 116 newly discovered snapshots from a Nazi officer's scrapbook donated to the Holocaust museum in Washington.

In the Shadow of Horror, SS Guardians Relax and Frolic*

Neil A. Lewis

The author is a freelance journalist and contractor who writes for
the New York Times.

1 Last December, Rebecca Erbelding, a young archivist at the United States Holocaust Memorial Museum, opened a letter from a former United States Army Intelligence officer who said he wanted to donate photographs of Auschwitz he had found more than 60 years ago in Germany.

2 Ms. Erbelding was intrigued: Although Auschwitz may be the most notorious of the Nazi death camps, there are only a small number of known photos of the place before its liberation in 1945. Some time the next month, the museum received a package containing in 16 cardboard pages, with photos pasted on both sides, and their significance quickly became apparent.

3 As Ms. Erbelding and other archivists reviewed the album, they realized they had a scrapbook of sorts of the lives of Aushwitz's senior SS officers that was maintained by Karl Höcker, the adjutant to the camp commandant. Rather than showing the men performing their death camp duties, the photos depicted, among other things, a horde of SS men singing cheerily to the accompaniment of an accordionist, Höcker lighting the camp's Christmas tree, a cadre of young SS women frolicking and officers relaxing, some with tunics shed, for a smoking break.

4 In all there are 116 pictures, beginning with a photo from June 21, 1944, of Höcker and the commandant of the camp, Richard Baer, both in full SS regalia. The album also contains eight photos of Josef Mengele, the camp doctor notorious for participating in the selections of arriving prisoners and bizarre and cruel medical experiments. These are the first authenticated pictures of Mengele at Auschwitz, officials at the Holocaust museum said.

5 The photos provide a stunning counterpoint to what up until now has been the only major source of preliberation Auschwitz photos, the so-called Auschwitz Album, a compilation of pictures taken by SS photographers in the spring of 1944 and discovered by a survivor in another camp. Those photos depict the arrival at the camp of a transport of Hungarian Jews, who at the time made up the last remaining sizable Jewish community in Europe. The Auschwitz Album, owned by Yad Vashem, the Israeli Holocaust museum, depicts the railside selection process at Birkenau, the area where trains arrived at the camp, as SS men herded new prisoners into lines.

[1]New York Times, September 29, 2007, B1 and B6.

6   The comparisons between the albums are both poignant and obvious, as they juxtapose the comfortable daily lives of the guards with the horrific reality within the camp, where thousands were starving and 1.1 million died.

7   For example, one of the Höcker pictures, shot on July 22, 1944, shows a group of cheerful young women who worked as SS communications specialists eating bowls of fresh blueberries. One turns her bowl upside down and makes a mock frown because she has finished her portion.

8   On that day, said Judith Cohen, a historian at the Holocaust museum in Washington, 150 new prisoners arrived at the Birkenau site. Of that group, 21 men and 12 women were selected for work, the rest transported immediately to the gas chambers.

9   Those killings were part of the final frenetic efforts of the Nazis to eliminate the Jews of Europe and others deemed undesirable as the war neared its end. That summer the crematoriums broke down from overuse and some bodies had to be burned in open pits. A separate but small group of known preliberation photos were taken clandestinely of those burnings.

10   Auschwitz was abandoned and evacuated on Jan, 18, 1945, and liberated by Soviet forces on Jan. 27. Many of the Höcker photos were taken at Solahütte, an Alpine-style recreation lodge the SS used on the far reaches of the camp complex alongside the Sola River.

11   Though they as yet have no plans to exhibit the Höcker album photos, curators at the Holocaust Memorial Museum have created an online display of them on the museum's Web site (ushmm.org).

9 How does an analysis of the rhetorical situations for Figures 2 and 3 help you perceive them as visual arguments? What is the effect of viewing these two photos together? What conclusions can you draw from these photos about the Holocaust, the Nazi death camps, the individuals imprisoned there, and the Nazi SS officers who worked there?

10 Fila did not grant permission to reproduce their advertisement for this text. However, Lewis does an excellent job of describing the layout, balance, color, key figures, diagonals, and background. In the margin of this essay, indicate those sentences where Lewis describes the advertisement, enabling us to clearly visualize it.

a. Parts of Lewis's essay describe and analyze the text that accompanies the advertisement, but she spends most of her time discussing the social, cultural, and gendered contexts of the advertisement. In the margin of the essay, indicate places where she analyzes the accompanying *text* and where she analyzes the *context* of the advertisement. Where in her analysis do you see her showing how text and context relate to each other? Explain.

b. Examine how Lewis *organizes* her analysis of the Fila advertisement. How does her organization reflect her thesis that the two figures, hers and his, are opposites? In other words, where and how does she use sentences and paragraphs to show that these two figures are "fundamentally different and total antonyms of each other"?

c. The genre of the Fila promotion is the clothing or fashion advertisement. Find at least three other advertisements for clothing or fashion. Use Lewis's strategy and analyze how the images, text, and context function together. How are the overall messages in these advertisements similar to or different from the messages that Lewis finds? Explain.

⓫ Choose an advertisement in a magazine and analyze it for how it works in the context of that particular magazine. First, research the magazine to profile its readers (typical income, class, occupations, or interests). Then examine several advertisements from this magazine to see which ads make the most effective appeals to this group of readers. Choose one particular ad and annotate it for appeals to audience as well as use of key images, color, graphics, balance, layout, diagonals, and accompanying text. Use the analysis of a Rosetta Stone advertisement in *Scientific American Mind* by student writer Sarah Kay Hurst as an example (see page 908).

A Portfolio of TV Commercials

The world's first television commercial was a ten-second Bulova watch ad broadcast in 1941. But it wasn't until the 1950s, when TV became a mass medium, that the commercial became a ubiquitous feature of popular culture. Before viewers had the technology to fast-forward through commercials, many probably regarded TV ads as annoying, occasionally informative or entertaining, but generally unnecessary accompaniments to their television experience. But of course, the commercial is not simply an extraneous byproduct of TV programming. It is television's very reason for existence. Before the age of public TV and of cable and satellite providers, television programs were financed entirely by the companies that created the commercials and that paid networks and local stations to broadcast them. Viewed from a marketing angle, the only purpose of commercial television is to provide a medium for advertising. The news, comedy, drama, game, and variety shows offered by TV are simply ways of luring viewers to watch the commercials.

Still, the unceasing deluge of commercials of every type means that advertisers have to figure out ways of making their messages stand out by being unusually creative, funny, surprising, or otherwise noteworthy.

The standard jingles, primitive animation, catch-phrases ("Winston tastes good like a cigarette should"), and problem-solution mini-dramas of TV commercials work for awhile but are quickly forgotten in the onslaught of new messages. It becomes the job of advertising agencies (of the type represented in *Mad Men*) that create both print and TV ads to make their clients' products stand out by ever more ingenious and striking ways of delivering their messages. To do this, these agencies rely not just on information about the product and clever audiovisual techniques; they attempt to respond to what they believe consumers crave, deep down. TV commercials, no less than print ads, rely on psychological appeals of the type discussed by Jib Fowles in his "Fifteen Basic Appeals."

The following portfolio includes some of the most noteworthy and successful TV commercials of the past sixty years. Many (though not all) of these commercials are featured in Bernice Kanner's *The 100 Best TV Commercials . . . and Why They Worked* (1999), where you will find additional description and commentary. To access the commercials, go to YouTube (YouTube.com), and enter the search terms provided under the commercial's title into the search box. In some cases, additional information is presented, in brackets, to help you navigate to the commercial. In cases where multiple versions of the same commercial are available, you may have to experiment to determine which one offers the best video and audio quality. In a few cases, uploaded commercials have been truncated, so you should generally select the longest version. In some cases, the indicated commercials may have been removed from the YouTube website. No matter; thousands more remain available for your observation and consideration.

As with the print ads, we provide two or three sets of specific questions for each TV commercial. These questions are intended to stimulate your thinking and writing process about the particular ways that the audio and visuals are intended to work. As you review these commercials, however, you might be thinking of the more general questions about advertisements raised by the preceding readings in the chapter. Here are some of those general questions:

1. What appears to be the target audience for this TV commercial? If it was produced more than two decades ago, how would this target audience likely react today to the ad?

2. What is the primary appeal made by the ad, in terms of Fowles's categories? What, if any, are the secondary appeals?

3. What is the chief attention-getting technique in the commercial?

4. How does the commercial make use of such tools as humor, surprise, fantasy, wonder, human interest, or social concern to achieve its goals?

5. What is the relationship between the visuals and the audio track? How do audio and video work together—or in contrast—to achieve the sponsor's purpose?

6. How do the commercial's visual techniques work to convey the message? Consider camera movement (or the lack of camera movement); the style and pace of editing (the juxtaposition of individual shots); and visual composition (the framing of the people and/or objects within the shot).

7. How do the expressions, the clothing, the postures of the person or people, and the physical objects in the shots help communicate the ad's message?

8. How do the words used by the actor(s) or by the voice-over narrator work to communicate the message of the commercial?

   Consider, also, the following evaluative questions[1]:

   - Is it a good ad? Why?
   - What do you like most about it? Why?
   - What do you dislike the most? Why?
   - Do you think it "works"? Why? Or Why not?
   - How could the ad be improved?
   - Could the sender have conveyed the same message using other strategies, other persuasive means? If so, explain.
   - Even if you don't believe that this particular ad works or persuades you, is there anything in the ad that still affects you or persuades you indirectly?
   - Does the ad have effects on you perhaps not intended by its creators?

[1]Lars Thoger Christensen, "How to Analyze an Advertisement." University of Southern Denmark—Odense. Jan. 2004. <http://wms-soros.mngt.waikato.ac.nz/NR/rdonlyres/ebabzr4hzmg5fr5p45ypc53mdvuxva5wxhe7323onb4ylelbaq3se5xjrslfc4mi3qg k6dmsx5dqbp/Advertisinganalysis.doc>

Note: Because Web content frequently changes without warning, not all of the listed videos may be available when you attempt to access them. It is possible that errant searches may lead to other videos with objectionable content. Such videos, as well as user-submitted comments under the specified videos below, do not reflect the views of the authors or of Pearson Publishing.

COMMERCIALS OF THE 1960S

Volkswagen: Snowplow

12 *YouTube Search Terms: vw snow plow commercial* [select black and white version]

   a. In the 1960s Volkswagen became famous in the United States not only for its funny-looking cars—so different in style from Detroit's massive passenger vehicles—but also for its "soft-sell" approach to print ads and TV commercials. How does that soft-sell approach work in this ad? What is the sales strategy, as embodied in the relatively primitive visuals and the voice-over track? What exactly is being sold?

   b. The closing shot of this commercial shows a snowplow driving past a Volkswagen. How does this image encapsulate the message of this ad? Write a sentence that expresses the message Volkswagen wants to communicate, without regard to the particular visuals of this ad.

Union Carbide: Chick

13 *YouTube Search Terms: union carbide chick*

   a. Based on the opening image, what is the essential psychological appeal (see Jib Fowles) of this ad?

   b. How does the visual (the commercial is unusual in consisting of a single, continuous shot) work *with* and work *against* the soundtrack voice-over? To what extent do you "hear" the narrator's voice—and his message—as you watch the image of the metal box in the beaker of boiling water? To what extent is there a danger that this commercial could backfire and create bad feeling about Union Carbide because of what is portrayed?

Alka Seltzer: Spicy Meatball

14 *YouTube Search Terms: alka seltzer meatball*

   a. Some TV commercials employ a "fake-out" strategy, based partially on our knowledge of other commercials. How does this approach work in the Alka Seltzer ad? Do you think it is likely to succeed in persuading viewers to buy the product?

   b. Like many successful TV commercials, this one relies on humor, grounded in human foibles and imperfections, and based on our experience that if things can go wrong, they generally will. How do the visuals and the audio track of the Alka Seltzer ad employ this kind of humor as a sales strategy?

COMMERCIALS OF THE 1970S

Chanel No. 5: Share the Fantasy

15 *YouTube Search Terms: Chanel 5 fantasy*

a. In many ways, this celebrated commercial—directed by filmmaker Ridley Scott (*Alien, Blade Runner, Thelma and Louise, Gladiator*)—is, stylistically, at the opposite pole from the gritty Volkswagen "Snowplow" commercial. Comment.

b. Chanel No. 5 is one of those products sold primarily on its "mystique." How do the visuals and the soundtrack of this commercial reinforce that mystique? "Read" the images and interpret them, in light of the product.

c. In terms of Fowles's categories, what are the central appeals of this ad?

Quaker Oats: Mikey

16 *YouTube Search Terms: quaker oats mikey*

a. Why don't the older kids want to try Life cereal? How does reluctance tie into Quaker Oats's larger marketing problem with the product? How does the commercial attempt to deal with this problem?

b. Many viewers came to hate this commercial because it was shown repeatedly and because it lasted so many years. Still, it endured because many other viewers found it endearing—and it did the job of publicizing the product. Do you think a commercial like this would work today? Explain.

Coca-Cola: Mean Joe Green

17 *YouTube Search Terms: coca cola joe green*

a. This commercial is a study in contrasts. Identify some of these contrasts (both visual and aural), and explain how they work as part of the sales strategy.

b. To what emotions does this commercial attempt to appeal? Did you find this appeal successful?

c. Like many commercials, this one is presented as a minidrama, complete with plot, character, setting, theme, and other elements found in longer dramas. Explain the way that the drama functions in this ad, particularly as it concerns the characterization of the two actors.

COMMERCIALS OF THE 1980S

Federal Express (FedEx): Fast-Paced World [with John Moschitta]

18 *YouTube Search Terms: federal express fast talker*

a. The actor in this commercial, John Moschitta, was for many years celebrated in the *Guinness Book of World Records* as the world's fastest talker (he was clocked at 586 words per minute). How does Moschitta's unique skill make him an ideal spokesperson for Federal Express?

b. There is always a danger that particularly striking ads may be counterproductive, in that they draw attention to their own cleverness or unusual stylistic qualities, rather than to the product being sold. Put yourself in the position of a Federal Express executive. To what extent might you be concerned that this commercial, clever as it is, would not succeed in making more people select Federal Express as their express delivery service? On the other hand, might any striking commercial for Federal Express be successful if it heightened public recognition of the brand?

Pepsi-Cola: Archaeology

19 *YouTube Search Terms: pepsi cola archaeology*
a. Summarize the main selling point of this commercial. How does this selling point relate to (1) the basic situation presented in the commercial and (2) Pepsi's slogan, as it appears at the end?

b. Pepsi-Cola and Coca-Cola have been engaged in fierce rivalry for more than a century. How does this commercial exploit that rivalry to humorous effect? How is each product visually represented in the ad?

c. As contrasted with the Volkswagen "Snowplow" ad or the Quaker Oats "Mikey" ad, this ad features lavish production values and is presented as if it were a science fiction film. How do the sets, costumes, props, and special effects help support the overall sales strategy of the ad?

Levi's: Launderette

20 *YouTube Search Terms: levi's laundrette*
a. What is the primary appeal of this British ad (in Jib Fowles's terms)? Do you think it is directed primarily to men or primarily to women? Explain.

b. How do the reactions of the various characters in this ad to the young man contribute to its overall effect? How does the young man's appearance figure into the overall effect?

c. What role does the musical track (Marvin Gaye's "I Heard It Through The Grapevine") play in this commercial?

COMMERCIALS OF THE 1990s

Jeep: Snow Covered

21 *YouTube Search Terms: jeep snow covered*
a. "This may have been the most arrogant commercial ever made," declared the creative director of the agency that produced it. In what way might this be so? Possible arrogance aside, is this an effective advertisement for Jeep? Explain.

b. How do the visuals support the message of the ad? What *is* that message?

c. Which appeals are most evident in this commercial?

Energizer: Darth Vader

22 *YouTube Search Terms: energizer darth vader*

a. The Energizer bunny was featured in numerous commercials of the 1990s, generally in settings where its sudden appearance was totally unexpected. How do the creators of this add draw upon the *Star Wars* mythology to support their sales pitch? In what way is the strategy of this ad similar to that of Alka Seltzer's "Spicy Meatball"?

b. In a sentence, summarize the message of this ad—without mentioning *Star Wars* or Darth Vader.

Got Milk? (California Milk Processor Board): Aaron Burr [Original Got Milk? Commercial]

23 *YouTube Search Terms: got milk burr*

a. The opening of this commercial is intended to convey a sense of culture and sophistication. How do the images and the soundtrack do this? Why is this "setup" necessary in terms of the ad's message? What is that message?

b. In the latter half of the commercial, how does the accelerated pace of the editing and camera work—and of the soundtrack—contribute to the ad's overall impact?

COMMERCIALS OF THE 2000S

The Gap: Pardon Our Dust

24 *YouTube Search Terms: gap dust*

a. This commercial was directed by filmmaker Spike Jonze (*Adaptation, Where the Wild Things Are*). Describe your reactions as you watched this ad. What did you think was happening as the mayhem within the store accelerated? What is the effect of the "Pardon Our Dust" title when it appears? What is the relationship of the prior visuals and the soundtrack (including the music of Grieg's "In the Hall of the Mountain King") to the last two titles?

b. In Jib Fowles's terms ("Fifteen Basic Appeals"), to what desires is this commercial intended to appeal?

c. According to the Web site "Top 10 Coolest Commercials by Movie Directors," Spike Jonze was asked by Gap executives to produce a commercial about the stores' new look. Bewildered by what Jonze delivered, the company ran the commercial in a few cities, then pulled it off the air after about a month. Did the company make the right decision (from a marketing standpoint)?

Honda: Physics

25 *YouTube Search Terms: honda physics*

a. Put yourself in the position of the ad agency copywriters for Honda *before* they conceived of this particular ad. What is your main selling point? Express, in a sentence, what you want to communicate to the public about Honda automobiles and engineering.

b. This commercial involves no computer graphics or digital tricks: everything that happens is real. All the components we see came from the disassembling of two Honda Accords. (The voice is that of *Lake Woebegon Days* author Garrison Keillor.) According to Honda, this single continuous shot required 606 takes—meaning that for the first 605 takes, something, usually minor, went wrong, and the recording team had to install the set up again and again. There is always a danger (for the client) that memorable commercials like this will amaze and impress viewers but will also fail to implant brand identification in their minds. Do you think there may be such a problem with this commercial? To what extent are viewers who have seen it likely, days or weeks later, to identify it with Honda and to associate whatever message (if any) they draw from the commercial with the particular qualities of Honda automobiles?

Sony Bravia: Bunnies

26 *YouTube Search Terms: sony bunnies*

a. Some of the same visual techniques used in this ad (to portray an unstoppable swarm of creatures that speedily overrun an urban area) have also been used—to very different effect—in horror films. What mood is conveyed—and how—by the visual and soundtrack elements of this commercial?

b. To what consumer desires (refer to Jib Fowles's categories) is this commercial designed to appeal?

c. Discuss how some of the visual techniques and special effects of this ad contribute to its effectiveness in conveying the benefits of the Sony Bravia.

Dove: Onslaught

27 *YouTube Search Terms: dove onslaught*

a. What is the message of this ad? How does the cinematic style of the visuals reinforce that message? Focus, in particular, on the contrasting visual styles used for the child and (later in the ad) her classmates, on the one hand, and the rest of the images, on the other. Consider, for example, how long the first image remains on screen, compared to those that follow.

   b. How many of Jib Fowles's fifteen basic appeals do you detect at work
      in this ad? How do these appeals work to convey the essential contrast
      of values underlying the ad?

Tide to Go: Interview

㉘ *YouTube Search Terms: tide to go interview*
   a. What is the message of this ad? How do the simple visuals and the
      more complex soundtrack work together (and against one another) to
      support that idea? How does that idea relate to one or more of
      Fowles's fifteen basic appeals?

   b. Like many contemporary TV ads, this one relies on humor. To what
      extent do you find humor used effectively here? What is the source
      of the humor? How do the two actors help create that humor? How
      is this humor rooted in common concerns and fears that we all
      share?

Planters Peanuts: Perfume

㉙ *YouTube Search Terms: planters perfume*
   a. Many of the elements in this ad are also found in perfume commercials.
      How are these elements used here to comic effect? Compare the mood
      and the visual style of this ad to that of a real perfume ad, the Chanel
      No. 5 "Share the Fantasy" commercial. Of what other commercials does
      this one remind you? Why?

   b. Like the Gap "Pardon Our Dust" commercial, the Planter's ad relies on
      the visual motif of comic mayhem. Do you think such visuals are an
      effective way of selling the product? Explain.

ADDITIONAL TV COMMERCIALS

Note: Unless otherwise indicated, all commercials listed were produced in the
United States.

Democratic National Committee: "Daisy Girl" (1964)
   YouTube Search Terms: democratic daisy ad

American Tourister Luggage: Gorilla (1969)
   YouTube Search Terms: luggage gorilla

Chevrolet: "Baseball, Hot Dogs, Apple Pie" (1969)
   YouTube Search Terms: america baseball hotdogs

Keep America Beautiful: "Crying Indian" (1970)
   YouTube Search Terms: America crying indian

Coca Cola: "Hilltop" ("I'd Like to Buy the World a Coke") (1971)
   YouTube Search Terms: buy world coke 1971

Hovis: "Bike Ride" (UK, 1973) [shot by Ridley Scott]
   YouTube Search Terms: hovis bike

Xerox: "Monks" (1975)
   YouTube Search Terms: xerox monks

Hebrew National: "Higher Authority" (1975)
   YouTube Search Terms: hebrew national higher

Basf: "Dear John" (New Zealand, 1979)
   Search Terms: basf dear john

Lego: "Kipper" (UK, 1980)
   YouTube Search Terms: lego kipper

Apple: Macintosh (1984)
   YouTube Search Terms: apple macintosh

Sony Trinitron: "Lifespan" (UK, 1984)
   YouTube Search Terms: sony trinitron advert

American Express: "Stephen King: (1984)
   YouTube Search Terms: american express king

The Guardian: "Points of View" (UK, 1987)
   YouTube Search Terms: guardian points of view

Volkswagen: "Changes" (UK, 1988)
   YouTube Search Terms: vw changes

Energizer: "Bunny Introduction" (1989)
   YouTube Search Terms: energizer bunny introduction 1989

Dunlop: "Tested for the Unexpected" (1993)
   YouTube Search Terms: dunlop tested unexpected

Swedish Televerket: "Noxin" (Sweden, 1993)
   YouTube Search Terms: Noxin

Little Caesar's Pizza: "Training Camp" (1994)
   YouTube Search Terms: caesar's training camp

Campbell's Soup: Winter Commercial (1995)
   YouTube Search Terms: campbell's soup winter

California Milk Processor Board: "Got Milk? Heaven" (1996)
   YouTube Search Terms: got milk heaven

Ameriquest Mortgage: "Plane Ride" (2008)
   YouTube Search Terms: ameriquest plane ride

Audi: "Oil Parade" (2009)
   YouTube Search Terms: audi oil parade

Blue Water Bridge
Port Huron, MI

21

What Is a Rebuttal?

T HERE ARE TWO BASIC APPROACHES TO REBUTTING AN ARGUMENT: YOU CAN REFUTE THE ARGUMENT, OR YOU CAN COUNTERARGUE. IN THE FIRST CASE, **REFUTATION**, YOU DEMONSTRATE THE SHORT-COMINGS OF THE ARGUMENT YOU WISH TO DISCREDIT, AND YOU may or may not offer a positive claim of your own. In the second case, **counterargument**, you focus on the strengths of the position you support,

Whaling is an ancient form of hunting that greatly expanded in the nineteenth century due to a worldwide demand for whale oil. By 1986 the worldwide whale populations were so seriously depleted that the International Whaling Committee banned commercial whaling to allow whale populations to replenish. Limited whaling continues for scientific research, but environmental organizations such as Greenpeace insist that "science" is a guise for the continuation of commercial whaling. Greenpeace protests all whaling vigorously—both by peaceful means and by open ocean confrontations with whaling vessels. Could their protests at sea be considered a rebuttal argument?

and spend little time on the specifics of the argument you are countering. There can be substantial overlap between these two tactics, and good rebuttal arguments often employ both refutation and counterargument.

Because they focus on the shortcomings in the opposition's argument, a refutation argument often takes much of its structure from the argument being refuted.

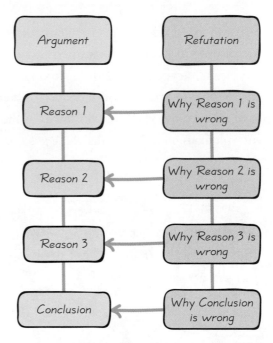

Many college students believe that using technology to "multitask" makes them more productive, believing that studying, texting a friend, and listening to music all at once is an efficient use of their time. But research shows that engaging in multiple tasks is distracting, interferes with memory, and makes it difficult to switch from one task to another, making multitaskers less productive than people focusing on one task at a time.

Counterarguments more often take up ideas the opposing claims has not addressed at all, or they take a very different approach to the problem. By largely ignoring the specifics of the argument being countered, they make the implicit claim that the counterargument is superior.

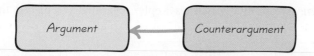

Those who argue for tariffs on goods from China claim that tariffs will protect American manufacturing jobs, but tariffs are a bad idea because they would increase prices on clothing, furniture, toys, and other consumer goods for everyone, and would cause the loss of retailing jobs as well.

Recognize Kinds of Rebuttal Arguments

REFUTATION

A refutation can either challenge the assumptions underlying a claim, or it can question the evidence supporting a claim. Until about five hundred years ago, people believed that the sky, and everything in it, moved, while the Earth remained still. They observed the stars moving from west to east in a regular, circular motion, and concluded that all the heavenly bodies orbited around an axis between Earth and Polaris, the northern star. This theory, however, did not explain the movement of the planets. If you watch the path of Mars over several nights, for example, you will notice that it moves, like the stars, from east to west. But occasionally, it will appear to move backward, from west to east, before reversing itself and resuming an east-to-west course. This phenomenon is called retrograde motion, and it is exhibited by all the planets in our solar system. In fact, our word *planet* derives from the Greek term *planetes*, meaning "wanderer." The ancient Greeks assumed that the planets and stars orbited the Earth, but that the planets sometimes wandered from their paths.

In the second century CE, the Greek astronomer Ptolemy made precise and detailed observations of the planets and created a model to predict their retrograde motion. In his treatise, the *Almagest*, he theorized that Mars and the other "wanderers" periodically deviated from their path around the Earth, making small circles, or epicycles, before moving on again. It was a complicated system, but it predicted the movements of the planets very accurately, and so it went unchallenged for over a thousand years.

In the early sixteenth century, the Polish astronomer Nicolaus Copernicus recognized that Ptolemy's observations could be explained more simply if the Earth and other planets circled the Sun. Copernicus's theory, later confirmed by the German astronomer Johannes Kepler, eventually replaced the Ptolemaic model of the solar system as the accepted explanation for observed planetary motion.

Copernicus did not question Ptolemy's evidence—the data he had collected showing where the stars and planets appear in the sky to an Earth-bound observer. Instead, he questioned Ptolemy's central assumption that Earth is the center of the solar system. Because evidence of the planet's retrograde motion had been observed by people over such a long period of time, it was unlikely to be wrong. Instead, it was the theory Ptolemy constructed to explain his data that was incorrect.

But sometimes evidence is wrong. Sometimes, too, evidence is incomplete or not representative, and sometimes counterevidence can be found. People who are bent on persuading others may leave out information that weakens their case, or employ evidence in questionable ways to try to bolster their claims. Dermatologists argue that indoor tanning is harmful to people's health because it exposes them to ultraviolet radiation, a known cause of cancer. The tanning industry, not surprisingly, disagrees, arguing that indoor tanning is safer than outdoor tanning because it assures safe levels of UV radiation exposure. While sunbathers often get sunburned, indoor tanners only get safe levels of radiation. This is an intriguing claim, but the AMA has discovered that in fact people who use tanning beds *do* get burned—as many of 50 percent of them. The tanning industry also claims indoor tanning provides people with a "protective" tan that reduces the amount of harmful UV radiation they absorb when they do go out in the sun. Doctors counter this claim by pointing out that a "base tan" provides only as much protection as a sunblock with a Sun Protection Factor, or SPF, of 3, and that the minimum recommended SPF for sunscreen is 15. The protection offered by an indoor tan is minimal at best. Both sides continue to argue over what evidence is valid, and accurate, when assessing the safety of indoor tanning.

COUNTERARGUMENT

Another way to rebut is to counterargue. In a counterargument, you might acknowledge an opposing point of view, but you might not consider it in detail. Rather, you put the main effort into your own argument. A counterarguer, in effect, says, "I hear your argument. But there is more to it than that. Now listen while I explain why another position is stronger." Counterargument is an effective way of persuading audiences, but sometimes it is used as a way to avoid addressing opposing views honestly. People's tendency to be persuaded by counterargument also makes them susceptible to red herrings, when an irrelevant but dramatic detail is put forward as if it were important, or *ad hominem* attacks, where someone makes spurious accusations about an opponent instead of engaging in real debate.

The counterarguer depends on the wisdom of his or her audience members to hear all sides of an issue and make up their own minds about the merits of the case. In the following short poem, Wilfred Owen, a veteran of the horrors of World War I trench warfare, offers a counterargument to those who argue that war is noble, to those who believe along with the poet Horace that "dulce et decorum est pro patria mori"—that it is sweet and fitting to die for one's country. This poem gains in popularity whenever there is an unpopular war for it rebuts the belief that it is noble to die for one's country in modern warfare.

Dulce Et Decorum Est

Bent double, like old beggars under sacks,
Knock-kneed, coughing like hags, we cursed through sludge,
Till on the haunting flares we turned our backs
And towards our distant rest began to trudge.
Men marched asleep. Many had lost their boots
But limped on, blood-shod. All went lame; all blind;
Drunk with fatigue; deaf even to the hoots
Of tired, outstripped Five-Nines that dropped behind.

Gas! Gas! Quick, boys! — An ecstasy of fumbling,
Fitting the clumsy helmets just in time;
But someone still was yelling out and stumbling,
And flound'ring like a man in fire or lime . . .
Dim, through the misty panes and thick green light,
As under a green sea, I saw him drowning.
In all my dreams, before my helpless sight,
He plunges at me, guttering, choking, drowning.

If in some smothering dreams you too could pace
Behind the wagon that we flung him in,
And watch the white eyes writhing in his face,
His hanging face, like a devil's sick of sin;
If you could hear, at every jolt, the blood
Come gargling from the froth-corrupted lungs,
Obscene as cancer, bitter as the cud
Of vile, incurable sores on innocent tongues,
My friend, you would not tell with such high zest
To children ardent for some desperate glory,
The old Lie; Dulce et Decorum est
Pro patria mori.

Owen does not summarize the argument in favor of being willing to die for one's country and then refute that argument point by point. Rather, his poem presents an opposing argument, supported by a narrative of the speaker's experience in a poison-gas attack, that he hopes will more than counterbalance what he calls "the old Lie." Owen simply ignores the reasons people give for being willing to die for one's country and argues instead that there are good reasons not to do so. And he hopes that the evidence he summons for his position will outweigh for his audience (addressed as "My friend,") the evidence in support of the other side.

Rebuttal arguments frequently offer both refutation and counterargument. Like attorneys engaged in a trial, people writing rebuttals must make their own cases based on good reasons and hard evidence, but they also do what they can to undermine their opponent's case. In the end the jury—the audience—decides.

Build a Rebuttal Argument

As you prepare to rebut an argument, look closely at what your opponent says. What exactly are the claims? What is the evidence? What are the assumptions? What do you disagree with? Are there parts you agree with? Are there assumptions you share? Do you agree that the evidence is accurate?

Knowing where you agree with someone helps you focus your rebuttal on differences. Having points of agreement can also help you build credibility with your audience, if you acknowledge that your opponent makes some logical points, or makes reasonable assumptions.

Consider using counterargument if you generally agree with a claim but do not think it goes far enough, if you feel an argument proposes the wrong solution to a problem, or if you think that, while accurate, it misses the "big picture." Counterargument lets you frame your own, stronger take on the question at hand without spending a lot of time trying to find flaws in the opposing position when there may not be many there.

If you do have serious objections to an argument, plan to refute it, and start by looking for the most important differences in your respective positions. What are the biggest "red flags" in the argument you disagree with? What are the weakest points of your opponent's argument? What are the strongest points of your own? You will probably want to highlight these differences in your rebuttal. You may find many problems with evidence and logic, in which case you will probably want to prioritize them. You do not necessarily need to point out the flaws in every single element of an argument. Direct your audience to the ones that matter the most.

You can also use counterargument in combination with refutation, first showing why an existing argument is wrong, and then offering an alternative. This is one of the more common forms of rebuttal. As you examine your opponent's claims and evidence, look closely for fallacies and faulty logic. How do these distort the problem or lead the audience to mistaken conclusions? Pointing them out to your readers will strengthen your position.

Look too at sources. Check your opponent's facts. Scrutinize the experts he or she relies on. And consider the purpose and motivation behind arguments you rebut. Groups funded by major industries, political parties, and special interest groups may have hidden or not-so-hidden agendas driving the arguments they make. Pointing these out to your readers can strengthen your own position.

CAN THE WEB BE TRUSTED FOR RESEARCH?

Most Web users are familiar with the huge and immensely popular Wikipedia, the online encyclopedia. What makes Wikipedia so different from traditional, print encyclopedias is that entries can be contributed or edited by anyone.

In 2007, Jimmy Wales, president of Wikimedia and one of its founders, debated the legitimacy of Wikipedia with Dale Hoiberg, editor-in-chief of *Encyclopedia Britannica.* Hoiberg's main criticism of Wikipedia is that its structure—an open-source wiki without the formal editorial control that shapes traditional, print encyclopedias—allows for inaccurate entries.

In response, Wales argues that *Britannica* and newspapers also contain errors, but Wikipedia has the advantage that they are easily corrected. Furthermore, he asserts that Wikipedia's policy of using volunteer administrators to delete irrelevant entries and requiring authors of entries to cite reliable, published sources ensures quality. Nonetheless, some universities including UCLA and the University of Pennsylvania along with many instructors strongly discourage and even ban students from citing Wikipedia in their work. (Wikipedia also cautions against using its entries as a primary source for serious research.)

1. If your college decided to ban the use of Wikipedia as a reference because it lacked the authority of a traditional encyclopedia, would you want to challenge it? Why or why not?

2. If you chose to challenge the college's policy, how would you do so? Would it be effective to refute the college's claims point by point, noting fallacies in logic and reasoning? Would it be effective to build a counterargument in which you examine the assumptions on which the college's claims are based? Which strategy would you choose, and why?

STEPS TO WRITING A REBUTTAL ARGUMENT

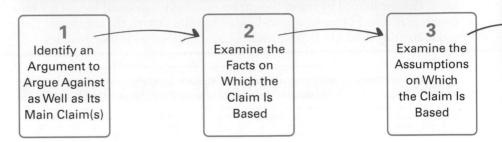

1 Identify an Argument to Argue Against as Well as Its Main Claim(s)

2 Examine the Facts on Which the Claim Is Based

3 Examine the Assumptions on Which the Claim Is Based

● **STEP 1 IDENTIFY AN ARGUMENT TO ARGUE AGAINST AS WELL AS ITS MAIN CLAIM(S)**

- What exactly are you arguing against?
- Are there secondary claims attached to the main claim?
- Include a fair summary of your opponent's position in your finished rebuttal.

EXAMPLES

- Arguing against raising taxes for the purpose of building a new sports stadium (examine how proponents claim that a new sports facility will benefit the local economy).
- Arguing for raising the minimum wage (examine how opponents claim that a higher minimum wage isn't necessary and negatively affects small-business owners).

● **STEP 2 EXAMINE THE FACTS ON WHICH THE CLAIM IS BASED**

- Are the facts accurate, current, and representative?
- Is there another body of facts that you can present as counterevidence?
- If the author uses statistics, can the statistics be interpreted differently?
- If the author quotes from sources, how reliable are those sources?
- Are the sources treated fairly, or are quotations taken out of context?

● **STEP 3 EXAMINE THE ASSUMPTIONS ON WHICH THE CLAIM IS BASED**

- What are the primary and secondary assumptions of the claim you are rejecting?
- How are those assumptions flawed?
- Does the author resort to name calling, use faulty reasoning, or ignore key facts?

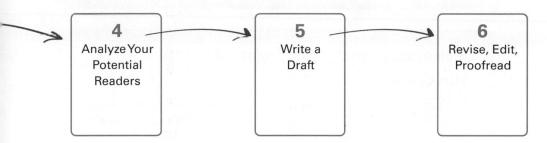

- **STEP 4 ANALYZE YOUR POTENTIAL READERS**
  - To what extent do your potential readers support the claim that you are rejecting?
  - If they strongly support that claim, how might you appeal to them to change their minds?
  - What common assumptions and beliefs do you share with them?

- **STEP 5 WRITE A DRAFT**

INTRODUCTION

Identify the issue and the argument you are rejecting.

- Provide background if the issue is unfamiliar to most of your readers.
- Give a quick summary of the competing positions even if the issue is familiar to your readers.
- Make your aim clear in your thesis statement.

BODY

Take on the argument that you are rejecting. Consider questioning the evidence that is used to support the argument by doing one or more of the following.

- Challenge the facts and the currency and relevance of examples.
- Present counterevidence and countertestimony.
- Challenge the credibility of sources cited.
- Question the way in which statistical evidence is presented and interpreted.
- Argue that quotations are taken out of context.

CONCLUSION

- Conclude on a firm note by underscoring your objections.
- Consider closing with a counterargument or counterproposal.

- **STEP 6 REVISE, EDIT, PROOFREAD**

READINGS

Minneapolis Pornography Ordinance

Ellen Goodman

Just a couple of months before the pool-table gang rape in New Bedford, Mass., *Hustler* magazine printed a photo feature that reads like a blueprint for the actual crime. There were just two differences between *Hustler* and real life. In *Hustler,* the woman enjoyed it. In real life, the woman charged rape.

There is no evidence that the four men charged with this crime had actually read the magazine. Nor is there evidence that the spectators who yelled encouragement for two hours had held previous ringside seats at pornographic events. But there is a growing sense that the violent pornography being peddled in this country helps to create an atmosphere in which such events occur.

As recently as last month, a study done by two University of Wisconsin researchers suggested that even "normal" men, prescreened college students, were changed by their exposure to violent pornography. After just ten hours of viewing, reported researcher Edward Donnerstein, "the men were less likely to convict in a rape trial, less likely to see injury to a victim, more likely to see the victim as responsible." Pornography may not cause rape directly, he said, "but it maintains a lot of very callous attitudes. It justifies aggression. It even says you are doing a favor to the victim."

If we can prove that pornography is harmful, then shouldn't the victims have legal rights? This, in any case, is the theory behind a city ordinance that recently passed the Minneapolis City Council. Vetoed by the mayor last week, it is likely to be back before the Council for an overriding vote, likely to appear in other cities, other towns. What is unique about the Minneapolis approach is that for the first time it attacks pornography, not because of nudity or sexual explicitness, but because it degrades and harms women. It opposes pornography on the basis of sex discrimination.

5   University of Minnesota Law Professor Catherine MacKinnon, who co-authored the ordinance with feminist writer Andrea Dworkin, says that they chose this tactic because they believe that pornography is central to "creating and maintaining the inequality of the sexes. . . . Just being a woman means you are injured by pornography."

They defined pornography carefully as, "the sexually explicit subordination of women, graphically depicted, whether in pictures or in words." To fit their legal definition it must also include one of nine conditions that show this subordination, like presenting women who "experience sexual pleasure in being raped or . . . mutilated. . . . " Under this law, it would be possible for a pool-table rape victim to sue *Hustler*. It would be possible for a woman to sue if she were forced to act in a pornographic movie. Indeed, since the law describes pornography as oppressive to all women, it would be possible for any woman to sue those who traffic in the stuff for violating her civil rights.

In many ways, the Minneapolis ordinance is an appealing attack on an appalling problem. The authors have tried to resolve a long and bubbling conflict among those who have both a deep aversion to pornography and a deep loyalty to the value of free speech. "To date," says Professor MacKinnon, "people have identified the pornographer's freedom with everybody's freedom. But we're saying that the freedom of the pornographer is the subordination of women. It means one has to take a side."

But the sides are not quite as clear as Professor MacKinnon describes them. Nor is the ordinance.

Even if we accept the argument that pornography is harmful to women—and I do—then we must also recognize that anti-Semitic literature is harmful to Jews and racist literature is harmful to blacks. For that matter, Marxist literature may be harmful to government policy. It isn't just women versus pornographers. If women win the right to sue publishers and producers, then so could Jews, blacks, and a long list of people who may be able to prove they have been harmed by books, movies, speeches or even records. The Manson murders, you may recall, were reportedly inspired by the Beatles.

10   We might prefer a library or book store or lecture hall without *Mein Kampf* or the Grand Whoever of the Ku Klux Klan. But a growing list of harmful expressions would inevitably strangle freedom of speech.

This ordinance was carefully written to avoid problems of banning and prior restraint, but the right of any woman to claim damages from pornography is just too broad. It seems destined to lead to censorship.

What the Minneapolis City Council has before it is a very attractive theory. What MacKinnon and Dworkin have written is a very persuasive and useful definition of pornography. But they haven't yet resolved the conflict between the harm of pornography and the value of free speech. In its present form, this is still a shaky piece of law.

Crossing the Line

Dan Stein

Dan Stein is president of the Federation for American Immigration Reform, a Washington D.C.-based nonprofit organization that seeks to stop illegal immigration. He frequently speaks and writes about immigration issues. He published "Crossing the Line" in the Los Angeles Business Journal *in February 2007.*

Stein uses a fact from a respected polling agency to bolster his assumption that the majority of Americans strongly oppose illegal immigration.

2

The timing could not have been worse for Bank of America to announce that it would begin issuing credit cards to illegal aliens in Los Angeles. News of Bank of America's decision was published in the *Wall Street Journal* on February 13, the same day that a new Harris Poll revealed that Americans perceive the two greatest threats to their security to be illegal immigration and the outsourcing of American jobs.

Even more than the prospect of the Iranians or the North Koreans with nukes, Americans believe that their security is threatened by millions of people pouring across our borders and by corporations that appear willing to sell out the interests of American workers. In one decision, Bank of America managed to pluck two raw nerves by appearing to encourage illegal immigration, while sending the message that it would not let any national interest stand in the way of it making a buck.

3

Stein connects his argument to other issues his audience is likely to relate to.

The Bank of America decision and the overwhelming negative public reaction to it illustrates the growing disconnect between the elite and everyone else in this country. To the elite—including the current occupant of the White House—the traditional idea of the nation has become a bothersome anachronism. To the extent that the entity known as the United States has any relevance at all to them, it is to secure their ability to conduct business and maximize their corporate bottom lines. Concepts of patriotism and loyalty are marketing tools and nothing more.

4

To Bank of America and other large corporations, illegal immigrants are a source of low wage labor and an untapped customer market. It matters not that illegal immigrants are breaking the laws of the United States, taking jobs from and driving down wages for middle class workers, burdening schools (not the ones the children of Bank of America executives attend, of course) and other vital public services. What matters to the banking industry is that the estimated 12 to 15 million illegal aliens living in the United States have purchasing power and that there is money to be made off of serving them.

5

It is true that Bank of America did not create the illegal immigration crisis in the United States, although banking industry decisions to allow illegal aliens to open bank accounts, take out home mortgages and now obtain credit cards has certainly added to the problem. But the fact that the federal government has done little to resolve the problem of illegal immigration does not mean that banks and other business interests have an unfettered right to profit from illegal immigration. Bank of America did not create the illegal drug problem in the United States, but that does not entitle it to market services to the drug cartels, even though it would be enormously profitable to do so.

Stein alludes to the drug industry to assert that corporations' obligation to respect the laws of the country trump their obligation to make a profit.

OVERTLY DISCRIMINATORY

6   The plan to issue credit cards to illegal aliens is also overtly discriminatory, giving a new meaning to their corporate slogan: "Bank of America, Higher Standards" (for some). While American citizens and legal U.S. residents are held to one standard in order to obtain credit, illegal aliens will be held to a lower standard. The plastic that any of us tote around in our wallets required us to open our entire lives to our creditors and to provide verification of our identities and credit-worthiness. In their hunger to make money off of illegal aliens Bank of America is prepared to accept easily counterfeited Mexican matricula cards as proof of identity, and maintaining a checking account for three months as a credit history.

7   Bank of America has obviously felt the sting of a public backlash, as evidenced by their sudden reluctance to discuss it in the media. Some people have gone so far as to pull their accounts out of Bank of America. But given the consolidation of the banking industry generally, and the fact that a handful of banks have corner on the credit card market, it will require government action to stop financial institutions from pursuing profits in blatant disregard of the law and the public interest.

8   Existing federal law clearly prohibits "encouraging or inducing unauthorized aliens to enter the United States, and engaging in a conspiracy or aiding and abetting" people who violate U.S. immigration laws. Products and services specifically marketed to illegal aliens, intended to make it easier to live and work in the U.S. illegally, violates the spirit if not the letter of the law.

Stein uses refutation heavily in his rebuttal, never straying too far from the issue: the legality and morality of Bank of America's new policy.

9   To Bank of America, illegal aliens are just customers and the United States nothing more than a market. To the American people, illegal immigration and corporate greed are seen as serious threats to their security. Bank of America has provided the proof that both are inexorably intertwined.

Stein summarizes his thesis in the conclusion.

Illegal Immigrants—They're Money

Gregory Rodriguez

Gregory Rodriguez is a Los Angeles-based Irvine Senior Fellow at the New America Foundation, a nonpartisan think tank in Washington, D.C. He has written widely about issues of national identity, social cohesion, assimilation, race relations, religion, immigration, demographics, and social and political trends. He published "Illegal Immigrants—They're Money," a rebuttal to Dan Stein's article about the Bank of America, as a column in the Los Angeles Times *on March 4, 2007.*

In paragraphs 2 and 3, Rodriguez defines his vision of the realities of the American dream.

Dan Stein, the premier American nativist and president of the Federation for American Immigration Reform, is shocked, shocked. He's mad at Bank of America for issuing credit cards to illegal immigrants. He says that to Bank of America "and other large corporations, illegal immigrants are a source of low-wage labor and an untapped customer market." You bet they are, and that's the American way.

2   Sure, I'm proud to be a citizen of a nation that portrays itself as a refuge for the "tired," "the poor" and the "huddled masses yearning to breathe free." But let's face it, Emma Lazarus, the poet who wrote those words, may have laid it on a bit thick. The truth, no less beautiful in its way, is a little more crass and self-serving. But it wouldn't have sounded nearly as poetic to say, "bring us your able-bodied, poor, hardworking masses yearning for a chance to climb out of poverty, establish a credit history and . . . ." We all love to rhapsodize about immigrants' embrace of the American dream, but it's more like a hard-nosed American deal— you come here, you work your tail off under grueling conditions, and you can try your damnedest to better your lot over time.

Rodriquez makes a transition to his thesis by pointing out that illegal immigration is a recent construct.

3   In their generational struggle for acceptance and security, from outsider to insider and, dare I say, from exploited to exploiter, immigrants could avail themselves of those inalienable rights that stand at the core of our national political philosophy—life, liberty and the pursuit of happiness.

4   But that, of course, was before the invention of illegal immigration.

5   Until the early 1900s, pretty much anybody who wasn't diseased, a criminal, a prostitute, a pauper, an anarchist or a Chinese laborer could gain entrance to the U.S. Between 1880 and 1914, only 1% of a total of 25 million European immigrants were excluded from this country. But after transatlantic crossings had already been halted by World War I, Congress buckled to anti-foreign sentiment and closed the proverbial Golden Door by passing a series of restrictionist laws in 1917, 1921 and 1924.

6   Yet even as the historical front door of the nation was being closed, business interests were busy prying open a new side-door. Only three months after the passage of the Immigration Act of 1917, which required all newcomers to pass a literacy test and pay a head tax, the U.S. Secretary of Commerce waived the regulations for Mexican workers. Thus began America's dishonorable relationship with Mexican immigrant labor.

7   For the next several decades, Mexican workers were brought in when the economy expanded and kicked out when times got bad. They were recruited in the 1920s, only to be deported in the 1930s. They were brought in again during the labor shortage in the 1940s. By the 1950s, one branch of the government recruited Mexican workers, under the illusion that they were "temporary," while another sought to keep them out.

Rodriquez establishes a longstanding tradition of fairweather treatment of Mexican immigrants by U.S. policy.

8   The *piece de resistance* in the creation of the illegal immigrant is the Immigration Act of 1965. Although touted as a great piece of liberal legislation that ended discriminatory immigration barriers, it imposed an annual cap on migrants from the Western Hemisphere that was 40% less than the number that had been arriving yearly before 1965. A decade later, Congress placed a 20,000 limit per country in this hemisphere.

9   In other words, after importing millions of Mexicans over the decades, particularly during the bracero guest-worker program from 1942 to 1963, and establishing well-trod routes to employment north of the border, the U.S. drastically reduced the number of visas available to Mexicans. This reduction, of course, coincided with a rapid rise in Mexico's population. And guess what? When jobs were available on this side of the border, Mexicans just kept coming, whether they had papers or not.

10   Clearly, today as ever, mass migration to the U.S. is being driven by economic need—the immigrants' and our economy's. But the hard-nosed American deal has become unfair because, on top of the handicaps we have always imposed on new arrivals, we've added a rather brutal one—criminal status. Good luck with that pursuit of happiness as you engage in backbreaking labor when your place in society is summed up with that one cutting word, "illegal."

Rodriguez asserts his thesis in this paragraph.

11   No, I'm not advocating open borders. Nor do I believe that immigrants should be guaranteed anything but a chance to achieve their end of the nation's cruel bargain. For hardworking illegal immigrants who've established roots here, we should uphold our end of the bargain and give them a chance to achieve their piece of the American dream. Bank of America is not wrong to give illegal immigrants the tools with which to compete legitimately in the marketplace. We as a nation are wrong for treating all these people as illegitimate.

Rodriquez addressed Stein only briefly in the introduction and here in the conclusion. Why?

STUDENT MODELS

Why Lawrence Summers Was Wrong: Culture Rather Than Biology
Explains the Underrepresentation of Women in Science
and Mathematics

Julee Christianson (student)

In 2005, Harvard University's president, Lawrence H. Summers, gave a controversial speech that suggested that the underrepresentation of women in tenured positions in math and science departments was partly caused by biological differences. In his address, Summers proposed three hypotheses explaining why women shy away from math and science careers. First, he gave a "high-powered job hypothesis," which stated that women naturally want to start a family and therefore will not have the time or desire to commit to the high-stress workload required for research in math and science. His second hypothesis was that genetic differences between the sexes cause more males than females to have high aptitude for math and science. Lastly, he mentioned the hypothesis that women are underrepresented because of discrimination, but he dismissed discrimination as a significant factor. It was Summers's second hypothesis about biological differences that started a heated national debate. The academic world seems split over this nature/nurture issue. Although there is some evidence that biology plays a role in determining math ability, I argue that culture plays a much larger role, both in the way that women are socialized and in the continued existence of male discrimination against women in male-dominated fields.

Evidence supporting the role of biology in determining math ability is effectively presented by Steven Pinker (2005), a Harvard psychologist who agrees with Summers. In his article "The Science of Difference: Sex Ed," Pinker focuses extensively on Summers's "variability" argument. According to Pinker, "in many traits, men show greater variance than women, and are disproportionately found at both the low and high ends of the distribution." He explains that males and females have similar average scores on math tests but that there are more males than females in the top and the bottom percentiles. This greater variance means that there are disproportionately more male than female math geniuses (and math dunces) and thus more male than female candidates for top math and science positions at major research universities. Pinker explains this greater variance through evolutionary biology: men can

Writing Arguments: A Rhetoric with Readings, Brief Eighth Edition by John D. Ramage,
John C. Bean, and June Johnson.

pass on their genes to dozens of offspring, whereas women can pass on their genes to only a few. Pinker also argues that men and women have different brain structures that result in different kinds of thinking. For example, Pinker cites research that shows that on average men are better at mental rotation of figures and mathematical word problems, while women are better at remembering locations, doing mathematical calculations, reading faces, spelling, and using language. Not only do males and females think differently, but they release different hormones. These hormones help shape gender because males release more testosterone and females more estrogen, meaning that men are more aggressive and apt to take risks, while women "are more solicitous to their children." One example Pinker uses to support his biological hypothesis is the case of males born with abnormal genitals and raised as females. These children have more testosterone than normal female children, and many times they show characteristically male interests and behavior. Pinker uses these cases as evidence that no matter how a child is raised, the child's biology determines the child's interests.

Although Pinker demonstrates that biology plays some role in determining math aptitude, he almost completely ignores the much larger role of discrimination and socialization in shaping the career paths of women. According to an editorial from *Nature Neuroscience* (2005) titled "Separating Science from Stereotype," "[t]he evidence to support [Summers's (2005)] hypothesis of 'innate difference' turns out to be quite slim" (p. 253). The editorial reports that intercultural studies of the variance between boys' and girls' scores on math tests show significant differences between countries. For example, in Iceland girls outscore boys on math tests. The editorial also says that aptitude tests are not very good at predicting the future success of students and that the "SATs tend to under-predict female and over-predict male academic performance" (p. 253). The editorial doesn't deny that men and women's brains work differently, but states that the differences are too small to be blamed for the underrepresentation of women in math and science careers.

If biology doesn't explain the low number of women choosing math and science careers, then what is the cause? Many believe the cause is culture, especially the gender roles children are taught at a very young age. One such believer is Deborah L. Rhode (1997), an attorney and social scientist who specializes in ethics and gender, law, and public policy. In her book *Speaking of Sex: The Denial of Gender Inequality*, Rhode describes the different gender roles females and males are expected to follow from a very young age. Gender roles are portrayed in children's books and television shows. These gender roles are represented by male characters as heroes and problem solvers, while the female characters are the "damsels in distress." Another example of gender roles is that only a very small number of these shows and books portray working mothers or stay-at-home fathers. Rhodes also discussed how movies and popular music, especially rap and heavy metal, encourage violence and objectify women. As girls grow up, they face more and more gender stereotypes from toys to magazines. Parents give their boys interactive, problem-solving toys such as chemistry sets and telescopes, while girls are left with dolls. Although more organizations such as the Girl Scouts of America (2004), who sponsor the Web site *girlsgotech.org*, are trying to interest girls in science and math and advertise careers in those fields to girls, the societal forces working against this encouragement are also still pervasive. For example, magazines for teenage girls encourage attracting male attention and the importance of looks, while being smart and successful is considered unattractive. Because adolescents face so many gender stereotypes, it is no wonder that they shape the career paths they chose later in life. The gender roles engraved in our adolescents' minds cause discrimination against women later in life. Once women are socialized to see themselves as dependent and not as smart as males, it becomes very difficult to break away from these gender stereotypes. With gender bias so apparent in our society, it is hard for females to have high enough self-confidence to continue to compete with males in many fields.

5   The effect of socialization begins at a very early age. One study by Melissa W. Clearfield and Naree M. Nelson (2006) shows how parents unconsciously send gendered messages to their infants and toddlers. This study examined differences in mothers' speech patterns and play behaviors based on the gender of infants ranging from six months to fourteen months. Although there was no difference in the actual play behavior of male and female infants, the researchers discovered interesting differences in the way mothers interacted with daughters versus sons. Mothers of daughters tended to ask their daughters more questions, encouraging social interaction, whereas mothers of sons were less verbal, encouraging their sons to be more independent. The researchers concluded that "the mothers in our study may have been teaching their infants about gender roles through modeling and reinforcement. . . . Thus girls may acquire the knowledge that they are 'supposed' to engage in higher levels of interaction with other people and display more verbal behavior than boys. . . . In contrast, the boys were reinforced for exploring on their own" (p. 136).

One of the strongest arguments against the biological hypothesis comes from a transgendered Stanford neurobiologist, Ben A. Barres (2006), who has been a scientist first as a woman and then as a man. In his article "Does Gender Matter?" Barres states that "there is little evidence that gender differences in [mathematical] abilities exist, are innate or are even relevant to the lack of advancement of women in science"

(p. 134). Barres provides much anecdotal evidence of the way women are discriminated against in this male-dominated field. Barres notes that simply putting a male name rather than a female name on an article or résumé increases its perceived value. He also describes research showing that men and women do equally well in gender-blind academic competitions but that men win disproportionately in contests where gender is revealed. As Barres says, "the bar is unconsciously raised so high for women and minority candidates that few emerge as winners" (p. 134). In one study reported by Barres, women applying for a research grant needed more than twice the productivity of men in order to be considered equally competent. As a female-to-male transgendered person, Barres has personally experienced discrimination when trying to succeed in the science and math fields. When in college, Barres was told that her boyfriend must have done her homework, and she later lost a prestigious fellowship competition to a male even though she was told her application was stronger and she had published "six high-impact papers," while the man that won only published one. Barres even notices subtle differences, such as the fact that he can now finish a sentence without being interrupted by a male.

Barres (2006) urges women to stand up publicly against discrimination. One woman he particularly admires as a strong female role model is MIT biologist Nancy Hopkins, who sued the MIT administration for discrimination based on the lesser amount of lab space allocated to female scientists. The evidence from this study was so strong that even the president of MIT publicly admitted that discrimination was a problem. Barres wants more women to follow Hopkins's lead. He believes that women often don't realize they are being discriminated against because they have faith that the world is equal. Barres explains this tendency as a "denial of personal disadvantage" (p. 134). Very few women will admit to seeing or experiencing discrimination. Until discrimination and sexism are addressed, women will continue to be oppressed.

As a society, we should not accept Lawrence Summers's hypothesis that biological differences are the reason women are not found in high-prestige tenured jobs in math and science. In fact, in another generation the gap between men and women in math and science might completely disappear. In 2003–2004, women received close to one-third of all doctorates in mathematics, up from fifteen percent of doctorates in the early 1980s ("Women in Mathematics," 2005). Although more recent data are not yet available, the signs point to a steadily increasing number of women entering the fields of math, science, and engineering. Blaming biology for the lack of women in these fields and refusing to fault our culture is taking the easy way out. Our culture can change.

References

Barres, B. A. (2006). Does gender matter? *Nature 44*(7), 133–136.

Clearfield, M.W. & Nelson N.M. (2006). Sex differences in mothers' speech and play behavior with 6-, 9-, and 14-month-old infants. *Sex Roles, 54,* 1–2, 127–137.

Girlsgotech. (2004). Retrieved from http://www.girlscouts.org

Pinker, S. (2005, February). The science of difference: Sex ed. *New Republic.* Retrieved from The New Republic.

Rhode D. L. (1997). *Speaking of sex: The denial of gender inequality.* Cambridge MA: Harvard UP.

Separating science from stereotype. (2005). *Nature Neuroscience, 8*(3), 253.

Summers, L. H. (2005). Remarks at NBER conference on diversifying the science and engineering workforce. *The Office of the President.* Retrieved from Harvard University.

Women in mathematics: Study shows gains. (2005). *American Mathematical Society.* Retrieved from American Mathematical Society.

Sample Student Rebuttal Argument

Oversimplifying the Locavore Ethic

Marta Ramos

Professor Jacobs

English 1010—April 30, 2010

Oversimplifying the Locavore Ethic

James McWilliams's (2008) argument in his essay "On Locavorism" is based on an overly simplistic understanding of the locavore ethic. His claim, that eating locally is an unrealistic goal, fails to take into account the flexibility of locavorism, the ways consumer food preferences drive the free market system, and the realities of food processing infrastructure.

Ramos identifies the source that she will refute and the source's claim in the first paragraph.

McWilliams's (2008) criticism of locavorism would make sense if, as he implies, locavores were a single-minded group of people demanding the complete conversion of the agricultural systems to uniform, regimented local production and consumption. In fact, there is no reason that locavorism has to completely replace the existing agricultural system, and hardly any locavores advocate this. Locavorism, the practice of eating food that is grown locally and in season, is not an all-or-nothing policy. It is a direction in which individuals and communities can move. Locavores.com, a Web site run by the chef Jessica Prentice, who coined the term "locavore," spells out local-eating strategies:

Ramos defines the term "locavore" and asserts that McWilliams misunderstands the movement.

> If not LOCALLY PRODUCED, then ORGANIC.
>
> If not ORGANIC, then FAMILY FARM.
>
> If not FAMILY FARM, then LOCAL BUSINESS.
>
> If not LOCAL BUSINESS, then TERROIR—foods famous for the region they are grown in. ("Guidelines," 2009, p. 23)

This hierarchy of food sources prefers local sources over distant ones, and prioritizes local farms and businesses to receive local food dollars. Eating locally, according to Locavores, represents "A step toward regional food self reliance" ("Top," 2009, p. 43). Given the political instability of many areas of the world that grow our food and the way energy costs can drastically affect food prices, it makes sense to reduce our dependence on distant food sources. As Jennifer Maiser (2007), one of the founders of the locavore movement, puts it,

Ramos uses a direct quotation from a respected voice in the locavore community to build credibility.

> Locavores are people who pay attention to where their food comes from and commit to eating local food as much as possible. The great thing

about eating local is that it's not an all-or-nothing venture. Any small

step you take helps the environment, protects your family's health and

supports small farmers in your area. (p. 11)

The goal is not to end completely our importation of food.

McWilliams (2008) cites Phoenix as an example of why locavorism won't

work. Certainly cities like Phoenix, which lacks the water to grow much food,

will always rely on external supply chains to feed their populations. But the

obstacles to local eating in Phoenix should not prevent residents of San

Francisco, Sarasota, or Charleston from eating locally grown foods. Locavorism

doesn't have to work everywhere to be beneficial. ◄————————

In her refutation Ramos addresses McWilliams's argument point by point.

In addition to misrepresenting locavorism's goals, McWilliams (2008)

illogically claims that it cannot meet people's food needs. "At current levels of

fruit production," he warns, "apples are the only crop that could currently feed

New Yorkers at a level that meets the U.S. Recommended Dietary Allowances"

(p. 12). McWilliams is wrong when he claims that if New Yorkers ate locally

grown fruits, they could "rarely indulge in a pear, peach, or basket of strawberries"

(p. 10). That might be the case if New York farmers continued to grow nothing

but apples and grapes. But if some of those crops were replaced with other

fruits, New York could have a very diverse supply of produce that would come

reasonably close to meeting the nutritional needs of its citizens. In fact, if

committed locavores seek out locally grown strawberries, peaches, and pears,

and are willing to pay more money for them than they do for apples, local

farmers will have sound economic reasons for replacing some of their aging

apple trees with peach and pear trees instead. McWilliams makes locavorism ◄————

Ramos quotes McWilliams and then disproves the quoted claim.

sound impractical because he tries to imagine it working within current

agricultural realities. In fact, locavores seek to change the way food is produced

and consumed. Moreover, locavorism works toward this change not, as

McWilliams suggests, by advocating laws that restrict food producers but by

encouraging consumers to vote with their wallets.

OVERSIMPLIFYING THE LOCAVORE ETHIC   4

Ramos questions McWilliams's assumptions and finds them lacking.

McWilliams's (2008) argument about New York also rests on the peculiar assumption that every person in the state has to eat the same fruits in the same amounts in order for locavorism to work. He points out that except for apples and grapes, "every other fruit the state produces is not being harvested at a level to provide all New Yorkers with an adequate supply." McWilliams implies that if you can't grow enough of a crop to supply every single person in the state, there is no point in growing it; however, the goal of locavorism is choice, not total local supply of all food, a fact McWilliams seems to willfully ignore.

Finally, McWilliams (2008) claims that the cost and inconvenience of processing food locally will prevent communities from moving toward local eating. He notes that "whereas the conventional system of production and distribution has in place a series of large-scale processing centers capable of handling these tasks in a handful of isolated locations" (p. 10), smaller communities do not. There are two problems with this argument. First, many of the "processing centers" McWilliams is thinking of aren't capable of handling the task of food production. The National Resources Defense Council reports that "from 1995 to 1998, 1,000 spills or pollution incidents occurred at livestock feedlots in 10 states and 200 manure-related fish kills resulted in the death of 13 million fish" ("Facts," 2005, p. 31). In 2009, Fairbank Farms recalled over half a million pounds of ground beef after nineteen people were hospitalized and two died from E. coli bacteria in the meat (United States, 2009). Also in 2009, the King Nut Companies of Solon, Ohio, sickened over 400 people, including three who died, by producing and distributing peanut butter infected with salmonella ("Virginia," 2009). Large-scale processing plants are not a solution to our food security needs. They are part of the problem.

Ramos addresses the claim that she takes greatest issue with last. She then gives it further emphasis by providing two distinct counterarguments.

Second, the cost of changing the country's food-processing system from large-scale to small-scale is not as prohibitive as McWilliams (2008) makes it sound. Factories age. Machines wear out and have to be replaced. Food production facilities are replaced all the time. Newer facilities could easily be built on a smaller, more regional scale. In fact, given the cost of recalls and

lawsuits when tainted food is distributed over a large area, food producers have

good reason to think about smaller, more localized production and distribution.

McWilliams (2008) either does not understand locavorism or understands

it and prefers to misrepresent its goals and methods. His arguments in favor of

our current food production system ignore both the very real benefits of local

eating, and the considerable cost of the existing system. ◄

Ramos closes with an appeal to the benefits of locavorism.

OVERSIMPLIFYING THE LOCAVORE ETHIC   6

References

Facts about pollution from livestock farms. (2005, July). *Natural Resources Defense Council*. Retrieved from http://www.americanrhetoric.com/speeches/barbarajordanjudiciarystatement.htm

Guidelines for eating well. (2009, June). *Locavores*. Retrieved from http://www.locavores.com/how/

Maiser, J. (2007, November). 10 steps to becoming a locavore. *PBS: NOW*. Retrieved from http://www.pbs.org/now/shows/344/locavore.html

McWilliams, J. (2008, August). Onlocavorism. *New York Times*. Retrieved from http://www.nytimes.com

Top twelve reasons to eat locally. (2009, June). *Locavores*. Retrieved from http://www.locavores.com/how/why.php

United States Dept. of Health and Human Services. (2009, November). Multistate outbreak of E.coli O157:H7 infections associated with beef from Fairbanks Farms. *Center for Disease Control and Prevention*. Retrieved from http://www.hhs.gov/

Virginia, Minnesota confirms salmonella deaths related to tainted peanut butter. (2009). *Fox News*. Retrieved from http://www.foxnews.com/story/0,2933,479624,00.html

PRACTICE

1. Individually or in groups, analyze the refutation strategies that Marybeth Hamilton employs in her argument, which appears in Chapter 16 on pages 699–701.

   a. Summarize each of the opposing reasons that Marybeth anticipates from her audience.

   b. How does she attempt to refute each line of reasoning in the opposing argument? Where does she refute her audience's stated reason? Where does she refute a warrant? Where does she concede to an opposing argument but then shift to a different field of values?

   c. How effective is Marybeth's refutation? Would you as a city resident vote for allotting more public money for this school? Why or why not?

2 Examine each of the following arguments. Attempt to refute each argument. Suggest ways to rebut the reason, or to concede to the argument.

a. Signing the Kyoto treaty (pledging that the United States will substantially lower its emission of greenhouse gases) is a bad idea because reducing greenhouse emissions will seriously harm the American economy.

b. Majoring in engineering is better than majoring in music because engineers make more money than musicians.

c. The United States should reinstitute the draft because doing so is the only way to maintain a large enough military to defend American interests in several different trouble spots in the world.

d. The United States should build more nuclear reactors because nuclear reactors will provide substantial electrical energy without emitting greenhouse gases.

e. People should be allowed to own handguns because owning handguns helps them protect their homes against potentially violent intruders.

South Haven Lighthouse
South Haven, MI

What Is a Proposal?

22

ALTHOUGH PROPOSAL ARGUMENTS ARE THE LAST TYPE WE EXAMINE, THEY ARE AMONG THE MOST COMMON ARGUMENTS THAT YOU WILL ENCOUNTER OR BE CALLED ON TO WRITE. THEIR ESSENCE IS THAT THEY CALL FOR ACTION. IN READING A proposal, the audience is enjoined to make a decision and then to act on it—to *do* something. Proposal arguments are sometimes called *should* or *ought* arguments because those helping verbs express the obligation to act: "We *should* do this [action]" or "We *ought* to do this [action]."

For instructional purposes, we will distinguish between two kinds of proposal arguments, even though they are closely related and involve the same basic arguing strategies. The first kind we will call *practical proposals,* which propose an action to solve some kind of local or immediate problem. A student's proposal to change the billing procedures for scholarship students would be an example of a practical proposal, as would an engineering firm's proposal for the design of a new bridge being planned by a city government. The second kind we will call *policy proposals,* in which the writer offers a broad plan of action to solve major social, economic, or political problems affecting the common good. An argument that the United States should adopt a national health insurance plan or that the electoral college should be abolished would be an example of a policy proposal.

The primary difference is the narrowness versus breadth of the concern. *Practical* proposals are narrow, local, and concrete; they focus on the nuts and bolts of getting something done in the here and now. They are often concerned with the exact size of a piece of steel, the precise duties of a new person to be hired, or a close estimate of the cost of paint or computers to be purchased. *Policy* proposals, in contrast, are concerned with the broad outline and shape of a course of action, often on a regional, national, or even international issue. What government should do about overcrowding of prisons would be a problem addressed by policy proposals. How to improve the security alarm system for the county jail would be addressed by a practical proposal.

Learning to write both kinds of proposals is valuable. Researching and writing a *policy* proposal is an excellent way to practice the responsibilities of citizenship, which require the ability to understand complex issues and to weigh positive and negative consequences of policy choices. In your professional life, writing *practical* proposals may well be among your most important duties on the job. Effective proposal writing is the lifeblood of many companies and also constitutes one of the most powerful ways you can identify and help solve problems.

Understand How Proposal Arguments Work

Proposal arguments make the case that someone should do something: "The federal government should raise grazing fees on public lands." "The student union should renovate the old swimming pool in Butler Gymnasium." "All parents should secure their children in booster seats when driving, even for short distances." Proposals can also argue that something should *not* be done, or that people should stop doing something: "The plan to extend Highway 45 is a waste of tax dollars and citizens should not vote for it." "Don't drink and drive."

The challenge for writers of proposal arguments is to convince readers to take action. It's easy for readers to agree that something should be done, as long as they don't have to do it. It's much harder to get readers involved with the situation or convince them to spend their time or money trying to carry out the proposal. A successful proposal argument conveys a sense of urgency to motivate readers, and describes definite actions they should take.

The key to a successful proposal is using good reasons to convince readers that if they act, something positive will happen (or something negative will be avoided). If your readers believe that taking action will benefit them, they are more likely to help bring about what you propose.

Proposal arguments take the form shown here.

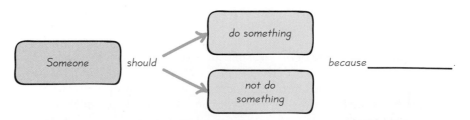

We should convert existing train tracks in the downtown areas to a light-rail system and build a new freight track around the city because we need to relieve traffic and parking congestion downtown.

Recognize Components of Proposal Arguments

Most successful proposals have four major components:

- **Identifying and defining the problem.** Sometimes, your audience is already fully aware of the problem you want to solve. If your city frequently tears up streets and then leaves them for months without fixing them, you shouldn't have much trouble convincing citizens that streets should be repaired more quickly. But if you raise a problem unfamiliar to your readers, first you will have to convince them that the problem is real. Citizens will not see the need to replace miles of plumbing lines running under the streets, for example, unless you convince them that the pipes are old and corroded and are a risk to everyone's safety. You will also need to define the scope of the problem—does every single pipe need replacing, or only those more than forty years old? Is this a job for the city, or do federal clean water regulations mean that other government officials must be involved? The clearer you are about what must be done, and by whom, the stronger your argument will be.

- **Stating a proposed solution.** A strong proposal offers a clear, definite statement of exactly what you are proposing. Vague statements that "Something must be done!" may get readers stirred up about the issue, but are unlikely to lead to constructive action. A detailed proposal also adds credibility to your argument, showing that you are concerned enough to think through the nuts and bolts of the changes to be made. You can state your proposed solution near the beginning of your argument, or introduce it later—for example, after you have considered and rejected other possible solutions.

- **Convincing readers that the proposed solution is fair and will work.** Once your readers agree that a problem exists and a solution should be found, you have to convince them that your solution is the best one. Perhaps you want your city to fire the planning committee members who are responsible for street repair. You will need to show that those officials are indeed responsible for the delays, and that, once they are fired, the city will be able to quickly hire new, more effective planners.

- **Demonstrating that the solution is feasible.** Your solution not only has to work; it must be feasible, or practical, to implement. You might be able to raise money for street repairs by billing property owners for repairs to the streets in front of their houses, but opposition to such a proposal would be fierce. Most Americans will object to making individuals responsible for road repair costs when roads are used by all drivers.

You may also have to show how your proposal is better than other possible actions that could be taken. Perhaps others believe your city should hire private contractors to repair the streets more quickly, or reward work crews who finish quickly with extra pay or days off. If there are multiple proposed solutions, all perceived as equally good, then there is no clear course of action for your audience to work for. Very often, that means nothing will happen.

Build a Proposal Argument

At this moment, you might not think that you feel strongly enough about anything to write a proposal argument. But if you write a list of things that make you mad or at least a little annoyed, then you have a start toward writing a proposal argument. Some things on your list are not going to produce proposal arguments that many people would want to read. If your roommate is a slob, you might be able to write a proposal for that person to start cleaning up more, but who else would be interested? Similarly, it might be annoying to you that where you live is too far from the ocean, but it is hard to imagine making a serious proposal to move your city closer to the coast. Short of those extremes, however, are many things that might make you think, "Why hasn't someone done something about this?" If you believe that others have something to gain if a problem is solved, or at least that the situation can be made a little better, then you might be able to develop a good proposal argument.

For instance, suppose you are living off campus, and you buy a student parking sticker when you register for courses so that you can park in the student lot. However, you quickly find out that there are too many cars and trucks for the number of available spaces, and unless you get to campus by 8:00 A.M., you aren't going to find a place to park in your assigned lot. The situation makes you angry because you believe that if you pay for a sticker, you should have a reasonable chance of finding a place to park. You see that there are unfilled lots reserved for faculty and staff next to the student parking lot, and you wonder why more spaces aren't allotted to students. You decide to write to the president of your college. You want her to direct parking and traffic services to give more spaces to students or else to build a parking garage that will accommodate more vehicles.

When you start talking to other students on campus, however, you begin to realize that the problem may be more complex than your first view of it. Your college has taken the position that if fewer students drive to campus, there will be less traffic on and around your campus. The administration wants more students to ride shuttle buses, to form car pools, or to bicycle to campus instead of driving alone. You also find out that faculty and staff members pay ten times as much as students for their parking permits, so they pay a very high premium for a guaranteed space—much too high for most students. If the president of your college is your primary audience, you first have to argue that a problem really exists. You have to convince the president that many students have no choice but to drive if they are to attend classes. You, for example, are willing to ride the shuttle buses, but they don't run often enough for you to make your classes, get back to your car that you left at home, and then drive to your job.

Next, you have to argue that your solution will solve the problem. An eight-story parking garage might be adequate to park all the cars of students who want to drive, but parking garages are very expensive to build. Even if a parking garage is the best solution, the question remains: who is going to pay for it? Many problems in life could be solved if you had access to unlimited resources, but very few people—or organizations—have such resources at their command. It's not enough to propose a solution that can resolve the problem. You have to be able to argue for the feasibility of your solution. If you want to argue that a parking garage is the solution to the parking problem on your campus, then you must also propose how to finance the garage.

Developing a Proposal Argument

Writers of proposal arguments must focus in turn on three main phases or stages of the argument: showing that a problem exists, explaining the proposed solution, and offering a justification.

CONVINCING YOUR READERS THAT A PROBLEM EXISTS

There is one argumentative strategy generic to all proposal arguments: calling your reader's attention to a problem. In some situations, your intended audience may already be aware of the problem and may have even asked for solutions. In such cases, you do not need to develop the problem extensively or motivate your audience to solve it. But in most situations, awakening your readers to the existence of a problem—a problem they may well not have recognized before—is your first important challenge. You must give your problem presence through anecdotes, telling statistics, or other means that show readers how the problem affects people or otherwise has important stakes. Your goal is to gain your readers' intellectual assent to the depth, range, and potential seriousness of the problem and thereby motivate them to want to solve it.

Typically, the arguer develops the problem in one of two places in a proposal argument—either in the introduction prior to the presentation of the arguer's proposal claim or in the body of the paper as the first main reason justifying the proposal claim. In the second instance the writer's first *because* clause has the following structure: "We should do this action *because* it addresses a serious problem."

Here is how one student writer gave presence to a proposal, addressed to the chair of the mathematics department at her school, calling for redesign of the first-year calculus curriculum in order to slow its pace. She wants the chair to see a problem from her perspective.

Example Passage Giving Presence to a Problem

For me, who wants to become a high school math teacher, the problem with introductory calculus is not its difficulty but its pace. My own experience in the Calculus 134 and 135 sequence last year showed me that it was not the learning of calculus that was difficult for me. I was able to catch on to the new concepts. My problem was that it went too fast. Just as I was assimilating new concepts and feeling the need to reinforce them, the class was on to a new topic before I had full mastery of the old concept. . . . Part of the reason for the fast pace is that calculus is a feeder course for computer science and engineering. If prospective engineering students can't learn the calculus rapidly, they drop out of the program. The high dropout rate benefits the Engineering School because they use the math course to weed out an overabundance of engineering applicants. Thus the pace of the calculus course is geared to the needs of the engineering curriculum, not to the needs of someone like me who wants to be a high school mathematics teacher and who believes that my own difficulties with math—combined with my love for it—might make me an excellent math teacher.

By describing the fast pace of the math curriculum from the perspective of a future math teacher rather than an engineering student, this writer brings visibility to a problem. What before didn't look like a problem (it is good to weed out weak engineering majors) suddenly became a problem (it is bad to weed out future math teachers). Establishing herself as a serious student genuinely interested in learning calculus, she gave presence to the problem by calling attention to it in a new way.

SHOWING THE SPECIFICS OF YOUR PROPOSAL

Having decided that there is a problem to be solved, you should lay out your thesis, which is a proposal for solving the problem. Your goal now is to stress the feasibility of your solution, including costs. The art of proposal making is the art of the possible. To be sure, not all proposals require elaborate descriptions of the implementation process. If you are proposing, for example, that a local PTA chapter buy new tumbling mats for the junior high gym classes, the procedures for buying the mats will probably be irrelevant. But in many arguments the specifics of your proposal—the actual step-by-step methods of implementing it—may be instrumental in winning your audience's support.

You will also need to show how your proposal will solve the problem either partially or wholly. Sometimes you may first need to convince your reader that the problem is solvable, not something intractably rooted in "the way things are," such as earthquakes or jealousy. In other words, expect that some members of your audience will be skeptical about the ability of any proposal to solve the problem you are addressing. You may well need, therefore, to "listen" to this point of view in your refutation section and to argue that your problem is at least partially solvable.

In order to persuade your audience that your proposal can work, you can follow any one of several approaches. A typical approach is to lay out a causal argument showing how one consequence will lead to another until your solution is effected. Another approach is to turn to resemblance arguments, either analogy or precedent. You try to show how similar proposals have been successful elsewhere. Or, if similar things have failed in the past, you try to show how the present situation is different.

THE JUSTIFICATION: CONVINCING YOUR READERS THAT YOUR PROPOSAL SHOULD BE ENACTED

The justification phase of a proposal argument will need extensive development in some arguments and minimal development in others, again depending on your particular problem and the rhetorical context of your proposal. If your audience already acknowledges the seriousness of the problem you are addressing and has simply been waiting for the right solution to come along, then your argument will be successful so long as you can convince your audience that your solution will work and that it won't cost too much. Such arguments depend on the clarity of your proposal and the feasibility of its being implemented.

But what if the costs are high? What if your readers don't think the problem is serious? What if they don't appreciate the benefits of solving the problem or the bad consequences of not solving it? In such cases you have to develop persuasive reasons for enacting your proposal. You may also have to determine who has the power to act on your proposal and apply arguments directly to that person's or agency's immediate interests. You need to know to whom or to what your power source is beholden or responsive and what values your power source holds that can be appealed to. You're looking, in short, for the best pressure points.

Proposal Arguments as Advocacy Posters or Advertisements

A frequently encountered kind of proposal argument is the one-page newspaper or magazine advertisement often purchased by advocacy groups to promote a cause. Such arguments also appear as Web pages or as posters or fliers. These condensed advocacy arguments are marked by their bold, abbreviated, tightly planned format. The creators of these arguments know they must work fast to capture our attention, give presence to a problem, advocate a solution, and enlist our support. Advocacy advertisements frequently use photographs, images, or icons that appeal to a reader's emotions and imagination. In addition to images, they often use different type sizes and styles. Large-type text in these documents frequently takes the form of slogans or condensed thesis statements written in an arresting style. To outline and justify their solutions, creators of advocacy ads often put main supporting reasons in bulleted lists and sometimes enclose carefully selected facts and quotations in boxed sidebars. To add an authoritative *ethos*, the arguments often include fine-print footnotes and bibliographies.

Another prominent feature of these condensed, highly visual arguments is their appeal to the audience through a direct call for a course of action: go to an advocacy Web site to find more information on how to support a cause; cut out a postcardlike form to send to a decision maker; vote for or against the proposition or the candidate; write a letter to a political representative; or donate money to a cause.

An example of a student-produced advocacy advertisement is shown in Figure 22.1. Here student Lisa Blattner joins a heated debate in her city on whether to close down all-ages dance clubs. Frustrated because the evening dance options for under-twenty-one youth were threatened in Seattle, Lisa directed her ad toward the general readership of regional newspapers with the special intention of reaching adult voters and parents. Lisa's ad uses three documentary-like, emotionally loaded, and disturbing photographs to give immediacy and presence to the problem. The verbal text in the ad states the proposal claim and provides three reasons in support of the claim. Notice how the reasons also pick up the ideas in the three photo images. The final lines of text memorably reiterate the claim and call readers to action. The success of this ad derives from the collaboration of layout, photos, and verbal text in conveying a clear, direct argument.

Now that you have been introduced to the main elements of a proposal argument, including condensed visual arguments, we explain in the next two sections two invention strategies you can use to generate persuasive reasons for a proposal argument and to anticipate your audience's doubts and reservations. We call these the "claim-type strategy" and the "stock issues strategy."

What Is Left for Teenagers to Do When the Teen Ordinance Bans Them from Dance Clubs?

Take Ecstasy
at Raves

Drink at Places with
No Adult Supervision

Roam the Streets

Is There an Answer to These Problems?

Yes! Through your support of the All Ages Dance Ordinance, teens will have a safe place to go where:

- No hard drugs, like ecstasy and cocaine, are present
- Responsible adults are watching over everyone
- All of their friends can hang out in one place indoors, instead of outside with drug dealers, criminals, and prostitutes

Give Your Child a Safe Place to Have Fun at Night

**Let the Seattle City Committee Know
That You Support the
All Ages Dance Ordinance**

Figure 22.1   Student Advocacy Advertisement

Using the Claim-Types Strategy to Develop a Proposal Argument

Evaluation and proposal claims often depend for their supporting reasons on claims about category, cause, or resemblance. This fact leads to a powerful idea-generating strategy based on arguments from category (which also includes argument from principle), on arguments from consequences, or on arguments from resemblance. This "claim-types" strategy is illustrated in the following chart:

Explanation of Claim-Types Strategy for Supporting a Proposal Claim		
Claim Type	Generic Template	Example from Biotechnology Issue
Argument from principle or category	We should do this action • because doing so adheres to this good principle [or] • because this action belongs to this good category	We should support genetically modified foods • because doing so values scientific reason over emotion [or] • because genetically modified foods are safe
Argument from consequences	• because this action will lead to these good consequences	• because biotech crops can reduce world hunger • because biotech crops can improve the environment by reducing use of pesticides
Argument from resemblance	• because this action has been done successfully elsewhere [or] • because this action is like this other good action	• because genetic modification is like natural crossbreeding that has been accelerated [or] • because genetic modification of food is like scientific advancements in medicine

Before we give you some simple strategies for using this approach, let's illustrate it with another example.

Insurance companies should pay for long-term psychological counseling for anorexia (proposal claim)

• because paying for such counseling is a demonstration of commitment to women's health. (principle/category)
• because paying for such counseling may save insurance companies from much more extensive medical costs at a later date. (consequence)
• because paying for anorexia counseling is like paying for alcoholism or drug counseling, which is already covered by insurance. (resemblance)

Note how each of these supporting reasons appeals to the value system of the audience. The writer hopes to show that covering the cost of counseling is within the class of things that the audience already values (commitment to women's health), will lead to consequences desired by the audience (reduced long-term costs), and is similar to something the audience already values (drug and alcohol counseling). The claim-types strategy for generating ideas is easy to apply in practice.

EXPLORING IDEAS

Because *should* or *ought* issues are among the most common sources of arguments, you may already have ideas for proposal issues. To think of ideas for practical proposals, try making an idea map of local problems you would like to see solved. For initial spokes, try trigger words such as the following:

- Problems at my university (dorms, parking, registration system, financial aid, campus appearance, clubs, curriculum, intramural program, athletic teams)
- Problems in my city or town (dangerous intersections, ugly areas, inadequate lighting, parks, police policy, public transportation, schools)
- Problems at my place of work (office design, flow of customer traffic, merchandise display, company policies)
- Problems related to my future career, hobbies, recreational time, life as a consumer, life as a homeowner

If you can offer a solution to the problem you identify, you may make a valuable contribution to some phase of public life.

To find a topic for policy proposals, stay in touch with the news, which will keep you aware of current debates on regional and national issues. Also, visit the Web sites of your congressional representatives to see what issues they are currently investigating and debating. You might think of your policy proposal as a white paper for one of your legislators.

IDENTIFYING YOUR AUDIENCE AND DETERMINING WHAT'S AT STAKE

Before drafting your argument, identify your targeted audience and determine what's at stake. Consider your responses to the following questions:

- What audience are you targeting? What background do they need to understand your problem? How much do they already care about it? How could you motivate them to care?
- After they read your argument, what stance do you imagine them holding? What change do you want to bring about in their view or their behavior?
- What will they find uncomfortable or threatening about your proposal? Particularly, what costs will they incur by acting on your proposal?

- What objections might they raise? What counterarguments or alternative solutions will you need to address?
- Why does your proposal matter? What is at stake?

ORGANIZING A PROPOSAL ARGUMENT

When you write your draft, you may find it helpful to have at hand an organization plan for a proposal argument. The plan shows a typical structure for a proposal argument. In some cases, you may want to summarize and rebut opposing views before you present the justification for your own proposal.

Organization Plan for a Proposal Argument

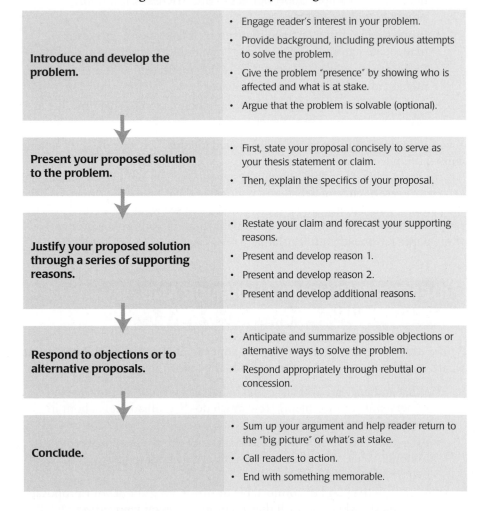

Introduce and develop the problem.	• Engage reader's interest in your problem.
	• Provide background, including previous attempts to solve the problem.
	• Give the problem "presence" by showing who is affected and what is at stake.
	• Argue that the problem is solvable (optional).
Present your proposed solution to the problem.	• First, state your proposal concisely to serve as your thesis statement or claim.
	• Then, explain the specifics of your proposal.
Justify your proposed solution through a series of supporting reasons.	• Restate your claim and forecast your supporting reasons.
	• Present and develop reason 1.
	• Present and develop reason 2.
	• Present and develop additional reasons.
Respond to objections or to alternative proposals.	• Anticipate and summarize possible objections or alternative ways to solve the problem.
	• Respond appropriately through rebuttal or concession.
Conclude.	• Sum up your argument and help reader return to the "big picture" of what's at stake.
	• Call readers to action.
	• End with something memorable.

QUESTIONING AND CRITIQUING A PROPOSAL ARGUMENT

As we've suggested, proposal arguments need to overcome the innate conservatism of people, the difficulty of anticipating all the consequences of a proposal, and so forth. What questions, then, can we ask about proposal arguments to help us anticipate these problems?

Will a skeptic deny that my problem is really a problem? The first question to ask of your proposal is "What's so wrong with the status quo that change is necessary?" The second question is "Who loses if the status quo is changed?" Be certain not to overlook this second question. Most proposal makers can demonstrate that some sort of problem exists, but often it is a problem only for certain groups of people. Solving the problem will thus prove a benefit to some people but a cost to others. If audience members examine the problem from the perspective of the potential losers rather than the winners, they can often raise doubts about your proposal.

Will a skeptic doubt the effectiveness of my solution? Assuming that you've convinced your audience that a significant problem exists and is worth solving, you then have to convince readers that your solution will work. Skeptics are likely to raise at least two kinds of questions about your proposed solution. First, they may doubt that you have adequately identified the cause of the problem. Perhaps you have mistaken a symptom for a cause or confused two commonly associated but essentially unlinked phenomena for a cause-effect relationship. For example, will paying teachers higher salaries improve the quality of teaching or merely attract greedier rather than brighter people? Maybe more good teachers would be attracted and retained if they were given some other benefit (fewer students? fewer classes? more sabbaticals? more autonomy? more prestige?). Second, skeptics are likely to invoke the phenomenon of unintended consequences—solving one problem merely creates a sequence of new problems. ("Now that we've raised teachers' salaries, we don't have enough tax dollars for highway maintenance; not only that, now firefighters and police are demanding higher salaries also.") As you anticipate audience objections, look again at the potential negative consequences of your proposed solution.

Will a skeptic think my proposal costs too much? The most commonly asked question of any proposal is simply, "Do the benefits of enacting the proposal outweigh the costs?" As we saw earlier, you can't foresee all the consequences of any proposal. It's easy, before the fact, to underestimate the costs and exaggerate the benefits of a proposal. So, in asking how much your proposal will cost, we urge you to make an honest estimate. Will your audience discover costs you hadn't anticipated—extra financial costs or unexpected psychological or environmental or aesthetic costs? As much as you can, anticipate these objections.

Will a skeptic suggest counterproposals? Once you've convinced readers that a problem exists, they are likely to suggest alternative solutions different from yours. If readers acknowledge the seriousness of the problem, yet object to your proposal, they are faced with a dilemma: either they have to offer their own counterproposals or they have to argue that the problem is simply in the nature of things and hence unsolvable. So, given the likelihood that you'll be faced with a counterproposal, it only makes sense to anticipate it and to work out a refutation of it before you have it thrown at you. And who knows, you may end up liking the counterproposal better and changing your mind about what to propose!

READINGS

The Declaration of Independence

Thomas Jefferson

The American Revolution had already begun with the battles of Lexington, Concord, and Bunker Hill, and George Washington had been named to head the colonial army by June 7, 1776, when the Continental Congress moved to draft a Declaration of Independence. Thomas Jefferson was given eighteen days to complete the task with the help of Benjamin Franklin and John Adams.

IN CONGRESS, JULY 4, 1776.

The unanimous Declaration of the thirteen united States of America,

When, in the Course of human events, it becomes necessary for one people to dissolve the political bands which have connected them with another, and to assume among the powers of the earth, the separate and equal station to which the laws of nature and of nature's God entitle them, a decent respect to the opinions of mankind requires that they should declare the causes which impel them to the separation.

We hold these truths to be self-evident: That all men are created equal; that they are endowed by their Creator with certain unalienable rights; that among these are life, liberty and the pursuit of happiness. That, to secure these rights, governments are instituted among men, deriving their just powers from the consent of the governed; that, whenever any form of government becomes destructive of these ends, it is the right of the people to alter or to abolish it, and to institute new Government, laying its foundation on such principles, and organizing its powers in such form, as to them shall seem most likely to effect their safety and happiness. Prudence, indeed, will dictate that governments long established should not be changed for light and transient causes; and accordingly all experience hath shown, that mankind are more disposed to suffer, while evils are sufferable, than to right themselves by abolishing the forms to which they are accustomed. But when a long train of abuses and usurpations, pursuing invariably the same object evinces a design to reduce them under absolute despotism, it is

Jefferson maintains that the drastic solution of declaring independence is justified if the problem is of great magnitude.

The rationale for the proposal is a definition argument. According to Jefferson, the purpose of a government is to ensure the rights of the governed. When a government fails to achieve its defined purpose—to ensure the rights of the people—the people have the right to abolish it. The British used similar arguments to justify the revolution against King James II in 1688.

...continued The Declaration of Independence, **Thomas Jefferson**

their right, it is their duty, to throw off such government and to provide new guards for their future security. Such has been the patient sufferance of these colonies, and such is now the necessity which constrains them to alter their former systems of government. The history of the present king of Great Britain is a history of repeated injuries and usurpations, all having in direct object the establishment of an absolute tyranny over these States. To prove this, let facts be submitted to a candid world.

He has refused his assent to laws, the most wholesome and necessary for the public good.

He has forbidden his governors to pass laws of immediate and pressing importance, unless suspended in their operation till his Assent should be obtained, and, when so suspended, he has utterly neglected to attend to them. He has refused to pass other laws for the accommodation of large districts of people, unless those people would relinquish the right of representation in the legislature–a right inestimable to them and formidable to tyrants only.

He has called together legislative bodies at places unusual, uncomfortable, and distant from the depository of their public Records, for the sole purpose of fatiguing them into compliance with his measures.

He has dissolved representative houses repeatedly, for opposing with manly firmness his invasions on the rights of the people.

He has refused for a long time, after such dissolutions, to cause others to be elected; whereby the legislative powers, incapable of annihilation, have returned to the people at large for their exercise; the State remaining in the mean time exposed to all the dangers of invasion from without, and convulsions within.

He has endeavored to prevent the population of these states; for that purpose obstructing the laws for naturalization of foreigners; refusing to pass others to encourage their migrations hither, and raising the conditions of new appropriations of lands.

He has obstructed the administration of justice by refusing his assent to laws for establishing judiciary powers.

He has made judges dependent on his will alone, for the tenure of their offices, and the amount and payment of their salaries.

He has erected a multitude of new offices, and sent hither swarms of officers to harass our people, and eat out their substance.

He has kept among us, in times of peace, standing armies without the consent of our legislatures.

He has affected to render the military independent of and superior to the civil power.

The burden for Jefferson is to convince others of the severity of the problem—that life is intolerable under the King. He goes on to detail a long list of complaints. His goal is to prove the need for change rather than to outline how the solution will work.

The legalistic list of charges is made more vivid by the use of metaphors such as "swarms of officers," which likens the British to a plague of insects.

He has combined with others to subject us to a jurisdiction foreign to our constitution, and unacknowledged by our laws; giving his assent to their acts of pretended legislation:

For quartering large bodies of armed troops among us;

For protecting them, by a mock trial, from punishment for any murders which they should commit on the inhabitants of these States;

For cutting off our trade with all parts of the world;

For imposing taxes on us without our consent;

For depriving us in many cases, of the benefits of trial by jury;

For transporting us beyond seas to be tried for pretended offences;

For abolishing the free system of English laws in a neighboring province, establishing therein an arbitrary government, and enlarging its boundaries so as to render it at once an example and fit instrument for introducing the same absolute rule into these colonies;

For taking away our charters, abolishing our most valuable laws, and altering fundamentally the forms of our governments;

For suspending our own legislatures, and declaring themselves invested with power to legislate for us in all cases whatsoever.

He has abdicated government here, by declaring us out of his protection and waging war against us.

He has plundered our seas, ravaged our coasts, burnt our towns, and destroyed the lives of our people.

He is at this time transporting large armies of foreign mercenaries to complete the works of death, desolation and tyranny, already begun with circumstances of cruelty and perfidy scarcely paralleled in the most barbarous ages, and totally unworthy the head of a civilized nation.

He has constrained our fellow citizens taken captive on the high seas to bear arms against their country, to become the executioners of their friends and brethren, or to fall themselves by their hands. ◀

The strongest charges against the king are placed at the end of the list.

He has excited domestic insurrections amongst us, and has endeavored to bring on the inhabitants of our frontiers, the merciless Indian savages, whose known rule of warfare is an undistinguished destruction of all ages, sexes and conditions.

In every stage of these oppressions we have petitioned for redress in the most humble terms; our repeated petitions have been answered only by repeated injury. A prince, whose character is thus marked by every act which may define a tyrant, is unfit to be the ruler of a free people.

Nor have we been wanting in attentions to our British brethren. We have warned them from time to time of attempts by their legislature to extend an unwarrantable jurisdiction over us. We have reminded them of the circumstances of our emigration and settlement

...continued The Declaration of Independence, **Thomas Jefferson**

here. We have appealed to their native justice and magnanimity, and we have conjured them by the ties of our common kindred to disavow these usurpations, which would inevitably interrupt our connections and correspondence. They too have been deaf to the voice of justice and of consanguinity. We must, therefore, acquiesce in the necessity, which denounces our separation, and hold them, as we hold the rest of mankind, enemies in war, in peace, friends.

We, therefore, the representatives of the United States of America, in general congress, assembled, appealing to the Supreme Judge of the world for the rectitude of our intentions, do, in the name, and by authority of the good people of these colonies, solemnly publish and declare, that these united colonies are, and of right ought to be free and independent states; that they are absolved from all allegiance to the British crown, and that all political connection between them and the state of Great Britain, is and ought to be totally dissolved; and that as free and independent states, they have full power to levy war, conclude peace, contract alliances, establish commerce, and to do all other acts and things which independent states may of right do. And for the support of this declaration, with a firm reliance on the protection of Divine Providence, we mutually pledge to each other our lives, our fortunes and our sacred honor.

To build credibility Jefferson makes a case that the colonists' frustration with the British government is justified. He argues that the colonists have tried the peaceful approach only to be rebuffed.

The proposal is that the colonies no longer have any political connection to Great Britain and possess all the rights of an independent country.

STUDENT MODELS

Why the United States Should Adopt Nuclear Power

Juan Vazquez

Professor Bean

English 210—July 15, 2008

Why the United States Should Adopt Nuclear Power

Thousands of studies conducted by scientists to measure climate change over the last one hundred years have accumulated substantial evidence that global warming is occurring unequivocally. According to the NASA *Earth Observatory* web site, greenhouse gas emissions have caused the average surface temperature of the Earth to increase by 0.6 to 0.9 degrees Celsius between 1906 and 2006. If fossil fuel energy continues to be burned relentlessly, scientists are predicting that the average surface temperatures could rise between 2°C and 6°C by the end of the twenty-first century (Riebeek, 2007). A prevalent consensus among scientists is that humans are a major culprit in global warming by burning fossil fuels such as coal and petroleum, with coal-fired power plants being one of the major problems. Lately, discussion has focused on what governments in developed countries can do to tackle climate change.

One solution, advocated by scientist William Sweet (2007) writing for the magazine *Discover*, is that the United States should expand its long-ignored nuclear power industry. However, many people—especially environmentalists—are afraid of nuclear power and believe that we can solve global warming through other alternatives. Despite these fears and counter-arguments, I believe that Sweet is right about nuclear energy. The United States should as quickly as possible phase out coal-burning power plants and replace them with nuclear power and other green technologies.

Before we look at the advantages of nuclear power, it is important to see why many people are opposed to it. First, opponents argue that nuclear power plants aren't safe. They regularly cite the Three Mile Island accident in 1979 and the disastrous Chernobyl meltdown in 1986. A more exhaustive list of recent small scale but worrisome nuclear accidents is provided by an editorial from the *Los Angeles Times,* which describes how a July 2007 magnitude 6.8 earthquake in Japan "caused dozens of problems at the world's biggest nuclear plant, leading to releases of radioactive elements into the air and ocean and an indefinite shutdown" ("No to Nukes," 2007, p. 4). Opponents also argue that nuclear plants are attractive terrorist targets. A properly placed explosive could spew radioactive material over wide swathes of densely populated areas. Nuclear power plants also provide opportunities for terrorists to steal plutonium for making their own nuclear weapons.

Second, while agreeing that nuclear power plants don't produce greenhouse gases, opponents remind us that radioactive waste cannot be stored safely and that radioactive waste remains hazardous for tens of thousands of years. The heavy walled concrete containers used to enclose nuclear waste will eventually develop cracks. If the planned disposal facility at Yucca Mountain, Nevada—where wastes would be stored in concrete and steel containers deep underground—ever becomes operational, it would ease the waste issue for the United States but would not eliminate it. The dangerous nuclear waste would still have to be trucked to Nevada, and even the Nevada site might not be completely impervious to earthquake damage or to the possibility that future generations would dig it up accidentally.

Finally, opponents claim that nuclear power plants are extremely expensive and the process of building them is extremely slow so that this method won't provide any short-term solutions for climate change. According to the "No to Nukes" (2007) editorial from the *Los Angeles Times*, the average nuclear plant is estimated to cost about $4 billion, making nuclear-generated energy about 25% to 75% more expensive than old-fashioned coal. At the same time, the regulatory process for building nuclear power plants is slow and unpredictable, making investors hesitant about supplying the capital needed. Opponents of nuclear energy

argue that these high costs and long waiting period would make it
impossible to launch a massive construction of nuclear power plants that
would have an immediate impact on global warming.

So in the face of these risks, why should we support Sweet's (2007)
proposal for expanding nuclear technology? One answer is that some of
the fears about nuclear plants are overstated, fabricated, or politicized. It
is true that in the past there have been accidents at nuclear power plants,
but improvements in technology make such disasters in the future very
unlikely. According to Sweet, changes in the design of nuclear reactors in
the United States make them "virtually immune to the type of accident
that occurred at Chernobyl in April 1986" (p. 62). Furthermore, Sweet
points out, the oft-cited Three Mile Island accident didn't injure a single
person and led to a better regulatory system that makes new reactors
much safer than old ones. According to Sweet, today's "coal fired power
plants routinely kill tens of thousands of people in the United States each
year by way of lung cancer, bronchitis, and other ailments; the U.S.
nuclear economy kills virtually no one in a normal year" (p. 62). In
addition, management of power plants has improved. As for the fear of
terrorist threats and nuclear proliferation, these concerns have been
blown out of proportion. As Sweet argues, if any terrorists are seeking to
produce bombs, their access to plutonium will not depend on how many
nuclear power plants the U.S. is building. Because nuclear power plants
must be housed within concrete containment barriers to prevent damage
from earthquakes, hurricanes, and floods, they are also resistant to
terrorist attacks. A study carried out by the Electric Power Research
Institute and reported in a major study of nuclear power by scientists from
MIT showed that an airplane crashing into a U.S. nuclear power plant
would not breech the containment barriers (*Future of Nuclear Power,*

2003). Moreover, nuclear scientists say that the safe containment of nuclear waste is not a technical problem but a political problem.

Although nuclear reactors are not risk free, they are much safer for people's health and for the environment than are coal-fired plants with their pollution-spewing greenhouse gases. According to the MIT (2003) study on nuclear power, since the first commercial nuclear reactor was built in the United States in 1957 (there are now currently 100 nuclear reactors in the United States), there has been only one accident that caused core damage (Three Mile Island). Using statistical analysis, the researchers estimate the current safety regulations and design specifications will limit core damage frequency to about 1 accident per 10,000 reactor years. They also believe that the technology exists to reduce the rate of serious accidents to 1 in 100,000 reactor-years (*Future of Nuclear Power, 2003*). The benefits of nuclear power for reducing global warming therefore outweigh the real but very low risks of using nuclear energy.

As to the problem of nuclear power's expense, it is true that nuclear plants are more expensive than coal, but it is important to understand that the high initial cost of building a nuclear power plant is being compared to the artificially low cost of coal power. If we were to tax coal-burning plants through a cap and trade system so that coal plants would have to pay for social and environmental costs of pollution and production of greenhouse gases, nuclear power would become more competitive. As Sweet (2007) argues, we need a tax or equivalent trading scheme that would increase the cost of coal-generated electricity to encourage a switch from cheap coal to more environmental friendly nuclear power plants.

Nuclear power plants are not the perfect or sole alternative to burning coal to generate energy, but they are certainly the most effective for combating global warming. Without nuclear power plants, we can't generate enough electricity to meet U.S. demands while also reducing carbon emissions. There are other alternatives such as wind technology, but this is also more expensive than coal and not nearly as reliable as nuclear power. Wind turbines only generate energy about a third of the time, which would not be enough to meet peak demands, and the problem of building enough wind towers and creating a huge distribution system to transmit the power from remote windy regions to cities where the power is needed is overwhelming. Currently wind power generates less than 1% of the nation's electricity whereas nuclear power currently generates 20 percent (Sweet, 2007). According to Jesse Ausubel (2005), head of the Program for the Human Environment at Rockefeller University,

> To reach the scale at which they would contribute importantly to meeting global energy demand, renewable sources of energy such as wind, water, and biomass cause serious environmental harm. Measuring renewables in watts per square meter, nuclear has astronomical advantages over its competitors. (p. 16)

10   To combat global warming we need to invest in strategies that could make a large difference fairly quickly. The common belief that we can slow global warming by switching to fluorescent light bulbs, taking the bus to work, and advocating for wind or solar energy is simply wrong. According to science writer Matt Jenkins (2008), the climate problem is solvable. "But tackling it is going to be a lot harder than you've been led to believe" (p. 39). Jenkins summarizes the work of Princeton researchers Stephen Pacala and Robert Socolow, who have identified a "package of greenhouse gas reduction measures" (p. 44), each measure of which they call a "stabilization wedge." Each wedge would reduce carbon gas emissions by one gigaton. Pacala and Socolow have identified 15 possible stabilization wedges and have shown that adopting 7 of these wedges

will reduce carbon emissions to the levels needed to halt global warming. One of Pacala and Socolow's wedges could be achieved by raising the fuel economy of 2 billion cars from 30 mpg to 60 mpg (Jenkins). Another wedge would come from building 50 times more wind turbines than currently exist in the world or 700 times more solar panels. In contrast, we could achieve a wedge simply by doubling the number of nuclear power plants in the world. Nuclear power is clearly not the only solution to climate change. In Pacala and Socolow's scheme, it is at most one-seventh of the solution, still forcing us to take drastic measures to conserve energy, stop the destruction of rain forests, develop clean-burning coal, and create highly fuel-efficient automobiles. But nuclear energy produces the quickest, surest, and most dramatic reduction of the world's carbon footprint. If we do not take advantage of its availability, we will need to get equivalent carbon-free power from other sources, which may not be possible and will certainly be more expensive. Therefore expanded use of nuclear technology has to be part of the solution to stop global warming. We should also note that other countries are already way ahead of us in the use of nuclear technology. France gets almost 80% of its electricity from nuclear power and Sweden almost 50% ("World Statistics," 2008). These countries have accepted the minimal risks of nuclear power in favor of a reduced carbon footprint and a safer environment.

In sum, we should support Sweet's (2007) proposal for adopting nuclear power plants as a major national policy. However, there are other questions that we need to pursue. Where are we going to get the other necessary wedges? Are we going to set gas mileage requirements of 60 mpg on the auto industry? Are we going to push research and development for ways to burn coal cleanly by sequestering carbon emissions in the ground? Are we going to stop destruction of the rain forests? Are we going to fill up our land with wind towers to get one more

WHY THE U.S. SHOULD ADOPT NUCLEAR POWER   8

wedge? If all these questions make climate change seem unsolvable, it

will be even more difficult if we cannot factor in nuclear technology as a

major variable in the equation.

WHY THE U.S. SHOULD ADOPT NUCLEAR POWER   9

References

Ausubel, J. H. (2005, March). Renewable and nuclear heresy. Plenary address,

    Nuclear Green. Retrieved from Canadian Nuclear Association.

The future of nuclear power: An interdisciplinary MIT study. Massachusetts

    Institute of Technology.

Jenkins, M. (2008, April–May). A really inconvenient truth. *Miller McClune.*

    38–49.

No to nukes. (2007, July). Editorial. *Los Angeles Times.* Retrieved from

    Los Angeles Times.

Riebeek, H. (2007, May). Global warming. *Earth Observatory.* Retrieved from

    NASA.

Sweet, W. (2007, August). Why uranium is the new green. *Discover.* 61–62.

World statistics: Nuclear energy around the world. *Resources and Stats.*

    Retrieved from Nuclear Energy Institute.

Running head: LET'S MAKE IT A REAL MELTING POT   1

Let's Make It a Real Melting Pot with Presidential Hopefuls for All

Kim Lee

Professor Patel

RHE 306—March 31, 2008

Let's Make It a Real Melting Pot with Presidential Hopes for All

The image the United States likes to advertise is a country that embraces diversity and creates a land of equal opportunity for all. As the Statue of Liberty cries out "give me your tired, your poor, your huddled masses yearning to breathe free," American politicians gleefully evoke such images to frame the United States a bastion for all things good, fair, and equal. As a proud American, however, I must nonetheless highlight one of the cracks in this façade of equality. Imagine an infertile couple decides to adopt an orphaned child from China. They follow all of the legal processes deemed necessary by both countries. They fly abroad and bring home their (once parentless) six-month-old baby boy. They raise and nurture him, and while teaching him to embrace his ethnicity, they also teach him to love Captain Crunch, baseball, and *The Three Stooges.* He grows and eventually attends an ethnically diverse American public school. One day in the fifth grade his teacher tells the class that anyone can grow up to be president. To clarify her point, she turns to the boy, knowing his background, and states, "No, you could not be president, Stu, but you could still be a senator. That's something to aspire to!" How do these parents explain this rule to this American-raised child? This scenario will become increasingly common. Senator Larry Craig of Idaho states that Americans adopt over 25,000 foreign-born children annually (Epstein, 2004). As the Constitution currently reads, only "natural-born" citizens may run for the offices of president and vice president. Neither these children nor the thousands of hardworking Americans who chose to make America their official homeland may aspire to the highest political position in the land. While the huddled masses may enter, it appears they must retain a second-class citizen ranking.

The "natural-born" stipulation regarding the presidency stems from the self-same meeting of minds which brought the American people the Electoral College. During the Constitutional Convention of 1787, the Congress formulated the regulatory measures associated with the office of the president. A letter sent from John Jay to George Washington during this period read as follows:

> "Permit me to hint," Jay wrote, "whether it would not be wise and seasonable to provide a strong check to the admission of foreigners into the administration of our national government; and to declare expressly that the Command in Chief of the American army shall not be given to, nor devolve on, any but a natural-born citizen" (as cited in Mathews, 2005, p. A1).

Shortly thereafter, Article II, Section I, Clause V of the Constitution declared that "No Person except a natural born Citizen, or a Citizen of the United States at the time of the Adoption of this Constitution, shall be eligible to the Office of President." Jill A. Pryor (1988) states in *The Yale Law Journal* that "some writers have suggested that Jay was responding to rumors that foreign princes might be asked to assume the presidency" (p. 881). Many cite disastrous examples of foreign rule in the eighteenth century are the impetus for the "natural born" clause. For example, in 1772—only fifteen years prior to the adoption of the statute—Poland had been divided up by Prussia, Russia, and Austria, (Kasindorf, 2004). Perhaps an element of self-preservation and *not* ethnocentrism led to the questionable stipulation. Nonetheless, in the twenty-first century this clause reeks of xenophobia.

The 2003 election of action film star Arnold Schwarzenegger as governor of California stirred up movement to change this Constitutional statute. Politicians such as Senators Orrin Hatch (R-Utah) and Ted Kennedy (D-Massachusetts and Arnold's uncle by marriage) have created a buzz for ratifying a would-be twenty-eighth amendment. In addition, grassroots campaigns like "Amend for Arnold" are trying to rally popular support as they dream of the Terminator-cum-president's political slogans ("I'll be back . . . for four more years" or "Hasta la vista, baby, and hasta la vista to high taxes").

Schwarzenegger has become the face—and the bulked-up body—of the viable *naturalized* president.

We as a nation should follow the lead set by those enamored of the action star, but distance the fight from this one extremely wealthy actor. We must instead take a stand against the discriminatory practice applied to all foreign-born American citizens by this obsolete provision of the Constitution. Congress has made minor attempts to update this biased clause. The Fourteenth Amendment clarified the difference between "natural-born" and "native born" citizens by spelling out the citizenship status of children born to American parents outside of the United States (Ginsberg, 1952). (Such a clause qualifies individuals such as Senator John McCain—born in Panama—for presidency.) This change is not enough. I propose that the United States abolish the "natural born" clause and replace it with a stipulation that allows naturalized citizens to run for president. This amendment would state that a candidate must have been naturalized and lived in residence in the United States for a period of at least twenty-five years. The present time is ideal for this change. This amendment could simultaneously honor the spirit of the Constitution, protect and ensure the interests of the United States, promote an international image of inclusiveness, and grant heretofore withheld rights to thousands of legal and loyal United States citizens.

In our push for change, we must make clear the importance of this amendment. It would not provide special rights for would-be terrorists. To the contrary, it would fulfill the longtime promises of the nation. The United States claims to allow all people to blend into the great stew of citizenship. It has already suffered embarrassment and international cries of ethnic bias as a result of political moves such as Japanese American internment and the Guantanamo Bay detention center. This amendment can help mend the national image as every American takes one more step toward equality. Naturalized citizens have been contributing to the United States for centuries. Many nameless Mexican, Irish, and Asian Americans sweated and toiled to build the American railroads. The public has welcomed naturalized Americans such as Bob Hope, Albert Pujols, and Peter Jennings into their hearts and living rooms. Individuals such as German-born Henry Kissinger and Czechoslovakian-born Madeleine Albright have held high posts in the American government and served as respected aides to its presidents. The amendment must make clear that it is not about one man's celebrity. Approximately 700 foreign-born Americans have won the Medal of Honor and over 60,000 proudly serve in the United States military today (Siskind, 2004). The "natural-born" clause must be removed to provide each of these people—over half a million naturalized in 2003 alone—with equal footing to those who were born into citizenship rather than working for it (U.S. Census Bureau, 2005).

Since the passing of the Bill of Rights, only seventeen amendments have been ratified. This process takes time and overwhelming congressional and statewide support. To alter the Constitution, a proposed amendment must pass with a two-thirds "super-majority" in both the House of Representatives and the Senate. In addition, the proposal must find favor in two-thirds (thirty-eight) of state legislatures. In short, this task will not be easy. In order for this change to occur, a grassroots campaign must work to dispel misinformation regarding naturalized citizens and force the hands of senators and representatives wishing to retain their congressional seats. We must take this proposal to ethnicity-specific political groups from both sides of the aisle, business organizations, and community activist groups. We must convince representatives that this issue matters. Only through raising voices and casting votes can the people enact change. Only then can every American child see the possibility for limitless achievement and equality. Only then can everyone find the same sense of pride in the possibility for true American diversity in the highest office in the land.

References

Epstein, E. (2004, October). Doubt about a foreign-born president. *San Francisco Chronicle 6,* A5. Retrieved from LexisNexis Academic.

Ginsberg, G. (1952). Citizenship: Expatriation: Distinction between naturalized and natural born citizens. *Michigan Law Review* 50, 926–929. Retrieved from JSTOR.

Kasindorf, M. (2004, December). Should the constitution be amended for Arnold? *USA Today.* Retrieved from LexisNexis Academic.

Mathews, J. (2005). Maybe anyone can be president. *Los Angeles Times,* A1. Retrieved from LexisNexis Academic.

Pryor, J. A. (1998). The natural born citizen clause and presidential eligibility: An approach for resolving two hundred years of uncertainty. *The Yale Law Journal* 97(5), 881–899.

Siskind, L. J. (2004, December). Why shouldn't Arnold run? *The Recorder,* 5. Retrieved from LexisNexis Academic.

United States Dept. of Commerce. Census Bureau. (2005, June). The fourth of July 2005. *Facts for Features.* Retrieved from US Dept. of Commerce.

A Proposal to Improve the Campus Learning Environment by Banning
Laptops and Cell Phones from Class

Submitted to Professor Ralph Sorento

Lucy Morsen
First-Year Student

If this were the actual proposal, it would begin on a new page following
the cover page.

1   Although I am generally happy as a first year student at this university, I wish to call the Faculty Senate's attention to a distracting problem:
classmates' frequent use of laptops and cell phones during class. In many
classes more than half the students have open laptops on their desks or
are openly text-messaging on cell phones. Inevitably, laptop users multitask between taking notes and checking email, perusing Facebook, surfing the Web, looking at YouTube videos, playing a game, or working on
an assignment for another class. (I have yet to see a student use his or her
laptop solely for note-taking.) Even though I try to focus on class lectures
and discussion, I find myself missing key points and ideas as my eyes are
drawn to the animations and flashing colors on neighboring laptop
screens. Other distractions come from the clicking of cell phone
keypads—or the momentary vibration of a phone on a desktop—which
can seem surprisingly loud in an otherwise quiet environment. When the
person next to me continually picks up and sets down her phone to send
and receive text messages, she not only distracts me from the lecture but
also lets me know that she is not engaged in class, and seemingly has no
interest in being so. My annoyance at my classmates and my frustration
at not being able to focus undercut my enjoyment of class.

2   Given the extensive use of laptops and cell phones in class, I question
the academic motivation of my classmates. As a student, I most enjoy
classes when I and my classmates are actively interested and engaged in
class lecture and discussion. Collective interest has a way of feeding on
itself. I mean, we as students do not operate in isolation from one
another, but instead we affect and influence one another in gross and
subtle ways. Together with our professor we create a collective environment in the classroom, and just as we as individuals affect this collective
environment, this collective environment influences us as individuals.
The broad effects and consequences of this dynamic interplay should not
be underestimated. Humans are highly social beings; we have the power
to influence each other in both positive and negative ways. I believe that
the distracting nature of laptops and cell phones is negatively affecting

classroom environments. Any steps we can take collectively to help each other learn and succeed should be considered.

3   To address this problem, I propose a campus-wide ban on laptops and cell phones during class. I believe a campus-wide ban would be more effective than more limited measures some institutions have adopted, such as blocking wireless access from classrooms or allowing each professor to choose whether or not to ban laptops in his or her classroom. Blocking wireless access does not address the problem of cell phones or non-Web-based laptop distractions (such as computer games or other class work). Leaving the decision up to professors creates an added difficulty for them. I can imagine that professors, fearing resentment and poor evaluations from their students, would be reluctant to enforce a ban in their classrooms, even if they feel it would improve the classroom experience.

4   A campus-wide ban, on the other hand, would be easy to enforce, and students would more easily establish new habits—namely, not using laptops and cell phones during class. Over time, this could become the new campus norm.

5   Although many students might at first object to a ban, the decision to ban all laptops and cell phones in class would bring benefits not only to distracted students like me but also to current users of laptops and cell phones as well as to professors.

6   For one thing, the banning of laptops and cell phones would improve the learning atmosphere of a classroom. These technologies simply create too many distractions for students, and the negative consequences of these distractions are significant enough to call for institutional intervention. While some of my classmates may begrudge the ban, I believe they would quickly get used to it and notice improvements in their own classroom interest and performance. Many of my classmates may actually welcome the ban because they—like myself—are aware of the negative distractions laptops and cell phones create. In fact, an informal survey by a Georgetown University law professor who bans laptops in his classroom indicated that 70% of his students welcomed the ban (Cole, 2008).

7   Second, a ban might directly improve academic performance of current users of laptops and cell phones. A recent study at the University of Winona (Fried, 2008) found that laptop use in the classroom had a significant negative effect on class performance. In Fried's study, students who brought laptops to class received lower grades than their classmates who did not bring laptops to class. Moreover, those who brought laptops to class reported using their laptops for non-class purposes for nearly a quarter of class time.

8   Many of my classmates will likely argue that this study doesn't apply to them. They believe that they are skilled multitaskers who can continue

to pay attention to a lecture while also engaging in these other activities. There is empirical evidence that they are in fact mistaken about their ability to multitask. A study by three Stanford University researchers found that persons who self-reported being heavy multitaskers were *more* easily distracted from a primary task than those who reported themselves as light multitaskers (Ophir, Nass, & Wagner, 2009). The researchers conducted this study in a lab by giving multitasking tasks to a group of self-identified heavy multitaskers and then to a group of light multitaskers. This study suggests that a person's own perception of how well he or she multitasks may not be reliable. Moreover it suggests that large amounts of daily multitasking may actually decrease a person's ability to concentrate on a single task and suppress irrelevant information.

9   A handful of students will likely argue that they only use their laptops for class-related purposes, and that an outright ban on laptops in the classroom would be unfair because they would be prohibited from using them for note taking. However, I am skeptical of any claims that students make of only using laptops for class-related purposes. I personally have never seen any evidence of this, and research is indicating that multitasking is overwhelmingly the common norm among laptop users in the classroom. In a study by Benbunan-Fich and Truman (2009), student laptop use was monitored for 28 classroom sessions of 80 minutes (with students' permission). The researchers analyzed how often the students toggled between screens, and whether the screens were class-related or non-class-related. They found that 76% of the time students toggled between screens that were non-class-related. On average, students toggled between computer-based activities 37.5 times per 80-minute session. This research suggests that the temptations of non-class-related activities are simply too great for students *not* to engage in multitasking in class—it is just too easy to do a brief check of email or a quick Facebook scan with a swift click of a mouse.

10   University institutions may feel reluctant to propose a campus-wide ban on laptops and cell phones in the classroom for fear of seeming overly authoritative and unnecessarily limiting student freedom. After all, students might rightly claim that they have a right to do whatever they want in the classroom as long as they aren't harming anyone else. (I have already shown they actually are harming others.) While I believe that individual rights are an important concern—in general I believe university institutions should allow for a great amount of autonomy for their students—I think that laptop use has too many negative consequences to be allowed simply in the name of student freedom. (Of course, a professor can always allow laptop use for students with special needs.)

11   For these reasons, I propose that a campus-wide ban on laptops and cell phones in the classroom should be considered. A campus-wide ban would help to create more positive, cohesive classroom experiences, and

it would provide a reprieve for students from the myriad of distractions this modern technological age presents us. A campus-wide ban would be easier on professors to enforce, and it would help to establish a new (and improved) norm.

References

Benbunan-Fich, R., & Truman, G. E. (2009). Multitasking with laptops during meetings. *Communications of the ACM, 52*(2), 139–141. doi:10.1145/1461928.1461963

Cole, D. (2008, October 23). Why I ban laptops in my classroom [Web log post]. Retrieved from http://www.britannica.com/blogs/2008/10/why-i-ban-laptops-in-my-classroom

Fried, C. B. (2008). In-class laptop use and its effects on student learning. *Computers and Education, 50,* 906–914. Retrieved from www.elsevier.com

Ophir, E., Nass, C., & Wagner, A. D. (2009). Cognitive control in media multitaskers. *Proceedings of the National Academy of Sciences.* PNAS Early Edition. Retrieved from www.pnas.org

PRACTICE

① Working individually or in small groups, use the strategies of principle/category, consequence, and resemblance to create *because* clauses that support each of the following claims. Try to have at least one *because* clause from each of the categories, but generate as many reasons as possible. Don't worry about whether any individual reason exactly fits the category. The purpose is to stimulate thinking, not fill in the slots. Repeat the exercise, taking a different position on each issue.

EXAMPLE

People should not own pit bulls (proposal claim)

- because pit bulls are vicious. (category)
- because owning a pit bull leads to conflicts with neighbors. (consequence)
- because owning a pit bull is like having a shell-shocked roommate—mostly they're lovely companions, but they can turn violent if startled. (resemblance)

    a. Marijuana should be legalized.

    b. Division I college athletes should receive salaries.

    c. High schools should pass out free contraceptives.

    d. Violent video games should be made illegal.

    e. Parents should be heavily taxed for having more than two children.

② a. What strategies does Lucy Morsen use to convince the Faculty Senate that a problem exists?

    b. What strategies does Lucy employ to persuade the Faculty Senate that her proposal is worth enacting and that it is more effective than alternative solutions?

    c. How does Lucy tie her proposal to the values and beliefs of her audience—college professors who are members of the Faculty Senate?

    d. How effective is Lucy's use of research evidence to support her proposal?

    e. If you were a faculty member, how effective would you find Lucy's proposal? How effective do you find it as a student? What are its chief strengths and weaknesses?

3 a. What are Juan Vazquez's major reasons for building more nuclear power plants? Which of these reasons do you feel is most persuasive?

b. What are your own major objections to building more nuclear power plants? Do you have any objections that Vazquez failed to summarize?

c. To what extent did Vazquez respond persuasively to your objections? Which of his refutations of the anti-nuke arguments is weakest?

d. How effective is Vazquez's use of audience-based reasons? How would you evaluate his overall appeal to *logos, ethos,* and *pathos*?

4 List three controversial topics currently in the news. Then choose one of those topics and explain the two "sides" of this argument. Now, imagine a third point of view. How is it different from the first two positions? Does coming up with a third position help you think creatively about how to resolve this dispute? Explain.

5 a. As she writes her essay, which appears in Chapter 15 on page 634, Tannen initially outlines the nature of the problem with the "argument culture" before she gives her solution. Which paragraphs most clearly demonstrate the problem? Which paragraphs explain her solution? Does she ignore any aspects of the problem? Would her solution really solve the problem she describes? Why or why not?

b. Critically analyzing the social, political, or cultural context is an important strategy for solving a problem. Where does Tannen explain the context(s) for the problem? Where does she argue that her solution will help resolve social, political, or cultural problems? Are there contexts where her solution might not work? Explain.

c. Read Tannen's advice in the final four paragraphs of her essay. Does she follow her own advice in writing this essay? Which pieces of advice does she follow and which does she ignore? Cite examples from the essay to support your analysis. Would her essay be more effective if she followed her own advice? Explain.

d. As a professor of linguistics, Tannen can write in a formal, academic style, but she can also write in an informal style for general audiences. In this essay, is Tannen writing for academics or for anyone interested in culture and communication? Find examples of Tannen's "academic" style as well as her informal style. Does she successfully integrate the two or is she too informal or too academic? Explain.

e. According to Tannen, the language we choose and the metaphors we use affect our perceptions of the world. Where does Tannen discuss how words or metaphors shape our perceptions? What examples does she give? In her own argument, does Tannen herself avoid language or metaphors referring to war, violence, or conflict?

f. The *New Yorker* cartoon by BEK, "This looks like a good spot for an argument," did not originally appear with Tannen's essay. Evaluate the appropriateness of this visual image for Tannen's essay. Does the cartoon support Tannen's thesis? Does it contribute to the essay's appeal, or does it distract from Tannen's argument? Citing details from the cartoon and passages from Tannen's essay, explain your response.

6 On the Internet, log on to the Web site of a national news magazine such as *Newsweek* or *Utne* magazine and read their e-mail letters in response to an essay on a controversial topic such as stem cell research, climate change, public transportation, educational testing, and so forth. Read several letters or responses. Can you find at least *three* positions on that issue—rather than just the standard "pro" and "con"? Explain the controversial topic and then write out at least three different positions or points of view which you discover in the responses.

7 In a group of three or four students, make a list of all the things you can think of that are problems: your roommate is a slob, the weather stays too hot or too cold for too long, store clerks are rude, and on and on. Share your list with the group. Then discuss the following.

- Which items turned up on more than one list?
- Which problems are the most important?
- Which are possible to solve?
- Which problems are the most interesting to your group?
- Which problems are the least interesting to your group?

Credits

Text Credits

Taken from *Reading and Writing in the Academic Community,* Kennedy, Smith, 4e.

Beaumont, Jeff. "Nunez and Beyond: An Examination of Nunez v. City of San Diego and the Future of Nocturnal Juvenile Curfew Ordinances." *Journal of Juvenile Law* 19 (1998): 84–122. *LexisNexis Academic.* Web. 3 Sept. 2008. Berry, Eleanor. "The Free Verse Spectrum" *College English* 59 (1997): 873–97. Print. Bloom, Benjamin. S., et al., eds. *Taxonomy of Educational Objectives; The Classification of Educational Goals, by a Committee of College and University Examiners.* New York: Longmans, 1956. Print. Carroll, Lee Ann. "Pomo Blues: Stories from First-Year Composition." *College English* 59 (1997): 916–33. Print. Elbow, Peter. *Writing With Power.* New York: Oxford, 1998. Print. Elbow, Peter. *Writing Without Teachers.* New York: Oxford, 1973. Print. Joy, Bill. "Why the Future Doesn't Need Us." *Wired* April 2000: 238. Print. Kellogg, Ronald T., and Bascom A. Raulerson III. "Improving the Writing Skills of College Students." *Psychonomic Bulletin & Review* 14.2 (2007): 237–43. *Academic Search Premier.* Web. 27 Aug. 2008. Knowles, John. *A Separate Peace.* New York: Macmillan, 1969. Print. Lamott, Anne. *Bird by Bird.* New York: Pantheon, 1994. Print. Lunsford, Andrea A., and Karen J. Lunsford. "'Mistakes are a Fact of Life': A National Comparative Study." *College Composition and Communication* 59:4 (2008): 781–806. Print. Turkle, Sherry. "Computational Technologies and Images of the Self." *Social Research* 64.3 (1997): 1093–112. *Academic Search Premier.* Web. 27 Aug. 2008. Turkle, Sherry. "Cuddling Up to Cyborg Babies." *UNESCO Courier* Sept. 2000: 43–45. *Academic Search Premier.* Web. 27 Aug. 2008. Budds, Michael J. "From Fine Romance to Good Rockin'—and Beyond: Look What They've Done to My Song." *Bleep! Censoring Rock and Rap Music.* Eds. Betty Houchin Winfield and Sandra Davidson. Westport: Greenwood, 1999. 1–8. Print. Friere, Paulo. *Pedagogy of the Oppressed.* Trans. Myra Bergman Ramos. New York: Seabury, 1970. Print. Kierkegaard, Søren. "Fear and Trembling." *Fear and Trembling and the Sickness unto Death.* Trans. Walter Lowrie. Princeton: Princeton UP, 1941. Print. Ong, Walter J., S.J. *The Presence of the Word: Some Prolegomena for Cultural and Religious History.* New York: Simon, 1967. 137. Print. Papalia, Diane, and Sally W. Olds. *Human Development.* New York: McGraw, 1978. Print. Selzer, Jack. "Rhetorical Analysis: Understanding How Texts Persuade Readers." Eds. Charles Bazerman and Paul Prior. *What Writing Does and How It Does It.* Mahwah: Erlbaum, 2004. Print. Bambara, Toni Cade. "The Lesson." *Gorilla, My Love.* New York: Random, 1972. 87–96. Print. Budds, Michael J. "From Fine Romance to Good Rockin'—and Beyond: Look What They've Done to My Song." *Bleep! Censoring Rock and Rap Music.* Eds. Betty Houchin Winfield and Sandra Davidson. Westport: Greenwood, 1999. 1–8. Print. Cooper, Rand Richards. "The Dignity of Helplessness: What Sort of Society Would Euthanasia Create?" *Commonweal* 25 Oct. 1996: 12–15. Print. Dickens, Charles. *A Tale of Two Cities.* 1859. New York: Pocket, 1957. Print. Drizin, Steven. "Juvenile Justice: A Century of Experience." *Current* Nov. 1999: 3+. Print. Dyson, Michael Eric. "2 Live Crew's Rap: Sex, Race, and Class." *Christian Century* Jan. 1991: 7–8. Print. Frude, Neil. *The Intimate Machine.* New York: New American Library, 1983. Print. Gates, David. "Decoding Rap Music." *Newsweek* 17 Mar. 1990: 60–63. Print. Goode, Stephen, and Timothy W. Maier. "Inflating the Grades." *Insight on the News* 25 May 1998: 8–11. *Proquest Research Library.* Web. 4 Sept. 2008. Goodwin, Doris Kearns. *The Fitzgeralds and the Kennedys.* New York: Simon, 1987. Print. Grant, Linda. "What Sexual Revolution?" *Sexing the Millennium: Women and the Sexual Revolution.* New York: Grove, 1994. Print. Heker, Liliana. "The Stolen Party." *Other Fires: Short Fiction by Latin American Women.* Ed. Alberta Manual. New York: Random, 1982. 152–58. Krauthammer, Charles. "First and Last, Do No Harm." *Time* 15 Apr. 1996: 83. Print. Laing, R. D. *The Politics of Experience.* New York: Ballantine, 1967. Print. Leo,

John. "When Life Imitates Video." *U.S. News and World Report* 3 May 1999: 14. Print. Luckman, Joan, and Karen C. Sorensen. *Medical-Surgical Nursing.* Philadelphia: Saunders, 1974. Print. Moffatt, Michael. "College Life: Undergraduate Culture and Higher Education." *Journal of Higher Education* Jan.–Feb. 1991: 44–61. Print. Monaco, James. *How to Read a Film.* New York: Oxford UP, 1977. Print. O'Donnell, Philip. "Ours and Theirs: Redefining Japanese Pop Music." *World and I.* July 1998: 186+. Print. Rothenberg, David. "Learning in Finland: No Grades, No Criticism." *Chronicle of Higher Education* 23 Oct. 1998: B9+. Print. Scherer, Joanna Cohan. "Historical Photographs as Anthropological Documents: A Retrospective." *Visual Anthropology* 3 (1990): 367–409. Print. "Should Children Be Tried As Adults?" *Jet* Nov. 1999: 52. Print. Stansky, Lisa. "Age of Innocence." *ABA Journal* Nov. 1996: 61–66. Print. Stephens, Gene. "High-Tech Crime Fighting: The Threat to Civil Liberties." *Futurist* July–Aug. 1990: 20–25. Print. Talbot, Margaret. "The Maximum Security Adolescent." *New York Times Magazine* 10 Sept. 2002: 41–47+. Print. Young, Lise A. "Suffer the Children: The Basic Principle of Juvenile Justice Is to Treat the Child, Not Punish the Offense." *America* 22 Oct. 2001: 19+. Print. Zuger, Abigail, and Steven H. Miles. "Physicians, AIDS, and Occupational Risk: Historical Traditions and Ethical Obligations." *Journal of the American Medical Association* 258 (1987): 1924–28. Print. Brown, Ann. L., and Jeanne D. Day. "Microrules for Summarizing Texts: The Development of Expertise." *Journal of Verbal Learning and Verbal Behavior.* 22.1 (1983): 1–14. Print. Sagan, Carl. "In Defense of Robots." *Broca's Brain.* New York: Ballantine, 1980. 280–92. Print. Stein, Victoria. "Elaboration: Using What You Know." *Reading-to-Write: Exploring a Cognitive and Social Process.* Eds. Linda Flower et al. New York: Oxford UP, 1990. 144–48. Print. Vidal, Gore. "The Four Generations of the Adams Family." *Matters of Fact and Fiction: Essays, 1973–1976.* New York: Random, 1978. 153–74. Print. August, Eugene. "Real Men Don't: Anti-Male Bias in English." *University of Dayton Review* Winter 1986–Spring 1987: 115–24. Print. Cooper, Rand Richards. "The Dignity of Helplessness: What Sort of Society Would Euthanasia Create?" *Commonweal* 25 Oct. 1996: 12–15. Print. Griffin, Pat. *Strong Women, Deep Closets: Lesbians and Homophobia in Sport.* Champaign: Human Kinetics, 1998. 16–18. Print. Henley, Nancy, Mykol Hamilton, and Barrie Thorne. "Womanspeak and Manspeak: Sex Differences and Sexism in Communication, Verbal and Nonverbal." *Beyond Sex Roles.* Ed. Alice Sargent. 2nd ed. St. Paul: West, 1985. 168–85. Print. Heywood, Leslie. *Pretty Good for a Girl: A Memoir.* New York: Free Press, 1998. Print. Richardson, Laurel. "Gender Stereotyping in the English Language." *The Dynamics of Sex and Gender: A Sociological Perspective.* 3rd ed. New York: Harper, 1988. 19–26. Print. Rothenberg, David. "Learning in Finland: No Grades, No Criticism." *Chronicle of Higher Education* 23 Oct. 1998: B9+. van den Haag, Ernest. "Make Mine Hemlock." *National Review* 12 June 1995: 60–62. Print. Aristotle. *The Rhetoric.* Trans. W. Rhys Roberts. *The Rhetoric and Poetics of Aristotle.* Ed. Friedrich Solomon. New York: Modern Library, 1954. Print. Corbett, Edward. *Classical Rhetoric for the Modern Student.* 3rd ed. New York: Oxford UP, 1990. Print. Elbow, Peter. *Writing Without Teachers.* New York: Oxford, 1973. Print. Goldberg, Jeffrey. "The Color of Suspicion." *New York Times Magazine* 20 June 1999: 51+. Print. Messner, Michael A. "When Bodies Are Weapons." *Sex, Violence, and Power in Sports: Rethinking Masculinity.* Eds. Michael A. Messner and Donald F. Sabo. Freedom: Crossing, 1994. 89–98. Print. Porter, Rosalie P. "The Newton Alternative to Bilingual Education." *Annals of the American Academy of Political and Social Science* Mar. 1990: 147–50. Print. Raspberry, William. "Racism in the Criminal Justice System Is Exaggerated." *Washington Post* Natl. weekly ed. 15–21 Apr. 1996. Print. Farber, Jerry. "A Young Person's Guide to the Grading System." *The Student as Nigger.* New York: Pocket, 1970. 67–72. Print. Flora, Stephen Ray, and Stacy Suzanne Poponak. "Childhood Pay for Grades Is Related to College Grade Point Averages." *Psychological Reports* 94 (2004): 66. Print. Mandrell, Liz. "Zen and the Art of Grade Motivation." *English Journal* Jan. 1997: 28–31. Print. Copyright 1997 by the National Council of Teachers of English. Reprinted with permission. Vogel, Steve. "Grades and Money." *Dissent* Fall 1997: 102–04. Print. Barlow, John Perry. "Cyberhood vs. Neighborhood." *Utne Reader* March–April 1995: 50–57. Print. Biever, Celeste. "Modern Romance." *New Scientist* 29 April–5 May 2006: 44–45. Print. © New Scientist Magazine. *Internet World Stats: Usage and Population Statistics.* n.d. Web. 8 Oct. 2008. Thompson, Clive. "I'm So Totally, Digitally Close to You: How News Feed, Twitter and Other Forms of Incessant Online Contact Have Created a Brave New World of Ambient Intimacy." *New York Times Magazine* 7 Sept. 2008: 42–47.

Print. Turkle, Sherry. "Cyberspace and Identity." *Contemporary Sociology* 28 (Nov. 1999): 643–48. Print. Weizenbaum, Joseph. "Technological Detoxification." *Technology Review* Feb. 1980: 10–11. Print. Cowley, Carol, and Tillman Farley. "Adolescent Girls' Attitudes Toward Pregnancy: The Importance of Asking What the Boyfriend Wants." *Journal of Family Practice* 50 (July 2001): 603–07. Print. Gibbs, Nancy. "Give the Girls a Break." *Time* 7 July 2008: 36. Print. Gulli, Cathy. "Suddenly Teen Pregnancy Is Cool?" *Maclean's* 28 Jan. 2008: 40–44. Print. Hymowitz, Kay S. "Gloucester Girls Gone Wild." *City Journal* 23 June 2008. Web. 4 Aug. 2008. Lessig, Lawrence. "Why Crush Them?" *Newsweek* 28 Nov. 2005: 48. Print. Bollier, David, and Laurie Racine. "Control of Creativity?" *Christian Science Monitor* 9 Sept. 2003: 9. Print. Helprin, Mark. "A Great Idea Lives Forever. Shouldn't Its Copyright?" *New York Times* (late edition (East coast)) 20 May 2007: 4.12. Print. Hajdu, David. "I, Me, Mine" *New Republic* 25 June 2008: 34–37. Print. Reprinted by permission of THE NEW REPUBLIC, © 2008, *The New Republic,* LLC. Lakoff, George. "Much More than Race: What Makes a Speech Great." *Open Left.* 24 March 2008. Web. 25 September 2008. Lopez, Ian F. Haney. "The Social Construction of Race: Some Observations on Illusion, Fabrication, and Choice." *Harvard Civil Rights-Civil Liberties Law Review* 29 (Winter, 1994). Print. Moses, Yolanda T. "Race, Higher Education, and American Society." *Journal of Anthropological Research* 55 (Summer 1999): 255. Print. Obama, Barack. "A More Perfect Union." Philadelphia: National Constitution Center. 18 March 2008. Address.

David Rockwood, "Letter to the Editor" from *The Oregonian,* January 1, 1993. Copyright © 1993 David Rockwood. Used with permission. From *Raids on the Unspeakable* by Thomas Merton. Copyright © 1966 by The Abbey of Gethsemani, Inc. Reprinted by permission of New Directions Publishing Corp. Reprinted by permission of International Creative Management, Inc. Copyright © 2008 by Michael Pollan for *The New York Times.* Stephanie Malinowski, "Questioning Thomas L. Friedman's Optimism in '30 Little Turtles.'" Copyright © 2007 Stephanie Malinowski. Reprinted with the permission of the author. James Gardiner, "The Effect of Online Social Networks on Communications Skills—Annotated Bibliography." Copyright © James Gardner. Used with permission. Shannon King, "How Clean and Green are Hydrogen Fuel-Cell Cars?" Copyright © 2008 Shannon King. Used with permission. Lauren Campbell, Charlie Bourain, and Tyler Nishida, "A Comparison of Gender Stereotypes in Spongebob Square Pants and a 1930s Mickey Mouse Cartoon," Reprinted by permission of the authors. "Everyday Use" from *In Love and Trouble: Stories of Black Women* by Alice Walker. Copyright © 1973 by Alice Walker. Reprinted by permission of Houghton Mifflin Harcourt Publishing Co. Elizabeth M. Weiler, "Who Do You Want to Be?" student essay. Reprinted with the permission of the author. Blog.thehill.com. Jake McIntrye, "Progressive Case Against the Immigration Bill" by Trapper John, posted on www.dailykos.com. Copyright © 2007. Used with permission. Ross Taylor, "Paintball: Promoter of Violence or Healthy Fun?" student essay. Reprinted with the permission of the author. William Sweet, "Better Planet: Dirty Coal Plants are Killers . . ." Copyright © 2007 William Sweet. Used with permission. Lucy Morsen, "A Proposal to Improve the Campus Learning Environment." Copyright © Lucy Morsen. Used with permission.

Reprinted with permission from Alan Blinder, "Outsourcing: Bigger Than You Thought," *The American Prospect,* Volume 17, Number 11: October 22, 2006. www.prospect.org. The American Prospect, 1710 Rhode Island Avenue, NW, 12th Floor, Washington, DC 20036. All rights reserved. Excerpted from "The US and China are Over a Barrel" by Michael T. Klare, published in the *Los Angeles Times,* Apr 28, 2008, p. 17. Michael Klare is a professor of Peace and World Security Studies at Hampshire College. Used by permission of the author. Graph of "Time to Depletion Midpoint of Oil Reserves, 2003 (Years)" from The Hubbert Peak for World Oil,

Taken from *Writing Arguments: A Rhetoric with Readings*, Rampage, Bean, 8e.

Taken from *Prentice Hall Essential Guide for College Writers*, Reid, Stephen, 9e.

Barbara Ehrenreich, "Teach Diversity with a Smile," *Time*, April 8, 1991. © 1991 Barbara Ehrenreich. Reprinted with permission of International Creative Management, Inc. Daniel M. Kammen, "The Rise of Renewable Energy," *Scientific American*, September 2006. Carolyn Kleiner Butler, "Coming Home," Appeared in *Smithsonian*, January, 2005, pp. 22–23. Reprinted by permission. Rebecca Moore Howard, "Should Educators Use Commercial Services to Combat Plagiarism?" CQ Researcher link at http://0-library.cqpress.com.catalog.library.colostate.edu/cqresearcher/document.php?id=cqresrre2003091906&type=hitlist. Deborah Tannen, "The Argument Culture," from *The Argument Culture*. Copyright © 1997 by Deborah Tannen. Used by permission of Random House, Inc. Electronically reproduced by permission of Deborah Tannen.

Photo Credits

Taken from *Allyn & Bacon Guide to Writing*, Ramage, Bean, 6e

Clockwise from top left: Jose Luis Pelaez Inc./Blend Images/Corbis; Corbis Premium RF/Alamy; Ken Seet Photography/Corbis; Richard G. Bingham II/ Alamy. Thomas Hannich/Bransch/NY Times. From left: Courtesy Manuel J. Cabrero; Courtesy Ron Taylor. Clockwise from top left: Karen Kasmauski/Corbis; Guillermo Arias/AP; Carlos Barria/Corbis; J. Emilio Flores/Corbis. Clockwise from top left: Steven James Silva/Reuters/Landov; Det. Greg Semendinger/NYPD/AP; David Turnley/Corbis. Peter Turnley/Corbis. Jean-Christophe Bott/Keystone/AP. Scala/Art Resource, NY. Albright-Knox Art Gallery/Art Resource, NY. June Johnson (2 images). Lars Halbauer/DPA/Landov. Coors Brewing Company. Advertising Archives. Advertising Archives (2 images). Stephen Crowley/The New York Times/Redux. Dorothea Lange.

Taken from *Good Reasons with Contemporary Arguments*, Faigley, Seltzer, 5e.

© MadV; © Rebecca Roth; © BP p.l.c.; © Dr. Michael Wesch; © Courtesy Hofstra University; © Lilly Lane/Corbis; © Los Angeles Daily News/Corbis; Courtesy of Mothers Against Drunk Driving (MADD).

Taken from *Writing Arguments: A Rhetoric with Readings*, Rampage, Bean, 8e.

Laura Rauch/AP (Kerry), AP (Clinton), Ron Haviv/VII/AP (Obama), Bill Ray/Time Life Pictures/Getty Images (Reagan). Seth Wenig/AP

Taken from *Writing: A Guide for College and Beyond*, Faigley, 2e.

Getty Images; Hoffmann/Getty Images; Gaslight Ad Archives; Volkswagen AG; Photofest; © 2006 Volkswagen of America, Inc.; National Archives; Vario images GmbH & Co.KG/Alamy.

Unless otherwise credited, all photos © Lester Faigley Photos.

Taken from *Perspectives on Argument*, Wood, 6e.

David Silverman/Getty Images; Shutterstock; Megan Kelso.

Taken from *Prentice Hall Essential Guide for College Writers*, Reid, Stephen, 9e.

Printed by permission of the Norman Rockwell Family Agency, Copyright © 1960 the Norman Rockwell Family Entities. Sal Veder\AP Wide World Photos.

Subject Index

Author and Title Index